FAULL & NIKPAY
THE EC LAW OF COMPETITION

FAULL & NIKPAY

THE EC LAW OF COMPETITION

Edited by

JONATHAN FAULL
Deputy Director General of Competition, European Commission

ALI NIKPAY
of the Inner Temple, Barrister

OXFORD
UNIVERSITY PRESS

OXFORD
UNIVERSITY PRESS

Great Clarendon Street, Oxford OX2 6DP

Oxford University Press is a department of the University of Oxford.
It furthers the University's objective of excellence in research, scholarship,
and education by publishing worldwide in

Oxford New York

Athens Auckland Bangkok Bogotá Buenos Aires
Cape Town Chennai Dar es Salaam Delhi Florence Hong Kong Istanbul
Karachi Kolkata Kuala Lumpur Madrid Melbourne Mexico City Mumbai
Nairobi Paris São Paulo Shangai Singapore Taipei Tokyo Toronto Warsaw

and associated companies in Berlin Ibadan

Oxford is a registered trade mark of Oxford University Press
in the UK and in certain other countries

Published in the United States
by Oxford University Press Inc., New York

British Library Cataloguing in Publication Data
Data available

Library of Congress Cataloging in Publication Data
Data available

ISBN 0–19–876538–X

5 7 9 10 8 6 4

Printed in Great Britain
on acid-free paper by
Biddles Ltd,
www.biddles.co.uk

EDITORS

Jonathan Faull
Deputy Director General of Competition, European Commission

Ali Nikpay
of the Inner Temple, Barrister*

CONTRIBUTORS

José Luis Buendia Sierra
Peder Christensen
Kevin Coates
Frances Dethmers
Brendan Devlin
James Dilley
Monika Ekstrom
Carles Esteva Mosso
Jonathan Faull
Mario Filipponi
John Finnegan
F. Enrique Gonzalez Diaz
Dan Kirk
Christian Levasseur
Linsey McCallum
Kirti Mehta
Ali Nikpay
Philip Owen
Luc Peeperkorn
Francisco Perez Flores
Henri Piffaut
Stephen Ryan
Marius Nino Schober
Dan Sjöblom
Cécile Verkleij
Charles Williams
David Wood
Donncadh Woods

* Non-practising.

FOREWORD

For almost four decades the Commission and the Community courts have developed a deep and comprehensive corpus of competition law principles, rules, procedures and analytical tools. The scope of EC competition law has broadened during that time to include merger control (introduced in 1990) and to apply to formerly closed sectors like financial services, energy, transport and communications (in all of which the Commission has been an effective accelerator of liberalization). Today EC competition law ranks in the first division of the world's antitrust regimes. Indeed, the EC system has been the model for many newly emerging antitrust jurisdictions, particularly in central and eastern Europe.

As the millennium approaches, EC competition law is at a crossroad.

The foundations of the present EC competition law procedural system were laid in the 1960s, notably with the adoption of Regulation 17 which unsurprisingly is no longer adequate for the next century, given the 37 years of economic and political changes in Europe since 1962. Similarly, the keystone of EC competition law and policy has been the market integration goal which underlies the Community courts' and the Commission's highly negative position toward territorial protections and conversely their passionate favoring of parallel imports. As the Community market becomes more integrated, it is questionable whether these positions should be modified.

Winds of change are blowing through the corridors of DGIV (now the Competition Directorate). First, economic analysis is playing a greater role in EC decisionmaking and legislation as reflected, for example, in the Commission's proposal for a new block exemption on vertical restraints. Second, dissatisfaction with Regulation 17, notably its notification system and the Commission monopoly over Article 81(3) (formerly 85(3)) exemptions, recently has resulted in the White Paper on Modernization which calls for a reformation (if not revolution) in EC competition law enforcement. Third, the much criticized bifurcation of Article 81 (formerly 85) and overly broad interpretation of a restraint of competition under 81(1) (formerly 85(1)) has caused considerable rethinking within the Commission.

As the Chinese saying goes, 'we live in interesting times'. Thus an in-depth treatment of EC competition law by authors responsible for the enforcement and policy of EC competition law comes at a particularly appropriate moment, both to describe the accomplishments of the past 40 years and to suggest avenues of future developments.

This presents a serious challenge to any author or set of authors. Jonathan Faull, Ali Nikpay and their team of contributors have more than met that challenge in *The EC Law of Competition*. They are lawyers and economists from the Competition Directorate who share with the public and bar their insights into the formation, application and future of EC competition law.

The EC Law of Competition contains numerous chapters whose depth of analysis and clarity of presentation make them candidates for free-standing scholarly law review articles. To cite only a few of many examples, the chapters on Article 81, Communications and Financial Services comprehensively describe and analyze the case law, administrative practice and notable trends in thinking. The opening chapter on the Economics of Competition provides an admirable précis for both novices and veterans. In sum, *The EC Law of Competition* should be at the right hand of every counselor.

The generation of EC competition law officials and advisors who cultivated, nurtured and matured what has become one of the most successful competition law systems in the world can take pride in the work of their younger colleagues who are carrying forward one of the finest traditions of DGIV—a willingness and openness to provide guidance to legal and business advisors. *The EC Law of Competition* provides that guidance and we are all the wiser for it.

Barry E. Hawk*

---

*Skadden, Arps, Slate, Meagher & Flom LLP; Director, Fordham Corporate Law Institute.

PREFACE

This book is the result of a joint effort by a large number of people. Therefore, breaking with tradition, we (that is the editors and contributors) will begin by thanking those who have helped us. First and foremost our thanks go to our partners, families and friends, all of whom suffered during the long hours these chapters were being discussed, written, rewritten, argued about and finalised. They deserve our heartfelt thanks.

Chris Rycroft, Rebecca Allen, and their colleagues at OUP have been remarkably patient and helpful. They understood what we were trying to achieve and gave us their full support throughout. They have worked very hard to turn a series of word-processed documents into a 1000 page book in the shortest possible time.

The editors and contributors are extremely grateful to Michael Albers, Julie Bon, Jason Cawley, Paolo Cesarini, David Deacon, Jonathan Dykes, Elke Graper, Dirk Van Erps, Eric Van Ginderachter, Julian Jappert, Nils Von Hinten, Giles Holman, Sir Robin Jacob, Fin Lomholt, Paul Malric-Smith, Bryan McGuire, Sam Momtaz, Nancy Peeters, Fay Poosti, Helmuth Schröter, Rostom Stepanian, Prof. Nicholas Stern, Georg Terhorst and Jim Venit. We are also grateful to Alexander Schaub, our Director General, for his support.

The names of Frances Dethmers, James Dilley, Monika Ekstrom and Marius Nino Schober appear on the list of contributors but not in the table of contents. Their names have been added to the list to reflect the important contribution each made at various times: James contributed substantially to the writing of section F of chapter 2; Monika wrote the first draft of section F of chapter 7; Nino worked, in one capacity or another, on several chapters. Special mention must be made of Frances Dethmers who read and commented on much of the book.

When we first set out to write this book our aim was not to provide another textbook or commentary in a well-supplied market, but rather to look behind the law at some of the competition policy issues in today's and tomorrow's European economy. As we began to discuss, dissect, write and rewrite, the project developed into something more substantial: what we hope the book now provides is a practical guide to European Competition law, economics and policy. Whilst providing a concise description of the law, we have also attempted to identify and, where possible, explain the rationale which underpins the law. Where appropriate we have also sought to identify some of the problems which may arise in the future (or in which the law is undecided). Additionally a great deal of space has been devoted to dealing with specific sectors of the economy. However, we realise that there are important issues which are not covered fully in the book and deserve attention in subsequent editions. Readers are invited to send comments or suggestions to us at alinikpay@hotmail.com.

Whilst we hope to provide a few fresh insights, readers will look in vain for secrets and indiscretions. In so far as we may be described as law enforcers and policy makers, those are the perspectives we bring to bear on the various subjects dealt with in the book. However we do not represent the Commission or its Competition Directorate General. The authors give their personal opinions and views in the book and nothing between its covers should be taken to reflect any official position whatsoever.

We have all been fortunate to work in the European Commission's Competition Directorate General at a time of fascinating change and development. While unafraid to be critical, we share a general pride in the maturity and capacity for change of the system of competition law and policy developed *ex nihilo* by our predecessors in the commission's Directorate General for Competition over the last 40 years.

It is therefore to the men and women of the Competition Directorate General throughout its short life that we dedicate this book.

Brussels, September 1999

Editors and
Contributors

CONTENTS—SUMMARY

CONTENTS

I GENERAL PRINCIPLES

1. The Economics of Competition

II SPECIFIC PRACTICES

6. Horizontal Agreements

III SPECIAL SECTORS

9. Financial Services

TABLE OF CASES

European Court of Justice and Court of First Instance

A. ALPHABETICAL

B. NUMERICAL

European Court of Justice

European Commission Decisions

A. ALPHABETICAL

B. NUMERICAL/CHRONOLOGICAL

Non-merger Decisions

Joint Venture Decisions

Merger Decisions

National Cases

France

Germany

Ireland

The Netherlands

UK

US

TABLE OF EU/EC TREATIES AND LEGISLATION

REGULATIONS (numerical/chronological)

DIRECTIVES (numerical/chronological)

NOTICES

TABLE OF NON-EU/EC TREATIES AND LEGISLATION

PART I

GENERAL PRINCIPLES

1

THE ECONOMICS OF COMPETITION

A. Introduction

1.01 There is a growing awareness among competition policy makers of the importance of economics for their daily work. In the EU, admittedly with some delay compared to the US, it is now normal to discuss competition cases in terms of market power, entry barriers, sunk costs, etc and to evaluate cases according to their effects on the market. Competition policy is an economic policy concerned with economic structures, economic conduct, and economic effects. It is for this reason that in a book on competition law an introduction to the economics of competition cannot be omitted.

1.02 The growing acceptance and importance of economics in competition policy also raises the question of the usefulness of economics for devising competition rules and deciding on competition cases. A word of caution may be in place in this respect. Economic thinking and economic models have not proven to be perfect guides.

1.03 Economic theories and economic models are built on and around assumptions. These assumptions by definition do not cover (all) real world situations. In addition, when the assumptions are changed the outcomes of the models may look strikingly different, changing for example the price from a monopoly level to a competitive price level. It is for these reasons that economics may often not be able to give a clear and definite answer on what will happen in a market when companies merge, when a company imposes a vertical restriction, or when companies try to collude.

1.04 The best economics can do in general is offer a number of useful concepts and models, exclude certain outcomes, and provide relevant arguments. In other words, it helps to tell the most plausible story. It may be useful by helping to formulate rules, devise safe harbours, indicate under what conditions anti-competitive outcomes are very unlikely or rather likely. In individual cases it will be necessary to find first the concepts and the model that fit best the description of the actual market conditions of the case and then to proceed with the analysis of the actual or possible competition consequences.

1.05 The competition policy practitioner is advised to follow the mainstream of economics, in order to avoid too much contradiction and untested assumptions. That is what this chapter sets out to do: to give a short introduction to the mainstream of industrial economics.[1] It has the following structure:

---

[1] Industrial economics or industrial organization can be described as applied microeconomics: it uses the models and concepts of microeconomics in an effort to understand the development of real world markets and company behaviour. For an excellent introduction see FM Scherer & D Ross, *Industrial Market Structure and Economic Performance* (3d edn, Boston: Houghton Mifflin Company, 1990). More technical and elaborate is the *Handbook of Industrial Organization* edited by R Schmalensee & R Willig (Amsterdam: North Holland, 1989).

— Section B describes some historical trends relevant for industrial economics;
— Section C describes the static welfare analysis of market power;
— Section D describes the dynamic welfare analysis of market power;
— Section E introduces the issues of market definition;
— Section F looks into the link between market power and dominance.

B. Structure, Conduct, Performance

(1) Early Developments

Interest in the issues of market power did not arise for the first time in the twentieth century. Descriptions of the dangers of monopoly can be found in ancient Greek written sources as well as in the Bible. Adam Smith made in his *Wealth of Nations* (1776) the famous remark that people of the same trade seldom meet, even for merriment and diversion, without it ending in a conspiracy to raise prices. More in general, Smith warned against the negative effects of (government inspired) monopoly.   **1.06**

In the nineteenth century neoclassical authors like Augustin Cournot and Alfred Marshall laid the basis for modern microeconomics with the development of simple models of perfect competition, monopoly, and duopoly. Especially the model of perfect competition was useful for developing theory on general equilibrium for the whole of the economy. However, these models did not seem in line with the developments at the end of the nineteenth/beginning of the twentieth century: concentration, the emergence of trusts, product differentiation, and advertising.   **1.07**

Research in the first half of the twentieth century also seemed to indicate that often companies were not producing against minimal average costs as the model of perfect competition would predict.[2] Instead they were producing on a decreasing cost curve, without, however, becoming much bigger. This, known as the Great Cost Controversy, led several authors like Sraffa, Chamberlin, and Robinson to write about imperfect and monopolistic competition, that is those situations in between the two extremes of perfect competition and monopoly. The authors tried to incorporate aspects like product differentiation and advertising in their models.   **1.08**

(2) The Harvard School

Not satisfied with the limited, rather simple, and theoretical models mentioned above, around World War II a number of economists like Mason and Bain started to look for more empirical explanations. They tried to develop a kind of applied   **1.09**

---

[2] For the concepts used see Section C, in particular paras 1.26–1.30 and 1.51–1.70.

microeconomics. Instead of deduction based on simple assumptions they wanted to incorporate the richness of the real world. Data were gathered and by induction they tried to develop general rules concerning likely company behaviour, effects on the market, and possibilities for government policy.

1.10 The main result of this so-called Harvard school,[3] that started and dominated the industrial economics scene for many years, is the Structure-Conduct-Performance (SCP) paradigm. In its simplest form it states that market structure determines companies' market behaviour which in turn determines market performance. Market structure, being the basis of the explanation, was seen as of paramount importance. In its most mechanistic form conduct becomes quite irrelevant to study. It is the structure that is responsible for the final market outcome. Studies were done for several sectors to collect market structure data like concentration ratios and height of entry barriers. These data were linked to performance indicators as profits, the general conclusion being that concentrated markets with entry barriers showed above average profitability. This approach fitted well in the general trend for structuralist theories and explanations developed in the social sciences in the forties, fifties, and sixties.

Figure 1: The simple S-C-P scheme

1.11 The main policy conclusion flowing from the simple S-C-P scheme has been that competition policy should concentrate on structural remedies. It should be avoided that markets become concentrated or entry barriers are erected. This was reflected, for example, in the use of concentration measures in assessing merger cases as in the 1968 Horizontal Merger Guidelines issued by the US Department of Justice. Behavioural remedies were seen as ineffective without the necessary structural changes.

(3) The Chicago School

1.12 A number of economists like Stigler, Demsetz, and Brozen questioned the S-C-P framework, its conclusion that concentration in general does lead to monopoly profits, and that competition policy should take structural measures. This group of scholars, also known as the Chicago school, criticized the empirical S-C-P studies. By using the same or improved data with different techniques or by using new data they showed that the relationship between concentration, entry barriers, and

---

[3] It is called the Harvard school because many of its originators like Mason worked in Harvard.

monopoly profits was not so stable or strong or even, at times, non existent. More important, however, was their theoretical attack on the S-C-P paradigm.

They argued that the causal link is not between high concentration and high prof- **1.13** its, but between firm size leading to increased efficiency leading to concentration and ultimately leading sometimes to increased profits. Central to this reasoning are economies of scale and scope and a general belief that competition forces some companies to become superior in terms of efficiency. These companies will grow quicker than others who may even go out of business. This at times may lead to higher concentration but this is desirable from a competition policy point of view as it leads to more efficient firms, even when it would also result in some mono- poly profits. Monopoly profits would not be very likely to arise and certainly not be durable, as it was argued that entry barriers are in general not very high and can be overcome in time. The more extreme members of the Chicago school are only willing to make an exception for government controlled entry barriers, thereby telling governments to clean up their own act instead of pursuing vigorous com- petition policy.

These attacks of the Chicago school, that started in the sixties but culminated in **1.14** the seventies and eighties, brought back a greater reliance on the self-healing forces of competition. High concentration is not necessarily bad and only in very particular circumstances is competition policy action called for. This fitted well with the general trend in the seventies and especially the eighties to see limits to the effectiveness of government interference.

(4) Latest Developments

The Chicago school returned in part to the deductive approach of the microeco- **1.15** nomic models, more concerned with theory than with empirical testing. It showed main theoretical weaknesses in the arguments of the Harvard school. It forced a reconsideration of the S-C-P framework that as a consequence has been extended and has been refined over the years. It has been recognized that a wide array of other basic conditions like consumer preferences and state of the techno- logy influence the market structure and that these basic conditions may them- selves change. As important, it has been accepted that conduct is not a negligible factor when it comes to explaining performance. In addition it is recognized that conduct and also performance may help shape the market structure. In other words that, although the main causal link may still run from market structure to market conduct to market performance, feed back mechanisms complicate the picture. The resulting extended S-C-P framework is illustrated in Figure 2.

This extended S-C-P framework is still important today in industrial economics **1.16** and in competition policy, not as the perfect explanatory framework but as a good way to organize one's thoughts. Market structure is still the starting point for

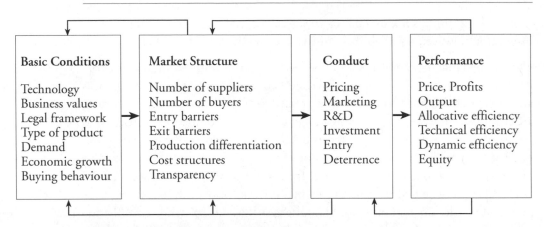

Figure 2: The extended S-C-P framework

competition policy arguments. It is generally accepted that certain market conditions are a prerequisite for anti-competitive conduct and performance. However, these necessary conditions may not be sufficient. Conduct like limit pricing or excess capacity creation may play its own role. Structural conditions can be used to describe safe harbours: situations in which anti-competitive behaviour or effects are highly unlikely. However, to find anti-competitive situations, usually structural, behavioural, and performance aspects will have to be taken account of. This is especially true under Articles 81 and 82 of the EC Treaty, where it is not enough to show that the market structure enabled anti-competitive conduct, but where also the conduct itself and/or the negative effects that with high likelihood resulted from this conduct have to be shown. It is only under the Merger Regulation that solely a structural analysis may suffice.

1.17 The renewed attention to the behaviour of companies is also reflected in the latest developments of industrial economics, sometimes called the new industrial economics. The centre of attention is the possible strategic behaviour of companies in oligopolistic situations. It tries to deduct, within the framework of more sophisticated microeconomic models and with the help of game theory, what the most likely company strategies are and whether collusion is likely or not. It fits in well with the more moderate, less ideological, and more technical approach of problems of the nineties. However, it has not led so far to very robust outcomes useful for competition policy.

C. Static Welfare Analysis of Market Power

(1) Introduction

In a nutshell, one could say that the economics of competition is about market **1.18**
power: what it is, how it is created or sustained, and what are its effects. The
answer given by economists on the first question—what is market power?—concentrates on the power to raise price above the competitive level. In the short run
this means the power to raise price above marginal cost and in the long run above
average total cost.[4] In other words a company has market power if it has a perceptible influence on the price against which it can sell and if by charging a price
above the competitive level it is able, at least for a significant period, to obtain
supra-normal profits.

This makes it very clear that market power is not a black and white concept and **1.19**
that companies can have different degrees of market power. In theory the appropriate measuring rod would be the net present value of the monopoly profits a
company can make. The net present value is today's value of the profit of this
period and all future periods. It depends therefore on the monopoly profit per
period, on the number of periods a monopoly profit can be sustained before entry
or expansion by competitors takes the profit away, and on the discount rate
against which future profits are evaluated.[5]

A firm with market power may raise its price by reducing its own output or by **1.20**
making competitors reduce theirs. As said, this price increase should increase its
profits and do so for a significant period of time. Under the current merger rules
dominance is, in practice, only established when the company involved will, with
high likelihood, be able to obtain supra-normal profits for a period longer than
two years. Under Articles 81 and 82 normally also shorter periods are taken into
account.

The second question about how market power is created or sustained brings us **1.21**
back to the question of the relevant elements of market structure and conduct.
And so does the third question about its effects. This section is devoted to a static
welfare analysis of these questions. By static it is meant that the level of technology
is assumed to be constant and effects of market power on innovation and vice
versa are ignored. The latter is dealt with in Section D, not surprisingly titled
dynamic welfare analysis of market power.

---

[4] The terminology used comes back and is explained in later parts.

[5] The present value of a stream of profits is given by: $\text{NPV} = \sum_{i=1}^{n} \frac{\pi i}{(1+r)}i$, where n is the number of
periods a monopoly profit is made, πi is the profit in period i, and πr is the discount rate. As discount
rate, usually the competitive rate of return on capital or the rate at which the company can lend
money is taken, since this measures the opportunity cost of using the company's own funds.

1.22 Welfare economics is the branch of microeconomics concerned with the efficiency of the company/the market/the economy.[6] A welfare economic analysis of the effects of market power concentrates on the effects on efficiency, both allocative and technical efficiency, and therewith the effect on total welfare. This is measured in terms of consumer surplus and company profits. The next subsection provides an explanation of these and other microeconomic concepts, followed by subsections analysing the market structure of perfect competition, monopoly, and oligopoly.

(2) Some Microeconomic Concepts

(a) Consumer Surplus

1.23 Consumer surplus is the net benefit consumers obtain by buying a certain good or service. It is the difference between their willingness to pay, sometimes called their reservation price, and the price actually paid. As consumers have different preferences and incomes some are normally willing to pay more than others for a certain good. Also, the higher the quantity of the good a particular consumer obtains the lower in general his willingness to pay for an additional unit. These characteristics mean that a demand curve, which shows for an individual or a whole market the relationship between the willingness to pay and the quantity bought, is normally downward sloping. This is shown in Figure 3, where the individual and collective consumer surplus at a market price of 5 are presented by the shaded areas.

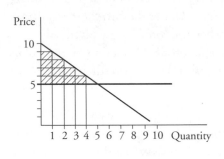
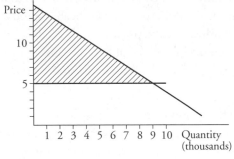

Figure 3: Individual demand curve   *Market demand curve*

(b) Production Costs

1.24 Production costs of a company can also be captured in curves. These cost curves are of course not the same for different companies and different industries. Some firms are capital intensive while others are labour intensive, some have high fixed costs while others have high variable costs, some experience economies of scale

---

[6] Tibor Scitovsky, *Welfare and Competition* (London: Unwin University Books, 1952).

while others have flat cost curves or even experience diseconomies of scale. However, some general characteristics can normally be assumed about cost curves.

These general characteristics depend very much on whether one looks at the short **1.25** or long run. In the short run many production factors may be fixed, that is the producer is not able to vary the quantity used of these factors in response to demand changes. This is usually true for the buildings and other main capital goods and the production process adopted. But it may also be true for labour, at least in a downward sense when rules on firing make adaptation difficult and slow, and sometimes in an upward sense when, for example, training for specific capabilities takes a long time. Other inputs like raw materials, intermediate goods, and energy may often be variable. In the long run all factors become variable as plants, production process, and personnel (including management) can be totally replaced.

(c) Short Run Production Costs

The general characteristics of the short run cost curves are best explained by what **1.26** economists call the law of increasing and decreasing returns. Let us assume for the moment that we have only two factors of production, capital and labour. The former is fixed while the latter is variable.

To produce, a company must employ labour to work with the available fixed **1.27** capital. At first, employing more labour will lead to a more efficient division of labour. By adding an employee the productivity of every employee will rise: the returns are increasing. In other words, the marginal product, that is the change in total output resulting from the use of one more employee, is increasing. This means that the costs of producing a unit of output are decreasing. This is so for the average total cost (ATC), that is all fixed and variable costs divided by total output, as well as for the average variable cost (AVC), that is all variable cost divided by total output. It is also true for marginal cost (MC), that is the cost of producing the last unit of output.

With the fixed capital as a constraint there comes a point where adding another **1.28** employee will lead to less extra output compared to adding the penultimate employee. The marginal product is declining, the returns start to decrease. The moment the marginal product starts to decline the marginal cost starts to increase: producing one more unit of output becomes more expensive than the previous unit of output in terms of employee time used.[7] By adding more employees the marginal cost will rise further and will cut the average variable and average total cost curves at their lowest point, as depicted in Figure 4.

---

[7] It is assumed that the price of the production factor, in this example the wage rate, is constant and not influenced by the quantity demanded by the company.

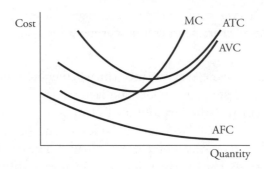

Figure 4: A company's short run cost curves ATC, AVC, AFC and MC

1.29 That the MC curve cuts the other two curves at their minimum is easily explained: when the extra costs incurred by producing one more unit of output are still lower than respectively the average variable or average total costs, producing this extra output will further sink these averages. However, the moment that producing this extra unit has marginal costs that are higher as the respective average, the average will start to rise.

1.30 In Figure 4, also, the average fixed cost curve (AFC) is depicted. This average will decline as long as output grows, as the fixed costs are spread over more units of output. In Figure 4 the cost curves are only drawn in so far as it is economically interesting. That means not too far left or right from the minimum of ATC. The further away from this minimum the less efficient the company produces. At its minimum the company reaches productive or technical efficiency. It is not relevant to see what happens if more and more employees are added to the fixed capital, making the average costs rise further and further and eventually leading to a decline in output. Nor is it interesting to see what happens when the company produces far below its optimal scale.

(d) Profit Maximization

1.31 What range of the cost curves is economically interesting is linked to the goal of the company. Usually it is assumed that this goal is profit maximization. Certainly in a competitive environment where profits are under pressure a company is best advised to try to maximize its profits in order to survive in the long run. In a situation of fierce competition profits will be rather low, just high enough to attract the required production effort, and a deviation from profit maximization will quickly lead to losses. It is only when a company has a certain degree of market power that it can afford to pursue such other goals as sales maximization with a minimum profit constraint.[8]

---

[8] Whether a company with market power actually will deviate from the goal of profit maximization will depend on the incentives of management, the control of ownership over management, and in general the restraining influence of the capital markets.

To maximize its profits or, when times are bad, to minimize its losses a company   **1.32**
should ensure that the additional costs of producing one extra unit of output are
still covered by the additional revenue earned by this extra unit of output: the marginal cost should equal the marginal revenue (MC=MR). This rule holds for companies with or without market power.

The MC curve is therefore the supply curve of the profit maximizing firm. The   **1.33**
MR curve will depend on the demand curve the company is facing. When the
company operates in a perfectly competitive market it is a price taker: its output
has no influence on the price on the market. If it raises its price above the market
price demand for its product will drop to zero. Its marginal revenue equals the
market price. Graphically this means the MR curve is a horizontal line at the level
of the market price. If, on the other hand, the company faces a downward sloping
demand curve, meaning that by varying its output it can change the price at which
it can sell, the MR curve will lie beneath the demand curve.[9]

Let us assume that the company is a price taker. In Figure 5 this means that as long   **1.34**
as the market price is below p1 the company is better advised not to produce at all:
the price does not even cover the average variable costs. With a price above p1 the
profit maximizing company will produce the amount where its MC equals the
price. Producing less would mean that MC is smaller than MR, indicating that
producing an extra unit of output will make it earn more. Producing more than
the amount that equals MC and MR would mean that MC is higher than MR,
indicating that reducing output will make it earn more. With a market price
between p1 and p2 the company is minimizing its losses, as the price does not yet
cover all average total costs. When the price rises above p2 the company will make

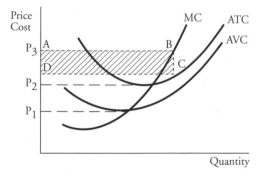

Figure 5: A company's cost curves and profit

---

[9] This will be explained in Section C(4), in particular paras 1.62–1.70, where the static effects of
monopoly are treated.

a profit, as the price exceeds the average total costs. With a price of p3 the profit will be the shaded area ABCD.

(e) Long Run Production Costs

1.35 It was said above that the cost curves depend very much on whether the short or long run is analysed. In the short run the law of increasing and decreasing returns indicates that the ATC, AVC, and MC curves will first decline and then increase. A flat bottom, an area where average costs are constant over a certain range of output, is possible but inevitably the cost curves will rise as more variable production factors are added to the fixed factors. The optimal capacity utilization will not vary much in the short run.

1.36 In the long run, when the fixed production factors are also variable, the picture looks different. If a company producing at its minimum short run ATC would like to double its output, it could do so by copying the existing plant and thus, by doubling all the necessary production factors, also double its output. This means that the long run ATC curve will have a flat part. The long run ATC is therefore in general depicted as in Figure 6. In the same picture different short run ATC curves are drawn belonging to different output levels. The long run ATC curve shows the lowest short run ATC achievable for every output.[10]

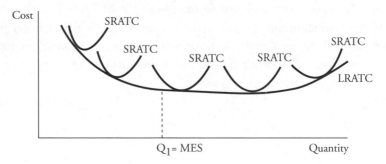

Figure 6: Long and short run ATC

(f) Economies of Scale and Minimum Efficient Scale

1.37 The long run ATC curve drawn in Figure 6 makes two other important concepts clear: that of economies of scale and the minimum efficient scale (MES). In Figure 6 an output below Q1 will be produced at higher average total costs than attainable when more than Q1 is produced. Up to Q1 increasing capacity will lead to

---

[10] The short run costs are, as it were, the real costs of a company, for example when it has to calculate its profit or loss. The long run costs indicate the possibility frontier in a static world where the level of technology is assumed to be constant (see Section C(1)).

economies of scale: a higher capacity reduces the average costs. These economies of scale result often from the indivisibility of certain production factors: the bigger truck that transports more while still requiring only one driver, the bigger company that can afford to have a full-time specialist employed for every relevant area, the bigger plant that requires not more spare parts to be kept in stock than the smaller plant. Economies of scale may also result from technical-physical relationships, like the bigger oil tanker that requires relatively less steel to be build, or from economies of increased dimensions, like the larger company that may obtain discounts when buying larger amounts of input or borrowing larger sums.[11] More in general, increased output brings a different, more efficient production process within reach.

Beyond Q1 no more economies of scale can be reaped. This point is called the **1.38** minimum efficient scale. Although in practice not always easy to establish, it is an important concept helping to explain concentration in a market. The MES makes clear what the maximum number of companies is that can operate efficiently in a market, at least when producing below MES level results in significantly higher costs per unit of output. To what extent it results in higher costs is measured by the cost gradient, that is the steepness of the slope of the cost curve. When the cost gradient is significant and the MES equals 5 per cent of total demand there is room for maximum twenty efficient companies.

In the example of a MES of 5 per cent of market demand it can be expected that **1.39** also a company having capacity to produce 20 per cent of the market will be able to produce at the same low ATC. In theory a company can have any size above MES and produce at the same low ATC. In order to produce more its management could simply copy MES size units. In practice, however, it can be expected that above a certain size diseconomies of scale will also appear. Management may become too complex, the number of management layers will increase and motivation may reduce. The long run ATC may creep up when size continues to increase.

Economies of scale, especially when they are substantial, are an important explan- **1.40** ation for concentration tendencies in a market. By indicating the maximum number of firms that can operate efficiently in the market the MES defines the minimum concentration degree. As some companies will be above MES scale the overall concentration in the market will usually be higher. This makes it quite clear that more companies in a market does not necessarily lead to a better market outcome and that protecting competitors is not the same as protecting competition or consumers' interests.

---

[11] In the latter case a distinction needs to be made between real economies, based on actual cost savings on the side of the input producer/bank, and pecuniary economies that merely reflect a benefit at the expense of the input producer/bank resulting from a different balance of power.

1.41 The economies of scale described above are sometimes referred to as static internal economies of scale. Internal because they are related to the plant or firm, static because they are not related to past production. A recent overview of the literature on economies of scale shows that estimates of the importance of these static internal economies of scale depend to a degree on the method of measurement.[12] Econometric studies based on cross section or times series data on costs and profits tend to find only limited positive economies of scale. For example, Lyons finds that in the UK for most of the studied 118 trades MES is below 250 employees.[13] However, engineering estimates, that is cost estimates by managers, engineers, etc, give more weight to economies of scale. In his study for the Commission, Pratten finds very important economies of scale in a number of sectors like motor vehicles, other means of transport, chemicals, machinery and instrument manufacturing and paper and printing, that is in particular in the production of industrial goods. Pratten estimates that 27 per cent of EU output is produced in industries whose MES is above 5 per cent of the whole EU market.[14]

1.42 In addition to static internal economies of scale, dynamic internal economies of scale are distinguished.[15] The latter refer to a lowering of the costs of production over time as a result of experience obtained on past cumulative output. They are also referred to as learning effects. In terms of Figure 6, these economies of scale lead to a downward shift of the long run ATC curve. These economies of scale are not so much an explanation for concentration tendencies but may be part of a first mover advantage. The company or companies that entered the market first were possibly able to recoup the higher original costs while latecomers may have to sell immediately at lower prices dictated by the first entrants having gained some experience in the market. Such learning effects are more likely in new industries, especially when operating with much skilled labour, and less likely in mature industries with known technologies, especially when operating with much fixed capital.

(g) Entry Barriers

1.43 As already alluded to in the previous paragraph economies of scale are also an important element when describing another main concept of industrial econom-

---

[12] Karsten Junius, *Economies of Scale: A Survey of the Empirical Literature*, Kiel Working Paper No 813 (Kiel Institute of World Economics, 1997). See also European Commission, *The Single Market Review*, Subseries V: Volume 4: Economies of Scale (1997).

[13] B Lyons, *A New Measure of Minimum Efficient Plant Size in the UK Manufacturing Industry* (Economica, 1980).

[14] C Pratten, *A Survey of the Economies of Scale*, Economic Papers of the European Commission, No 67 (1988).

[15] In the literature also (static and dynamic) external economies of scale are distinguished (see Karsten Junius, 1997). These refer to positive external effects resulting from firms being situated near each other. These economies are, however, less relevant for industrial economics and competition policy and play a role in regional economics and trade theory.

ics, the concept of entry barriers. It was Bain who stressed the importance of entry barriers as a condition for companies with a significant market share to have market power and turn this into monopoly profits. Without entry barriers easy entry would eliminate quickly such profits. Entry barriers, according to Bain, are 'the advantages of established sellers in an industry over potential entrant sellers, these advantages being reflected in the extent to which established sellers can persistently raise their prices above a competitive level without attracting new firms to enter the industry'.[16] In other words, the incumbent companies have certain advantages that allow them to increase their price above minimum ATC without attracting entry.

This definition of entry barriers is often used in competition policy as it indicates **1.44** situations in which a competition concern is likely to arise. In a market with entry barriers further concentration through mergers may have to be stopped, especially when the incumbent firms already experience reduced competition. A competition authority will also have to be more alert on abuse of a dominant position in case a market is shielded off by entry barriers.

The above definition of entry barriers, however, does not always give the right pol- **1.45** icy insights. When the question comes up whether a competition authority should stimulate or force entry in a particular market another definition, first proposed by Stigler, is superior. He defined entry barriers as costs that new entrants have but that the incumbents did not suffer.[17]

The difference with Bain's definition is most easily explained with the example of **1.46** economies of scale. Economies of scale qualify as an entry barrier under the definition of Bain. As new companies in general enter at a small scale they will experience a cost disadvantage compared to the incumbents. This will allow the latter, when competition between them already is reduced, to keep their price above their own minimum ATC and earn monopoly profits.[18] However, the incumbents were also faced with scale economies when they entered. In addition, new entrants might start immediately at MES size. Scale economies do therefore not qualify as an entry barrier under the definition of Stigler. Forcing entry by the competition authority will be inefficient when it increases the number of companies above the number of companies that can efficiently operate in the market, that is when the incumbents are not much bigger as MES.

In addition to economies of scale a number of other factors are sometimes men- **1.47** tioned in competition policy analysis as entry barriers, although these may not

---

[16] See J Bain, *Barriers to New Competition* (Cambridge: Harvard University Press, 1965) page 3.
[17] George J Stigler, 'Barriers to entry, economies of scale and firm size', in RD Irwin, *The Organization of Industry* (Homewood, 1968).
[18] In a case where the entrant considers entry at large scale it will seriously have to estimate the influence of its additional output on the market price. If it expects the price to drop to competitive levels entry may not be attractive.

always qualify as such under the definition of Stigler. Government regulations, especially when establishing exclusive rights, may work as an entry barrier, for example when only a limited number of licences is provided. State aid, when only available to incumbents, will work as an entry barrier. Import tariffs have the same effect on foreign suppliers. Intellectual property rights or ownership of absolutely scarce resources (for example, platinum mines) may also inhibit access by those that cannot avail themselves of these patents or scarce resources. Essential facilities, that is a facility that is required to be able to produce another good or service (the railway track and the railway service), may work as an entry barrier if access to the facility is not open to competitors. Vertical links or vertical integration may make access more difficult and foreclose potential competitors. Economies of scope, that is lower ATC as a result of producing a larger product range, may also make entry more difficult. The same can be said of brand loyalty of customers, for example stimulated by high advertising outlays, as it makes customers less willing to switch to comparable or better offers. More in general, when a customer will have to bear a high cost in order to switch to a new supplier, such switching costs may hinder entry of new suppliers. It may be added that many of these factors may not only work as an entry barrier but may also work as a barrier to expansion, preventing companies already in the market from expanding their output.

1.48 The question whether certain of the above mentioned factors should be described as entry barriers depends on whether the necessary outlays are sunk costs. Sunk costs are those costs that have to be made to enter or be active on a market but that are lost when the market is exited. Advertising costs to build consumer loyalty will work as an entry barrier if an exiting firm can not sell its brand name nor use it somewhere else without a loss. The more costs are sunk, the more potential entrants will have to weigh the risks of entering the market and the more credible incumbents can threaten that they will match new competition as they will not leave the market. High sunk costs invested in excess capacity may be an especially credible threat that the incumbent(s) cannot leave the market and will increase output and lower prices upon entry.

(h) Contestability

1.49 It were Baumol, Panzar and Willig who stressed the importance of sunk costs with their theory of contestable markets in the early 1980s.[19] A market is said to be contestable when there are no entry barriers and no sunk costs and consumers are willing to switch quickly, before incumbents can react, to the better offer of new entrants. Under these conditions so-called hit-and-run entry is possible. When

---

[19] William J Baumol, John C Panzar and Robert D Willig, *Contestable Markets and the Theory of Industry Structure* (New York: Harcourt Brace Jovanovich, 1982). For a brief introduction, see Derek Ridyard, 'Contestability Theory and its Practical Impact on Competition Policy Decisions', (1995) 26(2) *The Business Economist.*

the incumbents charge a price above minimum ATC it becomes profitable to enter, if not to stay on the market at least for the time it takes before the incumbents lower their price. The threat of such hit-and-run entry, in other words the existence of potential competition, will discipline the incumbents, even when they have very high market shares.

At a conceptual level the theory of contestable markets helped to underline and delineate the possible role of potential competition. In practice not many markets are truly contestable. The important question is how contestable markets are. In general, entry requires sunk costs, sometimes minor and sometimes major, and incumbents are often in the position to react quickly, that is before the consumer loyalty wears down. Even in transport markets, where it is possible in principle to redirect assets, like ships or planes, at short notice from one route to another, entry barriers like the non-availability of necessary slots may delay or impede entry. Actual competition is therefore still to be preferred above potential competition. **1.50**

(3) Perfect Competition

(a) The Model

When market models are put on a market power scale, perfect competition is the extreme at the low end. There is no company that holds market power and competition policy enforcers can quietly write books during office hours. Unfortunately, markets rarely fulfil the conditions of this model. However, the model is useful for two reasons. First, it highlights the two very important concepts of allocative and technical efficiency. Secondly, in certain respects it is useful as a benchmark against which to measure the competitiveness of actual markets. **1.51**

In order to be called perfectly competitive a market has to have a number of characteristics, the main ones of which are the following: there are many suppliers and many buyers, there are no entry barriers, the product is homogeneous, and there is full transparency. This means that the MES must be small compared to total market demand, so as to make it possible for many companies to operate on the market and produce at minimal costs. The last condition means that suppliers and potential suppliers are aware of every change in demand and price and, as there are no entry barriers, swiftly react by expanding or reducing supply. The last condition also implies that companies are aware of the most efficient production techniques and that no company is more efficient than the others. **1.52**

A company operating under such conditions will be a price taker, as briefly indicated in the previous section. The price is determined by the market and its own output is so small compared to total output that a change in the company's output has no perceptible influence on the market price. As entry and exit are swift and without costs the market will always quickly return to its equilibrium where the price exactly matches market demand and market supply, as shown on the **1.53** right-hand side of Figure 7. If demand rises, graphically this means the demand curve shifting to the right, the price will rise as the current output is not able to satisfy all demand. Immediately entry of new firms or expansion of existing firms will increase output until the equilibrium price is restored. A fall in demand, graphically the demand curve shifting to the left, leads to firms leaving the market until output is sufficiently reduced and equilibrium restored.

1.54 At the equilibrium market price every company in the market will produce at the same minimum ATC and makes no profits. This is shown in the left hand side of Figure 7. By no profits it is meant that the company's income is just enough to cover the rewards that all factors of production, including capital, need to make them stay in this company. In economic terminology they receive their opportunity cost. This means that the situation of no profits allows for normal accounting profits that are necessary to make capital stay in the company. These normal profits are part of the ATC cost curve. However, no excess profits are made.

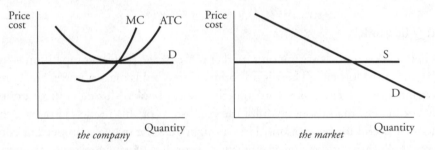

Figure 7: Perfect competition

1.55 Figure 7 deserves some further explanation as it shows a number of important issues. First, there is the difference between the market demand curve and the company's demand curve, that is the demand the company faces for its own output. The market demand curve is downward sloping, as explained in paragraph 1.23 (see Figure 3). The company's demand curve is (practically) horizontal at the level of the market price. At that price the company, given its small capacity, can sell as much as it wants. It does not need to lower its price to sell more. It is also not in the position to lower its price as this would lead to immediate losses as the price would be below average total cost. Increasing its price above the market price would lead to an immediate loss of all sales and exit of the market.

(b) **The Effects**

1.56 Figure 7 indicates that in perfect competition there is technical/productive efficiency: with given resources the maximum output is produced. This results from every company producing at the minimum ATC. If a company is less efficient it will make a loss and exit the market where its place will be taken by a new efficient

entrant. If a firm introduces a new cost saving technique this will be copied immediately by all the others, graphically represented by a downward shift of the supply curve, after which a new equilibrium will be realized at a lower price.

Figure 7 also indicates that in the equilibrium situation there is allocative effi- **1.57**
ciency: welfare is maximized as consumer surplus is at its largest. If less output
than the equilibrium quantity would be produced there would be buyers with a
reservation price above the equilibrium price. That means these buyers would be
willing to pay more than it costs to produce more units and welfare could thus be
increased by expanding output. Expanding output beyond the equilibrium would
also lower welfare as productive resources are used at the wrong place: elsewhere,
that is on other markets, they could be used to produce goods at cost equal to their
reservation price. The allocative efficiency is reflected at company level by every
company obtaining a price equal to its marginal costs (P=MC). Producing one
unit more would mean that the extra costs exceed the price it receives, in other
words the extra costs exceed the reservation price of the marginal consumer.

(4) Monopoly

(a) The Model

Monopoly is at the other extreme of the market power scale. In the full fledged **1.58**
monopoly model the monopolist has the maximum achievable market power.
One might expect that competition policy enforcers when such a situation occurs
have to give up the possibility to write books during office hours. However, this
may not be the case as the analysis of pure monopoly situations is rather straightforward, effective remedies like break-up are not available in EC competition policy, and markets rarely fulfil the conditions of this model. The model of monopoly
is, however, very useful as it helps to highlight a number of important concepts
and it provides the clearest example of what competition policy tries to prevent or
remedy.

In order to be called purely monopolistic a market has to have a number of char- **1.59**
acteristics, the main ones of which are that there is only one supplier while there
are many buyers and that there are entry barriers that practically prevent entry.

A company operating under such conditions will be a price setter. As it is the only **1.60**
company market demand is the demand for the company's product. By varying its
output the monopolist can determine the market price along the demand curve.
As entry is impossible it can quietly try to maximize its profits or pursue other
goals.

Assuming that profit maximization is the monopolist's goal it will produce that **1.61**
output where its marginal revenues equal its marginal costs (see paragraph 1.32).
In Figure 8 this is at quantity Qm. With a demand curve that is downward sloping its marginal revenue curve will also slope downward and lie beneath the

demand curve. The reason is simple. When the monopolist wants to sell an extra unit of output it has to lower the price somewhat. When price discrimination is assumed impossible the monopolist has to lower the price not only for this last unit but for all units it wants to sell. This means that the marginal revenue at a particular output is the new price minus the cumulative price loss it has to take on all other units. In Figure 8 it is further assumed that the ATC and MC curves of the monopolist are horizontal, that is there are no fixed costs and no economies of scale. This assumption simplifies the drawings without changing the principal outcome of the model.

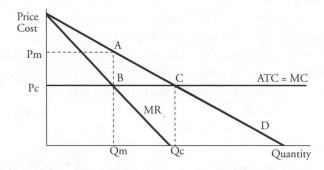

Figure 8: Pure monopoly

(b) The Effects

1.62 Figure 8 immediately shows the main disadvantages of monopoly. The monopolist sells Qm, which is less than the output Qc under competition. As a result the price the consumers have to pay is higher: Pm compared to Pc. This has two main welfare effects. First, there is a loss of welfare as part of the consumer surplus is lost. The area ABC is what is generally called the dead-weight welfare loss of monopoly. Secondly, there is a transfer of income from consumers to monopolist. The monopolist makes a profit of PmABPc. This amount used to be consumer surplus, but with the higher price the consumers have to pay it is turned into profits for the monopolist.

1.63 It can be debated whether the monopolist's profit should be counted as a welfare loss or not. One could argue that society's welfare as a whole does not change, as some gain what many lose. However, for a competition authority the case is quite straightforward. As the goal of competition policy is in general stated in terms of protection of competition to further the interests of the consumer, there can be no doubt that monopoly profits have to be seen as something negative which competition policy should try to avoid.

1.64 The allocative inefficiency is also evidenced by the difference between P and MC. As the price Pm is higher than the marginal costs, welfare could be increased by producing extra units. The consumers are willing to pay more for these units than it would actually cost to produce them.

Another question is whether the monopolist is technically efficient. In the example of Figure 8 the answer is 'yes'. The monopolist is producing at minimum ATC. But there are good reasons to believe a monopolist may not always be so efficient. Not feeling the heat of competition the company may become slow and inefficient. Slack eats away part of the possible monopoly profits. Taking life easy instead of profit maximization may have become important, especially when the owners (shareholders) do not exercise effective control. It was Leibenstein who coined this phenomenon with the term 'X-inefficiency', meaning internal inefficiency in the form of too high salaries, excessive corporate jets, too many employees, etc. That this leads to extra welfare loss is shown in Figure 9. **1.65**

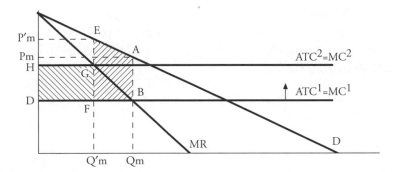

Figure 9: A monopolist with X-inefficiency

The X-inefficiency is reflected in higher ATC and higher MC cost curves. This results in a new equilibrium with the lower quantity Q'm and the higher price P'm. The consumer is paying for the higher costs with a higher price. There is an extra dead-weight welfare loss of EABF. In addition productive factors of the area HGFD are lost to society, as what was previously monopoly profit has now been used to produce inefficiently. **1.66**

A last loss of welfare caused by monopoly could be named 'the price of success'. A monopoly position is very attractive and many resources may be wasted by those that defend it and those that attack it. Those who defend it may try to erect and maintain entry barriers by keeping excess capacity, by excessive product differentiation, by political lobbying, by starting delaying lawsuits, etc. Those who attack the monopoly position have to spend resources to overcome these barriers. In theory all monopoly profits could be wasted in the struggle for the pie. **1.67**

Not everyone will recognize these costs as a welfare loss. When competition is seen as rivalry—a fight for temporary advantages, a struggle to gain market power **1.68** before being overtaken by the next wave of competition—at least part of these costs may be seen as the necessary price to be paid for vigorous competition. However, most competition authorities will, for example, be rather suspicious when finding dominant companies running up costs to maintain excess capacity.

1.69 Monopoly may not only have negative effects but may also lead to certain advantages for consumers. The first and, from a competition policy perspective, most relevant situation is when economies of scale require such a size that only one company in the market can produce at minimal cost. This is what is called a natural monopoly. Producing with more companies would necessarily lead to inefficient production. The dead-weight loss and the price asked by the monopolist may compare favourably with the welfare loss due to higher costs and the price level asked under competition.

1.70 A second possible positive effect has less relevance for competition policy. Some authors argue that the lower output and higher price of monopoly may counterbalance to a certain extent the short-sightedness of consumers. Less consumption of environmentally unfriendly products and less use of limited natural resources might actually increase welfare.

(5) Oligopoly

(a) **Introduction**

1.71 The models of monopoly and perfect competition may be on opposite sides of the market power scale, but they are remarkably similar in their emphasis on market structure and neglect of company behaviour. The only behavioural assumption that is introduced is that companies are profit maximizers. The C of the S-C-P paradigm can be ignored as the models are quite straightforward; the market structure leads *linea recta* to a specific market performance.

1.72 This is not the case for oligopoly, the most important intermediate market form on the market power scale. Oligopoly is the market structure in which there are a few suppliers, at least two while the maximum number of companies is not clearly determined. The main characteristic is that the companies on such a market realize or believe that their individual behaviour concerning output, price, etc influences the market outcome and that therefore each individual company realizes that its own actions may provoke reactions from its competitors. In the fisheries sector a fisherman rightly ignores the influence of his catch on the market price of fish. In the oligopolistic car market a large manufacturer cannot and will not ignore the impact its decisions have on the market and on its competitors and vice versa. This means that the C of the S-C-P scheme becomes important in oligopolistic markets. It also means that competition issues on such markets are rather complicated. Competition policy enforcers faced with such markets are forced to write their books in the evening hours.

Oligopolistic markets are difficult to analyse. The outcome of oligopolistic behaviour can vary to such an extent that one of the more popular statements is that 'with oligopoly anything goes'. The market price may be as low as under perfect competition or as high as under pure monopoly or anywhere between these two. The many economic models of oligopoly reflect well this diversity by being able to provide any outcome, often even within the same model by changing some of the specifications. A good example in question is provided by the oldest oligopoly model; Cournot's model from 1838 of a duopoly. Under the original model it is assumed that each rival decides on its profit maximizing output assuming the other's output will remain unchanged. This leads to a market price below the monopoly level but well above the competitive level. However, it can be shown that by relaxing the assumption that firms expect rivals not to change their output in response to their own output adjustments, the model can result in any price between the monopoly and the competitive level.[20]   **1.73**

This does not mean that competition policy has no task on oligopolistic markets. As many markets are oligopolistic and as anti-competitive outcomes may result these markets should probably be the focus of competition policy. However, given the complexity of these markets and the weak guidance offered by economic models its ambitions should be modest. Oligopoly cases are the clearest example of what was said in the introduction: that competition cases are concerned with writing the most plausible story or explanation of the market outcome. A good part of this story will consist of analysing the factors that either enhance or decrease the possibilities of collusion and choose the model and specifications that best fit the actual market conditions.   **1.74**

In the limited space of this chapter no more then a brief introduction to oligopoly theory can be provided.[21] The literature on oligopoly is vast and sometimes very technical. For a layman it may be disappointing to see that the various models are in general not very helpful to answer concrete policy questions. The models do not answer the question of which market conditions will lead companies in an oligopolistic market to compete fiercely on all important parameters (price, quality, and innovation) and of when competition will be replaced, on one or all parameters, by collusive behaviour. There is no super model that includes all possible relevant factors. Most models concentrate on the effects and interaction of a limited number of factors, sometimes under quite unrealistic conditions.   **1.75**

Collusion and collusive behaviour are used in this chapter as in the economic literature. Economists define collusion in terms of effects; it concerns oligopolistic   **1.76**

---

[20] See Scherer & Ross (n 1 above) 206.
[21] For more extensive introductions, see, for example, Scherer and Ross (n 1 above) or, more technical, A Koutsoyiannis, *Modern Microeconomics* (London: Macmillan, 1979) and J Tirole, *The Theory of Industrial Organisation* (Cambridge: MIT Press, 1988).

behaviour that leads to a price level above the competitive price. It therefore includes not only explicit collusion in the form of agreements or concerted action but also tacit collusion. The latter is what lawyers define as (conscious) parallel behaviour. Collusion is therefore possible without communication between the companies involved. This stands in contrast to legal definitions of collusion, which are usually limited to agreements and concerted practices, stressing the possibility for competition rules to provide a remedy for the situation.

(b) Non-Cooperative Game Theory

1.77 Most advances in oligopoly theory have been made since the Second World War by using game theory, especially non-cooperative game theory.[22] The main idea behind non-cooperative games, as opposed to co-operative games, is that the parties cannot make binding agreements. A non-cooperative game setting thus seems to be the appropriate framework to apply as competition rules make anti-competitive agreements unenforceable in court. Cartel members may make agreements, but these are not binding.

1.78 In non-cooperative game theory, fully rational oligopolistic behaviour requires an assessment of the potential actions of competitors. That is, the oligopolists take account of the interdependence of strategies. An equilibrium will therefore only exist when the decisions of companies lead to a 'self-reinforcing set of strategies in which each strategy is a best response to the other strategies'.[23] Such an equilibrium is called a Nash equilibrium, that is 'a set of actions is in Nash equilibrium, if, given the actions of its rivals, a firm cannot increase its own profit by choosing an action other than its equilibrium action'.[24] In other words, the game finds a stable outcome once every oligopolist sticks to its current strategy, for example concerning the price it sets for its own product, in the light of the strategies chosen by the other oligopolists.

(c) Non-Cooperative Game Setting with Prisoner's Dilemma

1.79 Within the non-cooperative game setting the game that provides most insight into the difficulties and possibilities of collusion is the prisoner's dilemma game. The original example used to explain the game went along the following lines. A murder is committed, and two suspects are arrested. Not having enough evidence, the police need them to confess in order to have a conviction for murder. If one of the prisoners testifies against the other, the first goes free if the other has not testi-

---

[22] Game theory as a formal theoretical analysis started with the book of the mathematician John von Neumann and the economist Oskar Morgenstern, *Theory of Games and Economic Behaviour* (Princeton: Princeton University Press, 1944).

[23] D Yao & S DeSanti, 'Game theory and the legal analysis of tacit collusion' (1993) Spring *The Antitrust Bulletin*, 113–141.

[24] J. Tirole (n 21 above) 206.

fied against him, and the second goes to jail for ten years. If neither testifies, both get a sentence of one year only for illegal possession of firearms. Lastly, if both testify, both go to prison for seven years.

The structure of the game can be presented in the diagram shown in Figure 10, **1.80** commonly referred to as the 'pay-off matrix', where in this case the pay-offs are negative as they represent years in prison.

		Player B		
		N	T	
Player A	N	1,1	10,0	N = not testify
	T	0,10	7,7	T = testify

Figure 10: The prisoner's dilemma game

In this case the pay-off matrix illustrates all the possible outcomes and pay-offs for **1.81** the different players (the first number provides A's jail sentence in years, the second B's sentence). It is clear upon close examination that the best strategy for both players in this case is to testify. If A does not testify it is better for B to testify and vice versa. If A testifies it is also better for B to testify and vice versa. In the jargon of game theory to testify is the dominant strategy. The result is that both go to jail for seven years as the two criminals testify against each other. The collectively optimal outcome of each serving the light sentence only is not attained as the criminals cannot make a binding agreement.

This analysis can easily be extended to the study of oligopolistic behaviour of **1.82** companies. Although oligopolists are normally not confined to choose between two prices, two quantities etc, it can be assumed that the basic choice to make is between competing or colluding. Instead of the decisions being 'not testify' and 'testify' they could be labelled 'co-operate' or 'defect' concerning collusive behaviour on the market. The pay-off matrix would then have the structure represented in Figure 11. The first figure provides company A's profit, the second company B's profit.

		Company B		
		C	D	
Company A	C	3,3	1,4	C = co-operate
	D	4,1	2,2	D = defect

Figure 11: The prisoner's dilemma applied to a duopoly

1.83 In the situation of Figure 11 the dominant strategy for both companies is to defect, in other words to compete. When the other company on the market will restrict output and thereby ensure a high market price it is advantageous not to co-operate. Similarly, when the other company will not restrict output it is against one's own interest to co-operate. As a result, the two companies will not co-operate and will forgo the collective optimal outcome and end up with the equilibrium with the lower collective profit. The latter is the Nash equilibrium of the prisoner's dilemma game.

(d) A Non-Cooperative Game Setting and Collusion: Some Arguments

1.84 If all oligopolistic markets would follow the simple rules of the prisoner's dilemma game just described there would not be many competition problems. Even Cournot's duopolists would compete each other down to the competitive price level.[25] The prisoner's dilemma shows the basic instability present in many situations of collusion. The collusive outcome creates the possibility to free ride or cheat on the co-operative behaviour of the others, as witnessed in practice by the breaking down and erosion of many cartel agreements.

1.85 However, competition policy practice and simulation experiments show that a collusive outcome is attainable. In practice, to co-operate does seem the dominant or chosen strategy in a not insignificant number of cases. This is explained by a number of factors.

1.86 First, the equilibrium outcome of the prisoner's dilemma game described above depends on the structure of the pay-off matrix. With a limited number of firms in the market, the game may be such that it is no longer a prisoner's dilemma type of game. An example of this is given by the pay-off matrix represented in Figure 12.

		Player B C	Player B D	
Player A	C	4,4	3,2	C = co-operate
	D	2,3	1,1	D = defect

Figure 12: A non-cooperative game with co-operation as the dominant strategy

1.87 By reducing its price each player loses more in profits on its current sales than it could gain in profits from newly attracted sales. In this setting, co-operation is the dominant strategy for both players and the collusive outcome ensues. Free riding

---

[25] Bertrand already in 1883 showed that if, instead of Cournot's assumption that the duopolists decide on their output, it is assumed that each duopolist sets its price assuming the other's price will remain unchanged, the competitive price will result. See Koutsoyiannis (n 21 above).

is not an attractive option. It is good to note that the oligopolists may actually take steps to worsen their possible gain from cheating, to make the pay-off structure change from a prisoner's dilemma to a setting where collusion is the dominant strategy. For example, the adoption by the oligopolists of a so-called most favoured customer plan, guaranteeing customers any possible discount the company will give within, for example, the next one year. Such a plan seriously undermines an oligopolist's gain from cheating, as the lower price offered to lure new customers away from its competitors will have to be awarded to all its customers of the past year.

1.88 A second factor that makes a collusive outcome more likely is that oligopolists usually do meet each other many times in the market place; the game is not played once but more than once. Intuitively this means that although the prisoner's dilemma pay-off structure may indicate it is rational to cheat if one only looks at one round, such cheating may spoil future profits that could possibly be attained by collusion. Past behaviour and possible future profits become important when formulating a strategy. In game theory one usually distinguishes between games that are infinite versus games that are played a finite number of times.

1.89 In a prisoner's dilemma setting that is played an infinite number of rounds the players might come to a collusive outcome. Such an infinitely repeated single-period game is called a supergame. Whether a collusive outcome results depends on the balance for each player of the gains from cheating in the first period against the loss of a part of the monopoly profit for every period or at least a number of periods thereafter. The incentive to cheat or free ride will be weighed by each player against the possible punishment the other players may inflict on him in the future. The punishment will in turn depend on the possibilities and rationality of punishing possible defectors. The players may try to reduce for all players the attractiveness of free riding by limiting the time or scope of possible free riding and/or increasing the possibilities of punishment.[26] The exchange of sensitive market information may be used by the players to help to detect free riding.

1.90 Also when the game is played a limited and not an infinite number of times a collusive outcome may result in a non-cooperative setting with a prisoner's dilemma pay-off matrix. Theoretically collusion becomes, however, more difficult. This is explained by backward induction. In a one-period prisoner's dilemma type non-cooperative game the best strategy for each player is, as explained before, not to co-operate. This means that in a multi-period game it is rational for both players not to co-operate in the last period. Given the certainty that both will not

---

[26] The punishment strategy that is chosen by the players influences the pay-off that results after the cheating has been found out. As the question of the best punishment strategy seems still unresolved this is not discussed further here.

co-operate in the last period it is also not rational to co-operate in the penultimate period, as there can be no reward in terms of co-operation in the last period etc.

1.91 However, as soon as the players do not have full information but instead have imperfect information and have to make up their minds about their best strategy in uncertainty—the common situation in real markets—collusion again becomes a possible outcome. Players may not know the number of times the game will be played, may have to guess about the costs and possibilities of the others to punish, may assign probabilities to the possible strategies of the others, etc. This may make it rational to co-operate, at least until someone starts to compete.

1.92 Different strategies can be imagined in repeated games. A most successful strategy in simulation that is also very simple is the so-called tit-for-tat strategy: co-operate on the first round and thereafter do whatever the other player did in the previous round. It has the advantage of starting with a co-operative strategy in the first round to try to reap the gains of collusion. In addition, it provides a quick reaction by hitting back when cheating is detected. After such punishment it offers the other the possibility to restore the collusive equilibrium.

1.93 A third factor that makes a collusive outcome more likely is that companies, also in a setting of a non-cooperative game like the prisoner's dilemma, may behave more as if they are in a co-operative game setting. Companies in general do not behave as nakedly rational as non-cooperative game theory usually assumes. Social constraints, moral codes of conduct, etc do influence behaviour. Business ethics may 'command' that oral non-binding agreements are kept; 'a man a man, a word a word'. This does not necessarily mean that players act irrationally, it may mean that their perspective becomes less 'self regarding' and more 'other regarding'.[27]

1.94 This also means that communication on future prices and output, sometimes described as 'cheap talk' as it does not change the pay-off matrix, may not be all 'cheap talk'. Whether companies do or do not come together in smoke filled back rooms to hammer out agreements detailing how much each will produce and what price will be charged may be quite vital as companies may become rather nervous about their co-operative attitude when there is not enough communication. Communication may be essential to 'prevent' companies from starting to behave as rationally as the underlying non-cooperative game assumes.

---

[27] One could be 'other regarding' and have as moral principle that one does not want to be the first who cheats. When applied rationally this leads to collusion. Also, sometimes certain deliberations do not enter the pay-off matrix; from a manager's point of view it may be very rational when he does not want to isolate himself on the green on Saturday by being the one who 'ruins' the market. See, for further details, H Pellikaan, *Anarchie, Staat en het Prisoner's Dilemma* (Delft: Eburon, 1996) ch 8.

From experiments with the prisoner's dilemma it is known that the narrow 'self-regarding' perspective is in general not realistic. Already the experiments of Flood and Dresher in the early fifties show this. In a 100-round prisoner's dilemma game they show that even highly qualified players let their choice, while non-collusion is the dominant strategy, be influenced by emotional considerations and feelings of revenge and that the players act in a surprisingly co-operative manner; in 60 rounds both co-operated at the same time while only in 14 rounds both defected at the same time.[28]   **1.95**

(e) A Non-Cooperative Game Setting and Collusion: Some Results

Real oligopoly situations are more complicated than the stylized games described above. In an oligopoly there are usually more than two players, and each company has the choice not just between competing or defecting but has to decide on a number of parameters that are important for competition; not just price or output, but also promotion activity, product differentiation, product and process innovation. On each of these parameters there are not just two options and two pay-offs but usually a range of options and pay-offs. It is therefore not surprising that there is no super oligopoly model that by incorporating all the parameters and strategies provides clear-cut solutions to the oligopoly game. However, game theory helps to understand the inherent tension between competition and collusion within oligopolistic markets.   **1.96**

It helps to understand why collusion becomes in general more difficult when the following factors increase: the number of firms in the market, product heterogeneity, inequality between companies concerning demand and costs, uncertainty about demand and costs, rate of technological development, and threat of entry. These factors are treated more in-depth in section F(5). Collusion becomes more difficult for three reasons. Firstly, each company's market share diminishes and therewith the interest to stay within a collusive arrangement. Secondly, differences between the companies and their products result in increased divergence of interests between them. Thirdly, more information is required in order to monitor each other's behaviour. In other words the incentives for free riding increase while the possibilities to detect and punish free riding diminish.   **1.97**

Game theory also puts in a clearer perspective the role played by so-called facilitating devices. Various of such practices that facilitate co-operation are described in the literature. Rees, for example, mentions the following facilitating devices: information exchange, trade associations, price leadership, collaborative research and cross-licensing of patents, most-favoured-customer (mfc) and meeting-competition (mc) clauses in sales contracts, resale price maintenance, basing point   **1.98**

---

[28] See W Poundstone, *Prisoner's Dilemma* (New York: Doubleday, 1992) 106–116.

pricing, common costing books.[29] What all these devices have in common is the exchange of information as the central element. This is obvious for the direct exchange of information between competitors or the exchange through an intermediary like a trade organization (collection and dissemination of data, forecasting studies, common costing books, etc). But it is also the case when the exchange runs via the customers (price leadership, mfc and mc clauses, resale price maintenance, basing point pricing). These devices may all be used to limit the influence of factors that destabilize co-operative outcomes or strengthen the factors that support co-operative outcomes. This is done by limiting the gains of free riding, by monitoring each other's behaviour thus making detection of free riding easier, by making the infliction of punishment better targeted, or by making it easier for firms to reach a consensus by reducing the effects of factors such as product heterogeneity, uncertainty about future cost, demand, or capacity, and technological change.

1.99 Although a well predicting encompassing oligopoly model does not yet exist, what can be concluded? The factor that is often taken as a starting point for competition policy analysis is the number of firms and their market shares and the resulting market concentration. The following seems a fair, though crude, summary based on theory and practice:

1.100 —A monopolist, assuming entry is not possible, will unlikely deviate much from the monopoly price. If entry is only partly blocked, limit pricing may become its strategy. Competition policy can sometimes prevent a monopoly from being created through merger control but once monopoly does exist competition policy has limited means to take effective action. Unless the authority can order the monopolist to break up or lower entry barriers it is confined to behavioural remedies and regulation.

1.101 —With a limited number of firms in the market the game theoretical situation may be one of a non-cooperative game without prisoner's dilemma. As explained above, in such a case co-operation is the dominant strategy for each company. In this situation of collective dominance the collusive outcome will normally result. As in the case of monopoly, competition policy is best advised to try to prevent such situations from arising as it has limited means to take effective action to redress such a situation.

1.102 It is not clear at which number such a situation may arise. As explained in section F whether it arises at any number depends on factors such as cost similarity, product homogeneity, etc. The 1992 Horizontal Merger Guidelines issued by the US Department of Justice and Federal Trade Commission presume that a merger is 'likely to create or enhance market power or facilitate its exercise' when the Herfindahl Hirschman Index (HHI) is above 1800 and the HHI increase result-

---

[29] R Rees, 'Tacit Collusion' (1993) 9 *Oxford Review of Economic Policy*, 27, 35–37.

ing from the merger exceeds 100.[30] The HHI threshold of 1800 implies there are roughly five or six equally large firms in a market. However, this does not mean that, in the US, mergers in such situations are systematically forbidden, as other factors like entry barriers, countervailing power, efficiencies, etc also play a role in the assessment. Likewise EC competition policy practice has been more cautious by attacking collective dominance mainly in cases where there are two or at maximum three main companies on the market.[31] The economic literature does not provide specific thresholds.[32]

—Once the number of firms or the other factors relevant for collusion increases **1.103** the situation changes into a non-cooperative game with the prisoner's dilemma characteristics. This means that each company has the incentive to free ride. Whether a collusive outcome will result depends on the trade-off between this incentive and the chance to be found out and the resulting punishment. The likelihood of reaching a collusive outcome lowers as the number of firms increases. It is likely to become rather small above a certain number, possibly when there are more than ten or twelve main firms on the market.[33]

In these oligopolistic markets competition authorities are to concentrate on the **1.104** detection of explicit collusion and in addition on the detection and analysis of facilitating practices. Investigation of facilitating devices offers the possibility to scrutinize conscious parallelism as closely as possible and take remedial action where possible. In terms of the US antitrust practice it means (de)fining the 'plus' in 'conscious parallelism plus something else' that together restrict competition.

---

[30] The HHI is a measure of concentration defined as the sum of the squared market shares of all the firms in the market.

[31] See the following merger cases: *Nestlé/Perrier* (Case IV/M190) [1992] OJ L356/1; *Kali & Salz* (Case IV/M308) [1994] OJ L186/38 and [1998] OJ C275/3; *Gencor/Lonhro* (Case IV/M619) [1997] OJ L11/30.

[32] A specific number is mentioned by Selten in an article of 1973 and Phlips in more recent work which builds upon the ideas of Selten. See: R Selten, 'A simple model of imperfect competition where four are few and six are many' (1973) 2 *International Journal of Game Theory* 141–201; L Phlips, *Competition Policy: a Game-Theoretic Perspective* (Cambridge: Cambridge University Press, 1995) and L Phlips, 'On the detection of collusion and predation' (1996) 40 *European Economic Review* 495–510. Their conclusion is that '4 are few and 6 are many', that is when there are four firms or less in a market the likelihood of collusion will be 1 while this likelihood drops to close to 0 when the number of firms becomes six or more. However, their conclusion is only valid with the restrictive assumptions underlying their model. The model of Selten, which is also the basis of Phlips's work, excludes the possibility of cheating. Each company decides beforehand whether it will co-operate or not. Once it has decided to co-operate it sticks to its promise. This therefore resembles the situation of a co-operative game with enforceable agreements. The model shows that such binding agreements will be formed with a likelihood of 1 as long as the number of firms does not exceed four.

[33] Scherer and Ross (n 1 above) 277 state: 'As a very crude general rule, if evenly matched firms supply homogeneous products in a well-defined market, they are likely to begin ignoring their influence on price when their number exceeds ten or twelve.' This does not exclude that, on oligopolistic markets with less than 10 or 12 main companies, also fringe companies and companies supplying niche markets can be active which do not exert an important competitive pressure.

(f) The Commission's Practice

1.105 Many of the negative decisions on cartels taken under Article 81 seem to corroborate the above analysis. Although it is not always easy to establish the number of competitors on the relevant market(s) in past decisions as it was not always considered necessary to carefully define the market(s) in cases of clear-cut price fixing and market sharing cartels, the number of main competitors seems in general to have been below twelve.[34] Exceptions to this rule are mainly found in decisions involving trade associations,[35] liner conferences,[36] or previously regulated industries such as the steel industry,[37] where for different reasons effective cartels were able to operate with a higher number of main players.

1.106 The Commission has also sometimes shown an understanding of the game theoretic background of its cases. For example, in the *Fatty Acids* case and the *UK Tractors* case, two cases where exchange of information as a facilitating device for parallel behaviour was the sole competition infringement, important elements of the above analysis can be found.[38]

The Fatty Acids *Case*

1.107 This was the first case where the Commission decided Article 81 was infringed while it could only prove that the companies involved were exchanging information.

1.108 The case concerned the oleochemicals oleine and stearine, the principal fatty acids produced by splitting natural oils and fats into raw fatty acids and glycerol. The decision describes the oleochemical industry as comprising about forty companies with three big integrated firms, Unichema, Henkel, and Oleofina. The large integrated companies do not only produce fatty acids for third parties but also have an important captive use. Unichema, with a share of the market for sales to third parties in Western Europe of over 30 per cent, is described as the market leader. Henkel and Oleofina had some 16 per cent and 14 per cent respectively.[39]

---

[34] See the following cases: *Polypropylene* [1986] OJ L230/1; *Meldoc* [1986] OJ L348/50; *Belasco* [1986] OJ L232; *Fatty Acids* [1987] OJ L3/17; *Italian flat glass* [1989] OJ L33; *Soda ash—Solvay* [1991] OJ L152/21; *UK Tractors* [1992] OJ L68/19; *Cement* [1994] OJ L343/1; *Carton Board* [1994] OJ L243/1.

[35] See the following cases: *SPO* [1992] OJ L92; *CNSD* [1993] OJ L203/27; *SCK/FNK* [1995] OJ L312/79.

[36] See the following cases: *TAA* [1994] OJ L376; *Far Eastern Freight Conference* [1994] OJ L378/17.

[37] See the following cases: *Welded Steel Mesh* [1989] OJ L260/1; *Steel Beams* [1994] OJ L116/1.

[38] See n 34. For a more extensive treatment of information exchange agreements, see L Peeperkorn, 'Competition Policy Implications from Game Theory: an Evaluation of the Commission's Policy on Information Exchange', CEPR/European University Institute Workshop, Florence, November 1996.

[39] It is left open in the decision whether the relevant product market concerns fatty acids or whether separate markets exist for stearine (market share of the three of around 60%) and oleine (market share of the three of around 80%).

According to industry sources, the European market was suffering from structural overcapacity and low or stagnant growth rates.

The three companies orally agreed in 1979 firstly to establish their respective total annual sales to third parties over the preceding three-year period and secondly to exchange as from 1980 onwards the same information on a quarterly basis. After the Commission had pointed out to the companies that the information exchange might constitute an infringement of Article 81 the companies terminated the agreement with effect from 1 January 1983.   **1.109**

The motivation of the companies, as described in the decision, is quite revealing: **1.110**

> In 1979 Unilever was planning the acquisition of Emery's 50% shareholding in Unilever-Emery and the integration of its operations with the wholly owned Unichema subsidiary. The merger would inevitably involve rationalisation and the reduction of fatty acid capacity. According to Unichema, there was a possibility of its competitors 'misinterpreting' its merger plans as a first indication of an intention to withdraw from the fatty acid sector, 'thus setting off even more competition and loss of market share for Unichema'.

> The Unichema representative, who proposed the agreement to his colleagues, has explained to the Commission that the object—also indicated to the other parties— was to enable the participants to monitor possible major changes in their relative positions as a result of any unilateral capacity reduction by Unichema which would follow the acquisition of Unilever-Emery by Unichema.

> Unichema has stated that, owing to the fragmented nature of the market and conditions of intense competition, it considered that the major producers had a duty to 'sanitize' the market. The solution to the problems of the industry, as perceived by Unichema's senior management, was 'orderly marketing'.

> Unichema's conception of its own responsibilities in this direction involved the need to adopt marketing policies which did not provoke its major competitors into blaming it for being 'destructive'. As the leading producer of a commodity product, Unichema considered it was entitled to maintain its traditional market share and, if competitors were to attempt to take from it established business by means of aggressive price cutting, it would consider such conduct as 'stealing'. If it were to lose business as a result of price cutting it would have to recoup that business in another market and so bring about a general price instability which it believed would be destructive to the interests of the trade as a whole.

> Unichema also considered that the major producers should bear the responsibility for capacity reductions. For its part, it had expressed a readiness to purchase the goodwill of smaller competitors and thereby facilitate the closure of uneconomic units. This opinion was shared by the other large producers.

The described motivation contains many elements of a non-cooperative game like the prisoner's dilemma. Companies are afraid to be misunderstood by their competitors, afraid to provoke price cutting which again would make retaliation necessary, when business is stolen recouping it elsewhere would be detrimental to the   **1.111**

35

current equilibrium, output needs to be controlled, monitoring of respective market positions is essential to allow orderly marketing.

1.112 The Commission made use of the provided motivation but took an opposing view on the competition distorting effect of the agreement:

> The agreement between Unichema, Henkel and Oleofina to exchange historic individual sales figures for the years 1976–1978 enabled the parties to determine their traditional respective position on a given market. The subsequent regular exchange of information gave each of the parties the opportunity of identifying the individual businesses of his two major competitors and thus to measure on a quarterly basis their future performance on that market.

> Despite the alleged general nature of the information exchanged it did improve their knowledge of market conditions in a way which strengthened the connection between them so that they would be able to react more rapidly and efficiently to one another's actions.

> In view of the market stabilisation which the parties undoubtedly wanted to achieve, this inevitably lessened the intensity of competition that would otherwise have existed between them.

> Although there is no evidence to suggest that, in this particular case, the parties to the exchange of information agreement did fix quotas directly, the Commission nevertheless considers that the object of the agreement bears a strong resemblance to that of an outright quota-fixing agreement since it clearly aimed at dissuading the parties from adopting aggressively competitive behaviour towards each other and also at achieving stabilisation of their relative positions on the market.

1.113 Also the Commission's assessment contains elements from non-cooperative game theory, especially that the monitoring of each other's behaviour allows the companies to react more rapidly. However, a number of elements indicate that the Commission did not base itself on or was not aware of the apparent underlying non-cooperative prisoner's dilemma game setting of the case. The decision does not make clear that the main effect of up-to-date monitoring is that punishment becomes more effective while the incentive to free ride is reduced.

The UK Tractors *Case*

1.114 This second case centres on the exchange of information identifying the volume of retail sales and market shares between the eight main producers and importers of agricultural tractors in the UK. The Commission started its investigation in 1984 and discovered the exchange in the course of inspections at the offices of some of the companies and the Agricultural Engineers Association Ltd (AEA), the UK trade association of manufacturers and importers of agricultural machinery. The information exchange had existed at least since 1975. In 1992 the Commission took a prohibition decision which was upheld by the Court of First Instance and the Court of Justice.

For the assessment of the information exchange agreement the Commission took **1.115**
account of:

— The market structure, ie:

— high concentration: the eight companies (Ford New Holland, Massey-
Ferguson, Case, John Deere, Renault, Watveare, Fiat and Same-
Lamborghini) that participated in the agreement held 88 per cent of the UK
tractor market. The first four companies mentioned shared 77 per cent of the
market and this increased to 80 per cent after Ford New Holland was taken
over by Fiat. The remaining 12 per cent was taken by several small manufacturers. This high concentration was further enhanced by the fact that not all
small suppliers were active in all regions and/or all horsepower categories;
— high barriers to entry: the need for an extensive distribution and service
network, a stagnant/declining market, the importance of brand loyalty, and
the effects of the information exchange;
— the absence of significant imports in the UK by third parties.

— The nature of the information exchanged: exact quantities of retail sales and
market shares of the participants with detailed breakdowns by model, product group, region (including dealer territories), and by yearly, quarterly,
monthly, and daily time periods. In addition to this information the AEA also
provided to each manufacturer information on sales by its own dealers. This
allowed monitoring of the own dealers' 'import and export' into each other's
territories within the UK and parallel import into the UK.
— The fact that the members met regularly within the AEA, giving a forum for
contacts.

Based on the above, the Commission concluded that for two reasons the informa- **1.116**
tion exchange led to a restriction of competition. First, the exchange prevented
hidden competition in a highly concentrated market. Secondly, it increased the
barriers to entry for non-members. The following quotations are instructive:

> The exchange restricts competition because it creates a degree of market trans-
> parency between the suppliers in a highly concentrated market which is likely to
> destroy what hidden competition there remains between the suppliers in that mar-
> ket on account of the risk and ease of exposure of independent competitive action.
> In this highly concentrated market, 'hidden competition' is essentially that element
> of uncertainty and secrecy between the main suppliers regarding market conditions
> without which none of them has the necessary scope of action to compete efficiently
> . . . This reasoning, however, in no way undermines the positive competitive bene-
> fits of transparency in a competitive market characterized by many buyers and sell-
> ers. Where there is a low degree of concentration, market transparency can increase
> competition in so far as consumers benefit from choices made in full knowledge of
> what is on offer. It is emphasized that the United Kingdom tractor market is neither
> a low concentration market nor is the transparency in question in any way directed
> towards, or of benefit to, consumers.

... the high market transparency between the suppliers on the United Kingdom tractor market which is created by the Exchange takes the surprise effect out of a competitor's action thus resulting in a shorter space of time for reactions with the effect that temporary advantages are greatly reduced ... This effect of neutralizing and thus stabilizing the market positions of the oligopolists is in this case likely to occur because there are no external competitive pressures on the members of the Exchange except parallel imports which are however also monitored.

It allows them ... to see at once whether there has been any increase in the retail sales of a rival, to see the territory in which such an increase takes place, to detect the models which contribute such an increase and finally to follow whether and to what extent any price or other marketing strategies of rivals are successful, ... to limit price competition as far as possible by allowing suppliers and dealers to react to any price-cutting or other market strategies selectively by limiting their response to the absolute minimum degree necessary in terms of product and territory and by being sure to hit the right target.

In the absence of the Exchange, firms would have to compete in a market with some measure of uncertainty as to the exact place, degree and means of attack by rivals. This uncertainty is a normal competitive risk bringing about stronger competition because reaction and reduction of prices cannot be limited to the absolute minimum degree necessary to defend an established position. Uncertainty would lead the firms to compete more strongly than if they knew exactly how much of a response was necessary to meet competition. They would have to exceed a minimum response, for instance by offering more favourable discounts to move their stock or by offering discounts for more products and in more territories.

1.117 In this decision the Commission more profoundly understood the apparent non-cooperative prisoner's dilemma game setting of the case. The emphasis on the context of a concentrated market, hidden competition and uncertainty about competitors' actions, a shortened reaction lag, eliminating the advantage of a company that tries to undercut, making targeted punishment possible, the possible effect that a reduction of intra-brand competition may have on inter-brand competition, etc all fit very well in such a game theoretical explanation.

D. Dynamic Welfare Analysis of Market Power

(1) The Time Dimension

1.118 In the static welfare analysis of market power, it follows from the discussion in section C above that a consumer surplus loss will occur where the consumers willing to pay the marginal cost are not supplied. Indeed this normally occurs when there is an unregulated monopoly that raises price above marginal cost of supply. A measure of the static inefficiency that results is analysed in terms of actual cost of production in comparison with the minimum production cost (productive inefficiency) and in terms of price set above marginal cost of supply (allocative ineffi-ciency).[40]

In this static analysis there is a clear total welfare loss associated with the exercise of market power. The static analysis, however, has no time dimension because it is looking at an equilibrium situation. It is unable to explain or incorporate techno-logical development or product and process innovation: it is concerned solely with the allocation of resources in the context of fixed technology and a given cost situation. However, in the real world product markets evolve over time because of new technological discoveries and the introduction of new and improved prod-ucts. Such innovation generates welfare gains due to dynamic efficiencies, and hence the question naturally arises whether the market structure affects the rate of innovation over the long run, since if it does then a proper welfare analysis of mar-ket power needs to take into account both the static and dynamic efficiencies—and any trade-off between them.   **1.119**

The introduction of quality improvements and of new products generates welfare gains because new wants are satisfied and many consumers may have reservation prices for the new product that exceed the price actually charged. The producer will expect to make profits to cover the initial losses, investment outlay, and any risk premium. Dynamic efficiency is analysed in terms of how total surplus, con-sumer plus producer, evolves over time with the introduction of product and process innovation.   **1.120**

A new product satisfies a demand that was not catered for before. If it were sup-plied at its short run marginal production cost then none of the suppliers would recover their original research and development investment and the anticipation of this by suppliers would mean that there would be no incentive to incur the investment and develop the new product. Even in a competitive market situation, we only expect a firm to invest in a project if the net present value of future returns match the investment outlay and initial losses. It should also be obvious that the competitive firm's assessment will include the need for at least a normal rate of profit as an equilibrium condition. Suppliers are indifferent between investing and not, if they subsequently earn profits to exactly recover their outlay as well as the normal return on the investment. Product innovation will only occur if firms earn more than just enough to offset their investment. They will only actually invest if they anticipate making profits in excess. Such profits, however, mean pricing above short run minimal average total costs either because there are barri-ers to entry or because the innovating firm has market power. As we have seen   **1.121**

---

[40] It is necessary to bear in mind some qualifications on the concepts of productive and allocative efficiency. Where economies of scale and MES are much larger than market demand, then clearly productive inefficiency will persist until demand grows; similarly when cost is falling over the rele-vant industry output range, pricing at marginal cost, ie allocative efficiency, can only be attained if overall losses of production are recovered from general taxation.

above, pricing above minimal average total costs is associated with static welfare losses. In addition, it would not be optimal if firms were to earn considerably more profit than would be necessary to induce them to develop the new product. The market, when it is functioning well, solves this difficult balance by accommodating the creation of temporary positions of market dominance, the resulting super profits attracting all manner and types of enterpreneurial factor which bids away the excessive profit such that in equilibrium the marginal investment will be just offset by the present value of future normal profit.

(2) Market Structure and Innovation

1.122 The argument that market power is much more important than competition in providing the circumstances under which innovation occurs was propounded long ago by JA Schumpeter. In his view, in competitive market situations without important barriers to entry there will be little incentive to make innovations, since both the profits of innovating and the losses from not innovating ahead of other firms will be very short-lived. If, however, there are major barriers to entry then there will also be firms with market power who will have the resources and the incentives to make major innovations that will generate large short run profits. Such profits then act as a beacon in turn for entry from many firms producing other products or with totally new technology, in order to whittle away the large profits through what was termed a 'process of creative destruction'. In this view the misallocation of resources consequent upon market power is contrasted with the benefits to growth and living standards associated with innovations, thereby coming to the conclusion that short-term resource misallocation is much the smaller welfare loss. While to an important extent the acceptance of the entry barrier presented by absolute patent protection recognizes the need to temporarily protect the innovator from profit-dissipating competition, can one conclude in general that dynamic efficiencies override static welfare losses?

1.123 A number of crucial elements in the Schumpeterian analysis have been investigated to test whether firm size, industry concentration, and market power systematically account for the greater part of innovation across industrial sectors. In a study based on a direct measure of innovation, analysing reports in specialized technical literature covering the entire manufacturing sector, Acs and Andretsch[41] report that the average small-firm innovation rate was higher than the large-firm innovation rate, although the study did not distinguish between major and minor innovations (ie between innovations that permit a very large cost reduction through the replacement of existing technology and those that improve only incrementally the industry's production economics). A sectoral analysis by the same study also revealed that industries that are concentrated, capital intensive,

---

[41] Zoltan J Acs and David B Andretsch, 'Innovation, Market Structure and Firm Size' (1987) LXIX Review of *Economics and Statistics*.

and characterized by product differentiation tend to promote large-firm innovation while small firms' innovative advantage was primarily in the early stages of the product cycle. The nexus between market structure and firm size, on the one hand, and the rate of innovative activity, on the other, is thus persistent, but not for all industries. Furthermore, the evidence shows that 'the extent to which the market is characterised by imperfect competition accounts for at least some of this disparate innovation activity between large and small firms'. So innovation rates themselves have a significant effect on firm size and market structure, which in turn may affect innovation rates.

Another element of the Schumpeterian thesis is that imitation is not only possible but also rapid, thus limiting the market dominating position of any innovator. That imitation is a common feature seems to be a theory borne out by empirical research: Mansfield et al[42] reported that 60 per cent of successful innovations in their sample were imitated within four years. Levin et al[43] found similar evidence in their survey of R & D managers, even in relation to major patented innovations. Furthermore, there was evidence in these studies to suggest, that on average, imitators' costs were between 65–75 per cent of those incurred by the original innovator. It would also appear that licensing of patented and non-patented technological know-how is highly common in industries subject to rapid technological progress.[44] Much of this licensing is between competitors, reflecting the fact that the obvious clients for a cost saving innovation are the competitors of the innovator in the same industry. **1.124**

Analysing the range of empirical evidence available on the process of innovation leads Katz and Shapiro[45] to the following summary of their theory and conclusions: markets do not encourage non-appropriable research, most of which is undertaken by governments, universities and other non-profit institutions and made available as a public good. The 'D' in R & D is, on the contrary, often privately appropriable, given a system of protection of property rights, and hence development tends to be rapidly pursued. In general the industry's established major firms, which are the most successful at using the existing technologies, will also be the developers of new technology. However, this general rule changes in the presence of imitation and licensing. The dominant firm will tend to make all the minor innovations with or without imitation and licensing, but will have incentives to develop major innovations if and only if imitation is difficult. This **1.125**

---

[42] Edwin Mansfield, Mark Schwartz and Samuel Wagner, 'Imitation Costs and Patents: An Empirical Study' (1981) December *Economic Journal*; E Mansfield et al, *The Production and Application of New Industrial Technology* (1977).

[43] Richard Levin et al, *Survey Research in R & D appropriability* (Yale University 1986).

[44] R Wilson, 'International Licensing of Technology: Empirical Evidence' (1977) April *Research Policy*.

[45] Michael L Katz and Carl Shapiro, 'R & D Rivalry with Licensing or Imitation' (1987) June *American Economic Review*.

obviously follows, since the benefits of being the first to innovate are not entirely appropriable for a long enough period. Where imitation is easy or patent protection imperfect, smaller incumbents and entrants will tend to make the major innovations and the dominant firm will find it profitable to follow through imitation. As a result, rather than a simple link between market structure and firm size on the one hand and with the rate of innovative activity on the other, the economic reality would seem to support a more complex relationship. Whether a dominant firm or a currently small firm will develop an innovation depends on whether the innovation is minor or major and the extent to which it can be imitated. In addition, both the dominant firm and its smaller competitor have the incentive to develop innovations that will also significantly benefit the other firm's cost structure provided that competitor licensing is permitted by antitrust authorities and the licensing income is sufficiently high to permit the licensor to face a more efficient rival.

(3) Conclusion

1.126 Once intertemporal efficiency is introduced into the analysis, it is evident that the presumption that market power leads to a loss of allocative efficiency and to a loss in consumer welfare is crucially predicated on the assumptions that the costs of the firms concerned do not fall due to production rationalization or that product innovation does not occur. As we have noted, there is much empirical literature to suggest that these assumptions are not entirely realistic. However, the same literature also shows that while market structure may indeed have an important bearing on some innovative activity, not all socially beneficial innovation activity will be undertaken. Market power may also encourage exclusionary practices[46] in conditions where, absent market power, licensing and hence technology dissemination would be more vigorous. Finally, some of the parameters influencing licensing and imitation are affected by public policy, in particular antitrust policy,[47] which also needs to be applied in a way that avoids perverse consequences for the rate of innovative development.

1.127 The conclusion that can be drawn would seem to be the following: market power may speed productivity and growth and reduce the costs of the growth process despite a tendency to a less than optimal allocation of resources in static equilibrium.[48] Certain firms, those adept at tracking new technology, tend to prosper and grow at the expense of others; growth confers further advantages, while decline compounds the difficulties. Over time, then, there would be a tendency for con-

---

[46] John A Weinberg, 'Exclusionary Practices and Technological Competition' (1992) June *Journal of Industrial Economics*.

[47] See Katz and Shapiro (n 45 above).

[48] Partha Dasgupta and Joseph Stiglitz, 'Uncertainty, Industrial Structure and the Speed of R & D' (1980) *Bell Journal of Economics*, and WJ Baumol, 'Horizontal Collusion and Innovation' (1992) *Economic Journal*.

centration even in an industry initially composed of equal-sized firms. The protection of intellectual property rights or sunk costs may give innovators some temporary market power and rewards for innovation, but skilful and agressive imitators tend to drive prices to costs unless the innovator can successfully retain a first mover status for several subsequent technological advances. Thus, in general, it is not evident that a concentrated market structure as such tends necessarily to stimulate innovation or that it plays a role at all stages of the product cycle. But the welfare analysis of market power has to pay careful heed to the complex relationships concerning dynamic efficiencies; as regards the link, if any, between market structure and innovation, it is sensible to bear in mind that the socially efficient way to identify and select the most promising R & D avenues has a greater chance to surface under a competitive regime and to be expressed in a diversified portfolio of R & D projects.[49]

E. Market Definition

(1) Market Power and the Need to Define the Market

In any discussion of competition restriction, market abuse, or of market domination the obvious question is whether a useful analysis can be made without actually defining the market in a precise way. A little reflection makes it clear that as the focus of any competitive analysis is on market power, it is crucial to define the relevant market. One way of seeing this is to consider the clause-by-clause analysis of an agreement between independent economic agents. Such an analysis may provide a valuable indication of the restrictive agreements being undertaken or contemplated by the parties. However, the effects of the clauses at issue can only be expected to have a significant impact, on any relevant market and hence on market variables such as price or output, if the agents concerned possess some market power. Thus an initial conclusion must be that in order to identify the existence of market power it is necessary to proceed to a definition of the market.

1.128

One obvious factor underlying this conclusion is that the very useful concept of market power, like many other useful concepts such as dominance, demand substitutability etc in the economics of competition, is not an observable entity. Some empirical counterpart for market power is therefore essential to make the concept usable in practice. It is this which explains why, even in situations where the anticompetitive object of any behaviour is clear and does not require any market definition, it may nevertheless be necessary to proceed to a definition of the market

1.129

---

[49] RR Nelson and SG Winter, *An Evolutionary Theory of Economic Change* (1982). The authors also conclude that for this to be attained the basic research part of R & D is better financed by public authorities.

in order to get a measure of the market power involved and to evaluate the impact of the situation.

1.130 Economics suggests a number of different indicators for market power. One such is the Lerner index,[50] which is defined as the firm's margin in relation to the current price set by the firm. The firm's margin is a microeconomic datum, and while in principle ascertainable, it is usually not known. Use of this measure is therefore rarely practicable. If instead the elasticity of demand facing the firm is known with some precision, then this information would enable us to say something about the firm's margin, since at its profit-maximizing equilibrium a firm's margin will equate to the reciprocal of the elasticity of demand facing it. Where the demand elasticity is low, the firm's margin is high, and vice versa. However, the elasticity of demand facing a firm is also usually not known, at least not with sufficient precision. In the absence of these elements it becomes necessary to proxy the market power of any firm by reference to the relative position of the firm *vis-à-vis* its competitors on the market. The market share is the obvious proxy measure, although not the only one. This line of reasoning, however, makes it clear that in the absence of a direct measure of market power of a firm, a very useful alternative is provided by identifying and evaluating all the products and firms that produce them, and which constrain the supply and price behaviour of the firm in question. This process of identifying all the firm's significant competitors is commonly referred to as market definition.

(2) The Relevant or Antitrust Market

1.131 We may begin with some basic considerations as to what constitutes a market. In the simplest case of a single homogeneous product market, definition is not a difficult issue. Outside of such simple situations the classic notion of a market for a good is thought of as the area in which buyers and sellers of the good come into contact with each other to transact their business.[51] An alternative definition, from the perspective of market failure, is the following: markets are institutions active over an area in which individuals (or firms) exchange not just commodities but the right to use them in particular ways for particular periods.[52] Neither of these definitions is particularly useful for antitrust analysis where the interest is in market power.

1.132 These textbook definitions assume, in common with most other theories that the price of a good converges to a common value range over the area. The reason for this tendency to price convergence may be surmised to be that each firm operating in the market is constrained by and subjected to external market forces. Firms

---

[50] Herbert Hovenkamp, *Federal Anti-trust Policy* (1994).
[51] P Hardwick, B Khan, J Langmead, *An Introduction to Modern Economics* (1992).
[52] H Gravelle and R Rees, *Microeconomics* (1988).

in a competitive market cannot choose to use inefficient production methods, since the competitive pressure of lower-cost, lower-priced rival offers of the product will drive them out of business. Similarly, they cannot choose to charge consumers an unduly high price, for if they do they will lose sales and ultimately fail. It is thus clear that where these external market forces are adequately constraining on the firm, the firm cannot have any market power. These elementary considerations suggest that market definition should therefore consist in defining those products and firms that must be studied together in order to understand the non-negligible constraints on the firm in question. If the approach adopted for the definition of the market does not achieve this, then the resulting proxy measure for the firm's market power is likely to be severely biased. By neglecting certain competitors through an over-narrow market definition, market power is exaggerated, while by including those supplying an inadequate substitute in an over-wide market definition one is left with a tool of limited value for the competitive analysis of market power.

To summarize, the concept of market that is most useful from the point of view of competition analysis is one that includes all the products and the firms that in fact do or could easily offer reasonable substitutes to the customers if the firm in question were to raise prices or supply inferior products. This concept of market is referred to in the market definition exercise as that of the 'relevant' or the 'antitrust' market. **1.133**

(3) The Product and Geographic Dimension

The operational description given to the concept of product market in the Regulations based on Articles 81 and 82 of the Treaty and in Regulation 4064/89 on the control of concentrations having a Community dimension is the following: **1.134**

> A relevant product market comprises all those products and/or services which are regarded as interchangeable or substitutable by the consumer, by reason of the products' characteristics, their prices and their intended use.

Similarly relevant geographic markets are defined as follows:

> The relevant geographic market comprises the area in which the undertakings concerned are involved in the supply and demand of the products or services, in which the conditions of competition are sufficiently homogeneous and which can be distinguished from neighbouring areas because the conditions of competition are appreciably different in those areas.

It may be argued that while these definitions of the 'relevant' product and the 'relevant' geographic market are consistent with the economic concept of the relevant market described above, the definitions themselves are not precise enough and do not contain the operational mechanism by which the relevant market is to be defined. This is also the criticism one could make of the classic notions of the **1.135** market outlined at the start of this section. In contrast, the 1984 US Department of Justice (DOJ) Guidelines formulated its definition of the relevant market paying heed to this aspect:

> Formally, a market is defined as a product or a group of products and a geographical area in which it is sold such that a hypothetical, profit-maximizing firm, not subject to price regulation, that was the only and future seller of those products in that area, would impose 'a small but significant and non-transitory' increase in price above prevailing or likely future levels.

(4) The Different Competitive Constraints on Firms

1.136 While one may debate the alternative formulations of the market definition, the essential point is that the market defined must include all the products and firms that represent competitive constraints on the firm in question. Often the difficult issue in market definition is that, whatever the operational formulation or the test employed, the appropriate boundaries of the market cannot be decided precisely. This merely recalls the fact that market definition is not a goal in itself but that competitive analysis of the market defined must take account of the products and the firms on the boundary as well as those retained in the market.

1.137 The foregoing introductory remarks suggest that the focus of market definition should be on the competitive constraints on the firm or firms in question. It is generally recognized that firms are subject to three major constraints: demand substitution, supply substitutability, and potential competition. A very useful way to approach the market definition process is to examine these distinct competitive constraints and assign a relative importance to them.

(5) Demand Substitution: The Main Constraint

1.138 One of the most immediate constraints upon the terms on which a firm supplies a product is the competitive pressure represented by perfect and near perfect substitutes available in the geographic area. The customer would readily shift to such products or to suppliers located in an alternative area, which are considered as perfect or near perfect substitutes. In practice, the problem thus reduces itself to determining the range of products and geographical areas that constitute substitutes for the customer or at least for a sufficiently important number of customers. It is clear that all customers are not alike and hence, to draw a line between products and areas in the market where the firm in question competes and those outside it, one needs to focus on the marginal customers, ie those who generally value the product at the price paid and not much more. Such consumers would likely shift completely to substitutes if the relative price increases. In contrast, the intra-marginal consumers' reservation price is higher than what they paid for the good and so they would substitute less or not at all if the relative price increases.

Since in many practical situations a simple observation of market circumstances **1.139** may not suffice, the foregoing considerations suggest a line of enquiry for delineating the market. This is by postulating a hypothetical, small but significant, lasting change in the terms on which the product is made available, for example relative price, and assessing the likely reactions of customers to that increase. An increase that was too significant would not capture the reactions of all the marginal customers while too large an increase may also capture intra-marginal as against marginal customers. For example, an important proportion of consumers may substitute beer for water if the price of water were to rise significantly (say 50 per cent) but only a negligible proportion would shift if the price of water were to rise by 5–10 per cent. Would one conclude that beer is in the same market as water? The larger price rise has induced reactions from intra-marginal as well as marginal consumers, and if used as a basis for defining the market would lead to very wide markets; in this case to all beverages being in the same market. Customer reactions to an appropriately calibrated relative price increase enables, in an iterative way, determination of those products and areas that sufficiently restrain the firm's pricing. Customer responses would show that a relative price increase would be profitable only when there is no significant shift to any other product or area. The products and area retained at that point would constitute the narrowest relevant market.

(6) Supply Substitution: The Second Constraint

Proceeding in this way would be a consistent approach when the individual con- **1.140** sumer can be expected to derive utility from all of the qualities of the product in terms of size, colour, brand, etc. Where, however, the individual consumer does not purchase, for example, all of the available sizes, but the representative consumer may be expected to do so, it is important to take account of the competitive constraints represented by a specific category of potential producers—namely, those having actual capacity to compete as demonstrated by their production of complementary sizes or varieties. Intuitively, supply substitution encompasses all of the products that can be considered to be substitutes for the representative consumer. If it is clear that the production of these supply substitutes uses the same fixed inputs and requires the same distribution network, then the costs of switching production from the supply substitutes to the product in question are negligible. For these reasons, supply substitution would constitute as immediate and as effective a competitive constraint as demand substitution, and hence should be incorporated into the market definition. In the straightforward cases of products of different sizes, colours, shapes, and other similar varietal differences, the identification of supply substitution is relatively clear. There are also other situations where, without new investment in fixed assets, tangible or intangible, there exist on the supply side a chain of substitution between the qualities and varieties that can be produced. These supply substitutes therefore also need to be taken into account in defining the market (see the relevant Commission Notice[53]). A very useful line of enquiry is suggested by the examination of the margins or gross returns in the production of supply substitutes as compared to the product in question. These margins should tend to equality if the supply substitutes are correctly identified, either because the prices and costs are the same or because quality-adjusted prices and costs tend to converge. Put differently, in the absence of barriers, the gross returns to the producers of the product in question cannot get out of line with those earned by producers of supply substitutes.

(7) Potential Competition: The Third Constraint

1.141   If supply substitution, as defined above, is taken into account in defining the market then the obvious question raised is why not also take into account the constraining influence of potential capacities in neighbouring geographic or product markets that could well become actual production after a period of say a year or so? The pragmatic difficulty with this approach is that, unlike supply substitution discussed above, it makes necessary the assignment of hypothetical market shares to potential producers, of whom only an indefinable proportion may become actual producers. From a theoretical point of view it is difficult to maintain a distinction between one category of potential producers (those who may enter after one year) and other categories of potential entrants who may enter later. These considerations suggest that potential competition should not be adopted as a criterion in defining the market. It is a competitive constraint that should be used to assess market power in the market thus defined. It is worth recalling that the purpose of market definition is to permit an indication of the concerned firms' market power, based on their market position *vis-à-vis* other incumbents. In consequence, potential competition needs to be considered at a later stage in the competitive analysis.

1.142   In conclusion, of the three major competitive constraints discussed it has been argued that two of them, demand substitutability and supply substitutability, represent the major immediate constraints and should therefore be adopted as the determining criteria for market definition, while the last one, that of potential competition, should not. This is not to say that the competitive constraint represented by potential entry is without importance: it is often the constraint that determines the outcome of competitive assessment on the relevant market thus defined. The Commission's Notice on market definition in fact adopts the approach outlined here; it also sets out what would constitute relevant evidence in respect of the competitive constraints, and how such evidence should be evaluated.

---

[53] Commission Notice on the definition of relevant market for the purposes of Community competition law [1997] OJ C372.

(8) Defining a Market in Practice

The starting point in terms of the practical implementation of the Notice is to **1.143** clearly describe the product or service in question. This then permits one to decide, from a summary examination of market share, whether in relation to the operation under analysis there are any competition issues, even on the narrowest conceivable market. Having determined that a market definition is needed, an enquiry into the opinions primarily of customers but also of competitors can be undertaken, in order to determine the following: what proportion of the customers would switch away entirely from the product in question if its price were to be raised by a small but significant proportion, to which substitutes would they switch, and what evidence do the customers provide of switching in the past.

For example, consider the following situation: gearboxes are produced captively by car manufacturers and are also manufactured/supplied by specialist component producers. Car manufacturers either depend entirely on captively produced or entirely on specialist supply or use a mixture of captively produced as well as specialist supply. It is true that it is not on a daily basis that car manufacturers decide whether to use captive or merchant supply: there will be some long-term agreement, but this does not necessarily mean that there is no flexibility at all between captive and merchant supply. The market definition question at issue might then be the following—does the captively produced gearbox product constrain the pricing of the specialist produced gearboxes or are the two gearboxes in distinct markets? One is therefore interested to see whether and under what conditions a car manufacturer would substitute between specialist produced and captively produced gearboxes. A priori one would expect switching costs: these, on the one hand, somewhat limit the possibility of substitution but, on the other, they also limit the specialist supplier from making unanticipated price increases, since any lost customers can only be recovered by price reductions large enough to compensate for the switching costs. If an increase in the relative price of specialist produced gearboxes induces no switch at all towards captive production over a reasonably short timescale, one would conclude that the current merchant suppliers are the only competitors to take into account, ignoring all the strictly captive producers. If, on the other hand, not a majority but a significant minority of the customers reply that they would, in response to a 5–10 per cent price increase, consider switching to captive production and have done so in the past, then it is clear that the market is wider. Furthermore, in this type of situation the captive production is likely to meet all of the conditions of supply substitutes: the only reason why it may not be treated as part of the market is because captive production is likely to require a higher gross return to be competitive with specialist production. In any case, a market enquiry would establish whether the specialist production was a distinct market or should be included because of supply substitution. The competitive assessment must certainly consider the competitive constraint represented by captive production capacities.

(9) Defining the Market: Not an End in Itself

1.144 A common complaint concerning the economic approach to defining the relevant market consists of the following: first, that the approach is too demanding of data which are not usually available; secondly, that it introduces complexity not compensated for by resulting clarity. The evident point of departure for this complaint is the question why should one not define a market in a way that is simple and obvious and without recourse to a price test. The best way to respond to this complaint is to start by recognizing that the way competition works in a market situation is not in itself affected by the way one classifies the products into the different 'markets'. Thus the competitive constraints on a firm's market power are to an extent determined by the market forces in the given situation irrespective of how one organizes the products of the various firms in particular markets. Recognition of this evident point, however, also implies that a market defined in an arbitrary even if 'obvious' way is not an end in itself, and so cannot and should not conclusively determine the outcome of the competitive assessment. If the market is defined too narrowly, then those producers representing a significant constraining influence who are not considered as incumbents must be treated as important potential entrants, since they are able effectively and immediately to respond to the needs of customers faced with increased prices or lower quality offered by the incumbents. Thus, arguably, the definition of the market adopted does not matter so long as it is employed in a consistent way and those constraining influences not included in the market are given their due weight in the assessment.[54]

1.145 It is a fact, however, that all too often a market definition adopted in an 'ad hoc' way has every semblance of becoming an end in itself. In contrast, the economic approach to defining the relevant market is different only in that it insists on consistency in the use of the market definition employed. The data required to determine which products and geographical areas are to be included in the relevant product market are precisely the data required in the alternative more 'obvious' approach in determining how significant entry is from different neighbouring products and geographical areas.

(10) Concluding Comments

1.146 Having defined the market, it is important for the subsequent competitive analysis to give consideration to the following. The customary economic approach dis-

---

[54] This is of course not correct where the market shares are used as legal tests, in which case it is vital to define the market appropriately since the shares as such trigger notification, such as in the R & D Block Exemption Regulation (EC) 418/85.

cussed above, as is well known,[55] does not lead to a relevant antitrust market that is unique. This is easy to see: if for a given collection of products over a geographic area a price increase is profitable, this is because the next best substitute does not exercise a sufficient constraining influence; hence a wider market including the next best substitute could also be deemed to be the relevant market as on this wider market too a price rise will be sustainable. It is for this reason that for competitive analysis the antitrust authorities seek to define the narrowest market. The approach of the Commission's Notice on market definition does not say explicitly that it seeks to define the narrowest market although in general this would be the tendency. It is also clear that a market definition approach that is based on evaluating substitution in response to an increase of price above the prevailing competitive level would systematically lead to overly wide markets being defined where the prevailing pricing is not competitive and the level is already above marginal costs. In such situations a number of products and firms that may normally be numbered amongst the potential rivals are likely already to be included in the market. This in itself is a useful element for competitive analysis since in the circumstances we know that the proper substitutes do not constrain pricing to converge towards marginal costs and we also learn from the firm's market share in the wider market how significant are the constraints represented by costlier and inferior substitutes. The resulting market share would tend to understate the firm's true market power.

In a more general way, a market definition will tell one who the immediate competitors of the firm are but not that all incumbents are of equal constraining influence on the firm. To learn this, it is necessary to enquire how rapidly and cost efficiently the current competitors can raise output to bid away the market share of the firm raising prices or offering products of reduced quality. The market shares of the firm's competitors can be expected to be a guide in this respect, but only reliably in the case of industries not undergoing a rapid pace of product and technological innovation. In the case of innovation products and emerging markets in general, it is indeed the relative difficulty of delineating the precise boundary between products 'in' and 'out', as well as judging whether the market shares of those in the market truly reflect their ability to expand quantity and quality of output, that poses the major issue for market definition. **1.147**

It is not just in the case of products undergoing innovation that such questions arise. Similar issues about the ability of incumbents to expand output also arise in the definition of the relevant market for intermediate products. Such situations are characterized by specialized producers as well as producers captively consuming a sizeable proportion of their output. Both these categories of producers are **1.148**

---

[55] See eg *Market Definition in UK Competition Policy* (OFT Research Paper, 1992) or GJ Werden and GA Rozanski 'The application of Section 7 to Differentiated products industries' (1994) 8(3) *Antitrust* 40–45.

competitors in the relevant market. The competitive constraints on a firm in such a market situation are not just the demand substitution possibilities of the non-captive customers, but also the supply possibilities of captive producers who are currently only participating in the merchant supply a little, if at all. The calculation of market shares should be undertaken for both the total market and separately for the merchant market.

1.149 At the outset of this section, it was suggested that the need for market definition is to be found in the role that market share has come to play as an observable proxy for market power. In these circumstances, it is not surprising that market definition has come to play a crucial role in antitrust analysis, albeit much more crucial in the analysis of mergers and acquisitions than in that of restrictive agreements. This difference in emphasis appears to arise because in appraising the restrictive nature of certain agreements like price fixing, market sharing, or resale price maintenance, most competition authorities do not consider it necessary to make an in-depth reference to the market power of the parties. It is somewhat different when the restrictive effects have to be assessed, at which point market definition becomes indispensable. The robustness of the subsequent competitive analysis will make it evident whether the market definition generated the market share or if the converse is true.

F. Market Power and Dominance

(1) Market Power and Market Price

1.150 It comes as no surprise that the basic element in the approach to identifying and assessing market power is to start by asking if the firm's output or price setting behaviour affects the market price or output. It may seem strange that those firms able to sell at the prevailing conditions on the market, whatever quantity they choose, have little or no market power, whereas those with market power can no longer do so or only to a limited extent. In this perspective dominance constitutes that degree of market power at which a firm sets, through its own output level, not only the equilibrium market price but also the output levels of the other incumbents. This notion of single dominance has to be contrasted with that of collective or joint dominance under which output is reduced and price increased through explicit or tacit collusion. Tacit collusion describes a situation when non-cooperative behaviour in an oligopoly leads to the collusive outcome.[56] It would be interesting, although beyond the scope of this chapter, to analyse how the equilibrium market outcome in terms of output, its quality, and average price attained under conditions of tacit collusion would compare with that attained under either

---

[56] See J Tirole (n 21 above) 207.

single dominance or collective dominance where there is explicit collusion. If, in the market in question, competition takes place in dimensions other than simply price or quantity of output, it is not at all evident that similar market outcomes would arise in each of these equilibria of dominance.

It is useful to look at market power from the point of view of the firm's ability to influence the market price, not only because this is methodically most straightforward, but also because it directs attention to the firm's incentive to set output at a level taking into account the elasticity of demand. In consequence the firm looks no longer at whether its price covers its costs at the margin, thereby satisfying all those customers ready and willing to pay a price that covers the marginal cost. Instead the firm as a profit maximizer will raise the price to a level at which it earns on each incremental sale at least as much as its marginal cost. The firm will thus set its output at a point where its marginal cost equals its marginal revenue. With a downward sloping demand curve, for any output level, marginal revenue is less than price; it follows that at its profit maximizing output, the firm's price will exceed it marginal cost (see section C(4) above). **1.151**

Such a pricing policy is, however, only possible for a firm that does not face such pressure from its competitors that any reduction in its own output is easily made up for by the competitors. It follows that a situation of market power cannot arise in markets where entry is easy or profitable or which are otherwise contestable, since in such conditions the pressure on prices to converge to average costs is rather persistent. A range of conditions on the production side such as economies of scale, joint production and cost indivisibilities (see paragraphs 1.37–1.42 above) may, however, imply that the most efficient plant size is relatively large in relation to demand so that production tends to be in the hands of a small number of players and entry subject to barriers of some significance. Given this precondition that entry either in the short term or in the longer term is constrained, market power will enable some incumbents to drive a wedge between prices and marginal costs. When this can be sustained, prices will also diverge from average costs. **1.152**

(2) Price Elasticities of Demand and Market Shares

1.153

The firms with market power in a market can be identified by assessing the own-price and cross-price elasticities of demand facing[57] each of the incumbents, as these reflect whether there is a potential to make profitable price increases taking account of the reactions of those producing the closest substitutes. A simpler but less certain approach is, having well defined the market, to focus on the market

---

[57] Paul Seabright, Robin Nutal, Damien Neven, *Merger in Daylight* (1993). The familiar concepts of own-price elasticity and cross-price elasticity are measures of the proportionate responses of demand to specific proportionate change in the product's own price and by prices of those of other substitutes or complements.

shares of the incumbents. In a competitive market, by definition each firm is a price taker, ie acts as if facing an infinitely elastic demand curve, and this irrespective of whether the total market demand is price elastic or inelastic. Similar technology, absence of scale or scope economies, and the commodity nature of products all combine to ensure that there is no great variability of market shares in such conditions. Where, however, certain firms have significant market shares this is certainly an indication that such firms are either cost leaders if the product is homogeneous or have both cost and product range advantages in a differentiated product market. A firm with 60 per cent market share would typically need, in order to double its sales, to cut its prices much more than a firm with 5 per cent market share in the same market. The practical approach based on market shares can be considered a heuristic way of taking into account price elasticities of demand and reaching a similar conclusion on the identity of the firms with market power. The assessment of single dominance essentially consists of showing whether or not the firm in question corresponds to the notion of a dominant firm in economic theory[58] and whether, given the barriers to expansion or entry, the other incumbents can expand output, or potential competitors could enter at the prices set by the dominant firm. It is also possible to refine the calculation of market power by considering the market shares as well as the degree of concentration of the market as measured by the market share of the top four or five firms (CR4 or CR5) or the HHI.[59] On the basis of information provided by these indicators it is possible to make an assessment whether or not the conditions for dominance may be attained.

(3) Single Dominance

1.154 For a firm to be considered dominant, it must have a large market share, conventionally more than 50 per cent of recent sales, its demand being the industry demand curve less the necessarily limited supply responses of the other smaller firms, and it must set market price.

1.155 The situation of a dominant firm in the total market is depicted to the right in Figure 13.[60] The effective demand curve (ED) facing the dominant firm is obtained by deducting from market demand DD, at each price, the necessarily limited supply responses of all the other firms (SS) in the market. The dominant firm would maximize profits by producing where its MC equals its MR; this is at the output OQ_1, which implies the price P_1, leaving the balance of the output being produced by smaller firms. The small firms accept the price set since in general their marginal costs exceed those of the dominant firm. The above situation would constitute single dominance if, in the first place, the other incumbents

---

[58] F Fisher, JJ McGowan, JE Greenwood (n 53 above).

[59] See, for example, the analysis in Encaoua and Jacquemin, 'Degree of Monopoly, indices of concentration and threat of entry' (1980) *International Economic Review*.

[60] P Hardwick, B Khan, J Langmead (n 51 above).

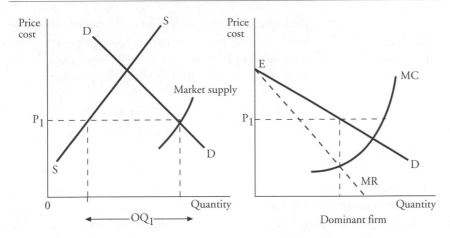

Figure 13: A dominant firm

could not easily expand their output given the pricing above marginal cost or the offering of inferior products by the dominant firm. In the second place, there must exist important entry barriers significantly impeding potential entry which would otherwise make unsustainable the pricing above competitive level by the dominant firm.[61] In assessing potential entry, allowance has to be made for the fact that entry may involve costs and new capacity may only come on stream over time (two to three years). This means that dominance is said to exist only when the situation of substantial market share together with pricing above cost is expected to be sustained over a period of time during which incumbents and entrants cannot be expected to bid away the dominant firm's market share through lower pricing and superior quality products. Under the Merger Regulation a period of less than one to two years is generally not assessed as a dominant position. A high market share in the absence of entry barriers, or where there is evidence of entry and exit of other firms as well as of expansion by incumbents, would tend to suggest that the significant market position is due to the firm in question being more cost competitive and innovative than its competitors.

A firm dominant in a market may have incentives to reinforce its dominance by **1.156** acquiring, merging, or through joint venture to expand its activities on the same or neighbouring markets. A number of scenarios of reinforcement of dominant position can be imagined; it is advisable to maintain a balanced appreciation of the different possibilities. A dominant firm can certainly acquire other incumbents on the market, but it is evident from the above that its position is reinforced only when it acquires the maverick firm which as a rule would have a cost structure similar or lower than its own at some output rate. Similarly, a dominant firm

---

[61] Compare with this the ECJ's similar definition of dominance eg in Case 85/76 *Hoffmann-La Roche* [1979] ECR 461.

may have buying power in the input market: its acquisition of a major input supplier to a large extent dissipates its buying power, and hence its dominant position
can only be reinforced if the operation leads to raising rivals' costs because the
rivals cannot shift to other input supplier firms or turn to captive production.

(4) Oligopolistic Competition and Collective Dominance

1.157   In contrast to the situation of a market with a dominant firm, in the situation of
competition amongst a few, each firm believes that the outcome of its decisions
depends significantly on the decisions taken by one or more of the other identifiable sellers. (See the discussion above in section C(5).) Each firm therefore faces a
residual demand curve and will formulate its own price and output decision on the
basis of its best prediction of the reactions of other firms, emphasizing particularly
the reactions of the firms producing the closest substitutes. Formally, then, one
could describe the situation facing the firm as implying that the effect on its own
price of a change in its own output is composed by two components: first, the
responsiveness of the demand for its own product to a change in its price and, secondly, the impact on its own price of any reaction in the outputs or prices of its
competitors. The firm usually does not know the output variation of its competitors and hence, in order to make a decision on its own profit maximizing output,
it must also make an estimate of how the other firms will react, which is commonly
called, in this static setting, the conjectural variation of the firm in question.[62]

1.158   Without some simplifying assumptions regarding the conjectural variation of
each firm in the market it is not possible to say how competition takes place in the
market. Two simplifying and ultimately unsatisfactory hypotheses are to be found
in the duopoly literature. At one extreme is the Cournot assumption that each
firm determines its own profit maximizing output on the basis that the other
would hold its short-term output constant. At the other extreme is the assumption associated with Bertrand, that each firm assumes that the other would keep
its price constant and then set its own profit maximizing price to undercut its
rival. Neither intense quantity competition nor intense price competition seem to
adequately explain all real world situations. It has to be recognized that firms that
survive in a market would come to realize that intense price competition is relevant when demand is below expected levels leaving them with unused capacity to
serve a large part of the market. Similarly when market demand is at the level commensurate with their capacities and expanding production takes time, firms may
engage in quantity competition. Furthermore, firms in an oligopoly situation may
also focus on competition in certain dimensions such as quality, branding, product innovation, etc, rather than purely in output or in prices. Such individually
optimizing behaviour may in certain specific market situations lead to a collusive

---

[62] See H Gravelle and R Rees (n 52 above).

market outcome (tacit collusion) despite there being no communication or agreement between the firms. The co-ordination may of course also be reached, albeit illegally, by explicit collusion, that is with the help of communication, agreements, etc.

(5) Relevant Factors for Collusion

The objective of explicit collusion is usually joint profit maximizing. Whether this **1.159** objective is attained depends for obvious reasons on the incentives to co-operate and cheat as well as the opportunities for monitoring and enforcement which all vary with the characteristics of the firms, markets, and products. The more important of these characteristics are the following:

1. The smaller the number of sellers, the easier it is to agree and monitor and the more evident is the incentive since each cannot individually gain sales without rivals retaliating. If, furthermore, production technologies are similar, giving rise to similar plant capacities, then the incentive is reinforced.

2. The tendency to joint profit maximization is greater the more homogeneous are the products of each seller. Each firm is engaged in close rivalry for customers and so will have greater difficulty in obtaining a lasting advantage by unilateral action. Sharply differentiated products on the other hand make monitoring of commitments more difficult and tend to give rise to opportunistic behaviour, which consists in defecting from the cartel.

3. Joint profit maximization is more sustainable in a growing rather than a stagnant market; the absence of excess capacity is an element limiting the tendency to alter the basis of allocation of customers. The converse argument may be relevant in an industry of high sunk costs relative to variable costs where stagnant demand creates conditions for collusive behaviour as a means of minimizing joint losses.

4. The existence of a dominant firm acting as a price leader can be materially important in maintaining price discipline and in acting as a swing producer, should changes in demand conditions require it.

5. The stability of joint profit maximizing is undermined when the market or product characteristics do not undergo innovation and do not sustain various forms of non-price competition such as advertising, promotions, quality changes, and the like, which increase marketing costs and also make necessary price renegotiations.

6. The incumbents can only successfully subscribe to joint profit maximization if entry barriers are high or at least significant and other firms attracted by the high profits are not able to easily and rapidly enter and take a significant market share. Thus the market cannot be contestable.

(6) Evaluation of Collusion

1.160 To the extent that, in a particular situation, the conditions above coincide in favouring collusion between rivals on their prices and outputs, the welfare consequences are more serious than in the case of monopoly.[63] A monopoly would reduce output by closing the inefficient plants. In the case of a temporary alliance of rivals each would need to retain their plants for the period after, and hence the output reduction would be prorated between efficient and inefficient plants. There is also the dead-weight loss of valuable management resources in co-ordinating competitor reactions. With the exception of the loss of management resources, the above conclusion and analysis applies possibly with less force to tacit collusion, especially if there exist facilitating devices such as information exchange or price announcements or capacity signalling. In view of these strictures on the consequences of collusion and oligopolistic dominance, it is important that major structural operations in medium to highly concentrated markets are analysed with particular attention to see if they facilitate the creation of an oligopolistic dominant position.

1.161 On quite general grounds, an examination of the potential for the creation of oligopolistic dominance is certainly indicated when the structural operation itself would lead to the similar market shares of two or three operators dominating the scene in a concentrated market, or if the consequence of an acquisition would be the removal of a significant, albeit small, competitor in such a market context. Even with less similarity in market shares, incentives for collusion may nevertheless be quite strong when there are up to five major operators. As the number of producers increase beyond this the short run gains from undercutting the collusive price increases quite rapidly thus making the collusion less stable, unless the price elasticity of demand facing each participant is extremely low.

1.162 It is possible to summarize the foregoing as follows: a situation with balanced market shares combined with no competitor having the capacity to practically serve the whole market provides the essential indication that price competition between the major incumbents is unlikely to be intense. Similarity market shares also lends support to the premise that product technology and cost economics do not substantially vary for the firms in question. If the remaining supply is fragmented among a number of small competitors then it would be important to rule out any capacity on their part to rapidly expand output. Other factors that have been considered indicative of the potential creation of oligopolistic dominance have been high barriers to entry, a stagnant market, product homogeneity, price

---

[63] WJ Baumol (n 48 above).

transparency, and a low rate of product innovation.[64] Clearly, product homogeneity and a low rate of product innovation tend to make monitoring and enforcement easier as well as contributing to price transparency.

The nature and evolution of demand and its price elasticity are ambivalent factors **1.163** for the assessment of oligopolistic dominance. First, it could be important whether the product is a final consumer product or an intermediate input in a complex production process, since market power at the level where consumer surplus can be extracted is more of an incentive: if the firm faces a competitive intermediate customer sector, it may find it difficult to exploit its market power. Intermediate inputs may also be characterized by strong countervailing power and professional buyers. In the second place, a market with stagnant demand would seem to suggest that a concentration may aim at joint dominance by eliminating a maverick producer or limiting price competition. This reasoning, however, demands that the other remaining small competitors are not able to bid away market share by better utilization of their capacity and by competing on price. Thirdly, firms able to set price would not be at their profit-maximizing output level if the demand facing them, that is the firm demand curve, is inelastic. They will find that it pays to increase price and reduce output, thus simultaneously increasing their total receipts and hence their profits. On the other hand, an inelastic *market* demand curve certainly provides incentives for collective output cuts, but it also provides much incentive for each individual member to defect from the output cut.

It follows from the foregoing review that, aside from key market structural factors **1.164** such as high market concentration, balanced market shares, no extravagant excess capacity, and similar technology and cost functions, it would be more indicative of the creation of joint dominance if there was a pattern of links between the major incumbents to facilitate price transparency, monitoring, and enforcement. Important joint ventures in related markets, supply relations, and collaborative product development are all possible indicators of commitment mechanisms that the firms concerned have put in place to contribute to the durability of any successful joint dominance.

It also has to be recognized that oligopolistic dominance may not result in the **1.165** same reduction in output and increase in price that would occur under single dominance. A possible result is an output level higher than under sole dominance, with accordingly smaller welfare losses for consumers and other producers, but nevertheless welfare losses as compared with the competitive output. How significant these losses are is indeed a crucial question in the analysis of individual cases.

---

[64] See for example the following merger cases: *Nestlé/Perrier* (Case IV/M190) (1992); *Kali & Salz* (Case IV/M308) (1993); *Pilkington/SIV* (Case IV/M358) (1993); *Rhône-Poulenc/SNIA* (Case IV/M206) [1992] OJ C319.

(7) Conclusion

1.166 Situations of single dominance and of oligopolistic dominance tend to lead to a high degree of market power where the firm or firms concerned account for a high share of the market output, are able to set the level of market prices and hence also the supply responses of the remaining necessarily small competitors, and are also able to limit entry. The question may be posed as to whether the concept of a degree of market power that is significant but below that of dominance has a useful role in competition economics. An equivalent way to look at this question is to ask how interventionist antitrust policy should be: should the authority only intervene when there is the creation or reinforcement of a dominant position, and when such a position is defined rather narrowly as in EC competition policy in terms of independence *vis-à-vis* others on the market, thereby having the possibility to clearly drive a wedge between price and average total costs? Or should the authority also intervene in situations where the power to price independently above average total costs is less clear?

1.167 An affirmative answer on the first question would accord with competition regimes that consider behaviour such as tying, predation, price discrimination, refusal to supply, foreclosure, and so on, as abusive only when practised by dominant firms. However, this is only a partial picture. Firms without such a high degree of market power may try to mimic that situation through explicit collusion. In addition, most goods and services markets have just a few firms that account for a significant part of output, for example because conditions of production and technology are such that the minimum efficient scale is large relative to market demand. Such firms often have significant market power. While *per se* prohibitions like price fixing or market sharing make no reference to market power, it is clear from the economic viewpoint that restrictive agreements could have appreciable anti-competitive effects on the relevant markets when the agreements are between firms with significant market power or between those who acquire it through the agreements. The notion of significant market power is, however, not precisely definable; in consequence, antitrust policy based on this notion is likely to be more effective when intervening to limit clear inefficiencies of resource allocation not offset by static or dynamic efficiency gains, rather than fine tuning agreements to improve the so-called 'efficiencies' beyond those implicit in mutually convened arrangements between independent entrepreneurs.

2

ARTICLE 81

A. Introduction

The purpose of the following overview of Article 81 (former Article 85) is to con- **2.01** sider some general features of that provision as it is interpreted and applied. Detailed analysis of its application is contained in other chapters of this book.

It is not intended here to provide a comprehensive textbook analysis of the provi- **2.02** sion, but rather to highlight some of the key legal and policy issues arising from its application, in order to introduce and underpin the substantive chapters.

On 28 April 1999, the Commission issued a white paper on modernisation of the **2.03** rules implementing Article 81 and Article 82 (former Article 86) of the EC Treaty.[1] This is a document of the utmost importance which has already given rise to intense debate and is intended to lead to legislation radically altering the way in

---

[1] White Paper on modernisation of the rules implementing Articles 85 and 86 [now Articles 81 and 82] of the EC Treaty COM (1999) 101 final, http://europa.eu.int/comm/dg04/entente/other.htm.

which EC competition law is applied. It contains a thoroughgoing analysis of the current system under Council Regulation 17 and discusses options for reform before setting out proposals for a entirely new system. It is beyond the scope of this edition of this book, and would be premature, to offer a full analysis of the white paper. The book concentrates on the law as it stands in 1999. However, the analysis and diagnosis set out in the white paper are of crucial importance for an understanding of the way competition law in Europe has developed these last forty years.

2.04 Today an understanding of how markets operate is a prerequisite for competition analysis. Markets must be defined in terms of their geographic extent and the relevant products or services before the activities of undertakings within them can be assessed. Examination of agreements under Article 81(1) requires rigorous attention to market structure. Thus, for example, an agreement to acquire a minority shareholding in a competitor, a joint venture agreement, various types of distribution agreement, or an information exchange system may be found to be restrictive of competition after proper analysis of the relevant markets and the role and position of the undertakings concerned in those markets. Although some restrictions of competition are easily identified without much economic analysis, most commercial agreements are neither good nor bad in themselves on first reading by a competition policy enforcer. Knowledge of their economic context is essential for an understanding of their impact on competition and therefore their treatment under Article 81(1).

B. General Scope of Article 81

2.05 Pursuant to Article 3 of the EC Treaty, 'the activities of the Community shall include, as provided in this Treaty and in accordance with the timetable set out therein: . . . (g) a system ensuring that competition in the internal market is not distorted'. Article 81 is interpreted and applied, together with other Treaty provisions, in order to create and sustain that system.

2.06 In general Article 81 applies to all sectors of the economy except where the Treaty itself grants exceptions. In accordance with Article 36 the competition rules apply to the production of and trade in agricultural products only to the extent determined by the Council within the framework of Article 37(2) and (3) and in accordance with the procedure laid down therein, account being taken of the objectives set out in Article 33. These products are listed in Annex II of the Treaty. Regulation 26 of 4 April 1962,[2] which was adopted on the basis of Articles 36 and

---

[2] Regulation 26 of 4 April 1962 on applying certain rules of competition to production of and trade in agricultural products [1962] OJ 30 as amended by Council Regulation 49 of 29 June 1962 [1962] OJ 53.

37, provides that Articles 81 to 86 of the Treaty and all the provisions adopted to implement them are also applicable to agriculture, but grants three exceptions. Under Article 2(1) of the Regulation, Article 81(1) of the Treaty does not apply to agreements, decisions, and practices which form an integral part of a national market organization or are necessary for the attainment of the objectives set out in Article 33 of the Treaty. In particular it does not apply to agreements, decisions, and practices of farmers, farmers' associations, or associations of such associations belonging to a single Member State which concern the production or sale of agricultural goods or the use of joint facilities for the storage, treatment, or processing of agricultural products, and under which there is no obligation to charge identical prices. This is so unless the Commission finds that competition is thereby excluded or that the objectives of Article 33 of the Treaty are jeopardized.[3]

Coal and Steel

Under Article 305(1) the provisions of the EC Treaty, including the competition **2.07** rules, shall not affect the provisions of the Treaty establishing the European Coal and Steel Community, in particular as regards the rights and obligations of Member States, the powers of the institutions of that Community, and the rules laid down by that Treaty for the functioning of the common market in coal and steel. Arrangements which restrict competition are therefore to be evaluated on the basis of Articles 65 and 66 of the ECSC Treaty in so far as they relate to the coal and steel market of the Community.[4] This will be the case until the expiry of the Treaty in 2002. They will then fall under the EC Treaty. The EC Treaty's provisions must also not derogate from those of the Treaty establishing the European Atomic Energy Community (Euratom) Treaty.

Defence

Particular attention must be paid to the applications of the rules on competition **2.08** to the defence sector. Article 296 provides that:

> 1. The provisions of this Treaty shall not preclude the application of the following rules:
>
> (a) no Member State shall be obliged to supply information the disclosure of which it considers contrary to the essential interests of its security;
> (b) any Member State may take such measures as it considers necessary for the protection of the essential interests of its security which are connected with the production of or trade in arms, munitions and war material; such measures shall not adversely affect the conditions of competition in the common market regarding products which are not intended for specifically military purposes.

---

[3] See also Council Regulation (EEC) 2077/92 of 30 June 1992 concerning inter-branch organiszations and agreements in the tobacco sector [1992] OJ No L215/80.

[4] Coal and steel products are defined in Annex I of the ECSC Treaty. Undertakings for the purposes of the ECSC Treaty are defined in Article 80 of that Treaty.

2. The Council may, acting unanimously on a proposal from the Commission, make changes to the list, which it drew up on 15 April 1958, of the products to which the provisions of paragraph 1(b) apply.

2.09   Pursuant to Article 298:

If measures taken in the circumstances referred to in Articles 223 and 224 [now Articles 296 and 297] have the effect of distorting the conditions of competition in the common market, the Commission shall, together with the State concerned, examine how these measures can be adjusted to the rules laid down in the Treaty. By way of derogation from the procedure laid down in Articles 226 and 227, the Commission or any Member State may bring the matter directly before the Court of Justice if it considers that another Member State is making improper use of the powers provided for in Articles 223 and 224.

2.10   In a number of merger cases,[5] the Commission has noted that Governments of Member States have instructed the undertakings notifying a concentration not to notify information relating to their military activities. The Commission considered information supplied by the Governments concerned and noted that:

- the unnotified part of the concentration related only to the production of or trade in arms, munitions and war material mentioned in the list referred to in Article 296(2);

- the measures taken by the Member States were necessary for the protection of essential security interests;

- there were no spill-over effects from military to non-military applications of dual use products;

- the merger would have no significant impact on suppliers and sub-contractors of the undertakings concerned or defence Ministries in other Member States;

- intermediate consumers would be little affected.

2.11   In these circumstances, the Commission declared itself satisfied with the measures taken by the Governments concerned and saw no need to invoke Article 298. It limited its decisions to non-military applications of dual use products.

2.12   It seems from the above analysis that the Commission will defer to Member States' refusal to allow undertakings to notify concentrations relating to solely military products. However, the Commission reserves the right to invoke Article 298 if these conditions are not met. The same principles apply, *mutatis mutandis*, to the other competition rules.

---

[5] See eg *British Aerospace/VSEL* (Case IV/M528) (1994) (United Kingdom); *GEC/VSEL* (Case IV/M529) (1994) (United Kingdom); *British Aerospace/Lagardère SCA* (Case IV/M820) (1996) (United Kingdom/France).

In other cases[6] in which no Member State invoked Article 296, the Commission **2.13**
has applied the Merger Regulation in the normal way to defence or military markets. Recently the Commission has pointed out that 'markets for defence equipment have shown a move towards a more international approach to procurement
over recent years'.[7] This suggests that competition in defence markets is ceasing to
be a purely national concern. This of course reflects general trends in defence policy in Europe in recent years. Again these principles apply, *mutatis mutandis*, to
the other competition rules.

Environment and Culture

In addition to these provisions there are also a number of other rules which are rel- **2.14**
evant to a discussion of the scope of the Article 81. In particular, environmental
and cultural issues must be taken into account in the application of the competition rules. However, they will be relevant only to policy considerations, arising
under Article 81(3), as they do not have any impact on the notion of restriction of
competition for the purposes of Article 81(1).

Article 6 provides: 'Environmental protection requirements must be integrated **2.15**
into the definition and implementation of the Community policies and activities
referred to in Article 3, in particular with a view to promoting sustainable development.' This integration requires the Commission and other bodies applying
Article 81 to take account of the impact of the agreements, etc under consideration on the promotion of sustainable development, and of the impact of their
decisions on that goal. This will be particularly important in applying Article
81(3). It does not mean that, in the event of a clash between policies, an agreement
which should be prohibited on competition grounds but which promotes sustainable development must be allowed to proceed. The Treaty does not prescribe
any such hierarchy and an anti-competitive agreement should not be allowed on
environmental grounds alone. There are other ways of protecting the environment and promoting sustainable development. Similarly, an agreement which is
innocent in competition terms, but favours unsustainable development, should
be dealt with by other means than the prohibition of Article 81(1).

Article 151 provides: 'The Community shall contribute to the flowering of the **2.16**
cultures of the Member States, while respecting their national and regional diversity and at the same time bringing the common cultural heritage to the fore . . . 4.
The Community shall take cultural aspects into account in its action under other
provisions of this Treaty, in particular in order to respect and to promote the

---

[6] *Matra Marconi Space/British Aerospace Space Systems* (Case IV/M437) (1994); *CGI/Dassault*
(Case IV/M571), (1995); *Thomson CSF/Teneo/Indra* (Case IV/M620) (1995); *Thomson/CSF/
Finmeccanica/Elettronica* (Case IV/M767), (1996); *Matra BAe Dynamics/DASA/LFK* (Case
IV/M945) (1998); *Snecma/Messier Dowty* (Case IV/M1159) (1998).
[7] *Matra BAe Dynamics/DASA/LFK* (Case IV/M945) (1998), para 23.

diversity of its cultures.' The interface between culture and competition has proved controversial in recent years as the Commission has grappled with resale price maintenance for books and the activities of public television companies. Here again, the most relevant consideration will occur under Article 81(3) as the promotion of cultural diversity takes its place among the benefits for the general welfare which an agreement may bring about despite its restrictive impact on competition.

C. Article 81(1)

2.17 Article 81 provides:

1. The following shall be prohibited as incompatible with the common market: all agreements between undertakings, decisions by associations of undertakings and concerted practices which may affect trade between Member States and which have as their object or effect the prevention, restriction or distortion of competition within the common market, and in particular those which:

(a) directly or indirectly fix purchase or selling prices or any other trading conditions;
(b) limit or control production, markets, technical development, or investment;
(c) share markets or sources of supply;
(d) apply dissimilar conditions to equivalent transactions with other trading parties, thereby placing them at a competitive disadvantage;
(e) make the conclusion of contracts subject to acceptance by the other parties of supplementary obligations which, by their nature or according to commercial usage, have no connection with the subject of such contracts.

2. Any agreements or decisions prohibited pursuant to this Article shall be automatically void.
3. The provisions of paragraph 1 may, however, be declared inapplicable in the case of:

— any agreement or category of agreements between undertakings;
— any decision or category of decisions by associations of undertakings;
— any concerted practice or category of concerted practices,

which contributes to improving the production or distribution of goods or to promoting technical or economic progress, while allowing consumers a fair share of the resulting benefit, and which does not:

(a) impose on the undertakings concerned restrictions which are not indispensable to the attainment of these objectives;
(b) afford such undertakings the possibility of eliminating competition in respect of a substantial part of the products in question.

2.18 Article 81 deals with the impact of a particular category of business behaviour on competition. Contractual and other consensual arrangements between undertakings are of course essential features of a market economy. Where the undertakings concerned are actual or potential competitors, what they decide to do together may be of interest to competition authorities. Even if they are not competitors, those authorities may legitimately take an interest in the impact of their commercial arrangements on the competitive process and on third parties.

The competitive relations with which Article 81 deals are thus traditionally divided into two categories: horizontal (between undertakings competing in respect of research, development, production, purchase, or sale of different goods or services) and vertical (between undertakings engaged in the research, development, production, purchase or sale of one and the same set of goods or services, but operating at different economic levels). This useful simplification is followed in Community policy and will be used in this chapter where necessary. **2.19**

The following sections will consider the constituent elements of Article 81. Before doing so it should be recalled that Community law has its own definitions for a number of the terms found in Article 81. Thus, for example, the meaning of '*undertaking*' or '*agreement*' in Article 81(1) is different from both the ordinary meaning of those words in English and any special meaning which may have been ascribed to them in legal systems in Member States of the Community (or elsewhere) which use the English language. The terms of Article 81 have the same meaning in all the Community's official languages. Article 81(1) contains a number of conditions, all of which have to be fulfilled if its prohibition is to apply. **2.20**

(1) Undertakings

Article 81(1) only applies to *undertakings*. The Court has repeatedly defined the concept of an undertaking as 'any entity engaged in an economic activity, regardless of its legal status and the way in which it is financed';[8] an economic activity is 'any activity consisting in offering goods and services on a given market'.[9] The Commission has followed the wide definition of this concept. For example, in *Film Purchases by German Television Stations*,[10] the Commission stated that the term 'covers any activity directed at trade in goods or services irrespective of the legal form of the undertaking and regardless of whether or not it is intended to earn profits'. **2.21**

An entity does not have to be incorporated under company law or take any other legally recognized form to be deemed an undertaking; it is the entity's engagement in commercial activity which makes it an undertaking for the purposes of the **2.22**

---

[8] Case C–41/90 *Klaus Höfner and Fritz Elser v Macrotron GmbH* [1991] ECR I–1979, para 21; Case C–35/96 *Commission v Italian Republic* [1998] ECR I–3851, para 49; Case C–244/94 *Fédération Française des Sociétés d'Assurances and Others v Ministère de l'Agriculture et de la Pêche* [1995] ECR I–4013, para 14; and Case C–55/96 *Job Centre coop arl* [1997] ECR I–7119, para 21.
[9] Case C–118/85 *Commission v Italy* [1987] ECR 2599, para 7.
[10] [1989]OJ L284/36.

competition rules. Pursuit of profit is not essential.[11] In *Fédération Française des Sociétés d'Assurances and Others v Ministère de l'Agriculture et de la Pêche*,[12] the Court held that a non-profit-making organization which managed a voluntary supplementary pension scheme under rules laid down by public authorities was an undertaking because it carried on an activity in competition with life assurance companies. The definition is therefore wide and includes not only companies and partnerships but also the self-employed,[13] including performing artists,[14] agricultural co-operatives,[15] protection and indemnity (P and I) clubs,[16] and sports associations. For example, in *Distribution of Package Tours during the 1990 World Cup*,[17] the Commission held that FIFA, football's world governing body, and the Italian Football Association carried out activities of an economic nature and were therefore undertakings.

Public Bodies

2.23   In cases involving public bodies, or other entities operating under State aegis, a distinction is drawn 'between a situation where the State acts in the exercise of official authority and that where it carries on economic activities of an industrial or commercial nature by offering goods or services on the market'.[18] In general, the rule outlined in paragraphs 2.21 and 2.22 above also applies to public bodies in so far as they engage in commercial activity. For example, in *Klaus Höfner and Fritz Elser v Macrotron*,[19] the ECJ held that the Federal German Employment Agency was an undertaking as the service it provided, employment procurement, was an economic activity and one which did not necessarily have to be provided by the state. A Soviet trading organization forming part of a Ministry[20] has been found to be an undertaking.

---

[11]   Case 7/82 *GVL v Commission* [1983] ECR 483.

[12]   Case C–244/94 [1995] ECR I–4013, para 17.

[13]   *Coapi* [1995] OJ L122/37, para 32. On the other hand individuals acting solely in their capacity as employees are not considered to be undertakings. See, for example, Joined Cases 40 to 48, 50, 54 to 56, 111, 113 and 114–173 *Coöperatieve Vereniging 'Suiker Unie' UA and others v Commission* [1975] ECR 1663. Similarly agents may, in certain circumstances, not be undertakings. See Section G of Chapter 7 of this book.

[14]   *RAI/UNITEL* [1978] OJ L157/39.

[15]   Case 61/80 *Coöperatieve Stremsel-en Kleurselfabriek v Commission* [1981] ECR 851.

[16]   *P & I Clubs* [1985] OJ L376/2, [1999] OJ L125/12. In its decision of 19 May 1999, the Commission stated at para 50: 'The Pooling Agreement and the IGA are agreements between the P & I Clubs. These must be considered non-profit-making undertakings performing an economic activity. In fact, they compete between themselves as well as with other mutuals and profit-making insurers in some segments of the P & I insurance business.'

[17]   *Distribution of Package Tours during the 1990 World Cup* [1992] OJ L326/31.

[18]   Case C–343/95 *Diego Calì & Figli Srl v Servizi ecologici porto di Genova SpA (SEPG)* [1997] ECR I–547; [1997] 5 CHLR 484, para 16. See also Case 118/85 *Commission v Italy* [1987] ECR 2599, para 7.

[19]   Case C–41/90 *Höfner and Elser* [1991] ECR I–1979.

[20]   *Aluminium imports from Eastern Europe* [1985] OJ L92/1.

However, in *Diego Calì & Figli Srl v Servizi ecologici porto di Genova SpA (SEPG)*, **2.24**
the ECJ held that the activities of a limited company which had been granted the
exclusive right to carry out anti-pollution services on the Genoa Port Authority's
behalf were not of an economic nature, notwithstanding the fact that the company charged vessels a fee, albeit one set unilaterally by the Port Authority, for its
services. The Court found that:

> The anti-pollution surveillance for which SEPG was responsible . . . *forms part of the*
> *essential functions* of the State as regards protection of the environment in maritime
> areas. Such surveillance is connected by its nature, its aim and the rules to which it
> is subject with the exercise of powers relating to the protection of the environment
> which *are typically those of a public authority*. It is not of an economic nature justify-
> ing the application of the Treaty rules on competition. The levying of a charge by
> SEPG for preventive anti-pollution surveillance is an integral part of its surveillance
> activity in the maritime area of the port and cannot affect the legal status of that
> activity.[21]

Similarly, in *Eurocontrol*,[22] the ECJ held that Eurocontrol's activities were connected with the exercise of powers relating to the control and supervision of air
space 'which are typically those of a public authority'. They were therefore 'not of
an economic nature justifying the application of the Treaty rules of competition'.[23]

While the pursuit of profit is not essential, regard must also be had to the way an **2.25**
entity is financed. In *Christian Poucet v Assurances Générales de France and Caisse*
Mutuelle Régionale du Languedoc-Roussillon,[24] the ECJ was asked whether an
organization charged with managing a special social security scheme is to be
regarded as an undertaking for the purposes of Articles 81 and 82 of the Treaty. In
response the Court stated that '[s]ickness funds, and the organisations involved in
the management of the public social security system, fulfil an exclusively social
function. That activity is based on the principle of national solidarity and is
entirely non-profit-making . . . The benefits paid are statutory benefits bearing no
relation to the amount of the contributions. Accordingly, that activity is not an
economic activity and, therefore, the organisations to which it is entrusted are not
undertakings.' The crucial fact in this case seemed to be the way the scheme was
financed, based as it was on the principle of '*solidarity*'. Solidarity was 'embodied
in the fact that the contributions paid by active workers serve to finance the pen-
sions of retired workers. It is also reflected by the grant of pension rights where no
contributions have been made and of pension rights that are not proportional to
the contributions paid. It follows', the Court said, 'that the social security

---

[21] Case C–343/95 [1997] ECR I–547, paras 22–24; emphasis added by the authors.
[22] Case C–364/92 [1994] ECR I–43.
[23] Case C–364/92 [1994] ECR I–43, para 30.
[24] Joined Cases C–159/91 and C–160/91 *Christian Poucet v Assurances Générales de France and*
Caisse Mutuelle Régionale du Languedoc-Roussillon [1993] ECR I–637, paras 4, 18, 19, 11, and 13.

schemes, as described, are based on a system of compulsory contribution, which is indispensable for application of the principle of solidarity and the financial equilibrium of those schemes.'

2.26   However, in *Fédération Française des Sociétés d'Assurances and Others v Ministère de l'Agriculture et de la Pêche*,[25] the ECJ reaffirmed that a non-profit-making organization managing a supplementary pension scheme under rules laid down by public authorities could be an undertaking. It rejected the French Government's argument that the scheme was based on the principle of 'solidarity', drawing attention in particular to the fact that the pension scheme under review was one that beneficiaries entered into on a voluntary, rather than a compulsory, basis.

(2) Agreements

2.27   The concept of an 'agreement' under Article 81(1) is widely drawn. For an agreement to exist it 'is sufficient if the undertakings in question should have expressed their joint intention to conduct themselves on the market in a specific way'.[26] This 'expression of a joint intention' does not have to take the form of a legally binding contract to qualify as an agreement under Article 81(1). In fact the form the agreement takes is irrelevant. It can be written or oral,[27] signed or unsigned.[28] 'Gentlemen's agreements' have been held to be agreements for the purposes of Article 81(1).[29] In SSI,[30] the Commission even held that a mere 'understanding' between an association of cigarette manufacturers and the representatives of cigarette wholesalers and retailers in The Netherlands was an agreement within the meaning of Article 81(1).

2.28   An arrangement does not cease to be an agreement because it does not prescribe in detail the conduct to be undertaken or because the parties have not agreed to each and every part of it; in order to qualify as an agreement it is sufficient for it to set the broad framework under which the parties will cease to operate independently. In *Polypropylene*,[31] the Commission decided that the fifteen firms involved had reached an agreement even though some had not been to every meeting or been involved in every decision that had been made. The Commission held that an agreement exists 'if the parties reach a consensus on a plan which limits or is likely to limit their commercial freedom by determining the lines of their mutual action or abstention from action in the market . . . In the present case the produc-

---

[25]   Case C–244/94 *Fédération Française des Sociétés d'Assurances and Others v Ministère de l'Agriculture et de la Pêche* [1995] ECR I–4013.
[26]   Case T–7/89 *SA Hercules Chemicals NV v Commission* [1991] ECR II–1711, para 2.
[27]   Case 28/77 *Tepea BV v Commission* [1978] ECR 1391.
[28]   *BP Kemi—DDSF* [1979] OJ L286/32.
[29]   Case 41/69 *ACF Chemiefarma NV v Commission* [1970] ECR 661.
[30]   [1982] OJ L232/1.
[31]   [1986] OJ L230/1.

ers, by subscribing to a common plan to regulate prices and supply in the polypropylene market, participated in an overall framework agreement which was manifested in a series of more detailed sub-agreements worked out from time to time.' Similarly, in its *Pre-Insulated Pipes Cartel* decision, the Commission held that as a matter both of evidence and of substantive law it was not necessary for every participant to have participated in, given its express consent to, or even to have been aware of each and every individual aspect or manifestation of an arrangement for an agreement to exist for the purposes of Article 81(1).[32]

An agreement is reached even if one or more of the undertakings involved intends **2.29** to ignore its provisions.[33] In *Roofing Felt Cartel*,[34] the Commission found that seven members and two non-members of a trade association had fixed prices. The non-members argued that they had joined the cartel for fear of retaliation. They had given the impression of going along with the cartel's plans, while having no real intention of abiding by its disciplines. They also argued that there was no evidence of their having observed the agreements in practice. However, the Commission held that 'neither the state of mind of the non-members when they entered into such agreements as to their intention of abiding by them, nor the fact that the non-members did not in fact observe the agreements (as some evidence suggests) would affect the Commission's finding that the agreements were made and that the non-members were parties to them'. Even cheating or occasional outbreaks of fierce competition do not prevent an arrangement from constituting an agreement for the purposes of Article 81(1) where there is a common and continuing objective to co-operate.[35]

The formal termination of an agreement does not necessarily mean that there is **2.30** no longer a violation of Article 81. In *EMI Records Limited v CBS United Kingdom Limited*,[36] the ECJ held that for Article 81 to apply 'it is sufficient that such agreements continue to produce their effects after they have formally ceased to be in force'. However, the Court added that '[a]n agreement is only to be regarded as continuing to produce its effects if from the behaviour of the parties concerned there may be inferred the existence of elements of concerted practice and of coordination peculiar to the agreement and producing the same result as that envisaged by the agreement'.[37] Thus, the agreement must continue to influence the conduct of the parties on the market.[38]

---

[32] [1999] OJ L24/1, para 134.
[33] Joined Cases 209 to 215 and 218/78 *Heinz van Landewyck SARL and others v Commission* [1980] ECR 3125.
[34] [1986] OJ L232/15, para 86, upheld on appeal: Case 246/86 *SC Belasco and others v Commission* [1989] ECR 2117.
[35] *Pre-Insulated Pipe Cartel* [1999] OJ L24/1, para 124.
[36] Case 51/75 [1976] ECR 811, para 30.
[37] ibid, para 31.
[38] *Soda-ash—Solvay, ICI* [1991] OJ L152/1, para 54.

2.31 The fact that the terms of, or the parties to, an arrangement change over time does not mean that as a result it ceases to be an agreement under Article 81(1). In *Pre-Insulated Pipes Cartel*, the Commission decided that each such change did not imply that a new 'agreement' had come into force for the purposes of Article 81(1).[39]

2.32 Agreements made before accession of a Member State will be deemed to be agreements for the purposes of Article 81(1) if they continue to produce their effects within the European Community after the date of accession.[40] In any event, the fact that an agreement was concluded outside the EC does not prevent Article 81(1) applying to it if the general rules on Community jurisdiction apply.[41]

At least two undertakings must be party to an arrangement for it to qualify as an agreement for the purposes of Article 81(1)

2.33 This means that unilateral conduct does not, in most instances, fall within the scope of the prohibition. Nevertheless, action which at first glance may seem to be unilateral may, in certain circumstances, be caught by Article 81(1). This is particularly true when the conduct takes place in the context of an existing vertical agreement. In *BMW Belgium SA et al v Commission*,[42] BMW Belgium had notified its standard form distribution agreement with its dealers to the Commission. The agreement contained no general export prohibition but prevented Belgian BMW dealers from selling BMW vehicles to non-approved dealers. At the time, the prices of BMW cars were appreciably lower in Belgium than in several other Member States. This brought about an increase in re-exports of BMW vehicles from Belgium. Some sales were made to non-approved dealers who were not acting on behalf of consumers. In response, BMW Belgium, with the support of the BMW Belgium dealers' association, sent a circular stating that 'henceforth no BMW dealer in Belgium will sell cars outside Belgium or to firms who propose to export them'. A number of dealers acknowledged, in writing, receipt of the circular. The ECJ held that an agreement had been made between BMW Belgium, the members of the Belgian dealers' association and, the Belgian dealers who had acknowledged receipt of the circular.

2.34 In *Ford-Werke AG and Ford of Europe Inc v Commission*,[43] the ECJ found that admission to Ford's dealer network in Germany necessarily implied acceptance by the dealer of Ford's policy with regard to the models which it chose to deliver to the German market. The Court therefore held that Ford's refusal to supply right-

---

[39] *Pre-Insulated Pipe Cartel* [1999] OJ L24/1, paras 129–138.
[40] Case 40/70 *Sirena Srl v Eda Srl and others* [1971] ECR 69.
[41] On jurisdiction, see below Section D.
[42] Joined Cases 32/78, 36 to 82/78 [1979] ECR 2435.
[43] Joined Cases 25 and 26/84 [1985] ECR 2725.

hand-drive cars to these dealers was not a unilateral act but part of the contractual relations between them and was subject to the prohibition of Article 81(1).

The Single Economic Unit Doctrine (No Intra-Enterprise Conspiracy in EC Law)

As already noted above, for the purposes of Article 81(1) at least two undertakings **2.35** must be party to an agreement. However, two or more legally separate entities may be treated as a single undertaking under the competition rules if their relationship justifies regarding them as a single economic unit. In this case, agreements between them, even legally enforceable ones, will usually be regarded as an internal allocation of functions within a corporate group rather than an agreement between independent undertakings capable of falling within the prohibition of Article 81(1). This means that Article 81 will not apply to arrangements between them, however anti-competitive they may seem to be.[44] However, it also means that parent companies, including those based outside the Community, can be held liable under Article 81 for the behaviour of their subsidiaries operating within the EU, since the undertaking *as a whole* is active there.[45]

In *Centrafarm v Sterling Drug*,[46] the ECJ held that an agreement between under- **2.36** takings belonging to the same group and having the status of parent and subsidiary was not caught by Article 81(1) 'if the undertakings form an economic unit within which the subsidiary has no real freedom to determine its course of action on the market, and if the agreements or practices are concerned merely with the internal allocation of tasks as between the undertakings'. In *Viho Europe BV v Commission*,[47] the ECJ held that Article 81(1) could not apply where a subsidiary did not freely determine its conduct on the market, but instead carried out the instructions given to it directly or indirectly by the parent company.

Determining whether related firms are independent in their decision making can, **2.37** in practice, be difficult. The Commission's decisions under the EC Merger Regulation, and its Notice on the concept of concentration,[48] provide perhaps the best guidance on this issue. In general, where a subsidiary is wholly owned, or where a parent company has a majority shareholding in a subsidiary, there is a presumption that the subsidiary is controlled by its parent.[49] Minority holdings may

---

[44] Article 82 may, however, apply.
[45] Case 48/69 *ICI v Commission* [1972] ECR 619.
[46] Case 15/74 *Centrafarm v Sterling Drug* [1974] ECR 619, para 1147.
[47] Case C–73/95 *Viho Europe BV v Commission* [1996] ECR I–5457.
[48] [1998] OJ C66/5.
[49] See para 13 of the Commission Notice On The Concept Of Concentration under Council Regulation (EEC) No 4064/89 on the control of concentrations between undertakings. See also *Zürich/MMI* (Case IV/M286) (1993) OJ C112/0; *Crédit Lyonnais/BFG Bank* (Case IV/M296) (1993) OJ C45/0.

also give the parent company control[50] where specific rights are attached to the minority shareholding which enable the minority shareholder to determine the strategic commercial behaviour of the other company (such as the power to appoint more than half of the members of the supervisory board or the administrative board). A minority shareholder may also be deemed to have control if it is likely to achieve a majority at the shareholders' meeting, given that the remaining shares are widely dispersed.

2.38   The situation is more complex where a subsidiary is jointly controlled by two companies or persons. In *Gosme/Martell*,[51] DMP was a joint subsidiary of Martell and Piper-Heidsieck. The Commission found that Martell was not in a position to control DMP's commercial activities because the parent companies each held 50 per cent of DMP's capital and voting rights; half the supervisory board members represented Martell shareholders and half Piper-Heidsieck shareholders; DMP also distributed brands not belonging to its parent companies; Martell and Piper-Heidsieck products were invoiced to wholesalers on the same document; and DMP had its own sales force and alone concluded the conditions of sale with the buying syndicates. The Commission therefore concluded that DMP, the subsidiary, and Martell, a parent company, were independent undertakings.

2.39   Similarly, in *Ijsselcentrale*,[52] four electricity generation companies had established a joint subsidiary to act as a vehicle for co-operation between them. The parties had argued that the subsidiary and the electricity generators formed an economic unit because they were components of one indivisible public electricity supply system. The Commission rejected this argument. It held that the four participants did not belong to a single group of companies. They were separate legal persons, and were not controlled by a single person, natural or legal. Each generating company determined its own conduct independently. The fact that the generators formed an indivisible part of the public electricity supply system did not mean that they were part of the same economic unit. The Commission also held that the subsidiary was not part of the same economic unit as its parents but rather a joint venture controlled by them together.

2.40   While property rights and shareholders' agreements are the most important factors in determining whether undertakings belong to the same economic unit, they are not the only ones. The fact that a company does not legally belong to a group is not decisive. Account must also be taken of the nature of the relationship between the undertakings belonging to that group.[53] Purely economic relationships may also play a role. In certain circumstances, a situation of economic

---

[50] See para 14 of the Commission Notice On The Concept Of Concentration under Council Regulation (EEC) No 4064/89 on the control of concentrations between undertakings.

[51] *Gosme/Martell—DMP* [1991] OJ L185/23.

[52] *Ijsselcentrale and others* [1991] OJ L28/32.

[53] Case 30/87 *Corinne Bodson v SA Pompes funèbres des régions libérées* [1988] ECR 2479.

dependence may lead to control on a *de facto* basis where, for example, important long-term supply agreements or credits provided by suppliers or customers, coupled with structural links, confer decisive influence on one party over another.[54]

(3) Judicial Settlement

It is not certain whether a settlement reached before a national court which constitutes a judicial act is an agreement capable of falling within the prohibition of Article 81(1). In *Bayer AG and Maschinenfabrik Hennecke GmbH v Heinz Süllhöfer*, the ECJ held that '[i]n its prohibition of certain "agreements" between undertakings, Article 85(1) [now Article 81(1)] makes no distinction between agreements whose purpose is to put an end to litigation and those concluded with other aims in mind'. However, it went on to note that 'this assessment of such a settlement is without prejudice to the question whether, and to what extent, a judicial settlement reached before a national court which constitutes a judicial act may be invalid for breach of Community competition rules.'[55] There is no doubt that agreements between undertakings to settle actual or potential litigation, for example on matters of intellectual property, may fall under Article 81(1).[56] **2.41**

(4) Decisions by Associations of Undertakings

Article 81(1) explicitly recognizes that collusion can take place through the medium of an association. As with the other terms of Article 81(1), the word 'association' is defined widely and is not restricted to trade associations. Thus such bodies as agricultural co-operatives,[57] associations entrusted with statutory functions,[58] and associations of trade associations[59] have been held to be 'associations of undertakings' under Article 81(1). **2.42**

Similarly the word 'decision' has a wider meaning under Article 81(1) than might appear at first glance. Thus where an association of undertakings is found to exist, its 'decisions' do not need to be binding on its members to bring them within the scope of Article 81(1). All that is required is that the 'decision' be made with the object or effect of influencing the commercial behaviour of the association's members. In *Verband der Sachversicherer eV v Commission*,[60] an association of German insurers issued a recommendation to its members to raise premiums. **2.43**

---

[54] See, eg, para 9 of Notice On The Concept Of Concentration; see also *CCIE/GTE* (Case IV/M258) [1992] OJ C265; *Lockheed Martin/Loral Corporation* (Case IV/M697) [1996] OJ C314/9.

[55] Case 65/86 *Bayer AG and Maschinenfabrik Hennecke GmbH v Heinz Süllhöfer* [1988] ECR 5249, paras 1 and 15.

[56] See, eg, *Toltecs-Dorcet* [1982] OJ L379/19.

[57] *MELDOC* [1986] OJ L348/50.

[58] *Pabst & Richarz/BNIA* [1976] OJ L231/24; *Coapi* [1995] OJ L122/37.

[59] *Milchförderungsfonds* [1985] OJ L35/35.

[60] Case 45/85 [1987] ECR 405.

The association had argued that this recommendation had been made by a committee which was not competent to adopt decisions binding on the association or its members. The recommendation therefore fell outside the scope of the prohibition. The ECJ held that the recommendation was a decision as it reflected the association's resolve to co-ordinate the conduct of its members on the German insurance market in accordance with the terms of the recommendation.

2.44 It should be noted that if a recommendation is carried out or, indeed, if it merely influences the behaviour of the members of the association, this can also amount to an agreement or a concerted practice as between the members themselves.[61] The importance of the concept of 'decisions by associations of undertakings' therefore lies in the fact that it enables those applying Article 81(1) to hold associations liable for the anti-competitive behaviour of their members.

(5) Concerted Practice

Definition

2.45 A concerted practice is a form of co-ordination where undertakings, without concluding any sort of agreement or establishing a plan of action, 'knowingly substitute practical co-operation between them for the risks of competition'.[62] The aim of the Treaty, in establishing the concept of concerted practice, is to prevent undertakings from evading the application of Article 81(1) by colluding in an anti-competitive manner which falls short of an agreement by, for example, informing each other in advance of the attitude each intends to adopt, so that each may regulate its commercial conduct in the knowledge that its competitors will behave in the same way.[63]

2.46 In *Imperial Chemical Industries Ltd (ICI). v Commission*, the ECJ held that, although undertakings were free to alter their behaviour to take into account the present or foreseeable conduct of their competitors, it was nevertheless 'contrary to the rules on competition contained in the treaty for a producer to cooperate with his competitors, in any way whatsoever, in order to determine a co-ordinated course of action . . . and to ensure its success by prior elimination of all uncertainty as to each other's conduct regarding the essential elements of that action'.[64]

2.47 The ECJ confirmed and developed this definition in *Coöperatieve Vereniging 'Suiker Unie' and others v Commission*.[65] The Commission had decided that sugar producers in Belgium, Germany, and Holland had engaged in a concerted prac-

---

[61] *Roofing Felt Cartel* [1986] OJ L232/15, upheld on appeal: Case 246/86 *SC Belasco and others v Commission* [1989] ECR 2117.

[62] Case 48/69 *ICI v Commission* [1972] ECR 619, para 64.

[63] *Pre-Insulated Pipe Cartel* [1999] OJ L24/1, paras 129–134.

[64] Case 48/69 *ICI v Commission* [1972] ECR 619, para 118.

[65] Joined Cases 40 to 48, 50, 54 to 56, 111, 113 and 114/173 [1975] ECR 1663.

tice to control the supply of sugar into The Netherlands. The producers had argued that for a concerted practice to exist it would have been necessary for them to have established a plan which removed in advance any doubt as to their future conduct; otherwise, they asserted, every attempt by an undertaking to react intelligently to the acts of its competitors could be portrayed as an offence. In their case no plan had been worked out, so no concerted practice had taken place.

The Court again acknowledged that the law did not deprive economic operators **2.48** of the right to adapt themselves intelligently to the conduct of their competitors. However, the underlying notion of competition in the EC Treaty was that each economic operator had to 'determine independently the policy which he intends to adopt on the common market including the choice of the persons and undertakings to which he makes offers or sells'. The law therefore strictly precluded 'any direct or indirect contact between such operators, the object or effect whereof is either to influence the conduct on the market of an actual or potential competitor or to disclose to such a competitor the course of conduct which they themselves have decided to adopt or contemplate adopting on the market'. Thus the law 'in no way require[d] the working out of an actual plan'[66] for a concerted practice to exist.

In *SA Hercules Chemicals NV v Commission*,[67] the CFI applied the tests laid down **2.49** in *ICI* and *Suiker Unie*. The Commission had found that the applicant had participated in meetings during which it discussed with its competitors matters such as the prices they wished to see charged on the market, the prices they intended to charge, their profitability thresholds, they judged to be necessary, their sales figures and the identity of customers. The CFI confirmed that the applicant, through its participation in those meetings, had taken part, together with its competitors:

> in concerted action the purpose of which was to influence their conduct on the market and to disclose to each other the course of conduct which each of the producers itself contemplated adopting on the market. Accordingly, not only did the applicant pursue the aim of eliminating in advance uncertainty about the future conduct of its competitors but also, in determining the policy which it intended to follow on the market, it could not fail to take account, directly or indirectly, of the information obtained during the course of those meetings. Similarly, in determining the policy which they intended to follow, its competitors were bound to take into account, directly or indirectly, the information disclosed to them by the applicant about the course of conduct which the applicant itself had decided upon or which it contemplated adopting on the market.[68]

---

[66] Joined Cases 40 to 48, 50, 54 to 56, 111, 113 and 114/73 [1975] ECR 1663, paras 4 and 5.
[67] Case T–7/89 [1991] ECR II–1711.
[68] Case T–7/89 [1991] ECR II–1711 paras 259–260. See also *Pre-Insulated Pipe Cartel* [1999] OJ L24/1, paras 129–138.

Thus it would seem that to prove a concerted practice a number of elements will usually need to be identified. First, some form of direct or indirect contact between undertakings is required. Secondly, there must some meeting of minds or consensus between the parties to co-operate rather than compete. Thus, for example, if A unilaterally tells its competitor, B, that it will be raising its price in a month's time, with the aim of getting B to do so as well, a concerted practice can be found to have taken place if B responds by increasing the price of its goods. If A, instead of telling its competitor direct, make a public announcement of its intention to behave in a particular manner, a concerted practice may be held to have taken place if A did so in the knowledge that its competitors would follow and they do so. Any direct or indirect contact between competitors which is designed or has the effect of reducing uncertainty about their future conduct is likely to be found to be a concerted practice.

2.50   In its *Anic* judgment of 8 July 1999, the ECJ further clarified a number of important issues in relation to concerted practices.[69] It held that a concerted practice had three elements: contact between undertakings, be it direct or indirect; subsequent behaviour in the market; and causality between the two. It went on to say that once concertation had been established, behaviour on the market could be presumed. The burden of rebuttal would then fall on the undertakings concerned since a concerted practice could fall under Article 81(1) by virtue of its object alone, whatever its effect. The behaviour in the market did not necessarily have to give rise to an actual restrictive effect on competition for Article 81(1) to apply.

Can a Concerted Practice be Inferred from Circumstantial Evidence Alone?

2.51   Although in most cases involving concerted practices there will be evidence of contact and a common intent to co-operate rather than compete, in certain circumstances a concerted practice may be inferred from circumstantial evidence alone. The test, however, is strict and hard to meet. In *ICI*,[70] the Commission found that the major producers of aniline dyes in the Community, who had all raised their prices by similar amounts on three separate occasions between 1964 and 1967, had engaged in a concerted practice. The parties appealed arguing that the increases could be explained by the oligopolistic nature of the markets concerned. Dismissing the appeal, the ECJ held that while parallel behaviour by itself did not constitute a concerted practice 'it may however amount to strong evidence of such a practice if it leads to conditions of competition which do not correspond to the normal conditions of the market having regard to the nature of the products, the size and number of undertakings, and the volume of the said market'.[71] The Court found that the market for aniline dyes was not oligopolistic. It was

---

[69]   Case C–49/92P *Commission v Anic Partecipazioni SpA* [1999].
[70]   Case 48/69 *ICI v Commission* [1972] ECR 619.
[71]   ibid, para 66.

national in scope with clear differences in characteristics between the different geographic markets. It was therefore 'hardly conceivable that the same action could be taken spontaneously at the same time, on the same national markets and for the same range of products'[72] as a result of independent decision making.

In *Ahlström Osakeyhtiö et al v Commission (Wood Pulp II)*,[73] the Court clarified fur-   **2.52**
ther the standard of proof required. It noted that Article 81 did not deprive economic operators of the right to adapt themselves intelligently to the existing and anticipated conduct of their competitors. Thus parallel conduct in itself 'cannot be regarded as furnishing proof of concertation unless concertation constitutes the only plausible explanations for such conduct. Accordingly, it is necessary in this case to ascertain whether the parallel conduct alleged by the Commission cannot, taking account of the nature of the products, the size and the number of the undertakings and the volume of the market in question, be explained otherwise than by concertation.'[74]

In *Compagnie Royale Asturienne des Mines SA and Rheinzink GmbH v*   **2.53**
Commission,[75] the Commission had held that two zinc producers had engaged in a concerted practice to prevent parallel imports from Belgium to Germany by terminating deliveries to their Belgian distributor within a week of each other. To refute this argument the ECJ held that it would be sufficient for the applicants to prove circumstances which cast the facts established by the Commission in a different light and which thus allow another explanation of their parallel behaviour. In this case the termination of deliveries could be explained by non-payment of invoices by the distributor over the preceding few months.

(6) Distinction between Agreement and Concerted Practice

It can be difficult to identify exactly where an agreement ends and a concerted   **2.54**
practice starts. Many types of collusive behaviour, which in the past would have been more appropriately termed a concerted practice, may today be found to be an agreement. The concepts are fluid and may overlap. An infringement may begin in one form and, as it evolves over time, progressively assume some or all the characteristics of another. In fact it often makes little sense to try to draw a distinction between the two concepts as an infringement may present simultaneously the characteristics of an agreement and a concerted practice.[76] Indeed, in cartel cases, the Commission often alleges that an agreement and/or concerted practice has taken place without distinguishing between the two. Nothing turns

---

[72] ibid, para 109.
[73] Joined Cases C–89/85, C–104/85, C–114/85, C–116/85, C–117/85 and C–125/85 to C–129/85 [1993] ECR I–1307.
[74] ibid, paras 71–72.
[75] Joined Cases 29/83 and 30/83 [1984] ECR 1679.
[76] *Pre-Insulated Pipe Cartel* [1999] OJ L24/1, paras 129–138.

on the precise distinction for the purposes of the substantive analysis under Article 81(1).[77] This is clear from the Commission's *Pre-Insulated Pipes Cartel* decision, in which it held that:

> where the various concerted practices followed and agreements concluded form part of a series of efforts made by the undertakings in pursuit of a common objective of preventing or distorting competition, the Commission is entitled to find that they constitute a single continuous infringement. As the Court of First Instance observed on this point in Case T–7/89: it would be artificial to split up such continuous conduct, characterised by a single purpose, by treating it as a number of separate infringements: 'The fact is that the (undertakings) took part—over a period of years—in an integrated set of schemes constituting a single infringement, which progressively manifested itself in both unlawful agreements and unlawful concerted practices.[78]

2.55 In fact, the concept of 'concerted practice' is important mainly in cases where the Commission or the Courts are forced to rely on circumstantial evidence alone. This will, for example, be the case where there is little 'hard' evidence of collusion and therefore it has to be argued that a particular outcome (for example, similarly timed price increases by competitors) necessarily implies that anti-competitive behaviour has taken place.

(7) 'which have as their object or effect the prevention, restriction or distortion of competition within the common market'

2.56 There is much debate about the central notion of Article 81(1): an agreement's object or effect to prevent, restrict, or distort competition. What is the competition which the provision is supposed to protect? This question has been put in many ways: the relationship between competition policy and other Community policies, the interplay between the competition provisions of the EC Treaty and its other rules, academic definitions of competition, lists of concerns distilled from the case law, argument about the merits of protecting competitors' interests as opposed to those of consumers, economic welfare considerations or the competitive process itself, the relevance of the EU's single market imperative, contrasts between the European and US approaches in various locations or at particular moments in time,[79] etc.

2.57 The debate is further complicated by a dispute about the notion of 'restriction of competition'. The critics' position may be summarized as follows. The Commission's application of Article 81(1) is too broad and/or fundamentally misconceived. Arrangements which are pro-competitive in the given market situation of a case are sometimes brought under Article 81(1) and exempted under

---

[77] *Polypropylene* [1986] OJ L230/1, para 85.

[78] [1999] OJ L24/1, para 131.

[79] For a brief account, see F Souty, *Le droit de la concurrence de l'Union Européenne* (2nd edn, Paris: Montchrestien, 1999) 23 *et seq.*

Article 81(3), when it would be simpler and less burdensome for all concerned if Article 81(1) were not applied to them in the first place. To make matters worse, most of this unnecessary exemption activity is not carried out in the proper procedural way foreseen by Regulation 17 by decisions which confer legal certainty, but by the ersatz, extra-regulatory, informal, and legally fragile comfort letter system. The fundamental misconception lying at the heart of this excessive application of Article 81(1) is said to be the view that a restraint on commercial freedom of action is a restriction of competition. This leads to examination of individual clauses rather than economic analysis and unnecessarily widens the scope of Article 81(1). The moves towards a 'rule of reason' analysis in the case law of the Court of Justice have been received unenthusiastically by the Commission, which has sought to distinguish subsequent cases from the judgments concerned.

In what follows, we will answer some of these points, consider the notion of competition in the EC context, and examine the notions of object and effect. It will be necessary to look into the important issue of the status of a pure economic test (price/output analysis) under Article 81(1). In practice little, if anything, turns on the terms *prevention, restriction, and distortion*, which tend to be used interchangeably.   **2.58**

At the outset, it must be recalled that the Community's competition law serves the essential goal of creating and sustaining a single market. This statement may seem trite, but it bears repetition because of its central importance to an understanding of the way in which competition law has developed in the EC. It is tempting to take for granted what has been achieved, but the elimination of barriers between Member States and the establishment of economic conditions across the EU more and more resembling those of a domestic national market are the result of forty years of effort, legal development, and policy insistence. This has profoundly affected the Commission's approach to the application of Article 81, particularly in the field of vertical restraints.   **2.59**

For an agreement or concerted practice to be caught by Article 81(1) it must have the object or effect of restricting competition to an appreciable extent. Three introductory points can be made. First, these are alternative and not cumulative requirements.[80] Thus if an agreement restricts competition by object, it is not necessary to show that it is also restrictive by effect and vice versa.[81] Secondly, while Article 81(1) does not contain the word 'appreciable', it is clear from the jurisprudence of the Court and administrative practice of the Commission that a restriction of competition will not fall within the scope of Article 81(1) unless it has an   **2.60**

---

[80] Case 56/65 *Société Technique Minière v Maschinenbau Ulm GmbH* [1966] ECR 235, at 249.
[81] Case 56/65 *Société Technique Minière v Maschinenbau Ulm* [1966] ECR 235; Case 45/85 *Verband der Sachversicherer v Commission* [1987] ECR 405.

appreciable impact on competition in the relevant market.[82] The concepts of, 'object', 'effect', and 'appreciability' are further discussed below. Thirdly, Article 81 is applicable both to horizontal and vertical agreements.[83]

Restriction by Object

2.61   Restrictions by object are restrictions which by 'their very nature'[84] or 'of them-selves' constitute a restriction of competition. The determination whether an agreement has as its object a restriction of competition is not dependent on the subjective intent of the parties but on 'its terms, the legal and economic context in which it was concluded and the conduct of the parties'.[85] Thus even if the parties are able to show that restricting competition was not their aim, or that their agree-ment had other laudable aims as well, the natural tendency of an agreement to restrict competition will suffice for a finding that the object is to restrict competi-tion. Conversely the courts and the Commission cannot find that a particular agreement has as its object a restriction of competition merely because the aim of the parties is to restrict competition.

2.62   In *IAZ International Belgium v Commission*,[86] the parties challenged a decision in which the Commission had held that the object of an agreement between them was to restrict competition. The parties were manufacturers and exclusive importers of washing machines affiliated to certain trade organizations in Belgium. They had agreed that one of them would carry out checks on appliances and grant a conformity label to machines fulfilling the relevant criteria. According to the parties the purpose of the agreement was to monitor the conformity of washing machines in order to preserve the quality of drinking water. After con-sidering the terms of the agreement, the legal and economic context in which it was concluded, and the conduct of the parties, the ECJ held that the object of the agreements was to restrict competition within the common market, notwith-standing the fact that it also pursued the objective of protecting public health and reducing the cost of conformity checks . The Court further held that it did not matter for this purpose that it had not been established that the intention of all the parties was to restrict competition.

2.63   In practice few types of agreement have as their object the restriction of competi-tion. Typically these are agreements which, *prima facie*, do not appear to have any significant beneficial effects and are entered into solely to restrict competition. For

---

[82]   Case 56/65 *Société Technique Minière v Maschinenbau Ulm* [1966] ECR 235.
[83]   Joined Cases 56 and 58/64 *Consten and Grundig v Commission* [1966] ECR 299.
[84]   Case 19/77 *Miller International Schallplatten v Commission* [1978] ECR 131.
[85]   Joined Cases 96 to 102,104,105,108 and 110/82 *NV IAZ International Belgium and others v Commission* [1983] ECR 3369, paras 23–25.
[86]   Joined Cases 96 to 102, 104, 105, 108 and 110/82 *NV IAZ International Belgium and others v Commission* [1983] ECR 3369; see also, eg, *AROW/BNIC* [1982] OJ L379/1.

agreements between undertakings at the same level of the market (horizontal agreements), essentially only those which have the obvious consequence of price fixing[87] or market sharing[88] are likely to be held to be restrictive by object. For vertical agreements, only those which impede parallel trade within the Community[89] or enforce resale price maintenance[90] are likely to be considered restrictive by object.[91]

Beyond these, the European Courts and the Commission are unlikely to find that **2.64** an agreement or restraint is restrictive by object. This means, for example, that where one party grants another party an exclusive right, this will not be considered as being 'of its nature' restrictive of competition.[92] The effect on competition of an agreement containing exclusivity clauses will therefore almost always have to be investigated. This is an important point to note as it is sometimes assumed that mere exclusivity is sufficient to bring an agreement within the prohibition of Article 81(1).

Agreements which are restrictive by object are caught by Article 81(1). The ECJ **2.65** has stated clearly on several occasions that, once an anti-competitive object has been shown, 'there is no need to take account of the concrete effect of an agreement'.[93] Thus if the object of an agreement is to fix prices it will not be necessary to show that actual prices were in fact affected. Similarly, arguments which purport to show that such agreements may also have pro-competitive effects will not usually be considered under Article 81(1)[94] but, where appropriate, may be examined under Article 81(3).

Restriction by Object and Appreciability

An agreement which has as its object the restriction of competition can neverthe- **2.66** less escape the prohibition of Article 81(1). The *Völk v Vervaecke* case, which

---

[87] See, eg, Case 123/83 *BNIC v Guy Clair* [1985] ECR 391.

[88] Case 41/69 *ACF Chemiefarma NV v Commission* [1970] ECR 661; Joined Cases T–68/89, T–77/89 and T–78/89 *Società Italiana Vetro SpA, Fabbrica Pisana SpA and PPG Vernante Pennitalia SpA v Commission* [1992] ECR II–1403; Case T–142/89 *Usines Gustave Böel SA v Commission* [1995] ECR II–867.

[89] See, eg, Joined Cases 56 and 58/64 *Consten and Grundig v Commission* [1966] ECR 299; Case 19/77 *Miller International Schallplatten v Commission* [1978] ECR 131.

[90] Case 234/83 *SA Binon & Cie v SA Agence et messageries de la presse* [1985] ECR 2015, para 44.

[91] This policy is reflected in para 276 of the Green Paper on Vertical Restraints, where it is stated that: 'The policy of treating *resale price maintenance* and *impediments to parallel trade* as serious violations of the competition rules would continue. It is proposed that they be treated as per se contrary to Article 85(1) [now Article 81(1)], as long as the agreement, concerted practice or decision concerned may affect trade between Member States. They are also unlikely to benefit from an exemption under Article 85(3).' See Section A of Chapter 7 of this book.

[92] Case 56/65 *Société Technique Minière v Maschinenbau Ulm* [1966] ECR 235.

[93] Joined Cases 56 and 58/64 *Consten and Grundig v Commission* [1966] ECR 299.

[94] See, eg, Joined Cases 56 and 58/64 *Consten and Grundig v Commission* [1966] ECR 299; Case 19/77 *Miller International Schallplatten v Commission* [1978] ECR 131.

concerned absolute territorial protection, established the principle that even in relation to restrictions by object it remains necessary to analyse the actual or potential effect of the agreement involved so as to rule out the possibility that it may only have an 'insignificant effect'[95] on the market or on trade.[96]

2.67 However, in *Società Italiana Vetro, Fabbrica Pisana and PPG Vernante Pennitalia v Commission*, the Commission sought to argue that the evidence of the agreements between the parties was so unambiguous and explicit that any investigation whatsoever into the structure of the market was entirely superfluous. While acknowledging that the Commission was not required to discuss in its decisions all the arguments raised by undertakings, the Court explicitly disagreed with the Commission's approach. It said that the Commission ought to have examined more fully the structure and the functioning of the market in order to show why the conclusions drawn by the applicants were groundless.[97] Most recently, in *Javico*, the ECJ reaffirmed this position. It held that:

> anti-competitive conduct may not be struck down under Article 85(1) [now Article 81(1)] of the Treaty unless it is capable of affecting trade between Member States . . . Moreover, that effect must not be insignificant . . . Thus, even an agreement imposing absolute territorial protection may escape the prohibition laid down in Article 85 if it affects the market only insignificantly, regard being had to the weak position of the persons concerned on the market in the products in question.[98]

This reference to 'affects the market' shows that this reasoning applies to the effect on competition as well as to effect on trade between Member States.

2.68 What is an '*insignificant effect*'? In its submission to the Court in *Völk v Vervaecke*, the Commission stated that the production of washing machines by Mr Völk's company represented 0.08 per cent of the total production of the common market and 0.2 per cent of production in the Federal Republic of Germany. Its market share of sales in Belgium and Luxembourg, the territory of its exclusive distributor Vervaecke, was approximately 0.6 per cent. On the basis of these small market shares the Commission admitted that even an agreement guaranteeing strict 'territorial protection' did not appreciably restrict competition. Neither did the Commission believe that the 'may affect trade between Member States' criterion was fulfilled. On the other hand in *Miller*,[99] which concerned a territorial restriction by object, the Court found that the company concerned, which had a market share of the German market in sound recordings which varied between 5

---

[95] Case 5/69 [1969] ECR 295, para 5/7.
[96] Not all commentators accept this view. Paragraph 7.34 of this book, for example, argues that once an agreement is caught by object, appreciability only applies to the effect on trade.
[97] Joined Cases T–68/89, T–77/89 and T–78/89 [1992] ECR II–1403, para 159.
[98] Case C–306/96 *Javico International v Yves Saint Laurent Parfums* [1998] ECR I–1983, paras 15–17.
[99] Case 19/77 *Miller International Schallplatten GmbH v Commission* [1978] ECR 131.

per cent and 6 per cent could not be compared with the undertakings in the *Völk* case and that Article 81(1) was infringed.

While market share is not the only criterion for assessing the impact of a vertical **2.69** restraint, for restrictions by object it is suggested that below 1 per cent market share the effect on the market is likely to be insignificant and Article 81(1) is unlikely to apply, while above 5 per cent the effect is likely to be appreciable and Article 81(1) is likely to apply. Between 1 per cent and 5 per cent is best described as a grey area. This is reflected in the Commission's Notice on Agreements of Minor Importance (the so-called *de minimis* Notice), which offers little comfort to undertakings in this grey area. The current Notice states that the applicability of Article 81(1) cannot be ruled out below the *de minimis* threshold, defined solely in terms of market share, for 'horizontal agreements which have as their object to fix prices or to limit production or sales; or to share markets or sources of supply' and for 'vertical agreements which have as their object to fix resale prices, or to confer territorial protection on the participating undertakings or third parties'.[100] Therefore, even companies with little market power who enter into restrictions by object run the risk of infringing Article 81(1).

Notwithstanding the terms of the current *de minimis* Notice, the Commission **2.70** rarely challenges agreements, even those which are restrictive by object, below 5 per cent market share for horizontal restrictions or 10 per cent for vertical restrictions. In economic terms, the impact of most restrictive agreements would be muted at low market share levels and the allocation of resources to such cases would, it is submitted, be questionable. If the Commission did challenge such agreements, the most likely reason for doing so would be pedagogical—to help ensure that a 'competition culture' was developed or maintained in a particular sector of the economy.

Appreciable Restriction by Effect

If an agreement does not have the object of restricting competition:

> the consequences of the agreement should then be considered and for it to be caught by the prohibition it is then necessary to find that those factors are present which show that competition has *in fact* been prevented or restricted or distorted to an appreciable extent. The competition in question must be understood within the actual context in which it would occur *in the absence of the agreement in dispute.*[101]

If there is appreciably less competition as a result of the agreement Article 81(1) will apply.

---

[100] The earlier 1986 Notice, which defined a *de minimis* threshold in terms of both market share (ie 5%) and turnover (ie ECU 200 million, increased to 300 million in 1994), applied to both restrictions by object and effect.

[101] Case 56/65 *Société Technique Minière v Maschinenbau Ulm GmbH* [1966] ECR 235, at 249 and 250.

2.72 This apparently simple formulation, however, masks a heated debate. What does 'appreciably less competition' mean and how is it to be measured? One way would be to look for evidence of actual anti-competitive consequences on the market. For example, market data could be analysed to determine whether the agreement has resulted in higher prices or lower output. Yet, even where the data exist, establishing causality will often be difficult in practice. The test becomes more complicated when an agreement is analysed before it has been put into practice, requiring assessment of future effects on prices or output. In many such cases the Courts or the Commission would have to balance the potential anti-competitive risks of the agreement against its likely pro-competitive benefits to determine its likely overall effect on price or output. In certain circumstances, potential cost savings resulting from an agreement may be large enough to offset any price increases, at least in the short run, which might take place as a result of the increased market power of the parties. It could be argued that this would need to be taken into account under Article 81(1) if such an approach were to be adopted.

2.73 This approach, which some have described as 'a rule of reason', has been regularly rejected by the Commission. The most recent exposition of this view came in the 1999 White Paper on Modernisation of the Rules Implementing Articles 85 and 86 [now Articles 81 and 82] of the EC Treaty in which the Commission argued that 'the structure of Article 85 is such as to prevent greater use being made of this approach: if more systematic use were made under Article 85(1) of an analysis of the pro-and anti-competitive aspects of a restrictive agreement, Article 85(3) would be cast aside, whereas any such change could be made only through revision of the Treaty'.[102]

2.74 Apart from the structure and wording of Article 81(1), the Commission's rejection of this approach is due to the assumptions it has made regarding the role of competition in the economy and the policy considerations which have underpinned its application of the rules.

2.75 The first, and perhaps most significant, assumption the Commission has made is that the process of competition itself, or, to be more precise, the process of rivalry between undertakings, produces the best results. For example, in its *Report on Competition Policy 1971* (Vol I), the Commission described competition as 'the best stimulant of economic activity'. It went on to argue that competition, '[t]hrough the interplay of decentralised decision-making machinery', enabled enterprises 'continuously to improve their efficiency which is the sine qua non for a steady improvement in living standards and employment prospects. From this point of view, competition policy is an essential means for satisfying to a great extent the individual and collective needs of our society.' Over a decade later, in its Fifteenth Report, the Commission described the role of competition, and thus of

---

[102] Commission programme 99/27 approved on 28 April 1999, COM/99/101 final, para 57.

Article 81(1), as preserving 'the freedom and right of initiative of the individual economic operators' and fostering 'the spirit of enterprise'. Thus for the Commission the protection of rivalry has been an end in itself.

The Commission has found some support for its view in the European Court of **2.76** Justice. For example in *Coöperatieve Vereniging 'Suiker Unie' v Commission*, the ECJ held that it is an 'inherent' concept in the provisions of the Treaty relating to competition 'that each economic operator must determine independently the policy which he intends to adopt on the common market',[103] while in *Béguelin* the Court held that 'in order to come within the prohibition imposed by Article 85 [now Article 81], the agreement must affect . . . the free play of competition'.[104] Similarly, in *Windsurfing International v Commission*, the ECJ spoke of the 'freedom of competition'.[105] In other words, as a general rule, undertakings should compete rather than co-operate. This applies as much to vertical agreements which restrict rivalry between distributors, as to horizontal ones which restrict competition between suppliers. In *Consten and Grundig* the European Court stated explicitly that:

> The principle of freedom of competition concerns the various stages and manifestations of competition. Although competition between producers is generally more noticeable than that between distributors of products of the same make, it does not thereby follow that an agreement tending to restrict the latter kind of competition should escape the prohibition of Article 85(1) [now Article 81(1)] merely because it might increase the former.[106]

In practice this philosophy has often led to an examination of the clauses in agree- **2.77** ments to identify whether restraints have been placed on the commercial conduct of the parties or third parties. This approach is also reflected in the information the Commission requires undertakings to provide when making a notification: section 4.2 of Form A/B specifically asks for the identification of 'any provisions contained in the agreements which may restrict the parties' freedom to take independent commercial decisions'.

However, the fact that an agreement contains clauses which limit the commercial **2.78** freedom of the parties is *neither a necessary nor a sufficient* condition for Article 81(1) to apply.

Restrictive Clauses not a Necessary Condition for the Application of Article 81(1)

Both the Commission and the European Courts have recognized that agreements which do not contain clauses restricting the commercial freedom of the parties **2.79**

---

[103] Joined Cases 40 to 48, 50, 54 to 56, 111, 113 and 114/73 [1975] ECR 1663, paras 173–174.
[104] See Case 22/71 *Beguelin* [1971] ECR 949, para 16 of the judgment.
[105] Case 193/83 [1986] ECR 611, para 85.
[106] Joined Cases 56 and 58/64 *Consten. and Grundig v Commission* [1966] ECR 299, at 342.

can restrict rivalry between them or adversely affect the position of third parties, and therefore fall within Article 81(1). For example, in *UK Agricultural Tractor Registration Exchange*,[107] an information sharing system had been set up which had the effect of revealing to all competitors the market positions and strategies of individual undertakings. The system did not contractually limit the participants' freedom to take independent commercial decisions. The Commission and subsequently the ECJ found that, on a highly oligopolistic market, uncertainty about the future conduct of competitors was one of the only remaining spurs to competition. The exchange of information which reduced this uncertainty was therefore likely to impair substantially competition between them. Thus the agreement fell within Article 81(1) even though it did not explicitly limit the parties' commercial freedom. Similarly, in *British-American Tobacco Company and RJ Reynolds Industries v Commission*,[108] the ECJ held that an acquisition of a minority shareholding in a competitor could fall within Article 81(1) if, *inter alia*, it served as an instrument for influencing the commercial conduct of the companies in question or created a structure likely to be used for such co-operation between them.

2.80 A comparable logic has been used by the Commission in its assessment of joint ventures. In its 1977 decision *GEC Weir Sodium Circulators*, the Commission held that:

> [e]ven in the absence of express provisions, the creation of a joint venture generally has a notable effect on the conduct of parent parties who have a significant holding in the joint venture. Within the field of the joint venture and in related fields such parties are likely to co-ordinate their conduct and be influenced in what would otherwise have been their independent decisions and activities. Where the parent parties are actual or potential competitors, their participation in a joint venture is accordingly likely to impair free competition between them, regardless of the existence of explicit restrictive provisions to that effect.[109]

2.81 Similarly, in its Notice concerning the assessment of cooperative joint ventures pursuant to Article 85 [now Article 81] of the EEC Treaty, the Commission acknowledged that 'competition between parent companies can be prevented, restricted or distorted through co-operation in a JV'.[110] Contractual terms in the agreement which limit the participants' freedom to take independent commercial decisions are just one of the factors taken into account when this analysis is made.

---

[107] [1992] OJ L68/19, paras 36–37; Case C–7/95 *John Deere Ltd v Commission* [1998] ECR I–3111; Case C–8/95 *New Holland Ford Ltd v Commission* [1998] ECR I–3175.
[108] Joined Cases 142 and 156/84 [1987] ECR 4487, paras 37–39.
[109] [1977] OJ L327/26, section II, para 2.
[110] [1993] OJ C43/2, para 18.

Restriction of Rivalry not a Sufficient Condition for the Application of Article 81(1)—Appreciability

Even where clauses in agreements restrict the commercial conduct of the parties, **2.82** or where the agreement in some other way restricts rivalry, the ECJ has held that an agreement will still need to affect competition[111] 'to an appreciable extent'[112] if it is to be caught by Article 81(1). This means that an agreement will fall outside the prohibition of Article 81(1) if it has 'only an insignificant effect'[113] on competition. Thus the ECJ has recognized the fact that even if an agreement limits rivalry between competitors, this may not affect the competitive pressures which exist on the market.

The Commission has issued a Notice on agreements of minor importance to pro- **2.83** vide some guidance on this issue. The Notice states that agreements between undertakings engaged in the production or distribution of goods or in the provision of services do not fall under the prohibition in Article 81(1) if the aggregate market shares held by all of the participating undertakings[114] do not exceed, on any of the relevant markets:

(a) 5 per cent, where the agreement is made between undertakings operating at the same level of production or of marketing ('horizontal' agreement); or

(b) 10 per cent, where the agreement is made between undertakings operating at different economic levels ('vertical' agreement).

In the case of a mixed horizontal/vertical agreement or where it is difficult to clas- **2.84** sify the agreement as either horizontal or vertical, the 5 per cent threshold is

---

[111] There will also have to be an effect on trade. This will be dealt with in Section D below.

[112] See Case 22/71 *Beguelin* [1971] ECR 949, para 16 of the judgment.

[113] Case 5/69 *Völk v Vervaecke* [1969] ECR 295, para 7; Case C–7/95 *John Deere Ltd v Commission* [1998] ECR I–3111.

[114] [1997] OJ C372/13. For the purposes of this Notice, 'participating undertakings' are:

(a) undertakings being parties to the agreement;.

(b) undertakings in which a party to the agreement, directly or indirectly,

— owns more than half of the capital or business assets, or
— has the power to exercise more than half of the voting rights, or
— has the power to appoint more than half of the members of the supervisory board, board of management or bodies legally representing the undertakings, or
— has the right to manage the undertaking's business;

(c) undertakings which directly or indirectly have over a party to the agreement the rights or powers listed in (b);

(d) undertakings over which an undertaking referred to in (c) has, directly or indirectly, the rights or powers listed in (b).

Undertakings over which several undertakings as referred to in (a) to (d) jointly have, directly or indirectly, the rights or powers set out in (b) shall also be considered to be participating undertakings.

applicable. The Notice goes on to state that agreements will not fall under the prohibition of Article 81(1) if the market shares given in the Notice are exceeded by no more than one-tenth during two successive financial years.[115]

2.85 However, it is important to recognize that agreements which breach the thresholds of the Notice do not necessarily fall within the scope of Article 81(1). Section I.3 of the 1997 Notice states that:

> The quantitative definition of appreciability, however, serves only as a guideline: in individual cases even agreements between undertakings which exceed the threshold set out below may still have only a negligible effect on trade between Member States or on competition within the common market and are therefore not caught by Article 85 (1) [now Article 81(1)].

2.86 Furthermore, the European Courts have explicitly rejected attempts to argue that Article 81(1) applies automatically to agreements when the market share of the parties exceed the thresholds. In *European Night Services v Commission*, the Court held that the 'mere fact that [the] threshold may be reached and even exceeded does not make it possible to conclude with certainty that an agreement is caught by Article 85(1) [now Article 81(1)] of the Treaty'.[116] Thus, even where agreements exceed the thresholds set out in the Notice 'the Commission must provide an adequate statement of its reasons for considering such agreements to be caught by the prohibition'[117] of Article 81(1).

Restriction of Rivalry not Sufficient Condition for the Application of Article 81(1)—Ancillary Restraints Doctrine

2.87 In a small but growing number of decisions the European Courts have held that clauses which restrict rivalry may nevertheless fall outside the prohibition of Article 81(1) if they are objectively necessary to secure the implementation of a lawful agreement. This line of reasoning was first used in *Metro (No 1)* where the

---

[115] Furthermore these thresholds do not in general apply to agreements between small and medium-sized undertakings (for a definition of SMEs see Annex to Commission Recommendation 96/280/EC). With regard to SMEs the Notice states that such undertakings are 'rarely capable of significantly affecting trade between Member States and competition within the common market. Consequently, as a general rule, they are not caught by the prohibition in Article 85(1) [now Article 81(1)]. In cases where such agreements exceptionally meet the conditions for the application of that provision, they will not be of sufficient Community interest to justify any intervention. This is why the Commission will not institute any proceedings, either upon request or on its own initiative, to apply the provisions of Article 85(1) to such agreements, even if the thresholds set out in points 9 and 10 above are exceeded. The Commission nevertheless reserves the right to intervene in such agreements:

(a) where they significantly impede competition in a substantial part of the relevant market,
(b) where, in the relevant market, competition is restricted by the cumulative effect of parallel networks of similar agreements made between several producers or dealers.'

[116] Case T–374/94 [1988] ECR II–3141, para 102; see also Case T–7/93 *Langnese-Iglo Gmbh v Commission* [1995] ECR II–1533, para 98.

[117] Case T–374/94 *European Night Services v Commission* [1998] ECR II–3141, para 102.

Court held that suppliers in sectors covering the production of high-quality and technically advanced consumer durables could refuse to supply distributors who did not fulfil 'objective criteria of a qualitative nature'.[118] Similarly in *Coditel 2,*[119] having regard to the specific characteristics of the cinematographic market, the ECJ rejected the argument that a licence for the exclusive right to exhibit a film in a territory of a Member State necessarily restricted competition.

This approach is also partly reflected in *Pronuptia,*[120] where the ECJ held that 'pro- **2.88** visions which are strictly necessary in order to ensure that the know-how and assistance provided by the franchisor do not benefit competitors do not constitute restrictions of competition for the purposes of Article 85(1) [now Article 81(1)]'.[121] For example, the Court stated that this would cover 'a clause prohibiting the franchisee, during the period of validity of the contract and for a reasonable period after its expiry, from opening a shop of the same or a similar nature in an area where he may compete with a member of the network'.[122]

The Commission has, albeit to a lesser extent, also applied the doctrine. The best **2.89** example of this is *Elopak/Metal Box—Odin,* in which the Commission considered the overall effect of the agreement and came to the conclusion that:

> as the parties could not realistically be regarded as competitors, actual or potential, and the creation of the joint venture entails no foreclosure risk, and the agreement does not involve the creation of a network of competing joint ventures, the agreements to establish Odin do not fall within the terms of Article 85 [now Article 81]. The specific provisions of the agreement must however be examined to ascertain whether such provisions restrict competition within the meaning of Article 85(1), or whether they are no more than is necessary to ensure the starting up and the proper functioning of the joint venture.[123]

Analysing the clauses, the Commission found that they were either:

> provisions not restricting competition in the sense of Article 85(1), or provisions which in other contexts might restrict competition but which in the context of the present case do not. Since such provisions cannot be disassociated from the creation of Odin without undermining its existence and purpose and since the creation of Odin does not fall within the scope of Article 85(1), these specific provisions also fall outside the scope of Article 85(1).[124]

---

[118] Case 26/76 *Metro SB-Großmärkte GmbH & Co KG v Commission* [1977] ECR 1875, paras 20–21. The law on selective distribution system is discussed in detail in Chapter 7.
[119] Case 262/81 *Coditel SA, Compagnie générale pour la diffusion de la télévision v Ciné-Vog Films* [1982] ECR 3381.
[120] Case 161/84 *Pronuptia de Paris v Pronuptia de Paris Irmgard Schillgalis* [1986] ECR 353.
[121] Case 161/84, para 16.
[122] Case 161/84, para 16.
[123] [1990] OJ L209/15, paras 28–29.
[124] [1990] OJ L209/15, para 36.

Ancillary Restraint Doctrine Difficult to Use for Taking Restrictive Clause outside Article 81(1)

2.90 However, companies and their advisers should take care in using this doctrine to take restraints outside Article 81(1). The *Pronuptia* case itself provides a warning that the ancillary restraint doctrine does not automatically apply to all restraints, particularly those which afford territorial protection. Thus the ECJ held that since a franchise agreement typically results:

> in a sharing of markets between the franchisor and the franchisees or between franchisees and thus restricts competition within the network . . . a restriction of that kind constitutes a limitation of competition for the purposes of Article 85(1) [now Article 81(1)] if it concerns a business name or symbol which is already well-known. It is of course possible that a prospective franchisee would not take the risk of becoming part of the chain, investing his own money, paying a relatively high entry fee and undertaking to pay a substantial annual royalty, unless he could hope, thanks to a degree of protection against competition on the part of the franchisor and other franchisees, that his business would be profitable. That consideration, however, is relevant only to an examination of the agreement in the light of the conditions laid down in Article 85(3).[125]

2.91 A more fundamental problem arises from the imprecise definition given to ancillary restraints under European competition law. Ancillary restraints are those which are 'directly related' to the agreement and objectively 'necessary for its existence'. However, they must also 'remain subordinate in importance to the main object' of the agreement.[126] Thus for an R&D joint venture the 'main object' of the agreement would be the complete or partial integration of the R&D operations of the parties in a particular field of research. An obligation on the parties not to carry out research independently in this area for the lifetime of the joint venture could, if it were objectively 'necessary' for the implementation of the agreement, be described as a subordinate clause. On the other hand, it would be difficult to argue persuasively that a clause which prevented these parties from competing with each other in another, unrelated field is directly related to the agreement or objectively necessary for its existence.

2.92 It is clear that the concept begs more questions than it answers. It is very difficult, if not impossible, to identify in the abstract whether a particular restraint will be treated as ancillary to a particular type of agreement. Of course, similar problems exist when applying the concept of indispensability under Article 81(3).[127]

---

[125] Case 161/84, at para 24.

[126] Notice concerning the assessment of cooperative joint ventures pursuant to Article 85 [now Article 81] of the EEC Treaty [1993] OJ C43/2. In *Metro v Commission* the ECJ referred to 'the corollary of the principal obligation': Case 26/76 [1977] ECR 1875, para 27.

[127] Is this different from the indispensability test under Article 81(3)? Under Article 81(3) the test is whether the clause is necessary for the attainment of the benefits identified. Under Article 81(1), the question is whether the clause is necessary for the existence and implementation of the agreement.

However, in such cases, advisers can often turn to the 'black lists' in the various block exemptions or the existing case law. Unfortunately, there is little case law under Article 81(1)[128] to guide companies and their advisers. The doctrine cannot therefore be applied with certainty by those who wish to argue that a particular restrictive clause in an agreement falls outside Article 81(1).

On the other hand, as will be seen below,[129] the development of the ancillary **2.93** restraint doctrine also means that even where an agreement itself is found to fall outside Article 81(1), restrictive clauses within it may still infringe the prohibition.

Restriction of Rivalry not a Sufficient Condition for the Application of Article 81(1)—New Economic Approach

The very existence of an ancillary restraints approach reveals a willingness on the **2.94** part of the European Courts and the Commission to apply a more economic approach to the analysis of cases under Article 81. For example, in holding, in *Metro (No 1)*, that a particular type of distribution system which limited price competition could, in certain circumstances, fall outside the prohibition, the ECJ took into account the economic advantages of the system under Article 81(1). In doing so it implicitly balanced the potential pro- and anti-competitive effects of the system.

In fact, in a growing number of cases, the European Courts have looked beyond **2.95** the negative elements of agreements in their analysis under Article 81(1) and have sought to determine what the actual or potential economic impact on the market of agreements hampering rivalry could be. For example, in *Breeders' rights—maize seed*,[130] the Commission had decided that by licensing a single undertaking to exploit a particular type of intellectual property in a given territory, the licensor had deprived itself for the duration of the contract of the ability to issue licences to other undertakings in the same territory, thereby eliminating them as competing suppliers. Further, by undertaking not to produce or market the product in the territory the licensor had likewise eliminated itself as a supplier in that territory. Applying its orthodox thinking, the Commission decided that competition was restricted by this agreement. This decision was challenged in *Nungesser v Commission*.[131] The Court adopted a different approach. While acknowledging that one form of competition might be restricted by such an agreement (ie that coming from other potential licensees or the licensor), the ECJ considered the overall impact of the agreement on competition. It found that an undertaking

---

[128] Nor can the decisions under the Merger Regulation be relied on under Article 81 except, perhaps, for structural operations.

[129] See para 2.99 below.

[130] [1978] OJ L286/23.

[131] Case 258/78 *Nungesser v Commission* [1982] ECR 2015.

might be deterred from accepting the risk of entering the new market without the protection from competition offered by the exclusive territory, and found that 'such a result would be damaging to the dissemination of a new technology and would prejudice competition in the Community between the new product and similar existing products'.[132] It therefore held that an open exclusive licence of the sort under consideration did not fall within Article 81(1). In reaching this conclusion the Court was once again conducting a balancing exercise which has traditionally been undertaken under Article 81(3).

2.96 In *Delimitis v Henninger*,[133] the Court of Justice stated that:

> the existence of a bundle of similar contracts, even if it has a considerable effect on the opportunities for gaining access to the market, is not, however, sufficient in itself to support a finding that the relevant market is inaccessible, inasmuch as it is only one factor, amongst others, pertaining to the economic and legal context in which an agreement must be appraised (Case 23/67 *Brasserie De Haecht*, cited above). The other factors to be taken into account are, in the first instance, those also relating to opportunities for access.

Therefore, in the presence of a positive element, (real opportunities for access), Article 81 would not have applied to the negative element (the network of similar beer supply agreements).[134]

2.97 In *European Night Services v Commission*,[135] the undertakings concerned challenged a Commission decision granting them a conditional exemption for a limited period of time. The Court of First Instance annulled the Commission decision, finding that the Commission 'must be regarded as not having made a correct and adequate assessment in the contested decision of the economic and legal context in which the ENS agreements were concluded'.[136] During proceedings before the Court of First Instance, the applicants argued, *inter alia*, that as regards the overall assessment of the notified agreements:

> the Court of Justice has consistently held (Case 56/65 *Société Technique Minière v Maschinenbau Ulm* [1966] ECR 235, Joined Cases 56/64 and 58/64 *Consten and Grundig v Commission* [1966] ECR 299, Case 26/76 *Metro v Commission*, cited above, Case 258/78 *Nungesser v Commission* [1982] ECR 2015, Case 161/84 *Pronuptia* [1986] ECR 353 and Case C–234/89 *Delimitis v Henninger Bräu* [1991] ECR I–935) that the pro-competitive effects of an agreement must be weighed up against its anti-competitive effects. If the pro-competitive effects outweigh the anti-competitive effects and the latter are necessary in order to implement the agreement, then the agreement cannot be regarded as having as its object or effect the preven-

---

[132] Case 258/78 *Nungesser v Commission* [1982] ECR 2015, para 57.
[133] Case C–234/89 [1991] ECR I–935, para 20.
[134] See also Case T–7/93 *Langnese Iglo v Commission* [1995] ECR II–1533.
[135] Joined Cases T–374/94, T–375/94, T–384/94 and T–388/94 [1998] ECR II–3141.
[136] para 206 of the judgment.

tion, restriction or distortion of competition within the common market within the meaning of Article 85(1) [now Article 81(1)] of the Treaty.[137]

For its part the Commission challenged the argument that the case law cited by the applicants and the United Kingdom established that it was bound to apply a 'rule of reason' and to balance the competitive benefits and harms of an agreement under Article 81(1). The Commission argued that 'such an approach is required in the context of Article 85(3) [now Article 81(3)] of the Treaty but not in respect of the appraisal of restrictions of competition under Article 85(1)'.[138]

In commenting on this issue the Court of First Instance chose its words very carefully, and appears to have left the door open for such a 'rule of reason' approach where restrictions by effect are involved. This, it is submitted, is because the Court in the last sentence of paragraph 136 of the judgment expressly excluded the weighing up of the pro-competitive effects of an agreement against its anti-competitive effects *only* where restrictions by object were involved. Given the importance of this issue the full text of paragraph 136 is quoted below: **2.98**

> Before any examination of the parties' arguments as to whether the Commission's analysis as regards restrictions of competition was correct, it must be borne in mind that in assessing an agreement under Article 85(1) [now Article 81(1)] of the Treaty, account should be taken of the actual conditions in which it functions, in particular the economic context in which the undertakings operate, the products or services covered by the agreement and the actual structure of the market concerned (judgements in *Delimitis*, cited above, *Gøttrup-Klim*, cited above, paragraph 31, Case C–399/93 *Oude Luttikhuis and Others v Verenigde Coöperatieve Melkindustrie* [1995] ECR I–4515, paragraph 10, and Case T–77/94 *VGB and Others v Commission* [1997] ECR II–759, paragraph 140), unless it is an agreement containing obvious restrictions of competition such as price-fixing, market-sharing or the control of outlets (Case T–148/89 *Tréfilunion v Commission* [1995] ECR II–1063, paragraph 109). In the latter case, such restrictions may be weighed against their claimed pro-competitive effects only in the context of Article 85(3) of the Treaty, with a view to granting an exemption from the prohibition in Article 85(1).

Ancillary Restraints Doctrine Limits Value of New Economic Approach

Ironically the usefulness in practice of this new economic approach is limited by the insistence of both the Commission and the Court on analysing the restrictive clauses in agreements falling outside Article 81(1) to ascertain whether they are necessary to secure the implementation of a lawful agreement. For example, in *Gøttrup-Klim v Dansk Landbrugs*,[139] the ECJ was asked to consider whether a joint buying co-operative which prevented its members from buying through other similar arrangements fell within Article 81(1). The Court stated that this was not **2.99**

---

[137] para 119 of the judgment.
[138] para 130 of the judgment.
[139] Case C–250/92 [1994] ECR I–5641, paras 32–34.

a matter which could be assessed in the abstract as the effects of the restraint depended on the economic conditions prevailing on the markets concerned. It therefore held that:

> in a market where product prices vary according to the volume of orders, the activities of cooperative purchasing associations may, depending on the size of their membership, constitute a significant counterweight to the contractual power of large producers and make way for more effective competition. Where some members of two competing cooperative purchasing associations belong to both at the same time, the result is to make each association less capable of pursuing its objectives for the benefit of the rest of its members, especially where the members concerned, as in the case in point, are themselves cooperative associations with a large number of individual members. It follows that such dual membership would jeopardize both the proper functioning of the cooperative and its contractual power in relation to producers. Prohibition of dual membership does not, therefore, necessarily constitute a restriction of competition within the meaning of Article 85(1) [now Article 81(1)] of the Treaty and may even have beneficial effects on competition.

However, somewhat paradoxically, the Court went on to say that:

> in order to escape the prohibition laid down in Article 85(1) [now Article 81(1)] of the Treaty, the restrictions imposed on members by the statutes of cooperative purchasing associations must be limited to what is necessary to ensure that the cooperative functions properly and maintains its contractual power in relation to producers.

Thus even where an agreement may have beneficial effects on competition, it will still be necessary to ensure that the restrictive clauses are objectively necessary.

D. Jurisdiction

2.100 There are two jurisdictional criteria for the application of Articles 81 and 82: effect on trade between Member States and the impact (to use a neutral term) on the Community necessary to justify jurisdiction under public international law.

(1) Effect on Trade between Member States

2.101 Both Articles 81 and 82 require that there may be an effect on trade between Member States before they can be applicable.[140] This has been analysed in two principal ways. The first relates to the flow or pattern of trade (trade means all economic activities relating to goods and services). The second test is the alteration of the 'competitive structure'.

---

[140] See Faull, 'Effect on Trade between Member States and Community-Member State Jurisdiction' [1989] Annual Proceedings of the Fordham Corporate Law Institute (B Hawk ed) 485.

Flow or Pattern of Trade

The European Courts have consistently held that, in order that an agreement   **2.102**
between undertakings may affect trade between Member States, 'it must be possible
to foresee with a sufficient degree of probability on the basis of a set of objective factors of law or fact that it may have an influence, direct or indirect, actual or potential, on the pattern of trade between Member States'.[141] Thus the flow or pattern of
trade must be caused, or be foreseeably likely, to develop differently from what
would have been the case in the absence of the agreement or conduct concerned.

Despite discrepancies in the language versions of the Treaty, this effect on trade   **2.103**
does not have to be 'harmful' or 'negative'.[142] Nor is it even necessary to establish
that trade between Member States is actually affected; it is sufficient merely to
show that the restrictive practice is capable of having such an effect.[143] For example, in *AEG-Telefunken v Commission*,[144] it had been argued that the way in which
the selective distribution system under review was applied could not affect trade
because the dealers were not engaged, at that moment in time, in trade. The ECJ
rejected this, holding that possible changes in the market situation had to be considered. Since it was reasonably foreseeable that dealers engaged in or capable of
engaging in trade between Member States might apply for admission to the selective distribution network, or might benefit or suffer from the restriction of competition caught by Article 81, there was an effect on trade between Member States.
Similarly in *BNIC v Aubert* the ECJ found that an agreement covering intermediate products, which were not themselves traded between Member States, could
affect trade because the final product in which they were used was traded.
Furthermore, it is not necessary to show that each restrictive clause of an agreement has or may affect trade; rather it is the effect on trade of the agreement as a
whole which must be considered.[145]

This criterion is easily fulfilled in cases of goods and services traded between   **2.104**
Member States or by arrangements between undertakings situated or operating in
more than one Member State. However, it used to be thought that an agreement
covering the entire territory of a Member State necessarily affected trade because,
by its very nature, it separated national markets from each other, thereby undermining the Community's market integration goal.[146] The *locus classicus* for this
was the ECJ's judgment in *Vereeniging van Cementhandelaren v Commission* where
the Court held that 'an agreement extending over the whole of the territory of a

---

[141]   Case 42/84 *Remia and Others v Commission* [1985] ECR 2545, para 22.
[142]   Joined Cases 56 and 58/64 *Consten and Grundig v Commission* [1966] ECR 299.
[143]   See Case C–219/95P *Ferriere Nord v Commission* [1997] ECR I–4411, para 19.
[144]   Case 107/82 *AEG-Telefunken AG v Commission* [1983] ECR 3151, para 60.
[145]   Case 193/83 *Windsurfing International Inc v Commission* [1986] ECR 611, para 96.
[146]   See, eg, Case C–35/96, *Commission v Italy* [1998] ECR I–3851, para 48.

member state by its very nature has the effect of reinforcing the compartmentalisation of markets on a national basis, thereby holding up the economic interpenetration which the treaty is designed to bring about and protecting domestic production'.[147]

2.105 Both the European Courts and the Commission have regularly applied this test in the past. For example, in *Pronuptia de Paris v Schillgallis*,[148] the Court held that franchise agreements which contained provisions sharing markets between the franchisor and the franchisees or between the franchisees themselves were 'in any event liable to affect trade between Member States, even if they are entered into by undertakings established in the same Member State, in so far as they prevent franchisees from establishing themselves in another Member State'.

2.106 However, in *SC Belasco v Commission*, the ECJ's approach became more circumspect: rather than holding that an agreement extending over the whole of the territory of a Member State 'by its very nature' affected trade, the Court stated that the fact that an agreement related only to the marketing of products in a single Member State was not sufficient to 'exclude the possibility' that trade between Member States 'might be affected'.[149]

2.107 The Court clarified its approach in *Bagnasco v Banca Popolare di Novara*,[150] where the question was whether national agreements in the financial services sector covering a whole Member State should be considered to affect trade. The Court held that uniform bank conditions laid down by the Italian Banking Association in relation to contracts for the opening of current account credit facilities were not liable to affect trade between Member States. In reaching this conclusion the Court had regard to the Commission's findings that the banking service in question involved economic activities which have a very limited impact on inter-state trade and that there was limited participation of subsidiaries or branches of non-Italian banks. The Court did not follow its Advocate General who had proposed that the conditions in question, applied by the quasi-totality of banks operating in Italy, reduced competition between banks and should be considered contrary to Article 81.[151] The effect of the *Bagnasco* judgment would seem to be that the mere fact that an agreement covers a particular Member State is no longer sufficient in itself for a finding that trade has been affected.

2.108 The case law has therefore come a long way from the simplicities of a *per se* analysis regarding 'national' agreements. Indeed, while the principal approach to considering effect on trade under Article 81 has not changed much over the years (*an*

---

[147] Case 8/72 [1972] ECR 977, para 29.
[148] Case 161/84 [1986] ECR 353, para 26.
[149] Case 246/86 [1989] ECR 2117, para 33.
[150] Joined Cases C–215 and C–216/96 *Carlo Bagnasco v Banca Popolare di Novara* and *Cassa di Risparmio di Genova e Imperia* [1999] ECR I–135, paras 47 *et seq.*
[151] Opinion of Ruiz-Jarabo AG, 15 January 1998.

influence, direct or indirect, actual or potential, on the structure of competition and pattern or flow of trade between Member States), the analysis necessary to establish such an effect has been clarified and gradually hardened. Today, the Commission, national authorities or courts applying Article 81(1) must satisfy themselves on the basis of evidence or prospective analysis based on economic data that the conduct in question is genuinely capable of affecting the pattern or flow of trade appreciably.[152]

2.109 A particular question arises concerning the possible effect on trade between Member States of agreements regarding activities in foreign countries.

2.110 In the *Javico* case,[153] the issue was as follows. Where a producer in one Member State has agreed with a distributor in another Member State that the latter will distribute the former's goods in a third country, can the latter be obliged not to sell the goods outside the third country in question, without violating Article 81?

2.111 The Court of Justice held that Article 81 would apply where the Community market for the product concerned is oligopolistic *or* where there is an appreciable difference between Community prices for the product and the price in the foreign country concerned *and* where the producer's market position for production and sales in the EC is such that the prohibition on sales outside the third country concerned entails a risk of an appreciable effect on the pattern of trade between Member States so as to undermine the attainment of the objectives of the single market.

Competitive Structure

2.112 The second approach used to establish an effect on trade is to consider whether there is any change to the structure of competition. For example, in *Commercial Solvents v Commission*[154] the Court held that:

> when an undertaking in a dominant position within the common market abuses its position in such a way that a competitor in the common market is likely to be eliminated, it does not matter whether the conduct relates to the latter's exports or its trade within the common market, once it has been established that this elimination will have repercussions on the competitive structure within the common market.

2.113 Similarly, in Case 27/76 *United Brands v Commission* [1978] ECR 207 para 201 the ECJ held that:

> if the occupier of a dominant position, established in the common market, aims at eliminating a competitor who is also established in the common market, it is immaterial whether this behaviour relates to trade between member states once it has been

---

[152] See discussion of appreciability above, paras 2.66–2.70 and 2.82–2.86.
[153] See Case C–306/96 *Javico International and Javico v Yves Saint Laurent Parfums* [1998] ECR I–1983.
[154] Joined Cases 6 and 7/73 *Commercial Solvents v Commission* [1974] ECR 223, para 33.

shown that such elimination will have repercussions on the patterns of competition in the common market.

2.114 While this test is more likely to be used in Article 82 cases, its application under Article 81(1) cannot be excluded. For example, agreements relating to joint ventures, restructuring agreements, or minority shareholdings which are potentially caught by Article 81(1) can be found to affect trade by means of their impact on the structure of the market. Indeed, in *Hugin v Commission*[155] the Court referred explicitly to Article 81, holding that the:

> interpretation and application of the condition relating to effects on trade between Member States contained in Articles 85 and 86 [now Articles 81 and 82] of the Treaty must be based on the purpose of that condition which is to define, in the context of the law governing competition, the boundary between the areas respectively covered by Community law and the law of the Member States. Thus Community law covers any agreement or any practice which is capable of constituting a threat to freedom of trade between Member States in a manner which might harm the attainment of the objectives of a single market between the Member States, in particular by partitioning the national markets or by affecting the structure of competition within the Common Market.

(2) International Jurisdiction

2.115 In addition to the 'internal' effect on trade criterion, international law requires that there be a *sufficient connection between the activity concerned and the territory of the European Community*.[156] European Community competition law establishes this connection in three ways, any one of which is sufficient as a ground of jurisdiction:

- the single entity doctrine,[157] whereby the presence and activities of a subsidiary in the European Community bring the entire group to which it belongs (parent company and fellow subsidiaries) under European Community jurisdiction as a single undertaking;

- the implementation doctrine,[158] whereby the implementation in the EC of agreements, concerted practices, decisions of associations of undertakings, or abuses of dominant position conceived abroad by foreign undertakings brings them within EC jurisdiction; and

---

[155] Case 22/78 *Hugin v Commission* [1979] ECR 1869, para 17.

[156] It is sometimes argued that the nationality doctrine of jurisdiction may also apply in competition cases, enabling the European Community to exercise jurisdiction over companies incorporated in a Member State. Since competition law is essentially concerned with effects on markets, it is preferable to base jurisdiction on the territorial doctrine or doctrines of jurisdiction.

[157] Case 48/69 *ICI v Commission* [1972] ECR 619, Case 15/74 *Centrafarm v Sterling Drug* [1974] ECR 619, and Case C–73/95 *Viho Europe BV v Commission* [1996] ECR I–5457.

[158] Joined Cases 89, 104, 114, 116, 117 and 125 to 129/85 *A Ahlström Osakeyhtiö and others v Commission* [1988] ECR 5193.

- the effects doctrine, whereby agreements, concerted practices, decisions of associations of undertakings, or abuses of dominant position conceived abroad by foreign undertakings which have effects in the European Community are brought under its jurisdiction.

Until recently the European Courts had refused to apply the effects doctrine **2.116** despite invitations to do so by Advocates General[159] and the Commission.[160] In *Woodpulp* the ECJ adopted the 'implementation' doctrine, rather than the effects-based approach advocated by the Commission:

> [a]n infringement of Article 85 [now Article 81], such as the conclusion of an agreement which has had the effect of restricting competition within the common market, consists of conduct made up of two elements, the formation of the agreement, decision or concerted practice and the implementation thereof. If the applicability of prohibitions laid down under competition law were made to depend on the place where the agreement, decision or concerted practice was formed, the result would obviously be to give undertakings an easy means of evading those prohibitions. The decisive factor is therefore the place where it is implemented.[161]

However in the recent *Gencor* judgment,[162] which arose under the Community **2.117** Merger Regulation,[163] the CFI explicitly used the language of the effects doctrine, including adjectives ('foreseeable, substantial and immediate') usually associated with the noun 'effect'. It held that:

> [a]pplication of the Regulation is justified under public international law when it is *foreseeable* that a proposed concentration will have an *immediate* and *substantial* effect in the Community. In that regard, the concentration would, according to the contested decision, have led to the creation of a dominant duopoly on the part of Amplats and Implats/LPD in the platinum and rhodium markets, as a result of which effective competition would have been significantly impeded in the common market within the meaning of Article 2(3) of the Regulation. *It is therefore necessary to verify whether the three criteria of immediate, substantial and foreseeable effect are satisfied in this case.*[164]

The ECJ did not overrule *Woodpulp* in *Gencor* and it is not possible to say that the **2.118** effects doctrine has superseded the implementation doctrine. However, the *Gencor* judgment means that exploration of possible gaps between implementation and

---

[159] See, for example, opinion of Advocate General Mayras in Case 48/69 *Imperial Chemical Industries v Commission* ECR [1972] 619.

[160] See for example *Dyestuffs* [1969] OJ L195/11.

[161] Joined Cases 89, 104, 114, 116, 117 and 125 to 129/85 *A Ahlström Osakeyhtiö and others v Commission* [1988] ECR 5193, para 16.

[162] Case T–102/96 *Gencor Ltd v Commission* paras 90–92.

[163] It is submitted that this endorsement of the effects doctrine is equally applicable to agreements falling under Article 81(1) since the jurisdiction issues arising in international law are identical and the language of Article 81(1) itself ('. . . object or effect the prevention, restriction or distortion of competition within the common market. . .') is clearly no obstacle to an effects-based concept of jurisdiction.

[164] Emphasis added.

effects is now an academic exercise, since even if only one and not the other is established, Article 81(1) will still apply, all other things being equal.

2.119 These are controversial issues, the ramifications of which go beyond the realms of competition law. The Commission and others responsible for applying Article 81(1) are bound in the years to come to face the dilemma of globalization in a world of sovereign states using legal doctrines developed in different times. The international law of jurisdiction was conceived in and for a pre-industrial world. Many of today's competition issues straddle national borders and no one 'sovereign' can hope to find all the information in its territory, let alone devise remedies which can be effected only there without impact on what another sovereign has done in the same case. The answers lie in strengthened international co-operation, both bilateral and multilateral, and in the sensitive exercise of jurisdiction tempered with proper regard to comity and the emerging instrument of positive comity.

E. Article 81(2)

2.120 Pursuant to Article 81(2), 'any agreements or decisions prohibited pursuant to this Article shall be automatically void'. The agreements and decisions as a whole are unenforceable, unless the restrictive elements (ie what is prohibited by Article 81(1) and not saved by Article 81(3)) can be separated from the remainder. If so, only those restrictive elements are void and unenforceable. Severability is a matter for the national court applying its own contract law as long as the Community law requirement that no effect be given to the restrictive elements is respected. The ECJ has held[165] that 'the automatic nullity decreed by Article 85(2) [now Article 81(2)] of the Treaty applies only to those contractual provisions which are incompatible with Article 85(1). The consequences of such nullity for other parts of the agreement, and for any orders and deliveries made on the basis of the agreement, and the resulting financial obligations are not a matter for Community law. Those consequences are to be determined by the national court according to its own law.'

It is beyond the scope of this chapter to delve into the many interesting questions which arise in respect of Article 81(2). Similarly, we have decided not to examine the issue of provisional validity and the impact of accession to the Community, which are dealt with extensively in other works.

---

[165] Case 319/82 *Société de Vente de Ciments et Bétons de l'Est SA v Kerpen & Kerpen GmbH und Co KG* [1983] ECR 4173, paras 11 and 12.

F. Article 81(3) Individual Exemption

(1) Introduction

For an exemption to be granted by the Commission the net effect of the agree- **2.121**
ments must be beneficial. The benefit must be to general welfare, not merely to
the parties involved. The burden of proof to establish the net benefit of an agreement is on the parties.

Activities which jeopardize the single market or put the competitive process at risk **2.122**
are unlikely to meet the requirements of Article 81(3). Price fixing,[166] quota setting,[167] and market sharing[168] are all clear examples of such activities.

Since Article 81(3) provides for an exception from a general prohibition, it must **2.123**
be construed strictly and is subject to the general requirement of proportionality.
Only indispensable restrictions of competition may be exempted and only for the
minimum period of time necessary to enable the parties to achieve the benefits
justifying the exemption. The CFI has held[169] that:

> the duration of an exemption granted under Article 85(3) [now Article 81(3)] . . .
> must be sufficient to enable the beneficiaries to achieve the benefits justifying such
> exemption, namely, in the present case, the contribution to economic progress and
> the benefits to consumers provided by the introduction of new high-quality trans-
> port services . . . Since, moreover, such progress and benefits cannot be achieved
> without considerable investment, the length of time required to ensure a proper
> return on that investment is necessarily an essential factor to be taken into account
> when determining the duration of an exemption, particularly in a case such as the
> present, where it is undisputed that the services in question are completely new,
> involve major investments and substantial financial risks and require the pooling of
> know-how by the participating undertakings.

(2) 'contributes to improving the production or distribution of goods or to promoting technical or economic progress'

General

The first condition for an individual exemption to be granted is that the agree- **2.124**
ment, decision, or concerted practice must contribute to 'improving the production or distribution of goods or to promoting technical or economic progress'.
Four elements can be identified within this condition and are used as the headings
below. Given the complex nature of many commercial arrangements, there is
often a significant overlap between the four elements and more than one may be

---

[166] *Papiers peints de Belgique* [1974] OJ L237/3.
[167] *Cimbel* [1972] OJ L303/24.
[168] *Quantel International Continuum/Quantel SA* [1992] OJ L235/9.
[169] Joined Cases T–374/94, T–375/94, T–384/94 and T–388/94 *European Night Services Ltd and others v Commission* [1988] ECR II–3141, para 230.

found to be applicable. Although only 'goods' are mentioned in relation to improvements in production and distribution, the rule applies by analogy to services.[170]

2.125 Below the four elements of the first condition for exemption are set out. Within each element there are a number of identifiable, if loose, explanatory groupings. These groupings are not exhaustive of all the potential circumstances which may satisfy the condition.

Element 1: 'improving the production . . . of goods' (or services)

General

2.126 Research and development agreements, specialization agreements, and joint venture manufacturing agreements may fall within this category. Some such agreements are covered by the block exemption Regulations 417/85[171] and 418/85.[172]

Efficiency and Cost Reduction

2.127 Increased industrial efficiency will, all other factors being equal, benefit the European economy. Cost reductions and productivity increases will be covered.[173] Co-operation where neither party could with its own resources and capabilities alone develop a product as effectively, economically, or quickly as both parties jointly may also suffice.[174] Arrangements that allow more detailed planning of supply may also lead to an improvement in production.[175]

Quality and Choice of Goods

2.128 Improvements in production may consist in bringing a new product to the market,[176] increasing the range of products available to consumers,[177] or improving the quality of existing products.[178] The introduction of an improved manufacturing process also falls within this limb of Article 81(3).[179]

---

[170] *P & I Clubs* [1985] OJ L376/2.

[171] Commission Regulation (EEC) 417/85 of 19 December 1984 on the application of Article 85(3) of the Treaty to categories of specialization agreements; as amended by Commission Regulation (EEC) 151/93 of 23 December 1992 and Commission Regulation (EC) 2236/97 of 10 November 1997.

[172] Commission Regulation (EEC) 418/85 of 19 December 1984 on the application of Article 85(3) of the Treaty to categories of research and development agreements; as amended by Commission Regulation (EEC) 151/93 of 23 December 1992 and Commission Regulation (EC) 2236/97 of 10 November 1997.

[173] *Vacuum Interrupters Ltd* [1977] OJ L48/32.

[174] *GEC/Weir (Sodium Circulators)* [1977] OJ L327/26.

[175] Case 26/76 *Metro SB-Großmärkte GmbH & Co KG v Commission* [1977] ECR 1875.

[176] *Optical Fibres* [1986] OJ L236/30.

[177] *Sopelem/ Vickers* [1978] OJ L70/47.

[178] *Soplem/ Vickers* [1978] OJ L70/47.

[179] Case T–17/93 *Matra Hachette SA v Commission* [1994] ECR II–595.

Overcapacity

An agreement to bring production capacity more into line with demand has been **2.129** held to improve production. In the admittedly exceptional *Synthetic Fibres* case,[180] technological advances had led to overcapacity, exacerbated by sluggish growth in demand. The Commission stated that: 'In a free market economy it ought to be principally a matter for the individual undertaking to judge the point at which overcapacity becomes economically unsustainable and to take the necessary steps to reduce it.' However, it then continued:[181] 'In the present case, however, market forces by themselves had failed to achieve the capacity reductions necessary to re-establish and maintain in the longer term an effective competitive structure within the common market. The producers concerned therefore agreed to organise for a limited period and collectively, the needed structural adjustment.'

Whether this is a reliable precedent for so-called 'crisis cartels' is questionable. An appeal to the ECJ against the Commission's decision was withdrawn.

Elements 3 and 4 are also relevant in considering the possible benefits of reducing overcapacity.

Employment

In the *Metro* case,[182] the ECJ held that employment was a matter which could be **2.130** considered under the first condition of Article 81(3). The agreement in question constituted: 'a stabilizing factor with regard to the provision of employment which, since it improves the general conditions of production, especially when market conditions are unfavourable, comes within the framework of the objectives to which reference may be had pursuant to Article 85(3) [now Article 81(3)]'.

In a wider social context, in the *Ford/Volkswagen* case[183] the Commission **2.131** exempted a joint venture to produce a new vehicle in Portugal. The Commission made it clear in this case that the creation of jobs, in a relatively poor area, was a consideration in the granting of the exemption.

Others

Patent and know-how licences providing for exclusive production rights may be **2.132** held to improve production and indeed some are exempted under Regulation 240/96[184] relating to certain categories of technology transfer agreements. The rationale of this exemption is the need to encourage the dissemination of technical knowledge in the Community and to promote the manufacture of technically

---

[180] *Synthetic Fibres* [1984] OJ L207/17, para 30.
[181] *Synthetic Fibres* [1984] OJ L207/17, para 31.
[182] Case 26/76 *Metro SB-Großmärkte GmbH & Co KG v Commission* [1977] ECR 1875, para 43.
[183] *Ford/Volkswagen* [1993] OJ L20/14.
[184] Commission Regulation (EC) 240/96 of 31 January 1996 on the application of Article 85(3) [now Article 81(3)] of the Treaty to certain categories of technology transfer agreements.

sophisticated products. Licences to manufacture under trade marks may also be held to improve production[185] where, for example and subject to the other terms of the licence, they permit a sufficient return to allow production to go ahead.

Element 2: 'improving the . . . or distribution of goods' (or services)

Exclusive Distribution and Purchase

2.133 Some exclusive distribution arrangements are block exempted by Regulation 1983/83.[186] This block exemption gives examples of improvements in production, which may also be relevant to individual exemption, including: allowing the parties to concentrate sales activities, more effective sales activities, rationalization of distribution systems, continuity of supply, easier access to markets (especially for small and medium-size undertakings), and proper provision of sales and guarantee services.

2.134 Regulation 1984/83,[187] the block exemption Regulation for exclusive purchasing agreements, lists the following as benefits of exclusive purchase, which again may be relevant to individual exemption: allowing precise and secure planning of future supplies, allowing a reduction of costs and risks, encouraging the supplier to improve the structure of the distribution network and intensify marketing efforts, increasing market access (especially for small and medium-sized undertakings).

2.135 Care should, however, be taken in relation to the benefits listed in the block exemptions. In the ice cream cases, *Langese-Iglo v Commission*[188] and *Schöller v Commission*,[189] the Court of First Instance stated:

> Although it is apparent from the fifth recital in the preamble to Regulation No 1984/83 that exclusive purchasing agreements lead in general to an improvement in distribution . . . in view of the fact that the applicant holds a strong position on the relevant market, the contested agreements do not, contrary to the expectation expressed in the sixth recital in the preamble to Regulation No. 1984/83, have the effect of intensifying competition between different brands of products.[190]

Franchising

2.136 Franchising agreements may also improve distribution. Regulation 4087/88[191] lists some of the potential benefits as: establishment of a uniform network which

---

[185] *Campari* [1978] OJ L70/69.
[186] Commission Regulation (EEC) 1983/83 of 22 June 1983 (Exclusive Distribution), amended by Commission Regulation (EC) 1582/97 of 30 July 1997.
[187] Commission Regulation (EEC) 1984/83 of 22 June 1983 (Exclusive Purchasing), amended by Commission Regulation (EC) 1582/97 of 30 July 1997.
[188] Case T–7/93 *Langnese-Iglo v Commission* [1995] ECR II–1533 and Case C–279/95 *Langnese-Iglo GmbH v Commission* [1998] ECR I–5609.
[189] Case T–9/93 *Schöller v Commission* [1995] ECR II–1611.
[190] Case T–7/93 *Langnese-Iglo v Commission* [1995] ECR II–1533, paras 181 and 182.
[191] Commission Regulation (EEC) 4087/88 of 30 November 1988.

may improve market access (especially for small and medium-sized undertakings), allowing traders a more rapid and secure method of setting up new outlets.

Selective Distribution

Selective distribution agreements limiting sales to dealers who meet certain criteria may improve distribution by improving the continuity of supply, increasing the range of products offered, and increased sales promotion. The benefits of selective distribution are more likely to accrue in the case of technically complex goods and/or high-quality and luxury goods. **2.137**

Others

Improvements in distribution may be found in a variety of other circumstances such as the collective purchasing of raw materials which may allow a more flexible distribution system.[192] In the *EBU/Eurovision* case,[193] the Commission decided that the joint negotiation, acquisition, and sharing of broadcast rights as well as the exchange of the signal and its transport on a common network provided a number of improvements to both production and distribution. The Commission stated that joint negotiations reduced transaction costs and the sharing of broadcast rights allowed fuller coverage of events and facilitates cross-border broadcasting. The exchange of the television signals, the Commission stated, resulted in considerable rationalization and cost savings in that it allowed other members to use the originating member's signal free of charge. The Commission also found enhanced reliability and further cost saving benefits. Finally, the possibility of contractual access for non-members reduced the restriction of competition against non-members. **2.138**

Element 3: 'promoting technical . . . progress'

General

This third category is often applicable in the same circumstances as the first, namely 'an improvement in production'. **2.139**

Technical Advances and Dissemination of Existing Technology

The most obvious benefit here is direct technical progress. Licences of new technology,[194] specialization and joint manufacture agreements,[195] and joint research and development agreements[196] may all lead to improvement in specific technologies and technological progress. **2.140**

---

[192] *National Sulphuric Acid Association* [1980] OJ L260/24.

[193] *EBU/Eurovision* [1993] OJ L179/23 although this has now been annulled, on other grounds, by the CFI in Joined Cases T–528, T–542, T–543 and T–546/93 *Métropole Télévision and Others v Commission* [1996] ECR II–649.

[194] *Olivetti/Canon* [1988] OJ L52/51.

[195] *Jaz-Peter (No 2)* [1978] OJ L61/17.

[196] *Carbon Gas Technologie* [1983] OJ L376/17.

2.141 Technical progress may also be found where existing technologies are combined in a new product. In *Matra*,[197] both the Commission and the Court found that technical improvements made to the vehicle fell within the scope of Article 81(3), since they brought together in a single product techniques which, where they existed, were used in isolation, on different models.

2.142 The rapid dissemination of computer hardware technology has been accepted by the Commission as promoting technical progress by encouraging the development of software.[198]

Improved Safety and Consumer Protection

2.143 A technological improvement may include better service or increased safety[199] for the consumer.

Social and Environmental Considerations

2.144 A reduction in pollution has been held to be a technological improvement.[200] In its *Report on Competition Policy 1995* (Vol XXV) the Commission stated that 'improving the environment is regarded as a factor which contributes to improving economic or technical progress'.

2.145 The Treaty of Amsterdam has reinforced the European Union's commitment to the environment by inserting the concept of sustainable development in the preamble and in the objectives of the EU Treaty and in Article 2 of the EC Treaty, which lays down the tasks of the Community. The new Article 6 EC Treaty states that environmental protection requirements will be integrated into the definition and implementation of other policies. This new article also cites such integration as one means of promoting sustainable development. These amendments should result in environmental considerations being given greater weight by the Commission when it considers the applicability of Article 81(3) to agreements with an impact on the environment.

Overcapacity

2.146 A reduction of overcapacity has been held to be technical progress.[201] This rationale may, as the categorization under Element 1 above shows, also be considered an improvement in production.

---

[197] Case T–17/93 *Matra Hachette v Commission* [1994] ECR II–595, para 110: the CFI upheld the Commission's decision.
[198] *Olivetti/Digital* [1994] OJ L309/24.
[199] *BMW* [1978] OJ L46/33, *Asahi/St Gobain* [1994] OJ L354/87.
[200] *Exxon/Shell* [1994] OJ L144/20.
[201] *Synthetic Fibres* [1984] OJ L207/17.

Element 4: 'promoting . . . or economic progress'

Rationalization and Cost Reduction

As early as 1969 the Commission noted that rationalization achieved by special-   **2.147**
ization would increase competition and thereby lead to technical improvements
and economic progress.[202]

The Commission has found[203] that joint investments, allowing the co-ordination   **2.148**
of investments, may, depending on the surrounding circumstances, ensure that
uneconomic plants will not be set up and enable the parties to wait until market
conditions are most favourable before setting up high-capacity plants thus reducing costs. The co-ordination of investments may also have a decisive impact on
cost by improving the load factor of existing and future plants and by reducing in
the same proportion the burden of fixed costs, if these account for a major proportion of the total cost of the relevant industrial process.

Benefits of Dissemination of Technology

The benefits flowing from the dissemination of technologies via exclusive licens-   **2.149**
ing arrangements may encourage economic progress as well as technical progress
by enabling new technologies.[204] Similarly, agreements for joint research and
development may contribute to economic as well as technical progress.[205]

Overcapacity and Restructuring

Agreements for the reduction of overcapacity may contribute to, *inter alia*, tech-   **2.150**
nical progress[206] (see also Element 3 above). The Commission has also found that
economic progress may be made by permitting necessary restructuring of an
industry under acceptable social conditions.[207]

Improving Financial Systems

Economic progress is clearly linked to the effectiveness of financial systems.   **2.151**
Improving the security and effectiveness of the Eurocheque payments system has
been held to constitute economic progress.[208] The Commission has also found
that co-operation between two banks could lead to an improvement in cross-
border payment systems and again constituted economic progress.[209]

---

[202] *Clima Chappée-Buderus* [1969] OJ L195/1.
[203] *United Reprocessors* [1976] OJ L51/7.
[204] *Boussois/Interpane* [1987] OJ L50/30.
[205] *Beecham/Parke Davis* [1979] OJ L70/11.
[206] *Synthetic Fibres* [1984] OJ L207/17.
[207] *Stichting Baksteen* [1994] OJ L131/15.
[208] *Uniform Eurocheques* [1985] OJ L35/43 and *Uniform Eurocheques* [1989] OJ L36/16.
[209] *Banque Nationale de Paris/Dresdner Bank* [1996] OJ 188/37.

5.152 In the insurance sector the Commission has exempted arrangements to pool the expertise in the insurance sector.[210] Regulation 3932/92[211] provides a block exemption for agreements for co-operation between insurance providers for the collation of data and standardization of terms.

Viability of Requisite Finance

2.153 The Commission exempted a number of agreements relating to the operation of services through the Channel Tunnel on the basis, *inter alia*, that the agreements contributed to the project's financial stability by helping to protect the very large investment necessary for the envisaged services and provided a guaranteed revenue stream without which private finance would have been difficult or impossible to obtain.[212] In the *European Night Services* case,[213] the Court of First Instance accepted the applicant's argument that the duration of the exemption granted by the Commission was insufficient to achieve a return on the requisite investment and should indeed be longer.

(3) 'allowing consumers a fair share of the resulting benefit'

Introduction

2.154 The second positive condition is that the agreement must allow 'consumers a fair share' of the benefits identified under the first heading of Article 81(3). The parties must show a reasonable probability that at least some of the benefit that accrues will be passed on to the consumer. Generally the transmission of the benefit will depend on the intensity of competition within the relevant market. The more intense the competition, the higher the probability that the benefits will be passed on to the consumer as the various undertakings compete for business. The relevant market must be analysed to show that competition is sufficiently intense for this to be so.[214]

2.155 Account must be taken of the consumers' purchasing power and expertise to assess the probability of transmission of the benefit to the consumer. For example, in the *Vacuum Interrupters* case,[215] the Commission decided that: 'vacuum interrupters are sold to sophisticated buyers whose technical and economic requirements are demanding and whose expertise and bargaining strength will ensure that a fair

---

[210] *Nuovo CEGAM* [1984] OJ L99/29.

[211] Commission Regulation (EEC) 3932/92 of 21 December 1992 on the application of Article 85(3) of the Treaty to certain categories of agreements, decisions and concerted practices in the insurance sector.

[212] *Eurotunnel* [1994] OJ L354/66 and Joined Cases T–79/95 and 80/95 *SNCF and British Railways v Commission* [1996] ECR II–1491.

[213] Joined Cases T–374/94, T–375/94, T–384/94 and T–388/94 *European Night Services Ltd and Others v Commission* [1998] ECR II–3141.

[214] Case 75/84 *Metro v Commission (No 2)* [1986] ECR 3021, per van Themaat AG.

[215] *Vacuum Interrupters* [1980] OJ L383/1, section III, para 5.

share of the benefit is passed to the user'. Similarly in *GEC/Weir Sodium Circulators*,[216] the Commission took into account under this condition the negotiating strength of consumers in determining whether they would gain a fair share of the benefits.

In general this condition has received less consideration than the other criteria of Article 81(3). Often, provided that the first positive condition is satisfied and there is a sufficiently competitive market, the Commission will assume that the *consumers will receive* 'a fair share' *of the benefits.*   **2.156**

Consumer

The term 'consumer' in this context is widely defined. It clearly covers private individuals purchasing as typical end-users. It also covers undertakings purchasing in the course of their own trade or business.[217]   **2.157**

The Commission considers the benefit accruing to consumers throughout the Community and not only the benefit to the consumers within the Member States concerned by the agreement.[218]   **2.158**

Benefit

The benefit to the consumer is the same improvement in production or distribution, or technical or economic progress that satisfied the first positive condition of Article 81(3) or the effect of that improvement on prices, availability, quality, and other demand-side parameters.   **2.159**

The following benefits have been held by the Commission to accrue to consumers: higher quality of the products offered,[219] introduction of new[220] and improved products,[221] more favourable prices,[222] greater range of goods,[223] lower costs and hence lower costs for consumers,[224] efficient operating of customer service,[225] or ensuring regularity of supply.[226]   **2.160**

---

[216]   *GEC/Weir (Sodium Circulators)* [1977] OJ L327/26.
[217]   *Kabelmetal/Luchaire* [1975] OJ L222/34.
[218]   *Ford Werke AG* [1983] OJ L327/31, Joined Cases 25 and 26/84 *Ford v Commission (No 2)* [1985] ECR 2725.
[219]   *EBU/Eurovision* [1993] OJ L179/23.
[220]   *Moosehead/Whitbread* [1990] OJ L100/32.
[221]   *Jaz/Peter (No 2)* [1978] L61/17.
[222]   *BT/MCI* [1994] OJ L223/36.
[223]   *Soplem/Vickers* [1978] OJ L70/47.
[224]   *P&I Clubs* [1985] OJ L376/2.
[225]   *Grundig II* [1994] OJ L29/15.
[226]   *Eurotunnel II* [1994] OJ L354/66, para 100.

Fair Share

2.161 In the absence of any precise definition of the term 'fair share' the Commission seems to have a wide discretion in determining what constitutes a fair share. There must be a demonstrable likelihood that consumers will derive benefit from the agreement under examination.

2.162 The time frame within which the benefit accrues should be examined. In *Screensport/EBU*,[227] the Commission accepted the parties' arguments as to consumer benefit in that: 'in the short term at least, consumers benefit from the introduction of a new, dedicated sports channel enabling them to have much more extensive coverage of sports events shown on national television . . . [and] . . . the viewer may be able to see, possibly for the first time, certain new events previously shown only to other national audiences'. However, the Commission went on to say that consumers would be better served by the 'autonomous development of a dedicated sport channel by the Sky group' giving consumers the choice of two European sports channels.

2.163 Clearly if the alleged benefit of the agreement is merely to restrict competition consumers cannot obtain a fair share. In *SPO and others v Commission*,[228] a Dutch building association applied for exemption for a set of rules to protect itself from 'ruinous competition'. The Court of First Instance upheld the Commission's decision that a fair share of the benefits could not be conveyed to the consumers where the agreement was designed to eliminate competition in the industry. As the Court said: 'by taking action to counteract what they regard as ruinous competition, the applicants necessarily restrict competition and therefore deprive consumers of its benefits'.

2.164 If some consumers are denied the benefit of the agreement an exemption will not be granted.[229]

(4) First Negative Condition—Article 81(3)—Indispensability

2.165 An agreement caught by the prohibition of Article 81(1) must generate benefits, a fair share of which are passed on to consumers. Its restrictive clauses must also be indispensable to the attainment of *those* benefits. In other words, the agreement must not give rise to any restrictions of competition which are not absolutely necessary for the positive benefits identified under the first condition of Article 81(3).

2.166 A clause or agreement falling within the prohibition of Article 81(1) would meet the requirements of this criterion if the benefits identified under the first condi-

---

[227] *Screensport/EBU* [1991] OJ L63/32, paras 72 and 73.
[228] Case T–29/92 *SPO v Commission* [1995] ECR II–289, para 294 (upheld on appeal, Case C–137/95P [1996] ECR I–1611).
[229] *Prym/ Beka* [1973] OJ L296/24.

tion of Article 81(3) would either not arise at all, or not occur within the same period of time or to the same extent or with the same degree of probability in its absence. For example, in *Computerland*[230] the Commission decided that the restrictive clauses in the franchise agreement in question were indispensable because potential franchisees would not have made the investments necessary for opening up a new outlet without them; similarly, in *Olivetti-Digital*[231] the Commission decided that the restrictive obligations were indispensable because they were the only way in which the identified benefits to consumers could be ensured. In *Ford Volkswagen*[232] the Commission decided that the co-operation between two major car manufacturers to produce a new type of vehicle would enable them to offer a high-quality product, designed for the specific needs of European consumers, in a relatively new and low volume segment of the market in a comparatively short time. The Commission accepted the parties' arguments that each, acting on its own, could not develop and produce the vehicle so rapidly and efficiently.

2.167 As in many areas of competition law, however, it is difficult, a priori, to determine whether a particular clause would be considered to be indispensable. Even the most restrictive provisions can, in the right circumstances, be indispensable. Two categories of restrictions will, almost invariably, fail to fulfil this criterion. The first are those which are restrictive by object. For example, absolute territorial protection will, almost certainly, not be considered indispensable, even if the parties were to bring forward convincing arguments showing that major benefits would flow from the provision for the European economy. The single market imperative would trump such arguments. The second are clauses which appear on the black lists in the various block exemptions the Commission has adopted. Indeed, perusal of these black lists is often a good starting point for determining whether the Commission is likely to decide that a particular clause is indispensable.

2.168 It should also be noted that in practice the test applied by the Commission is not always one of 'absolute necessity'; rather it will often seek to determine whether there are less restrictive means available to the parties which would allow the identified benefits to be achieved. In *Philips-Osram*,[233] two manufacturers of lead glass for lamps agreed to modernize, operate, and control jointly a factory initially owned by one of them. An older factory belonging to the other party was to be closed down. The Commission decided that the operation would lead to rationalization, greater flexibility in production, savings in energy use, and reduced costs. In deciding that the agreement was indispensable to the attainment of these

---

[230] [1987] OJ L222/12.
[231] [1994] OJ L309/24.
[232] [1993] OJ L20/14, para 29.
[233] [1994] OJ L378/37.

benefits, the Commission specifically considered less restrictive alternatives which the parties could have adopted. In particular it examined whether the parties could have set up new facilities or upgraded their existing ones independently. It concluded that these options would have resulted in a disproportionately high and risky investment for the parties to shoulder independently, given the limited size and the mature character of the market. In *P&O Stena Line*,[234] the parties, who operated ferries across the English Channel, notified the formation of a joint venture in which, *inter alia*, they had combined their operations on a particular route. The Commission decided that the creation of the joint venture fell within the prohibition of Article 81(1) but that it would also have a number of benefits, which consumers would share, such as an increase in the frequency of crossings and major cost savings. Turning to the issue of indispensability, the Commission decided that it fulfilled this criterion as less restrictive forms of co-operation between P&O and Stena, such as joint scheduling, or pooling, would be unlikely to lead to the benefits which would be achieved by the joint venture.

(5) Second Negative Condition—Article 81(3)—Elimination of Competition

2.169 The agreement, decision by associations of undertakings, or concerted practice must not afford the undertakings the possibility of eliminating competition in respect of a substantial part of the products (or by analogy, services) in question.

2.170 Commission decisions have not always given this condition as much considera-tion as some of the other conditions of Article 81(3). This is often either because an assessment of the level of competition on the market will already have been car-ried out, in determining whether the agreement would result in a net benefit and whether this benefit would be transmitted to the consumers, or because the agree-ment has failed to fulfil one of the three preceding conditions. Nevertheless it is an important condition and must be fulfilled if an exemption is to be granted.

2.171 Analysis will focus on the effect on competition both between the parties to the arrangements and also in the market as a whole. The more restrictive the arrange-ments between the parties, and therefore the higher the degree of elimination, the more vigorous competition will need to be on the market in question for an exemption to be granted. To make this assessment a structural analysis of the mar-ket is necessary.

2.172 One must first define the relevant market (by reference to the Commission Notice on the definition of the relevant market under Community competition law[235]). Then market shares can be considered. It should be noted that market share is not

---

[234] [1999] OJ L163/61.
[235] Commission's Notice on the definition of the relevant market under Community competi-tion law [1997] OJ C372/5.

the only relevant criterion. The type of product in question,[236] the number and strength of the remaining competitors,[237] the existence of potential competitors,[238] and barriers to entry[239] are all relevant factors together with other factors relating to market power familiar from other competition law analyses. However, in general, it would seem that agreements between parties with market shares of up to one-third[240] will not fail this condition of Article 81(3). Beyond this it is difficult to give precise guidance. A key question is the relationship between this last requirement of Article 81(3) and Article 82. An agreement which gives rise to a dominant position on the part of the undertakings concerned can clearly be said to afford them the possibility to eliminate competition in respect of a substantial part of the products in question. In its draft Guidelines on Vertical Restraints the Commission notes that: 'The last criterion of elimination of competition is related to the question of dominance. In case an undertaking is dominant or becoming dominant as a consequence of the vertical agreement, a vertical restraint that has appreciable anti-competitive effects can in principle not be exempted.'[241]

---

[236] Case 26/76 *Metro v Commission* [1977] ECR 1875.

[237] eg *Olivetti/Digital* [1994] OJ L309/24.

[238] *BBC Brown Boveri* [1988] OJ L301/68.

[239] *Vacuum Interrupters I* [1977] OJ L48/32.

[240] eg *ENI/Montedison* [1987] OJ L5/13; *Enichem/ICI* [1988] OJ L50/18, para 48; *Exxon/Shell* [1994] OJ L144/20, para 81.

[241] para 42 Draft Guidelines on Vertical Restraints (not yet published).

3

ARTICLE 82—ABUSE OF A DOMINANT POSITION

A. Introduction

(1) General

Article 82 (former Article 86) of the EC Treaty provides as follows:　　　　**3.01**

> Any abuse by one or more undertakings of a dominant position within the common market or in a substantial part of it shall be prohibited as incompatible with the common market insofar as it may affect trade between Member States.
>
> Such abuse may, in particular, consist in:
>
> a) directly or indirectly imposing unfair purchase or selling prices or other unfair trading conditions;
>
> b) limiting production, markets or technical development to the prejudice of consumers;
>
> c) applying dissimilar conditions to equivalent transactions with other trading parties, thereby placing them at a competitive disadvantage;

d) making the conclusion of contracts subject to acceptance by the other parties of supplementary obligations which, by their nature or according to commercial usage, have no connection with the subject of such contracts.

3.02 Together with Article 81 (former Article 85), which is analysed in Chapter 2, Article 82 constitutes a basic provision of EC competition law. Both articles pursue one of the main objectives of the EC Treaty which, according to Article 3(g) thereof, consists in establishing: 'a system ensuring that competition in the internal market is not distorted'.

3.03 It is clear from the wording of Article 82 that it regulates the unilateral behaviour of one or, in certain cases, more undertakings. This is in contrast with Article 81, which deals with situations involving collusive behaviour between several undertakings, ie agreements, decisions of an association of undertakings, or concerted practices.

3.04 Article 82, also differently from Article 81, cannot be applied to any undertaking. It only applies to particular ones, namely those holding a 'dominant position'. As will be explained below (see paragraphs 3.28 and following), undertakings in a dominant position are, in essence, firms holding a substantial amount of market power in one or more of the markets in which they operate.

3.05 Article 82, however, does not prevent the mere creation or possession of a dominant position. As its wording clearly states, it prohibits 'abuses' of such a dominant position. These abuses may consist in one of the four different actions listed in the second paragraph of Article 82. The list contained in this paragraph is not, however, exhaustive. As the Court of Justice clarified in *Continental Can,*[1] its first decision concerning Article 82, this list is merely indicative. Abuses may also consist, as will be explained below (see paragraph 3.111), in any kind of behaviour by a dominant undertaking that appreciably distorts competition or exploits customers in the market in question.

3.06 Finally, abuses of a dominant position will only be prohibited in so far as they may affect trade between Member States. This condition, also included in Article 81, limits the sphere of application of EC competition law. Its precise meaning will be detailed below (see paragraph 3.312).

3.07 From what has already been explained, it can be inferred that Article 82 makes a distinction between two types of undertakings, those which hold a dominant position and those which do not. It places particular obligations upon the former category. As the Court of Justice said in *Michelin:*[2]

---

[1] Case 6/72 *Europemballage Corporation and Continental Can v Commission* [1973] ECR 215, para 26.
[2] Case 322/81, *NV Nederlandsche Baden-Industrie Michelin v Commission* [1983] ECR 3461 para 57 (emphasis added by the authors).

A finding that an undertaking has a dominant position . . . simply means that, irrespective of the reasons for which it has such a dominant position, the undertaking concerned has a *special responsibility* not to allow its conduct to impair genuine undistorted competition in the common market

In other words, undertakings which do not hold a dominant position will only have to comply with the generally applicable provisions contained in Article 81, while the firms which do hold one will have to comply with those of Article 82, in addition to the provisions of Article 81. The relationship between the two articles is further developed below (see Section E of this chapter). **3.08**

The wording of Article 82 does not make any reference to the consequences of the violation of the prohibition that it establishes. As is explained in more detail below (see paragraph 3.349), an abuse of a dominant position may have the consequence that agreements concluded in exercise of such abuse are void. In addition, competition authorities applying the EC competition rules may order that the infringement be terminated and may be permitted to impose fines on undertakings found to have breached Article 82. Damages arising from harm suffered as a result of infringements of this article can moreover be sought from national courts. **3.09**

(2) Rationale for Article 82

Methods of Regulating Firms Holding Substantial Market Power

Article 82, as explained, is a provision that places particular obligations on undertakings holding substantial market power. Several methods of regulation are available to public authorities to limit the potentially detrimental effects for consumers of the existence of firms holding substantial market power. One of these methods is public ownership, which may ensure that public interests are pursued by the management of such firms. Public authorities may also seek to protect public interests through the direct regulation of output and/or prices of these firms. **3.10**

Other methods preserve to a greater extent the autonomy of firms holding market power. Public authorities will prohibit certain types of conduct by these firms and will only intervene when these prohibitions are breached. This is the approach normally adopted by competition regulations and authorities. The conduct prohibited may be either customer exploitation or exclusionary practices, or both. **3.11**

Prohibition of Customer Exploitation

By prohibiting customer exploitation, competition regulations and authorities focus on the effects of the exercise of market power. The exercise of market power, indeed, often leads to direct exploitation of customers, principally in the form of excessive prices, reduction of output, or various types of customer discrimination. **3.12**

3.13 This approach presents, however, several problems.[3] First, it is difficult to distinguish the exercise of market power from its possession. Indeed, firms with market power will, by behaving in a 'commercially sensible' manner (ie trying to maximize their profits), inevitably charge higher prices and produce less output than firms in a competitive market structure. Therefore, the prohibition of customer exploitation may lead, if broadly interpreted, to the prohibition of the very existence of firms holding market power.

3.14 Secondly, the exercise of market power by incumbents will normally attract new entrants into the market (at least, in industries with limited barriers to entry).[4] Incumbents, by charging higher prices than would be possible in a competitive market, obtain supra-competitive profits that other firms will want to share. The entry of the latter firms will normally in turn increase competition, reduce prices, and automatically improve consumer welfare. It can legitimately be enquired whether a competition authority should intervene in such situations.

3.15 Finally, intervention by authorities to curb exploitative behaviour normally requires them, as the case may be, to determine what are the characteristics of output that should be provided, or what is the price that should be charged, by the dominant undertaking. This involves, in some cases, direct regulation of prices and output for the industry in question. Neither competition authorities nor courts are particularly well suited to this task.

Prohibition of Exclusionary Practices

3.16 A second possible approach to dealing with firms holding substantial market power consists in prohibiting conduct which, not being based on normal business performance, excludes or seeks to exclude competitors from the market. The approach does not seek to prohibit the mere possession of market power or the effects of such possession, but the increase or maintenance of such power by anti-competitive means.

3.17 This approach avoids direct regulation of the prices and output of dominant firms. It relies on the self-regulating mechanism of the market for preventing dominant undertakings from reducing consumer welfare. That is why its main aim is to ensure that the market functions properly and that competition is not distorted by anti-competitive conduct.

3.18 This is the approach adopted by US Courts in interpreting section 2 of the Sherman Act, which prohibits monopolization. As Judge Hand said in *Alcoa*,[5] this

---

[3] See, V Korah, *EC Competition Law and Practice* (fifth edn, 1994) 97; L Gyselen, 'Abuse of monopoly power within the meaning of Article 86 of the EEC Treaty: recent developments' [1989] Fordham Corporate Law Institute and TE Kauper, 'Whither Article 86? Observations on excessive prices and refusals to deal' [1989] Fordham Corporate Law Institute.

[4] Unless the supra-competitive profit earned is used by the incumbent to strengthen dominance.

[5] *US v Aluminium Co* 148 F 2d 416 (2d Cir, 1945).

provision does not prevent undertakings from excluding competitors by 'superior skill, foresight and industry'. It prevents, as also stated by the US Supreme Court,[6] 'the wilful acquisition or maintenance of monopoly power as distinguished from growth or development as a consequence of superior product, business acumen or historic accident'.

The difficulty inherent in this approach is to distinguish competition on the mer- **3.19**
its, which is allowed, from exclusion by anti-competitive means, which is not. This question is analysed in detail below (see paragraphs 3.126–3.130).

Methods of Regulation permitted by Article 82 of the EC Treaty

The wording of Article 82 is not clear enough to enable an automatic determina- **3.20**
tion as to which of the prohibition methods described above is prescribed by the provision. Indeed, although Article 82 prohibits abuses of a dominant position, no definition of what amounts to an abuse is to be found in this or in any other article of the EC Treaty.

The first commentators on Article 82 were divided on this issue. Some[7] tended to **3.21**
the view that the provision involved a clear prohibition of exploitative behaviour alone. They supported this view with reference to the types of prohibited conducts itemized in Article 82 (ie unfair prices and terms of trade, limitation of output, discrimination, and tying practices) which refers to instances where market power is exercised to the detriment of customers or suppliers, independently of the effects on competition. Others,[8] on the other hand, supported an interpretation of Article 82 which extended its ambit to a prohibition of exclusionary practices.

Both the practice of the Commission as well as the decisions of the Court of **3.22**
Justice have followed the latter school of thought and interpreted Article 82 as also embodying a prohibition of exclusionary practices. In *Continental Can*[9] the Court took an early opportunity to say that Article 82 'is not only aimed at practices which may cause damage to consumers directly, but also at those which are detrimental to them through their impact on an effective competition structure'.

---

[6] *US v Grinnell Corp* 348 US 563 (1966).

[7] R Joliet, *Monopolization and abuse of dominant position, a comparative study of the American and European approaches to the control of economic power* (Liège: Faculté de Droit, 1970).

[8] EEC Commission, *Concentration of Enterprises in the Common Market, Memorandum to the Governments of the Member States* (1965). It largely reproduced the conclusions of a group of professors appointed by the Commission two years earlier to study the problems raised by the interpretation of Article 82. See also, M Siragusa, *Application of Article 86: Tying arrangements, refusals to deal, discrimination and other cases of abuse* (Bruges, 1974). In 1974 he already considered that Article 82 should mainly apply to exclusionary behaviour and be interpreted so as only prohibiting the exploitative abuses listed in the second para of the article.

[9] Case 6/72 , *Europemballage Corporation and Continental Can v Commission* [1973] ECR 215, para 26.

Most of the cases in which Article 82 has been applied (for example exclusive deal-ing, refusals to deal, tying, pricing practices) fall into this second category.

3.23 The exploitative practices explicitly mentioned in the wording of Article 82 are still prosecuted in certain circumstances but less frequently than would be expected given the wording of the provision. This is probably explained by the self-policing character of these abuses (see paragraph 3.14 above) as well as by the fact that authorities applying the provision may well balk at the subjectivity involved in deciding that a particular course of conduct is either unfair or unreas-onable.

3.24 There are circumstances, however, in which exploitative abuses continue to be pursued for sound economic reasons. First, there is some economic sense in pur-suing such abuses in markets with high barriers to entry, where supra-competitive profits will not attract new entrants, and which are not regulated at a national level. Secondly, Article 82 is sometimes used to pursue exploitation in conjunc-tion with Article 86 (former Article 90) in order to liberalize markets subject to exclusive rights.[10] Thirdly, in some cases, this type of abuse has been pursued because the practice in question facilitated the dominant undertakings in ques-tion infringing other principles of the EC Treaty, in particular where the practice created obstacles to the establishment of the single European market.[11]

B. Dominant Position

(1) General

Market Power Defined—What is Dominance?

3.25 Dominance is a position of considerable economic power held for a period of time by a firm/s over customers and/or suppliers in a market. More specifically, it is the ability of a firm/s to restrict output and thus raise prices above the level that would prevail in a competitive market, without existing rivals or new entrants in due time taking away its customers (a detailed economic discussion of market power is contained in Chapter 1).

3.26 Dominance is not an absolute concept, but is a matter of degree. Market power may be found to exist to a greater or lesser extent, or for longer or shorter periods of time. Dominance is not synonymous with monopoly. To be considered domin-

---

[10] See C–41/90 *Höfner and Elser v Macrotron* [1991] ECR I–1979, where the Court considered that the Bundesanstalt für Arbeit, a German agency with a monopoly in the provision of placement services, had failed to meet the demand for its services, and that it had, therefore, abused its domi-nant position. This was considered an infringement of both Articles 86 and 82.

[11] See Case 26/75 *General Motors Continental NV v Commission* [1975] ECR 1367, where a sur-charge applied by General Motors in Belgium to certifications of imported cars which prevented imports from other Member States was considered an excessive price caught by Article 82.

ant, an undertaking should hold a substantial amount of market power and be able to behave independently from its competitors. It is not however necessary that it eliminates all competitors from the relevant market. Monopolies— whether *de jure* or *de facto*—however, are by definition dominant undertakings within the meaning of Article 82.

The temporal element is crucial. In the absence of substantial barriers to entry, **3.27** market forces would ensure that dominance vanishes in the long term. Indeed, new companies would inevitably enter the market, attracted by the supra-competitive profits obtained by the incumbent, and would erode the latter's market power and position. During the period of time needed for new entrants to establish a presence in the market, however, the dominant undertaking may engage in exclusionary or abusive practices aimed at securing its position. Competition policy is concerned with impeding such practices during this period, even if market forces alone would over the longer term restore consumer welfare. A company will therefore normally be considered dominant if it holds market power for a period of time long enough to enable it to operate independently of competitors and customers, and which allows it to obtain an economic benefit from that position.

The Court of Justice's Definition

The classic definition of the nature of a dominant position within the meaning of **3.28** Article 82 is contained in the ECJ's judgment in the *United Brands* case, where it was described as follows:

> a position of economic strength enjoyed by an undertaking which enables it to prevent effective competition being maintained on the relevant market by giving it the power to behave to an appreciable extent independently of its competitors, customers and ultimately of consumers.[12]

The Court has, in successive judgments, essentially retained this definition.[13] The **3.29** Court emphasizes the notion of a dominant firm's independence from the competitive forces normally constraining a supplier in the market.[14] This does not mean that a firm must, in order to be dominant, be able to ignore competition entirely and simply do as it wishes by, for example, raising prices without any constraint. Indeed, a firm can be dominant even in circumstances where it must sometimes take competitive factors into account in determining its

---

[12] Case 27/76 *United Brands v Commission* [1978] ECR 207.
[13] Cases 85/76 *Hoffman-La Roche v Commission* [1979] ECR 461, Case 322/81 *NV Nederlandsche Baden-Industrie Michelin v Commission* [1983] ECR 3461.
[14] Note that the Commission's definition of a dominant position used to refer to independence from competitors and suppliers; reference to the latter was abandoned in the *ABG* case where BP was found to be dominant on the Dutch petrol market notwithstanding its dependence on the OPEC cartel for supplies.

commercial behaviour.[15] If, however, a firm can substantially disregard, and keep safely at bay, its competitors over a long period of time, this is a clear indication of dominance.

3.30 The same idea of independence of behaviour is also found in Article 66(7) of the ECSC Treaty, which enables the Commission to address recommendations to dominant undertakings in the coal and steel sectors. Indeed, this provision defines dominant undertakings as:

> public or private undertakings which, in law or in fact, hold or acquire in the market for one of the products within its jurisdiction a dominant position shielding them against effective competition in a substantial part of the common market [.]

The Merger Regulation's Concept of Dominant Position

3.31 Article 2 of the Merger Regulation[16] states that 'a concentration which creates or strengthens a dominant position as a result of which effective competition would be significantly impeded in the common market or in a substantial part of it shall be declared incompatible with the common market'.

3.32 There is no reason to believe that the concept of dominant position in the Merger Regulation has a meaning different from the concept in Article 82 of the EC Treaty.[17] However, the scope and purpose of the two provisions being substantially different, this same concept is necessarily applied from different perspectives. First, while Article 82 applies to existing dominant positions, and requires fundamentally a retrospective analysis, the Merger Regulation, which assesses the possibility of a dominant position being created or strengthened, necessitates a prospective analysis. Secondly, Article 82 is not primarily concerned with the reduction of competition which results from the existence of a company occupying a dominant position, but with the abuses that this company may engage in. The Merger Regulation, on the other hand, is primarily concerned with the effects on competition of the creation or strengthening of such a dominant position (see a detailed analysis of the Merger Regulation in Chapter 4).

(2) Determining Dominance

3.33 The existence of a dominant position in a particular market is normally inferred from a variety of factors, some of which tend to carry more weight than others. These factors relate to the structure of the market, in particular the barriers to

---

[15] See Temple-Lang, 'Some aspects of abuse of dominant positions in European Community anti-trust law' (1979) 3 Fordham International Law Forum.

[16] Council Regulation 4064/89 of 21 December 1989 on the control of concentrations between undertakings [1989] OJ L395.

[17] See C–395/96P and C–396/96P *Compagnie Maritime Belge and Dafra-Lines v Commission* 29 October1998 paras 26 and 27 (Opinion of Fenelly AG).

entry thereto and to the firm's position on the market as well as to its own structure and competitive conduct.[18]

The Relevant Market

In determining the existence of a dominant position, it is first necessary to iden- **3.34**
tify the relevant product and geographic markets. Dominance can only be
appraised by reference to a defined category of products within a specified geographical area; it is thereby possible to establish whether or not an allegedly dominant firm is facing competitive pressures that enable it to behave in relative
disregard of its competitors.[19] Market definition is dealt with in detail at Chapter
1 above.

Measurement of Market Power

Market Shares

As also explained in Chapter 1, there are various methods of assessing market **3.35**
power. The primary—albeit imperfect—indicator of dominance is usually the
allegedly dominant company's share of the relevant market (ie the percentage that
the sales of the undertaking represent in relation to the whole market turnover). If
a company is dominant on that market, it is logical that it will have succeeded in
gaining a large share of it. The Court of Justice in *Hoffmann-La Roche*[20] stated
that:

> the existence of a dominant position may derive from several factors which taken
> separately are not necessarily determinative but among these factors a highly impor-
> tant one is the existence of very large market shares.

Absolute market share levels.   It is not possible to point to a specific share of the **3.36**
market above which a firm is conclusively dominant, and below which it is not.
Neither have the Commission or Court of Justice taken such a simplistic line.
Certain levels will, however, give rise to strong presumptions one way or the other.

Very high market shares provide in themselves virtually conclusive proof that a **3.37**
firm is dominant. The Court of Justice in *Hoffmann-La Roche* stated that:

> although the importance of the market shares may vary from one market to another
> the view may legitimately be taken that very large market shares are *in themselves,
> and save in exceptional circumstances,* evidence of the existence of a dominant posi-
> tion [emphasis added].

---

[18] In analysing these factors, this chapter will focus on analysis conducted by the Commission
and the Court of Justice when applying Article 82 of the EC Treaty. In some cases, however, decisions adopted under the Merger Regulation assessing the existence of a dominant position may also
be referred to.

[19] See Commission Notice on the definition of the relevant market for the purposes of
Community competition law [1997] 97/C 372/5.

[20] Case 85/76 *Hoffman-La Roche v Commission* [1979] ECR 461.

3.38   In that case, Hoffmann-La Roche held very high shares of a number of markets. These very high shares ranged from approximately 75 per cent to approximately 87 per cent of a series of specific Community vitamin markets, and the Court considered that the shares were so high as to require no further examination of other factors before concluding that dominance existed. In *Hilti*,[21] the Court of Justice upheld the Commission's view that market shares of between 70 per cent and 80 per cent were so high as not to require further corroboration. The same situation arose in *Tetra Pak II*,[22] where the undertaking concerned held a market share of around 90 per cent.

3.39   High market shares (of over about 50 per cent), held over a period of time, are considered to be strong prima facie evidence of dominance and effectively create a presumption that a firm is dominant. In *Michelin*,[23] market shares of 57 per cent and 65 per cent were considered, in the absence of any countervailing indications, sufficient evidence of dominance. In *AKZO*,[24] a market share of 50 per cent over at least three years was considered strong evidence of the existence of a dominant position. If, however, high market shares are only held for relatively short periods of time, they may not be sufficient in themselves to establish the existence of dominance.

3.40   Low market shares, on the other hand, (less than 40 per cent or so) are generally considered to be indicative of a firm not occupying a dominant position. In the case of market shares of between about 25 per cent and 40 per cent, it must be considered unlikely that a single company could be held to occupy a dominant position, unless the shares of the firm's competitors are very fragmented. In *Grundig*,[25] the Commission did not find dominance with market shares of 23 per cent and 33 per cent for the two leaders in the German colour TV market.

3.41   Market shares of less than 25 per cent are very unlikely to be associated with dominance by a company. By analogy, it should be noted that recital 15 to the Merger Regulation indicates that concentrations 'where the market share of the undertakings concerned does not exceed 25% either in the common market or in a substantial part of it' are presumed to be compatible with the common market.

3.42   Finally, very low shares of the relevant market are considered definitive indicators of the absence of dominance. In the *SABA II* case,[26] for example, a market share of 10 per cent was considered by the Court to be conclusive of a lack of dominance.

---

[21]   T–30/89 *Hilti v Commission* [1992] ECR II–1439 and C–53/92P.
[22]   T–83/91 *Tetra Pak International v Commission* [1994] ECR II–755.
[23]   Case 322/81 *NV Nederlandsche Baden-Industrie Michelin v Commission* [1983] ECR 3461.
[24]   C–62/86 *AKZO Chemie BV v Commission* [1991] ECR I–3359.
[25]   *Grundig* [1985] OJ L233/1.
[26]   *SABA II* [1986] 6 ECR 3021.

Market share levels over time. Market shares should be held over a certain   **3.43**
period of time to constitute evidence of a dominant position. The Court, in
Hoffmann-La Roche,[27] has stressed the importance of this temporal element:

> an undertaking which has a very large market share *and holds it for some time* . . . is
> by virtue of that share in a position of strength which makes it an unavoidable trad-
> ing partner and which, already because of this secures for it, *at the very least during
> relatively long periods*, that freedom of action which is the special feature of a domi-
> nant position [emphasis added].

The length of the period of time over which large market shares should be main-   **3.44**
tained in order to prove dominance will vary in accordance with the specifics of
each individual case, principally as a function of the barriers to entry in the relevant market. In *Hoffmann-La Roche*, the Court of Justice considered that the company's fluctuating share of the vitamin B3 market (ranging from 29 per cent to 51
per cent over a three-year period) could not be considered sufficient evidence of
dominance. Large market shares in a market which is in a first stage of development, and where barriers to entry are low, would not normally be considered sufficient evidence of a dominant position.[28]

Market share levels relative to competitors. In the case of large market shares   **3.45**
which are nevertheless not so great that they provide more or less conclusive proof
of dominance, it is usually necessary to also examine the shares of the company's
closest rivals. The Court of Justice in *Hoffmann-La Roche* accepted the
Commission's finding of dominance in relation to the company in the vitamin A
market (where its share was 47 per cent), in particular because of the smaller relative size of the company's competitors' shares (27 per cent, 18 per cent, 7 per cent,
and 1 per cent) in what the Court described as a 'narrow oligopolistic market'. A
share of between 40 per cent and 45 per cent in another vitamin market was also
found to amount to a dominant position. The Court pointed out that this share
was 'several times greater' than that of the company's nearest rival, and that its
other rivals were considerably further behind again in terms of market share.

Price Elasticity of Demand

The market power held by a particular undertaking can also be directly measured   **3.46**
by estimating the price elasticity of demand of the enterprise in question. Price
elasticity of demand is the percentage by which the output sold by the undertaking decreases in relation to an increase in its price. In general, the lower price
elasticity of demand is, the higher the market power held by the firm in question.

Estimating price elasticity of demand, however, requires a substantial amount of   **3.47**
detailed data, on levels of prices and output sold, which is rarely available. In view

---

[27] Case 85/76 *Hoffman-La Roche v Commission* [1979] ECR 461.
[28] *MSG Media Services*; 9 November 1994, para 55.

of this difficulty, authorities enforcing competition regulations, as explained above, normally define a market, and then assess the position of the undertakings in question on that market, as a surrogate means of assessing market power.

Profitability Measurement

3.48 Measuring the levels of profits of an undertaking has sometimes also been considered an alternative means of inferring market power. It can be, however, a very misleading tool and so is best avoided. It is true that supra-competitive profits can be associated with a dominant position, but this correlation is easily severed. Indeed, non-dominant firms can be particularly profitable, due to superior performance in terms, for example, of greater innovation, risk taking, or efficiency than the firm's rivals. Conversely, low profits or even losses can sometimes be explained by poor performance in the market, and are not necessarily inconsistent with dominance.[29]

Barriers to Entry

3.49 In addition to determining the position that a company holds in a particular market, an element of particular importance in determining whether such a company holds a dominant position is the existence of barriers to entering that market. Indeed, a company will only be able to exert market power (ie increase prices without losing output) if potential competitors are prevented from easily entering the market. If entry is easy, companies which increase prices will not be able to retain their share of the market, no matter how large this share is, and will inevitably lose output in relation to new entrants.

Types of Barriers to Entry

The case law does not provide a clear definition of the concept of barrier to entry.

3.50 There are, however, several elements that constitute barriers to entry and these have been taken into account by case law in determining dominance. Below, these elements are classified into four different categories and discussed in detail.

Legal or administrative barriers.   Any exclusive right to operate in a certain

3.51 market, granted by a legal or administrative provision, constitutes a barrier to entry. Case law has dealt with several of those barriers: national monopolies in certain sectors[30] or the need to obtain an administrative authorization.

A particular type of legal barrier to entry consists in the possession of *intellectual*

3.52 *property rights* (patents, trade marks, designs, or copyrights). These confer on their

---

[29] In Case 27/76 *United Brands v Commission* [1978] ECR 207, the Court did not consider relevant the fact that the company had suffered losses for a number of years; those losses had been due to extraneous factors (climatic conditions, accidents, etc); see also *Irish Sugar* [1997] OJ L258/1.

[30] Merger Decision *Elf/Ertoil* (Case IV/M63) (1991).

holders the exclusive ownership for a period of time of certain intellectual creations. These rights may allow their holders, therefore, to exclude competitors from certain activities that cannot be performed without the exercise of the intellectual property rights in question.

Some types of intellectual property rights will be more likely than others to confer dominant positions. Patents covering a new production method, for instance, have been considered several times by the jurisprudence as conferring dominance in the market in question.[31] The same reasoning could apply to copyrights for certain information needed in order to provide a product or service.[32] Trade marks, in themselves, are less likely to confer dominance. They will contribute to it only when they refer to a well-established brand (see paragraphs 3.62 and 3.63 below). **3.53**

Sunk costs of entry. Sunk costs of entry are those costs that cannot be recovered if entry fails. The Court has already recognized that they constitute barriers to entry. In *United Brands*,[33] for instance, it stated that: **3.54**

> The barriers to competitors entering the market are the exceptionally large capital investments required . . . the economies of scale from which newcomers to the market cannot derive any immediate benefit and the actual cost of entry made up inter alia of all the general expenses incurred in penetrating the market such as the setting up of an adequate commercial network, the mounting of very large-scale advertising campaigns, all those financial risks, the costs of which are irrecoverable if the attempt fails.

Sunk costs which are fixed (ie which do not depend on the amount of output to be produced) lead to the existence of *economies of scale*. The larger the output produced, the larger the spread of the fixed sunk costs between those units produced and the lower the average costs obtained, ie the larger the economies of scale. The existence of such economies of scale, therefore, also constitutes a barrier to entry.[34] **3.55**

Different types of sunk costs have normally to be incurred in order to enter a new market. They can be distinguished according to the functional area of the company concerned (production, research and development (R&D), distribution, and marketing costs). **3.56**

As far as production costs are concerned, investments in plants and other production facilities, which could not be recovered if entry fails, constitute barriers to entry. **3.57**

---

[31] T–83/91 *Tetra Pak International v Commission* [1994] ECR II–755. See also Merger Decisions *ATT/NCR* (Case IV/M50) (1991) and *Boeing/McDonnell Douglas* (Case IV/M877 [1997] OJ L336/16.

[32] T–69/89 *Radio Telefis Eireann v Commission* [1991] ECR II–485; T–70/88 *BBC Enterprises Ltd v Commission* [1991] ECR II–535; and T–76/89 *Independent Television Publications v Commission* [1991] ECR II–575.

[33] Case 27/76 *United Brands v Commission* [1978] ECR 207, para 122.

[34] Merger Decisions *Procter & Gamble/Schickedanz* (Case IV/M430) [1994] OJ L354/32 or *Nestlé/Perrier* (Case IV/M190) [1992] OJ L356/1.

3.58 With regard to R&D, in markets where innovation plays an important role, a lead in R&D or a technological advantage would normally constitute a factor contributing to dominance. Indeed, in order to replicate such a lead, new entrants have to incur substantial costs which, by definition, are sunk, because it cannot be known in advance whether such investment will lead to effective results.

3.59 The Court of Justice has already mentioned the possession of a technical lead as constituting a barrier in *United Brands*, where it indicated that UBC's rivals could not 'develop research at a comparable level and are in this respect at a disadvantage'. It has also been relied on as a relevant factor by the Commission and Court in some other cases.[35] Merger decisions have also often referred to technological advantage in order to determine whether a dominant position is being created.[36]

3.60 In low technology markets, or in markets where the relevant patents have expired (as was the case in *Hoffmann-La Roche*), this factor should not play an important role.[37] It is also arguable that technology which can easily be replicated by competitors should not be treated as a barrier. The dominant firm may have had to make considerable investments in order to develop such a technology, but this level of investment might not need to be replicated by newcomers to the same extent.

3.61 Sunk costs in distribution facilities also constitute barriers to entry. The Court of Justice, in *Hoffmann-La Roche* for instance, considered the fact that the company had an extensive sales network to be a factor contributing to dominance. In *Van den Bergh Foods*, the Commission placed reliance on the company's nationwide distribution network.

3.62 Finally, as far as marketing is concerned, investments in building a reputation and in particular in promoting a trade mark are also normally sunk. A brand signals the quality and origin of a product and, in markets for non-homogeneous products, and particularly luxury products, amounts to one of the basic parameters of competition. A leading trade mark, therefore, is an additional factor to be taken into account when evaluating dominance.

3.63 In *United Brands* the strength of UBC's brands was taken into account in the Commission and Court's assessment of the existence of dominance. In *Van den Bergh Foods*, the strength of Unilever's ice cream brands in Ireland was relied on by the Commission as being one of the considerations relevant to the finding of

---

[35] Case 85/76 *Hoffman-La Roche v Commission* [1979] ECR 461, para 48; Case 322/81 *NV Nederlandsche Baden-Industrie Michelin v Commission* [1983] ECR 3461, para 58; T–30/89 *Hilti v Commission* [1992] ECR II–1439 and C–53/92P.

[36] *Saint Gobain/Wacker-Chemie/Nom* (Case IV/M774) (1996) [1997] OJ L247/1.

[37] V Korah, *EEC Competition Law and Practice* (1990).

dominance. Several decisions assessing the compatibility of a concentration within the common market have also referred to this factor.[38]

Switching costs for customers.   Barriers to entry derive not only from the costs   **3.64** that the entrant would have to support, but also from costs that new entry would create for the customers. Indeed, a barrier to entry will exist when a customer would have to bear a high cost in order to switch to a competitor. This will be the case when, for instance, it has to invest in new facilities in order to be supplied by the competitor, or when it has to train its workforce to use the new entrant's product. In all these cases, the new entrant will often have to support part of these switching costs in order to make its way into the market, while the incumbent company will not have to face them.

The Commission acknowledged that switching costs can constitute a barrier to   **3.65** entry in the *Tetra Pak I* case.[39] In order to determine whether Tetra Pak, a producer of milk packaging systems, held a dominant position, the Commission examined whether customers of Tetra Pak would easily switch to its competitors. It considered that the choice for a dairy of the type of packaging system it will use is an important investment decision, because not only must packaging machinery specific to the package employed be purchased, but milk-treating and storing equipment has also to be adapted.

Strategic behaviour.   Finally, barriers to entry can derive from the behaviour of   **3.66** the firm holding a dominant position. The threat to engage in a price war, or to expand output, in response to a new entry can amount to a barrier sufficient to deter new entrants. Excessive investments in publicity or product range, for instance, may also raise the cost of entry for rivals, thereby constituting barriers.

The existence of *excess capacity*[40] could, in particular, constitute a barrier, because   **3.67** it allows the dominant company to prevent entry through strategic behaviour. Indeed, the fact that a company is able to increase its output at short notice, because it is not using all of its production capacity, allows it to respond to a competitive move of its competitors, and may thereby contribute to the company's dominance.[41] Conversely, the existence of several competitors with substantial excess capacity may lead to the conclusion that a company with large market share

---

[38] *Coca Cola/Amalgamated Beverages* (Case IV/M794) (1997); *Guiness/Grand Metropolitan* (Case IV/M938) (1997).

[39] *Tetra Pak I* [1988] OJ L272/37, para 37.

[40] It is important to distinguish 'excess' capacity from 'idle' capacity. The former allows a firm to increase its level of production at short notice and without substantial capacity maintenance costs. The latter, often the result of the advent of new technology, is capacity whose usage is expensive and usually not economically viable. It should not therefore be taken into account as a factor supporting a finding of dominance.

[41] The Court of Justice, in Case 85/76 *Hoffman-La Roche v Commission* [1979] ECR 461, accepted that the company's overcapacity was a factor relevant to the issue of dominance.

is not dominant, as any attempt to exploit its position could be met by an increase in production by its competitors.[42]

3.68 It is not necessary to determine whether strategic behaviour constitutes in itself an abuse in order to consider it a barrier to entry, and thereby to conclude as to the existence of a dominant position. Indeed, an exclusionary abuse often gives rise to a certain extent to a barrier to entry. That is not to say, however, that any strategic behaviour intended to raise the cost of entry for rivals may be deemed to constitute an abuse within the meaning of Article 82 of the EC Treaty.

Barriers to expansion

3.69 A final concept to take into consideration in this context is the notion of a barrier to expansion. Instead of preventing companies not present in the market from entering it, barriers to expansion prevent firms already present in the market from expanding their output. This type of barrier is also relevant for the determination of a dominant position because, in the absence thereof, a dominant firm will not be able to exert market power: if it raises prices, output will be easily lost to its competitors.

3.70 The term 'barriers to expansion' has not yet been used as such in case law, but the concept has been taken into account by the Courts in order to determine dominance. For instance, the Court of Justice has considered that dominance could be established when competitors having smaller market shares than the leading undertaking were not 'able to meet rapidly the demand from those who would like to break away from the undertaking which has the largest market share'.[43]

3.71 Most of the barriers to entry just detailed could also be considered barriers to expansion. So, for example, sunk costs, switching costs, and strategic behaviour can constitute also barriers to expansion. Legal rights, on the other hand, are exclusively barriers to entry: once acquired, they do not limit the expansion of the company in the market in question.

3.72 Generally speaking, barriers to expansion tend to be high in sectors where an increase in capacity requires large investment (for example, in building production plants, finding new sources of supply, expanding distribution networks), but tend to be low in those sectors where, once a large entry investment has been made, the marginal cost of supplying a new product unit is very low.

---

[42] See Merger Decisions *Mannesmann/Vallourec/Ilva* (Case IV/M 315), (1994) or *Aérospatiale/MBB* (Case IV/M 17), (1991).

[43] Case 85/76 *Hoffmann-La Roche v Commission* [1979] ECR 461.

Other Factors Taken into Account to Determine Dominance

The Courts sometimes have taken other factors into account in order to deter-   **3.73**
mine dominance. It should be stressed that these are factors *additional* to market
share and do not—taken alone—constitute sufficient evidence of the existence of
dominance. There follows a non-exhaustive list of a number of factors taken into
account by the Commission and/or the Court in assessing dominance within the
meaning of Article 82.

Structural Factors

Size of operations.   Sheer size, established on the basis of turnover or any other   **3.74**
similar measure (for example volume of assets), has sometimes been considered as
a relevant factor in finding dominance. However, large size can result from the fact
that a company is operating in several different markets, a fact which does not normally have any particular bearing on the appreciation of whether the undertaking
concerned has market power in one of these markets. Indeed, the Court of Justice
in *Hoffmann-La Roche*[44] dismissed this as a valid criterion, even for the purpose of
corroborating apparent dominance based on high market shares.

Wide geographical presence.   Wide geographical presence is a factor that could   **3.75**
be relevant for establishing dominance, particularly when large multinational
conglomerates benefit from group synergies at different levels (purchasing, technological development, distribution channels, etc), which can allow them to
behave, to some extent, independently from competitors. In the absence of such
synergies, mere presence in different geographic markets is not particularly helpful in determining whether the company in question holds market power in one
of those markets.

In *Michelin*,[45] the Court accepted as relevant to the issue of dominance that the   **3.76**
company appeared to gain advantages from the fact that it had subsidiaries operating throughout Europe and the world. The Commission has sometimes also
mentioned this factor,[46] both in Article 82 and in Merger decisions, in determining the existence of a dominant position.[47] Conversely, competitors with large

---

[44] Case 85/76 *Hoffman-La Roche v Commission* [1979] ECR 461.

[45] Case 322/81 *NV Nederlandsche Baden-Industrie Michelin v Commission* [1983] ECR 3461.
However, the Court of Justice, in Case 85/76 *Hoffman-La Roche v Commission* [1979] ECR 461,
did not consider relevant to the issue of dominance the fact that Roche was the biggest producer of
vitamins in the world, noting that several of its competitors were also companies with a wide geographical presence.

[46] *United Brands*, Case T–83/91 *Tetra Pak International v Commission* [1994] ECR II–755, *Van
den Bergh Foods* [1998] OJ L246/1.

[47] *BT/MCI* (Case IV/M856) [1997] OJ L336/1; *Nestlé/Perrier* (Case IV/M190 [1992] OJ
L356/1; *Boeing/McDonnell Douglas* (Case IV/M877) [1997] OJ L336/16.

market shares have sometimes not been found dominant when they face competitors belonging to large multinational groups.[48]

3.77 **Financial resources.**   Ready access to considerable finance (ie deep pockets) has been cited by the Commission[49] and the Court of Justice[50] as an additional factor relevant to the establishment of dominance under Article 82. Article 2 of the Merger Regulation also refers to financial power as one of the elements to be taken into account in assessing whether a concentration creates or strengthens a dominant position, and several Merger decisions have mentioned it.[51] As some economists have pointed out,[52] however, if financial markets are efficient in allocating capital resources, it is not obvious why this should be a factor relevant to an assessment of dominance.

3.78 **Vertical integration.**   If vertical integration allows a firm to have exclusive access, or better access than its rivals, to raw materials or other inputs, particularly scarce ones, this could no doubt constitute a factor relevant to a finding of dominance.

3.79 In *United Brands*, for instance, the Commission pointed to the vertical integration within UBC of the various stages in bringing bananas to market as a further supporting factor indicating the company's dominance. Vertical integration has also been mentioned in several Merger Decisions[53] as a factor contributing to dominance.

3.80 **Product range or differentiation.**   A wide range of products is not always an indicator of dominance. It should only be so when it allows the firm in question to obtain significant cost savings by exploiting economies of scope, or when there are consumers interested in purchasing the whole range of products. In this case, a company offering the full range will reduce the transaction and supply costs for the customers and will also be able to maximize its promotion campaigns (by, for instance, offering discounts across the range). This advantage for a firm offering a full range of products is sometimes referred to as a 'portfolio effect'. In cases where such effects do not exist, the fact that a company is present in different product markets does not say anything about its dominance in one of them.

---

[48]   *Unilever France/Ortiz Miko* (Case IV/M422) (1994).
[49]   See, for instance, C–310/93P *BPB Industries plc & Anor v Commission* [1995] ECR I–865, para 115.
[50]   Case 27/76 *United Brands v Commission* [1978] ECR 207.
[51]   *Lyonnaise des Eaux/Suez* (Case IV/M916) (1997).
[52]   C Baden Fuller, 'Article 86 EEC: Economic analysis of the Existence of a Dominant Position' (1979) 4 ELR 423.
[53]   *Mannesman/Hoesch* (Case IV/M222) [1992] OJ L114/34; *Nestlé/Perrier* (Case IV/M190) [1992] OJ L356/1; *Nordic Satellite Distribution* (Case IV/M490) [1995] OJ L53/20.

The Commission has referred several times to a large range of products as a factor **3.81**
contributing to dominance. In *Tetra Pak II*,[54] for instance, it pointed out that 'the
diversity of its products' increased market power. In *Van den Bergh Foods*, the
breadth of the dominant company's range of products compared to those of its
rivals is also mentioned by the Commission as a factor influencing the finding of
dominance. The Court of Justice has, in several cases, also taken product range
into account in addressing the question of dominance.[55] Likewise, several Merger
decisions point to this factor in considering the existence of dominance.[56]

Behavioural Factors—conduct of the allegedly dominant firm

It should finally be considered whether a dominant position could also be inferred **3.82**
from the conduct of the allegedly dominant firm. It has been explained that a
dominant position is a position that allows a company to behave independently
from its competitors and customers. It could be argued, therefore, that the very
evidence of such independent behaviour could also be used to prove the existence
of a dominant position.

Both the Court of Justice and the Commission have, sometimes, used behavioural **3.83**
elements to justify the existence of a dominant position. For instance, in *Hoffman
La Roche*,[57] the Court analysed whether the company could behave to a large
extent independently of competitors. It considered that, should the company
have been forced to reduce its prices in reaction to competitors' discounts, it
would not have been possible to conclude that it behaved independently and,
therefore, that it held a dominant position.[58]

In none of the cases involving the application of Article 82 has the assessment of **3.84**
behavioural factors provided a substitute for the analysis of the structure of the
market and of the position of the allegedly dominant company on that market,
but rather has complemented it.[59] It is in fact difficult to imagine a situation where
different conclusions would be reached by using a structural and a behavioural
analysis.

---

[54] Case T–83/91 *Tetra Pak International v Commission* [1994] ECR II–755.
[55] Case 322/81 *NV Nederlandsche Baden-Industrie Michelin v Commission* [1983] ECR 3461,
para 55; C–62/86 *AKZO Chemie BV v Commission* [1991] ECR I–3359, para 58; in Case 85/76
Hoffman-La Roche v Commission [1979] ECR 461, the Court considered that Roche's wide range of
vitamins was not relevant to any of its findings of dominance. However, this seems to have been
because the company's rivals also supplied a range of vitamins, and any advantage that might otherwise have accrued to Hoffmann-La Roche was thereby neutralized.
[56] *Guiness/Grand Metropolitan* (Case IV/M938) (1997); *Nestlé/Perrier* (Case IV/M190) [1992]
OJ L356/1; *Kimberly-Clark/Scott* (Case IV/M623) [1996] OJ L183/1, among others.
[57] Case 85/76 *Hoffman-La Roche v Commission* [1979] ECR 461, para 71.
[58] See, also, Case 27/76 *United Brands v Commission* [1978] ECR 207, paras 67 and 68 or case
85/76 *Hoffman-La Roche v Commission* [1979] ECR 461, para 71.
[59] M Waelbroeck and A Frignani, *Comentaire J Megret. Volume 4. Concurrence* (1997) 244

(3) Particular Situations of Dominance

3.85 Several particular situations of dominance will be described below. First, those situations will be dealt with in which undertakings, due to a particular characteristic, will always be considered to be in a dominant position. This is the case for statutory monopolies. The question of whether a company is always dominant in its aftermarkets (for example markets for the supply parts of a certain brand) and markets for which it holds intellectual property rights will also be discussed here. Secondly, it will be analysed whether Article 82 can also be applied to oligopolies or, in other words, whether dominant positions can be held by several undertakings. The notion of a so-called 'collective dominant position' will be described in this context. Thirdly, it will be considered whether Article 82 can apply to the behaviour of firms in a market where they do not have a proper dominant position, being markets neighbouring ones to those in which the firm holds a dominant position. Finally, the question of whether a dominant buyer can also be considered to hold a dominant position, and therefore be subject to Article 82, will also be discussed.

Undertakings always Found to Be in a Dominant Position

Statutory Monopolies

3.86 Public monopolies or undertakings that have been granted an exclusive right to operate in a particular market will always be considered to be in a dominant position, if such a market constitutes a relevant market for competition purposes. Many examples of these kinds of monopolies are to be found in the case law. Statutory monopolies have been found, *inter alia*, in the markets for certificates of conformity for imported cars;[60] telecom services;[61] provision, maintenance, and repair of telecom equipment;[62] recruitment services;[63] postal delivery;[64] harbour pilot and other services;[65] as well as broadcasting.[66]

3.87 Such statutory monopolies, for so long as they do not operate as public authorities, are subject to Article 82 of the EC Treaty in the same way as any other undertaking holding a dominant position. In fact, Article 5 of the EC Treaty imposes an obligation on Member States not to adopt any measure that can deprive this or other Treaty articles of their effectiveness. Furthermore, if the state measure grant-

---

[60] Case 26/75 *General Motors Continental v Commission* [1975] ECR 1367.

[61] Case 41/83 *Italian Republic v Commission* [1985] ECR 880.

[62] Case C–202/88 *French Republic v Commission* [1991] ECR I–1223 and C–18/88 *RTT v GB-Inno-BM* [1991] ECR I–5941.

[63] Case C–41/90 *Klaus Hofner and Fritz Elser v Macrotron Gmbh* [1991] ECR I–1979.

[64] Case C–320/91 *Corbeau v Belgian Post Office* [1993] ECR I–2533.

[65] C–179/90 *Porto di Genova* [1991] ECR I–5889; C–18/93 *Corsica Ferries Italia Srl v Corpo dei piloti del porto di Genova* [1994] ECR I–1812.

[66] Case 311/84 *Télémarketing* [1985] ECR 3261.

ing the exclusive right leads the monopoly to abuse its dominant position, it might also infringe Article 86 of the EC Treaty (former Article 90) (see a detailed analysis of this article in Chapter 5). Even if the statutory monopoly has been entrusted with the operation of services of general economic interest, Article 82 will apply, according to Article 86 (2), in so far as it does not obstruct the performance, in law or in fact, of the particular tasks assigned to the undertaking in question.

Dominance in aftermarkets

In some instances, the Commission and the Court of Justice have considered that **3.88** a company held a dominant position in the aftermarkets (or secondary markets) of the products it provides. By aftermarket (or secondary market) is normally meant the markets for products or services complementary to the main product that the undertaking provides (primary market), such as spare parts or repair and maintenance services.

Two main examples of this can be mentioned. In *General Motors*[67] it was consid- **3.89** ered that this firm, which was not dominant on the market for car manufacture (primary market), held a dominant position in the market for delivery of certificates of conformity for imported cars into Belgium (secondary market). This certificate was necessary for cars the subject of parallel imports (ie not imported by the manufacturer itself but by other car dealers) in order to be registered in the country, and car manufacturers were authorized by law only to deliver such certification to cars of their own brand. The second example, the *Hugin* case,[68] involved a producer of cash registers (primary market), which did not hold a dominant position on this market, but was found to be in such a position on the market for spare parts to be used for the repair or maintenance of Hugin cash registers.

It cannot be inferred from these cases, however, that a manufacturer will always be **3.90** considered to hold a dominant position on its aftermarkets. Indeed, in most cases the relevant market for competition purposes comprises both the basic product market and the aftermarkets. If the manufacturer is not dominant in the primary market it will not be considered as such in the secondary one. Consumers are supposed to take into account the conditions in the aftermarkets at the moment of purchasing the primary product and, therefore, a producer will avoid abusing its position in the aftermarkets in order not to damage its competitive position on the primary market. In some cases, however, consumers might not take into account the behaviour of the producers in the aftermarkets when purchasing the primary product. This will be particularly the case when there are difficulties in finding

---

[67] Case 26/75 *General Motors Continental v Commission* [1975] ECR 1367. See also 226/84 *British Leyland v Commission* [1986] ECR 3263.
[68] 22/78 *Hugin v Commission* [1979] ECR 1869. See also T–30/89 *Hilti v Commission* [1992] ECR II–1439 and C–53/92P.

compatible secondary products, as well as when the lifetime of the primary product is relatively long.[69] This could also be the case when the cost of the secondary product is a small fraction of the cost of the primary product and, therefore, is not taken into account when the primary product is purchased.[70] In these cases, manufacturers of the main product might be considered as holding a dominant position in the aftermarkets.[71]

Collective Dominant Positions

3.91 Article 82 refers to abuses by 'one or more undertakings'. This wording implies that Article 82 is addressed not only to single dominant firms, but also to more than one undertaking holding together a dominant position. The issue at stake is to determine in what circumstances several firms can be considered as holding together a dominant position.

Concept of Collective Dominant Positions

3.92 The concept of a collective dominant position was formulated in the jurisprudence, for the first time, in *Flat Glass*,[72] where the Court of First Instance stated that:

> There is nothing, in principle, to prevent two or more independent economic entities from being, on a specific market, united by some economic links that, by virtue of that fact, together they hold a dominant position vis-à-vis the other operators in the same market.

This was supplemented by the Court of Justice in the *Almelo* case,[73] where it stated that:

> In order for such a collective dominant position to exist, the undertakings must be linked in such a way that they adopt the same conduct on the market.

---

[69] Commission Notice on the definition of the relevant market for the purposes of Community competition law [1997] OJ C372/5, para 56.

[70] *Digital*, Report on Competition Policy 1997 (Vol XXVII) point 69, where Digital was considered dominant in the maintenance of computers it had sold. See also Philip Andrews, 'Aftermarket power in the computer Services market: the Digital undertaking' [1998] ECLR. On the contrary, in *Pelycan v Kyocera, Report on Competition Policy 1995* (Vol XXV) 140, Kyocera was not considered dominant in the market for toner cartridges for its printers because it was not dominant in the printer market.

[71] See also *Eastman Kodak Co v Image Technical Services Inc* 112 S Ct 2072 (1992), a landmark case where the US Supreme Court rejected Kodak's contention that lack of market power in service and replacement parts for copying equipment must be assumed when such power is absent in the primary equipment market.

[72] Cases T–68/89, T–77/89 and T–78/89 *Societa Italiano Vetro SPA, Fabrica Pisana SPA and PPG Vernante Pennitalia SPA v Commission* [1992] ECR II–1403. The CFI considered that the Commission had not proved the existence of a collective dominant position and, therefore, partially annulled its Decision.

[73] Case C–393/92 *Almelo* [1994] ECR I–1477.

Both the Court of Justice and the CFI have followed this definition in all subsequent judgments where the concept of a collective dominant position has been discussed.[74]

From these case law definitions, the elements required to determine the existence **3.93** of a collective dominant position can be inferred. First, the entities occupying the collective dominant position must be independent economic entities. A collective dominant position is not a concept which applies to firms belonging to the same group, and therefore constituting a single economic unit,[75] but rather applies to undertakings independent one from the other. Secondly, such undertakings must be united by economic links. And thirdly, by virtue of these economic links, the undertakings must hold together a dominant position. The characteristics necessary to define a position as dominant are the same as those which apply to single dominant positions.

The crucial element needed to infer the existence of a collective dominant posi- **3.94** tion is, therefore, the existence of links between the undertakings in question. The case law has only specified that the links should unite the undertakings in such a way that they adopt the same conduct on the market. The Commission has developed this by requiring that, for two or more companies to be in a joint dominant position, they must first together have the same position *vis-à-vis* their customers and competitors as a single company would have if it were in a dominant position. In addition, it is necessary that there be no effective competition between the companies on the relevant market.[76]

The most obvious examples of collective dominant positions are those where the **3.95** link between the undertakings is of a contractual nature. In *Flat Glass*,[77] the CFI cited as an example of undertakings with economic links those which jointly have licences which give them a technological lead over the remaining competitors in the market. It has also been suggested that football clubs involved in the organization of a professional league,[78] or two air carriers sharing an air route constituting a separate market,[79] hold together a dominant position. The Commission has also applied this concept to two companies jointly managing a port and jointly

---

[74] Case C–96/94 *Centro Servizi Spediporto* [1995] ECR I–2883; C–140/94, C–141/94, C–142/94 *Dip SpA v Commune di Bassano del Grappa* [1995] ECR I–3257; T–24/93, T–25/93, T–26/93, T–28/93 *Compagnie Maritime Belge Transports SA, Dafra-Lines A/S, Deutsche Afrika-Linien GmbH & Co and Nedlloyd Lijnen BV v Commission* [1996] ECR II–1019.

[75] This was the position adopted by the UK Government in its intervention in the *Flat Glass* case.

[76] Notice on the application of the Competition Rules to access agreements in the telecommunications sector [1988] OJ C265/3, paras 78–79.

[77] Cases T–68/89, T–77/89 and T–78/89 *Societa Italiano Vetro SPA, Fabrica Pisana SPA and PPG Vernante Pennitalia SPA v Commission* [1992] ECR II–1403.

[78] Case C–415/93 *Bosman* [1995] ECR I–4921, Opinion of Lenz AG.

[79] Case 66/86 *Ahmed Saeed Flugreisen v Zentrale zur Bekampfung Unlauteren Wettbewerbs* [1989] ECR 803, Opinion of Lenz AG.

poperating ferry services from it,[80] as well as to insurance companies participating in a reinsurance pool which covers a substantial share of the relevant market.[81]

3.96　Collective dominant positions could also exist when the undertakings in question are not linked by contractual relationships, but where there is a structural link that leads them to behave as a single undertaking. Cross-shareholdings or common directorships could constitute such types of links.[82]

3.97　There are some cases where the contractual link between undertakings holding a collective dominant position consists in an agreement or concerted practice which falls under Article 81(1) of the EC Treaty.[83] The clearest example of this situation is found in the Commission decisions concerning maritime conferences.[84] These are agreements between shipowners to share a particular route and agree on uniform rates and transport conditions for that route. These agreements are caught by Article 81(1) but benefit from a block exemption regulation.[85] This has not prevented, however, the Commission from considering that the members of such conferences, by virtue of the agreements concluded between them, hold a collective dominant position in the maritime route in question, and that they abuse it by engaging in exclusionary practices. This position has already been confirmed by the CFI.[86]

Oligopolies

3.98　It should also be discussed whether Article 82 can be applied to simple oligopolistic situations. In such cases, a limited number of undertakings hold significant market power in a given market. Depending on the characteristics of the industry in question, the interdependence between the members of the oligopoly could lead to a worse situation for consumers, in terms of excessive prices or output restrictions, than would result from competition.[87] From an economic point of view, there does not seem to be any reason to treat these situations differently from the ones resulting from the existence of a single dominant firm.

---

[80]　*Port of Rodby* [1994] OJ L55/52.

[81]　*International Group of P&I Clubs* [1999] OJ L125.

[82]　Joined cases C–395/96P and C–396/96P *Compagnie Maritime Belge NV and Dafra-Lines v Commission* [1998] Opinion of Fennelly AG.

[83]　For a detailed analysis of the relationship between Articles 81 and 82 in situations of collective dominance, see Soames, 'An analysis of the principles of concerted practice and collective dominance: A distinction without a difference?' [1996] 1 ECLR 24–39.

[84]　*French-West African Shipowners' Committees* [1992] OJ L134/1 and *CEWAL* [1993] OJ L34/20. See also *P&O/Nedlloyd* (Case IV/M831) (1996), para 53.

[85]　Council Regulation (EEC) 4056/86 on the determination of modalities for the application of Articles 85 and 86 of the EC Treaty to maritime transports [1986] OJ L378.

[86]　T–24/93, T–25/93, T–26/93, T–28/93 *Compagnie Maritime Belge Transports SA, Dafra-Lines A/S, Deutsche Afrika-Linien GmbH & Co and Nedlloyd Lijnen BV v Commission* [1996] ECR II–1019. See also C–395/96P and C–396/96P *Compagnie Maritime Belge and Dafra-Lines v Commission* [1998] Opinion of Fennelly AG.

[87]　See a seminal article from J Stigler, 'A Theory of Oligopoly' (1964) 72 *J Pol Econ* 44.

The European Courts, in applying the Merger Regulation (see Chapter 4), have **3.99** already concluded that the concept of a collective dominant position could also be extended to oligopolistic situations.[88]

In *Kali & Saltz*,[89] the Court of Justice confirmed the Commission's view[90] that **3.100** mergers creating an oligopolistic market structure (duopolistic in the case in question) could be covered by Article 2(3) of the Merger Regulation, which prohibits concentrations which create or strengthen a dominant position as a result of which effective competition would be impeded. The Court defined a collective dominant position under the Merger Regulation as follows:

> a situation in which effective competition in the relevant market is significantly impeded by the undertakings involved in the concentration and one or more other undertakings which together, in particular because of corrective factors giving rise to a connection between them, are able to adopt a common policy on the market and act to a considerable extent independently of their competitors, their customers, and also of consumers.[91]

The Court of Justice considered that such a situation could be found when several **3.101** characteristics are met. In particular, it referred to the factors mentioned by the Commission in its decision, such as the homogeneity of the product; the maturity and transparency of the market; the high degree of concentration; the similar market share of the members of the oligopoly. It also referred to structural links between the companies in question, such as participation in the same export cartel and use in one Member State, by one of the companies, of the distribution network of the other. It was not clear from this case, however, whether such structural links are an indispensable element in concluding as to the existence of an oligopolistic structure, or merely an additional element increasing the likelihood of parallel behaviour between the companies in question.

This issue was clarified in the decision *Gencor/Lohnro*.[92] Indeed, according to the **3.102** CFI:

> there is no reason whatsoever in legal or economic terms to exclude from the notion of economic links the relationship of interdependence existing between the parties

---

[88] See also Schodermeier, 'Collective dominance revisited: an analysis of the EC Commission's new concepts of oligopoly control' [1990] 1 ECLR 28–34; Barry J Rodger, 'The oligopoly problem and the concept of collective dominance' [1995] 2 Columbia Journal of European Law, 25–47.

[89] Cases C–68/94 and C–30/95 *French Republic, Société Commerciale des Potasses et de l'Azote and Entreprise Minière et Chimique v Commission* [1998] ECR I–1375.

[90] *Kali & Salz/MdK/Treuhand* (Case IV/M308) [1994] OJ L186/38, but also previous decisions such as *Alcatel/AEG/Kabel* (Case IV/M165) (1991); *Nestlé/Perrier* (Case IV/M190) [1992] OJ L356/1; *Dalmine/Mannesmann/Vallourec* (Case IV/M315) [1994] OJ L102/15 among many others.

[91] Cases C–68/94 and C–30/95 *French Republic, Société Commerciale des Potasses et de l'Azote and Entreprise Minière et Chimique v Commission* [1998] ECR I–1375, para 221.

[92] T–102/96 *Gencor Ltd v Commmission* [1999], para 276.

to a tight oligopoly within which, in a market with the appropriate characteristics, in particular in terms of market concentration, transparency and product homogeneity, those parties are in a position to anticipate one another's behaviour and are therefore strongly encouraged to align their conduct in the market, in particular in such a way as to maximise their joint profits by restricting production with a view to increasing prices.

3.103 Structural links, therefore, do not need to be proved in order to determine collective dominance. In *Gencor/Lohnro,* the Commission relied on several other elements to prove such dominance. These elements were the following: market concentration, similarity of cost structures of the undertakings holding the collective dominant position, market transparency, product homogeneity, moderate growth in demand, price inelastic demand, mature production technology, high entry barriers, and lack of negotiating power of purchasers.[93]

3.104 It has been submitted that the concept of a dominant position under Article 82 and the Merger Regulation is fundamentally similar (see paragraphs 3.31 and 3.32 above). The *Gencor/Lohnro* judgment confirms that its findings on collective dominant positions also apply to Article 82.[94] The Commission has already indicated that this is the interpretation of Article 82 that it considers appropriate.[95] It can, therefore, be concluded that several companies in an oligopolistic market fulfilling the characteristics described in the previous paragraphs could be found to be in a collective dominant position and, therefore, to infringe Article 82 if they engage in abusive practices.

Dominance and Neighbouring Markets

3.105 Normally, abuses within the meaning of Article 82 can only be committed in the market where the dominant position is established. However, in special circumstances, a dominant undertaking may commit an abuse in neighbouring markets to those where it holds a dominant position.

3.106 In particular, in *Tetra Pak II,* the CFI[96] and the Court of Justice[97] confirmed the Commission's finding that Tetra Pak had committed abuses in the markets for non-aseptic packaging machines and non-aseptic cartons, while Tetra Pak's dominant position had only been established in the markets for aseptic packaging

---

[93] T–102/96 *Gencor Ltd v Commmission* [1999], para 159.

[94] T–102/96 *Gencor Ltd v Commmission* [1999], paras 273–277. See also C–395/96P and C–396/96P *Compagnie Maritime Belge and Dafra-Lines v Commission* [1998] Opinion of Fennelly AG, para 27, where it considers that there is no fundamental difference in the requirement of 'economic links' under Article 82 case law and of 'factors giving rise to a connection' under Merger Regulation case law.

[95] Notice on the application of the Competition Rules to access agreements in the telecommunications sector [1988] OJ C265/3, para 79.

[96] Case T–83/91 *Tetra Pak International v Commission* [1994] ECR II–755.

[97] Case C–333/94P *Tetra Pak International v Commission* [1996] ECR I–5951.

machines and aseptic cartons (where it had a market share of nearly 90 per cent).
The Court[98] acknowledged that:

> the application of Article 86 [now Article 82] to conduct found on the associated,
> non-dominated market and having effects on that associated market can only be jus-
> tified by special circumstances.

In this case, it was justified by the leading position that Tetra Pak held in these
markets (even if it did not amount to a dominant position), and because of the
strong links existing between the aseptic and non-aseptic packaging machines and
cartons markets. In particular, the Court referred to the fact that both aseptic and
non-aseptic products were used for packaging the same products (ie fruit juices
and dairy products); that a substantial proportion of Tetra Pak's customers operated in both sectors; and that its main competitors also operated in both sectors.

In *Interbrew*,[99] the Commission indicated that Article 82 would be applicable to   **3.107**
an abuse in the same product market, but outside the geographic market where
dominance was held. In that case, Interbrew subsidiaries outside Belgium (where
the company is dominant) pursued a policy of not supplying beer to customers
likely to export outside their territory, including to Belgium. The fact that the
abuses had the effect of protecting the Belgian market would appear to provide the
necessary link between the latter market, where dominance was held, and those
where the abuses were allegedly committed.

It has been questioned whether it is reasonable to sanction under Article 82 an   **3.108**
undertaking's exclusionary behaviour in a market in which it is not dominant.[100]
Indeed, an exclusionary practice will normally not be successful if the undertaking engaging in it cannot rely on a certain amount of market power. Nevertheless,
it may be true that in some exceptional cases the mere possession of market power
in neighbouring markets will suffice to make such a practice succeed or, as the
Court stated, to enjoy a freedom of conduct compared with the other economic
operators on those markets. In that case, the application of Article 82 might be
justified.[101]

---

[98] Case T–83/91 *Tetra Pak International v Commission* [1994] ECR II–755, para 27.
[99] *Report on Competition Policy 1996* (Vol XXVI) para 53.
[100] R Subiotto, 'The special responsibility of dominant undertakings not to impair genuine
undistorted competition' (1995) 18(3) *World Competition*.
[101] Notice on the application of the Competition Rules to access agreements in the telecommunications sector [1988] OJ C265/3, paras 65–67: the Commission applies this analysis to the
telecommunications sector. Another example of this is found in a merger case, *Guinness-Grand
Metropolitan* (Case IV/M938) (1997), where the Commission applied the portfolio effects theory.
This suggests that companies might exert market power in several linked markets, even if they only
hold a dominant position in one of them, because of the combined effects of their position in all
these markets.

Buyer's Dominance

3.109 An undertaking may hold a dominant position in relation either to its customers or to its suppliers. In the latter case, it is referred to as buyer's dominance.[102] The Commission has acknowledged the possibility of applying Article 82 to abuses of a buyer's dominant position but there is little case law actually applying this concept.

3.110 Most cases of buyer's dominance will arise in relation to companies that hold a monopolistic position in their own markets and, therefore, are also the single buyer for certain components of the products or services they supply. In the guidelines for the application of the competition rules to the telecommunications sector,[103] the Commission has already indicated that monopolist telecom operators might abuse their dominant purchasing position by imposing on suppliers excessively favourable prices or other trading conditions. The *Tabacalera/Filtrona* case[104] constitutes another example: Tabacalera was the dominant producer of cigarettes in Spain and it decided to stop buying filters from Filtrona, because it had started to produce them on its own. The Commission considered that Tabacalera had a dominant position on the filters buying market and that a refusal to buy from a certain competitor could constitute an abuse within the meaning of Article 82. Nevertheless, the Commission accepted that the refusal was justified by the economies of scale and reduction of costs that Tabacalera would achieve by producing filters of its own.

3.111 This issue is also of particular relevance in relation to the business of retailing. The increasing concentration of this sector in most European markets may lead to situations of buyer's dominance, and so to a more frequent application of Article 82. Merger control has already taken buyer's market power into account in the assessment of concentration between retailers.[105]

(4) Dominant Position in a Substantial Part of the Common Market

3.112 There is an additional criterion specified in Article 82 in relation to the geographic scope of a finding of dominance, namely that the relevant geographic market must constitute the whole of the common market or at least 'a substantial part' thereof. The Court of Justice has had a number of opportunities to interpret this further requirement. In *Suiker Unie*, the Court said that:

---

[102] If it is a case of a single buyer, in economic terms it is referred to as a monopsony.

[103] Guidelines for the application of competition rules to the telecommunications sector [1991] OJ C233, paras 116–120.

[104] European Commission, *Report on Competition Policy 1989* (Vol XIX), para 61.

[105] *Kesko/Tuko* (Case IV/M784) (1996). See also, in other sectors, *Crown Cork/Carnaud Metalbox* (Case IV/M603) [1995] OJ L75/38.

for the purpose of determining whether a specific territory is large enough to amount to 'a substantial part of the common market' within the meaning of Article 86 [now Article 82] of the Treaty, the pattern and volume of the production and consumption of the said product as well as the habits and economic opportunities of vendors and purchasers must be considered.

This means that an analysis, not just of the geographic extent of the market but also of the product market in that geographic area, is required. Such an analysis involves essentially a quantitative assessment of the economic importance of the market relative to the total Community market. The Court found in the instant case that the sugar market in Belgium and Luxembourg constituted such a substantial part of the common market. In reaching that conclusion, it took account of the volumes of production and consumption of sugar in the area, and of the proportion of the Community market that these represented: production levels amounted to some 9 per cent of total Community production and consumption accounted for about 5 per cent of total consumption in the Community. **3.113**

The borderline between what is substantial and what is not is not always obvious. It seems that the entire territory of a Member State, even the smallest ones,[106] will usually be considered a substantial part of the common market. The Court has also held that large areas falling short of the entire territory of a Member State can also be substantial.[107] In a number of recent cases, the Commission has considered several major transport terminals as constituting substantial parts of the common market. The ports of Genoa in Italy,[108] Rodby in Denmark,[109] Holyhead in the UK,[110] Roscoff in France, as well as Brussels Airport,[111] have all been placed into this category. By contrast, the English and Irish courts have found respectively that the North of England[112] and County Kerry[113] in Ireland do not constitute substantial parts of the common market. **3.114**

---

[106] In the *Magill* [1989] 4 CMLR 749 case, the Commission found that the market for TV licences in Ireland was substantial (c 1% of total Community licences); in *BP v Commission* [1978] ECR 1513, AG Warner indicated that Luxembourg would be likely to be considered a substantial part of the common market.

[107] In Case 40–48 and others *Suiker Unie v Commission* [1975] ECR 1663, and in *BP v Commission*, the Court found that southern Germany was a substantial part of the common market; in *Hugin* [1979] ECR 1869, the City of London was held to be such a substantial part.

[108] *Porto di Genova* [1997] OJ L301.

[109] *Report on Competition Policy 1994* (Vol XXIV) point 226.

[110] *Report on Competition Policy 1993* (Vol XXIII) point 234.

[111] *Report on Compeition Policy 1995* (Vol XXV) point 120.

[112] *Cutsforth v Mansfield Inns* [1986] 1 WLR 558 (QBD).

[113] *Cadbury Ltd v Kerry Co-op* [1982] ILRM 77.

C. Abuse

(1) General

3.115 The holding of a dominant position is not in itself objectionable under Article 82. It is the abuse of that position which contravenes the provision.

3.116 Article 82 itself does not provide any definition of what constitutes an abuse of a dominant position. As explained in detail in the introduction to this chapter (see above) there was some uncertainty regarding the nature of the concept of abuse in the early years of the application of EC competition law. It is now established, however, that this is a multi-faceted concept, covering both exclusionary and exploitative practices by dominant undertakings.

3.117 Exclusionary abuses are those practices, not based on normal business performance, which seek to harm the competitive position of the dominant company's competitors, or to exclude them from the market altogether. Exploitative abuses, on the other hand, involve the attempt by a dominant company to exploit the opportunities provided by its market strength in order to harm customers directly.

3.118 In contrast to exploitative abuses, exclusionary ones may not have a directly harmful effect on the customers of the dominant firm, and may indeed result in at least short-term benefits for them. Most exclusionary abuses are, however, likely to indirectly result in long-term harm to the dominant firm's customers or trading partners. The harm done to competition by the exclusionary behaviour may provide the dominant firm with the opportunity to exploit that position at the expense of consumers. For that reason, exploitative abuses will sometimes follow exclusionary ones. A firm might, for example, exclude it competitors via predatory pricing (an exclusionary abuse which provides short-term benefits to consumers), only to raise its prices to a supra-competitive level subsequently, thereby engaging in exploitative behaviour. Other abuses may be at the same time both exclusionary and exploitative.

3.119 A simple definition encompassing both concepts would be too broad-ranging to constitute a useful analytical tool. Some elements of the notion of abuse, however, are common to both exclusionary and exploitative conducts. These are analysed below (see paragraphs 3.120 to 3.123). The main characteristics and types of exclusionary and exploitative abuses are then described.

Abuse as an Objective Concept—Intent not Required

3.120 The concept of abuse is an objective one, not requiring any subjective dimension as to the mindset of the dominant firm.[114] It is simply a question of fact to be deter-

---

[114] Case 85/76 *Hoffman-La Roche v Commission* [1979] ECR 461, para 91.

mined, and it is therefore not necessary to prove that an abuse was intentionally committed.

Notwithstanding the fact that lack of intent cannot be put forward as a defence, **3.121** evidence relating to intent is one of the factors to be taken into account in assessing the exclusionary (or otherwise) purpose of an alleged abuse; such evidence sheds light on the motivation of an undertaking (see below paras. 3.126–3.130).

Furthermore, the mental element is relevant to the level of fine which may be **3.122** imposed by the Commission. Negligent or unconscious behaviour will attract a less severe fine than will intentional conduct. Indeed, the Commission guidelines on the method of setting fines consider as an attenuating circumstance the fact that the infringements were committed as a result of negligence or unintentionally.[115]

Abuse by an Undertaking in a Dominant Position

A particular practice may only be considered to constitute an abuse when it has **3.123** been carried out by an undertaking in a dominant position. Exactly the same behaviour would not constitute an abuse, and would therefore probably be perfectly legal, if performed by any other undertaking. The concept of abuse, therefore, even if it is an objective one, only applies to particular entities, those undertakings which occupy a dominant position. As explained in the introduction to this chapter, this is because these companies have a 'special responsibility not to allow their conduct to impair genuine undistorted competition on the common market'.[116]

(2) *Exclusionary Abuses*

General Characteristics

The Court of Justice has, on several occasions, defined exclusionary abuses using **3.124** the following words:

> The concept of an abuse is an objective concept relating to the behaviour of an undertaking in a dominant position which is such as to influence the structure of a market where, as a result of the very presence of the undertaking in question, the degree of competition is weakened and which, through recourse to methods different from those which condition normal competition in products or services on the basis of the transactions of commercial operators, has the effect of hindering the maintenance of the degree of competition still existing in the market or the growth of that competition.[117]

---

[115] Guidelines on the method of setting fines imposed pursuant to Article 15(2) of Regulation No 17 and Article 65(5) of the ECSC Treaty [1998] OJ C9.
[116] Case 322/81 *NV Nederlandsche Baden-Industrie Michelin v Commission* [1983] ECR 3461, para 57.
[117] Case 85/76 *Hoffman-La Roche v Commission* [1979] ECR 46, para 91.

3.125   This definition starts by describing the characteristics common to all abuses, in particular the fact that an abuse is an objective concept and that it can only be committed by a dominant undertaking. It then spells out the two particular elements of exclusionary abuses. First, it refers to the fact that an abuse only takes place when 'methods different from those which condition normal competition' are used. Secondly, such methods should have the effect of 'hindering the maintenance of the degree of competition still existing in the market or the growth of that competition'.

Competition on the Merits Distinguished

3.126   The key element in defining exclusionary abuses by firms in a dominant position is the need to distinguish anti-competitive behaviour from the pro-competitive behaviour which the competition rules are intended to foster. The primary question to be considered in determining whether a practice that excludes competitors from the market is abusive or not is whether the practice has been the result of competition on the merits. Any firm will try to exclude its competitors from the market by performing more effectively than them. A firm only abuses its position when the exclusion of competitors is not the consequence of better performance.

3.127   In order to distinguish competition on the merits from exclusionary abuses, it is essential to analyse whether the practice in question may be justified by any reason other than a simple attempt to exclude competitors. If the practice reduces the costs of the dominant undertaking or otherwise increases its efficiency, it will normally be considered as an example of normal competition, even if it contributes to the elimination of competitors not able to match this increase in performance. If, on the other hand, a practice leads to the exclusion of competitors without increasing at all the efficiency of the dominant undertaking, it is much more likely that such a practice would be considered an abuse within the meaning of Article 82.

3.128   An example can be used to clarify this issue. The granting of volume rebates (ie rebates granted when customers reach a certain volume of purchases from the dominant undertaking) can in some cases be an abuse and in others a straightforward instance of competition on the merits. If the market concerned enables the achievement of important economies of scale, a dominant undertaking might be interested in offering volume rebates in order to attract new business, increase its output, thereby profiting from its economies of scale and lower average costs. If no such economies of scale are attainable, however, volume rebates could not contribute to an increase in the dominant undertaking's efficiency. In both cases the rebates may have as an effect the exclusion of competitors from the market, but only in the latter circumstances should their granting be considered an abuse.

3.129   An otherwise abusive practice can be justified by reasons other than proving that the practice enhances efficiency. These reasons may relate to the need for the dominant company to protect its rights, or for other reasons of an objective nature. For example, a dominant undertaking that refuses to supply an existing customer, which customer is, as a consequence, excluded from the market, normally contravenes Article 82. The refusal may be justified, however, if it is made in reaction to a breach of contract by the customer. Indeed, in such a case, the general interest of ensuring that contractual obligations can be enforced (and, therefore, that a breach can be sanctioned) may prevail over the objectives pursued by competition rules. Other objective justifications for each of the most common abuses are described below.

It could be argued that, in substantive terms, the possibility of justifying otherwise   **3.130**
abusive conduct on the basis of its benefits for general economic welfare is equivalent to the possibility provided for in Article 81(3) to exempt agreements prohibited under Article 81(1). Some commentators[118] even consider the fact that Article 81 and 82 have a different structure as irrelevant in this regard, and take the view that the same legal analysis could be adopted under both articles. This is, however, a largely theoretical discussion because, in practical terms, the scope for justifying behaviour of an otherwise abusive nature is necessarily rather limited.

Exclusionary Effect

The second specific element included in the definition of exclusionary abuse   **3.131**
reproduced above is that the behaviour of the dominant undertaking 'has the effect of hindering the maintenance of the degree of competition still existing in the market or the growth of that competition'.

In order to analyse this element of the definition, it must be first said that the effect   **3.132**
required by the definition of the Court of Justice can be either actual or potential. Indeed, in order for conduct by a dominant undertaking to be considered abusive, there is no need to prove that it has actually hindered competition. It is enough to demonstrate that the conduct is likely to produce such an effect or, as the Court said in *Commercial Solvents*,[119] that it 'risks' producing it. This is the same interpretation that the Court has adopted for the equivalent provision of Article 81.

Secondly, the definition of the Court of Justice requires that the behaviour by the   **3.133**
dominant undertaking 'hinders the degree of competition' in the relevant market. It appears that this should be understood as demanding that the behaviour in question be liable to alter the structure of the market, by weakening or eliminating competitors. There is no need, however, to prove that such an effect is substantial. Indeed, in markets where an undertaking holds a dominant position, competition is already weakened and any further modification of the market

---

[118]   L Gyselen, 'Abuse of monopoly power within the meaning of Article 86 of the EEC Treaty: recent developments' [1989] Fordham Corporate Law Institute, 637.
[119]   See, for instance, Cases 6–7/73 *Commercial Solvents v Commission* [1974] ECR 223, para 25.

structure could strengthen the market power of this undertaking. In this respect, therefore, the interpretation of Article 82 differs from the interpretation of Article 81, which requires the existence of a substantial anti-competitive effect.

3.134   In practice, and depending on the characteristics of the market analysed, the Court of Justice has applied Article 82 to practices affecting market structure in different ways. In some cases, the weakening of one competitor has been sufficient for the Court to consider that the conduct producing such effect was abusive. In other cases, the Court has required, at least, the exclusion of a competitor,[120] even though other competitors could remain in the market. Finally, more recently, the Court has required proof that the conduct would completely eliminate any competition from the market in question.[121] In all these cases, the likely result of the behaviour pursued would have been the maintenance or strengthening of the market power of the dominant undertaking.

3.135   In some cases, however, the Court of Justice has applied Article 82 to behaviour not at all likely to affect market structure and, therefore, the degree of competition in the market.[122] These different approaches adopted by the case law might be explained by the fact that Article 82 can be used in order to pursue different objectives. As explained before, it sometimes attempts, not only to protect the degree of competition in a particular market, and therefore the final customers, but also to ensure fairness between the different companies operating in that market.

3.136   Exclusionary behaviour can take diverse forms. Indeed, any type of behaviour by a dominant undertaking that can, directly or indirectly, affect the competitive position of a competitor is liable to be caught by Article 82. Theorists have suggested a whole variety of different denominations or classifications of types of abusive behaviour.[123]

3.137   Below, the different possible types of exclusionary abuses are classified in a few broad categories according to the methods used to commit the abuse. Abuses committed by means of a refusal to deal will be developed first. This category includes different types of 'pure refusals' to deal, unilaterally engaged in by the dominant undertaking (for example refusals to supply, refusals to grant a licence, refusals to grant access to an essential facility). It also covers refusals to deal resulting from contracts between the dominant undertaking and its customers or suppliers (ie exclusive dealing). Finally, the category of abuse also includes refusals by a dominant undertaking to deal with customers who do not accept the imposition

---

[120]   See, for instance, *Commercial Solvents*, para 25.
[121]   Case C–7/97 *Oscar Bronner GmbH & Co v Mediaprint Zeitungs* [1998] ECR I–7791, para 41.
[122]   See, for instance, Case 27/76 *United Brands v Commission* [1978] ECR 207.
[123]   See, for instance, M Waelbroeck and A Frignani, *Comentaire J Megret. Volume 4. Concurrence* (1997) 244.

of supplementary obligations not having any connection with the supply of the product or service for which the undertaking in question is dominant (ie tying).

The second broad category developed below concerns abuses committed by means **3.138** of pricing practices. These include predatory practices (ie pricing below cost), as well as practices aimed at squeezing competitors (ie pricing intermediate components so as to impede competition in the final product market) or at discriminating between customers. As discounts and rebates are one of the main methods used to price discriminate between customers, abuses committed through these practices (for example fidelity rebates, target discounts) are also covered under this section. Finally, a pricing policy could also be used by a dominant undertaking to incite customers to accept a tying arrangement, namely bundling.

Thirdly, different possible types of abuses attempting to directly raise the costs of **3.139** competitors will be described. In particular, this section will deal with legal harassment, a practice aimed at increasing the legal costs of competitors. Fourthly, abuses committed by means of allocating costs from the activity where the undertaking is dominant to activities where it faces competition (ie cross-subsidization) will be dealt with.

Finally, some types of structural abuses will be discussed. Structural abuses consist **3.140** in those types of commercial actions by dominant firms, or transactions involving them, which produce an immediate change in the structure of the market to the detriment of competition. They include, for instance, acquisitions by the dominant undertaking of control in another undertaking (or of minority shareholdings).

(a) Refusal to Deal

Refusal to Deal (1): Unilateral Refusals to Deal

General Principles

In most EC Member States, the legal order embodies the principles of a market **3.141** economy and the freedom to engage in business activities. A corollary of these principles is the freedom granted to undertakings to deal with whom they will. Nevertheless, in some cases, legal provisions may oblige undertakings to engage in certain business activity in order to protect the public interest.

Article 82 of the EC Treaty is one of these provisions. In particular circumstances, **3.142** it imposes on undertakings holding a dominant position the obligation to deal, either with customers or with competitors. In other words, a refusal to deal may constitute an abuse of a dominant position within the meaning of Article 82. It will only constitute an abuse, however, when the refusal not only harms a consumer or a competitor, but substantially weakens competition in the relevant market and is not objectively justified.

3.143 The prohibition of a refusal to deal is justified by the need to protect short-term competition in certain markets. This is a need particularly acute in those cases where a dominant undertaking controls the inputs (for example raw materials, transport facilities) which are necessary to operate in particular markets. By refusing access to such inputs to competitors or customers, the dominant undertakings might restrict or completely eliminate competition in these markets. At the same time, it must be borne in mind that freedom to deal is a principle which is justified by economic considerations. Indeed, ensuring that companies will be able to freely use their output fosters long-term competition. If companies fear that they may be obliged to give competitors access to their output, for instance a facility that they have built or a new production process that they have developed and patented, the incentive to engage in these activities might be reduced. Therefore, applying Article 82 to a refusal to deal will always involve a trade-off between short-term and long-term competition, and so should be handled very carefully.

Elements of the Abuse

3.144 **Refusal to deal.**   The concept of refusal to deal covers a wide range of practices. Without being exhaustive, all the following types of refusal might be caught by Article 82: refusal to supply both products and services; refusal to provide information; refusal to license intellectual property rights; refusal to grant access to an essential facility or refusal to become part of a network. Different examples of the actual application of Article 82 to refusals to deal will be discussed in detail below (see paragraph 3.161 et seq).

3.145 A refusal to deal can take the form both of a refusal to start dealing, as well as of the unilateral termination of an ongoing business arrangement (for example, a withdrawal of supply). Both are treated in an equivalent manner under Article 82, because both can have the same effects on competition. However, the unilateral termination of an ongoing deal would normally be more difficult to objectively justify than a simple refusal to start dealing; a sudden change of behaviour by a dominant monopolist, consisting in the unilateral termination of a deal, would be more difficult to explain objectively (see below a detailed analysis of different justifications for a refusal to deal).

3.146 The concept of a refusal to deal covers not only a pure refusal, but also an acceptance by a dominant company to deal but under unreasonable conditions. In this regard, price and non-price conditions should be distinguished. As to the latter, the Commission has acknowledged that non-refusal conditional upon acceptance of other unrelated products or services would be considered an abuse.[124] An oblig-

---

[124] Notice on the application of the EC competition rules to cross-border credit transfers [1995] OJ C251/3 para 26.

ation, imposed by a dominant supplier, to indicate the geographical destination of the goods supplied, and/or the identity of the final customers, might also be considered an abuse of a dominant position.[125]

As to pricing conditions, the dominant company should charge a reasonable and non-discriminatory price.[126] Excessive prices, as well as being abusive in themselves, may also amount to an effective refusal[127] (see, below, a detailed analysis of the concept of excessive prices). **3.147**

Finally, the Commission has acknowledged that undue, inexplicable or unjustified delays in responding to a request for access to essential infrastructure may also constitute an abuse.[128] **3.148**

Weakening of competition.   A refusal to deal will, in principle, only be covered by Article 82 when it weakens competition in a particular market. The market in question may be either the market where the dominant undertaking is present (referred to as a primary line abuse) or any other market (referred to as a secondary line abuse). **3.149**

In the first case, the refusal directly harms competitors. The most obvious example is that of a dominant undertaking in an upstream market (for example managing harbour facilities), which also operates in a market downstream (for example operating ferries) from the market where it is dominant. The dominant undertaking abuses its position if it refuses to deal, in the upstream market, with undertakings competing in the downstream market, in order to strengthen its position in this second market. **3.150**

In the second case (secondary line abuse), a refusal to deal with particular customers operating in a market where the dominant undertaking is not present may discriminate between them, thereby potentially weakening competition in this market. The refusal, however, may also be addressed to customers (for example distributors) who favour competitors to the dominant undertaking. In this case the refusal would also indirectly harm competition in the market where the dominant undertaking is present. **3.151**

In order to determine whether competition will be weakened by a refusal to deal, the key question is to estimate the extent of the handicap imposed on an actual or potential competitor by such a refusal. If the competitor remains able to operate in the market by other means (for example to obtain the inputs required to **3.152**

---

[125] *Polaroid/SSI Europe, Report on Competition Policy 1983* (Vol XIII), paras 155–157.

[126] Notice on the application of the competition Rules to access agreements in the telecommunications sector [1998] OJ C265/3, para 91.

[127] Notice on the application of the competition Rules to access agreements in the telecommunications sector [1998] OJ C265/3 , para 97.

[128] Notice on the application of the competition Rules to access agreements in the telecommunications sector [1998] OJ C265/3, para 95.

operate in such a market from another supplier or to replicate the essential facility by itself) it is clear that the refusal should not be considered an abuse.

3.153 The case law is less clear about whether it would be sufficient that the position of the competitor would have been more advantageous in the absence of the refusal. As far as access to an essential facility is concerned, the Commission considers that the refusal must lead to the competitor's activities being made either impossible, or at least seriously and unavoidably uneconomic.[129] In *Oscar Bronner*[130] the Court confirmed this point. It held that the refusal to grant access to a distribution facility would constitute an abuse only if there was no real or potential substitute to it. It remains to be seen whether this precedent also applies to other types of refusal to deal.

3.154 In order to weaken competition, however, it is not enough that a refusal to deal weakens a competitor or excludes it from the market; the weakening or exclusion of this competitor should also reduce the degree of competition in the market in question. This might be the case if, for example, the refusal to deal blocks the emergence of a new service or product, if it reduces substantially the number of players in the market, or if it weakens substantially the main remaining competitors. For instance, when several competitors are already present in a market, a refusal to deal which excludes a further competitor will have less effect on competition than a refusal to deal which would exclude the only competitor of the dominant undertaking remaining in the market.

3.155 The case law on this point, too, is not completely clear. In some cases, of which *United Brands* is probably the most obvious example (see a description of the facts below), dominant undertakings have been obliged to deal with a particular undertaking even if the refusal would not have excluded the undertaking from the market in question or changed substantially the level of competition existing in the market.

3.156 **Absence of an objective justification.** A refusal to deal by a dominant undertaking will not be considered an abuse under Article 82 of the EC Treaty if it is objectively justified. This will be the case if the refusal can be justified on business grounds other than the intention to eliminate a competitor from the market.

3.157 The justifications may relate, first, to the characteristics of the dominant undertaking. For instance, such an undertaking cannot be required to supply a customer or a competitor if it does not have enough capacity to satisfy its own needs, or if the costs of dealing render its business unprofitable. It should also be possible

---

[129] Notice on the application of the competition Rules to access agreements in the telecommunications sector [1998] OJ C265/3, para 91.
[130] Case C–7/97 *Oscar Bronner GmbH & Co v Mediaprint Zeitungs* [1998], para 41. See also, Opinion of the Advocate General in the same case.

to refuse to supply a competitor if, for efficiency reasons, the dominant undertaking decides to stop providing such product or service independently. It should be noted, however, that such efficiency considerations have featured to only a limited extent in the case law. For instance, in *Commercial Solvents*,[131] the Court condemned a refusal to supply an intermediate product to a competitor, even where the dominant undertaking had decided to integrate vertically and itself produce the final product.

Secondly, the justifications may refer to the behaviour of the undertaking requesting the deal. For instance, a dominant undertaking cannot be obliged to deal with a company which is at risk of bankruptcy, which does not respect the agreed conditions of the deal, or which might put in danger the quality and reputation of the supplier. **3.158**

Neither can a dominant undertaking be obliged to treat its clients equally in all circumstances. In times of shortage, for instance, a dominant firm is allowed to favour its more permanent customers over its occasional ones.[132] It is not permitted, however, to favour those exclusively dealing with it over those also dealing with competitors.[133] **3.159**

It should moreover be permitted for a dominant undertaking to refuse to supply a customer who is damaging its legitimate distribution policy. Not to permit refusal in such circumstances would impede dominant undertakings from introducing or developing efficiency-enhancing distribution methods. However, the case law is contradictory on this point. In *United Brands*[134] the Court admitted that a dominant undertaking is entitled to defend its commercial interests, provided that the measures taken are proportionate. Also, in *BBI/Boosey and Hawkes*,[135] the Commission specified that when the customer transfers its principal activity to the promotion of a competing brand, the dominant undertaking may even be entitled to protect its commercial interests by terminating, with a timely announcement, a special supply relationship with a customer. Nevertheless, in both cases (see a description of the relevant facts below) the refusals to supply by the dominant undertakings were considered not to be proportionate and were deemed to be an infringement of Article 82 of the EC Treaty. **3.160**

Types of Unilateral Refusals to Deal

Refusal to supply products or services. The most obvious instance of a refusal to deal is the refusal to supply a raw material needed by a competitor in order to be present in its own market. The classic case in this field is *Commercial* **3.161**

---

[131] Cases 6–7/73 *Commercial Solvents v Commission* [1974] ECR 223.
[132] Case 77/77 *BP v Commission* [1978] ECR 1513, para 34.
[133] C–310/93P *BPB Industries plc & Anor v Commission* [1995] ECR I–865.
[134] Case 27/76 *United Brands v Commission* [1978] ECR 207.
[135] *BBI/Boosey & Hawkes* [1987] OJ L286/36, para 19.

Solvents.[136] This US company had a dominant position on the market for aminobutamol, a chemical input for the production of ethambutol and drugs based on this component. Through its Italian subsidiary it sold aminobutamol to an Italian company, Zoja, for more than three years. The Italian subsidiary then modified its strategy and started to produce drugs based on ethambutol; it therefore decided no longer to supply aminobutamol, the intermediate product. Zoja complained and both the Commission and the Court considered the refusal to deal to be an abuse within the meaning of Article 82 of the EC Treaty. The Court did not accept that the fact that the Italian subsidiary of Commercial Solvents started to produce the final product could justify its termination of supplies, which termination had excluded from the market one of its main competitors.

3.162 In other cases, the refusal does not concern the supply of a raw material, but the supply of the final product to a competitor present in the market for the distribution of such product. The Commission prohibited, for instance, the refusal by British Sugar to supply industrial sugar to Napier Brown, an established customer, after the latter had attempted to compete with British Sugar in the retail sugar market.[137] The Commission also adopted interim measures against the refusal by Boosey & Hawkes, the leading UK manufacturer of brass instruments, to supply two of its customers, resellers of brass instruments, when it discovered that they had created BBI, a competing manufacturer of brass instruments.[138]

3.163 Finally, a refusal to supply competitors may also involve secondary products, such as spare parts. In *Hugin*,[139] for instance, the Court considered that a Swedish manufacturer of cash registers abused its dominant position by terminating its supply of spare parts to Lipton, a UK company operating in the market for repair and maintenance of cash registers, a market in which Hugin was also present. A similar abuse was found in *Hilti*.[140]

3.164 The refusal to supply competitors could refer both to products or to services. As to the latter, the Court considered that CLT, a television broadcaster from Luxembourg, infringed Article 82 by refusing to provide broadcasting time to a Belgian telemarketing company.[141] The reason for such refusal was to reserve the telemarketing business (TV advertisement of products that can be purchased immediately by calling a telephone number) to one of its subsidiaries, which also operated in this market.

3.165 In some other cases, the refusal to supply concerns customers who are not competitors of the dominant undertaking. In *United Brands*, the Court condemned a

---

[136] Cases 6–7/73 *Commercial Solvents v Commission* [1974] ECR 223.
[137] *Napier Brown/British Sugar* [1988] OJ L284/41.
[138] *BBI/Boosey & Hawkes* [1987] OJ L286/36.
[139] Case 22/78 *Hugin v Commission* [1979] ECR 1869.
[140] Case T–30/89 *Hilti v Commission* [1992] ECR II–1439 and C–53/92P [1994] ECR I–667.
[141] Case 311/84 *Telemarketing v CLT* [1985] ECR 1869.

producer of bananas for refusing to supply to Olesen, a Danish distributor which had taken part in an advertising campaign by one of United Brands' competitors. Surprisingly, the Commission did not prove that Olesen would be eliminated from the market and did not consider the refusal justified by the fact that Olesen was promoting a brand competing with United Brands'. The Court confirmed this finding.

Refusal to provide information.   In some cases, companies cannot have access **3.166** to certain markets unless they obtain proprietary information from their competitors. In such cases, refusal to provide this information can constitute an abuse under Article 82 of the EC Treaty.

The Commission obliged IBM,[142] for instance, to provide technical information **3.167** to manufacturers of computer peripheral products (for example printers) in sufficient time to allow them to compete with IBM in the market for such products. In other cases, the modification of technical standards without informing competitors has also been considered an abuse. In *Decca Navigator System*,[143] for instance, the dominant manufacturer of electronic equipment for maritime navigation modified the electronic signals produced by its equipment, without informing manufacturers of competing equipment, with the consequence that all competing equipment produced unreliable results. The Commission considered that this practice constituted an abuse within the meaning of Article 82 of the EC Treaty.

Not only technical information has been the subject of this type of abuse. In *ITT* **3.168** *Promedia/Belgacom*,[144] the Commission considered that the refusal by the dominant telecom operator in Belgium to provide, on reasonable terms, data about customers of telephone services to a new entrant in the telephone directories market also constituted an abuse of dominant position.

Refusal to license intellectual property rights.   As has been explained before, **3.169** the existence of a patent, trade mark, or copyright is not sufficient to establish a dominant position. Nevertheless, when it is established that the existence of such rights confers a dominant position, the refusal to license those rights may in exceptional circumstances, constitute an abuse of this dominant position.

Intellectual property rights are established in order to reward the creativity, qual- **3.170** ity, or innovation of their holders. They grant to their holders the exclusive use of an intellectual creation, a trade mark, or a patent for a certain period of time. This may lead to the elimination of competition in the market for which the right was

---

[142] Undertakings offered by IBM [1984], *Report on Competition Policy 1984* (Vol XIV) paras 94–95.
[143] *Decca Navigator System* [1988] OJ L43/27, paras 108–110.
[144] IP/97/292.

granted, but this is a consequence of the existence of such a right and a refusal to license it cannot be considered an abuse of the dominant position occupied by the holder of the right. If this were to be the case, those rights would no longer fulfil their main purpose, and creativity or innovation would no longer be rewarded. Nevertheless, in some cases the refusal to license such rights may go beyond what is necessary to fulfil their essential function and may hinder competition in a neighbouring market other than the one for which the right was granted.[145] In such exceptional cases, Article 82 may oblige the holder of the right to license it.

3.171 One example of a case where the refusal to grant a licence of an intellectual property right was not considered an abuse is provided by *Volvo v Veng*.[146] In that case, independent producers of spare parts for cars were prevented from competing with car manufacturers because they held design rights and refused to license them. The Court set out the basic principle that it is lawful for a dominant company to obtain exclusive rights under intellectual property law, and that a refusal to license them does not constitute an abuse in the meaning of Article 82.

3.172 In a more recent case, however, the Court has confirmed the Commission's view that, in certain circumstances, a refusal to grant an intellectual property right could amount to an abuse of a dominant position. In *Magill*,[147] the Commission considered that RTE and BBC, the main television broadcasters in Ireland, held dominant positions on the markets for the supply of their programme lists (protected by a copyright) and that they were abusing this dominant position by refusing to give details of their programmes to other magazines more than a day in advance. This made it impossible for independent publishers to produce a weekly magazine covering all broadcasters' programmes. Both the CFI[148] and the Court of Justice[149] confirmed this view. They pointed to the fact that the refusal to license had prevented the appearance of a new product for which there was a potential consumer demand; that there was no justification for such refusal, either in the activity of television broadcasting, or in that of publishing television magazines, and that the broadcasters, by their refusal, had reserved to themselves the secondary market of weekly television guides by excluding all competition on that market.

---

[145] See interpretation of previous case law by Jacobs AG in his Opinion in case C–7/97 *Oscar Bronner GmbH & Co v Mediaprint Zeitungs* [1998], para 43.

[146] Case 238/87 *Volvo AB v Erik Veng* [1988] ECR 6211. See also Case 53/87 *Consorzio Italiano della Componentistica di Ricambio per Autoveicoli v Régie Nationale des Usines Renault* [1988] ECR 6039.

[147] T–69/89 *Radio Telefis Eireann v Commission* [1991] ECR II–485; T–70/88 *BBC Enterprises Ltd v Commission* [1991] ECR II–535; and T–76/89 *Independent Television Publications v Commission* [1991] ECR II–575.

[148] T–69/89 *Radio Telefis Eireann v Commission* [1991] ECR II–485; T–70/88 *BBC Enterprises Ltd v Commission* [1991] ECR II–535; and T–76/89 *Independent Television Publications v Commission* [1991] ECR II–575.

[149] C–241 and 242/91 *RTE and ITP v Commission* [1995] ECR I–743.

The position of the CFI and the Court of Justice in *Magill* was the subject of con-   **3.173**
siderable criticism for eroding the content of intellectual property rights.[150] In a
more recent case, *Tiercé Ladbroke*,[151] the CFI confronted this criticism by specifying the exceptional circumstances in which a refusal to license an intellectual
property right may infringe Article 82. The case concerned the Commission's
rejection of a complaint by the leading operator in the Belgian horse betting market against the refusal by undertakings holding the video and audio rights to
French horse races to license such rights for use by the complainant's betting shops
in Belgium. The CFI considered that, whereas in *Magill* the refusal to grant intellectual property rights had impeded the complainant from entering a market, in
the present case the complainant was not only present, but was the leading operator in the market for which the use of the right was necessary. In addition to this,
the refusal to grant a licence applied to all Belgian betting operators and, therefore, did not entail any discrimination. It concluded by saying:

> The refusal to supply the applicant could not fall within the prohibition laid down
> by Article 86 [now Article 82] unless it concerned a product or service which was
> either essential for the exercise of the activity in question, in that there was no real or
> potential substitute, or was a new product whose introduction might be prevented,
> despite specific, constant and regular potential demand on the part of consumers.

Refusal to grant access to an essential facility.   The Commission defines an   **3.174**
essential facility as a 'facility or infrastructure which is essential for reaching customers and/or enabling competitors to carry on their business, and which cannot
be replicated by any reasonable means'.[152] A refusal to grant access to such an
essential facility, which has anti-competitive effects or in some cases also exploitative ones, and which is not objectively justified, is prohibited by Article 82.[153]

As its name indicates, the basic characteristic of the concept of essential facility is   **3.175**
that access to it is essential in order to operate in a particular market. In other
words, it is not sufficient that the dominant undertaking's control over the facility
gives it a competitive advantage; it should give it a genuine stranglehold on the
market in question. The duplication of the facility must be impossible or

---

[150] See Opinion of Gulman AG on cases C–241 and 242/91 *RTE and ITP v Commission* [1995]
ECR I–797 and also I Forrester, 'Software Licensing in the light of current EC competition law con-
siderations' [1992] 5 ECLR 5–20 and R Subiotto, 'The right to deal with whom one pleases under
EEC Competition Law: small contribution to a necessary debate'.

[151] T–504/93 *Tiercé Ladbroke v Commission* [1997] ECR II–923; appeal pending (C–300/97P).

[152] Notice on the application of the Competition Rules to access agreements in the telecommunications sector [1988] OJ C265/3, para 68.

[153] See, on essential facilities in general: J Temple Lang, 'Defining legitimate competition: companies' duties to supply competitors and access to essential facilities' [1994] Fordham International
Law Journal 2; D Glasl, 'Essential Facilities Doctrine in EC Anti-trust Law: a contribution to the
current debate' [1994] 6 ECLR; JS Venit and JJ Kallaugher, 'Essential Facilities – A comparative
Law approach' [1994] Fordham Corporate Law Institute; R Derek, 'Essential facilities and the
obligations to supply competitors under UK and EC competition law' [1996] ECLR 8

extremely difficult owing to physical, geographical, or legal constraints.[154] As to the latter, it must be demonstrated that it is totally uneconomical to duplicate the facility, in other words that the total income generated in the market in question would not make investment in two facilities profitable. It is not enough to prove that it would not be economical for a given competitor to duplicate the facility, on account of the limited turnover of that competitor.[155]

3.176 The concept of essential facility was first used by the Commission in relation to transport infrastructure and, in particular, in relation to harbour facilities. In *Sea Containers v Stena Sealink*,[156] an interim measures decision concerning the port of Holyhead in Wales, the Commission concluded that Stena Sealink, the port operator, had abused its dominant position in the market for port services by refusing access to its harbour to a potential competitor in the market for ferry services. Through this refusal, Stena Sealink, which was also a ferry operator, protected its position in this market.[157]

3.177 Access to harbour facilities has become a frequent subject of cases concerning essential facilities. The Commission has also adopted a decision concerning access to the Port of Rodby (Denmark),[158] and has intervened in relation to access to the Ports of Elsinore (Denmark), and Roscoff (France).[159] It has moreover, applied Article 82 to the imposition of non-equitable conditions in relation to access to the Port of Genoa (Italy).[160] In some of these cases, where ports are operated by public companies or companies entrusted with special rights, the Commission found that Article 86 had been infringed together with Article 82 of the EC Treaty.

3.178

Several cases involving access to essential facilities have also arisen in the air transport field. In *London European-Sabena*[161] the Commission declared the refusal by Sabena to grant a competing airline access to its computer reservation system to be an abuse of the dominant position that the former held in the Belgian market for computer reservation services. Sabena had engaged in this conduct in order to force the competing airline to raise its fares on the London–Brussels route, on

---

[154] See Opinion of Jacobs AG in C–7/97 *Oscar Bronner GmbH & Co v Mediaprint Zeitungs* [1998].

[155] Case C–7/97 *Oscar Bronner GmbH & Co v Mediaprint Zeitungs* [1998], para 45. See also the opinion of the Advocate General in the same case.

[156] *Sea Containers v Stena Sealink—interim measures* [1993] OJ 1994 L15/8.

[157] The evolution of this particular market may have proved the Commission wrong in defining such a harbour as an essential facility. Indeed, competition on the same route seems to have been developed from Liverpool harbour, which had been excluded by the Commission decision from the relevant market. See National Economic Research Associates (NERA), Competition Brief no 4, January 1999.

[158] *Port of Rodby* [1994] OJ L55/52.

[159] *Report on Competition Policy 1996* (Vol XXVI) point 131.

[160] *Porto di Genova* [1997] OJ L301.

[161] *London European-Sabena* [1988] OJ L317/47.

which there was limited competition. Also in the aviation sector, landing and take-off slots,[162] the ramp (or apron) of the airport (to which access is required for the provision of ground-handling services),[163] and underground pipes used for refuelling aircrafts[164] have also been considered essential facilities. By contrast, locomotives or train crews were considered not to be such essential facilities by the Court in *European Night Services.*[165]

Essential facilities cases may also arise in recently liberalized markets, where for-   **3.179**
mer monopolists have retained ownership of infrastructure, access to which is necessary for new entrants to the market. This is the case for telecommunications markets, where the dominant telecommunications operators own the main net-works, as well as for energy markets, where former monopolists control electricity lines, pipelines, and other facilities to which access is required in order to compete in the energy distribution market. The Commission has adopted a Notice on the application of the competition rules to access agreements in the telecommunica-tions sector,[166] which clarifies how it intends to apply Article 82 to these issues.

In addition to transport and liberalized markets, essential facilities can be found   **3.180**
in other sectors. In the financial services sectors, payment systems (ie systems established between financial entities in order to allow their customers to use non-cash payment instruments such as credit transfers, cheques, or cards) can also sometimes be considered essential facilities. In the Notice on the application of competition rules to cross-border credit transfers, the Commission considers that such a system is an essential facility when participation in it is necessary for banks to compete on the relevant market; this would be the case if a new competitor could not feasibly gain access to another system, or create its own system, in order to compete on the relevant market.[167]

The Commission has taken the view that certain cross-border transfer systems   **3.181**
that had been notified to it were essential facilities,[168] but that access to them was granted on a non-discriminatory basis and that, therefore, the competition rules had not been infringed. In one case, concerning the refusal to allow La Poste to have access to Swift, a network for processing and transmitting cross-border bank

---

[162] See Council Regulation 95/93 on common rules for the allocation of slots at Community air-ports [1993] OJ L14/1.

[163] *Flughafen Frankfurt/Main AG* [1998] OJ L72/30.

[164] *Disma, Report on Competition Policy 1994* (Vol XXIV) 80.

[165] Joined Cases T–374–375/94; T–384/94 and T–388/94 *European Night Services v Commis-sion* [1998] ECR II–3141.

[166] Notice on the application of the competition rules to access agreements in the telecommun-ications sector [1998] OJ C265/3.

[167] Notice on the application of the EC competition rules to cross-border credit transfers [1995] OJ C251/3.

[168] See Luc Gyselen, 'EU antitrust law in the area of financial services—capita selecta for the cau-tious shaping of a policy' [1986] Fordham Corporate Law Institute, 359–361.

operations, the Commission appeared ready to apply Article 82 to a refusal to deal in this sector. However, when Swift introduced non-discriminatory access conditions, the case was closed without a final decision.[169]

3.182 Finally, in *Oscar Bonner*[170] the Court analysed whether a newspaper national home delivery service could be considered an essential facility. It concluded that it was not because, firstly, another nationwide distribution system could be established. The Court did not consider it material that it would be uneconomical for a newspaper with limited circulation to establish a nationwide distribution system. Rather, for the system to be qualified as an essential facility, it would have to have been demonstrated that the market could not sustain a competing system at all. Secondly, the Court pointed out that there were alternative, even if less convenient, means of distributing newspapers, such as mail deliveries or conventional newspaper retail outlets.

3.183 **Other unilateral refusals to deal.**   The most frequent cases of refusals to deal have been detailed above, but the refusal to conclude any type of deal that substantially weakens competition might be covered by Article 82. The Commission Decision in *British Midland/Aer Lingus*[171] can be mentioned as an example of a particular refusal to deal not explicitly covered by any of the previous categories. The case concerned the refusal to interline, which is an airline practice consisting in issuing tickets on behalf of other airlines, allowing passengers to use a single ticket for a journey made by two different airlines. In the case at issue, Aer Lingus, the dominant operator on the Dublin–London route, terminated its agreement to interline with British Midland when the latter started to compete on the Dublin–London route. It should be noted that the absence of interlining would not have impeded British Midland from operating on the route, but would probably have forced it to offer more flights and incur additional costs. The Commission considered that the significant handicap imposed on British Midland sufficed for it to consider the refusal to interline an abuse of a dominant position.

Refusal to Deal (2): Exclusive Dealing

3.184 The imposition of exclusivity obligations by a dominant firm on its trading partners (ie customers, suppliers) obliges them to refuse to deal with any party other than the dominant undertaking. Such exclusivity imposed by a dominant firm

---

[169] Publication of an undertaking. *La Poste v Swift + GUF* [1997] OJ C335/3.
[170] Case C–7/97 *Oscar Bronner GmbH & Co v Mediaprint Zeitungs* [1998], para 41. See also, Opinion of the Advocate General in the same case.
[171] *British Midland/Aer Lingus* [1992] OJ L96/34. See also *Lufthansa/Air Europe. Report on Competition Policy 1991* (Vol XXI) 83.

will attract the sanction of Article 82 where it has as its consequence that the market is substantially foreclosed to the dominant company's competitors.

In *Hoffmann-La Roche*, the Court of Justice made a comprehensive statement **3.185** about when exclusivity obligations of this kind, imposed on, or agreed with, customers, would infringe Article 82, saying that 'an undertaking which is in a dominant position on a market and ties purchasers—even if it does so at their own request—by an obligation or promise on their part to obtain all or most of their requirements exclusively from the said undertaking abuses its dominant position within the meaning of Article 86 [now Article 82]'.

Elements of the Abuse

Legal or *de facto* exclusivity. Article 82 applies to exclusivity obligations imposed **3.186** either legally or *de facto*. The Commission's decision in *Van den Bergh Foods*[172] provides a good example of the latter. Van den Bergh Foods, the dominant supplier of 'impulse' ice cream in Ireland, supplied freezer cabinets to retail outlets, on condition that only its ice cream would be stored in them. The Commission considered that such a prohibition led to *de facto* exclusivity, at least in those outlets where it would not be economically viable to install a second freezer.

Substantial foreclosure effect. The imposition of an exclusivity obligation only **3.187** constitutes an abuse if it forecloses a substantial share of the market to competitors, thereby, weakening competition in it. In *Van den Bergh Foods* for instance, the part of the market foreclosed represented around 40 per cent of the relevant market.

Absence of objective justification. The imposition of exclusivity arrangements **3.188** may in certain circumstances be considered objectively justifiable. This will normally only be the case where the anti-competitive effects are kept to the minimum necessary for the attainment of some economic advantage. Exclusive supply contracts of a limited duration have, for example, been accepted by the Commission on the grounds that they provide the customer with the benefit of security of supply. In an earlier case concerning the European soda-ash market,[173] for example, the Commission had originally objected (in a proceeding terminated informally) to contracts between ICI and Solvay, on the one hand, and their customers, on the other, which provided for exclusive supply. The Commission accepted amendments to those contracts, however, which provided for supply of fixed tonnage, but for periods not exceeding two years. The Commission took the view that this amendment amounted to a balance between the customer's need for security of supply and the freedom to turn elsewhere for supplies.

---

[172] *Van den Bergh Foods* [1998] OJ L246/1.
[173] *Report on Competition Policy 1981* (Vol XI) paras 73–76.

Types of Exclusive Dealing Abuses

3.189 **Requirements contracts (imposition of exclusive obligations on customers).** Dominant companies infringe Article 82 if they oblige their customers to purchase from them all or most of their requirements, if this can be demonstrated to have a substantially foreclosing effect on competing suppliers. In *Hoffmann-La Roche*, exclusivity obligations of this kind were contained in some of the company's agreements with customers. The same cases also concerned agreements imposing on customers the obligation to obtain quantities which were close to their total requirements, thereby producing a level of foreclosure similar to that produced by total requirements contracts. In the *Soda Ash* cases, Solvay and ICI used similar mechanisms, including the use of 'tonnage contracts' (where the tonnage more or less corresponded to a customer's total requirements) ensuring virtual *de facto* exclusivity.

3.190 **Imposition of exclusive obligations on distributors.** In *Hachette*,[174] a case which did not result in a formal decision, the Commission objected to the imposition, by the two dominant newspaper distributors in France, of exclusive distribution arrangements on French publishers seeking to export newspapers/periodicals to other Member States, as well as on foreign publishers wishing to import such publications into France from other Member States. The Commission was of the view that the exclusive obligations rendered access to these import and export markets very difficult. In another case resolved without a formal decision, Visa International abandoned a plan to introduce exclusivity obligations in its arrangements with banks. These arrangements, which would have prohibited the banks from issuing competing cards, had been objected to by the Commission on account of their probable anti-competitive consequences.[175]

3.191 **Imposition of exclusive obligations to suppliers.** In the *IRI/Nielsen* case,[176] the Commission provisionally concluded (this case was resolved informally) that Nielsen had abused its dominant position on the European market for retail tracking services by concluding exclusivity contracts with retailers. These contracts were patently exclusionary, in that they prevented those retailers from providing certain kinds of market data, the raw information crucial to produce retail tracking reports, to competitors of Nielsen.

3.192 **'English clauses'.** So-called 'English clauses' or 'most favoured customer clauses' included in supply contracts allow the purchaser to switch from one supplier to another if that other supplier is able to offer more favourable terms which the dominant supplier is not willing to match. These clauses, when included in

---

[174] *Report on Competition Policy 1978* (Vol VIII) paras 114–115.
[175] *Report on Competition Policy 1996* (Vol XXVI) para 63.
[176] *Report on Competition Policy 1996* (Vol XXVI) para 64.

contracts between dominant suppliers and their customers, may impede other suppliers from attracting customers through a more attractive offer, unless the dominant supplier is not willing to match it. In *IRI/Nielsen*,[177] the Commission objected to such clauses.

English clauses enhance transparency in the market, and increase the likelihood **3.193** that a competitor lowering prices will not gain market share but will prompt the incumbent supplier to match the lower price. The proliferation of such clauses in highly concentrated markets, therefore, could lead to a parallelism of conduct between different players, thereby resulting in a reduction of price competition between them. Should it be possible to prove that a collective dominant position exists in such a market, challenging such clauses as abusive would be one means for competition authorities to remedy the anti-competitive effects of oligopolies.

Refusal to Deal (3): Tying

Concept of Tying

According to Article 82(d) of the EC Treaty an abuse may, in particular, consist **3.194** in:

> making the conclusion of contracts subject to acceptance by the other parties of supplementary obligations which, by their nature or according to commercial usage, have no connection with the subject of such contracts.

This provision covers those cases where a company which holds a dominant posi **3.195** tion forces its customers to purchase the goods or services for which it is dominant together with other goods or services for which it is not (the first products or services are commonly referred to as the tying market and the second ones as the tied market). Such a practice might distort competition in the tied market by driving out of the market those providers who only sell the tied products. Indeed, if most of the tied product consumers are also in need of the tying product, they would inevitably obtain the tied product together with the tying one and would not need, therefore, to obtain the former from other suppliers.

The classic example of tying in EC competition case law is found in the *Hilti* case. **3.196** This case concerned a company trading in nail guns and their accessories (cartridge strips and nails) which attempted to eliminate independent producers of nails compatible with its guns by, first, selling its cartridge strips only to those customers who agreed to buy its own nails and, secondly, by reducing discounts to the customers who only ordered its cartridge strips and bought compatible nails from independent manufacturers. The Commission[178] considered that these practices constituted abuses within the meaning of Article 82 of the EC Treaty and imposed

---

[177] *Report on Competition Policy 1996* (Vol XXVI) para 64.
[178] *Eurofix-Bauco/Hilti* [1988] OJ L65/19.

a 6 million Ecu fine upon Hilti. Both the CFI[179] and the ECJ[180] upheld the Commission's decision.

Elements of the Abuse

3.197 **Dominance in the tying market.** In general, only a company which holds a dominant position in a given market can successfully impose tying on its customers. A company is only able to force its customers to purchase two independent products or services together if the customers are dependent on this company for the supply of one of these products. If this is not the case, customers might buy these products from suppliers other than the dominant company.

3.198 **Tying of two independent products or services.** Tying exists, by definition, when a dominant company forces its customers to buy two independent products or services together. In order to conclude that the abuse of tying has been committed it must be demonstrated therefore, that the two products or services are independent one from the other. While it is generally agreed, for example, that a car and its tyres constitute a single product, or that an air flight and the meal served on it are a single service, it is less obvious whether, for instance, a computer operating unit and its screen should also be considered a single product.

3.199 According to Article 82, this should be determined either by analysing the nature of the products or services in question or by assessing if they are normally sold together ('according to commercial usage'). These two criteria allow for a determination in most cases of whether two or more products or services sold together are indeed a single unit. These criteria have been sufficient for the ECJ and the CFI to decide the main tying cases brought before them. In *Tetra Pak II*,[181] for instance, it was concluded that the packaging machines and the packaging materials used by these machines were two independent products, not linked by their nature, which could perfectly well be manufactured and sold separately.

3.200 Nevertheless, in some cases and, in particular, in relation to new products brought to the market, nature and commercial usage will not always be the most appropriate criteria to apply. Indeed, deciding whether a new product is by nature a single unit, or whether each of its components should be considered an independent product, may become a rhetorical question. Indeed, where the product is new, there is no commercial usage to look at. In these cases, the weight of the analysis shifts from the question of whether the products sold together are independent, to the question of whether it is objectively justified to sell them together (see paragraph 3.208 below).

---

[179] Case T–30/89 *Hilti AG v Commission* [1991] ECR II–1439.
[180] Case C–53/92P *Hilti AG v Commission* [1994] ECR I–667.
[181] Case T–83/91 *Tetra Pak International v Commission* [1994] ECR II–755.

It should also be noted that the characterization of products as independent from   **3.201**
each other evolves over time. What at a certain stage of technological development
might be considered as two separate products might, at a later stage, be viewed as
a single integrated product. A good example of this is provided by the *IBM System*
370 case,[182] where the Commission considered that selling central computer units
together with memory devices and basic software applications amounted to illegal tying. Not much later, integrating and selling these components as a single
product became commonplace in the computer industry. The application of
Article 82 in these cases should be careful not to hinder technological development by preventing such integration.

Coercion to purchase two products or services together.   This is a crucial ele-   **3.202**
ment of the abuse. Any company, even a dominant one, is free to sell two or more
products together. The abuse will only occur when the customers of a dominant
company are coerced to purchase two products together against their will.

The coercion may have different degrees. The most extreme coercion would con-   **3.203**
sist in making the purchase of the tied products or services an absolute condition
for the selling of the tying ones. This condition may be embodied in the contract
concluded between the dominant company and its customers[183] or in the contract
concluded between the dominant company and its distributors.[184] The condition
can also be applied *de facto* by the dominant company, if it does not sell the tying
products unless customers also buy the tied ones.[185]

Coercion could also be applied by withdrawing some benefits from customers   **3.204**
who purchase the two products or services separately. The most obvious example
of this is the withdrawal of the guarantee for a product if the customers do not use
spare parts or accessories from the same manufacturer. A recent example of this
type of tying is provided by *Novo Nordisk*,[186] a case where a manufacturer of an
insulin-injecting pen disclaimed liability for the malfunction of its pen products,
or refused to guarantee such products when they were used in conjunction with
compatible components (for example, disposable needles) manufactured by its
competitors.

A degree of coercion could also be exercised through pricing incentives. A domin-   **3.205**
ant company could reduce rebates to customers purchasing both products separately[187] or could increase rebates to customers purchasing both the tying and the

---

[182] *Bull CE* 10/84, para 3.4.1. See also the ongoing US litigation opposing the US Department
of Justice and Microsoft, concerning whether integrating the internet navigator software with the
operating system software constitutes an instance of unlawful tying.
[183] Case T–83/91 *Tetra Pak International v Commission* [1994] ECR II–755.
[184] *Windsurfing* [1983] OJ L229/1.
[185] Case T–30/89 *Hilti AG v Commission* [1991] ECR II–1439.
[186] European Commission, *Report on Competition Policy 1996* (Vol XXVI) 35.
[187] Case T–30/89 *Hilti AG v Commission* [1991] ECR II–1439.

tied product[188] (see also below the analysis of exclusionary pricing abuses). If these pricing incentives are so powerful that no rational customer would choose to buy the products separately, their effect can be similar to tying. Some commentators refer to this less stringent form of tying as 'bundling'.

3.206 **Distortion of competition in the tied market.** In order to be considered an abuse, tying should affect or be able to affect competition in the tied market. This will be the case if the tying practice forecloses the tied market to suppliers of the tied product or service alone, which will only happen when the majority of customers for the tied product are also customers purchasing the tying one. If this is not the case, the suppliers of the tied product or service alone will be able to remain in the market selling to those customers which are not in need of the tying product.

3.207 In *Hilti*, for instance, the tying practice was intended to prevent independent nail manufacturers from entering the market for Hilti-compatible nails by tying these nails to Hilti cartridge strips. As most consumers of Hilti-compatible nails were the purchasers of Hilti cartridge strips, the tying practice was effective and may have foreclosed independent nail manufacturers completely from the market for such nails.

3.208 **Absence of an objective justification.** A tying practice will not constitute an abuse if it can be justified on objective grounds. The most obvious reason is likely to be that the tying practice enhances efficiency, in other words, that it would be more costly to produce or distribute the tied products or services independently. As to productive efficiency, the example (at paragraph 3.201) of integrating the different components of a computer in a single unit is a good one. As to distributive efficiency, this results from selling together products that people normally would buy together (for example right and left shoes), thereby saving the extra costs (ie packaging, storage) that would derive from selling each unit independently.

3.209 Other possible justifications may include a guarantee of the quality, safety, and good usage of the products provided. A tying practice may help the provider to ensure the quality of all the elements of the system it provides and be able to guarantee the good functioning of the whole system. However, in several cases where this justification has been advanced,[189] the Commission concluded that the use of elements manufactured by third parties would not damage the systems in question and that tying could, therefore, not be justified. In any case, the tying would be justified only if it was the least restrictive means of ensuring the quality of the

---

[188] Case 85/76 *Hoffman-La Roche v Commission* [1979] ECR 461, para 71 and *IRI/Nielsen, Report on Competition Policy 1996* (Vol XXVI) 144–148.

[189] Case T–30/89 *Hilti AG v Commission* [1991] ECR II–1439, Case T–83/91 *Tetra Pak International v Commission* [1994] ECR II–755, *Novo Nordisk*, European Commission, *Report on Competition Policy 1996* (Vol XXVI) 35.

products sold. In *Hilti*, for instance, the Commission remarked that a selective distribution system (that Hilti had already notified) would have been a less restrictive means of ensuring that its products were sold together with the appropriate components.

Types of Tying

As explained, a tying practice may involve any combination of separate product or services. Below, the most common types of tying are described.　**3.210**

Tying of products with their accessories. Several examples of tying already **3.211** mentioned, such as *Hilti*, *Tetra Pak II*, and *Novo Nordisk*, involve a product and the accessories needed for its functioning. In these cases, one of the main issues is whether the market for the accessories is a relevant product market in itself (see above a discussion about dominance in aftermarkets).

Tying of complementary products. Tying often involves the sale of two com- **3.212** plementary products, that is two products intended to be used together. In *Windsurfing*[190] (a case involving the application of Article 81), for instance, the Commission and the ECJ considered that selling windsurf boards and sails together constituted tying. It is in such cases, in particular, that the tying might be justified by efficiencies in distribution.

Tying of products in the same range. In *Hoffmann-La Roche* the Commission **3.213** condemned a practice consisting in the granting of particular rebates to customers purchasing the whole range of vitamins supplied by this dominant company. If such rebates are not justified by economies of scope (ie reduction in the average cost of producing the whole range of products), they may constitute tying contrary to Article 82 of the EC Treaty.

Tying of a product and related services. This is the type of tying that arises **3.214** when a dominant company only sells a product if the customer also purchases some related services from it. For instance, such tying occurs in cases where a dominant company only sells spare parts if it is also allowed to perform the repairing service. A similar situation arose in *British Sugar*,[191] where, in certain instances, the dominant company only agreed to sell sugar if it could also transport it to the final destination.

Tying of the same product in different geographic markets. A tying practice **3.215** may not only involve different product markets, but could also concern different geographic markets for the same product. In *IRI/Nielsen*[192] the Commission considered that Nielsen had abused its dominant position in the market for retail

---

[190] Case 193/83 *Windsurfing International v Commission* [1986] ECR 611.
[191] *Napier Brown/British Sugar* [1988] OJ L284/41.
[192] European Commission, *Report on Competition Policy 1996* (Vol XXVI) 36.

tracking services by applying discounts in exchange for commitments from customers to call upon its services in a wide range of countries. This involved the
bundling of countries where Nielsen was the sole provider of these services with
countries that IRI was entering, thereby preventing the latter company from
establishing a presence in Europe.

(b) Pricing Practices

Pricing Practices (1): Predatory Pricing

3.216   Predatory pricing is a commercial strategy by which a dominant firm first lowers
its price to a level which will ultimately force its rivals out of the market. When the
latter have been successfully expelled, the company can raise the price again and
reap the rewards. The logic is that the company chooses to incur short-term losses
in an attempt to obtain long-term profit gains.

Elements of the Abuse

3.217   **Level of prices.**   Not every price below cost will be considered predatory. The
US Courts have developed a relatively simple, objective, cost-based rule for dealing with cases of predatory pricing. The so-called Areeda & Turner rule[193] states
that a price at or above average variable cost (cost which varies according to the
quantity produced) benefits from a presumption of legality, while a price below
that level may be unlawful. As described below, the Commission and Court of
Justice have, in contrast, evolved an approach based not solely on a cost analysis
but partly on the subjective intent of the dominant firm.

3.218   The Commission made its first finding of predatory pricing in 1985, in the *AKZO*
case.[194] The case involved a complaint to the Commission by ECS, a competitor
of AKZO's in the supply of organic peroxides to millers in the UK and Ireland.
Initially, ECS did not supply these products outside the flour industry, but in
1979 it decided to expand its activities and approached a German plastics' manufacturer (BASF) with a view to supplying it. When AKZO learned of this, it met
with ECS and threatened to eliminate it from the market, unless ECS would agree
to withdraw from supplying the plastics industry. When ECS failed to do so,
AKZO proceeded to offer organic peroxides to ECS's regular customers at prices
well below those which it offered its normal customers. ECS alleged to the
Commission that the prices were below average variable cost and that their only
rationale could be the elimination of ECS from the market. As a consequence,
ECS suffered considerable loss of market share, and only managed to sustain a
foothold in the market by reducing prices to below cost for those customers which
it retained. A surprise Commission inspection uncovered internal documents at

---

[193]   So called after the two US economists who proposed the test in a seminal academic publication.
[194]   *Akzo* [1985] OJ L374/1.

AKZO's premises which appeared to confirm ECS's allegations of below-cost selling and of a deliberate attempt to oust it from the market.

In finding that AKZO's behaviour in offering below-cost prices to ECS's customers was abusive, the Commission expressly rejected the need to adopt a purely cost-based rule for establishing the existence of predatory pricing.[195] Instead, the Commission emphasized that a deliberate attempt to impair competition in the market, by seeking to eliminate or harm the competitive position of a competitor/s, must be demonstrated. **3.219**

Although the Court of Justice upheld the Commission's finding[196] of predatory pricing by AKZO, it rejected the test which the Commission had employed. The Court emphasized that the concept of an abuse is an objective one, although the test which it devised retains an element of subjectivity. The test is a two-pronged one: **3.220**

(i) prices set at *below* average *variable* cost[197] are presumed to be predatory and thus abusive, such a price necessarily implies a loss of all the fixed costs[198] and at least some of the variable costs. This amounts to a *per se* presumption of abusive behaviour;

(ii) prices set at *below* average *total* cost,[199] *but above* average *variable* cost, are also presumed to be predatory, but only if some evidence of intention to eliminate a weaker competitor/s can be demonstrated; the Court made it clear that for such prices to be abusive they must have been set within the framework of a specific plan aimed at eliminating the competitor/s.

In the instant case, the Court found, applying the test just described, that all but one of the prices offered to AKZO's customers were between average variable and average total cost; the other price was below even average variable cost. Principally because the prices had not also been offered to AKZO's normal customers, the Court found that AKZO must have intended to exclude ECS from the market, or at least severely harm its competitive position. **3.221**

The Court's approach is open to criticism. One problem with applying a test which relies, even in part, on evidence of an intention to exclude rivals is that such an intention is not in itself anti-competitive; indeed, it is often inherent in the competitive process that firms will seek to eliminate each other. A further **3.222**

---

[195] The Commission's rejection of the need for a thorough cost-based analysis might be explicable by the fact that the case appeared to be such a clear-cut one on the facts.

[196] It reduced the level of the fine by 25%, however, in view of the novelty of predatory pricing as an abuse.

[197] ie costs which vary according to the quantity produced.

[198] ie costs which are constant irrespective of the quantity produced.

[199] ie variable costs plus fixed costs.

disadvantage of this approach is that it provides less legal certainty than a completely objective cost-based rule.

3.223 Since *AKZO* there have been two further Commission decisions[200] involving predatory pricing: *Napier Brown/British Sugar*[201] and *Tetra Pak II*.[202] In *Napier Brown* the Commission found that British Sugar had abused its dominant position by charging predatory prices to sugar packers for raw sugar (see further in paragraph 3.230 below). In *Tetra Pak II* the Commission appears to have taken into account the Court's judgment in *AKZO* in that it made a detailed cost analysis before finding that the company had engaged in predatory pricing in the market for non-aseptic cartons in Italy. The prices considered abusive had been set at below average total cost over a period of seven years, and at some stages during that time they even fell below average variable cost.

3.224 *Limit pricing.* Limit pricing, whereby a firm sets prices (and output) at a level which ensures that there is not enough demand left for another firm to profitably enter the market, is not regarded as abusive, even if it might have the effect of keeping out potential market entrants. Indeed, the test for determining whether a price is predatory appears not to be whether it allows a competitor to remain profitably in the market but whether it allows it to cover, at least, its variable costs.

3.225 **Objective justification.** A real difficulty from the point of view of applying Article 82 to allegations of predatory pricing is to distinguish legitimate, competitive conduct from predatory, anti-competitive behaviour.[203] A price below cost may moreover be consistent with a number of other competitively legitimate explanations such as, for example, the need to clear stocks or to meet a competitor's offer. It is likely that the presumptions of abuse contained in the Court's test will be rebutted in the light of evidence that the prices charged were objectively justified by these or similarly legitimate commercial considerations.

3.226 **Need to recoup losses.** As explained before, a firm engaging in predatory pricing, to be successful, must keep the price at the level at which its rivals are forced to withdraw from the market. It must therefore be able to survive the low price levels for longer than its competitors can. The firm would then be able to raise its price to a level sufficiently high, and for a sufficiently long period of time, to

---

[200] In the *Report on Competition Policy 1987* (Vol XVII) paras 334–336, the Commission detailed its policy (on the basis of a study which it had commissioned) in relation to predatory pricing, largely reaffirming its rejection of a purely cost-based rule and in particular of a rule providing for *per se* legality for prices above marginal cost. The Commission emphasized that 'predatory pricing practices must be regarded as part of an abusive global strategy aimed at eliminating other producers in an anti-competitive manner'.

[201] *British Sugar* [1988] OJ L284/41.

[202] *Tetra Pak II* [1992] OJ L72/1.

[203] AG Lenz noted that the Commission seemed to have ignored the defence of 'meeting competition' in C–62/86 *AKZO Chemie BV v Commission* [1991] ECR I–3359.

enable it not only to recoup the losses incurred by the predation, but also to secure higher profits than it would have obtained had it not engaged in the predatory behaviour. The lower the barriers to entering the market are, the more difficult it will be for the predator to recoup its losses and then reap the monopoly profits.

It seems that to establish this abuse there is no need to demonstrate that the dominant company will be able to raise prices following the expulsion of its competitors sufficiently to enable it to recoup its losses and then enjoy supra-competitive profits.[204] In *Tetra Pak II* the Court stated that it is not necessary for the Commission to prove conclusively that the predator will be able to raise its prices following the elimination of its rivals. It will suffice for the Commission to simply demonstrate that the predatory price is likely to eliminate the dominant firm's rivals.[205]   **3.227**

This is probably explained by the fact that the authorities' intervention will likely occur before the victims of predation have been excluded altogether from the market, and probably before the dominant firm will have succeeded in fully recouping its losses. For this reason, proving the abuse will generally involve a degree of conjecture as to the behaviour's likely ultimate consequences.   **3.228**

Particular Types of Predatory Pricing

'Fighting Ships'.   This is a strategy, sometimes adopted by the members of a shipping 'conference', in order to harm non-member shipping companies. The abuse consists in the predatory shipping conference sailing a ship (a so-called 'fighting ship') in competition with a non-member (ie on the same route and on approximately the same date), and charging rates which are below those which the conference normally charges, with the aim of eliminating the non-member. The members then share the loss of revenue. The Commision found in *CEWAL*,[206] that the conference in question used the strategy over an eighteen-month period and that it formed part of a deliberate plan aimed at eliminating its principal competitor on routes between the North Sea and Zaïre. The special characteristic of the abuse is that it presupposes a finding of joint dominance on the part of the members of the shipping conference, which the Commission did find in this case. The decision has been upheld by the Court of First Instance.   **3.229**

---

[204] This is in contrast with US case law which requires that the alleged predator be shown to have a reasonable likelihood of recouping the losses it suffered by predation—see *Brooke Group v Brown and Williamson Tobacco* (1993) 509 US 940.

[205] The Court said that 'it must be possible to penalize predatory pricing whenever there is *a risk* that competitiors will be eliminated' (emphasis added).

[206] *CEWAL* (1993) OJ L34/20.

Pricing Practices (2): Price Squeezing

3.230 A price squeeze is a form of pricing behaviour by a company which, being dominant in both an upstream and a downstream market, charges a price in the upstream market that does not enable its competitors to operate profitably in the downstream one. Even if neither the upstream nor the downstream price is in itself abusive (ie excessive or predatory) the combination of the two (the squeeze) is contrary to Article 82.

3.231 Pursuing an abuse of this kind requires establishing that the margin between the two prices is insufficient for the dominant firm's competitor to achieve an acceptable rate of return. This presents a particular difficultly for the regulator, in the sense that it requires information about the cost structures of both the dominant and squeezed companies, in order to establish that the requisite margin is too narrow.

3.232 In *Napier Brown*, British Sugar was dominant in both the upstream (industrial sugar) and downstream (retail sugar) markets. Napier Brown was dependent on supplies of industrial sugar from British Sugar in order for it to be able to operate in the retail sugar market. The margin between the two prices was below British Sugar's own repackaging and selling costs, and did not allow Napier Brown to remain viable as a packer and seller of retail sugar. The Commission also relied on evidence that the behaviour formed part of a deliberate price-cutting campaign by British Sugar aimed at excluding Napier Brown from the retail market.

Pricing Practices (3): Discriminatory Pricing

Price Discrimination Generally

3.233 Price discrimination occurs when a firm charges different prices to different customers for identical goods or services. Firms often discriminate between customers for legitimate commercial reasons. In some cases they charge different prices for the same product to different customers (eg medical or legal services are sometimes priced according to the wealth of the patient or client). In most cases, however, discriminatory pricing is effected through rebates and discounts. Customers who obtain a rebate for buying a large quantity of a given good will pay a lower overall price for the goods purchased than customers buying the same product but in less quantity.

3.234 Discrimination can only occur if three conditions are fulfilled. First, the firm engaging in it must have market power. Firms are not able to discriminate in a competitive market. Secondly, there must be different groups of customers with different elasticities of demand (ie ready to buy the products at different prices), and, finally, arbitrage between these groups of customers must not be possible.

3.235 Discrimination is not always economically harmful. To the extent that discrimination enhances output, by enabling a firm to sell more than it would have in the absence of the discrimination, it increases consumer welfare. In some cases, however, price discrimination produces anti-competitive effects. In analysing the exclusionary effects produced by price discrimination, it is useful to distinguish between what is termed 'primary line price discrimination', which harms the direct competitors of the dominant company by foreclosing access to the market where the dominant firm is present, and 'secondary line price discrimination', which harms customers of the dominant company who are competing with each other. In addition to these two forms of discrimination, Article 82 is arguably also concerned with price discrimination which simply exploits the dominant firm's customers (see exploitative abuses below).

Elements of the Abuse

Article 82(c) states that an abuse may consist in 'applying dissimilar conditions to equivalent transactions with other trading parties, thereby placing them at a competitive disadvantage'. It is established that this provision also implies a ban on the equal treatment of non-equivalent transactions.[207]   **3.236**

Equivalent transactions.   In order to fulfil the first criterion of Article 82(c), it is **3.237** necessary to decide in what circumstances transactions are 'equivalent'. This involves an evaluation of the nature of the products and/or services concerned, and may necessitate consideration *inter alia* of their composition, quality, variety, of the speed or time of delivery, of marketing costs, or of any other relevant factors. The most obvious means of concluding that two transactions are not equivalent is to show that the dominant company's costs in providing the products and/or services were not the same.

It should be noted that both the Commission and the Court have been particu- **3.238** larly careful not to differentiate otherwise equivalent transactions on the basis of nationality. More controversially, in some cases they have also regarded transactions involving identical goods, but where the goods are sold in different geographic markets, as equivalent (see the *United Brands* and *Tetra Pak II* cases, discussed below under geographical price discrimination). However, in recent cases a more detailed analysis of transport costs has been made before considering two transactions as equivalent. In the Commission's decision in *Deutsche Bundesbahn*,[208] for example, the Commission did not accept the German rail operator's assertion that its freight carriage costs to Dutch and Belgian ports were higher than to North German ports. This is also the case for quantity discounts based on cost savings, as will be seen below.

---

[207] See the bundled pricing cases discussed at 3.260 below: *Napier Brown* and *Van den Bergh Foods*.
[208] *Deutsche Bundesbahn* OJ 1994 L104, p 34.

3.239 **Placing trading parties at a competitive disadvantage.** The second condition of Article 82(c) requires that the dominant firm's trading parties be placed at a competitive disadvantage as a result of the discrimination. This condition is somewhat ambiguous. First, it is not clear whether it requires that the customer of the dominant firm be placed at a competitive disadvantage *vis-à-vis* the dominant firm itself (primary line discrimination), in relation to other customers of the dominant firm (secondary line discrimination), or simply that it must suffer commercially in such a way that its ability to compete in whatever market is impaired

3.240 Perhaps on account of this ambiguity, the requirement to demonstrate that trading parties have been placed at a competitive disadvantage has been substantially neglected by the Commission and by the Courts. In most of the principal cases dealing with price discrimination (*United Brands* and *Hoffmann-La Roche*, for example), this aspect, or at least the precise wording, was entirely neglected, while in others (*Suiker Unie* and *Irish Sugar*, for example) only brief reference was made thereto. It is, however, implicit in these rulings that the Commission and Courts regard both primary and secondary line discrimination as covered by the provision.

3.241 **Objective justification.** As a general rule, it will be a legitimate defence to the application of Article 82 to discrimination by dominant firms to demonstrate that the behaviour can be objectively justified. The most obvious instance of objective justification in this context is to show that the dominant company has been forced to discriminate in order to meet a competitor's offer. The extent to which the Commission and Courts will be prepared to admit the defence of meeting competition is unclear, though there are some indications that a dominant firm will be given greater leeway in more competitive markets. In *BPB Industries*,[209] for example, the Commission considered that specific price discounts, accorded to customers in a geographic market where competition was particularly vigorous, were justifiable.

Discounts and Rebates

3.242 **General.** Price discrimination does not consist in direct pricing abuses alone, but can also (and in fact more usually does) occur as a result of indirect pricing practices, principally by means of the granting of discounts or rebates. Discounts are generally offered on individual transactions, while rebates are normally deductions or cash payments made retrospectively to a customer in accordance with the latter's purchases over a period of time.[210]

3.243 Discounts and rebates are often used as instruments of healthy and legitimate price competition. The difficulty for the competition authority or other enforcer

---

[209] C–310/93P *BPB Industries plc & Anor v Commission* [1995] ECR I–865.
[210] Sometimes, however, the words are used interchangeably.

of the competition rules is, as with so many alleged abuses of market power, to distinguish such genuinely pro-competitive behaviour from anti-competitive or exploitative conduct. At one end of the spectrum, where the discount/rebate is a direct reflection of the dominant company's efficiency, it will be unobjectionable. At the other end, where the only commercially rational explanation for the discount/rebate is in terms of an attempt to exclude competitors or exploit customers, it will fall foul of Article 82.

In deciding whether a firm is objectively justified in granting the discount or rebate, it is normally necessary to have regard to whether the discount/rebate bears a relation to an economic saving made by the dominant firm, arising from its supply to the recipient of the discount, as well as to the objectivity of the rules governing the discount scheme. It is also necessary to examine the extent to which the discount/rebate has the effect of restricting the customer's commercial likelihood of deciding to purchase from another supplier. Finally, the likely harm to the dominant firm's rivals needs to be assessed, as well as the extent to which the discounts/rebates will be likely to shore up its dominant position. **3.244**

Non exclusionary discounts or rebates.   The most common types of discounts and rebates do not fall foul of Article 82. First, discounts or rebates based on the volume purchased are normally not exclusionary. In economic terms, quantity discounts/rebates are more accurately described as an instance of non-uniform pricing rather than pricing which is discriminatory between customers. Where such discounts/rebates, normally based on quantities purchased, are based on cost efficiencies directly flowing from the purchases in question, they will be unobjectionable. This, however, needs to be qualified. When the volume required to obtain the discount or rebate represents a large share of the customer's needs, the discount may be objectionable (see below under target rebates). **3.245**

Although the Commission has rarely required the direct correlation with efficiencies to be quantified, it seems logical that such schemes should only be permitted to the extent that they correspond to actual cost savings on the part of the dominant company. Not to require such a link would effectively amount to discrimination against smaller companies, and could accordingly be regarded as an exploitative abuse. The Commission has rarely condemned quantity rebate schemes where all customers are treated equally, ie where the scheme is entirely objective in terms of its qualification criteria. However, a volume discount scheme specifically targeted to favour a particular customer might have exclusionary effects for the favoured customer's competitors. This was the case in *Brussels Airport*,[211] where the Commission found such a scheme to be contrary to Article 82, because it seems to have been tailored so that only the airport's largest customer, Sabena, would benefit. Other rebates which are likely to be accepted, **3.246**

---

[211] See Commission's *Nineteenth Report on Competition Policy 1989* (Vol XXVI) point 50.

because they normally confer an economic benefit on the dominant supplier, include: discounts corresponding to services rendered by the customers, for example 'functional discounts' sometimes granted to wholesalers;[212] discounts given for cash payment; discounts given for prompt payment, and rebates given because of quality defects.

3.247 **Discounts or rebates not permissable under Article 82.** Some other types of discounts or rebates would normally fall foul of Article 82. They are discussed below.

3.248 *Fidelity/loyalty rebates.* Fidelity rebates seek to reward customers for their pattern of purchases from a dominant firm. They normally reward customers for *de facto* exclusive purchasing but, as they are not based on cost savings by that firm, are normally considered objectionable under Article 82. Although it is arguable that fidelity rebates amount to no more than vigorous price competition, the Commission and Court have come close to establishing a presumption of illegality for such schemes. US law, by contrast, tends to take a more robust view of the merits of rebates/discounts of this kind.

3.249 Fidelity rebates are often used by a dominant company so as to make it difficult, or commercially irrational, for the customer to switch to another supplier. This can have the effect, on the one hand, of foreclosing a substantial part of the market in question to the competitors of the dominant firm. Indeed, the dominant firm's competitors would have to match the level of rebates granted by their more powerful competitor in order to be able to sell to the customer in question. On the other hand, where the dominant supplier's customers are competitors of each other, those not receiving the rebate are thereby placed at a competitive disadvantage *vis-à-vis* those who do.

3.250 The Commission first objected to fidelity rebates in *Suiker Unie*, where the dominant sugar supplier granted rebates to loyal customers, namely those who met the totality of their requirements from the dominant supplier. The Commission found that, even though the dominant supplier's competitors were offering lower prices, these were not sufficient to match the rebate and attract customers receiving the rebate. The Commission's findings were upheld by the Court of Justice.

3.251 In *Hoffmann-La Roche*, the Court gave its most comprehensive indication that fidelity rebates would infringe Article 82. It said that not only will a firm in a dominant position on a market infringe Article 82 when it ties purchasers *de jure* through exclusivity obligations (as described above at para 3.185), but that 'the same applies if the said undertaking [the dominant firm], without tying the pur-

---

[212] In the *Coca-Cola* case ((Case IV/M794) [1997] OJ L218/15), for example, the Commission indicated that rebates granted in return for distributors' use of Coca-Cola's advertising material would be objectively justified.

chasers by a formal obligation, applies, either under the terms of agreements concluded with these purchasers or unilaterally, a system of fidelity rebates, that is to say discounts conditional on the customer's obtaining all or most of its requirements, whether the quantity of its purchases be large or small, from the undertaking in a dominant position'.

In the instant case, the fidelity rebates were progressive with regard to the proportion of the customer's purchases taken from Hoffmann-La Roche; that is to say that the greater the proportion of requirements accounted for by such purchases, the greater the rate of rebate accorded to the customer. This had a clear tying effect on the dominant supplier's customers, making it more difficult for them to turn elsewhere with every additional unit which they purchased. As with *de jure* exclusivity obligations, the Court also made it clear that such rebates were caught by Article 82 even if they had been expressly requested by the customer.   **3.252**

Target and long-term rebate schemes.   Article 82 can also be infringed where dominant companies grant rebates on the basis of the customer having reached a specified sales target, if this has the effect of inducing the latter to purchase larger quantities from the former. Such rebates are often fixed bilaterally between the dominant supplier and its customer and do not usually depend on the customer achieving all or most of his requirements from the supplier. The compatibility of such schemes with the Treaty will depend *inter alia* on the length of the reference period upon which the rebate is calculated, and on the degree to which the criteria for granting the rebate are objective and transparent.   **3.253**

These so-called 'target rebates' were discussed at length by the Court of Justice in *Michelin*.[213] In that case, specific targets were fixed between Michelin and its customers at the beginning of each year, based on the latter's purchases in the previous year. If the target was reached or exceeded, an individually negotiated discount would be granted. In finding the rebate system abusive, the Court placed particular emphasis on the length of the reference period (one year), pointing out that the supplier would be unlikely to switch suppliers at any point during the year (but particularly as the year progressed) for fear of not qualifying for the rebate. The Court also relied, though to a lesser extent, on the secret manner in which the rebates were agreed, and the general lack of uniformity and transparency characterizing the system.   **3.254**

Target rebates will, however, only be objectionable if they have an appreciable tying effect on customers (ie if they impede them from switching to a competitor). In the *Coca-Cola* case,[214] which was resolved without the need for a formal decision, the Commission objected to Coca-Cola's target rebate scheme for its   **3.255**

---

[213] Case 322/81 *Michelin* [1983] ECR 3461.
[214] Case IV/M794 [1997] OJ L218/15.

customers in Italy, which used a reference period of one year for the calculation of the rebate. As in *Michelin*, the Commission felt that such a scheme had a tying effect on purchasers, thereby substantially foreclosing the market to Coca-Cola's competitors. When the company volunteered to reduce the reference period to three months, however, the Commission accepted that the scheme no longer substantially impeded the company's customers from switching suppliers.

3.256 Target rebates were also the subject of the Commission's decision in *Irish Sugar*.[215] A number of small companies had entered the Irish retail sugar market as sugar packers, and sourced most of their requirements from Irish Sugar. The dominant company was at that time the only domestic sugar packer operating on the Irish market. The Commission found that Irish Sugar was abusing its position of dominance by offering selective target rebates to certain wholesalers and retailers, based on target increases in their total sugar purchases from Irish Sugar. The scheme was not governed by objective award criteria and it had the effect of discouraging the recipient wholesalers and retailers from purchasing sugar from Irish Sugar's sugar packaging competitors.

3.257 Several of these packers also complained to the Commission that they were the only bulk sugar customers of Irish Sugar who did not receive any non-volume-related discounts.[216] The Commission found that this too amounted to an abuse of Irish Sugar's dominance, in that it placed those sugar packers (the ones sourcing from Irish Sugar) at a competitive disadvantage *vis-à-vis* both Irish Sugar itself as a sugar packer, and *vis-à-vis* other sugar packers sourcing from elsewhere.

3.258 *Top slice rebates.* A so-called 'top slice rebate' is a specific form of rebate resulting from the fact that purchasers sometimes obtain the bulk of their requirements (or their 'core requirements') from a single supplier and the rest from elsewhere. In such circumstances, dominant firms may seek to induce the purchaser to additionally purchase that remnant (the so-called 'top slice') from it by offering a special discount on the top slice tonnage. In the *Soda Ash* cases, the Commission penalized the chemical company ICI for pursuing such pricing policies, relying also on the fact that the rebates were not granted at a uniform rate to all recipients.

3.259 *Tying or aggregated rebates.* If a discount is granted only on condition that the customer agrees to buy several different types of products and/or services, this will not normally be permitted under Article 82. Such rebates can have exclusionary effects in a number of markets simultaneously. In *Hoffmann-La Roche*, for example, the Court held that the dominant company's system of fidelity rebates, calculated on a customer's purchases of a variety of products in different product

---

[215] *Irish Sugar* [1997] OJ L258, 1.
[216] These were primarily so-called 'promotional' discounts.

markets, also constituted an infringement of Article 82(d)[217] (see also an analysis of tying in paragraph 3.194 *et seq* above)

Pricing Practices (4): Bundled Pricing

Another form of exclusionary pricing practice, similar to a tying practice and to **3.260** discriminatory pricing, is bundling through the pricing of a product or service (see also below). This is an instance of applying equivalent conditions to non-equivalent transactions. In *Napier Brown*, the Commission found British Sugar's policy of 'delivered pricing' to be discriminatory. This policy involved charging all purchasers of sugar a bundled price (a 'delivered price') which included the cost of delivery, even when buyers did not wish to have the sugar delivered by British Sugar. The Commission's intervention ensured that British Sugar introduced an alternative 'ex factory' price for customers not taking delivery from the company.

In *Van den Bergh Foods*,[218] the Commission indicated[219] that Unilever's former **3.261** policy of so-called 'inclusive pricing', whereby the costs of freezer cabinet provision and of the ice cream products themselves were bundled together in a single price charged to all retailers, would amount to an abuse within the meaning of Article 82. The pricing policy had the effect of discriminating against retailers who bought Unilever's ice cream but did not take its cabinets. No formal finding was made, however, because the alleged abuse had been terminated following the Commission's statement of objections.

(c) Other Abusive Practices

Raising Rivals' Costs

General

The notion of 'raising rivals' costs' arises in those cases in which a dominant **3.262** undertaking engages in a practice that increases its own costs as well as those of any other competitor present in, or attempting to enter, the market.[220] Normally, the dominant company, which holds a substantial market share, will be able to absorb the increase in costs much more easily than small new entrants. For some of them, the increase in costs may even make the difference between a profitable and a non-profitable entry, thereby keeping them out of the market.

Raising rivals' costs will only be considered an abuse if there are no objective jus- **3.263** tifications for the increase in costs other than the exclusion of a competitor from

---

[217] Similar abuses were the subject of the *Digital* case, which was resolved with undertakings— see *Report on Competition Policy 1997* (Vol XXVII) para. 69.

[218] *Van den Bergh Foods* [1998] OJ L246, 1.

[219] *Van den Bergh Foods* [1998] OJ L246, 76.

[220] Most of the exclusionary practices would have the effect of raising rivals' costs and, at the same time, creating or strengthening barriers to entry. For instance, refusing to deal with a competitor would normally increase its costs as it would have to find or develop alternative sources of supply.

the market. The problem with this type of abuse is that it is very difficult to prove that the expenses incurred by the dominant undertaking (for example in legal costs) are not in fact objectively justified. In most cases, this can only be demonstrated by evidence of exclusionary intent.

Types of Abuses Raising Rivals' Costs

3.264 There are numerous courses of action that a dominant company can resort to in order to raise its costs at the same time as raising the costs of its rivals. The following are a number of examples:

—Engaging in a publicity campaign so as to oblige one's rivals to spend heavily on publicity before entering the market.

—Increasing research expenditure, and registering patents even on any marginal invention, in order to force competitors to either match the research efforts or to challenge the patents' validity.

—Lobbying in favour of regulations that have a more heavy impact on small new entrants than on established market incumbents.

—Negotiating market-wide wage increase with trade unions, which would have a heavier impact on small and wage intensive new entrants.

3.265 There is, however, little or no case law on this type of abuse. The jurisprudence has only explicitly considered legal harassment as a practice contrary to Article 82. The Commission has, in addition, made a reference to raising input costs as an abuse covered by Article 82 in a case concluded by informal means. Both of these 'raising rivals' costs'-type abusive practices are dealt with in detail below.

Legal harassment

3.266 An undertaking may abuse its dominant position by an excessive use against competitors of the instruments that the legal order puts at its disposal to defend its rights. Two different types of this abuse can be distinguished:

—abuse of legal proceedings, and

—abuse of claims for performance of a contract.

3.267 **Abuse of legal proceedings.** The fact that an undertaking with a dominant position on a particular market brings legal proceedings against a competitor on that market may constitute an abuse within the meaning of Article 82 of the EC Treaty. Nevertheless, as the CFI pointed out in *ITT Promedia*:[221]

> As access to the Court is a fundamental right and a general principle ensuring the rule of law, it is only in wholly exceptional circumstances that the fact that legal

---

[221] T–111/96 *ITT Promedia NV v Commission* [1998] ECR II–2937 para 60.

proceedings are brought is capable of constituting an abuse of a dominant position within the meaning of Article 82 of the EC Treaty.

The Commission[222] has laid down two cumulative criteria for determining in what cases bringing such legal proceedings would constitute an abuse: first, the legal action cannot reasonably be regarded as an attempt to establish the rights of the undertaking concerned, and can therefore only serve to harass the competitor; and, secondly, the legal action must have been conceived in the framework of a plan whose goal is to eliminate competition. Since the two criteria constitute an exception to the general principle of access to the courts, they must be construed and applied strictly. **3.268**

As to the first criterion, the CFI specified[223] that it should not be interpreted as a question of determining whether the rights that the dominant undertaking was asserting actually existed or whether the action was well founded. It is a question of simply assessing whether the legal action is intended to assert what the dominant undertaking could reasonably consider to be its rights. In view of this interpretation, the first criterion will probably only be satisfied if it can be shown that the only purpose of the action is to harass a competitor. As to the interpretation of the second criterion, although there is no particular guidance provided by the case law, it can be assumed that it will only be satisfied if there is evidence of intention to eliminate competition through the legal action. **3.269**

Abuse of claims for performance of a contract. In the same *ITT Promedia* case[224] the CFI ruled that a claim for performance of a contractual obligation may also constitute an abuse for the purposes of Article 82 of the EC Treaty if, in particular, that claim exceeds what the parties could reasonably expect under the contract, or if the circumstances applicable at the time of the conclusion of the contract have changed in the meantime. In any other case, if the conclusion of the contract in itself was not deemed to be abusive, it would not be possible to rule that a claim for performance of that contract is contrary to Article 82 of the EC Treaty. **3.270**

Raising Rivals' Input Costs

The Commission considered, in a recent case resolved informally, that Nielsen, the dominant provider of retail tracking services in Europe, had abused its dominant position by concluding contracts with retailers, stipulating that data should not be sold to Nielsen's competitors at more favourable prices than those offered to Nielsen.[225] As retailers' data is an essential input for the provision of retail **3.271**

---

[222] *ITT Promedia/Belgacom* (IV/35.258) [1996] IP/97/292 not published. Mentioned in *ITT Promedia* (see n 221 above), para 55. The CFI did not explicitly confirm that the two criteria were well founded because the claimant did not challenge them, but gave some indications as to how they should be interpreted.

[223] T–111/96 *ITT Promedia NV v Commission* [1998] ECR II–2937, paras 72–73 and 93.

[224] T–111/96 *ITT Promedia NV v Commission* [1998] ECR II–2937, para 140.

[225] *IRI/Nielsen, Report on Competition Policy 1996* (Vol XXVI) 144–148.

tracking services, these contracts allowed Nielsen to directly raise its rivals' costs by raising the price that it paid to retailers.

Cross-Subsidization

Concept

3.272 Cross-subsidization occurs when one undertaking allocates all or part of the costs of its activity in one or more product or geographic market to its activity in another product or geographic market.

3.273 If an undertaking in a dominant position engages in cross-subsidization from the market where it is dominant to a market where it is not, it could benefit from its position in the first market in order to reduce its costs in the second market. It would not, therefore, compete purely on the basis of efficiency in this second market, thereby distorting competition there. Cross-subsidization, therefore, may constitute an abuse within the meaning of Article 82 of the EC Treaty.

3.274 Cross-subsidization will normally allow the dominant company to charge lower prices than it would have charged in the absence thereof. The existence of a cross-subsidization abuse, however, is independent of the level at which these prices are set. There is no need to prove that the prices are predatory in order for cross-subsidization to be considered abusive. Indeed, evidence that the lower prices can be explained by the existence of cross-subsidies is enough to conclude that the dominant company is not competing on the merits. It is only when such evidence does not exist that the absence of competition on the merits needs to be inferred from the price levels themselves (ie it will have to be demonstrated that the prices are set below average variable cost).

Types of Cross-Subsidization

3.275 To date, cross-subsidization has only been considered an abuse when it takes place in markets reserved to monopolies and, in particular, when the activities in these markets subsidize activities in markets open to competition.

3.276 In the Guidelines on the application of the EC competition rules in the telecommunications sector[226] the Commission considered that 'subsidising activities under competition, by allocating their costs to monopoly activities, is likely to distort competition in violation of Article 86 [now Article 82]'.

3.277 Equally, in the Notice on the application of the Competition rules to the Postal Sector and on the assessment of certain state measures relating to postal services, the Commission claims that 'cross-subsidisation in the postal sector, where nearly all operators provide reserved and non-reserved services, can distort competition and lead to competitors being beaten by offers which are made possible not by

---

[226] [1991] OJ C233/2 paras 102–110.

efficiency and performance but by cross-subsidies'. The Commission concludes by saying that 'subsidising activities open to competition by allocating their costs to reserved services is likely to distort competition in breach of Article 86 [now Article 82]'.

According to the Commission,[227] this type of cross-subsidization can take differ- **3.278** ent forms. It can be carried out, either by funding the activities in question with capital remunerated substantially below the market rate, or by supplying those activities' premises, equipment, experts, and/or services at a remuneration substantially lower than the market price.

Such cross-subsidization is substantially easier to detect if monopolies are obliged **3.279** to keep separate financial records, identifying separately costs and revenues associated with the provision of services supplied under their exclusive rights and those provided under competitive conditions. EC law imposes such an obligation on telecommunications operators and the Commission considers that Members States should also require it of postal operators.[228] In certain other cases,[229] such as where a condition was required for the grant of an exemption pursuant to Article 81(3), the Commission has imposed separated cost accounting and transparency requirements.

Other types of cross-subsidization also involving telecommunications or postal **3.280** monopolies would not be considered restrictive of competition. Cross-subsidies between reserved activities are allowed, not only because they cannot restrict competition, but also because they might be necessary in order to enable the monopolists to perform their obligation to provide a universal service (for example profitable mail delivery in urban areas may subsidize unprofitable delivery in rural ones). The role played by such cross-subsidies in ensuring the financial viability of monopolies entrusted with a service of general interest may even justify maintaining an exclusive right in relation to activities that should, otherwise, be provided under competitive conditions.[230]

As to cross-subsidies from non-reserved activities to reserved ones, these rarely **3.281** occur. Such cross-subsidies would not normally make commercial sense as, unless it is more efficient than its competitors, the cross-subsidies would impede the monopolist from offering a competitive price for its non-reserved activities. Even if they did occur, they would not be restrictive of competition because they would only affect the market already reserved to the monopolist.

---

[227] Guidelines on the application to EC competition rules in the telecommunications sector, [1991] OJ C233/2, para 104.

[228] Notice on the application of the competition rules to the postal sector and on the assessment of certain state measures relating to postal services, para 8(b).

[229] *Atlas and Phoenix* [1996] OJ L239/57 and *Unisource* [1997] OJ L381/1.

[230] See Case C–320/91 *Procureur du Roi v Corbeau* [1993] ECR I–2533.

Structural Abuses

General Principles

3.282   The notion of a structural abuse consists in a commercial action by, or transaction involving, a dominant firm which produces an immediate change in the structure of the market to the detriment of competition. Structural abuses are distinct from the other exclusionary abuses detailed above, in that the latter are essentially behavioural in nature, and generally result from a course of conduct over a period of time. Structural abuses, by contrast, are usually one-off occurrences. Such an abuse might consist in, for example, the acquisition by a dominant company of a minority shareholding or of a technology licence. The creation by a dominant firm of a co-operative joint venture or other long-term co-operation agreement might also be considered to constitute a structural abuse.

3.283   The notion of a structural abuse was first recognized by the Court of Justice in its seminal 1973 ruling in *Continental Can*. The Court established the principle that any commercial practices which are damaging to the maintenance of an effective competitive structure are prohibited by Article 81. The Court said that the Article

> is not only aimed at practices which may cause damage to consumers directly, but also at those which are detrimental to them through their impact on an effective competition structure, such as is mentioned in Article 3(f) [now 3(g)] of the Treaty. Abuse may therefore occur if an undertaking in a dominant position strengthens its position in such a way that the degree of dominance reached substantially fetters competition, ie that only undertakings remain in the market whose behaviour depends on the dominant one.

The Court goes on to stress that 'the strengthening of the position of an undertaking may be an abuse and prohibited by Article 86 [now Article 82] of the EC Treaty, regardless of the means and procedure by which it is achieved, if it has the effects mentioned above'. In other words, Article 82 applies to structural operations, as well as to behavioural practices.

Acquisition of Control of Another Undertaking

3.284   *Continental Can* established that Article 82 is applicable to concentrations which strengthen an already existing dominant position. It is not clear, however, whether it could also be applicable to concentrations which create a dominant position.[231] This discussion has, however, become largely academic because the Commission

---

[231] Although the Court of Justice has never addressed this question, it is very questionable whether Article 82 could be extended to include the prohibiton of such operations; note that in its decision in *Metaleurop* [1990] OJ L179/41, a decision taken before the Merger Regulation came into force, the Commission seemed to imply (see para 18) that Article 82 could be applicable to concentrative operations which created a dominant position.

can no longer take action on the basis of Regulation 17 against such operations.[232] Since the adoption of the Merger Regulation in 1989, concentrations (as defined in the Regulation) with a 'Community dimension' (as defined in the Regulation) are assessed by the Commission on the basis of that Regulation (see Chapter 4).

Acquisition of Minority Shareholdings

It is established that Article 82 may be applicable to acquisitions of shareholdings **3.285** which do not confer on the acquirer sole or joint control of the enterprise in which the acquired shareholding represents a stake. In *BAT and Reynolds*,[233] the Court stated that, where a company in a dominant position acquires a minority share-holding in another company, 'an abuse of such a position can only arise where the shareholding in question results in *effective control* of the other company *or at least in some influence on its commercial policy*' (emphasis added).[234]

The Commission appears to have gone further than that by finding Article 82 **3.286** applicable to the acquisition by a dominant firm of minority shareholdings which confer little if any determinative control over the company in which the stake was acquired. In *Warner-Lambert/Gillette*,[235] the Commission held that the acquisi-tion by Gillette, which was dominant in the wet-shaving market in Europe, of a minority shareholding in its principal competitor, was contrary to Article 82. The Commission reached this conclusion notwithstanding the fact that the 22 per cent stake in question conferred on Gillette very few formal powers, it obtained no voting rights or board representation. The Commission pointed out that 'the structure of the wet-shaving market in the Community had been changed by the creation of a link between Gillette and its leading competitor', and that the change would have an adverse effect on competition. Referring to *BAT and Reynolds*, the Commission concluded that the management of Gillette's competitor would be 'obliged to take into account' the position of Gillette, and that the minority stake would thereby influence its commercial conduct. The Commission ordered Gillette to dispose of the minority shareholding.

---

[232] It could, however, act on the basis of Article 85 (former Article 89), either on its own initia-tive or at the request of a Member State/s. Nor is that to say that national courts cannot apply Article 82 to such operations: the applicability of the Treaty provision, being directly applicable, is not affected by secondary legislation such as the Merger Regulation. It should also be noted that Member State authorities can apply Article 82 to concentrations without a Community dimen-sion—see Recital 29 to the Merger Regulation, and Article 84 (former Article 88) of the Treaty; the latter provision provides that Member State authorities can apply the competition rules in the absence of implementing legislation pursuant to Article 83 (former Article 87); since neither Regulation 17, nor the Merger Regulation, apply to concentrations without a Community dimen-sion, there is no such implementing legislation for these operations.

[233] Cases 142 and 156/84 *BAT and Reynolds* [1986] ECR 1899.

[234] Cases 142 and 156/84 *BAT and Reynolds* [1986] ECR 1899, para 65.

[235] Case 93/252 *Warner-Lambert/Gillette* L116, 12 May 1993, p 21.

Acquisition of a Licence

3.287 In *Tetra Pak I*,[236] the firm, which was dominant in the markets for aseptic milk cartons and filling machinery, acquired a competitor, thereby also acquiring an exclusive licence to a new technology for filling packages. The Court of First Instance held that, in doing so, Tetra Pak had abused its dominant position. The abuse, according to the Court, did not consist in the concentrative aspect of the operation but in the fact that the transaction gave Tetra Pak access to a technology which would strengthen its dominance, and have a substantial foreclosure effect on the company's rivals for a long period of time.

3.288 In *Carlsberg/Interbrew*,[237] a case which did not result in a formal decision, the Commission objected to an exclusive licence from Carlsberg, to the Belgian brewer Interbrew, for the distribution of the former company's beer products in Belgium. The Commission was of the view that the licence would result in a strengthening of Interbrew's dominance on the Belgian beer market by increasing the portfolio of beers it could offer to consumers, as well as by making it more difficult for its competitors to make a comparable offer. In response to the Commission's objections, Carlsberg rendered the licence non-exclusive, and created a second distributor for its products in partnership with a local wholesaler.

3.289 The Commission has even acted against licensing arrangements which have been in operation for a long time. In *Svenska Tobaks*,[238] also a case resolved informally, the Commission expressed doubts as to the compatibility with Article 82[239] of a long-standing[240] exclusive licensing arrangement between the dominant cigarette company in Sweden (the licensee) and a Danish cigarette company (the licensor). The licence concerned the manufacture, distribution, and sale of one of the major cigarette brands in Sweden. The Commission was of the view that such a long-term licensing arrangement produced anti-competitive effects, thereby strengthening the licensee's dominance on the Swedish cigarette market. Following the Commission's intervention, the licence was essentially reduced to a subcontracting arrangement.

Co-operative Joint Ventures/Co-operation Agreements

3.290 In line with the approach taken towards the applicability of Article 82 to licensing arrangements, it would seem that the same principles would apply in relation to co-operative joint ventures or long-term co-operation agreements between competitors. There appears to be no case law relating specifically to this question,

---

[236] Case T–51/89 *Tetra Pak I* [1990] ECR II–309.
[237] See *Report on Competition Policy 1994* (Vol XXIV) paras 209 and 213.
[238] See *Report on Competition Policy 1997* (Vol XXVII) para 66.
[239] The Commission also considered that the arrangements infringed Article 81.
[240] The original licence was granted in 1961.

which may be explained by the fact that Article 81 is almost invariably sufficient to deal with such cases.

(3) Exploitative Abuses

General Characteristics

The term 'exploitative abuses' normally refers to those practices engaged in by **3.291** dominant undertakings which, while not directly harming competitors in the market, nonetheless reduce the welfare of consumers. This reduction of welfare or exploitative effect can take various forms, such as excessive prices, insufficient quality or diversity of products, reduction of innovation, or discriminatory treatment of customers.

Exploitative Effects

As already explained in the introduction to this chapter, the assessment of **3.292** exploitative effects presents some substantial conceptual and practical difficulties. The main conceptual problem is that, theoretically, an exploitative abuse could be committed every time that a company with market power operates in the market. Indeed, according to economic theory, companies with market power will invariably charge a higher price or produce lower output than companies operating in a pure competitive situation and, therefore, reduce the welfare of customers.

This conceptual problem is closely linked to a practical difficulty in assessing **3.293** exploitative effects: in order to determine whether a particular firm is exploiting its customers, it must be determined at what level of prices and/or output it would not be doing so. The level of prices and output that would prevail in a competitive situation is the appropriate objective reference, but in most cases it will be impossible for competition authorities and courts to determine what that reference is. Other more subjective references, therefore, have been used, such as a comparison with the situation pertaining in similar markets, or an assessment of the level of satisfaction of demand in the market in question.

The determination of an exploitative effect necessarily involves, therefore, the **3.294** need to make a subjective judgement as to the appropriate level of prices and output in a particular market. It is notable that, probably in order to limit the risks inherent to any subjective judgement, competition authorities and courts tend to exercise restraint in this area and only pursue exploitative behaviour in cases where the reduction of consumer welfare is particularly clear.

Unfair or Excessive Prices

Article 82(a) of the EC Treaty expressly states that an abuse may, in particular, **3.295** consist in indirectly imposing unfair purchase or selling prices or other unfair trading conditions. Generally speaking, such abuses will consist in the charging of unfairly high prices by dominant suppliers, but could also include the extraction of unfairly low prices by dominant buyers.

Excessive Prices

3.296 **General.** In economic terms, excessive prices are those which are set at above the competitive level as a result of the exercise of market power. It is often pointed out that excessive prices are not anti-competitive, that is to say that in a functioning market economy they should have the effect of attracting new entrants who will force the price down, and that they consequently should not be the concern of antitrust authorities. Indeed, excessive prices do not reduce overall economic welfare, but merely affect the distribution thereof. It is also often argued that to prohibit a dominant company from charging high prices amounts to unfairly penalizing the company's competitive success in achieving dominance by depriving it of its just reward for that endeavour. This, broadly speaking, is the approach adopted by the US courts,[241] who have repeatedly refused to countenance a 'reasonable price' test, principally on account of the inherent uncertainty of such a test.

3.297 The EC Treaty, however, is expressly concerned with a dominant firm's ability to exploit consumers by charging them unfairly high prices. Intervention against excessive pricing can moreover be supported by a number of economic and public policy justifications.[242] While economic theory may predict that new firms should enter a market, the reality may prove otherwise, particularly where a market is characterized by structural problems; thus the need for intervention. Protecting consumers is, moreover, a legitimate policy objective of antitrust law. Where, for example, the barriers to entering a market are particularly high, such a policy interest may be particularly compelling. Furthermore, while competition rules should not deprive a firm of the fruits of its genuine success in the market place, it is legitimate to prevent the undue exploitation of its market power. It should also be added that, in some instances, a firm's dominance came about as a result of forces other than competition.

3.298 Excessive pricing has, however, proved to be a notoriously difficult abuse to prosecute, principally on account of the complexity involved in calculating what amounts to an unreasonably high price. Taking such cases is also unsatisfactory in the sense that the intervening authority is expected to take on the role of a quasi-price regulator, with the task of second-guessing the market as to what should be the correct price level. Conversely, from a dominant company's point of view, the

---

[241] The approach is also favoured by some commentators on EC law—see Korah, *EEC Competition Law and Practice* (1990).

[242] See more generally Conor Hanley, *Pricing—a behavioural approach to abuses of market power* (1994) Ph.D thesis, UCD, unpublished.

control of excessive pricing poses a problem of legal certainty: how high can its prices lawfully be set? It is perhaps not surprising, therefore, that the Commission has only rarely taken decisions making a finding of excessive pricing, notably in the *General Motors* and in the *United Brands* cases and, even then, the findings were in both instances subsequently struck down by the Court of Justice.

General Motors.   In this case, the Commission held that General Motors had   **3.299** abused its dominant position on the market for granting Opel car conformity certificates in Belgium by charging excessively high fees for the service. The Court of Justice struck down the finding, however, in view of the relative triviality of the allegations, and because General Motors had terminated the alleged abuse even before the Commission's intervention. Nevertheless, the Court made it clear that excessive pricing could in principle constitute an abuse[243] if the price was excessive in relation to the economic value of the service provided, and if it had the effect of either curbing parallel trade (thereby eliminating the possibility of competition from the lower prices charged elsewhere) or of unfairly exploiting customers.

United Brands.   The prices charged by UBC in the various Member States   **3.300** where it operated varied considerably: the biggest price difference was between Ireland and Denmark, the level being 138 per cent higher in the latter than in the former. Using the Irish prices as a base, the Commission concluded that the prices charged by UBC were 'excessive in relation to the economic value of the product supplied',[244] that the differences could not be accounted for by transport costs, and that the prices were excessive by comparison with those charged by UBC's competitors. No detailed cost/price analysis was, however, carried out. The Commission proceeded to require UBC to reduce its prices by a fixed percentage in certain Member States.

The Court of Justice's test.   The Court of Justice, while reiterating that excessive   **3.301** prices would fall foul of Article 82 where they bore no reasonable relation to the economic value of the product supplied and resulted in harm being caused to consumers, nevertheless held that the Commission's economic analysis in the instant case had been flawed. The Court made it clear that it was necessary for a detailed cost analysis to be made, stating that the question to be determined is 'whether the difference between the costs actually incurred and the price actually charged is excessive and, if the answer to this question is in the affirmative, to consider whether a price has been imposed which is either unfair in itself or when compared to competing products'.

---

[243] The Court had given earlier signals that it was prepared to entertain findings of excessive pricing—see the *Sirena* and *Deutsche Grammophon* cases.

[244] They were 30–40% higher than the prices charged for unbranded bananas, which were only of slightly inferior quality.

3.302 This is a twofold test: the first part requires a cost/price analysis, followed by a determination as to whether the difference is excessive; the second part necessitates determining whether a price is either excessive in itself or by comparison to competitors' products. Applying the test in the instant case, the Court found that UBC's prices were only 7 per cent greater than those of its main competitiors, and so annulled the Commission's finding of excessive pricing.

3.303 It is submitted that the Court's failure to articulate a more objective, and perhaps a more workable, test is to be regretted. In applying both parts of the test, the notion of what is meant by 'excessive' arises, and the Court provides no real guidance which might relieve this uncertainty. The Court does not describe exactly what costs should be taken into account in making the cost/price analyis. Nor does it shed light on when a price should be considered 'in itself' excessive. The requirement to make a comparison with the prices of competing products is, moreover, potentially unreliable in that the prices compared may themselves be unfair.

3.304 The *United Brands* case highlights the major difficulties of proof associated with finding an abuse of excessive pricing, and probably explains the relative dearth of instances in which the Commission has intervened in such cases.

Unfairly Low Prices Extracted by Dominant Buyers

3.305 Although instances appear to be rare, it has been established that Article 82 can also be applied in relation to the behaviour of a company (or companies in the case of joint dominance) which is a dominant purchaser in the relevant market, and which exercises its buying power to extract unfairly low prices from its suppliers. In particular, concern is increasingly being expressed by suppliers and consumers about the power of the major retail groups in certain Member States.[245]

3.306 In the *CICCE* case,[246] the Commission rejected a complaint from a film distributors' association against the three French TV stations, in which the complainants alleged that the stations charged unfairly low broadcasting fees for the airing of their films. While accepting that the TV stations did possess the requisite buying power to enable them to commit an abuse by charging excessively low fees, the Commission's rejection of the complaint was upheld by the Court on the grounds that the allegation was unsupported by sufficiently detailed evidence demonstrating that the fees bore no reasonable relation to the economic value of the films, a value which would vary according to each individual film. Once again, the difficulty of proving unfair pricing abuses is evident.

---

[245] See *Report on Competition Policy 1986* (Vol XVI) paras 345–348, regarding the increasing buying power of large retail chains and the increasing incidence of purchasing associations.
[246] Case 298/83 *CICCE* [1985] ECR 1105.

Imposing Other Unfair Terms

In addition to condemning excessive prices, Article 82(a) also considers that the **3.307** imposition of other unfair trading conditions may constitute an abuse. Determining whether a trading condition imposed by a dominant undertaking is unfair presents the same problems as determining whether a price is fair or excessive.

As explained above, determining whether a price or trading condition is unfair **3.308** requires the authorities applying Article 82 to assess what would be the prices or conditions that would prevail in a competitive environment.

In exceptional cases, however, the Commission and the Court have considered **3.309** that conditions imposed by dominant undertakings were unfair and, therefore, contrary to Article 82. In *BRT v SABAM*,[247] a case concerning a performing rights society, it was considered that restrictions imposed on the authors who were members of the society were unfair in so far as they were not necessary to allow the performing rights society to properly conduct its business (ie to negotiate with radio and TV stations over copyright licences).

In other cases, the criteria for determining whether a trading condition was fair **3.310** have focused on the burden that the condition places on customers. In *Alsatel*,[248] a case concerning the rental of telecommunication equipment, the Court considered that a clause allowing the dominant company to increase unilaterally the rent and automatically extend for fifteen years the rental contract was excessive. Similarly, in *Tetra Pak II*,[249] a clause obliging the payment of a rent, at the beginning of the contract, of almost the same amount as the value of the machine was considered unfair. Indeed, it would force the customer to pay as much as if it had purchased the machine, but would deprive it of the legal benefits of being the owner.

Finally, excessive conditions have also been considered abusive when imposed by **3.311** dominant buyers. In *Eurofima*[250] (a company created by the main European rail operators in order to develop new rail passenger carriages), the Commission considered that a dominant buyer of railway stock was abusing its dominant position by inviting tenders for development contracts on condition that unlimited patent licences should be granted to it without further remuneration.

---

[247] Case 127/73 *BRT v SABAM* [1974] ECR 51.
[248] Case 247/86 *Alsatel* [1988] ECR 5987, para 10.
[249] *Tetra Pak II* [1992] OJ L72/1, paras 135–138.
[250] *Eurofima, Report on Competition Policy 1973* (Vol III) para 68.

Limiting Production, Markets, or Technical Development

3.312 Another example of exploitative abuse is contained in Article 82(b) of the EC Treaty, which states that an abuse may, in particular, consist in limiting production, markets, or technical development to the prejudice of consumers.

3.313 As with other exploitative abuses, there are no simple criteria for determining what should be the amount and quality of output produced by an undertaking occupying a dominant position (or the level of technical development that it should attain) in order not to prejudice consumers and, therefore, not to engage in an abuse within the meaning of Article 82.

3.314 Theoretically, it could be said that an undertaking holding a dominant position abuses this position when it produces a lower level of output or innovation than a competitive environment would produce. However, authorities applying competition rules do not have the means to perform such an analysis and, therefore, are obliged to find other, less perfect, criteria for determining when Article 82(b) of the EC Treaty is being infringed.

3.315 The most straightforward situation to assess is that in which a company holding a dominant position ceases to provide a product or service that it was providing previously. In such a case, if the interruption prejudices customers and is not justified by any reasonable business objective (for example to eliminate the losses that such a product generated) it may be deemed to constitute an abuse of a dominant position. In *British Leyland*,[251] for instance, the refusal by a British car manufacturer to renew the certifications for left-hand drive cars that it had been granting in the past was considered to be an abusive limitation of output. In this particular case, British Leyland could not advance any business justification for its decision because it was obvious that the main motivation behind the refusal to renew certification was to foreclose the British market from parallel imports.

3.316 More generally, it can be assessed whether the output produced by the dominant undertaking, both in qualitative and quantitative terms, leaves a substantial amount of the demand unsatisfied. If this is the case, the undertaking may be found to have infringed Article 82 of the EC Treaty.

3.317 The Court has applied this type of analysis to undertakings entrusted by Member States with an exclusive right to perform certain activities. In *Höfner and Elser v Macrotron*,[252] it considered that the Bundesanstalt für Arbeit, a German agency with the monopoly for the provision of placement services, had failed to meet the demand for its services and that it had, therefore, abused its dominant position.

---

[251] Case 226/84 *British Leyland* [1986] ECR 3263, paras 12–21.
[252] C–41/90 *Höfner and Elser v Macrotron* [1991] ECR I–1979.

Similarly, in *Port of Genoa*,[253] the Court considered that the undertaking with the exclusive right to organize dock work had abused its dominant position by failing to use modern technology, thereby resulting in increased costs and longer service delays. In both cases the Court found that granting exclusive rights under such conditions constituted an infringement of Article 82 together with Article 86 of the EC Treaty.

This analysis has not only been used in the case of legal monopolies, but also in relation to private undertakings holding a dominant position. The Commission has considered, for instance, that the *International Group of P&I Clubs*,[254] which covers around 90 per cent of the market for maritime third-party liability insurance, had abused its dominant position by only providing a single level of insurance cover, thereby leaving a substantial proportion of the demand unsatisfied. **3.318**

Discriminatory Practices

Article 82(c) prohibits discriminatory practices and, in particular, discriminatory pricing. The elements of this abuse have been discussed above (see paragraph 3.233 *et seq*) in so far as it may amount to an exclusionary practice. Discrimination can, however, also be exploitative. Some particular types of exploitative discriminatory pricing are discussed below. **3.319**

Discrimination Based on Nationality

Nationality can never constitute an admissible ground for discrimination. To do so would fly in the face of a fundamental tenet of Community law, enshrined in Article 12 of the Treaty, namely that discrimination on the basis of nationality is absolutely prohibited. Discrimination on the basis of nationality has the effect of impeding the development of the single market. The European competition rules serve the purpose not only of protecting competition, but also of ensuring the integration and proper functioning of that market. For that reason, this form of discrimination can legitimately be penalized by Article 82. **3.320**

The prohibition covers both direct and indirect discrimination, and so extends to discrimination on the basis, for example, of domicile or place of establishment. In *Corsica Ferries*,[255] the Court of Justice found that pilot tariffs had been set in such a way as, indirectly, to discriminate against certain ships on the basis of nationality. In *GVL*,[256] the Court held that a refusal by a dominant company to supply a category of customers, defined according to those customers' nationality or domicile, was contrary to Article 82. **3.321**

---

[253] C–179/90 *Port of Genoa v. Gabrielli* [1991] ECR I–5889.
[254] *International Group of P&I Clubs* [1999] OJ L125.
[255] *Corsica Ferries* [1989] ECR 4441.
[256] Case 7/82 *GVL* [1983] ECR 2327.

Geographical Price Discrimination

3.322 The *United Brands* and *Tetra Pak* cases demonstrate that for a dominant firm to charge different prices in different Member States can also attract the sanction of Article 82. It seems clear that, in these cases, the Commission and Court have been motivated by the desire to prevent the segmentation of the market along national lines. These cases are less straightforward, however, than the cases involving discrimination on the basis of nationality, because it is not clear whether it is the discrimination as such which has been condemned, or the discrimination combined with other factors specific to those cases.

3.323 In *United Brands*, UBC had a long-standing policy of supplying bananas to ripener-distributors in the various Member States where it operated, at considerably varying price levels. The bananas were of identical quality, were sold in an identical condition, and in the same place (usually Bremerhaven or Rotterdam). The Commission, in a decision upheld by the Court of Justice, found this to be an infringement of Article 82(c).

3.324 It seems rather far-reaching, on the face of it, that Article 82 should be extended to apply to a company which pursues a different pricing policy in different national markets. It should be noted, however, that the Commission and Court appear to have been particularly influenced by what they saw as UBC's deliberate attempt to partition the Community along national market lines, in particular by imposing obligations on its customers not to resell green bananas. This additional restriction had the effect of rendering more difficult the possibilities for arbitrage via the development of a cross-border wholesale trade in bananas. The resale restrictions and discriminatory pricing were separately condemned by the Commission and Court.

3.325 UBC argued that its pricing policy was objectively justified in that it was charging what the market would bear, and that this differed significantly from one geographic market to the other. The reasons for these differences depended, according to UBC, on a variety of locally-specific factors such as seasonal demand variations and so on.

3.326 The Commission and Court refused to accept that different market conditions pertaining in the various Member States could amount to an objective justification for the price differences. In reaching this conclusion, the Commission placed particular emphasis on the fact that identical bananas were usually sold in the same place at widely varying prices. The Court appeared also to rely on the fact that UBC was not itself directly selling in the markets concerned, but only to resellers who were selling there; only the latter were bearing the risks inherent in the local markets, and so only they would need to take into account local market specificities in setting price levels.

In *Tetra Pak II*, however, the Commission and Court condemned geographical   **3.327**
price discrimination by a vertically integrated dominant firm selling directly to
customers in a variety of national markets. In that case, also, the differences
between the prices charged in the various Member States were very considerable.
The Commission and Court did not accept that the price differences could have
any legitimate explanation other than as an attempt to partition the common
market along national lines. Again, as in *United Brands*, the Commission and
Court placed reliance on the fact that resale restrictions were imposed on Tetra
Pak's customers and, again, the resale restrictions and discriminatory pricing were
separately condemned.

This approach has, with a degree of justification, been sharply condemned by   **3.328**
some commentators.[257] It can be argued that, in cases such as those just described,
it is the resale restrictions alone which should be condemned. The possibility of
arbitrage should ensure that markets become more integrated notwithstanding
the price discrimination (though in the case of integrated firms selling directly to
consumers, this would be more difficult).

It is certainly unreasonable to prohibit geographical price discrimination, at least   **3.329**
by integrated firms, where selling costs (advertising, promotional, or fiscal costs,
for example) in the various national markets differ to any great extent. It is even
arguable that the approach adopted by the Commission and Court in *United
Brands* and *Tetra Pak II* amounts to giving dominant companies the responsibility for the implementation of public policy. The approach might be seen as requiring such firms to charge more or less uniform prices across all Member States,
thereby depriving them of the possibility of pricing optimally (availing of the differing price levels in the different Member States) in the same way as non-dominant companies can.

In *Irish Sugar*, the Commission impugned a series of abuses aimed at protecting   **3.330**
the Irish sugar market from imports. These included an *ad hoc* rebate scheme
operated periodically by the dominant supplier of sugar in Ireland, whose purpose was patently protectionist. The scheme sought to restrict imports from
Northern Ireland (where sugar prices were usually lower than in the Republic),
including reimports of Irish Sugar's own products, by offering so-called 'border
rebates' to customers on the Irish side of the border area, the clear aim being to
discourage them from importing sugar from Northern Ireland. The company
also indulged in 'selective pricing' of Irish Sugar's own retail brand, offering it to
some customers at lower prices than others—particularly where those customers

---

[257] See Mario Siragusa, *The application of Article 86 to the pricing policy of dominant companies:
discriminatory and unfair prices*; Michael Waelbroek, *Price discrimination and rebate policies under
EU Competition Law.*

had started to stock, or had expressed an interest in stocking, imported sugar brands.[258]

3.331 Finally, a peculiar form of geographical price discrimination was also sanctioned by the Commission in *Irish Sugar*. The dominant supplier had been operating a system of so-called 'sugar export rebates', whereby rebates were granted on sales of industrial sugar to companies exporting the final processed products from Ireland to other Member States. The Commission found that this scheme of rebates was a clear example of discrimination with trade distorting consequences. Irish Sugar claimed that domestic processors were not placed at a competitive disadvantage *vis-à-vis* the exporters, as the two were competing on different markets. However, the Commission pointed out that the rebate scheme also discriminated against the local processors by placing them at a competitive disadvantage *vis-à-vis* third parties, such as importers into Ireland of processed sugar products from other Member States.[259] It remains to be seen whether the Courts will uphold the Commission's interpretation of what is meant by the notion of 'competitive disadvantage' in this context.

D. Effect on Trade between Member States

3.332 The same principle outlined regarding Article 81 applies to Article 82. Indeed, it will be considered that an abuse of a dominant position affects trade between Member States when it is capable of influencing, either directly or indirectly, actually or potentially the patterns of trade in goods or services between Member States. (See Chapter 2 for a more detailed analysis of this question.)

3.333 A circumstance specific to Article 82 should, however, be considered here. In the case of elimination of a competitor by an undertaking holding a dominant position it is not necessary to analyse whether this elimination would have an impact on trade patterns within the common market. It is not necessary to analyse, therefore, whether the eliminated competitor's presence in the market would have had a substantial impact on export or import activity. The ECJ considers that even if trade between Member States is not directly affected, it is sufficient to show that there will be repercussions on the competitive structure of the common market.[260]

---

[258] Similar rebates were also impugned by the the Commission and Courts in *BPB Industries*.
[259] See *Irish Sugar* [1997] OJ L258/1, para 140.
[260] Cases 6 and 7/73 *Commercial Solvents v Commission* [1974] ECR 223.

E. Relationship between Article 81 and Article 82

(1) A Common Purpose

Both Articles 81 and 82 serve the principles set out in Articles 2 and 3(g) of the **3.334** Treaty. That is to say, they are both instrumental in facilitating the establishment and maintenance of a common market, and they together comprise 'a system ensuring that competition . . . is not distorted'[261] in that market. The two provisions are aimed at policing the market behaviour of commercial undertakings. Article 86 and Articles 88–90 (former Articles 92–94), by contrast, are concerned with public measures which have the effect of distorting competition in the common market.

The Court of Justice clearly sees Articles 81 and 82 as the two branches of a single **3.335** bifurcated antitrust system. In *Continental Can*,[262] the Court stressed that, because the two articles ultimately pursue the same basic objective, they 'cannot be interpreted in such a way that they contradict each other'. This means that care must be taken to ensure that Articles 81 and 82 are applied in a coherent fashion.

Articles 83–85 (former Articles 87–89) of the EC Treaty, as well as the relevant **3.336** implementing legislation, in particular Council Regulation No. 17, apply to both Articles 81 and 82. Article 83 provides the legal basis for such implementing rules, while Article 85 specifically prescribes an enforcement function for the Commission in respect of Articles 81 and 82. Article 84 is concerned with transitional arrangements.

(2) Differences

While Articles 81 and 82 serve the same basic purpose, they are nevertheless inde- **3.337** pendent instruments, designed to remedy broadly different commercial situations. The principal differences between them can be summarized as follows.

First, Article 82 is essentially concerned with unilateral conduct by a single dom- **3.338** inant firm,[263] while Article 81 is addressed to concerted behaviour or agreements between companies. Secondly, a finding that Article 81 has been infringed must involve establishing that the agreement has an anti-competitive object or effect, whereas conduct falling foul of Article 82 need not have been intended to restrict competition or to have had such effect. It is sufficient to demonstrate that the dominant company has behaved in an exploitative manner. Thirdly, unlike in the case of Article 81, the relevant market for the application of Article 82 must constitute the whole or at least a substantial part of the common market. Finally,

---

[261] Article 3(g) EC Treaty.
[262] [1973] ECR 215, para 25.
[263] Or, in the case of collective dominance, by more than one dominant company.

Article 82 contains neither a provision for automatic nullity equivalent to Article 81(2), nor a provision for exemption equivalent to Article 81(3).

(3) Parallel Application of the Two Articles

3.339 The Court of Justice made it clear in *Hoffmann-La Roche*[264] that, where an agreement appears to infringe both Articles 81 and 82, either Article may be applied. It also now seems clear that both Articles 81 and 82 can simultaneously be applied to the same agreement or conduct. The Commission sought to do this in *Italian Flat Glass*, a case involving the notion of collective dominance (discussed in detail at paragraph 3.95 above). Although the Commission's decision was struck down on other grounds, the Court of First Instance recognized that the same conduct could be both incompatible with Article 81(1) and Article 82. It went on to say, however, that 'for the purposes of establishing an infringement of Article 86 [now Article 82], it is not sufficient . . . to "recycle" the facts constituting an infringement of Article 85 [now Article 81]'.

3.340 There had initially been some doubt as to the Court of Justice's attitude towards the simultaneous application of both articles to the same subject matter. In *Ahmed Saeed*,[265] the Court seemed to consider that it would only be possible to apply Article 82 to an agreement falling foul of Article 81 where the agreement 'simply constitutes the formal measure setting the seal on an economic reality characterized by the fact that an undertaking in a dominant position has succeeded in having the . . . [agreements] . . . in question applied by other undertakings'. This seemed to imply that, in order for there to be simultaneous application of the two articles, it would be necessary to demonstrate that the abuse in reality consisted in a unilateral imposition by the dominant company of the agreements in question. In *Almelo*,[266] however, the Court of Justice clearly held that the application by a group of companies holding a collective dominant position of an exclusive purchasing obligation could be at the same time contrary to both Articles 81 and 82.

(4) Relationship between Articles 81(3) and 82

3.341 It is clear that Articles 81 and 82 operate independently of each other, and that the application of one cannot prevent the application of the other. The fact that Article 81(3) may be applicable to an agreement falling under Article 81(1) does not preclude the application of Article 82 to the same agreement.

3.342 A conflict between exemption and abuse is most likely to arise in the context of an agreement which benefits from a block exemption, it being unlikely that an individual exemption would be granted to an agreement infringing or likely to in the

---

[264] Case 85/76 *Hoffman-La Roche v Commission* [1979] ECR 461, para 116.
[265] Case 66/86 [1989] ECR 803.
[266] Case C–393/92 [1994] ECR I–1477.

future infringe Article 82. In deciding whether to grant such an exemption, the Commission can be assumed to have given consideration to the applicability of Article 82. Moreover, the final condition for the granting of an exemption pursuant to Article 81(3), namely that an exempted agreement should not facilitate the elimination of competition in respect of a substantial part of the products in question, amounts to a test which is largely equivalent to the application of Article 82. The applicability of a block exemption does not, however, contain the same implication that Article 82 is not infringed, and it therefore provides no protection against its application. Apart from the fact that no individual assessment will have been made of the agreement in question, a block exemption is a piece of secondary legislation and cannot therefore override a Treaty provision.

In *Tetra Pak I*, the Court of First Instance confirmed the Commission's finding that the acquisition by Tetra Pak of an exclusive patent licence was contrary to Article 82. The fact that the licence containing the exclusivity provision benefited from an exemption by virtue of the patent licensing block exemption (Regulation 2349/84) did not affect the possibility of finding such an infringement. The Commission in any event made it clear that, had Tetra Pak not renounced all claims to the exclusivity before the Commission Decision was taken, it would have withdrawn the benefit of the block exemption and found an infringement of Article 81. Indeed, in a block exemption concerning shipping conferences,[267] the Regulation explicitly provides that, where the Commission finds that the conduct of the conferences benefiting from the exemption has effects which are incompatible with Article 82, it may withdraw the benefit of the block exemption and take measures to terminate the infringements. **3.343**

F. Remedies

Article 82 prohibits the abuse of a dominant position but it does not make any reference to the remedies to be applied once such abuse has been found to have taken place. Remedies that have been imposed by the Commission and the Courts are described below. **3.344**

(1) Termination of the Infringement

Article 3 of Regulation No. 17 provides for the Commission to adopt a decision requiring undertakings to terminate their infringements of the competition rules in the EC Treaty. This decision is binding on the undertakings to which it is addressed and it normally takes effect immediately, even if in some cases the Commission may grant a delay for the termination of such infringements.[268] **3.345**

---

[267] Commission Regulation 4056/86, Article 8.
[268] For instance, in *Magill TV Guide* [1989] OJ L78/43, the parties were given two months to bring the infringements to an end

3.346 A decision ordering the termination of an abuse within the meaning of Article 82 will normally consist in an order to cease an action. The order can also extend to any future behaviour having a similar effect to the conduct deemed to be abusive.[269]

3.347 The decision may also require the undertaking having abused its dominant position to adopt a certain course of action. As the Court of Justice held in *Commercial Solvents*,[270] the decision can include:

> an order to do certain acts or provide certain advantages which have been wrongfully withheld, such as prohibiting the continuation of certain actions, practices or situations which are contrary to the EC Treaty.

3.348 An order to adopt a certain course of action will be more likely in the case of a refusal to deal. It may oblige a resumption of supply, if this had been interrupted by the dominant undertaking,[271] or it might require the granting of access to any facility or information which had been denied. In both cases, the Commission can order that the access terms be reasonable,[272] but should not interfere in the principle of freedom to contract, except to the extent that this is strictly necessary.[273]

(2) Nullity of Agreements Concluded in Breach of Article 82

3.349 Article 82 does not include a provision equivalent to Article 81(2), which prescribes that any agreements or decisions prohibited by Article 81(1) shall be automatically void. Nevertheless, the ECJ has stated that a similar consequence applies to any breach of Article 82.[274] The nullity of contracts concluded in breach of Article 82 can be enforced by national courts, in view of the direct applicability of Article 82.

(3) Structural Remedies

3.350 Article 3 of Regulation 17 only allows the Commission to issue an order to terminate the abuse. There is no provision enabling the Commission to avoid such an abuse being repeated by imposing a modification in the market structure, for example by requiring a divestiture by the dominant undertaking.

3.351 Structural remedies, however, could probably be adopted in cases where the abuse derives directly from the market structure (see above under structural abuses). For instance, in *Continental Can*,[275] the Commission considered that the acquisition of a competitor by a dominant undertaking amounted to an abuse of Article 82,

---

[269] *Hilti* [1988] OJ L65/19.
[270] Cases 6 and 7/73 *Commercial Solvents v Commission* [1974] ECR 223.
[271] Cases 6 and 7/73 *Commercial Solvents v Commission* [1974] ECR 223.
[272] As it did in *Magill TV Guide* [1989] OJ L78/43.
[273] See Case T–24/90 *Automec v Commission II* [1992] ECR II–2223.
[274] Case 172/73 *BRT v SABAM* [1974] ECR 51.
[275] Case 6/72 *Europemballage and Continental Can v Commission* [1973] ECR 215.

and required the dominant company to dispose of the acquired company. The order was not applied, however, because the ECJ annulled the decision on substantive grounds.

(4) Fines

Article 15 of Regulation 17 allows the Commission to impose fines on under- **3.352** takings that infringe Article 82. Fines can be applied for infringements made either intentionally or negligently. They may range from ECU 1,000 to ECU 1,000,000, or a sum in excess thereof but not exceeding 10 per cent of the turnover in the preceding business year of each of the undertakings participating in the infringement.

According to the Guidelines on the method of setting fines adopted by the **3.353** Commission[276] an abuse of a dominant position will normally constitute a serious infringement, and so will normally result in the imposition of a fine ranging between ECU 1 million and ECU 20 million. Clear-cut abuses of a dominant position by undertakings holding a virtual monopoly, however, might be considered very serious infringements, and may attract fines above ECU 20 million.

Within each of these categories, the fine will be set according to the nature of the **3.354** infringement committed, the effective economic capacity of offenders to cause significant damage to other operators, the deterrent effect, and the size of the undertaking committing the infringement. In addition, for infringements of medium duration (one to five years) the fine could be increased by up to 50 per cent, and for infringements of long duration (more than five years) by up to 10 per cent per year. Aggravating and attenuating circumstances will also be taken into account.

To date, the largest fines in a case involving an abuse of a single dominant position **3.355** were imposed in *Tetra Pak II*[277] and amounted to ECU 75 million. The largest fines for abuse of a collective dominant position were imposed in *TACA*[278] and amounted to 273 million euros. Other large fines in Article 82 cases have been imposed in *AKZO*,[279] where they amounted to ECU 7.5 million, in *British Sugar*[280] and *BPB Industries/British Gypsum*,[281] in each of which a fine of ECU 3 million was imposed.

---

[276] Guidelines on the method of setting fines imposed pursuant to Article15(2) of Regulation 17 and Article 65(5) of the ECSC Treaty [1998] OJ C9.

[277] Case T–83/91 *Tetra Pak International v Commission* [1994] ECR II–755.

[278] *TACA* [1998] OJ L95/1.

[279] Case C–62/86 *Akzo v Commission* [1991] ECR I–3359.

[280] *British Sugar* [1988] OJ L284/41.

[281] Case T–65/89 *BPB Industries/British Gypsum* [1993] ECR II–389.

4

MERGERS

A. Introduction to the Merger Regulation

European Merger Control

4.01 Council Regulation (EEC) 4064/89 on the control of concentrations between undertakings[1] ('the Merger Regulation') provided the Community, for the first time, with an adequate instrument for the control of cross-border concentrations.

4.02 From the outset the Merger Regulation has had two goals: first, to provide a means to prevent anti-competitive concentrations and, secondly, to provide a single framework within which such transactions may be assessed. This single framework operating at a Community level arrives at definitive conclusions on a timely basis. This 'one-stop shop' assessment of mergers has replaced the numerous national legislative regimes for those operations that have a Community dimension subject to the exceptions that are discussed below.

4.03 Council Regulation (EC) 1310/97 amending Regulation (EEC) 4064/89 on the control of concentrations between undertakings[2] ('the Amending Regulation') was adopted following broad discussions with industry, the legal profession,

---

[1] [1989] OJ L395/1 (amended [1990] OJ L257/13).
[2] [1997] OJ L180/1.

Member States, the European Parliament, and the Economic and Social Committee, including the issue of a Green Paper.[3]

Legal Requirement for the Review

4.04 The legal requirements for the review of the Merger Regulation, which are set out in Article 1(3), required that the threshold criteria be reconsidered; similarly Article 9(10) required that Article 9 be reappraised; finally Article 22(6) required a reassessment of Article 22 in the light of any changes made to Article 1. The Commission's proposal in 1993 in its Report from the Commission to the Council[4] had concluded that further experience of the operation of the Merger Regulation was required before any proposals for change were made. However, the proposal also concluded that a review would take place before the end of 1996.

Specific Items Requiring Review

4.05 In addition to the legal requirement to review thresholds and the mechanism for the referral of cases to and from the Member States, the Commission also reviewed the question of multiple notifications (ie transactions without a Community dimension but requiring notification under the laws of several Member States); the treatment of joint ventures; the acceptance of remedies in first phase investigations; the definition of banking income; and the application of Article 7 concerning a suspension of the concentration.

The Main Changes Made by the Amending Regulation

4.06 The main changes brought about by the Amending Regulation were as follows:

— multiple notifications: thresholds have been amended so that multiple notifications may, in certain circumstances, have a Community dimension;

— joint ventures: full-function joint ventures (and not simply concentrative joint ventures) are brought under the Merger Regulation. Co-ordination of competitive behaviour of undertakings remaining independent is to be assessed under the EC Treaty Article 81 (former Article 85);

— the use of assets to determine banking income is replaced by a test based on gross banking income;

— remedies may be accepted in first phase cases;

— Article 7 is amended so that the concentration is suspended until either an Article 6 or an Article 8 decision is adopted;

— the 'serious damage' test under Article 7 has been removed;

— Article 9 has been changed to make the referral of a case to a Member State more flexible.

---

[3] COM (96) 19 final.
[4] COM (93) 385 final.

(It should be noted that all references to articles in this chapter are to articles of the Merger Regulation.)

B. The Merger Regulation:
Matters of Jurisdiction and Substance

(1) Introduction

The Merger Regulation applies exclusively to *concentrations with a Community* **4.07** *dimension*. This exclusivity is multifaceted. First, it means that the Merger Regulation cannot be applied to any type of transaction which does not meet its definition of a concentration. Secondly, it means that only Community legislation applies to concentrations.[5] Consequently, the competition authorities in the Member States have no jurisdiction over operations that fulfil the conditions of the Merger Regulation.[6] It should, however, be noted that a concentration, which falls to be assessed under the Merger Regulation, may also be subject to one or several extra-Community jurisdictions.

In 1994, in an effort to increase the efficiency and transparency of the Merger **4.08** Regulation, the Commission adopted four Interpretative Notices.[7] Following the adoption of the Amending Regulation each of these four Notices has been updated.[8] Their purpose is to set out the principles relating to the main jurisdictional criteria relating to the Merger Regulation. The logic of the four Notices is as follows: the Notices on the concept of 'concentration' and on the concept of a 'full-function joint venture' provide the basis for deciding if a given operation meets the definition of a concentration. If it does, the other two Notices, on the concept of 'undertakings concerned' and 'calculation of turnover', help determine whether it has Community dimension.

Each of the four Notices and their interaction is discussed below.

---

[5] Article 22(1) and (2). Theoretically, the Commission could apply the EC Treaty Articles 81 (former Article 85) and 82 (former Article 86) by means of Article 85 (former Article 89). However, the Commission has stated that it normally does not intend to use this possibility (see Commission Notes on Council Regulation (EEC) 4064/89, published together with the Merger Regulation itself). In practice, the Commission has not intervened against any concentration on the basis of Article 85.

[6] Article 21(2) and (3). For exemptions from this principle relating to the protection of legitimate interests other than those protected by the Merger Regulation, see below para 4.121.

[7] The fifth Interpretative Notice, on restrictions ancillary to concentrations, is not intended for jurisdictional purposes as such. It is discussed separately below, see para 4.123.

[8] [1998] OJ C66.

(2) A Concentration: Article 3 of the Merger Regulation

4.09   According to Article 3 a concentration is defined as an operation whereby two previously independent parties merge, or whereby control is acquired over the whole
or parts of another undertaking. The purpose is to include only operations that
bring about a lasting change in the structure of the undertakings concerned.[9] The
main principles for deciding whether a given operation meets this definition are
set out in the Notice on the concept of concentration under Council Regulation
(EEC) 4064/89 on the control of concentrations between undertakings.[10] This
Notice is of general applicability to all mergers and acquisitions of control.
Additional guidance on the application of Article 3(2), in the specific cases of joint
ventures, is provided in the Notice on the concept of full-function joint ventures
under Council Regulation (EEC) 4064/89 on the control of concentrations
between undertakings.[11]

Mergers—Article 3(1)(a)

4.10   The distinguishing feature of a true merger is that one or more pre-existing undertakings, as a result of the transaction, cease to exist as individual economic entities.

4.11   In the sense of Article 3(1)(a), a merger occurs when two or more independent
undertakings amalgamate into a new undertaking and cease to exist as separate
legal entities. A merger may also occur when an undertaking is absorbed by
another, the latter retaining its legal identity while the former ceases to exist as a
legal entity. Even in the absence of a legal merger, an operation resulting in the
legal or *de facto* creation of a single economic unit into which the activities or
interests of previously independent undertakings are transferred may be considered to be a merger.[12] A prerequisite for a finding of a common economic unit is
the existence of a permanent, single economic management. Other relevant factors may include internal profit and loss compensation as between the various
undertakings within the group, and their joint liability externally. The *de facto*
amalgamation may be reinforced by cross-shareholdings between the undertakings forming the economic unit.

4.12   Perhaps surprisingly a relatively small proportion of cases notified under the
Merger Regulation are mergers. Overall, in the first eight years of application
(1990–1997) fewer than 3 per cent of all notified cases fell into this category.
From a jurisdictional viewpoint mergers tend to be relatively uncomplicated.
First, these cases clearly constitute concentrations within the meaning of the

---

[9]   See Recital 23 to the Merger Regulation.
[10]   [1998] OJ C66/5.
[11]   [1998] OJ C66/1.
[12]   See, eg, *RTZ/CRA* (Case IV/M660) (1995).

Merger Regulation. Secondly, the Community dimension test is normally straightforward, since the merging companies will always be considered as the undertakings concerned for the purposes of the turnover thresholds.

The Acquisition of Control (Article 3(3))

An acquisition of control is characterized by one or more undertakings attaining, **4.13** on a legal or *de facto* basis, the ability to make the strategic decisions for one or more other undertakings.

The vast majority of all cases notified under the Merger Regulation are acquisi- **4.14** tions of control. Such acquisitions can be made by one company ('sole control'), or by two or more companies ('joint control'). Joint control distinguishes itself primarily by providing its holders with a negative form of control, for example the right to *veto* strategic decisions proposed by one or more of the jointly controlling partners. By way of contrast, sole control confers the positive ability to impose strategic decisions on the controlled entity.[13]

It follows that the concept of 'control' is central to the application of the Merger **4.15** Regulation. The definition of control in Article 3(3) does not distinguish between sole and joint control. In both cases control is defined as the:

> rights, contracts or any other means which, either separately or in combination and having regard to the considerations of fact or law involved, confer the possibility of exercising decisive influence on an undertaking, in particular by:
>
> (a) ownership or the right to use all or part of the assets of an undertaking;
> (b) rights or contracts which confer decisive influence on the composition, voting or decisions of the organs of an undertaking.

Decisive Influence

The Merger Regulation's aim is to provide an efficient system for pre-merger con- **4.16** trol. It therefore necessarily takes a structural approach to the question whether a transaction will enable the acquirer(s) to exercise control over the target company.

The key expression in Article 3(3) is 'the possibility of exercising decisive influ- **4.17** ence on an undertaking'. Therefore, for the purposes of the Merger Regulation, it is irrelevant whether the acquirer of control will actually exercise the decisive influence, or indeed whether the acquisition of control was the intended result of the arrangement. This is consistent with the Merger Regulation's aim to provide a system for pre-merger control, as it would be impractical for notifying parties if they were obliged to show that a notified operation actually led to the new acquirer(s) exercising control over the target company.

---

[13] The question whether an operation gives rise to the acquisition of sole or joint control has important consequences for the definition of the 'undertakings concerned', and therefore for the question whether an operation has Community dimension. See below para 4.85.

4.18 It should also be noted that the concept of control is based on qualitative rather than quantitative criteria. This means that considerations of both law and fact will be taken into account when considering whether a certain operation amounts to a concentration in the meaning of the Merger Regulation. The existence and consequences of shareholders' agreements are always taken into account. Control may also be conferred by other agreements relating to intellectual property rights, long-term supply arrangements, or credits.

The Identity of the Acquirer

The Main Rule

4.19 In most cases the identity of the acquirer is unimportant as to whether an operation constitutes a concentration. This is the case in all circumstances when control is acquired by a company, or some other private legal entity, in which case normally no difficulties arise.

Natural Persons

4.20 The Merger Regulation is, however, also applicable if one or more natural persons acquire control over an undertaking, provided that they already control at least one undertaking.[14] In *EDFI/Graninge*,[15] joint control over Graninge was acquired by the Electricité de France group (EDF) and a number of individuals, who were all descendants of the founder of the company. None of these individuals held economic interests outside Graninge. The question of whether these individuals could be considered as undertakings concerned was, however, left open, since EDF would in any case acquire (joint) control over Graninge, which meant that the operation, regardless of the position of the family members, constituted a concentration with a Community dimension.[16]

State or Other Public Bodies

4.21 Another particular situation is when both the acquiring and the acquired undertakings are owned by the same State or other public body. Such operations fall under the Merger Regulation only if the two undertakings have been parts of different economic units with independent powers of decision.[17] A recent example of this was the merger between the two Finnish State controlled companies Neste and IVO. Although the companies previously had been controlled by the same Member State, the operation was considered to constitute a concentration in the meaning of the Merger Regulation since the companies had had separate and independent management structure.[18]

---

[14] See Article 3(1)(b).
[15] Case IV/M1169 (1998).
[16] See also *Asko/Jakobs/Adia* (Case IV/M82) (1991).
[17] See recital 12 of the Merger Regulation.
[18] *Neste/IVO* (Case IV/M931) (1998) and *Pechiney/Usinor* (Case IV/M97) (1991).

Acquisition Vehicles

Article 3(4)(b) provides the possibility to 'see through' the formal acquirer of con- **4.22** trol if it can be established that the formal acquirer is used as a vehicle by another person or undertaking, which will in fact exercise that control.

The Object of Control

The target of a notified operation is in most cases one or several undertakings **4.23** which each constitute legal entities. In those cases it is immaterial whether the operation concerns the acquisition of the legal entity itself or its assets. However, the object of an acquisition of control can also be a part of a company's assets, for example its brands or licences, provided that the assets in question constitute a business to which a market turnover can be attributed.[19]

The Concept of Sole Control

An operation involving the acquisition of sole control can take two forms. The **4.24** acquirer can, prior to the operation, be in a position of having no decisive influence over the target company (a change from no control to sole control). Alternatively, the acquirer may already, prior to the operation, have joint control over the target company (a change from joint to sole control). The latter situation, which was first considered in *ICI/Tioxide*,[20] is a concentration in the meaning of the Merger Regulation because decisive influence exercised alone is substantially different from decisive influence exercised jointly.

Sole control is normally based on the ownership of an amount of shares in a target **4.25** company sufficient to control that company. Such ownership rights may be coupled with contractual arrangements between two or more shareholders. Finally, other contractual arrangements such as options or financing arrangements may be of importance in assessing the control structure of a company.

Considerations Based on Ownership of Shares

As indicated earlier, sole control confers the positive ability to impose strategic **4.26** decisions on the controlled entity. In the normal case of the acquisition of shares, the test is what proportion of voting rights the acquirer will hold after the operation. If the Memorandum or Articles of Association of the target company do not contain any specific requirements regarding qualified majorities for strategic decisions, an acquisition of shares that will give the acquirer more than 50 per cent of the votes will be seen as an acquisition of sole control.

In particular in publicly quoted companies, an acquisition of a qualified minority **4.27** holding of less than 50 per cent of the voting rights will often be sufficient to

---

[19] See *Saint-Gobain/Wacker Chimie/NOM* (Case IV/M774) (1996) [1997] OJ L247/1.
[20] Case IV/M23 (1990).

confer *de facto* sole control. This is the case since, in such companies, it is unlikely that all the smaller shareholders will be present or represented at a shareholders' meeting. Based on evidence of the presence of shareholders at such meetings in previous years (normally the last three years), an assessment must be made to determine whether the holder of a qualified majority will be likely to achieve a majority at future meetings. If that is the case, then sole control is deemed to exist. For example see *Anglo American Corporation/Lonrho*,[21] where a holding of 27.5 per cent of the share capital and votes was considered to give Anglo American sole control over Lonrho.[22]

4.28 On the other hand, an acquisition of shares that will not give the acquirer a legal or *de facto* majority of the voting rights cannot in itself confer control over the target company. This is so, even if more than 50 per cent (or possibly even 100 per cent) of the share capital will be held by the acquirer. In particular, it is necessary to ascertain that factors such as different voting rights or shareholders' agreements do not alter the impression given by the size of the shareholding.[23]

Considerations Based on Contractual Arrangements

4.29 The most common type of contractual arrangement conferring control over another company is the shareholders' agreement. As is indicated by the term, the parties to such agreements are normally shareholders in the target company. If such an agreement is concluded between shareholders, accounting together for the required majority of voting rights, and provides one shareholder with the ability to manage or determine the strategic behaviour of the target, or to appoint the majority of the managing body of the target, that shareholder will be considered to have sole control over the company. Apart from shareholders' agreements, any other legally binding agreement conferring on a given party the rights indicated above could in principle form the basis for an acquisition of sole control. Theoretically, sole control could even be acquired by a company that does not hold any shares at all in the target company.

Options and Other Financial Arrangements

4.30 Put and call options are contractual arrangements whereby two or more parties agree to the terms of a future transaction. Although such agreements may, at the time of their exercise, be of relevance for the control of the target company, they do not normally, prior to their exercise, lead to a change in the control structure. Option agreements are therefore normally not considered as triggering a concentration in the sense of the Merger Regulation.[24]

---

[21] Case IV/M754 (1997) [1988] OJ L149/21.
[22] See also *Société Generale de Belgique/Generale de Banque* (Case IV/M343) (1993).
[23] See, eg, *Crédit Lyonnais/BFG Bank* (Case IV/M296) (1993).
[24] Case T–2/93 *Air France v Commission* [1994] ECR II–323.

However, in situations where it is clear that the option will be exercised in the near **4.31** future, in accordance with legally binding arrangements, the option agreements are taken into consideration along with other elements, such as contractual arrangements or minority acquisitions. Thus, if based on an overall assessment, it is concluded that *de facto* a change of control will occur prior to the exercise of the option, a notifiable concentration will be deemed to arise at that earlier date. For example, in *KLM/Air UK*,[25] the Commission found that KLM had acquired *de facto* joint control of Air UK through a minority holding (14.9 per cent) and option agreements coupled with a complex package of financial arrangements. KLM was able to demonstrate that it had, partly due to the option agreements, in practice had the possibility to exercise a joint decisive influence over the target company.

The Concept of Joint Control

Under the Merger Regulation a company that is jointly controlled by two or more **4.32** parents is referred to as a joint venture. As indicated above, joint control distinguishes itself by the fact that the jointly controlling companies (the parent companies) must all agree on the major decisions concerning the joint venture. The decisive influence exercised by the parents of a joint venture means the power to veto actions which are decisive for the strategic, commercial behaviour of the joint venture. The power to veto such actions will result in deadlock unless an agreement between the parent companies is reached. Since the joint venture would not be able to function properly in that deadlock situation, the parent companies will be forced to reach an agreement, or simply to terminate the joint venture. Therefore, each parent company has decisive influence over the joint venture.

Joint control is only relevant for the purposes of the Merger Regulation if it can be **4.33** seen to be acquired on a lasting basis. In *BS/BT*,[26] the Commission concluded that a situation of joint control that would last only for a start-up period of, at most, three years gave rise to an acquisition of sole control for the parent that will retain its decisive influence after the start-up period. The same case also illustrates the principle that, while joint control is clearly incompatible with the existence of casting votes for either parent company, a casting vote can be accepted if it applies only after a series of arbitration procedures, or in a very limited field.

Equality between Parent Companies

The classical scenario, where two parent companies share the voting rights on a **4.34** 50/50 basis, is the only situation where joint control will be presumed to exist even in the absence of any agreement to that effect. It should, however, be noted that, even in this scenario, any contractual arrangements that deviate from the

---

[25] Case IV/M967 (1997).
[26] Case IV/M425 (1994).

principle of equality, for example by entitling one parent to a larger number of board representatives, is liable to rebut this presumption. Consequently a conclusion would be reached that sole control exists.[27]

4.35 In other situations, where three or more parents share the voting rights in the joint venture on an equal basis, joint control will normally be established through a shareholders' agreement or simply by an indication in the Memorandum or Articles of Association of the joint venture that decisions of strategic, commercial importance will require approval of all parent companies. Thus, when a joint venture has more than two parents with equal voting rights, additional elements will have to be present to establish joint control. These additional elements follow the same principle as in situations of inequality between parent companies described below.

Inequality between Parent Companies

4.36 In cases where two parent companies have unequal voting rights in a joint venture, or where there are more than two parent companies, joint control is normally established by provisions conferring veto rights on each parent. Such veto rights are generally set out in a shareholders' agreement or in the Memorandum or Articles of Association of the joint venture. A provision that certain decisions require a quorum of shareholders' votes, including the minority shareholder(s') votes as well as those of the majority shareholder, will in effect constitute a veto right. For example, where the voting rights in a company are held by three parties (Company A: 50 per cent, Company B and C: 25 per cent each), a quorum of 80 per cent of the voting rights will effectively constitute a veto right for each shareholder.[28]

4.37 The veto rights may relate to decisions to be taken at the shareholders' meeting, the board of directors, the supervisory board, etc. The decisive question is, regardless of the level where the veto rights may be exercised, whether they will afford each parent the ability to exercise decisive influence on the strategic, commercial decisions of the joint venture.

Strategic, Commercial Veto Rights

Management, Budget, and Business Plan

4.38 In general, the most important strategic decisions relating to the joint venture's commercial behaviour are those relating to the appointment of its management, and approval of its budget and business plan. Where a minority shareholder holds

---

[27] See, eg, *Matra/Cap Gemini Sogeti* (Case IV/M272) (1993).

[28] If, in the same example, no quorum rules exist, the shareholder with 50% will effectively enjoy the type of negative, or veto-based, influence that is characteristic of joint control. This shareholder will therefore be considered to acquire control in the meaning of the Merger Regulation.

a veto over these matters, there is a strong indication of the existence of joint control. Although joint venture agreements often involve veto rights in all these areas, joint control can be found even if only some, or one, have been included, provided that this veto right is sufficient to confer a decisive influence. A veto over the appointment of management may be sufficient in itself, in particular if the budget and business plan are of a relatively general nature, thus leaving strategic decisions to the management of the company. On the other hand, if the budget and business plan provide details of the aims of the joint venture as well as the means to achieve them, the role of the management may be more of a day-to-day than strategic nature. In such situations a veto right relating to the budget and/or business plan of the joint venture may confer control on its holder.

Market Specific Rights

In some circumstances joint control may be conferred by veto rights on matters **4.39** other than the appointment of the joint venture's management, and approval of its budget or business plan. This may, for example, be the case if the joint venture will be active on a market where continuous investments are essential. This is normally more likely to be the case in emerging, technology driven markets than in mature markets. If it can be shown that continuous investments will be essential for the strategic market behaviour of the joint venture, a veto on such investments may be sufficient to confer joint control.[29] On the other hand, where a veto on investments only applies to investments of an exceptional value, the veto right may come closer to a normal minority protection right. As in the case of investments, if it can be demonstrated that the decisions as to which technology the joint venture will use are of decisive importance for its future market behaviour, a veto on these decisions may be sufficient to confer joint control.

Overall Assessment

Whether or not, in a specific case, existing veto rights are sufficient to constitute **4.40** joint control will be assessed on the basis of the total 'package' of such rights, having regard also to the business of the joint venture. Where no veto is provided for the traditional areas of appointment of management and approval of budgets and business plans, the notifying parties will have to substantiate a claim of joint control with other specific, conclusive evidence.

Minority Protection

Certain types of veto rights are insufficient to confer joint control. These are, for **4.41** example, the veto rights that a minority shareholder may have in order to protect its financial investment, over questions such as changes to the company's statutes, increases or decreases in the share capital, sale or liquidation of the company.

---

[29] See, eg, *Bell Cablemedia/Cable & Wireless/Videotron* (Case IV/M853) (1996).

Normally these types of veto right are neither intended to, nor have the effect of, allowing the minority shareholders to exercise decisive influence on the strategic, commercial decisions of the joint venture.

Joint Exercise of Voting Rights

4.42 Where two or more minority shareholders agree to pool their voting rights, this may confer on them jointly decisive influence over the target company. In this scenario the same principles will apply as described above concerning sole control at certain levels of shareholding. If the combined shareholding is indeed sufficient to control the target company, the parties to the pooling agreement will be considered to have joint control.

4.43 Even in the absence of a pooling agreement, a strong common interest could be sufficient to establish joint control between minority shareholders. This is the case if it can be demonstrated that strong common interests will mean that the minority shareholders will act together in exercising their voting rights. In two cases notifying parties have unsuccessfully claimed that their respective transactions, on the basis of strong common interests, would result in notifiable concentrations.[30] In both cases the Commission concluded that there was insufficient evidence that the minority shareholders would act together in exercising their voting rights.

Shifting Alliances

4.44 With the exception of the above mentioned possibility of joint control arising on a *de facto* basis between minority shareholders, situations where no stable voting majority can be attributed to two or more minority shareholders will not constitute a concentration. For example, where two shareholders each hold 40 per cent in the target company, but no quorum rules are laid down in its statute and no pooling agreement exists, each party will in future voting situations have to rally support from other smaller shareholders, with the result that neither of the 40 per cent shareholders has a lasting majority. However, as an operation that creates such a structure would not constitute a concentration, in the meaning of the Merger Regulation, no obstacles would exist against applying the EC Treaty Article 81 and/or national competition rules to the operation (see Articles 22(1) and 21(2), Merger Regulation). In addition, if the two shareholders with 40 per cent in the above example subsequently were to conclude a shareholders' agreement, the conclusion of this agreement would confer joint control to both of them, and therefore constitute a concentration under the Merger Regulation.

---

[30] See *Channel Five* (Case IV/M673) (1995) and *Nokia Oy/SP Tyres* (Case IV/M548) (1995).

Changes to the Structure of Control

The Main Rule

As explained above, the Merger Regulation defines the concept of a concentration **4.45**
in terms of an acquisition of control. Moreover, control exercised solely is different in nature from control exercised jointly. The Merger Regulation will therefore
normally apply to transactions leading to a change from sole to joint control, and
vice versa. It will further apply to increases as well as to reductions in the number
of jointly controlling parents.[31]

Exceptions to the Main Rule

Article 3(5) of the Merger Regulation contains three exceptions to the principle **4.46**
that an acquisition of control constitutes a concentration. These exceptions relate
to temporary acquisitions by financial institutions, liquidation and similar proceedings and acquisitions by financial holding companies within the meaning of
Council Directive (EEC) 78/660 based on Article 44(3)(g) of the Treaty on the
annual accounts of certain types of companies.[32]

The purpose of these exceptions is to avoid the notification of transactions which **4.47**
have neither as their object nor their effect acquisition of control over the target
company. As these are exemptions from the general principle, they have been
interpreted strictly. Rescue operations, where banks and other financial institutions transform the debt of an existing company into shares, will typically not fall
within the exception, since, even though the intention may be to transform and
resell the target company, the process of doing so will normally involve taking
control of its commercial strategic behaviour for a period exceeding the one year
allowed in Article 3(5)(a). Rescue operations are therefore normally considered to
constitute concentrations in the meaning of the Merger Regulation.[33]

(3) Full-Function Joint Venture (Articles 3(2) and 2(4))

The Merger Regulation applies to transactions with a structural effect on the mar- **4.48**
ket. A joint venture fulfils this criterion, provided that its actions are not merely
auxiliary to its parent companies, and that it operates on a market in its own right.

The Amending Regulation

The Amending Regulation introduced changes for deciding whether a joint **4.49**
venture falls within the Merger Regulation. The basic change in Article 3(2) is
that the definition of the concept of concentration has been enlarged, so that

---

[31] See, eg, *Avesta (III)* (Case IV/M504) (1994).
[32] [1978] OJ L222/11.
[33] See, eg, *Kelt/American Express* (Case IV/M116) (1991) and *Deutsche Bank/Commerzbank/J.M. Voith* (Case IV/M891) (1997).

full-function joint ventures are no longer excluded from the scope of the Merger Regulation, even if they lead to co-operation between the parent companies outside the joint venture ('spill-over effects').[34] The other main change relating to joint ventures is found in Article 2(4), which provides the legal basis for making an Article 81 assessment of the co-operative aspects resulting from the establishment of a joint venture. Article 2(4) does not *strictu sensu* deal with a jurisdictional distinction (ie whether the Merger Regulation is applicable), but sets out the substantive test to be applied to the spill-over effects resulting from joint ventures. However, it will, for the sake of coherence, be treated in this section.

Full-Function Joint Ventures

4.50 If a company becomes controlled by two or more parent companies, in the meaning set out above, it may fall to be assessed under the Merger Regulation. However, while the colloquial use of the term 'joint venture' may encompass a broad range of operations, ranging from cartel-type to merger-type operations, the applicability of the Merger Regulation is restricted to *full-function joint ventures*. An operation resulting in the creation of such a joint venture is defined in Article 3(2) as 'the creation of a joint venture performing on a lasting basis all the functions of an autonomous economic entity'.

Auxiliary Function

4.51 If a joint venture is not fully equipped to operate on a market, it will be considered auxiliary to one or more of its parent companies. This type of joint venture only undertakes a limited part of the value chain necessary to market a product or service. Joint ventures limited to research and development, production, or sales are therefore normally not considered to be full-function, and consequently fall outside the scope of the Merger Regulation.[35]

Lasting Basis

4.52 Equally, the Merger Regulation will not be applicable unless the joint venture is intended to operate on a lasting basis. Joint ventures of a short, finite duration will not be considered as bringing about a structural change in the companies concerned, and, therefore, on the market. This does not mean that a provision in the joint venture agreement providing for certain contingencies in case of the failure of the venture or of fundamental disagreement between the parents will cause the transaction to be considered as non-structural. In cases where the agreement setting up the joint venture is concluded for an indefinite term, the lasting basis is normally clear. On the other hand, if this indefinite period is subject to possible

---

[34] For an analysis of the applicability of Article 81 to spill-over effects, see in particular Section E of Chapter 6.
[35] Such transactions are consequently subject to Article 81.

early termination by either party, the agreements should provide for a sufficiently long minimum period to bring about a lasting change. In *John Deere Capital/Lombard*,[36] an indefinite joint venture agreement that could be terminated by either party after four years was considered sufficient to bring about a lasting change. Whether a specified duration will be sufficiently long to bring about a structural change in cases where the joint venture agreement defines its duration will depend on the features of the markets in question. An agreement establishing a five-year term may be significant and not easily reversed in certain high-technology industries, where the life cycle of a product can be very short. On the other hand, in more mature markets, a similar period may have significantly less impact in terms of market structure.

Ability to Operate on a Market

A joint venture is considered to be full-function if it is fully equipped to operate **4.53** on a market. This criterion is mainly of interest in cases where the joint venture is created by the operation. In cases concerning the acquisition of a joint control in an existing company, full-functionality can often be presumed to exist.

Basis for the Assessment

A full-function joint venture is normally based on a joint venture agreement **4.54** between the parent companies. Such an agreement will set out the joint venture's business objectives. This is normally the first source of information, describing the parent companies' intentions when setting up the joint venture. The agreement will normally indicate the joint venture's field of commercial activity, the resources allocated for the attainment of its objectives, its management structure, and the extent to which the joint venture will continue to be dependent on its parent companies, for example, in terms of supply and purchase relationships.

Field of Activity and Resources

A joint venture is considered equipped to operate on a market if, in comparison **4.55** with other companies active on that market, it has all the appropriate resources. Such a comparison is necessary, since the required resources will vary significantly between different economic sectors. However, even though relative needs may vary, a full-function joint venture should have the financial resources, the staff, and the tangible and intangible assets needed to meet its objective as stated in the joint venture agreement.

Access to Resources

From an economic perspective it may not be essential that the joint venture owns **4.56** these resources. Alternative solutions whereby certain assets are owned by the

---

[36] Case IV/M823 (1996).

parent company, or a third party, may be equally valid. In *Thomson/Deutsche Aerospace AG*,[37] the licensing of certain intellectual property rights was considered equivalent to the transfer of those rights. Similarly, in *British Gas Trading/Group 4 Utility Services*,[38] one of the parent companies sold certain assets to a financial institution, which subsequently leased the assets to the joint venture. This was considered equivalent to the transfer of those assets to the joint venture.

4.57 The importance of ownership of certain assets may also depend on the degree of independence given to the management of the joint venture. For example, in *Nokia/Autoliv*,[39] the joint venture was dependent for a start-up period on sales to one parent, and also relied on its parents for supplies and certain services. However, since it could be demonstrated that the joint venture would have an independent management, which was genuinely able to terminate these agreements, the company was considered to be a full-function joint venture.

Management of the Joint Venture—'Autonomy'

4.58 The parent companies' control over the joint venture will normally include the appointment of its management, as this clearly represents a strategic decision. This does not, however, normally mean that employees of the parent companies will actually run the day-to-day operations of the joint venture. Instead, for a joint venture to constitute an autonomous economic entity, operational decisions on competitive issues, such as pricing, production volumes, sources of supply and demand, should normally be taken by the joint venture itself.

4.59 If the parent companies are directly involved in its day-to-day operations, a question arises whether the joint venture can be seen to operate on a market, or whether its functions are more properly attributed to the parent companies. Indeed, unless the joint venture has a management that is dedicated to its own operations, the joint venture may resemble a non-structural operation, such as a joint selling agency. In contrast, cases where the joint venture's management has been granted a sufficient degree of independence in the implementation of its business objectives will normally result in a structural change in the companies concerned, and, therefore, on the market. The importance of management having a high degree of independence will normally be greater in cases where the joint venture will continue to have a large number of contractual arrangements with its parent companies.[40]

---

[37] Case IV/M527 (1994).
[38] Case IV/M791 (1996).
[39] Case IV/M686 (1996).
[40] See *Nokia/Autoliv* (Case IV/M686) (1996) and *VAI/Davy International* (Case IV/M585) (1995).

Continued Dependency on Parent Companies

Start-up Periods

It is relatively common that joint ventures, in the start-up period, will be largely **4.60** dependent on one or more parents for administrative services or even for commercial relationships (up- or downstream). Thus, during the initial period, before the joint venture has been able to establish itself on the market, the fact that it will be largely dependent on its parent companies will not disqualify it as a full-function joint venture. However, in such circumstances it must be demonstrated, for example by reference to the joint venture's business plan and the surrounding market characteristics, that this dependency will be substantially reduced, normally within a three-year period.[41] Adaptation of this general principle may be necessary in cases such as *Siemens/Italtel*,[42] where the joint venture was to sell large parts of its products (telecommunication equipment) to one of its parent companies (Telecom Italia). Since this situation was caused by Telecom Italia's downstream, infrastructure monopoly, rather than commercial considerations, the joint venture was still considered to be full-function.

Where the dependency on the parent companies is not limited to a start-up **4.61** period, a distinction must be made between situations where the joint venture will be active on markets upstream or downstream of the parent companies.

Upstream of Parent Companies

When the joint venture will be active on upstream markets, the relative propor- **4.62** tion of its sales to its parent companies will be an important factor in determining its dependency on its parents. When such sales, on a continuous basis, will make up a significant proportion of the joint venture's total production, the operation comes closer to that of a production joint venture. In such cases, other factors may be of importance in deciding whether the joint venture can be considered full-function. These will include the question as to which company assumes financial risk and whether sales to its parent companies are made on normal commercial terms.[43] In exceptional cases one or more parent companies may act as sales agencies for the joint venture. The role of an agent does not include the assumption of commercial risk. The joint venture will therefore in such situations be seen as the real market player. Consequently a joint venture may in such circumstances be considered as full-function, even though a large part of its sales are made through the parent companies. See, for example, *TNT/Canada Post, DBP Postdienst, La*

---

[41] See, eg, *EDS/Lufthansa* (Case IV/M560) (1995) and *RSB/Tenex/Fuel Logistic* (Case IV/M904) (1997).

[42] Case IV/M468 [1995] OJ L161/27.

[43] See, eg, *Zeneca/Vanderhave* (Case IV/M556) (1996) and *Bayer/Hüls-Newco* (Case IV/M751) (1996).

Poste, PTT Post and Sweden Post,[44] where an exclusive agency agreement was accepted for an initial start-up period of two years.

Downstream of Parent Companies

4.63   When the joint venture will be active on a market which is downstream of its parent companies, the question whether it can be characterized as full-function will not solely depend on the relative proportion of its sales that will be made up by products supplied by its parent companies. Of equal importance is the question whether the joint venture will add significant value to its parents' products. This may be the case where the parent companies supply semi-manufactured materials to the joint venture, which will then further process these materials and provide additional service elements, such as installation. On the other hand, if the activities of the joint venture are limited to mere assembly of the materials supplied by the parent companies, it may in reality be closer to a sales agency.

Trade Markets

4.64   A special situation exists, when the joint venture will be active on a trade market. An example of such a trade market is *Texaco/Norsk Hydro*.[45] A trade market is characterized by the presence of companies specialized in sales and distribution, without being active at the upstream production level. Moreover, a trading company can normally be distinguished from a sales agency by its ability to obtain deliveries from a large number of suppliers. Any quasi-exclusivity provision between the parent companies and the joint venture is therefore prima facie incompatible with the finding that the joint venture will act as a trading company. A joint venture active on a trade market will be considered as full-function, if it has all the functions of companies active on that market.

Jurisdictional Conclusion

4.65   Full-function joint ventures under the Merger Regulation are defined in Article 3(2) as 'the creation of a joint venture performing on a lasting basis all the functions of an autonomous economic entity'. In practice, this excludes certain operations where the joint venture is created for a short, finite duration. It also excludes operations where a joint venture is not equipped to function on the market in its own right. This assessment will focus mainly on whether the joint venture has been given sufficient assets to carry out a business activity, or where it, rather than the parent companies, will *de facto* act on the market. Joint ventures that fulfil this requirement normally bring about a lasting change in the structure of the undertakings concerned, as well as a change in the structure of the market. It is therefore proper to examine them under the Merger Regulation.

---

44   Case IV/M102 (1991).
45   Case IV/M511 (1995).

(4) Co-operative Aspects of Joint Ventures

As previously stated, the Amending Regulation has expanded the scope of the **4.66** Merger Regulation in the field of joint ventures. Prior to 1 March 1998 certain operations were excluded from its application on the grounds that they could lead to co-operation between the parent companies outside the joint venture. The fact that these operations now will be assessed in the framework of the Merger Regulation does not, however, diminish the importance of such co-operation.

The co-operation between the parent companies outside the joint venture that **4.67** may appear in connection with the creation of a full-function joint venture can be grouped into three main categories:

— ancillary restrictions;
— spill-over effects;
— other co-operative aspects.

The classification of any existing co-operation between the parent companies out- **4.68** side the joint venture into the above categories will have no impact on the assess- ment of the joint venture itself. As long as it fulfils the full-function criteria the joint venture will be considered under the dominance test of the Merger Regulation, provided that the turnover thresholds in Article 1 are met. From an administrative viewpoint, the classification of the co-operation with the parent will have a direct impact on the question of how it is treated. As with any other type of concentration under the Merger Regulation, restrictions that are directly related to and necessary for the implementation of the concentration (ancillary restrictions) will be assessed together with the operation itself. The second cate- gory of restriction, spill-over effects, will also be assessed in the same procedure as the concentration, however, in accordance with the criteria of the EC Treaty Articles 81(1) and (3). Finally, restrictions that do not fall into either of these cat- egories will normally be assessed under Council Regulation (EEC) 17/62 First Regulation implementing Articles 85 and 86 of the Treaty.[46]

Each of these three categories will be further described and discussed below.

Ancillary Restrictions

As with any other type of concentration, the Commission decision will also cover **4.69** restrictions flowing from contractual arrangements that are directly related to and necessary for the implementation of the concentration. The specific features of joint ventures will normally mean that some non-compete clauses, and licensing and other provisions may be regarded as an integral part of the concentration rather than as ancillary restrictions. For a full discussion on the concept of ancil- lary restrictions, see below, paragraph 4.123 et seq.

---

[46] [1962] OJ Spec Ed 87.

Spill-over Aspects

Those not Resulting from the Contractual Arrangement

4.70 Prior to the entry into force of the Amending Regulation, full-function joint ventures which had as their object or effect a co-ordination of the competitive behaviour of their parent companies were excluded from the scope of the Merger Regulation (Article 3(2)(1)). This has, however, changed with the introduction of the Amending Regulation, which provides that all full-function joint ventures satisfying the turnover thresholds will be assessed under the Merger Regulation. In other words, the question of co-operative, or *spill-over aspects,* will no longer be a jurisdictional barrier. Instead, a substantive assessment of these aspects will be carried out within the same procedure as the merger analysis. The recent nature of this amendment inevitably means that a degree of uncertainty remains concerning its practical application. Although it is probably premature to attempt a definition of the term 'spill-over', it should be possible to distinguish such effects from ancillary restrictions. Whereas the latter are based on contractual provisions related to a concentration, the former are likely to flow more or less automatically from the structure that is created by the concentration. Spill-over effects are therefore unlikely to be based on contractual arrangements.

4.71 In order to achieve this broadening of the scope of the Merger Regulation, Article 2(4) has been introduced providing the Commission with the legal basis to apply the criteria of the EC Treaty Article 81 to the co-operative aspects of a joint venture's establishment. The Commission's Notice on the concept of full-function joint ventures under Council Regulation 4064/89 on the control of concentrations between undertakings[47] is a jurisdictional Notice, relating to the applicability of the Merger Regulation to different types of transactions. It is therefore logical that this Notice should not deal with the substantive analysis of spill-over aspects. The above-mentioned uncertainty is another reason why the Commission did not consider it appropriate to issue further guidance on the application of Article 2(4) until some experience had been gained through handling such cases. The Commission has indicated in the Commission Notice on the concept of full-function joint ventures[48] that it intends, in due course, to provide such guidance. Consequently pending the adoption of such guidance, some direction may be found in the jurisdictional principles set out in paragraphs 17–20 of the Commission Notice on the distinction between concentrative and co-operative joint ventures under Council Regulation (EEC) 4064/89 on the control of concentrations between undertakings.[49]

---

[47] [1998] OJ C66/1.
[48] [1998] OJ C66/1.
[49] [1994] OJ C385/1.

The New Provisions

Article 2(4) provides the following: **4.72**

> To the extent that the creation of a joint venture constituting a concentration pursuant to Article 3 has as its object or effect the co-ordination of the competitive behaviour of undertakings that remain independent, such co-ordination shall be appraised in accordance with the criteria of Articles 85(1) and (3), with a view to establishing whether or not the operation is compatible with the common market.
>
> In making this appraisal, the Commission shall take into account in particular:
>
>> whether two or more parent companies retain to a significant extent activities in the same market as the joint venture or in a market which is downstream or upstream from that of the joint venture or in a neighbouring market closely related to this market;
>> whether the co-ordination, which is the direct consequence of the creation of the joint venture, affords the undertakings concerned the possibility of eliminating competition in respect of a substantial part of the products or services in question.

The principles contained in Article 2(4) are further expanded in recital five of the **4.73** Amending Regulation. It follows that the joint venture will be subject to the dominance test of Article 2(1)–(3). In addition, to the extent that, as a direct consequence, it will bring about co-operative *spill-over aspects*, these will be assessed according to the criteria of the EC Treaty Article 81(1) and (3).

Spill-over Markets

Normally spill-over effects would be found between two or more parent compan- **4.74** ies when they retain significant activities either in the market of the joint venture or in a closely related market. This impression is strengthened by the fact that recital five states that the EC Treaty Article 81(1) *may* apply when the parents retain activities in the market of the joint venture, or *possibly* in upstream, downstream or neighbouring markets. However, none of the new provisions excludes a finding of spill-over aspects outside these more likely areas. Therefore, significant effects on potential competition between the parent companies could fall under this provision.

Causality

Textual analysis of the second indent would seem to indicate a strong requirement **4.75** of causality ('direct consequence') and that the appraisal of the competitive impact may require a substantial impact to be shown ('possibility of eliminating competition'). It is apparent that the latter part is similar to the fourth criterion in EC Treaty Article 81(3), and probably at least partly related to the dominance test. Again, it may, however, be useful to note that these are the factors that the Commission must *in particular* take into account. Consequently other factors (such as the other three criteria in EC Treaty Article 81(3)) may in specific cases be considered.

Centre of Gravity

4.76 Another interesting point is that the fifth recital contains one further element that is not included in Article 2(4), namely that 'if the effects of [full-function] joint ventures on the market are primarily structural, Article 81(1) does not as a general rule apply'. This would seem to imply a weighting of the structural impact of the joint venture against the non-structural effects of the spill-over. It should be noted that recital five uses the general terminology 'market', rather than 'relevant market'. This would seem to be of some importance as spill-over effects would appear to be most likely when the parents retain activities on the same market as the joint venture. Therefore, a 'centre of gravity assessment' could be made of the economic importance of the joint venture compared to the spill-over aspects flowing from activities retained by the parent companies. In such an assessment it would appear more likely that the parents would use a small joint venture to co-ordinate large retained activities rather than the other way around.

Assessment Criteria

4.77 From the above analysis it would seem that the investigation of spill-over aspects under Article 2(4) is likely to include identification of the following issues: the spill-over markets, the parent companies' incentives to co-ordinate (possibly with a centre of gravity analysis), and the causality between the creation of the joint venture and the spill-over aspects.

4.78 In cases where such an analysis shows that no spill-over effects will arise, only the dominance test—applied to the joint venture itself—will determine whether or not the transaction can be declared compatible with the common market. However, if spill-over aspects are established, this could, unless appropriate remedies can be found, lead to a decision of incompatibility for the whole transaction. Finding appropriate remedies may raise difficult questions, in particular if such spill-over concerns a market other than that of the joint venture. In such cases it would not only appear difficult to find remedies related to the joint venture's activities, but also to consider the possible pro-competitive effects of the joint venture in an EC Treaty Article 81(3) analysis of the spill-over aspects. Such an assessment would imply balancing the negative impact on one group of customers with the positive effects for another group, which in normal circumstances would be difficult to justify.

The First Cases

4.79 The first example where the issue of spill-over effects were significantly discussed was in *Telia/Telenor/Schibsted*.[50] In this case the joint venture was to be active in the

---

[50] Case IV/JV1 (1998). Subsequent cases (until 15 September 1998) including an Article 2(4) assessment are *Enel/FT/DT* (Case IV/JV2), *BT/AirTouch/Airtel* (Case IV/JV3), *Viag/Orange* (Case

provision of various services linked to the use of the Internet. The creation of the joint venture was assessed under the dominance test of Article 2, and raised no serious doubts. The Commission also made an Article 2(4) assessment of the impact on the 'candidate markets' for spill-over effects. These markets were indicated as the market for web site production, where the joint venture and two of the parent companies were active, and in addition, the market for the provision of 'dial-up' access to the Internet, a market upstream to that of the joint venture, where at least two of the parent companies would remain active.

For the web site production market, the Commission concluded that the com- **4.80** bined market share of the parent companies and the joint venture would be so low that, even if the parent companies were to co-ordinate their activities, this co-ordination could not lead to an appreciable restriction of competition. Therefore it was not necessary to consider whether there was a causal link between the creation of the joint venture and the behaviour of the parent companies outside the joint venture. The 'dial-up' Internet access market was competitive and growing, and therefore not likely to be conducive to co-ordination of competitive behaviour. The fact that this market was substantially larger than the markets of the joint venture was considered to reduce the likelihood of co-ordination further. In conclusion, there was no likelihood that the parent companies would co-ordinate on the 'dial-up' Internet access market. Consequently it was not necessary to examine any causal link between the creation of the joint venture and the behaviour of the parent companies outside the joint venture on that market.

The analyses in the other cases examined under Article 2(4) have followed broadly **4.81** the same lines. It is notable that all these cases have concerned new technology markets in the telecommunication field. For companies involved in transactions raising possible Article 2(4) aspects, the inclusion of this provision in the Amending Regulation offers significant advantages, as all full-function joint ventures subsequently will be assessed in the framework of the Merger Regulation. It, however, also raises a number of novel questions. Answers to these questions will only become clear when more experience has been accumulated in applying this new provision.

Other Co-operative Aspects

Co-operative aspects that fall outside the two above mentioned areas will nor- **4.82** mally have to be examined outside the Merger Regulation procedure, by means of Council Regulation (EEC) 17/62 First Regulation implementing Articles 81 and

---

IV/JV4), *Cegetel/Canal+/AOL/Bertelsmann* (Case IV/JV5), *Ericsson/Nokia/Psion* (Case IV/JV6), *Telia/Sonera/Lietuvos Telekomas* (Case IV/JV7), *Telia/Sonera/Motorola/UAB Omnitel* (Case IV/JV9), and *@Home Benelux* (Case IV/JV11).

82 of the Treaty.[51] In terms of contractual arrangements that are too broad to be considered as ancillary restrictions, the situation is not changed by the Amending Regulation. In relation to spill-over aspects an assessment outside the Merger Regulation could be necessary, for example, if the required causality link cannot be established. In the latter respect, and in line with general principles, a company could only invoke Article 2(4) as a defence against possible future measures under Council Regulation (EEC) 17 First Regulation implementing Articles 81 and 82 of the Treaty if it has made full and honest disclosure of all relevant facts at the time of the Merger Regulation proceedings.

(5) Community Dimension

4.83 The Merger Regulation is intended to apply to concentrations of a significant size, the basic assumption being that such operations have an impact in more than one Member State, and therefore can be more effectively assessed at a European level.

4.84 After having established that a certain transaction constitutes a concentration in the meaning of Article 3 of the Merger Regulation, the second part of the jurisdictional test is to see whether the transaction is of a Community dimension. This analysis requires, first, the identification of the 'undertakings concerned' and, secondly, to establish that the turnover attributable to these undertakings meets the thresholds laid down in Article 1 of the Merger Regulation. In this respect it is irrelevant whether or not the undertakings concerned are located in the Community. The important issue is only whether they achieve turnover in the Community and whether the operation has an impact on competition in the Community. In *Gencor/Lonrho*,[52] the concentration took place in South Africa. However, the companies' turnovers met the turnover thresholds of the Merger Regulation, and, since platinum was a global market, the Community was also affected by the concentration. The Court of First Instance[53] accepted that the Commission was justified to block this merger. This was due to the fact that the merger would have led to the creation of a dominant oligopoly on a global level and therefore have an effect on competition in the Community.

Identifying the Undertakings Concerned (Article 1)

4.85 As an introductory remark it should be noted that the purpose of these rules is to measure the total amount of resources being combined through a concentration. It follows from this objective that the seller of a business will not be considered as an undertaking concerned, unless it retains a jointly controlling interest in the divested business. Consequently, the turnover of the seller (and its group) is only of interest if it retains such joint control.

---

[51] See also Regulations (EEC) 1017/68, (EEC) 4056/86 and (EEC) 3975/87.
[52] Case IV/M619 (1996) [1997] OJ L11/30.
[53] T–102/96 *Gencor v Commission* judgment of 25 March 1999, not yet reported.

Mergers

In this most straightforward scenario, the undertakings concerned will be each of **4.86** the merging entities.

Acquisition of Sole Control

Here, the undertakings concerned will be the company acquiring control and the **4.87** target of the acquisition.

In cases of sole control there can only be one undertaking concerned on the **4.88** acquiring side, the entity that is the actual acquirer. However, in cases where the undertaking concerned is a special purpose vehicle for the acquisition, or otherwise a subsidiary, the Commission will normally accept that the concentration is notified by the parent company.

The other undertaking concerned, the target of the acquisition, can be one or **4.89** more whole companies, or parts thereof. Obviously the Merger Regulation is not intended to apply to acquisitions of ordinary business assets, such as machinery or office equipment. However, since the transfer of a business may be structured as a sale of all its business assets, the Merger Regulation applies also where the target of the acquisition is not a legal entity, but rather a division, a unit, or certain assets (for example brands or licences). In such cases it must be shown that these assets constitute a business to which a market turnover can be attributed.

Acquisition of Joint Control

When a new joint venture is created, the undertakings concerned will be each of **4.90** its controlling parents. The joint venture, which at the time of the transaction does not exist, will not be considered as an undertaking concerned.

In cases where a pre-existing company or business comes under the joint control **4.91** of two or more parents, each of the controlling parents will be considered as an undertaking concerned, regardless of whether or not they also, prior to the transaction, were solely or jointly controlling the target company.

The target company will be considered an undertaking concerned in all situations **4.92** except one. If, prior to the transaction, it was solely controlled by one parent company, and this parent will retain joint control, the economic reality is that the target prior to the transaction was part of the initial parent's group. To avoid making an artificial separation of the initial group, the target company will not, in this situation, be considered as an undertaking concerned.

Acquisition of Control by a Joint Venture

Even in this situation, the main rule will normally apply, ie the undertakings **4.93** concerned are usually the joint venture and the target company. However, if there are strong indications that the parents of the joint venture are in reality the real players behind the operation, they will, to the exclusion of the joint venture, be regarded as undertakings concerned. This will always be the case if the joint venture has been set up as a vehicle for making a certain acquisition. Other cases where the parents could be seen as the real players behind the operation may be if the joint venture is not a full-function company or if there appears to be little industrial logic for the joint venture to invest in the business of the target company. In *TNT/Canada Post, DBP Postdienst, La Poste, PTT Post and Sweden Post,*[54] five national postal administrations had set up a company (GD Net), specifically for the purpose of participating in the notified transaction. The Commission found that each of the five postal administrations had joint control over GD Net, and therefore looked through the veil of GD Net and considered each of the postal administrations as undertakings concerned.

Change in Shareholdings in Cases of an Existing Joint Venture

4.94 If one existing parent acquires (whether by shares or contract) sole control over a company that had until then been a joint venture, the undertakings concerned are the acquiring company and the target company (which ceases to be a joint venture).

4.95 Any other change in the structure of control over a joint venture, by which one or more undertakings acquire (whether by shares or contract) joint control will be deemed to constitute a concentration. In this case the undertakings concerned will be each controlling parent company and the target company.[55]

Other Situations

4.96 A demerger, ie an operation reversing a previous merger or joint venture, will normally constitute two or more separate concentrations. In *Solvay/Laporte,*[56] the Commission concluded that the break-up of a previous joint venture constituted two separate operations, and issued a combined Article 6(1)(a) and 6(1)(b) decision for both operations. Moreover, the Commission accepted that both operations were notified in a single notification. Thus, even if, at least in theory, it is conceivable that a demerger could be totally symmetrical, for example that each original party regains exactly the same assets as it had previously contributed to the joint venture, the demerger would nevertheless constitute a (second) change in the quality of control over those assets. In demerger cases the undertakings concerned for each concentration will normally be, on the one hand, the original party and, on the other hand, the assets that are acquired by that original party. If, at the time of the break-up, some of the assets are acquired by a party that was not involved in the original transaction, that party's acquisition will be treated as a normal acquisition of sole or joint control as the case may be.

---

[54] Case IV/M102 (1991).
[55] See, eg, *Synthomer/Yule Catto* (Case IV/M376) (1993).
[56] Case IV/M197 (1992).

A swap agreement, ie where two or more undertakings agree to exchange certain **4.97**
assets with one another, will be considered to constitute as many concentrations
as there are acquisitions of control. In each such acquisition of control the undertakings concerned will be the acquiring company and the acquired assets.

According to Article 3(1) of the Merger Regulation an individual can be regarded **4.98**
as an undertaking concerned only if he/she prior to the transaction under consideration already controls at least one other undertaking.[57]

A specific case of acquisition by individuals is the management buyout. The man- **4.99**
agers will normally not be considered as undertakings concerned as they normally
do not previously control any other undertaking. Even if the managers pool their
interests in a joint venture, it is likely that this will simply be the vehicle used for
the transaction. Therefore, unless the management buyout is supported by an
investment partner (normally a bank or a venture capital company), which
acquires sole or joint control over the target company, the management buyout
may not constitute a concentration in the meaning of the Merger Regulation.

The fact that two companies ultimately are controlled by the same State (or **4.100**
regional or local public entity) does not automatically mean that a merger or an
acquisition between them should be seen as internal reorganization, falling outside the Merger Regulation. The decisive criterion is whether the two companies
are part of different economic units with independent power of decision. If that is
indeed the case the Merger Regulation will be applicable, and each of the companies involved in the concentration will be regarded as undertakings concerned.[58]

Calculation of Turnover (Article 5)

After the undertakings concerned have been identified, the question of whether a **4.101**
concentration has a Community dimension will depend on a purely quantitative
test of whether or not the turnover attributable to those undertakings is sufficient
to reach the thresholds set out in Article 1(2) or 1(3).[59]

These two sets of thresholds are alternative. Article 1(2) contains the threshold **4.102**
included in the Merger Regulation (ie the threefold test of worldwide turnover
greater than ECU 5 billion, Community-wide turnover greater than ECU 250
million for two parties, and less than two-thirds of that Community-wide
turnover in a single Member State). Only in cases where these thresholds are *not*

---

[57] See *Asko/Jacobs/Adia* (Case IV/M82) (1991).
[58] See, eg, *CEA Industrie/France Telecom/SGS-Thomson* (Case IV/M216) (1993) and *Neste/IVO* (Case IV/M931) (1998).
[59] For more details, see Commission Notice on calculation of turnover under Council Regulation (EEC) 4064/89 on the control of concentrations between undertakings [1998] OJ C66/25 ('the turnover Notice').

met, do the parties need to consider the new set of thresholds of Article 1(3), which was introduced by the Amending Regulation.

4.103   The reason for introducing this new provision was to include concentrations that otherwise would have had to be notified in several Member States. In addition to including a lower level for the worldwide and Community-wide turnover (ECU 2.5 billion and ECU 100 million respectively), Article 1(3) contains an additional requirement that a minimum level of turnover be achieved in at least three Member States (combined turnover of ECU 100 million and greater than ECU 25 million for at least two parties). The two-thirds requirement is maintained in Article 1(3). In accordance with Article 1(4) this new set of thresholds will be reviewed in the year 2000.

4.104   In relation to the EEA agreement it should be noted that the turnover thresholds relate to the Community as such. This means, *inter alia,* that it is not possible to apply Article 1(3) by fulfilling the requirement of ECU 25 million and ECU 100 million in one EFTA State and two Member States. Such a case would not have a Community dimension.

Turnover: An Accounting and a 'Net' Concept

4.105   In order to provide the intended reflection of the economic strength of the undertakings concerned, the Merger Regulation's turnover concept is based on 'net sales'. The main rule is therefore that, regardless of whether the undertaking's activities consist of the sale of products or the provision of services, the financial resources combined through the concentration—as indicated by the invoiced amounts—will determine the jurisdictional issue. In this context it is of no consequence what proportion of the turnover is actually affected by the transaction.

4.106   Companies will often not include sales rebates, VAT or other indirect taxes in their accounts under the heading 'sales'. However, to the extent that the undertakings concerned do this it will be necessary to exclude such items in order to arrive at the 'net sales'. Moreover, sales between companies in the same group should also be excluded in order to avoid double counting.

Adjustments to Turnover

4.107   The Commission will normally base itself on audited accounts for the last financial year. However, if more recent figures are available in a final form, and if the result of using these figures would be decisive for the jurisdictional question, the Commission may take the unaudited figures into account. The undertakings concerned would, however, in order to achieve this, have to provide sufficient evidence that the unaudited figures may be relied on.

4.108   The turnover thresholds should reflect the economic strength of the undertakings concerned at the date of the event that triggered the notification. The turnover attributable to the acquirer(s) as well as to the target company should therefore be adjusted in the case of acquisitions or disposals that have taken place between the last audited accounts and the triggering date. Moreover, if a divestiture or closure of existing operations is a precondition for the notified transaction, it is appropriate to deduct the turnover attributable to such operations.[60]

The Turnover of Groups—The Application of Article 5(4)

In order to reflect accurately the financial strength of an undertaking concerned, **4.109** its turnover will be combined with that of all other companies in the same group. Subject to the above-mentioned exception where a divestiture or closure of existing operations is a precondition for the notified transaction, the assessment of which entities form part of the group of an undertaking concerned will look at the situation as of the date of the event triggering the notification. Basically the group will include parent and sister companies as well as subsidiaries. Control in a legal or economic sense, rather than any formal requirement of a certain level of ownership, will decide whether a company should be considered to fall into one of these categories.

In the specific case of pre-existing joint ventures between a company in the group **4.110** and one or more third parties, the turnover of that joint venture should be allocated to the group in proportion to the number of controlling parents.[61]

Geographical Allocation of Turnover

Often the accounts of an undertaking will not contain a precise breakdown of **4.111** turnover for each Member State. This normally does not cause a problem, since in most cases it can be clearly shown that the Community-wide threshold is exceeded. In such cases it is not necessary to provide exact figures for each Member State. If a detailed breakdown should be necessary in order to settle the jurisdictional test, the main principle is to attribute turnover to the location of the customer, which provides the best indication of where competition to achieve the sales actually took place. If the Community-wide turnover thresholds are satisfied on this basis, no further investigation is normally required.

In the field of air transport and telecommunication, the nature of the services in **4.112** question have caused certain questions to arise as to the most proper method to geographically allocate turnover. In *Delta Airlines/Pan Am*,[62] the Commission considered, in addition to the method of allocating the turnover to the area where the sales actually took place, also what would be the effect of allocating the turnover to the place of the destination or by allocating the turnover on a 50/50 basis between the place of departure and the place of arrival. As the relevant

---

[60] Case T–2/93 *Air France v Commission* [1994] ECR II–323.
[61] See *Ameritech/Tele Denmark,* (Case IV/M1046) (1997).
[62] Case IV/M130 (1991).

turnover thresholds were met irrespective of the method employed, this question was left open. Similar alternatives for the geographic allocation of turnover were considered in *British Telecom/MCI (II)*.[63]

Credit and Other Financial Institutions and Insurance Undertakings

4.113 Following the Amending Regulation, Article 5(3)(a) specifies that the calculation of turnover for financial institutions will follow Council Directive (EEC) 86/635 on the annual accounts and consolidated accounts of banks and other financial institutions.[64] The turnover Notice sets out these rules in detail.

4.114 The changes introduced by the Amending Regulation do not affect the established rules for calculating the turnover of insurance companies.

(6) Extension and Reduction of Community Competence

4.115 The one-stop shop principle of the Merger Regulation has a limited number of exceptions, by which the Commission's exclusive competence to deal with concentrations of a Community dimension may either be extended (Article 22) or reduced (Article 9). In addition, in spite of the exclusive competence it is possible for Member States to apply national legislation designed to protect legitimate interests (Article 21).

Article 22

4.116 Article 22 allows a Member State to refer a concentration which is not of Community dimension to the Commission, if that concentration threatens to create or strengthen a dominant position within its territory. Following the Amending Regulation such a referral can be made jointly by two or more Member States. The request must be made within one month of either the date when the concentration was effected or when the Member State was informed of the concentration. In the case of a joint request this deadline runs from the date when all the relevant Member States were so informed.

4.117 Following the Amending Regulation, the suspensive effect of Article 7 will apply to cases assessed in accordance with Article 22, unless the concentration has already been effected when the Commission informs the parties about the request.

4.118 Article 22 serves an important objective, in particular for Member States which do not have the proper instruments to assess certain concentrations. This is clearly indicated by the fact that two cases notified in accordance with Article 22 were, after examination, prohibited by the Commission.[65]

---

[63] Case IV/M856) (1997).
[64] [1986] OJ L372/1.
[65] See *Kesko/Tuko* (Case IV/M784) (1996) [1997] OJ L110/53 and *Blokker/Toys 'R' Us (II)* (Case IV/M890) (1997) [1998] OJ L316/1.

Article 9

Article 9 allows a Member State to ask the Commission to refer a concentration **4.119** with a Community dimension for assessment at national level. A Member State wishing to make such a request must inform the Commission within three weeks after receiving a copy of the notification. If a request is made the initial deadline for the Commission is extended to six weeks (Article 10(1)).

Following the entry into force of the Amending Regulation, a presumption has **4.120** been introduced in Article 9 that whole or partial referrals to a Member State will be made on request, if the market concerned does not constitute a substantial part of the Community. In this sense Article 9 can be seen as an expression within the Merger Regulation of the general principle of subsidiarity. So far the Commission has made a full referral to a Member State in five cases (one in 1993, three in 1996, and one in 1997).

Article 21

Article 21(3) recognizes that Member States may apply national legislation **4.121** designed to protect legitimate interests in the fields of public security, plurality of the media, and prudential rules. As an exception from the general rule on exclusive competence for the Commission, this provision should be interpreted narrowly and cannot be used by Member States as a means to reopen the competitive analysis made by the Commission. Consequently, in the three cases where this provision has been invoked, the Commission has insisted on being informed of any measures proposed by a Member State in accordance with this provision.[66]

EC Treaty Article 296

In a number of cases concerning military products a Member State has instructed **4.122** the undertakings concerned not to notify certain aspects of the case, since such a notification could reveal national security secrets. The Commission has accepted this on the condition that the Member State concerned demonstrates that the non-notified part of the concentration relates to the production of, or trade in, arms, munitions, and war material that are mentioned in the list referred to in Article 296(2).[67] In addition, the measures must be necessary for the protection of the essential interests of the Member State's security and there must not be any spill-over effects from the military to the non-military activities. Finally, the merger must not have a significant impact on suppliers and subcontractors of the under-takings concerned and on the Ministries of Defence of other Member States.[68]

---

[66] See *Newspaper Publishing* (Case IV/M423) (1994), *Lyonnaise des Eaux/Northumbrian Water* (Case IV/M567) (1995), and *Sun Alliance/Royal Insurance* (Case IV/M759) (1996).
[67] See Chapter 2, paras 2.05–2.16.
[68] See, eg, *British Aerospace/VSEL* (Case IV/M528) (1994).

(7) *Ancillary Restrictions*

4.123 Ancillary restrictions are contractual arrangements agreed between the parties to a concentration. Acknowledging that such restrictions may be necessary for the implementation of a concentration, the Merger Regulation provides a system whereby such restrictions can be assessed together with the concentration itself. However, in order to benefit from this possibility, notifying parties are obliged to demonstrate that any such clauses are necessary and directly related to the transaction, in the sense that the concentration could not, or could only with significant difficulty, be implemented in their absence.

4.124 The purpose of assessing ancillary restrictions under the same procedure as the concentration itself is to reduce the time and cost that would otherwise be incurred by the notifying parties and the Commission. In addition, it allows for an assessment of those restrictions in their correct economic context. It must, however, be stressed that it is for the notifying parties to indicate in the notification any contractual arrangements that they want to have assessed as ancillary restrictions. Form CO contains a specific question to that effect. If notifying parties do not indicate that they want to have certain arrangements treated as ancillary restrictions, the Commission will generally not on its own initiative search the documents annexed to the notification for possible ancillary restrictions. Moreover, Article 22(1) of the Merger Regulation provides that Council Regulation (EEC) 17/62 First Regulation implementing Articles 81 and 82 of the Treaty still applies in respect of ancillary restrictions. The effect of this is that any restrictions not covered by the Merger Regulation decision remain, in principle, subject to the application of EC Treaty Article 81.

4.125 Originally the concept of ancillary restrictions was included only in Article 8 of the Merger Regulation. The Amending Regulation introduced a similar provision in Article 6(1), thereby codifying the Commission's long-established practice of also assessing ancillary restrictions in connection with its first phase Article 6(1)(b) decisions.

Restriction of Competition

4.126 As the term ancillary restriction indicates, the measure in question must constitute a restriction of competition in the sense of Article 81(1). In view of the severe time constraints imposed by the Merger Regulation, in particular in the first phase investigation, it is, however, not always possible to conduct a detailed investigation in order to determine if, from an economic viewpoint, a certain provision will result in an appreciable restriction of competition.

Necessary and Directly Related

Therefore, in practice, the assessment of ancillary restrictions is often carried out **4.127** while presuming such restrictive effects. If, based on such a presumption, it can still be concluded that the 'restriction' is necessary and directly related to the concentration, it will be covered by the merger decision. Equally, if it is clear that a presumed 'restriction' is not necessary or directly related to the concentration, it will not be covered by the decision.

Non-Restrictive Clauses

It follows from the above that the main test applied to assess ancillary restrictions **4.128** under the Merger Regulation might be said to be whether or not such 'restrictions' are ancillary. Nevertheless, the contractual arrangements concluded in relation to a concentration will obviously regularly include a number of provisions that do not bring about any restriction of competition. As these provisions do not infringe Article 81(1), they will obviously not need to be covered by the decision. It is therefore useful to provide a few examples of clauses that normally can be considered as non-restrictive. One example is a clause in an agreement to sell a certain business, specifying that the seller will not take any measures adversely affecting the business between the date of the agreement and the closing date.[69] Another type of measure that cannot in itself be considered restrictive is one that constitutes the concentration. Examples of the latter are contractual arrangements that organize the control structure of the target company following the concentration. In the specific case of a joint venture, non-compete clauses in favour of the joint venture will normally be an integral part of the concentration, as they organize the lasting withdrawal of the parent companies from the joint venture's market (see further below).

Burden of Proof

Moreover, it is for the parties to demonstrate that a restriction is directly related to **4.129** and necessary for the implementation of the concentration. Restrictions that are to the detriment of third parties will not be considered ancillary.[70] Furthermore, it is not sufficient that the restriction has been agreed between the parties to the concentration at the same time as the concentration itself. Unless it can be demonstrated that the restriction results from the concentration, it will not be considered ancillary. Finally, it must be demonstrated that a restriction is necessary for the implementation of the concentration. This will normally be based on an assessment of the proportionality of the restriction in terms of its duration, and its

---

[69] See, eg, *Textron/Valois* (Case IV/M721) (1996).
[70] See, eg, *Cable & Wireless/Maersk Data-Nautek* (Case IV/M951) (1997).

product and geographic scope. A restriction that relates to matters outside the scope of the concentration will not be considered ancillary.[71]

Ancillary Restrictions in Acquisitions

Non-Compete Clauses

4.130 The most common type of restrictive arrangement in relation to acquisitions of undertakings is the non-compete clause, by which the seller undertakes not to compete with the divested business or otherwise solicit its clients (or employees). Such clauses are accepted as ancillary to the concentration, as they allow for the transfer of the full value of the acquired business. However, for it to be considered ancillary, the legitimate protection of the buyer may not exceed what is necessary. Therefore, the product and geographic scope of the non-compete clause should be limited so as to correspond to the activities of the divested business. Finally, in terms of the acceptable duration, the Commission's practice is well established. If the operation involves a transfer of substantial technical and commercial know-how, a period up to five years may be accepted. If the parties do not succeed in showing such a transfer of know-how, a period of two to three years is normally accepted if a significant transfer of goodwill is involved. Whereas these principles will in general be followed, they are not absolute rules. The periods allowed may therefore in specific cases be adjusted, depending on the features of the market and the justification submitted by the parties.

4.131 The fact that a non-compete clause is directly aimed at removing one potential entrant from the market makes the presumption of a restrictive effect justified. This is the case even if, in reality, a non-compete clause may only have a *de minimis* effect on competition within the meaning of Article 81(1) and the Commission's Notice on Restrictive Agreements of Minor Importance.[72] This may be the case, in particular, if the seller has a very limited position on the market in question or if barriers to entry are insignificant.

Purchase, Supply, and Distribution Agreements

4.132 The second most common form of ancillary restriction is the purchase, supply, or distribution agreement. These can be in favour of either the seller or the acquirer and are normally acceptable as they allow for a smooth transition from established intra-group relationships to the new situation where the seller and the divested business will form separate economic entities. The underlying reasons justifying such clauses cannot, however, legitimately be extended to a period going beyond a transitional period required to establish new purchase, supply, or distribution relationships for each of the two groups. A three-year period will normally be

---

[71] See, eg, *Dupont/ICI* (Case IV/M984) (1997).
[72] See Chapter 2, para. 2.56 et seq.

accepted for this transition. If, in the view of the parties, a longer period would be justified, they will be required to justify that assertion with reference to specific market conditions, such as the scarcity of alternative sources of supply or specific reasons why a change of suppliers would require a longer period. Finally, to be considered necessary for the implementation of the concentration, the purchase, supply, or distribution agreement should not amount to an exclusive arrangement.

Intellectual Property Rights

The third broad category of arrangements that are often included in the transfer of businesses are those related to intellectual property rights (patents, trade marks, know-how, etc). If the divested business has been using such rights that are owned by the selling company, which will continue to use these rights in other fields, a licence will normally serve as a substitute for an outright transfer. Such licences may therefore often be seen as an integral part of the concentration, and consequently should not need to be considered as ancillary restrictions. However, if the licensing arrangements provide for limitations on the field of use allowed for the licensee (in terms of product or geographic scope), these limitations may effectively amount to a market sharing arrangement. Therefore any such arrangements must be justified by the notifying parties. **4.133**

Ancillary Restrictions in Joint Venture Cases

Non-Intra-Group Arrangements

Contractual arrangements between a parent company and a joint venture cannot be viewed as intra-group relationships, which are incapable of infringing Article 81(1). First, a full-function joint venture is defined by the Merger Regulation as a company 'performing on a lasting basis all the functions of an autonomous economic entity'. This is clearly very different from the normal intra-group relationship between a parent company and its subsidiary. Secondly, the fact that a joint venture has at least two controlling parent companies indicates that most contractual arrangements between them and the joint venture may also be seen as restrictions between the parent companies. However, as described above, the assessment under the Merger Regulation may not call for a conclusion on these intricate questions. Instead the decisive issue will often be whether a contractual arrangement between a parent company and the joint venture can be regarded as directly related to and necessary for its creation. **4.134**

The creation of a full-function joint venture in the meaning of Article 3(2) of the Merger Regulation will normally entail contractual arrangements between the parent companies that may constitute integral parts of the concentration or ancillary restrictions. **4.135**

Non-Compete Clauses as an Integral Part of the Concentration or Forming Ancillary Restrictions

4.136 A non-compete clause which merely reflects the lasting withdrawal of the parent companies from the markets of the joint venture will be considered as an integral part of the concentration, and may therefore be concluded on an indefinite basis. In cases where, prior to the establishment of the joint venture, the parent companies were not competitors these clauses do not raise any difficulties.

4.137 However, in cases where the parent companies have been active on the same market, further considerations may have to be taken into account. If all previously competing parent companies enter into non-compete clauses covering the same product and geographic dimensions, it will be clear that the non-compete provisions are in favour of the joint venture. If, however, one of the parent companies accepts a more limited restriction than one or more other parent companies, the restriction imposed on the latter will in effect not only apply in favour of the joint venture, but also in favour of the parent whose restriction is more limited. In such cases, the parties should demonstrate that this restriction between the parent companies is directly related to and necessary for the creation of the joint venture.

Licensing Intellectual Property Rights to the Joint Venture

4.138 Normally an agreement where one of the parent companies licenses certain intellectual property rights to the joint venture will be seen as an alternative to an outright transfer. As such it could be considered an integral part of the concentration, and not as a restrictive agreement. The same applies when an intellectual property right is transferred to the joint venture and subsequently licensed back to the parent. These principles will apply even if the licence is exclusive, and regardless of whether or not it contains restrictions in the permitted fields of use. It should, however, be noted that licensing agreements between the parent companies, whether this is done either directly or through the joint venture, cannot normally be considered necessary for and directly related to the concentration.

Supply Arrangements between the Joint Venture and its Parent Companies

4.139 The creation of a joint venture will often involve questions concerning contractual arrangements between the parent companies and the joint venture relating to purchase, supply, or distribution obligations. Such arrangements may or may not be seen as restrictive, and to the extent that they are restrictive they may or may not be regarded as ancillary to the concentration. The assessment of such purchase, supply, or distribution obligations will normally follow the same principles as described above in relation to acquisitions of businesses. That is to say provisions that can be regarded as transitory will normally be considered ancillary, whereas provisions with a broader scope will need to be justified in the light of specific circumstances. In this connection it should also be remembered that contractual obligations of this kind may, if their scope and duration is excessive, lead to a conclusion that the joint venture is not full-function (see above, section on continued dependency on parent companies).

(8) The Creation or Strengthening of a Dominant Position: Article 2(3)

The Merger Regulation sets out in Article 2(3) the creation or strengthening of **4.140** 'a dominant position as a result of which effective competition would be impeded in the common market or in a substantial part of it' as the test for whether a concentration is or is not compatible with the common market. However, the Merger Regulation does not provide a definition of dominance.

For the purpose of the Merger Regulation the Commission employs the defini- **4.141** tion of dominance as defined by the European Court of Justice in past EC Treaty Article 82 cases:

> The dominant position referred to (in Article 86 [now Article 82]) relates to a position of economic strength enjoyed by an undertaking which enables it to prevent effective competition being maintained on the relevant market by giving it the power to behave to an appreciable extent independently of its competitors, customers and ultimately of its consumers.[73]

and:

> such a position does not preclude some competition, which it does where there is a monopoly or quasi-monopoly, but enables the undertaking which profits by it, if not to determine, at least to have an appreciable influence on the conditions under which that competition will develop, and in any case to act largely in discard of it so long as such conduct does not operate to its detriment.[74]

Consequently, according to the Court of Justice, a company is dominant if it has **4.142** the power to act to an appreciable extent independently of its competitors, customers, and ultimately of consumers. However, a dominant position is 'less' than a monopoly or quasi-monopoly. It is enough that an undertaking have an appreciable influence on the conditions under which competition can develop and be able to act largely in disregard of such competition. For example, in an industry consisting of one large and a number of smaller firms, the large firm could under certain circumstances be dominant within the meaning of the Merger Regulation.

The concept of dominance as defined by the Court of Justice is a legal and not an **4.143** economic concept. However, the assessment of the impact on competition of a merger is necessarily an economic analysis focusing on the potential increase in market power resulting from a merger. In other words, the relevant question is whether a merger increases the market power of the merging parties to such an

---

[73] Case 27/76 *United Brands Company and United Brands Continentaal BV v Commission* [1978] ECR 207.
[74] Case 85/76 *Hoffmann-La Roche & Co AG v Commission* [1979] ECR 461.

extent that they will have the possibility 'to act to an appreciable extent independently of [their] competitors, customers and ultimately of consumers'. In this respect, in standard economic theory, the focus of the analyses of market power is whether a company is able to increase prices (or reduce output and thereby increase prices) above marginal costs. In accordance with standard economic theory, the Commission has in its assessment of dominance normally analysed whether it would be possible for an undertaking to increase prices or restrict output following the implementation of a concentration.

4.144 However, while the possibility of price increases is often one of the main concerns in the assessment of the negative effects of dominance, the Commission's assessment goes further. For example, the possibility of a company to establish a 'gatekeeper' function, whereby it would be in a position to control entry to a market, has played an important role in a number of cases.[75] This concern is not only with the possibility to earn monopoly profits, but also with the negative impact of reduced consumer choice over time (for example with respect to television programmes[76] or soft drinks).[77] Further concerns could include, for example, increased scope for predatory pricing or the negative effects of a refusal to deliver to third parties. These are examples of possible market behaviour, which may become possible as a consequence of a merger resulting in the creation or strengthening of a dominant position. They are not exhaustive. Ultimately, potential negative effects resulting from a merger can only be established on a case-by-case basis.

4.145 In contrast with cases of abuse under the EC Treaty Article 82, the assessment of dominance in merger cases is necessarily forward-looking, since the objective of merger control is to prevent the creation or strengthening of dominant positions as a result of merger operations. In other words the focus is on future market structures rather than how competition has evolved in the past. Consequently, the assessment of dominance under the Merger Regulation involves a market forecast of how competition will develop in the future.[78] Industry dynamics may, for example, lead to a change in the supplier structure within the near future, which could lead to a higher level of potential competition. Such developments could also be a result of changes in regulatory regimes on a market or technological innovation (see section on potential competition below).[79]

---

[75] eg *The Coca-Cola Company/Carlsberg a/s* (Case IV/M833) (1997) [1998] OJ L145/41; *MSG Media Service* (Case IV/M469) [1994] OJ L364/1; and *Nordic Satellite Distribution* (Case IV/M490) (1995) [1996] OJ L53/20.

[76] *MSG Media Service* and *Nordic Satellite Distribution* (see n 75 above).

[77] *The Coca-Cola Company/Carlsberg a/s* (see n 75 above).

[78] In a market forecast it is normally necessary to decide on the relevant forecast period. In merger cases, as a rule of thumb, the relevant forecast period is often considered to be some five years. However, the actual relevant forecast period will depend on the specific market.

[79] Dynamics on the demand side are considered in the market definition. The geographic market may, for example, at present be national, but is expected for various reasons to develop into an EU

In its assessment the Commission weighs a number of factors such as market posi- **4.146**
tion, countervailing buyer power, and potential competition simultaneously
against each other in reaching a conclusion on whether a dominant position is created or strengthened. In academic economics literature, methods have been suggested by means of which market power can be assessed quantitatively, for
example by estimating the residual demand elasticity of an undertaking following
a concentration. The main problem is that these analyses normally require a large
amount of data, and still in most cases can only be expected to give a certain indication of whether a merger significantly increases market power. While the
Commission will use quantitative evidence, whenever it is available and sufficiently sound, the assessment of dominance is still, in the large majority of cases,
a qualitative analysis based on a mix of quantitative and qualitative evidence. The
Commission will normally first assess current competition between existing competitors. If need be, the Commission will subsequently analyse countervailing
buyer power and potential competition.

The Assessment of Current Competition among Existing Suppliers

In its assessment of whether a company will become dominant, the Commission **4.147**
will initially look at market shares as the indicator of market power. A merger leading to high market shares would normally result in a strong presumption of dominance, whereas low market shares would indicate no dominance and normally
lead to a rapid clearance of a case.

Normally, market shares of below 25 per cent indicate that dominance does not **4.148**
exist. In previous cases the Commission has not found dominance where market
shares have been less than 40 per cent, even though it cannot be excluded that
dominance could be found even with market shares of less than 40 per cent. Very
high market shares of, for example, 70–80 per cent have normally been interpreted as a strong indication of dominance.[80] However, it is not possible to provide any general rule as to what precise level of market share would lead to a
finding of dominance. This will depend on the structural features of the market in
question such as the size of other competitors in the market. As an example, the
Commission is likely to be concerned about, say, a 40 per cent market share in a
market where the rest of the suppliers are highly fragmented, and therefore more
likely to simply follow the actions of the market leader, say by acting as price tak-
ers. In contrast a more limited number of sizeable suppliers, that could challenge
the market leader, could mean that even a 40 per cent market share will not lead
to the creation or strengthening of a dominant position.

---

market within a relative short time period, and the relevant market may, therefore, be considered an
EU market.

[80]   *Tetra Pak/Alfa-Laval* (Case IV/M68) [1991] OJ L290/35.

4.149 In the assessment of current competition in a market it is sometimes the case that a company has joint control or some other degree of influence over another supplier. The Court of First Instance recognized in *Gencor v Commission*[81] that in such a situation there can be competition between such entities even though one company has some degree of control over the other. Therefore, in such cases the Commission needs to assess the extent to which there is competition between such entities. However, no firm rules can be given in this respect: the analysis has to be completed on a case-by-case basis.

The Assessment of Countervailing Buyer Power

4.150 In cases where the merger has resulted in high market shares for the merging parties and where competition from existing competitors in the market has been found to be insufficient to prevent the creation or strengthening of a dominant position, the Commission has proceeded to an assessment of the strength of countervailing buyer power and potential competition as means to constrain the actions of the merging parties.

4.151 In its assessment of countervailing buyer power the Commission will normally first look at the structure of the buyers. The assumption is that buyers are more likely to have countervailing buyer power if the buyer structure is concentrated rather than fragmented. In this respect the Commission has in previous decisions attached little importance to the simple fact that the buyers may be large, sophisticated, and resourceful corporations.[82] Large, sophisticated and resourceful corporations may, for example, have insignificant countervailing buyer power, if they only buy small volumes of a given product. In *Enso/Stora*,[83] countervailing buyer power was an important issue in finding the operation compatible. The proposed operation resulted in a concentrated supply situation with Enso/Stora achieving market shares above 60 per cent in the market for liquid packaging board used for applications such as milk and juice cartons. However, the new entity was faced with a very concentrated buyer structure, with notably Tetra Pak as the main buyer accounting for more than 60 per cent of the purchases of liquid packaging board. It should also be noted that Tetra Pak had been instrumental in growing this market and had developed several of the suppliers of liquid packaging board. Consequently it was concluded that the purchasers were sufficiently powerful and had sufficient countervailing buyer power, for example through an ability to develop alternative suppliers and therefore, if need be, prevent the creation or

---

[81] T–102/96 *Gencor v Commission* [1999] not yet reported.

[82] eg *Shell/Montecatini* (Case IV/M269) [1994] OJ L332/48; *Orkla/Volvo* (Case IV/M582) [1996] OJ L66/17; *Crown Cork & Seal/Carnauld Metalbox* (Case IV/M603) (1995) [1996] OJ L75/38; *Kimberley-Clark/Scott Paper* (Case IV/M623) [1996] OJ L183/1; and *The Coca-Cola Company/Carlsberg a/s* (Case IV/M833) (1997), [1998] OJ L145/41.

[83] Case IV/M1225 (1998).

strengthening of a dominant position. Nevertheless, the Commission has in the past only accepted that a company has countervailing buyer power if specific reasons for the existence of such power can be identified.

The crucial question in respect of countervailing buyer power is to what extent it **4.152** neutralizes the effect of the possible creation or strengthening of a dominant position. It is, for example, clear that large supermarket chains have more buyer power than small independent grocery stores. Consequently, the former are able to purchase on more favourable conditions than the latter. However, this does not necessarily mean that the buyer power of large supermarket chains is sufficient to neutralize the effect of the creation of a dominant position in the sense that it brings the overall price level in the market down to its pre-merger level or even competitive level. It may only mean that supermarket chains are able to buy more cheaply than small grocery stores. The overall price level in the market can still be such that it implies dominance. While not excluding the possibility of taking countervailing buying power into account in its assessment, it should be noted that, in the past, the Commission has only taken countervailing buying power into account to the extent that it could be proved that it neutralized the effect of the creation or strengthening of a dominant position.

The Assessment of Potential Competition

The assessment of whether potential competition is a constraining force on com- **4.153** panies in a given market relies basically on the assessment of entry barriers for the likely potential entrants. If entry barriers are low and consequently entry is easy and rapid then, normally, potential competition would be considered in the assessment of the degree of effective competition in a market. On the other hand, if entry barriers are high, and consequently entering the market will be difficult and slow, then potential competition would not be considered as a source of competition.

The assessment of potential competition depends on the specific case. However, **4.154** the Commission has normally only accepted taking potential competition into account, if potential competitors could enter the market within one year. The Commission thus partly relied on potential competition in its decision to clear *Mercedes-Benz/Kässbohrer*.[84] In this case the question was how quickly potential competitors could enter the German bus market. Resourceful competitors such as Volvo and Renault were already in the process of entering the German market for buses, and it was forecast that potential competitors would have an impact on the market within a relatively short time period. In *Saint Gobain/Wacker Chemie/NUM*,[85] on the other hand, the question was whether potential Chinese

---

[84] Case IV/M477 [1995] OJ L211/1.
[85] Case IV/M774 (1996) [1997] OJ L247/1.

and Eastern European producers would be able to enter the EEA markets for sili-
con carbide. It was found that entry was likely only to take place after a period of
several years. Potential competition was not considered a sufficiently strong constraining force on the merging parties in this case. Similar arguments were considered in two aerospace mergers.[86] In *Boeing/McDonnell-Douglas* it was in
particular noted that research and development costs for a new large jet aeroplane
amounted to some US $10 billion and production involved large-scale advantages
in the form of learning curve effects. Finally, in *Kesko/Tuko*,[87] it was even concluded that the merger led to an increase in entry barriers (and consequently a
decrease in potential competition).

4.155 Entry barriers vary from market to market and can take numerous forms such as
regulatory barriers, for example concerning packaging, or purely economic barriers, such as the need to build brands requiring heavy advertising expenditures,
access to distribution, access to technology, or high research and development
costs. In its assessment of entry barriers the Commission has attached importance
to the existence of sunk costs.[88] A typical example has been the case where it was
necessary to build a brand in order to compete in a market; such brand building
required heavy advertising expenditure. These expenditures would be sunk costs
and would therefore increase the risk of entering a market.[89] The impact of sunk
costs as an entry barrier could be even higher in cases where the market leader
already has high market shares, since the market leader may be able to increase further its advertising expenditures and thereby raise entry barriers for potential
entrants.

Vertical Mergers

4.156 Vertical mergers involve mergers between companies at two different stages of a
production process. A producer of a certain product may, for example, decide to
buy one of its distributors. In such cases no addition of market shares within a
given market takes place, and any increases in market power which will lead to the
creation or strengthening of a dominant position within a particular market will
have to come through the vertical links between markets.

4.157 The Commission has, in a number of cases, found that vertical integration leads
to the creation or strengthening of a dominant position.[90] In these cases, the competition problems arose mainly because the vertical integration resulted in domin-

---

[86] *Aerospatiale-Alenia/de Havilland* (Case IV/M53) [1991] OJ L334/42 and *Boeing/McDonnell-Douglas* (Case IV/M877) [1997] OJ L336/16.

[87] Case IV/M784 (1996) [1997] OJ L110/53.

[88] eg *Aerospatiale-Alenia/de Havilland*—see n 86 above.

[89] eg *Procter & Gamble/VP Schickedanz (II)* (Case IV/M430) [1994] OJ L354/32, and *Kimberley-Clark/Scott Paper* (Case IV/M623) (1996).

[90] *MSG Media Service, Nordic Satellite Distribution, RTL/Veronica/Endemol* (Case IV/M553) [1996] OJ L294/14, and *The Coca-Cola Company/Carlsberg a/s* (n 75 above).

ance due to the creation or strengthening of foreclosure effects to one or more markets. On the other hand in vertical mergers where no foreclosure effects are found, the Commission has not normally been concerned about the vertical aspects of the merger.

Conglomerate Mergers

Conglomerate mergers are mergers where several different relevant product markets are affected. The markets may or may not be neighbouring markets. In cases where the affected markets are completely different in terms of physical product characteristics, customer groups, production facilities, distribution, etc, they would normally be assessed completely separately and no consideration of any links between the markets would be considered.   **4.158**

In cases involving related relevant product markets, the Commission will include   **4.159** the relationships between the involved markets in its assessment. Such effects have been analysed in detail in several cases. In *Tetra Pak/Alfa-Laval*,[91] it was found that the dominant position of Tetra Pak in aseptic packaging processing machines would not be reinforced nor could this position be leveraged by Tetra Pak to the markets for food processing machines in which Alfa-Laval was active. For other consumer products such conglomerate effects have, on the other hand, been found to be important. In consumer products markets such as beers, soft drinks, or spirits the ability to offer a portfolio of products such as a portfolio of spirits or a portfolio of beers and soft drinks has thus been found to be a distinct advantage.[92] Such conglomerate effects are often of particular importance in cases where the merging parties are already dominant in one market, and where this dominant position through various means can be leveraged into a neighbouring market or the dominant position even reinforced by the creation of a dominant position in a neighbouring market. Such leverage can take place through various means like the ability to push products in neighbouring markets by insisting that these products will only be sold as part of a portfolio or through the ability to obtain status as exclusive supplier to customers of a portfolio of products.

In conglomerate mergers the Commission has in some cases such as *Magneti*   **4.160** *Marelli/CEAC*,[93] *Accor/Wagon-Lits*,[94] *ABB/Daimler-Benz*,[95] and *Boeing/McDonnell-Douglas*[96] included the financial strength of the parties to a merger in its assessment of the merger. It is not excluded that a merger involving a financially strong

---

[91] Case IV/M68 [1991] OJ L290/35.
[92] *The Coca-Cola Company/Carlsberg a/s* (n 75 above) and *Guinness/Grand Metropolitan* (Case IV/M938) (1997) [1998] OJ L288/24.
[93] Case IV/M43 [1991] OJ L222/38.
[94] Case IV/M126 [1992], OJ L204/1.
[95] Case IV/M580 (1995) [1997] OJ L11/1.
[96] *Boeing/McDonnell-Douglas* (Case IV/M877) [1997] OJ L336/16.

company could lead to a finding of a strengthening or a creation of a dominant position, simply due to the fact that one of the merging companies is financially strong.

Oligopolistic Dominance

4.161 Oligopolistic markets, where only a few large suppliers account for most of the market supply, can be highly competitive. However, under certain circumstances oligopolistic markets may also be characterized by no or insignificant competition. In this situation a mere adaptation to market conditions causes anti-competitive parallel behaviour whereby the oligopoly becomes dominant. Active collusion is, therefore, not required for members of the oligopoly to become dominant. Similar negative effects which arise from a dominant position held by one firm arise from a dominant position held by an oligopoly.

4.162 The Commission has in several previous decisions examined oligopolistic dominance, for example *Nestlé/Perrier*,[97] *Kali-Salz/MDK/Treuhand*,[98] and *Gencor/ Lonrho*.[99] *Nestlé/Perrier* and *Kali-Salz/MDK/Treuhand* were cleared subject to conditions, whereas *Gencor/Lonrho* was prohibited. The French Government appealed against the Commission's decision in *Kali-Salz/MDK/Treuhand* arguing that oligopolistic dominance was not covered by the Merger Regulation, since there was no explicit reference to oligopolistic dominance therein. Judgment was given in the case by the European Court of Justice on 31 March 1998.[100] The European Court of Justice annulled the Commission's decision, but concluded that oligopolistic dominance was covered by the Merger Regulation subject to due consideration for the rights of defence of third parties.

4.163 In its assessment of oligopolistic dominance the Commission has in previous cases tended to analyse, first, whether the structural features of the market were such that the market was prone to oligopolistic dominance. In this regard the Commission has looked at whether the market was transparent, involved a homogeneous product, had a moderate level of growth and a low rate of technological change, high barriers to entry, no countervailing buyer power, and so on. While not excluding that oligopolistic dominance could also exist in other market environments, it is believed that markets with such characteristics are prone to tacit coordination, particularly if the concentration of the industry is high. Having established that a market is prone to oligopolistic dominance, the Commission has analysed the level of past competition to see whether there was already oligopolistic dominance and simply to understand the nature of past competition.

---

[97] Case IV/M190 [1992], OJ L356/1.
[98] Case IV/M308 (1993) [1994] OJ L186/38.
[99] Case IV/M619 (1996) [1997] OJ L11/30.
[100] Joined cases C–68/94 and C–30/95 *French Republic and Société commerciale des potasses et de l'azote (SCPA) and Entreprise minière et chimique (EMC) v Commission* [1998] ECR I–1375.

Finally, as the last step in the analysis, the Commission has then looked at how the proposed concentration would affect competition in the oligopoly. This analysis will normally involve both the impact an operation may have on the market, for example by increasing the transparency or entry barriers, as well as the impact the operation has on competition between the oligopolists in terms of the incentives to compete and the possibilities of retaliation. Under certain circumstances the merger will result in a situation where there will be few incentives for the members of the oligopoly to compete. In the past the Commission has concluded that a merger which gives rise to such a situation amounts to the creation or strengthening of a dominant oligopolistic position.

In the judgment given by the Court of First Instance on 25 March 1999 in *Gencor* **4.164** *v Commission*,[101] the Court confirmed the Commission's decision and dismissed the appeal. In the judgment the Court accepted that the Commission can look at factors such as market transparency, product homogeneity, a moderate level of growth, a low rate of technological change, high barriers to entry, etc in its analysis of whether a market is prone to tacit co-ordination. Furthermore, of particular interest is that the Court interpreted the judgment in *Società Italiana Vetro SpA, Fabbrica Pisana SpA and PPG Vernante Pennitalia SpA v Commission* (*'Flat Glass'*)[102] as far as the role of structural links between members of an oligopoly is concerned. The Court explicitly said that the reference to structural links in *Flat Glass* was merely by way of example, and that structural links are not necessary for a finding of oligopolistic dominance. Therefore, according to this judgment, it can be concluded that the focus of analysis in the assessment of oligopolistic dominance is the likelihood of tacit co-ordination and not whether there are structural links between the members of an oligopoly.

Failing Company

The failing company defence was applied in *Kali-Salz/MDK/Treuhand*, where a **4.165** dominant position was found to be created in the German market for potash. However, the case was cleared because it was considered that a prohibition would have led to the same market outcome as a clearance. In the reasoning of the decision the following three criteria were in particular set out in this respect:

— the company will go bankrupt within the immediate future;
— the market shares of the company would in any case go to the merging party; and
— there is no less anti-competitive way of selling the company.

---

[101] T–102/96 *Gencor v Commission* [1999] not yet reported.
[102] Joined cases T–68/89, T–77/89 and T–78/89 *Società Italiana Vetro SpA, Fabbrica Pisana SpA and PPG Vernante Pennitalia SpA v Commission* [1992] ECR II–1403.

4.166 In the past the failing company defence has been considered in other cases involving companies in financial difficulties. However, so far the Commission has only
applied the failing company defence in *Kali-Salz/MDK/Treuhand* where it could
be shown that the market outcome was not likely to be different, even if the case
was prohibited. The Commission has not in the past accepted an extension of the
failing company defence to failing divisions[103] or to companies having entered a
so-called 'death spiral'.[104]

Efficiency Defence

4.167 In some merger proceedings the parties have brought forward arguments related
to technical and economic progress resulting from the merger. The Commission
has in some of these cases included a discussion of the impact of technical and economic progress in its decision in the case.[105] However, the Merger Regulation does
not allow for an efficiency defence in the sense that the negative effects of a merger
are weighed up against the positive effects of the merger. The Merger Regulation
only allows efficiency considerations to be included in the assessment 'provided
that it is to the consumer's advantage and does not form an obstacle to competition.' (Article 2(1)(b)).

Remedies

4.168 If in a particular case the Commission has established that a merger will lead to the
creation or strengthening of a dominant position, it is often still possible to proceed with the merger, if a satisfactory remedy to the competition problem created
by the merger can be found. In this respect the Commission has always been willing to consider remedies and works constructively with the merging parties in
order to solve the competition problems otherwise created by a merger. A prohibition decision has been taken only if no satisfactory remedy could be found.
Consequently, most cases which were likely to lead to a creation or strengthening
of a dominant position have in the past been cleared with one or more remedies.

4.169 In order for the Commission to take proposed remedies into account they normally have to be of a structural nature. 'Structural' refers to the need for the remedy to re-establish the market structure in such a way that the creation or
strengthening of a dominant position resulting from the merger has been eliminated. The focus of the remedy is, therefore, the maintenance of competitive market structures. An example of a structural remedy could be a divestiture of a
business or sale of assets such as brands or production capacity. In contrast so-
called 'behavioural' remedies have not been accepted under the Merger

---

[103] eg *Saint Gobain/Wacker Chemie/NUM* (Case IV/M774) (1996) [1997] OJ L247/1.
[104] *Boeing/McDonnell-Douglas* (Case IV/M877) [1997] OJ L336/16.
[105] eg *Nordic Satellite Distribution* (Case IV/M490) (1995) [1996] OJ L53/20.

Regulation. By behavioural undertakings are meant remedies which amount to statements of intent or promises not to abuse a dominant position. They could for example involve undertakings not to increase prices or to continue to supply competitors on a non-discriminatory basis following a merger. In past decisions, where the parties have offered such undertakings, the Commission has noted the existence of the undertakings. While recognizing that such behavioural undertakings may not be without value in particular market circumstances, they have not been taken into account in merger decisions. This is a logical approach, since the purpose of the Merger Regulation is to maintain competitive market structures by preventing dominant positions from being created or strengthened as a result of mergers.[106]

There have been several cases which have been cleared subject to divestiture remedies. Some of the most recent are *Guinness/Grand Metropolitan*,[107] *Anglo American Corporation/Lonrho*,[108] *The Coca-Cola Company/Carlsberg a/s*,[109] *Kimberley-Clark/Scott*,[110] *Procter & Gamble/Schickedanz (II)*,[111] *ABB/Daimler-Benz*,[112] *Crown Cork & Seal/Carnauld Metalbox*,[113] and *Orkla/Volvo*.[114] The Commission has in these cases insisted that the undertaking given by the merging parties must be an absolute commitment to divest the required asset within a given time period. A sale must be made by the end of the divestiture period without regard to the price for the assets. The Commission has also normally emphasized that a divestiture must be relatively speedy, ie within six to twelve months. Furthermore, in order to secure the viability in the market place of the assets to be sold, the Commission has in some cases insisted on the appointment of a trustee to manage the assets in the interim period. However, the particular circumstances of a specific case must be taken into account in deciding on the appropriate time frame for and the structuring of the sales procedure. **4.170**

Remedies Accepted under Article 6

It has been the Commission's practice to accept remedies in first phase cases where the competition concern: **4.171**

---

[106] In the judgment in T–102/96 *Gencor v Commission* (not yet reported) the CFI specifically stated that the decisive point is not whether a remedy is behavioural or structural in nature, but whether it prevents the creation or strengthening of a dominant position. This is not in contradiction with the above, since it cannot be completely excluded that a behavioural undertaking under certain circumstances can prevent the creation or strengthening of a dominant position.

[107] Case IV/M938 (1997) [1998] OJ L288/24.

[108] Case IV/M754 (1997) [1998] OJ L149/21.

[109] Case IV/M833 (1997).

[110] Case IV/M623 (1996).

[111] Case IV/M430 (1994).

[112] Case IV/M580 (1995).

[113] Case IV/M603 (1995).

[114] Case IV/M582 (1996).

— is clear cut;

— is easily remedied; and

— where the fulfilment of the remedy can be easily monitored.

4.172 The Commission has considered that this approach provides an appropriate regulatory response which is proportionate to the size of the competition problem. The Commission's policy has been to give Member States and interested third parties the opportunity to comment on proposed remedies before an Article 6(1)(b) decision has been adopted.

The Position to Date

4.173 From 1990 to 1997, the Commission has accepted remedies in sixteen Article 6(1)(b) cases. The nature of these remedies varies widely: some cases involve disposals, others open the market to potential competitors, while yet others are examples of distribution restrictions being erased thereby relaxing the market structure. Finally, a number of cases give assurance to customers and competitors that they will be treated equitably by the merging parties.

4.174 The Commission has always striven to ensure that remedies are 'structural' because of the need to re-establish the market structure in such a way as to eliminate the anti-competitive effects of the concentration. By way of contrast, 'behavioural' remedies, promises by companies not to abuse the market through their dominant position, have been rejected. Naturally the definition of what forms a structural or a behavioural remedy is open to interpretation. This lack of distinction may be seen in the different forms of remedy which are discussed further below.

Disposals

4.175 The first, *Courtaulds/SNIA*,[115] concerned the disposal by Courtaulds of its minority interest in INACSA, the third-ranking competitor on the market, if defined as Western Europe. No further details, including timing of the sale, were disclosed. In *Elf Atochem/Rütgers*,[116] the Commission accepted an engagement from Rütgers that it would end its structural link with a major competitor, to allow competition to take place between Bitmac (in which Rütgers held 48 per cent of the shares) and Rütgers. In *Repola/Kymene*,[117] the parties would have become the only operator on the Finnish market for paper sacks. However, a structural remedy was devised whereby 'the operation [would] not result in an addition of market shares since . . . will be divested'. This divestiture was considered sufficient in order to approve the operation.

---

[115] Case IV/M113 (1991).
[116] Case IV/M442 (1994).
[117] Case IV/M646 (1995).

In the subsequent *Bank Austria/Creditanstalt* Case,[118] the Commission identified **4.176** two areas of concern: banking and the construction sector. In the former the Commission accepted Bank Austria's engagement to sell its stake in GiroCredit and to reduce the merging parties' shareholding in OeKB, an export insurance operation. As concerns the construction sector, Bank Austria committed itself to selling its stake in either Universale or Stuag. No information is provided in the decision as regards the timing or details of the disposal process.

Finally, the Commission approved the operation in *Lyonnaise des Eaux/Suez*,[119] **4.177** following a commitment by Lyonnaise des Eaux to divest most of its interests in the disposal and cleaning services sectors in Belgium. Details of the disposal process are contained in the decision which set out:

— the period allowed for the disposal;
— details of a trustee, approved by the Commission, who would oversee the sales process; and
— the requirement that the purchaser must be a viable, independent competitor.

Clearly this approach reflects that followed in a number of Article 8(2) decisions.

Market Entry

The question of market entry has been clearly addressed in three cases concerning **4.178** the airline industry when finding the operations compatible in terms of Article 6(1)(b). In *Air France/Sabena*,[120] *British Airways/TAT*,[121] and *Swissair/Sabena*[122] the Commission concluded that dominant positions would arise due to the operations in connection with certain city pairs, for example Paris/Brussels, Paris/London, and Brussels/Zürich respectively. In order to resolve such problems the airlines agreed to assist any potential, new entrant competitors. If such competitors were unable to obtain sufficient slots through normal allocation channels the airlines committed to give up a number of their existing slots.

The terms and conditions of these commitments, together with related matters, **4.179** are clearly detailed in the decisions.

Elimination of Distribution Restrictions

In the first case of this nature, *Grand Metropolitan/Cinzano*,[123] the operation **4.180** would have led to Grand Metropolitan controlling the whole vermouth market, at a distribution level, in Greece. However, Grand Metropolitan agreed to give up the distribution of Martini brands and accordingly the problem was resolved. In

---

[118] Case IV/M873 (1997).
[119] Case IV/M916 (1997).
[120] Case IV/M157 (1992).
[121] Case IV/M259 (1992).
[122] Case IV/M616 (1995).
[123] Case IV/M184 (1992).

Unilever France/Ortiz Miko (II),[124] the Commission was concerned by the question of 'freezer exclusivity'. Consequently Unilever made known to the Commission that the Frigecreme network of wholesale distributors would be opened to competition. This was achieved by the suppression of an exclusivity clause in the relevant contracts.

4.181 On the other hand, in *Elf Aquitaine-Thyssen/Minol*,[125] the Commission was confronted with numerous comments from competitors. They were concerned as to their degree of dependence (in the former East Germany) on Minol for their oil supplies. Accordingly, the Commission accepted a commitment by Elf that it would grant competitors throughput rights and supplies from Minol's depots on commercially acceptable terms based on local conditions.

Customer and Competitor Assurance

4.182 In a number of cases the Commission has accepted remedies which appear to be a means by which customers or competitors have been reassured, as to potential action by the merging parties, rather than to be remedies to dispel the possible creation of dominant positions. Consequently the remedies received have not resolved competition concerns but rather have allowed the Commission to respond to customer, supplier, and competitor concerns voiced as a result of the announcement of the concentration.

4.183 For example, in *Elf Aquitaine-Thyssen/Minol*,[126] competitors argued that Elf's right to manage existing refineries in the former East Germany would give it a competitive advantage as the refineries' losses would be borne by the Treuhandanstalt. However, the Treuhandanstalt stated, to the Commission, that it would exercise its inspection rights to verify that the refineries' production was priced according to market data. Accordingly Elf would not gain access to products on more favourable terms than would otherwise be the case. The purpose of this statement is therefore to assure competitors rather than to resolve a competition concern.

4.184 Similarly in the three cases concerning international courier services,[127] competitors to the merging parties appeared to be concerned that they may be charged higher prices for access to the distribution network than those available to the parties due to cross-subsidization from the parties' exclusive concessions. Accordingly a remedy was offered in the first case (and repeated in the others) to allay this fear.

---

[124] Case IV/M422 (1994).
[125] Case IV/M235 (1992).
[126] Case IV/M235 (1992).
[127] *TNT/Canada Post, DBP Postdienst, La Poste, PTT Post and Sweden Post* (Case IV/M102) (1991), *PTT Post/TNT-GD Net* (Case IV/M787) (1996), and *PTT Post/TNT/GD Express Worldwide* (Case IV/M843) (1996).

The Interpretation of Article 6(2)

The Amending Regulation allows the Commission expressly to accept remedies **4.185**
which resolve competition concerns identified during the first phase investigation. The provisions of Article 6(2) and (3) mirror, in many ways, the provisions
of Article 8: the Commission may attach conditions and obligations to the remedies entered into by the merging parties to ensure compliance therewith; similarly
the Commission may revoke a decision based on Article 6(2).

Given the established history of the Merger Regulation there is no reason to sup- **4.186**
pose that the Commission will depart from its earlier practices of accepting disposals and allowing the entry of potential competitors as the main types of
remedy. Undoubtedly there will be an increase in merging parties' interest in first
phase remedies to ensure 'quick-fix' solutions; however, what may well change is
the level of transparency in the decision.

Since the entry into force of the Amending Regulation, the Commission has **4.187**
adopted a number of decisions on the basis of Article 6(2). The first was *Owens-
Illinois/BTR Packaging*.[128] This case concerned the acquisition of BTR's Packaging
Business Group by Owens-Illinois Inc, which gave rise to a significant overlap for
the production of glass containers for use in the food and beverage industries in
the UK and Ireland. On the widest possible market definitions, Owens-Illinois
would achieve a market share of 'less than 60%'; one competitor would have a
market share of 'between 10% and 20%' and four other competitors market
shares of 'less than 10%'.

The Commission concluded that the 'operation as notified would threaten to cre- **4.188**
ate a dominant position' and accepted a remedy in order to approve the operation.
The remedy comprised the proposed sale of the glass container manufacturing
business carried on by BTR Packaging, together with a 50 per cent share in a glass
recycling business. This remedy will eliminate an overlap between the parties in
these businesses.

The remedy is subject to strict terms which are clearly set out in the annex to the **4.189**
decision. These terms are, broadly:

— divestment within . . . of completion—which was to take place . . . after the
  adoption of the Article 6(1)(b) decision;
— the purchaser is to be 'a viable existing or prospective competitor unconnected
  to and independent of Owens-Illinois';
— the appointment of a trustee to oversee the disposal process;
— reporting to the Commission by both the trustee and Owens-Illinois;

---

[128] Case IV/M1109 (1998).

— the trustee to receive an irrevocable mandate to find a purchaser for the business if Owens-Illinois has not entered into a binding letter of intent to sell within . . . of completion. Owens-Illinois would have to sell to a purchaser found by the trustee within . . . of completion.

4.190 The degree of clarity and transparency in this remedy clearly indicates the path the Commission intends to follow and sets a valuable precedent for the future.

Timing for First Phase Remedies: The Implementing Regulation

4.191 Article 18 of the Commission Regulation (EC) 447/98 on the notifications, time limits and hearings provided for in Council Regulation (EEC) 4064/89 on the control of concentrations between undertakings[129] ('the Implementing Regulation') lays down the time period in which remedies must be submitted: this is within three weeks from the date of the receipt of the notification. While this period may appear clear from the wording of the Implementing Regulation, a reading of Article 3 of Council Regulation (EEC, EURATOM) 1182/71 determining the rules applicable to periods, dates and time limits[130] may imply that the three week period should be extended:

— to allow an extra day at the beginning of the period; and
— to allow the last day of the period to fall on a working day if the last day was otherwise a Commission holiday or weekend.

4.192 However, it is likely that the Commission will interpret the three-week deadline strictly and, to avoid doubt, remedies should be submitted within this period. Similarly the Commission can be expected to adopt a decision in an Article 6(2) case strictly within the six week period foreseen by Article 10(1) of the Merger Regulation.

4.193 However, another aspect is of relevance: should it be necessary to develop remedies to counter the Article 81 aspects of a joint venture case, and if the parties are seeking a first phase clearance, these also must be submitted within the same time period provided for in the Implementing Regulation.

C. The Merger Regulation: Procedure

(1) The Pre-Notification Stage

Confidentiality

4.194 It is sometimes said there is a fear of parties to a possible or probable merger that news of their operation will become public prior to its notification to the

---

[129] [1998] OJ L61/1 (amended by [1998] OJ L66/25).
[130] [1971] OJ Spec Ed 354.

Commission. This reason is frequently referred to when companies, or their lawyers, avoid pre-notification meetings with the Commission. This fear is unfounded: the relevant legislation contained in the EC Treaty, Article 286, requires that officials do not reveal business secrets. Similarly Article 17(2) of the Merger Regulation forbids officials (and other servants) from disclosing information acquired through the application of the Merger Regulation.

The Commission has a solid record of maintaining confidential, pre-notification **4.195** contacts. However, within certain limits, a degree of confidentiality may be retained until notification takes place. For example, in all written correspondence between the parties and the Commission code names may be employed to conceal the identities of the parties. Obviously the case team will have to be aware of these identities in order to appreciate the nature, scope, and potential problems that the operation initiates.

It must be appreciated that the less the case team knows of the parties to the oper- **4.196** ation, the less able it will be to provide constructive advice leading to a satisfactory outcome for both the parties and the Commission.

The Role and Purpose of Pre-Notification Meetings

The role and purpose of the pre-notification meeting is: **4.197**

— to inform the Commission about the background to a possible or probable merger;
— to discuss the timing of the notification and of the subsequent decision;
— for the Commission to provide guidance to the parties on technical, jurisdictional, and other aspects of the Merger Regulation;
— for the Commission to indicate the type and quantity of data that will be necessary in the notification; and
— for the parties to gain some idea as to the likely attitude of the Commission on substantive issues arising from the operation.

Waivers

Article 3(2) of the Implementing Regulation empowers the Commission to dis- **4.198** pense with the obligation on the parties to provide some of the information or documents required by the notification form. The Implementing Regulation does not require that the parties formally request a waiver from submitting data; neither does it require the Commission to respond formally to such a request. Consequently careful note should be taken at pre-notification meetings to ensure that both the parties and the Commission agree as to the exact extent and nature of the waiver. With such an agreement the notifying parties have a legitimate expectation that a submitted notification would be deemed complete. However, it must also be recalled that a waiver given by the Commission is conditional on a full and complete disclosure of the relevant facts. Otherwise, a notification may still be declared incomplete.

Short Form Notification

4.199 In the case of a concentration leading to the creation of a joint venture company with a *de minimis* presence in the EEA, notification is permitted in an abbreviated format. The *de minimis* presence is based on the anticipated turnover of the joint venture and the value of assets that are to be transferred to the future operation. The test is cumulative: the anticipated turnover must be less than ECU 100 million and the assets transferred must not exceed ECU 100 million.

4.200 The Commission, however, reserves the right to require a full or, where appropriate, partial notification where the operation does not conform to the above thresholds or where necessary for an adequate investigation of the operation.

(2) Notification—First Phase

The Obligation to Notify and its Timing

4.201 Article 4 of the Merger Regulation requires that concentrations with a Community dimension be notified to the Commission not more than one week after the conclusion of the agreement giving rise to the concentration; or the announcement of the public bid; or the acquisition of a controlling interest. The Commission has, however, always distinguished between the obligation to notify and the possibility of allowing operations to be notified prior to the date when it becomes obligatory.

4.202 This approach has allowed companies some flexibility in the planning of their operations in order that they may meet deadlines for shareholders' meetings, fiscal year-ends etc. However, the Commission has insisted in cases where notification has taken place at a date prior to when it becomes obligatory that the companies should have entered into binding contracts to complete the operation, subject, of course, to Commission approval. The Commission will also insist that the investigation cannot be hindered by claims of confidentiality concerning the merger plans. On the other hand, it will not accept notifications in cases where companies or consortia are bidding for future contracts, for example as mobile telephone operators. This is simply because a great number of companies or consortia bid for such contracts without any knowledge of the outcome. To accept all such notifications would impose an intolerable burden on the Commission's scarce resources.

Completeness: The Application of Article 4 of the Implementing Regulation

4.203 Article 4 of the Implementing Regulation allows the Commission to declare a notification incomplete, thereby postponing the start of the time period for the assessment of a notified operation. However, it is common for the Commission to allow the notifying party several days to submit the required data in cases where the notification is less than 'materially' incomplete. Such action does not extend the Commission's deadline for adopting a decision.

'Material incompleteness' is hard to define but the concept is unlikely to be **4.204** invoked if the notifying parties have made their best efforts to answer fully all questions contained in the notification Form CO. Consequently, in order to be sure that a notification is complete, the notifying parties should discuss notification requirements with the Commission at a pre-notification meeting and obtain appropriate waivers for the submission of specific data.

The procedural steps that take place on notification are as follows. Upon receiving **4.205** the notification the registry of the Commission will issue a receipt. Should the notification then be found to be incomplete, the Commission must inform the notifying parties, in writing, without delay (Article 4(2)) and set a deadline for the submission of the missing information. Upon receipt of the missing information, a further letter will be issued acknowledging receipt of the missing information, stating that the notification is complete, and giving the effective date on which the data were received (Articles 3(3) and 4(2)). This last point sets the starting point for the deadline by which the Commission must adopt a decision.

Two other points are important. First, Article 4(4) states that misleading or incor- **4.206** rect information shall be considered as being incomplete information. Should such information be supplied, either negligently or intentionally, the Merger Regulation provides that fines may be levied on the responsible party. Secondly, Article 4(5) requires the Commission to publish the date of the receipt of the notification. Should an incomplete notification mean that this date is no longer valid, the date on which the notification becomes effective (following the receipt of the missing data) must also be published.

Calculation of Legal Deadline

Article 10(1) of the Merger Regulation states that a decision taken pursuant to **4.207** Article 6(1) must be taken within one month. The period of one month starts on the day following the receipt of the notification, or the day following the receipt of additional information should the Commission deem the notification to be incomplete. The Implementing Regulation (Article 6(4)) specifies that the first day of the period has to be a working day. Consequently weekends and Commission holidays are adjusted for in calculating the start of the one-month period.

The period of one month ends on the same date, one month after the first day of **4.208** the period. Should this date not appear in the month the period ends, it falls instead on the last day of that month (Article 7(4)). However, if the last day of the period is not a working day, the period ends on the expiry of the following working day (Article 7(8)). Should Commission holidays (the dates of which are published annually in the *Official Journal*) fall into the one-month period, the relevant number of days are added to the period.

4.209 An example:

—Notification	1 April 1998
First working day after notification (assuming that the notification is complete)	2 April 1998
—End of period therefore	2 May 1998
However, 2 May 1998 is a Saturday	
Therefore end of period becomes following working day	4 May 1998
However 9, 10 , 13 April, and 1 May are Commission holidays	
—Therefore add four days making the deadline	8 May 1998

Requests for Information: The Article 11 Letter

4.210 The Commission requests information, on the basis of Article 11 letters, from two principal sources: the notifying parties and their customers, suppliers, and competitors. The power to request such information is contained in Article 11 of the Merger Regulation. However, the request for information, in the form of a letter, is only the first step in a two-stage procedure.

4.211 The request for information must set out the legal basis for and purpose of the request; identify the information required; set out the penalties that may be levied if the information provided is incorrect, and specify the date for a response. Should the requested information not be provided within the stated time period or if only an incomplete response is given, the Commission may, by way of a decision, require that the information be provided. Should this decision be ignored the Commission may impose fines on the recalcitrant undertaking.

4.212 The deadline given for a response may often appear short. However, it must be understood that the Commission only has one month in which to reach a conclusion on a notified operation: two-thirds of this time will comprise the actual investigation.

4.213 In connection with Article 11 letters it should be noted that the Commission may levy fines by virtue of Articles 14(1) and 15(1) of the Merger Regulation. Such fines may be imposed for a non-response within the specified period; or the supply of incorrect information; or the supply of incomplete information. By virtue of Form CO (Introduction Section B) this power extends to the notifying parties wherever they are situated. On the other hand this power only extends, as regards requests for information, to suppliers, customers, competitors, trade associations, etc located within the EEA. This is because while the Merger Regulation is only applicable in the European Union its scope is extended into the EEA countries by virtue of the EEA Agreement.

The language regime of requests for information is also of importance. It is to be **4.214** expected that the formal request would be in the case language chosen by the noti- fying parties or that of the country where the addressee is located. However, the detailed questions would normally be drafted in the language of the case. Consequently recipients may approach the Commission to seek clarifications if the language used is not one with which they are familiar. The language of the case (Article 2(4) of the Implementing Regulation) must be an official language of the Community and is used throughout the proceeding by the parties and the Commission.

Other Form of Investigation: Articles 12 and 13

These provisions form the legal basis for the Commission to carry out inspections **4.215** ('dawn-raids') under the Merger Regulation and these powers are equivalent to those under Council Regulation (EEC) 17/62 First Regulation implementing Articles 81 and 82 of the Treaty. Inspections are carried out in co-operation with the competent authority of the Member State. In the course of such inspections the authorized officials are empowered to enter the premises of the company, examine all business records, take copies thereof, and to ask for oral explanations on the spot. Should the company resist the inspection order, measures to enforce this order will be taken by the national authorities, in accordance with national law.

Under the Merger Regulation the Commission will not normally have to resort to **4.216** using these measures as most companies involved in notifiable mergers provide the requested information voluntarily, in order to obtain, as speedily as possible, the legal certainty that is provided by a decision under the Merger Regulation. However, if there are indications that the involved companies are not providing the required information in full, the Commission will not hesitate to use its pow- ers under these provisions in appropriate cases. This has, to date been carried out on two occasions: in one case there were indications that a notifiable transaction had not been notified voluntarily, and, in another case, there were indications that the provided information was not materially complete.

Articles 14 and 15—penalties

The provisions of Articles 14 and 15 allow the Commission to impose fines or **4.217** periodical penalty payments for a number of offences relating to companies' duties under the Merger Regulation. For certain grave offences such fines could potentially be very significant, ie up to 10 per cent of the aggregate turnover of the companies concerned.

The Merger Regulation provides for the mandatory notification of all concentra- **4.218** tions with a Community dimension. In order to maintain a level playing field it is

essential that this obligation be respected by all companies involved in such concentrations. The Commission is therefore particularly vigilant in applying the
fining provisions of the Merger Regulation to ensure that companies do not create advantages for themselves by intentionally or negligently failing to notify
transactions.

4.219 In the first case where a fine was imposed under the Merger Regulation, the South
Korean company Samsung was fined ECU 33,000 for its failure to notify the
acquisition of AST Research Inc and for implementing the transaction without
Commission approval.[131]

4.220 The Commission will not hesitate to impose significantly larger fines if it learns of
a failure to notify a case with more significant effects on competition, if the failure
to notify was intentional, or if the company concerned would not co-operate with
the Commission when its failure to notify has been discovered.

Article 7

4.221 Article 7 of the Merger Regulation effects a suspension of a concentration unless
the Commission adopts a decision derogating from the suspensive effect.

Impact of the Amending Regulation

4.222 The Amending Regulation has made two fundamental changes to Article 7. The
first is that the suspensive effect of notification is no longer simply valid for the
three weeks following notification but lasts until a decision of compatibility is
adopted on the basis of either Article 6 (1)(b) or Article 8(2).

4.223 Secondly, an applicant for a derogation from the suspensive effect of notification,
or to vote shares acquired by way of public bid, no longer has to prove that serious
damage would be caused to an undertaking concerned or to a third party. Instead
the Commission will assess the effect of the suspension on one or more of the
undertakings concerned or on a third party or on the threat to competition posed
by the concentration. However, it is to be anticipated that derogations from the
suspensive effect will continue to be the exception.

Article 7(4) Derogation: When to Apply

4.224 When wishing to obtain a derogation from the suspensive effect of notification,
on the basis of Article 7(4) it is clear that the earlier the application is made the better it is for all concerned. The reason for this is the somewhat burdensome procedure imposed by Article 18 of the Merger Regulation and Article 12 of the
Implementing Regulation.

---

[131] Commission press release IP/98/166 of 18 February 1998.

The procedural steps may be summarized as follows. The notifying parties make **4.225** a reasoned application for a derogation on the basis of Article 7(4). If the Commission concurs with their views it takes a provisional decision on the basis of Article 18(2). This provisional decision gives the notifying parties the opportunity to make known their views on the decision: should no comments arise that decision would become final.

On the other hand, should the Commission object to the application the situa- **4.226** tion becomes more complex. It must be appreciated that even in such cases the Commission has a wish to act speedily. Accordingly, a provisional decision on the basis of Article 12(2) of the Implementing Regulation would be adopted allowing the parties to make known their views and permitting an oral hearing to be held. Once such views have been made known, and/or an oral hearing has been held, the Commission would adopt a final decision annulling, amending, or confirming the provisional decision. Should no comments be made within the allotted time, the provisional decision would become final.

It is important to note that, in so far as they would be affected, other involved par- **4.227** ties to a concentration (ie the vendor and the target) are entitled to receive and comment on the provisional decision and to receive the final decision. The Commission may also deem it necessary to hear other third parties, for example in a contested takeover. However it must be appreciated that a delay may occur between the dispatch of the original decision to the notifying parties and that to the involved parties. This is due to the potential need to eliminate any business secrets of the notifying parties.

The Article 6 Decision

The first phase procedure is ended by the adoption of a decision in accordance **4.228** with Article 6 of the Merger Regulation. Such a decision may find that the concentration does not fall within the scope of the Merger Regulation; that the concentration is compatible with the common market; that the second phase should be initiated; or that, following the receipt of appropriate modifications, the concentration may be found to be compatible.

Conversion of Article 6(1)(a) Decisions

An Article 6(1)(a) decision can arise either because the concentration does not **4.229** attain the turnover thresholds requiring notification and therefore granting the Commission the competence to assess the operation or because the operation does not form a concentration within the meaning of the Merger Regulation. In the latter case the operation may be assessed on the basis of the EC Treaty Article 81.

The ability to convert a notification under the Merger Regulation into a notifica- **4.230** tion for the EC Treaty Article 81 purposes requires that the notifying parties have answered positively Section 11.2 of the notification Form CO. However, the notifying parties should be prepared to provide further information to the Commission as required by Article 5(2) of the Implementing Regulation.

Who Receives the Decision?

4.231 The Article 6 decision is addressed to the notifying party or parties, or their representatives if so appointed, who receive a copy on the day of its adoption. Similarly the competition authorities of the Member States receive the decision soon after its adoption.

4.232 The Commission has generally interpreted Article 6(2) restrictively in contradiction to the Commission Notice on the concept of undertakings concerned under Council Regulation (EEC) 4064/89 on the control of concentrations between undertakings.[132] The Commission services' view is that Article 6(5) restricts the dissemination of the decision to the undertakings concerned which have notified the operation and not to other undertakings concerned by the operation, ie the target or the acquired business.

4.233 In several cases the Commission services have been prepared to provide a copy of the Article 6 decision to target and even vendor companies. However, the distribution of decisions in such isolated cases presupposes the elimination of the notifying parties' business secrets.

Elimination of Business Secrets: The Hearing Officer's Mandate—Commission Decision of 12 December 1994 on the Terms of Reference of Hearing Officers in Competition Procedures before the Commission[133]

4.234 In the vast majority of cases the elimination of any business secrets contained in a decision is readily achieved by way of dialogue between the Commission services and the notifying parties. However, in some cases even extended dialogue cannot resolve the totality of these differences.

4.235 In such cases it is arguable whether the Hearing Officer should become involved in the dispute. Without doubt the Commission services would consult the Hearing Officer, on an informal basis, where serious conflicts arose; however, Article 5 of the mandate probably also permits a formal procedure for consultation by the parties.

4.236 Article 5(3) requires that the undertaking be informed of the fact that a business secret will be disclosed together with the reasons therefor. A time limit is also fixed for the undertaking's response. Following the receipt of the undertaking's comments, and assuming that the Commission considers that disclosure is still required, a reasoned decision adopted by the Hearing Officer would be drafted

---

[132] [1998] OJ C66/14.
[133] [1994] OJ L330/67.

and notified to the undertaking concerned. This decision would specify the date on which the information would be disclosed (Article 5(4)). The decision must allow at least a week between the dates of notification and future disclosure. This is to allow the undertaking leave to appeal the Hearing Officer's decision.

Publication of the Decision

Following the elimination of business secrets the public version of the decision **4.237** becomes available. The general public is informed of this fact by way of the publication of a summary notice in the *Official Journal*; moreover, the full text of the public version becomes available on the Internet.

(3) Notification—Second Phase

Timetable

The Commission has four months, from the start of the working day following **4.238** the day on which the second phase proceeding was initiated, in which to adopt a decision pursuant to Article 8. The four-month period may be broken down as follows.

Broadly speaking the Commission services have six weeks in which to raise further **4.239** questions with the parties, their suppliers, customers, and competitors and to analyse their responses. Two weeks are then, if appropriate, given over to the preparation of the Statement of Objections and its discussion with services which are associated to Directorate General for Competition. Upon the dispatch of the Statement of Objections the parties are permitted approximately two weeks for the preparation of the response to the Statement of Objections and to allow time to prepare for the Oral Hearing.

Subsequent to the Oral Hearing, the Commission services have a further week to **4.240** prepare a draft of the final decision. This must be sent to the Member States at least two weeks prior to the meeting of the Advisory Committee (Article 19(5)). Following the Advisory Committee the Commission services must make the appropriate changes to the draft final decision, consult associated services, and submit the draft decision to the Secretariat General of the Commission. This requires some two weeks. Finally a gap of around a further ten days is necessary between the submission of the draft decision to the Secretariat General and its adoption by the Commission.

The Statement of Objections

In cases where, following the initiation of the second phase procedure, and further **4.241** investigation and analysis, the Commission's doubts on the compatibility of a concentration with the common market persist, a statement pursuant to Article

18 of the Merger Regulation (the 'Statement of Objections') is prepared and dispatched to the notifying parties.

Purpose, Form, and Context of the Statement of Objections

4.242 The purpose of the Statement of Objections is to fulfil the Commission's obligations, contained in Article 18(1) of the Merger Regulation, of allowing the undertakings concerned to make known their views on the objections levelled against them. This requirement is reiterated in Article 13(2) of the Implementing Regulation. The Statement of Objections takes the form of a reasoned letter, which addresses all the points that could be expected to be found in the final decision. Therefore the operation/nature of the concentration are described, the product and geographic markets, and details of the creation or strengthening of a dominant position. In addition, should the parties have already submitted a remedy that has been found to be insufficient, this would also be included.

4.243 The Statement of Objections must contain all the objections against the parties that the Commission intends to employ in its final decision (Article 18(3)). A copy is also addressed to each party against whom objections are raised. The introduction of further objections, subsequent to the sending of the Statement, would require a second Statement of Objections.

Non-Confidential Version and Communication to Third Parties

4.244 On the dispatch of the Statement of Objections, the Commission will require that the notifying parties identify any business secrets contained in the Statement of Objections in order that they may be eliminated. This is necessary in order to allow the Commission to inform other involved parties of the objections (Article 13(2)) and, similarly, any third parties identified in accordance with Article 18(4) of the Merger Regulation of the same objections (Article 16(1)).

4.245 The notifying parties, other involved parties, and third parties may respond to the Statement of Objections in writing. However, a response is not obligatory. In addition, the Commission services have adopted a policy of making such parties' responses available to the other parties, after an elimination of business secrets. While the notifying parties may wish to have their response distributed, in order to present their view of the effects of the operation, the Commission cannot enforce such action.

Rights of Notifying, Involved, and Third Parties, Management and Union Bodies

4.246 The right of the notifying parties to be heard is established in Article 18(1) of the Merger Regulation; similarly Article 18(4) allows the Commission to hear other third parties and specifically members of the administrative or management bodies of the undertakings concerned and representatives of their employees. The right of representatives of employees' organizations to be heard has been confirmed in two cases[134] brought before the Court of First Instance concerning the acquisition of Perrier by Nestlé.

The Implementing Regulation is, however, more specific as regards the various parties' rights as Table 1 shows.   **4.247**

Table 1

	Receipt of Statement of Objections	Right of response to Statement	Access to the file	Attendance at Oral Hearing	Right to speak at Oral Hearing
Notifying parties	Yes	Yes	Yes	Yes	Yes
Involved parties	After deletion of business secrets	Yes	In so far as is necessary in order to exercise their rights of defence	Yes	Yes
Third parties	Limited to 'nature and subject matter of the procedure'	Yes	No	Yes	Yes

Third parties should expect that 'nature and subject matter of the procedure' be limited to a summary of the contents of the Statement of Objections although in some cases the Commission has disseminated the whole Statement subsequent to the elimination of business secrets.   **4.248**

Access to the File

The Commission has codified its policy on access to the file in its Notice on the internal rules of procedure for processing requests for access to the file in cases under Articles 81 and 82 of the EC Treaty, Articles 65 and 66 of the ECSC Treaty and Council Regulation (EEC) 4064/89.[135]   **4.249**

---

[134] Case T–12/93 *Comité Central d'Entreprise de la Société Anonyme Vittel and Comité d'Etablissement de Pierval and Fédération Générale Agroalimentaire v Commission* [1995] ECR II–1247. Case T–96/92 *Comité Central d'Entreprise de la Société Générale de Grandes Sources and Others v Commission* [1995] ECR II–1213.

[135] [1997] OJ C23/3.

4.250 The Merger and Implementing Regulations are clear on who has access to the file: only notifying and involved parties as defined in Article 11 of the Implementing Regulation. The notifying parties may have access as soon as they have received the Statement of Objections, although a slight delay, to allow a digestion of its contents, may be appropriate thus permitting a more thorough understanding of the contents of the file.

4.251 Involved parties would have access to the file at a later date. This is due to the need to eliminate business secrets from the Statement of Objections, allowing its later dispatch to the involved parties. Involved parties would need to see the Statement in order to motivate their request because Article 13(3) of the Implementing Regulation allows them access only in so far as is necessary for the purposes of preparing their observations.

What to Expect: Commission Procedure and Appeals

4.252 The transparency regarding access to the file has been greatly improved by the Commission's Notice. However, it is useful to repeat what may take place when a company's representatives arrive at the Commission to review the contents of the file.

4.253 At this point in time the contents of the file will have been split between those to which the parties can have access (or partial access) and those which are inaccessible. Accessible papers will comprise the data submitted by the parties themselves together with information in the public domain: press articles, independent statistical data, Commission reports on the industry/sector in question, etc. Partially accessible data will generally comprise those parts of third party responses submitted to the Commission which do not contain business secrets or which have had business secrets contained therein deleted. Similarly, notes of meetings, from which names etc have been deleted, would form partly accessible data.

4.254 Non-accessible papers include internal Commission documents, correspondence with the Member States, and business secrets data submitted by third parties.

4.255 The notifying parties' representatives are permitted to photocopy the accessible and partially accessible papers.

4.256 It could be that a dispute arises over access to certain documents where a notifying party to whom a Statement of Objections has been addressed believes that the Commission has documents in its possession which have not been disclosed. In such a situation the recipient of the Statement of Objections may turn to the procedure contained in the Commission's decision on the terms of reference of hearing officers in competition procedures before the Commission.[136]

---

[136] [1994] OJ L330/67.

Article 5(1) thereof permits the recipient of the Statement of Objections to issue   **4.257**
a reasoned request to the Hearing Officer indicating which documents it believes
are in the Commission's possession, which have not been disclosed, and which are
necessary for a proper exercise of the right to be heard. Article 5(2) requires that a
reasoned decision be adopted by the Hearing Officer in respect of any such
request. Such a decision could of course be challenged before the Court of First
Instance.

The Oral Hearing

An oral hearing is provided for in Article 18(1) of the Merger Regulation, when   **4.258**
persons, undertakings, and associations of undertakings, against whom the
Commission has levelled objections, are granted the right to be heard. Third parties must apply to the Hearing Officer in order to be granted leave to attend the
Hearing.

The Purpose and Timing of the Oral Hearing

The purpose of the oral hearing is to give the notifying parties, against whom a   **4.259**
Statement of Objections has been issued, the right to respond formally, setting out
their counter arguments to the Commission's objections. In addition, the oral
hearing provides the forum for other involved parties and for interested third
parties to comment on the positions of both the Commission and the notifying
parties.

The oral hearing takes place some two weeks after the dispatch of the Statement   **4.260**
of Objections and some three weeks before the meeting of the Advisory
Committee.

Who Attends?

The meeting is chaired by the Hearing Officer who has the responsibility for   **4.261**
deciding who should be admitted to the meeting. Normally the Commission services associated with the case are present together with the notifying parties, their
representatives, and other involved and interested third parties. Representatives of
the Member States are also present.

The Role of the Hearing Officer

Apart from deciding who should be admitted, the Hearing Officer also presides   **4.262**
over the meeting. He is responsible for the orderly running of the meeting, deciding whether any part of a statement contains business secrets, thereby requiring
part of the session to be held in camera. He may also be approached, prior to the
Oral Hearing, by the notifying parties in order to ascertain which third parties are
attending the hearing.

The Procedure

4.263 The procedure for the Oral Hearing is as follows: first, the Commission services make a presentation of the case, summarizing the objections against the concentration. Subsequently the Oral Hearing is given over to the notifying parties in order that they may present their appreciation of the concentration and answer the Commission's objections.

4.264 Once the notifying parties' presentation has been given, the Member States' representatives, third parties, and the Commission services are invited to pose questions. Obviously the notifying parties are expected to respond.

4.265 The next rounds of presentations are made by the involved parties followed by the third parties: questions are raised on their presentations by the Member States, other parties, and Commission services in turn. The final stage of the Oral Hearing is left to the notifying parties to make concluding remarks.

Rights of Notifying, Involved, and Third Parties, Management and Union Bodies

4.266 Article 11 of the Implementing Regulation distinguishes between notifying parties, involved parties, and third parties. Article 18(4) of the Merger Regulation specifically identifies members of management or employee bodies.

4.267 The Commission requests whether an oral hearing is required when sending the Statement of Objections to the notifying parties and, if appropriate, informing other involved parties of the objections. A hearing has to be held if requested in accordance with Article 14 of the Implementing Regulation.

4.268 The position of third parties is somewhat different. If such third parties request the right to be heard, they may be heard at the same time as the notifying or involved parties at the Oral Hearing. However, they may also be heard separately, in a meeting chaired by the Hearing Officer.

The Role of the Advisory Committee

4.269 Article 19(2) of the Merger Regulation requires the Commission to maintain a close and constant liaison with the competent authorities of the Member States. More specifically, Article 19(3) requires the Commission to consult the Advisory Committee prior to adopting a decision on the basis of Article 8 (termination of the second phase procedure), rendering a fine on an undertaking (Articles 14 and 15), or adopting implementing rules in respect of the Merger Regulation. The Advisory Committee comprises one or two representatives of each of the Member States' authorities. At least one representative from each Member State has to be competent in competition affairs.

4.270 The Advisory Committee is provided with a copy of the Commission's proposed decision, together with an 'indication of the most important documents' relevant for an appreciation of the case. In addition, a representative from one of the Member States' delegations is responsible for the presentation of the case, an indication of the questions that the meeting must address, and for drawing up the Member States' conclusions. This responsibility revolves around the Member States in alphabetical order.

Normally the meeting will address whether the concentration is of Community **4.271** dimension, whether the relevant product and geographic markets have been properly defined, whether the concentration creates or strengthens a dominant position, and whether the remedies proposed by the parties to counter the negative competitive effects are appropriate.

The Commission services associated with the case are represented at the meeting and **4.272** members of the Advisory Committee may pose questions in relation to the case.

The Committee members indicate their agreement or otherwise to the questions **4.273** posed by the Member States' representative; opinions formed are thus adopted either by unanimity or by majority. The Commission is bound by Article 19(6) to take the utmost account of the Committee's opinion and must inform the Committee in what manner its opinion has been taken into account.

In a number of cases[137] more than one Advisory Committee has been held due to **4.274** the Merger Regulation's requirements that the Commission maintains a 'close and constant liaison' with the Member States. Given the rapid evolution of the *Boeing* case such meetings were necessary on three occasions.

The Commission Procedure after the Advisory Committee

Normally there are some three to four weeks between the meeting of the Advisory **4.275** Committee and the Commission decision which is shortly followed by the legal deadline for the case.

Translation and Publication of the Decision

The decision is adopted by the Commission in the language of the case as chosen **4.276** by the notifying parties. Should this language not be English, French, or German, these three working languages of the Commission must also be available at the time of the decision's adoption. Consequently it may still be necessary to ensure the translation of the decision into seven or eight languages prior to publication.

Furthermore, the decision must be adjusted for any business secrets contained **4.277** therein. The parties are requested to identify any such secrets and the Commission services will ensure their erasure or, in the case of figures, replacement by an indicative range. Should a debate arise, the parties' final recourse is to the Hearing Officer in accordance with his mandate.

---

[137] eg *Boeing/McDonnell Douglas* (Case IV/M877) (1997).

4.278 Once the decision has been translated and business secrets have been deleted, the Commission services will forward the decision for publication in the *Official Journal.* The period between adoption of the decision and its publication may be between six and twelve months.

Availability of the Decision before Publication

4.279 Given the length of time between the adoption of a decision and its publication in the *Official Journal*, it has become the practice of the Commission services to make decisions available once business secrets have been deleted. However, the person requesting the decision must demonstrate a legitimate interest in gaining access to the decision. It is also probable, however, that the decision would only be made available in the case language.

D. Statistics 1990–1998

4.280 The number of cases examined under the Merger Regulation has grown over its period of operation. As Table 2 shows, second phase cases form a relatively small proportion of the overall total.

Table 2: Cases considered under the Merger Regulation 1990–1998

	1990	1991	1992	1993	1994	1995	1996	1997	1998	Total
Cases notified	12	63	60	58	95	110	131	172	235	936
Cases withdrawn	0	0	3	2	6	4	6	9	9	39
Net number of notifications	12	63	57	56	89	106	125	163	226	897
Decisions:										
Article 6(1)(a)	2	5	9	4	5	9	6	4	6	50
Article 6(1)(b)	5	50	47	49	80	93	109	118	217	768
Article 6(1)(b) with conditions and obligations								2	12	14
Article 6(1)(c)	0	6	4	4	6	7	6	11	12	56
Article 8(2) with conditions and obligations	0	3	3	2	2	3	3	7	5	28
Article 8(2) without conditions and obligations	0	1	1	1	2	2	1	1	2	11
Articles 8(3)/(4) prohibition	0	1	0	0	1	2	3	3	2	12
Final decisions adopted	7	60	60	56	90	109	122	135	244	883

5

ARTICLE 86—EXCLUSIVE RIGHTS AND OTHER ANTI-COMPETITIVE STATE MEASURES

A. Introduction

Competition Law Normally Deals Only with the Behaviour of Undertakings

Competition Law has traditionally dealt with anti-competitive behaviour of **5.01** undertakings. The private or public nature of ownership is irrelevant in that respect. In principle both public (ie, State controlled) and private undertakings are subject to competition rules.

State Defence Doctrine

5.02 The normal competition rules (ie, Articles 81 and 82 (former Articles 85 and 86) of the EC Treaty) only apply to the autonomous behaviour of undertakings. Such rules can only be infringed (and the undertaking held responsible) when the behaviour is the result of an autonomous decision of the undertaking. The autonomous character of the behaviour is not excluded by mere persuasion or encouragement from the State. However, binding State measures imposing particular behaviour on an undertaking do exclude such autonomy of decision. In principle, a State imposed behaviour cannot constitute an infringement of normal competition rules by the undertaking. The undertaking may invoke this 'State defence doctrine' to avoid antitrust liability when the behaviour is imposed by law. This lack of liability on the part of the undertaking is to some extent compensated for by State liability under Article 86(1) (former Article 90(1)) of the EC Treaty.[1]

State Liability under Competition Law

5.03 Even if competition law has traditionally been seen as dealing only with the behaviour of undertakings, it is obvious that State measures imposing anti-competitive behaviours may easily undermine the effectiveness of EC competition rules. This led the European Court of Justice (following the example of the US Supreme Court) to establish a doctrine that allows for a limited application of antitrust rules to State measures which force or induce undertakings to behave anti-competitively.

Application of Articles 3(g), 10, and 81/82 of the EC Treaty to Anti-Competitive State Measures

Initial Position (Broad Interpretation)

5.04 This doctrine was based on the combined application of Article 3(g),[2] Article 10,[3] and Articles 81 and/or 82 (former Articles 3(g), 5, and 85/86) of the EC Treaty and was established in the *Inno/ATAB* case.[4] The basic reasoning was as follows: Article 10 prevents Member States from adopting measures depriving EC rules of

---

[1] See para 5.55 below.

[2] Article 3 of the EC Treaty reads as follows: 'For the purposes set out in Article 2, the activities of the Community shall include, as provided in this Treaty and in accordance with the timetable set out therein: . . . (g) a system ensuring that competition in the internal market is not distorted . . .'.

[3] Article 10 (former Article 5) of the EC Treaty reads as follows:

'Member States shall take all appropriate measures, whether general or particular, to ensure fulfilment of the obligations arising out of this Treaty or resulting from action taken by the institutions of the Community. They shall facilitate the achievement of the Community's tasks.

They shall abstain from any measure which could jeopardise the attainment of the objectives of this Treaty.'

[4] Case 13/77 *Inno v ATAB* [1977] ECR 2144, paras 31–33.

their 'effet utile'. Article 3(g) establishes undistorted competition as one of the main Community goals and Articles 81 and 82 prohibit anti-competitive behaviours of undertakings. Taken together, all these provisions were interpreted by the Court of Justice as prohibiting Member States from depriving competition rules of their 'effet utile' by adopting measures that would allow the undertakings to ignore the limits imposed by Articles 81 and 82 of the Treaty.[5] At one point this case law seemed to imply that every State measure producing restrictive effects on competition would have *effects* similar to those of a cartel (or to those of an abuse of a dominant position). As a consequence every State measure producing restrictive *effects* on competition would be contrary to Articles 3(g), 10, and 81 (or 82) of the EC Treaty, even in the absence of any behaviour by the undertaking. This would mean that every measure taken by the State having an impact on the price or the quantity of goods or services would be prohibited. Such an approach would have greatly reduced the ability of Member States to intervene in the economy.

Court Narrows Interpretation

Although the theoretical implications of this doctrine were far-reaching, its prac- **5.05** tical impact has been much more limited. The reasons are twofold. First of all, the Court of Justice has subsequently interpreted this 'effet utile' in a restrictive way. According to this recent and more restrictive case law, which started in 1993 with the *Meng, Reiff* and *Ohra* cases, a mere anti-competitive effect cannot in the absence of *behaviours* of undertakings mean that the State measure is contrary to Articles 3(g), 10, and 81 or 82 of the EC Treaty.[6] Only those State measures that impose or induce anti-competitive behaviour by undertakings, reinforce the

---

[5] The leading cases of the Court of Justice were: Case 229/83 *Leclerc v Au blé vert* [1985] ECR 1; Case 231/83 *Cullet* [1985] ECR 305; Case 123/83 *BNIC v Clair* [1985] ECR 391; Joined Cases 209–213/84 *Nouvelles Frontières* [1986] ECR 1425; Case 311/85 *Vlaamse Reisbureaus* [1987] ECR 3801; Case 267/86 *Van Eycke* [1988] ECR 4769. For some of the literature on the subject see Y Galmont & J Biancarelli, 'Les réglementations nationales en matière de prix au regard du droit communautaire' [1985] RTDE ii 299; G Marenco, 'Le Traité CEE interdit-il aux Etats membres de restreindre la concurrence?' [1986] CDE année XXII, iii–iv 294–295; G Marenco, 'Effets des règles communautaires de concurrence (art 85 et 86) sur l'activité des Etats membres' in J Schwarze, (ed), *Les pouvoirs discrétionnaires des EE.MM. de la CE dans le domaine de la pol . économique et leurs limites en vertu du TCEE*, Contributions to an International Colloquium of the European University Institute, Florence 14–15 May 1987 (Baden-Baden: Nomos Verlagsgesellschaft, 1988) 53–67; P Pescatore, 'Public and Private Aspects of Community Competition Law' [1986] FCLI 381–430; M Waelbroeck, 'Les rapports entre les règles sur la libre circulation des marchandises et les règles de concurrence applicables aux entreprises dans la CEE' in Various, *Du droit international au droit de l'intégration—Liber Amicorum Pierre Pescatore* (Baden-Baden: Nomos Verlagsgesellschaft, 1987) 781–803; R Joliet, 'Réglementation étatiques anticoncurrentielles et Droit communautaire' [1988] CDE 363–382; L Gyselen, 'Anticompetitive State measures under the EC Treaty: towards a substantive legality standard' [1994] ELR Competition checklist 55 *et seq*; JF Verstrynge, 'The Obligations of Member States as Regards Competition in the EEC Treaty' [1988] FCLI 17.1–17.43; U Bøegh Henriksen, *Anti-Competitive State Measures in the European Community* (Copenhagen: Handelshøjskolens Forlag, 1994) 21–29.

[6] Case C–2/91 *Meng* [1993] ECR I–5797, para 14; Case C–185/91 *Reiff* [1993] ECR I–5847, para 14, and Case C–245/91 *Ohra* [1993] ECR I–5878, para 10.

effects of anti-competitive behaviour or delegate regulatory powers to private operators can be considered as violating these provisions. This very strict test dramatically reduces the scope of application of Articles 3(g), 10, and 81/82 as regards anti-competitive State measures.[7]

5.06 Moreover, this case law on Articles 3(g), 10, and 81/82 of the EC Treaty has never given any significant value-added to EC law. The reason is that EC competition law, contrary to many other competition systems (such as US antitrust), has always had specific provisions dealing with the most significant anti-competitive State measures, such as State Aids or exclusive rights. The need for 'creative' jurisprudence was therefore much less marked and its re-definition in a restrictive way has meant that it has had, in practice, a very limited impact.

Application of Articles 86, 87, and 88 to Anti-Competitive State Measures

5.07 Therefore, EC competition law includes not only Articles 81 and 82, the rules addressed to undertakings, but also Articles 86, 87, and 88 (former Articles 90, 92, and 93), the rules addressed to the Member States. Articles 87 and 88 deal with one of the more characteristic instruments for State intervention in the market: State aids. Due to their specific character, State aids fall outside the scope of this book.[8] The other provision, Article 86, refers to exclusive rights granted by the State in favour of certain undertakings and also to other kinds of restrictive State measures related to public or privileged undertakings. This provision also contains a limited exception from competition and other EC rules in favour of services of general economic interest. Finally, Article 86 also provides for a special procedure. These three dimensions of Article 86 are examined in this chapter.

B. Article 86(1): State Measures in Respect of Public or Privileged Undertakings

(1) Addressees and Regulatory Content

5.08 Article 86(1) (former Article 90(1)) provides:

> In the case of public undertakings and undertakings to which Member States grant special or exclusive rights, Member States shall neither enact nor maintain in force any measure contrary to the rules contained in this Treaty, in particular those rules provided for in Articles 12 and 81 to 89.

---

[7] N Reich, 'The "November Revolution" of the European Court of Justice: Keck, Meng and Audi revisited' [1994] 21 CMLRev 459–492; B Van Der Esch, 'Loyauté fédérale et subsidiarité: à propos des arrêts du 17 novembre 1993 dans les affaires C–2/91 (Meng), C–245/91 (Ohra) et C–185/91 (Reiff)', [1994] CDE v–vi 536; A Bach, 'Judgments of the Court, cases C–185/91 Reiff, C–2/91 Meng and C–245/91 Ohra' [1994] CMLRev 1357–1374.

[8] See L Hancher, T Ottervanger & PJ Slot, *EC State Aids*, European Practice Library (London: Chancery Law Publishing, 1993) for a general overview of State aid rules.

Article 86(1) of the EC Treaty is only addressed to Member States.[9] As interpreted by the Court of Justice this provision prohibits Member States from adopting or maintaining in force any measures contrary to the Treaty:

- when such measures benefit Public undertakings or undertakings to which Member States grant exclusive or special rights, or

- when these undertakings are the instrument used by the Member State for the implementation of the measures.[10]

Article 86(1) is also interpreted as applying to the *granting* of exclusive rights to any undertaking when such a grant is contrary to another Article of the EC Treaty.[11]

State measures which are related to public or privileged undertakings only fall **5.09** under Article 86(1) if they are 'contrary to the rules contained in this Treaty, in particular those rules provided for in Articles 12 and 81 to 89'. This means that Article 86(1) is not entirely self-contained, and cannot be applied alone. In order to establish a specific obligation for Member States the provision has always to be applied 'in combination with' another rule of the EC Treaty. This implies that Article 86(1) has a multiplicity of legal contents with different scopes of application.

(2) State Measures

Whilst Articles 81 and 82 refer to the behaviour of undertakings, Article 86(1) **5.10** refers to State measures. A State measure is an act undertaken by a public entity in

---

[9] Case C–41/90 *Höfner* [1991] ECR I–2015, para 16; Case C–320/91 *Corbeau* [1993] ECR I–2533, paras 10–12.

[10] See JL Buendia Sierra, *Exclusive Rights and State Monopolies in EC Law*, (Oxford University Press, 1999) chapters 4–6. Different collective works have dealt with Article 86: Various, *Concorrenza tra settore pubblico e privato nella CEE*, Colloquio di Bruxelles della 'Ligue Internationale contre la concurrence déloyale' 5–6 March [1963] RDI anno XII 1–256; Various, *L'entreprise publique et la concurrence. Les articles 90 et 37 du Traité CEE et leurs relations avec la concurrence*, Semaine de Bruges 1968 (De Temple, Bruges, 1969); Various, *Equal treatment of public and private enterprises*, 1978 FIDE Congress in Copenhagen [1978] FIDE Copenhagen volume 2; Various, *Le processus de libéralisation d'activités économiques et de privatisation d'entreprises face au Droit de la concurrence*, XVI Congrès de la FIDE [1994] FIDE Rome iii. Among the individual contributions see: R Joliet, 'Contribution à l'étude du régime des entreprises publiques dans la CEE' [1965] AFDL i 23–92; G Marenco, 'Public Sector and Community Law' [1983] 20 CMLRev 495–527; J Temple Lang, 'Community Antitrust Law and Government Measures relating to Public and Privileged Entreprises: Article 90 EEC Treaty' [1984] FCLI 543–581; H Papaconstantinou, *Free Trade and Competition in the EEC. Law, Policy and Practice* (London/New York: Routledge, 1988); LM Pais Antunes, 'L'Article 90 du Traité CEE—Obligations des Etats Membres et pouvoirs de la Commission' [1991] RTDE ii 187–209; D Edward & M Hoskins, 'Article 90: deregulation and EC Law. Reflections arising from the XVI FIDE Conference' [1995] 32 CMLRev 157–186; R Kovar, 'Droit communautaire et service public: esprit d'orthodoxie ou pensée laïcisée' [1996] RTDE xxxii (ii) 215–242, xxxii (iii) 493–533; F Blum & A Logue, *State Monopolies under EC Law* (Chichester: Wiley, 1998).

[11] Paras 5.42–5.44 below.

its role as a public authority. However, the distinction between State measures and behaviour of undertakings cannot solely be based on the private or public nature of the entity. Even if private entities cannot, as a general rule, adopt State measures, public entities may undertake economic activities. In this case, the commercial activities of the public entities are clearly subject to Articles 81 and 82, even if fulfilled directly by a public body.[12] It is therefore necessary to differentiate between the different acts of public entities, ie between 'State measures', to which Article 86(1) may apply, and the 'behaviour of public undertakings', to which Articles 81 and 82 may apply.

Formal Criteria are Not Decisive in Defining 'State Measures'

5.11   It is very tempting to rely solely on formal criteria to make the distinction referred to above. According to this approach, public law instruments would be examined under Article 86(1) and private law instruments under Articles 81 and 82.[13] This has the advantage of being a rather simple and easy to use criterion. It is also a reasonably realistic one. After all, State measures are normally adopted through laws, acts, regulations, administrative rules, or other instruments of public law. Private law contracts are normally used by public entities when exercising a commercial activity.

The Function of the Act is the Decisive Factor in Defining 'State Measures'

5.12   However, although the form of the relevant instrument is an important factor, it cannot be the sole factor. EC law has always been reluctant to rely on formal criteria in order to define the scope of its different provisions. The reason for this reluctance is that, very often, the different Member States use different legal instruments to achieve the same results. In order to be credible, EC law must be able to apply similar rules to situations that are similar from a substantive point of view. This means that the criterion of the private or public law form of the relevant act has to be complemented with another criterion: that of its functional nature. An act whose function is to regulate the market place from the perspective of the public interest would be a 'State measure'.[14] This would be the case even if adopted under the form of a private law contract.[15] An act of a purely commercial nature would fall under Articles 81 and 82 even if adopted under a public law form.[16]

---

[12]   Case C–393/92 *Almelo* [1994] ECR I–1517, para 31.
[13]   In Case C–18/93 *Corsica Ferries* [1994] ECR I–1825, para 43, the Court of Justice applied Article 86 to an act as commercial in nature as a tariff. The criterion used was obviously a formal one.
[14]   Case 30/87 *Bodson* [1988] ECR 2479.
[15]   For instance, local authorities in Germany usually grant public service concessions to electricity distributors by means of private law contracts. It is submitted that these concessions should be treated as State measures to the extent that their aims are to regulate the market place from a perspective of public interest.
[16]   Case 41/83 *British Telecommunications* [1985] ECR 873, paras 19–20.

The Form of the Act Creates a Presumption, but its Function is the Decisive Criterion in Defining it as a 'State Measure'

It follows from this that the functional nature of the act—rather than its form— **5.13** should, at least in theory, be the decisive criterion in determining the borderline between Article 86(1) on the one hand and Articles 81 and 82 on the other hand. In practice, however, a private law form will create a strong presumption that one is dealing not with a State measure but with a 'behaviour' of a public undertaking. It would nevertheless still be possible—but not easy—to destroy this presumption by relying on the regulatory nature of the act.

State Measures May Be Adopted by any Type of Public Authority

State measures can be adopted by any public entity of a Member State provided **5.14** that the entity is invested with some kind of public authority role. Local or regional authorities, for instance, can adopt State measures like national authorities.[17]

(3) Related to Public or Privileged Undertakings

In order to fall under Article 86(1), a State measure has to have a link with one or **5.15** more 'undertakings' (ie, entities exercising an 'economic activity'). In principle, this undertaking has to be either a 'public undertaking' or an 'undertaking to which the Member State grants exclusive or special rights'. These different concepts, and the precise nature of this link between the measure and the undertaking, are examined below.

'Economic Activity'

Article 86(1) Applies to State Regulation of Economic Activities

Article 86(1) only applies if the State measure relates to one or more entities that **5.16** exercise an 'economic activity'. The State *measure* itself must of course have a regulatory nature, but the *activity*, which is being regulated by that measure, must be of an economic nature. In other words, Article 86(1) applies to State regulation of economic activities. Regulatory measures relating to non-economic activities (such as 'exclusive rights' in respect of national defence, public security, etc) are not covered by Article 86(1).

Definition of 'economic activity'

The existence of an 'economic activity' is a prerequisite for the application, **5.17** not only of Article 86(1), but of any competition rule. This notion embraces all activities of a commercial or industrial nature. Unfortunately, the borderline

---

[17] Case 30/87 *Bodson* [1988] ECR 2479; Case C 323/93 *Lu Crespelle* [1994] ECR I–5077.

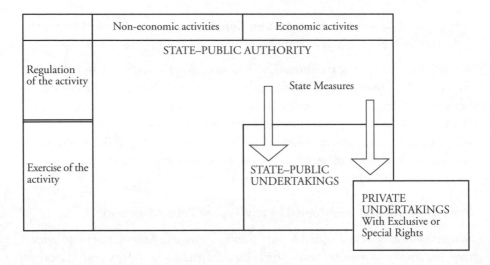

Figure 1: The dual nature of the State: public authority and public undertaking

between economic and non-economic activities is particularly difficult to draw in the public sector. Indeed, the State provides its citizens with many 'services' in areas such as utilities, health, social security, education, or defence and it is not always easy to determine which ones are 'economic' (and whose regulation is therefore subject to Article 86(1)) and which ones are not. Utilities, such as telecommunications, energy, transport, or postal services, are clearly economic activities. However, other public sector activities, such as health, social security or education, have a less clear status. This makes it necessary to find rational criteria by which to differentiate between the two groups.

Criteria Used by the European Court of Justice

5.18 In its *Höfner* judgment, the Court of Justice seemed to imply that any activity that may conceivably be exercised by a private undertaking should be considered as an economic activity, irrespective of its actual mode of financing.[18] This far-reaching interpretation would have implied that activities such as health or social security were 'economic' and would, therefore, be subject in principle to the competition rules.

5.19 However, the Court of Justice has subsequently modified this interpretation in the *Poucet* judgment by making clear that 'compulsory social security systems' cannot be considered as economic activities.[19] The reason seemed to be the mode of financing, based on 'solidarity' amongst contributors. Other more recent

---

[18] Case C–41/90 *Höfner* [1991] ECR I–2015, paras 20–22.
[19] Cases C–159 and 160/91 *Poucet* [1993] ECR I–637, paras 17–19.

judgments, by relying on criteria such as the exercise of public prerogatives[20] or the pursuit of objectives of general interest,[21] have made the definition of economic activity even more confused.

Thus, the Court of Justice seems to consider that activities whose financing is **5.20** based on solidarity or which are exercised with public power prerogatives are non-economic activities. *A contrario*, all the other activities should in principle be considered as economic. There is not, however, a clear definition of these concepts.

A Critical View

It is submitted that the criterion used in *Höfner* to determine which activities are **5.21** 'economic' seems the most appropriate as it is based on the objective nature of the activity rather than on the particular regime applying to that activity. These regimes (concerning the mode of financing, for instance) may be different for the same activity in the different Member States. It is therefore difficult to use them as a basis for a Community definition. It is easier to determine, by examining the situation in the different countries, whether an activity can actually be exercised by a private undertaking.

One should not forget that the mere qualification of an activity as 'economic' does **5.22** not automatically imply an obligation to open that activity to competition. Issues such as the 'solidarity' in the financing or the character of 'general interest', if they do not exclude the 'economic' nature of the activity, may justify the application of the exception set out in Article 86(2).[22]

'Public' Undertaking

Article 86(1) applies, first of all, to State measures having a link with one or more **5.23** 'public undertakings'. The notion of a public undertaking embraces all undertakings that are subject to the dominant influence of the public administrations of a Member State (at national, regional, or local level).

Definition of Public Undertaking

The Commission defined 'public undertaking' as any undertaking in which the **5.24** public administrations may exercise, directly or indirectly, a dominant influence.[23] This dominant influence may be the result of ownership, of financial participation, or of the rules governing the undertaking. Dominant influence is presumed when the public administrations, directly or indirectly, either control

---

[20] Case C–364/92 *Eurocontrol* [1994] ECR I–43, paras 24–30.
[21] Case C–343/95 *Calì* [1997] ECR I–1547, paras 22–23.
[22] See para 5.122 *et seq* below. See Buendia Sierra (n 10 above) paras 1.141–1.201, for a detailed study of the concept of 'economic activity'.
[23] Article 2 of Commission Directive (EEC)80/723 concerning the transparency of financial relations between Member States and their public undertakings [1980] OJ L195/35.

the majority of the capital of the undertaking, or the majority of the places on the governing or controlling bodies of the undertaking. This notion of 'dominant influence' has many similarities with the notion of 'control' under the Merger Regulation.[24]

A Separate Legal Entity Is not Necessary

5.25 Public undertakings are often organized as autonomous entities with a distinct legal personality. However, this is not always the case. A public administration can also be considered as a public undertaking to the extent that it is directly involved in the operation of an economic activity.[25]

Public Undertakings after Privatization

5.26 The 'public' character of undertakings has rarely been controversial in the past, but privatization may have changed this. Even if privatization normally implies that a 'public undertaking' becomes a 'private undertaking', this is not always the case. In some cases the Government loses ownership but retains a 'golden share' in the privatized company. The powers connected with this 'golden share' may in some cases be so important as to lead to 'dominant influence' by the public authorities. In such a scenario a privatized undertaking may well remain a 'public undertaking' at least from the point of view of Article 86(1).

'Privileged' Undertakings

5.27 Article 86(1) also applies to State measures concerning 'undertakings to which Member States grant exclusive or special rights'. These 'privileged' undertakings may be public or private.[26] This means that Article 86(1) may well apply to State measures concerning a certain kind of private undertaking. What characterizes these undertakings is the granting by the Member State of 'special or exclusive rights'. It is therefore necessary to examine these concepts.

Exclusive Rights

5.28 **Notion of 'exclusive right'.** An 'exclusive right' is the right granted by a State measure to one undertaking to exercise an economic activity on an exclusive basis. The legal notion of 'exclusive right' roughly corresponds with the popular notion of 'monopoly'.

---

[24] Article 3(3) of Council Regulation (EEC) 4064/89 concerning the control of concentrations between undertakings [1989] OJ L395/1.

[25] Case 118/85 *Commission v Italy* (transparency) [1987] ECR 2599 para 11.

[26] The expression 'privileged enterprises' was used by J Temple Lang, 'Community Antitrust Law and Government Measures relating to Public and Privileged Enterprises: Article 90 EEC Treaty' [1984] FCLI 543–581.

The definition of exclusive rights means that, for each economic activity and in a   **5.29**
given territory, there is a single beneficiary, a monopolist.[27] It is also possible to
have exclusive rights granted in parallel to different undertakings provided that
they operate in different territories.[28] In this case, each of the operators is a
monopolist within its reserved territory. However, when the activity is reserved to
more than one competing undertaking one is faced, not with an exclusive right,
but with a 'special' right.[29]

Exclusive right and dominant position are different things.   Some judgments   **5.30**
of the Court of Justice[30] and some decisions of the Commission[31] suggest that the
mere existence of an exclusive right automatically puts its holder in a dominant
position. However, it is submitted that such an automatic link does not exist. The
concept of an exclusive right is closely connected to but independent from the
concept of 'dominant position' under Article 82 of the EC Treaty. The existence
of an exclusive right entirely depends on legal factors. The existence of a dominant
position depends on a number of economic factors. It is true that in most cases the
protection from competition granted by the exclusive right puts the undertaking
in a dominant position, as the Court said in *Telemarketing*,[32] but this is not always
the case. The key question, as the Court explained in *Bodson*,[33] is whether the
scope of the exclusive right embraces a substantial part of a market which is 'relevant' from an economic point of view. If this is the case, the exclusive right will
lead to a dominant position on that market (and Article 82 may apply). If this is
not the case, the holder of the exclusive right may fall short of having a dominant
position within the meaning of Article 82. In any event, contrary to some inter-
pretations, it is clear that the mere existence of an exclusive right does not automatically imply the existence of a dominant position.

Exclusive rights are created by State measures.   In order to fall under Article   **5.31**
86(1), the exclusive right has to be created by a State measure.[34] This means that
it has to be granted by a public administration acting in its role as a public authority. Exclusive rights granted by a public undertaking acting as an economic operator do not fall under Article 86(1) but under Article 81. For instance, in the
Almelo case, an exclusive purchase contract between a local council (acting in
its capacity as undertaking in charge of distribution of electricity) and a regional

---

[27] Case T–260/94 *Air Inter* [1997] ECR II–997, para 120–121. See Buendia Sierra (n 10 above)
Chapter 1, for a detailed study of the concept of 'exclusive right'.
[28] Case 30/87 *Bodson* [1988] ECR 2479; Case C–323/93 *La Crespelle* [1997] ECR I–5077, para 17.
[29] Paras 5.34–5.37 below.
[30] Case C–41/90 *Höfner* [1991] ECR I–2015, para 28; Case 260/89 *ERT* [1991] ECR I–2925,
para 31; Case C–179/90 *Port of Genoa* [1991] ECR I–5889, para 14; Case C–18/93 *Corsica Ferries*
[1994] ECR I–1783, paras 39–41; Case C–323/93 *La Crespelle* [1997] ECR I–5077, paras 17 and 24.
[31] *British Telecommunications* [1982] OJ L360/36, para 26.
[32] Case 311/84 *Télémarketing* [1985] ECR 3261, para 16.
[33] Case 30/87 *Bodson* [1988] ECR 2479, paras 26–29.
[34] The notion of 'State measure' has been examined in paras 5.10–5.15.

distributor was examined within the framework of Article 81.[35] The Commission seems to consider that Article 86(1) only applies if the exclusive right is granted through law, administrative regulation, or other act with a public law form.[36] However, although State measures normally have a public law form, this is not essential. An exclusive right granted by a public authority thought a private law contract may fall under Article 86(1) if its regulatory rather than commercial function can be proved.[37]

5.32 **Need for a discretionary decision by the State.**   The granting of the exclusive right must be the result of a *discretionary* decision by the public authority. This may consist in an artificial limitation of the number of players to a single one and/or in the discretionary choice of the single operator when a natural monopoly exists. In both cases the undertaking may feel obliged towards the public authority whose discretionary decision is at the origin of its monopoly position. This may give the public authority some influence over the behavior of the undertaking. This is not the case in respect of patents and other intellectual property rights, which are automatically granted once the various legal conditions are fulfilled. The Court of justice considers that intellectual property rights are not 'exclusive rights' within the meaning of Article 86.[38]

5.33 As explained below[39] exclusive rights play a dual role within Article 86(1). On the one hand, the provision refers to State measures concerning undertakings to which Member States *have previously granted* exclusive rights. On the other hand, Article 86(1), as interpreted by the Court of Justice, also applies to the *original* granting of an exclusive right to an undertaking.

Special Rights

5.34 The notion of 'special rights' and its relationship with that of 'exclusive rights' has for a long time been controversial. The Court of Justice condemned the Commission for its failure to differentiate between these categories,[40] and the Commission has finally provided, in its 'satellites' Directive (1994), a definition of 'special rights':[41]

---

[35] Case C–393/92 *Almelo* [1994] ECR I–1517, paras 30–31.

[36] See the definition of 'exclusive rights' contained in Article 2(1) of Commission Directive (EC)94/46 on satellite communications [1994] OJ L268/15.

[37] For instance, it is submitted that electricity concessions in Germany could be treated as State measures, despite their private law form, to the extent that the aim of the granting authorities is to regulate the market place from a perspective of public interest.

[38] Case 13/77 *Inno v ATAB* [1977] ECR 2115, para 41.

[39] See paras 5.42–5.44 below.

[40] Case C–202/88 *Terminal equipment for telecommunications* [1991] ECR I–1223, paras 45–47; Cases C–271, 281 and 289/90 *Telecommunications services* [1992] ECR I–5883, paras 28–32.

[41] See definition of 'special rights' contained in Commission Directive (EC)94/46 on satellite communications [1994] OJ L268/15.

'Special rights' means rights that are granted by a Member State to a limited number of undertakings, through any legislative, regulatory or administrative instrument, which, within a given geographical area,

—limits to two or more the number of such undertakings, otherwise than according to objective, proportional and non-discriminatory criteria, or

—designates, otherwise than according to such criteria, several competing undertakings, or

—confers on any undertaking or undertakings, otherwise than according to such criteria, any legal or regulatory advantages which substantially affect the ability of any other undertaking to import, market, connect, bring into service and/or maintain telecommunication terminal equipment in the same geographical area under substantially equivalent conditions[.]

The Commission includes in this definition two different kind of rights. 'Special rights' are, first of all, the rights to exercise an economic activity in a given territory granted by a State measure *only to a limited number of undertakings.* If the legal notion of 'exclusive right' finds its parallel in the popular notion of 'monopoly', these 'special rights' roughly correspond with the popular notion of 'oligopoly'.

It is important to underline that the Commission also considers as 'special rights' **5.35** the legal advantages granted by State measures only to some of the undertakings that are active in a market which is, in principle, open to competition. In this second scenario, public authorities do not restrict the number of operators but give some of them other legal privileges implying a competitive advantage. An example of this kind of special right is the right granted to some telecommunication operators to manage the numbering system in a Member State. The qualification of these rights as 'special rights' means that Article 86 would continue to apply as regards these undertakings, even if they no longer enjoy either exclusive rights or special rights of the first category.

Special rights only exist if there is a *discretionary* decision by the public Authority. **5.36** This may consist in an artificial limitation of the number of players and/or in the discretionary choice of the operators. No special rights exist when the access to an activity (such as a profession) is restricted to those fulfilling certain predetermined conditions, as long as there is no limitation on the number of operators.[42]

In order to fall under Article 86(1), the special rights have to be created by State **5.37** measures. This means that they have to be granted by a public administration acting in its role as a public authority. The Commission seems to consider that Article 86(1) only applies if the special rights are granted through law, administrative regulation, or other act with a public law form. However, as has already been explained when examining the notions of 'State measure' and 'exclusive right', this is not an absolute requirement.

---

[42] Case 13/77 *Inno v ATAR* [1977] ECR 2115, para 41.

The Connection between the Measure and the Undertaking

Kinds of Connection Required by Article 86(1)

5.38 Article 86(1) only applies to State measures that have some kind of connection with public or privileged undertakings. General measures affecting all undertakings (public and private—privileged or not) in the same manner do not fall within Article 86(1).

5.39 However, the precise nature of the connection required by Article 86(1) is not explained. Article 86(1) merely says that 'in the case of' these undertakings, Member States shall neither adopt nor maintain in force measures contrary to the rules of the Treaty. As interpreted by the Court of Justice and the Commission, this means that a State measure falls under Article 86(1):

(a) when such *measures benefit* public undertakings or undertakings to which Member States grant exclusive or special rights; and/or

(b) when these public or privileged *undertakings are the instrument* used by the Member State for the implementation of the measures; and/or

(c) when the measure consists of the granting or maintenance in force of an *exclusive right*.

State Measures which Benefit the Undertaking

5.40 Most State measures fall under Article 86(1) because they benefit a public undertaking or an undertaking to which a Member State grants exclusive or special rights. The granting of an exclusive right to an undertaking, for instance, obviously benefits that undertaking.

State Measures which Use the Undertaking as an Instrument

5.41 This kind of beneficial effect is not essential in order for Article 86(1) to apply, however. The provision also applies to measures that use public or privileged undertakings as instruments by imposing on them certain behaviours, even when the measures do not benefit the undertakings in question. For instance, in the *Corsica Ferries* case, the Court of Justice found that Article 86(1) applied to a measure imposing on an undertaking having an exclusive right for 'pilotage' services in the Port of Genoa a system of tariffs, which discriminated according to the national or foreign origin of each transport service.[43] This discrimination was not beneficial for the undertaking having the exclusive right but was nevertheless found to be an Article 86(1) State measure.

---

[43] Case C–18/93 *Corsica Ferries* [1994] ECR I–1783.

State Measures Granting an Exclusive Right

As has been seen, the general rule is that State measures fall under Article 86(1) **5.42**
when such measures benefit public undertakings or undertakings to which
Member States grant exclusive or special rights and/or when these undertakings
are the instrument used by the Member State for the implementation of the measures. However, State measures consisting in the granting or maintenance in force
of *exclusive rights* have a particular regime.

It was thought by some commentators that exclusive rights would only be con- **5.43**
sidered State measures falling under Article 86(1) when they were granted to
either a *public* undertaking or to a private undertaking to which a Member State
had previously granted an exclusive or special right. However, the Court of Justice
has interpreted Article 86(1) as applying to the *original* granting of an exclusive
right to an undertaking as well, even if the undertaking in question is neither a
public undertaking nor a private undertaking to which Member States had previously granted an exclusive right. In the *Port of Genoa* case, for instance, the Court
found that the only exclusive right granted to a private undertaking, the company
of dockers, fell under Article 86(1).[44] In *La Crespelle* the exclusive rights granted to
various private undertakings were also examined under Article 86(1).[45]

The Dual Role of Exclusive Rights within Article 86(1)

This approach means that the exclusive right may be, in respect of Article 86(1), **5.44**
both the *State measure* and/or the element that makes the *undertaking* fall under
that provision. Indeed, exclusive rights play a dual role within Article 86(1). On
the one hand, the provision refers to State measures concerning undertakings to
which Member States *have previously granted* exclusive rights. On the other hand,
Article 86(1), as interpreted by the Court of Justice, also applies to the *original*
granting of an exclusive right to an undertaking. The original granting of an
exclusive right is a 'State measure' under Article 86(1) even if the undertaking in
question is neither a public undertaking nor a private undertaking to which
Member States have previously granted an exclusive right.

General Measures Do not Fall under Article 86(1)

Article 86(1) only applies to State measures to the extent that these measures are **5.45**
connected—in one of the above-mentioned ways—with public or privileged
undertakings. When such a link or connection does not exist (because the measure applies in the same way and with similar effects to all of the undertakings
in a particular sector), we are concerned with 'general' measures to which
Article 86(1) does not apply.[46] This does not exclude the possible application of

---

[44] Case C–179/90 *Port of Genoa* [1991] ECR I–5889, para 2.
[45] Case C–323/93 *La Crespelle* [1997] ECR I–5077, paras 15–22.
[46] Temple Lang, (n 10 above) 552; Pais Antunes (n 10 above) 200.

other provisions of the EC Treaty, such as Articles 28 or 49 (former Articles 30 and 59).

(4) Contrary to Another Provision of the EC Treaty

5.46 State measures which are related to public or privileged undertakings only fall under Article 86(1) if they are 'contrary to the rules contained in this Treaty, in particular those rules provided for in Articles 12 and 81 to 89'. This means that Article 86(1) cannot be applied alone—in order to establish a specific obligation for Member States, it has always to be applied 'in combination with' another rule of the EC Treaty. Article 86(1) is therefore a 'règle de renvoi' whose legal content depends on that of the rule which is applied in combination with it.

5.47 This means that Article 86(1) has a multiplicity of legal contents with different scopes of application. As a result, a State measure may in some cases violate both Article 86(1) in combination with Article 82 and Article 86(1) in combination with Article 28[47] or with Article 49.[48] In other cases, a State measure may be compatible with Article 86(1) in combination with Article 82 while being incompatible with Article 86(1) in combination with Articles 28 or 49,[49] or vice versa.[50]

It is therefore necessary, in order to analyse the legal content of Article 86(1), to distinguish between its application in combination with the antitrust rules and its application in combination with the free movement rules.

(5) Article 86(1) in Combination with the Competition Rules Addressed to Undertakings

5.48 Article 86(1) not only reminds Member States of their obligation to respect the rules of the EC Treaty that are addressed to them, but also prohibits Member States from adopting measures contrary to Articles 81 and 82 of the EC Treaty, rules that are in principle addressed not to the Member States but to undertakings. As Articles 81 and 82 have as their object the behaviour of undertakings and not State measures,[51] their application to Member States through Article 86(1) in some cases requires an adaptation of their logic.[52] In other words, when applied in combination with Article 86(1) as regards State measures, the contents and scope of Articles 81 and 82 are not necessarily the same as when these Articles are directly applied to the behaviour of undertakings.

---

[47] Case C–179/90 *Port of Genoa* [1991] ECR I–5889, paras 21 and 24; Case C–18/88 *RTT* [1991] ECR I–5941, paras 28 and 36.

[48] Case 260/89 ERT [1991] ECR I–2925, paras 26 and 38.

[49] Case C–323/93 *La Crespelle* [1997] ECR I–5077, paras 22 and 29.

[50] Case C–41/90 *Höfner* [1991] ECR I–2015, paras 34 and 40.

[51] See section A of this chapter.

[52] Buendia Sierra (n 10 above) Chapters 4 and 5; A Pappalardo, 'Régime de l'Article 90 du Traité CEE: les aspects juridiques', in Various, *L'entreprise publique et la concurrence. Les articles 90 et 37 du Traité CEE et leurs relations avec la concurrence*, Semaine de Bruges 1968 (De Temple, Bruges, 1969), 94; Papaconstantinou (n 10 above) 76.

(a) Article 86(1) in Combination with Article 82

According to the case law of the Court of Justice and the doctrine of the European **5.49** Commission, a State measure concerning a public or privileged undertaking will infringe Article 86(1) in combination with Article 82 when the following conditions are met:

(1) the undertaking must be in a dominant position on a market which is relevant from an economic point of view and which embraces a substantial part of the common market;

(2) the measure must

—either actually lead the undertaking to behave in such a way as to abuse its dominant position,

—or have the potential to lead the undertaking to behave in such a way as to abuse its dominant position,

—or produce effects similar to those of an abusive behaviour;

and

(3) the effects of the abuse or the effects of the State measure must be capable of affecting intra-Community trade.

Dominant Position

For Article 86(1) to apply in combination with Article 82, the public or privileged **5.50** undertaking has to be in a dominant position on a market which is relevant from an economic point of view and which embraces a substantial part of the common market.

This dominant position may well be the result of State measures, such as an **5.51** exclusive right, but the mere existence of an exclusive right does not automatically imply the existence of a dominant position.[53] The notion of 'dominant position' is an economic one. In principle, this notion does not vary when Article 82 is applied in combination with Article 86(1). It is true that in most cases the protection from competition granted by the exclusive right puts the undertaking in a dominant position, as the Court said in *Telemarketing*,[54] but this is not always the case. The key question, as the Court explained in *Bodson*,[55] is whether the scope of the exclusive right embraces a substantial part of a market which is 'relevant' from an economic point of view. If this is the case, the exclusive right will imply a dominant position on that market. If this were not the case, Article 86(1) might not be

---

[53] See para 5.30 above.
[54] Case 311/84 *Telemarketing* [1985] ECR 3261, para 16.
[55] Case 30/87 *Bodson* [1988] ECR 2479, paras 26–29.

applied in combination with Article 82. In practice, however, both the Court of Justice and the Commission often presume the existence of a dominant position from the existence of an exclusive right.[56] It is submitted that it should be possible to reverse that presumption with economic analysis showing that, despite the exclusive right, the undertaking is not in a dominant position.

State Measures Leading to Actual Abusive Behaviour of the Undertakings

5.52 Article 86(1) in combination with Article 82 applies first of all to State measures that lead, or may lead, a public or privileged undertaking to behave in such a way as to abuse its dominant position. Any behaviour which would normally be considered as an abuse contrary to Article 82 if spontaneously adopted by a dominant undertaking, will fall under Articles 86(1) and 82 when it is imposed or induced by a State measure.

Different Kinds of Abuses

5.53 Among the more typical abuses under Articles 86(1) and 82 are those related to prices. Price regulation is a common instrument for State intervention in the utilities sector, where the presence of public undertakings or undertakings with exclusive or special rights is also normal. The tariffs applied by these undertakings are often established and/or approved by the public authorities. In some cases these State approved tariffs may lead the undertaking to engage in discriminatory,[57] excessive,[58] and/or predatory pricing which, if adopted spontaneously, would infringe Article 82. If this is the case, the State approved tariff would infringe Article 86(1) in combination with Article 82. The substantive criteria to determine the discriminatory, excessive, or predatory character of a price are the same irrespective of whether Article 82 is applied alone or in combination with Article 86(1).

5.54 Other typical abuses under Articles 86(1) and 82 are those implying a 'refusal to deal' resulting, not from an autonomous behaviour of the monopolist, but from a State measure. A typical variety is the refusal to grant access to an 'essential facility' such as the refusal to grant a ferry operator access to a port.[59]

---

[56] Case C–41/90 *Höfner* [1991] ECR I–2015, para 28; Case 260/89 *ERT* [1991] ECR I–2925, para 31; Case C–179/90 *Port of Genoa* [1991] ECR I–5889, para 14; Case C–18/93 *Corsica Ferries* [1994] ECR I–1783, paras 39–41; Case C–323/93 *La Crespelle* [1997] ECR I–5077, paras 17 and 24; *British Telecommunications* [1982] OJ L360/36, para 26.

[57] Case C–18/93 *Corsica Ferries* [1994] ECR I–1781, para 43; Case C–242/95 *GT Link* [1997] ECR I–4449; *Zaventem* [1995] OJ L216/8.

[58] Case C–179/90 *Port of Genoa* [1991] ECR I–5889, para 19; Case C–242/95 *GT Link* [1997] ECR I–4449.

[59] *Rødby* [1994] OJ L55/52.

Only the State is Responsible for State Imposed Abuses

It has always been accepted that Article 86(1) in combination with Article 82 pro-   **5.55**
hibits Member States from *obliging* their public or privileged undertakings to
abuse their dominant position.[60] One should keep in mind that Article 82 taken
in isolation can only be infringed (and the undertaking held liable) when the
behaviour is the result of an autonomous decision of the undertaking. In principle, a State imposed behaviour cannot constitute an infringement by the undertaking of normal competition rules. Thus, by interpreting Articles 86(1) and 82
as an obligation upon Member States to refrain from imposing abusive behaviours
on their public or privileged undertakings, the lack of liability of the undertaking
under Article 82 is compensated for by the liability of the State under Articles
86(1) and 82.

Both the State and the Undertaking are Liable for State Induced Abuses

In general, Article 86(1) in combination with Article 82 prohibits Member States   **5.56**
from legally obliging public or privileged undertakings to abuse their dominant
position. However, in the absence of a binding imposition to abuse, it is generally
agreed that Article 86(1) in combination with Article 82 also prohibits Member
States from merely *inducing* their public or privileged undertakings to abuse their
dominant position. Of course, the mere presence of State inducement does not
exclude either the autonomous character of the behaviour of the undertaking or
its potential liability under Article 82.[61] This might at most be considered as a mitigating factor in the establishment of fines.[62] These non-binding inducements
may, however, have a very severe anti-competitive impact on the market. It is
therefore logical to establish in these cases two parallel potential liabilities: one for
the State under Articles 86(1) and 82 for having induced the undertaking to abuse
and one for the undertaking under Article 82 for having responded when it was
not bound to do so.[63]

State Inactivity

Some authors even suggest that the simple *inactivity* of the Member State when   **5.57**
faced with an abusive behaviour by a public or privileged undertaking should be

---

[60] Case 30/87 *Bodson* [1988] ECR 2479, para 33.
[61] Temple Lang (n 10 above) 558.
[62] The Guidelines on the method of setting fines imposed pursuant to Article 15(2) of
Regulation No 17 and Article 65(5) of the ECSC Treaty, [1998] OJ C9/3, consider that the 'existence of reasonable doubt on the part of the undertaking as to whether the restrictive conduct does
indeed constitute an infringement' is an attenuating factor. It is submitted that such a 'reasonable
doubt' would often exist when a Member State induces the undertaking to act in such a way.
[63] A Pappalardo, 'Measures of the States and Rules of Competition of the EEC Treaty' [1984]
FCLI 527–528.

enough for Article 86(1) in combination with Article 82 to apply.[64] However, nothing in the case law of the Court of Justice or in the practice of the Commission suggests that a mere failure to prevent an abuse engages the responsibility of the Member State.[65]

State Measures Affecting the Structure of Competition and Leading to Potential Abusive Behaviour of Undertakings

No Need for Actual Abuses

5.58 Even if some kind of positive action by the Member State is always required for Article 86(1) to apply, this positive action does not need to be related to one specific abuse. Article 86(1) also applies as regards State measures affecting the structure of the market if the resulting structure leads an undertaking to abuse. This means that, for Articles 86(1) and 82 to apply, there is not an obligation to establish first that an actual abuse has been committed. What is required is to establish that the State measure is such as could lead an undertaking to abuse. Of course, being able to prove that actual abuses have been committed will help in establishing that a measure leads an undertaking to abuse, but this is not an absolute requirement. In the *RTT* judgment, the Court of Justice clearly said that Articles 86(1) and 82 may apply even in the absence of actual abuses.[66]

The Granting of Regulatory Powers to an Undertaking

5.59 There is broad consensus that Article 86(1) in combination with Article 82 is violated when a Member State entrusts a public undertaking active in a competitive market with regulatory tasks. Such a measure places the undertaking in a situation of conflict of interest between its regulatory mission and its commercial objectives. As a regulator of the market place, this undertaking can easily use its regulatory powers to inflict competitive disadvantages on its competitors. The combination of the granting of regulatory power with the objective situation of a conflict of interest creates a situation inevitably leading the public undertaking to abuse of its dominant position. The accumulation of commercial and regulatory functions in the same entity is therefore incompatible with Articles 86(1) and 82

---

[64] I Hochbaum, 'Commentaire de l'Article 90 du Traité CEE' in Thiesing, Schröter, Hochbaum, *Les ententes et les positions dominantes dans le Droit de la CEE*, updated translation of the 2nd German edn 1974 (Paris: Editions Jupiter, Editions de Navarre, 1977) 284; P Mathijsen, 'Egalité de traitement des entreprises dans le Droit des Communautés européennes', in Various, *Equal treatment of public and private enterprises*, volume 2 (Copenhagen: FIDE, 1978), 11.4; A Deringer, 'Equal treatment of public and private enterprises. General report' in Various, *Equal treatment of public and private enterprises*, volume 2 (Copenhagen: FIDE, 1978), ch 1, 1.19; AC Page, 'Member States, Public Undertakings and Article 90', [1982] ELR 24; CD Ehlermann, 'Managing Monopolies: The Role of the State in Controlling Market Dominance in the European Community' [1993] 2 ECLR 65–66.

[65] Temple Lang (n 10 above) 559.

[66] Case C–18/88 *RTT* [1991] ECR I–5941, paras 23–24.

of the EC Treaty. The validity of this interpretation has been confirmed in the *RTT* case and in other judgments of the European Court of Justice.[67]

The 'Bundling' of Regulatory and Commercial Activities

Thus Article 86(1) in combination with Article 82 prohibits the 'bundling' of, on the one hand, the regulatory functions of the State and, on the other hand, the entrepreneurial activities of the State. In other words, public undertakings must be 'independent' from the bodies that regulate their markets and vice versa. The key question is the degree of separation necessary to achieve such 'independence'. The Court of Justice has already made clear that two directorates within the same administration cannot be considered as being independent.[68] This implies at least that a mere functional unbundling within a single entity (public undertaking or administration) is not enough to fulfil the obligation of independence. The Commission considers that the independence requirement is fulfilled, first of all, where a former public undertaking belongs to private shareholders and not to the State. It is obvious that, in such a situation, the exercise of regulatory functions by the public administration does not raise any concern about conflict of interest. The requirement is also fulfilled where the State keeps its financial interest in the commercial undertakings but transfers the regulatory functions to a body 'independent from the relevant Ministry'.[69]

5.60

The Granting of an Exclusive Right

The granting of an exclusive right is a positive State measure that may, in some circumstances, 'lead' the undertaking to abuse its dominant position. In a way, this might be seen as a wide interpretation of the notion of inducement: by assuring a dominant position through the granting of an exclusive right, the State would 'induce' the undertaking to abuse of this dominant position. However, not every exclusive right necessarily leads the beneficiary to abuse. The Court of Justice has restricted this reasoning by requiring some additional circumstances also to be present.

5.61

The Demand Limitation Doctrine

First of all, an exclusive right is found to 'inevitably lead' the undertaking to abuse when the undertaking is not in a position to satisfy properly existing demand for that type of service. This demand limitation doctrine was established in the

5.62

---

[67] Case C–202/88 *Terminal equipment for telecommunications* [1991] ECR I-1223, paras 48–52; Case C–18/88 *RTT* [1991] ECR I–5941, paras 25–28; Cases C–46/90 and C–93/91 *Lagauche* [1993] ECR I–5267; Case C–69/91 *Decoster* [1993] ECR I–5335; Case C–92/91 *Taillandier* [1993] ECR I–5383.

[68] Case C–69/91 *Decoster* [1993] ECR I–5335, para 21.

[69] Commission Communication on the status and implementation of Directive (EEC) 90/388 on competition in the markets for telecommunications services [1995] OJ C275/2, see p 10.

Höfner case.[70] The issue was that the exclusive rights enjoyed by the German federal office for employment placed that entity in a dominant position in the executive recruitment market, however, the entity was clearly not capable of satisfying the existing demand in the market for this type of activity. Article 82(b) defines as abusive the behaviour of undertakings which consists in 'limiting production, markets or technical development to the prejudice of consumers'. The fact that an activity is reserved to an entity which is not in a position to carry it out is necessarily going to lead to abuses of this type being committed. In the circumstances, the grant of exclusive rights would be contrary to Articles 86(1) and 82. This, then, is what can be referred to as the 'demand limitation doctrine'.[71]

The Conflict of Interest Doctrine

5.63 The *RTT* case made clear that Article 86(1) in combination with Article 82 is violated when a State measure creates a situation of conflict of interest between the regulatory mission entrusted to an undertaking and its commercial objectives. This is not, however, the only kind of conflict of interest that may occur. A conflict of interest may also be created between two different commercial activities of a single undertaking. This approach was established in the *ERT* case,[72] which concerned the Greek television monopoly. The Greek authorities had granted ERT the exclusive right both to broadcast programmes produced by itself and programmes produced abroad. It was obvious that in such a situation the monopoly would logically tend to prefer the programmes which it had produced itself over programmes from other Member States. This would constitute an abuse of a dominant position contrary to Article 82. As the judgment said, Article 86(1) of the Treaty prohibits the granting of an exclusive right to retransmit television broadcasts to an undertaking which has an exclusive right to transmit broadcasts, where those rights are liable to lead that undertaking to infringe Article 82 of the Treaty by virtue of a discriminatory broadcasting policy which favours its own programmes.

5.64 In *ERT* the circumstance which led the beneficiary of the exclusive rights to act in an abusive manner was the existence of a conflict of interests. Although the grant of the exclusive rights did not legally oblige the undertaking benefiting from them to discriminate in favour of its own programmes, it is obvious that the temptation would be very difficult to resist in practice. The grant of exclusive rights to an undertaking with such a conflict of interests creates a structure favouring abusive behaviour. This is what can be called 'the conflict of interests doctrine'.

---

[70] Case C–41/90 *Höfner* [1991] ECR I–2019.
[71] The Commission had previously used the same approach in two other decisions: *Dutch Courier Services* [1990] OJ L10/50, paras 14–15, *Spanish Courier Services* [1990] OJ L233/22, para 11.
[72] Case 260/89 *ERT* [1991] ECR I–2925.

No Smoke without Fire

In very rare cases, the Court of Justice has concluded, on the basis of the gravity **5.65**
and repetition of particular abuses, that they were an inevitable consequence of
the existence of an exclusive right. The judgment in *Port of Genoa* is the clearest
example.[73] The facts were as follows: the undertaking Sidelurgica had applied to
Merci, holder of exclusive rights for the organization of dock works, for a ship to
be unloaded in the port of Genoa. Various problems arose, including a strike in
the dock work company, Compagnia. As a result, delays occurred and Sidelurgica
suffered losses. In the subsequent litigation, the question arose as to the compatibility of the exclusive rights enjoyed by Merci and Compagnia with Articles 86(1)
and 82. The Court listed no fewer than four different types of abuse which had
occurred (demanding payment for unrequested services, charging excessive
prices, engaging in discriminatory pricing, and not using technologically
advanced unloading equipment). The surprising point is that the Court moved
from the existence of these abuses of a dominant position to the conclusion that
the abuses were the result of the exclusive rights without examining the causal relationship.[74] It seems that the variety, seriousness, and repeated nature of the abuses
committed led the Court to the presumption that the very structure of the market
(the operation of exclusive rights) favoured the commission of abuses and for that
reason was incompatible with Articles 86(1) and 82 of the Treaty.

Effects Similar to Those of an Abusive Behaviour

Article 86(1) in combination with Article 82 also applies to some State measures **5.66**
having effects similar to those of an abusive behaviour, even in the absence of any
actual or potentially abusive behaviour by the undertaking.

The Doctrine of the Extension of a Dominant Position

This doctrine holds that the grant to an undertaking, which is already dominant **5.67**
in one market, of exclusive rights in another adjacent but distinct market is contrary to Articles 86(1) and 82, unless such a grant can be objectively justified.

The doctrine of the extension of a dominant position was used for the first time in **5.68**
the framework of Articles 86(1) and 82 in the *RTT* case.[75] In this judgment the
Court considered that an exclusive right was contrary to Articles 86(1) and 82 not

---

[73] Case C–179/90 *Port of Genoa* [1991] ECR I–5889.

[74] The Court limited itself to stating that: 'it appears from the circumstances described by the
national court and discussed before the Court of Justice that the undertakings enjoying exclusive
rights in accordance with the procedures laid down by the national rules in question are, as a result,
induced either to demand payment for services or to commit the rest of the abuses mentioned
above'. Case C–179/90 *Port of Genoa* [1991] ECR I–5889.

[75] Case C–18/88 *RTT* [1991] ECR I–5941. This theory had previously been used by the
Commission in its two decisions based on Article 86 concerning courier postal services in The
Netherlands and Spain.

because it resulted in real or potential abuse of a dominant position, but rather because it produced a similar effect to such abuse.

5.69 The undertaking GB-Inno-BM had imported and sold telephones in Belgium without having them approved by RTT, the public telecommunications operator. The Court appears to have assumed that RTT had not independently decided to exclude competitors but rather that such exclusion was a direct consequence of the legislation. The Court also appears to have identified RTT's power to approve its competitors' telephones with a true exclusive right for the sale of terminals. RTT, which already enjoyed a monopoly in the operation of the network, thus received a second exclusive right from the State, for the sale of telephones. On this basis, it was considered that there was an extension of RTT's dominant position from one market to another. The extension was not the result of abuses committed by RTT but instead was due to the State granting RTT the exclusive power to approve competitors' telephones. Such extension by law of a dominant position is illegal not because it induces or favours abuse, but rather because it produces identical effects to those which would be produced by abusive behaviour contrary to Article 82.

5.70 In this way, on the basis of effects rather than behaviour, the Court established its doctrine of the extension of a dominant position. This doctrine, which was used again by the Court of Justice in its 1992 judgment concerning the telecommunications services directive,[76] has come to play a key role in the liberalization process.

5.71 Of course, apart from exclusive rights, other State measures may extend the dominant position of a public or privileged undertaking, thus falling under Article 86(1) in combination with Article 82.[77]

The Automatic Abuse Doctrine

5.72 Although the Court has subsequently retreated from this position, in the *Corbeau* case[78] the Court of Justice seemed to consider that, even in the absence of these circumstances, an exclusive right would automatically lead the beneficiary to abuse, therefore falling under Articles 86(1) and 82.

5.73 The facts of the case were as follows. Paul Corbeau provided services consisting in the collection and delivery of mail in the city of Liège, Belgium. Despite the services offered being superior to those of the State postal service, the charges were slightly lower. Belgian legislation imposed on the Régie des Postes a universal obligation to ensure basic postal services throughout Belgian territory at a uni-

---

[76] Cases C–271, 281 and 289/90 *Telecommunications Services Directive* [1992] ECR I–5868, paras 35–36.
[77] *GSM Italy* [1995] OJ L280/49; *GSM Spain* [1997] OJ L76/19.
[78] Case C–320/91 *Corbeau* [1993] ECR I–2533.

form tariff. In exchange, the Régie des Postes was granted an exclusive right over postal services without distinguishing between basic postal services and more profitable services such as courier services. The Régie des Postes started criminal proceedings against Paul Corbeau for breach of the exclusive rights and the matter was referred to the Court of Justice.

In the judgment, the Court did not regard it as necessary to look for even the **5.74** slightest hint of abusive behaviour. It limited itself to stating the obligation of Member States not to compromise the 'effect utile' of Article 82. It is submitted that this expression has to be understood as a general reference to the effects theory. Without ever reaching any specific conclusions as to what the obligations of Member States are under Article 86(1), the Court surprisingly went on to examine the scope of the exception contained in Article 86(2).[79] While the reasoning may be scant, the conclusion the Court reached was clear: if the grant of exclusive rights was only permitted under Article 86 to the extent that it came within the exception contained in Article 86(2), that meant that in principle all grants of exclusive rights were contrary to Article 86(1) unless they were objectively justified.[80]

Corbeau was simply the final consequence of the effects theory. If the role of **5.75** Article 82 was to prevent the distortion, restriction, or elimination of competition caused by the behaviour of undertakings, a State measure which totally eliminated competition would have the same effects, if not worse, as such behaviour. Since the behaviour of undertakings would have been contrary to Article 82, such State measures were contrary to Article 86(1) in conjunction with Article 82.

The overall effect of *Corbeau* was simply to reverse the burden of proof. Until **5.76** *Corbeau*, the starting point had been that exclusive rights were prima facie legal (*Sacchi*). They would only be contrary to Articles 86(1) and 82 if it was shown that they led undertakings to engage in abusive behaviour (*Höfner, ERT*, and *Port of Genoa*) or if they constituted an extension of a dominant position (*RTT, Telecommunications Services*). Following *Corbeau*, exclusive rights were presumed to be illegal, unless they could be objectively justified or unless they were necessary to guarantee the effective carrying out of a project of general economic interest. The effect of *Corbeau* was simply to bring the approach in relation to Articles 86(1) and 82 into line with that concerning the free movement of goods. That is,

---

[79] Article 86(2) reads as follows: 'Undertakings entrusted with the operation of services of general economic interest or having the character of a revenue-producing monopoly shall be subject to the rules contained in this Treaty, in particular to the rules on competition, in so far as the application of such rules does not obstruct the performance, in law or in fact, of the particular tasks assigned to them. The development of trade must not be affected to such an extent as would be contrary to the interest of the Community.'

[80] It is therefore no coincidence that this new approach coincided with a new emphasis on the exception under Article 86(2), which would permit, *inter alia*, those exclusive rights which were indispensable to ensure objectives of general economic interest being allowed.

restrictions on trade and free competition were in principle prohibited unless they existed because of mandatory requirements of general interest and they respected the principle of proportionality.

The Pendulum Swings Back

The La Crespelle Case

5.77 The automatic abuse doctrine established in *Corbeau* has subsequently been abandoned by the Court of Justice. In October 1994 the judgment in *La Crespelle*[81] heralded a change of approach. A local monopolist brought proceedings against the La Crespelle centre for breach of its exclusive right to artificially inseminate cattle. According to this judgment, while the legislation in question authorized the insemination centres to freely establish their charges, it did not incite them to demand exorbitant prices. Therefore it could not be concluded that such legislation led undertakings to abuse their dominant positions. This last statement involved a radical change of direction in the interpretation of the expression 'led to abuse'. Until that moment, the case law had suggested that if a monopoly 'facilitated' the possibility of abuse, that was sufficient to constitute 'leading' the undertaking to abuse. Given that all monopolies, by definition, facilitated the charging of abusive prices, the logical conclusion was that all monopolies were prima facie contrary to Articles 86(1) and 82. This was the position taken in *Corbeau*. However, faced with a similar situation in *La Crespelle* the Court reacted in a different way and held that the presence of possible abuses derived from the exercise of the exclusive right could not automatically be imputed to the mere existence of the exclusive right. The fact that the monopolist had abused its dominant position by demanding excessive prices could justify the application of Article 82 to such behaviour, but could not on its own lead to an action against the Member State under Articles 86(1) and 82. Such action would only be justified if a causal relation between the State measure and the abuse were demonstrated.

The judgment in *Banchero* confirmed the Court of Justice's change of approach to the application of Articles 86(1) and 82 to exclusive rights.[82]

What Remains?

5.78 While it is clear that the case law has taken a step backwards with the judgments in *La Crespelle* and *Banchero*, quite how far backwards has yet to be determined. In any case, it appears that the Court has decided to retreat from the general presumption of incompatibility of all exclusive rights with Articles 86(1) and 82 which had been precariously established in *Corbeau*. Of course, that does not mean that there has been a return to the old theory of the absolutely sacrosanct

---

[81] Case C–323/93 *La Crespelle* [1997] ECR I–5077.
[82] Case C–387/93 *Banchero* [1995] ECR I–4663.

nature of exclusive rights. From both *La Crespelle* and *Banchero* it is clear that in certain circumstances exclusive rights can come into conflict with Articles 86(1) and 82. The problem is to know in which circumstances.

It is significant that in the *La Crespelle* and *Banchero* judgments *Corbeau* is not **5.79** cited but *Höfner* and *Port of Genoa* are. The Court appears to be at ease with the behaviour theory, which prohibits those State measures which lead undertakings to carry out abusive behaviour. The problem, again, is how to interpret the word 'lead'. Despite continuing to approve *Port of Genoa*, it is clear that today the Court is less willing to consider that a given structure 'led' an undertaking to commit abuse than it was in 1991. Nevertheless, the limitation of demand theory in *Höfner* appears to remain in force given that it was applied in *Banchero*.[83] It is further submitted that in conflict of interest situations such as that arising in *ERT* the Court would continue to consider that monopolies are led to abuse and therefore infringe Articles 86(1) and 82. As far as the theory of the extension of the dominant position is concerned, there is no good reason why the Court should go back on the theory so clearly established in *RTT* and, above all, in *Telecommunications Services*. The impression is that the Court has gone back on the theory it established in *Corbeau*, and no longer considers that all exclusive rights which are not objectively justified must necessarily be contrary to Articles 86(1) and 82 of the Treaty. However, apart from this the Court does not appear to have modified its theoretical approach, Both the behaviour theory (in its different guises) and the theory of the extension of a dominant position remain in force. What does appear to have changed is the general attitude of the Court, which now appears much more ready to give the benefit of the doubt to monopolies. This will probably be reflected by the Court adopting a more reserved attitude when considering whether a particular measure led an undertaking to engage in abusive behaviour, together with a more generous approach in applying the exception contained in Article 86(2) to justify exclusive rights.

Effect upon Intra-Community Trade

For Article 86(1) to apply in combination with Article 82 the effects of the abuse **5.80** or the effects of the State measure should be capable of affecting intra-Community trade.[84] It is not necessary to prove that trade is actually been affected, a mere potential effect being enough for the condition to be fulfilled.[85] The condition is an objective one: it does not prevent an undertaking from invoking Articles 86(1) and 82 *vis-à-vis* a measure of its own Member State.[86]

---

[83] Case C–387/93 *Banchero* [1995] ECR I–4663, para 53.
[84] Case 30/87 *Bodson* [1988] ECR 2479, paras 24–25.
[85] Case C–41/90 *Höfner* [1991] ECR I–2015, paras 32–33; Case C–179/90 *Port of Genoa* [1991] ECR I–5889, para 20.
[86] Case C–320/91 *Corbeau* [1993] ECR I–2533, L Hancher, 'Case C–320/91, Corbeau' [1994] 21 CMLRev 114.

(b) Article 86(1) in Combination with Article 81

5.81 In theory Article 86(1) may apply in combination with the prohibition of anti-competitive agreements between undertakings contained in Article 81 (former Article 85). In practice, however, there are few examples so far of such application in the case law of the Court of Justice and in the practice of the Commission.

5.82 The most obvious situation in which Article 86(1) could in theory apply in combination with Article 81 would be a State measure inducing one or more public or privileged undertakings to agree between themselves and/or with other undertakings in order to restrict competition. However, there are no examples of such a 'compulsory cartel' in the case law or in the practice of the Commission.

5.83 In the *Ahmed Saeed* case, the Court of Justice found that Article 86(1) in combination with Article 81 applied to the approval by a Member State of tariffs agreed by the two air carriers operating on a given route as a result of a bilateral Treaty.[87] This suggests that Articles 86(1) and 81 combine to prohibit Member States from adopting measures reinforcing the effects of anti-competitive agreements in which at least one public or privileged undertaking takes part.

5.84 An analogy with the case law of the Court of Justice in respect of Articles 3(g), 10, and 81 suggests that Article 86(1) in combination with Article 81 would also prohibit State measures that either impose or induce anti-competitive agreements in which at least one public or privileged undertaking takes part.[88]

(6) Article 86(1) in Combination with the Treaty Rules Addressed to the Member States

(a) The Double Function of Article 86(1)

5.85 Article 86(1) can also be applied in combination with the rules of the Treaty that are addressed to the Member States, such as the rules on free movement of goods, the rules on freedom to provide services, and the rules on freedom of establishment. When applied in combination with these rules, Article 86(1) may play two different roles. First of all, it serves as a reminder to Member States that these rules must also be respected when adopting measures concerning public or privileged undertakings. Secondly, Article 86(1) prevents Member States from using their public or privileged undertakings as instruments in order to circumvent the application of these rules.

---

[87] Case 66/86 *Ahmed Saeed* [1989] ECR 803, paras 47–58.
[88] Opinion of Van Gerven AG , point 23, Case C–179/90 *Port of Genoa* [1991] ECR I–5889.

Article 86(1) as a 'Reminder' of Prohibitions

As stated above, when applied in combination with the rules of the Treaty **5.86** addressed to the Member States, Article 86(1) reminds them that these rules must also be respected when adopting measures concerning public or privileged undertakings.[89] From a substantive point of view this reminder is totally redundant. Whether applied in combination with Article 86(1) or not, the measures in question would in any event infringe the rules of the Treaty. The value-added provided by Article 86(1) is of a procedural nature. When the State measures are contrary to one of the rules of the Treaty addressed to the Member States but also have a link with a public or privileged undertaking so as to fall under Article 86(1), this opens up the possibility of using the special procedures established in Article 86(3).

The 'Lifting of the Veil'

Although Article 86(1) is in principle addressed to the Member States, it also has **5.87** some impact on public and privileged undertakings. Thus, Article 86(1) in combination with the rules of the Treaty addressed to the Member States prohibits behaviours of public or privileged undertakings that, if done directly by the State, would infringe the rules of the Treaty addressed to the Member States. This simply means that Member States cannot do *indirectly* (through their influence over these undertakings) what they cannot do *directly* (through behaviours of Public Authorities). Article 86(1) allows one to 'lift the veil' of apparent autonomy of the undertaking so as to attribute to the Member State responsibility for the acts of the undertaking that do not fit into an entrepreneurial logic.

It is well known that if a *public* undertaking transfers funds to another undertak **5.88** ing, these funds may well be State aids within the meaning of Article 92, even if they come from a public undertaking and not directly from the Member State itself. This same logic may apply, by virtue of Article 86(1), as regards other rules addressed to Member States. For instance, if a public or privileged undertaking follows a 'buy national' procurement policy which is irrational from a purely entrepreneurial point of view, the Member State may be found responsible for this behaviour under Articles 86(1) and 28.[90]

A good example of the attribution to a Member State of responsibility for the **5.89** behaviour of a public undertaking can be found in the *Transmediterranea* case. In 1987 the Commission adopted a decision, based on Articles 90(1) and 7 of the EEC Treaty (now Articles 86(1) and 12 of the EC Treaty), against a Spanish law

---

[89] Buendia Sierra (n 10 above) paras 6.06–6.13; Temple Lang (n 10 above) 550.
[90] Buendia Sierra (n 10 above) paras 6.02–6.05; Commission, *Report on Competition Policy 1972* (Vol II) para 129; *Report on Competition Policy 1976* (Vol VI) para 275.

obliging transport operators to give discounts only to Spanish nationals on trips to the Canary and Balearic islands.[91] After the abrogation of these legal provisions, a public undertaking called Transmediterranea started offering similar discounts in favour of nationals. The undertaking claimed that these were the result of an autonomous commercial decision and therefore immune from former Article 7, which was a rule addressed solely to the Member State. The Commission found, however, that this behaviour could not be explained on a commercial basis, but only on a governmental one. It therefore concluded that the behaviour of Transmediterranea constituted a new State measure contrary to former Articles 90(1) and 7.[92]

5.90 Having examined in general terms how Article 86(1) functions in combination with the rules of the Treaty addressed to the Member States, it is now necessary to examine how the provision works in combination with each particular category of rules.

(b) Article 86(1) in Combination with the Rules on Free Movement of Goods—Articles 28 and 31

5.91 Measures taken by a Member State that restrict access to its markets for goods imported from other Member States will often conflict with the rules of the Treaty on free movement of goods.[93] When this type of restrictive State measure is linked with a public or privileged undertaking, then the rules of the Treaty on free movement of goods will apply in combination with Article 86(1), and the special procedures of Article 86(3) may be used.

5.92 When considering the Treaty rules on free movement of goods, a distinction has to be drawn between the general regime based on Article 28 (former Article 30) and the special regime under Article 31 (former Article 37) applying to State monopolies of a commercial character.

The General Regime: Measures of Equivalent Effect and Article 28

5.93 Article 28 prohibits so-called 'measures of equivalent effect to quantitative restrictions on imports'. This notion was traditionally interpreted by the Court of Justice, notably in its *Dassonville* judgment, in a very broad manner, including all State measures restricting imports irrespective of their discriminatory or non-discriminatory character.[94] According to the *Cassis de Dijon* doctrine, only measures

---

[91] *Spanish transport tariffs* [1987] OJ L194/28.

[92] Commission, *Report on Competition Policy 1991* (Vol XXI) para 334.

[93] See P Oliver, *Free Movement of Goods in the EEC under Articles 30 to 36 of the Rome Treaty* (2nd edn, London: European Law Centre Limited, 1988) Buendia Sierra (n. 10 above) paras 6.14–6.115; A Mattera, *Le marché unique européen. Ses règles, son fonctionnement* (Paris: Jupiter, 1988) , for a general overview.

[94] Case 8/74 *Dassonville* [1974] ECR 87, para 5.

that are equally applicable to both national and foreign products and that are necessary to guarantee certain 'mandatory requirements' may avoid failing under the prohibition contained in Article 28.[95]

However, the interpretation of Article 28 has subsequently been restricted by the **5.94** Court of justice in its *Keck* judgment.[96] The Court distinguishes between two groups of measures. As regards measures concerning the characteristics of products (composition, packaging, labelling, etc), nothing has changed: measures that restrict imports, even if they are non-discriminatory, can only avoid prohibition under Article 28 if they are necessary to guarantee 'mandatory requirements'.[97] The change comes when considering measures related to the circumstances in which the products are traded (the so-called 'modalités de vente'): irrespective of their restrictive effect these measures would only fall under Article 28 if they discriminate, in law or in fact, against imported products.[98] Of course, the borderline between measures concerning the characteristics of products and measures related to the circumstances in which the products are traded is not at all easy to draw.[99]

Although a more detailed analysis of Article 28 is beyond the scope of this book, **5.95** it is in any event clear that State measures related to public or privileged undertakings dealing in goods would in many cases fall under the prohibition of Article 28. Such State measures may assume various forms: obligations to purchase, special rights, etc.

In principle, exclusive rights relating to goods can also be considered as 'measures **5.96** of equivalent effect' contrary to Article 28[100] and there are plenty of examples of this in the case law of the Court of Justice and in the practice of the Commission, both before[101] and after[102] the *Keck* judgment. However, the application of this rule has to take into account the existence of a specific provision, Article 31, which applies to State measures concerning the functioning of State monopolies of a commercial character. Although the precise borderline between Articles 28 and 31 is difficult to determine (because of the hesitations of the Court of Justice on

---

[95] Case 120/78 *Cassis de Dijon* [1979] ECR 649, para 8.
[96] Cases C–267 and 268/91 *Keck* [1993] ECR I–6097.
[97] Cases C–267 and 268/91 *Keck* [1993] ECR I–6097, para 15.
[98] Cases C–267 and 268/91 *Keck* [1993] ECR I–6097, paras 16–17.
[99] N Reich, 'The "November Revolution" of the European Court of Justice: Keck, Meng and Audi revisited (1994) 21 CMLRev 470, A Mattera, 'De l'arrêt Dassonville à l'arrêt Keck: l'obscure clarté d'une jurisprudence riche en principes novateurs et en contradictions' [1994] RMUE i 153.
[100] M Van Der Woude, 'Article 86: "Competing for Competence" ', (1991) ELR Competition Law Checklist 72.
[101] Commission Directive (EEC) 88/301 on competition in the markets for telecommunication terminal equipment [1988] OJ L131/73, para 3, confirmed by the Court of Justice in the judgment of Case C–202/88 *Terminal equipment for telecommunications* [1991] ECR I–1223, paras 33–39; Case C–179/90 *Port of Genoa* [1991] ECR I–5889, para 21.
[102] Cases C–277, 318 and 319/91 *Ligur Carni* [1993] ECR I–6621, paras 35–38, Case C–323/93 *La Crespelle* [1997] ECR I–5077, paras 28–29.

this issue),[103] it seems clear that exclusive rights would in many cases have to be examined under Article 31.[104]

The Special Regime: State Monopolies and Article 31

5.97 Article 31 provides:

1. Member States shall adjust any State monopolies of a commercial character so as to ensure that no discrimination regarding the conditions under which goods are procured and marketed exists between nationals of Member States.

The provisions of this Article shall apply to any body through which a Member State, in law or in fact, either directly or indirectly supervises, determines or appreciably influences imports or exports between Member States. These provisions shall likewise apply to monopolies delegated by the State to others.

2. Member States shall refrain from introducing any new measure which is contrary to the principles laid down in paragraph 1 or which restricts the scope of the Articles dealing with the prohibition of customs duties and quantitative restrictions between Member States.

3. If a State monopoly of a commercial character has rules which are designed to make it easier to dispose of agricultural products or obtain for them the best return, steps should be taken in applying the rules contained in this Article to ensure equivalent safeguards for the employment and standard of living of the producers concerned.

Article 31 corresponds with former Article 37 although a few changes have been introduced. The old Article 37 was as follows:

1. Member States shall progressively adjust any State monopolies of a commercial character so as to ensure that when the transitional period has ended no discrimination regarding the conditions under which goods are procured and marketed exists between nationals of Member States.

The provisions of this Article shall apply to any body through which a Member State, in law or in fact, either directly or indirectly supervises, determines or appreciably influences imports or exports between Member States. These provisions shall likewise apply to monopolies delegated by the State to others.

---

[103] This question is analysed later in this section.
[104] See JL Buendia Sierra, *Exclusive Rights and State Monopolies in EC Law* (Oxford University Press, 1999) chapter 3. On the doctrine see: Pierre-Alex Franck, 'Les entreprises visées aux articles 90 et 37 du Traité CEE' in Various, *Les articles 90 et 37 du Traité CEE et leurs relations avec la concurrence*, Semaine de Bruges 1968 (De Temple, Bruges, 1969), 44; CA Colliard, 'Régime de l'Article 37 du Traité CEE: les aspects juridiques' in Various, *L'entreprise publique et la concurrence. Les articles 90 et 37 du Traité CEE et leurs relations avec la concurrence*, Semaine de Bruges 1968 (De Temple, Bruges, 1969), 143; R Franceschelli, 'Rapport sur l'Article 37 du Traité CEE (présenté le 26 octobre 1967 à la Ligue Internationale contre la concurrence déloyale)' in Various, *L'entreprise publique et la concurrence. Les articles 90 et 37 du Traité CEE et leurs relations avec la concurrence*, Semaine de Bruges 1968 (De Temple, Bruges, 1969), 481; GC Rodriguez Iglesias, *El régimen jurídico de los monopolios de Estado en la Comunidad Económica Europea* (Madrid: Instituto de Estudios Administrativos, 1976); F Burrows, 'State Monopolies' [1983] YEL 25–47.

2. Member States shall refrain from introducing any new measure which is contrary to the principles laid down in paragraph 1 or which restricts the scope of the Articles dealing with the abolition of customs duties and quantitative restrictions between Member States.

3. The timetable for the measures referred to in paragraph 1 shall be harmonised with the abolition of quantitative restrictions on the same products provided for in Articles 30 or 34 [now Articles 28 and 29].

If a product is subject to a State monopoly of a commerical character in only one or some Member States, the Commission may authorise the other Member States to apply protective measures until the adjustment provided for in paragraph 1 has been effected; the Commission shall determine the conditions and details of such measures.

4. If a State monopoly of a commercial character has rules which are designed to make it easier to dispose of agricultural products or obtain for them the best return, steps should be taken in applying the rules contained in this Article to ensure equivalent safeguards for the employment and standard of living of the producers concerned, account being taken of the adjustments that will be possible and specialisation that will be needed with the passage of time.

5. The obligations on Member States shall be binding only in so far as they are compatible with existing international agreements.

6. With effect from the first stage the Commission shall make recommendations as to the manner in which and the timetable according to which the adjustment provided for in this Article shall be carried out.

Thus, the Treaty of Amsterdam has repealed paragraphs 3, 5 and 6 of former Article 37 because these paragraphs had become redundant once the transitional period ended. Paragraphs 1, 2 and 4 of former Article 37 are now paragraphs 1, 2 and 3 of Article 31. The only substantive change is the elimination of the word 'progressively' and of the reference to the transitonal period, which had become redundant.

'State Monopolies of a Commercial Character'

This concept of 'State monopolies of a commercial character' has traditionally **5.98** been interpreted in a very restrictive and formalistic way, as referring only to public undertakings that have been conferred, by law, with exclusive rights for the production, commercialization, importing and/or exporting of goods. A careful reading of the two paragraphs of Article 31(1) shows, however, that the concept embraces all situations in which a Member State can influence imports or exports through an undertaking. What is essential is, on the one hand, the existence of an undertaking (the 'monopoly')[105] which can appreciably[106] influence the import or

---

[105] Article 31 also applies to situations where the State influences imports through a greater number of undertakings: Case 30/87 *Bodson* [1988] ECR 2479, paras 12–14.

[106] Complete control over imports or exports is not necessary for Article 31 to apply. In Case C–347/88 *Greek oil monopoly* [1990] ECR I–4747, para 41, the Court of Justice found that control over 65% of imports implied an appreciable influence.

export of goods[107] between Member States.[108] This ability to influence may result from exclusive rights for import[109] or export, from exclusive rights over other activities (commercialization, production, etc), from special rights,[110] or simply from the existence of a dominant position.[111] The other essential element for a State monopoly to exist is that the Member State[112] should either control the undertaking (in this case it would be a public undertaking) or have an appreciable influence over its behaviour. This influence can be presumed when the undertaking is a private undertaking that has been granted exclusive or special rights by the State.[113] This notion of 'monopolies delegated by the State to others' under Article 31(1), paragraph 2, corresponds with the notion of privileged undertakings under Article 86(1).

Obligations Contained in Article 31

5.99 Once the notion of 'State monopolies of a commercial character' is defined, it is necessary to determine what the obligations are that Article 31 imposes on Member States. A distinction has to be made, in that respect, between the obligations that apply during the transitional period and those that apply thereafter.[114] Former Article 37 contained some provisions that were applicable only

---

[107] In principle, Article 31 only applies to goods, not to services: Case 155/73 *Sacchi* [1974] ECR 409, para 10; Case 271/81 *Mialocq* [1983] ECR 2057, para 8; Case 30/87 *Bodson* [1988] ECR 2479, para10; Case C–17/94 *Gervais* [1995] ECR I–4353, para 35. However, Article 31 may apply to cases where an undertaking can appreciably influence the trade in certain goods because it has a monopoly over certain services: Case 271/81 *Mialocq* [1983] ECR 2057, para 10; Case C–17/94 *Gervais* [1995] ECR I–4353, paras 36–37. A monopoly over funeral services, for instance, might in some cases allow the undertaking to influence the trade in coffins: Case 30/87 *Bodson* [1988] ECR 2479, para 10. Electricity is considered a good, not a service, and therefore electricity monopolies are subject to Article 31, as confirmed by the Court in Case C–393/92 *Almelo* [1994] ECR I–1517, para 28 and Case C–158/94 *Italian electricity monopoly* [1997] ECR I–5789, para 17.
[108] Imports coming directly from third countries are not covered by Article 31: Case 91/78 *Hansen* [1979] ECR 935, para 19.
[109] Case C–157/94 *Dutch electricity monopoly* [1997] ECR I–5699, para 20.
[110] Case C–157/94 *Dutch electricity monopoly* [1997] ECR I–5699, paras 17–18.
[111] This clearly results from the text of Article 31(1), second para. However, the Court of Justice seems reluctant to admit it: Case 271/81 *French artificial insemination monopoly* [1983] ECR 2079, paras 14–18, Case C–393/92 *Almelo* [1994] ECR I–1517, paras 29–32. Most commentators also restrict the application of Article 31 to *de jure* monopolies: Franck (n 104 above) 47; Rodriguez Iglesias (n 104 above) 32; De Cocborne (n 104 above) 313.
[112] The notion of Member State is not restricted to the national government but includes all the public authorities of the country (regional governments, local councils, etc): Case 30/87 *Bodson* [1988] ECR 2479, para 13.
[113] Case C–157/94 *Dutch electricity monopoly* [1997] ECR I–5699, para 20. Opinion of Roemer AG, point 63, Case 82/71 *SAIL* [1972] ECR 119.
[114] The transitional period ended on the 31 December 1969 for the original Member States, on 31 December 1977 for the United Kingdom, Ireland, and Denmark, on 31 December 1985 forGreece, on 31 December 1991 for Spain, and on 31 December 1992 for Portugal. No transitional period was foreseen for Finland, Sweden, and Austria (except a three-year transitional period for the Austrian tobacco monopoly).

during the transitional period. As the transitional period has ended these provisions have become redundant and the new Article 31 does not include them.

Obligations during the Transitional Period

During the transitional period, former Article 37 contained an obligation for Member States to *progressively* adjust their State monopolies of a commercial character, (b) a provisional exemption from other Treaty provisions, and (c) an obligation to maintain a position of standstill as regards new restrictive measures.

5.100

The progressive adjustment of State monopolies is the main obligation arising out of former Article 37(1) during the transitional period. This provision obliged Member States to 'progressively adjust' their State monopolies 'so as to ensure that when the transitional period has ended no discrimination regarding the conditions under which goods are procured and marketed exists between nationals of the Member States'. The 'adjustment' was presented in this provision as a *process* that had to take place during the transitional period, in order to achieve a *result* by the end of that period. This result was 'to ensure that . . . no discrimination regarding the conditions under which goods are procured and marketed exists between nationals of the Member States'. The precise meaning of this obligation of non-discrimination will be discussed later. One must focus first upon how this process of adjustment had to be managed. Ideally, the adjustment should have been realized by the Member State in a progressive way. However, former Article 37 left Member States with a wide margin of discretion in determining the rhythm and the manner in which the adjustment had to take place.[115] The Commission could only formulate non-binding recommendations in relation to these questions. What was essential was that the result of non-discrimination was achieved by the end of the transitional period. Before that moment the obligation to progressively adjust the monopolies did not have direct effect.[116]

5.101

Former Article 37 provided a transitory exception during the transitional period. The definitive regime applying to monopolies only apply at the end of the transitional period.[117]

5.102

Article 31(2) (and former Article 37(2)) contain a standstill clause which prohibits Member States from adopting new discriminatory or restrictive measures during the transitional period. This standstill obligation has direct effect.[118]

5.103

Obligations after the Transitional Period

Once the transitional period has ended, Article 31 obliges Member States 'to ensure that no discrimination regarding the conditions under which goods are

5.104

---

[115] Case C–361/90 *Portuguese alcohol monopoly* [1993] ECR I–95, paras 12–18.
[116] Case C–76/91 *Caves Neto Costa* [1993] ECR I–117, para 8.
[117] Case 45/75 *Rewe* [1976] ECR 196, para 24; Case 86/78 *Peureux I* [1979] ECR 897, para 31.
[118] Case 6/64 *Costa v ENEL* [1964] ECR 1141.

procured and marketed exists between nationals of the Member States'. This obligation has direct effect.[119] The precise content of this obligation is to some extent still controversial, as it depends on how the notion of 'discrimination' is interpreted[120] and also on the interpretation given to the expression 'to ensure that no discrimination exists'.

5.105 **State measures that directly discriminate** against imported goods are clearly prohibited by Article 31(1). This is the case in respect of measures imposing quantitative limits on imports, by the monopoly, discriminatory fiscal measures,[121] or measures fixing the price of products in such a way as to discriminate against imports.[122]

5.106 **Discriminatory behaviours of the monopoly** as regards imported goods, even in the absence of any explicit State measure, also seem to fall under Article 31(1),[123] although this interpretation is controversial.[124]

5.107 **Exclusive rights** granted to a State monopoly are clearly affected by Article 31. However, the precise impact of the provision is still to some extent controversial. Some commentators have argued in the past that, since Article 31 did not require the *abolition* of State monopolies but only *adjustment*, this meant that any exclusive rights that they held were legal. It is clear that even if the provision does not impose the elimination of all exclusive rights, it does require the elimination of exclusive rights having a discriminatory character.[125] The question is how to determine which exclusive rights are discriminatory and which are not.

5.108 Since the *Manghera* case[126] the Court of Justice has held that exclusive rights over the activities of importing,[127] exporting,[128] and/or the wholesale distribution[129] of goods are *per se* discriminatory and therefore contrary to Article 31.

---

[119] Case 45/75 *Rewe* [1976] ECR 196, para ,4.

[120] MG Ross, 'Article 37—Redundancy or Reinstatement' [1982] 7(4) ELR 281–299.

[121] Case 13/70 *Cinzano* [1970] ECR 1089; Case 91/75 *Miritz* [1976] ECR 217; Case 45/75 *Rewe* [1976] ECR 196.

[122] Case 91/78 *Hansen* [1979] ECR 935; Case 78/82 *Italian tobacco monopoly* [1983] ECR 1955.

[123] Case 91/78 *Hansen* [1979] ECR 935, para 14; *Report on Competition Policy 1971* (Vol I) para 196; De Cockborne (n 104 above) 322 and 342. See JL Buendia Sierra, *Exclusive Rights and State Monopolies in EC Law* (Oxford University Press, 1999) paras 3.117–3.126.

[124] The Court of Justice seems to reject this interpretation in its more recent cases: Case 30/87 *Bodson* [1988] ECR 2479, para 14; Case C–393/92 *Almelo* [1994] 1 ECR I–1517, paras 29–32.

[125] Rodriguez Iglesias (n 104 above) 87–88.

[126] Case 59/75 *Manghera* [1976] ECR 91.

[127] Case 59/75 *Manghera* [1976] ECR 91, paras 9–13; Case C–347/88 *Greek oil monopoly* [1990] ECR I–4747, paras 42–44; Case C–157/94 *Dutch electricity monopoly* [1997] ECR I–5699, paras 15 and 17; Case C–158/94 *Italian electricity monopoly* [1997] ECR I–5789, paras 23 and 32; Case C–159/94 *French electricity and gas monopolies* [1997] ECR I–5815, paras 33, 39, and 40.

[128] Case C–158/94 *Italian electricity monopoly* [1997] ECR I–5789, paras 24 and 25; Case C–159/94 *French electricity and gas monopolies* [1997] ECR I–5815, paras 34 and 35.

[129] Case C–347/88 *Greek oil monopoly* [1990] ECR I–4747, paras 43, 44, and 56.

Much less clear is the status of exclusive rights over sales at the retail level. The   **5.109**
recent *Franzén* judgment suggests that such exclusive rights do not fall under
Article 31 if the monopoly is organized in such a way as to avoid discrimination
between national and foreign goods.[130] However, this approach seems incompatible with the traditional interpretation of Article 31 and also with three other
judgments adopted by the Court of Justice that same day.[131] Indeed, the *Franzén*
judgment ignores the fact that Article 31 not only bans discrimination between
national and foreign *goods* but also discrimination between national and foreign
operators and customers. A retail monopoly, by preventing foreign producers from
reaching the customers of that Member State directly and by preventing national
consumers from reaching foreign operators directly, clearly discriminates between
national and foreign *operators and customers*. It is therefore submitted that exclusive rights for sales at the retail level should also be considered as contrary to Article
31.[132]

It has traditionally been thought that exclusive rights in respect of the production   **5.110**
of certain types of goods do not fall under Article 31 due to their 'industrial' (as
opposed to 'commercial') character.[133] This highly questionable interpretation has
never been either confirmed or denied by the Court of Justice. It seems clear,
however, that, even if these exclusive rights of production were not caught by Article
31, they may fall under other provisions (such as Article 43 (former Article 52)).

The Borderline between the General and Special Regimes

In principle, Article 31 only applies as regards State measures (such as exclusive   **5.111**
rights) that are closely 'linked' with the existence and the functioning of a monopoly. Measures that do not have such a close link are considered as 'detachable' or
general measures that are subject to Article 28.[134]

This dual regime is not always applied in a coherent way. First of all, the distinc-   **5.112**
tion between 'linked' and 'detachable' measures is not a clear one. In addition, the

---

[130] Case C–189/95 *Franzén* [1997] ECR I–5909, paras 37–66.

[131] Case C–157/94 *Dutch electricity monopoly* [1997] ECR I–5699, paras 21–23; Case C–158/94
Italian electricity monopoly [1997] ECR I–5789, paras 23 and 32; Case C–159/94 *French electricity
and gas monopolies* [1997] ECR I–5815, paras 33 and 38–40.

[132] See JL Buendia Sierra, *Exclusive Rights and State Monopolies in EC Law* (Oxford University
Press, 1999) paras 3.162–3.172.

[133] This is the dominant opinion: RC Beraud, 'L'aménagement des monopoles nationaux prévu
à l'Article 37 du Traité CEE à la lumière des récents développements jurisprudentiels' [1979]
RTDE iv 586; F Wooldridge, 'Some recent decisions concerning the ambit of Article 37 of the
EEC Treaty' [1979] LIEI i 120; Oliver (n 93 above) 320; Mattera (n 93 above) 36; M Bazex,
'L'entreprise publique et le Droit européen—Public Enterprise and European Law' [1991]
RDAI—IBLJ iv 471.

[134] Case 91/78 *Hansen* [1979] ECR 935, para 9; Case 86/78 *Peureux I* [1979] ECR 897, paras
35–37; Case C–387/93 *Banchero* [1995] ECR I–4661, para 29, Case C–189/95 *Franzén* [1997]
ECR I–5909, paras 35–36.

Court of Justice has in the past often applied Article 28 as regards exclusive rights, which are the measures most closely 'linked' with the existence and the functioning of a monopoly.[135] Happily, these ambiguities have a rather limited practical impact. The reason is that the prevailing interpretation of Article 31 as prohibiting discrimination between national and foreign operators and customers makes this provision very similar in substance to the prohibition contained in Article 28.

(c) Article 86(1) in Combination with the Rules on Freedom to Provide Services and on Establishment—Articles 43 and 49

5.113 State measures that restrict the provision of services by undertakings established in other Member States will often conflict with Article 49 (former Article 59), the Treaty rule on freedom to provide services. State measures that restrict the establishment of undertakings coming from other Member States will often conflict with Article 43 (former Article 52), the Treaty provision on freedom of establishment.[136] When restrictive State measures of this type are linked with a public or privileged undertaking, then the Treaty rules on freedom to provide services and establishment will apply in combination with Article 86(1), and the special procedures of Article 86(3) may be used.

Article 86(1) in Combination with Article 49

5.114 Article 49 of the EC Treaty, as interpreted by the Court of Justice, prohibits Member States from adopting measures that unduly restrict the provision of cross-border services by undertakings established in other Member States. Of course, this provision clearly prohibits restrictions having a discriminatory character, either in law or in fact, against foreign service providers and in favour of national ones. However, Article 49 also prohibits certain non-discriminatory but clearly restrictive State measures. Indeed, the *Mediawet* judgment has made it clear that State measures restricting the provision of services that on the face of it apply equally to both foreigners and nationals still fall under Article 49 unless they can be justified as being necessary to guarantee certain 'mandatory requirements'.[137]

5.115 Exclusive rights in the field of services would normally impede the access of foreign service-providers to the relevant national market for services.[138] Special rights

---

[135] Case C–347/88 *Greek oil monopoly* [1990] ECR I–4747; Case C–202/88 *Terminal equipment for telecommunications* [1991] ECR I–1223, paras 33–43; Case C–323/93 *La Crespelle* [1994] ECR I–5077, paras 28–39.

[136] See G Marenco, 'The Notion of Restriction on the Freedom of Establishment and Provision of Services in the Case-law of the Court' [1991] 11 YEL 111–150, for an interesting study of both Articles. See also Buendia Sierra (n 10 above) paras 6.116–6.275.

[137] Case C–353/89 *Mediawet* [1991] ECR I–4069, pars 14–19; Case C–288/89 *Stichting Collectieve Antenne Gouda* [1991] ECR I–4007, paras 10–15.

[138] Case 352/85 *Bond van Adverteerders* [1988] ECR 2085, paras 24–26; Case C–3/88 *Commission v Italy* (*data services*) [1989] ECR 4035, paras 8–9; Case C–353/89 *Mediawet* [1991] ECR I–4069, para 25; Case 260/89 *ERT* [1991] ECR I–2925, paras 19–26.

may also restrict market access for foreign undertakings. Such exclusive or special rights would only be compatible with Article 49 if they could be proven to be proportional.[139]

Article 86(1) in Combination with Article 43

Article 43 obliges Member States to authorize the establishment within their territories of undertakings from other Member States on the same terms as apply to their own nationals. This means that, unlike Article 49, Article 43 in principle only prohibits restrictive State measures that discriminate against foreigners.[140] **5.116**

However, the Court of Justice, interprets the notion of discrimination in this context in a very broad manner. It embraces not only formal but also material discrimination. Even measures that on their face apply equally to both nationals and foreigners are considered discriminatory if in fact they make establishment more difficult for foreigners than for nationals.[141] **5.117**

Exclusive rights were at first considered to be non-discriminatory measures, as (apart from the monopolist) all national and foreign undertakings were treated on equal footing.[142] The Court of Justice has subsequently made clear that a measure that discriminates in favour of a single national undertaking (and therefore against all the other undertakings, national and foreign) is also considered to be a discriminatory restriction of establishment contrary to Article 43.[143] **5.118**

Thus, the granting of an exclusive right to a national undertaking may in principle fall under Article 43. The application of this provision should be excluded, however, when the Member State can prove that the selection of the undertaking that benefits from the exclusive right has been made in an objective and transparent way. **5.119**

Need for a Cross-Border Element

Article 86(1) in combination with Articles 43 and 49 only applies to situations where a cross-border element exists. This is the case where an undertaking wants to establish in another Member State, or wants to provide services to customers residing in that Member State, and is prevented from doing so by the existence of **5.120**

---

[139] Case C–3/88 *Commission v Italy* (*data services*) [1989] ECR 4035, paras 10–11; Case C–353/89 *Mediawet* [1991] ECR I–4069, para 42; Case C–288/89 *Stichting Collectieve Antenne Gouda* [1991] ECR I–4007, para24.

[140] Marenco (n 136 above) 111–128. There are, however, some judgments about non-discriminatory restrictions: Case 107/83 *Klopp* [1984] ECR 2971; Case 96/85 *Commission v France* [1986] ECR 1475; Case 143/87 *INASTI* [1988] ECR 3877. See also *Greek insurances* [1985] OJ L152/25.

[141] Case C–3/88 *Commission v Italy* (*data services*) [1989] ECR 4035, paras 8–9.

[142] Case 6/64 *Costa v ENEL* [1964] ECR 1141; Case 90/76 *Van Ameyde* [1977] ECR 1091, paras 26–30.

[143] Case C–3/88 *Commission v Italy* (*data services*) [1989] ECR 4035, paras 8–9.

an exclusive right. However, in contrast to the way that Article 86(1) operates in combination with Article 82, Article 86(1) in combination with Articles 43 and 49 cannot be invoked by a national against an exclusive right granted by the authorities of his own Member State.[144]

(7) Direct Effect

5.121 Article 86(1), when applied in combination with Articles 82, 28, 31, 43, or 49 has direct effect.[145] It can therefore be applied not only by the European Commission, but also by national courts.

C. Article 86(2): Services of General Economic Interest and Other Public Interest Objectives

5.122 The strict regime contained in Article 86(1) as regards anti-competitive State measures has to be balanced by the exceptions foreseen in the Treaty for those restrictions that may be justified by public interest objectives. Article 86(2) (former Article 90(2)), in particular, may allow derogation from the prohibitions contained in Article 86(1) when this is necessary for the achievement of a purpose of general economic interest (public service) that has been entrusted by the State to one undertaking.[146]

5.123 Article 86(2) provides:

> Undertakings entrusted with the operation of services of general economic interest or having the character of a revenue-producing monopoly shall be subject to the rules contained in this Treaty, in particular to the rules on competition, in so far as the application of such rules does not obstruct the performance, in law or in fact, of the particular tasks assigned to them. The development of trade must not be affected to such an extent as would be contrary to the interest of the Community.

---

[144] Case C–41/90 *Höfner* [1991] ECR I–2015, paras 35–41; Case C–17/94 *Gervais* [1995] ECR I–4353, paras 23–28.

[145] Temple Lang (no 10 above) 544; Case C–179/90 *Port of Genoa* [1991] ECR I–5889, para 23.

[146] See JL Buendia Sierra, *Exclusive rights and State Monopolies in EC Law* (Oxford University Press, 1999) chapter 8. For discussion of the underlying theory see: Various, *Concorrenza tra settore pubblico e privato nella CEE*, Colloquio di Bruxelles della 'Ligue Internationale contre la concurrence déloyale' 5–6 March [1963] RDI anno XII 1–256; L Hancher, 'Case C–320/91, Corbeau' [1994] 21 CMLRev 105–122; A Wachsmann & F Berrod, 'Les critères de justification des monopoles: un premier bilan après l'affaire Corbeau' [1994] RTDE xxx (i) 39–61; R Kovar, 'Droit communautaire et service public: esprit d'orthodoxie ou pensée laïcisée' [1996] RTDE xxxii (ii) 215–242, xxxii (iii) 493–533; D Simon, 'Les mutations des services publics du fait des contraintes du Droit communautaire', in R Kovar & D Simon, D (dir) *Service public et Communauté européenne: entre l'intérêt général et le marché, Actes du colloque de Strasbourg, 17–19 octobre 1996* (Paris: La Documentation Française, 1998) 65; JL Buendia Sierra, 'La Communication sur les services d'intérêt général en Europe et la politique communautaire de concurrence' in R Kovar & D Simon (dir) *Service public et Communauté européenne: entre l'intérêt général et le marché, Actes du colloque de Strasbourg, 17–19 octobre 1996* (Paris: La Documentation Française, 1998) 461–473.

During the 1997 Intergovernmental Conference there were attempts to modify **5.124** Article 86(2) of the EC Treaty.[147] This led to the adoption in the Treaty of Amsterdam of new Article 16 (former Article 7D) of the EC Treaty which reads as follows:

> Without prejudice to Articles 73, 86 and 87, and given the place occupied by services of general economic interest in the shared values of the Union as well as their role in promoting social and territorial cohesion, the Community and the Member States, each within their respective powers and within the scope of application of this Treaty, shall take care that such services operate on the basis of principles and conditions which enable them to fulfil their missions.

It is submitted that, as the text itself makes clear, this provision does not modify Article 86(2) but rather reaffirms the logic behind the provision.

(1) The Undertakings to which Article 86(2) Relates

Article 86(2) refers to two different categories of undertakings: undertakings **5.125** entrusted with the operation of services of general economic interest and revenue producing monopolies.

Undertakings Entrusted with the Operation of Services of General Economic Interest

Article 86(2) applies, first of all, to undertakings, public or private, that have been **5.126** entrusted by the public authorities of the Member State with a service of general economic interest. This is a Community law concept that more or less corresponds with the notion of 'public services' that exists in some Member States. In 1996, the Commission gave an interpretation of the concept in its communication on services of general interest in Europe.[148]

The activity in question has to have an economic character. Otherwise, the prohi- **5.127** bitions contained in Article 86(1) would not apply and the application of the exception contained in Article 86(2) would be totally unnecessary. The role should first have been defined by the Member State, and then entrusted through an express act to a single undertaking.[149]

Of course, in the absence of Community harmonization, Member States have a **5.128** wide margin of freedom when defining the relevant role.[150] However, the exception contained in Article 86(2) will only apply if these nationally defined roles fit

---

[147] S Rodrigues, 'Comment intéger les principes du service public dans le droit positif communautaire. Quelques propositions' RFD adm xi (ii) 335–342.

[148] Commission communication on 'Services of General Interest in Europe' OJ C281/3.

[149] Case 7/82 *GVL* [1983] ECR 483, para 31; Case C–159/94 *French electricity and gas monopolies* [1997] ECR I–5815, paras 69–70.

[150] This freedom was perhaps exaggerated by the CFI in Case T–106/95 *La Poste* [1997] ECR II–233, paras 108 and 192.

within the Community concept of 'service of general economic interest'.[151] This is a flexible framework, but nevertheless a framework that has to be respected for Article 86(2) to apply. The concept is an evolving one:[152] it will develop according to the evolution of societal needs, technological developments, etc.

Revenue Producing Monopolies

5.129 Apart from undertakings entrusted with services of general economic interest, Article 86(2) also refers to another category of undertakings: revenue producing monopolies. There is a general consensus, however, that exclusive rights whose only objective is the generation of revenues would never be justified under Article 86(2).[153] The reason is that revenue producing monopolies would normally fail to satisfy the proportionality test, as there are less restrictive means available for obtaining such revenues, such as fiscal measures.[154]

(2) Article 86(2) as an Exception Applicable to the Behaviour of Undertakings and to State Measures

5.130 Articles 81 and 82 are provisions addressed to undertakings. As such, they apply directly not only to private but also to public undertakings. The point of departure is therefore that these provisions apply to all undertakings. Article 86(2), however, expressly provides for a limited exemption: Articles 81 and 82 will only apply to the behaviour of an undertaking that has been entrusted with a service of general economic interest to the extent that their application does not endanger the fulfilment of the undertaking's specific role. It follows from this that Article 86(2) can be invoked by these undertakings in the context of procedures based on Articles 81 and/or 82 of the EC Treaty.[155]

5.131 Despite some early doubts,[156] it is now clear that the exception provided for in Article 86(2) can also apply to State measures that are contrary to a rule of the Treaty addressed to the Member States,[157] such as Article 86(1) in combination with Articles 28, 31, 43, 49, or 82, or the rules on State aids (Articles 87 and 88).[158]

---

[151] This has always been the position of the Court of Justice, see, for instance, Case C–179/90 *Port of Genoa* [1991] ECR I–5889, para 27.

[152] Case C–18/88 *RTT* [1991] ECR I–5941, para 16.

[153] Franck (n 104 above) 39, Papaconstantinou (n 10 above) 90; R Wainwright, 'Public Undertakings under Article 90', [1989] FCLI 249.

[154] This position was adopted by the Commission in Recommendation 62/1500 *French tobacco monopoly* [1962] OJ 48 and Recommendation 62/1502 *French matches monopoly* [1962] OJ 48.

[155] Case C–393/92 *Almelo* [1994] ECR I–1517, paras 33–50; Case 41/83 *British Telecommunications* [1985] ECR 873, paras 28–35.

[156] Case 72/83 *Campus Oil* [1984] ECR 2727, para 19.

[157] Case C–157/94 *Dutch electricity monopoly* [1997] ECR I–5699, paras 27–31; Case C–158/94 *Italian electricity monopoly* [1997] ECR I–5789, paras 38–44; Case C–159/94 *French electricity and gas monopolies* [1997] ECR I–5815, paras 44–50.

[158] Case T–106/95 *La Poste* [1997] ECR II–233, para 172.

(3) Conditions for the Application of Article 86(2)

One has to keep in mind that Article 86(2), as with any exception, will be inter-   **5.132**
preted strictly.[159] It goes without saying that the mere invocation of Article 86(2)
by a Member State or by an undertaking does not automatically entail that the
exception will be applied. This would only happen if all the conditions foreseen in
the provision are fulfilled. The first condition, that a service of general economic
interest must have been entrusted by the State to one undertaking, has already
been examined. The other two conditions are that the restriction must be proportional (or necessary) and the interest of the Community must be respected.

The Necessity of the Measure

Article 86(2) only applies to the extent that the restriction is *necessary* for the ful-   **5.133**
filment of the relevant purpose of general economic interest. In other words, the
exception will only apply if the *proportionate* character of the restriction can be
proved. Thus, the legality of many State measures or behaviours of undertakings
will depend on the interpretation given to this condition. It goes without saying
that this fact makes its interpretation highly controversial.

The Proportionality Principle

The proportionality test contained in Article 86(2) is no different from those   **5.134**
existing in other areas of EC law. The proportionality test is considered to be fulfilled when the following three elements are proven:[160]

1) that a causal link exists between the measure and the objective of general interest,

2) that the restrictions caused by the measure are balanced by the benefits for the
   general interest, and

3) that the objective of general interest cannot be achieved through other less
   restrictive means.

The Old Approach: A Strict Interpretation of the Proportionality Test

This test has traditionally been applied, at least within the framework of Article   **5.135**
86(2), in a very strict way.[161] Not surprisingly, the exception contained in this
Article was rarely found to apply. At the time, this did not raise concerns, as the
prohibitions contained in Article 86(1) were also interpreted in a restrictive way.

---

[159] Case 127/73 *BRT II* [1974] ECR 313, paras 20–21; Case T–260/94 *Air Inter* [1997] ECR
II–997, para 135.

[160] J Schwarze, *European Administrative Law* (Office for Official Publications of the European
Communities, Sweet and Maxwell, 1992), 854; G De Burca, 'The Principle of Proportionality and
its Application in EC Law' [1993] YEL xiii 113.

[161] *Navewa-Anseau* [1982] OJ L167/39, para 66; *British Telecommunications* [1982] OJ
L360/36, para 41; Case C–18/88 *RTT* [1991] ECR I–5941, para 22.

However, the traditional approach seems difficult to accept in the current context, when the scope of the prohibitions contained in Article 86(1) has been greatly enlarged. As many exclusive rights now fall under the prohibition contained in Article 86(1), it is necessary to examine whether they can be justified for public service reasons. The Court of Justice has therefore adopted in its recent judgments a less rigid interpretation of the proportionality test as regards exclusive rights.[162] The precise implications of this new approach are not totally clear.

The Need for a More Flexible Interpretation

5.136 The need for a more flexible interpretation of Article 86(2) mainly arose as regards certain exclusive rights in the utilities sector (electricity, gas, telecommunications, postal services, etc). These exclusive rights had been established for public service reasons. However, new technological, economic, and/or social developments challenged the *status quo*. Legally speaking, the new interpretation of Article 86(1) in combination with Articles 28, 31, 43, 49, and 82 meant that many of the exclusive rights were in breach of these provisions and therefore illegal unless justified by Article 86(2).

The 'Cherry-Picking' Problem

5.137 The problem was particularly acute as regards exclusive rights linked with the provision of a universal service. Universal service obligations are a particular category within the general concept of roles of general economic interest. Undertakings entrusted with a universal service obligation are requested by the Member State to provide certain services or goods to all the citizens, irrespective of their place of residence, at an affordable cost. In many cases the State also imposes a uniform tariff applicable in the territory, the so-called 'postalization'. This postalization necessarily implies cross-subsidization[163] from low-cost customers (ie, those residing in urban areas) to high-cost customers (ie, those residing in rural areas). In other words, low-cost customers are paying a relatively high price to allow the undertaking to offer an affordable (below-cost) price to high-cost customers.

5.138 Of course, this cross-subsidization would be difficult to sustain in a fully competitive environment. Newcomers could easily target the incumbent's low-cost customers by offering them attractive tariffs. This 'cherry-picking' strategy (also called 'cream-skimming') would deprive the incumbent of its most profitable customer base and endanger the provision of the universal service to high-cost customers. In order to avoid this, undertakings entrusted with universal service obligations are often granted exclusive rights for the provision of these services (or part of these services, the so-called 'reserved area'). The idea is that the

---

[162] Case C–320/91 *Corbeau* [1993] ECR I–2533.
[163] See L Hancher & JL Buendia Sierra, 'Cross-subsidization and EC Law' [1998] 35 CMLRev 901–945.

monopoly profits so generated will serve to finance the provision of the universal service.

The 'Cherry-Picking' Problem under the Old Approach

The 'cherry-picking' argument would hardly satisfy the traditional version of the   **5.139**
proportionality test. Strictly speaking, an exclusive right is not indispensable in order to guarantee the provision of a universal service. A Member State could achieve the same objective by using instruments less restrictive than a monopoly (for instance, by directly subsidizing the provision of the service to high-cost customers).[164] This suggests that, in principle, Article 86(2) would never justify exclusive rights, even those that are granted for the provision of universal services.

The New Approach to Proportionality: The Corbeau Case

However, neither the Commission nor the Court of Justice have always followed   **5.140**
such a strict approach. In the *Corbeau* case, the Court of Justice accepted that Article 86(2) did justify an exclusive right which served to finance the universal service obligation of the Belgian postal operator.[165] However, the Court made a distinction between the 'basic' postal service, which could be reserved to the incumbent, and 'value-added' services, which should be open to competition unless the economic impact would be such as to endanger the financial equilibrium of the universal service.[166] In the *Almelo* case, the Court of Justice held that Article 86(2) applied in respect of the anti-competitive behaviour of a Dutch local electricity distributor.[167] The reason behind this behaviour was the need to finance a universal service obligation. The exception in Article 86(2) was also found to apply in the telecommunications sector. In its early directives, the Commission considered that the financing of a universal telecommunication network was a valid justification for the maintenance of exclusive rights for voice telephony.[168]

Need for an Economic Analysis

Even if the proportionality test is applied in a flexible way, an economic analysis   **5.141**
will be necessary in order to apply the exception in Article 86(2). This analysis should be conducted as follows:[169]

— the net cost of providing a universal service must be evaluated in an objective manner;

---

[164] Opinion of Rozes AG, Case 172/82 *Used Oils* [1983] ECR 555, point 3.
[165] Case C–320/91 *Corbeau* [1993] ECR I–2533, paras 15–18.
[166] Case C–320/91 *Corbeau* [1993] ECR I–2533, para 19.
[167] Case C–393/92 *Almelo* [1994] ECR I–1517, paras 46–49.
[168] Directive (EEC) 90/388 on competition in the markets for telecommunications services [1990] OJ L192/10, para 18.
[169] Case T–260/94 *Air Inter* [1997] ECR II–997, paras 138–140.

— the economic advantages inherent to the exclusive right also have to be evaluated;

— the two figures should then be compared;

— due account must be taken of State aids and other advantages also received by the undertaking as compensation for the universal service cost.

The Dynamic Character of Proportionality

5.142 The proportionality of the means used to perform a role of general economic interest must be evaluated according to the circumstances at the relevant time. An exclusive right may have been fully justified in the past, but following developments of a technological, economic, legal, social, or other nature, may cease to be justified in the future.[170] For example, starting in the mid-nineties, the Commission began to change its approach to the telecommunications sector. Once the universal coverage of the telecommunication networks was assured, the justification for the voice telephony monopolies disappeared. For that reason, following a review of the situation in the sector, the Commission decided to modify its directives in order to liberalize also the services.[171] In the future, universal telecommunications services will have to be assured without exclusive rights. Cross-subsidization (ie, from long-distance to metropolitan calls) will, no longer be sustainable (thus leading to the re-balancing of tariffs by incumbents). Universal telecommunication services will have to be financed by other mechanisms, more neutral from a competitive point of view. The net cost of providing a universal service will have to be calculated in an objective way. The provider of the universal service could for instance be compensated for these net costs with money coming from a 'universal service fund'. Such a fund could be established with contributions from all the operators that are active in the market and the contributions calculated following an objective and non-discriminatory method. This example illustrates the dynamic character of the exemption contained in Article 86(2).

Different Approaches Depending on the Sector

5.143 The Court of First Instance, in the *Air Inter* case, rejected the application of Article 86(2) to justify exclusive rights in the air transport sector. The undertaking invoked the 'cherry-picking' argument to defend its exclusive rights over some profitable air routes which were allegedly used to cross-subsidize other non-profitable routes (it was a universal service type of argument). The Court, however, relying on a strict interpretation of the proportionality test, suggested that

---

[170] Case C–18/88 *RTT* [1991] ECR I–5941, para 16.
[171] Directive (EC) 96/19 on full competition in telecommunications [1996] OJ L74/13, paras 13–24.

there were means less restrictive than exclusive rights to achieve the objective of integrating the territory.[172]

The Strict Approach and the Flexible Approach

The previous examples show that, when evaluating the legality of exclusive rights **5.144** for the provision of universal services, Article 86(2) has sometimes been applied in a traditional, strict way and sometimes in a more flexible way. It is submitted[173] that this apparent inconsistency can be explained by taking into account two factors: the traditional or newly created character of the universal service in question, and the presence or lack of Community intervention in the sector.

A more flexible approach is followed as regards existing exclusive rights that have **5.145** traditionally served to finance a classical universal service.[174] This 'acquired rights' approach no longer applies once the Commission uses its discretionary powers under Article 86(3) to opt for the stricter approach,[175] or when other Community legislation liberalizes the sector.[176] Of course, the greater flexibility implicit in the 'acquired rights' approach should never benefit newly created (or extended) exclusive rights or newly designed universal service obligations.

Universal Services and Other Services of General Economic Interest

Universal service is the most typical justification of exclusive rights, but exclusive **5.146** rights may be justified for reasons other than universal service.[177] It is only one among the various kinds of services of general economic interest to which Article 86(2) refers. In principle, there is nothing to prevent a Member State from establishing exclusive rights for the provision of other kinds of (non-universal) public services. It is submitted that in all these cases the proportionality test under Article 86(2) must be applied strictly.[178]

Proportionality and Other Measures

Exclusive rights are the most typical measures to be covered by Article 86(2). **5.147** However, other State measures and conduct of undertakings may also benefit from this exemption provided that all the conditions of Article 86(2), including the proportionality test in its stricter version, are fulfilled.

---

[172] Case T–260/94 *Air Inter* [1997] ECR II–997, paras 138–140.

[173] See JL Buendia Sierra, *Exclusive Rights and State Monopolies in EC Law* (Oxford University Press, 1999) paras 8.238–8.243 for more details.

[174] This was the case of the postal and electricity monopolies at the time of the *Corbeau* and *Almelo* cases.

[175] This is the case in the telecommunication sector.

[176] This is the case in the air transport sector.

[177] Commission communication on 'Services of General Interest in Europe' OJ C281/31; Kovar (n 146 above) 242 and 515.

[178] See JL Buendia Sierra, *Exclusive Rights and State Monopolies in EC Law* (Oxford University Press, 1999) para 8.244; V Hatzopoulos, 'L'Open Network Provision (ONP) moyen de la dérégulation' [1994] RTDE xxx (i) 87 and 96.

The Interest of the Community

5.148 The second sentence of Article 86(2) makes clear that, for the exemption to apply, the development of trade must not be affected in a manner contrary to the Community interest. The majority view is that this is not an additional condition, but merely a clarification concerning the proportionality requirement contained in the previous sentence.[179] On this view, Article 86(2) as a whole has direct effect and national courts can directly apply the exemption without a previous decision by the Commission.

5.149 It is submitted that there is also another plausible interpretation: that direct effect is restricted only to the first sentence of Article 86(2).[180] This would mean that national courts are competent to apply the exemption as regards national measures that they consider to be proportional. However, the Commission would retain the exclusive competence to declare, subject to the review of the Court of Justice, that the 'interest of the Community' is being infringed. The second sentence of Article 86(2) would therefore be 'an exception to the exception'.

(4) Invocation of Article 86(2) and Burden of Proof

5.150 Article 86(2) is an exception. This means that it can only be applied to a case if it is invoked by the Member State or by the undertaking which is in charge of the service of general economic interest.[181] Neither the Commission nor the Courts can be obliged to apply this provision *ex officio*.

5.151 In principle, those invoking the exception have the burden of proving that all the conditions of Article 86(2) are fulfilled.[182] The Member State and/or the undertaking would have to prove that a role of general economic interest had been entrusted to the undertaking and that the measure or behaviour concerned was proportional. This is logical, as these elements fall within their sphere of knowledge. It would be absurd to require the Commission to prove the lack of proportionality of a measure every time that somebody invoked Article 86(2). Such an approach would transform the provision into a quasi-automatic scapegoat. However, the Court of Justice has to an extent nuanced the issue of the burden of

---

[179] Wainwright (n 153 above) 251; Wachsman & Berrod (n 146 above) 53; Case C–202/88 *Terminal equipment for telecommunications* [1991] ECR I–1223, paras 11–12.

[180] This position was defended by Van Gerven AG in Case C–179/90 *Port of Genoa* [1991] ECR I–5889, paras 26–28, and by the CFI in Case T–16/91 *Rendo* [1992] ECR II–2417. The Court of Justice, however, refused to endorse this position in its appeal judgment, Case C–19/93P *Rendo* (appeal) [1995] ECR I–3319, paras 18–19.

[181] *Zaventem* [1995] OJ L216/8, para 20; *GSM Italy* [1995] OJ L280/49, paras 26–27; *GSM Spain* [1997] OJ L76/19, para 30.

[182] Case 155/73 *Sacchi* [1974] ECR 409, para 15; Case 41/83 *British Telecommunications* [1985] ECR 873, para 33; Case T–260/94 *Air Inter* [1997] ECR II–997, para 138.

proof, by making clear that the Commission is obliged to respond to the legal and economic arguments put forward by the State or undertaking.[183]

(5) Relationship between Article 86(2) and Other Exceptions
'Mandatory Requirements' in the Framework of Article 86(2)

Under the 'Cassis de Dijon' doctrine, general measures falling within the rules on **5.152** free movement could only be justified on the basis of 'non-economic' objectives such as the protection of human health, culture, etc.[184] Economic objectives, such as the promotion of national industry, were clearly not admissible. The only Treaty exception allowing 'economic' objectives to be taken into account was Article 86(2) (objectives of general 'economic' interest).

Furthermore, Article 86(2) has traditionally been interpreted as referring *only* to **5.153** objectives of an 'economic' nature.[185] According to this view, the notion of objectives of 'general economic interest' did not include 'non-economic' objectives.

Today it is obvious that many restrictions concerning public or privileged under- **5.154** takings (and therefore falling within Article 86(1)) may be justified for non-economic reasons, such as the protection of public health (this may be the case of alcohol monopolies) or the promotion of culture (television monopolies). The Court of Justice has made clear that these restrictions can also in some cases benefit from the exception in Article 86(2).[186] This means that these non-economic objectives (or 'mandatory requirements') may also be objectives of general interest under Article 86(2). Strictly speaking, therefore, the adjective 'economic' used in this provision refers to the means (a commercial activity) not necessarily to the objectives.

Article 81(3)

It follows from the *Eurovision* case that the exception provided by Article 86(2) **5.155** may overlap from a substantive point of view with the exemption that the Commission may grant on the basis of Article 81(3) (former Article 85(3)).[187] A notifying party may therefore invoke Article 86(2) within the framework of a notification to the Commission under Article 81(3). It does not seem possible, however, to invoke Article 86(2) to avoid the notification requirement.[188]

---

[183] Case C–157/94 *Dutch electricity monopoly* [1997] ECR I–5699, paras 48–64; Case C–158/94 *Italian electricity monopoly* [1997] ECR I–5789, paras 46–60; Case C–159/94 *French electricity and gas monopolies* [1997] ECR I–5815, paras 90–107.

[184] Case 120/78 *Cassis de Dijon* [1979] ECR 649, para 8.

[185] Opinion of Tesauro AG, Case C–320/91 *Corbeau* [1993] ECR I–2531, para 14.

[186] Case C–18/88 *RTT* [1991] ECR I–5941, para 22.

[187] Cases T–528, 542, 543 and 546/93 *Eurovision* [1996] ECR II–649, paras 114–126.

[188] See, however, Case C–393/92 *Almelo* [1994] ECR I–1517.

D. Article 86(3): Procedural Rules Applying to Anti-Competitive State Measures

5.156   Article 86(3) (former Article 90(3)) provides:

> The Commission shall ensure the application of the provisions of this Article and shall, where necessary, address appropriate directives or decisions to Member States.

Thus Article 86 contains in its third paragraph procedural rules for the application of the substantive provisions contained in the first two paragraphs. Article 86(3) gives the Commission, on the one hand, the power to adopt *decisions* declaring that a Member State has infringed Article 86(1) and obliging this Member State to put an end to the infringement. On the other hand, it also gives the Commission the power to adopt *directives* with binding effects on all Member States, in order to specify the obligations contained in Article 86(1) and/or to prevent future infringements of the obligations.[189]

(1) Article 86(3) Decisions

General Issues

5.157   Article 86(3) gives to the Commission the power to adopt *decisions* declaring that Article 86(1) has been infringed and obliging the Member State to put an end to the infringement. This procedure constitutes an exception to the general procedure of Article 226 (former Article 169), in which it is up to the Court of Justice to declare that the Treaty has been infringed), but is not a revolutionary idea. Indeed, the Commission has similar powers as regards anti-competitive behaviour of undertakings (Articles 81 and 82)[190] and as regards State aids (Articles 87 and 88). This suggests a design giving the Commission similar powers to react quickly against all restrictions of competition, irrespective of their public or private origin.[191]

---

[189] On the doctrine see: JL Buendia Sierra, *Exclusive Rights and State Monopolies in EC Law* (Oxford University Press, 1999) chapter 10; C Hocepied, 'Les directives Article 90, paragraphe 3. Une espèce juridique en voie de disparition?' [1994] RAE ii 49–63; A Pappalardo, 'State Measures and Public Undertakings: Article 90 of the EEC Treaty Revisited' [1991] 1 ECLR 29–39; M Kerf, 'The Policy of the Commission of the EEC Toward National Monopolies. An Analysis of the Measures Adopted on the Basis of Article 90(3) of the EEC Treaty' (September 1993) 17(1) *World Competition* 73–111; LM Pais Antunes, 'L'Article 86 du Traité CEE—Obligations des Etats Membres et pouvoirs de la Commission' [1991] RTDE ii 187 *et seq*; H Papaconstantinou (n 10 above); F Melin-Soucramanien, 'Les pouvoirs spéciaux conférés à la Commission en matière de concurrence par l'Article 86.3 du Traité de Rome' [1994] 382 RMCUE 601–610.

[190] L Ortiz Blanco, *EC Competition Procedure* (Oxford: Clarendon Press, 1996) ch 7 *et seq*.

[191] Papaconstantinou (n 10 above) 102–104.

Analogy with Other Procedures

There is no supplementary text that specifies Article 86(3) procedure in greater **5.158** detail. The obvious temptation is to turn to the analogy with other procedures, such as the antitrust procedure,[192] the State aids procedure,[193] or the Article 226 procedure.[194] However, these analogies have to be handled with care, taking due account also of the differences between these rules and Article 86.

Discretionary Character of the Procedure under Article 86(3)

Even if the Commission always has the ability to act (*ex officio* or following a com- **5.159** plaint) on the basis of Article 86(3), the provision does not oblige the Commission to commence infringement proceedings whenever a violation of Article 86(1) comes to light. The Commission has a wide margin of discretion in this respect.[195] This margin also exists as regards the choice between the different procedures.[196] The Commission is not obliged to use Article 86(3) to act against infringements of Article 86(1). The possibility of using the Article 226 procedure always remains open, although Article 86(3) would normally be preferred due to its characteristics.

Lodging of Complaints and *Ex Officio* Cases

The Commission may act *ex officio* or following a complaint. Complaints and *ex* **5.160** *officio* cases based on Article 86 are registered and examined during a preliminary phase. During this phase, the Commission may request additional information from the complainant or from the Member State. At the end of the preliminary phase, the Commission decides whether an infringement procedure should be opened and informs the complainant of its decision.

Dismissal of Complaints

The Commission has a wide margin of discretion in deciding whether to open an **5.161** infringement procedure under Article 86(3). The Commission may therefore reject a complaint not only on substantive grounds, but also on opportunity grounds (because the case is considered as non-priority). Of course, complainants confronted with a refusal from the Commission always have the right to invoke the direct effect of Article 86(1) before national courts. However, even if the

---

[192] Rejected by the CFI in Case T–32/93 *Ladbroke I* [1994] ECR II–1015, para 38.
[193] Case C–18/88 *RTT* [1991] ECR I–5941, para 31; Opinion of La Pergola AG, Case C–107/95P *Expert accountants* [1996] ECR I–957, paras 14–21.
[194] Opinion of Van Gerven AG, Case C–18/88 *RTT* [1991] ECR I–5941, para 8.
[195] Case T–32/93 *Ladbroke I* [1994] ECR II–1015, paras 37–38; Case T–548/93 *Ladbroke II* [1995] ECR II–2565, para 45; Case T–84/94 *Expert accountants* [1995] ECR II–101, para 31, confirmed by Case C–107/95P *Expert accountants* (appeal) [1996] ECR I–957, para 27.
[196] Papaconstantinou (n 10 aboe) 113; J Flynn & E Turnbull, 'Joined Cases C–48/90 and C–66/90, (the "Dutch Couriers" Case)' [1993] CMLRev 402; Hoçepied (n 189 above) 55.

Court of Justice has left the door open to this alternative approach in 'exceptional situations',[197] complainants cannot in principle either bring an Article 230 (former Article 173) action against the Commission's refusal to open a procedure[198] or bring an Article 232 (former Article 175) action against the Commission's failure to act following a complaint based on Article 86.[199]

The Infringement Procedure

Interim Measures

5.162 The infringement procedure is normally opened by a letter of formal notice. However, an analogy with the procedure of Regulation 17/62 suggests that it should be possible for the Commission to adopt interim measures in cases where there is a clear urgency and a serious and irreparable risk for the complainant or for the general interest.[200]

Letter of Formal Notice

5.163 The Court of Justice in its *Dutch PTT* case made clear that, before the adoption of an Article 86(3) decision, the Commission must inform the Member State of its intention and the legal reasoning supporting them and give this Member State the opportunity to make observations.[201] These requirements arise as a result of the rights of defence of the Member State. This communication normally takes the form of a letter of formal notice addressed by the Commission to the Member State. The letter must clearly identify the State measures that are the object of controversy and explicitly announce the possibility of a future Article 86(3) decision.

The Rights of the Member State and of the Undertaking that Benefits from the Measure

5.164 According to the *Dutch PTT* case, as the Member State is the sole addressee of an Article 86(3) decision, it is also the sole party having rights of defence within the framework of the procedure. The undertaking that benefits from the State measure at stake does not have such a right of defence, but merely a right to be heard.[202] This right implies a right to receive a copy of the letter of formal notice and a right to make comments to the Commission.

End of the Procedure without a Formal Decision

5.165 The infringement procedure may conclude without a formal decision. This happens when the Member State decides to put an end to the infringement before the

---

197 Case C–107/95P *Expert accountants* (appeal) [1996] ECR I–957, para 25.
198 Case T–84/94 *Expert accountants* [1995] ECR II–101, para 31, confirmed by Case C–107/95P *Expert accountants* (appeal) [1996] ECR I–957, para 27.
199 Case T–32/93 *Ladbroke I* [1994] ECR II–1015, paras 34–36.
200 Case 792/79R *Camera care* [1980] ECR 119.
201 Cases C–48 and 66/90 *Dutch PTT* [1992] ECR I–565, para 45.
202 Cases C–48 and 66/90 *Dutch PTT* [1992] ECR I–565, paras 50–51.

adoption of a decision, and also when the Commission changes its mind as a result of the comments made by the Member State.

The Formal Decision and its Effects

If the dispute remains after the answer to the letter of formal notice, then the **5.166** Commission may adopt a formal decision based on Article 86(3). The Commission retains a wide margin of discretion to decide whether or not to adopt such a decision.

An Article 86(3) decision is a normal decision within the meaning of Article 249 **5.167** (former Article 189) of the EC Treaty. As such, it must contain a statement of its legal basis and of the steps requested to be taken by the Member State. When a choice exists as regards the means to put an end to an infringement, the Commission has the power to ask for one specific means rather than the others.[203] An Article 86(3) decision is notified by the Commission to the recipient Member State, and produces its effects from the date of notification. The decision must also establish a deadline for the notification by the Member State of the implementing measures.

Binding Effects

Article 86(3) decisions are, as with any other decision, obligatory for the Member **5.168** States to which they are addressed, as made clear by the *Greek insurances* case.[204] This means that their direct effect can probably be invoked before a national court once the deadline has expired without the measures being implemented.[205]

Action for Annulment against an Article 86(3) Decision

If the Member State disagrees with the decision, it has to bring an action for **5.169** annulment (Article 230, former Article 173) before the Court of Justice within two months of its notification. An Article 230 action may also be introduced before the Court of First Instance by third parties that are directly and individually affected by the decision (such as the undertaking that benefits from the State measure at stake) within two months of their knowing of the decision (ie two months from notification or of publication, depending on the case).[206] In principle, an action for annulment does not suspend the obligatory character of the decision, although the Member State may ask the Court to adopt an interim

---

[203] Cases C–48 and 66/90 *Dutch PTT* [1992] ECR I–565, para 28; Case C–107/95P *Expert accountants* (appeal) [1996] ECR I–947, pars 23.

[204] Case 226/87 *Greek insurances* [1988] ECR 3611, para 12.

[205] Pais Antunes (n 189 above) 205–206; Hocepied (n 189 above) 55.

[206] Case C–107/95P *Expert accountants* (appeal) [1996] ECR I–957, para 24; Cases C–48 and 66/90 *Dutch PTT* [1992] ECR I–565, para 50, and Opinion of Van Gerven AG in that case, para 5.

suspension. If no action is brought within the two months or if the action is rejected by the Court the decision becomes final and its legality cannot be further challenged, unless there are devices available such as to declare it non-existent.[207]

Action for Failure to Implement an Article 86(3) Decision

5.170   Once the deadline given to the Member State expires without the decision having been correctly implemented (and unless the Court has adopted an interim suspension), the Commission may open an Article 226 action against the Member State for failure to respect the decision. The Commission is obliged to send first a letter of formal notice and then a reasoned opinion to the Member State before bringing the case to the Court of Justice. It must be stressed that the substance of the case (the legality of the decision) cannot be further argued at this stage (unless as referred to above, there are devices available such as to seek a declaration of non-existence).[208]

5.171   As well as facing the intervention of the Commission and the Courts, a Member State that has been found to be in breach of its Community obligations under Article 86 may face actions from particular bodies asking for indemnities under the 'Francovitch' doctrine.[209]

(2) Article 86(3) Directives
Preventive Functions of Article 86(3) Directives

5.172   The Commission is entrusted with a mission of vigilance as regards the respect by Member States of the Treaty rules and of Article 86 in particular. In view of this mission, Article 86(3) grants the Commission not only powers to act against concrete infringements but also *preventive* powers as regards future infringements. Indeed, apart from the power to adopt individual decisions addressed to a Member State, Article 86(3) also gives to the Commission the power to adopt *directives* with binding effects on all Member States. The objective of these directives is to prevent future infringements of the obligations contained in Article 86(1). Unlike Article 86(3) decisions, the directives based on this provision do not have a repressive function: they do not constitute a declaration that actual infringements have been committed.[210]

5.173   The prevention of future infringements operates in two ways. First of all, the Commission may use an Article 86(3) directive to create instrumental obligations aimed at making possible the detection of future infringements. Secondly, the Commission may also use an Article 86(3) directive to specify the meaning and

---

[207] Case 226/87 *Greek insurances* [1988] ECR 3611, paras 12–16.
[208] Case 226/87 *Greek insurances* [1988] ECR 3611, paras 12–16.
[209] Cases C–6 and 9/90 *Francovitch* [1991] ECR I–5357, paras 36–37.
[210] Case C–202/88 *Terminal equipment for telecommunications* [1991] ECR I–1223, para 17.

extent of the obligations that already exist under Article 86(1) of the Treaty. This means that under Article 86(3) the Commission has certain quasi-legislative powers, even if it is subject to strict limits and under the legal control of the Court of Justice. This raises delicate legal and political issues.

Article 86(3) Directives as Instruments for Detecting Future Infringements

The most obvious example of the use of Article 86(3) directives as an instrument **5.174** for detecting future infringements is the 'transparency' Directive, originally adopted in 1980 and subsequently modified in 1985 and 1993.[211] This Directive creates an obligation on Member States to set up transparent accounting systems reflecting the financial relationships between the public administrations and public undertakings. The idea was to make possible the detection of State aids in favour of public undertakings. The obligation to set up transparent accounts did not exist prior to the adoption of the Directive. It was created as an new obligation ancillary to the State aid rules. Thus, this new obligation was an instrument to guarantee that existing rules were respected. The Court of Justice confirmed in 1982 that Article 90(3) (now Article 86(3)) gave the Commission the power to adopt this kind of preventive measure.[212]

Article 86(3) Directives as Instruments for 'Specifying' the Obligations Imposed by the Treaty

Article 86(3) directives may also be used to 'specify' the meaning and extent of the **5.175** obligations that already exist under Article 86(1) of the Treaty. The first example of this approach was the 'telecom terminals' Directive, in which the Commission 'specified' that the exclusive rights granted to the telecommunications operators for the import and commercialization of terminal equipment were incompatible with Article 86(1) in combination with Articles 28, 31, 49, or 82.[213] On the basis of this 'specification', the Directive obliged Member States to abolish these exclusive rights. A similar approach has been used in many other Article 86(3) directives. The Court of Justice fully confirmed the legality of this approach in 1991 and 1992.[214]

In situations where a Treaty obligation can be implemented in different ways, the **5.176** power to 'specify' these obligations implies a power to impose on Member States one specific means of implementation.[215]

---

[211] Commission Directive (EEC) 80/723 concerning the transparency of financial relations between Member States and their public undertakings [1980] OJ L195/35.

[212] Cases 188, 189 and 190/80 *Transparency directive* [1982] ECR 2545.

[213] Comission Directive (EEC) 88/301 on competition in the markets for telecommunication terminal equipment [1988] OJ L131/73, para 3.

[214] Case C–202/88 *Terminal equipment for telecommunications* [1991] ECR I–1223, para 17, Cases C–271, 281 and 289/90 *Telecommunications services* [1992] ECR I–5883, para 12.

[215] Cases C–271, 281 and 289/90 *Telecommunications services* [1992] ECR I–5883, paras 17 and 22; L Hancher, 'Judgments of the Court Lagauche, Decoster & Taillandier' [1994] 21 CMLRev 857–873.

Legal Regime of Article 86(3) Directives

The Exclusive Competence of the Commission

5.177 The Commission has the exclusive competence to adopt Article 86(3) directives and has a total discretion as to when to use this power. Even if the Treaty does not require the intervention of any other institution, in practice the Commission normally consults the European Parliament, the Member States, and the interested parties. Often, a draft Article 86(3) directive is published first in the C series of the *Official Journal* to invite comments from institutions and bodies who may wish to intercede. The directive is only adopted by the Commission after taking into account the results of this consultation.[216]

Limits to the Commission's Competence

5.178 Irrespective of this policy of searching for consensus, the Commission has from a legal point of view the sole responsibility for the adoption of Article 86(3) directives. However, this power to adopt directives under Article 86(3) is not a general legislative competence but a precisely defined competence which is exercised under the legal control of the Court of Justice. Some of the limits to the regulatory power of the Commission are examined in the following paragraphs.

Article 86(3) Directives Cannot Deal with the Autonomous Behaviour of Undertakings

5.179 In principle the object of Article 86(3) directives must be State measures, not the behaviour of undertakings.[217] Moreover, these State measures must be connected in one way or another with public or privileged undertakings or with public services (ie, falling within Article 86(1) or 86(2)).

Formal Limits to the Commission's Power under Article 86(3)

5.180 The power that Article 86(3) grants to the Commission of creating obligations (either preventive or mandatory) must be exercised using the legal form of a directive. The use of other instruments, such as a communication, would undermine legal certainty and would be illegal.[218]

5.181 An Article 86(3) directive has all the characteristics of a normal directive within the meaning of Article 249 (former Article 189) of the EC Treaty. It must contain a clear legal basis.[219] In accordance with Article 254(2) (former Article 191(2)) the

---

[216] *Report on Competition Policy 1995* (Vol XXV) para 100.

[217] Case C–202/88 *Terminal equipment for telecommunications* [1991] ECR I–1223, paras 55–57; Cases C–271, 281 and 289/90 *Telecommunications services* [1992] ECR I–5883, paras 24–26.

[218] Case C–325/91 *Transparency communication* [1993] ECR I–3283.

[219] Case C–202/88 *Terminal equipment for telecommunications* [1991] ECR I–1223, paras 45–47; Cases C–271, 281 and 289/90 *Telecommunications services* [1992] ECR I–5883, paras 28–31.

directive will be published in the L series of the *Official Journal* and will enter into force twenty days after its publication, unless otherwise specified.

Binding Effects

Article 86(3) directives are obligatory for the Member States to which they are addressed. This obligatory effect is independent of the obligatory effect of the Treaty rules on which the directive is based.[220]

5.182

Lack of Direct Effect

In principle, directives are not directly applicable but require the adoption of implementing measures at national level. However, provisions having an unconditional and precise enough content may be recognized as having direct effect once the deadline has expired without their being implemented.[221]

5.183

Relationship between Directives under Article 86(3) and Harmonizing Directives

Even though the Court of Justice has repeatedly confirmed its legal validity, the quasi-legislative competence that Article 86(3) gives to the Commission has been the object of political controversy. Those powers, however, fit well into the logic of the EC Treaty where the provisions addressed to the Member States, such as Article 86, are not of a programmatic nature but rather directly obligatory rules. This makes it difficult to distinguish between 'creating law' and 'applying existing law'. Article 86 directives are simply a witness of this ambiguity.

5.184

Article 86(3) Overlaps with Other Treaty Provisions

The competence of the Commission under Article 86(3) coexists with the legislative competences of the Council of Ministers and the European Parliament under Article 95 (former Article 100A) and many other provisions. The Court of Justice has confirmed that certain matters may be regulated either by a directive of the Council and the Parliament or by a directive of the Commission.[222] This happens in particular as regards the liberalization of the utilities sectors.

5.185

The Dissuasive Role of Article 86(3)

The political implications of this overlapping of competences are delicate. The participation of the European Parliament in the legislative procedure under Article 95 gives to the relevant directives a democratic legitimacy that does not

5.186

---

[220] Edward & Hoskins (n 10 above) 184; Pais Antunes (n 189 above) 203.

[221] Cases C–46/90 and C93/91 *Lagauche* [1993] ECR I–5267, and Opinion of Lenz AG on this case at paras 13–19; Case C–69/91 *Decoster* [1993] ECR I–5335, and Opinion of Tesauro AG on this case; Case C–92/91 *Taillandier* [1993] ECR I–5383.

[222] Cases 188, 189 and 190/80 *Transparency directive* [1982] ECR 2545, paras 11–14; Case C–202/88 *Terminal equipment for telecommunications* [1991] ECR I–1223, paras 23–26; Cases C–271, 281 and 289/90 *Telecommunications services* [1992] ECR I–5883, para 14.

exist in the case of Article 86(3) directives. This clearly reduces, from a political point of view, the margin of discretion of the Commission in choosing the appropriate legal basis for its liberalization directives. This may explain the restraint shown by the Commission in the use of Article 86(3) directives: so far this instrument has only been used in the telecommunications sector and not in the liberalization of the electricity, gas, air transport, railways and postal sectors. It would be a mistake, however, to think that Article 86(3) has not played any role in these liberalization processes. It is clear that the mere possibility for the Commission to adopt an Article 86(3) directive has had an influence upon the attitudes of the actors in the legislative process. It is submitted that this 'dissuasive' role of Article 86(3) is an essential factor in achieving a balanced Community approach to liberalization.

PART II

SPECIFIC PRACTICES

6

HORIZONTAL AGREEMENTS

A. Introduction

(1) Definition of Horizontal Agreements and Practices

6.01 In this context horizontal agreements refer to agreements between companies operating at the same level in the production/distribution chain, for example research or production. In the majority of cases the focus of the antitrust rules will be on horizontal agreements between actual and/or potential competitors. However, agreements between companies that have complementary skills or technology may also be of concern to the antitrust authorities to the extent that such agreements harm the competitive position of third parties, for example by foreclosing market entry.

(2) Classification of Horizontal Agreements and Practices

6.02 Depending on their effects on competition horizontal agreements can be classified in two broad categories, 'per se' and 'non-per se'.

6.03 Agreements falling under the so-called 'per se' category, such as price-fixing cartels etc, are considered as illegal in themselves, without regard to any anti-competitive effects that they might produce. The underlying idea being that *per se* offences are invariably harmful to competition.

6.04 The assessment of 'non-per se' co-operation agreements is quite different. The principle involved here is that these cases are not necessarily harmful to competition. Their effect on competition depends, *inter alia*, on the nature of the agreement and market conditions. Therefore their assessment is primarily carried out on a case-by-case basis.

(3) Use of Commission Decisions

6.05 The Commission generally publishes decisions when it wishes to establish points of principle and give greater clarity as to how it assesses individual cases. However, it is important also to realize that the Commission policy has developed over time. This is in part a reaction to changing markets as well as a refining of the analytical approach and techniques open to it, and experience. There is also a variation in the level of analysis in different cases. This chapter does not attempt to provide a detailed review of Commission decisions; rather it discusses general points of principle and illustrates these points, where possible, with recent Commission decisions.

B. Hard Core Cartels

(1) Introduction

6.06 It is commonly accepted that not all the restrictions of competition resulting from private arrangements among competitors are capable of being identified with the same degree of certainty. The EC Treaty, by listing in sub-paragraphs (a) to (e) of Article 81(1) (former Article 85(1)) typical restrictions of competition, acknowledged this fact and the Court ruled that the fact that the infringement of Article 85(1) [now Article 81(1)] of the EEC Treaty, in particular subparagraphs (a), (b) and (c), is a clear one precludes the application of a rule of reason, assuming such a rule to be applicable in Community competition law, since in that case it must be regarded as an infringement *per se* of the competition rules'.[1]

On the other hand, although not all the agreements restrictive of competition deserve the same degree of censure, the EC Treaty does not differentiate among them as far as the legal consequences are concerned: according to Article 81(2), they are all equally void. Over the years, however, the practice developed by the Commission has acknowledged the fact that agreements which lead to price-fixing, establishment of quotas, and market sharing are the most detrimental to competition.[2] As they represent a direct attack to the heart of the process of competition they are called 'hard core' cartels. The OECD defines a hard core cartel as: **6.07**

> an anticompetitive agreement, anticompetitive concerted practice or anticompetitive arrangement by competitors to fix prices, make rigged bids (collusive tenders), establish output restrictions or quotas, or share or divide markets by allocating customers, suppliers, territories or lines of commerce.[3]

These agreements have as their object a restriction of competition and therefore in Community law there is no need to examine their actual effects on competition provided that they can affect trade between Member States. Concerning an agreement fixing prices the Court ruled that 'for the purposes of Article 85(1) [now Article 81(1)] it is unnecessary to take account of the actual effects of an agreement where its object is to restrict, prevent or distort competition';[4] agreements concerning market sharing[5] and quotas[6] are considered similarly.

The Commission does not rule out the possibility that hard core cartels of 'minor importance' (ie where aggregate market shares held by all of the participating undertakings do not exceed 5 per cent on the relevant market) can restrict competition in an appreciable way. It reserves the right to institute proceedings against them.[7]

---

[1] Case T–14/89 *Montedipe SpA v Commission* [1992] ECR II–1155, para 265.

[2] See eg *Report on Competition Policy 1971* (Vol I) para 1ff.

[3] Recommendation of the Council of March 1998 concerning Effective Action against Hard Core Cartels.

[4] Case 123/83 *BNIC v Guy Clair* [1985] ECR 391.

[5] Case *ACF Chemiefarma NV v Commission* [1970] ECR 661 (para 128 'the sharing out of domestic markets has as its object the restriction of competition and trade within the Common Market'); Joined Cases T–68/89, T–77/89 and T–78/89 *Società Italiana Vetro SpA, Fabbrica Pisana SpA and PPG Vernante Pennitalia SpA v Commission* [1992] ECR II–1403('agreements the purpose of which *was price-fixing and market-sharing, are caught by Article 85(1)(a) and (c) [now Article 81(1)(a) and (c)], without its being necessary to examine whether they actually affected competition. The Court cannot accept the argument advanced by the applicants . . . that those agreements should be regarded as de minimis'*). (Emphasis added.)

[6] Case T–142/89 *Usines Gustave Böel SA v Commission* [1995] ECR II–871.

[7] Commission's Notice on agreements of minor importance [1997] OJ C372 pp 13–15.

6.08   The undisputed illegality in Community law of the so-called hard core cartels is shown by the fact that, in the vast majority of appeals against Commission decisions that condemned them, the issues at stake were the standard of proof and the amount of the fines imposed on the undertakings. For instance, in the numerous judgments[8] concerning the *Cartonboard* decision,[9] the Court dealt with the following issues: the rights of the defence, liability of the undertakings, standard of proof, lawfulness of the order to refrain from exchanging some statistical information, and the amount and statement of reasons for the fines imposed.

6.09   In any event, notwithstanding their anti-competitive nature, the Court has ruled that even hard core cartels can be exempted from the prohibition established in Article 81(1) 'provided that all the conditions laid down in Article 85(3) [now Article 81(3)] of the Treaty are satisfied and the practice in question has been properly notified to the Commission'.[10] The fact, however, that most of them are kept secret excludes this possibility and even when they are notified to the Commission, their possible (rare) efficiencies are highly unlikely to compensate the restrictions involved and a prohibition decision is to be expected. Furthermore, the Commission considers that price-fixing and market-sharing quotas constitute very serious infringements of competition law and they can attract fines of at least ECU 20 million (the amount is commensurate with the duration of the infringement and the aggravating and mitigating circumstances, as well as the undertakings' co-operation with the Commission)[11] with a ceiling, however, of 10 per cent of the undertaking's turnover.

6.10   As stated above, hard core cartels normally operate in secrecy. The subject of proof, albeit an issue of capital importance for the authorities entrusted with the enforcement of competition law, will not be dealt with in this book. In the following paragraphs we will try to summarize the Commission's practice on hard core cartels.

(2) Fixing of Prices and Terms of Trade

6.11   The first example of prohibited agreements given by Article 81(1) is the direct or indirect fixing of purchase or selling prices or any other trading conditions. Although in many cases agreements on trading conditions complement agreements on prices they can be dealt with separately.

---

[8] Cases T–295/94, T–304/94, T–308/94, T–309/94, T–310/94, T–311/94, T–317/94, T–319/94, T–327/94, T–334/94, T–337/94, T–338/94, T–339/94, T–340/94, T–341/94, T–342/94, T–347/94, T–348/94, T–352/94, T–354/94, not yet reported.

[9] [1994] OJ L243/1.

[10] Case T–17/93 *Matra Hachette SA v Commission* [1994] ECR II–595, para 85.

[11] Guidelines on the method of setting fines imposed pursuant to Article 15(2) of Regulation 17 and Article 65(5) of the ECSC Treaty [1998] OJ C9 pp 3–5.

Price-Fixing

Since price competition is the essential form of competition, price-fixing consti-   **6.12**
tutes the most obvious infringement to competition law. Besides agreements on
common selling prices,[12] on the *amount of a price increase*,[13] or on the *amount of
rebates*,[14] price-fixing can adopt several other forms:

(a) Agreement on Recommended or Target Prices

In *Vereeniging van Cementhandelaren v Commission*, the Court ruled that the fix-   **6.13**
ing of a target price 'affects competition because it enables all the participants to
predict with a reasonable degree of certainty what the pricing policy pursued
by their competitors would be'. Similarly, in *Polypropylene*,[15] the Commission
stated: 'The setting of a particular price level which has been presented to the
market as "the list price" or "the official price" meant that the opportunities for
customers to negotiate with producers were already circumscribed and that they
were deprived of many of the benefits which would otherwise be available from
the free play of competition forces.' On appeal, the CFI decided that 'for the purposes of the application of Article 85(1) [now Article 81(1)] of the EEC Treaty the
fixing of target prices constitutes direct or indirect fixing of selling prices as mentioned, by way of example, in point (a) of that provision . . . The purpose of Article
85(1), and in particular of point (a) thereof, is to prohibit undertakings from distorting the normal formation of prices on the markets.'[16] In *SCK/FNK*, the
Commission established that 'jointly recommended prices, which may or may
not have been observed in practice, make it possible to predict with reasonable
certainty what the pricing policy of competitors would be'.[17] The CFI upheld the
Commission's position on this issue.[18] Likewise in *Fenex* the Commission stated

---

[12] See eg *Scottish Salmon Board* [1992] OJ L246/37 ('An agreement to fix prices *per se* limits competition within the meaning of Article 85(1) [now Article 81(1)]'); *Building and construction industry
in the Netherlands* [1992] OJ L92/1, upheld by the CFI in Case T–29/92 *Vereniging van samenwerk-
ende prijsregelende organisaties in de bouwnijverheid and others v Commission* [1995] ECR II–289.

[13] See eg *Cartonboard* (n 9 above).

[14] See eg *Vimpoltu* [1983] OJ L200/44, which dealt with a decision of the Dutch association of
agricultural tractor wholesalers prohibiting importers from selling tractors to dealers at a total discount per tractor exceeding 25% of the recommended retail price.

[15] [1986] OJ L230/1.

[16] Case T–13/89 *Imperial Chemical Industries plc v Commission* [1992] ECR II–1021, para 310.

[17] [1995] OJ L132/79.

[18] Joined Cases T–213/95 and T–18/96 *Stichting Certificatie Kraanverhuurbedrijf (SCK) and
Federatie van Nederlandse Kraanbedrijven (FNK) v Commission* [1997] ECR II–1739, para 164: 'It
follows from the above that the system of recommended and internal rates was a system of imposed
prices which enabled FNK's members, even if some of them did not always adhere to the prices set,
to predict with a reasonable degree of certainty the pricing policy pursued by the other members of
the association. In addition, it has been established that it had the object of increasing market prices.
The Commission was therefore right in finding that that system restricted competition for the purposes of Article 85(1) [now Article 81(1)] of the Treaty' (*Vereeniging van Cementhandelaren v
Commission*, paras 19 and 21, and *Verbund der Sachversicherer v Commission*, para 41).

that: 'The circulation of recommended tariffs by a trade organisation is liable to prompt the relevant undertakings to align their tariffs, irrespective of their cost prices. Such a method dissuades undertakings whose cost prices are lower from lowering their prices and thus creates an artificial advantage for undertakings which have the least control over their production costs'.[19]

(b) Agreement on an Element of the Price

6.14 In *Ferry operators currency surcharges*,[20] the Commission condemned an agreement between several ferry operators concerning the amount and the introduction date of a surcharge on freight shipments following the devaluation of the pound. In *VOTOB*,[21] the Commission objected to a uniform 'environmental charge'.

(c) Adoption of a Collective Resale Price Maintenance Policy

6.15 In *VBBB/VBVB*,[22] the Commission condemned an agreement between the Dutch and the Flemish associations of booksellers, publishers, and members of allied trades by which anyone selling books or offering them for sale must respect the prices fixed by Dutch or Flemish publishers. The Court upheld the Commission's position as to collective resale price maintenance stating that the effect of such a system is 'to deprive distributors of all freedom of action as regards the fixing of the selling price up to the level of the final price to the consumer. Such an arrangement would indeed infringe Article 85(1)(a) [now Article 81(1)(a)].'[23]

(d) Alleged 'Fair Trade' Practices on Prices

6.16 In the decisions *IFTRA Glass Containers*[24] and *IFTRA Virgin Aluminium*,[25] the Commission considered incompatible with Article 81(1) the establishment of an open price system (by which each undertaking informed the others of the prices, rebates, and selling terms that it applied, as well as the amendments to be made from a given date and individual exceptions granted to certain customers); the setting up of a delivered price system; the use of a uniform joint cost calculation formula; the prohibition of discriminatory prices, secretly departing from published offers or prices, departing from price lists, selling below cost, dumping in each other's territory, undercutting prices offered by competitors; and the obligation to express prices in the currency of the country of destination.

---

[19] [1996] OJ L181/28, 61.

[20] [1996] OJ L26/23.

[21] *Report on Competition Policy 1992* (Vol XXII) 177–186.

[22] [1982] OJ L54/36.

[23] Joined Cases 43/82 and 63/82 *Vereniging ter Bevordering van het Vlaamse Boekwezen, VBVB, and Vereniging ter Bevordering van de Belangen des Boekhandels, VBBB v Commission* [1984] ECR 19.

[24] [1974] OJ L160/1.

[25] [1975] OJ L228/3.

Agreements on Trading Conditions Other than Prices

Since trading conditions play a major role in competition, agreement on these **6.17** conditions can be assimilated to agreement on prices. Article 81(1) defines such agreements at the same level as price-fixing. The Commission has consistently prohibited these agreements. Some examples of decisions condemning them are as follows:

— In *Fedetab,* the association of Belgian and Luxembourg producers of manu-factured tobacco (Fedetab) issued a recommendation which *inter alia* estab-lished that 'the normal rule is that payment should be made cash; special periods of credit may be agreed on between a manufacturer and one or more of his customers but they may not extend beyond a fortnight from the invoice date';[26] a similar decision by Belgian wallpaper manufacturers had been con-demned by the Commission in *Papiers peints de Belgique.*[27]

— In *Vereeniging van Cementhandelaren,*[28] the Commission condemned a series of agreements and decisions taken by the Dutch cement dealers' association concerning the sale of cement in The Netherlands which *inter alia* strictly limited the commercial benefits which might be granted to purchasers and prevented any services being provided for customers which fell outside the framework of what was regarded as 'normal'. Likewise, in *Roofing Felt,* several Belgian roofing felt manufacturers agreed among other things on banning gifts to customers or selling them other products at a loss.[29]

— Other trading practices of the Belgian wallpaper manufacturers found to be illegal by the Commission in *Papier peints de Belgique*[30] included the follow-ing: the requirement that the General Conditions of sale must be standard-ized; the agreements on the opening and closing of marketing years; the fixing of a minimum amount to be purchased by customers; the prohibition on Saturday deliveries and the understanding on the annual closing of supply depots; and the fixing of dates, prices, and conditions for clearance sales.

(3) *Output Restrictions or Quotas; Restructuring Agreements*

Since the price of a product is a function of output and demand, a restriction **6.18** in output will affect prices. It is therefore not surprising if participants in an

---

[26] [1978] OJ L224/29. On appeal, *Heintz van Landewyck SARL and others v Commission* [1980] ECR 3125.

[27] [1974] OJ L237/3. On appeal, Case 73–74 *Groupement des fabricants de papiers peints de Belgique and others v Commission* [1975] ECR 1491.

[28] [1971] OJ L13/34. On appeal, Case 8/72 *Vereeniging van Cementhandelaren v Commission* [1972] ECR 977.

[29] [1986] OJ L232/15.

[30] See n 27 above.

agreement on prices also enter into an agreement to *limit production* in order to support the agreed prices. Two examples of decisions adopted by the Commission against this practice are as follows:

— *Zinc Producer Group*:[31] the members of the cartel, in order to support the common agreed price, also agreed to curtail production and to notify investment projects to all the members of the group.

— *Cartonboard*:[32] several producers of cartonboard co-ordinated their down time in order to restrain supply and keep prices up. The CFI confirmed the Commission's view.[33]

6.19 Output restrictions are most commonly achieved through *delivery quotas* which, in most cases, consist of the participants in the cartel setting a maximum permissible volume of deliveries allocated to each of them. In *Italian Cast Glass*,[34] for instance, three Italian producers of cast glass agreed on quotas for sales on the Italian market. In *Welded Steel Mesh*,[35] the participants established delivery quotas for welded steel mesh for the French, German and Benelux markets. These quotas are often fixed according to the market shares of the members of the cartel. In *Cartonboard*,[36] for instance, the participants reached an understanding on maintaining the market shares of the major producers at constant levels.

6.20 *Limitation or control of investments* is likely to have a similar effect to limitation of production. In *Cimbel*,[37] the Commission condemned an agreement which provided, among other things, that the establishment of new cement plants must be subject to prior approval of all the contracting parties.

6.21 Limitation of output or investments is a common feature of *restructuring agreements* between undertakings in order to deal with overcapacity. In principle, the Commission considers that in a market economy it is up to the individual undertakings to decide when overcapacity becomes economically unsustainable and to take the necessary measures to reduce it. Nevertheless, the Commission recognizes that in the case of structural overcapacity, market forces are very slow at bringing about the necessary radical changes needed to maintain an effective competitive structure in the longer term. Although consumers seem to be better off in situations of excess of supply, this is not the case when there exists overcapacity of a structural nature (since they must pay for the increased costs caused by ineffi-

---

[31] [1984] OJ L220/27.
[32] See n 9 above.
[33] See n 8 judgments, above.
[34] [1980] OJ L383/19.
[35] [1989] OJ L260/1. On appeal, Cases T–141,142,143,144,145, 147, 148, 149, 150, 151 and 152/89 [1995] ECR II–791.
[36] See n 9 above.
[37] [1972] OJ L303/24.

ciencies). In the longer term, a competitive structure is therefore to the consumer's advantage.

Structural overcapacity exists where, over a prolonged period, an entire economic **6.22** sector has been experiencing a significant reduction in the rates of capacity utilization, a drop in output accompanied by substantial operating losses (this condition was not fulfilled, however, in *Stichting Baksteen*,[38] where the Commission only detected a sharp fall in the firms' operating profits), and where the situation is not likely to change in the medium term.[39] In these circumstances the Commission has adopted a favourable approach towards concerted reductions of capacity provided that the agreement fulfils the following conditions:[40]

— the agreement must contain a detailed and binding programme of closures and must prevent the creation of any new capacity;

— consumers must not be deprived of the freedom of choice between competitors or the benefits of continued competition between the participating companies;

— any information exchange ancillary to the agreement must be solely with a view to supervising capacity reductions; and

— the agreement must be for a specifically stated period.

Besides the benefits accruing from the competitive structure of a sector in the long term, the Commission takes into account the fact that the co-ordination of plant closures ensures that restructuring is carried out in acceptable social conditions, including the redeployment and retraining of workers made redundant.

In *Synthetic fibres*,[41] nine European producers accounting for more than 60 per cent **6.23** of the European production of several synthetic fibres entered into an agreement to reduce capacity which was exempted by the Commission. The Commission stated that 'by committing themselves to reduce capacity, the parties accept restrictions on the scale of their production capacities and hence on their investment'.

The chemical industry has made extensive use of bilateral restructuring agree- **6.24** ments, as seen in the following decisions: *BPCL/ICI*,[42] *Bayer/BP Chemicals* (in this case, however, older capacity was to be replaced by modern capacity),[43] *ENI/Montedison*,[44] *Enichem/ICI*.[45]

---

[38] [1994] OJ L131/15.
[39] *Report on Competition Policy 1982* (Vol XII) point 38.
[40] *Report on Competition Policy 1982* (Vol XII) point 39.
[41] [1984] OJ L207/17.
[42] [1984] OJ L212/1.
[43] [1988] OJ L150/35 amended by decision (EC) 94/384 ([1994] OJ L174/34).
[44] [1987] OJ L5/13.
[45] [1988] OJ L50/18.

6.25 In *Stichting Baksteen*,[46] the Commission exempted an agreement entered into by sixteen Dutch brick producers in order to finance the definitive and irreversible closing down of seven production units owned by four of them. The Commission recognized that since demand for bricks was highly rigid with respect to price levels in the short or medium term (bricks represent only 2–3 per cent of the cost of a building) the producers' pricing policies were not likely to increase the rate of construction or total demand for building materials. In these circumstances market forces were not capable of achieving the necessary capacity cuts to restore and eventually maintain an efficient competitive structure. The reduction of capacity would lead to an increased utilization rate, a crucial factor in industries with high fixed costs and very little flexibility in the production process. In addition, because the closures were co-ordinated, restructuring could be carried out in acceptable social conditions. Consumers would also benefit from the improvement in production since in the long term they would be dealing with a healthy industry offering competitive supplies. The Dutch brick industry would therefore increase its profitability and restore its normal competitiveness.

(4) Market Sharing

Allocation of Customers

6.26 The allocation of customers can adopt the form of respecting the other party's customers. In *Roofing Felt*,[47] for instance, several Belgian producers of roofing felt agreed to supply only their own customers. Customers can be allocated through objective criteria: in *European Sugar Industry*,[48] the Belgian producers of sugar could only sell to the dairy industry in Holland; in *BP Kemi/DDSF*,[49] BP agreed to supply all of DDSF's requirements of ethanol and granted DDSF the exclusive right for sales of ethanol in Denmark. BP however reserved for itself those customers whose annual consumption exceeded 100,000 litres. Finally, one single customer can be the object of market sharing: in *Flat Glass*,[50] two producers of flat glass decided to share on an equal basis their supplies to a large consumer.

Allocation of Territories

6.27 The 'home market' rule constitutes the most obvious means of allocating territories. Since it runs contrary to one of the fundamental objectives of the Treaty, namely the establishment of a common market, it has consistently been condemned by the Commission with fines being levied on the companies involved.

---

[46] [1994] OJ L131/15.
[47] See n 29 above.
[48] [1973] OJ L140/17.
[49] [1979] OJ L286/32.
[50] [1989] OJ L33/44.

In *Cement*,[51] for instance, the Commission condemned the arrangements between more than thirty cement producers and their associations intended to protect the companies' home markets. The Commission imposed fines totalling more than ECU 120 million.

Besides the outright sharing of markets by competitors, the same result can be achieved through: **6.28**

(a) *Exclusive Distribution Agreements between Competitors*

They can be reciprocal as in *European Sugar Industry*,[52] where the Belgian and Dutch producers channelled all their cross-border deliveries through each other, or in *CSK/Gist-Brocades*,[53] where CSK became, in The Netherlands, the exclusive distributor of rennet produced by Gist-Brocades while outside The Netherlands Gist-Brocades was, *de facto*, the exclusive distributor of Rennet produced by CSK. They can be unilateral with the same result of isolating a market, as in *Vegetable Parchment*[54] where the continental manufacturers of vegetable parchment refrained from supplying other UK users while at the same time agreeing to supply the main UK producer with the quantities of the product it needed to fill its production gap and thus meet the entire British demand; or in *Aluminium Imports from Eastern Europe*,[55] where all the primary aluminium producers of the EC agreed to purchase the entire supplies of aluminium offered by the State Trading agencies of the Eastern bloc countries, which in turn agreed to sell exclusively to the EC primary aluminium producers. **6.29**

(b) *Reciprocal Exclusive Selling Rights between Competitors*

In *Siemens/Fanuc*,[56] Siemens and Fanuc granted each other exclusive selling rights of numerical controls in Europe and Asia respectively; thus Siemens neutralized the direct impact of an important competitor in Europe and prevented all other undertakings in the common market from buying direct from Fanuc. **6.30**

(c) *Reciprocal Cross-Supply Contracts between Competitors*

In *Agreement between manufacturers of nitrogenous fertilisers*, the Commission objected to a cross-supply contract between two producers of fertilizer by which each producer delivered products to the other producer's customers. The Commission considered 'it quite inconceivable for long-term reciprocal supplies between competing manufacturers to continue if one of the two parties were to **6.31**

---

[51] [1994] OJ L343/1; on appeal, Case T–25/95 (not yet decided).
[52] See n 48 above.
[53] *Report on Competition Policy 1996* (Vol XXVI) 143.
[54] [1978] OJ L70/54.
[55] [1992] OJ L92/1.
[56] [1985] OJ L376/29.

compete with the other on the latter's domestic market so as to cause fear for part of its market share'.[57]

Allocation of Lines of Commerce. Specialization Agreements

6.32   An agreement whereby one party refrains from producing certain products in favour of the other party constitutes a market sharing agreement. In *Welded Steel Mesh*,[58] for instance, the Commission condemned an agreement between three welded steel mesh producers whereby one of them would not produce catalogue mesh while the other two would not produce standard mesh. The Court upheld the Commission's view and stated that because of its intrinsic gravity and obviousness, that agreement constitutes an infringement of Article 85(1) [now Article 81(1)] of the Treaty, in particular subparagraph (c) thereof'.[59] Community law, however, has always adopted a favourable view towards certain specialization agreements since they can contribute to efficiencies in the form of cost reductions or output increase. If effective competition exists in the markets concerned, consumers are likely to receive a fair share of the resulting benefits of the specialization agreement. Under certain conditions, Article 4.2(3) of Regulation 17 exempts them from the prohibition of Article 81(1). Moreover, Regulation (EEC) 417/85[60] exempts certain bilateral specialization agreements together with other exclusive purchasing, supply and distribution obligations which normally accompany these agreements. Finally, specialization agreements that are not caught by any of these Regulations may benefit from individual exemption provided that the conditions established in article 81(3) are met.

(5) Rigged Bidding

The Commission's position on rigged bidding was clearly stated in *European*
6.33   *Sugar Industry*:[61] 'In a system of tendering, competition is of the essence. If the tenders submitted by those taking part are not the result of individual economic calculation, but of knowledge of the tenders by other participants or of concertation with them, competition is prevented, or at least distorted or restricted.' In *Building and construction in the Netherlands*,[62] the Commission condemned the rules and regulations of the Association of associations of Dutch builders and contractors SPO which provided, among other things, for exchanges of information prior to tendering procedures and for concerted action on price tenders for building and construction contracts. Moreover it shared between members the

---

[57] *Report on Competition Policy 1976* (Vol VI) point 126.
[58] See n 35.
[59] Case T–141/89 *Tréfileurope Sales SARL v Commission* [1995] ECR II–797, para 97.
[60] [1985] OJ L53/1.
[61] See n 48 above.
[62] [1992] OJ L92.

demand side of the market through the prior designation of successful tendering undertakings and the protection of the entitled undertakings. The Court of First Instance, which rejected the appeal by the undertakings, stated that 'concertation by contractors regarding the manner in which they intend responding to an invitation to tender is incompatible with Article 85(1) [now Article 81(1)] of the Treaty, even where the invitation sets unreasonable conditions. It is for each contractor to determine independently what he regards as reasonable or unreasonable and to conduct himself accordingly.'[63]

C. Exclusionary Practices

(1) Collective Exclusive Dealing

On the basis of these agreements a group of competitors agree to sell exclusively through certain distribution channels. In *SCK/FNK*,[64] SCK closed off the crane-hire market in and around The Netherlands by prohibiting its members from hiring extra cranes from non-members; in *Hudson's Bay—Dansk Pelsdyravler-forening*,[65] DPF, the leading auctioneer of furs in Europe compelled its members to sell their entire production to a DPF subsidiary. **6.34**

(2) Collective Refusal to Supply

In *Papiers peints de Belgique*,[66] the Commission condemned the decision of the Belgian association of wallpaper manufacturers to cease supplying an independent dealer that had supplied a retailer which had not complied with the obligation to charge the prices fixed by the association and did not observe the prohibition on displaying price reductions. **6.35**

In *Bronbemaling/Heidemaatschappij*,[67] the Commission condemned the agreements concluded between four Dutch building undertakings not to grant licences for a drainage system without the consent of a majority of them. **6.36**

In *Fedetab*,[68] the Commission condemned the agreement between Belgian and Luxembourg producers of manufactured tobacco not to supply several large distribution firms which did not stock a minimum range of brands. **6.37**

---

[63] See n 12 above.
[64] See n 17 above.
[65] [1988] OJ L316/43; on appeal, C–13/89 *Dansk Pelsdyravlerforening v Commission* [1992] ECR II–1931.
[66] [1974] OJ L237/3.
[67] [1975] OJ L249/27.
[68] See n 26 above.

(3) Aggregated Rebate System

6.38　A collective pricing system by which the customers' rebates depend on their total purchases from all participating manufacturers[69] leads to a concentration of orders with the parties to the agreement restricting in this way competition from other producers who are not parties to the agreement.

D. Co-operation Agreements

Introduction

6.39　It is increasingly common in today's economic environment for companies to choose to co-operate with each other. This is usually for beneficial pro-competitive reasons. It allows companies to spread the costs and risks associated with investment in R&D or new production facilities. It also allows them to pool expertise or market information necessary to launch new products or enter new geographic markets. Such co-operations are often a response to the increasing competitive pressure of modern global and high technology markets. They can lead to significant advantages for consumers if the efficiencies achieved through co-operation are passed on through lower prices, or if new products are brought to market more quickly.

6.40　If the *per se* or 'hard core' restrictions discussed earlier are avoided then experience has shown that such agreements are less likely to raise competition concerns. However, the Commission's policy has for many years been to apply Article 81(1) very widely to co-operation agreements, even if ultimately they are frequently exempted unchanged. This has led many firms to notify their agreements to the Commission for the sake of legal security and to avoid the potential problem of litigation under Article 81(2).

6.41　Several statements by the Commission have, however, referred to the need for a greater economic analysis in assessing competition cases.[70] In recent times enforcement practice and experience have also tended to focus on a more substantial analysis of the application of Article 81(1). If this trend continues perhaps fewer agreements should be expected to fall within the competition rules in the future. The Commission also announced in the XXVIIth Annual Report on Competition (1997), that it had launched a review of its policy towards horizontal agreements aimed at clarifying the various regulations and notices dealing with these agreements. While this is generally to be welcomed it does mean that a certain degree of caution should be maintained in interpreting current Commission policy from earlier decisions.

---

[69]　*Supexie* [1970] OJ L10/12; *Papiers peints de Belgique* [1974] OJ L237/3.
[70]　*Report on Competition Policy 1983* (Vol XIII).

There is no precise definition of what constitutes a co-operation agreement. **6.42** Agreements are sometimes structured as joint ventures, sometimes as looser co-operation arrangements. Generally it is only agreements between actual or potential competitors that will cause competition problems, although agreements between non-competitors but which significantly affect the position of third parties, by perhaps foreclosing a market, can also fall within Article 81(1). In the following sections most types of co-operation will be covered apart from vertical agreements and technology licensing agreements which are covered elsewhere.[71]

The legal form of an agreement should not fundamentally alter the assessment **6.43** under the competition rules. However, there are certain elements of assessment that are peculiar to different forms of agreement and therefore the assessment of the main forms of agreement, principally *joint ventures*, is discussed in the next section. The subsequent sections consider other 'types' of co-operation agreement that commonly occur. These can be broadly identified as co-operation at the various stages of industrial activity ie *R&D, production, specialization, distribution*, or *buying* as well as other forms of co-operation such as *exchanges of information*.

An agreement concerning each of these activities can raise different issues and will **6.44** require variations in the analytical approach. Therefore for each type of agreement we consider the general Commission policy towards such agreements, the likelihood of an agreement falling under Article 81(1), and the criteria for exemption. Other factors such as particular problems of market definition that can arise and the attitude of the Commission to certain common restrictions are also discussed.

However, agreements rarely fall very precisely in these categories. Often they **6.45** involve elements of co-operation at more than one level such as production plus joint distribution. As a general rule an agreement that is primarily concerned with one area of co-operation, such as joint R&D, will be assessed as such. The provisions related to co-operation in other areas, such as joint exploitation of this R&D, will be looked at in the light of their importance to the main co-operation.

There are several Notices and Regulations in the field of horizontal co-operation. **6.46** These, together with relevant decisions, are referred to in the context of the individual agreements and what they say about the Commission's approach to any restrictions involved.

---

[71] Article 5 of Commission Regulation (EC) 240/96 of 31 January 1996 on the application of Article 85(3) [now Article 81(3)] of the Treaty to certain categories of technology transfer agreements, discussed under technology licensing agreements in the context of JVs.

E. Joint Ventures

(1) Definition and Constitution of a Joint Venture

Definition

6.47 Joint ventures have been defined in several different ways, in fact, virtually any commercial arrangement involving two or more firms could be called a 'joint venture'. As it has been pointed out,[72] in defining joint ventures one must focus on those factors that make these kinds of business transaction a distinctive subject of antitrust concern. For the purposes of this chapter joint ventures will be defined as agreements by which two or more independent undertakings proceed to the partial integration of their business operations which are put under joint control in order to achieve some commercial goal.[73] In practice, joint ventures encompass a broad range of operations, from merger-like operations to co-operation for particular functions such as R&D, production, or distribution.

Constitution of a Joint Venture

6.48 A joint venture can be the result of the pooling of two companies' potential capacity to produce, distribute, etc,[74] a specific product or service through the setting up of a new business entity (whether or not endowed with the corporate form). This type of joint venture may bring about not only the potential benefits derived from integration of commercial activities or technological expertise but also the addition, at least in principle, of a new competitive force to the market (*ex novo* creation) and in this respect it differs from the categories that follow.

6.49 A second possibility consists of the pooling of two companies' existing capacity to produce, distribute, etc, a specific product or service short of a complete merger between them but entailing the total and irreversible withdrawal of their independent activities at least in a particular product and geographic market.

6.50 And finally, although not significantly different from the last option, the pooling of existing assets might affect either one (for example through the acquisition of shares of an existing enterprise) or all the undertakings party to the agreement *without* giving rise to their total withdrawal, actual or potential, from the markets concerned.

6.51 All these varied forms of constitution share the same common denominator: a limited integration of operations coupled with the preservation of the economic

---

[72] Brodley, 'Joint Ventures and Antitrust Policy' (1982) 95 Harv L Rev at 1525.

[73] The Commission's Notice on co-operative and concentrative JVs describes them as 'undertakings controlled by two or more other undertakings'. Commission Notice on the distinction between concentrative and cooperative joint ventures [1994] OJ C385/1 (para 2).

[74] Carry out R&D, buy, sell, etc.

independence of the companies party to the joint venture agreement (the parent companies). Because of these two common features these sorts of arrangement can give rise to both a positive and a negative presumptive attitude of the antitrust laws.

In effect, it could be argued that, as mergers, joint ventures have a potential for the generation of efficiencies and other economic benefits and therefore should deserve the more favourable treatment dispensed to mergers. If in addition to that it is considered that, as opposed to mergers, some joint venture agreements do not entail the total elimination of the parent companies as actual or potential competitors in the market of the joint venture, preserving thus their independence as economic agents, and that in a majority of cases they also give rise to the creation of a new competitive force in the market, it could be concluded that they even deserve a more permissive approach than that granted to mergers.[75] **6.52**

However, as seen below, the very fact that the undertakings party to the joint venture agreement remain independent after its setting up can rather give rise to competition concerns to the extent that the existence of the joint venture may unite the economic interests of the parent companies thus facilitating the conclusion of restrictive arrangements or the creation of anti-competitive spill-over effects. **6.53**

These are some of the reasons why joint ventures have caused and continue to cause so much legal debate on both sides of the Atlantic.

(2) Distinction Between Co-operative and Concentrative Joint Ventures

There is an important distinction between the so-called concentrative joint ventures, ie joint ventures falling under the Merger Regulation[76] and subject exclusively to the dominance test, and co-operative joint ventures, ie joint ventures to which Article 81 applies. Within this latter category a further distinction must be made as between those joint ventures falling under Merger Regulation, the so-called co-operative full-function joint ventures, which are subject both to the dominance test and Article 81, and those falling under Regulation 17 and other implementing Regulations, the so-called co-operative non-full-function joint ventures, to which only Articles 81 and 82 apply. **6.54**

Indeed, under the amendments to the Merger Regulation which entered into force in 1998 a joint venture falls outside the provisions of Regulation 17/62 if it can be regarded as a concentration under Article 3 of the Merger Regulation, that is to say if it performs on a lasting basis all the functions of an autonomous **6.55**

---

[75] In relation to this see Brodley, n 72 above, at 1523 *et seq.*

[76] Council Regulation (EEC) 4064/89 of 21 December 1989 on the control of concentrations between undertakings, [1989] OJ L385, [1990] OJ L257 with amendments introduced by Council Regulation (EC) 1310/97 of 30 June 1997, [1997] OJ L180/1.

economic entity.[77] However, whenever the creation of full-function joint ventures leads to the co-ordination of the competitive behaviour of companies that remain independent the Commission must apply the test of Article 81 to this aspect of the transaction.[78]

(3) The Rationale behind the Difference in Treatment between Concentrative and Co-operative Joint Ventures

6.56 Concentrative joint ventures are subject to a more benign regulatory framework in terms of substance than co-operative full-function joint ventures since the former are only subject to the dominance test while the latter are subject to both the dominance test and to Article 81.

6.57 This difference in treatment has given rise to a considerable number of criticisms from the legal community.[79] The main criticism levelled at the distinction between co-operative and concentrative joint ventures, in particular with regard to co-operative full-function joint ventures, is that the Commission is treating differently economically similar transactions, thus deterring the formation of desirable joint ventures, and that this ultimately leads to less competitive markets in European industries.[80] According to Professor Hawk,[81] the principal rationale for

---

[77] Article 3(2) of Council Regulation (EEC) 4064/89 of 21 December 1989 on the control of concentrations between undertakings as amended by Council Regulation 1310/97of 30 June 1997. See also Commission Notice on the Concept of full-function joint ventures under Council Regulation (EEC) 4064/89 on the control of concentrations between undertakings [1998] OJ C66.
[78] Article 2(4) of the amended Merger Regulation reads:

'To the extent that the creation of a joint venture constituting a concentration pursuant to Article 3 has as its object or effect the coordination of the competitive behaviour of undertakings that remain independent, such coordination shall be appraised in accordance with the criteria of Article 85(1) and (3) [now Article 81(1) and (3)] of the Treaty, with a view to establishing whether or not the operation is compatible with the common market.

In making this appraisal, the Commission shall take into account in particular:.

— whether two more parent companies retain to a significant extent activities in the same market as the joint venture or in a market which is downstream or upstream from that of the joint venture or in a neighbouring market closely related to this market;.
— whether the coordination which is the direct consequence of the creation of the joint venture affords the undertakings concerned the possibility of eliminating competition in respect of a substantial part of the products or services in question.

[79] See Hawk, 'A Bright Line Shareholding Test to End the Nightmare Under the EEC Merger Regulation' (1993) 30 CMLR 1155.
[80] Firms are encouraged to merge their competing operations fully and permanently rather than engage in limited duration/partial function joint ventures that create fewer long-term risks of competitive harm. Other criticisms levelled at the co-operative/concentrative distinction are the following: the cost, unpredictability, and time-consuming nature of applying the distinction to individual cases, the risk of forum shopping and of alteration of private transactions to fit the definition of concentrative joint venture, and the corruption of substantive antitrust principles when used for jurisdictional purposes. Hawk, 'A Bright Line', 1162–1167.
[81] Relying on the seminal work of Joseph Brodley, op cit, 1521.

the distinction between co-operative and concentrative joint ventures, ie that co-operative joint ventures create greater risks of competitive harm and fewer opportunities for competitive benefits than full mergers and acquisitions and that these competitively 'worse' transactions can be adequately regulated only under the stricter enforcement regime of Article 81, does not survive close analysis. This is so, the argument goes, because most joint ventures, especially those with a limited duration or only partial contribution of their parents' operations, (a)typically create lower (and certainly no greater) risks of competitive harm than full mergers and acquisitions involving the same parties;[82] and (b) are often equally likely to involve functional integration of economic resources (and thus result in economic efficiencies and other competitive benefits).[83]

However, in order fully to understand the rationale for this difference in treatment **6.58** between concentrative and co-operative joint ventures, one needs to bear in mind why mergers and acquisitions of single control are given a more favourable treatment under EC competition law. The reasons appear to be twofold. First of all, this type of transaction is considered to be more likely to produce efficiency gains through the integration of resources of previously independent companies than other kinds of transactions such as co-operative joint ventures, licensing agreements, cartels, etc where the level of economic integration is either less important or practically non-existent. Secondly, one would expect the risk of such efficiencies not being fully exploited to the benefit of consumers to arise only in cases where the concentration in question would create or strengthen a dominant position.

Under EC law, the 'concentration privilege' is thus only reserved for those trans- **6.59** action, which could be presumed to give rise to a significant level of efficiency in terms of economic integration between undertakings.

As far as joint ventures are concerned, the need to bring about a considerable **6.60** degree of economic integration in order to qualify as a concentration has been essentially embodied in the legal requirement that the joint venture under

---

[82] This would be so because a joint venture can never eliminate competition more than a full merger between the same parties since full mergers totally and permanently eliminate all actual and potential competition between the parties. In comparison, joint ventures (especially limited duration and/or partial function ventures) often create lower risks of competitive harm than full mergers because joint ventures may preserve some degree of competition between the parents in the joint venture's market and may be more likely to break up at some later date, which could either maintain or reintroduce both parents as independent competitors in the joint venture's market. Even if the joint venture creates a very high spill-over risk, the total harm to competition can never be greater than that which would occur if the same parties entered into a full merger.

[83] The types and magnitude of economic integration created by a (non-sham) joint venture would often equal those created by a full merger between the same parties in terms of scale or scope economies, risk allocation, facilitation of new product development or geographic entry, and synergies resulting from combining complementary operations.

scrutiny be full-function, ie it must perform on a lasting basis all the functions of an autonomous economic entity.

6.61 However, this rationale does not explain the reason why some co-operative joint ventures—and in particular those bringing about the creation of a full-function joint venture—were excluded from the scope of application of Article 3 (2), second sub-paragraph, of the Merger Regulation prior to the entry into force of Regulation 1310/97.

6.62 The answer lies not in the inability of a co-operative full-function joint venture to bring about a significant degree of economic integration in such cases but, rather, in its ability to give rise to the co-ordination of the competitive behaviour of undertakings which remain independent in areas which have not been 'merged' within the joint venture.

6.63 Thus the Council's rationale for not applying the Merger Regulation appears to be based on the Commission's belief that joint ventures which could lead to the co-ordination of the competitive behaviour of undertakings with regard to business activities which are not pooled within the joint venture, and which consequently are not integrated within a single economic entity, do not deserve the benefit of the 'concentration privilege'. In other words, the argument goes, there is no reason to give the benefit of the dominance test to a restriction of competition in areas of business activity of the parent companies which do not give rise to an increase in the level of economic integration and which consequently cannot compensate its anti-competitive effects with the creation of significant efficiencies.

6.64 In addition to that, and in particular in cases where the parent companies operate in the same market as the joint venture, the co-ordination of the competitive behaviour of the parent companies and the joint venture could also potentially lead to a decrease in the level of efficiency generated by the integration of economic activities within the joint venture. This is because the joint venture might not act as a profit maximizing company, given the need to take into account the interests of the parent companies in deciding its pricing and output strategies.

6.65 In sum, a considerable number of full-function joint ventures were subject to the strictures of Article 81, Regulation 17, and other implementing Regulations, since they had the potential to give rise to the co-ordination of the competitive behaviour of undertakings that remain independent in areas of business activity where the parent companies had not pooled their activities and, consequently, had not created any significant efficiency gains.

6.66 In this regard, Professor Hawk's comparison between a full-function joint venture, leading to the co-ordination of the competitive behaviour of the parent companies with regard to business activities which are not the subject of any integration other than that resulting from collusion, and a merger of the same parent companies in respect of the same activities, does not seem appropriate. Indeed, the first scenario produces co-ordination without any redeeming virtue. In the second scenario, however, although there is an elimination of competition, this is accompanied by an integration of economic activity likely to give rise to significant efficiencies. Against this background, it is difficult to accept the contention that the Commission incorrectly applied a different treatment to equivalent business transactions.

However, Professor Hawk is right to point out that, by applying Article 81(1)   **6.67** not only to the co-ordination of the competitive behaviour of the parent companies, but also to the actual pooling of activities within the joint venture, the Commission was likely to treat the potential for efficiencies created by a co-operative full-function joint venture more harshly than the equivalent potential for efficiencies stemming from the setting up of a concentrative joint venture.[84]

(4) The Application of Article 81(1) by the Commission to Co-operative Joint Ventures prior to the Entry into Force of the Amended Merger Regulation

This section will describe the way in which the Commission has assessed under   **6.68** Article 81 those joint ventures which, in spite of involving a significant degree of integration (R&D, production and/or distribution of goods or services), do not qualify, under its approach, as concentrative joint ventures.

One of the most complete descriptions of the competitive risks associated with   **6.69** the formation of a joint venture under Article 81 can be found in the *GEC-Weir Sodium Circulators* decision of 21 November 1977.[85] This decision concerned a joint venture agreement entered into between General Electric Company Ltd of London (UK) and Weir Group Ltd of Glasgow (UK), for the purposes of joint development, production, and sale by the parties of sodium circulators and for the allocation between the parties of work for the development and production of such circulators. In finding that the joint venture had as its object or effect the prevention, restriction, or distortion of competition within the meaning of Article 81(1) the Commission stated that:

First—from a structural point of view, the mere setting up of a joint venture between two undertakings which were, prior to the occurrence of this event, at least potential competitors in the field of activity of the joint venture is to be

---

[84] This potential for discrimination has been acknowledged by the Commission in its Green Paper on the Review of the Merger Regulation and, as will be seen below, was at the basis of its proposal to the Council to modify the Merger Regulation with regard to joint ventures.
[85] [1977] OJ L327/26.

considered a restriction of competition due to the replacement of two under-takings by one, the joint venture.[86]

Second—the collusive effect, either in the joint venture's market or in related ones where the parents are in competition, arising out of the joint management of their offspring, is also a restriction of competition as such: the joint fixing of prices, pro-duction targets, etc, of the joint venture normally leads, in the absence of an express agreement, to the alignment of the commercial policies of the parties involved thereto and in any case the joint management of the joint venture gener-ates a kind of co-operative atmosphere giving rise to a decrease of the competitive zeal between the parent companies in other related areas.

Third—even in the absence of an express agreement not to compete, the parent companies of a joint venture will normally not compete with it.

Fourth—in the case of joint ventures vertically related to the parent companies the position of third parties will be affected to the extent that the joint venture will be preferred as a source of supply or as an outlet, producing a foreclosure effect restrictive of competition.

These three last restrictions identified by the Commission represent what has been characterized above as the so-called spill-over effect.

6.70 In more recent cases,[87] Article 81(1) has also been applied to the network effect resulting from the setting up of the so-called interlocking joint ventures, ie joint ventures with at least one common parent company.

6.71 The Commission's analysis of spill-over effects under Article 81(1) to date[88] can be thus summarized as follows: once a joint venture has been characterized as a co-operative joint venture the Commission assesses the anti-competitive effects aris-ing out of its creation not only with regard to spill-over effects as defined above but also with regard to the pooling of activities within the joint venture.

6.72 For example, if company A and company B, both active in the manufacture and sale of say widgets and gadgets, decided to pool their widget operations within a joint venture, the Commission would examine under Article 81(1) not only the possible spill-over effects stemming from the setting up of the joint venture on the gadget market (where both parent companies would remain competitors) but also

---

[86] The Commission applies thus a merger-like assessment of the transaction under Article 81 with regard to the loss of competition resulting from the integration of activities of the parent com-panies.

[87] See for example *Optical Fibres* [1986] OJ L236/30 and *Night Services* [1994] OJ L259/20.

[88] For more recent cases following the same basic approach see: *Lufthansa/SAS* [1996] OJ L54 p. 28; *Atlas* [1996] OJ L239/23; *Exxon/Shell* [1994] OJ L144/20; *Philips/Osram* [1994] OJ L378/34; *IPSP* [1994] OJ L354/75; *Pasteur Merieux/Merck* [1994] OJ L309/1; *Asahi/Saint-Gobain* [1994] OJ L354/87; *Night Services* [1994] OJ L259/20; *ACI* [1994] OJ L224/28; *BT/MCI* [1994] OJ L223/36; *Astra* [1993] OJ L2/23; *Ford/VW* [1993] OJ L20/14; *Gosme/Martell* [1991] OJ L185/23.

the anti-competitive effects resulting from the addition of market share (or the loss of potential competition) arising out of the combination of their activities on the widget market. In other words, once the joint venture was characterized as a co-operative joint venture the Commission would proceed not only to the assessment of the anti-competitive effects of the joint venture on the market where collusion was likely to occur but also on the market where the parties had merged their activities thus carrying out a limited form of merger control under Article 81(1).

In addition to that, and despite the fact that the co-ordination of the competitive **6.73** behaviour of the parent companies and the joint venture was abandoned, in the 1994 Notice, as a jurisdictional criterion to determine whether or not a joint venture had to be characterized as concentrative or co-operative, if the Commission came to the conclusion that the joint venture fell under the latter category then the co-ordination of the competitive behaviour of the parent companies and the joint venture was also assessed under Article 81. For instance, if in our example only company A had transferred its widget activities to the joint venture, then the Commission would have examined separately under Article 81 the possible co-ordination of the competitive behaviour between company B and the joint venture on the widget market.[89]

Finally, the Commission also assesses under Article 81 the possible foreclosure **6.74** effect stemming from the creation of the joint venture wherever the parent companies and the joint venture are in a vertical relationship. For instance, if in our example company A was also a manufacturer of an input for the production of widgets, the Commission would examine the possible foreclosure effects in terms of *de facto* exclusivity granted to the joint venture,[90] resulting from the setting up of the joint venture.

The most striking feature of the Commission's analysis of co-operative joint ven- **6.75** tures (both full-function and not full-function) under Article 81 was, despite its stated policy in point 26 of the 1993 Notice on cooperative joint ventures[91] and some isolated cases,[92] the almost automatic conclusion that once the parent companies of the joint venture and the joint venture itself were in any of the situations described above the joint venture would lead to an appreciable restriction of competition provided the thresholds of the Notice on agreements of minor importance[93] were exceeded.

---

[89] See for example *Mitchell Cotts/Sofiltra* [1987] OJ L41/31 and *Gosme/Martell—DMP* [1991] OJ L185/23.

[90] See for example *Night Services* [1994] OJ L259/20.

[91] See Commission Notice concerning the assessment of cooperative joint ventures pursuant to Article 85 [now Article 81] of the EEC Treaty [1993] OJ C43/2.

[92] See cases cited by Hawk in 'Joint Ventures Under EEC Law' op cit and Pathak op cit.

[93] Notice on agreements of minor importance, which do not fall under Article 85(1) [now Article 81(1)] of the Treaty establishing the European Community [1997] OJ C372.

6.76 There was some tension, it is submitted, between this policy and the analysis developed both by the Court of Justice in dealing with the appreciability of alleged anti-competitive effects of agreements likely to produce significant efficiency gains[94] and with the need to show a sufficient degree of causality between the creation of a structure which might be presumed likely to lead to anti-competitive effects and actual anti-competitive effects,[95] and by the Commission itself in some areas of its decisional practice including some joint venture cases[96] and, in particular, in the context of exchange of information agreements[97] in dealing both with the issue of appreciability and with the conditions likely to lead to the co-ordination of competitive behaviour among competitors, in the absence of an express agreement to collude.

The following section will develop in more detail the notion and role of potential competition in assessing the validity of joint ventures under Article 81.

(5) The Notion and Role of Potential Competition in Assessing the Validity of Joint Ventures under Article 81

6.77 In its early decisions considering joint ventures under Article 81,[98] the Commission seemed to be quite willing to embrace a rather broad conception of the conditions required to assert that one or more companies were in a situation of potential competition (defined in this setting as the ability to enter the joint venture market). In effect, the Commission adopted this approach not only where the partners would have been able independently to engage in the activities exercised by the joint venture, but also where the joint venture enabled the parties to develop a new product or to enter a new market which neither of them would have been able to develop or enter into independently. Such competitive benefit is taken into consideration by the Commission only when assessing whether the

---

[94] See for example, Case C–234/89 *Stergios Delimitis v Henninger Bräu AG* [1991] ECR I–935 and Case C–306/96 *Javico AG v Yves Saint Laurent Parfums SA (YSLP)* [1998] ECR I–1983, Case C–250/92 *Gøttrup—Klim ea Grouvareforeninger* [1994] ECR I–5641, and Case C–399/93 *HG Oude Luttikhuis ea* [1995] ECR I–4515.

[95] Joined Cases C–68/94 and C–30/95 *French Republic and Société commerciale des potasser et de l'azote (SCPA) and Enterprise minière et chirnique (EMC) v Commission* [1998] ECR I–1375.

[96] See cases cited by Hawk and Pathak op cit.

[97] Commission decision of 17 February 1992, *UK Agricultural Tractor Registration Exchange* [1993] OJ L68/19. The Commission's approach towards the co-ordination of the competitive behaviour resulting from the setting up of an exchange of information system among competitors has been recently endorsed both by the Court of First Instance (Case T–34/92 *Fiatagri and New Holland Ford v Commission* [1994] ECR II–905 and Case T–35/92 *John Deere Ltd v Commission* [1994] ECR II–957 and by the Court of Justice (Case C–7/95P *John Deere Ltd v Commission* [1998] ECR I–1311, and Case C–8/95P *New Holland Ford Ltd v Commission* [1998] ECR I–3175).

[98] *KEWA* [1976] OJ L51/15; *Vacuum Interrupters* [1976] OJ L48/32; *GEC-Weir Sodium Circulators* [1977] OJ L327/26; *Beecham/Parke Davis* [1979] OJ L70/11; *Langenscheidt-Hachette* [1982] OJ L39/25; *Amersham-Buchler* [1982] OJ L314/34, 35; *Rockwell-Iveco* [1983] OJ L224/19; *VW-MAN* [1983] OJ L376/11; *Carlsberg* [1984] OJ L207/26.

conditions of Article 81(3) were fulfilled.[99] The Commission in these decisions based its determination of the existence of potential competition as between the parent companies on presumptions related to the previous activities and expertise of the parent companies, their theoretical access to the necessary technology, and their financial resources.[100]

This approach gave rise to an easy and sometimes cursory consideration of many **6.78** joint ventures as restrictive of competition and to the consequent increase of the Commission's powers of supervision under Article 81 of the Treaty. This led the Commission to reconsider its gauging of the potential competition issue. In this connection the Commission stated in the *Thirteenth Report on Competition Policy* that to evaluate, in an individual case, whether the formation of a joint venture in the production field restricts potential competition, it may use the following checklist of questions with respect to each of the partners. The basic point is that the degree of potential competition depends largely on the nature of the product manufactured or the services offered by the joint venture.

The following individual questions may be relevant:

(a) Input of the Joint Venture

Does the investment expenditure involved substantially exceed the financing **6.79** capacity of each partner? Does each partner have the necessary technical know-how and sources of input products?

(b) Production of the Joint Venture

Is each partner familiar with the process technology? Does each partner itself pro- **6.80** duce inputs for or products derived from the joint venture's product and does it have access to the necessary production facilities?

(c) Sales by the Joint Venture

Is the actual or potential demand such that it would be feasible for each of the **6.81** partners to manufacture the product on its own? Does each have access to the necessary distribution channels for the joint venture's product?

(d) Risk Factor

Could each partner bear the technical and financial risks associated with the pro- **6.82** duction operations of the joint venture alone?[101]

---

[99] See Waelbroeck, 'Antitrust Analysis under Article 85(1) and (3)' [1987] *Annual Proceedings of the Fordham Corporate Law Institute* 716.

[100] For a commentary on this issue see FL Fine, *Mergers and Joint Ventures in Europe* (Graham & Trotman, 1989) 60.

[101] It is patent the way in which the Commission avoids any reference to the perceptive potential competition as a decisive element in order to decide whether or not the formation of the joint venture leads to a lessening of competition on the relevant market.

6.83 This relaxation in the Commission approach has manifested itself in some decisions (*Optical Fibres*,[102] *Mitchell Cotts/Sofiltra*,[103] *Olivetti/Canon*[104]) where, for example, it has not deemed the considerable technological and financial resources of the parties sufficient to establish that the parent companies were in a position to enter the joint venture market independently.[105]

6.84 This apparently more lenient stance towards the potential competition issue could diminish the relevance of one of the more thorny legal problems, at least from the point of view of a coherent antitrust analysis and enforcement, posed by the Commission implementation of Article 81(1) and (3) to joint ventures.

6.85 Indeed, once it is established that the formation of the joint venture restricts competition because of the substitution of one competitor, the joint venture, for two, the Commission in order to grant an exemption under Article 81(3) has to show that the agreement does not impose on the undertakings concerned restrictions which are not indispensable to the attainment of objectives such as the improvement of the production or distribution of goods, the promotion of technical or economic progress, etc.

6.86 If the parents were able to enter the market independently, if the constitution of a joint venture represented therefore a loss of competition, which in a system of market economy is considered to be the best mechanism to achieve all the economic objectives above-mentioned, then, how could the Commission justify the indispensability of the joint venture under Article 85(3)?

6.87 In essence, the Commission examines whether the parent companies could with their own resources and capabilities alone develop the joint venture products and whether other forms of co-operation such as a licence agreement, a specialization agreement, etc[106] could be expected to lead to the same type of benefits.

(6) Conditions Leading to the Incentive to Co-ordinate (Spill-Over Effects)

6.88 Although not discussed in the 1990, 1993, and 1994 Commission Notices, economic theory appears to support the view that the setting up of a joint venture can lead either to anti-competitive parallel behaviour (tacit collusion) by the parent

---

[102] [1986] OJ L236/30. See Korah, 'Critical Comments on the Commission's Recent Decisions Exempting Joint Ventures to Exploit Research that Needs Further Development' [1987] European Law Review 18, 37.

[103] [1987] OJ L41/31.

[104] [1988] OJ L52/51.

[105] However, the Commission has also developed additional means of establishing potential competition. In several decisions, the Commission has considered: (i) whether the joint venture partner is a potential competitor of the joint venture itself (*Iveco/Ford* [1988] OJ L230/39 and *Mitchell Cotts/Sofiltra*); and (ii) whether there are joint ventures in competition with each other (*Optical Fibres*).

[106] For a recent example see *Atlas* [1996] OJ L239/23.

companies[107] (or by the parent companies and third companies) or to independent behaviour having equivalent effects.[108]

Generally, the parent companies of a joint venture can be presumed to have an **6.89** incentive to co-ordinate their competitive behaviour where this co-ordination is likely to be profitable, ie economically rational. Such a situation may arise, in particular, when the parent companies in question, either on their own or in combination with third parties, acquire and/or increase their ability to raise prices above the competitive level and/or to exclude competitors, ie whenever they acquire or increase their market power beyond some significant level.

In the context of homogeneous products, this would normally be the case when- **6.90** ever the establishment of a joint venture leads to the creation of a market setting in which anti-competitive parallel behaviour becomes a rational option for the parent companies or for the parent companies and third parties.[109]

For heterogeneous products, be they in the same or in neighbouring relevant mar- **6.91** kets, co-ordination may become a rational option, in particular, where the parent companies, as a result of the creation of the joint venture, can acquire or increase their market power by taking advantage of the product range effect deriving from the co-ordination of their competing brands,[110] for instance by resorting to anti-competitive price discrimination or by favouring their joint venture to the detriment of third parties.

One of the key issues in deciding whether the setting up of a joint venture would **6.92** lead to the co-ordination of the competitive behaviour of the parent companies or of the parent companies and their joint venture is precisely the causal link between the creation of the joint venture and this putative co-ordination. In other terms, in what way does the creation of a joint venture modify the incentive of the parent companies to collude?

There are a number of factors, other than the ability to exercise market power, that **6.93** can have a bearing on the incentive of the parent companies to compete after the creation of a joint venture. Such factors include the ownership and control structure operating within the new entity,[111] the size of the joint venture compared to

---

[107] Or with the joint venture in cases where the parent companies operate on the same market as the joint venture.

[108] Stephen Martin, 'Joint Ventures and Market Performance in Oligopoly', EUI Working Papers No 88/368, Florence, 1988, 1.

[109] The need for tacit co-ordination with third parties would be required in those situations where the parent companies (and the joint venture where the parents operate in the same product and geographic market as the joint venture) do not jointly have market power.

[110] For a recent application of the product range effect theory in the context of merger control see *Guinness/Grand Metropolitan* (Case IV/M938) (1997) [1998] OJ L288/24.

[111] Variations in the ownership and control of the joint venture may significantly affect the incentives of the parent companies to continue competing with each other or with the joint venture. The greater the parent's stake in the joint venture, the less likely the parent will continue to compete

that of the parents' independent operations,[112] the duration of the agreement,[113] the degree and the extent of the exchange of commercially sensitive information,[114] etc.

Spillovers on the Same Market as a Joint Venture

6.94   If the parents are present on the same market as the joint venture (JV) the first question to address is whether the JV will lead to a co-ordination of the behaviour of the parents' interests on that market.

6.95   The likelihood of co-ordination will depend other than on the structural characteristics of the relevant market upon the economic importance of the JV to the parents. Thus if the JV produces a significant proportion of the parents' output it can lead to a co-ordination of all their interests on that market. The 1993 Notice on co-operative joint ventures includes, in paragraph 26, reference to the criteria to be applied in assessing whether a JV leads to an appreciable restriction of competition, and in particular to the co-ordination of the parents' behaviour. However, these are only qualitative indications. The Commission's practice to date has been to apply Article 81(1) almost automatically to a JV between competitors and to aggregate their market share in the assessment.

6.96   The *Exxon/Shell* decision of 1994 is a rare example where the co-ordination effect is discussed in more detail. Exxon and Shell agreed to create a JV, Cipen, to produce certain grades of polyethylene (PE) in Europe. This PE would be supplied back exclusively to the parents who would then sell on to final consumers. Shell and Exxon had a combined share of 20 per cent of the EU production capacity for

---

against the venture in the relevant market. See Robert Pitofsky, 'Joint Ventures Under the Antitrust Laws: Some Reflections on the Significance of Penn-Olin' (1969) 82 HarvLRev 1007, 1012. Similarly, the parent's ability to co-ordinate its independent business decisions with those of the joint venture increases as its control over the venture increases. A controlling parent may attempt to ensure that the joint venture does not cannibalize the parent's independent sales in the joint venture market. See Timothy F Bresnahan and Steven C Salop, 'Quantifying the Competitive Effects of Production Joint Ventures' (1986) 4 Intl J Ind Org 155, 156.

[112]   For example, a 50% stake in a venture that is five times larger than the parent's independent operations in the relevant market will reduce the incentive of the parent to compete against the joint venture. See Edmund Kitch, 'The Antitrust Economics of Joint Ventures' (1987) 54 Antitrust LJ 957, 962.

[113]   The shorter the duration, the more likely the parties will continue to compete against each other in markets affected by the joint venture. Indeed, when the duration of the joint venture is limited, the parents will continue to compete in the relevant market knowing that their collaboration's end is on the near horizon. See A Piriano, 'Beyond Per Se, Rule of Reason or Merger Analysis: A New Antitrust Standard for Joint Ventures' (1991) 76 Minn L Rev 1, 65.

[114]   Joint ventures may serve as conduits for co-ordinating the participant's market behaviour or for exchanging competitively sensitive information. See Joseph Kattan, 'Antitrust Analysis of Technology Joint Ventures: Allocative Efficiency and the Rewards of Innovation' (1993) 61 Antitrust LJ 937, 949.

these grades of PE and the JV represented 17 per cent of this combined capacity. Thus the Commission argued that:

> the flow of information between Exxon and Shell allowed by the JV structure is the basis on which each partner can plan its polyethylene production and adapt it to the choices of the other partner . . . In fact any increased reduction or halt in production decided by one partner in order to adjust its behaviour to one other partner's choices in the joint venture entails a general reconsideration of the production plans of all (polyethylene) sites belonging to that partner's group.[115]

As a result the Commission concluded that the parents would be likely to co-ordinate their behaviour on the EU market for these grades of PE through the JV. Therefore the agreement fell under Article 81(1).

It is not just the relative importance of a JV to the parents' activities on the **6.97** market that will determine whether they will co-ordinate their behaviour. The greater the parents' combined market share on the market the stronger the incentive there is for them to co-ordinate and hence a smaller JV can be the source of anti-competitive co-ordination.

The Commission has stated on several occasions that it is necessary to undertake **6.98** an economic analysis of the incentives on the parents to co-ordinate their behaviour, as well as the effects of doing so in order to assess whether a JV will lead to an 'appreciable' restriction of competition.

This was reconfirmed by the court in the recent judgment on the *European Night* **6.99** *Services* decision.[116] In the original decision,[117] in 1994, the Commission exempted, with certain conditions, a JV, European Night Services, between several European rail companies to provide train services through the Channel Tunnel to cities beyond London, Paris, and Brussels. However the parties appealed against this decision arguing that the JV in fact did not fall under Article 81(1) at all and that the Commission had not demonstrated sufficient reasoning for its decision. The Court upheld the appeal on a variety of grounds including the fact that the Commission had not demonstrated sufficient economic reasoning in its original decision that the agreements fell under Article 81(1).[118]

Spillovers on to Other Markets

The second question to answer is whether the JV may provide a means for co- **6.100** ordination of the parties' behaviour on an adjacent product or geographic market. Typically these markets will be upstream or downstream of the co-operation.

---

[115] *Exxon/Shell* [1994] OJ L144/20, para 63.
[116] Joined Cases T–373/94, T–375/94, T–384/94 and T–388/94 *European Night ServicesLtd (ENS)*, judgment of 15 September 1998.
[117] *European Night Services* [1994] OJ L259/20.
[118] See in particular paras 135–160 of the judgment.

Spillovers on to Downstream Markets

6.101   In particular joint production of an element that represents a significant proportion of the costs of the final product may significantly reduce the scope for competition on the downstream product market.

6.102   The *Philips/Osram* decision of 1994[119] illustrates the possible link of a JV with a downstream market. The case concerned a JV to manufacture lead glass tubing for incandescent and fluorescent lamps. The parties had approximately 65 per cent of the EEA capacity for producing lead glass, which was the basis of the assessment under Article 81. However, the parties also produced, separately, the final lamps and produced over two-thirds of the European market for lamps. They were also competitors in most segments of this downstream lamp market. However, the lead glass tubing represented only 0.67 per cent of the final costs of the lamp, and therefore even though there were other small elements of common cost structure the Commission concluded that: 'given the very small importance of lead glass on the manufacturing costs of lamps, such standardisation is not considered relevant enough as to constitute a restriction of competition'.

Spillovers on to Adjacent Product Markets

6.103   If the parties are competitors on other markets to that of the JV the mere fact of having made significant investment in a JV on one market may reduce the incentive to compete as actively in these markets. However, it is only likely if these markets are closely related. The Commission Notice on co-operative joint ventures[120] notes in paragraph 41 that:

> Where the JV operates on a market adjacent to that of its parents, competition can only be restricted when there is a high degree of interdependence between the two markets. This is especially the case when the JV manufactures products that are complementary to those of its parents.

6.104   The Commission has never yet taken a formal decision in which a co-operation has been adjudged as falling under Article 81(1) solely because of these potential spill-over effects. In the *Ford/Volkswagen* decision of 1992,[121] concerning a JV to develop a range of multi-purpose vehicles, so-called 'people carriers', the Commission in its assessment of whether Article 81(1) applied noted that:

> the co-operation between Ford and VW will furthermore lead to an extensive exchange and sharing of, *inter alia*, technical know-how which could affect the competitive behaviour of the two partners in neighbouring market segments like those of estate cars or light vans.

---

[119]   *Philips/Osram* [1994] OJ L378/37.
[120]   Notice Concerning the Assessment of co-operative joint ventures pursuant to Article 85 [now Article 81] of the EEC treaty [1993] OJ C43/2.
[121]   *Ford/Volkswagen* [1993] OJ L20/14.

However, the main reason that the Commission argued this JV fell within Article 81(1) remained the effect of two major competitors on the EU car market jointly developing a major new product.

Spillovers on to Adjacent Geographic Markets

The argument that a JV can limit competition on adjacent markets applies equally to adjacent geographic markets as well as adjacent product markets. In the *Atlas* decision of 1996,[122] the Commission exempted a JV, Atlas, between France Telecom (FT), and Deutsche Telekom (DT), to provide international telecom services to corporate customers. However, several conditions were imposed upon the parents. In particular, there was concern that neither parent would enter each other's domestic market after full telecoms liberalization from 1 January 1998. Under the JV agreement each parent would distribute Atlas services within its own national market and refrain from active selling of such services into each other's home market. While it was impossible to impose conditions that the parents would compete the Commission did require disposal of a FT subsidiary in Germany, present on the German market for corporate communications.

6.105

Network Effect

A JV may also be one of several JVs between the parents in the same or related markets. Individually these JVs may not be regarded as sufficient to lead to a restriction of competition but the combined effect of several such JVs may be. These are commonly referred to as *Network Effects.*

6.106

The situations in which networks of JVs may give rise to concern are well described in the Notice on co-operative joint ventures between paragraphs 27 and 31. In essence a JV should not be assessed without taking account of all other relevant interests of the parents on that market or on related markets.

6.107

The *Optical Fibres* decision of July 1986[123] usefully illustrates the concern. In this case the Commission ultimately granted an exemption to a series of JV agreements between Corning, a US producer of glass fibre for fibre optic cable, and a number of EU cable manufacturers. The agreements were designed to develop and produce fibre optic cable for EU markets. While the Commission noted that neither Corning nor its individual European partners were actual or potential competitors for the manufacture of fibre optic cables the individual JVs were. Therefore, as a condition for exemption, Corning's individual influence on each JV was reduced and they were required to meet passive sales requests into each other's territory. The Commission argued that Corning's presence as a common party to each JV would restrict competition between them, hence Article 81(1) applied.

6.108

---

[122] *Atlas* [1996] OJ L239/23.
[123] [1986] OJ L236/30.

6.109   In the *European Night Services* judgment of 1998, overturning the earlier Commission Decision of 1994, the Court rejected the Commission's argument that the fact that the parents had interests in a series of other JVs to transport goods and passengers through the Channel Tunnel would lead to a restriction of competition. In particular the Commission was concerned about the ACI JV between BR and SNCF to transport goods through the tunnel and the Autocare Europe JV between BR and SNCB to transport motor vehicles. In rejecting the Commission's arguments the Court noted that these JVs were not in the same market as ENS, passenger services, but in related markets. The 1993 Notice states that when parent undertakings set up JVs for 'non-complementary' services competition may be restricted when these 'non-complementary' services are marketed by the parent undertakings themselves. However in this case none of the parents sell the services of these JVs themselves and the Commission in its decision did not explain how the participation of the parents in such a network of JVs would lead to a restriction of competition. Therefore the Court rejected this element of the Commission decision.

(7)   Direct Restrictions between Parents

6.110   There can be an express restriction of competition between the parents of a JV resulting from direct contractual agreements between them. Thus, agreements to fix prices or share markets would fall automatically within Article 81(1). Other restrictions would have to be assessed on an individual basis taking into account the presence of the parties on all affected markets. These restrictions would be assessed under the procedures in Regulation 17/62 as for all other co-operation agreements. However, those restrictions that are directly related to the setting up and functioning of a JV and are regarded as necessary for the operation of the JV may be ancillary to the JV and as such assessed together with the JV.[124]

(8)   Spillovers under the Amended Merger Regulation

6.111   As outlined above the Amended Merger Regulation still allows for the co-ordination effects arising from a full-function co-operative JV to be assessed under Article 81, see Article 2(4) of the Regulation. Since the entry into force of the Amended Merger Regulation in March 1998 the Commission has examined a significant number of full function JVs where there were possible co-ordination effects.[125] The majority of these JVs have been in the telecoms, internet, or related industries. Due to the number of closely related markets in these sectors JVs are perhaps more likely to lead to the possibility of spillovers.

---

[124]   1993 Notice on co-operative JVs, part V; see also Commission Notice regarding restrictions ancillary to a concentration [1990] OJ C203/5.

[125]   (October 1998) 3 *Competition Policy Newsletter*, 30.

It should be stressed from the outset that the Commission has chosen not to issue **6.112**
guidelines on the application of Article 2(4) to the spill-over effects stemming
from the setting up of a joint venture. Indeed, at footnote 3 of its Notice on the
concept of full-function JVs it stated that it intended, in due course, to provide
guidance on the application of Article 2(4). Pending the adoption of such guidance, interested parties are referred to the principles set out in paragraphs 17 to 20
of its 1994 Notice on the distinction between concentrative and co-operative
joint ventures.[126]

However, the first months of application of Article 2(4) have proved to be **6.113**
extremely fruitful in providing guidance as to the way in which the Commission
intends to apply this provision of the Merger Regulation. Moreover, if the incipi-
ent case law consolidates itself as the basis for the future application of both
Articles 2(4) and 81(1) to spill-over effects, the adoption of Regulation 1310/97
might constitute a significant departure from the Commission's traditional
approach to the notion of restriction of competition, at least with regard to the
spill-over effect generated by structural operations, and the consolidation of a
more economic driven analysis of this type of economic phenomena.

The first case in which the Commission had the opportunity to develop its **6.114**
new approach towards the spill-over effects stemming from the creation of a
full-function joint venture under Article 2(4) was *Telia/Telenor/Schibsted* (Case
IV/JV1) (1998).[127]

This case concerned the setting up of a JV (Scandinavia OnLine) between **6.115**
Schibsted Multimedia AS,[128] Telenor Nextel AS,[129] and Telia AB[130] for the provi-
sion of certain Internet services to consumers and business customers mainly in
Sweden. The JV company was to take over the assets and activities of Telia

---

[126] [1994] OJ C385/1.

[127] This novel way of numbering JVs is due to the new allocation of tasks within DGIV. For the
moment JVs requiring a more in-depth analysis under Article 2 (4) are dealt with by the operational
Directorate/s responsible for the economic sector/s affected by the putative spill-over effects in liaison with the MTF (Directorate B).

[128] Telia AB, wholly owned by the Swedish State, is the main telecommunications operator in
Sweden, providing a broad range of telecommunications services both in Sweden and abroad,
including enhanced services through its shareholding in Unisource. Telia is also an Internet Service
Provider (ISP). Internet services in the Swedish language are provided by Telia InfoMedia
Interactive AB.

[129] Telenor AS is the main Norwegian telecommunications operator. Its subsidiary, Telenor
Nextel AS, offers a number of Internet related services. It is a shareholder in Telenordia (33%, the
other parent companies are BT and TeleDanmark), which provides telecommunications services in
the Swedish market. Telenordia's subsidiary Algonet is an ISP on the Swedish market.

[130] The Norwegian Schibsted group is involved in a range of media related activities such as news-
papers, television, films, and multimedia. Its subsidiary Schibsted Multimedia AS has a number of
Internet related activities, including the provision of content, in Sweden via Scandinavia On-Line
AB, which is jointly owned by Telenor AS. Schibsted also has a stake in Aftonbladet, a newspaper in
Sweden, which also has an Internet edition.

InfoMedia and Scandinavia On-Line AB (SOL) and to operate on the market for web site production for third parties, including design of web sites and related programming (services were to be provided in the Swedish language).

6.116 After finding that the operation constituted a concentrative joint venture within the meaning of Article 3 of the Merger Regulation, the Commission proceeded to the definition of the relevant product and geographic markets for the purposes of its assessment under the dominance test (Article 2(3) of the Merger Regulation). The Commission defined three relevant markets, all of them having a national dimension or possibly a linguistic dimension: the markets for Internet advertising, paid-for content provision, and web site production. It found that the operation did not create a dominant position in all of these markets.

6.117 With regard to Article 2(4), the Commission stated, at point 28 of the decision, what appears to be a new, more economic-driven, approach to the treatment of spill-over effects under Article 81(1). Indeed, according to the Commission, 'In order to establish a restriction of competition in the sense of Article 85(1) [now Article 81(1)] EC-Treaty, it is necessary that the co-ordination of the parent companies' competitive behaviour is likely and appreciable and that it results from the creation of the joint venture, be it as its object or its effect.'

6.118 In this regard, it should be noted that, although the requirement of appreciability was already part of the Commission's normal practice in dealing with spill-over effects, the need to show likelihood on more than a purely theoretical basis and, above all, the requirement to prove causality constitute two significant and welcome developments in the Commission's approach to the applicability of Article 81(1) to JVs.

6.119 Having defined the framework for analysis under Article 81(1), the Commission proceeded to the identification of the so-called candidate markets for co-ordination, ie those on which the joint venture and at least two parent companies are active, or closely related neighbouring markets where at least two parent companies remain active. The Commission identified two candidate markets for co-ordination: (i) web site production and related services and (ii) dial-up Internet access.[131]

---

[131] See points 29 to 37 of the decision. With regard to geographic market definition, the Commission found that for web site production the relevant geographic market was at least as wide as Sweden or Sweden plus the Swedish language communities in other Nordic countries. However, the Commission indicated there is no technical barrier to these services being provided outside Sweden and the Nordic countries. The Internet services of the JV will be offered in the Swedish language for private and business users in Sweden. Although access to Internet content in Sweden is available from outside Sweden, this does not widen the market definition as the content offered is aimed specifically at consumers in Sweden. Therefore, the relevant geographic market for dial-up Internet access was defined as Sweden.

dial-up internet access was considered a candidate market for co-ordination **6.120** because Telia and Telenordia (Algonet) provide dial-up internet access to users and because access to the internet is a necessary prerequisite for any use of the internet. This market was thus considered as a market upstream to the JV's markets and thus as closely related to the JV's markets.[132]

As far as the assessment under Article 2 (4) is concerned, the Commission reached **6.121** the following conclusions:

(1) In the absence of clear indications to prove that the object of the creation of the JV is the co-ordination of the competitive behaviour of the parent companies, an intended co-ordination of the parent companies' behaviour cannot be established (decision at point 38). However, the effect of the operation might be to give way to the co-ordination of competitive behaviour.

(2) On the web site production market, the Commission indicated that the combined market share of the parent companies did not exceed [. . .][133] per cent and the JV would have a market share of [. . .][134] per cent. The Commission considered that this total market share of [. . .][135] per cent on the Swedish market, which is the narrowest and most unfavourable to the parties, in any event, would not allow the conclusion that any restriction of competition is appreciable.

Therefore, the Commission concluded that in the light of the above, even if the parent companies were to co-ordinate their activities on the web site production market this co-ordination could not lead to an appreciable restriction of competition and it was therefore not necessary to establish a causal link between the creation of the JV and the behaviour of the parent companies outside the JV on this closely related market.

(3) With the regard to the dial-up internet access market, the Commission found that it is characterized by high growth[136] and relatively low barriers to entry. The costs of starting a small ISP providing a dial-up service are low and small companies can and do provide dial-up internet access. According to the information supplied by the parties, there were around 100 such ISPs in Sweden. Entry is also possible from both local start-up ISPs and global ISPs entering the Swedish market. In addition, as the market is very price-sensitive, in particular given low switching costs, this would prevent higher

---

[132] It is to be noted that the impact of the JV on the web site and related services market was already assessed and cleared under the dominance test.

[133] Business secret: less than 5%.

[134] Business secret: less than 5%.

[135] Business secret: less than 10%.

[136] According to information obtained during the Commission's investigation, the growth rate in Sweden in the next three years will be around 30%.

prices through co-ordination from being sustained. Any increase in prices would result in the parties quickly losing market share to rival companies as new subscribers opted for lower price offerings.

Telia was present on this market. Telenor, through Telenordia (33 per cent, the other parent companies are BT and TeleDanmark), was also present. Telia and Telenordia held substantial market shares.[137] However, the Commission considered that market shares were of limited significance in relation to this growing market. In any case, the combined market share of Telia and Telenordia had fallen by between 15 and 20 per cent of the total market over the last nine months.

Given the characteristics identified above, the Commission concluded the market structure was not conducive to co-ordination of competitive behaviour. The Commission also stated that the relative size of the markets for internet advertising, content and web site production (the markets of the JV), compared with that of dial-up internet access, was relevant to the likelihood of co-ordination. The dial-up internet access market was substantially larger than the other markets mentioned above[138] and, therefore, given the relative sizes of the markets concerned, the likelihood of co-ordination was reduced further.[139]

---

[137] Telia has a 30–40% market share and Telenordia has 15–20% of the market defined above. The largest service provider offering dial-up Internet access in Sweden is Tele2 (a telecommunications company which is a member of the Kinnevik Group, a leading Nordic media company), which has a 40–50% market share. However, on the basis of other information received, it appears that if the market share of Telenordia were to be attributed to Telenor, their total market share would be 45–60%. This data is based on information obtained from the notifying parties and other third parties during the investigation. Other third party estimates have put the leading three companies' market shares as being lower than these figures.

[138] According to information obtained by the Commission during its investigation, the proportion of revenues derived from access is 93% in Sweden compared with 7% from all other Internet revenue sources.

[139] In *Cegetel/Canal+/AOL/Bertelsmann* (Case IV/JV5) (1998) the Commission took into account, in excluding the likelihood of co-ordination in a vertically related market, the provision of network distribution services, the fact that, according to the parties, the JV would not be the main customer for the network distribution services provided by these parent companies. Their infrastructures were to be used primarily for telecommunications and TV distribution and not for dial-up Internet access services respectively, so they would not create economically meaningful incentives for co-ordination in network distribution service offerings to ISPs. In *Ericsson/Nokia/Psion* (Case IV/JV12) (1998) the Commission found that the creation of a JV would not lead to the co-ordination of the competitive behaviour of the parent companies on the downstream markets for wireless information devices and mobile phones. With regard to wireless information devices, the Commission based its analysis on the lack of commonality of costs, the fact that the cost of the operating system produced by the JV was likely to be relatively low as an overall proportion of the costs of the wireless information devices, the presence of actual or potential competition and the need to establish the new operating system on the market, and the ongoing development of this kind of device (decision, points 31, 32, and 33) and the wide scope for product differentiation (decision, points 34 and 35). With regard to mobile phones, the Commission's analysis rested on the fact that the operating system to be developed by the JV would not be included

The Commission thus found that, even on the basis of the narrowest market definition, there was no likelihood that the parent companies would co-ordinate their competitive behaviour on the dial-up internet access market and it was therefore not necessary to establish a causal link between the creation of the JV and the behaviour of the parent companies outside the JV on this related market.

6.122

To sum up the Commission's approach can be described as follows:

6.123

(1) The Commission determines first whether the JV performs on a lasting basis the functions of an autonomous economic entity. If it does the Merger Regulation applies. In reaching this conclusion account must be taken of the Notice on the notion of full-function joint ventures of 2 March 1998.

(2) Once the JV has been characterized as a concentration the Commission will examine whether it creates or strengthens a single or collective dominant position on any of the relevant markets affected by the operation. The Commission will apply in this context its traditional approach under Article 2(3) of the Merger Regulation.

(3) The Commission will proceed then to examine whether the creation of the JV will lead to the co-ordination[140] of the competitive behaviour of the parent

---

in mobile phones, on the lack of direct connection between the JV and the technology used in mobile phones, on the existence of sufficient actual competition (despite the fact that Nokia and Ericsson account together for around 50% of the market), on market performance (prices have decreased steadily over the past five years) and on the relative sizes of the markets (revenue from the JV would be extremely small in proportion to the overall revenue generated by their mobile telephony activities (decision, points 37 and 38).

[140] In assessing the likelihood of co-ordination the Commission will take into account both actual and potential competition. See in this sense *ENEL/FT/DT* (Case IV/JV2) (1998). This case concerned the creation of a JV, WIND Telecomunicazioni SpA (Wind) between ENEL SpA (ENEL), France Telecom SA (FT), and Deutsche Telekom (DT) for the provision of a full range of domestic and international telecommunications services combining mobile and fixed line telecommunications activities to business and residential customers located in Italy, in competition with the incumbent telecommunications operator, Telecom Italia, and other new market entrants. Following the methodology laid down in its *Telia* decision, the Commission identified the following candidate markets for co-ordination of the competitive behaviour of FT and DT: fixed line telephony, ie domestic and international voice and data telecommunications services in Italy, France, and Germany, advance international services, and mobile telephony in Italy and in Western Europe. As to the domestic and international voice and data telecommunications services in Italy, the Commission considered that in view of the substantial investments in Wind which both FT and DT had already made or would need to make, it was unlikely that they would enter these markets on their own in the future. The markets for domestic and international voice and data telecommunications services in France and Germany were considered as closely related markets within the meaning of Article 2(4) in view of their geographic proximity and their importance to Italy. (Germany and France are the two most important countries for Italy in terms of bilateral traffic. In 1997, for example, bilateral traffic between Italy and Germany alone amounted to around 700 million minutes.) Both DT and FT hold a strong (if not dominant) position in these markets in their respective countries. FT has not so far expanded its operations to Germany to any important degree since it sold its shares in Info AG in the context of the Atlas/GlobalOne transaction. Neither has DT entered the French markets to any noticeable extent. FT and DT could be considered as at least potential competitors on the French and German markets.

companies on the JV market or on related markets (upstream, downstream, or neighbouring).

(4) In doing so; the Commission will identify first the candidate markets for co-ordination, ie those markets in which the parent companies either compete or are on a vertical or conglomerate relationship.[141] Secondly it will determine

---

[141] In *NC/Canal+/CDPQ/BankAmerica* (Case IV/M1327) (1998), the Commission had the opportunity to examine the effects of the setting up of a JV in the French pay TV market on a neighbouring market (the Spanish pay TV market) under Article 2(4) of the amended Merger Regulation. This case concerned the acquisition of joint control by Canal+, Caisse de dépôt et placement du Québec, and BankAmerica Corporation over Numéricable (NC), a French cable television network operator previously controlled by Canal+. After concluding that the notified operation did not give rise either to the creation or strengthening of a dominant position or to the co-ordination of the competitive behaviour of the parent companies in the French pay TV market, the Commission assessed the impact of the notified transaction on the Spanish pay TV market including the wholesale supply of films and sports channels for retail pay TV under Article 2(4). This assessment was based on the fact that: a) the BankAmerica and CDPQ's groups have controlling interests (joint control) in Cableuropa, a future significant network cable operator in the Spanish pay TV market and a buyer of pay TV rights, and b) Sogecable (a significant supplier of pay TV rights in Spain) is under joint control of Prisa and Canal+. Therefore, all the undertakings concerned were active both in the same product/service market as NC (pay television) and in the vertically related market (the wholesale supply of films and sports channels for retail pay TV) in a neighbouring geographical market (Spain). The Commission had thus to examine the potential anti-competitive spill-over effects arising out of the newly created link between Canal+/Sogecable and BankAmerica-CDPQ/Cableuropa in the Spanish pay TV market. In making this assessment the Commission took into account the significant position of Sogecable in the Spanish TV market and the highly concentrated nature of this market. As to the possibility of vertical co-ordination between Canal+/Sogecable and BankAmerica-CDPQ/Cableuropa (a buyer of pay TV rights in Spain), the Commission concluded that, as a result of the NC deal, there were strong indications (amounting to serious doubts within the meaning of Article 6 (1) (c) of the Merger Regulation) that both companies had a significant incentive to co-ordinate their competitive behaviour at least with regard to access to Sogecable's content. In particular, the Commission deemed that Canal+ had a strong incentive to favour Cableuropa in its supply arrangements to the detriment of other players in the cable segment of the pay TV market in Spain. The Commission based its conclusion on Cableuropa's significant and real power to retaliate against Canal+ in France if it was not given favourable conditions in the access to the audio-visual rights that it needs to develop its pay TV activities in Spain and on the fact that some days after the NC deal was signed, Sogecable and Cableuropa reached a content distribution agreement on a non-exclusive basis.

Although the notifying parties contested this analysis they submitted undertakings to the Commission in order to remove the competitive concerns raised by the Commission with regard to the Spanish pay TV market. These undertakings consisted essentially of the obligation not to discriminate in the granting of access to pay TV rights for as long as the conditions in the Spanish market and the shareholdings of Canal+, BankAmerica, and CDPQ in Sogecable, Cableuropa, and NC remain substantially the same. The Commission concluded that the undertakings were sufficient to remove its serious doubts within the meaning of Article 6(1)(c) of the Merger Regulation and to render the concentration compatible with the common market.

This case illustrates how the Commission will not limit its assessment under Article 2(4) of the amended Merger Regulation to potential spill-over effects on the same product and geographic markets as those of the JV or to horizontal co-ordination between the parent companies. Indeed, as shown in the *NC/Canal+/CDPQ/BankAmerica* decision, the Commission will also examine the effects resulting from the creation of a JV in neighbouring markets both at the horizontal and vertical/conglomerate levels. Obviously, the Commission's findings in this case were strongly conditioned by the very strong position held by Sogecable in the Spanish pay TV market and by the need to limit the creation of further links, or of their effects, in an already highly concentrated market.

whether the co-ordination of the parent's competitive behaviour is likely, appreciable, and results from the creation of the JV be it as its object or its effect. If any of these tests are not met Article 2(4) does not apply and the Commission does not examine the other ones.

(5) With regard to the likelihood of co-ordination test, the Commission seems to focus on the question whether the market characteristics, including the market position of the JV and its size, are conducive to co-ordination of the competitive behaviour. As to the appreciability test, the Commission seems to go beyond the strict limits imposed by the Notice on agreements of minor importance. Finally, as regards the causality test, the Commission examines whether or not the creation of the JV, and not any other factor such as the existence of previous links as between the parent companies, is the real cause of the putative co-ordination of the competitive behaviour as between the parent companies.[142] The Commission has followed this basic approach in various cases to date.[143]

---

[142] In *ENEL/FT/DT* (Case IV/JV2) (1998) the Commission found that the creation of Wind would not lead to the co-ordination of the competitive behaviour of FT and DT in each other's markets (ie the restriction of potential competition) on grounds of lack of causality. Indeed, according to the Commission: 'As mentioned above, DT and FT have already so far (at least since the Atlas/GlobalOne transaction) not competed strongly with each other in their respective home countries despite the possibilities to do so which the liberalisation of the telecommunications sector has created. The two companies have, through their joint venture Atlas, entered into a joint venture with Sprint Corporation (GlobalOne) for the purpose of providing advanced telecommunications services which has already been mentioned. The lack of competition on their respective home markets in the past therefore appears to stem from a deliberate choice on the part of these companies. It is not possible to claim with the requisite degree of certainty that such lack of competition (if it were to continue in the future) would be the result of the creation of Wind.'

The lack of causality argument has also been used by the Commission to conclude that the creation of a JV will not lead to the co-ordination of the competitive behaviour of two parent companies active on the same market as the JV in *BT/Air Touch/Grupo Acciona/Airtel* (Case IV/JV3) (1998) at point 25 and in *Viag/Orange* (Case IV/JV4) (1998) at point 32.

In *Cegetel/Canal+/AOL/Bertelsmann* (Case IV/JV5) (1998) the Commission concluded that although, according to the notifying parties, only Vivendi, one of the parent companies (via its Info On-Line site), had declared its intent to offer paid-for content in France, and had suspended its sole product line earlier that year, it could be stated that after the creation of the JV all four parties and the JV were also potential competitors on the paid-for content market, either because they developed content or because they were active in the traditional media market, and were therefore likely to use proprietary content to provide paid-for content. Therefore the Commission considered this market as a candidate market for co-ordination. With regard to network distribution services, the Commission equally considered the issue of potential competition in the following terms: 'Cegetel is the second long distance carrier on the French telecommunications market, as well as the second French mobile GSM operator. The notifying parties submitted that no other party to the concentration is active in France in the market for network distribution services for ISPs. However, Canal+ is active in the broadcasting (both analogue and digital), and the distribution of television services by cable and satellite. CanalSatellite, a general partnership managed by Canal+, has started testing a dial-up Internet access service via DTH satellite transmission. NC Numéricâble, a subsidiary of Canal+, operates cable networks for the provision of CA-TV in various locations in France. In particular, Télériviera, a company jointly owned by NC Numéricâble and TDS, a subsidiary of Cegetel, has experimented a dial-up Internet access service via its cable in the Nice area. In any case,

F. Research and Development Agreements

(1) Introduction

6.124 In many industries a company's level of innovation has become a key competitive factor. From pharmaceuticals to computing and electronics it is not just price and quality that give firms a competitive edge but their technical know-how and ability to develop new products.

6.125 Co-operation at the level of research and development is therefore increasingly important to many companies. The costs, and risks, associated with R&D can be very high, therefore many companies choose to co-operate to spread these risks. There are also potentially enormous benefits in avoiding expensive duplication of effort and in the cross-fertilization of ideas and experience that come from R&D co-operation. It is for these reasons that the Commission has taken a generally positive view of R&D co-operation.

6.126 Co-operation in R&D can take place at many levels. In some cases the co-operation is in fundamental research projects far from the market often in collaboration with universities or publicly funded research programmes. In other cases the R&D is basically no more than incremental improvements to existing products and may be an adjunct to a joint production arrangement.

6.127 R&D agreements are equally structured in many different forms. These may range from JVs with provisions on exploitation and sales to subcontracting

---

cable modems allowing cable networks to be used as local loops have been developed, and although Numéricâble's cable network has not been used for this purpose yet, it is likely to be in the future.' However, the Commission cleared the transaction on grounds of lack of appreciable effect given the low market shares of the parties (below 10%).

¹⁴³ *Telia/Telenor/Schibsted* (Case IV/JV1) (1998); *ENEL/FT/DT* (Case IV/JV2) (1998); *BT/AirTouch/Grupo Acciona/AirTel* (Case IV/JV3) (1998); *Cegetel/Canal+/AOL/Bertelsmann* (Case IV/JV5) (1998); *Ericsson/Nokia/Psion* (Case IV/JV6) (1998); *Viag/Orange UK* (Case IV/JV4) (1998); *Telia/Sonera/Lithuanian Telecommunications* (Case IV/JV7) (1998); *Telia/Sonera/Motorola/Omnitel* (Case IV/JV9) (1998); *@ Home Benelux BV* (Case IV/JV11) (1998); *Deutsche Telekom/Springer/Holtzbrink/Infose* (Case IV/JV8) (1998); *Panagora/DG Bank* (Case IV/JV14) (1998); *NC/Canal+/CDPQ/BankAmerica* (Case IV/M1327) (1998); *Wintershall/EnBW/MVV/WV/DED* (Case IV/JV13) (1998); and *BT/AT&T* (Case IV/JV15) (1998). The Commission decided to open detailed inquiry into a proposed JV between British Telecommunications and AT&T, two of the world's largest telecommunications operators. The joint venture will provide a broad range of telecommunications services to multinational corporate customers as well as international carrier services to other carriers. The Commission decided to carry out a second-phase inquiry into the effects of the JV on several global telecommunications markets and also some in UK. Subsequent to its preliminary inquiry, the Commission has expressed concerns in the following areas: the parties' combined market position on the markets for the provision of global telecommunications services to large multinational companies and for international carrier services, the effect of the creation of the JV leading to the possible creation or strengthening of a dominant position for certain telecommunications services in the UK, and the possible co-ordination effects of the proposed JV in the UK between ACC, a wholly owned subsidiary of AT&T, and between BT and Telewest, in which AT&T through TCI will have a jointly controlling stake.

arrangements. However, fundamentally the assessment should not depend upon the legal form of the agreement.

The Commission has identified three types of competition problems in R&D **6.128** agreements. The first is that the contractual terms around the exploitation of the results of the R&D may limit competition in the application of the R&D. The second is that following the co-operation there may not be sufficient competition at the level of R&D itself. The third is that as a result of the co-operation third parties may be foreclosed from access to necessary technology or R&D.

In most of the Commission's published Notices and decisions it is the first problem that has most concerned the Commission.

(2) *Application of Article 81(1) to R&D Agreements*

The Commission has often stated that it sees little problem with co-operation in **6.129** R&D[144] and indeed over recent years through the various Community research programmes it has actively encouraged co-operation in R&D and in the dissemination of its results. R&D agreements are also one of the few types of horizontal agreements to benefit from a block exemption.[145] However, despite this there remains some confusion as to when co-operation in R&D will fall under Article 81. Many companies find particular difficulty in assessing the potential effect of such agreements on markets when there may not yet be an actual product and there is no guarantee as to whether the R&D will be successful.

Potential Competition

Article 81(1) applies, in particular, to agreements where the parties are actual or **6.130** potential competitors. The notion of a potential competitor has been discussed earlier in the context of JVs. As shown below this notion is particularly important in the context of R&D co-operation.

The Commission policy towards potential competition in R&D is usefully set out **6.131** in the 1990 *Elopak/Metal Box—Odin* decision.[146] Elopak and Metal Box agreed to set up a JV, Odin, to research, develop, and ultimately manufacture and distribute a new type of packaging involving a carton base and a separate closure that could be filled with UHT and processed food. The technology was new and involved contributions of existing know-how from both parents. In the Commission's view 'neither party could in the short term enter the market alone as such entry would require a knowledge of the other party's technology which could not be developed without significant and time consuming investment'.

---

[144] *Report on Competition Policy 1984* (Vol XIV), *Report on Competition Policy 1985* (Vol XV).
[145] Commission Regulation (EEC) 418/85 of 19 December 1984 ([1985] OJ L53/5) as amended by Commission Regulation (EEC) 151/93 of 23 December 1992.
[146] *Elopak/Metal Box—Odin* [1990] OJ L209/15.

Therefore it did not regard the parties as potential competitors and the JV did not fall within Article 81(1).

6.132 Similarly, in the 1990 *Konsortium ECR 900* decision[147] the Commission issued a negative clearance to a development agreement between AEG, Alcatel, and Nokia, to respond to calls for tender to systems and equipment related to the GSM mobile telephone system in Europe. The Commission concluded that the parties were effectively not credible potential competitors. None of the parties individually would have been able to comply with the timetable set in the tender documents if they were to proceed individually and nor would they have been able to bear the considerable financial risk involved.

6.133 It is therefore clear that as far as R&D co-operation is concerned there must be some reasonable likelihood that the parties could undertake the R&D effort independently and that they already have the essential background know-how to do so.

6.134 The *KSB/Goulds/Lowara/ITT* decision[148] of 1990 set out some of the limits to this approach. The parties, who were all existing manufacturers of pumps with significant presence in European and US markets, had argued that without co-operation they would not have invested in the necessary development work on a new generation of chrome nickel steel pumps, and therefore negative clearance was appropriate. The Commission, however, decided that due to the size of each of the parties they would have been capable of bearing the necessary financial cost of the development work. The parties also argued that they needed the technical know-how belonging to one of the parties, Lowara. However, the Commission also argued that such basic technology was available under licence from other manufacturers. Indeed the Commission went on to argue that there were other ways to recover the development costs such as licensing to third parties rather than producing jointly.

6.135 The agreement fulfilled all the criteria of the block exemption except for the market share threshold of 20 per cent, and therefore the Commission granted an individual exemption. Interestingly in the Commission's analysis under Article 81(3) it argued that the restrictions inherent in the agreement were indispensable to the project since the development costs could be justified economically only if a minimum level of production of units was attained.

6.136 In the 1994 *Asahi/Saint Gobain* decision,[149] the Commission also rejected the parties' arguments that they were not potential competitors for the R&D. The companies had set up an R&D JV to develop a new type of safety glass for use in the

147 *Konsortium ECR 900* [1990] OJ L228/31.
148 *KSB/Goulds/Lowara/ITT* [1991] OJ L19/25.
149 *Asahi/Saint Gobain* [1994] OJ L354/87.

automotive industry. They argued that as they carried out R&D efforts in different regions, Asahi in Japan, St Gobain in Europe, and there were certain key patents in Europe that blocked entry into that market, they were not potential competitors. However, both companies had already developed pilot plants and submitted samples to potential customers, thus the Commission argued that they could continue with their R&D programmes independently.

In the 1994 *Pasteur Mérieux/Merck* decision,[150] exempting a JV in the field of child **6.137** vaccines, the Commission made some attempt to analyse potential competition in R&D. The JV was established to develop, produce, and distribute the parties' existing and future vaccines in Europe. The Commission identified several restrictions of competition related to the development of future products resulting from the JV.

In particular they argued that: **6.138**

> as regards future products in an advanced stage of clinical trials ('pipeline products'), it is realistic to assume that the parties, in view of their past performance, financial strength and existing vaccine knowledge, can be considered as potential competitors for those new [products] for which their actual R&D portfolio shows an overlap.

However, for R&D programmes more distant from the market the Commission recognized the difficulty of assessing whether the parties were potential competitors:

> An assessment of the restriction of competition between the parties for other new [products] in earlier stages of R&D ('future pipeline products') is far more difficult, in view of the extremely broad range of such future research and the lack of precise indications as to the chances of bringing successful products to the markets.

More specifically the Commission argued that:

> It is, furthermore, not accepted that the parties could be considered as potential competitors for the development of these [new products] simply because of their ability to obtain access to the missing (antigens) via licences to proprietary know-how and/or patents, and possibly bulk supplies from other manufacturers.

While the assessment of potential competition clearly varies with the specific **6.139** details of each case, the inherent uncertainty in any R&D project makes the assessment of whether companies are potential competitors for that R&D extremely difficult. It is notably difficult to be conclusive as to whether a company could have successfully completed an R&D project without the co-operation. However, as the decisions referred to above have illustrated, it is essentially when the R&D effort has led to some successful outcome, such as a prototype or perhaps drugs entering the later stages of clinical trials, that the Commission has found that the companies involved have been considered as being potential competitors.

---

[150] *Pasteur Mérieux/Merck* [1994] OJ L309/1.

Market Position on R&D and Related Markets

6.140 In common with most agreements, assessment of the parties' market position should be made by the Commission as part of the assessment as to whether Article 81(1) applies.

6.141 Market definition in R&D cases can be extremely difficult. The R&D co-operation may relate to improvements in existing products, to the development of new products that will compete on an existing market, or to new products that will create a completely new market. In some cases it is therefore not straightforward to apply the Commission's Notice on market definition to such agreements.

6.142 It can also be difficult to identify at what level of market power an R&D co-operation is likely to lead to an appreciable restriction of competition. Markets where R&D and technological development are important are often characterized by both high and large fluctuations in market shares as a new product may arrive on the market and temporarily have very high market shares. If the R&D leads to a completely new product market the parties may, initially, have 100 per cent market share.

Market Definition in the R&D Block Exemption

6.143 The R&D block exemption, in common with most block exemptions, does not explicitly define when an R&D agreement falls within Article 81(1). Instead it states that to the extent that agreements covered by the block exemption do fall within Article 81(1) they would be exempted.

6.144 However, it recognizes the importance of market power to an assessment of R&D agreements and it therefore gives some useful guidance as to which markets should be considered when assessing R&D co-operation.

6.145 The block exemption states in Recital 8 that:

> In order to guarantee that several independent poles of research can exist in the common market in any economic sector, it is necessary to exclude from the block exemption agreements between competitors whose combined share of the market for products capable of being improved or replaced by the results of the research and development exceeds a certain level at the time agreement is entered into.

As a result, Article 3 of the block exemption sets out limits in its application depending upon the market share of the parties on possibly affected markets.

6.146 Article 3(1) of the block exemption states:

> Where the parties are not competing manufacturers of products capable of being improved or replaced by the contract products, the exemption provided for in Article 1 shall apply for the duration of the research and development programme

and, where the results are jointly exploited for five years from the time the contract products are first put on the market within the common market.

This article grants the benefit of the block exemption to those R&D agreements **6.147** where the parents are not already present on the product markets likely to be affected by the results of the R&D. Thus an R&D agreement covering a completely new product in a new market would be covered by the Regulation. Similarly a new product that might compete in an existing market on which the parents were not present would also be covered. There is *no* market share limit for the duration of the R&D programme and for the first five years after the product is first put on the market.

Article 3(3) sets out the conditions of application of the block exemption after the **6.148** end of five years:

> the exemption shall continue to apply as long as the production of the contract products together with the parties' combined production of other products which are considered by users to be equivalent in view of their characteristics, price and intended use does not exceed 20% of the total market for such products in the common market or a substantial part thereof'.

Thus a 20 per cent market share threshold only applies once the products have been brought onto the market.

However, if the R&D relates to improvements to existing products or to new **6.149** products that are capable of replacing the parties' existing products on a market, then the Commission imposes a market share threshold in Article 3(2):

> the exemption . . . shall apply . . . only if at the time the agreement is entered into, the parties' combined production of the products capable of being improved or replaced by the contract products does not exceed 20% of the market for such products in the common market or a substantial part thereof.

The Commission assumes that if the parties have market power on the 'existing' product market they may be able to reduce or delay innovation on this market.

R&D and Innovation Markets, 'Poles of Research'

The block exemption thus relates power in R&D or innovation to market shares **6.150** in a downstream product market. However, the Commission has also referred on several occasions to the need to ensure sufficient competing 'poles of research', both in the recitals to the block exemption and in the 1993 Notice on co-operative JVs.

More specifically the Notice in referring to R&D JVs states that these: **6.151**

> do not in principle fall within Article 85(1) [now Article 81(1)]. The non-application of the prohibition is justified by the combination of complementary knowledge . . . in the JV. That is, however, subject to the reservation that there remains room for a sufficient number of R&D centres . . . in the respective area of economic activity of the JV.

6.152 The Notice does not give any guidance as to what a sufficient number should be or how these could be assessed. But in some cases it may be possible to identify these poles without reference to market shares. This requires an assessment of what is sometimes referred to as an 'R&D' market or a 'potential' market. In essence this requires an assessment of the numbers of alternative research efforts directed at a particular market that are likely to be successful within a short period of time and therefore provide a credible constraint on the co-operation of the parties.

6.153 The Commission has not published any decisions under Article 81 explaining this concept in detail. However, the *Pasteur Mérieux/Merck* decision[151] did discuss the effects of the JV on the development of vaccines in the future. In this case the Commission noted that the JV might lead to a reduction in the incentives of the parties to improve existing products, and to a co-ordination of their R&D programmes.

6.154 Recent Merger Decisions have also provided a useful insight into the Commission's assessment of R&D markets.

6.155 In the *Glaxo/Wellcome* decision,[152] the Commission included R&D projects in its competitive assessment of the concentration. In the pharmaceutical sector the Anatomical Therapeutic Classification 'ATC' system is used to group medicines according to their composition and therapeutic properties. This system applies to both medicines in clinical trials as well as those already on the market. It therefore provides a method for assessing whether R&D efforts are 'competing poles of research' as well as whether they are likely to compete with existing medicines.

6.156 The decision argues, in paragraph 9, that:

> In the pharmaceutical sector, in order to be complete a competition assessment will require scrutiny of products which are not yet on the market but which are at an advanced stage of development (normally after a very considerable investment of resources of time and money). The potential of such products to compete with other products either in development or already on the market can only be assessed by reference to their characteristics and intended use.

6.157 The Commission found when it applied the ATC classification to Glaxo and Wellcome's existing range of drugs and to those undergoing research and in clinical trial that there were some overlaps, in particular in the market for anti-migraine products. Both Glaxo and Wellcome had strong existing products in these markets and R&D programmes in the latter stages of clinical trials. Several other major pharmaceutical firms had anti-migraine research programmes and at least two of these had drugs in Phase III clinical trials. Therefore in assessing the

---

[151] *Pasteur Mérieux/Merck* [1994] OJ L309/1.
[152] Case IV/M555 *Glaxo/Wellcome* [1995] OJ C–065/3.

market position of the parties the Commission took into account both the market shares of any existing products and the number of research programmes aimed at the same market.

The Commission did not argue that Glaxo/Wellcome had a dominant position **6.158** for migraine remedies but, to remedy any possible concern, the parties agreed to grant an exclusive licence to one of their drugs in clinical trials at that time to a third party.

It seems reasonable to assume that in Article 81 cases the same approach could be **6.159** taken. Thus market definition may look not just at existing market shares but also at R&D programmes.

The Commission is not explicit about how many 'competing poles of research' **6.160** would be necessary to maintain competitiveness in the R&D market. It is clear that research is inherently uncertain and it is difficult to judge whether one pole is more likely to succeed than another. While a co-operation between companies undertaking similar or competing R&D may conceivably fall within Article 81(1) if as a result of it there are too few independent R&D efforts, the Commission has never yet explicitly indicated how many competing R&D efforts are appropriate.

Technology Licensing Markets

The other market definition issue relevant for R&D is the question of markets **6.161** for technology, or more specifically the licensing of technology. In the *Shell/Montecatini* decision,[153] the Commission considered the worldwide market for the necessary technology to produce polypropylene (PP) from propylene. As the decision noted:

> it appears that the licensing of advanced PP technology and other associated services . . . constitutes a distinct product market upon which the effects of the proposed joint venture should be assessed. . . . Dominance in the PP technology market would enable a PP technology provider to exercise market power with regard to an essential element of PP production.

The decision went on to conclude that the resulting JV would lead to a dominant **6.162** position on the PP technology market and to require Montecatini's subsidiaries to transfer their PP technology business, including related R&D facilities and staff, out of the JV into a separate company.

This decision illustrates that the licensing of technology can constitute a distinct antitrust market.

---

[153] *Shell/Montecatini* (Case IV/M269) [1996] OJ L332/48, para 44.

Restriction of Competition

6.163 In its policy statements on co-operation in R&D the Commission has usually taken the line that R&D agreements that do not impose restrictions on the parties' use of the results of that R&D or on their activities in other areas do not represent a restriction of competition.

6.164 Thus the 1968 Notice on co-operation agreements,[154] states that:

> Agreements having as their sole object:
>
> a) the joint implementation of research and development projects ,
> b) the joint placing of research and development contracts,
> c) the sharing out of research and development projects among participating enterprises

do *not* fall under Article 81(1). It goes on to note that the mere exchange of information on experience in or results of R&D will not lead to a competition problem and nor will agreements on the joint execution of research work up to the stage of industrial application.

6.165 This is repeated in Recital 2 of the R&D block exemption, which notes that:

> agreements on the joint execution of research work or the joint development of the results of the research, up to but not including the stage of industrial application, *generally* do not fall within the scope of Article 85(1) [now Article 81(1)] of the Treaty. In certain circumstances, however, such as where the parties agree not to carry out other research and development in the same field thereby foregoing the opportunity of gaining competitive advantage over other parties, such agreements may fall within Article 85(1) . . .

6.166 Therefore those agreements that do impose restrictions on the parties' freedom to carry out competing R&D projects or on the exploitation of the results of the R&D such as how the parties may grant licences to each other or third parties, *may* fall within Article 81(1).

6.167 Clearly, in practical terms, most agreements involving R&D co-operation include contractual terms on the exploitation of the results of that R&D. They may also include other restrictions relating to the use of any know-how contributed, etc. It is these contractual terms that have often been at the basis of much of the Commission's analysis of co-operation in R&D. This is discussed further under the section related to exemption under Article 81(3).

6.168 However, it is important to recognize that if the parties are not actual or potential competitors and do not have an appreciable effect on competition then the agree-

---

[154] Notice concerning agreements, decisions and concerted practices in the field of co-operation between enterprises [1968] OJ C75 pp 3–6.

ments do not fall under Article 81(1) and nor do any associated contractual restrictions.

Foreclosure Effects

Agreements may fall under Article 81(1) if they have significant foreclosure effects **6.169** on the market. Thus if a company with a key, or dominant, technology enters into an exclusive co-operation in R&D with another company, third parties will be restricted in their access to the necessary technology to compete on the relevant R&D and downstream markets.

The 1993 Notice on co-operative JVs, referring to JVs between non-competitors, **6.170** states that: 'This group rarely causes problems for competition . . . one must simply examine whether market access of third parties is significantly affected by the co-operation'.

The 1994 *Pasteur Mérieux/Merck* decision discusses in some detail the effect of the **6.171** JV on third parties. In this case, the Commission considered that the exclusivity granted to the JV with regard to existing technology and 'pipeline products', together with the parties' strong position in the relevant markets, could affect the position of third parties, and hence a restriction of competition was found:

> Other producers will, in view of these arrangements, be limited in their possibilities to collaborate either with the parent companies or with the JV as a source for them to get access to 'missing' [elements for new products] or vaccine technologies. This outside sourcing could become important for the development of [new products].[155]

However, when the Commission considered the market for future vaccines, some **6.172** way into the future, it did not find a restriction of competition. Although R&D efforts in vaccine technology were carried out in Europe by only four firms, two of which were the parties, spending more than ECU 25 million a year on vaccine related R&D, many other bodies carried out research in this area:

> There are, therefore, in view of the number of potential competitors for the wide range of future vaccines and vaccine technology, no indications that the creation of the JV will lead to appreciable restrictions of competition by reducing the sourcing-out possibilities of third producers for future vaccines and vaccine technology.

Thus the Commission appears only to be concerned with foreclosure effects when the degree of remaining actual and/or potential competition is considered to be insufficient.

---

[155] *Pasteur Mérieux/Merck* [1994] OJ L309/1, para 69.

(3) Grounds for Exemption

The R&D Block Exemption

6.173 In 1994 the Commission published a block exemption covering certain forms of R&D co-operation.[156] In contrast to other block exemptions, such as those for distribution agreements, the R&D Regulation was not a response to a problem of mass notifications but an attempt to encourage more R&D co-operation. By attempting to clarify the Commission's policy in this area the aim was to encourage more co-operation at a time when Europe was felt to be falling behind Japan and the US in key technological areas.

6.174 While the policy statements in the recitals emphasize the benefits of R&D co-operation, the substance of the Regulation is fairly narrowly drawn and can be difficult to interpret.

6.175 The Regulation sets out in detail the precise restrictions within an R&D agreement that will allow it to fall within the block exemption, the so-called 'White List' of clauses in Articles 4 and 5, and those absolutely prohibited, the 'Black List' in Article 6. It also includes a limitation of the exemption based on the market power of the parties to the agreement, based on their market share, which has been discussed earlier.

Necessary Elements of an R&D Agreement

6.176 There are several key elements of an R&D agreement that are necessary for it to fall within the terms of the block exemption, these are set out in Article 2 of the Regulation.

6.177 The R&D, which is defined very broadly in Article 1(2)(a), must be carried out within a defined framework setting out the objectives for the work, Article 2(a). Any joint exploitation must relate only to results which are protected by intellectual property, or constitute know how, and which substantially contribute to technical or economic progress and which are decisive for the manufacture of any contract products, Article 2(d).

6.178 The Commission would appear to require some evidence to support the application of these criteria. In the *KSB/Goulds/Lowara/ITT* decision of 1990, the Commission accepted that the combined R&D programme of the four parties involved did meet these criteria. It referred in this respect to the various patents granted, awards for innovative research, and a clear description in the JV agreement of the R&D work that was to be jointly exploited.

---

[156] Commission Regulation (EEC) 418/85 of 19 December 1984 ([1985] OJ L53/5) as amended by Commission Regulation (EEC) 151/93 of 23 December 1992.

Restrictions on Exploitation

The block exemption is clearly aimed at a model of an R&D co-operation **6.179**
between equal partners. There are certain key elements required in any R&D
agreement that reflect this. Thus under Article 2(b) and (c) all parties must have
access to the results of the R&D and if there is no joint exploitation each party
must be allowed to exploit them separately.

However, many agreements are more one-sided. It is not completely clear how **6.180**
these would be treated under the block exemption. The definition of 'joint
exploitation' in Article 1(3) is deliberately wide, covering both the exploitation of
the results by a JV, 'allocation between the parties by way of specialisation in
research development or production', or in paragraph (b) 'collaboration in any
way in the assignment or the licensing of intellectual property rights or the communication of know-how'. To the extent that they do not fulfil the criteria in
Article 2(b) it is not explicitly clear that the agreements could fall under the block
exemption.

The provisions of Article 4(1)(a) allow for some exclusivity in the distribution of **6.181**
the 'contract products'. Equally Article 1(3)(a) and (b) extends the definition of
'joint exploitation' to a very broad range of contractual arrangements. However,
Article 2(b) and (c) appears to limit the scope for such co-operation to fall under
the block exemption.

Nevertheless, while such subcontracting or original equipment manufacturing **6.182**
(OEM) agreements may not always fall under the block exemption it is very likely
that they would benefit from an individual exemption, provided other elements
of the block exemption such as the market share thresholds were met.

Other Contractual Restrictions

Despite these limitations the Commission has tried to emphasize that it generally **6.183**
takes a liberal policy towards R&D co-operation and that in many cases individual exemption for agreements falling outside the block exemption is still possible
(Recital 10). There is also an opposition procedure in Article 7, although it is
apparent that this is rarely used.

Individual Exemption

To qualify for an exemption an agreement must fulfil the four criteria of Article **6.184**
81(3) EC. Namely it must contribute to technical or economic progress; allow
consumers a fair share of the resulting benefit; not impose restrictions which are
not indispensable; nor allow the parties the possibility of eliminating competition
in respect of a substantial part of the products in question.

6.185   In practice for R&D agreements the first condition is usually fulfilled. The Commission's analysis generally focuses on the question of elimination of competition and on the nature and effect of any restrictions imposed.

Elimination of Competition

6.186   The issue of market definition for agreements related to R&D has been discussed earlier. In many cases the parties' position in existing markets is assessed in line with the principles set out in the R&D block exemption. In the *Asahi/St Gobain* decision and the *KSB/Goulds/Lowara/ITT* decision, the parties all had strong existing market shares; in both cases above the 20 per cent threshold in the block exemption.

6.187   In these cases the result of the R&D was likely to be a product that would compete directly with the parties' existing products, in one case autoglass, and in the other liquid pumps. However, more recently the Commission has recognized that in R&D leading to new products and possibly new markets this is not the appropriate measure. In cases such as *Elopak*, reference has been made to the fact that a significant number of firms with the relevant or competing technologies remain outside the co-operation. This concept of a 'pole' of research has been used in the US for some years and in some recent Merger decisions from the Commission. It is difficult to define it precisely but it is a useful tool for the parties wishing to demonstrate the limited anti-competitive effects of their co-operation.

6.188   However, an analogy with the 20 per cent threshold might suggest that if at least five other 'poles' of research were identifiable an R&D co-operation might well be exemptable even if it did not benefit explicitly from the R&D block exemption. This is probably a very conservative assessment. It is hard to imagine the Commission finding that such a collaboration breached Article 81(1) at all.

Contractual Restrictions

6.189   The type and scope of the contractual restrictions that can be accepted as part of an R&D agreement is one of the key issues to industry and its advisers. As has been discussed in earlier sections, if an agreement falls within Article 81(1) the restrictions imposed must be indispensable to the achievement of the objectives of the agreement, ie they must go no further than is necessary to achieve these objectives.

6.190

This section deals with the commonest contractual restrictions and the Commission's likely response. As with earlier discussions, the Commission's move towards a more economic and therefore market structure based approach is perhaps likely to limit its concern with individual restrictions in the future.

Joint R&D Together with Joint Exploitation

The extension of an R&D collaboration into joint production, and sometimes **6.191** joint distribution and sales, is increasingly common. It is also increasingly common that the parties wish to set out the terms of these arrangements at the beginning of the R&D collaboration. This raises difficulties of assessment of the effect the agreement has on the market.

The block exemption specifically allows joint exploitation, whether in the form of **6.192** joint manufacture or joint licensing of the results, Articles 1(1)(b) and (2)(d). However, this is constrained by a market share limit of 20 per cent, Article 3. The block exemption was extended in 1992 to include joint distribution, this time within a market share limit of 10 per cent, Article 3a.

The market shares refer to the market for 'products which are considered by users **6.193** to be equivalent in view of their characteristics, price and intended use'. Individual exemptions are clearly possible above this market share limit and many of the Commission's published decisions in this area relate to R&D together with joint production. For example, in the *Olivetti/Canon* decision of 1987,[157] the Commission argued that a JV to develop, design, and produce copying machine products, laser beam printer products, and facsimile products, fell under Article 81(1) as the parents were existing competitors for some products and potential competitors for others. The parties' combined market share in some of the product categories was as high as 30 per cent. However, an exemption under Article 81(3) was appropriate, among other reasons because, as stated in paragraph 54:

> The expansion of production in the EEC which is the effect of the joint venture enables the parties to spread the costs of these investments [in R&D] over a larger number of products: otherwise the costs of these products would be too high for producers to be able to sell them at a competitive price.

Similarly, in the *Fujitsu/AMD Semiconductor* decision,[158] the Commission stated **6.194** that an R&D and production JV was exemptable, *inter alia* because 'new product lines require considerable investment. This investment is risky . . . The JV will allow each parent substantially to reduce these costs and risks.'

In these cases the market to be assessed seems to be that for the final product rather **6.195** than that for the R&D itself. However, as discussed earlier, the Commission is more and more likely to consider R&D markets and therefore parties to an agreement may need to consider their position on both the R&D and downstream product markets.

---

[157] *Olivetti/Canon* [1988] OJ L52/51.
[158] *Fujitsu/AMD Semiconductor* [1994] OJ L341/66.

Joint Exploitation of Joint R&D between Non-Competitors

6.196 There is also a question of how to treat joint exploitation of the results of R&D when the parties were not actual competitors for that R&D. For example, if there would have been no product without the co-operation, is it still a restriction of competition to exploit the results of the co-operation jointly?

6.197 The Commission's approach to this question is not completely clear. However, the *Mitchell Cotts/Sofiltra* decision of 1986[159] argues that although the parties to the agreement are not potential competitors for the production of the product in question, high quality air filters, they are potential competitors for its distribution therefore territorial restrictions are restrictions of competition caught by Article 81(1). The implication of this decision is that although the parties are not competitors initially once they have collaborated and therefore both have access to the results of the R&D they are potential competitors and Article 81(1) may apply.

Joint Marketing

6.198 The block exemption was amended in 1992 to include provisions related to joint marketing or the allocation of sole marketing to one party or a third party (Article 3a). This is limited to agreements where the parties have a market share of under 10 per cent.

6.199 Two decisions have illustrated the generally favourable approach taken towards joint marketing in those industries where complex tendering procedures are required. In the *Alcatel Espace/ANT Nachrichtentechnik* decision[160] in 1990, the Commission accepted that a joint R&D, production, and marketing agreement was exemptable as competition in the procurement industry for satellites generally took place by customers calling for tenders which are then submitted by consortia. Therefore joint R&D, joint manufacture, and separate marketing is impractical. The decision noted that: 'in this particular case the benefits of joint R&D and joint manufacture can only be achieved if they are combined with a degree of joint marketing'.

6.200 In the *Konsortium ECR 900* decision,[161] also in 1990 the Commission actually decided that the agreements to set up a consortia to bid for tendered contracts for mobile phone technology did not in fact fall under Article 81(1) at all as the parties would not have been able to tender independently.

Territorial Restrictions on Manufacturing or Sales

6.201 It is also extremely common for the parties to an agreement to allocate exclusive territories to each other, whether within Europe or worldwide. In principle this is

---

[159] *Mitchell Cotts/Sofiltra* [1987] OJ L41/31.
[160] *Alcatel Espace/ANT Nachrichtentechnik* [1990] OJ L32/19.
[161] See n 147 above.

allowed under the block exemption (Article 4(1)(d) and (f)). A ban on active sales into a specified territory is only allowed for a period of five years. Passive sales into and out of the exclusive territory must be allowed. Absolute territorial protection banning such passive sales is a *per se* prohibited restriction (Article 6(h)).

The block exemption appears to reflect a certain relaxation of the Commission's **6.202** policy towards territorial restrictions. For example, in *Beecham/Parke Davis*[162] the Commission states that:

> To qualify for an exemption in these circumstances joint research co-operation can only be admitted if the results of such joint research can be used by both parties freely and independently without any territorial or other restrictions on production or marketing within the common market

However, some territorial restrictions are clearly not allowed. The *Siemens Fanuc* **6.203** decision of 1985[163] concerned an R&D agreement between Siemens and Fanuc, a subsidiary of Fujitsu, for the development and sale of numerical controls for machine tools. The parties entered into an exclusive distribution agreement whereby Siemens sold Fanuc's products in Europe and Fanuc sold Siemens's in Asia. The agreement was never notified and on investigation the Commission found that prices for Fanuc's products were higher in Europe than in Asia but that it was almost impossible for third parties to purchase direct from Fanuc. The result was that the exclusivity led to higher prices in Europe. As a result the parties were fined almost ECU one million each. The R&D elements of the agreement were secondary to the exclusivity arrangements and in no way justified them.

This was reaffirmed by the *Quantel International-Continuum/Quantel SA* deci- **6.204** sion of 1992.[164] This concerned an import restriction in the context of the sale of a business whereby the seller agreed not to sell the products in question, lasers, into the European market. The Commission reaffirmed that such absolute territorial restrictions are not allowed. It also confirmed that the limited territorial exclusivity permitted by the block exemption must be limited to five years after products come onto the market and must refer to the results of a specific R&D programme. Not, as in this case, to an agreement with some limited extra elements of R&D co-operation but whose primary purpose is something else, in this case the sale of a business.

Prohibitions on Engaging in Competing R&D

These are common contractual restrictions and are usually regarded as ancillary to **6.205** the main agreement. They generally cover both individual efforts outside the co-operation and co-operation with third parties. Such restrictions are allowed by the

---

[162] *Beecham/Parke Davis* [1979] OJ L70/11.
[163] *Siemens/Fanuc* [1985] OJ L376/29.
[164] *Quantel International-Continuum/Quantel SA* [1992] OJ L235/9.

R&D block exemption, Article 4(1)(a) and (b). The clear limitation on such non-compete restrictions is that they must be limited to the field of the co-operation. The *Fujitsu/AMD Semiconductor* decision[165] illustrates these principles. A basic non-compete clause for the life of the JV is:

> a restriction of competition which is ancillary to the JV in so far as it has to be considered necessary to the setting up and proper operation of the JV. In view of the difficulty, risks and costs involved in successfully developing NVMs, [microchips], this non-competition clause is necessary to allow each party to obtain the benefit of its investment.

6.206 In principle short periods of post-term non-compete obligations may also be allowed. For example, if a JV is created the parties may be required not to compete for a period of typically three years after they sell their interest. This ensures that a buyer can be found as any purchaser has a protected limited period to recoup their investment.

Prohibition from Engaging in Unconnected R&D

6.207 These would not be regarded as acceptable restrictions and are specifically included as a black clause in Article 6(a) of the block exemption. The strict interpretation of such clauses will depend on the nature of the parties' R&D interests. If they are not actual or potential entrants into adjacent R&D then it is possible that such an arrangement would not fall under Article 81(1). However, such restrictions are not likely to be ancillary to the main agreement and therefore a notification for a separate assessment by the Commission could be necessary for clarification.

6.208 It is clear that for the parties to an agreement these restrictions can be similar in object and scope to 'field of use' restrictions discussed below. While the Commission has generally taken a more positive approach to the latter, specific prohibitions on unrelated activity are too close to blatant 'market sharing' restrictions to be generally acceptable.

Field of Use Restrictions

6.209 Again it is common for companies entering a co-operation agreement to wish to limit the co-operation to a fairly specific field of operation. They may see advantages in a collaboration in one area but do not want the technology they provide to the co-operation to be used by their partner in another unrelated field. To a certain extent such restrictions are covered by normal intellectual property rules. Thus if a company grants a licence for its know-how, it can impose certain restrictions on the use of that technology.

---

[165] See n 158 above.

The block exemption allows specific field of use restrictions in Articles 4(1)(e) and **6.210**
5(1)(b). However, in the context of a R&D co-operation or JV the parties cannot
impose restrictions on product markets or other R&D co-operations that its partners can enter into in other areas (Article 6(a)).

Granting of Licences to Partners, JVs; Grant Backs of Technical Improvements; and
Cross-Licensing after Termination of a Co-Operation

It is frequently the case that the parties to an agreement, or a JV, wish to grant **6.211**
licences for all necessary technology to the JV on an exclusive basis. This may
often include provisions on further technical developments from either of the parents. These provisions do not come under Article 81(1) if the co-operation does
not. The exclusivity is merely a guarantee that the parties will commit all efforts
and investment to the success of the JV.

Conditions imposed on a JV that it will grant back any improvements made to its **6.212**
parents during its life are also not restrictions of competition. Nor are agreements
to cross license any necessary technology after the termination of a co-operation
to ensure that each parent has the necessary technology to use the results satisfac-
torily. However, any post term links or exchanges of information would need to
be considered in the light of market structure as they may limit subsequent competition as between the parties.

Royalties

The block exemption allows various contractual agreements on the allocation of **6.213**
royalties between the parties to an agreement (Article 5(1)(f) and (g)). In general
these will not lead to a restriction of competition unless they significantly distort
the incentive on the parties to compete with each other in the exploitation of the
R&D co-operation. That assessment will depend upon the nature of the market
and the structure of the royalty payments. In particular any uneven royalty payments may distort the incentives on the parties to compete.

(4) Duration of Exemption

Until recently there has been no standard Commission policy towards the dura- **6.214**
tion of an exemption granted under Article 81(3). Article 3 of the R&D block
exemption grants an initial five years' exemption from the point at which the
products arising from an R&D collaboration arrive on the market. This will continue to apply after the five-year period provided the market share of the parties
concerned does not exceed 20 per cent.

In several decisions, notably *Asahi/St Gobain* in 1994 and *KSB/Goulds/Lowara/* **6.215**
ITT in 1990, the Commission has accepted a similar duration. However, the
recent decision by the Court of First Instance in the *European Night Services*

case[166] held that the Commission, in granting exemptions for limited periods, should take account of the period necessary for the parties to recoup their investment. In paragraph 230 of this decision the court states that: 'the length of time required to ensure a proper return on that investment is necessarily an essential factor to be taken into account when determining the duration of an exemption'. It is too early to tell how this will affect the Commission's policy towards the duration of exemption decisions. However, for R&D agreements where the costs can be significant and there can be a period of several years before the R&D even results on a product coming to market it is likely that a significant change will be necessary.

(5) Future Policy

6.216 The original R&D block exemption was due to expire at the end of 1997. It has, however, been extended for a period of three years to allow the Commission to continue its wider policy review in this area. It is too early to tell what the outcome of this will be.

It seems clear that the Commission generally regards R&D co-operation, in whatever form, as bringing economic benefits and it is only likely to be concerned where significant restrictions on markets occur.

G. Joint Production Agreements

(1) Legislation

6.217 The Commission has published two useful pieces of legislation relevant to the treatment of production arrangements. These are the block exemption on specialization agreements[167] and the Notice on co-operative joint ventures.[168] The Specialization Regulation is restricted to a fairly limited form of co-operation, and while it has been amended on several occasions it is of limited use. The Notice on co-operative JVs while providing less legal certainty than a Regulation does give some useful explanation of how production JVs should be analysed under Article 81. It has, however, been superseded to a certain extent by the recent amendments to the Merger Regulation.[169]

---

[166] Judgment of the Court of First Instance 15 September 1998 in Joined Cases T–373/94, T–375/94, T–384/94 and T–388/94 *European Night Services v Commission* [1998] ECR II–3141, para 230.

[167] Commission Regulation (EEC) 417/85 of 19 December 1984 on the application of Article 85(3) [now Article 81(3)] of the Treaty to categories of specialization agreements [1985] OJ L53/1. As amended by Commission Regulation (EEC) 151/93 of 23 December 1992 [1993] OJ L21/8.

[168] Notice concerning the assessment of co-operative joint ventures pursuant to Article 85 [now Article 81] of the EEC Treaty [1993] OJ C43/2.

[169] Council Regulation (EC) 1310/97 of 30 June 1997 [1997] OJ L180/1.

Specialization Block Exemption

The rationale for this block exemption is set out in its recitals. Namely that:　　**6.218**

> Agreements on specialisation in production generally contribute to improving the
> production or distribution of goods, because undertakings concerned can concen-
> trate on the manufacture of certain products and thus operate more efficiently and
> supply the products more cheaply.

The Regulation is primarily aimed at small and medium enterprises, on the basis　**6.219**
that it will allow them to compete more effectively with larger companies by using
their assets more efficiently. The basic concept is set out in Article 1 of the
Regulation, which requires that the undertakings concerned must:

> accept reciprocal obligations:
>
> a) not to manufacture certain products or have them manufactured, but to leave it
> to other parties to manufacture the products or have them manufactured; or
> b) to manufacture certain products or have them manufactured only jointly.

Although the reciprocal nature of the obligations appears to narrow the scope of
the Regulation it does cover the creation of production JVs, provided that both
parties withdraw from production in favour of the JV.

There are no explicit cross-supply obligations imposed under the block exemp-　**6.220**
tion but if the parties wish to impose an exclusive supply/purchase obligation on
each other then these are covered by Article 2(1)(b). Article 2(c)(d)(e) and (f) also
allows for various exclusive distribution arrangements within the EU, with the
usual provision that parallel imports must be allowed.

There are two main limitations to the scope of the block exemption. The first is　**6.221**
that in common with the R&D Regulation it is restricted to agreements between
undertakings whose combined share in the relevant product market is less than 20
per cent (Article 3(1)(a)). The second is that it is limited to agreements between
undertakings whose combined aggregate annual turnover does not exceed ECU
1,000 million[170] (Article 3(2)(b)). The aim of the latter restriction is to limit the
application of the regulation to small or medium-sized enterprises (SMEs) but
clearly it does severely restrict the usefulness of the Regulation. There is an opposition procedure set out in Article 4 for agreements exceeding these turnover and
market share thresholds but it is rarely if ever used.

The Regulation was amended in 1992 to include provisions on joint distribution　**6.222**
of the contract products. However, this is limited to cases where the participating

---

[170] According to Article 6 of the Regulation, for the purpose of calculating total annual turnover
within the meaning of the Regulation, the turnovers achieved during the last financial year by the
participating undertakings in respect of all goods and services excluding tax are added together. For
this purpose, no account is taken of dealings between the participating undertakings or between
these undertakings and a third undertaking jointly charged with manufacture or sale.

undertakings have less than 10 per cent of the relevant product market, and again a combined turnover of less than ECU 1,000 million. These restrictions are set out in Article 3(2)(a) and (b).

Notice on Co-Operative Joint Ventures

6.223 This Notice provides a general overview of the Commission's policy towards JVs. However, it has particular relevance to production agreements as these are frequently organized through JVs and many JVs also include an element of joint production.

6.224 This Notice was drafted at the time when the Commission's policy debate focused on the distinction between co-operative and concentrative JVs, and hence on whether or not the provisions of the Merger Regulation[171] applied. Since then the Merger Regulation has been revised. The main policy distinction now rests on the question whether the JV is full function and autonomous from its parents. This is discussed in more detail in Section E above.

6.225 The Notice on co-operative JVs, however, provides some guidance as to the Commission's policy towards production JVs under Article 81. Clearly, for Article 81(1) to apply, the creation of the JV must restrict actual or potential competition between the parents or the creation of the JV must have a significant detrimental effect on third parties' ability to compete on the market. The restriction of competition must, of course, be appreciable.

6.226 Not only must the effect of the JV itself be assessed, but also the competitive relationship between the JV and its parents and between the parents themselves. This assessment will depend, *inter alia*, on whether they are present on the same markets as the JV, adjacent markets (upstream or downstream), and the economic importance of the JV to the parents.

6.227 For full-function JVs, where the JV is autonomous from the parents and is actively engaged in selling on the market, the possible competitive restrictions are more complex. Full function JVs are either considered under the Merger Regulation, or by Member State authorities. This section is therefore concerned primarily with those co-operative production JVs, where the JV is not independently active on the market. However, it should be noted that the question of co-ordination of the behaviour of the parents as a result of such full-function JVs still falls under Article 81, and to that extent it is discussed here.

---

[171] Council Regulation 4064/89 of 21 December 1989 on the control of concentrations between undertakings [1989] OJ C395/1.

(2) Application of Article 81(1)

As with all co-operation agreements the initial analysis of the applicability of **6.228** Article 81(1) must be whether the parties are actual or potential competitors. The Commission has generally applied Article 81(1) to the creation of JVs among actual or potential competitors despite policy claims to the contrary. One of the most significant exception being the *Elopak* decision.[172]

The second step in assessing the applicability of Article 81(1) must be whether the **6.229** agreement will lead to an appreciable restriction of competition. Whilst many early decisions of the Commission focused more on the question whether the JV agreements restricted the freedom of action of the undertakings involved in the market, the Commission has emphasized the importance of a more economic approach on several occasions. This will be the focus of the analysis in this section.

Market Definition

The principles behind market definition for production agreements are the same **6.230** as for all other markets, and are set out in the Commission's Notice on market definition. However, there are certain aspects that are peculiar to production agreements.

One of the most important difficulties in assessing production JVs is to distin- **6.231** guish between captive and free production. In many sectors such as the chemical industry a proportion of the output of plant is used internally by a company and a proportion is sold on the free market. Therefore when considering the market position of the parties to an agreement it is not always clear whether it is the share of the free market or of total production that is relevant. This can be further complicated by swap arrangements between companies and by the difference between the theoretical capacity of a manufacturing facility and what it actually produces.

In assessing market power the Commission focuses on those products, or produc- **6.232** tion facilities, that act as a competitive constraint on the behaviour of an undertaking. Thus captive production that could easily be switched to the free market if prices rose would be included in the market calculations. Similarly if there is overcapacity in an EU market such that not all plants run at full capacity then there may be a competitive constraint provided that the marginal costs of increasing production are not too high.

Production Joint Ventures

The Notice on co-operative JVs discussed, in paragraph 40, two possible types **6.233** of non-full-function production JV. In the first scenario 'the JV manufactures

---

[172] *Elopak/Metal Box—Odin* [1990] OJ L209/15.

primary or intermediate products for competing parent companies, which are further processed by the parents into the final product'. A restriction of competition may arise depending, *inter alia*, upon the importance of the initial product to the price of the finished product. Thus the higher the price of the input product the more significant the commonality of cost between the competing parents and the less scope they have for effective competition.

6.234 In the second scenario:

> the JV undertakes the processing of basic materials supplied by the parents, or the processing of half-finished into fully-finished products, with the aim of resupplying the parents, then competition between the participating undertakings, taking into consideration the market proximity of their co-operation and the inherent tendency to align prices, will usually exist only in a weaker form. This is particularly so when the entire production activities of the parents are concentrated in the JV and the parents withdraw to the role of pure distributors. This leads to the standardisation of manufacturing costs and the quality of the products so that essentially the only competition between the parents is on trade margins. This is a considerable restriction of competition, which cannot be remedied by the parents marketing the products under different brand names.

6.235 These scenarios are usefully illustrated by two recent decisions. In the *Philips/Osram* decision of 1994,[173] the parents created a JV to manufacture lead glass tubing for incandescent and fluorescent lamps. This tubing was an intermediate product, which was to be sold back to the parents for incorporation in the lamps and also onto the free market for those manufacturers without their own production facilities. The JV involved the combination of the parties' existing production facilities in the EEA together with investment in new plant. However, outside the EEA the parties continued to produce independently.

6.236 The Commission argued that there was likely to be no effect on the market for lamps as the lead glass represented typically only 2 per cent of the cost of the final product. The Commission therefore concluded that there was no restriction of competition on the market for lamps: 'given the very small importance of lead glass on the manufacturing costs of lamps, such standardisation is not considered relevant enough as to constitute a restriction of competition'. However, Article 81(1) did apply to the JV given the likely effect on the market for lead glass, as prior to the JV the parties accounted for approximately 66 per cent of production capacity on the EEA market for lead glass.

6.237 In the *Ford/Volkswagen* decision of 1992,[174] Ford and Volkswagen agreed to set up a JV to design, develop, and manufacture a 'People Carrier' or Multi Purpose Vehicle, MPV. These vehicles would be supplied exclusively to the parents for distribution and sale. The parents agreed to make some attempt to differentiate the

---

[173] *Philips/Osram* [1994] OJ L378/37.
[174] *Ford/Volkswagen* [1993] OJ L20/14.

products though the use of different engines in most models and through different exterior design and appearance.

The Commission was clearly concerned about the very limited possibility for **6.238** competition between the two companies' final products given the virtual identity of the final product. However, the analysis under Article 81(1) was limited to the fact that both firms were potential entrants onto the MPV market and that by investing in this project they effectively preclude separate entry. The Commission also examined the possible spill-over effects on the adjacent markets for 'estate cars and light vans'. The substantive analysis of whether there was in practice any scope for competition between the parents was discussed under Article 81(3).

The *Exxon/Shell* decision of 1994[175] provides a more detailed analysis of why **6.239** Article 81(1) applies to a production JV. The two companies agreed to set up a JV to construct and operate a new plant to manufacture Linear Low Density Polyethylene (LLDPE) on the EU market.

The EC market for LLDPE and its substitutes, various other forms of PE and **6.240** polypropylene, is oligopolistic. Together Exxon and Shell have approximately 20 per cent of the EC capacity for producing LLDPE. The JV represented 17 per cent of the parents' EC capacity.

As the JV would effectively source all its raw materials exclusively from the parents **6.241** and then supply all its output to the parents, the JV was not full function. It was also under the joint control of the parents who, through the management structure, had an active role in the JV's commercial decisions.

Exxon and Shell remained competitors on the LLDPE market and were capable **6.242** of building plants separately. Therefore in assessing whether Article 81(1) applies the Commission argued that 'account must be taken of the legal and economic context, in particular in the light of the situation on the relevant market and the position of the parties thereon'. It also stated that in line with the Notice on co-operative JVs:

> As the joint venture processes feedstock provided by the parent companies into polyethylene (which continues also to be individually produced and marketed by Exxon and Shell) to be supplied back to them, competition between undertakings—taking into account the market proximity of their co-operation and the inherent tendency to align prices—will exist in a weaker form only.

More specifically the decision argues that decisions on investment, either within **6.243** the JV or separately, will inevitably take into account the interests of the other party. Similarly the parents will be led to co-ordinate their production with the other party and the JV. The fact that the parents continue to market the LLDPE products independently does not reduce the anti-competitive effect: 'As sales

---

[175] *Exxon/Shell* [1994] OJ L144/20.

prices are largely similar, the major competition parameter is the overall strategy on investment and production which is precisely the concern of the co-ordination within the joint venture.'

(3) Application of Article 81(3)

6.244 In common with Commission decisions in many areas the analysis of production agreements under Article 81(3) is not always consistent and rigorous. However, an attempt is made here to emphasize the more recent and hopefully more relevant points in various exemption decisions.

Improvement of Production and Promotion of Technical Progress

6.245 This condition is rarely given much weight and is usually fulfilled by the parties investing in new production facilities or reorganizing existing plants or capacities.

Benefits to Consumers

6.246 This condition also does not receive much analysis. In such cases as it does, reference is made to the benefits of improved products, greater energy efficiency, or other environmental advantages.

Indispensable Restrictions of Competition

6.247 There appear to be two main focuses of analysis in the Commission's assessment of this condition. The first one, as developed in part in the *Ford/Volkswagen* and *Exxon/Shell* decisions, is to assess whether the overall arrangement is the least restrictive way to achieve the objectives of the collaboration.

6.248 Thus in the *Ford/Volkswagen* decision the Commission accepted the parties' argument that 'the partners each acting on its own could not develop and produce the MPV in the same conditions so rapidly and so efficiently as their co-operation will enable them to do'. Similarly in *Exxon/Shell* the Commission considered the possibility of alternative arrangements such as a toll manufacturing agreement and accepted that for technical reasons and reasons of investment they would not have achieved the same advantages as the JV.

6.249 The second relates to the assessment of individual restrictions such as exchanges of information, length of supply agreements, or non-compete obligations. The Commission's position is that none of these restrictions should go any further or last longer than is appropriate.

Elimination of Competition

6.250 As in the assessment of other types of agreements the upper limit of market share or market concentration at which the Commission has indicated it would prohibit a production agreement would be that of dominance. The Commission frequently takes into account the restraining effect of potential competition from imports outside the EU, and of countervailing buying power from customers.

(4) Future Policy

There are likely to be two important future developments with regard to the **6.251** Commission's policy towards production agreements. First, the Specialization Regulation expires at the end of 1999. The Commission has announced that this Regulation together with the R&D Regulation will be reviewed. It is not yet clear what the outcome of this review will be. The second important change will be the impact of the revisions to the Merger Regulation. Full-function JVs are now no longer be primarily dealt with under Article 81. It remains to be seen what impact this will have on the way business chooses to structure its production co-operation agreements but it is expected that more and more will take advantage of the accelerated procedures available under the Merger Regulation.

H. Joint Selling Agreements

(1) Introduction

Definition.   The agreements covered in this section involve co-operation in the **6.252** selling of products or services between companies operating at the same level of the supply chain. Joint selling covers a range of different forms of co-ordination of sales policy: market prospecting, reciprocal assistance at the distribution stage (reciprocal supply arrangements), and joint selling as such. In the latter situation, producers grant to a common agent or a joint sales organization, whether or not on an exclusive basis, the right to sell their products or services in either all markets or on a number of markets. In this section joint selling will be used in this sense, but will also include reciprocal supply arrangements.

A distinction can be drawn between those agreements where the selling of a prod- **6.253** uct or service is an adjunct to another co-operation, for example the joint selling of the output resulting from joint production which has already been or can be challenged under Article 81(1), and those agreements where joint selling is the main joint activity of the partners involved. Where joint selling is the adjunct of an anti-competitive practice, its assessment under Article 81(1) must be carried out in combination with that practice. This section thus analyses agreements having joint selling as their sole or principal object. Full-function joint ventures performing the functions of an autonomous economic entity engaged in joint selling will not be considered here as they fall either under the EC Merger Regulation or, in a case where they fall below the thresholds thereof, under the jurisdiction of Member States' competition rules.

6.254 **Potential or actual competitors.**   In the 1968 Notice concerning agreements, decisions, and concerted practices in the field of co-operation between enterprises,[176] it is pointed out under heading II (6) that Article 81(1) does not apply to:

> Agreements having as their sole object:
>
> (a) joint selling arrangements,
> (b) joint after-sales and repairs service, provided the participating enterprises are not competitors with regard to the products or services covered by the agreement.

Thus, competition problems are only likely to arise when the parties to the joint selling agreement are actual or potential competitors.

6.255 **Horizontal or vertical nature.**   A distinction can be made between the horizontal and vertical nature of a selling agreement between what appear to be potential competitors. An undertaking may choose a competing undertaking to sell its products in a particular market. Provided the selling undertaking controls prices and other distribution aspects, he acts as a reseller and the relationship is of a vertical nature. However, if the supplying undertaking keeps control over the price of the product the other undertaking sells, the relationship is of a horizontal nature between competitors and must be assessed as such.

6.256 **Consortium.**   If a consortium is being set up for the joint supply of goods or services, and the parties are not competitors as regards these goods or services, the whole operation falls outside the scope of Article 81. For example, in a case where a consortium allows the undertakings involved to introduce a tender for a project that they would not be able to fulfil, or would not have bid for, individually, the parties are not considered to be potential competitors.[177] However, the Commission has also indicated in its 1968 Notice that 'if the absence of competition between the enterprises and the maintenance of this situation are based on agreements or concerted practices, there may be a restraint of competition'.[178]

6.257 **No joint sales.**   There is no restraint of competition, even if they are competitors, in a case where 'several manufacturers, without acting in concert with each other, arrange for an after-sales and repair service for their products to be provided by an enterprise which is independent of them'.[179] The reason is that such an activity is not considered to fall within the category of joint selling activities, as parties do not act together.

6.258 **Main competition issues.**   Joint sales agreements normally lead to the co-ordination of prices and sales conditions, and sometimes even to output restrictions

---

[176] [1968] OJ C75/3, rectified in [1968] OJ C84/14.
[177] *Eurotunnel* [1988] OJ L311/86.
[178] Heading II(5) of the 1968 Notice.
[179] Heading II(6), last para, of the 1968 Notice.

and market sharing. These issues can therefore be considered as the main competition problems in respect to these agreements. As a result such agreements will normally be prohibited, in particular as regards price-fixing and market sharing, both regarded as hard core restrictions.

(2) Joint Selling

Joint Selling Considered as a Classic Horizontal Cartel

The Commission's attitude towards joint selling by competing parties has **6.259** changed since the late sixties and early seventies, as is clearly shown in its Notice concerning the assessment of co-operative joint ventures pursuant to Article 81 of the EC Treaty.[180] This Notice is very explicit on the issue of joint selling and the European competition rules. It states that:

> Sales JVs belong to the category of classic horizontal cartels. They have as a rule the object and effect of co-ordinating the sales policy of competing manufacturers. In this way they not only close off price competition between the parents but also restrict the volume of goods to be delivered by the participants within the framework of the system of allocating orders. The Commission will therefore in principle assess sales JVs negatively.[181]

In principle all joint selling arrangements between competitors, not being SMEs, are caught by Article 81(1) as they normally lead to the co-ordination of prices and sales conditions, and sometimes even to output restrictions or market sharing.

Selling Market

Size of the Undertakings Concerned

SMEs. The 1968 Notice indicates that very often there is no appreciable restriction **6.260** of competition if joint selling is undertaken by small or medium-sized enterprises (SMEs), even if they are competing with each other. However, no definition of SMEs is given in the Notice. It is only since 1996 that a Community definition of SMEs exists.[182] Nonetheless, even in the presence of such a definition, it should be borne in mind that the Notice does not exclude the application of Article 81(1) in a case where joint selling is agreed upon between a number of SMEs. Indeed, the Notice says that *very often* no appreciable restriction of competition will occur in a case of joint selling by SMEs, but this cannot be totally excluded. In this context the 1986 Commission Notice on agreements of minor importance which do not fall under Article 81(1)[183] (known as the 'De Minimis Notice') also defines the field of application of Article 81(1) with regard to co-operation between SMEs

---

[180] [1993] OJ C43–C43/2.
[181] Points 38 and 60 of the 1993 Notice.
[182] [1996] OJ L107/4.
[183] [1986] OJ C231, pp 2–4.

and between other undertakings. It can thus be applied in the area of joint selling agreements. The De Minimis Notice[184] builds on the 1968 Co-operation Notice and refers essentially to the appreciable effect on competition. Agreements concluded between undertakings having a market share of not more than 5 per cent (horizontal or mixed agreements) or 10 per cent (vertical agreements) of the relevant product and geographical markets do generally not have an appreciable effect on competition within the meaning of Article 81(1). In view of the 5 per cent market share threshold, SMEs are likely to benefit from this Notice when engaging as competitors in horizontal co-operation agreements like joint selling. However, the applicability of Article 81(1) cannot be ruled out in the case of agreements representing serious restrictions of competition, including the sharing of sources of supply. Yet, the Commission will only act upon such agreements if the Community interest so requires and in particular if they affect the proper functioning of the single market.[185]

6.261 The Commission's policy towards joint selling carried out by competing SMEs is illustrated in the *SAFCO* (Société Anonyme des Fabricants des Conserves alimentaires) decision.[186] It is the first decision where a joint selling agency, responsible for sales to other Member States, was granted a negative clearance because of the small size of the undertakings concerned.

Oligopolistic Markets

6.262 In general, joint sales organizations set up by the biggest undertakings in a concentrated market infringe Article 81(1) and are very unlikely to be exempted, because they exclude competition to a very large extent. Furthermore, co-operation through joint selling will not be exempted if it injures competition by reducing the level of potential competition, especially if competition in the relevant market is already weak and the potential competitors are the only credible entrants, as for example in the *Floral* case.

6.263 The Commission's *Floral* decision[187] relates to the sales of compound fertilizers produced by the three leading French manufacturers of fertilizers. Their production counted for more than two-thirds of total French production. Moreover, at the time France was second only to the United Kingdom in production of compound fertilizers in the Community. French exports to Germany in the mid-seventies accounted for two-thirds of intra-Community exports. Large quantities

---

[184] First issued in 1970, [1970] OJ C64/1 (5% market share and aggregate annual turnover of ECU 15 million) and amended for the first time in 1977, [1977] OJ C313/3 (5% market share and ECU 50 million). The 1986 Notice contained a turnover threshold of ECU 200 million, last amended in 1994 (ECU 300 million), [1994] OJ C368. In 1997 the turnover threshold was abandoned.

[185] *Report on Competition Policy 1996* (Vol XXVI) point 38.

[186] *SAFCO* [1972] OJ L13/44.

[187] *Floral* [1980] OJ L39/51.

of compound fertilizers were imported both into France and Germany, which were also major exporters. The customers were around thirty co-operatives and fertilizer wholesalers.[188] All the parties' products for export to Germany passed through Floral. Although they had not explicitly undertaken to channel all their exports to Germany exclusively through Floral, they nevertheless did so for a period of more than five years. Later on the bulk of such exports was channelled through Floral. Exports to other Member States took place on an individual basis. The three French manufacturers sold their products to Floral at varying prices. However, the products were resold at uniform prices (including identical rebates) and on uniform terms.[189] The prices were aligned on those of German manufacturers which were on average 5 per cent to 10 per cent, and sometimes as much as 15 per cent, higher than in France. German buyers were thus faced with identical prices and identical sales conditions for products of the same type.

The Commission concluded that the organization of export sales in this manner, ie channelled and standardized through Floral, amounted to an export sales agency. The parties thus refrained from exporting to Germany otherwise than through Floral, thereby excluding competition between them on the German market.   **6.264**

In order to measure the impact of Floral on the relevant market, the Commission took into account the following factors: (i) the three manufacturers were France's largest manufacturers, (ii) they also were large manufacturers in relation to total Community production, ie representing together more than 10 per cent, (iii) they had a substantial exportable output and their plants were capable of exporting on their own to Germany, (iv) freight costs for Germany were to a large extent not higher than those for destinations in France, (v) the competition structure on the German market, where the number of competitors was very small, ie dominated by three companies. The Commission thus concluded that the market concerned had an oligopolistic structure. The Commission also concluded that, if on such a market three of the few suppliers channel and standardize their supply through a joint sales organization, the oligopoly becomes even tighter. Individual sales, even in relatively small quantities, can, in such a market, have an appreciable impact on market conditions.   **6.265**

The Commission took a similar approach in *Ansac*.[190] Ansac (American Natural Soda Ash Corporation) was the export cartel of the United States natural soda ash industry. Between 1982 and 1990, imports of US natural soda ash into the Community were restricted by anti-dumping measures. In 1983 the US producers concluded a membership agreement under which they agreed to make all   **6.266**

---

[188] Point 5 of the decision, 53.
[189] Point 6 of the decision, 53 and 54.
[190] *Ansac* [1991] OJ L152/54.

export sales by them through Ansac. Ansac would decide on the products to be sold, the choice of customers, and the prices to be charged. This agreement would allow for only one new entrant on the European market, as its American members were obliged to sell soda ash on this market only through Ansac. However, the members were all large undertakings, capable of selling regularly on an individual basis within the Community. If Ansac were allowed to enter the Community market, this would not lead to the improvement of the market structure nor improve competition in the Community's soda ash market in general, as there would be no possibility between Ansac's members to compete between themselves and between them and Community producers. The Community soda ash market at the time could be characterized as having a rigid and oligopolistic structure, not characterized by active competition. The Commission took the view that the anti-competitive agreements between Community producers did not as such keep out competition from third parties. If their collusive prices were set above the market level, competitors outside these agreements could still enter the European market by applying a lower price. In such a market it was not necessary for the US producers to combine their sales in the Community in order to be able to enter into this rigid market. The principal obstacles to the entry of US natural soda ash were the Community anti-dumping measures and the exclusionary rebates systems operated by a couple of Community producers, both of which were removed.

Market Entry

6.267   In *SAFCO*,[191] it was shown that a joint sales agency of SMEs can facilitate and increase new export activities to markets outside the normal spheres of activity of the undertakings involved, which can be seen as desirable from a competition point of view. The economic rationale behind this decision is to encourage market entry by facilitating this kind of co-operation between SMEs, thus making them become more competitive and strengthening also the competitive structure of the market.

6.268   Encouragement of market entry by facilitating joint sales was also the underlying rationale in *Cekanan*,[192] which concerned a co-operation agreement concluded between two packaging companies in Sweden and in Germany. The object of the agreement was to extend throughout Europe the use of a new packaging, known as Cekacan. In this respect the parties envisaged to set up a new company, Ceka Europe, allowing the parties to introduce and market the new process in other Member States. The agreement appeared to be aimed solely at co-operation in an initial phase for the introduction of the new product, taking advantage of the experience obtained by the German partner in using the processes in question. The introduction of the processes concerned on other Member States' markets,

---

[191]   *SAFCO* [1972] OJ L13/44.
[192]   *Cekanan* [1990] OJ L299/64.

including Germany where the German partner had been using the processes in question, would thus be undertaken only through the joint venture Ceka Europe. It would also be the sole supplier of materials and services required in the production of Cekanan. The establishment of Ceka Europe would prevent the German partner from developing its practice as regards the use of the relevant processes, thereby removing an independent competitor from the market. Secondly, the joint sales of materials and services related to the production of Cekanan by the JV again would affect the position of the German partner. Indeed, the exclusive supply clauses contained in the agreement would remove any incentive for the German party to manufacture the necessary materials, since it would not be able to sell them for Cekacan products. This would also restrict its competitive position towards third parties manufacturing such materials which were free to market them to Cekacan customers.

In its assessment of the agreement under of Article 81(3), the Commission took **6.269**
into account that the agreement allowed for the extension of the use of the Cekacan product, which represented a substantial technological innovation. The agreement was also necessary to enable the participants to establish an efficient distribution system in a new market. Thus, the agreement would help to improve production and in particular the distribution of this product within the single market, using the experience of the German partner. This should result in a faster increase in the number of customers using Cekacan packaging.

Types of Seller Behaviour

Price Restrictions

Price competition is expressively covered in Article 81(1) (a) in the sense that **6.270**
agreements or concerted practices that directly or indirectly fix selling prices are prohibited. Price is directly linked to supply, and thus is of special importance in case of joint selling agreements. With regard to these agreements, attention will naturally focus on jointly setting prices through joint sales organizations.

Belgian-German fertilisers[193] constitutes an example of such a case. It concerned a **6.271**
reciprocal supply arrangement, operated by a Belgian and two German manufacturers of fertilizers. The Belgian manufacturer sold each of the German parties every month an agreed quantity. The fertilizer was then delivered, not in Germany, but to the Belgian clients of the German manufacturers. The German manufacturers sold equivalent quantities to their Belgian partner, but supplied them directly to the latter's customers in Germany. Manufacturers of fertilizers sell their products at prices including transport costs, ie the cost of carriage to the station or port of destination. At the time German prices were around 12 per cent higher than Belgian prices. The price for the reciprocal sales between the Belgian

---

[193] *Report on Competition Policy 1976* (Vol VI) points 126–128.

and the two German producers was the same. Although the parties did not sell directly to their foreign customers, they nonetheless compared actual freight costs with the higher transport costs that would have been incurred if they had sold directly to those customers. The companies then shared the difference. Moreover, the price for sales to their own customers was the same as the one charged in the country of destination for their foreign customers. Yet the arrangement left the parties free to determine this price. Although there was no formal agreement to align prices, the Commission considered that this system in practice led to price co-ordination between the three parties.

Output Restrictions

6.272 Joint selling agreements may influence the parties' output. Any limitation thereof, for example through sales quotas, necessarily has an impact on the volume of goods to be delivered and hence limits the choice of purchasers. These output restrictions may also be a means of controlling prices through controlling supply. Output restrictions intended to reduce overcapacity are not being dealt with in this chapter, but are being considered in relation to crisis cartels.

6.273 *Ansac*[194] can also serve as a good example of the effect joint selling can have on output. Its overall goal was to market the natural soda ash produced by its members in Europe and to this end to enter the European market, but only as a second supplier to glass manufacturers, by limiting its sales in the Community to 5 per cent of total demand. At the time of the Ansac membership agreement, the few Community producers of soda ash were involved in collusive pricing and marketing agreements.[195]

6.274 In general terms, the Ansac membership agreement restricted competition with respect to output and prices in an oligopolistic market. It was Ansac's intention to limit its sales in the Community to 5 per cent of total demand, thereby accepting the role of a secondary supplier and leaving the soda ash market in the hands of the European producers. This would minimize the competitive effect Ansac's supplies might have on the sales of Community producers and clearly restricted output. Moreover, as a result of the arrangements, Ansac would apply uniform prices and conditions. Furthermore, if the US producers would sell their soda ash through a single agency, this would facilitate the opportunity for collusion with the Community producers. Even in the case of absence of collusion, Ansac would become a price follower as it envisaged limiting its sales to 5 per cent of total demand. This meant that the customers of the Community soda ash producers were not offered a real alternative in terms of supply.

---

[194] *Ansac* [1991] OJ L152/54.
[195] *Solvay/ICI* [1991] OJ L152/1; *Solvay/CFK* [1991] OJ L152/16; *Solvay* [1991] OJ L152/21; *ICI* [1991] OJ L152/40.

Exclusivity Clauses

In particular, it should be noted that it is not important whether or not the agree-   **6.275**
ment commits the parties to sell exclusively through the joint sales agency. What
counts is whether, as was shown in both the *Floral* and soda ash decisions, in practice they do so, irrespective of whether this is done in order to obtain the rationalization benefits of a single organization.

Efficiencies

As indicated in the 1968 Co-operation Notice,[196] the Commission gives   **6.276**
favourable consideration to agreements for reasons of economies of scale, such as
joint storage and transport facilities. However, it is considered that in general joint
selling arrangements largely exceed what might be necessary to achieve economies
of scale by the parties concerned. It is therefore unlikely that they can be exempted
under Article 81(3). In particular, joint sales organizations established among the
biggest producers in a market are highly unlikely to be exempted.

In both the soda ash and the *Floral* cases, the Commission prohibited joint sales,   **6.277**
among other reasons, because of the size of each of the parties to the agreements.
If the parties to a joint selling agreement are capable of selling on an individual
basis, they will have to provide strong justifications in order to demonstrate the
need for their co-operation, especially in terms of efficiencies.

Also, when joint selling arrangements like the Ansac membership agreement   **6.278**
largely exceed what might be necessary to achieve economies of scale, resulting
from joint storage and transport facilities, these efficiencies cannot outweigh the
anti-competitive effects resulting from the joint selling agreement. In any event,
no efficiencies can justify a joint selling agreement that leads to price fixing and
also otherwise does not introduce any additional competition in an oligopolistic
market already characterized by notable lack of competition.

Specific Circumstances Allowing for an Exemption

Although joint selling arrangements are rarely exemptable, specific circumstances   **6.279**
may allow for an exemption to be granted.

The 1993 Notice indicates that:

> The Commission takes a positive view however of those cases where joint distribu-
> tion of the contract products is part of a global cooperation project which merits
> favourable treatment pursuant to Article 85(3) [now Article 81(3)] and for the suc-
> cess of which it is indispensable. . . . In other cases, an exemption can be envisaged
> only in certain specific circumstances.[197]

---

[196] [1968] OJ C75/3, point II (4).
[197] Point 60 of the 1993 Notice.

6.280 In this respect attention should be drawn to *UIP*,[198] which is the most obvious example of such a situation of specific circumstances. As an exception to the rule that sales JVs do not qualify for exemption, it is worthwhile to take a closer look and analyse the elements that have led the Commission to adopt this decision.

6.281 The decision concerns the distribution and licensing by United International Pictures (UIP) on an exclusive basis of feature motion pictures, short subjects, and trailers produced and/or distributed by three production companies (Paramount, MCA, and MGM), all engaged in the production and distribution of feature films and other entertainment programmes for exhibition in cinemas, on television, and through other media. The parent companies originally distributed their own films within the Community through their own separate distribution organizations.

6.282 A first important feature of the market for the exhibition of films is that there are a number of means to measure its size. The decision mentions the following ones: (a) the number of films, (b) the number of tickets sold or admissions, (c) box-office receipts, ie the amount paid by the public to see a film, (d) rentals, ie the part of box-office receipts paid by the cinemas to the distributor for the right to show a film.[199] Of these possibilities, the Commission has chosen the box-office receipts as the most meaningful in order to measure the size of the relevant market. On this basis the three parent companies accounted for some 22 per cent of Community gross box-office receipts. However, their market share sometimes varied considerably from one Member State to the other, as the decision shows (from 13 per cent in Greece up to 35 per cent in the UK). A second important characteristic of this market is the wide variation in market share from year to year depending on the success of the films shown. In this respect the Commission notes that the cinema industry has suffered from 'a remarkable decline both in admissions and in box-office receipts in the years prior to the agreements'.

6.283 UIP was granted a right of first refusal to distribute its parents' films. However, UIP must distribute a film if a parent, holding the distribution rights in any territory, so directs.

6.284 The parties to the agreements indicated that the purpose in forming UIP was to enhance efficiencies by reducing fixed overhead costs while maximizing for each parent the gross receipts from the films distributed.[200]

6.285 **The specific characteristics of the cinema industry** played an important, even decisive role in the Commission's considerations to grant an exemption. Indeed, the Commission attached particular importance to the important changes in the

---

[198] *UIP* [1989] OJ L226/25.
[199] Point 12 of the decision, 26.
[200] Point 15 of the decision, 27.

market which had occurred with regard to the cinema industry over a period of more than fifteen years preceding the conclusion of the agreements concerned. During that period (1970–1986) cinema admissions fell by an average of 40 per cent. Box-office revenue fell by around 26 per cent. This decline resulted from structural changes in the market. The introduction of new technologies associated with television, such as cable, satellite television, and video cassettes, allowed for a growth of film presentation through these media to the detriment of cinemas. In addition costs related to production and distribution had risen sharply. Within this economic environment, the Commission found the JV indispensable for the continuation of the international distribution of films of the parents.

These characteristics also strongly influenced the economic power UIP could **6.286** exercise on the relevant market, normally measured in terms of market share. Although it has an average market share of 22 per cent in the Community, the Commission considered that competition in this market tends to be localized due to language barriers, national regulations, and different patterns of distribution. However, more important were the wide variations in market share from year to year depending on the success of the films shown in a given Member State, which the Commission has observed. Thus, the market share UIP held in various Member States did not necessarily reflect its economic power in these countries.

The 1993 Notice cited above indicates two situations where the Commission **6.287** grants a favourable treatment to joint selling agreements pursuant to Article 81(3). The decisional practice of the Commission shows, however, that a third situation also exists, namely when the joint sales agency is necessary to enter a new (product) market, as was shown in *Cekanan*.

Practices Restricted to a National Market

The Cobelaz doctrine. The initial position taken by the Commission with **6.288** regard to joint sales agencies set up by competing undertakings, not being SMEs, was expressed in its *Report on Competition Policy 1971* (Vol I). A couple of decisions taken at the end of the sixties and early seventies reflect this position, known as the Cobelaz[201] doctrine. At the time, the Commission granted a couple of negative clearances[202] after joint selling systems were altered by the parties so that they were restricted to national markets and to markets outside the then EEC. Thus joint sales agencies could no longer be used within the Community, but were accepted as long as their scope did not go beyond a national scale. It was considered that purely national sales organizations did not affect trade between Member States and therefore were not caught by Article 81(1). However, at the same time the Commission indicated that it would undertake investigations in order to find

---

[201] *Cobelaz/Febelaz* [1986] OJ L276/13; *Cobelaz Cokeries* [1986] OJ L276/19.
[202] *SEIFA* [1969] OJ L173/8; *Supexie* [1970] OJ L10/10.

out whether the maintenance of national joint sales agencies would not lead to a protection of national markets which is incompatible with the competition rules.[203]

6.289 **The CSV doctrine.** In contrast with the *Report on Competition Policy 1971* (Vol I), the 1993 Notice concerning the assessment of co-operative joint ventures pursuant to Article 81 of the EC Treaty[204] does not make a distinction between national joint sales agencies and those which co-ordinate sales from and to markets of Member States. After the Commission decision in the *CSV* case, it is accepted case law that nationwide joint sales agreements may affect trade between Member States.

6.290 *CSV*[205] marks the second stage in the case law relating to joint selling agreements applied on the territory of a single Member State. As in the *Cobelaz* case, which concerned a Belgian joint sales agency of fertilizers, the CSV sales agency was granted an exclusive right to sell for the territory of a single Member State, this time The Netherlands. In both cases each of the parties retained its individual right to sell in other Member States. In the *Cobelaz* case this led the Commission to grant a negative clearance, as it considered such an agreement, confined to a national market, not to affect trade between Member States. However, in the *CSV* case, the Commission shifted its position considerably.

6.291 CSV (Centraal Stikstof Verkoopkantoor) was a joint sales agency of two Dutch manufacturers of straight nitrogenous fertilizers. Between them they accounted for 80 per cent of Dutch production and 16 per cent of Community production of this type of fertilizer. Moreover, their major competitors in the Community each accounted for between 7 and 8 per cent of total Community production. Under the CSV agreement the sales agency was responsible for marketing all straight nitrogenous fertilizers manufactured by the two parties in The Netherlands and on export markets outside the Community. To this extent, the parties notified to CSV their production and sales forecasts before the beginning of each marketing year. On the basis of the information collected by CSV, the parties monthly adjusted their figures on volumes produced and sold on the various markets in the previous month and corrected the forecasts for the remaining months of the year. Every month a planning committee discussed stocks, production, and sales in order to verify whether the parties were in line with the forecasts. This system also included exports within the Community. Due to the monthly planning, export levels for exports within the Community set by the parties at the beginning of the year were not exceeded. Additional quantities were made available to the joint sales agency, in order to avoid the risk of these quantities being

---

[203] *Report on Competition Policy 1971* (Vol I) point 13.
[204] [1993] OJ C43, p 2.
[205] *CSV* [1978] OJ L242/15.

sold twice. A steering group discussed, every two months, questions relating to sales in The Netherlands, prices, rebates, deliveries to competitors, imports, exports, etc. As regards prices, uniform prices were applied, since the other sellers aligned their prices on those of CSV.

Despite the fact that exports to other Member States were not handled by CSV, **6.292** the co-operation between the two parties affected their entire production and distribution policy. Although, at the beginning of each marketing year the parties were free to decide on the quantities they would sell through CSV and the quantities they would sell themselves, in practice the planning system led to the co-ordination of their plans. Corrections to these plans were also harmonized in the course of the year. In such a situation the effect of the agreement on trade between Member States could be considered as appreciable, also because the parties accounted for some 16 per cent of Community production of the product concerned.

I. Joint Buying Agreements

(1) Introduction

Definition. Joint buying covers a wide range of different forms of co-ordination **6.293** of purchase policy. Joint buying can take place through central buying organizations, by means of a JV, or on the basis of looser forms of joint purchasing. Experience shows that joint buying is most likely to happen in the retail sector, especially the food retail sector.

Associations of retailers. Joint buying by so-called associations of retailers such **6.294** as co-operatives, whereby the central buying organization is owned by the members of the co-operative, can contain both horizontal and vertical elements. Depending on the specific features of the case, such agreements will be considered either as vertical arrangements or horizontal agreements.

Co-operatives. A co-operative may have an effect on competition in two ways. **6.295** First, a co-operative, by reason of the very principles that govern it, may affect the free play of competition as regards the activity constituting its object as a co-operative. Secondly, the obligations imposed on the members of a co-operative, and in particular the obligations associated with the principle of 'fidelity to the co-operative', by virtue of which the co-operative generally imposes on its members obligations to supply to it or to take supplies from it in return for the particular advantages which it grants them, are liable to influence both the economic activity of the co-operative and the free play of competition between its members and *vis-à-vis* third parties. Thus, it cannot be considered that the exercise of an economic activity by a co-operative society is, as a matter of principle, not subject to the provisions of Article 81(1) of the Treaty or that the conditions for the applicability of the Community competition rules, as such, to the co-operative sector are of a different nature from those applying to the other forms of organizing economic activity. In assessing the effects on a given market of the presence of a co-operative, account will be taken of the particular features of that form of association of undertakings, but that exercise must be carried out *inter alia* in the light of Article 81(3) of the Treaty.[206]

6.296 **Potential or actual competitors.** For joint buying to constitute a real competition problem the parties to the joint buying agreement must be either potential or actual competitors. In *Screensport/EBU*,[207] the Commission considered that the Eurosport Consortium members and Sky could be qualified as potential competitors in the market for transnational television sports channels. In deciding so, it attached much importance to the fact that the Eurosport Consortium members (an association of broadcasting organizations which are also members of the European Broadcasting Union, as well as Sky Television and News International) decided to establish a new satellite television sports channel, while at the same time Sky actively tried to acquire rights to sports events and also was contemplating the establishment of a satellite sports channel. Sky thus had the potential to become a direct competitor to the satellite sports channel the interested EBU members wanted to establish.

6.297 **Main competition issues.** Competition problems may arise on the purchasing market when the parties to the agreement pool their buyer power and co-ordinate their purchase prices and other purchase conditions. Joint buying might also lead to co-ordination between the parties on the downstream market. Furthermore, account has to be taken of efficiencies realized through joint buying.

6.298 Contrary to joint selling arrangements, the 1968 Notice does not deal with joint buying as such. Reference is made to 'agreements, which have as their sole object the joint use of . . . storing and transport equipment'.[208] However, joint buying agreements cannot benefit from this Notice, as they normally do not have as their sole object joint storing and transport of the goods bought. Joint buying agreements go well beyond these organizational and technical aspects.[209] It is not uncommon for parties to a joint buying agreement to engage also in developing products under a common label. In this respect the 1968 Notice indicates that 'agreements having as their sole object the use of a common label to designate a certain quality, where the label is available to all competitors on the same condi-

---

[206] Case T–61/89 *Dansk Pelsdyravlerforening v Commission* [1992] ECR II–1931 (exclusive supply obligations).

[207] *Screensport/EBU* [1991] OJ L63/32.

[208] Heading II (4) of the 1968 Notice.

[209] See, for example, the case mentioned in the *Report on Competition Policy 1983* (Vol XIII) point 130.

tions' do not restrict competition.[210] Again, the parties to a joint buying agreement normally do not limit themselves to this joint activity.

The main competition issues arising out of joint buying agreements are briefly set out in the 1993 Notice concerning the assessment of co-operative joint ventures pursuant to Article 81.[211] Compared to the position taken by the Commission towards joint selling, the position reflected in its 1993 Notice is less negative towards joint purchasing co-operative JVs that according to the Notice: **6.299**

> Purchasing JVs contribute to the rationalisation of ordering and to the better use of transport and store facilities but are at the same time an instrument for the setting of uniform purchase prices and conditions and often of purchase quotas. By combining their demand power in a JV, the parents can obtain a position of excessive influence vis-à-vis the other side of the market and distort competition between suppliers. Consequently, the disadvantages often outweigh the possible benefits, which can accompany purchasing JVs, particularly those between competing producers.
>
> The Commission is correspondingly prepared to grant exemptions only in exceptional cases and then only if the parents retain the possibility of purchasing individually.[212]

Two views of buyer power.   Two contrasting views can be identified when it comes to the possible consequences of buyer power.[213] The first one is a positive or benign view of buyer power. It takes as a starting point the fact that retailers' buyer power can be used to counter the market power of suppliers, thus preventing the latter from fully exploiting their market position. Buyer power could then lead to lower prices which, as a result of effective competition on the downstream market, would be passed on to consumers. The contrary or deleterious view is that buyer power may have damaging effects in the longer run for a couple of reasons. First, because of the effects it may have on the profitability of suppliers, which may result in lower investments in branded products and in the development of new products. Secondly, it might lead to a weakening of smaller retailers, as wholesale prices for them may rise as a response of suppliers to the lower wholesale prices the bigger retailers are able to obtain. The fear is that brands might disappear and that only a small number of retailers would mainly supply own brands. This would finally mean reduced choice and possibly in some cases higher consumer prices.   **6.300**

The economic welfare trade-offs.   It seems useful to keep these two views in mind when examining buyer power, as they allow consideration of a number of trade-offs. The first trade-off is a short run trade-off between increased buyer   **6.301**

---

[210] Heading II(8) of the 1968 Notice.
[211] [1993] OJ C43, p 2.
[212] Point 61 of the 1993 Notice.
[213] CD Ehlermann and LL Laudati (eds), *Proceedings of the European Competition Forum* (New York: John Wiley & Sons, 1997).

power of a retailer (as a result of a merger) or a group of retailers (as a result of a joint buying agreement) on the upstream market and increased retailer power on the downstream market where it operates as a seller. If a retailer increases its market share, it may use its increased buyer power to put downward pressure on wholesale prices. At the same time, its stronger position on the downstream market could be used to raise rather than lower final prices. The second trade-off is a trade-off between the short run benefits of lower final prices and the longer term damage to manufacturer competition from weakened brands and greater own-label penetration and the distortion of retail competition on the downstream market in favour of large retailers. Given these trade-offs, it cannot be anticipated what will be the net economic welfare effect of buyer power.

(2) Buyer Power—General
The Concept of Buyer Power

6.302   Buyer power enables an undertaking to influence the price and other terms at which it obtains its products from suppliers.[214] The concept of buyer power in this very broad definition is analogous to the concept of market power.

6.303   In 1981 the OECD defined buyer power as 'a situation which exists when a firm or a group of firms, either because it has a dominant position as a purchaser of a product or service or because it has strategic or leverage advantages as a result of its size or other characteristics, is able to obtain from a supplier more favourable terms than those available to other buyers'.[215] This definition relies mainly on whether a buyer or a group of buyers have favourable terms compared to other buyers. It has the disadvantage that it ignores an obvious source of price differences, namely those that arise from cost-related discounts. If, for example, a retail chain, by setting up its own central depot, absorbs a part of the distribution costs that was borne before by suppliers, one would expect the retailer to obtain a lower purchasing price as a result thereof.

6.304   The OECD definition also does not catch the situation where the members of a purchasing group are competitors at the downstream level. In such a situation, joint buying may also affect their behaviour as suppliers on the retail market. For the analysis of buyer power it makes a difference whether there is a situation of power on both the upstream (procurement) and downstream (retail) markets, or whether there only exists a situation of power on the procurement market but not on the retail market.

---

[214] CD Ehlermann and LL Laudati (eds), *Proceedings of the European Competition Forum* (New York: John Wiley & Sons, 1997) 176.

[215] OECD, *Buying Power: The Exercise of Market Power by Dominant Buyers*, Report of the Committee of Experts on Restrictive Business Practices (Paris, 1981).

The research paper on the welfare consequences of the exercise of buyer power, **6.305** prepared for the OFT in 1998,[216] also refers to the more favourable terms an undertaking or a group of firms can obtain from suppliers when describing buyer power. However, compared to the OECD definition, it is a broader one. It distinguishes between more favourable terms in general, namely more favourable terms than those available to other buyers, and those terms that are more favourable than 'would otherwise be expected under normal competitive conditions'. The latter part of the definition is interesting in the sense that it seems to suggest that in some cases the exercise of buyer power might be the result of lack of sufficient competition in the market concerned. However, this definition also shows the same deficiencies as the one of the OECD in so far as it is also based on the more favourable terms approach without singling out cost-related discounts.

In 1998 another attempt within the OECD was made to define buyer power.[217] **6.306** This time, the definition says that:

> a retailer is defined to have buyer power if, in relation to at least one supplier, it can credibly threaten to impose a long term opportunity cost which, were the threat carried out, would be significantly disproportionate to any resulting long term opportunity cost to itself. By disproportionate, we intend a difference in relative rather than absolute opportunity cost, eg Retailer A has buyer power over Supplier B if a decision to de-list B's product could cause A's profit to decline by 0.1 per cent and B's to decline by 10 per cent.

Again, the 1998 OECD definition does not catch the situation where members of **6.307** a purchasing group are downstream competitors. The situation described in its paper also seems to point towards a dependency relation, where a retailer is exploiting the state of economic dependence of a supplier, which has no real alternative. In terms of competition the relationship between a retailer and a supplier can be described as asymmetric. Indeed, a retailer, by the sheer fact that he/she sells a broad range and a great diversity of products (on average a supermarket may offer 18,000 different products), often represents a significant proportion of the overall sales of a supplier, whereas the products of the supplier may represent a much smaller percentage of the retailers' turnover. The example given by the OECD would also indicate that concerns about buying power relate to the distribution of economic rents, namely the division of profits and not to the impact of the retailers' behaviour on economic welfare. However, when buyer power is mainly a matter of distribution of economic rents, it may be better dealt with as an issue of unfair competition. Under traditional antitrust law, economic dependence may be of concern if it results in adverse welfare effects in terms of underinvestment by suppliers or higher consumer prices.

---

[216] PW Dobson, M Waterson and A Chu, *The Welfare Consequences of the Exercise of Buyer Power*, Research Paper 16 (London: Office of Fair Trading, 1998).

[217] OECD, *Buyer Power of Large Scale Multiproduct Retailers*, Background Paper by the Secretariat, Round Table on Buying Power (Paris, 1998).

6.308 The foregoing shows that the concept of buyer power is not easy to define. This seems at least partly related to the confusion that may arise out of the concept of most favourable terms in relation to buyer power. Indeed, although buyer power inevitably translates itself into more favourable supply contracts, the fact that some buyers are successful in obtaining more favourable purchasing terms than others does not automatically mean that there might be a case of buyer power. Especially in case of cost-related discounts this seems not always the case. More favourable terms as such are therefore not sufficient evidence of buyer power. Thus, it seems more appropriate to distinguish at least between cost-related discounts and more favourable purchasing terms not related to cost savings. This distinction can also serve as an indicator of competition problems, especially with regard to the question whether buyer power generates efficiencies or not. It seems also appropriate to identify those cost-related discounts that are the result of a high volume of products bought. In such a case, depending on the volume bought, more favourable discount can be the result of buyer power. Thus, some cost-related discounts can serve as evidence of buyer power and some cannot.

6.309 Another problem in relation to the concept of buyer power is the issue of a supplier's economic dependence on a retailer. It is not clear under which circumstances the exploitation of a supplier's economic dependence can be considered as an expression of buyer power. It is particularly difficult to determine whether there is a case of unfair competition or loss of economic welfare. For this reason, examples of economic dependence are often used in order to describe buyer power, but they might well fail to show any real detrimental impact on competition in terms of damage to economic welfare.

(3) The Existence of Buyer Power

6.310 The existence of buyer power in a given market depends on a number of factors. Some of these factors have already been mentioned briefly in relation to the concept of buyer power. They relate to the structure of the markets, the degree of commonality of costs among the members to a joint buying agreement and the parties' conduct in terms of pricing and strategic buyer behaviour.

6.311 Competition concerns may arise if a joint buying agreement allows the buying group to gain or increase market power over suppliers and if the agreement facilitates the co-ordination of the parties' competitive behaviour on the downstream selling market where they are active as suppliers.

6.312 There is no absolute threshold to measure buyer power. It is a matter of degree. Buyer power depends on a number of factors, such as the market position of the parties and their competitors on the relevant market(s), the concentration of the market(s), barriers to entry, the countervailing power of suppliers, the nature of the products, and the degree of elasticity of supply. Due to the potential asymmetric relation between suppliers and retailers (see the concept of buyer power), the market share threshold at which joint buying might have a negative effect on competition might be lower than the threshold indicating a supplier's seller power.

Direct Measurement of Buyer Power

Elasticity of Supply

BPI. The Buying Power Index of Blair and Harrison[218] is based on the elasticity **6.313** of supply. The underlying idea is that if the supply of a good is perfectly elastic, a monopsonist, ie a monopoly buyer, cannot exert buyer power through a restriction of supply. The less elastic the supply, the greater the possibility for a monopsonist to exert buyer power. This index thus examines the scope for a single buyer to use buyer power. However, it can only be used in a monopsony type of situation. Within monopsony situations, the index can be especially relevant if the supply side is perfectly competitive. In other situations, demand interferes as a factor and supply no longer can serve as the overall factor determining the measurement of buyer power. Furthermore, elasticities of supply are difficult to measure and this index seems therefore of limited use in practice in order to draw conclusions with regard to buyer power. It requires a substantial amount of detailed data on levels of prices and output sold rarely available. In view of this difficulty, other methods are used for assessing buyer power.

Indirect Measurement of Buyer Power

Market Shares

As in the case for market power in general, buyer power is most likely to occur **6.314** when one or a few undertakings dominate as buyers on the procurement market. Although buyer concentration is no definitive proof of the existence of buyer power and other factors need to be taken into consideration, it can serve as a useful indicator of the existence of buyer power. In this respect, buyer concentration relates both to the number of undertakings and to the difference in size between them. For example, buyer concentration may arise when in a given market three dominant buyers operate, each of them having 30 per cent of the market. In another situation, buyer concentration may arise when one player holds 40 per cent of the market and its competitors each only around 5 per cent. Especially in the latter situation it seems desirable to pay attention to the leading undertakings' market share, as well as to the direction in which it has developed over a number of years. Changes in market share can serve as an indicator for the dynamics of the market concerned and point at an increase, stabilization, or decrease of buyer concentration.

---

[218] OFT Research Paper, 50, endnote 7.

6.315 **Buyer concentration ratio.** There are several ways to measure buyer concentration using market share. One of them is the buyer concentration ratio. It focuses on the market share of the largest buyers in the market. The ratio depends on the number of undertakings one wants to take into account. Thus, if the ratio is four, this means that the market share of the four largest buyers serves as an indicator of buyer power on the market. The advantage of this method is that it is easy to apply. The disadvantage is that it does not take account of all the market players and therefore may not always present a complete picture of the situation.

6.316 **HHI.** The Herfindahl-Hirschmann Index measures the sum of the squared market shares of undertakings buying a particular product. The advantage of this index is that it takes account of the market share of each of the competitors in the market. However, a problem might arise if not all market shares are known, but the extent of this problem depends on which undertakings' market share data are missing.

Performance Measures

6.317 A third method to measure buyer power is to measure output or performance variables such as profitability or the price-cost margin. Taking a competitive price and competitive purchasing conditions as a basis, buyer power would then be measured in terms of the size of the discount compared to the competitive price and the value of special purchasing conditions obtained from suppliers compared to competitive purchasing terms. As with the Buying Power Index, this system has the disadvantage that it would be difficult to put in practice, as it requires a lot of data that are not readily available.

6.318 Price-cost margins of undertakings are a more available source of information. However, it is not an indicator of buyer power alone (see also under concept of buyer power). Price-cost margins may reflect cost savings obtained as a result of the efficient operation of an undertaking or cost savings handed over by the supplier to the buyer as a result of cost savings related to the handling of the goods bought. For these reasons price-cost margins as such are not a very useful indicator of buyer power.

Other Variables

6.319 Additional methods to measure buyer power, used in combination with the above-mentioned measures, are the weighted annual average purchases per undertaking, in order to capture the impact of large buyers having strong bargaining power, and a measure of the dispersion of sales across industries, reflecting the relation between the dependency and the bargaining power of suppliers.[219]

---

[219] OFT Research Paper, 53, endnote 27.

Relevant Markets

The effects on competition of buying power must be assessed on two categories of **6.320** markets. First, on the relevant upstream (procurement) market. Secondly, on the relevant downstream (selling) market, ie the market where the parties to the joint buying agreement are active as suppliers. Indeed, co-operation in the field of buying can lead to competition problems on the selling market, although the initial co-operation is undertaken on the procurement market.

Definition of substitutability. The definition of the relevant product and geo- **6.321** graphic markets is carried out on the basis of the methodology laid down in the Commission's Notice on Market Definition.[220] However, it has to be noted that the definition of substitutability on a procurement market is different. Whereas substitutability in a selling market is being defined from the viewpoint of consumers, in a procurement market it is being defined from the viewpoint of suppliers. Thus, the alternatives suppliers have in the case of a small but lasting price *decrease* are decisive to identify the competitive restraints on purchasers.

Calculation of market share. The market share held by an undertaking in a pro- **6.322** curement market can be calculated as the percentage of purchases made by the parties concerned of the total sales of the purchased product or service in the relevant market.

Procurement Market

Buyer power on a procurement market can be assumed if a buying agreement **6.323** accounts for a sufficiently large proportion of the total volume of a procurement market, so that the buyer, by restricting demand, can drive prices down below the competitive level. *Socemas*[221] is a good example of lack of buyer power in relation to joint purchasing. The members of Socemas used their organization in order to import products from other Community countries for sale on the French market. Socemas operated primarily as an intermediary. The parties to the agreements together had a market share of 9 per cent of the French food market. The products imported through Socemas represented no more than 0.1 per cent of their aggregated turnover. This percentage had not changed over the years. In view of these facts the Commission concluded that the agreements had no appreciable effect on competition.

A similar position was taken in *Intergroup*.[222] Intergroup is a co-operation between **6.324** SPAR chains established in a number of Community countries. The chains are composed of food retailers and wholesalers entitled to use the SPAR symbol. In

---

[220] [1997] OJ C372, pp 5–13.
[221] *Socemas* [1968] OJ L201/4.
[222] *Intergroup* [1975] OJ L212/23.

1973, these chains comprised about 35,000 retailers and 180 wholesalers. In the same year, the total volume of imports carried out by each SPAR chain via Intergroup accounted for between 0.06 and 0.89 per cent of the total turnover of all the SPAR wholesalers. Their 1973 turnover was less than 4 per cent of the total EC food retail turnover. Although Intergroup concluded in most cases the contracts in the name of the SPAR members, the latter remained free to determine the resale prices of the product purchased through or after negotiation by Intergroup. Since imports effected by the members through or after negotiation by Intergroup represented only a small part of their total turnover, and because purchases effected or negotiated by Intergroup accounted for a relatively small proportion of the total turnover in the retail food trade in each of the Member States of the then EEC, the agreements fell outside Article 81(1).

6.325 At first sight lower prices resulting from buyer power might be seen as pro-competitive, as long as they are passed on to final consumers due to competition in the selling market. However, this does not automatically mean that in such a situation there is effective competition on these markets. In particular, buyer power exercised by a group of undertakings may lead to raising rivals' costs because suppliers will try to recover price reductions or other advantages for one group of buyers by increasing prices or reducing favourable purchasing conditions for other buyers. Furthermore, in a case where prices are forced below competitive level by buyer power, the consequence thereof might be inefficiencies with the supplier such as quality reductions or less innovation.

Retailer-Supplier Relationship

6.326 A clear distinction should be made between situations where buyer power is being exercised against suppliers that have no seller power (unilateral power situation) as opposed to situations where suppliers have countervailing power (bilateral power situation).

Unilateral Power Situation

6.327 **Upward sloping supply function.** In this situation, the competition analysis is similar to the one applied in the case of a monopsony, ie a single buyer, or an oligopsony, where a number of sellers are confronted with a few buyers. Some conditions have to be fulfilled if such a situation is to appear. First, the buying agreement should account for a substantial proportion of the total volume of a procurement market. In case of oligopsony, the higher the concentration level in terms of buyers, the greater the impact will be. Secondly, there are barriers to entry into the buyer's market. Thirdly, and this is very important, the supply curve of the product or service has to be upward sloping, indicating an increase in the unit cost of production in the case of an increase of production due to increased demand. Thus, each marginal unit costs more than the average cost. This leads to diminishing returns as output increases. Under these circumstances buyer power means that the buyers are able to depress the price paid for a product or a service to a level that is below the competitive level, thereby depressing output. The social welfare consequence is that too few production resources are being employed. Moreover, the lower the elasticity of supply, the steeper the supply curve will be.

Dynamic effects.   Joint buying may offer the participants an opportunity to   **6.328** obtain more favourable purchasing conditions from suppliers. The parties to the agreement may be better off, but some of the suppliers concerned might be worse off. Thus, attention needs to be paid to the consequences of buyer power on the position of suppliers, especially in a case where the prices at which they sell are forced below competitive level by buyer power. Possible detrimental welfare effects may relate to a reduction in the ability of suppliers to invest, for example in innovation or rationalization, and an increased concentration on the supply level as some suppliers might be driven out of the market. These considerations relate to the possible dynamic effects of buyer power and are more difficult to assess, as they are likely to occur only in the medium or long term, if they occur at all.

Efficiencies.   At the same time, attention should be drawn to the fact that joint   **6.329** buying can contribute to efficiencies, for example in terms of lower prices, product variety or availability, better use of transport and store facilities, and possible other economies of large-scale purchases. The economic benefits resulting from joint buying may outbalance the above-mentioned competition problem, but this depends on the circumstances of each case. However, these benefits have to be scrutinized carefully in case of buyer power. Special attention will be paid to situations where joint buying agreements mainly have the objective of gaining or increasing buyer power while having only limited efficiencies. It is highly unlikely that these agreements will be exempted under Article 81. On the basis of the above competition analysis joint buying cannot be considered as presenting the simple 'mirror' situation of joint selling.

Bilateral Power Situation

In a situation of bilateral power, the undertakings exercising buyer power are con-   **6.330** fronted with seller power on the side of suppliers. Bilateral power can range from a bilateral monopoly (ie a monopoly exists on both the upstream and downstream markets) or bilateral oligopoly to a lesser but still sufficiently concentrated number of undertakings on both the buying and selling sides. A bilateral power situation is even less clear cut in competition terms than a unilateral power situation, because the detrimental social welfare effects are much less obvious due to the more complicated situation as a result of mutual interdependence between the two sides. Neither of them can dominate in terms of price, as is the case in a unilateral power situation. It is therefore not unlikely that both buyer(s) and seller(s) will try to set a price that maximizes their profits. However, if the buyer is a monopolist on the downstream market, the buyer can use this position in order to restrict quantity below the competitive level.

6.331 **Original versus opposing power.**[223]   Sometimes it is claimed that buyer power is a response to selling power of suppliers. In this view, selling power is the original power, whereas buyer power is opposing power, countervailing the selling power of suppliers. It is also claimed that in such a situation the opposing power may be beneficial to competition, as it weakens the original power. Two observations can be made in this respect. First, it seems too general a statement to say that buyer power has developed as a response to suppliers' selling power. Concentration on the suppliers' side has certainly occurred in certain product segments, but not in others. Secondly, even if buyer power in some cases can be considered as opposing selling power, competition concerns cannot be excluded, especially if the buyer, as already indicated above, has seller power in the downstream market.

6.332 **SMEs.**   Joint buying is often carried out by SMEs to achieve similar volumes and discounts to their bigger competitors. If large suppliers dominate the procurement market, joint buying by SMEs normally does not present a case of bilateral power. *EEIG Orphe*[224] shows that if joint buying is undertaken by SMEs, this is very likely to fall outside the scope of Article 81(1). The European Economic Interest Group (EEIG) Orphe was set up by seven SMEs, most of them co-operatives, specialized in the wholesale distribution of pharmaceuticals. Because of the fact that very large wholesalers dominated the market concerned, the Commission considered that joint buying enabled the SMEs concerned to obtain a better place in the market. This can be considered as desirable from a competition point of view. It is important to note that the parties remained free to determine the prices and conditions of sale of their products, including those bought through their central purchasing organization. Moreover, market entry may be encouraged by facilitating this kind of co-operation between SMEs, thus making them become more competitive and strengthening at the same time the competitive structure of the market.

6.333 **Efficiencies.**   In *National Sulphuric Acid Association*,[225] the members of the joint buying pool were allowed to jointly purchase 25 per cent of sulphur for sulphuric acid production. The members of the pool accounted for more than 80 per cent of the UK and 100 per cent of the Irish output of sulphuric acid. The 25 per cent should enable the pool to maintain sufficient buyer power towards the major suppliers, only eight worldwide. Since sulphur accounts for up to 80 per cent of sulphuric acid production cost, cost and distribution benefits resulting from the

---

[223] OFT Research Paper, 19.
[224] *EEIG Orphe, Report on Competition Policy 1990* (Vol XX) 80, point 102.
[225] *National Sulphuric Acid Association* [1980] OJ L260/24 and [1989] OJ L190/22.

pool were taken into account, especially for those requiring only small amounts of sulphur.

Retailers' Gatekeeper Role

As a result of considerable concentration on retail markets in Europe, accompan- **6.334** ied by technological changes such as scanning, retailers have obtained a consider- able advantage over suppliers in terms of controlling access to consumers, both in terms of access to sales outlets and access to information on consumers' buying behaviour. This has led to a shift in the balance of power away from suppliers to retailers. In this respect mention should also be made of the rise and success of retailers' brands or own-label products as opposed to suppliers' brands. They rep- resent a key factor in the relation between retailers and suppliers. First, own-label products will not suffer from practices such as de-listing, as suppliers' brands sometimes might. Secondly, in setting the final price for his own-label products, a retailer can more easily take into account the consumer price of a competing prod- uct set by a supplier.

Selling Market

Commonality of costs. In cases where the parties to a joint buying agreement **6.335** are also downstream competitors on their selling market, joint buying may also affect their behaviour as suppliers on this market. This effect is explained by the commonality of costs and its influence on the total output of the parties in the seller market. As to the effect on the market, the following principle applies: the higher the proportion the parties buy together, the higher the degree of com- monality of costs and the more competition between them is restricted. If a high proportion (for example 40 per cent) of goods is bought jointly, co-ordination of the parties' behaviour as market suppliers may be inevitable and competition will be substantially reduced. On the other hand, if the parties only buy a small proportion (for example 5 per cent) of their needs jointly, and the remaining 95 per cent are still bought independently, a restrictive effect on their competitive behaviour as suppliers is unlikely. Thus, joint buying may lead to a significant degree of commonality of costs among the participants of the buying group, provided that joint buying amounts to a sufficient proportion of their total costs. Commonality of costs facilitates the co-ordination of the parties' compet- itive behaviour as suppliers in their selling markets. However, this is only a prof- itable strategy if the parties would gain or increase market power by co-ordinating their behaviour. The restrictive effect between the parties should therefore not be seen in isolation from the issue of market power. The possibil- ity to achieve a higher degree of market power provides an incentive to co- ordinate competitive behaviour, even if the effects caused by commonality of costs are moderate. Consequently, the higher the degree of market power held in the market, the lower the degree of commonality of costs which is regarded as sufficient for a restrictive effect to be assumed. The effects of joint buying can be therefore rather similar to joint production.

6.336 In *Screensport/EBU*,[226] the Commission not only looked at the degree of market power held by EBU members on the market for the acquisition of rights to sports events, but also to the effect thereof on the market for the supply of television sports programmes. Although the agreements primarily concerned joint buying of rights to sports events, they strengthened at the same time the position of the parties on the market for the provision of television sports programmes.

Types of Buyer Behaviour

Strategic Buyer Behaviour

6.337 Through joint purchasing, buyers may employ a number of practices,[227] other than pricing behaviour, to exploit their joint forces. The OFT research paper mentions the following examples of strategic buyer behaviour: (a) slotting allowances,[228] (b) exclusive distribution, (c) conditional purchase behaviour,[229] (d) exclusivity contracts, (e) cloning behaviour,[230] (f) joint marketing by seller and buyer, (g) predatory buying of inputs,[231] (h) strategic purchasing of facilities,[232] (i) reciprocal dealing, and finally (j) terms of business. These practices may serve a number of different purposes. Some can enhance efficiencies, some can distort competition, while others allow buyers to obtain a greater share of profits, so-called rent shifting.

6.338 A number of these practices concern vertical restraints, such as exclusive distribution, exclusivity contracts, and reciprocal dealing which are dealt with in other chapters in this book. However, in dealing with the possible anti-competitive effects resulting from vertical restraints, it might be argued that, due to the asymmetric relation between suppliers and retailers, the market share threshold at which joint buying might have a negative effect on competition might be lower than the threshold applied in case of a supplier's selling power. Other practices come close to unfair competition, like cloning behaviour and slotting allowances, often observed in the context of the economic dependency of a supplier. In all these examples, it has to be examined whether there is any detrimental impact on

---

[226] *Screensport/EBU* [1991] OJ L63/32.

[227] OFT Research Paper 16, 22.

[228] Payments of a supplier to a buyer in order to obtain the right to have one's goods displayed at all or in a particular place on the shelves in the latter's shops.

[229] The purchase of a good only on the condition that significant concessions are made by the supplier of such goods.

[230] Close copy or 'look-alike' of trade marks and similar devices.

[231] Cost raising strategy in order to induce exit and eventually to deter market entry.

[232] Retail outlets, in particular large store formats such as super- and hypermarkets, have become the dominant form of access for suppliers to reach consumers, thus control of such facilities provides retailers with bargaining power over suppliers.

economic welfare. Experiences drawn from Member States' competition authorities show that this proves to be a difficult exercise in practice.

Exclusive purchasing obligations.   The Commission has challenged joint buy-   **6.339**
ing agreements covering a significant part of the market, that include exclusive
purchasing   obligations.[233]   In   *Rennet*[234]   the   Cooperatieve   Stremsel-   en
Kleurselfabriek accounted for 90 per cent of the Dutch market for the production
of rennet. Its members were under the obligation to buy all their rennet from the
co-operative. The purchasing obligation was further strengthened by a penalty
provision in case this obligation was not met. The Commission considered that
the efficiencies resulting from the joint production, such as improvement of the
quality of rennet and cost saving, could still be obtained if the members were
allowed greater freedom of choice in terms of buying.

In *National Sulphuric Acid Association*,[235] the exclusive purchase clause obliging all   **6.340**
pool members to buy their total requirements of imported sulphur for sulphuric
acid production through the pool had to be abolished before an exemption could
be granted. The members of the pool accounted for over 80 per cent of the UK
and 100 per cent of the Irish sulphuric acid output. The purchasing obligation
was brought down to 25 per cent, allowing the pool to maintain a strong negotiation position with the major suppliers, of which only eight existed worldwide. In
ARD/MGM[236] joint buying of exclusive television broadcasting rights for films
was exempted after so-called 'windows' allowing broadcasting by third parties
during certain periods had been accepted by the parties.

Possibility of purchasing individually.   In *National Sulphuric Acid Association*   **6.341**
and *ARD/MGM*, joint buying was associated with a restriction of the freedom to
buy independently. In *Socemas* and *Intergroup*, the parties' freedom to buy was not
restricted. Although the existence of such an express restriction is important, what
matters is whether or not the parties in practice buy exclusively or partly through
the joint buying organization.

Common Trade mark.   In *Orphe*,[237] its members engaged in joint buying of   **6.342**
pharmaceutical and parapharmaceutical products and created a common trade
mark, which would appear beside the trade mark of each member on the products
distributed by the members. Since the members were SMEs and very large wholesalers dominated the procurement market, the agreement was considered beneficial, among other things because it would allow for wider product choice.

---

[233] *GISA* [1972] OJ L303/45.
[234] *Rennet* [1979] OJ L51/19.
[235] *National Sulphuric Acid Association* [1980] OJ L260/24 and [1989] OJ L190/22.
[236] *ARD/MGM* [1989] OJ L284/36.
[237] *EEIG Orphe, Report on Competition Policy 1990* (Vol XX) 80, point 102.

J. Information Exchange Agreements

(1) Introduction

6.343 **Definition.** An information exchange agreement is an arrangement whereby undertakings organize themselves in such a way that they can gather and exchange certain information between them or supply such information to a common agency responsible for centralizing, compiling, and processing this information before returning it to the participants in the form and at the frequency agreed. The information exchanged can contain different kinds of data. Information exchange agreements can relate to the collection of individual data and/or aggregate data. Individual data are data relating to a designated or directly or indirectly identifiable undertaking. Aggregate data are data relating to at least three undertakings. Data relating to only two undertakings cannot be regarded as aggregate, since it enables each of the two undertakings concerned to know precisely, by subtraction, the data relating to the other.

6.344 A distinction should be drawn between those cases where the exchange of information is the adjunct of an anti-competitive practice which has already been or can be challenged under Article 81(1) and those cases where the system as such constitutes a threat to competition. Where an exchange of information is the adjunct of an anti-competitive practice, its assessment will be carried out in combination with that practice.[238] The Commission in *VVVF and IFTRA* clarified this.[239]

6.345 This kind of information exchange agreement will not be dealt with in this section. This section analyses information exchange, which might constitute a threat to competition in its own right. This comprises cases where, without there being evidence of other collusive practice that is caught by Article 81(1), the information exchange agreement causes undertakings to change their conduct in a way which damages competition. *Fatty Acids*[240] is the first example of a prohibition of an information exchange agreement that is not the adjunct of an otherwise demonstrated, illegal practice but which in itself already infringes EC competition law. It therefore marks the first important stage in the case law concerning information exchange and EC competition law.

6.346 **Internal and external effects.** Information exchanges have two main effects. First, there is an internal effect, namely information sharing increases the information available within the group of undertakings participating in the information sharing. This, in turn, is likely to reduce the uncertainty among its

---

[238] Case T–1/89 *Rhône-Poulenc* [1991] ECR II–867.
[239] *VVVF* [1969] OJ L168; *IFTRA-Glass containers* [1974] OJ L160 and *IFTRA-Aluminium* [1975] OJ L228; *Cement* [1994] OJ L343, in particular Article 2 thereof.
[240] *Fatty Acids* [1987] OJ L3/17.

members. Secondly, there are external effects, which will depend on the nature of the market in which they operate. These effects can vary but are likely to include price and output setting. Of course, the consequences for economic welfare will depend on the extent to which prices or quantities are the main strategic variables used by the undertakings concerned.

Public versus private market transparency.   It is important to distinguish **6.347** between public and private market transparency.[241] Public market transparency is transparency for consumers, while private market transparency is transparency for undertakings. It has been argued that public market transparency is essential for competition, since it allows consumers to effectively compare products and services. This kind of exchange of information will therefore intensify competition. Therefore, the publication of prices, for example, via advertisements will increase both public and private market transparency. On the other hand, private market transparency only increases market transparency for the undertakings involved and may, through collusive behaviour on prices and output, have an adverse effect on competition. Indeed, in terms of effect on competition, public market transparency can be seen as the opposite of private market transparency. As a consequence thereof, private market transparency will be the main concern of competition authorities.

Price announcements.   In view of the foregoing, it can be said that price **6.348** announcements made by producers to users do not constitute a concerted practice within the meaning of Article 81(1), since the producers who made them have no guarantee regarding the conduct that will be adopted by their competitors, as was shown in *Wood Pulp*.[242]

Main competition issues.   The main reason for competition authorities to be **6.349** concerned with information exchange agreements lies in the potential of these agreements to facilitate collusive behaviour among competing undertakings, since they are likely to improve the monitoring of activities of competitors.

In the 1968 Co-operation Notice, the Commission takes the view that the fol- **6.350** lowing agreements do not restrict competition:

Agreements having as their sole object:

(a) an exchange of opinion or experience,
(b) joint market research,
(c) the joint carrying-out of comparative studies of enterprises or industries,
(d) the joint preparation of statistics and calculation models.[243]

---

[241] European Commission, *Information exchanges among firms and their impact on competition* (1995), 92.
[242] Case C–89/85 *Wood Pulp* [1993] ECR I–1307.
[243] [1968] OJ C231, heading II(1).

The Commission thus considered information exchange agreements as a form of co-operation that can be assessed under the EC competition rules. The Notice is a first attempt to develop criteria for such an assessment. As regards agreements not falling under Article 81(1), it indicates that:

> Agreements whose sole purpose is the joint procurement of information which the various enterprises need to determine their future market behaviour freely and independently, or the use by each of the enterprises of a joint advisory body, do not have as their object or effect the restriction of competition.

(2) Information Exchange—Criteria for Assessment

6.351 The assessment of an information exchange agreement depends mainly on three factors: (i) market structure, (ii) the type of information exchanged, and (iii) the frequency of information exchange.

6.352 **Guidelines.** In its *Report on Competition Policy 1977* (Vol VII), the Commission established guidelines for the assessment of exchanges of information along the lines indicated by the Court of Justice in the *Sugar case*.[244] The Commission stated that it had no fundamental objection to the exchange of statistical information either direct or through trade associations or reporting agencies, even when they provide a breakdown of the figures, as long as the information exchanged does not enable the identification of individual undertakings.[245] The Commission went on to say that it would generally regard the organized exchange of individual data from individual undertakings, such as figures or quantities produced and sold, prices and terms for discounts, higher and lower rates, credit notes, and general terms of sale, delivery, and payment, as practices which have as their object or effect the restriction or distortion of competition and which are therefore prohibited. The Commission also explained that the distinction between good and bad information exchange systems can be made only on a case-by-case basis in the light of all features of each agreement, having regard in particular to the structure of the market and the nature of the information exchanged.

6.353 As the Commission stated very clearly in its *Report on Competition Policy 1977* (Vol VII):

> the area between permissible and prohibited exchange of information is defined by the distinction between a purely statistical arrangement with a breakdown of data by product, country and period of time which is not conducive to collusion, and the kind of arrangement which clearly relates to individual firms.[246]

---

[244] Joined Cases 40–48/73 *Suiker Unie and others v Commission* [1975] ECR 1663.
[245] *Report on Competition Policy 1977* (Vol VII) point 7.
[246] *Report on Competition Policy 1977* (Vol VII) point 7.

The Market Structure

The exchange of sensitive individual data on an atomistic market does not enable **6.354**
undertakings to predict or anticipate the conduct of all of their competitors
because of the fragmented nature of the market. The concentration ratio of the
market concerned is of particular importance for the assessment of information
exchange agreements, as this element greatly influences the competitive structure
of the market. The market can be more or less concentrated in itself, or alternatively the number of participants to the agreements may be such as to cover a
substantial part of the market. In this respect the Court in *New Holland Ford*
observed that:

> on a truly competitive market transparency between traders is in principle likely to
> lead to the intensification of competition between suppliers, since in such a situation
> the fact that a trader takes into account information made available to him in order
> to adjust his conduct on the market is not likely, having regard to the atomized
> nature of the supply, to reduce or remove for the other traders any uncertainty about
> the foreseeable nature of its competitors' conduct.[247]

The Court further states that:

> general use, as between main suppliers, of exchanges of precise information at short
> intervals, identifying registered vehicles and the place of their registration is, on a
> highly concentrated oligopolistic market such as the market in question and on
> which competition is as a result already greatly reduced and exchange of informa-
> tion facilitated, likely to impair considerably the competition which exists between
> traders. In such circumstances, the sharing, on a regular and frequent basis, of
> information concerning the operation of the market has the effect of periodically
> revealing to all the competitors the market positions and strategies of the various
> individual competitors.

The Type of Information Exchanged

The Level of Detail

The level of aggregation of data. To analyse the effects of an information **6.355**
exchange agreement from a competition point of view, it is important to determine the level of aggregation of data. Indeed, the harmfulness in terms of competition depends on the possibility to identify sensitive data. Identification of such
data is possible where the data exchanged are individual data. Identification is also
possible sometimes in the case of aggregate data. When confronted with an apparently general data system, one has to ensure for oneself that the degree of aggregation of data is sufficient to prevent any identification.

Statistics. A first group of data which is very often the subject of exchange of **6.356**
information comprises statistics. Statistical material which sets out production

---

[247] Case C–7/95 *New Holland Ford*, not yet reported.

and other figures for the industry or trade in question without identifying individual undertakings, as is the practice in official statistics, is a fine example of aggregate data which do not allow for the identification of individual undertakings. The exchange of these data is perfectly legitimate.

6.357 A second group of data which can be identified in information exchange agreements comprises statistical data, broken down by product, country, or period of time. Depending on whether the breakdown of figures enables a party to the information exchange to identify or not the competitive behaviour of the other parties, the data will or will not be regarded by the Commission as restricting or distorting competition.

6.358 **Individual data.** A third group of data concerns individual data from individual undertakings, such as figures on prices, production, sales, customers, delivery, and payment. Under this heading we can distinguish a number of elements which undertakings are interested in for the purpose of information exchange: (i) prices, production, sales, market share, and customers, (ii) costs and demand structure, (iii) capacity, and (iv) R&D. Some of these elements can be refined. Prices, for example, include not only prices as such, but also price changes and price factors such as discounts, rebates, and reductions. As far as customers are concerned, lists of customers as well as information on the order book are relevant elements in this respect. In relation to capacity, one can identify information on investments as well as on capacities and production-capacity utilization rates. With regard to R&D, not only R&D programmes but also the results thereof can be of interest to undertakings. The Commission will generally regard the organized exchange of this kind of data as likely to restrict or distort competition. It should be noted that individual data not only enable the parties to identify the nature of each other's commercial strategies, they also facilitate the enforcement of a cartel as it will be easier to identify an undertaking deviating from the cartel strategy.

6.359 The organized exchange of individual data from individual companies will generally be regarded by the Commission as likely to restrict or distort competition, as shown by *UK Tractor* and related Court cases.[248]

6.360 The Commission's *UK Agricultural Tractor Registration Exchange* decision[249] marks the second stage in the case law relating to information exchange agreements. It is a concrete example of the application of the Commission's competition policy towards the exchange of aggregate data which nonetheless allow for identification of the conduct of competitors. Furthermore, the case is the first one in which the information exchange system did not directly concern prices.

---

[248] Joined Cases T–34 and 35/92 *Fiatagri and John Deere* [1994] ECR II–905 and 957; Joined Cases C–7 and 8/95 *New Holland Ford (formally Fiatagri) and John Deere*, not yet reported.
[249] *UK Agricultural Tractor Registration Exchange* [1992] OJ L68/19.

The agreement concerned an exchange of information identifying the volume of   **6.361**
retail sales and market shares of eight, later seven, manufacturers and importers of
agricultural tractors on the UK market. The exchange was managed by the
Agricultural Engineers Association Ltd (the AEA), the UK trade association of
manufacturers and importers of agricultural machinery.

The members could obtain three sets of data. First, they were offered information   **6.362**
on aggregate industry sales. This information could be broken down by geographic areas, land use, counties, dealer territories, and postcode sectors. It could
be made available for yearly, quarterly, monthly, and weekly time periods. In addition to these data, each member could obtain information identifying the volume
of retail sales and market shares of each individual member to the agreement, with
detailed breakdowns by model, product groups, geographic areas, and by yearly,
quarterly, monthly, and daily time periods. Finally, a third group of data was provided for and concerned information on sales by dealers belonging to the dealer
network of each member, in particular the imports and exports in their respective
territories. In the Commission's view this permitted each party to monitor every
other party's sales.

With regard to the first group of data, the aggregate industry sales data, the   **6.363**
Commission observed in its decision that it did not in principle object to the availability of these data because they do not identify the retail sales of the individual
members. However, in this particular case the Commission did object to the
exchange of these data. Since there were a small number of producers by category
or product or geographic area, or the number of units sold in a given period was
low, or the frequency of exchanges was high, the information exchange allowed
for the identification of undertakings.

The Age of the Information Exchanged

The age of data can be grouped in three categories: (i) historical information,   **6.364**
being more than one year old, (ii) recent information, being less than one year old,
and (iii) future information. Depending on the age of the information, the
exchange thereof will be more or less harmful for competition. As a rule, it can be
said that the exchange of historical information is usually not caught by Article
81(1), unless it is the adjunct of another anti-competitive arrangement.

It is sometimes argued that the exchange of information about past conduct can-   **6.365**
not be anti-competitive and that only the exchange of information about future
conduct may be anti-competitive. This argument cannot be accepted, as it would
be impossible to sustain collusion in the absence of information about past behaviour.[250]

---

[250] European Commission, *Information exchanges among firms and their impact on competition*
(1995), 99.

The Frequency of Information Exchange

6.366 The frequency of information exchange plays an important role in affecting the scope of collusion. The effect will certainly grow with the frequency at which data are being exchanged. This also strongly influences the age of the information, as a frequent exchange of data normally implies that the most recent information is being exchanged. This may further strengthen collusion.

7

VERTICAL AGREEMENTS

A. General Principles

(1) Applicability of Article 81 to Vertical Restraints

7.01 The early jurisprudence of the Court of Justice confirmed that Article 81 (former Article 85) of the Treaty applies not only to horizontal agreements between traders operating at the same level in the chain of supply but also to vertical agreements between traders at different levels in the chain of supply. The first case submitted to the Court of Justice under Article 234 (former Article 177) of the Treaty concerned vertical restraints whereby a German manufacturer, Bosch, had in 1903 granted its Dutch distributor, van Rijn, an exclusive right of sale of all its products on the Netherlands market.[1] In his Opinion Advocate General Lagrange stated, *inter alia*: 'The first point which seems clear, and does not seem to have been contested in the main action, is that Article 85 [now Article 81] refers as much to "vertical" as to "horizontal" agreements . . .'.[2]

7.02 This view was endorsed by the Court in that it did not 'exclude the possibility that the restrictions on export . . . come within the words "agreements . . . which may affect trade between Member States" '.[3] Nevertheless, in *Italy v Council & Commission*,[4] the Government of Italy argued, *inter alia*, that Article 81 'covers dealings between persons trading on the horizontal level, whereas Article 86 [now Article 82] governs the relationships between persons trading at successive stages, vertically'. In its judgment the Court definitively rejected the view that only Article 82 applied to vertical restraints:

> Neither the wording of Article 85 [now Article 81] nor that of Article 86 [now Article 82] justifies interpreting either of these Articles with reference to the level in the economy at which the undertakings carry on business. Neither of these provisions makes a distinction between businesses operating in competition with each other at the same level or between businesses not competing with each other and operating at different levels. It is not possible to make a distinction where the Treaty does not make one.

> It is not possible either to argue that Article 85 can never apply to an exclusive dealing agreement on the ground that the grantor and grantee thereof do not compete with each other. For the competition mentioned in Article 85 (1) means not only any possible competition between the parties to the agreement, but also any possible competition between one of them and third parties.

---

[1] Case 13/61 *de Geus v Bosch & van Rijn* [1962] ECR 45.

[2] ibid, at 69.

[3] ibid, at 53.

[4] Case 32/65 *Italy v Council & Commission* [1966] ECR 389. See the related judgments in Joined Cases 56/64 and 58/64 *Consten and Grundig v Commission* [1966] ECR 299.

The Court has also upheld the application of Article 81 to vertical restraints **7.03** affecting both inter-brand and intra-brand competition.[5] In the *Consten & Grundig* case,[6] the Commission had restricted its analysis of the effects of the vertical restraints relating to exclusive distribution and non-compete in terms of their effects on intra-brand competition. Grundig and Consten and the German Government argued that Article 81(1) only applied to vertical restraints which have a negative economic effect on inter-brand competition. It was argued that exclusive distribution agreements of the type granted to Consten are not only not harmful to competition but have the beneficial effect of increasing inter-brand competition.

The Court rejected the view that Article 81 did not apply to vertical restraints **7.04** relating to intra-brand competition:

> Although competition between producers is generally more noticeable than that between distributors of products of the same make, it does not thereby follow that an agreement tending to restrict the latter kind of competition should escape the prohibition of Article 85(1) [now Article 81(1)] merely because it might increase the former.

(2) The Two-Stage Analysis under Article 81 and the Commission's Monopoly over the Granting of Exemptions under Article 81(3)

The analysis of whether an agreement infringes Article 81 of the Treaty takes place **7.05** in two stages. First, it is examined to establish whether it falls within the scope of the prohibition in Article 81(1). Where the application of the first test is positive, then it is necessary to proceed to the second test to see if the agreement is eligible for a declaration (commonly referred to as an exemption) under Article 81(3). The prohibition in Article 81(1) can be declared inapplicable by the Commission providing the four substantive conditions set out in Article 81(3) are fulfilled.

The necessity for a declaration from the Commission, in the event of Article 81(1) **7.06** being applicable, is central to an understanding of the way in which vertical restraints have been assessed under the provisions of Article 81 over the past thirty years. The Commission's monopoly[7] over the granting of exemptions under Article 81(3), to the exclusion of courts of law and national competition authorities, has had a profound impact on the interpretation of Article 81. It has enabled the Commission to interpret Article 81(1) very broadly and to apply a regulatory

---

[5] For an analysis of the economic importance of intra-brand competition see Steiner, 'How manufacturers deal with the price-cutting retailer: when are vertical restraints efficient?' (1997) 65 Antitrust Law Journal 407.

[6] Joined Cases 56/64 and 58/64 *Consten and Grundig v Commission* [1966] ECR 299, 342.

[7] Article 9.1 of Council Regulation (EEC) 17/62 of 6 March 1962, First Regulation Implementing Articles 81 and 82 of the Treaty [1962] OJ 13/204 ([1959–62] Spec Edn 87), states that 'Subject to review of its decisions by the Court of Justice, the Commission shall have sole power to declare Article 85(1) [now Article 81(1)] inapplicable pursuant to Article 85(3) of the Treaty.'

approach to Article 81(3). However, it has also resulted in a mass of notifications to the Commission seeking the application of Article 81(3).

(3) History of the Application of Article 81 to Vertical Restraints

7.07 The unique character of EC competition policy towards vertical restrictions can in good part be explained by its double goal. EC competition policy not only aims to ensure undistorted competition but also market integration. This latter aim has led to a two-way tug on policy makers. On the one hand vertical restraints, including territorial exclusivity, were recognized as necessary for both producers and distributors to grasp the opportunities of the common market. The penetration of new markets takes time and investment and is risky. The process is often facilitated by agreements between the producer who wants to break into a new market and a local distributor.

7.08 On the other hand territorial exclusivity in particular was considered as contrary to the fundamental aim of the creation of a real internal/single market. Arrangements between producers and distributors can be used to continue the partitioning of markets or exclude new entrants who would intensify competition and bring about downward pressure on prices. Therefore, agreements between producers and distributors (vertical restraints) can be used pro-competitively to promote market integration and efficient distribution or anti-competitively to block integration and competition.

7.09 The Community's response to the two-way tug in vertical restraints may be summarized as twofold. Firstly, the Commission adopted a wide interpretation of the application of Article 81(1) coupled with a regulatory approach of block exemptions laying down the types of agreements and detailed clauses that would be permitted or not permitted.

7.10 This approach is reflected in the *First Report on Competition Policy 1971*, where it is stated that:

> During the first stage in the application of the rules on competition set out in the EEC Treaty, the problem of exclusive dealing[8] agreements was in the foreground of the Commission's competition policy . . . The attention given to the exclusive dealing agreements was fundamentally due to the fact that such agreements are particularly likely to create obstacles with regard to the integration of national markets into a single market, to the extent that they guarantee to the holder of the concession not only the exclusive right to obtain supplies direct from the manufacturer but also to be the only distributor allowed to introduce the relevant products into the territory allocated to him.[9]

---

[8] The term 'exclusive dealing' is no longer used by the Commission. It was used primarily to describe what is now more commonly referred to as exclusive distribution; however, it was also used to describe exclusive purchasing. See in particular the 8th preamble of Commission Regulation (EEC) 67/67 of 22 March 1967 [1967] OJ 57/849.

[9] *First Report on Competition Policy 1971* point 45.

Theory of Active/Passive Sales

To counteract absolute territorial protection arising from territorial exclusivity, **7.11**
the Commission developed the theory of active/passive[10] sales and parallel trade.
While distributors and producers may be allowed to agree not to sell actively outside their allotted territory, the possibility for passive (ie unsolicited) sales outside
the exclusive territory and parallel trade must never be excluded. This mechanism
was seen as a safety or pressure valve. It was believed that if price differences
between Member States became excessive, then parallel traders would start to
exploit the possibilities of arbitrage. The possibility of passive sales was also seen
as necessary to protect what was seen as the fundamental right of consumers or
their agents to purchase wherever they wanted. This right is a symbol of the internal market. Such was the strength of feeling with respect to the right to make parallel trade and passive sales, that any attempt in a distribution system to frustrate
these rights was almost treated as a *per se* infringement of Article 81.

This approach of the Commission was first given concrete expression in its deci- **7.12**
sion in the *Grundig & Consten* case,[11] which was confirmed in its essential points
by the judgment of the Court of Justice.[12] Both the decision and judgment
showed that the exclusive distribution agreement concluded between the German
manufacturer and his distributor for the sale of those products in France fell
within the scope of Article 81(1) and did not qualify for exemption under Article
81(3) because the concession of exclusivity was combined with absolute territorial protection.[13]

---

[10] Article 2.2(c) of Commission Regulation (EEC) 1983/83 of 22 June 1983 on the application
of Article 81(1) of the Treaty to categories of exclusive distribution agreements [1983] OJ L173/1,
exempts, *inter alia*, the imposition on the exclusive distributor of 'the obligation to refrain, outside
the contract territory and in relation to the contract goods, from seeking customers, from establishing any branch and from maintaining any distribution depot'. This obligation is commonly referred
to as a prohibition on active sales. The imposition of such a prohibition on active sales outside the
appointed territory does not restrict the freedom of the exclusive distributor to respond to unsolicited orders received from parties outside his appointed territory, commonly referred to as passive
sales.

[11] [1964] OJ 2545/64.

[12] Joined Cases 56/64 and 58/64 *Consten and Grundig v Commission* [1966] ECR 299, 342.

[13] Absolute territorial protection occurs where a dealer faces no intra-brand competition within
his territory. Such competition could arise from passive sales by other network dealers, or imports
by parallel traders/consumers. The concept of absolute territorial protection as used by the Court
appears to be somewhat wider than the use of the word 'absolute' might suggest. In *Consten and
Grundig* the Court used this term to refer to the 'wish to eliminate any possibility of competition at
the wholesale level in Grundig products in the territory specified'(343). Therefore, it would appear
that the absence of arbitrage at the wholesale level is sufficient to establish absolute territorial protection despite the possibility for arbitrage by consumers. An example of the narrow definition of
absolute territorial protection, where even arbitrage by consumers was impossible, is to be found in
the *BMW leasing* case (see n 92 below). In any event the dividing line between absolute territorial
protection and an intra-Community export ban is not so important given that under current case

System of Block Exemption Regulations

7.13 The Commission's approach to vertical restraints together with the notification system provided for in Council Regulation 17/62[14] gave rise to a 'mass' problem with almost 30,000 notifications concerning vertical agreements.[15]

7.14 Under the complex procedures laid down in Regulation 17 the Commission is unable to adopt many formal decisions (currently no more than around twenty a year). The possibility of closing cases informally is also limited. Therefore an approach of 'block exemptions' was adopted.

7.15 Under Council Regulation 19/65,[16] the Commission is empowered to adopt block exemption regulations which define certain categories of agreements which generally fulfil the conditions of exemption under Article 81(3). Council Regulation 19/65 requires that Commission block exemption regulations define the types of agreements covered and specify the restrictive clauses which must not be included. In addition, Council Regulation 19/65 required, until its amendment in June 1999, that the block exemption specify the clauses which must be present, or other conditions which must be satisfied. It was restricted to vertical restraints relating to exclusive distribution of goods for resale, exclusive purchase of goods for resale, obligations in respect of exclusive supply and exclusive purchase for resale, and restrictions imposed in relation to the assignment or use of industrial property rights. It was also limited to agreements entered into between two parties. It did not empower the Commission to adopt block exemption regulations relating to the distribution of goods which are not for resale or the distribution of services. The amendments effected to Council Regulation 19/65 in June 1999 are described in Section H of this chapter.

7.16 The Commission block exemption Regulations in the field of distribution, which were adopted pursuant to Council Regulation 19/65 prior to its amend-

---

law they both constitute restrictions by object. In April 1998 the Court of Justice reaffirmed in para 14 of the *Javico* case (see n 31 below) that 'an agreement which requires a reseller not to resell contractual products outside the contractual territory has as its object the exclusion of parallel imports within the Community and consequently restriction of competition in the common market. . . . Such provisions, in contracts for the distribution of products within the Community, therefore constitute by their very nature a restriction of competition.'

[14] This Regulation not only gave the Commission its exclusive competence to grant exemptions under Article 81(3) but also set up a system of notification to the Commission for agreements for which an exemption or negative clearance is sought.

[15] *First Report on Competition Policy 1971* point 48.

[16] Council Regulation (EEC) 19/65 of March 1965 [1965] OJ 36/533.

ment in 1999, relate to exclusive distribution,[17] exclusive purchasing,[18] franchising,[19] and motor vehicle distribution.[20]

Where an exclusive distribution, purchasing, or franchising agreement conforms **7.17** to the relevant block exemption, no notification to the Commission is necessary for the granting of a declaration pursuant to Article 81(3), such declaration emanates automatically from the block exemption Regulation itself. This has considerably reduced the administrative burden on the Commission services and provided legal certainty to the companies that can clearly fit their agreements within the terms of a block exemption Regulation.

No block exemption regulation has been adopted for selective distribution, where **7.18** distributors are chosen on the basis of criteria necessary for the efficient distribution of the goods in question. Selected distributors normally provide some pre- or after-sales services and may only sell to final consumers or other approved dealers. Because it was found difficult to define in advance which categories of goods would justify a selective distribution system, Commission policy has been set out in individual decisions. In the future policy on vertical restraints described in Section H of this chapter selective distribution will be covered by a wide and flexible block exemption covering all vertical restraints up to the level of a single market share threshold. The future block exemption is unlikely to retain the nature of the product criteria as a condition for coverage by the block exemption, but this criteria will be relevant for withdrawal. It will also remain relevant above the threshold of the future block exemption.

(4) When is a Vertical Restraint Likely to Fall within the Scope of Article 81(1)?

General

Article 81(1) prohibits 'all agreements between undertakings, decisions by associ- **7.19** ations of undertakings and concerted practices which may affect trade between Member States and which have as their object or effect the prevention, restriction or distortion of competition within the common market'. A vertical restraint will only fall within the scope of Article 81(1) where all of these criteria are fulfilled. While in Article 81(1) the criteria of effect on trade between Member States

---

[17] Commission Regulation (EEC) 1983/83 of 22 June 1983 on the application of Article 85(3) [now Article 81(3)] of the Treaty to categories of exclusive distribution agreements [1983] OJ L173/1.

[18] Commission Regulation (EEC) 1984/83 of 22 June 1983 on the application of Article 85(3) [now Article 81(3)] of the Treaty to categories of exclusive purchasing agreements [1983] OJ L173/5.

[19] Commission Regulation (EEC) 4087/88 of 30 November 1988 on the application of Article 85(3) [now Article 81(3)] of the Treaty to categories of franchise agreements [1988] OJ L359/46.

[20] Commission Regulation (EC) 1475/95 of 28 June 1995 on the application of Article 85(3) [now Article 81(3)] of the Treaty to certain categories of motor vehicle distribution and servicing agreements [1995] OJ L145/25.

appears before that of restriction of competition, it is common practice both in the decisions of the Commission and judgments of the Community Courts to examine the issue of restriction of competition prior to that of effect on trade.

Agreement between Undertakings

7.20 This concept is dealt with in greater detail in paragraphs 2.27–2.41 of this book. In summary Article 81 does not apply to unilateral acts or to agreements between traders which do not constitute separate undertakings.

7.21 In vertical cases the distinction between the concept of agreement and unilateral act is not always so clear-cut. The Commission may well find that what appear at first glance to constitute unilateral actions if looked at in isolation are in fact agreements or concerted practices because they form part of wider business relations. For example, in Joined Cases 25/84 and 26/84 *Ford v Commission*,[21] the Court held that the refusal by a motor vehicle manufacturer to supply its authorized dealers in Germany with right-hand-drive vehicles did not constitute a unilateral act which fell outside the scope of Article 81(1) but was an agreement within the meaning of that provision if it formed part of a set of continuous business relations governed by a general agreement drawn up in advance. Commenting on the *Tretorn* case in 1994,[22] the Commission stated that 'the general ban on exports and the barriers which Tretorn placed in the way of parallel imports were not just the result of unilateral action by Tretorn, but formed an integral part, though not committed to paper, of Tretorn's distribution or sales agreements, or were at any rate the result of a concerted practice on the part of Tretorn and its distributors'. The Commission's decision[23] in the *Tretorn* case was upheld on appeal to the Court of First Instance[24] which agreed with the Commission's finding that the Dutch distributor 'had participated in the reporting and investigating of parallel imports of Tretorn tennis balls in order to enforce Tretorn's policy'[25] of protecting its distributors from parallel imports.

7.22 The issue of separate undertakings arose in the *Viho* case.[26] This case concerned the dismissal by the Commission of a complaint lodged with it concerning the distribution by Parker pen and its subsidiaries of its products throughout the European Union. The Court stated as follows at paragraphs 16–18 of its judgment:

> 16 Parker and its subsidiaries thus form a single economic unit within which the subsidiaries do not enjoy real autonomy in determining their course of action in the

---

[21] [1985] ECR 2725, para 21.
[22] *Report on Competition Policy 1994* (Vol XXIV) 360.
[23] *Tretorn* [1994] OJ L378/45.
[24] Case T–49/95 *Van Megen Sports Group BV v Commission* [1996] ECR II–1799.
[25] para 52 of the judgment in Case T–49/95.
[26] Case C–73/95 [1996] ECR I–5457.

market, but carry out the instructions issued to them by the parent company controlling them . . .

17 In those circumstances, the fact that Parker' s policy of referral, which consists essentially in dividing various national markets between its subsidiaries, might produce effects outside the ambit of the Parker group which are capable of affecting the competitive position of third parties cannot make Article 85(1)[now Article 81(1)] applicable, even when it is read in conjunction with Article 2 and Article 3(c) and (g) of the Treaty. On the other hand, such unilateral conduct could fall under Article 86 [now Article 82] of the Treaty if the conditions for its application, as laid down in that article, were fulfilled.

18 The Court of First Instance was therefore fully entitled to base its decision solely on the existence of a single economic unit in order to rule out the application of Article 85(1) to the Parker group.

7.23 Finally, while 'intra-group' distribution agreements normally fall outside of the scope of Article 81 because of the absence of an agreement between undertakings, they may, as stated by the Court in *Viho*, fall within the scope of Article 82 where the undertaking concerned is in a dominant position.[27]

Object or Effect of Restricting Competition and Appreciability

7.24 For an agreement or concerted practice to be caught by Article 81(1) it must also have either the object or effect of restricting competition. These are alternative and not cumulative requirements.[28] In assessing the compatibility of a distribution system with Article 81 it is essential to identify whether there are any restrictions by object. This is because restrictions by object can be held to infringe Article 81 without the requirement for a detailed economic analysis required to establish a restriction by effect. Therefore, even undertakings with relatively small market shares have been found to infringe Article 81, when restrictions by object are involved.[29]

7.25 Vertical restraints with the object of resale price maintenance, absolute territorial protection, or exclusion of parallel imports/exports[30] constitute, by their very nature, restrictions of competition and will fall within the prohibition of Article 81(1) unless the effects on competition and trade between Member States are insignificant. The concepts of restriction by object and restriction by nature are

---

[27] In the settlement in the *Interbrew* case reported in the *Report on Competition Policy 1996* (Vol XXVI), the Commission states, *inter alia*, 'DG IV's intervention in this case confirms its policy of prohibiting any barrier to parallel trade resulting either from an agreement between undertakings or from an abuse of a dominant position.'

[28] Case 56/65 *Societe Technique Miniere v Maschinenbau Ulm GmbH* [1966] ECR 235, 249.

[29] Case 19/77 *Miller International Schallplatten GmbH v Commission* [1978] ECR 131. This case is summarized in para 7.50 of this chapter.

[30] The distinction between absolute territorial protection and exclusion of parallel imports is not clear-cut. See n 13 above.

synonomous.[31] The jurisprudence does not support the assertion that all impediments to parallel trade constitute restrictions by object. For example a purely qualitative selective distribution system will normally not fall within the scope of Article 81(1) even though the inherent nature of a selective distribution system is that parallel trade by non-network dealers is excluded. Common distribution formats such as exclusive distribution, exclusive purchasing, and selective distribution have never been held by the Community Courts to constitute restrictions by object unless implemented with the objective of achieving absolute territorial protection, exclusion of parallel trade, or resale price maintenance. While there is no definitive list of those vertical restraints which constitute restrictions by object, providing these three latter elements are absent from the distribution system, the vertical restraints will, in all likelihood, be assessed as restrictions by effect and not restrictions by object.[32]

7.26 While Article 81(1) does not contain the word 'appreciable', it is clear from the jurisprudence of the Court and administrative practice of the Commission that a restriction of competition will not fall within the scope of Article 81(1) unless it has an appreciable impact on competition in the relevant market. The concepts of 'object', 'effect', and 'appreciability' are further discussed below.

Restriction by Object and Appreciability

7.27 The concept of restriction by object is also dealt with in paragraphs 2.61–2.70 of this book. This section concentrates on the vertical aspects of these restrictions. According to the Commission no effect on the market is required for Article 81(1) to apply, if the restriction is already the object of the arrangement.[33] This statement requires clarification in three respects.

7.28 **Subjective Intent.** Firstly, the existence of a restriction by object is not dependent on the subjective intent of the parties to the restriction. While subjective intent is relevant, the determination as to whether an agreement has as its purpose a restriction of competition is dependent on 'its terms, the legal and economic context in which it was concluded and the conduct of the parties'.[34] The vast majority of distribution systems have as their purpose the competitive distribution of goods and services and not the restriction of competition or restoration of

---

[31] See paras 14, 20, & 21 of the judgment of the Court of Justice in Case C–306/96 *Javico International and Javico AG v Yves Saint Laurent Parfums SA* [1998] ECR I–1983.

[32] See cases summarized in para 7.48–7.89 of this chapter.

[33] *Report on Competition Policy 1994* (Vol XXIV) point 145. This statement finds support in the case law of the Court. In *Consten and Grundig* cited above the Court of Justice states at 342 of its judgment that 'for the purposes of applying Article 85(1) [now Article 81(1)], there is no need to take account of the concrete effects of an agreement once it appears that it has as its object the prevention, restriction or distortion of competition'.

[34] Joined Cases 96–102, 104, 105, 108 & 110/82 *NV IAZ International Belgium and others v The Commission* [1983] ECR 3369, paras 23–25.

national divisions in trade between Member States.[35] Of the wide range of vertical restraints available to distributors very few have been held by the European Courts to constitute restrictions by object. For example, in *Delimitis* the Court was of the opinion that a beer supply agreement involving both an exclusive purchase and non-compete obligation did not constitute a restriction by object and that it was necessary to analyse its effects.[36] In *Javico*,[37] the Court stated that 'an agreement in which the reseller gives to the producer an undertaking that he will sell the contractual products on a market outside of the Community cannot be regarded as having the object of appreciably restricting competition within the common market'.

Restriction by nature. Secondly, restrictions by object are restrictions which by   **7.29**
their very nature constitute a restriction of competition. In the absence of horizontal elements,[38] vertical restraints have only been held to constitute restrictions by object where they are used to impede parallel trade within the Community or enforce resale price maintenance. In *Consten and Grundig* the Court was of the opinion that 'the agreement thus aims at isolating the French market for Grundig products'.[39] In *Miller*,[40] the Court held that 'by its very nature, a clause prohibiting exports constitutes a restriction on competition'. In *Binon*,[41] a case which involved the selective distribution of newspapers, the Court stated that 'provisions which fix the prices to be observed in contracts with third parties constitute, of themselves, a restriction on competition within the meaning of Article 85(1) [now Article 81(1)]'.

This policy is reflected in paragraph 276 of the Green Paper on Vertical Restraints,   **7.30**
where it is stated that:

> The policy of treating *resale price maintenance* and *impediments to parallel trade* as serious violations of the competition rules would continue. It is proposed that they be treated as per se contrary to Article 85(1) [now Article 81(1)], as long as the

---

[35] '[A]n agreement between producer and distributor which might tend to restore the national divisions in trade between Member States might be such as to frustrate the most fundamental objections [objectives] of the Community. The Treaty, whose preamble and content aim at abolishing the barriers between states, and which in several provisions gives evidence of a stern attitude with regard to their reappearance, could not allow undertakings to reconstruct such barriers. Article 85(1) [now Article 81(1)] is designed to pursue this aim, even in the case of agreements between undertakings placed at different levels in the economic process.' (Joined Cases 56/64 and 58/64 *Consten and Grundig v Commission* [1966] ECR 299, 340.)

[36] Case C–234/89 *Stergios Delimitis v Henniger Brau AG* [1989] ECR 935, 984, para 13.

[37] Case C–306/96 *Javico International and Javico AG v Yves Saint Laurent Parfums SA* [1998] ECR I–1983.

[38] It is important to recognize that vertical distribution arrangements may also have horizontal aspects which contain restrictions by object, particularily where there is territorial or customer allocation as between the parties to the vertical restraint—see *BP Kemi—DDSF* [1979] OJ L286/32.

[39] See n 12.

[40] Case 19/77 *Miller International Schallplatten v Commission* [1978] ECR 131.

[41] Case 234/83 *SA Binon & Cie v SA Agence et messageries de la presse* [1985] ECR 2015, para 44.

agreement, concerted practice or decision concerned may affect trade between Member States. They are also unlikely to benefit from an exemption under Article 85(3).

7.31 **Agreements of minor importance.** The third clarification relates to *agreements of minor importance.* The *Volk v Vervaeke* case,[42] which concerned absolute territorial protection, established the principle that even in relation to restrictions by object it remains necessary to analyse the actual or potential effect of the vertical restraint involved so as to rule out the possibility that it may only have an insignificant effect on the market.[43]

7.32 It is not possible to give a precise quantitative definition of 'insignificant effect'. While the Court did not say that distribution arrangements for Volk's products in Belgium had an insignificant effect on the market, because the case arose from an Article 234 reference, this is the clear inference of the judgment. In its submission to the Court the Commission stated that the production of washing machines by Mr Volk's company represented 0.08 per cent of the total production of the common market and 0.2 per cent of production in the Federal Republic of Germany. Its market share of sales in Belgium and Luxembourg, the territory of its exclusive distributor Vervaeke, was approximately 0.6 per cent. On the basis of these small market shares the Commission 'admitted that even when an agreement guaranteeing strict "territorial protection" is concluded, the manufacturer does not appreciably restrict competition'. Neither did the Commission believe that the criteria 'may affect trade between Member States' was fulfilled.

7.33 In the *Miller* case,[44] which concerned a territorial restriction by object, the Court found that the company concerned, which had a market share of the German market in sound recordings which varied between 5 and 6 per cent could not be

---

[42] Case 5/69 *Volk v Vervaeke*, [1969] ECR 295, 302, paras 5–7, where the Court stated: 'If an agreement is to be capable of affecting trade between Member States it must be possible to foresee with a sufficient degree of probability on the basis of a set of objective factors of law or of fact that the agreement in question may have an influence, direct or indirect, actual or potential, on the pattern of trade between Member States. Moreover, the prohibition in Article 85(1) [now Article 81(1)] is applicable only if the agreement in question also has as its object or effect the prevention, restriction or distortion of competition within the Common Market. These conditions must be understood by reference to the actual circumstances of the agreement. Consequently an agreement falls outside the prohibition of Article 85 when it has only an insignificant effect on the markets, taking into account the weak position which the persons concerned have on the market of the product in question. Thus an exclusive dealing agreement, even with absolute territorial protection, may, having regard to the weak position of the persons concerned on the market in the products in question in the area covered by the absolute protection, escape the prohibition laid down in Article 85(1).'

[43] The 'insignificant effect' doctrine of *Volk v Vervaeke* applies to both the restriction of competition and effect on trade criteria—see n 42 above. However, as will become apparent from the case law analysed below, the real litmus test for restrictions by object appears not to be one of appreciability of the restriction but rather whether it is capable of having an appreciable affect on trade between Member States.

[44] Case 19/77 *Miller International Schallplatten GmbH v Commission* [1978] ECR 131.

compared with the undertakings in the *Volk* case and that the probibition of Article 81(1) was infringed. While market share is not the only criteria for assessing the impact of a vertical restraint, it can be stated as a general rule for restrictions by object that below 1 per cent market share the effect on the market is likely to be insignificant and Article 81(1) is unlikely to apply, while above 5 per cent the effect is likely to be appreciable and Article 81(1) is likely to apply. Between 1 per cent and 5 per cent is best described as a grey area. Unlike earlier *de minimis* Notices, the current Notice of the Commission offers no comfort to undertakings in this grey area.[45] Therefore, even companies with little market power who enter into restrictions by object run the risk of infringing Article 81(1).

While restrictions by object are subject to the appreciability doctrine, it will be seen from the cases summarized in paras 7.48–7.89 below that the doctrine does not appear to have been consistently applied to both the restriction of competition and affect on trade. In many cases the appreciability of the restriction appears to be assumed (ie restriction by nature), with the analysis of appreciability concentrating upon affect on trade between Member States.   **7.34**

Restriction by Effect and Appreciability

In *Technique Miniere*,[46] the Court, states that where the analysis of the clauses of an agreement, in the economic context in which it is to be applied, does not reveal the effect on competition to be sufficiently deleterious as to constitute a restriction by object: **7.35**

> the consequences of the agreement should then be considered and for it to be caught by the prohibition it is then necessary to find that those factors are present which show that competition has in fact been prevented or restricted or distorted to an appreciable extent.

> The competition in question must be understood within the actual context in which it would occur in the absence of the agreement in dispute. In particular it may be doubted whether there is an interference with competition if the said agreement seems really necessary for the penetration of a new area by an undertaking.

In the 1971 *Beguelin case*, concerning the legality of an exclusive distribution agreement, the Court ruled that the effect on competition must be appreciable: 'in order to come within the prohibition imposed by Article 85 [now Article 81], the agreement must affect trade between Member States and the free play of   **7.36**

---

[45] The current 1997 Notice states that the applicability of Article 81(1) cannot be ruled out below the *de minimis* threshold, defined solely in terms of market share, 'for vertical agreements which have as their object—to fix resale prices, or—to confer territorial protection on the participating undertakings or third parties'. The earlier 1986 Notice, which defined a *de minimis* threshold in terms of both market share (ie 5%) and turnover (ie ECU 200 million, increased to 300 million in 1994), applied to both restrictions by object and effect.

[46] See n 28 above.

competition to an appreciable extent'.[47] The Court also gave some guidance on the elements to be examined when applying the criteria of appreciability:

> 17. In order to examine whether this is the case, these factors must be considered in the light of the situation which would have existed but for the agreement in question.

> 18. It follows that, in order to determine whether a contract which contains a clause conferring an exclusive right of sale is caught by that Article, account must be taken in particular of the nature and quantity, restricted or otherwise, of the products covered by the agreement; the standing of the grantor and of the grantee of the concession on the market in the products concerned; whether the agreement stands alone or is one of a series of agreements; the stringency of the clauses designed to protect the exclusive right or on the other hand, the extent to which any openings are left for other dealings in the products concerned in the form of re-exports or parallel imports.[48]

7.37 The Court of Justice has further narrowed the scope of application of Article 81(1) to vertical restraints which are not restrictions by object, by applying the concept of necessity (the 'ancillary restraints doctrine'). This approach of the Court is partly reflected in its judgment in *Pronuptia*,[49] where it ruled, *inter alia*, that 'provisions which are strictly necessary in order to ensure that the know-how and assistance provided by the franchisor do not benefit competitors do not constitute restrictions of competition for the purposes of Article 85(1) [now Article 81(1)]'.[50] The Court stated that this would cover 'a clause prohibiting the franchisee, during the period of validity of the contract and for a reasonable period after its expiry, from opening a shop of the same or a similar nature in an area where he may compete with a member of the network'.[51]

7.38 Nevertheless, extreme caution must be taken in applying an entirely effects based approach where the distribution system affords territorial protection. In the *Pronuptia* case the Court, basing itself on its judgment in *Consten and Grundig*, was of the opinion that franchise agreements typically result:

> in a sharing of markets between the franchisor and the franchisees or between franchisees and thus restricts competition within the network . . . a restriction of that kind constitutes a limitation of competition for the purposes of Article 85(1) [now Article 81(1)] if it concerns a business name or symbol which is already well–known. It is of course possible that a prospective franchisee would not take the risk of becoming part of the chain, investing his own money, paying a relatively high entry fee and undertaking to pay a substantial annual royalty, unless he could hope, thanks to a degree of protection against competition on the part of the franchisor

---

[47] See the judgment of the Court of Justice of 25 November 1971 in Case 22/71 *Beguelin* [1971] ECR 960, para 16.

[48] Case 22/71 at paras 17 and 18.

[49] Case 161/84 *Pronuptia de Paris v Pronuptia de Paris Irmgard Schillgalis* [1996] ECR 374.

[50] Case 161/84, 388.

[51] Case 161/84, para 16.

and other franchisees, that his business would be profitable. That consideration, however, is relevant only to an examination of the agreement in the light of the conditions laid down in Article 85(3).[52]

Finally, in its judgment in *Case T–374/94 European Night Services [ENS] & Others*   **7.39**
v The Commission,[53] the Court of First Instance has further reduced the scope of application of Article 81(1), leaving the door open for a balancing of positive and negative effects under Article 81(1). This judgment which is essential reading for those wishing to understand the scope of Article 81, is discussed in some detail in paragraphs 2.97–2.98 of this book.

This approach of the Court contrasts with that of the Commission which has   **7.40**
been to apply Article 81(1) relatively widely to vertical restraints and exempt them from Article 81(1).[54] For example Regulation 1983/83 on exclusive distribution gives almost no legal justification as to why exclusive distribution agreements fall within the scope of Article 81(1) but justifies their exemption on the grounds, *inter alia*, that they are 'often the most effective way and sometimes the only way, for the manufacturer to enter a market and compete with other manufacturers already present'. Providing an exclusive distribution agreement does not impede parallel trade within the Community or enforce resale price maintenance, it is clearly arguable, under the jurisprudence of the Community Courts that such agreements do not fall under Article 81(1) in the first place.[55]

May Affect Trade between Member States and Appreciability

This concept is dealt with in chapter 2, paragraphs 2.100–2.114.   **7.41**

De Minimis Notices of the Commission

The concept of *de minimis* is also dealt with in paragraphs 2.66–2.86 of this book.   **7.42**
This section concentrates on the vertical aspects of this concept. It is important to stress that the *de minimis* notices are only binding on the Commission,[56] however they can be of persuasive influence before national courts.[57]

---

[52] Case 161/84, para 24.
[53] [1998] ECR II 3141.
[54] See paragraphs 7.07 *et seq* above.
[55] In addition to *Pronuptia*, cited above, see also Case 258/78 *Nungesser* [1982] ECR 2015, para 58: 'Having regard to the specific nature of the products in question, the Court concludes that, in a case such as the present, the grant of an open exclusive licence, that is to say a licence which does not affect the position of third parties such as parallel importers and licensees for other territories, is not in itself incompatible with Article 85(1) [now Article 81(1)] of the Treaty'.
[56] para 7 of 1997 Notice.
[57] See judgment of the UK Court of Appeal of 22 July 1998 in *Gibbs Mew plc v Graham Gemmell*, where the national court gave considerable weight to the Commission's definition of *de minimis* in the beer sector (as set out in the Commission's Notice concerning Regulations (EEC) 1983/83 and 1984/83 [1984] OJ C101/2) in rejecting the application of Article 81(1) to certain beer tie (ie exclusive purchase and non-compete) agreements.

7.43 The 1997 Notice[58] represents a complete revision of three earlier Notices which had been broadly similar in content and format. Subject to the exceptions described below, it establishes the principle that vertical agreements between undertakings whose market share on the relevant market does not exceed 10 per cent, do not fall under the prohibition of Article 81(1). It is extremely important not only in terms of how it defines *de minimis* but also because it gives important insights into the current thinking of the Commission's services as to when vertical restraints fall under Article 81(1).[59] This notice clearly confirms the application of the condition of 'appreciability' to both restrictions of competition and affect on trade between Member States, irrespective of whether a restriction by object or effect is involved. In this context it is interesting to note that the legal assessments of the Commission in the 1992 *Parker Pen* case[60] and 1994 *Tretorn* case,[61] both involving an export ban, a restriction by object, contain no analysis of the condition of appreciability in relation to the restriction on competition although it is referred to in relation to effect on trade. On the other hand, the Commission's 1998 decision in the *VW-Audi* case,[62] which found both restrictions by object and effect, analysed both the restriction on competition and effect on trade in terms of their appreciability.[63] Neither has it been clear from the jurisprudence of the Community Courts that the concept of 'appreciability' applied to both of these conditions.[64] Nevertheless, for the purposes of the latest *de minimis* Notice the Commission has interpreted the jurisprudence of the Court of Justice as having 'clarified that this provision [ie Article 81(1)] is not applicable where the impact of the agreement on intra-community trade or on competition is not appreciable'.[65] While the interpretation of the Commission is helpful, it should, as regards restrictions by object, be treated with some caution.[66]

---

[58] [1997] OJ C372/13.

[59] Section I(2) of the Notice reads as follows: 'Article 85 (1) [now Article 81(1)] prohibits agreements which may affect trade between Member States and which have as their object or effect the prevention, restriction or distortion of competition within the common market. The Court of Justice of the European Communities has clarified that this provision is not applicable where the impact of the agreement on intra-Community trade or on competition is not appreciable. Agreements which are not capable of significantly affecting trade between Member States are not caught by Article 85. They should therefore be examined on the basis, and within the framework, of national legislation alone. This is also the case for agreements whose actual or potential effect remains limited to the territory of only one Member State or of one or more third countries. Likewise, agreements which do not have as their object or their effect an appreciable restriction of competition are not caught by the prohibition contained in Article 85 (1).'

[60] *Viho/Parker Pen* [1992] OJ L233/27.

[61] *Tretorn and others* [1994] OJ L378/45.

[62] *VW-Audi* [1998] OJ L124/60, on appeal.

[63] *VW-Audi* [1998] OJ L124/60, paras 149 and 150, on appeal.

[64] See paras 37–41 of the Opinion of Advocate General Mischo in Case 27/87 *SPRL Louis Erauw-Jacquery v La Hesbignonne SC* [1988] ECR 1919.

[65] para 2 of the 1997 *de minimis* Notice [1997] OJ C372/13.

[66] See conclusion in para 7.92 below.

Both the 1986 and 1997 Notices state that agreements which fall outside the **7.44**
Notice do not necessarily fall within the scope of Article 81(1).[67] Surprisingly,
these statements have not prevented the Commission from arguing that Article
81(1) applied by virtue of the mere fact that the thresholds were exceeded.[68] The
Community Courts have rejected such argument pointing out that the mere fact
that the thresholds are exceeded does not make it possible to conclude with certainty that an agreement is caught by Article 81(1).[69]

Paragraph 11 defines certain vertical restraints which cannot benefit from the **7.45**
Notice. These are vertical restraints having as their object the fixing of resale prices
or the conferring of territorial protection. Unfortunately, the concept of 'territorial protection' is not defined in the Notice. It is hardly conceivable that all distribution arrangements involving an element of territorial protection would not be
covered by the Notice. If such was the case, then the appointment of an exclusive
distributor protected from active but not passive sales by other exclusive distributors within the same network, could not be covered by *de minimis*. What the
Commission appears to be attempting to do here is to define those vertical
restraints which, subject to the *Volk v Vervaeke* jurisprudence,[70] would be treated
as almost *per se* infringements of Article 81(1) and unlikely to qualify for individual exemption under Article 81(3). As regards vertical restraints, this finds clearer
expression in paragraph 276 of the Green Paper on Vertical Restraints where it is
stated that:

> The policy of treating *resale price maintenance* and *impediments to parallel trade* as
> serious violations of the competition rules would continue. It is proposed that they
> be treated as per se contrary to Article 85(1) [now Article 81(1)], as long as the agree-
> ment, concerted practice or decision concerned may affect trade between Member
> States. They are also unlikely to benefit from an exemption under Article 85(3).

---

[67] Section I(3) of the 1997 Notice states that: 'The quantitiative definition of appreciability,
however, serves only as a guideline: in individual cases even agreements between undertakings
which exceed the threshold set out below may still have only a negligible effect on trade between
Member States or on competition within the common market and are therefore not caught by
Article 85(1) [now Article 81(1)]. This notice does not contain an exhaustive description of restic-
tions which fall outside Article 85(1). It is generally recognized that even agreements which are not
of minor importance can escape the prohibition on agreements on account of their exclusively
favourable impact on competition.' The 1986 Notice, which had a lower market share threshold for
vertical restraints, contained a similar statement in its section I(3), namely: 'The quantative definition of "appreciable" given by the Commission is, however, not appreciable: in fact, in individual
cases even agreements between undertakings which exceed these limits may still have only a negligible effect on trade between Member States or on competition, and are therefore not caught by
Article 85(1) [now Article 81(1)].'
[68] Case T–7/93 *Langnese-Iglo Gmbh v Commission* [1995] ECR II–1533, para 97 and Case
T–374/94 *European Night Services & Others v Commission*, [1998] ECR II–314, para 102.
[69] Cases T–7/93 *Langnese-Iglo Gmbh v Commission* [1995] ECR II–1533, para 98 and Case
T–374/94 *European Night Services & Others v Commission*, unreported of 15 September 1998, para
102.
[70] Case 5/69 *Volk v Vervaeke*, [1969] ECR 295.

7.46   Therefore, it is submitted that paragraph 11 of the Notice should, in so far as it relates to vertical restraints, be interpreted in the light of paragraph 276 of the Green Paper.

7.47   Section III of the Notice states that 'agreements between small and medium-sized undertakings, as defined in the Annex to Commission recommendation 96/280/EC[71] are rarely capable of significantly affecting trade between Member States and competition within the common market. Consequently, as a general rule, they are not caught by the prohibition in Article 85 (1) [now Article 81(1)].' Nevertheless, the Commission reserves the right to intervene in respect of agreements between SMEs where there are significant impediments to competition or where competition is restricted by the cumulative effect of parallel networks. The SME provisions of the Notice are particularly important for the distribution sector which accounts for one third of all EU enterprises, 95 per cent of which contain fewer than ten employees.[72]

Analysis of Leading Cases on Vertical Restraints

7.48   In the following section we will try to provide readers with the clearest possible picture of what Community Courts have considered to amount to restriction by object or restriction by effect.

Restrictions by Object

7.49   *Consten and Grundig*[73]—**exclusive distribution combined with absolute territorial protection (1966).**   This case arose from proceedings in France taken by Consten, the exclusive distributor in France of Grundig electrical appliances, against a French parallel importer UNEF who had been sourcing Grundig appliances from German wholesalers and reselling them in France to retailers at prices below those of Consten. The national proceedings were stayed following UNEF's March 1962 application to the Commission for a declaration that the distribution arrangements between Consten and Grundig infringed Article 81 of the Treaty. In January 1963, Grundig notified, *inter alia*, its agreements with Consten. The

---

[71]   Article 1 of the Annex to Commission recommendation (EC) 96/280 [1996] OJ L107/8 states as follows: 'Small and medium-sized enterprises, hereinafter referred to as "SMEs", are defined as enterprises which:

— have fewer than 250 employees, and
— have either,

an annual turnover not exceeding ECU 40 million, or
an annual balance-sheet total not exceeding ECU 27 million,

— conform to the criterion of independence as defined in para 3.'

[72]   Green Paper on Commerce, 3.
[73]   Joined Cases 56/64 and 58/64 *Consten and Grundig v Commission* [1966] ECR 299.

decision of the Commission in the *Grundig and Consten* case,[74] which was confirmed in its essential points by the judgment of the Court of Justice,[75] showed that the exclusive distribution agreement fell within the scope of Article 81(1) and did not qualify for exemption under Article 81(3) because absolute territorial protection was combined with the concession of exclusivity. The Court clearly assessed the distribution arrangements as a restriction by object because of the absolute territorial protection granted to Consten.[76] Absolute territorial protection arose from Consten's agreement not to deliver directly or indirectly to the markets of other countries, the imposition by Grundig on its German wholesalers and distributors in other countries of the obligation to refrain from making deliveries from their contract territories to other contractual territories, and the exclusive assignment to Consten of certain trade mark rights for the duration of the distribution agreement.[77]

Miller[78]—**prohibition on exports (1978).** This case is an appeal against a **7.50** Commission decision in which it was found that the prohibitions on the exports of records, tapes, and cassettes inserted by Miller, a German producer of sound recordings, in an exclusive dealing agreement with a French distributor infringed Article 81(1) of the Treaty. What is interesting about this case is that Miller did not dispute the facts but maintained 'that they cannot have appreciably affected trade between Member States in view of the insignificance of the undertaking on the market in sound recordings, the nature of its products, which are chiefly intended for the German-speaking public, and the nature of its customers'. Between 1970 and 1975 the market share of Miller on the total German market in sound recordings varied between 5 and 6 per cent in terms of volume.

While Miller did not challenge the appreciability of the export ban as a restriction **7.51** of competition (it did claim that 'it did not correspond to a blameworthy objective') the Court of Justice held at paragraph 7 that:

> by its very nature, a clause prohibiting exports constitutes a restriction on competition, whether it is adopted at the instigation of the supplier or of the customer since the agreed purpose of the contracting parties is the endeavour to isolate a part of the market.

Miller supports the thesis that export prohibitions are restrictions by object which **7.52** constitute *per se* restrictions of competition within the meaning of Article 81(1) with no evidence being required as to the appreciability of the restriction.

---

[74] [1964] OJ 161.
[75] Joined Cases 56/64 and 58/64 *Consten and Grundig v Commission* [1966] ECR 299.
[76] Joined Cases 56/64 and 58/64 *Consten and Grundig v Commission* [1966] ECR 299, 342.
[77] Joined Cases 56/64 and 58/64 *Consten and Grundig v Commission* [1966] ECR 299, 343.
[78] Case 19/77 *Miller International Schallplatten GmbH v Commission* [1978] ECR 131.

7.53   With regard to effect on trade the Court concluded at paragraphs 10 to 15 that:

> Miller, far from being comparable to the undertakings concerned in the judgments of 30 June 1966 (*Technique Miniere v Maschinenbau Ulm*, case 56/65 (1965) ECR 235), of 9 July 1969 (*Volk v Vervaeke*, Case 5/69 (1969) ECR 295) and of 6 May 1971 (*Cadillon v Hoss*, Case 1/71 (1971) ECR 351), is an undertaking of sufficient importance for its behaviour to be, in principle, capable of affecting trade.

> . . . In prohibiting agreements which may affect trade between Member States and which have as their object or effect the restriction of competition Article 85 (1) [now Article 81(1)] of the Treaty does not require proof that such agreements have in fact appreciably affected such trade, which would moreover be difficult in the majority of cases to establish for legal purposes, but merely requires that it be established that such agreements are capable of having that effect.

> The Commission, basing its assessment on Miller's position on the market, its scale of production, ascertainable exports and price policy, has provided appropriate proof that in fact there was a danger that trade between Member States would be appreciably affected.

7.54   Therefore, where a restriction by object is involved, *Miller* is authority for the applicability of the appreciability test to potential effects on trade between Member States. However, as demonstrated by this case, the actual or potential effects do not have to be economically significant before the appreciability criteria are satisfied. It is likely that the Court was particularly influenced by the fact that Miller was trying to protect its home market 'against the re-importation of products exported at low prices'.

7.55   *Binon*[79]—**resale price maintenance (1985).**   This case, an Article 234 reference to the Court of Justice, concerned the distribution of newspapers in Belgium by way of a selective distribution system. SA Binon & Cie, an undertaking which carried on a business in Charleroi selling books, stationery, and educational toys, had brought a case before the national court against SA Agence et messageries de la presse (hereinafter referred to as AMP). The purpose of the action was to obtain an order directing AMP to cease refusing to sell or deliver to Binon the newspapers and periodicals, both Belgian and foreign, which it distributed in Belgium. AMP was responsible for the distribution to retailers of close to 70 per cent of Belgian newspapers and periodicals and virtually all newspapers and periodicals published abroad.

7.56   In relation to resale price maintenance the Court stated as follows :

> 44. It should be observed in the first place that provisions which fix the prices to be observed in contracts with third parties constitute, of themselves, a restriction on competition within the meaning of article 85(1) [now Article 81(1)]which refers to agreements which fix selling prices as an example of an agreement prohibited by the Treaty.

---

[79] Case 243/83 *SA Binon & Cie v SA Agence et messageries de la presse* [1985] ECR 201.

Therefore, it can be concluded that restrictions on resale prices are restrictions by **7.57** object and constitute a *per se* restriction of competition within the meaning of Article 81(1). However, they do not fall within the scope of Article 81(1) unless they may appreciably affect trade between Member States.

While the Court did not expressly apply the criteria of appreciability to the restric- **7.58** tions by object in this case, the criteria were probably fulfilled given the high market shares involved. Paragraph 46 of the judgment is important in that it provides for the possibility for exemption, albeit under very limited conditions:

> 46. If, in so far as the distribution of newspapers and periodicals is concerned, the fixing of the retail price by publishers constitutes the sole means of supporting the financial burden resulting from the taking back of unsold copies and if the latter practice constitutes the sole method by which a wide selection of newspapers and periodicals can be made available to readers, the Commission must take account of those factors when examining an agreement for the purposes of Article 85(3) [now Article 81(3)].

Following this reasoning, the Commission's statement at paragraph 276 of the **7.59** Green Paper on Vertical Restraints that resale price maintenance and impediments to parallel trade are 'unlikely to benefit from an exemption under Article 85(3) [now Article 81(3)]', appears to be going slightly further than the case law of the Community Courts permits. As the Court of First Instance has stated 'in principle, no anti-competitive practice can exist which, whatever the extent of its effects on a given market, cannot be exempted, provided, that all the conditions laid down in Article 85(3) [now Article 81(3)] of the Treaty are satisfied and the practice in question has been properly notified to the Commission'.[80] In other words, there is always the possibility for exemption even for so called *per se* infringements.

Erauw-Jacquery[81]**—export prohibition and minimum resale prices (1988).** **7.60** Like *Nungesser* this case concerns plant breeders' rights; however, unlike *Nungesser* it does not concern the exclusive assignment of those rights for a particular territory but rather the use of those rights by its holder to control the propagation and sale of seed by a third party grower. This case arose from proceedings before the Belgian courts between SPRL Louis Erauw-Jacquery (the breeder), the holder of plant breeders' rights, and La Hesbignonne SC (the grower), a co-operative authorized by it to propagate basic seed and to sell seed of the first or second generation produced from that basic seed and intended for cereal production. The licence agreement contained a provision prohibiting the sale and export of basic seed and a minimum resale price obligation. The grower did not abide by the minimum resale price communicated to it by the breeder. In the national proceedings

---

[80] Case T–17/93 *Matra Hachette SA v Commission* [1994] ECR II–595, para 85.
[81] Case 27/87 *SPRL Louis Erauw-Jacquery v La Hesbignonne SC* [1988] ECR 1919.

the breeder claimed that this had in turn obliged other growers to lower their prices, causing them to incur losses for which they claimed compensation. Therefore, the breeder was seeking to pass on those claims in the national proceedings. In response to an Article 234 reference the Court of Justice ruled:

> (1) A provision, of an agreement concerning the propagation and sale of seed, in respect of which one of the parties is the holder of certain plant breeders' rights, which prohibits the grower from selling and exporting the basic seed, is compatible with Article 85(1) [now Article 81(1)] of the treaty in so far as it is necessary in order to enable the breeder to select the growers who are to be licensees.

> (2) A provision in an agreement such as that described in paragraph 1, which obliges the grower to comply with minimum prices fixed by the other party falls within the prohibition set out in Article 85(1) only if it is found, having regard to the economic and legal context of the agreement containing the provision in question, that the agreement is capable of affecting trade between Member States to an appreciable degree.

7.61 In relation to the first ruling the Court refers at paragraph 10 of the judgment to its earlier judgment in the *Nungesser* case and describes the circumstances in which a sale and export probibition may fall outside of the scope of Article 81(1):

> the development of the basic lines may involve considerable financial commitment. Consequently, a person who has made considerable efforts to develop varieties of basic seed which may be the subject-matter of plant breeders' rights must be allowed to protect himself against any improper handling of those varieties of seed. To that end, the breeder must be entitled to restrict propagation to the growers which he has selected as licensees. To that extent, the provision prohibiting the licensee from selling and exporting basic seed falls outside the prohibition contained in Article 85 (1) [now Article 81(1)].

7.62 Advocate General Mischo gives a much clearer insight as to why the sale and export prohibition for basic seed does not fall within Article 81(1):

> 11. Basic seed is to a certain extent comparable to a manufacturing process protected by a patent, since certified seed of the first and second generation intended for sale to farmers for use in cereal production is produced from it. The breeder (or his agent) must therefore remain in a position to control the destination and the use of the basic seed; otherwise he would risk the de facto loss of the exclusive rights granted to him in respect of the new varieties which he has developed. The Commission is right to point out that the propagation agreement is an agreement where the identity of the other party is essential.

> 12. The situation of a breeder or his agent therefore resembles in certain respects the situation of a franchisor, in respect of whom the Court has stated that he 'must be able to communicate his know-how to the franchisees and provide them with the necessary assistance in order to enable them to apply his methods, without running the risk that know-how and assistance might benefit competitors, even indirectly. It follows that provisions which are essential in order to avoid that risk do not constitute restrictions on competition for the purposes of Article 85(1) [now Article 81(1)]' (judgment of 28 January 1986 in Case 161/84 *Pronuptia* (1986) ECR 353, paragraph 16).

In relation to the second ruling the Court states at paragraph 12 of the judgment **7.63** that the minimum resale price provision constitutes both a restriction by object and effect. The Court then proceeded to find that the agreement may affect trade between Member States but recalled that 'an agreement is subject to the prohibition contained in Article 85 [now Article 81] only if it appreciably affects trade between Member States'.[82] This case also supports the thesis that where a restriction by object is concerned the test of appreciability applies to the 'effect on trade' but not to the restriction. The Court gave the following guidance on assessing appreciability in this case:

> 18 In this respect it must be stressed that the impact of the contested agreement on intra-community trade depends, in particular, on whether it forms part of a cluster of similar agreements concluded between the breeder and other licensees, on the breeder's market share in respect of the seed concerned and on the ability of the producers bound by those agreements to export that seed.

> 19 It is for the national court to decide, on the basis of the relevant information at its disposal and taking into account the economic and legal context of the agreement of 26 February 1982, whether that agreement is capable of affecting trade between member states to an appreciable degree.

Advocate General Mischo, while of the opinion that the test of appreciability **7.64** should be applied to both the restriction of competition and effect on trade in this case, points out that in two earlier judgments involving resale price maintenance[83] the Court appears not to have used that criterion, and 'after having found that an agreement of the type in question in the main proceedings entailed a restriction on competition and was capable of affecting trade between Member States, immediately concluded that such an agreement was incompatible with Article 85(1) [now Article 81(1)] of the Treaty and prohibited by that article'. It is interesting to note that despite the observations of Advocate General Mischo on appreciability, the Court, in its judgment, appears only to have applied the criterion to effect on trade.

Parker Pen[84]—**export prohibition (1994).** This case arose from an appeal by **7.65** Parker Pen Ltd against a decision of the Commission[85] fining Parker Pen ECU

---

[82] See para 17 of the judgment.

[83] Case 311/85 *ASBL Vereniging van Vlaamse Reisbureaus v ASBL Sociale Dienst van de Plaatselijke and Gewestelijke Overheidsdiensten* [1987] ECR 3801 and Case 123/83 *BNIC v Clair* [1985] ECR 391, at 425. The latter case concerned an agreement which, *inter alia*, fixed the price of spirits used in the manufacture of cognac, that is to say an intermediate product which is not normally sent outside the Cognac region. The Court declared in that context that: 'any agreement whose object or effect is to restrict competition by fixing minimum prices for an intermediate product is capable of affecting intra-Community trade, even if there is no trade in that intermediate product between the Member States, where the product constitutes the raw material for another product marketed elsewhere in the Community'.

[84] Case T–77/92 *Parker Pen Ltd v Commission* [1994] ECR II–549.

[85] *Viho/Parker Pen* [1992] OJ L233/27.

700,000 for including an export ban in an agreement with a German distributor Herlitz. Parker did not deny the existence of the clause prohibiting exports, but claimed that it was not capable of affecting trade between Member States to an appreciable extent and also that the clause was not implemented. Relying on *Volk v Vervaeke*, and *Miller*, Parker Pen argued that an agreement which by its nature restricts competition falls outside the prohibition of Article 81(1) if it has only an insignificant effect on the markets. It further argued that the relevant geographic market was Community-wide and that the relevant market share was that of Herlitz in the Community. While the market shares have been deleted from the public version of the judgment it would appear that Herlitz's market share on the Community market was below that of 5 per cent, which was considered in the *Miller* case as being of sufficient importance for Miller's conduct to be, in principle, capable of affecting trade to an appreciable extent. Parker Pen also relied on the argument that the agreement's 'potential effect on intra-Community trade was practically nil because the wholesale prices charged by Parker were similar in the various Member States'.

7.66 In its appraisal, the Court of First Instance confirmed that a clause prohibiting exports constitutes a *per se* restriction of competition without any need to assess the appreciability of its actual or potential impact on competition:

> The Court of Justice has consistently held that 'by its very nature, a clause prohibiting exports constitutes a restriction on competition, whether it is adopted at the instigation of the supplier or of the customer, since the agreed purpose of the contracting parties is to endeavour to isolate a part of the market' (see the judgments of the Court of Justice in *Miller v Commission*, cited above, paragraph 7, and, most recently, in Cases C–89/85, C–104/85, C–114/85, C–116/85, C–117/85 and C–125/85 to C–129/85 *Ahlstroem Osakeyhtioe and Others v Commission* [1993] ECR I–1307, paragraph 176 ('Woodpulp')).[86]

7.67 The Court of First Instance also confirmed the application of the test of appreciability to effect on trade but clarified that the test of 'appreciability' is not any greater than that of 'insignificant effect' used in the *Volk* case:

> To be capable of affecting trade between Member States, a decision, an agreement or a concerted practice must make it possible to foresee with a sufficient degree of probability, on the basis of a set of objective elements of law or fact, that it may have an influence, direct or indirect, actual or potential, on the pattern of trade between Member States capable of hindering the attainment of the objectives of a single market between States. That influence must also be appreciable (Volk, cited above, paragraph 5, and, most recently, the judgment of the Court of First Instance in Case T–66/89 *Publishers Association v Commission* [1992] ECR II–1995, paragraph 55). Accordingly, even an agreement according absolute territorial protection escapes the prohibition laid down in Article 85 [now Article 81] of the Treaty where it affects the market only insignificantly, regard being had to the weak position of

---

[86] Case T–77/92, see n 84 above, para 37.

those concerned on the market for the products in question (judgment of the Court of Justice in Joined Cases 100/80 to 103/80 *Musique diffusion française and Others v Commission* [1983] ECR 1825, paragraph 85).[87]

The Court of First Instance also rejected the claim that the relevant market share **7.68** for assessing the appreciability of the effect on trade was solely that of Herlitz, it being sufficient that the sales of one of the parties are not inconsiderable:

> The influence which an agreement may have on trade between Member States is to be determined by taking into account in particular the position and importance of the parties on the market for the products concerned (judgment of the Court of Justice in Case 99/79 *Lancôme v ETOS* [1980] ECR 2511, paragraph 24).[88]

> The Court of Justice has held that when it is evident that the sales of at least one of the parties to an anti-competitive agreement constitute a not inconsiderable proportion of the relevant market, Article 85(1) [now Article 81(1)] of the Treaty should be applied (see the judgment in Miller, cited above, paragraph 10).

Unfortunately the market shares of Parker Pen and Herlitz on the German and **7.69** Community markets are deleted from the public version of the judgment. Nevertheless, the Court of First Instance states that the 'figures show that Parker and Herlitz are undertakings of sufficient importance for their conduct to be, in principle, capable of affecting intra-Community trade. Moreover, it is not disputed that Herlitz is a major client of Parker on the German market'.[89] 'Having regard to the importance of the position which Parker holds, the size of its production, its sales in the Member States and the proportion of sales of Parker products made by Herlitz', the Court found that the export prohibition was 'capable of affecting appreciably patterns of trade between Member States in such a way as to jeopardize the attainment of the objectives of the common market'.[90]

Interestingly, the Court of First Instance did not go into detail as regards Parker **7.70** Pen's argument relating to similarity in wholesale prices charged by Parker in the various Member States, simply noting at paragraph 42 that the Commission had observed 'price differences between the Member States which might give rise to a parallel trade'. However, it did reduce the level of the fine from ECU 700,000 to 400,000, 'having regard in particular to the low turnover to which the infringement relates'.[91]

BMW Leasing case[92]—**absolute territorial protection (1995)**. This case, an **7.71** Article 234 reference to the Court, arose from national proceedings between

---

[87] Case T–77/92, see n 84 above, para 39.
[88] Case T–77/92, see n 84 above, para 40.
[89] Case T–77/92, see n 84 above, para 45.
[90] Case T–77/92, see n 84 above, para 46.
[91] Case T–77/92, see n 84 above, para 95.
[92] Case C–70/93 *Bayerische Motorenwerke AG v ALD Auto-Leasing D GmbH* [1995] ECR I–3439.

Bayerische Motorenwerke AG (BMW) and ALD Auto-Leasing D GmbH (ALD) concerning a circular letter sent by BMW, a motor vehicle manufacturer, to its authorized dealers in Germany, in which it called upon them not to supply leasing companies that made vehicles available to customers residing or having their seat outside the contract territory of the dealer in question. The Court found that the letter constituted an agreement granting absolute territorial protection to the BMW dealer on whose territory the customer of ALD is established. Interestingly, while the Court stated that for the agreement to fall within the scope of Article 81(1), 'it must be considered whether the ban on supplies resulting from the agreement has as its object or effect the restriction to an appreciable extent of competition within the common market and whether it may affect trade between Member States',[93] the judgment contains no reference to the position of BMW on the German or other markets. In fact there is no economic assessment of the word 'appreciable'. With regard to effect on trade, the Court states that 'the agreement in question, since it relates to vehicles of the BMW mark, which are the subject of significant international trade, may affect trade between Member States'.[94]

7.72 In this case the Court applied the criterion of appreciability to both the 'object' and 'effect' of the restriction. Surprisingly, the Court does not appear to have applied this criterion to effect on trade.

Restrictions by Effect

7.73 *Béguelin*[95]—**exclusive distribution (1971).**   This case arose from proceedings in France taken by Béguelin, the exclusive distributor in France for cigarette lighters of the mark 'WIN' against a parallel importer which had imported a consignment of the lighters from Germany and the exclusive distributor for the mark in Germany from whom it had sourced the lighters. Based on the exclusivity granted by the distribution agreement Béguélin sought an injunction preventing sale of the imported lighters and damages. The defendants pleaded before the national court that the exclusive agreement infringed Article 81. In response to an Article 234 reference the Court of Justice ruled:

> An exclusive dealing agreement . . . comes within the prohibition imposed under Article 85 [now Article 81] of the Treaty in cases when, *de jure* or *de facto* it prevents the distributor from re-exporting the products in question to other Member States or prevents the products from being imported from other Member States into the protected area and from being distributed therein by persons other than the exclusive dealer or his customers.

7.74 It is not clear from the case that the distribution contract granted Béguelin absolute territorial protection,[96] which probably explains why the Court assessed

---

[93] Case C–70/93, see n 92 above, para 18.
[94] Case C–70/93, see n 92 above, para 20.
[95] Case 22/71 *Béguelin Import Co v SAGL Import Export* [1971] ECR 949.
[96] See Opinion of Advocate General Dutheillet de Lamothe, 965.

this case in terms of its 'effect' and not 'object'. This is evident from paragraphs 13 and 14 of the judgment :

> 13 In order to determine whether this is the position [ie prevention of imports or exports], account must be taken not only of the rights and obligations arising from the clauses of the agreement but also of the economic and legal conditions under which it operates and particularly of the existence of any similar agreements entered into by the same producer with exclusive dealers established in other Member States.
>
> 14 More especially, an exclusive dealing agreement is liable to affect trade between Member States and may have the effect of impeding competition if, owing to the combined effects of the agreement and of national legislation on unfair competition, the dealer is able to prevent parallel imports from other Member States into [a] territory covered by the agreement.

The Court also confirmed that 'in order to come within the prohibition imposed by Article 85 [now Article 81], the agreement must affect trade between Member States and the free play of competition to an appreciable extent'.

Nungesser[97]—**territorial protection in the form of 'open exclusivity' (1982).** **7.76**
This case arose from an appeal by Nungesser and others against a decision of the Commission which found an infringement of Article 81(1) as a result of the content and application of two contracts relating to the assignment of plant breeders' rights for certain maize seeds in the Federal Republic of Germany. The decision also rejected an application for the exemption of the agreements under Article 81(3).

While the judgment of the Court is limited to the licencing of plant breeders' **7.77**
rights, it is submitted that the reasoning of the judgment is also relevant to the consideration of territorial protection relating to the distribution of goods and services where substantial levels of investments are involved and distributors may be deterred from making such investments unless they have assurances that they will not face active competition from other distributors of the same product. First, the Court rejected the submission that the Commission had failed to take into account the particular nature of plant breeders' rights, the exercise of which demands strict observance of territorial protection:

> It is therefore not correct to consider that breeders' rights are a species of commercial or industrial property right with characteristics of so special a nature as to require, in relation to the competition rules, a different treatment from other commercial or industrial property rights. That conclusion does not affect the need to take into consideration, for the purposes of the rules on competition, the specific nature of the products which form the subject-matter of breeders' rights.[98]

---

[97] Case 258/78 *LC Nungesser KG and Kurt Eisele v Commission* [1982] ECR 2015.
[98] Case 258/78, see n 97 above, para 43.

7.78 Secondly, the Court accepted the argument that the Commission was wrong to consider that every exclusive licence of breeders' rights by its nature falls within the terms of Article 81(1). The Court drew a distinction between two types of territorial protection, namely *open exclusivity* and *closed exclusivity*.

> the first case concerns a so-called open exclusive licence or assignment and the exclusivitiy of the licence relates solely to the contractual relationship between the owner of the right and the licensee, whereby the owner merely undertakes not to grant other licences in respect of the same territory and not to compete himself with the licensee on that territory. On the other hand, the second case involves an exclusive licence or assignment with absolute territorial protection, under which the parties to the contract propose, as regards the products and the territory in question, to eliminate all competition from third parties, such as parallel importers or licensees for other territories.[99]

7.79 Having drawn this distinction the Court proceeded to analyse the former in terms of its effects on competition, rather than treating it as a restriction by object.

> 57. In fact, in the case of a licence of breeders' rights over hybrid maize seeds newly developed in one Member State, an undertaking established in another Member State which was not certain that it would not encounter competition from other licensees for the territory granted to it, or from the owner of the right himself, might be deterred from accepting the risk of cultivating and marketing that product; such a result would be damaging to the dissemination of a new technology and would prejudice competition in the community between the new product and similar existing products.

> 58. Having regard to the specific nature of the products in question, the court concludes that, in a case such as the present, the grant of an open exclusive licence, that is to say a licence which does not affect the position of third parties such as parallel importers and licensees for other territories, is not in itself incompatible with Article 85(1) [now Article 81(1)] of the Treaty.

7.80 Much the same arguments could be used in relation to the distribution of goods and services which require considerable levels of investment. If the Commission were to permit all forms of distribution to avail of this reasoning the parties to a distribution agreement could agree territorial sales restrictions as between themselves without falling within the scope of Article 81(1). Article 81(1) would then only apply where distributors were granted territorial protection from other distributors or parallel traders.

7.81 *Binon*[100]—**qualitative selective distribution (1985).** This case, an Article 234 reference to the Court of Justice, concerned the distribution of newspapers in Belgium by way of a selective distribution system. SA Binon & Cie, an undertaking which carried on a business in Charleroi selling books, stationery, and educational toys, had brought a case before the national court against SA Agence et

---

[99] Case 258/78, see n 97 above, para 53.
[100] Case 243/83 *SA Binon & Cie v SA Agence et messageries de la presse* [1985] ECR 201.

messageries de la presse. The purpose of the action was to obtain an order directing AMP to cease refusing to sell or deliver to Binon the newspapers and periodicals, both Belgian and foreign, which it distributed in Belgium. AMP was responsible for the distribution to retailers of close to 70 per cent of Belgian newspapers and periodicals and virtually all newspapers and periodicals published abroad.

In relation to qualitative selective distribution the Court stated as follows in paragraphs 31 and 32 of the judgment: **7.82**

> 31. It must be noted that according to the Court's decisions and in particular its judgment of 25 October 1977 in case 26/76 (*Metro SB-Grossmarkte GmbH and Co Kg v Commission*, (1977) ECR 1875) selective distribution systems constitute an aspect of competition which accords with Article 85(1) [now Article 81(1)], provided that re-sellers are chosen on the basis of objective criteria of a qualitative nature relating to the technical qualifications of the re-seller and his staff and the suitability of his trading premises in connection with the requirements for the distribution of the product and that such criteria are laid down uniformly for all potential re-sellers and are not applied in a discriminatory fashion.

> 32. Such a system may be established for the distribution of newspapers and periodicals, without infringing the prohibition contained in Article 85(1), given the special nature of those products as regards their distribution . . .

Therefore, qualitative selective distribution, where justified by the nature of the product, can never constitute a restriction by object but only by effect.[101] This contrasts with the position of quantitative selective distribution in respect of which the Court, at paragraph 35, appears, at first sight, to find a restriction by object: **7.83**

> a selective distribution system for newspapers and periodicals which affects trade between Member States is prohibited by Article 85(1) [now Article 81(1)] of the Treaty if re-sellers are chosen on the basis of quantitative criteria. However, the Commission may, within the framework of an application for exemption under Article 85(3), examine whether, in a particular case, criteria of that kind may be justified.

In a selective distribution system the right of resale of members of the network is normally restricted to final users or other network members. Intermediaries are excluded from the distribution of the particular branded product or service which is distributed by way of selective distribution. Therefore, it can be used to isolate national markets and impede parallel trade. Where, as is the case for the vast majority of consumer goods, search costs are high, arbitrage by network dealers is the only feasible mechanism to ensure parallel trade in a selective distribution network. However, the tighter the control which a supplier has over its distribution network the greater the potential to block parallel trade between network **7.84**

---

[101] See also Case 75/84 *Metro v Commission* [1986] ECR 3021, para 40.

members. While a qualitative system could be used for the same purpose, in theory the higher number of potential network dealers should limit the control exercised over individual network dealers and the potential for isolation of national markets. It is submitted that these factors, together with the high market share of AMP (close to 70 per cent) explains the Court's finding on quantitative selective distribution in this case. It is further submitted that in the absence of market power a quantitative selective distribution system should only be assessed as a restriction by effect.

7.85 *Javico*[102]—**export prohibition from a third country (1998).** Vertical restraints can be used to prevent the reimportation of products into the Community. This is evidenced by the judgment of the Court of Justice in the *Javico* case. This case arose from national proceedings brought by Yves Saint Laurent Parfums SA (YSLP) against Javico International and Javico AG (Javico) for breach of the terms of two contracts for the distribution of its products, one covering the territory of Russia and Ukraine and the other the territory of Slovenia, in which Javico had agreed to confine its sales activities to the relevant territories. The contract for Russia and Ukraine stated, *inter alia*, 'our products are intended for sale solely in the territory of the Republics of Russia and Ukraine. In no circumstances may they leave the territory of the Republics of Russia and Ukraine'.[103] The distribution contract for Slovenia stated, *inter alia*, 'in order to protect the high quality of the distribution of the products in other countries of the world, the distributor agrees not to sell the products outside the territory or to unauthorised dealers in the territory'.[104] Shortly after the conclusion of those contracts, YSLP discovered in the United Kingdom, Belgium, and The Netherlands products sold to Javico which should have been distributed in Russia, Ukraine, and Slovenia.

7.86 The Court confirmed that an export prohibition of the type at issue would if contained in a contract relating to the distribution of goods within the Community constitute by its very nature a restriction of competition and fall within the scope of the prohibition of Article 81(1) if it was capable of affecting trade between Member States. In other words, an export prohibition in an agreement relating to the supply of goods within the Community is a restriction by object.

7.87 However, the Court did not treat the export prohibition in this case as a restriction by object because it was not 'intended to exclude parallel imports and marketing of the contractual product within the Community but as being designed to enable the producer to penetrate a market outside the Community by supplying a sufficient quantity of contractual products to that market . . . it follows that an agree-

---

[102] Case C–306/96 *Javico International and Javico AG v Yves Saint Laurent Parfums SA (YSLP)* [1998] ECR I–1983.
[103] Case C–306/96, see n 102 above, para 5.
[104] Case C–306/96, see n 102 above, para 6.

ment in which the reseller gives to the producer an undertaking that he will sell the contractual products on a market outside the Community cannot be regarded as having the object of appreciably restricting competition within the common market or as being capable of affecting, as such, trade between Member States'.[105]

The Court stated that to constitute a restriction by effect the agreement must be **7.88** examined in its economic and legal context and in particular the fact that YSLP had a selective distribution system in the Community which had been exempted by the Commission. In paragraphs 23–26 it gave some guidance as to the other economic and legal factors which should be taken into account:

> 23 In that regard, it is first necessary to determine whether the structure of the Community market in the relevant products is oligopolistic, allowing only limited competition within the Community network for the distribution of those products.
>
> 24 It must then be established whether there is an appreciable difference between the prices of the contractual products charged in the Community and those charged outside the Community. Such a difference is not, however, liable to affect competition if it is eroded by the level of customs duties and transport costs resulting from the export of the product to a non-member country followed by its re-import into the Community.
>
> 25 If that examination were to disclose that the contested provisions of the agreements concerned had the effect of undermining competition within the meaning of Article 85(1) [now Article 81(1)] of the Treaty, it would also be necessary to determine whether, having regard to YSLP's position on the Community market and the extent of its production and its sales in the Member States, the contested provisions designed to prevent direct sales of the contractual products in the Community and re-exports of them to the Community entail any risk of an appreciable effect on the pattern of trade between the Member States such as to undermine attainment of the objectives of the common market.
>
> 26 In that regard, intra-Community trade cannot be appreciably affected if the products intended for markets outside the Community account for only a very small percentage of the total market for those products in the territory of the common market.[106]

The application of the effects principle to this type of vertical restraint is likely to **7.89** make it difficult for parallel importers to source goods outside the EEA.[107] However, the situation of parallel importers will be even more difficult in respect of branded goods where the brand owner is able to rely on the principle of EEA

---

[105] Case C–306/96, see n 102 above, paras 19–20.

[106] The judgment is unclear as to whether the economic factors of oligopolistic Community market (para 23) and appreciable price difference (para 24) are alternative or cumulative conditions. In para 24 the words 'it must then' indicate that the factors are cumulative while in the dispositive of the judgment in para 28 the word 'or' indicates that they are alternative.

[107] While the judgment of the Court of Justice in *Javico* only distinguishes intra- from ex-Community trade, it is submitted that an intra-EEA export prohibition is likely to be assessed as a restriction by object, in the same way as an intra-Community export prohibition.

exhaustion of trade mark rights. EEA exhaustion, when incorporated into national trade mark legislation, enables trade mark owners to block the importation of products which they have put on the market outside the EEA. The judgment in the *Silhouette* case,[108] emphasizes the obligation upon Member States to provide for EEA exhaustion in their national legislation implementing the Trade Marks Directive.[109] This case arose from proceedings brought in Austria by Silhouette against Hartlauer, to block the sale by Hartlauer on the Austrian market of 21,000 out-of-fashion spectacle frames which Silhouette had placed on the market in Bulgaria and the former USSR.

Conclusion

7.90 Vertical restraints with the object of resale price maintenance, absolute territorial protection, and exclusion of parallel imports/exports constitute *per se* restrictions of competition and will fall within the prohibition of Article 81(1) unless they fail to satisfy the doctrine of appreciability established in the *Volk v Vervaeke* case. The jurisprudence does not support the assertion that all impediments to parallel trade constitute *per se* restrictions. For example a purely qualitative selective distribution system will normally not fall within the scope of Article 81(1) even though the inherent nature of a selective distribution system is that parallel trade by non-network dealers is excluded. Common distribution formats such as exclusive distribution, exclusive purchasing, and selective distribution have never been held by the Community Courts to constitute restrictions by object unless implemented with the objective of achieving absolute territorial protection, exclusion of parallel imports/exports, or resale price maintenance. While there is no definitive list of those vertical restraints which constitute restrictions by object, providing these three latter elements are absent from the distribution system, the vertical restraints will, in all likelihood, be assessed as restrictions by effect and not restrictions by object.

7.91 The Community Courts have never quantified appreciability, but have confirmed the application of Article 81(1) in cases involving relatively low market shares. The greater the anti-competitive nature of the restriction of competition the greater the likelihood that the criteria of appreciability will be satisfied. Therefore it is not surprising to find the Community Courts upholding the application of

---

[108] Case C–355/96 *Silhouette International Schmied GmbH & Co KG v Hartlauer Handelsgesellschaft mbH* [1998] ECR I–4799. In response to questions from the Austrian court pursuant to Article 234 of the Treaty, the Court responded, *inter alia*: 'National rules providing for exhaustion of trade-mark rights in respect of products put on the market outside the EEA under that mark by the proprietor or with its consent are contrary to Article 7(1) of First Council Directive (EEC) 89/104 of 21 December 1988 to approximate the laws of the Member States relating to trade marks, as amended by the Agreement on the European Economic Area of 2 May 1992.'

[109] First Council Directive (EEC) 89/104 of 21 December 1988 to approximate the laws of the Member States relating to trade marks [1989] OJ L40/1, as amended by the EEA Agreement.

Article 81(1) in a case involving absolute territorial protection even though the parties to the vertical restraint had market shares not exceeding 6 per cent.[110]

As highlighted in the Opinion of Advocate General Mischo, in the *Erauw-* **7.92** *Jacquery* case, the Court's application of the appreciability doctrine has not been consistent. Of the cases analysed above, the Court appears to have (1) not applied the criterion in the *Binon* judgment, (2) applied the criterion to both the restriction of competition and effect on trade in the *Béguelin* judgment, (3) applied the criterion to only the restriction of competition in the *BMW* judgment, and (4) applied the criterion only to the effect on trade in the *Miller, Erauw-Jacquery,* and *Parker Pen* judgments. Therefore, it would appear that in many cases involving restrictions by object, the appreciability of the restriction is assumed (ie restriction by nature), with the analysis of appreciability concentrating upon effect on trade between Member States.

(5) Exemption from the Prohibition of Article 81(1)

The prohibition in Article 81(1) can be declared inapplicable by the Commission **7.93** providing the four substantive conditions set out in Article 81(3) are fulfilled.[111] In simplistic terms the conditions laid down in Article 81(3) are fulfilled where 'the advantages of the system for competition outweigh the disadvantages'.[112]

Given the Commission's monopoly over the granting of declarations under **7.94** Article 81(3) (so called exemptions) and the wide scope of application of Article 81(1) to vertical restraints, vertical restraints policy has been largely decided under Article 81(3) and not 81(1). It should be borne in mind that the Commission has a wide margin of discretion in the application of Article 81(3). Since exemptions are granted after an analysis of complex economic facts, judicial review of the legal characterization of the facts is limited to the possibility of the Commission having committed a manifest error of assessment. This was confirmed by the Court of First Instance in the *Matra* case,[113] which also confirmed that, in principle, no anti-competitive practice can exist which, whatever the extent of its effects on a given market, cannot be exempted, provided that all the conditions laid down in Article 81(3) of the Treaty are satisfied and the practice in question has been properly notified to the Commission.[114] The onus is on notifying undertakings to

---

[110] Case 19/77 *Miller International Schallplatten GmbH v Commission* [1978] ECR 131.

[111] See section F of Chapter 2 for a detailed consideration of these conditions.

[112] Case 75/84 *Metro v Commission* [1986] ECR 3021, para 49.

[113] Case T–17/93 *Matra Hachette SA v Commission* [1994] ECR II–595, paras 104 & 157.

[114] Case T–17/93, see n 113 above, para 85 which reads as follows: 'The Court observes that such reasoning presumes that there are adverse effects on competition which, by their nature cannot qualify for an exemption under Article 85(3) [now Article 81(3)]. In other words, as the Commission rightly points out, such reasoning presumes acceptance of the view that there are infringements which are inherently incapable of qualifying for an exemption but Community competition law, the applicability of which is subject to the existence of a practice which is

provide the Commission with evidence that the conditions laid down by Article 81(3) are met.[115]

7.95 The pro- and anti-competitive effects of an agreement or concerted practice are balanced under Article 81(3) and not to establish whether Article 81(1) applies in the first place. This approach was criticized by Advocate General Roemer in the 1966 *Grundig and Consten* case, who, when commenting on the US requirement for a comprehensive economic analysis before ruling on the acceptability of a system of exclusive dealings, stated, *inter alia*:

> It seems to me wrong to have regard to such observation only for the application of paragraph (3) of Article 85 [now Article 81], because that paragraph requires an examination from other points of view which are special and different. But in particular (as shown by *Societe Technique Miniere v Maschinenbau Ulm GmbH*) it would be artificial to apply Article 85(1), on the basis of purely theoretical considerations, to situations which upon closer inspection would reveal no appreciable adverse effects on competition, in order to grant exemption on the basis of Article 85(3).

7.96 In the light of the history of vertical restraints as described in paras 7.07–7.18 above, it is all too easy to side with Advocate General Roemer and to criticize the Commission for having adopted such an approach to vertical restraints. However, it must be remembered that in 1965 progress towards the establishment of a common market was nowhere near as advanced as it is today. The landmark decisions of the Court of Justice on free movement of goods in the 'Dassonville'[116] and 'Cassis de Dijon'[117] cases only occurred in the mid to late 1970s.[118] It is submitted that Advocate General Roemer's comments are more valid in today's environment

---

anti-competitive in intent or has an anti-competitive effect on a given market, certainly does not embody that principle. On the contrary, the Court considers that, in principle, no anti-competitive practice can exist which, whatever the extent of its effects on a given market, cannot be exempted, provided that all the conditions laid down in Article 85(3) of the Treaty are satisfied and the practice in question has been properly notified to the Commission.' This statement of the Court of First Instance presupposes, in the case of a notification seeking a declaration under Article 81(3), an obligation on the part of the Commission to carry out a detailed analysis under each of the conditions of Article 81(3). While it is submitted that the Commission is obliged to carry out such an analysis in all cases seeking the application of Article 81(3), the legal position is not entirely settled for restrictions by object. In this regard reference is made to para 46 of the judgment of the Court of Justice of 17 September 1985 in Joined Cases 25 and 26/84 *Ford-Werke AG and Ford of Europe Inc v Commission* [1985] ECR 2725, where the Court stated, *inter alia*, that '[t]he Commission is not obliged to carry out a detailed examination of all the advantages and disadvantages likely to flow from a selective distribution system when it has good reason to believe that a manufacturer has used such a system to prevent parallel imports and thus artificially to partition the Common Market'.

[115] Case T–17/93, see n 113 above, para 104.

[116] Judgment of the Court of 11 July 1974 in Case 8/74 *Procureur du Roi v Benoît and Gustave Dassonville* [1974] ECR 837.

[117] Judgment of the Court of 20 February 1979 in Case 120/78 *Rewe-Zentral AG v Bundesmonopolverwaltung für Branntwein* [1979] ECR 649.

[118] For a history of the case law of the Community Courts on the free movement of goods see Oliver, *Free Movement of Goods in the European Community* (London: Sweet and Maxwell, 1996).

where the creation of a single market is much closer to completion than it was in 1965. The policy issue which needs to be decided is whether the single market is sufficiently well established so that market integration can be downgraded from a primary to a secondary objective of EC competition policy. It is only when this happens that EC competition policy can totally discard its current legalistic form based system for one based on purely economic criteria relating to effects on inter-brand competition.

This raises the question as to whether the current or near-future state of the inter- **7.97** nal market justifies a relaxation of the market integration aim of competition pol-icy. There are still very significant price differences within the European Union, sometimes even for the same products manufactured by the same company.[119] Transport costs, regulatory constraints, and the relations between producers and distributors in the various Member States account for these differences. While there are examples of distributors moving outside their 'home' market and there are some European-wide chains emerging, distribution, particularly at the retail level, is still largely national.[120] It also seems that 'many retailers do not take advan-tage of opportunities to exploit price differences between Member States, for fear of spoiling long-term relations with manufacturers or, possibly, being faced with retaliatory actions, such as boycotts or price discrimination. Cross-border pur-chasing groups do not yet seem to have had a significant impact.'[121]

While the internal market is undoubtedly further advanced than it was in 1965 **7.98** and Economic and Monetary Union (EMU) will further facilitate cross-border trade, it is submitted that it is too early to relax this objective. Account also has to be taken of forthcoming enlargement which will require a further process of mar-ket integration. Some commentators have criticized the market integration objective of EC competition policy:

> [EU]competition policy is intended to facilitate trade between Member States, even if trade between Member States were in some circumstances to be antithetical to other goals such as efficiency of distribution or competition within Member States . . . In theory there is no reason why the prevention of parallel imports should be antithetical to market integration (let alone efficiency), since it might be only under the guarantee of absolute territorial exclusivity that a distributor would be willing to take the risk of distributing. However, the form-based nature of the interpretation of Article 85(1) [now Article 81(1)] has in practice guaranteed that an agreement that prevents parallel imports can be construed as being anti-competitive in object even if not anti-competitive in effect . . .[122]

---

[119] For example, see biannual reports of the Commission on car prices and *VW-Audi* [1998] OJ L124/60, on appeal.

[120] See para 29 of Green Paper on Vertical Restraints.

[121] See para 236 of Green Paper on Vertical Restraints.

[122] Neven, Papandropoulos and Seabright, *Trawling for Minnows—European Competition Policy and Agreements Between Firms* (Centre for Economic Policy Research, 1998) 37–38.

7.99 Moreover, assuming that competition policy was to drop the single market object-ive and permit absolute territorial protection from intra-brand competition in the presence of a sufficient level of inter-brand competition, this would result in the abolition of the right of European consumers to purchase goods in the country of their choice. Cases such as *Ford*[123] and *VW-Audi*,[124] which upheld the right of European consumers to purchase cars in Member States in which they were not resident at lower prices, would no longer be pursued. It is worth noting that in the *VW-Audi* case the Commission had received a large number of complaints from consumers who had had difficulty buying new cars from authorized dealers in Italy.[125] Judging by the criticism[126] which followed upon the judgment of the Court of Justice in the *Silhouette* case,[127] which upheld the use of trade marks to prevent parallel trade into the Community, an even stronger reaction would be likely were traders and consumers prevented from effecting parallel trade within the Community. Irrespective of the economic logic, ie increased levels of market entry, more efficient distribution, greater inter-brand competition, consumers would feel that they are being denied the benefits of the internal market. It is sub-mitted that this consumer right is so fundamental that its abolition, at this stage in the development of the Community, would be politically unacceptable.

7.100 The issue that remains is how to balance these two concepts at the current stage of development in the single market. In the near to medium future it is likely that the Commission will continue to rely upon two imperfect safety valves against signif-icant price differences between Member States. The first being the distinction between active and passive sales, with exclusive distribution arrangements only being exempted on condition that the exclusive dealer remains free to make unsol-icited sales outside of his territory. The second is parallel trade by intermediaries and consumers. However, it is also possible that advances in information techno-logy which can be used to 'copperfasten' the isolation of national markets[128] may ultimately revolutionize distribution and make redundant the concept of exclus-ive territories. The Internet is an advertising and selling medium which extends beyond the scope of exclusive territories as is evidenced by the growth in Internet car sales in the US.[129] Therefore, it may be important to protect the right of exclus-ive dealers to advertise on this medium.

---

[123] Case 26/84 *Ford v Commission* [1985] ECR 2745.
[124] *VW-Audi* [1998] OJ L124/60, on appeal.
[125] Commission press release of 28 January 1998. DN:IP/98/94.
[126] See article entitled 'Grey import whitewash', *Financial Times*, 17 July 1998, 8 & 15.
[127] Case C–355/96 *Silhouette International Schmied Gmbh & Co KG v Hartlauer handelsge-sellschaft mbH*, unreported of 16 July 1998.
[128] paras 45 and 52 of the Green Paper on Vertical Restraints.
[129] See 'Death of a salesman', *Economist*, 8 March 1997, 76.

(6) Cumulative Effect

An individual agreement which when looked at in isolation has neither an appre-   **7.101**
ciable effect on competition or trade between Member States may nevertheless fall
within the scope of the prohibition of Article 81(1) where the overall impact of
that agreement and similar agreements have such an appreciable effect. In other
words agreements must be assessed in their economic and legal context. Where
the anti-competitive effects on a market arise not from the agreements of one
undertaking but from the cumulative effects of similar agreements of a number of
undertakings, the Community Courts have ruled that the prohibition of Article
81(1) applies to the agreements of those companies which make a significant contribution to the cumulative effect.

Foreclosure

The anti-competitive effect most likely to arise from a parallel series of vertical   **7.102**
agreements is foreclosure. While neither the Community Courts nor the
Commission have defined the concept of foreclosure, paragraph 21 of the judgment of the Court of Justice in the *Delimitis* case offers some guidance in that it
refers to the 'necessity to examine whether there are real concrete possibilities for
a new competitor to penetrate the bundle of contracts'[130] and enter the market.
Therefore, foreclosure can only be said to occur when the cumulative effect of a
parallel series of agreements makes it difficult to enter the market and there are no
concrete ways of bypassing those agreements such as by acquisition or use of other
distribution formats.[131]

**Assessment Required to Find a Cumulative Effect which Falls within the
Scope of Article 81(1)**

In practice, this assessment is carried out under three headings, namely the effect   **7.103**
of the network, other factors, and significant contribution.[132] Each of these three
headings is considered below.

Effect of the Network

In the case *Brasserie De Haecht v Wilkin*,[133] the Court of Justice held that the effects   **7.104**
of an exclusive purchase agreement for beer had to be assessed in the economic
and legal context in which they occur and where they might combine with others
to have a cumulative effect on competition:

---

[130] Case C–234/89 *Delimitis v Henninger Bräu* [1991] ECR I–935, para 21.
[131] Case C–234/89, see n 130 above, paras 21–22.
[132] Case C–234/89, see n 130 above, paras 19–24.
[133] Case 23/67 [1967] ECR 407.

by basing its application to agreements, decisions or practices not only on their subject-matter but also on their effects in relation to competition, Article 85(1) [now Article 81(1)] implies that regard must be had to such effects in the context in which they occur, that is to say, in the economic and legal context of such agreements, decisions or practices and where they might combine with others to have a cumulative effect on competition. In fact, it would be pointless to consider an agreement, decision or practice by reason of its effects if those effects were to be taken distinct from the market in which they are seen to operate and could only be examined apart from the body of effects, whether convergent or not, surrounding their implementation. Thus in order to examine whether it is caught by Article 85(1) an agreement cannot be examined in isolation from the above context, that is, from the factual or legal circumstances causing it to prevent, restrict or distort competition. The existence of similar contracts may be taken into consideration for this objective to the extent to which the general body of contracts of this type is capable of restricting the freedom of trade.[134]

Other Factors

7.105 The Court of Justice has also held that the effect of the network of exclusive purchasing agreements is only one factor, among others, pertaining to the economic and legal context in which an agreement must be appraised.[135] The other factors to be taken into account are, in the first instance, those also relating to opportunities for access and, secondly, the conditions under which competitive forces operate on the relevant market.

Opportunities for Access

7.106 Paragraph 21 of the *Delimitis* judgment referred to the

> real concrete possibilities for a new competitor to penetrate the bundle of contracts by acquiring a brewery already established on the market together with its network of sales outlets, or to circumvent the bundle of contracts by opening new public houses. For that purpose it is necessary to have regard to the legal rules and agreements on the acquisition of companies and the establishment of outlets, and to the minimum number of outlets necessary for the economic operation of a distribution system. The presence of beer wholesalers not tied to producers who are active on the market is also a factor capable of facilitating a new producer's access to that market since he can make use of those wholesalers' sales networks to distribute his own beer.

7.107 Therefore, assuming that the untied independent outlets on a particular market are insufficient to facilitate entry, this is not sufficient in itself to support a finding that the relevant market is foreclosed. It is also necessary to examine whether there are real concrete possibilities for a new competitor to enter the market such as by purchasing or opening new retail outlets. This also raises the issue as to whether new entrants are confined to existing distribution formats. Other forms of entry must be taken into account in the assessment of foreclosure.

---

[134] Case 23/67, see n 133 above, at 415.

Competitive Forces on the Market

Account must be also taken of competitive forces on the market, including num- **7.108**
ber and size of producers, degree of market saturation, consumer fidelity, and
dynamics of the market.[136]

Significant Contribution

Where it has been established that competition has been restricted because of a **7.109**
cumulative effect the prohibition of Article 81(1) can only be applied to those
undertakings which make a significant contribution to the restriction. As the
Court clarified in paragraph 24 of the *Delimitis* judgment:

> Under the Community rules of competition, responsibility for such an effect of
> closing off the market must be attributed to the breweries which make an appreci-
> able contribution thereto. Beer supply agreements entered into by breweries whose
> contribution to the cumulative effect is insignificant do not therefore fall under the
> prohibition under Article 85(1) [now Article 81(1)].

This principle was applied by the Commission in the *Van Den Bergh* decision[137] **7.110**
(hereinafter referred to as the Irish ice cream decision), where the Commision
applied Article 81(1) to the network of a dominant supplier with a market share
exceeding 75 per cent of the relevant market for single-wrapped items of impulse
ice cream in Ireland, and not to similar networks of other suppliers because they
did not make a significant contribution to the foreclosure of the relevant market.[138] This case is also interesting because unlike the *Langnese-Iglo*[139] and
Schöller[140] cases (hereinafter referred to as the German ice cream cases), the foreclosure arose not from *de jure* exclusive purchase contracts but from freezer cabinet agreements[141] which were said to result in *de facto* exclusivity.[142]

---

[135] Case C–234/89, see n 130 above, para 20.

[136] Case C–234/89, see n 130 above, para 22.

[137] *Van Den Bergh Foods Limited* [1998] OJ L246/1. This decision which prohibits the practice
of freezer exclusivity by Van Den Bergh Foods Limited was suspended by the President of the Court
of First Instance on 7 July 1998 pending the hearing of an appeal in the matter.

[138] See para 204 of the decision.

[139] Case T–7/93 *Langnese-Iglo GmbH v Commission* [1995] ECR II–1533.

[140] Case T–9/93 *Schöller Lebensmittel GmbH & Co KG v Commission* [1995] ECR II–1610.

[141] The freezer cabinet agreements contain provisions requiring the cabinets to be used exclusively for the storing of products for sale which are supplied by Van Den Bergh Foods (ref para 142
of the decision).

[142] See para 184 of the decision. The economic implications of freezer exclusivity are examined
by Aidan Robertson and Mark Williams, 'An Ice Cream War: The Law Economics of Freezer
Exclusivity I' [1995] 1 ECLR 7. See also Valentine Korah, 'Exclusive Purchasing Obligations: Mars
v langnese and Schöller' [1994] 3 ECLR 171; Julian Maitland-Walker, 'Ice-cream Wars: An
Honourable Peace or the Beginning of a Greater Conflict?' [1995] 8 ECLR 451 ,and Michael Rowe,
'Ice Cream: The Saga Continues' [1998] ECLR 479.

7.111   The principle of significant contribution was also applied in the *Greene King* decision,[143] where, while considering the UK on-trade beer market to be foreclosed, the Commission was of the opinion that Greene King, a regional brewer with a tied market share of 1.3 per cent, was too small to contribute significantly to the foreclosure.

7.112   The finding of a restrictive effect for a network of an undertaking would apply equally to each of its constituents.[144]

Quantification of Contribution

7.113   Quantification of the contribution primarily takes account of overall market share, tied market share, and duration. The Court has ruled in the *Delimitis* judgment[145] that 'the extent of the contribution made by the individual agreement depends on the position of the contracting parties in the relevant market and on the duration of the agreement'. In paragraphs 25 and 26 of the judgment, the Court has clarified that 'that position is not determined solely by the market share held by the brewery and any group to which it may belong, but also by the number of outlets tied to it or to its group, in relation to the total number of premises for the sale and consumption of drinks found in the relevant market'.

7.114   As to the duration, the Court states at paragraph 26 of the judgment that 'if the duration is manifestly excessive in relation to the average duration of beer supply agreements generally entered into on the relevant market, the individual contract falls under the prohibition under Article 85(1) [now Article 81(1)]. A brewery with a relatively small market share which ties its sales outlets for many years may make as significant a contribution to a sealing-off of the market as a brewery in a relatively strong market position which regularly releases sales outlets at shorter intervals.'

7.115   In the German ice cream cases, the Court of First Instance, in assessing the significant contribution of the companies in question to 'the closing-off of the market',

---

[143]   Rejection of complaint by Commission Decision of 6 November 1998 in Case IV/36511, not yet published. At time of writing available on DG IV's Internet site at *http://europa.eu.int/comm/dg04/entente/closed/en/1998.htm#563*. The Commission's press release IP/98/967 of 6 November 1998 states that '[t]he Commission continues to consider the UK on-trade beer market as foreclosed. However, the Commission concludes that Greene King is too small to contribute significantly to the foreclosure. Indeed, Greene King's sales in its managed, tenanted and loan-tied estate account for only 1.3% of the UK on-trade market. This is considerably less than the 5% (or more) that each of the big UK brewers (Scottish & Newcastle, Bass, Whitbread and Carlsberg-Tetley) realises in their tied network (including the restrictive agreements with non-brewing pub companies).'

[144]   The Court of First Instance pointed out in Cases T–7 & 9/93 *Langnese-Iglo & Schöller* [1995] ECR I–1539 & 1611, para 129/95 that 'where there is a network of similar agreements concluded by the same producer, the assessment of the effects of that network on competition applies to all the individual agreements making up the network'. The judgment of the Court of First Instance was upheld on appeal by the Court of Justice in its judgment of 1 October 1998 in case C–279/95P.

referred to 'the strong position occupied by the [company concerned] in the relevant market, and, in particular, its market share'.[146] Therefore, it would appear that in this case the Court of First Instance, when taking into account all the factors referred to in *Delimitis*, placed greater emphasis on the overall market share as opposed to the tied market share. This was probably because of the highly concentrated nature of the market.[147]

The general rule is that the longer the duration of the exclusive purchase arrangement the greater the foreclosure effect. In the Irish ice cream decision Van Den Bergh Foods argued that freezer exclusivity agreements which can be terminated on two months' notice are evidence of a temporary relationship and cannot lead to a *de facto* tie which foreclosed other suppliers from the market. The Commission did not agree pointing out that the cabinet agreements were of indefinite duration and that market research showed that the relationship was not temporary.[148] The argument of temporary relationship also appears in the *Whitbread* decision,[149] where it was argued that since it was possible to terminate a loan tie upon three months' notice, such ties should no longer be considered as hindering any opportunities for access to the market. The Commission considered that the average duration of four years for such loan ties indicated that the contractual relationship was not a temporary one.[150] **7.116**

It should be noted that in assessing the contribution to foreclosure made by a supplier the Commission takes into account any retail/buyer outlets owned by the supplier. Therefore, in the beer sector, while the managed estate of the brewer does not of itself fall under Article 81(1) as it does not concern an agreement between independent operators, the brewer's market share acquired via its managed estate is assessed as a part of its tied market share and taken into account in the Commission's assessment of foreclosure.[151] **7.117**

Exemption under Article 81(3)

Non-Exemptable Foreclosure

In the Irish ice cream case the Commission refused to exempt the freezer exclusivity agreements because (1) any improvements in distribution arising from the freezer exclusivity agreements did not outweigh the restrictive effects of those agreements and in particular the limitation they place on access by competing ice **7.118**

---

[145] Last sentence of point 1 of the operative part of the judgment.

[146] See para 87 of *Schöller* case and para 112 of *Langnese-Iglo* case.

[147] The two leading companies had between them a tied market share exceeding 30% (ref para 105 of the *Langnese-Iglo* case) and a total market share exceeding 70% (ref para 96 of *Langnese-Iglo* and para 73 of *Schöller*).

[148] See para 208 of the decision.

[149] *Whitbread plc* [1999] OJ L88/26. See also press release IP/99/104 of 11 February 1999.

[150] para 115 of the decision.

[151] para 134 of the decision.

cream suppliers, (2) there was no guarantee that benefits will be passed on to consumers, (3) the exclusivity condition was not indispensable for the attainment of the alleged benefits, and (4) they constitute an important barrier to entry which in combination with the strength of the supplier's position on the relevant market, contributes substantially to an elimination of competition on the relevant market.[152] In the German ice cream cases the Court of First Instance rejected a plea that the exclusive purchase agreements satisfied the conditions of Article 81(3) on the grounds that it had not been shown that the Commission had committed a manifest error of assessment in considering that the contested agreements did not fulfil the first condition laid down by Article 81(3). Commenting on this first condition the Court of First Instance stated that 'it is settled law that the improvement cannot be identified with all the advantages which the parties obtain from the agreement in their production or distribution activities. The improvement must in particular display appreciable objective advantages of such a character as to compensate for the disadvantages which they cause in the field of competition.'[153] The Court considered that the applicant had 'failed to produce any factual evidence such as seriously to challenge the Commission's analysis regarding the barriers to entry to the market raised by the supply agreements and, consequently, the resulting weakening of competition'.[154]

Exemptable Foreclosure

7.119 This contrasts with the *Whitbread* decision[155] where the Commission exempted the exclusive purchase contracts with pubs in the United Kingdom despite the fact that they were considered to result in foreclosure effects. It should be noted that the exclusive purchase contracts in this case relate to premises which are owned by the brewer and which are rented to tenants by way of leasehold/tenancy agreements. In respect of the first condition of Article 81(3) the Commission concluded that the notified leasehold agreements, including the tying restrictions, contributed to an improvement of distribution on the UK on-trade beer market. This conclusion was justified by a complex analysis of a number of factors[156] including recognition of the fact that:

- Beer supply agreements generally lead to an improvement in distribution as they make it significantly easier to establish, modernize, maintain and operate premises used for the sale and consumption of drinks;

7.120
- the letting of premises at an agreed rent, particularly in view of the restrictive UK licensing system, is a method of providing the means for a lessee to operate

---

[152] See paras 221–254 of the decision.
[153] Case T–7/93, see n 139 above, at para 180.
[154] Case T–7/93, see n 139 above, at para 182.
[155] See n 149 above.
[156] See paras 150–170 of the decision.

premises and, as such, allows a low-cost entry of a newcomer on the on-trade market for the distribution of beer;

• the incentive on the reseller, following from the exclusive purchasing and the non-competition obligation, to devote all the resources at his disposal to the sale of the contract goods will generally lead to an improvement in the distribution of the contract goods;

• they allow long-term planning of sales and consequently a cost-effective organization of production and distribution and the pressure of competition between products of different makes obliges the undertakings involved to determine the number and character of premises used for the sale and consumption of drinks in accordance with the wishes of customers; and

• the higher prices for beer payable by tied tenants *vis-à-vis* untied or free tenants do not negate the improvements in distribution because they are compensated for by countervailing benefits arising from the overall business relationship with the tying brewer.

It is submitted that analysis of the fourth and final criteria of Article 81(3) (ie pos- **7.120** sibility of eliminating competition in respect of a substantial part of the market in question) is why the exclusive agreements were looked at more favourably in this case than in the ice cream cases discussed above. In this case there was sufficient inter-brand competition[157] so that the benefit of efficiencies were likely to be passed on to consumers. In paragraph 177 of the decision the Commission states:

> It is evident that Whitbread cannot eliminate competition from a substantial part of the market, as they account for only 13% of the UK on-trade beer market in 1997. Moreover, even taking into account the fact that in 1997 at most 58% of the UK on-trade market for beer was foreclosed through the parallel networks of brewers' agreements, Whitbread's notified agreements do not lead to the elimination of competition in respect of a substantial part of the UK on-trade beer market.

It should be noted that the Commission applied a narrow test of foreclosure in the **7.121** *Whitbread* case. This related to the possibility for independent access to the market. What is surprising about the application of this narrow test is that the Commission recognized that other forms of access were possible:

> It is not disputed that the tied volume might still offer indirect access for other brewers in so far as the (property or loan) tying brewer/wholesaler is prepared to supply to its tied outlets beer from other brewers. However, the assessment on foreclosure focuses on opportunities for independent access for other brewers which clearly does not result from 'horizontal' cooperation between actual competitors. Such

---

[157] The Herfindahl-Hirschmann Index (hereinafter HHI), used to help describe market concentration, for the UK beer market increased, on the basis of the market shares of the national brewers, from 1350 in 1991 to 1678 in 1996. With an HHI of between 1000 and 1800, the market is described as 'moderately concentrated' (ref para 19 of the decision).

cooperation may limit the level of inter-brand competition between the brewers in question and the tying brewer will only allow another brewer's beer in his outlets when this is in the tying brewer's interest.[158]

7.122 The narrow test of foreclosure applied in the *Whitbread* case focuses primarily on the pure vertical aspects of entry, ie the ability of a foreign brewer to get its beers directly into retail outlets rather than indirectly through the network of an incumbent brewer. Access via the network of an incumbent brewer will normally have horizontal aspects. The Commission takes these horizontal aspects of entry into account when deciding whether to grant an exemption to the vertical aspects of foreclosure.

B. Exclusive Distribution

(1) Regulation 1983/83

7.123 Both in the administrative practice of the Commission and case law of the Court of Justice, exclusive distribution has been considered to fall within the scope of Article 81(1). This is due to its ability to restrain intra-brand competition by means of the reduction in the number of distributors for a given good.[159] In *Consten/Grundig*,[160] the Court of Justice said:

> Although competition between producers is generally more noticeable than that between distributors of the same make, it does not thereby follow that an agreement tending to restrict the latter kind of competition should escape the prohibition of Article 85(1) [now Article 81(1)] merely because it might increase the former.

7.124 Nevertheless, exclusive distribution is also perceived as a very efficient form of distribution since as specified in recitals 5 to 7 of Regulation 1983/83,[161] these agreements 'lead in general to an improvement in distribution because the undertaking does not need to maintain numerous business relations with a larger number of dealers and is able, by dealing with only one dealer, to overcome more easily distribution difficulties in international trade resulting from linguistic, legal and other differences'. They 'facilitate the promotion of sales of a product and lead to intensive marketing and to continuity of supplies while at the same time rationalising distribution . . . they stimulate competition between the products of different manufacturers'; such an agreement is 'often the most effective way, and sometimes indeed the only way, for the manufacturer to enter a market . . . this is particularly so in the case of small and medium sized undertakings'. As a result

---

[158] para 116 of the decision.
[159] Recent developments in economic thinking have now shown that exclusive distribution can also harm competition by facilitating foreclosure at the distribution level.
[160] *Consten/Grundig* [1966] ECR 229.
[161] Regulation 1983/83 [1983] OJ L173/1.

consumers 'can obtain products manufactured in particular in other countries more quickly and more easily'.

For these reasons exclusive distribution agreements are likely, under the **7.125** Commission's practice, to qualify for an exemption, subject to the condition that they do not establish absolute territorial protection in favour of the distributor.[162] In line with this perspective, the Commission has issued, on the basis of the powers granted by the Council in Regulation 19/65, the block exemption Regulation 1983/83. This Regulation declares inapplicable, on the basis of Article 81(3), the provision of Article 81(1) to certain formats of exclusive distribution agreements.

(2) Scope of Application of Regulation 1983/83

An exclusive distribution contract can be defined as the agreement under which **7.126** one party, the supplier, undertakes to supply certain goods exclusively to the other party, the distributor, within a given territory. Nevertheless, it must be borne in mind that the presence of such an obligation on the supplier is only a necessary but not sufficient condition for an agreement to fall within the scope of the block exemption. Regulation 1983/83, in fact, does not provide a generalized exemption to all the agreements drafted on the basis of the above-described framework. In order to fall within its scope of application, exclusive distribution agreements must fulfil the specific requirements established in Article 1 and partially in Article 3.

Only Two undertakings

In the first place Regulation 1983/83 only covers bilateral exclusive distribution **7.127** agreements. Article 1, following the provisions of Regulation 19/65, establishes that the exemption of Article 81(3) is only applicable to agreements to which only two undertakings are party.

The exclusion of multilateral agreements from the coverage of the block exemp- **7.128** tion Regulation, is mainly based on the Commission's suspicion of contracts concluded between the supplier and various distributors operating at the same level of the supply chain (ie a producer appoints, with the same agreement, several exclusive distributors in different Member States). The ratio of this exclusion lies in the wish to reduce the possibility of collective negotiation of exclusive distribution agreements, a practice which might easily result in an opportunity to facilitate horizontal collusion at the distribution level. However, the very strict formulation of Article 1 also excludes from the coverage of the block exemption multilateral agreements entered into by firms operating at different levels of the supply chain (ie a producer appoints an exclusive distributor and an exclusive retailer).

---

[162] *DRU/Blondel* [1965] OJ 2194; *Hummel/Isbeque* [1965] OJ 2581. This approach has also been confirmed by the jurisprudence of the Court (in particular *Consten/Grundig*).

7.129 On the other hand, this provision of Article 1 does not apply when the supplier enters into parallel (and formally separated) exclusive distribution agreements covering the same goods with several distributors. Paragraph 14 of the Commission Notice concerning Commission Regulations (EEC) 1983/83 and (EEC) 1984/83,[163] in fact, establishes that the limitation on the number of undertakings only applies to individual agreements. This point is of extreme importance in commercial practice since it allows the supplier to set up an exclusive distribution network without losing the benefit of the block exemption.

7.130 Another important aspect of this provision that must be clarified is the concept of 'undertaking'. In particular it is of interest to understand the circumstances in which 'collective parties' can be defined as 'single' undertakings. In this regard some guidance can be obtained both from the Commission Notice and Court jurisprudence. In the first place, paragraph 13 of the Commission's Notice stipulates that for the purpose of the applicability of Article 1, several undertakings which are separate legal entities but form an economic unit, are considered as a single undertaking.[164] This could be the case of a supplier that enters into an exclusive agreement with a distributor and one of his subsidiaries. This hypothesis must be distinguished from the situation in which one of the parties to an exclusive distribution agreement is an association of independent undertakings. In *Salonia*,[165] the Court of Justice established that an agreement between two trade associations could not be covered by Regulation 67/67[166] since the parties could not be regarded as two undertakings within the meaning of Regulation 19/65.

7.131 The requirement of 'two undertakings only' is also respected, according to paragraph 15 of the Commission Notice, when the supplier delegates the performance of the obligations arising from the contract to a connected or independent undertaking which he has entrusted with the distribution of his goods.

Agreements between Competitors

7.132 The second limitation on the scope of Regulation 1983/83 concerns exclusive distribution agreements between competitors. This hypothesis is regulated by the first two paragraphs of Article 3.

7.133 According to these provisions, agreements entered into between competitors[167] are covered by the block exemption only if non-reciprocal and if the total annual

---

[163] [1984] OJ C101/7.

[164] This view was confirmed by the Court of Justice in Case 170/83 *Hydrotherm/Andreol* [1984] ECR 2999.

[165] Case 126/80 *Salonia/Poidomani* [1981] ECR 1563. The same view was upheld by the Commission in *Flower Auction Aalsmeer I* [1988] OJ L262/27, 42.

[166] OJ 057 25/03/1967, p 0849.

[167] Article 3(a) defines a competitor as the 'manufacturer of identical goods or of goods which are considered by users as equivalent in view of their characteristics, price and intended use'. In this

turnover of each party does not exceed ECU 100 million.[168] The justification for such a provision lies in the intention to avoid the situation where a reciprocal exclusive distribution agreement might be used to partition the market between competitors. On the other hand, the exemption granted to non-reciprocal agreements takes into account the fact that the appointment of a competitor as a distributor can be the most efficient way to penetrate a new geographic market.

Goods for Resale

The third limitation imposed on the applicability of the block exemption regards the subject matter of the contract. In accordance with the enabling powers of Regulation 19/65, Regulation 1983/83 only covers agreements concerning the distribution of goods for resale.   **7.134**

The first and most evident consequence of such a provision is the exclusion from the scope of the block exemption of those agreements relating primarily to services.[169] The only case in which Regulation 1983/83 covers the provision of services is when they can be considered 'incidental' to the distribution of goods.[170] A borderline case which the block exemption is intended to cover is the one described in paragraph 12 of the Commission Notice, which specifies that the hiring of goods, which prima facie may be considered as a service, is economically speaking closer to the resale of goods than to the provision of services.   **7.135**

The second point of interest which arises from the analysis of this part of Article 1 is the limitation in the scope of the block exemption to the distribution of goods for resale only. The Commission Notice defines goods for resale as those goods which the purchasing party does not transform or process into other goods, which he does not use or consume in manufacturing other goods, or which he does not combine with other components into a different product.[171] In other words, in order to qualify as goods for resale, the distributed goods must retain their own   **7.136**

---

respect, the Commission Notice specifies that the provisions of Article 3(a) and (b) are applicable regardless of whether the parties are based in the Community and whether they are actual competitors. If the parties are competitors in a different product market from the one affected by the agreement, the Regulation will still apply.

[168] Article 5 gives guidance on the calculation of the total annual turnover. In particular it is specified that the block exemption is still applicable even if during a period of two consecutive financial years, the turnover exceeds the threshold of ECU 100 million provided the excess is no more than 10% (in other words, at the end of the two financial years the turnover of each party must not exceed the amount of ECU220 million).

[169] These agreements will be dealt with on an individual basis, as confirmed by the Commission in *RAI/Unitel* [1978] OJ L157/39.

[170] Commission Notice concerning Regulations 1983/83 and 1984/83, para 11. The same para specifies that a case where 'the charge for the service is higher than the price of the goods would fall outside the scope of the regulation'.

[171] Commission Notice, para 9.

economic identity.[172] The criterion the Commission established in order to define if an additional operation performed by the retailer affects the economic identity of the goods, is based on how much value this operation adds to the goods. The Notice, in fact, stipulates that 'only a slight addition in value can be taken not to change the economic identity of the goods'. The assessment of what amounts to a 'slight addition in value' in individual cases must be based on trade usage.[173]

Exclusivity of the Supply

7.137 The fourth pillar on which is based the delimitation in scope of Regulation 1983/83, is the exclusivity of the supply obligation. In order to benefit from the block exemption the agreement must also provide that the supplier will supply the contract goods exclusively to the distributor in the contract territory. The precise content of the exclusive supply obligation is clarified by the Commission in paragraph 27 of its Notice. Here it is stated that this obligation does not prevent the supplier from providing the contract goods to other resellers, established outside or inside the territory, who wish to sell within the contract territory. The only conditions which must be respected are that a) the supply must be made at the request of the reseller (the supplier cannot actively sell to other distributors within the contract territory), b) the delivery must take place outside the territory, and c) transport costs into the territory have to be paid by the reseller and not by the supplier. On the other hand, a distribution agreement appointing directly more then one distributor in the same territory is considered to fall outside the coverage of the block exemption.[174]

---

[172] ibid.

[173] In this regard, in para 10 of the Commission Notice it is said that the Regulation applies in the case of pre-sale operations such as the breaking up and packaging of goods in smaller quantities or mere repackaging. On the other hand, additional operations to improve the quality, durability, appearance, or taste of the goods such as rustproofing of metals, sterilization of food, or the addition of colouring matter or flavouring of drugs, bring the agreement outside the scope of the block exemption Regulation. In respect of this issue, of particular relevance is the position held by the Commission in *Campari* [1978] OJ L70/69.

[174] In *Junghans* [1977] OJ L30/10, the Commission declared inapplicable Regulation 67/67 to a distribution agreement that appointed three distributors for Junghans watches in Belgium. The exclusion from the scope of the Regulation of what might be defined as semi-exclusive distribution agreements, could appear prima facie surprising and inconsistent with the ratio which lies behind the exemption of this category of agreements. If, in fact, the main concern about exclusive distribution agreements is the restriction of intra-brand competition due to the limitation in the number of distributors in a given territory, it seems illogical that agreements, which are from this point of view less restrictive, are not covered by the exemption. The ratio for such a provision can be based on the assessment of the efficiencies which justify the exemption of exclusive distribution agreements. As already pointed out above (see para 1) this form of distribution is considered compatible with the competition rules because, even though drastically limiting the number of commercial entities which can distribute a certain product, it brings about efficiencies. In particular it is meant to facilitate distribution allowing the supplier to deal with only one distributor for a given territory and to facilitate the penetration of new markets by protecting the distributors from free riders. In the case of the simultaneous presence of more than one distributor within the same territory the aforesaid efficiencies would be strongly reduced and the restriction of competition deriving from the presence of a sole distributor would be less justifiable.

Nevertheless, it is worth noting that non-exclusive distribution agreements are often likely to fulfil the requirements for an individual exemption under Article 81(3).[175]

Extent of the Territory

The territory granted by the supplier to the distributor can extend to the whole of **7.138** the common market.[176] Agreements which grant an exclusive territory which is wider than the common market might still benefit from the block exemption.[177]

If a supplier established in the common market grants exclusive distribution **7.139** rights in third countries Article 81(1) does not apply even if associated with a prohibition on reimport into the common market unless it is possible to prove anticompetitive effects within the common market.[178] Article 1 does not impose any maximum or minimum limit on the size of the territory.[179]

(3) Additional Obligations that Can be Imposed on the Parties to an Exclusive Distribution Agreement

Whereas in the previous section we have tried to define the basic requirements **7.140** which an exclusive distribution contract must provide for in order to be covered by Regulation 1983/83, it is now our intention to describe the additional obligations the parties can undertake without losing the benefit of the block exemption.[180]

---

[175] *Report on Competition Policy 1987* (Vol XVII) point 28.

[176] The possibility to allocate the whole of the common market as an exclusive territory represented a new element in comparison with Regulation 67/67 in which the maximum extent of the territory was a defined area of the common market.

[177] Case 170/83 *Hydrotherm/Andreol* [1984] ECR 2999.

[178] With regard to the treatment of this contractual provision (known in commercial practice as *destination clause*) some more guidance has been recently provided by the Court in the judgment in Case C–306/96 *JAVICO/YSLP* ECR I–1983. In this case the Court established, in the first place, that destination clauses do not have as their object the restriction of competition within the common market, since they are not aimed at preventing parallel imports and the distribution of the relevant product within the territory of the Community but only to ensure an effective penetration of a geographic market located outside the Community by distributing in this market a sufficient quantity of products. However, destination clauses may be considered to have the effect of restraining competition within the common market. In order to assess the restrictive effect of these clauses, the Court set out the following criteria. First, it is necessary to establish whether the structure of the Community market for the relevant products is oligopolistic allowing only a limited degree of competition. Secondly, there must be an appreciable price difference between the price of the products sold within the Community and the price of those sold outside the Community. Thirdly, if the first two criteria are met, it is also necessary to determine whether, based on the supplier's position on the Community market and the extent of its production and sales in the Member States, destination clauses are capable of affecting the trade between Member States.

[179] The absence of a minimum area for the exclusive territory can be of particular importance in commercial practice. The possibility to allocate very small territories to distributors allows manufacturers to use exclusive distribution to set up retailing networks.

[180] In this context, it seems important to specify that the absence of the following obligations on the parties to the agreement does not affect the applicability of the block exemption.

Obligation that Can be Imposed on the Supplier

7.141 Article 2(1) stipulates that, apart from the exclusive supply obligation referred in Article 1, no other restriction can be imposed on the supplier other than not to supply directly to final users within the contract territory.[181] The supplier will always remain free to supply the contract goods to users that are resident in the territory subject to the condition that the delivery is made outside the territory.[182] In other words, the supplier can be obliged not to compete directly with the distributor within the contract territory. This kind of obligation on the supplier might also assume a non-absolute dimension. The agreement, in fact, will be still compatible with the block exemption where the supplier undertakes to supply certain customers only in the territory, with or without payment of compensation to the exclusive distributor.[183]

Obligations that Can be Imposed on the Distributor

7.142 Article 2(2) and (3) provides the list of obligations that the supplier may impose on the distributor without losing the benefit of the block exemption. The Commission in drafting Article 2 made a distinction between the 'restrictions of competition' which can be block exempted in the context of an exclusive distribution agreement (paragraph 2) and the 'additional obligations' which the supplier can impose on the distributor (paragraph 3). Such a distinction was based on the assumption that the first category of clauses always restricts competition while the second one normally does not.[184]

7.143 More recent developments in economic thinking have shown that the aforesaid assumption is not entirely correct because, when assessed in terms of their economic rather than legal effects, the obligations referred in paragraph 2 may not necessarily restrict competition and the obligations listed in paragraph 3 are not always inoffensive from a competition point of view. For this reason, in the present section we will not respect the nomenclature used in the Regulation and we will refer in general to the 'obligations'.

---

[181] It is important to avoid confusing overlaps between this provision and the content of the exclusive supply obligation provided in Article 1. Article 2 only makes reference to the restriction on direct supplies to *final users*. Article 1, on the other hand, concerns the limitation on the supplies to other distributors (for the content of this obligation see para 1.2.4).

[182] *Report on Competition Policy 1984* (Vol XIV) and paragraph 30 of the Commission Notice.

[183] Commission Notice, para 30.

[184] Paragraph 19 of the Commission Notice in this regard states that: 'The obligations cited in this provision [Article 2(3)] are examples of clauses which generally do not restrict competition. Undertakings are therefore free to include one, several or all of these obligations in their agreements. However the obligation may not be formulated or applied in such a way as to take on the character of restrictions of competition which are not permitted.'

(a) Non-Compete Obligation

The first obligation the supplier can impose on the distributor is 'the obligation **7.144** not to manufacture or distribute goods, which compete with the contract goods'. By means of this obligation the supplier can prevent other manufacturers from distributing their products through the exclusive distributor. The duration of this non-compete obligation is limited to the duration of the exclusive distribution agreement.[185] The importance of this provision lies in the possibility given to the supplier to set up a single-branded distribution network.

(b) Exclusive Purchasing Obligation

According to Article 2(2)(b) the supplier may oblige the distributor to purchase **7.145** the contract goods only from him and not from alternative sources. This provision assumes a particular importance in the context of an exclusive distribution system since it allows the supplier to stop cross-supplies between dealers belonging to the same network.[186] Even if, in fact, the supplier cannot impose on the distributor an obligation not to sell to other dealers belonging to the network, he may always oblige the distributor, by means of this provision, not to buy the contract goods from other dealers.[187]

(c) Ban on Active Sales

Article 2 allows the supplier to impose on the distributor a ban on active sales out- **7.146** side the contract territory. In this respect, paragraph (2)(c) provides that the distributor may be obliged by the supplier 'to refrain, outside the contract territory and in relation to the contract goods, from seeking customers, from establishing any branch and from establishing any distribution depot'.

This provision is of particular importance within the framework of Regulation **7.147** 1983/83 because it introduces what can be considered as a peculiarity of EC competition law: the distinction between passive and active sales.[188] As clearly stated in

---

[185] The previous Regulation 67/67 allowed the extension of the non-compete obligation for one year after the end of the agreement.

[186] Among practitioners there seems to be a certain confusion between the non-compete obligation and the exclusive purchasing obligation, probably due to the fact that in the commercial practice they are often used jointly. The first permits the supplier to prevent the distributor from distributing goods produced by other manufacturers, while the distributor remains free to buy the producer goods wherever he prefers. The second allows the supplier to oblige the distributor to buy its goods only from him, but the distributor remains free to distribute competing goods.

[187] Paragraph 17 of the Commission Notice mentions among the obligations that are not normally covered by the block exemption the restriction imposed on the distributor in the choice of his customers.

[188] The introduction of such a distinction, and the consequent prohibition of absolute territorial protection, is not based on pure competition concerns but is due to the market integration goal. According to the current interpretation of Article 2 and Article 3(g) of the Treaty of Rome, EC competition rules have also the object to promote the integration of national economies in view of the implementation of the single market. The distinction between passive and active sales has also been

the text of Article 2(2)(c), the distributor can be obliged not to make any sales effort outside the contract territory, but it cannot be prevented from responding to unsolicited requests from buyers based outside the territory.[189]

(d) Obligation to Purchase a Complete Range of Goods or Minimum Quantities

7.148 The supplier may impose on the distributor the obligation to purchase complete ranges of goods or minimum quantities (Article 2(3)(a)). The first part of this provision refers to the possibility for the supplier to expand the coverage of a single exclusive distribution contract to several categories of goods.[190] In this respect some doubt arises from the formulation of Article 2. In particular it is not clear if the supplier may introduce within the 'complete range of goods' products that belong to a non-homogeneous category of goods. The answer to this question is of crucial importantion, because the permissibility of such a conduct could give the supplier the possibility to extend the exclusive purchasing and non-compete obligations to a group of products having different natures.[191] Neither the Commission nor the Court of Justice seem to have ever taken a position in this respect. However, we think that an answer to this question is suggested on the basis that when the Commission intended to prevent the supplier from covering in the same agreement goods of different natures, it stated so clearly. An example is given in Article 3(c) Regulation 1984/83, where the Commission stipulates that the block exemption is not applicable to those agreements where 'the exclusive purchasing obligation is agreed for more than one type of goods where these are neither by their nature nor according to commercial usage connected to each other'. As far as the obligation to purchase minimum quantities of goods is con-

---

introduced in order to accommodate the political objective of defending the right of consumers, and buyers in general, to purchase wherever they want within the Community.

[189] Ban on passive sales is in the Commission practice considered as a 'hard-core' restriction. This means that the presence of such a provision not only brings the agreement outside the scope of the block exemption Regulation, but also makes the contract unlikely to be exempted on an individual basis. Moreover, the implementation by the supplier of vertical restraints giving rise to absolute territorial protection is a circumstance in which the Commission is likely to impose heavy fines. See *VW-Audi* [1998] OJ L124/60.

[190] The ratio of such a provision is to ensure for the supplier that the distributor offers to his customers a wide selection of products. This view was already expressed by the Commission in *Omega Watches* [1970] OJ L242/22.

[191] This conduct is commonly known as 'tying'. From a competition point of view it is considered a very dangerous practice because it allows the supplier to expand its market power to different product markets. A typical example of tying is represented by the latest Microsoft case in the US. Microsoft, which holds approximately 95% of the market for operating systems for personal computers, tied in an exclusive dealing agreement (exclusive purchasing and non-compete) entered into with the main PC producers its latest operative system together with its Internet browser. As a result Microsoft, exploiting its market position in the market for operative systems, raised its market share in the Internet browser market from 5% to 50%.

cerned, it seems reasonable to argue that this obligation is extendable to all the goods comprised in the 'complete range'.[192]

(e) Use of Trade Marks and Presentation

The supplier can oblige the distributor 'to sell the contract goods under trade **7.149** marks or packed and presented as specified' (Article 2(3)(b)). This provision allows the supplier to exercise a certain degree of control[193] on the distributor's sales activity establishing the use of trade marks under which the product must be displayed and sold. The supplier can also determine conditions relating to the presentation of the goods such as the way they are packed and displayed. It should be noted that the possibility for the supplier to establish the conditions of packaging must be reconciled with the provision of Article 1 concerning the requirement of 'goods for resale'. If the supplier imposes packaging conditions which go beyond the limits set out in the Notice and by Commission practice the agreement might be brought outside the scope of the block exemption.

(f) Promotion Activity

Article 2(3)(c) allows the supplier to impose on the distributor the obligation 'to **7.150** take measures for promotion of sales, in particular:

to advertise,
to maintain a sales network or stock of goods,
to provide customer and guarantee services,
to employ staff having specialised or technical training'.

This obligation is designed to be the counterpart, together with the non-compete **7.151** obligation, of the exclusive territory granted to the distributor. If in fact the exclusivity is justified to induce the distributor to concentrate his sales efforts on the contract goods, these obligations are the legal tools by which the supplier can ensure the achievement of this goal.

In the context of this provision, particular attention must be paid to the obliga- **7.152** tion to maintain a sales network. In this regard the Commission Notice specifies in paragraph 20 that as part of this obligation a distributor can be requested not to supply unsuitable dealers. However, in order to maintain the benefit of the

---

[192] It is important to emphasize that the obligation to purchase minimum quantities of goods, although exempted by Regulation 1983/83, could be perceived by the Commission, in the context of an individual procedure, as a serious restriction of competition. Such an obligation could be used as a close substitute for a non-compete obligation, particularly where the minimum quantities imposed equate approximately to the distributor's annual requirement.

[193] It has been correctly noted that when control by the supplier over the sales activity of the distributor exceeds a certain limit, the agreement comes close to the concept of franchising (see V Korah, WA Rothnie, *Exclusive Distribution and EEC Competition Rules* (London: Sweet & Maxwell, 1992). However, the current jurisprudence does not provide any guidance in determining the level of control required for such a shift.

exemption the agreement must provide objective admission criteria 'of qualitative[194] nature relating to the professional qualification of the owner of the business or his staff or the suitability of his business premises'. The Notice also states that these criteria must be the same for all the potential dealers and must be applied in a non-discriminatory manner.

(4) Obligations that are not Covered by the Block Exemption

7.153 The text of the Regulation clearly states that the only obligations imposed on the parties which will be covered by the block exemption are those mentioned in Article 1 and Article 2.[195] In order to further clarify this concept, Recital 8 of the Preamble to Regulation 1983/83 provides some specific examples of obligations the presence of which brings the agreement outside the coverage of the block exemption.

Restrictions on the Distributor's Freedom to Choose his Customers

7.154 The first case is related to the presence in the agreement of clauses that limit the freedom of the distributor to choose his customers. This provision is specifically designed to protect the freedom of the distributor to supply independent intermediaries (wholesalers or retailers not belonging to the supplier distribution network). Independent intermediaries are in fact the only economic entities within the supply chain which, by buying and selling huge quantities of goods in different exclusive territories, can make arbitrage on prices possible.[196] It must be noted, however, that two limitations to this principle are admissible. In the first place, the possibility for the supplier to prevent the distributor from selling actively outside its contract territory.[197] Secondly, the possibility for the supplier to forbid the distributor from supplying the contract goods to 'unsuitable dealers', subject to the respect for the conditions mentioned in paragraphs 7.151–7.152.

Restrictions on the Distributor's Freedom to Determine the Resale Price

The second hypothesis mentioned in recital 8 concerns possible limitations on the freedom of the distributor to determine the resale price. Such a restriction brings the agreement outside the coverage of the block exemption independently of the

---

[194] The adoption of quantitative criteria would not be covered by the block exemption and would require an individual exemption, *Ivoclar* [1985] OJ L369/1.

[195] In other words, the list provided by Articles 1 and 2 must be considered an exhaustive list that cannot be extensively interpreted.

[196] In most of the product markets, the mobility of final consumers is insufficient to avoid the exploitation by the supplier of the territorial exclusivity in order to price discriminate among different geographic areas. This is particularly true in relation to low priced goods where search costs normally outweigh price savings.

[197] See above paras 7.146–7.147.

legal form used to achieve it.[198] The Commission and the Court challenged both agreements embodying a price-fixing clause[199] and indirect practices intended to push the distributors to respect a fixed price level.[200] The same applies to the case in which the supplier imposes upon the distributor a maximum resale price.[201]

Whereas resale price maintenance is not covered by the block exemption, the sit- **7.156** uation may be different in relation to recommended prices. This is the case when the supplier does not impose the resale price but simply indicates the prices the distributor should adopt. This practice is normally considered to fall outside the scope of Article 81(1) unless it amounts to a concerted practice aimed at fixing prices.[202]

(5) *Circumstances that are not Covered by the Block Exemption*

Article 3(c) and (d)[203] provides a list of circumstances to which the block exemp- **7.157** tion Regulation does not apply. The main difference from the examples quoted in recital 8 and analysed in the previous paragraphs is that these circumstances do not refer to specific obligations imposed by one party on the other but they relate to objective market situations obtained by means of the implementation of the exclusive distribution agreement.

Impossibility of Parallel Imports

Paragraph (c) of Article 3 stipulates that the block exemption is inapplicable **7.158** when 'users can obtain the contract goods in the contract territory only from the exclusive distributor and have no alternative source of supply outside the contract territory'. Such a provision is essentially aimed to exclude from the coverage of the block exemption those exclusive distribution agreements that provide the distributor with protection from sales of other distributors established outside the contract territory (so-called absolute territorial protection).[204] This is confirmed by paragraph 31 of the Commission Notice that says: 'The block

---

[198] This is one of the few cases in which the Commission, drafting the block exemption Regulations, abandoned the typical formalistic approach and adopted an effect based assessment.

[199] *Polistil/Arbois* [1984] OJ L136/9, *Hennessey/Henkell* [1980] OJ L383/11.

[200] Case 107/82 *AEG/Telefunken* [1983] ECR 3151.

[201] The reason for such a ban on maximum resale prices is that even if they could help the supplier to prevent the distributor from exploiting the market power deriving from its territorial exclusivity, they could also amount to fixed prices. This is particularly the case when the distributor margin is reduced and the maximum price becomes the minimum resale price the distributor can afford.

[202] Cae 161/84 *Pronuptia* [1986] ECR 353.

[203] The provisions of Article 3(a) and (b) have been already described in paragraphs 7.132 *et seq* in relation to the definition of the scope of application of Regulation 1983/83.

[204] It is in fact a natural condition in the context of an exclusive distribution agreement that the distributor is the only source of supply within the contract territory. However, it must be underlined that if the supplier agrees to supply users directly within the exclusive territory he can represent an alternative source of supply: Commission Notice , para 31.

exemption can not be claimed for agreements that give the exclusive distributor absolute territorial protection.' The Notice continues specifying the measures the parties must take in order to remedy the occurrence of such a situation: '[i]f the situation described in Article 3(c) obtains, the parties must ensure either that the contract goods can be sold in the contract territory by parallel importers or that users have a real possibility of obtaining them from undertakings outside the contract territory'.

7.159 The possibility for parallel importers to sell within the contract territory is, in our view, closely linked to the effective freedom of exclusive distributors to choose their buyers. An agreement that prevents the distributor from selling to customers (final users or resellers) who are likely to export the contract goods in other territories would be certainly contrary to the provision of Article 3(c). At the same time, both the Commission and the Court have repeatedly affirmed that the distributor cannot impose any export ban on its customers.[205] On the other hand the possibility for users to obtain the contract good from alternative sources of supply outside the contract territory relates to the freedom of exclusive distributors to passively sell outside the contract territory. In this respect, any restriction on passive sales would be contrary to Article 3(c)[206] and result in loss of coverage of the block exemption. From this point of view also a limitation on the quantity of supplies to exclusive distributors established outside the contract territory might be considered to prevent re-export unless otherwise justified.[207]

(6) Withdrawal Procedure

7.160 Article 6 stipulates that the Commission has the power, pursuant to Article 7 Regulation 19/65, to withdraw the benefit of the block exemption in respect of agreements that, although covered by Regulation 1983/83, do not satisfy at least one of the conditions established by Article 81(3). Article 6 provides a non-exhaustive list of situations which may induce the Commission to implement a withdrawal procedure:

(a) the contract goods are not subject, in the contract territory, to effective competition from identical goods or goods considered by users as equivalent in view of their characteristics, price and intended use;

(b) access by other suppliers to the different stages of distribution within the contract territory is made difficult to a significant extent;

(c) for reasons other than those referred in Article 3(c) and (d) it is not possible for intermediaries or users to obtain supplies of the contract goods from dealers outside the contract territory on the terms there customary;

---

[205] *Tretorn and others* [1994] OJ L378/45; *Gosme/Martell-DMP* [1991] OJ L185/23; *Johnson & Johnson* [1980] OJ L377/16; *Sandoz Prodotti v Commission* Case C–277/87 [1990] ECR I–0045.

[206] See above paras 7.146–7.147.

[207] Having regard to this issue it must be noticed that the main concerns do not arise from the conclusion of a single agreement but from the conclusion of a number of parallel agreements establishing an exclusive distribution network.

(d) the exclusive distributor:

(i) without any objectively justified reason refuses to supply in the contract territory categories of purchasers who can not obtain contract goods elsewhere on suitable terms or applies to them differing prices or conditions;

(ii) sells the contract goods at excessively high prices.

From a procedural point of view, there are two main features of the withdrawal **7.161** procedure. In the first place, the Commission can only withdraw the benefit of the block exemption by means of an individual decision under Regulation 17, which 'may be coupled with an individual exemption subject to conditions or obligations or, in an extreme case, with the finding of an infringement and an order to bring it to an end'.[208] Secondly, this decision cannot have retroactive effect. In other words, the Commission, on the basis of a withdrawal procedure cannot attack the agreement for the period comprised between its entry into force and the adoption of the decision.

The withdrawal procedure differs from the provisions of Article 3 concerning the **7.162** non-applicability of Regulation 1983/83. In the latter case, there is no need for a declaratory decision since agreements not conforming with Article 3 have never been covered by the block exemption. Accordingly, in such cases the Commission remains free to challenge the agreement under Article 81 from the date of its entry into force.

(7) Guarantees and After-Sales Services

The Commission has repeatedly stated that a manufacturer's guarantee must be **7.163** applicable throughout the Community, irrespective of the Member State where the product was purchased.[209] The same principle applies to the provision of after sales services and 'essential services'.[210] This is because limitations imposed on the provision of such services might be used to prevent or impede parallel imports. In its *Report on Competition Policy 1986* (Vol XVI) the Commission stated that a 'refusal to honour a guarantee in respect of a product which has not been imported or exported through the manufacturer's established network may constitute a substantial barrier to trade within the Community . . . [and felt it necessary to] warn manufacturers that unless consumers could obtain Communitywide guarantees on products purchased in any Member State, the distribution arrangements covering such product might be declared to be incompatible with the competition rules'.[211]

---

[208] Commission Notice, para 24.

[209] *Matsushita Electrical Trading, Report on Competition Policy 1982* (Vol XII) points 77–78; *Report on Competition Policy 1986* (Vol XVI) point 56; *Sony, Report on Competition Policy 1987* (Vol XVII) point 67; *Grundig's EC Distribution System* [1994] OJ L20/15.

[210] *AKZO Coatings, Report on Competition Policy 1989* (Vol XIX) point 45.

[211] *Report on Competition Policy 1986* (Vol XVI) point 56.

7.164 In a series of decisions concerning clocks and watches,[212] motor vehicles,[213] consumer electronics,[214] electrical appliances,[215] and personal computers,[216] the Commission has required that where the manufacturer gave a guarantee on branded goods, the service covered by that guarantee would be available from any approved dealer, not merely the dealer from which it was purchased. This position has been confirmed by the Court of Justice in the *Hasselblad*[217] and *Swatch*[218] cases. In the latter case the Court held that clauses inserted in an exclusive distribution agreement, whereby the producer is obliged to grant final consumers a manufacturer's guarantee but which is to be withheld from customers of parallel importers, infringe Article 81(1) in so far as the restriction of competition resulting therefrom is likely to restrict trade between Member States.

No Requirement for Uniformity of Guarantees

7.165 It should be noted that this does not necessarily mean that the manufacturer is obliged to provide the same guarantee and after sales assistance coverage all over the Community. In this respect the service standard applicable will be that of the Member State in which the product is used rather than that of the Member State in which the product was sold.[219] In the case in which the imported product needs to comply with particular local safety legislation, the manufacturer can make the provision of guarantee and after sales services dependent on the payment of adaptation costs.[220] Similarly, the buyer can be asked to bear the costs of returning the imported product to the country in which it was sold when 'the model concerned is not of the same type as those marketed in the country of use and the spare parts needed for the repair are unavailable'.[221]

Selective Distribution

7.166 The only case in which a derogation to the above-described principles may be envisaged relates to the distribution of goods through a selective distribution system. Requirements relating to the protection of the integrity of a selective distribution network may justify the imposition of an obligation on the distributors to

---

[212] *Omega* [1970] OJ L242/22; *Report on Competition Policy 1971* (Vol I) point 56.

[213] *Bayerische Motoren Werke* [1975] OJ L29/1; *Report on Competition Policy 1974* (Vol IV) point 86.

[214] *SABA* [1976] OJ L28/19; *Report on Competition Policy 1975* (Vol V) point 54.

[215] *Zanussi* [1978] OJ L322/26; *Report on Competition Policy 1978* (Vol VIII) point 116.

[216] *IBM Personal Computer* [1984] OJ L118/24; *Report on Competition Policy 1984* (Vol XIV) point 63.

[217] Case 86/82, *Hasselblad Ltd. v Commission* [1984] ECR 883.

[218] Case 31/85, *ETA Fabriques d'Ebauches v DK Investment* [1985] ECR 3933.

[219] *Zanussi* [1978] OJ L322/26.

[220] *Moulinex*, *Report on Competition Policy 1980* (Vol X) point 70; *Matsushita Electrical Trading Report on Competition Policy 1982* (Vol XII) points 77–78.

[221] ibid.

provide guarantee and after-sales services only in respect of those goods which have been sold by an authorized outlet.[222] It should also be noted that these principles relate to conditions under which a manufacturer provides guarantee and after-sales services. They do not apply when these services are provided autonomously by the distributor. Nor do they apply where a distributor grants additional services to its customers over and above those required by the manufacturer.[223]

C. Exclusive Purchasing

(1) Regulation 1984/83: Exclusive Purchasing Agreements

An exclusive purchasing agreement can be defined as the agreement under which **7.167** one party, the distributor, undertakes to purchase certain goods for resale exclusively from the other party, the supplier. The first element of reflection in the analysis of this Regulation is that such an obligation, together with most of the additional obligations that the parties can embody in the text of the agreement, is also present within the framework of the above described Regulation 1983/83. The only substantial difference between the two block exemptions is represented by the possibility provided to the supplier by Regulation 1983/83 to grant an exclusive territory to the distributor. From this point of view, Regulation 1984/83 may be described as a diminished version of the block exemption dedicated to exclusive distribution agreements. This partial overlap between the two block exemption Regulations finds its justification in the concept of the Commission that exclusive distribution and exclusive purchasing are meant to be used at different levels of the supply chain. Regulation 1983/83 was designed having in mind the relationship between producer and importer while Regulation 1984/83 was supposed to regulate the relation between the wholesaler and the retailer. Experience has clearly shown that such a concept is not really founded in commercial practice and that parties often use the two distribution formats independently of the distribution level concerned.

(2) Scope of Application of Regulation 1984/83

As already noted in relation to exclusive distribution, the scope of application of **7.168** Regulation 1984/83 is defined by means of the requirements established in the text of the block exemption. In this respect, Article 1 stipulates that the Regulation will only be applicable to agreements 'to which only two undertakings are party and whereby one party, the reseller, agrees with the other, the supplier, to purchase certain goods specified in the agreement for resale only from the supplier

---

[222] Case C–376/92 *Metro SB Großmärkte Gmbh v Cartier* [1994] ECR I–15.
[223] Case 86/82 *Hasselblad Ltd v Commission* [1984] ECR 883, para 34.

or from a connected undertaking or from another undertaking which the supplier has entrusted with the sale of his goods'. On the other hand, Article 3(1) and (2) provides that the exemption will not be applicable to exclusive purchasing agreements entered into by competitors unless non-reciprocal and unless the turnover of each of the parties does not exceed ECU 100 million. Requirements relating to 'two undertakings', the destination of goods for resale, and the inapplicability to agreements between competitors, have already been dealt with in the context of Regulation 1983/83.

Exclusive Purchasing Obligation

7.169 The main element used by the Commission in order to define the scope of application of Regulation 1984/83 is the presence in the agreement of an exclusive purchasing obligation. The exclusive purchasing obligation can be defined as the obligation by which one party undertakes to purchase certain goods only from the other party. This obligation requires clarification in at least two respects. In the first place, it is important to recall the distinction made in footnote 186 between an exclusive purchasing obligation and a non-compete obligation. The first one affects exclusively intra-brand competition since it provides, in relation to the contract goods, that the distributor can only purchase from the appointed distributor and, accordingly, can be prevented from obtaining the goods from alternative sources of supply. In this context the distributor remains completely free to distribute goods which are in competition with the contract goods but are manufactured by a different producer. On the other hand, a non-compete obligation is meant to affect inter-brand competition. Such an obligation is in fact designed to oblige the distributor to purchase and distribute the contract goods only without restricting his freedom to choose the source of supply. It is not uncommon for confusion to arise in the use of the two terms. This is because the term 'exclusive purchase' is sometimes used to define both an exclusive purchasing obligation and a non-compete obligation. Both Regulation 1983/83 and Regulation 1984/83 allow a combination of these obligations.

7.170 The second important element to be stressed concerns the exclusivity of the obligation. As we have already noted in relation to exclusive distribution, the block exemption is only applicable to distribution agreements under which the purchasing party is obliged to source the contract good exclusively from the other party. Agreements that provide for semi-exclusive purchasing obligations fall outside the scope of the Regulation.[224] This view is confirmed by the Commission Notice which states in paragraph 35 that 'the regulation only covers agreements whereby the reseller agrees to purchase all his requirements for the contract goods

---

[224] As for semi-exclusive distribution, reasons for such obligations not being covered by the block exemption are related to a presumption of reduced efficiencies. See n 174 above.

from the other party. If the purchasing obligation relates to only part of such requirements, the block exemption does not apply.' Nevertheless, the second part of the same paragraph mentions two limited derogations to this principle. In the first place, the Notice clarifies that the parties can introduce in the agreement, without falling outside the scope of the block exemption, what in commercial practice is known as an 'English clause'. This is a provision which allows the purchasing party to obtain the contract goods from alternative sources of supply 'should these sell them more cheaply or on more favourable terms than the other party'. In this respect, it represents a derogation to the principle of the exclusivity of the purchasing obligation because it permits the distributor to source the contract goods simultaneously from two different suppliers. The second relaxation of the exclusivity mentioned in paragraph 35 of the Notice relates to the clause where a distributor tied by an exclusive purchasing obligation is free to obtain the contract goods from alternative sources when the supplier is not able to supply.

Absence of an Exclusive Territory

A second element used to define the scope of application of Regulation 1984/83 **7.171** is the absence of an exclusive territory. The block exemption, in fact, does not cover those exclusive purchasing agreements under which the distributor is granted an exclusive territory. In this respect, Article 16 establishes that the Regulation is not applicable 'to agreements by which the supplier undertakes with the reseller to supply only to the reseller certain goods for resale, in the whole or in a defined part of the Community, and the reseller undertakes with the supplier to purchase these goods only from the supplier'. Agreements providing at the same time territorial protection and an exclusive purchasing obligation may be able to qualify as exclusive distribution agreements and might fall within the scope of application of Regulation 1983/83. This provision is important in that territorial exclusivity is the only clear element that contributes to define the uncertain border between the scope of application of Regulation 1984/83 and Regulation 1983/83.

(3) Additional Obligations that Can be Imposed on the Parties to an Exclusive Purchasing Agreement

Respecting the structure of Regulation 1983/83, Article 2 of Regulation 1984/83 **7.172** provides a list of obligations the parties are free to accept without losing the benefit of the block exemption. It is worth repeating that the absence of these obligations from the content of the agreement does not prejudice the applicability of the block exemption.

Additional Obligations which Can be Imposed on the Supplier

7.173 The only obligation that can be imposed on the supplier is the obligation 'not to distribute the contract goods or goods which compete with the contract goods in the reseller's principal sales area and at the reseller's level of distribution'. This provision requires qualification. In the first place it seems important to determine the precise content of the obligation the supplier may assume. In this respect it is crucial to emphasize that this provision does not prevent the supplier from supplying other distributors located in the distributor's principal resale area even if operating at the same level of trade. This view is reinforced by paragraph 37 of the Commission Notice according to which 'this provision allows the reseller to protect himself against direct competition from the supplier in his principal sales area' and the supplier remains free 'to appoint other dealers in the area'.[225] In other words, a supplier may be prevented only from selling directly to his reseller's customers.

7.174 A second point of interest in the analysis of this provision is the definition of those elements that the Commission adopted in order to determine the borders of the supplier obligation: the reseller's principal sales area and the same level of trade. As far as the first element is concerned, it must be noted that the Regulation does not provide a definition of principal sales area. Nevertheless, some guidance can be obtained from paragraph 37 of the Commission Notice which in its second part states that 'the reseller's principal sales area is determinated by his normal business activity', that means the area in which the reseller is normally expected to seek customers and to make its sales. This flexible concept can be further specified by the parties. Paragraph 37 continues by stating that the principal resale area 'may be closely defined in the agreement'. With regard to the negative requirement of the 'same level of trade' on the basis of which the supplier may be obliged to refrain from competing at the same commercial stage as the purchasing party, it has been correctly noted that this provision, although apparently clear, can in practice give rise to some confusion.[226] This is due to the fact that in commercial reality the distinction between the different levels of trade can be unclear and difficult to detect. In particular difficulties could arise where the purchasing party operates at more then one level of the supply chain (ie the distributor operates both as a distributor and as a retailer). In such a case it could be problematic to define the precise limits of the supply obligation.

---

[225] Paragraph 37 of the Commission Notice goes further by specifying that the supplier cannot be forbidden to supply dealers who obtain the contract goods outside this area and afterwards resell them to customers inside it .

[226] V Korah and WA Rothnie, *Exclusive Distribution and EC Competition Rules*, see n 193 above.

Additional Obligations which Can be Imposed on the Distributor

Repeating the structure of Regulation 1983/83, Article 2 of Regulation 1984/83 **7.175**
lists the additional obligations the distributor may assume without losing the benefit of the block exemption.

(a) Non-Compete Obligation

Pursuant to Article 2, the purchasing party may accept an obligation not to pro- **7.176**
duce or distribute goods which are in competition with the contract goods. As
already has been stressed,[227] the possibility to embody in the agreement a non-
compete obligation, allows the supplier to obtain a high degree of control over the
distributor, permitting the parties to mimic a vertical integration process. In particular, it must be stressed that, like in the framework of the block exemption for
exclusive distribution, this provision allows the distributor to set up a single
branding distribution network. However, comparing the provisions of
Regulation 1984/83 with Regulation 1983/83 on this issue, an important distinction must be made. Regulation 1983/83 permits the extension of the non-
compete obligation for the entire duration of the exclusive distribution
agreement. Regulation 1984/83 limits to five years the duration for exclusive purchasing and non-compete obligations falling within its scope of application.[228]
Such a limited duration for an exclusive purchase and non-compete obligation
could act as a disincentive for the parties (at least for the supplier who normally
has got an interest in preventing his competitors from using his own distribution
channels) in the use of this distribution format and instead encourage parties to
adopt exclusive distribution agreements. It should be noted that the exclusive distribution block exemption gives the parties the possibility to achieve the same
result as an exclusive purchasing agreement without the limits of Regulation
1984/83. The requirement of Regulation 1983/83 for the granting of an exclusive
territory to the distributor may not represent a substantial obstacle since, as
observed before, the parties are completely free in the determination of the territorial scope.

(b) Other Additional Obligations

Article 2(3) of Regulation 1984/83 provides a list of some further obligations the **7.177**
parties may undertake without losing the benefit of the block exemption. These
are the obligations to purchase a complete range of goods or minimum quantities,
the obligation to use trade marks or to adopt a particular presentation, and the
obligation to engage in promotion activity. Given that this provision does not

---

[227] See above para 2.169.
[228] Regulation 1983/83 does not lay down any duration limit for exclusive distribution agreements.

differ substantially from Article 2(3) of Regulation 1983/83, the remarks made in the previous section are applicable.

(4) Obligations which are not Covered by the Block Exemption

7.178 Article 3(c) and (d) provide a list of obligations the presence of which brings the agreement outside of the scope of the block exemption.[229]

Obligation to Purchase more than One Type of Goods

7.179 The first 'black clause' mentioned in Article 3 concerns limits on the freedom of the parties to extend the exclusive purchasing obligation (together with the other permissible obligations) to products belonging to different types of goods. In this respect, paragraph (c) specifies that the block exemption is inapplicable where the exclusive purchasing obligation 'is agreed for more than one type of goods where these are neither by their nature nor according to commercial usage connected to each other'. The ratio which lies behind such a provision is the desire of the Commission not to exempt what in commercial practice is known as tying. As already stated above,[230] the possibility to tie products belonging to different categories of goods is perceived by the Commission as a very harmful practice due to its ability to extend the producer's market power to non-related markets.[231] However it is evident from the text of this provision that Regulation 1984/83 does not completely exclude the possibility of tying different products within the same contract. Article 3(c), in fact, sets out the limits within which the implementation of this practice does not preclude the applicability of the block exemption. In particular, in order to identify the different types of products which it is permissible to tie in the same exclusive purchasing agreement, reference is made to the criteria of connection by nature or by commercial usage. These criteria are commented upon in paragraph 38 of the Commission Notice which states that a relationship among the tied goods 'can be found on technical (eg a machine, accessories and spare parts for it) or commercial grounds (eg several products used for the same purpose) or in usage in the trade (eg different goods that are customarily offered for sale together). In the latter case, regard must be had to the usual practice at the reseller's level of distribution on the relevant market, taking into account all relevant dealers and not only particular forms of distribution.' Unfortunately, the parameters provided in the Commission Notice do

---

[229] The provisions of Article 3(a) and (b) of Regulation 1984/83 concerning the exclusive purchasing agreements between competitors are similar to Article 3(a) and (b) of Regulation 1983/83 discussed above.

[230] See n 191.

[231] This view is confirmed by the fact that Article 81(1)(e) EC mentions as an example of a practice that can restrict competition 'the conclusion of contracts subject to the acceptance by the other parties of supplementary obligations which, by their nature or according to commercial usage, have no connection with the subject of such contracts'.

not provide sufficient guidance in the assessment of the relationship which would justify tying different products in the same contract. They are in fact vague and dependent on subjective evaluation.[232] A point of interest which arises from the analysis of Article 3(c) is the link of this provision with Article 2(3)(a) which allows the supplier to oblige the distributor to purchase a complete range of goods. Having regard to the content of Article 3(c) it would appear that the limits established by this provision are also subject to the obligation to purchase a complete range of goods.[233]

Exclusive Purchasing Agreements Exceeding Five Years

Article 3(d) sets a duration limit beyond which exclusive purchasing agreements **7.180** are not covered by the block exemption. This provision stipulates that the block exemption is inapplicable when 'the agreement is concluded for an indefinite duration or for a period of more than five years'. The justification for such a provision can be found in the intention of the Commission to limit the impact, both at intra-brand and inter-brand level, of the foreclosure effect related to the implementation of an exclusive purchasing agreement.[234] This provision, limiting the duration of the exclusive purchasing and non-compete obligations, is in fact supposed to give the retailer every five years the possibility to switch to a different supplier for the contract goods or to a supplier of competing goods.[235] A crucial point of interest in the analysis of Article 3(d) concerns the condition under which an exclusive purchasing agreement, originally concluded for a fixed term of five years or less, can be renewed without losing the benefit of the block exemption. In this

---

[232] The parties could overcome the difficulties resulting from the uncertain formulation of the criteria by concluding separate exclusive purchasing agreements for products belonging to different product categories.

[233] In this respect it should be noted that in the context of the exclusive distribution block exemption we have interpretated in a less restrictive manner the provision of Article 2(3)(c) concerning the obligation to purchase a complete range of goods. Such an approach is justified by the absence in the text of Regulation 1983/83 of a provision, similar to Article 3(c) Regulation 1984/83, which specifically forbids the parties from extending the coverage of the agreement to products belonging to different categories of goods.

[234] Regulation 1984/83, Recital 11.

[235] It is interesting to note that Regulation 1983/83, although allowing the use of both an exclusive purchasing and a non-compete obligation, does not establish any time limit for exclusive distribution agreements. It seems that the Commission when drafting Regulation 1983/83 was not concerned by the possiblity of a foreclosure effect in the context of an exclusive distribution network. The reason for such a divergence of treatment probably lies in the Commission's concept that exclusive distribution was meant to regulate the relationship at the first stage of the distribution chain (eg producers/importers) where foreclosure is unlikely to become a serious concern. On the other hand, exclusive purchasing was supposed to be the legal form commonly adopted to regulate the relationship at the lower stage of the distribution chain (eg wholesalers/dealers) where foreclosure is more likely to be a serious issue. In our view such a difference of treatment under EC competition law between the two distribution formats could result in an incentive to parties to expand the use of so-called exclusive distribution and to limit the adoption of exclusive purchasing agreements. Of crucial importance is the fact that the legal framework permitted under Regulation 1984/83 can also be obtained through the application of the block exemption on exclusive distribution.

respect, a first indication is given by paragraph 39 of the Commission Notice according to which: 'Agreements that specify a fixed term but are automatically renewable unless one of the parties gives notice to terminate are to be considered to have been concluded for an indefinite period.' This provision is justified by the fact that the Commission wishes to provide the parties, and particularly resellers, with the possibility to effectively renegotiate the exclusive purchasing contract. From this point of view, automatic renewal could have been used to avoid the intended effect of a duration provision.

(5) Withdrawal Procedure

As regards withdrawal of the block exemption, the comments made in relation to exclusive distribution in paragraph 7.160 are also relevant.

D. Selective Distribution

The Commission's policy on selective distribution is expected to undergo substantial change in the near future. This is dealt with in Section H of this chapter.

(1) Introduction

7.181 As we have already seen in the previous sections of this chapter, the main distribution formats (exclusive distribution, exclusive purchasing, and franchising) are regulated by means of block exemption regulations defining the conditions under which distribution agreements are compatible with EC competition rules. The only exception to this principle in the current policy concerns selective distribution. In this area the conditions of compatibility with competition rules are not 'codified' in a legislative tool but must be inferred from a number of Court judgments and Commission decisions,[236] describing the application in individual cases of both Article 81(1) and Article 81(3).[237]

7.182 Such a different approach will also be reflected in the structure of the present section. In the first place we will try to provide a definition of selective distribution, to identify the commercial reasons which may induce a supplier to set up a selective distribution network, and to describe all the possible forms and nuances that

---

[236] In addition to formal decisions, the Commission's position on selective distribution may also be defined through the analysis of a large number of comfort letters granted in relation to cases identical to those settled by formal decision and through the examination of comments published in several Annual Competition Reports (see in particular the *Reports on Competition Policy 1979, 1980, and 1983* (Vols IX, X, and XIII)).

[237] The choice of the Commission not to issue a specific block exemption regulation for selective distribution, and to adopt an approach based on the analysis of a number of relevant cases, is usually justified by the fact that this distribution format is normally adopted in a limited number of areas of the economy and only at certain level of trade.

this format can assume. Secondly, on the basis of an analysis of the jurisprudence and of the Commission decisions we will attempt to clarify the conditions that render a selective distribution agreement compatible with the provision of Article 81(1) or, alternatively, bring it into compliance with the conditions of Article 81(3).

(2) Nature and Reasons for Selective Distribution

Selective distribution can be defined as a distribution system under which the sup-   **7.183**
plier limits the number of dealers distributing his products according to certain selection criteria and under which he prevents selected dealers from selling to dealers not belonging to the selective network. Such a method of distribution could prima facie seem in contradiction with the normal interest of a supplier to obtain the widest possible diffusion of his products throughout the market in order to reach the highest possible number of potential purchasers. In practice, the choice to approach the market through a limited number of points of sales may be justified on several grounds. The supplier could in fact have an interest to ensure that at the distribution level qualified staff are hired to advise customers on the choice of products, that a high standard of after-sales service and repair is provided, that the product is presented and displayed under optimum conditions, or that the exclusive image of the product is preserved.[238] In order to achieve these goals, the supplier must be able to maintain a certain degree of control over the characteristics of the points of sales for his products, preventing unsuitable distributors from entering into the distribution network. The main instruments by which a supplier can obtain such control over the distribution of his products are the selection criteria for authorized dealers and the ban on sales to non-authorized dealers. The first one is designed to select a priori, among the mass of dealers that are potentially able to undertake the distribution, those who are the most suitable in relation to the inborn characteristics of the product. The second one is aimed to preserve, once the selective distribution network has been implemented, the integrity of the system, avoiding the possibility that dealers originally excluded from the network may obtain the contract goods from authorized dealers.

It is self-evident that such a selection policy results inevitably in a reduction in the   **7.184**
number of dealers that effectively distribute the supplier's goods.[239] Such a reduc-

---

[238] All these interests might be perceived to be of particular importance in the context of the distribution of technically sophisticated goods (such as clocks and watches, cameras and photographic equipment, TVs, videos, hi-fis, computers) or goods which are characterized by a particularly strong image (perfumes, jewellery, *haut couture*, and branded or luxury goods in general).

[239] This view has been confirmed by the Commission which in its *Report on Competition Policy 1979* (Vol IX), para 5 says: 'Manufacturers that operate such [selective] distribution systems determine general rules governing sales with the aim of ensuring that specialised or complex products are properly marketed by the trade. With this in mind, they restrict the number of independent dealers and the location of sales points to degrees that vary according to the stringency of the requirements to be met by dealers seeking appointment . . .'

tion represents the main element of concern for competition authorities, which are called upon to assess whether the reduction in intra-brand competition might result in an opportunity for the creation of market power at the distribution level.

(3) 'Nature of the Good' Requirement

7.185 Both the Commission and the Community Courts share the view that the supplier has a legitimate interest in keeping under control the distribution of his products, requiring from dealers the fulfilment of certain requirements, only when this is required by the specific nature of the good to be distributed.[240] On the basis of this criteria the Commission and the Court have found the following categories of products to deserve the applicability of a selective distribution system: photographic products,[241] clocks and watches,[242] small household electrical goods,[243] jewellery,[244] personal computers,[245] dinner services,[246] consumer electronic goods,[247] newspapers and periodicals,[248] and cosmetics.[249]

7.186 In other cases the Commission and the Court denied the possibility to adopt a selective distribution system. It assumed, in fact, that the intimate nature of the following categories of goods did not justify the implementation of a selection policy: plumbing fixtures[250] and low price watches.[251]

7.187 The above-described case law seems to indicate a tendency to permit the applicability of selective distribution to the commercialization of goods, primarily consumer durables, characterized by certain elements such as technological complexity, luxury and sophisticated image and high quality.[252] Nevertheless, it must

---

[240] In this regard the Commission in one of its more recent decisions on selective distribution stated that: 'certain products which are not ordinary products or services have properties such that they cannot properly be supplied to the public without the intervention of specialised distributors'—*Givenchy* [1992] OJ L236/11. More guidance on the 'nature of the good' requirement can be found in the following decisions: *Yves Saint Laurent* Commission Decision 16 December 1991 [1992] OJ L12; *Vichy* [1991] OJ L75/57.

[241] *Kodak* [1970] OJ L147/24 and *Dupont de Nemours Deutschland* [1973] OJ L194/27.

[242] *Junghans* [1977] OJ L30/10.

[243] *Krups* [1980] OJ L120/26.

[244] *Murat* [1983] OJ L348/20.

[245] *IBM* [1984] OJ L118/24.

[246] *Villeroy & Boch* [1985] OJ L376/5.

[247] Case 107/82 *AEG—Telefunken v Commission* [1983] ECR 3151; Case 26/76 *Metro I* [1977] ECR 1875.

[248] Case 243/83 *Binon* [1985] ECR 2015; Case 126/80 *Salonia* [1981] ECR 1563.

[249] Case T–19/9, *Vichy* [1992] ECR II–415.

[250] *Ideal Standard* [1985] OJ L20/38; *Grhoe* [1985] OJ L19/17.

[251] Case 31/85 *ETA Fabriques d'Ebauches v DK Investment* [1985] ECR 3933.

[252] In Case T–19/92 which concerned the selective distribution of Yves Saint Laurent perfumes the Court of First Instance stated, *inter alia*, that 'While the Court of Justice has held in particular that such selective distribution systems on qualitative criteria may be accepted in the sector covering production of high quality and technically advanced consumer durables without infringing Article 85(1) . . . it is also apparent from its case law that selective distribution systems which are justified

be emphasized that from the analysis of the jurisprudence of the Court and of the relevant Commission decisions it is, unfortunately, impossible to abstract a general rule providing a secure guidance in assessing the applicability of the nature of the good requirement.

(4) Different Forms of Selective Distribution

7.188 Selective distribution may assume different forms in relation to the different criteria adopted in the selection process and in relation to the contractual obligations stipulated in the agreement. The distinction between different forms of selective distribution is extremely important in the context of the assessment of compatibility of this distribution format with EC competition rules. Both the Commission and the Court of Justice apply different parameters when evaluating the impact of the different forms of selective distribution.

Unilateral Selective Distribution

7.189 Unilateral selective distribution might be defined as an atypical form of selective distribution. In this case, in fact, the selection process is not based on criteria set up in an agreement. The supplier, on a pure unilateral basis, enters into a mere distribution agreement with a limited number of distributors upon which he does not impose any contractual restraints concerning the resale activity and with whom he does not assume any obligation other than to supply the contract goods.

7.190 The main characteristic of unilateral selective distribution is that the distributors do not undergo a proper selection process based on criteria fixed by the counterpart but they are simply unilaterally chosen by the supplier to undertake the distribution of his products. This kind of selective distribution is considered not to fall within the scope of Article 81 since it does not result from a contractual relationship between the supplier and the distributor. On the other hand, unilateral selective distribution might be identified with refusal to supply and, as such, it might be caught by Article 82 of the Treaty when implemented by an enterprise enjoying a dominant position in the relevant market.

Qualitative Selective Distribution

7.191 The first type of selective distribution that we can identify in the panorama of the current case law is so-called 'simple selective distribution'.[253] This form of selective distribution is normally reached when the process for selecting dealers is based on objective qualitative criteria.

---

by the specific nature of the products or the requirements for their distribution may be established in other economic sectors without infringing Article 85(1) [now Article 81(1)].

[253] The attribution of 'simple' to this form of selective distribution was given by the Court of Justice in Case 75/84 *Metro II* [1986] ECR 3021.

7.192 These criteria may be defined as criteria aimed to select dealers in view of their objective suitability to distribute a particular kind of good. In this context, the suitability is normally assessed on the basis of the professional qualification of the dealers and/or of the characteristics of the premises from which the distribution is carried out.[254] As regards the compatibility of these criteria with EC competition rules, the Court of Justice has constantly defined them as falling outside the scope of Article 81(1). Nevertheless, it must be specified that such a compatibility with Article 81 is subject to the respect of two basic principles elaborated by the jurisprudence: the principle of necessity and the principle of proportionality.[255]

7.193 The principle of necessity requires that the qualitative criteria implemented to select the dealers are characterized by a close relation with the nature of the product to be sold through the selective distribution system. The application of this principle is meant to define the scope within which the selection criteria for the distribution of a given type of product must be chosen in order to qualify as objective and qualitative.[256] An important aspect of the application of the principle of necessity is that the same selection criteria may be compatible with Article 81(1) when applied for the distribution of a certain type of product while it might be found incompatible in the context of the distribution of different kind of product.[257] On the other hand, the principle of proportionality requires that the criteria used in the selection process do not go beyond what may be thought necessary for the distribution of a given product.[258] Such a principle is aimed to define the 'threshold' above which the selection criteria, even if fulfilling the necessity requirement, are no longer considered to be compatible with the provisions of Article 81(1).

7.194 However, it must be emphasized that beyond the respect of the aforesaid principles, the compatibility of objective qualitative selection criteria with Article 81 may also depend on factors which are outside the control of the parties. In particular, the Court of Justice has stressed the relevance in such an assessment of the

---

[254] Having regard to the professional qualifications of the dealers and of their staff, the following are generally considered as objective qualitative criteria: a degree or a professional certificate; a minimum level of sales experience in a specific sector; specific training concerning the contract goods; capability of providing customers with technical assistance, presale services or guarantee services; bank guarantees. As concerns the suitability of the sale premises, the following are the most common requirements: establishment of particular sales condition within the point of sale; availability of an appropriate surface for display and demonstration of the contract goods; availability of a service outlet; possibility of appropriate display conditions; conformity of the outlet conditions to the product's reputation.

[255] See Paolo Cesarini, Les system de distribution sélective en droit communautaire de la concurrence, in Revu du Marché Unique Européen, 2–1992.

[256] See *Vichy* and *Metro II*, nn 249 and 253 above respectively.

[257] I Van Bael and JF Bellis, *Competition Law of the ECC* (CCH Editions Limited, 1987).

[258] See *IBM* (n 245 above) and *Villeroy and Boch* (n 246 above) where the Commission judged disproportionate the criteria on the basis of which the authorized point of sale was required to be located in a central area.

market structure in the framework of which the selective distribution system is meant to be implemented. In this regard the Court has stated that:

> It must be borne in mind that, although the Court has held in previous decisions that 'simple' selective distribution systems are capable of constituting an aspect of competition compatible with Article 85(1) [now Article 81(1)] of the Treaty, there may, nevertheless be a restriction or elimination of competition where the existence of a certain number of such systems does not leave any room for other form[s] of distribution based on [a] different type of competition policy or results in a rigidity in price structure which is not counterbalanced by other aspects of competition between products of the same brand or by the existence of effective competition between different brands.[259]

The Court essentially refers to the hypothesis of the simultaneous presence of numerous parallel networks of selective distribution agreements in a given market. Such a presence may induce a certain rigidity in the price structure, due both to the absence of less restrictive distribution channels and to the amplification of the inborn tendency of selective distribution to reduce intra-brand competition. Such a scenario, when in conjunction with an insufficient degree of inter-brand competition, may attract 'simple' selective distribution within the scope of application of Article 81(1).

Qualitative Selective Distribution plus Promotional Obligations

The supplier may decide to make the selection process more 'selective' by choosing its distributors not only on the basis of objective qualitative criteria but also by introducing a further requirement based on the acceptance by dealers of additional promotional obligations aimed at concentrating their efforts on the distribution of the supplied products. The acceptance of such obligation by the selected dealers may bring the agreement within the scope of Article 81(1). This is due to the fact that such obligations are normally perceived as not fulfilling the requirements established in the framework of the 'principle of necessity'[260] and, as such, representing a factor capable of introducing an undue restriction of competition.[261] Notwithstanding this restrictive nature, the Commission practice clearly

7.195

---

[259] *Metro II* (see n 253 above).

[260] In the case *Metro I* (see n 247 above), the Court of Justice explicitly mentioned the following obligations on the dealers as exceeding the threshold established by the principle of necessity: obligation to contribute to the establishment of distribution network; obligation to reach a given annual turnover; obligation to purchase minimum quantities or to maintain a sufficient stock.

[261] Promotional obligation can restrict competition both at intra-brand and inter-brand level. At intra-brand level by causing a further restriction in the number of authorized dealers; at inter-brand level by inducing the reseller to concentrate his commercial efforts on a single brand. It must be said, however, that in particular cases the Commission has assessed generic promotional obligations on the distributor as not falling within the scope of Article 81(1). This may be the case when these obligations do not concern the achievement of sales targets and minimum purchase quantities and when the structure of the relevant market is particularly competitive (see *Villeroy & Boch*, n 246 above). Nevertheless, the exceptional nature of this jurisprudence should be noted. The

shows that promotional obligations are likely to qualify for an individual exemption when there is sufficient evidence that they can result in an economic advantage by allowing the supplier to set up a more efficient distribution network.[262] In this regard, the Commission has highlighted that promotional obligations may help the supplier to design effective production and sales planning, to ensure continuity of supply, to rationalize distribution by concentrating his activity on the best performing distributors and to optimize the partitioning of distribution and marketing costs.[263]

Quantitative Selective Distribution

7.196 Quantitative selective distribution occurs when the supplier engages in a selection process which is not only aimed to identify the most suitable dealers for the distribution of his products but also to predefine the global number of points of sale which will be admitted to the distribution network.[264]

7.197 Independently of the nature of the criteria adopted to select the dealers,[265] quantitative selective distribution has always been perceived, from a competition point of view, as a very restrictive distribution method. This is mainly due to its ability to magnify the inherent capacity of selective distribution to reduce intra-brand competition by dramatically restricting the actual number of points of sale distributing a certain product and, consequently, by allowing the selected distributor to enjoy a market power position in respect of the supplied product. Consistently with this perspective, the Commission has always considered quantitative selective distribution as falling within the scope of application of Article 81(1).

7.198 As regards the possibility for an individual exemption under Article 81(3), the Commission approach, over the last two decades, has undergone an evolution process which has led to the present tendency to consider this distribution format

---

Commission, in fact, usually adopts a much more restrictive approach in the application of competition rules to promotional obligations, as clearly indicated in the case *Yves Saint Laurent,* Commission Decision, 16 December 1991, [1992] OJ L12.

[262] In this regard the Commission has made clear that promotional obligations accepted in the framework of a selective distribution agreement are likely to be exemptable under Article 81(3) only when they must be considered indispensable in order to achieve the above-described economic advantages. On this point see *SABA I,* Commission Decision 15 December 1975, [1976] OJ L28; *SABA II,* Commission Decision 21 December 1983 [1983] OJ L376.

[263] *SABA I* (see n 262 above); *SABA II* (see n 262 above).

[264] Alternatively, quantitative selective distribution may be defined as a selective distribution system where not all the distributors who meet the selective criteria may be admitted to the network, L Ritter, WD Braun and F Rawlinson, *EEC Competition Law—A Practitioner Guide* (Deventer: Kluwer, 1991) 212.

[265] Those might be abstract and uniform (as in the case of a selection process based on the potential purchase capacity of the targeted customers) or absolutely subjective and linked to the implementation of commercial strategies (as in the case of a selection based on the number or density of points of sale in respect of the network coverage area).

as a *per se* restriction and, as such, not exemptable.[266] Whereas, in fact, in the early seventies the Commission envisaged the possibility of granting an individual exemption to a quantitative selective distribution system when the products concerned where luxury goods produced in a limited quantity and addressed to a restricted clientele[267] or when the relevant market was sufficiently competitive,[268] nowadays a much more restrictive approach seems to have been adopted. This change of approach, due to the greater level of attention paid by the Commission to safeguard intra-brand competition in view of the achievement of the market integration objective, has resulted in a more severe application of Article 81 in respect of quantitative selective distribution systems.[269] However, it must be recalled that the Commission's attitude in respect of the exemptability of quantitative selective distribution may undergo a further evolution in the very near future. The recently adopted Commission Communication on the application of EC competition rules to vertical restraints[270] envisages the inclusion of selective distribution within the scope of a future block exemption regulation, irrespective of the qualitative or quantitative nature of the selection criteria.

(5) Application of the Selection Criteria

Irrespective of the qualitative or quantitative nature of the criteria adopted to **7.199** select dealers, selective distribution will (normally) be considered to infringe Article 81 when the selection process is implemented in a discriminatory manner.[271] The Commission and the Court have specified that discriminatory application occurs when a supplier refuses a priori to appoint certain dealers notwithstanding their objective ability to match the criteria established for the selection process,[272] or when the selection criteria are not applied uniformly to different categories of dealers.[273] It must be specified that in order to classify the

---

[266] Jean Dubois, *European Competition Forum, Selective Distribution—The European Community's Stance* (Brussels, 1995).

[267] *Omega* [1970] OJ L242/22.

[268] See the analysis of the cases *Dior* and *Lancôme* in the *Report on Competition Policy 1974* (Vol IV) para 96.

[269] A significant example of this new approach is reflected in *Yves Saint Laurent*, Commission Decision 16 December 1991 [1992] OJ L12, where the Commission made the grant of an individual exemption dependent on the definitive abandonment by the French company of the quantitative selective distribution system previously implemented.

[270] COM(98)544 final, 30 September 1998. For an overview of the policy proposal contained in this document see Section H.

[271] In its *Report on Competition Policy 1981* (Vol XI) the Commission stipulates: 'Where refusal to appoint a dealer results from a discriminatory application of a distribution system, its compatibility with Art 85 is brought into question..

[272] In particular the Commission takes the view that discriminatory application occurs when the supplier refuses to admit to his selective network: dealers which are likely to implement a low price strategy (discounters), certain forms of distribution (supermarkets, shopping centre, etc), and dealers who are likely to exploit the price differential between different Member States. On this point see the *Report on Competition Policy 1983* (Vol XIII), para 11.

[273] In *Binon* [1985] ECR 2015.

supplier's refusal to admit a qualified dealer to the selective network as a discriminatory application of selection criteria, the Commission must provide sufficient evidence that the refusal is part of a strategy aimed at excluding certain dealers. In this respect, the Court has stressed that 'refusals to approve distributors who satisfy the qualitative criteria mentioned above therefore supply proof of an unlawful application of the system if their number is sufficient to preclude the possibility that they are isolated cases not forming part of a systematic conduct'.[274]

7.200 As already stated above, the discriminatory application of selection criteria will normally result in the incompatibility of the selective distribution agreement, irrespective of its qualitative or quantitative nature, with Article 81. This does not mean that the Commission will have the power to oblige the supplier, unless it is a dominant firm as defined in the context of Article 82, to directly supply the excluded dealers.[275] However, the Commission will be able, under Article 81, to oblige the supplier to refrain from hindering the excluded dealers obtaining the contract goods from authorized distributors. In order to obtain the possibility to be supplied directly by authorized distributors, excluded dealers do not need to lodge a complaint with the Commission. Given the direct applicability of Article 81(1), excluded dealers are entitled to invoke the application of the above described measure before national courts.[276]

7.201 Discriminatory application of selection criteria seems to be a matter of particular concern for the Commission. This is clearly shown by its constant attempts to limit suppliers' control on the selection process. In *Villeroy & Boch*, the Commission said:

> The principle that the producer should himself verify the qualifications of specialised retailers admitted to the network is necessary to ensure that the selective distribution system is uniform and remains closed. Inasmuch as it is accessory to the main obligation of specialisation incumbent on the retailer, and contributes to ensuring compliance with that obligation, the principle that the producer should himself control the access of specialised retailers to the network does not go beyond what is necessary to maintain the network.[277]

Consistent with this principle, in *Murat* the Commission induced the notifying party to modify its standard selective distribution agreement to allow authorized

---

[274] Case 107/82 *AEG—Telefunken* (see n 247 above). In the same judgment the Court rejected the argument according to which the refusal to approve a dealer may be qualified as a unilateral act of the supplier falling outside the scope of application of Article 81. In this respect the Court said: 'The view must therefore be taken that even refusals of approval are acts performed in the context of contractual relations with authorised distributors inasmuch as their purpose is to guarantee observance of the agreements in restraint of competition which form the base of contracts between manufacturer and approved distributors.'

[275] As clarified in Case 210/81 *Demo-Studio Schmidt v Commission* [1983] ECR 3045. Article 81 cannot be the legal base for the imposition of an obligation to supply.

[276] *Yves Saint Laurent* Commission Decision, 16 December 1991, [1992] OJ L12.

[277] *Villeroy & Boch* [1985] OJ L376/15.

dealers to sell the contract product to retailers who, in their judgement, met the selection criteria.[278] In the second *SABA* decision the Commission established the concept that, where the selective distribution system provide for the existence of an intermediary level of selected wholesalers between the production (or import) stage and the retailing stage, these must be entitled to admit directly to the distribution network retailers matching the selection criteria.[279]

(6) Restrictions on Resale Activity

As we have already seen in paragraphs 7.183–7.184, restrictions on dealers' resale **7.202** activity represent a key element in the framework of a selective distribution system. The supplier, in fact, in order to preserve the integrity of the network can impose an obligation on his distributors not to sell to non-approved retailers. At the same time, these restrictions are also the main concern from a competition point of view, implying a reduction of competition at the intra-brand level. For this reason, the Commission has always adopted a very strict approach on the compatibility with EC competition rules of further resale restrictions.

Such an approach first of all requires that the approved distributors are kept free **7.203** to engage in cross-supplies within the selective network. In other words, approved distributors must be able to source the contract goods not only vertically from the supplier but also horizontally from any other network distributor (being importer, wholesaler, or retailer) located within the Community.[280] Accordingly, approved distributors must also be able to supply all the other members of the distribution network. In this respect, the inclusion in a selective distribution agreement of an exclusive purchasing provision according to which distributors are obliged to source the contract product only from a designated supplier would be considered to infringe Article 81. On the other hand, more flexible forms of supply sourcing may be considered to be compatible with the provisions of Article 81. In *Yves Saint Laurent Perfumes* the Commission took the view that an obligation on retailers to purchase from Yves Saint Laurent's exclusive agents a minimum quantity of contract products (amounting to at least 40 per cent of the average purchases figure during the previous year of all retail outlets in a given Member State) was exemptable under Article 81(3).[281] It should be noted that in the same decision the Commission drew attention to other contractual mechanisms capable of indirectly preventing selected distributors from implementing a

---

[278] *Murat* [1983] OJ L348/20.

[279] *SABA II* [1983] OJ L376/41.

[280] The maintenance of the possibility of cross-supplies within the selective network assumes particular importance with reference to trans-border transactions in view of the market integration objective. In the cases *Dior* and *Lancôme* the Commission obliged the parties to modify their agreement in order to allow cross-supplies among distributors located in different Member States. See *Report on Competition Policy 1974* (Vol IV).

[281] *Yves Saint Laurent*, Commission Decision 16 December 1991, [1992] OJ L12.

cross-supplies strategy. Monitoring activity aimed at controlling the flow of contract goods among members of the selective network can be implemented only
when the supplier has sufficient reason to fear the resale of products outside the
network. Contract provisions making it uneconomic for distributors to resell the
contract goods to other members of the network were not exempted. In the same
case the parties were induced to eliminate a clause according to which sales to
other members of the selective network were not counted in the calculation of the
annual minimum purchase requirement.

7.204 A second category of resale restriction which can result in a selective distribution
agreement infringing Article 81 is that which limits the ability of the appointed
distributor to choose its customers.[282] This is the case when a supplier imposes an
obligation on the appointed distributors to supply exclusively customers located
in a given territory or belonging to a particular customer group. Irrespective of the
criteria adopted, the Commission has always considered such a restriction as not
exemptable.[283] The ratio behind this Commission practice is the intention to
avoid that selective distribution's inherent ability to restrict intra-brand competition should be magnified by the presence of exclusivity granted to the appointed
distributor in respect of its customers.[284]

7.205 Lastly, the Commission has always adopted a negative approach in respect of steps
taken by the supplier to prevent its appointed distributors from selling products
which are in competition with the contract goods. In this respect, the presence in
a selective distribution agreement of a non-compete obligation on the distributor
may constitute an infringement of Article 81. The Commission takes the view
that competition among different products within the same point of sale (so
called in-store competition) may represent an efficient tool to counterbalance the
reduction of intra-brand competition arising from a selective distribution system.

E. Franchising

(1) Introduction

7.206 Franchising is not a heterogeneous phenomenon. In the English speaking world
the word 'franchise' is used to denote a liberty or privilege such as the right to hold
fairs and markets. At common law a franchise was a royal privilege which not only
authorized something to be done, but gave the holder of the franchise the right to

---

[282] Excluded the aforesaid ban on resale to other distributors not forming part of the network.
[283] *Ideal Standard* (see n 250 above); *Grohe* (see n 250 above).
[284] This approach seems to be confirmed by the recent Commission Communication on the
Application of EC Competition Rules to Vertical Restraints COM(98)544 final, which foresees the
inclusion, in the 'black list' of the future block exemption regulation, of the combination at the same
stage of the supply chain of selective distribution with exclusive distribution or customer allocation.

prevent others from interfering with the right. In relation to vertical restraints, the term can be used to describe contractual relationships between economic operators each acting at different levels of the supply chain. Kotler has defined a franchise organization as 'a contractual association between a franchiser (manufacturer, wholesaler, service organisation) and franchisees (independent business-people who buy the right to own and operate one or more units in the franchise system)'.[285] The main distinction between a franchise system and other types of contractual supply chains is that a franchise system is normally perceived as a vertically integrated entity and is based on some product or service; method of doing business; or some brand name, goodwill, or patent which the franchisor has developed. Franchising allows firms to expand into new areas without having to provide all the necessary capital and makes use of local expertise in new markets. The Court of Justice has distinguished between three forms of franchising:

> (i) service franchises, under which the franchisee offers a service under the business name or symbol and sometimes the trade-mark of the franchisor, in accordance with the franchisor's instructions, (ii) production franchises, under which the franchisee manufactures products according to the instructions of the franchisor and sells them under the franchisor's trade-mark, and (iii) distribution franchises, under which the franchisee simply sells certain products in a shop which bears the franchisor's business name or symbol.[286]

(2) The Pronuptia Judgment

7.207 Until 1986 the legal status of distribution and service franchises under Community competition law was unclear. Production franchising had been addressed in the 1978 decision of the Commission in the *Campari* case,[287] although the decision which analyses the notified trade mark licensing agreement and know-how licensing agreement does not classify the contractual arrangements as relating to a production franchise. Until the judgment in the *Pronuptia* case it had been thought that if distribution franchises fell within the prohibition of Article 81(1), they could be covered by the block exemption regulations for exclusive distribution and exclusive purchasing.

7.208 On 28 January 1986 the Court of Justice delivered a preliminary ruling in the *Pronuptia* case, the first franchising case submitted to it. The franchise system in this case related to the distribution of wedding dresses and other bridal wear under the trade mark 'Pronuptia de Paris'. In its judgment the Court ruled that many of the provisions in the Pronuptia contract, essential to the working of the franchise system, did not restrict competition. Other provisions, which afforded franchisees a degree of territorial protection from each other, were found to restrict

---

[285] Philip Kotler, *Principles of Marketing* (3rd edn) 1986 Prentice Hall 461.
[286] Case 161/84 *Pronuptia de Paris GmbH v Pronuptia de Paris Irmgard Schillgalis* [1986] ECR 374, at para 13.
[287] *Campari* [1978] OJ L70/69.

competition. The Court also made it clear that the existing block exemption for distribution agreements could not be applied to franchise contracts.

7.209 The case arose from proceedings before a national court in Germany in which Mrs Shillgalis, a Pronuptia franchisee, had invoked the invalidity of the agreements under Article 81(1) in order to escape her contractual obligation to pay arrears in royalties. The Court ruled that 'the compatibility of franchise agreements for the distribution of goods with Article 85(1) [now Article 81(1)] depends on the provisions contained therein and on their economic context'.[288] The judgment in this case relates to distribution franchises; however, in a later codification of the law in the franchising block exemption Regulation,[289] the Commission applies the same principles to service franchises. In paragraph 15 of the judgment the Court points out the differences between a franchise and other formats of distribution and explains why, subject to two conditions being met, distribution franchises without territorial protection[290] do not fall within the prohibition of Article 81(1):

> 15. In a system of distribution franchises of that kind an undertaking which has established itself as a distributor on a given market and thus developed certain business methods grants independent traders, for a fee, the right to establish themselves in other markets using its business name and the business methods which have made it successful. Rather than a method of distribution, it is a way for an undertaking to derive financial benefit from its expertise without investing its own capital. Moreover, the system gives traders who do not have the necessary experience access to methods which they could not have learned without considerable effort and allows them to benefit from the reputation of the franchisor's business name. Franchise agreements for the distribution of goods differ in that regard from dealerships or contracts which incorporate approved retailers into a selective distribution system, which do not involve the use of a single business name, the application of uniform business methods or the payment of royalties in return for the benefits granted. Such a system, which allows the franchisor to profit from his success, does not in itself interfere with competition. In order for the system to work two conditions must be met.

7.210 The two conditions are set out in paragraphs 16 and 17 of the judgment:

> 16. First, the franchisor must be able to communicate his know-how to the franchisees and provide them with the necessary assistance in order to enable them to apply his methods, without running the risk that that know-how and assistance might benefit competitors, even indirectly. It follows that provisions which are essential in order to avoid that risk do not constitute restrictions on competition for

---

[288] Case 161/84 (see n 286 above), at para 27.

[289] Commission Regulation (EEC) 4087/88 of 30 November 1988 on the application of Article 85(3) [now Article 81(3)] of the Treaty to categories of franchise agreements [1988] OJ L357/46.

[290] Note that 'requirements relating to the location of the shop' were not considered as amounting to territorial protection (ref para 19 of the judgment). This should not be understood as support for the thesis that location clauses do not fall under Article 81(1). It is clear from a full reading of para 19 that the Court used the term 'location' in the sense of its effect on the reputation of the network and not in terms of affording protection to franchisees from intra-brand competition.

the purposes of Article 85(1) [now Article 81(1)]. That is also true of a clause prohibiting the franchisee, during the period of validity of the contract and for a reasonable period after its expiry, from opening a shop of the same or a similar nature
in an area where he may compete with a member of the network. The same may be
said of the franchisee's obligation not to transfer his shop to another party without
the prior approval of the franchisor; that provision is intended to prevent competitors from indirectly benefiting from the know-how and assistance provided.

17. Secondly, the franchisor must be able to take the measures necessary for maintaining the identity and reputation of the network bearing his business name or
symbol. It follows that provisions which establish the means of control necessary for
that purpose do not constitute restrictions on competition for the purposes of
Article 85(1).

Therefore vertical restraints which are '*essential*' to protect the know-how trans- **7.211**
ferred to the franchisee and which are '*necessary*' to protect the identity and reputation of the network do not constitute restrictions of competition. In paragraph
16, quoted above, the Court gives examples of vertical restraints relating to non-
compete and transfer of ownership which are deemed essential to avoid disclosure
of the know-how. The examples given by the Court are not exhaustive. In paragraphs 18 to 22 the Court assesses vertical restraints relating to the franchisee's
obligation to (1) use the know-how provided, (2) follow instructions on layout,
decoration, and location of shop,[291] (3) seek approval for any assignment of his
rights and obligations, (4) follow instructions on the quality of goods sold, and (5)
seek approval for any advertising. In relation to the sourcing of goods the Court
specifically recognized that in certain cases it may be permissible for franchisors to
go beyond specifying merely the quality of the goods to be sold by the franchisee:

21. . . . It may in certain cases—for instance, the distribution of fashion articles—be
impractical to lay down objective quality specifications. Because of the large number of franchisees it may also be too expensive to ensure that such specifications are
observed. In such circumstances a provision requiring the franchisee to sell only
products supplied by the franchisor or by suppliers selected by him may be considered necessary for the protection of the network's reputation. Such a provision may
not however have the effect of preventing the franchisee from obtaining those products from other franchisees.

The Court then proceeded to give an example of a category of vertical restraints **7.212**
common to many franchise systems which are not necessary for the protection of
the know-how provided or the maintenance of the network's identity and reputation, and which constitute a restriction of competition for the purposes of Article
81(1). These are vertical restraints which impact not on inter-brand competition
but on intra-brand competition and which in the words of the Court 'restrict
competition between the members of the network'.[292] As an example the Court

---

[291] On location, see n 290 above.
[292] Case 161/84, see n 286 above, at para 23.

referred to 'provisions which share markets between the franchisor and franchisees or between franchisees or prevent franchisees from engaging in price competition with each other'.[293] Basing itself on its judgment in *Consten and Grundig*, the Court was of the opinion that a franchise agreement typically results:

> in a sharing of markets between the franchisor and the franchisees or between franchisees and thus restricts competition within the network . . . a restriction of that kind constitutes a limitation of competition for the purposes of Article 85(1) [now Article 81(1)] if it concerns a business name or symbol which is already well-known. It is of course possible that a prospective franchisee would not take the risk of becoming part of the chain, investing his own money, paying a relatively high entry fee and undertaking to pay a substantial annual royalty, unless he could hope, thanks to a degree of protection against competition on the part of the franchisor and other franchisees, that his business would be profitable. That consideration, however, is relevant only to an examination of the agreement in the light of the conditions laid down in Article 85(3).[294]

7.213 It is interesting to note that having cleared so many vertical restraints which impact on inter-brand competition the Court should have applied Article 81(1) to franchising systems solely on the basis of restraints relating to intra-brand competition,[295] even where they were necessary for the commercial viability of the franchise system because franchisees would not have invested without a degree of exclusivity. It is clear that the doctrine of 'necessity'[296] has its limits, particularly where the single market objective is called into question. Korah opines that the Court may have been reluctant to overrule *Consten and Grundig* and 'seem to have assumed that a network of exclusive territories, coupled with a requirement that each franchisee sell only from its shop, would confer absolute territorial protection'.[297] This thesis is supported by paragraph 26 of the judgment where the Court states that:

> franchise agreements for the distribution of goods which contain provisions sharing markets between the franchisor and the franchisees or between the franchisees themselves are in any event liable to affect trade between Member States, even if they are entered into by undertakings established in the same Member State, in so far as they prevent franchisees from establishing themselves in another Member State.

---

[293] Case 161/84, see n 286 above, at para 23.

[294] Case 161/84, see n 286 above, at para 24.

[295] It could be argued that the requirement for the business name to be 'well-known' implies that the franchise system must have achieved a certain level of market power.

[296] Valentine Korah, *Franchising and the EEC Competition Rules Regulation 4087/88* (Oxford: ESC Publishing Limited, 1989) 21. Korah also argues that the doctrine of necessity appears to be an example of the ancillary restraint doctrine adopted in the USA and not an application of the rule of reason as originally applied in the USA as no balancing is required between the pro- and anti-competitive effects of the agreement.

[297] Supra n 296 at 21.

The Court took a favourable view of recommended prices in the context of fran-   **7.214**
chising:

> 25 Although provisions which impair the franchisee's freedom to determine his own
> prices are restrictive of competition, that is not the case where the franchisor simply
> provides franchisees with price guidelines, so long as there is no concerted practice
> between the franchisor and the franchisees or between the franchisees themselves for
> the actual application of such prices. It is for the national court to determine
> whether that is indeed the case.

In the context of the application of Article 81(1) to franchise agreements the   **7.215**
Court went on to say that Regulation 67/67[298] on the application of Article 81(3)
to certain categories of exclusive dealing agreements is not applicable to franchise
agreements for the distribution of goods.[299] While this was consistent with the
Court's assessment as to the difference in nature between franchising and exclusive dealerships it placed franchise systems affording territorial protection to franchisees in a position of legal uncertainty. This was because they were liable to fall
within the prohibition of Article 81(1) where they had an appreciable effect on
competition and on trade between Member States and could only be removed
from this provision by way of an individual exemption decision on the part of the
Commission. To allay such fears and avoid a flood of unnecessary notifications,
the then Commissioner for competition policy, Peter Sutherland, issued a statement in March 1986 in which he communicated the Commission's positive attitude to franchising agreements and stressed the priority being given to the
drafting of a block exemption.[300]

(3) Decisions of the Commission

Between 1986 and 1988 the Commission adopted five formal decisions concern-   **7.216**
ing franchise systems. The Commission used these decisions as the basis for drafting the franchising block exemption adopted in November 1988.

Yves Rocher [301]

This case arose from the notification of a system of standard form franchise con-   **7.217**
tracts for the retailing of cosmetics. Franchisees were given know-how and
granted the exclusive right within an area defined in the contract, to use in a retail
shop the trade marks and designs of Yves Rocher for the sale of its products. In its
legal assessment the Commission, while recognizing the closely integrated form

---

[298] This block exemption Regulation on exclusive dealing, which expired on 30 June 1983, was
replaced by Regulations 1983/83 on exclusive distribution agreements and 1984/83 on exclusive
purchasing.
[299] Case 161/84, see n 286 above, at para 33.
[300] Statement by Mr Peter Sutherland—Euro Conferences 25 March 1986—Franchise
Agreements under EEC Competition Rules, IP/86/150.
[301] *Yves Rocher* [1987], OJ L8/49.

of the distribution system, found that the franchise contracts were agreements between undertakings within the meaning of Article 81(1) because the franchisees are the owners of their business of which they bear the financial risk.[302] The obligation on the franchisees to sell only products bearing the Yves Rocher trade mark was recognized as being inherent in the nature of the distribution system and did not constitute a restriction of competition. The Commission recognized that this implied that supplies could only be obtained from Yves Rocher or other franchisees. It is noted that resale price maintenance provisions were deleted from the notified contract 'as a result of observations made by the Commission'.[303] In its analysis of a post-termination non-compete clause, under which former franchisees were forbidden to carry on a retail cosmetics business within the exclusive contract territory for one year after termination of the contract, the Commission noted that it did not go beyond what was strictly necessary to protect the know-how and assistance provided. However, the clearance of this provision seemed to depend on the possibility for former franchisees to compete with Yves Rocher as soon as the contract expires by setting up in business outside their former exclusive territory.[304] This contrasts with the judgment in *Pronuptia* where the Court recognized a clause preventing, for a reasonable period, a former franchisee from opening a shop of the same or a similar nature in an area where he may compete with a member of the network as not constituting a restriction of competition. Consistent with the judgment in *Pronuptia* the system was found to fall within the prohibition of Article 81(1) because the territorial protection given to franchisees (neither the franchisor nor other franchisees were permitted to open up another beauty centre in the franchisee's territory—unlike in the *Computerland* decision discussed below no indication is given as to the size of the exclusive territory) constituted a restriction of competition within the distribution network, but these were exempted under Article 81(3). The legal assessment contains no assessment as to the appreciability of the effects of the restriction on competition but the appreciability of the effect on trade is justified primarily by the fact that Yves Rocher had a market share exceeding 5 per cent in two of the Member States concerned.

Pronuptia [305]

7.218 In contrast to *Yves Rocher* the Commission in *Pronuptia* followed the Court's assessment of the non-compete provision and recognized that a prohibition on a franchisee from competing with other members of the network for a period of one year after termination of the contract was essential to prevent the know-how from

---

[302] See para 38.
[303] See para 30.
[304] See para 48.
[305] *Pronuptia* [1987] OJ L13/39.

benefiting competitors and did not constitute a restriction of competition. Obligations relating to sourcing of goods from the franchisee or nominated suppliers, payment of royalties, and holding of stocks were assessed as not constituting restrictions of competition. Referring to the Court's acknowledgement that franchising is different in nature than other distribution formats, the decision states that the latter two of these obligations could constitute restrictions of competition in the context of a selective distribution system.[306] As in *Yves Rocher* the system was found to fall within the prohibition of Article 81(1) because of the territorial protection given to franchisees (each franchisee is granted the exclusive right to use the Pronuptia de Paris trade mark in a defined sales territory—unlike in the *Computerland* decision discussed below no indication is given as to the size of the exclusive territory), but this was exempted under Article 81(3). Again the legal assessment contains no assessment as to the appreciability of the restriction of competition but refers to the Court's statement at paragraph 27 of the judgment that 'provisions which share markets between the franchisor and the franchisees or between franchisees constitute restrictions of competition for the purposes of Article 85(1) [now Article 81(1)]'. Unlike *Yves Rocher* there is no reference to the appreciability of the effect on trade, with the Commission relying on the Court's statement at paragraph 26 of the judgment (see above), although reference is made to Pronuptia's significant share of the French market ('about 30% of the bridal wear market'). In respect of clauses granting territorial protection, the Commission exempted an obligation undertaken by the franchisor to pay the franchisee 10 per cent of any mail order sales to customers located in the franchisee's territory.

Computerland [307]

This decision concerned a franchise network involving (1) the sale of goods not **7.219** manufactured by the franchisor, (2) end-users who were predominantly business-users (as opposed to home-users), and (3) the provision of a number of pre- and after-sales services to end-users, under the franchisor's name, trade marks and systems. In this case the franchisees played an active role in establishing the product range. Each franchisee was afforded territorial protection within a radius of less than one kilometre from the approved location (in the first year the radius was doubled). Within this protected area no other Computerland franchisees could set up a franchise outlet. There were no restrictions on selling to end-users in the protected area of another franchisee. The non-compete clause provided that during the term of the agreement the franchisee would not operate in any competing business and for one year following termination would not operate any competing business within a 10-kilometre radius of the ex-franchisee's former outlet (as originally notified the post-termination ban was for a period of three years). In its

---

[306] See para 27.
[307] *Computerland* [1987] OJ L222/12.

legal assessment the Commission found, despite the small size of the 'protected area' that the territorial protection afforded to franchisees was a restriction of competition because 'the exclusivity clause, which assures him of a protected zone in which no other Computerland outlets can be established . . . results in a certain degree of market sharing'.[308] The prohibition on resale other than to end-users and other franchisees was also considered to constitute a restriction of competition in the context of this franchise system because 'the Computerland name and trademark cover the business format as such, but not the microcomputer products being sold, which bear the name and trademark of each individual manufacturer'.[309] The inference being that such a prohibition only fails to constitute a restriction where the franchisee sells goods bearing the trade mark of the franchisor and the prohibition is based on the legitimate concern that the name, trade mark, or business format could be damaged if the contract products were sold by non-network resellers. The issue of appreciability is only addressed in the context of effect on trade and not in respect of the restrictions of competition. The effect on trade was found to arise from the fact that franchisees could not extend their operations to other Member States. The effect was deemed to be appreciable because of the anticipated expansion of the franchise system which at the time of the decision had not yet reached a market share of 5 per cent (in 1986 the largest market share in any given Member State was approximately 4 per cent; however, the then market share in the USA exceeded 20 per cent).

ServiceMaster[310]

7.220 This decision concerned a service franchise network involving the supply of housekeeping, cleaning, and maintenance services to commercial and domestic customers according to the instructions of ServiceMaster. It also concerned, on an ancillary basis, the supply of goods directly linked to the provision of those services. The notified ServiceMaster franchise included a uniform presentation of the contract services based on the use of a common name, a substantial package of technical, commercial, and administrative know-how relating to the provision of the services, and continuing assistance provided by ServiceMaster. The Commission considered that service franchises show strong similarities to distribution franchises and can therefore basically be treated in the same way. However, it recognized that service franchises have certain characteristics which distinguish them from distribution franchisees:

> know-how is often more important in the [supply] apply of service[s] than in the supply of goods because each service requires the execution of particular work and creates a close personal relationship between the provider of the service and the

---

[308] See para 25.
[309] See para 26.
[310] *Servicemaster* [1988] OJ L322/38.

receiver of the service. Therefore, the protection of the franchisor's know-how and reputation can be even more essential for service franchises than for distribution franchises where mainly the goods advertise the business by carrying the trademark of the producer or distributor. Also certain services, as for instance the ServiceMaster services, are executed at the customer's premises, while goods are usually sold at the premises of the retailer. Services of this type further reinforce the link between the provider of the services and the customer.[311]

7.221 Provisions which the Commission considered as being aimed at preventing the know-how from benefiting competitors, and therefore as not falling within Article 81(1), included the franchisee's obligation (1) to preserve, before and after the termination of the agreement, the secrecy of all information and know-how and to impose a similar obligation on his employees, (2) to use the know-how and intellectual property rights licensed solely for the purposes of exploitation of the ServiceMaster franchise, (3) after termination of the agreement, to cease using the know-how package of ServiceMaster, (4) during the term of the agreement, not to be engaged in a competing business, (5) after the termination of the agreement, not to be engaged, for a period of one year, in a competing business within any territory within which he has provided services prior to the termination of the agreement, (6) not to solicit, for a period of one year, customers who have been, during the period of two years prior to the termination of the agreement, his customers, and (7) not to sell or assign the franchised business without ServiceMaster's approval.

7.222 Provisions which the Commission considered as allowing the franchisor to safeguard the common identity and reputation of the franchise network, and therefore as not falling within Article 81(1), included the franchisee's obligation (1) to use ServiceMaster's know-how and to apply the trading methods developed by ServiceMaster, (2) to communicate to ServiceMaster any improvements he makes in the operation of the business, (3) to obtain ServiceMaster's prior approval for the location of his franchise premises, (4) to devote the necessary time and attention to ServiceMaster business and to use his best endeavours to promote and increase the turnover of that business, (5) to purchase certain cleaning equipment and certain chemicals used in the operation of the business from ServiceMaster or other suppliers nominated or approved by ServiceMaster,[312] (6) to obtain the approval of ServiceMaster for the carrying out of advertising, and (7) to submit to inspections of his premises by ServiceMaster and to present financial statements.

---

[311] See para 6.

[312] This obligation is qualified by the statement, at para 17 of the decision. that it 'does not prevent franchisees from obtaining supplies of equipment and goods of equivalent quality from third-party suppliers. ServiceMaster will not withhold its approval of suppliers proposed by franchisees if the goods of those suppliers chemicals [apply with] the requirements of safety, non-toxicity, bio-degradability and effectiveness. The franchisee is also free to purchase the required goods from any other ServiceMaster franchisee.'

7.223 Provisions which the Commission considered to fall within Article 81(1) were those affording territorial protection to franchisees.[313] As in the *Computerland* decision the issue of appreciability is only addressed in the context of effect on trade and not in respect of the restrictions of competition. The effect on trade was found to arise from the fact that franchisees could neither set up outlets in other Member States nor actively seek customers in territories of franchisees of other Member States. As in *Computerland*, the effect was deemed to be appreciable because of the anticipated expansion of the franchise system, which at the time of the decision had an EEC market share of less than 5 per cent.[314]

Charles Jourdan [315]

7.224 This decision concerned the distribution by the Charles Jourdan Group of its shoes and leather goods in France. Distribution was carried out through four types of retail shops, namely, (1) branches owned and managed by the Group, (2) franchised shops, (3) franchise-corner retailers, and (4) traditional retailers chosen on the basis of their competence and reputation. The distinction between franchised shops and franchise-corner retailers being that in respect of the former the franchise and shop sign relates to the whole of the premises while in respect of the latter the franchise and shop sign relates to an interior and separate part of the premises, with other brands of competing goods being sold on the same premises. Both types of franchised outlet were allocated a specific territory. Franchisees received know-how and assistance from the Charles Jourdan Group relating to purchasing and fashion trends, decoration and layout, management, sales and business activities of other network members, and advertising. The Commission classified this know-how as primarily commercial in nature, while also recognizing that it covered aspects of management. It also recognized the know-how as being substantial and giving traders a clear advantage over competitors.[316]

7.225 The supply arrangements were amended, at the request of the Commission, to permit cross-supplies between members of the distribution network of the

---

[313] It is stated at para 22 that 'the combined effect of the clause which prohibits the franchisee from setting up further outlets outside his own territory, and the territorial protection clause which prevents the franchisee from actively seeking customers outside his territory, results in a certain degree of market-sharing between the franchisees, thus restricting competition within the ServiceMaster network. This territorial protection is, however, limited by two elements: the franchisee holds a non-exclusive right only within his territory with regard to ServiceMaster itself and each franchisee is entitled to provide services to non-solicited customers outside his territory.'

[314] It is stated at para 23 that 'ServiceMaster is an important competitor in the market which is capable of setting up a great number of outlets throughout the EEC as it has done before in the United States and Canada where ServiceMaster has over 2,900 franchisees. ServiceMaster already has a 6% market share in the United Kingdom and reckons that its EEC market share will exceed 5% in the near future.'

[315] *Charles Jourdan* [1989] OJ L35/ 31.

[316] See para 11 of the decision.

Charles Jourdan Group, even where such a member is a traditional retailer.[317] Upon termination of a franchise agreement, franchisees are not subject to any restrictions on their business activities. They may continue to distribute similar or competing products within the same geographic area and in the same shop. They are merely required to remove all shop signs and advertising displays and to modify the fittings associated with the franchise activity.[318] Consistent with its earlier decisions the Commission listed a number of clauses of the notified contracts which it classified as either being aimed at preventing the know-how from benefiting competitors or as allowing the franchisor to safeguard the common identity and reputation of the franchise network, and therefore as not falling within Article 81(1). A ban on the franchisee reselling the Charles Jourdan Group's goods to traders other than franchisees, franchise-corner retailers or retailers supplied by the Group, appears in the latter classification. The Commission stated that 'this clause is intended to maintain the unity of the network and the link, in the consumer's mind, between the Charles Jourdan Group's product and the place where it is sold'.[319] What is interesting about this provision is that the exemption of the limitation on sales to resellers extends to each of the distribution formats of the Charles Jourdan Group and not just the franchise format.

Consistent with its earlier decisions and the *Pronuptia* judgment, the Commission held that Article 81(1) applied to the agreements relating to the franchise shops because 'the clauses that involve market sharing between the Charles Jourdan Group and its partners or between its partners themselves constitute restrictions of competition within the meaning of Article 85(1) [now Article 81(1)] . . . [and] [t]he franchise agreements may affect trade between Member States as they constitute the basis of a network w[h]ich is bound to spread over the whole Community and as the franchisees are not allowed to become established in another Member State'.[320] This was despite the fact that the territorial protection afforded to franchisees was of a limited nature, ie while there may be only one franchise shop in a given area, there may be several franchise-corner retailers and traditional retailers within the area. The issue of appreciability is assessed neither in relation to the restriction of competition nor the effect on trade, although the decision does estimate the market share of the Charles Jourdan Group in the market for medium to top quality shoes at nearly 10 per cent of the French market and around 2 per cent of the Community market.[321] The Commission held that Article 81(1) did not apply to the franchise-corner retailer agreements as, due to their limited number, they were not likely to affect trade between Member States or significantly restrict competition. The Commission granted a ten-year

7.226

---

[317] See para 16 of the decision.
[318] See para 21 of the decision.
[319] See para 28 of the decision.
[320] See paras 32 & 33 of the decision.
[321] See para 5 of the decision.

exemption to the retail franchise agreements primarily on the grounds that 'few prospective franchisees would be willing to undertake the necessary investment, to pay an initial lump-sum fee or a guarantee deposit and to pay royalties in proportion to their turnover in order to belong to such a distribution system, if they did not enjoy some territorial protection against competition from other franchisees and from the Charles Jourdan Group'.[322]

(4) Analysis of Commission Regulation (EEC) 4087/88[323]

7.227 The Commission drafted this block exemption on the basis of the judgment of the Court of Justice in the *Pronuptia* case and its experience in the five key decisions outlined above.

7.228 While it does not lay down a mandatory regime for the regulation of franchise agreements, compliance with its provisions affords the parties the benefit of an automatic exemption from Article 81(1) of the Treaty. The block exemption covers distribution and service franchises but does not cover industrial franchises involving the manufacture of products (Article 1). It specifies those obligations which are exempted (Article 2) and those which do not infringe Article 81(1) (Article 3—so called white list). It lays down conditions for the application of the block exemption (Article 4) and conditions which result in the non-application of the block exemption (Article 5—so-called black list). It also provides for an opposition procedure (Article 6) and for the possibility of withdrawal (Article 8). Set out below is a summary and analysis of the main elements of the block exemption.

Definition of a Franchise for the Purposes of the Block Exemption (Article 1.3)

7.229 Article 1.3(b) defines a franchise agreement for the purposes of the Regulation as:

> an agreement whereby one undertaking, the franchisor, grants the other, the franchisee, in exchange for direct or indirect financial consideration, the right to exploit a franchise for the purposes of marketing specified types of goods and/or services; it includes at least obligations relating to:
> — the use of a common name or shop sign and a uniform presentation of contract premises and/or means of transport,
> — the communication by the franchisor to the franchisee of know-how,[324]
> — the continuing provision by the franchisor to the franchisee of commercial or technical assistance during the life of the agreement[.]

---

[322] See para 39 of the decision.
[323] Commission Regulation (EEC) 4087/88 of 30 November 1988 on the application of Article 85(3) [now Article 81(3)] of the Treaty to categories of franchise agreements [1988] OJ L359/46.
[324] Article 1.3(f) defines 'know-how' as 'a package of non-patented practical information, resulting from experience and testing by the franchisor, which is secret, substantial and identified'. The terms 'secret', 'substantial', and 'identified' are also defined in Article 1.3.

Five Key Elements of a Franchise

From this definition it is possible to identify the following five key elements of a **7.230** franchise for the purposes of the block exemption:

— marketing specified types of goods and/or services,

— direct or indirect financial consideration,

— the use of a common name or shop sign and a uniform presentation of contract premises and/or means of transport,

— the communication by the franchisor to the franchisee of know-how,

— the continuing provision by the franchisor to the franchisee of commercial or technical assistance during the life of the agreement.

(a) Marketing Specified Types of Goods and/or Services

Only franchises relating to the sale of goods and/or supply of services to end- **7.231** users[325] are covered by the block exemption. Korah argues that use of the words 'for the purposes of marketing' implies that other forms of supply, such as agency and hire, can fall within the scope of the Regulation.[326] Franchises relating to the manufacture of goods are not covered. The fourth preamble to the Regulation distinguishes the latter category on the grounds that such agreements 'which usually govern relationships between producers, present different characteristics than the other types of franchise. They consist of manufacturing licences based on patents and/or technical know-how, combined with trade-mark licences.' The fifth preamble clarifies that the exclusion for manufacturing franchises does not relate to sales or service franchises which process or adapt goods to fit the specific needs of customers. Neither are the concepts of sale and service mutually exclusive. While the definition of a 'franchise' in Article 1.3 of the Regulation states that it must relate to 'the resale of goods *or* the provision of services to end users' (emphasis added), the fifth preamble to the Regulation specifically mentions the possibility for 'a combination of these activities'. Wholesale franchises are not covered by the block exemption, although master franchise agreements are. The distribution of motor vehicles cannot avail of the franchise block exemption.[327]

---

[325] The limitation relating to 'end users' is apparent from the definition of the term 'franchise' in Article 1.3(a) and from the fifth preamble to the Regulation which states that '[t]his Regulation covers franchise agreements between two undertakings, the franchisor and the franchisee, for the retailing of goods or the provision of services to end users . . .'.

[326] Korah, *Franchising and the EEC Competition Rules—Regulation 4087/88* (Oxford: ESC Publishing Limited, 1989) 41.

[327] Article 12 of Regulation 1475/95.

(b) Direct or Indirect Financial Consideration

7.232 The *Pronuptia* case arose from non-payment by the franchisee of an annual franchise fee calculated at 10 per cent of total sales.[328] It is worth noting that this
annual fee was in addition to the payment of a single entry fee of DM 15,000. The
payment of financial consideration for the right to use the franchise is one of the
factors which is considered to differentiate franchising from other distribution
formats where the buyer normally already has the know-how and only pays for the
goods. While there is no express indication as to what the level of the consideration should be, it is likely to impact on the assessment as to whether the know-how
is substantial. Use of the word 'indirect' gives some flexibility in the way in which
the fee is calculated, for example it could be included in the purchase price of the
goods rather than payable as a separate fee. However, in such cases, it should be
clearly identifiable and quantifiable.

*(c) Use of a Common Name or Shop Sign and Uniform Presentation of Contract
Premises and/or Means of Transport*

7.233 The franchise network must have a uniform and common network with which
consumers can readily identify. The eighth preamble of the Regulation refers to
the homogeneity of the network and co-operation between network members as
ensuring constant quality. This ensures that consumers identify with the franchise
network rather than with individual outlets. The eighth preamble also implies
that the homogeneity of the network increases inter-brand competition. While
Article 4(c) requires the franchisee to indicate its status as an independent undertaking, it is also specified that this indication must not interfere with the common
identity of the franchised network. The twelfth preamble states that the requirement on the franchisee to indicate its independent status is to 'better inform consumers' and not to 'jeopardize the common identity of the franchised network'. In
the *Computerland* decision the Commission stated that '[t]he franchisee's obligation to post a sign on the premises indicating that he is the independent owner
thereof, operating under a franchise . . . ensures that the public is in no way mis-
led as to the true ownership of and responsibility for each individual outlet'.[329]

(d) Communication of Know-How

7.234 The seventh preamble states that franchise agreements 'allow independent traders
to set up outlets more rapidly and with higher chances of success than if they had
to do so without the Franchisor's experience and assistance'. This statement is a
recognition of the fact that a franchise concept represents a business format which
will normally have been successfully developed and applied by the franchisor itself

---

[328] Case 161/84, see n 286 above, para 6.
[329] See *Computerland* decision, n 307 above, para 24(iii).

prior to its extension to franchisees.[330] To enable the franchisee to duplicate the business format and increase its chances of success, a franchisor wishing to be covered by the block exemption is required to communicate know-how to the franchisee. Know-how is defined as 'a package of non-patented practical information, resulting from experience and testing by the franchisor, which is secret, substantial and identified'.[331] The terms 'secret', 'substantial', and 'identified' are also defined.[332] The secrecy required is that the know-how must not be generally known or easily accessible. It is not required that each individual component of the know-how be totally unknown or unobtainable outside the franchisor's business. To be substantial the know-how must include information which is of importance for the sale of goods or the provision of services to end-users and be 'capable, at the date of conclusion of the agreement, of improving the competitive position of the franchisee'. The know-how must be identified in a comprehensive manner by way of a sufficient description which 'can either be set out in the franchise agreement or in a separate document or recorded in any other appropriate form'.

(e) The Continuing Provision of Commercial or Technical Assistance

The seventh preamble refers to franchise agreements assisting the entry of new **7.235** competitors, particularly SMEs, and that these new entrants have a higher chance of success because of the 'franchisor's experience and assistance'. The eighth preamble refers to 'constant cooperation between the franchisor and the franchisees'. Given that the Commission wished to facilitate the entry of SMEs to the market, it is not surprising that the Regulation provides for the continuing provision of commercial or technical assistance during the life of the agreement. In the *Computerland* decision the franchisor's 'continuing support services include training, information, advice, guidance and know-how regarding the Computerland methods [of] in store management, operation, financing, advertising, sales and inventory'.[333]

---

[330] See also para 15 of the *Pronuptia* judgment, where the Court states, *inter alia*, that 'rather than a method of distribution, it [ie franchising] is a way for an undertaking to derive financial benefit from its expertise without investing its own capital. Moreover, the system gives traders who do not have the necessary experience access to methods which they could not have learned without considerable effort and allows them to benefit from the reputation of the franchisor's business name. Franchise agreements for the distribution of goods differ in that regard from dealerships or contracts which incorporate approved retailers into a selective distribution system, which do not involve the use of a single business name, the application of uniform business methods or the payment of royalties in return for the benefits granted.'

[331] Article 1.3(f) of the Regulation.

[332] See Article 1.3(g)–(i) of the Regulation.

[333] See *Computerland* decision, n 307 above, para 2.

Protection from Intra-Brand Competition (Granting of an Exclusive Territory—Prohibition on Active Sales outside Allotted Territory) (Article 2)

7.236 In the *Pronuptia* judgment the Court of Justice confirmed the application of Article 81 to a franchise system because of the presence of vertical restraints impinging on intra-brand competition, even when they are necessary for the commercial viability of the franchise system.[334] The ninth preamble to the Regulation identifies the granting of an exclusive territory to franchisees combined with a prohibition on actively seeking customers outside that territory as such a restriction of competition, but which may be exempted because it allows franchisees to concentrate their efforts on their allotted territory. Article 2 of the block exemption lists the following intra-brand restrictions as being covered by the exemption:

> (a) an obligation on the franchisor, in a defined area of the common market, the contract territory, not to:
>
> grant the right to exploit all or part of the franchise to third parties,
> itself exploit the franchise, or itself market the goods or services which are the subject-matter of the franchise under a similar formula,
> itself supply the franchisor's goods to third parties;
>
> (b) an obligation on the master franchisee not to conclude franchise agreements with third parties outside its contract territory;
> (c) an obligation on the franchisee to exploit the franchise only from the contract premises;
> (d) an obligation on the franchisee to refrain, outside the contract territory, from seeking customers for the goods or the services which are the subject-matter of the franchise[.]

Protection from Inter-Brand Competition (Non-Compete and Exclusive Purchasing) (Articles 2(e); 3.1(a)–(c) and (f); 5.1(b) and (c))

7.237 In the *Pronuptia* judgment the Court of Justice confirmed the non application of Article 81 to vertical restraints which impact on inter-brand competition, where necessary for the protection of the know-how or reputation of a franchise system.[335] The Court gave a non-exhaustive list of such vertical restraints, including:

> a clause prohibiting the franchisee, during the period of validity of the contract and for a reasonable period after its expiry, from opening a shop of the same or a similar nature in an area where he may compete with a member of the network.[336]

In relation to the sourcing of goods the Court specifically recognized that in certain cases it may be permissible for franchisors to go beyond specifying merely the quality of the goods to be sold by the franchisee:

---

[334] See above summary of *Pronuptia* case.
[335] See above summary of *Pronuptia* case.
[336] See para 16 of the judgment.

It may in certain cases—for instance, the distribution of fashion articles—be impractical to lay down objective quality specifications. Because of the large number of franchisees it may also be too expensive to ensure that such specifications are observed. In such circumstances a provision requiring the franchisee to sell only products supplied by the franchisor or by suppliers selected by him may be considered necessary for the protection of the network's reputation. Such a provision may not however have the effect of preventing the franchisee from obtaining those products from other franchisees.[337]

Non-Compete for Franchise

In relation to a non-compete obligation relating to the franchise, the block **7.238** exemption follows the *Pronuptia* judgment in relation to the scope of the non-compete provision during the term of the agreement, but narrows it following termination. Article 3.1(c) provides that the exemption shall continue to apply in the presence of an obligation[338] on the franchisee 'not to engage, directly or indirectly, in any similar business in a territory where it would compete with a member of the franchised network, including the franchisor; the franchisee may be held to this obligation after termination of the agreement, for a reasonable period which may not exceed one year, in the territory where it has exploited the franchise'.

Non-Compete for Goods which are the Subject Matter of the Franchise

In relation to non-compete obligations for goods competing with the franchisor's **7.239** goods, despite the Courts ruling that such obligations may not fall within the scope of Article 81, Article 2(e) of the block exemption classifies these as a restriction of competition covered by the exemption:

> an obligation on the franchisee not to manufacture, sell or use in the course of the provision of services, goods competing with the franchisor's goods[339] which are the subject-matter of the franchise; where the subject-matter of the franchise is the sale or use in the course of the provision of services both certain types of goods and spare parts or accessories therefor, that obligation may not be imposed in respect of these spare parts or accessories.

It is submitted that this paragraph applies both to service and distribution fran- **7.240** chisees. Nevertheless, it is important to note that there is no comma after the word 'sell', as there is in Article 3.1(a) and (b). On a literal interpretation, it could be argued that this paragraph relates solely to service franchises and not to distribution franchises. If such a literal interpretation were adopted, then a similar non-compete provision relating to goods, which are the subject matter of a distribution franchise, would not be covered by the block exemption and the Regulation could

---

[337] Judgment, para 21.
[338] The obligation must be 'necessary to protect the franchisor's industrial or intellectual property rights or to maintain the common identity and reputation of the franchised network'.
[339] 'Franchisor's goods' means goods produced by the franchisor or according to its instructions, and/or bearing the franchisor's name or trade mark (re. Article 1.3(d)).

not be used to limit the use of non-compete obligations for spare parts and accessories. It could then be argued, on the basis of the *Pronuptia* judgment, that such a provision would not fall under Article 81 where necessary to protect the know-how, identity, or reputation of the franchise network. Korah argues against the limitation of Article 2(e) to service contracts on the grounds that she has 'insufficient faith in the care with which the Commission uses its commas'.

7.241 It is submitted that Korah's interpretation is correct. Had the Commission wished to make such a distinction between service and distribution franchises, it is likely to have done so in a clearer manner and given some justification for the same in the preamble to the Regulation.[340] Nevertheless, it should be noted that the comma is also omitted from the ninth preamble to the Regulation[341] and the French text of Article 2(e).

Additional Non-Compete Obligations

7.242 Article 2(e) must be read in conjunction with subparagraphs (a), (b), and (f) of Article 3.1 which provide that the exemption shall continue to apply in the presence of an obligation[342] on the franchisee:

> (a) to sell, or use in the course of the provision of services, exclusively goods matching minimum objective quality specifications laid down by the franchisor;

> (b) to sell, or use in the course of the provision of services, goods which are manufactured only by the franchisor or by third parties designated by it, where it is impracticable, owing to the nature of the goods which are the subject-matter of the franchise, to apply objective quality specifications;

> . . .

> (f) to use its best endeavours to sell the goods or provide the services that are the subject-matter of the franchise; to offer for sale a minimum range of goods, achieve a minimum turnover, plan its orders in advance, keep minimum stocks and provide customer and warranty services[.]

7.243 While Article 3.1(b) above describes the circumstances in which the franchisor is able to impose an obligation to sell only goods manufactured or designed by it, it

---

[340] It should be noted that it would be possible to draw a distinction between service and distribution franchises. In the *ServiceMaster* decision (see above) the Commission recognized that know-how is often more important to service franchises than distribution franchises where the goods advertise the business.

[341] The ninth preamble to the Regulation states that 'where the franchisees sell or use in the process of providing services, goods manufactured by the franchisor or according to its instructions and or bearing its trade mark, an obligation on the franchisees not to sell, or use in the process of the provision of services, competing goods, makes it possible to establish a coherent network which is identified with the franchised goods. However, this obligation should only be accepted with respect to the goods which form the essential subject-matter of the franchise. It should notably not relate to accessories or spare parts for these goods.'

[342] The obligation must be 'necessary to protect the franchisor's industrial or intellectual property rights or to maintain the common identity and reputation of the franchised network'.

cannot impose an exclusive purchase obligation upon the franchisee, who must remain free to source the goods from other network members. In this regard Article 4(a) provides that the block exemption shall only apply on condition that the franchisee is free to obtain the goods that are the subject matter of the franchise from (1) other franchisees, and (2) members of any other authorized distribution network.

Article 2(e) affords the franchisor greater control over the goods sold in the franchised outlet providing the goods are (1) manufactured by it, (2) manufactured according to its instructions, or (3) bear its name or trade mark. Although substantial, subparagraphs (a), (b), and (f) of Article 3.1 represent weaker forms of non-compete. **7.244**

Foreclosing Suppliers

Article 5(b) and (c) of the Regulation provides that the imposition of any of the following obligations on the franchisee will result in the non-application of the block exemption: **7.245**

> without prejudice to Article2(e) and Article3(1)(b), the franchisee is prevented from obtaining supplies of goods of a quality equivalent to those offered by the franchisor; without prejudice to Article2(e), the franchisee is obliged to sell, or use in the process of providing services, goods manufactured by the franchisor or third parties designated by the franchisor and the franchisor refuses, for reasons other than protecting the franchisor's industrial or intellectual property rights, or maintaining the common identity and reputation of the franchised network, to designate as authorized manufacturers third parties proposed by the franchisee[.]

The regulation draws a distinction between franchisor's goods which are the subject matter of the franchise and other goods, including spare parts and accessories. Pursuant to Article 5(c) the exemption will not apply where the franchisor refuses to designate third party manufacturers for the supply of these latter goods, unless such refusal is justified by the legitimate objective of protecting the identity and reputation of the network. **7.246**

Protection of Know-How (Articles 3.2 and 5(d) and (f))

Article 3.2 provides that the exemption shall apply notwithstanding the presence of any of the following obligations on the franchisee relating to the protection of know-how: **7.247**

(a) not to disclose to third parties the know-how provided by the franchisor; the franchisee may be held to this obligation after termination of the agreement;

(b) to communicate to the franchisor any experience gained in exploiting the franchise and to grant it, and other franchisees, a non-exclusive licence for the know-how resulting from that experience;

    (c) to inform the franchisor of infringements of licensed industrial or intellectual property rights, to take legal action against infringers, or to assist the franchisor in any legal actions against infringers;

    (d) not to use know-how licensed by the franchisor for purposes other than the exploitation of the franchise; the franchisee may be held to this obligation after termination of the agreement providing the know-how has not become generally known or easily accessible.

7.248 Article 5(d) and (f) of the Regulation provides that the imposition of any of the following obligations on the franchisee will result in the non-application of the block exemption:

    (d) the franchisee is prevented from continuing to use the licensed know-how after termination of the agreement where the know-how has become generally known or easily accessible, other than by breach of an obligation by the franchisee;

    (e) the franchisor prohibits the franchisee from challenging the validity of the industrial or intellectual property rights which form part of the franchise, without prejudice to the possibility for the franchisor of terminating the agreement in such a case.

Resale Price Maintenance (Article 5(e))

7.249 Article 5(e) provides that the block exemption shall not apply where the franchisee is restricted in the determination of sale prices for the goods or services which are the subject matter of the franchise, without prejudice to the possibility for the franchisor of recommending sale prices.

Customer Restrictions (Article 3.1(e))

7.250 Where, as in *Computerland*, the goods are not the subject matter of the franchise, the prohibition on resale other than to end-users and other franchisees may constitute a restriction of competition. In the *Computerland* case this was because the Computerland name and trade mark covered the business format, but not the computer products being sold, which bore the name and trade mark of each individual manufacturer.[343]

7.251 Article 3.1(e) stipulates, subject to certain conditions, that the block exemption shall continue to apply where an obligation is imposed on the franchisee to sell the goods which are the subject matter of the franchise only to end users, to other franchisees, and to resellers within other channels of distribution supplied by the manufacturer of these goods or with its consent.

---

[343] See para 26 of the decision. Supra n 309.

Parallel Imports and Guarantees (Article 4(a) and (b))

The twelfth recital of the block exemption refers to the necessity that parallel **7.252**
imports remain possible, as a means of guaranteeing that competition is not eliminated for a substantial part of the goods which are the subject of the franchise. To
maintain the possibility for parallel trade, Article 4(a) of the Regulation provides
that (1) cross-deliveries between franchisees should always be possible, and (2)
where a franchise network is combined with another network of authorized distributors, franchisees should be free to obtain supplies from such authorized distributors. Under Article 4(b) where the franchisees have to honour guarantees for
the franchisor's goods, this obligation must also apply to goods supplied by other
franchisees, the franchisor, or other distributors who give similar guarantees.

Opposition Procedure (Article 6)

Recital 14 makes it clear that agreements which are not automatically covered by **7.253**
the exemption because they contain provisions that are not expressly exempted by
the Regulation, while not being expressly excluded from exemption may none the
less generally be presumed to be eligible for exemption under Article 81(3).
Article 6 of the Regulation facilitates the notification of such agreements pursuant
to an opposition procedure. Such agreements are automatically covered by the
block exemption where they are notified to the Commission and it does not
oppose the application of the exemption within six months.

Withdrawal of Block Exemption (Article 8)

Article 8 provides that the Commission may withdraw the benefit of the **7.254**
Regulation where it finds that individual agreements exempted by the Regulation
have effects which are incompatible with Article 81(3). This applies in particular
where the relevant market is foreclosed or lacking in effective competition.

Duration of Block Exemption (Article 9)

Regulation 4087/88 expires on 31 December 1999.[344] In its September, 1998 **7.255**
Communication on the application of the EC competition rules to vertical
restraints[345] the Commission makes it clear that its proposal to adopt a wide block
exemption complemented by guidelines will cover franchising. Therefore, it is
likely that the duration of Regulation 4087/88 will be extended pursuant to transitional arrangements for franchise contracts in existence on the date of entry into
force of the new wide block exemption, and that the franchise block exemption

---

[344] ref Article 9 of Regulation.
[345] COM(1998) 544 final.

will ultimately be subsumed by the wider non-sectorial block exemption. This is described in greater detail in Section H of this chapter.

F. Application of Article 81(3) to Vertical Restraints in Particular Sectors

(1) Introduction

7.256 The block exemption Regulations described in this chapter relating to exclusive distribution (Regulation 1983/83), exclusive purchasing (Regulation 1984/83), and franchising (Regulation 4087/88) are not limited to specific sectors, but are applicable to all sectors of the economy.[346] However, the Commission has also adopted special rules for the application of Article 81(3) for three specific sectors of industry, namely the beer sector, the service station sector, and the motor vehicle sector. In the area of exclusive purchasing, the Commission has added specific provisions applicable to beer supply agreements and service station agreements respectively (Titles II and III of Regulation 1984/83). The Commission has also adopted a special block exemption regulation, Regulation 1475/95, applicable to motor vehicle distribution agreements.

(2) Specific Rules for Beer Supply Agreements—Title II of Regulation 1984/83

7.257 Regulation 1984/83[347] is divided into four titles. While Title I (Articles 1–5) contains the general provisions for exclusive purchasing agreements, Title II (Articles 6–9) contains special provisions for beer supply agreements. Regulation 1984/83 came into force on 1 July 1983. Like Regulation 1983/83, it was due to expire on 31 December 1997, but was extended until 31 December 1999. The Commission has issued a Notice which provides guidelines on the interpretation of Regulations 1983/83 and 1984/83.[348] Regulation 1983/83 does not apply to beer supply agreements.[349]

---

[346] As an exception, Regulation 4087/88 is not applicable to the motor vehicle sector (Article 12 of Regulation 1475/95 relating to motor vehicle distribution).

[347] Commission Regulation (EEC) 1984/83 of 22 June 1983 on the application of Article 85(3) [now Article 81(3)] of the Treaty to categories of exclusive purchasing agreements ('Regulation 1984/83') [1983] OJ L173/5; corrigendum [1983] OJ L281/24.

[348] Commission Notice concerning Commission Regulations (EEC) 1983/83 and (EEC) 1984/83 of 22 June 1983 on the application of Article 85(3) [now Article 81(3)] of the Treaty to certain categories of exclusive distribution and exclusive purchasing agreements [1984] OJ C101/2 ('the Notice').

[349] Commission Regulation (EEC) 1983/83 of 22 June 1983 on the application of Article 85(3) [now Article 81(3)] of the Treaty to categories of exclusive distribution agreements ('Regulation 1983/83'), Article 8.

The Commission's policy concerning vertical restraints is currently under review. **7.258**
In its Green Paper on Vertical Restraints,[350] the Commission proposed to replace
the existing block exemption Regulations listed above by one single block exemption Regulation which would cover all sectors of industry.[351] As a result, the beer
sector would be governed by the general provisions applicable to all sectors. This
is described in Section H of this chapter.

Justification for Sector-Specific Rules

It has been considered justified to apply special rules to beer supply agreements, **7.259**
since exclusive purchasing obligations usually entail advantages for the supplier as
well as for the reseller. The supplier has the advantage of guaranteed outlets, the
possibility to plan his sales over the duration of the agreement, and the ability to
organize production and distribution effectively. The reseller has the advantage of
gaining access to the beer distribution market under favourable conditions and
with the guarantee of supplies. The reseller is also able to benefit from the supplier's assistance in guaranteeing product quality and customer service.[352]

The Scope of Title II

Title II (Articles 6–9) of Regulation 1984/83 applies to: **7.260**

> agreements to which only two undertakings are party and whereby one party, the
> reseller, agrees with the other, the supplier, in consideration for the according of spe-
> cial commercial or financial advantages, to purchase only from the supplier, an
> undertaking connected with the supplier or another undertaking entrusted by the
> supplier with the distribution of his goods, certain beers, or certain beers and certain
> other drinks specified in the agreement for resale in premises used for the sale and
> consumption of drinks and designated in the agreement.

Title II of Regulation 1984/83 applies only to on-licensed premises, ie premises **7.261**
that are licensed to sell alcoholic beverages for consumption on and off the
premises. It does not apply to off-licensed premises, such as supermarkets which
are licensed for off-premises consumption only.[353] Moreover, it applies only to
agreements concluded between brewers or wholesalers and resellers. Agreements
between brewers and wholesalers are therefore not covered by Title II, but by the
general provisions in Title I.[354] Title II does not apply to agreements between competitors (Article 3(b)). Another requirement is that the supplier grants the reseller
special commercial or financial advantages. Such advantages are those going

---

[350] Green Paper on Vertical Restraints in EC Competition Policy, COM(96) 721 final, adopted
by the Commission on 22 January 1997.
[351] The only sector not affected would be the motor vehicle sector (footnote 2 of the Green
Paper).
[352] Recital 15 of Regulation 1984/83.
[353] Notice, para 42.
[354] Notice, para 44.

beyond what the reseller could normally expect under the agreement and may for example include financial contributions, the granting for the reseller of a loan on favourable terms, the equipping of the reseller with a site or premises for conducting his business and with equipment or fittings.[355]

Permitted Restrictions

7.262 The following restrictions are exempted according to Articles 6 and 7 of Regulation 1984/83:

(a) An Exclusive Purchasing Obligation

7.263 An obligation imposed on the reseller to purchase certain beers, or certain beers together with certain other drinks, only from the supplier is exempted under the following conditions (Article 6(1)):

- The exclusive purchasing obligation must cover all, and not only part of the requirement (paragraph 35 of the Notice).

- The exclusive purchasing obligation must be specified in several ways. First, the beers and other drinks covered by the obligation must be specified by brand or denomination in the agreement (paragraph 41 of the Notice). Secondly, if the supplier wants to extend the obligation to other drinks, this must be done in an additional agreement (paragraph 42 of the Notice). Thirdly, the name and location of the premises must be stated in the agreement (paragraph 42 of the Notice).

(b) A Non-Compete Obligation

7.264 An obligation on the reseller not to sell beers and other drinks which are of the same type as beers or other drinks supplied under the agreement is exempted (Article 7(1)(a)). The possibility to impose such an obligation depends on the supplier's ability to supply the beers and other drinks in sufficient quantities (para 48 of the Notice).

(c) An Obligation to Sell Different Types of Beer in Bottles or Cans

7.265 It is permitted to impose an obligation on the reseller who sells different types of beer in the premises to do so only in bottles, cans, or other small packages, unless the sale of such beers in draught form is customary or necessary to satisfy a sufficient demand from consumers (Article 7(1)(b)).

(d) An Obligation on Advertising

7.266 The supplier may impose on the reseller an obligation only to advertise other goods in proportion to the share of such goods in the total turnover realized in the premises (Article 7(1)(c)).

---

[355] Notice, para 44 and Recital 13 of Regulation 1984/83.

(e) Other Permitted Obligations

A supplier may impose on a reseller an obligation to purchase complete ranges **7.267** (Article 2(3)(a)), to maintain stocks and to promote sales (Article 2(3)(d)). The supplier may also impose on the reseller an obligation to sell the contract goods under trade marks and in the supplier's packaging (Article 2(3)(c)). It is also permitted to impose a minimum sales obligation on the reseller (Article 2(3)(b)). However, the reseller must always have the right to obtain drinks other than beer from other undertakings offering them on more favourable terms and from other undertakings if the supplier does not offer them (Article 8(2)(b)).

Duration of the Tie

If the Reseller Does not Lease the Premises from the Supplier

- If the exclusive purchasing obligation relates to specified beers and other drinks, **7.268** the agreement may not be concluded for more than five years (Article 8(1)(c)).

- If the exclusive purchasing obligation relates only to specified beers, the agreement may not be concluded for more than ten years (Article 8(1)(d)).

- Agreements concluded for an unlimited time are thus not exempted (Article 8(1)(c–d)).

Special Rules if the Reseller Leases the Premises from the Supplier

- An exclusive purchasing obligation as well as a non-compete obligation may be **7.269** imposed on the reseller for the whole period for which the reseller operates the premises if the supplier leases the premises to the reseller (Article 8(2)(a)).

- However, in such cases the reseller must have the possibility of purchasing drinks, with the exception of beers supplied under the agreement, from other undertakings, which can supply on more favourable terms than the supplier. The supplier must, however, be given an opportunity to match those more favourable conditions (so-called 'English clause') (Article 8(2)(b) in conjunction with paragraph 55 of the Notice). The tenant must also be permitted to purchase drinks other than beer of a different trade mark from other suppliers if the supplier does not offer them (Article 8(2)(c)).

Restrictions not Exempted

The following restrictions are not exempted under Regulation 1984/83: **7.270**

(a) Tie Pass Over

The supplier may not require the reseller to impose an exclusive purchasing oblig- **7.271** ation on his successor for a longer period than the reseller himself remains tied to the supplier (Article 8(1)(e)).

(b) A Tying-in Clause to Other Goods or Services

7.272 The supplier may not impose an exclusive purchasing obligation for goods other than drinks or for services (Article 8(1)(a)).

(c) A Restriction on Other Goods

7.273 An exclusive purchasing obligation and a non-compete obligation may not extend to goods other than drinks or to services. Moreover, the reseller must have the freedom to obtain goods other than drinks or related services from undertakings of his choice (Article 8(1)(a) and (b)). However, the installation of amusement machines in tenanted public houses may be made subject to the owner's permission. The permission may be withheld if it would impair the character of the premises.[356]

Withdrawal of the Benefit of the Block Exemption

7.274 Pursuant to Article 14 of Regulation 1984/83, the Commission is entitled to withdraw the benefit of the Regulation, when it finds that an agreement which is exempted by the Regulation nevertheless has certain effects which are incompatible with the conditions set out in Article 81(3). This could, for example, be the case where the beer or other drinks are not subject to effective competition in a substantial part of the common market. The term 'effective competition' is not defined, but seems to indicate at least that the market in question should not be foreclosed or dominated by brewers holding a dominant position.

Individual Exemption under Article 81(3)

7.275 Beer supply agreements which do not comply with the provisions of Title II of Regulation 1984/83 may be notified to the Commission in order to benefit from an individual exemption under Article 81(3). Whitbread, the fourth largest brewer in the UK, notified in 1994 three standard forms of leases with a duration of twenty years. In a Notice pursuant to Article 19(3) of Regulation 17,[357] the Commission stated that the notified agreements did not fall under the scope of Regulation 1984/83, due to the fact that the brewer had specified the tie by reference to the type of beer, instead of by reference to the brand. This gave the brewer the freedom to unilaterally change the brands of the same type which the reseller had to purchase from him. However, Title II of Regulation 1984/83 requires that such change must be made by mutual agreement between the parties. The lessees which were tied to Whitbread had to pay considerably more for their beer purchases than individual operators who bought the same beer from Whitbread.

---

[356] Notice, para 53.
[357] *Whitbread* (Notice pursuant to Article 19(3) of Regulation 17) [1997]OJ C294/2. See also press release IP/97/821 of 29 September 1997.

However, Whitbread offered its lessees certain countervailing benefits, such as lower rents, professional assistance, and bulk purchasing rebates, which could compensate for the price differential and which enabled the Commission to grant an exemption under Article 81(1). The exemption decision is commented on in paragraphs 7.119–7.122 of this chapter.

(3) Application of Article 81(3) to Service Station Agreements

Introduction

Service station agreements contain in general an exclusive purchasing obligation **7.276** on behalf of the reseller to purchase, for a predetermined period, fuels and other petroleum products for resale exclusively from the supplier. This obligation is generally backed by a prohibition on selling competing products. In consideration for this, the supplier generally affords the reseller certain benefits, such as the letting of premises and furniture and necessary equipment.

Special Rules Applicable to Service Station Agreements (Title III of Regulation 1984/83)

Title III (Articles 10–13) of Regulation 1984/83[358] contains specific rules applic- **7.277** able to service station agreements. Regulation 1983/83[359] does not apply to service station agreements (Article 8 of Regulation 1983/83). The provisions in Title III shall be read in conjunction with the Commission Notice on Regulation 1984/83.[360] Regulation 1984/83 is due to expire on 31 December 1999. The Green Paper on Vertical Restraints adopted by the Commission on 22 January 1997 foresees that the existing block exemption Regulations governing vertical restraints, *inter alia* Regulation 1984/83, will then be replaced by one single block exemption Regulation.

It has been considered justified to apply special rules in this sector since the exclu- **7.278** sive purchasing obligation and non-compete obligation imposed on the reseller result in lasting co-operation between the parties which allows them to improve or maintain the quality of the contract goods and to make long-term planning of sales.[361]

---

[358] Commission Regulation (EEC) 1984/83 of 22 June 1983 on the application of Article 85(3) [now Article 81(3)] of the Treaty to categories of exclusive purchasing agreements ('Regulation 1984/83) [1983] OJ L173/5; corrigendum [1983] OJ L281/24.

[359] Commission Regulation (EEC) 1983/83 of 22 June 1983 on the application of Article 85(1) [now Article 81(1)] of the Treaty to categories of exclusive distribution agreements ('Regulation 1983/83').

[360] Section VI, paras 58–66 of Commission Notice concerning Commission Regulations (EEC) 1983/83 and (EEC) No 1984/83 of 22 June 1983 on the application of Article 85(3) [now Article 81(3)] of the Treaty to categories of exclusive distribution and exclusive purchasing agreements ('Notice').

[361] Recital 15 of Regulation 1984/83.

The Scope of Title III

7.279 Pursuant to Article 10 of Regulation 1984/83, Article 81(1) shall not apply to:

> agreements to which only two undertakings are party and whereby one party, the reseller, agrees with the other, the supplier, in consideration for the according of special commercial or financial advantages, to purchase only from the supplier, an undertaking connected with the supplier or another undertaking entrusted by the supplier with the distribution of his goods, certain petroleum-based motor vehicle fuels or certain petroleum-based motor vehicle and other fuels specified in the agreement for resale in a service station designated in the agreement.

7.280 In some Member States, service station operators act as agents for the purpose of the sale of petrol, and in some cases, lubricants, and as independent resellers for the sale of other products. Despite the fact the operators act partly as agents, the contracts have been considered to be subject to the rules in Title III of Regulation 1984/83. If these provisions were not applicable, it would not be possible to impose a maximum duration on the contracts with the effect of making it difficult for new operators to enter the market.

Permitted Restrictions

7.281 The following restrictions are exempted according to Articles 10 and 11 of Regulation 1984/83:

(a) An Exclusive Purchasing Obligation

7.282 An obligation on the reseller to obtain, on an exclusive basis, certain petroleum-based motor vehicle and other fuels specified in the agreement is permitted under certain conditions (Article 10). The obligation must cover all, and not only part of, the requirement.[362] The exclusive purchasing obligation can cover either motor vehicle fuels (for example, petrol, diesel, fuel, LPG, and kerosene) alone or motor vehicle fuels and other fuels (for example, heating oil, bottled gas, and paraffin). The goods must be petroleum-based products and be for use in motor-powered land or water vehicles or aircraft.[363]

(b) An Obligation not to Sell Competing Fuel

7.283 The reseller may be obliged not to sell motor-vehicle fuel and other fuels which are supplied by other undertakings in the service station designated in the agreement (Article 11(a)).

(c) An Obligation not to Use Competing Lubricants

7.284 The reseller may be obliged not to use lubricants and related petroleum-based products supplied by other suppliers. Related petroleum-based products are

---

[362] Notice, para 35.
[363] Notice, paras 59–60.

additives and brake fluids. It is important to note that the non-compete obligation only refers to the servicing and maintenance of motor vehicles, ie to the reseller's activity in the field of provision of services. It does not, however, affect the reseller's right to purchase such products from other undertakings for resale in the service station (Article 11(b)).[364]

(d) An Obligation to Advertise Other Goods only in Proportion of the Share

7.285 The reseller may be obliged to advertise competing goods within or outside the service station only in proportion to the share of such goods in the total turnover realized in the service station (Article 11 (c)).

(e) An Obligation to Have the Equipment Owned by the Supplier

7.286 The supplier may oblige the reseller to have equipment owned by him or by a connected undertaking (Article 11 (d)). Such a requirement may impose a heavy financial burden on the operators.

Restrictions not Exempted

7.287 The following restrictions are not exempted under Regulation 1984/83 pursuant to Article 12:

(a) An Exclusive Purchasing Obligation for Goods Other than Fuels

7.288 The supplier may not impose exclusive purchasing obligations on the reseller for goods other than motor vehicle and other fuels, such as for example batteries and tyres. The only exception to this would be an obligation not to use competing lubricants in servicing and maintenance and to purchase equipment from the supplier (Article 12(1)(a)).

(b) A Post-Term Competition Ban

7.289 The retailer must be free to switch to another supplier after the expiry of the contract (Article 12(1)(d)). This may be difficult if the supplier owns the service station's equipment, in particular the storage tank.[365]

(c) A Restriction on the Reseller's Freedom to Obtain Other Goods

7.290 It is not allowed to restrict the freedom of the reseller to obtain goods or services which are not covered by the exclusive purchasing obligation from other undertakings (Article 12(1)(b)).

---

[364] Notice, para 62.
[365] See *Report on Competition Policy 1988* (Vol XVIII) 22 where the Commission found that an obligation on the service station operator to return storage tanks to the petroleum company at the expiry of the contract fell under the scope of Article 81(1). The case was dealt with by the Paris Court of Appeal which judged that the obligation fell under Article 81(1) and was not exempted under Regulation 1984/83.

(d) Maximum Duration of Ten Years when Premises are not Leased

7.291   It is not allowed to conclude a service station agreement for an indefinite duration or for a period of more than ten years (Article 12(1)(c)). However, where the supplier makes available premises to the operator, it is permitted to impose exclusive purchasing obligations or non-compete obligations for as long as the reseller operates the premises (Article 12(2)).

Withdrawal of the Benefit of the Block Exemption

7.292   Pursuant to Article 14 of Regulation 1984/83, the Commission is entitled to withdraw the benefit of the Regulation, when it finds that an agreement which is exempted by the Regulation nevertheless has certain effects which are incompatible with the conditions set out in Article 81(3), for example where motor vehicle fuels are not subject to effective competition in a substantial part of the common market.

(4) Application of Article 81(3) to Vertical Restraints in the Motor Vehicle Distribution Sector

Introduction

7.293   Motor vehicles have certain specific features as compared to other consumer products. A motor vehicle is a technically complex product capable of causing physical as well as material damage. It is also an expensive product compared to other consumer products and the purchase of a car is typically the second most expensive purchase for most consumers after a house purchase. The prices of motor vehicles differ substantially between different Member States within the European Union. This part of the chapter will deal with the application of Article 81(3), in particular in the context of Regulation 1475/95 which is the special block exemption Regulation for car distribution.

Block Exemption Regulation 1475/95

7.294   In the *BMW* decision of 13 December 1974,[366] the Commission concluded that although the dealer agreement concluded between BMW and its dealers restricted competition in several respects, it nevertheless fulfilled the conditions set out in Article 81(3) and was therefore granted an individual exemption. In the light of the *BMW* decision, and to avoid a situation whereby all motor vehicle manufacturers notified their distribution and servicing agreements individually, the Commission adopted a block exemption for motor vehicle distribution and servicing agreements, Regulation 123/85.[367] Regulation 123/85 expired on 30 June

---

[366] *Bayerische Motoren Werke AG* [1975] OJ L29/1.
[367] Regulation (EEC) 123/85 of 12 December 1984 on the application of Article 85(3) [now Article 81(3)] of the Treaty to certain categories of motor vehicle distribution and servicing agreements [1985] OJ L15/16.

1995 and was replaced by Regulation 1475/95.[368] Regulation 123/85 continued to apply during a transitional period of one year for agreements concluded before 1 October 1995. From 1 October 1996 onwards, only Regulation 1475/95 applies.

Justification for Selective and Exclusive Clauses

Motor vehicle manufacturers are allowed under Regulation 1475/95 to conclude **7.295** distribution and servicing agreements with a limited number of dealers of their choice. The manufacturers may also prohibit the dealers from supplying new vehicles to independent resellers that do not form part of the authorized network. They may allot the dealers an exclusive territory and impose a ban on dealing in competing products. The supplier cannot impose such a ban when the sale of competing products is carried out in a manner which avoids confusion between makes. Regulation 1475/95 thus allows for a combination of selective and exclusive clauses. These restrictions have been considered indispensable on the ground that motor vehicles are consumer goods which at both regular and irregular intervals require expert maintenance and repair. Motor vehicle manufacturers should be able to co-operate with only those selected dealers who can provide such specialized servicing.[369] This argument seems to apply to favour selective distribution, but to a lesser extent the exclusivity clauses.

The Scope and Objective of Regulation 1475/95

Regulation 1475/95 applies to the distribution and servicing of new motor vehi- **7.296** cles with three or more wheels that are intended for use on public roads. It does not apply to the distribution of used vehicles, tractors, and motorcycles. The Regulation only applies to the combined sales of 'new motor vehicles . . . together with spare parts therefor' (Article 1). This means that the Regulation only applies if there is a link between the sales and servicing of motor vehicles. The separate distribution of spare parts without any connection to the distribution of vehicles is therefore not covered by the Regulation.[370] The same would apply to the separate distribution of motor vehicles without any connection to servicing.

In view of the experiences under Regulation 123/85, certain adjustments were **7.297** incorporated in Regulation 1475/95. The main objectives were to intensify competition in the car sector and to better balance the interests of the dealers and the

---

[368] Regulation (EEC) 1475/95 of 28 June 1995 on the application of Article 85(3) [now Article 81(3)] of the Treaty to certain categories of motor vehicle distribution and servicing agreements [1995] OJ L145. See also the explanatory brochure published by the Commission concerning Regulation 1475/95, 'Distribution of motor vehicles', Explanatory brochure, European Commission, DGIV, IV/9509/95.

[369] Recital 4 of Regulation 1475/95.

[370] *Rover/Unipart* [1988] OJ L45/34. See also *Distribution of Fiat spare parts in Italy, Twenty-third Report on Competition Policy*, 229 and press release of 24 February 1994, IP/94/159.

manufacturers. Thus, Regulation 1475/95 explicitly prohibits practices which directly or indirectly prevent parallel trade. The manufacturers may only lawfully prohibit sales to non-authorized dealers, but not to authorized dealers, final consumer, or authorized intermediaries acting on behalf of consumers. The Regulation also gives independent spare parts manufacturers an opportunity to sell via the authorized networks. Dealers are given a possibility to refer certain disputes with the dealers to a third party for arbitration. The notice of termination was extended from one to two years, to enhance the dealers' independence *vis-à-vis* the manufacturers. The Regulation also introduced a system of 'black clauses' and 'black practices' with obligations and restrictions that would not be exempted and which would result in an automatic loss of the benefit of the block exemption.

The Activities of Third Parties in the Light of Regulation 1475/95

Activities of Independent Dealers

7.298 Article 3(10) of Regulation 1475/95 provides that a manufacturer may oblige his dealers not to sell cars to resellers outside the distribution network, so-called independent dealers. However, Regulation 1475/95, like its predecessor Regulation 123/85, does not regulate or oppose the activities of independent dealers. Regulation 1475/95 only relates to the relation between the manufacturer and the dealer. The activities of an independent dealer therefore fall outside the scope of that Regulation. It is therefore not contrary to Regulation 1475/95 for an independent dealer to acquire new vehicles through parallel import and carry on business marketing such vehicles. Nor does that Regulation prevent independent dealers from carrying on business as an authorized intermediary within the meaning of Article 3(11) of that Regulation.[371]

Activities of Authorized Intermediaries

7.299 Regulation 1475/95 is not applicable to the activities of authorized intermediaries. Article 3(11) of Regulation 1475/95 merely provides that the manufacturer may require the dealer not to sell motor vehicles to intermediaries who act for final consumers unless the intermediary is able to show a prior written authority from the customer to purchase a specified motor vehicle. In *Ecosystem*,[372] Ecosystem carried on business as a professional intermediary in Belgium and Luxembourg on behalf of and with written authorizations from French final consumers wishing to purchase Peugeot vehicles. Peugeot claimed that Ecosystem was not an intermediary, but carried on activities equivalent to a reseller. However, the Court of First Instance found that Ecosystem had not exceeded its limits as intermediary, since

---

[371] Case C–309/94 *Nissan France SA et al* ECR [1996] I–677. See also Case C–226/94 *Grand Garage Albigeois SA et al* ECR [1996] I–551. Although these cases referred to Regulation 123/85, which was in force at that time, the reasoning still applies in the context of Regulation 1475/95.

[372] Case T–9/92 *Automobiles Peugeot SA and Peugeot SA v Commission* ECR [1993] II–493.

it did not carry any legal or financial risk normally inherent in selling motor vehicles, nor had it displayed advertisements that could create confusion as to its status.

The fact that Ecosystem acted as a professional intermediary and sold many vehi- **7.300**
cles was irrelevant according to the Court which held that a purely quantitative criterion based on the number of authorizations received by an intermediary acting in a professional capacity was irrelevant. The Court described the object of Article 3(11) of Regulation 123/85 as being: 'to prevent, by maintaining parallel imports, the partitioning of national markets, in the framework of a system of motor vehicle distribution, and thereby to contribute to the attainment of a single market'.[373] The same argument applies in the context of Regulation 1475/95. The Commission has also published guidelines on the activities of intermediaries.[374]

Activities of Independent Leasing Companies

The same reasoning has been applied in the context of independent leasing com- **7.301**
panies. In the *BMW* and *VW Leasing* cases, the manufacturers had required their dealers, by means of a circular letter, not to provide cars to independent leasing companies that made vehicles available to customers residing or having their seat outside the dealers' contract territories. BMW and VW argued that the independent leasing companies were in the same position as unauthorized dealers and that they were entitled not to supply such dealers pursuant to Article 3(10) of Regulation 123/85. The Court found the practices of BMW and VW in violation of Article 81(1). The Court went on to state that the practices could not be exempted under Regulation 123/85. First, the provisions in a block exemption cannot be interpreted widely in a way to extend the effects of the regulation beyond what is necessary to protect the interests which they are intended to safeguard. Secondly, leasing companies which do not offer an option to purchase cannot be regarded as independent dealers. Finally, the Court stated that Article 13(12) of Regulation 123/85 applied only to the relation between the manufacturer and the dealer and was irrelevant for the question whether the independent leasing companies were comparable to unauthorized resellers.[375]

---

[373] See above, para 61.
[374] In this context, see also Commission Notice concerning Regulation 123/85 on the application of art. 85(3) of the treaty to certain categories of motor vehicle distribution and servicing agreements 1985 OJ C17/4.
[375] Case C–70/93 *Bayerische Motorenwerke AG v ALD Auto-Leasing D GmbH* [1985] ECR I–3439 and Case C–266/93 *Bundeskartellamt v Volkswagen AG and VAG Leasing GmbH* [1995] ECR I–3477, paras 28–30.

Permitted Restrictions on the Suppliers (Articles 1 and 2)

An Obligation to Supply Contract Goods only to Certain Specified Dealers

7.302 The supplier may undertake, within a defined territory, to supply motor vehicles and associated spare parts only to the dealer or to the dealer and a specified number of other dealers for the purpose of resale (Article 1).

An Obligation not to Sell or Provide Services for the Contract Goods within the Contract Territory

7.303 The supplier may, in addition, undertake not to sell or provide services for the contract goods to final consumers within the contract territory (Article 2). In the absence of such clause, the manufacturer is entitled to supply final consumers, so-called 'direct sales'. The manufacturer is, however, not entitled to prevent the dealer from supplying the final consumers that the supplier wishes to supply through direct sales.

Permitted Restrictions on the Dealers (Articles 3 and 4)

An Obligation to Sell Competing Makes Separately

7.304 The manufacturer may oblige the dealer not to sell competing motor vehicles except on separate sales premises, under separate management, in the form of a distinct legal entity, and in a manner which avoids confusion (Article 3(3)). The separate sales premises may be located in the same building as the sales premises for the contract goods. A separate management implies separate records and accounts. A separate company must also be set up for each dealership. However, the dealer may be released from these obligations if he can show an objective reason to release him from the obligations, for example that they prevent him from operating on an economically viable basis (Article 5(2)(1) and Recital 18).

An Obligation not to Use Equipment Purchased by the Manufacturer for the Repair of Competing Makes

7.305 The dealer has the right to provide after-sales service on cars of other makes in the same workshop. However, the manufacturer may require that third parties are not able to benefit 'unduly' from the investments made by it and may thus require that the dealer does not use equipment purchased by the manufacturer for the repair of other makes (Article 3(4)).

An Obligation not to Supply Unauthorized Dealers

7.306 The manufacturer may impose on the dealer an obligation not to supply contract goods to independent dealers which are not part of the distribution network (Article 3(10)(a)). The dealer may, however, not be prevented from selling such goods to other authorized dealers in the same Member State or in other Member States (so-called 'cross-selling).

An Obligation to Verify the Authorization of an Intermediary

The dealers must always be able to sell motor vehicles within the contract range to **7.307** final consumers, whether they buy directly or via an intermediary. If an intermediary makes the purchase on behalf of a final consumer, he must be able to show a prior written authority that identifies the final consumer by name and address. The authorization shall also specify the vehicle and be signed by the consumer (Article 3(11)). If the intermediary fails to provide such authorization, the dealer may refuse to sell to him pursuant to Article 3(10).

An Obligation to Sell Competing Spare Parts only if They are of Matching Quality

The manufacturer may impose on its dealers an obligation to sell spare parts **7.308** which compete with the contract goods only if the parts are of matching quality. The manufacturer may also impose on the dealers a prohibition on using parts of lower quality for repair or maintenance of contract goods (Article 3(5)). The dealers must, however, be free to sell spare parts which do not compete with the contract goods. The dealers must also be able to sell spare parts to unauthorized resellers of spare parts provided the reseller uses them for repair or maintenance (Article 3(10)(b)).

An Obligation not to Use Competing Spare Parts in Guarantee Work

The dealers may be obliged to use only the spare parts within the contract range **7.309** for guarantee work, free servicing, and vehicle-recall work for contract goods (Article 4(1)(7)). These spare parts may be supplied either by the manufacturer or by another undertaking with the manufacturer's consent. The dealers are, however, free to use competing spare parts for the repair and maintenance of contract goods, on condition that the customers are informed about this (Article 4(1)(8)–(9)).

An Obligation not to Make Active Sales outside the Contract Territory

The dealers may not engage in active sales outside the contract territory, ie to set **7.310** up a distribution branch or depots, or actively solicit customers by means of personalized advertising, for example telephone or direct mail. The dealer must, however, remain free to seek customers outside his territory by means of for example media, posters, brochures, or newspaper advertisements (Article 3(8)(b)).

An Obligation to Fulfil Certain Minimum Standards

The manufacturer may require the dealer to fulfil certain qualitative requirements **7.311** regarding the equipment of the business premises, the technical training of the staff, the repair and maintenance of the contract, advertising, and the storage of the goods (Article 4(1)(1)). The manufacturers may also set up certain quantitative requirements that the dealers must fulfil, for example sales targets, to keep a certain level of stock, and to keep a certain number of demonstration vehicles

(Article 4(1)(2)–(5)). The sales targets are to be mutually agreed. In the event of disagreement between the parties, an expert third party can be appointed as an arbitrator (Article 4(1)(3)).

An Obligation to Provide Guarantee and Repair Work on Contract Goods

7.312 The manufacturers may be required to provide guarantee work, free servicing, and vehicle-recall work for contract goods (Article 4(1)(6)). An obligation to carry out repair and maintenance work or guarantee work must apply regardless of in which Member State the vehicle has been purchased, provided it was supplied by an authorized dealer (Article 5(1)(1)(a)).

Positive Conditions to be Satisfied by the Supplier[376]

7.313 Article 5 sets out certain positive conditions which must be fulfilled for the restrictions listed in Articles 1–4 to be exempted.

(a) Availability of Passenger Cars

7.314 The manufacturer must supply to a dealer any passenger car which corresponds to a model within the contract programme and which is marketed by the manufacturer or with the manufacturer's consent in the Member State in which the vehicle is to be registered (Article 5(1)(2)(d)). This situation arises in particular when it is advantageous for consumers from the United Kingdom or Ireland to purchase right-hand-drive cars on the Continent. The manufacturers must in such cases supply to a dealer who wishes to sell any passenger car within the contract range to a final consumer. The manufacturer is entitled to charge an objectively justifiable supplement for special distribution costs and any differences in equipment and specification.[377] The Regulation does not impose any obligation on the dealers to supply, since it is considered to be in the dealer's interest to maximize sales.

(b) Distinction between Different Sales in the Calculation of Discounts

7.315 When calculating the discounts to be granted to a dealer, the manufacturer must distinguish between the supplies to the dealer of (i) cars within the contract range (ii) spare parts within the contract range, and (iii) other goods, ie spare parts available outside the dealer network. If this distinction is not made, the dealer may be granted a high discount from the manufacturer that the independent spare part suppliers are unable to match (Article 5(1)(2)(c)).

(c) Duration of the Agreement and Notice of Termination

7.316 The parties may conclude an agreement for a definite period, or for an indefinite period of time. If the agreement is concluded for a definite period of time, each

---

[376] The positive conditions to be satisfied by the dealers under Article 5 have been treated above in conjunction with the restrictions in question.

[377] Commission Notice concerning Regulation 123/85 [1985] OJ C17/4, para II.2.

party must inform the other at least six months before the expiry if they do not wish to renew the agreement (Article 5(2)(3)). If the agreement is concluded for at least five years or for an indefinite period of time, the notice of termination is two years (Article 5(2)(2)). A notice of termination of one year may be applied if the manufacturer pays appropriate compensation to the dealer or where the dealer is a new entrant to the network (Article 5(2)(2)).

The manufacturer may also terminate the agreement on one year's notice where **7.317** this is necessary to reorganize the whole or a substantial part of the network. A party may also terminate the agreement without any notice for cause where the other party fails to perform one of its basic obligations. In case of disagreement, the parties may have recourse to an expert third party or an arbitrator, without prejudice to the parties' right to apply to a national court under national law (Article 5(3)).

Restrictions not Exempted

'Black Clauses'

The insertion of any of the following clauses are not exempted pursuant to Article **7.318** 6(1)(1)–(5) of Regulation 1475/95:

To link or apply the agreement to other products or services.   It is not permit- **7.319** ted to link a dealer agreement to products or services other than those referred to, ie new motor vehicles and spare parts. It would, for instance, not be allowed under Regulation 1475/95 to extend the obligations in the agreement to cover also insurance or leasing services (Article 6(1)(2)).

To include more far-reaching restrictions.   A restrictive clause which would go **7.320** beyond the restrictions expressly exempted under the Regulation would be prohibited, for example to impose a restriction on sales of cars to other authorized dealers (Article 6(1)(3)). It is also prohibited to agree on obligations which are permitted under Regulation 1983/83 on exclusive distribution or under Regulation 1984/83 on exclusive purchasing, but are more far-reaching than that which is exempted under Regulation 1475/95 (Article 6(1)(4)). It would, for example, not be permitted under Regulation 1475/95 to impose an exclusive purchasing obligation on the dealer, an obligation which would be permitted under Regulation 1984/83.

To unilaterally alter the contract territory.   A clause which gives the manufac- **7.321** turer or supplier a unilateral right to alter the contract territory or to conclude agreements with other dealers in the contract territory is not exempted (Article 6(1)(5)).

'Black Practices'

7.322 The following restrictions that are not exempted pursuant to Article 6(1)(7)–(12) of Regulation 1475/95:

7.323 **Resale price maintenance.**   A manufacturer may not restrict, directly or indirectly, the dealer's freedom to determine prices and discounts in reselling contract goods or corresponding goods (Article 6(1)(6)).

7.324 **Restrictions of parallel trade.**   The supplier may not, directly or indirectly, impede final consumers, their intermediaries, or authorized dealers from buying a vehicle where they consider it to be most advantageous. It is, for example, prohibited for a supplier to make the dealer's remuneration dependent on the destination of sale, such as reducing bonuses or margins. Parallel trade can either be prevented directly through export bans or indirectly by restricting availability of right-hand-drive cars to dealers or by refusing to honour guarantee services for motor vehicles purchased abroad. All the above restrictions constitute black practices pursuant to Article 6(1)(7) and (8).[378]

7.325 **Restrictions on the trade in spare parts from third parties.**   The manufacturer may not, directly or indirectly, restrict the freedom of the dealers to purchase spare parts from third parties, provided that the parts match the quality of the contract products (Article 6(1)(9)). Conversely, the manufacturer may not prevent the spare part suppliers from supplying such spare parts to the dealers or from placing their trade mark on the goods (Article 6(1)(10) and (11)).

7.326 **Restrictions on independent repairers.**   The manufacturer must make accessible, if appropriate on payment, the technical information required for the repair or maintenance to independent repairers, provided the information is not covered by the manufacturer's intellectual property rights or constitutes identified, substantial, secret know-how. Even in such cases, the information shall not be withheld improperly. The manufacturer must not discriminate or abuse its position in any other way (Article 6(1)(12) and Recital 28).

Automatic Loss of the Benefit in Cases of 'Black Clauses' or 'Black Practices'

7.327 The effect of including a 'black clause' in an agreement is that the benefit of Regulation 1475/95 is automatically lost. The loss applies not only to the clause in question, but to all other restrictions of competition which are included in the agreement, irrespective of whether they are imposed in favour of the manufacturer or the dealer (Article 6(2)).

---

[378] See the *VW/Audi* decision, para 187, in which the Commission declared that Regulation 1475/95 was automatically inapplicable as a result of the 'black practices' applied by the two manufacturers and their importer with the object and effect of restricting parallel trade.

The loss of the benefit is also automatic in case of a 'black practice' which is com-   **7.328**
mitted systematically or repeatedly. As a result, Regulation 1475/95 does not
apply to the restrictive clauses which are to the manufacturer's advantage. The
company in question loses the benefit of the block exemption in the area where
the practice has taken place and the benefit is lost only for so long as the conduct
lasts.[379] The Commission does not have to intervene, since the loss is automatic.
National courts have the power of establishing that a contract contains a black
clause. In contrast to the Commission, they are also able to grant injunctions and
award damages.

Withdrawal Procedure

Under Article 8 of Regulation 1475/95, the Commission has the power to with-   **7.329**
draw the benefit of the Regulation where it finds that in an individual case an
agreement which is drafted in accordance with the Regulation nevertheless has
effects which are incompatible with Article 81(3). In a non-exhaustive list, the following circumstances are listed:

- where motor vehicles and/or spare parts are not subject to competition within
  the whole or substantial parts of the common market (Article 8(1)),

- where prices or conditions of supply for contract goods are continually being
  applied which differ substantially between Member States, such differences
  being chiefly due to obligations exempted by the Regulation (Article 8(2)), and

- where a manufacturer or undertaking within the distribution system applies,
  unjustifiably, discriminatory prices or sales conditions when supplying distributors with contract goods (Article 8(3)).

The Commission has not yet made use of the possibility to withdraw the benefit   **7.330**
of the block exemption, a possibility which was also provided in Regulation
123/85. In the *Ecosystem* case, the Commission declared that it would withdraw
the benefit of Regulation 123/85, which was applicable at the time, if Peugeot SA
did not send out a new circular within two months whereby it cancelled the previous circular and in which it urged its dealers not to suspend supplies to the
intermediary Ecosystem. Since Peugeot complied with the order, a withdrawal
was not necessary.

It can be argued that the Commission has had opportunities to withdraw the ben-   **7.331**
efit of the block exemption pursuant to Article 8(2). It is clear that differences in
car prices remain high between different Member States. However, even where
important price differences exist, Article 8(2) requires that these differences
should be 'chiefly due' to obligations exempted by the Regulation. This seems

---

[379] See *VW/Audi* where the anti-competitive practice took place within Italy, Austria, and
Germany and where the loss of the benefit was automatic.

very difficult to prove, since a number of factors, both regulatory (differences in taxation, standards, right-hand-drive specifications for UK cars) and non-regulatory (monetary fluctuations and manufacturers' pricing policies) play a role in the setting of price.

7.332 It is possible that the scope for withdrawal of the benefit of the block exemption is also reduced in practice by the introduction of the 'black list' and 'black practices' in Regulation 1475/95. It is likely that the situations set out in Article 8(1) and Article 8(3) will in fact be covered by the prohibited practices and clauses listed in Article 6. In that case the loss of the benefit would be automatic and the Commission would not need to interfere.

The Application of Regulation 1475/95

7.333 It is difficult to establish whether Regulation 1475/95 has actually achieved its aims of facilitating parallel trade and creating a better balance between dealers and manufacturers. The fact that almost all motor vehicle manufacturers apply the system of distribution foreseen in Regulation 1475/95 and draft their standard dealer agreements in compliance with its provisions does not necessarily mean that its objectives are fulfilled. The *VW/Audi* decision shows a flagrant example where the provisions of Regulation 1475/95 on the right to parallel trade were not complied with. A number of consumers complain of problems in purchasing a right-hand-drive car on the Continent, a right which is in principle guaranteed by Regulation 1475/95, but which seems to cause problems in times of monetary fluctuations.[380]

7.334 Regulation 1475/95 also lays down rules with the aim to increase the dealers' independence *vis-à-vis* the manufacturers. Certain of these provisions, regarding the right of recourse to an arbitrator in case of dispute, or the very detailed rules on termination, seem to be a matter of private law rather than of competition law properly speaking. Whether they have achieved their objective is difficult to measure. While the regulation provides the dealers with some protection, it also provides the possibility for the manufacturer to terminate the contracts without cause, provided a notice of two years is respected. This is likely to maintain the dealers in a situation of dependence in relation to the manufacturers.

Regulation 1475/95 after the year 2002

7.335 It is not yet decided what will happen after the expiry of Regulation 1475/95 on 30 September 2002. The Commission is currently reviewing its policy concerning vertical restraints. However, this review does not cover the motor vehicle

---

[380] See eg press release of the Commission of 10 July 1998 IP/98/652 concerning, *inter alia*, the problems encountered by UK citizens in buying RHD cars in Ireland or in mainland Europe.

sector.[381] Therefore, a new block exemption regulation covering all vertical restraints would not be applicable in this sector. Regulation 1475/95 provides that the Commission shall draw up a report on the evaluation of the Regulation by 31 December 2000 (Article 11(3)). It will in particular take into account the impact the Regulation has had on price differentials between different Member States and on the quality of service to final users (Article 11(2)). On the basis of this report, a decision will be taken as to whether to renew the block exemption or not.

G. Agency

(1) Introduction

Agency contracts are commonly used for the distribution of goods and services. An agent is a natural or legal person who negotiates contracts with third parties on behalf of its principal. Once the contract is concluded the agent drops out, with performance of the contract being left to the principal or third party. The Commission has looked favourably upon such contracts where the principal appoints the agent as his sole agent for a given territory and the agent agrees to work exclusively for the principal for a certain period of time. The Commission considered such exclusivity provisions as being the natural result of the special relationship between a commercial agent and its principal which required them to protect each other's interests and therefore as not restricting competition. In such circumstances the exclusive agent is treated as an auxiliary of its principal. **7.336**

This thinking is expressed in part II of the Commission's 1962 Notice on Exclusive Dealing Contracts with Commercial Agents,[382] discussed below. This Notice has become somewhat outdated for a number of reasons, including the adoption of an EC Council Directive on self-employed commercial agents[383] and developments in the administrative practice of the Commission and case law of the Community Courts. However, perhaps the most fundamental change relates to changes in the systems of distribution. In 1962, goods were, in general, manufactured, stored, and pushed down the supply chain by way of arm's length transactions between independent manufacturers, wholesalers, and retailers. The **7.337**

---

[381] Commission's Green Paper on Vertical Restraints in EC Competition Policy (COM(96) 721 final), footnote 2.

[382] [1962] OJ 139 2921/62.

[383] Council Directive (EEC) 86/653 of 18 December 1986 on the coordination of the laws of the Member States relating to self-employed commercial agents [1986] OJ L382/17. For the purposes of the Directive a 'commercial agent' is defined as a 'self-employed intermediary who has continuing authority to negotiate the sale or the purchase of goods on behalf of another person hereinafter called the "principal", or to negotiate and conclude such transactions on behalf of and in the name of that principal' (it should be noted that services are excluded from this definition).

whole nature of distribution has been changed by the information technology revolution and the adoption of Just-in-time (JIT) principles.[384] The absence of risk relating to individual transactions, which was the main criterion used for differentiating an agent from an independent trader, is no longer the preserve of the commercial agent. Combined with modern technology, JIT has facilitated a shift from 'push' (ie where products were manufactured and stored in anticipation of demand) to 'pull' (ie where consumer demand pulls products towards the market and behind those products the flow of components is also determined by that same demand) in the supply chain.

7.338 One of the implications of the shift from push to pull is that manufacturers/ suppliers have less incentives to organize their distribution chains in a manner which requires their distributors to maintain stocks over which they hold legal title and act as resellers. With the reduction in risks relating to the holding of stocks, distributors will have greater scope to switch their legal status from that of resellers to agents. This is demonstrated by the 1996 *Ford Service Outlet* case[385] which related to Ford's reorganization of its European dealer network. As part of this reorganization smaller dealers who mainly do servicing and sell a small number of cars ceased to be Ford Dealers and instead became service outlets. What is interesting about this case is that the service outlets, while having no legal obligation to sell cars, could continue to 'do so in the name and on behalf of their affiliated main dealer with remuneration by way of commission on each sale'.[386] Therefore, in relation to the sale of new cars these service outlets bore no financial risk and were acting as commercial agents.

(2) The 1962 Notice on Exclusive Dealing Contracts with Commercial Agents[387]

7.339 As with many of the measures adopted by the Commission in the 1960s the 1962 Notice on exclusive dealing contracts with commercial agents was designed to contribute towards the alleviation of the 'mass' of notifications[388] made to the Commission following the adoption of Regulation 17 in February 1962.[389] The current Notice has been under review by the Commission since 1990.[390] It is now

---

[384] JIT is based on the principle that no products should be made, no components ordered, until there is downstream demand. For a useful summary of changes in distribution see paras 40–45 of the Green Paper on Vertical Restraints.

[385] The notification in this case is summarized in a notice published in [1996] OJ C227/11. The *Report on Competition Policy 1997* (Vol VII) 147 reports that the case was closed by way of comfort letter.

[386] See para 2 of the Notice.

[387] [1962] OJ 139 2921/62.

[388] See n 15 above.

[389] *Report on Competition Policy (1979)* point 2, n 2.

[390] *Report on Competition Policy 1990* (Vol XX) point 4. The *Report on Competition Policy 1991* (Vol XXI) point 133, indicated that a new notice should have been adopted in 1992. The 1997 Green Paper on Vertical Restraints, footnote 2, states that commercial agents are the subject of a separate exercise.

likely that the 1962 Notice will be replaced by a chapter in the forthcoming Guidelines on Vertical Restraints.[391]

To be covered by the 1962 Notice the principal must appoint the agent as his sole **7.340** agent for a given territory and the agent must agree to work exclusively for the principal for a certain period of time. In the 1962 Notice 'the Commission considers that contracts made with commercial agents in which those agents undertake, for a specified part of the territory of the common market, to negotiate transactions on behalf of an enterprise, or to conclude transactions in the name and on behalf of an enterprise, or to conclude transactions in their own name and on behalf of this enterprise, do not fall under the prohibition in Article 85(1) [now Article 81(1)] of the Treaty'. It should be noted that to be covered by the Notice the commercial agent must have a specified territory. It would also appear that there is a requirement for exclusivity. It is submitted that this arises from the use of the words 'exclusive dealing contracts' in title and text of the Notice. Moreover, the following statement in the second last paragraph of the Notice clearly supports the requirement for exclusivity on behalf of both the agent and principal:

> The obligation assumed by the agent—to work exclusively for one principal for a certain period of time—entails a limitation of supply on that market; the obligation assumed by the other party to the contract—to appoint him sole agent for a given territory—involves a limitation of demand on the market. Nevertheless, the Commission views these restrictions as a result of the special obligation between the commercial agent and his principal to protect each other's interests and therefore considers that they involve no restriction of competition.

The reason why the Commission does not consider such contracts to fall within **7.341** the prohibition of Article 81(1) is set out in section II, paragraph 2 of the Notice, namely:

> the Commission takes the view that the test for prohibition under Article 85(1) [now Article 81(1)] is not met by exclusive dealing contracts with commercial agents, since these contracts have neither the object nor the effect of preventing, restricting or distorting competition within the common market. The commercial agent only performs an auxiliary function in the market for goods. In that market he acts on the instructions and in the interest of the enterprise on whose behalf he is operating. Unlike the independent trader, he himself is neither a purchaser nor a vendor, but seeks purchasers or vendors in the interest of the other party to the

---

[391] Section II.2 of draft Guidelines on Vertical Restraints, as published on 24 September, 1999 on DG IV's Internet site at http://europa.eu.int/comm/dg04/antitrust/others/vertical_restraints/reform/consultation/draft_guidelines_en.pdf; Official Journal reference [1999] OJ C–270/07. It should be noted that paragraph 14 of the draft text states that 'The determinative factor in assessing whether Article 81(1) is applicable is the financial and commercial risk borne by the agent in relation to the contracts concluded under the agency agreement.' Therefore, it would appear that the Commission is in favour of retaining only the first of the two criteria of 'financial risk' and 'auxiliary organ' set out in the jurisprudence of the Court of Justice (see paragraphs 7.354–7.355 below).

contract, who is the person doing the buying or selling. In this type of exclusive dealing contract, the selling or buying enterprise does not cease to be a competitor; it merely uses an auxiliary, ie the commercial agent, to distribute or acquire products on the market.

7.342 From the foregoing paragraph it is submitted that the Commission does not apply Article 81(1) to agency contracts covered by the Notice for two reasons, either of which would on their own be sufficient for the non application of Article 81(1), namely the absence of (1) an agreement which is between undertakings,[392] and (2) a restrictive object or effect. The inference of the Notice is that where the first condition is not complied with then the second condition cannot be assumed. This explains why it is so important to distinguish a commercial agent from an independent trader. Use of the term 'agent' is not the determining factor. In distinguishing the two the Notice places strong reliance on the financial risks associated with the performance of the agency contract. Where the 'agent' bears the financial risks of the transactions conducted on behalf of its principal, other than the usual *del credere* guarantee, then it will be treated as an independent trader. The Notice states that a commercial agent will be treated as an independent undertaking particularly where he:

> is required to keep or does in fact keep, as his own property, a considerable stock of the products covered by the contract, or is required to organize, maintain or ensure at his own expense a substantial service to customers free of charge, or does in fact organize, maintain or ensure such a service, or can determine or does in fact determine prices or terms of business.

7.343 In addition to the activity of the commercial agent on the market of its principal in the purchase and sale of goods and services. It is also necessary to consider the various markets for the provision of agency services. For example a travel agent acting for a number of principals each offering different travel packages which may constitute different relevant markets for the purposes of an antitrust analysis is also operating on the market for the provision of travel agency services. It is clear from the second last paragraph of the Notice, as quoted above, that the Commission views the imposition of exclusivity on the agent as inherent in the nature of a true commercial agent and not involving a restriction of competition. An agency agreement in which the agent does not agree to work exclusively for its principal is not covered by the Notice.[393]

---

[392] This is because the two undertakings are deemed to constitute a single economic unit. See paragraphs 7.20–7.23 above and paragraph 7.352 below.

[393] In its decision in *European Sugar Industry* [1973] OJ L140/27, the Commission stated that the Notice 'defined the role of a commercial agent as that of a temporary employee integrated into the principal's undertaking and considered his obligation to work exclusively for a certain time for one employer as a consequence of the special obligation of mutual defence of interest as between commercial agent and principal, and thus not as a restriction on competition'.

(3) Relationship between Agency Contracts and EC Competition Law

Great caution must be taken in attempting to extend the principles in the Notice **7.344** to agency in general.

The Commission in its decision in *Pittsburg Corning Europe*,[394] refused to accord **7.345** the benefit of the Notice to an agreement whereby Pittsburg organized the distribution of its products in Belgium by way of an exclusive agency agreement. Looking beyond the form of the agreement the Commission refused to apply the Notice because the 'agent' was not in a position of economic dependence *vis-à-vis* Pittsburg.

In the *Vlaamse Reisbureaus* case,[395] the Belgian Government denied that Article **7.346** 81(1) could apply to the relationship between a tour operator and a travel agent, arguing that the relationship is one of principal and agent because travel agents operate in the name and on behalf of tour operators. A travel agent must therefore be regarded as an auxiliary organ of the tour operator.[396] This line of argument is based on the Court's case law under which agents may be categorized either as independent traders, in which case they constitute undertakings for the purposes of Article 81, or auxiliary organs forming an integral part of the principal's undertaking, in which case they constitute, together with that undertaking, a single economic unit to which Article 81 does not apply.[397] The Court of Justice did not accept this line of argument and ruled that:

> a travel agent of the kind referred to by the national court must be regarded as an independent agent who provides services on an entirely independent basis. He sells travel organised by a large number of different tour operators and a tour operator sells travel through a very large number of agents. Contrary to the Belgian government's submissions, a travel agent cannot be treated as an auxiliary organ forming an integral part of a tour operator's undertaking.[398]

---

[394] [1972] OJ L272/35.

[395] Case 311/85, *ASBL Vereniging van Vlaamse Reisbureaus v ASBL Sociale Dienst van de Plaatselijke en Gewestelijke Overheidsdiensten* [1987] ECR 3801.

[396] Case 311/85, n 395 above, at para 19.

[397] See the judgments in Joined Cases 56/64 and 58/64 *Consten and Grundig v Commission* [1966] ECR 299 and Joined Cases 40–48, 50, 54–56, 111, 113 and 114/73 *Cooperatieve Vereniging 'Suiker Unie' UA and others v Commission* [1975] ECR 1663.

[398] Case 311/85, n 395 above, at para 20. N Koch and G Marenco, 'L'Article 85 du Traité CEE et les contrats d'agence' [1987] *Cahiers de droit européen* 603, criticize the reasoning of the Court in the *Vlaamse Reisebureaus* case and earlier jurisprudence. They argue, *inter alia*, that agency contracts should escape the prohibition of Article 81 not because of the absence of an agreement between independent undertakings arising from the theory of 'auxiliary organ' but because such contracts do not restrict competition in so far as they relate to the market upon which the principal operates, as opposed to the market upon which the agent operates. See also B Van Houtte, 'Les contrats d'agence au regard de l'Article 85 CEE: Agir pour le compte d'autrui et integration dans son entreprise' [1989] *Cahiers de droit européen* 345, who argues, *inter alia*, that in the absence of some percieved element of assimilation between a principal and agent, the agent should be subject to the same competition rules as an independent trader.

7.347 The Court then proceeded to apply Article 81(1) to agreements whereby travel agents were prevented from competing on prices because they were unable to pass on to their customers some portion of the commission which they receive.

7.348 Agency contracts can be said to fall outside of the scope of Article 81 when the following two conditions are met:

- the agent must not bear any of the financial risks resulting from the contracts negotiated on behalf of its principal, and

- it must operate as an auxiliary organ forming an integral part of the principal's undertaking.

7.349 These two principles were confirmed by the Court of Justice in its 1995 judgment in the *Volkswagen Leasing* case.[399] In rejecting Volkswagen's and VAG's argument that Volkswagen's dealers, as intermediaries of VAG Leasing, form one economic unit with VAG and VAG Leasing, the Court of Justice ruled as follows at paragraph 19 of the judgment:

> Representatives can lose their character as independent traders only if they do not bear any of the risks resulting from the contracts negotiated on behalf of the principal and they operate as auxiliary organs forming an integral part of the principal's undertaking (see Joined Cases 40/73 to 48/73, 50/73, 54 to 56/73, 111/73, 113/73 and 114/73 *Suiker Unie and Others v Commission* [1975] ECR 1663, paragraph 539). However, the German VAG dealers assume, at least in part, the financial risks linked to the transactions concluded on behalf of VAG Leasing, in so far as they repurchase the vehicles from it upon the expiry of the leasing contracts. Furthermore, their principal business of sales and after-sales services is carried on, largely independently, in their own name and for their own account.

7.350 Finally, it should be noted that agency agreements can also be prohibited by Article 82.[400]

---

[399] Case C–266/93 *Bundeskartellamt v Volkswagen AG and VAG Leasing GmbH* [1995] ECR I–3508. See also the Opinion of Advocate General Tesauro in this case, [1995] ECR I–3479. The learned Advocate General attacks the use of the economic unit theory as a criteria for the applicability of Article 81 to agency contracts. He concludes in para 19 of his Opinion that 'an agency contract is indeed invariably concluded by two separate undertakings, with the result that, in principle, it has to comply with the competition rules. It follows that individual clauses of a contract escape the application of those rules only in so far as neither the object nor effect is to restrict competition.'

[400] In the 'Suiker Unie' case, see n 397 above, the Court identified two possible abuses in paras 482–486 of the judgment, namely: (1) '. . . if the agreements entered into between the principal and his agents, whom the contracting parties call "trade representatives", confer upon these agents or allow them to perform duties which from an economic point of view are approximately the same as those carried out by an independent dealer, because they provide for the said agents accepting the financial risks of the sales or the performance of contracts entered into with third parties. In fact in such a case the agents cannot be regarded as auxiliary organs forming an integral part of the principal's undertaking with the result that, if a clause prohibiting competition is agreed between principal and agent and the principal is an undertaking occupying a dominant position, that clause may constitute an abuse within the meaning of Article 86 as it is likely to consolidate that dominant position', and (2) '. . . clauses prohibiting competition imposed by an undertaking occupying a

H. The Commission's Radical Overhaul of EC Competition Policy towards Vertical Restraints

(1) Introduction

Distribution is a dynamic and constantly evolving sector.[400a] Almost all products pass from supplier to final consumer via the distribution system which thereby performs an important function within the European Union. It accounts for almost 13 per cent of the total Gross Domestic Product of the fifteen countries of the Union, employing more than 15 per cent of the active population and encompassing almost 30 per cent of enterprises.[401] All industries need distribution and the level of service provided by, and efficiency of, distribution are important elements of the competitive process to reach customers. To keep distribution channels open and competitive is therefore vital for any economy. **7.351**

Not only is distribution changing but also upstream, between manufacturers, relationships are changing with the increasing use of subcontracting, outsourcing, co-development, etc. The long-term viability of any individual member of a supply chain is becoming increasingly dependent on the ability of the entire chain to compete with the chains of other economic operators. Traditional production and distribution channels consisting of independent operators, each acting at arm's length and seeking to maximize their own profit rather than those of the channel, as a whole are in decline. There are two major reasons for this change. First, advances in information technology have enabled more tightly managed and efficient business practices between suppliers and buyers, like just-in-time production and more customized production, that require, however, more co-operation. Secondly, once involved in closer vertical relations the levels of trade become mutually more dependent on each other. For example, an efficient producer would lose its competitive advantage over a less efficient rival where its subcontractors or distributors are inefficient and have higher operating costs than those of its competitor. Similarly, an efficient distributor would lose its competitive advantage over less efficient rivals where those rivals are sourcing equivalent goods at lower prices. **7.352**

---

dominant position on trade representatives may constitute an abuse, if foreign competitors find that there are no independent operators who can market the product in question on a sufficiently large scale, and are in practice forced to apply to the said undertaking's trade representatives if they wish to sell this product in the latter's sales territory . . .'.

[400a] For a useful summary of changes in distribution see chapter 1 of the Green Paper on Vertical Restraints in EC Competition Policy, COM(96) 721 final. The reader is also referred to the Green Paper on Commerce, COM(96)530 final and to the section on distribution in the Commission's annual publication entitled *Panorama of EU Industry*.

[401] Annex A to the Green Paper on Commerce, COM(96)530 final.

It was against the background of these and other developments and a growing feeling of unease with the effectiveness of its own competition policy in the field of vertical restraints that the Commission started a thorough review of its policy in this field.[402] The Commission commenced this review by adopting the Green Paper on Vertical Restraints in EU Competition Policy on 22 January 1997.[403]

7.354 A number of points became clear during the consultation process that followed publication of the Green Paper:

(1) that the current Block Exemption Regulations on exclusive distribution/exclusive purchasing/franchising are too legalistic and formbased and create an unnecessary compliance burden, especially for companies without significant market power;

(2) that changes in the methods/formats of distribution make these Block Exemption Regulations work more and more as a straitjacket;

(3) that the current Block Exemption Regulations exempt clear cases of market power where vertical restraints can have serious negative effects;

(4) that for future policy a more economic approach is required, analysing vertical restraints in their market context and making the assessment dependent upon the (likely) effects on the market;[404]

(5) that a new policy should, to the extent possible, take account of the wish for legal certainty and limitation of compliance costs.

7.355 The Commission subsequently sketched the new policy approach it favours in its 1998 Communication on the Application of the EC Competition Rules to Vertical Restraints,[405] the follow-up to the Green Paper. The kernel of the approach is to create a safe harbour with a broad umbrella block exemption regulation covering all vertical restraints for the distribution of goods and services.[406] The regulation will use the concept of a market share threshold to distinguish

---

[402] A vertical restraint is a vertical agreement that falls within Article 81(1), that is a vertical agreement which has as its object or effect the prevention, restriction, or distortion of competition within the common market and which may affect trade between Member States.

[403] COM(96)721 final.

[404] For a useful summary of recent economic thinking on vertical restraints see chapter 2 of the Green Paper on Vertical Restraints in EC Competition Policy. The reader is also referred to Peeperkorn, 'The Economics of Verticals', (June 1998) EC Competition Policy Newsletter; Steiner, 'How manufacturers deal with the price-cutting retailer: when are vertical restraints efficient?', (1997), 65 Antitrust Law Journal 407; Dobson and Waterson, *Vertical Restraints and Competition Policy*, (London, 1996); Rey and Caballero-Sanz 'The Policy Implications of the Economic Analysis of Vertical Restraints', European Commission Directorate-General for Economic and Financial Affairs Policy Paper No 119, November 1996; and *Competition Policy and Vertical Restraints*, (Paris: OECD, 1994).

[405] COM(98) 544 final.

[406] Motor vehicle distribution is the only sector not covered by the policy review, see the Green Paper on Vertical Restraints, 2, n 2.

between agreements that are block exempted and agreements that are not block exempted. In addition the regulation will not any more contain a long 'white' list of clauses that may be contained in vertical agreements but will be based primarily on a 'black'-clause approach, ie a hard-core list will define what is not block exempted even when the relevant market share threshold is not breached. In the Communication the Commission also proposed that vertical agreements which are not in the hard-core list but fall outside the regulation, for example because of a too high market share, would not be presumed illegal.[407]

(2) Two New Council Regulations

When the Commission adopted the Communication it also submitted to the Council two draft Council amending regulations in order to enable it to adopt the described new policy approach. **7.356**

The Council adopted the two new Council Regulations on 10 June 1999.[408] Council Regulation (EC) 1215/99 amends Regulation (EEC) 19/65 and Council Regulation (EC) 1216/99 amends Regulation 17/62. Both Regulations have entered into force on 18 June 1999. **7.357**

The Possibility of Retroactive Exemption

The second Council amending Regulation relates to an amendment of Article 4(2) of Council Regulation 17/62, the first Regulation implementing Articles 81 and 82 of the Treaty. In the Communication it is stated that amendment 'is necessary because under the current system the date upon which an exemption can enter into effect cannot precede the date of notification. The Commission wants to change that system so as not to punish those companies which under the new more economic based system working with market share thresholds may make mistakes in the assessment of their market position.'[409] The proposed amendment was considered important to create a reasonable level of legal certainty for economic operators. The inability to exempt retro-actively combined with the automatic nullity of Article 81(2): **7.358**

> has the effect that many vertical agreements falling under Article 85(1), despite fulfilling the requirements for exemption under Article 85(3), are automatically void under Article 85(2) until they have been notified to the Commission. The fact that such agreements are automatically void, pending notification, has two negative effects. Firstly, it results in an unnecessary high number of notifications and secondly, it results in the competition rules being used as a strategic tool to avoid the enforcement of contracts, rather than as a means to address competition problems.

---

[407] Communication, 23–24.
[408] Council Regulation (EC) 1215/99 of 10 June 1999 amending Regulation (EEC) 19/65 and Council Regulation (EC) 1216/99 of 10 June 1999 amending Regulation 17[1999] OJ L148 1 and 5, respectively.
[409] Communication, 35.

The objective of the draft amending text is to enable the Commission to exempt retroactively when the notification takes place at a later date. The practical effect of such a legislative amendment is that companies would no longer have to notify vertical agreements which they do not believe to cause competition concerns, simply to ensure legal security. Instead, companies will place greater weight on their own analysis of the economic effects of the vertical restraints at issue, knowing that in the event of subsequent litigation it would not be too late to apply for an exemption under Article 85(3).[410]

Extension of the Power to Block Exempt

7.359 Council Regulation 1215/99 relates to an amendment of Council Regulation (EEC) 19/65. Amendment was required to extend the power of the Commission to block exempt categories of vertical agreements. Such extension was considered necessary:

> because the current enabling regulation[411] is restricted to a limited number of vertical restraints, namely, exclusive distribution of goods for resale, exclusive purchase of goods for resale, obligations in respect of exclusive supply and exclusive purchase for resale, and restrictions imposed in relation to the assignment or use of industrial property rights. It is also limited to agreements entered into between two parties.
> . . .
> The current Commission block exemption regulations in the field of distribution . . . cannot be satisfactorily amended to provide for the change in policy proposed in this Communication. Therefore, subject to the adoption of the two Council Regulations outlined above, a new Commission Regulation will be proposed. This regulation will extend to all vertical restraints in all sectors of distribution other than motor vehicles, covering, inter-alia, selective distribution, services, intermediate goods and agreements between more than two parties each operating at different levels in the distribution chain.[412]

Definition of a Vertical Agreement

7.360 Council Regulation (EC) 1216/99, by adapting Article 4(2) of Regulation 17/62, enables vertical agreements to be exempted retroactively when they are 'entered into by two or more undertakings, each operating, for the purposes of the agreement, at a different level of the production or distribution chain, and relate to the conditions under which the parties may purchase, sell or resell certain goods or services.' This is a rather wide definition of what is a vertical agreement.[413] It covers agreements between more than two undertakings as long as each of the undertakings operates at a different level of the production or distribution chain, for example between a manufacturer, a wholesaler, and a retailer. It also covers agree-

---

[410] Communication, 35.
[411] Council Regulation (EEC) 19/65 of 2 March 1965; [1965] OJ 36/533.
[412] Communication, 35 and 36.
[413] There is a strong analogy with the definition found in the withdrawn US Department of Justice Vertical Restraints Guidelines of 23 January 1985.

ments between competitors, as long as for the purposes of the agreement they are operating at different levels, for example when one manufacturer becomes the exclusive distributor for another manufacturer's products. Lastly, it covers such agreements when these relate to the conditions under which the parties may purchase, sell, or resell certain goods or services. These general terms mean that all forms of distribution agreements like exclusive distribution, selective distribution, exclusive purchasing, customer allocation, non-compete obligations, resale price maintenance, etc, are covered, for both final and intermediate goods and services.

In Article 1 of Council Regulation (EC) 1215/99 the same definition of vertical agreements is used. This makes it possible for the Commission to adopt a broad umbrella block exemption covering all distribution agreements. The new Council Regulation in Article 1 further amends Council Regulation 19/65 in such a way that the Commission is no longer obliged to specify a so-called white list of clauses that may be contained in the agreements. This opens the possibility for a block exemption regulation with a black list only. **7.361**

In addition to these two important amendments, Council Regulation (EC) 1215/99 contains two further amendments of Council Regulation 19/65. The first concerns disapplication of a block exemption regulation, the second concerns withdrawal of a block exemption regulation by Member States. **7.362**

Disapplication of a Block Exemption Regulation

Article 1(2), by inserting a new Article 1a into Regulation 19/65, gives the possibility to the Commission to include the power to disapply a block exemption regulation for parallel networks of similar agreements or concerted practices on a particular antitrust market. The block exemption regulation must stipulate the conditions which may lead to the exclusion of its application. It could, for example, specify a coverage ratio of 50 per cent: when more than 50 per cent of a particular market is covered by the same or similar vertical restraints the Commission may disapply the block exemption for such restraints relating to that market. **7.363**

This power to disapply is a new instrument, which the Commission may use for a certain market instead of withdrawing the block exemption for individual companies. The difference with an individual withdrawal is that the Commission, in the case of disapplication, does not need to prove Article 81(1) is violated and/or that Article 81(3) cannot be applied. It only needs to establish that in a certain market the specified condition, like the coverage ratio, is fulfilled for a particular type of agreement. Where a withdrawal decision normally contains the prohibition of certain restraints applied by a particular company, disapplication merely brings certain restraints applied by a group of companies in a particular market again under the direct applicability of Article 81. The Commission may subsequently take individual decisions to prohibit the agreements of individual **7.364** companies. Or it may, for example, try to solve a perceived competition problem through a settlement with the companies involved.

7.365 Procedural safeguards are provided in the Council Regulation in Article 1(2) and 1(3) for this new instrument. The Commission needs to establish the fulfilment of the specified condition by means of a regulation. It needs therefore to respect all the requirements for adopting a block exemption regulation, including consultation of the Advisory Committee on Restrictive Practices and Monopolies and all persons concerned by publication for comments of a draft text. The only difference with the procedure for a block exemption regulation is that the consultation of the Advisory Committee on Restrictive Practices and Monopolies is not required before publishing a draft regulation when no Member State requests such consultation. The Commission needs to fix a period in such a disapplication regulation at the expiry of which the block exemption regulation would no longer be applicable in respect of the relevant agreements. This period may not be shorter than six months.

Withdrawal of a Block Exemption Regulation by Member States

7.366 Article 1(4) of Council Regulation 1215/99, by inserting a new paragraph into Article 7 of Regulation 19/65, gives the possibility to the competent authority of a Member State to withdraw the benefit of any new, or already existing, block exemption regulation adopted under Council Regulation 19/65. This may be done when, in a particular case, agreements or concerted practices covered by the block exemption regulation have certain effects which are incompatible with Article 81(3) in the territory of that Member State, or in a part thereof, which has all the characteristics of a distinct geographic market.

(3) A New Block Exemption Regulation and a Set of Guidelines

7.367 Following adoption of the two new Council Regulations the Commission started the final stage of the reform of the legislative framework applicable to vertical restraints. It decided on 14 July 1999 to start the consultative procedure for the adoption of a new group exemption regulation and a set of guidelines in the field of vertical restraints. The Commission subsequently transmitted two draft documents, containing a draft regulation and a draft set of guidelines, to the Advisory Committee on Restrictive Practices and Monopolies for initial consultation. After meeting with the Committee the Commission will publish the documents for consultation of interested third parties.[414]

7.368 The Commission wants to create a safe harbour by way of the proposed umbrella block exemption regulation. But it will only do so for those situations where the

---

[414] At the time of writing of this chapter the publication was foreseen for the end of September 1999.

parties to a vertical agreement either have no market power or where the degree of market power held by the parties is such that the vertical agreement is unlikely to lead to net negative effects. While acknowledging that market share is not a perfect measuring rod for market power, it is assumed to be the best single indicator available. In a declaration, joined to the two Council Regulations, the Council supported the use of one market share threshold above which the general block exemption will not apply. Both the Council and the Commission in their respective declarations stated that a market share threshold of 30 per cent would be appropriate as a basis for consultation and this is also found in the draft text for the regulation.

For companies with a market share above the threshold of the block exemption it **7.369** must be stressed that there will be no presumption of illegality. The market share threshold will only serve to distinguish those agreements which are presumed to be legal from those that may require individual examination.

The proposed new policy is a radical overhaul of EC competition policy towards **7.370** distribution agreements. It solidifies a shift towards a more economic approach while increasing the overall level of legal security for companies by providing them with a safe harbour. Within the safe harbour, delineated by a market share threshold, it will no longer be necessary for companies to assess the validity of their agreements under the EC competition rules. Outside the safe harbour guidelines will assist companies in the assessment of their vertical agreements under Article 81.

The proposed guidelines describe the type of vertical agreements that fall outside **7.371** Article 81(1), clarify and explain the block exemption regulation, describe the procedures for withdrawal and disapplication, and shed light on particular market definition issues and on the future enforcement policy outside the scope of the block exemption regulation. For the latter purpose a framework of analysis is described and a number of specific vertical restraints are analysed.

The definitive texts of the new block exemption regulation and the guidelines **7.372** were not available when this book went to print. As draft texts usually undergo a number of sometimes not unimportant changes, it does not seem appropriate to describe here in detail the draft texts. Therefore, the remainder of this section will try to explain the economic rationale and analysis that underlie these proposals. While doing so, a number of the essential elements which will almost certainly be kept in the final texts will be pointed out.[415]

---

[415] The remainder of the section draws heavily on the two draft texts adopted by the Commission on 14 July 1999 and sent by the Commission to the Member States to start the consultation process (the Draft Guidelines on Vertical Restraints and the Draft Commission Regulation on the application of Article 81(3) of the EC Treaty to categories of vertical agreements and concerted practices). Aside from minor changes most of the following text is taken directly from the draft guidelines as

Vertical versus Horizontal Agreements

7.373 One of the elements underlying the policy change is the recognition that vertical agreements are generally less harmful for competition than horizontal agreements. The main reason for treating a vertical agreement more leniently than a horizontal agreement lies in the fact that the latter may concern an agreement between competitors producing identical or substitute goods/services. In such horizontal relationships the exercise of market power by one company (higher price of its product) may benefit its competitors. This may provide an incentive to competitors to induce each other to behave anti-competitively. In vertical relationships the product of the one is the input for the other. This means that the exercise of market power by either the upstream or downstream undertaking would normally hurt the demand for the product of the other. The undertakings involved in the agreement therefore usually have an incentive to prevent the exercise of market power by the other.

7.374 However, the Commission takes the view that this self-restraining character should not be overestimated. When there is sufficiently strong inter-brand competition, the efficiency gains arising from vertical restraints are likely to be passed on to consumers and net negative effects are unlikely. However, when an undertaking has market power and inter-brand competition is weakened it can also use vertical restraints to try to increase its profits at the expense of its direct competitors by raising their costs and at the expense of its final consumers by trying to appropriate some of their consumer surplus by charging a higher price or providing a lower quality. This can happen when the upstream and downstream company share the extra profits or when one of the two uses the vertical restraint to appropriate all the extra profits.

7.375 The more lenient approach towards vertical agreements is exemplified by the proposed market share cap of 30 per cent. This is appreciably higher than the market share threshold the Council and Commission might consider appropriate for horizontal agreements. Therefore, the draft block exemption regulation excludes from its application vertical agreements between competitors. An exception to this exclusion is, however, proposed for non-reciprocal agreements where the buyer has a total annual turnover not exceeding 100 million euros or where the buyer is a distributor and not a competing manufacturer. The first exception, of

---

sent to Member States. In addition, the section is based on the Communication, on the two declarations that were joined with the two Council Regulations 1215/99 and 1216/99 (Declaration of the Council on the Essential Elements of the new Competition Policy relating to Vertical Restraints and the Declaration of the Commission on the Essential Elements of its new Competition Policy in the field of Vertical Restraints, both available in the minutes of the Council, see document 8958/99 ADD 1 of 4 June 1999), and on Luc Peeperkorn, 'Commission's Policy Review on Vertical Restraints' in John Grayston (ed.), *European Economics and Law*, Isle of Wight: Palladian Law Publishing Ltd, (1999), 1–18).

which similar forms can be found in earlier block exemption regulations, indicates that below a certain turnover threshold the Commission expects little harm to competition. Through the latter exception, vertical agreements between a manufacturer and independent resellers of his product are covered by the block exemption regulation even when the manufacturer also acts himself as a distributor (situations of dual distribution).

Methodology of Analysis

In assessing cases above the proposed market share threshold of 30 per cent the **7.376** Commission will make a full competition analysis. This means that, first, it needs to be established whether the vertical restraint falls under Article 81(1), that is whether it is likely to have an appreciable negative effect on competition. To assess the likelihood of an anti-competitive effect, all the relevant factors enhancing or reducing the possibilities to use market power need to be taken into account. Once an anti-competitive effect has been established the question needs to be answered whether the conditions of exemption under Article 81(3) are fulfilled.

The assessment of a vertical restraint will, after adoption of the new Block **7.377** Exemption Regulation, involve the following five steps:

1. Does the vertical agreement contain a hard-core restriction as defined in the Block Exemption Regulation? If such a hard-core restriction exists and it violates Article 81(1), then the Block Exemption Regulation does not apply and individual exemption is unlikely.

2. If the answer to the first question is negative, the undertakings involved need to define the relevant market in order to establish the market share of the supplier or the buyer, depending on the vertical restraint involved.

3. If the relevant market share is below the threshold, the vertical agreement is covered by the Block Exemption Regulation subject to the conditions set out in that regulation.

4. If the relevant market share is above the threshold, it is necessary to assess whether the vertical agreement falls within Article 81(1).

5. If the vertical agreement falls within Article 81(1), it is necessary to examine whether it fulfils the conditions for exemption under Article 81(3).

Relevant Factors for the Assessment of Article 81(1)

The draft guidelines mention the following factors as the most important that **3.378** need to be taken into account in establishing whether a vertical restraint constitutes an appreciable restriction of competition under Article 81(1):

(a) market position of the supplier;
(b) market position of competitors;

(c) entry barriers;

(d) buying power;

(e) maturity of the market;

(f) level of trade;

(g) nature of the good or service;

(h) other factors.

7.379 The importance of individual factors may vary from case to case and depends on all other factors. For example, a high market share of the supplier is usually a good indicator of market power, but in a case of low entry barriers it may not indicate market power. It is therefore not possible to provide strict rules on the importance of the individual factors. However, the following can be said:

Market Position of the Supplier

7.380 The market position of the supplier is established first and foremost by its market share on the relevant product and geographic market. The higher its market share the higher its market power is likely to be. The market position of the supplier is further strengthened if it has certain cost advantages over its competitors. Competitive advantages may result from a first mover advantage (having the best site etc), holding essential patents, having superior technology, being the brand leader, or having a superior portfolio.

Market Position of Competitors

7.381 The same indicators, that is market share and possible competitive advantages, apply to describe the market position of competitors. The stronger the established competitors are and the greater their number, the less risk there is that the supplier or buyer in question will be able to foreclose the market individually and the less there is a risk of a reduction of inter-brand competition. However, if the number of competitors becomes rather small and their market position (size, costs, R & D potential, etc) is rather similar this may increase the risk of collusion. Fluctuating or rapidly changing market shares are in general an indication of intense competition.

Entry Barriers

7.382 Entry barriers are measured by the extent to which incumbent companies can increase their price above minimum average total cost and make a profit above the competitive level without attracting entry. Without any entry barriers, easy and quick entry would eliminate such profits. In as far as effective entry is likely to occur within one or two years entry barriers can be said to be low.

7.383 Entry barriers may result from a wide variety of factors like economies of scale and scope, government regulations especially when establishing exclusive rights, State aid, import tariffs, intellectual property rights, ownership of absolutely scarce resources, essential facilities, and brand loyalty of consumers created by strong advertising. Vertical links and vertical integration may also work as an entry barrier by making access more difficult and foreclose (potential) competitors. Entry barriers may be present at only the suppliers' or buyers' level or at both levels.

The question as to whether many of these factors should be described as entry bar- **7.384** riers depends on whether they are related to sunk costs. Sunk costs are those costs that have to be made to enter or be active on a market but that are lost when the market is exited. Advertising costs to build consumer loyalty are normally sunk costs unless an exiting firm could either sell its brand name or use it somewhere else without a loss. The more costs are sunk, the more potential entrants have to weigh the risks of entering the market and the more credibly incumbents can threaten that they will match new competition as it will be costly to leave the market. If, for example, distributors are tied to a manufacturer via a non-compete obligation the foreclosing effect will be more significant if setting up its own distributors will impose sunk costs on the potential entrant.

In general, entry requires sunk costs, sometimes minor and sometimes major. **7.385** Therefore actual competition is in general more effective and will weigh more in the assessment of a case than potential competition.

Buying Power

Buying power ensues from the market position of the buyer. The first indicator of **7.386** buying power is the market share of the buyer on the purchase (upstream) market. This share reflects the importance of its demand for its possible suppliers. Other indicators focus on the market position of the buyer on its downstream market including characteristics such as a wide geographic spread of its outlets, own brands of the distributor, and its image among final consumers. The effect of buying power on the likelihood of anti-competitive effects is not the same for the different vertical restraints. For single branding type of restraints buying power will often mitigate possible anti-competitive effects, while buying power may increase the negative effects in the case of restraints arising from the limited distribution and market partitioning groups such as exclusive supply, exclusive distribution, and selective distribution.[416]

Maturity of the Market

A mature market is a market that has existed for some time, where the technology **7.387** used is well known and widespread and not changing very much, where there are no major brand innovations, and in which demand is relatively stable or declining. In such a market negative effects are more likely than in more dynamic markets.

---

[416] The different types and groups of vertical restraints are described in paragraphs 7.394–7.403 the next subsection on the negative effects of vertical restraints.

Level of Trade

7.388 The level of trade is linked to the distinction between intermediate and final goods and services. As indicated earlier, negative effects are in general less likely at the level of intermediate goods and services. As far as the distribution of final goods and services is concerned, negative effects are in general less likely at the wholesale level than at the retail level.

The Nature of the Good or Service

7.389 The nature of the good or service plays a role for final goods and services in assessing both the likely negative and the likely positive effects. To address the first question it is important whether the goods or services on the market are more homogeneous or heterogeneous, whether the good or service is expensive, taking up a large part of the consumer's budget, or is inexpensive, and whether the good or service is a one-off purchase or repeatedly purchased. In general when the good or service is more heterogeneous, less expensive, and resembles more a one-off purchase, the more vertical restraints are likely to have negative effects.

Other Factors

7.390 In the assessment of particular restraints other factors may have to be taken into account. Among these factors would be the cumulative effect or coverage of the market by similar agreements between different parties, the duration of the agreements, whether the agreement is 'imposed' (mainly one party is subject to the restrictions or obligations) or 'agreed' (both parties accept restrictions or obligations), the regulatory environment and behaviour that may indicate or facilitate collusion like price leadership, pre-announced price changes, and discussions on the 'right' price, price rigidity in response to excess capacity, systematic price discrimination, and past collusive behaviour.

Negative Effects of Vertical Agreements

7.391 The negative effects on the market that may result from vertical restraints and that EC competition law aims to prevent are the following:

  (i) foreclosure of other suppliers or other buyers by raising barriers to entry;
  (ii) reduction of inter-brand competition between the companies currently operating on a market, including facilitation of collusion among suppliers or buyers;
  (iii) reduction of intra-brand competition between distributors of the same brand;
  (iv) the creation of obstacles to market integration, including, most of all, limitations on the freedom of the final consumers to purchase a good or service in any Member State they may choose.

Unlike most other competition law systems, the EC's competition policy on vertical restraints has not one but two principal objectives. The first, in common with all competition enforcement authorities, is the objective to keep markets open and competitive as reflected by (i), (ii), and (iii). The second, which is not common to other enforcement authorities, is the single market objective as reflected by (iv) above. The Community has progressively broken down government erected trade barriers between Member States. It is therefore considered that it would make no sense to prohibit such State measures if they could be replaced by agreements between companies that again hinder or delay market integration.

7.392

Normally the two objectives do not contradict each other but lead to the same policy outcome. When competition is not strong on a particular market, the geographic widening of such a market will increase the intensity of competition by adding competitors to the incumbent ones. The elimination of obstacles to market integration does help to remedy situations of insufficient competition. However, the possibility cannot be excluded that the Commission will also in the future sometimes take remedial action in situations of obstacles to market integration when the competitive situation of the market alone may not justify the priority given to such action. Such action will, however, in general also further improve the competitive situation of the market. This is partly why the proposed hard-core list (still) contains a general ban on resale restrictions. However, by excluding from the hard-core list such resale restrictions as the allocation of exclusive territories or customer groups and the restriction on resale to unauthorized distributors by the members of a selective distribution system it is acknowledged that resale restrictions may under certain conditions be positive for both competition and market integration. In the proposed guidelines this is also acknowledged, especially in the case of the introduction of a new product or in the case where an existing product is sold for the first time on a different geographic market. Vertical restraints linked to the opening up of new markets are considered to fall outside Article 81(1).

7.393

The described negative effects may result from various vertical restraints. Agreements that are different in form may have the same substantive impact on competition. To analyse these possible negative effects the guidelines are likely to divide vertical restraints into four groups: a single branding group, a limited distribution group, a resale price maintenance group, and a market partitioning group. The vertical restraints within each group have largely similar negative effects on competition. This classification is based upon what could be described as the basic elements of vertical restraints. In practice many vertical agreements contain a combination of these elements.

7.394

Single Branding Group

7.395 Under the heading of *single branding* come those agreements that have as their main element that the buyer is induced to concentrate his orders for a particular type of good or service with one supplier. This component can be found in, among others, non-compete and quantity forcing on the buyer, where an obligation or incentive scheme agreed between the supplier and the buyer makes the latter purchase its requirements for a particular good or service and its substitutes only or mainly from one supplier. The same component can be found in tying, where the obligation or incentive scheme relates to a good or service that the buyer is required to purchase as a condition of purchasing another distinct good or service. The first good or service is referred to as the 'tied' good or service and the second is referred to as the 'tying' good or service.

7.396 There are four main effects on competition: (1) other suppliers in that market cannot sell to the particular buyers and this may lead to foreclosure of the market, in case of tying to foreclosure of the market of the tied product; (2) it makes market shares more rigid and this may help collusion when applied by several suppliers; (3) as far as the distribution of final goods is concerned, the particular retailers will only sell one brand and there will therefore be no inter-brand competition in their shops (no in-store competition); and (4) in case of tying the buyer may pay a higher price for the tied product than it would otherwise do. All effects may lead to a reduction in inter-brand competition.

7.397 The reduction in inter-brand competition may be mitigated by stronger *exante* competition between suppliers to obtain the single branding contracts, but the longer the duration of the contract the more likely it will be that this effect will not be strong enough to fully compensate for the lack of inter-brand competition.

Limited Distribution Group

7.398 Under the heading of *limited distribution* come those agreements that have as their main element that the manufacturer is selling only to one or a limited number of buyers. This may be to restrict the number of buyers for a particular territory or group of customers, or to select a particular kind of buyer. This component can be found in, among others, exclusive distribution and exclusive customer allocation. The supplier limits its sales to only one buyer for a certain territory or class of customers. It is also found in exclusive supply and quantity forcing on the supplier, where an obligation or incentive scheme agreed between the supplier and the buyer makes the former to sell only or mainly to one buyer. Also selective distribution contains this element as the conditions imposed on or agreed with the selected dealers usually limit their number. After-market sales restrictions contain the same element by limiting the original supplier's sales possibilities.

There are three main effects on competition: (1) certain buyers within that mar- **7.399**
ket can no longer buy from this particular supplier and this may lead, in particular in the case of exclusive supply, to foreclosure of the purchase market; (2) when
most or all of the competing suppliers limit the number of retailers this may facilitate collusion, either at the distributors' level or at the suppliers' level; and (3)
since fewer distributors will offer the product it will also lead to a reduction of
intra-brand competition. In the case of wide exclusive territories or exclusive customer allocation the result may be total elimination of intra-brand competition.
This reduction of intra-brand competition can in turn lead to a weakening of
inter-brand competition.

Resale Price Maintenance Group

Under the heading of *resale price maintenance* come those agreements that have as **7.400**
their main element that the buyer is obliged or induced to resell not below a certain price, at a certain price, or not above a certain price. This group comprises
minimum, fixed, maximum, and recommended resale prices. Maximum and recommended resale prices, while as such not having negative effects, may work as
fixed resale price maintenance. As resale price maintenance relates to the resale
price it is mainly relevant for the distribution of final goods.

There are two main effects of minimum and fixed resale price maintenance on **7.401**
competition: (1) the distributors can no longer compete on price for that brand,
leading to a total elimination of intra-brand price competition; and (2) there is
increased transparency on price and responsibility for price changes, making horizontal collusion between manufacturers or distributors easier, at least in concentrated markets. The reduction in intra-brand competition may, as it leads to less
downward pressure on the price for the particular good, have as an indirect effect
a reduction of inter-brand competition.

Market Partitioning Group

Under the heading of *market partitioning* come agreements that have as their main **7.402**
element that the buyer is restricted in where it either sources or resells a particular
good or service. This component can be found in exclusive purchasing, where an
obligation or incentive scheme agreed between the supplier and the buyer makes
the latter purchase its requirements for a particular good or service exclusively
from the designated supplier, but leaves the buyer free to buy and sell competing
goods or services. The heading also includes territorial resale restrictions, the allocation of an area of primary responsibility, restrictions on the location of a distributor, customer resale restrictions, and prohibitions of resale.

The main effect on competition is a reduction of intra-brand competition that **7.403**
may help the supplier to partition the market and thus hinder market integration.
This may facilitate price discrimination. When most or all of the competing sup-

pliers limit the sourcing or resale possibilities of their buyers this may facilitate collusion, either at the distributors' level or at the suppliers' level.

Relevant Factors for Assessment under Article 81(3)

7.404 The draft guidelines mention four relevant criteria to assess a vertical restraint under Article 81(3):

— the vertical agreement must contribute to improving the production or distribution or to promoting technical or economic progress;

— the vertical agreement must allow consumers a fair share of these benefits;

— the vertical agreement may not impose on the undertakings concerned vertical restraints which are not indispensable to the attainment of these benefits;

— the vertical agreement may not afford such undertakings the possibility of eliminating competition in respect of a substantial part of the products in question.

7.405 The last criterion of elimination of competition is related to the question of dominance. In the case where an undertaking is dominant or becoming dominant as a consequence of the vertical agreement, a vertical restraint that has appreciable anti-competitive effects can in principle not be exempted. The vertical agreement may, however, fall outside Article 81(1), for example when necessary for the protection of client specific investments or for the transfer of substantial know-how without which the supply or purchase of certain goods or services may not take place.

7.406 Where the supplier (or, in the case of exclusive supply, the buyer) is not dominant, the other three criteria become important. The first, concerning the improvement of production or distribution and the promotion of technical or economic progress, refers to the type of efficiencies described in the next subsection. These efficiencies have to be substantiated and must produce a net positive effect. Speculative claims on avoidance of free riding or general statements on cost savings will not be accepted. Cost savings that arise from the mere exercise of market power or from anti-competitive conduct cannot be accepted. Secondly, efficiencies must also benefit the consumers. However, the criterion concerning the consumers' fair share can normally be assumed to be fulfilled if there is sufficient residual competition on the market. The third criterion will play a role in ensuring that the least anti-competitive restraint is chosen to obtain certain positive effects.

Positive Effects of Vertical Restraints

7.407 The Commission recognizes that vertical restraints often have positive effects. When a company has no significant degree of market power it can only try to increase its profits by optimizing its manufacturing or distribution processes. It is recognized that in a number of situations vertical restraints may be helpful in this respect as the usual arm's length dealings between supplier and buyer, determining only price and quantity of a certain transaction, can lead to a suboptimal level of investments and sales.

The following reasons that may justify the application of certain vertical restraints **7.408** are mentioned in the draft guidlines:[417]

1. *To solve a free rider problem.* One buyer may free ride on the promotion efforts of another buyer. This type of problem is most common at the wholesale and retail level, but less at the level of intermediate goods or services. Exclusive distribution or similar restrictions may be helpful in avoiding such free riding. Free riding can also occur between suppliers, for example where one invests in promotion at the buyer's premises, in general at the retail level, that may also attract customers for its competitors. Non-compete type restraints can help to overcome this second situation of free riding.

   For there to be a problem there needs to be a real free rider issue. Free riding between buyers can only occur on pre-sales services and not on after-sales services. The product will usually need to be relatively new or technically complex as the customer otherwise may very well know what he or she wants from past purchases. And the product must be of a reasonably high value as it is otherwise not attractive for a customer to go to one shop for information and to another to buy. Lastly, it must not be practical for the supplier to impose by contract on all buyers effective service requirements concerning the pre-sales services.

   Free riding between suppliers is also restricted to specific situations. A non-compete type agreement may help capture the full benefits where the promotion takes place in the retail outlets and is not brand specific.

2. *To open up or enter new markets.* In case where a manufacturer wants to enter a new geographic market, for example by exporting for the first time to another country, this may involve special 'first time investments' to establish the brand in the market. In order to convince a local distributor to make these investments it may be necessary to provide territorial protection to the distributor so that it can recoup these investments by charging temporarily a higher price. Distributors based in other markets should then be refrained for a limited period from trying to sell in the new market. This is a special case of the free rider problem described under 1 above.

3. *A different promotional strategy in different markets.* For example, assume a manufacturer does most brand promotion itself in its home market while it

---

[417] While trying to give a fair overview of the various justifications for vertical restraints, the draft guidelines do not claim to be complete or exhaustive.

leaves the promotion to be done by its (exclusive) distributor(s) in other markets. It may have good reasons of scale economies or market expertise for this. The manufacturer's promotion costs will be part of its ex-factory price in the home market, while it can and may have to apply, under competitive conditions, a lower ex-factory price in the other markets. The manufacturer may want to restrain to some extent its distributors in the latter markets from re-importing the product into its home market to prevent free riding on the promotional efforts of the manufacturer paid by the retailers through a higher ex-factory price.

4. *The certification free rider issue.* In some sectors, certain retailers have a reputation for stocking only 'quality' products. In such a case selling through these retailers may be vital for the introduction of a new product. If the manufacturer cannot initially limit its sales to the premium stores, it runs the risk of being de-listed and the product introduction may fail. This means that there may be a reason for allowing for a limited duration a restriction such as exclusive distribution or selective distribution. The duration must be enough to guarantee introduction of the new product but not so long as to hinder large scale dissemination. Such benefits are more likely with 'experience' goods or complex goods that represent a relatively large purchase for the final consumer.

5. *The so-called 'hold-up' problem.* Sometimes there are specific investments to be made by either the supplier or the buyer, such as in special equipment or training. For example, a component manufacturer that has to build/buy new machines and tools in order to satisfy a particular requirement of one of its customers. The investor may not commit the necessary investments before particular supply arrangements are fixed.

However, as in the other free riding examples, there are a number of conditions that have to be met before the risk of under-investment is real or significant. First, the investment must be sunk and brand specific. An investment is considered sunk when, upon exiting the market or after termination of the contract, the investment cannot be sold unless at a significant loss. An investment is brand specific if it can only be used to produce that particular component, to store that particular brand, etc and thus cannot be used profitably to produce or resell alternatives. Secondly, it must be a long-term investment that is not recouped in the short run. And thirdly, the investment must be asymmetric, ie one party to the contract invests more than the other party. When these conditions are met there is usually a good reason to have a vertical restraint for the duration it takes to depreciate the investment. The adequate vertical restraint will be of the non-compete type or quantity forcing type when the investment is made by the supplier and of the exclusive distribution, exclusive customer allocation, or exclusive supply type when the investment is made by the buyer.

6. *The specific hold-up problem that may arise from investments made at the premises of the other party to the contract.* The more costly it is to take the investments back the more it is necessary for the investor to sell the investment to the other party when the contract is terminated. However, this may give rise to transaction costs. If these costs are significant this may justify a vertical restraint with a limited duration; of the non-compete type or quantity forcing type when the investment is made by the supplier and of the exclusive distribution or exclusive supply type when the investment is made by the buyer. It may also help in avoiding free riding on the investment by competitors of the investor. An example could be a petrol tank at a petrol station financed or owned by the petrol company.

7. *The specific hold-up problem that may arise in the case of transfer of substantial know-how.* The know-how, once provided, cannot be taken back and the provider of the know-how may not want it to be used for or by its competitors. In as far as the know-how was not readily available to the receiver, is substantial, and necessary for the operation of the agreement such transfer may form a good reason to agree an exclusive relationship. Where the know-how is provided by the supplier this may justify a non-compete type of restriction. Where there is a continuing transfer of know-how or a continuing risk of losing know-how to competitors a restriction protecting the know-how may be necessary for the duration of the agreement.

8. *Economies of scale in distribution.* In order to have these economies exploited and thereby see a lower retail price for its product the manufacturer may want to concentrate the resale of its product with a limited number of distributors. For this it could use exclusive distribution, quantity forcing in the form of a minimum purchasing requirement, selective distribution containing such a requirement or exclusive purchasing. Such scale economies may be particularly potent at the wholesale level.

9. *Capital market imperfections.* The usual providers of capital (banks, equity markets) may provide capital suboptimally especially when they have imperfect information on the quality of the borrower or there is an inadequate basis to secure the loan. The buyer or supplier may have better information and be able, through an exclusive relationship, to obtain extra security for its investment. In a case where the supplier provides the loan to the buyer this may lead to non-compete or quantity forcing on the buyer. Where the buyer provides the loan to the supplier this may be the reason for having exclusive supply or quantity forcing on the supplier.

10. *Uniformity and quality standardization.* Another way in which a vertical restraint may help to increase sales is by creating a brand image and attractiveness to the final consumers by imposing a certain measure of uniformity

571

and quality standardization on the distributors. This can, for example, be found in selective distribution and franchising.

7.409 In addition to these ten reasons an eleventh reason that could have been mentioned but that is not found in the draft guidelines is the possibility of 'double marginalization'. It is not mentioned because of its hypothetical character. In a case where both the manufacturer and the distributor have market power each will set its price above marginal cost. They both add their margin that exceeds the one that would exist under competition. This may result in a retail price that even exceeds the monopoly price an integrated company would charge, to the detriment of their collective profits and consumers. In this case quantity forcing on the buyer or maximum resale price maintenance could help the manufacturer bring the price down to monopoly level.

7.410 The above-mentioned eleven situations make clear that under certain conditions vertical agreements are likely to help realize efficiencies and entry into new markets which may offset possible negative effects. The case is in general strongest for vertical restraints of a limited duration which help the introduction of new complex products or protect specific investments.

7.411 There is a large measure of substitutability between the different vertical restraints. This means that the same inefficiency problem can be solved by different vertical restraints. For example, as explained above, economies of scale in distribution may possibly be exploited by using exclusive distribution, selective distribution, quantity forcing, or exclusive purchasing. This is of importance as the negative effects on competition may differ between the various vertical restraints. This should play a role when indispensability is discussed under Article 81(3).

General Rules for the Evaluation of Vertical Restraints

7.412 Lastly, in evaluating vertical restraints from a competition policy perspective, some general rules are formulated in the draft guidelines:

1. For most vertical restraints competition concerns can only arise if there is insufficient inter-brand competition, ie if there exists a certain degree of market power at the level of the supplier or the buyer or both. Market power is the power to raise price above the competitive level and, at least in the short term, to obtain supra-normal profits. Companies may have market power below the level of market dominance as foreseen in Article 81.

2. Vertical restraints which reduce inter-brand competition are generally more harmful than vertical restraints that reduce intra-brand competition. For example, non-compete obligations are likely to have more net negative effects than exclusive distribution. The former, by possibly foreclosing the market to

other brands, may prevent these brands from reaching the market. The latter, while limiting intra-brand competition, does not prevent the good from reaching the final consumer.

3. Vertical restraints from the limited distribution group are particularly harmful when, in addition to a reduction in intra-brand competition, more efficient distributors or distributors having a different distribution format are foreclosed, as this denies consumers the particular service or a superior price-service combination of these distributors.

4. Exclusive dealing arrangements are generally worse for competition than non-exclusive arrangements. Exclusive dealing makes, by the express language of the contracts or their practical effects, one party satisfy all or practically all its requirements from another party. For example, under a non-compete obligation the buyer purchases only one brand, while quantity forcing leaves the buyer scope to purchase competing goods. The degree of foreclosure is therefore different.

5. Vertical restraints agreed for non-branded goods and services are in general less harmful than restraints affecting the distribution of branded goods and services. Branding tends to increase product differentiation and reduce substitutability of the product, leading to a reduced elasticity of demand and an increased possibility to raise price. The distinction between branded and non-branded goods or services will often coincide with the distinction between intermediate goods and services and final goods and services.

Intermediate goods and services are sold to undertakings and are used as an input to produce other goods or services and are generally not recognizable in the final good or service.[418] The buyers of intermediate products are professionals, able to assess quality and therefore less reliant on brand and image. The undertakings buying intermediate goods or services normally have specialist departments or advisers who monitor developments in the supply market. Because they effect sizeable transactions search costs are in general not prohibitive.

Final goods are, directly or indirectly, sold to final consumers that often are relying more on brand and image. As distributors (retailers, wholesalers) have to respond to the demand of final consumers, competition between distributors may suffer more when certain distributors are foreclosed from selling one or a number of brands than competition suffers when certain buyers of

---

[418] Intermediate goods and services are a broad category, including, for example, iron ore, steel, airplane engines, but also consultancy services. Sometimes the same good or service can be both an intermediate and a final good or service, depending on who is buying it. For example, soft drinks bought by a company for its own cafeteria are an intermediate good, while the same soft drinks bought for resale to final consumers are a final good.

intermediate products are foreclosed of certain sources of input. Also a loss of intra-brand competition is less important at the intermediate level.

6. In general a combination of vertical restraints aggravates their negative effects. However, certain combinations of vertical restraints are better for competition than their use in isolation from each other.

7. Possible negative effects of vertical restraints are reinforced when not just one supplier with its buyers practices a certain vertical restraint but when also other suppliers and their buyers organize their trade in a similar way. These so-called cumulative effects may be a problem in a number of sectors.

8. The more the vertical restraint includes the transfer of know-how the more reason there may be to expect efficiencies to arise and the more a vertical restraint may be necessary to protect the know-how transferred or invest-ment costs incurred.

9. The more the vertical restraint is linked to investments which are relatively specific and sunk, the more justification there is for certain vertical restraints. The justified duration will depend on the time necessary to depreciate the investment.

10. In the case of a new product or where an existing product is sold for the first time on a different geographic market it may be difficult for the company to define the market or its market share may be very high. However, this should not be considered a major problem as vertical restraints linked to opening up new markets, either by the introduction of a new product or by entering a new geographic market, in general do not restrict competition.

8

INTELLECTUAL PROPERTY

A. Introduction

(1) Overview

The application of the competition rules to the field of intellectual property (IP) **8.01** protection is complex. This is due in part to the varied scope and nature of that which can benefit from intellectual property right protection, and in part to the development over time of the jurisprudence on the relationship between intellectual property rights, often granted nationally, and Community law. This chapter sets out the application of EC competition law to licensing of, and refusals to license, intellectual property, and draws out the underlying principles governing the area as a whole.

8.02 A complete treatment of intellectual property licensing under Community law would require an analysis both under the Community competition rules, and the rules on free movement. As this book is concerned solely with the competition rules, the latter laws are beyond the scope of this chapter, save where there is a direct impact on the application of the competition rules. This is most notably the case in the discussion of the existence/exercise distinction and the consequent definition of the specific subject matter of an intellectual property right.

8.03 IP rights may be relevant to an appraisal under the competition rules in the absence of licensing issues or allegations of abusive behaviour, such as an analysis of barriers to entry on a particular market.[1] These issues are similarly beyond the scope of the present chapter.

(2) Purpose of Intellectual Property Rights

8.04 Intellectual property law confers certain exclusive rights in relation to the exploitation of intellectual endeavour—invention, design or expression—which would otherwise not be protected by traditional property laws. Intellectual property may be costly to develop: attempts to develop new intellectual property often fail and successful projects sometimes take a long time to complete. The end result of a successful development of intellectual property may often be easily reproduced at a fraction of the original development cost. This makes free riding on others' development commercially attractive, and protection of that development important if further development is to be encouraged.

8.05 The intellectual property right gives the developer certain rights over the exploitation of the work. The resulting profits earned by the owner may appear monopolistic compared to the costs of exploiting the work, even taking into account development costs. The relationship between legitimate exploitation of an intellectual property right, and abusive exploitation contrary to Article 82 (former Article 86) is far from clear.

8.06 For example, once a new drug has been developed and tested, manufacturing the drug is a relatively simple and low cost exercise. The researchers can only enjoy the reward for their successful work if they can prevent 'free riders' reproducing it at low cost. The profits earned by the manufacturer of a successful drug may seem high, even compared to the cost in time and resources of developing the drug. However, this is to examine the situation *ex post*. Given the high proportion of development projects that do not come to fruition, no development would take place were there not a right to recoup the development costs of both the failed and the successful drugs.

---

[1] Commission Regulation (EC) 447/98 of 1 March 1998 on the notifications, time limits and hearings provided for in Council Regulation (EEC) 4064/89 on the control of concentrations between undertakings (text with EEA relevance) [1998] OJ L61/1, Article 8(9).

The literature on the economic benefits of providing this legal protection for **8.07** intellectual property is extensive, although the optimum level and form of intellectual property protection for the various types of intellectual property remains controversial.

(3) The Relationship between Intellectual Property Protection and EC Law

Intellectual property rights interact with Community law mainly in the areas of **8.08** free movement and competition law. The position is complicated by intellectual property law remaining primarily the responsibility of the Member States. Article 295 (former Article 222) EC requires the Community to respect national systems of property ownership. Neither the single market rules nor Community competition law can be interpreted so as to negate nationally granted intellectual property rights.

Intellectual Property Protection and the Free Movement Provisions

The (still largely) national granting of intellectual property rights sits uneasily **8.09** with the single market objective of the European Community as most notably expressed in Article 28 (former Article 30) EC. This single market conflict, largely played out before the ECJ, is relevant to the application of the competition rules in that the scope and extent of intellectual property rights under Community law has largely been defined by the ECJ in the context of these cases. The ECJ developed the conceptual distinction between the existence of an intellectual property right, which could not be affected by EC law, and its exercise, which could: this necessitated an elaboration of the concept of the specific subject matter of the intellectual property right—that package of rights which together make up the intellectual property right itself. A separate means of addressing parts of this problem is through the harmonization of certain aspects of intellectual property rights at the Community level.[2]

Intellectual Property Protection and the Competition Rules

The second area where intellectual property rights and Community law interact **8.10** relates to the application of the EC competition rules to the licensing of intellectual property rights, or the refusal to do so. An intellectual property right gives its holder the ability to impose conditions on licensors, who may be actual or

---

[2] See, for example: Council Directive (EEC) 89/104 of 21 December 1988 to approximate the laws of the Member States relating to trademarks [1989] OJ L40/1; Council Directive (EEC) 92/100 of 19 November 1992 on rental right and lending right and on certain rights related to copyright in the field of intellectual property, [1992] OJ L346/61; Council Directive (EEC) 93/98 of 29 October 1993 harmonizing the term of protection of copyright and certain related rights, [1993] OJ L290/9; Council Directive (EEC) 93/83 of 27 September 1993 on the coordination of certain rules concerning copyright and rights related to copyright applicable to satellite broadcasting and cable retransmission [1993] OJ L248/15.

potential competitors of the right holder. Competition law limits the restraints to which actual or potential competitors can be subject, and imposes further obligations where the licensor has a position of dominance on a relevant market. This latter point is complicated by the fact that it may be the IP right itself which leads to the dominant position on the market. Article 81 (former Article 85) and Article 82 are therefore both relevant to a determination of the permissible restrictions which can be imposed on licencees. The existence/exercise distinction referred to above is also relevant here, the competition rules limiting the latter, and not the former.

8.11 **General Approach.**   The application of Article 81(1) to an intellectual property licence is therefore complicated by the need to determine whether the licence provisions are necessary to secure the specific subject matter of the intellectual property right. Use of an intellectual property right in a manner which ensures for the right holder the benefit of the specific subject matter of that right is regarded as preserving the existence of the right. Use of an intellectual property right in a manner which goes beyond the specific subject matter of the right is regarded as being an exercise of that right which must be analysed in light of the competition provisions of the Treaty. Therefore, only those provisions of a licence which go beyond the specific subject matter are potentially caught by Article 81(1).

8.12   The Commission has in the past taken the view that the permissible content of a licence has varied depending on the form of intellectual property right covered by the licence. This has required the Commission to determine what is the preponderant element of a licence (is it, for example, mostly a patent licence, with ancillary trade mark elements, or vice versa?), and then apply certain rules relevant to that intellectual property right.[3] This practice has been accused of artificiality given the complex package of rights often included in a single licence.

8.13 **Block Exemptions.**   This was also largely the approach taken in the earlier block exemption regulations. However, the technology transfer block exemption, discussed in detail below, takes a slightly different line, encompassing both patent and know-how rights, together with other ancillary intellectual property rights within a single approach.

Form of the Following Analysis

8.14   Given the substantial overlap between the specific subject matter of the various forms of intellectual property right, discussed below, it is arguable that it is the purpose of the licence arrangement, rather than the form of intellectual property right licensed, which should be the main element of an analysis under Article 81. To a large extent, this appears to be the approach adopted by the Commission

---

[3] See, for example, *Moosehead/Whitbread* [1990] OJ L100/32, at para 16 (only the English text is authentic).

under the technology transfer block exemption. The present text therefore approaches the analysis based more on the purpose of the licence, rather than on the intellectual property rights contained within it. There is an obvious correlation between this and the more traditional analysis—based on an identification of the preponderant type of intellectual property rights—licences to manufacturers tend to be of patents and know-how, licences to distributors tend to be of trade marks, and content licensing is essentially the same as copyright licensing. The advantage, however, is that the discussion becomes less arbitrarily focused on the notion of the preponderant element of the licence. This chapter therefore looks at licensing under the following headings:

- Manufacturing licences: licences of technology to a potentially competing manufacturer who will use the intellectual property in its production process (primarily patent and know-how licensing under the Technology Transfer Block Exemption, and, in certain circumstances, including patent pools);

- Distribution licences: licences of intellectual property to a distributor who will use the intellectual property in the distribution of goods manufactured by the owner of the intellectual property (primarily trade mark licensing);

- Content licences: licences of 'content' such as film and television programming which are used in the entertainment industries and the operation of performing rights societies (primarily copyright licensing, including collective licensing of copyright and its neighbouring rights carried out by rights societies).

The sections of this chapter are therefore as follows: **8.15**

Section B outlines the distinction in Community law between the existence of an   **8.16**
intellectual property right and its exercise. It then outlines the various types of
intellectual property right and their specific subject matter. It describes the common features of all types of intellectual property, and describes how the distinction between the existence of the intellectual property right (its specific subject matter) and its exercise is used to determine how competition law is applied to an intellectual property licence.

Section C analyses licences to manufacturers which, in practice, often will involve   **8.17**
the technology transfer block exemption,[4] and, decreasingly, the earlier block
exemptions.

Section D looks at licences to distributors.   **8.18**

Section E looks at content licensing, including collective licensing.   **8.19**

---

[4] Commission Regulation (EC) 240/96 of 31 January 1996 on the application of Article 85(3) [now Article 81(3)] of the Treaty to certain categories of technology transfer agreements (text with EEA relevance) [1996] OJ L31/2.

8.20 **Section F** examines the relatively new area of software licensing, including the software copyright directive[5] and the settlement in the *Microsoft* case.

8.21 **Section G** discusses the special considerations in applying Article 82 to the actions of owners of intellectual property.

B. Intellectual Property Rights and EC Law

(1) Introduction

8.22 Within the Community, the granting of intellectual property rights has historically fallen within the competence of the Member States. More recently EC legislation has given rise to new or harmonized intellectual property rights throughout the EU, for example in relation to trade marks,[6] rental and lending rights,[7] the harmonization of the term of protection of copyright,[8] satellite broadcasting and cable retransmission rights,[9] and the legal protection of databases.[10]

8.23 The relationship between EC law and Member State laws granting intellectual property rights has been most extensively explored in cases involving the free movement of goods. The EC Treaty provisions on the free movement of goods do not override national laws on intellectual property rights. First, Article 30 (former Article 36) EC provides a specific exception from the free movement provisions where they conflict with national intellectual property rights.[11] Secondly, Article 295 (former Article 222) EC[12] contains a general protection against the provisions of the Treaty undermining national systems of property ownership. The *Grundig*

---

[5] Council Directive (EC) 91/250 on the legal protection of computer programs [1991] OJ L122/42.

[6] Council Directive (EEC) 89/104 of 21 December 1988 to approximate the laws of the Member States relating to trademarks [1989] OJ L40/1.

[7] Council Directive (EEC) 92/100 of 19 November 1992 on rental right and lending right and on certain rights related to copyright in the field of intellectual property [1992] OJ L346/61.

[8] Council Directive (EEC) 93/98 of 29 October 1993 harmonizing the term of protection of copyright and certain related rights, [1993] OJ L290/9.

[9] Council Directive (EEC) 93/83 of 27 September 1993 on the coordination of certain rules concerning copyright and rights related to copyright applicable to satellite broadcasting and cable retransmission [1993] OJ L248/15.

[10] Directive (EEC) 96/9 of the European Parliament and of the Council of 11 March 1996 on the legal protection of databases [1996] OJ L77/20.

[11] Article 30: 'The provisions of Articles 28–32 shall not preclude prohibitions or restrictions on imports, exports or goods in transit justified on grounds of public morality, public policy or public security; the protection of health and life of humans, animals or plants, the protection of national treasures possessing artistic, historic or archaeological value; *or the protection of industrial and commercial property*. Such prohibitions shall not, however, constitute a means of arbitrary discrimination or a disguised restriction on trade between Member States.' Emphasis added.

[12] Article 295: 'This Treaty shall in no way prejudice the rules of Member States governing the system of property ownership.'

Consten case[13] established that Member State intellectual property rights were a form of property that enjoyed the protection of Article 295. This protection is limited, however. First, the Court is prepared to examine the extent of the rights granted at the national level to ensure that they do not conflict with the overall objectives of the Treaty. Secondly, the extent of Article 295 is unclear in that the use of the term 'system' of property ownership may imply that Article 295 is aimed more at the distinction between public and private ownership.

This section looks at the relationship between intellectual property rights and EC law under the following headings: **8.24**

— Existence v Exercise and the Specific Subject Matter of an Intellectual Property Right;

— The Specific Subject Matter of Intellectual Property Rights;

— Exhaustion of Intellectual Property Rights;

— Exhaustion Concept in EC Intellectual Property Legislation.

(2) Existence v Exercise and the Specific Subject Matter of an Intellectual Property Right

Existence and Exercise.   This distinction between existence and exercise of an **8.25** intellectual property right was initially drawn in the *Grundig Consten* case.[14] The existence of an intellectual property right is protected by Articles 30 and 295; its exercise falls to be examined under the Treaty.

This distinction has been attacked as being artificial, giving the EC institutions an **8.26** arbitrary ability to limit the scope of Member State law on intellectual property rights.[15] The converse, however, would appear equally arbitrary: were the existence of an intellectual property right to prevent any analysis of how that right were used in practice, then intellectual property rights would be effectively exempt from the free movement and competition law provisions of the Treaty.

Specific Subject Matter.   The distinction between the existence and exercise of **8.27** an intellectual property right is based on the 'specific subject matter' of the intellectual property right. Use of an intellectual property right in a manner which ensures for the right holder the benefit of the specific subject matter of that right is regarded as preserving the existence of the right and cannot be overruled by the free movement or competition provisions of the Treaty. Use of an intellectual property right in a manner which goes beyond the specific subject matter of the right is regarded as being an exercise of that right which must be analysed in light

---

[13] Joined Cases 56/64 and 58/64 *Consten and Grundig v Commission* [1966] ECR 299.
[14] Joined Cases 56/64 and 58/64 *Consten and Grundig v Commission* [1966] ECR 299.
[15] For example, V Korah, *Technology Transfer Agreements and the EC Competition Rules* (1st edn, Oxford: Clarendon Press, 1996) 2.1.1.

of the free movement and/or competition provisions of the Treaty. Once the intellectual property owner has received the benefit of the specific subject matter of the intellectual property right, the right is said to be 'exhausted'.

(3) The Specific Subject Matter of Intellectual Property Rights

8.28 The above distinction between the existence and exercise of intellectual property rights, and the doctrine of exhaustion, makes the definition of the specific subject matter of the right fundamental to any appraisal under the competition rules.

Patents

8.29 For the purposes of Community law, the specific subject matter of a patent has been defined as follows:

> the specific object of industrial property is inter alia to ensure to the holder, so as to recompense the creative effort of the inventor, the exclusive right to utilise an invention with a view to manufacture and first putting into circulation of industrial products either directly or by the grant of licences to third parties, as well as the right to oppose any infringement.[16]

Know-How

8.30 The technology transfer block exemption defines know-how as 'a body of technical information that is secret, substantial and identified in any appropriate form'.[17] Know-how is not a form of intellectual property right, but is closely analogous to patents. A firm which has certain knowledge or technology which is potentially patentable has a choice as to whether or not to seek patent protection. The firm may prefer not to disclose the information (required if a patent is sought), but instead to protect its investment in developing the technology by maintaining the confidentiality of the information. Such a decision would be appropriate, for example, where enforcement of the patent would be more difficult than maintaining the confidentiality.

8.31 Although such 'know-how' does not therefore enjoy a specific legal protection, owners of know-how can protect it through the general law on confidentiality. Conceptually, therefore, it may be appropriate to regard know-how as being protected not by virtue of it being an intellectual property right in itself, but by virtue of it being an aspect of the general law on confidentiality.

8.32 Presumably as a consequence of this, there is no clear definition of the specific subject matter of know-how in the case law of the Court.

8.33 One commentator suggests that in early Commission competition decisions, only the maintenance of confidentiality was regarded as being part of the specific sub-

---

[16] Case 15/74 *Centrafarm BV v Sterling Drug Inc* [1974] ECR 1147, at para 9.
[17] TTBE, at Article 10.

ject matter of know-how, which led to know-how licences being treated more strictly than patent licences. This position changed over time, and the know-how Regulation accepted that the weaker legal protection afforded to know-how under the general law was a reason for more contractual protection not less.[18]

It is likely that the specific subject matter of know-how would now be regarded as **8.34** essentially the same as that for patents. The common treatment of patents and know-how in the technology transfer block exemption suggests that this is at least the case for the purposes of the competition rules.

Copyright

Copyright takes the form not of giving the author an exclusive right to the ideas **8.35** in the work, as is the case with patents, but in giving the author rights over the expression of these ideas. The precise scope of the rights varies, however, and the specific subject matter of copyright cannot be stated with precision.

The specific subject matter of copyright comprises several different elements, **8.36** reflecting the different ways in which a copyrighted work can be exploited. There is no single definition of the specific subject matter of copyright, but the following elements emerge from the case law:

— a right to decide on the first placing of a work on the market;[19]

— a right to require fees for public performance;[20] and

— a right to rent out a work.[21]

A complicating factor is the variation between Member States as to what can be **8.37** copyrighted. One of the more controversial recent cases, the *Magill* decision discussed below, related to TV listings—copyrightable in the UK and Ireland, but not in other Member States. One commentator has identified this as the reason for the Court's controversial judgment[22] (despite the Court having explicitly said the contrary).

Trade marks

For the purposes of Community law, the specific subject matter of a trade mark **8.38** has been defined as the right:

---

[18] V Korah, *Technology Transfer Agreements and the EC Competition Rules* (1st edn, Oxford: Clarendon Press, 1996) at 4.1.3.

[19] Joined Cases 55 and 57/80 *Musik-Vertried Membran GmbH v GEMA* [1981] ECR 147.

[20] Case 62/79 *SA Compagnie Générale pour la Diffusion de la Télévision, Coditel v SA Ciné Vog Films* [1980] ECR 881.

[21] Case 158/86 *Warner Brothers and Metronome Video ApS v Christiansen* [1988] ECR 2605.

[22] WR Cornish, *Intellectual Property: patents, copyright, trade marks and allied rights* (3rd edn, London: Sweet & Maxwell, 1996).

inter alia to ensure to the holder the exclusive right to utilise the mark for the first putting into circulation of a product, and to protect him thus against competitors who would take advantage of the position and reputation of the mark by selling goods improperly bearing that mark.[23]

8.39   The EC has also issued a Directive harmonizing national trade mark protection[24] and established a Community trade mark system.[25]

Plant Breeders' Rights

8.40   Plant breeders who develop a new strain of plant are entitled to a monopoly in production and sale of seeds for this new variety of plant under a variety of Member State laws. In addition there is a separate Community-wide right established by EU law.[26]

8.41   There is no clear single definition of the specific subject matter of a plant breeder's rights, but the Court has held that the constant need to care for and monitor seed means the right extends beyond mere marketing.[27]

(4) Exhaustion of Intellectual Property Rights

Exhaustion Requires Consent

8.42   A holder (H) of intellectual property rights in Member State A cannot oppose the import of a product protected by those intellectual property rights into that Member State, where that product was put on the market of Member State B by H or with H's consent.

8.43   *Centrafarm v Sterling Drug.*[28]   This principle was set out in the context of pharmaceuticals protected by patent and trade mark law. Sterling Drug and its subsidiaries had registered the patent for a drug marketed as 'Negram' in several Member States including the UK and The Netherlands. The company had also registered the trade mark in a number of Member States including the UK and The Netherlands. The UK National Health Service purchases the majority of the human pharmaceuticals used in the UK, and has the power to obtain compulsory licences to pharmaceutical compounds. As a result it enjoys a position of considerable market power with respect to pharmaceutical companies operating in the UK. Perhaps as a result of this, Sterling Drug sold the Negram product in the UK

---

[23] Case 16/74 *Centrafarm BV v Winthrop BV* [1974] ECR 1183.
[24] Council Directive (EC) 89/104 to approximate the laws of the Member States relating to trade marks [1989] OJ L40/1.
[25] Council Regulation (EC) 40/94 on the Community trade mark [1994] OJ L11/1.
[26] Council Regulation (EC) 2100/94 of 27 July 1994 on Community plant variety rights [1994] OJ L227/1.
[27] *Breeders' rights—maize seed* [1978] OJ L286/23 at I.E(4) (only the German and French texts are authentic).
[28] Case 15/74 *Centrafarm BV v Sterling Drug* [1974] ECR 1147.

for approximately half of the price that it obtained for the product in The Netherlands.

Centrafarm obtained supplies of Negram from UK wholesalers and resold these **8.44** in The Netherlands, undercutting the prices in the Dutch market. Sterling Drug alleged that these sales were in breach of the Dutch patent and trade mark held by Sterling Drug and its subsidiaries. However, the ECJ held that the specific subject matter of Sterling Drug's intellectual property protection was to obtain a financial reward by ensuring that Sterling Drug had an exclusive right to be the first to market a product protected by the intellectual property rights. Sterling Drug had obtained this benefit by selling the product in question on the UK market. Sterling Drug had received the benefit of the specific subject matter of its intellectual property rights in the products in question by selling them in the UK, and had therefore exhausted its rights in the products. Its attempt to further limit transactions in these goods by relying on its Dutch intellectual property rights contravened Article 30 of the Treaty.

For a Sale to Exhaust Intellectual Property Rights it is not Necessary for that Sale to be Made in a Jurisdiction where it Enjoys Intellectual Property Right Protection

A holder (H) of intellectual property rights in Member State A cannot oppose the **8.45** import of a product protected by those intellectual property rights into that Member State, where that product was put on the market of Member State B by H or with H's consent, even where that product did not enjoy intellectual property protection in Member State B.

Merck v Stephar.[29]   A sale in a Member State where the good in question is not **8.46** protected by intellectual property rights can exhaust protection of the goods in other Member States where it would otherwise be so protected. Italian law did not allow pharmaceutical products to be patented. Despite this, a pharmaceutical called Monuretic, which was protected by patents owned by the Merck group in other Member States, including The Netherlands, was being sold in Italy by a subsidiary of Merck. Stephar purchased Monuretic in Italy and imported it into The Netherlands. The Court held that Merck had exhausted its rights in the Monuretic product in question by selling it in Italy, and that it could not invoke its Dutch patents to prevent the import of goods which had been produced and sold by it in Italy.

---

[29]   Case 187/80 *Merck & Co Inc v Stephar BV* [1981] ECR 2063.

Exhaustion Requires the Consent of the Right Holder even if the Goods were Lawfully Put on the Market in Another Member State without that Consent

8.47 A holder (H) of intellectual property rights in Member State A can oppose the import of a product protected by those intellectual property rights into that Member State, where that product was put on the market of Member State B without H's consent, even if the placing of the product on the market of Member State B was itself lawful (for example, because there was no intellectual property protection of the product in Member State B).

8.48 *EMI/Patricia.*[30] EMI UK and its German subsidiary owned the UK and German copyrights to certain recordings. A German company, Patricia, produced copies of these recordings in Germany without the consent of EMI. These were exported to Denmark and sold there. The Danish copyright on the recordings had expired so Danish law could not be used to prevent this sale. Some of the recordings were reimported into Germany. The Court held that EMI could invoke its German copyright to prevent the sale of these imported recordings despite the fact that they had first been sold on a market where EMI did not benefit from copyright, as EMI had not consented to this first sale.

8.49 *Keurkoop/Nancy Kean Gifts.*[31] Nancy Kean imported handbags of a particular design from Taiwan. As the first importer of goods of this design it was able to register the design in The Netherlands, despite not having been the original designer. Keurkoop imported handbags of the same design from Taiwan and sold them in The Netherlands. Some of the bags imported by Keurkoop were first imported from Taiwan into Germany and then re-exported to The Netherlands. Nancy Kean did not own design rights to the handbags in Germany, and could not own such rights as the German law only allowed the original designer of a product to register the design. Keurkoop argued that as the initial sale in Germany did not infringe any intellectual property rights, Nancy Kean could not invoke its rights under Dutch law to prevent the import of the bags to The Netherlands. The Court ruled that since Nancy Kean had not consented to the sale in Germany of the handbags, its intellectual property rights were not exhausted, despite the fact that the sale in Germany was legal.

Exhaustion Depends on the Specific Subject Matter of the Right in Question

8.50 A holder (H) of intellectual property rights in Member State A can oppose the import of a product protected by those intellectual property rights into that Member State, even if that product was put on the market of Member State B by

---

[30] Case 341/87 *EMI/Patricia* [1989] ECR 79.
[31] Case 144/81 *Keurkoop BV v Nancy Kean Gifts BV* [1982] ECR 2853.

H or with H's consent, provided that the putting on the market did not exhaust the specific subject matter of the right in question.

Exhaustion in any particular case can, by definition, only be analysed in light of **8.51** the specific subject matter of the intellectual property right. This is most clearly apparent in the area of copyright, where sale, public performance, and rental have all been identified as distinct elements of the subject matter of the right.

Warner v Christiansen.[32]   In *Warner v Christiansen* the Court of Justice recog-   **8.52** nized that the specific subject matter of copyright extended not only to the right to sell copies for home use, but also to the right to rent copies of the film. A sale for home use did not therefore exhaust the right to obtain revenue by renting the copy to several users.

Warner owned the copyright to certain films in both the UK and Denmark. UK   **8.53** law gave Warner the exclusive right to make the first sale of a video cassette record-ing, but once the sale had been made they could not prevent the recording from being rented out. The Danish law recognized a rental right, ie it had recognized that there was a market for short term rentals of video cassette recordings as well as one for the purchase of copies for personal use. In Denmark, Warner could sell a recording for home use and prohibit the purchaser from renting it out. Alternatively it could sell copies at a higher price to firms that wished to rent out the recording to third parties. Christiansen, a Danish operator of a video rental business, purchased video cassettes in the UK and imported them into Denmark where they rented them out. The Court held that the rental right created by the Danish law was a separate right, which was not exhausted by the purchase of a copy of the video cassette in the UK for home use.

The Court later clarified the nature of the rental right further: 'it is not contrary to   **8.54** Articles 30 and 36 [now Articles 28 and 30] of the Treaty . . . for the holder of an exclusive rental right to prohibit copies of a film from being offered for rental in a Member State even where the offering of those copies for rental has been author-ised in the territory of another Member State'.[33]

Exhaustion for the Purposes of EC Law Requires Use in the EEA

A holder (H) of intellectual property rights in Member State A can oppose the   **8.55** import of a product protected by those intellectual property rights into that Member State, where that product was put on the market outside the EEA, even

---

[32]   Case 158/86 *Warner Bros and Metronome v Christiansen* [1988] ECR 2605.
[33]   Case C–61/97, *Foreningen af danske Videogramdistributører, acting for Egmont Film A/S, Buena Vista Home Entertainment A/S, Scanbox Danmark A/S*, judgment delivered on 22 September 1988, not yet reported. See also, in relation to the right of public performance, Case 395/87 *Ministère Public v Tournier* [1989] ECR 2521.

if the placing of the product on the market outside the EEA was done by H or with H's consent.

8.56 A sale outside the EEA does not exhaust intellectual property rights for the purposes of Community law. In *EMI v CBS*,[34] the Court found that even if an owner of intellectual property rights in a Member State of the EC had consented to the sale outside the EC of goods covered by these rights they could invoke their rights to prevent the import of these goods into the EC.

8.57 As a result of agreements and transactions pre-dating the formation of the EC the 'Columbia' trade mark was owned by EMI and it subsidiaries in the EC, and by CBS in the United States. CBS had a UK subsidiary which imported goods bearing the Columbia trade mark from the United States and placed them on the market in several Member States. Despite the fact that these goods had been legitimately produced and sold in the US by CBS, and that CBS's ownership of the trade mark in the United States was as the result of an agreement between EMI and CBS, EMI could invoke its trade mark rights in the Member States of the EC to prevent the import of these goods from the United States.

8.58 In the more recent *Silhouette* case,[35] the Court's interpretation of the 1988 trade mark Directive maintained this position. Hartlauer is an Austrian discount retailer of spectacles. Silhouette is an Austrian producer of high-quality and high-price spectacles, which it sells throughout the EEA under its own registered trade mark. Silhouette had in the past refused to supply Hartlauer with its spectacles on the grounds that to do so would damage Silhouette's brand image. In 1995 it had sold a single consignment of old model Silhouette spectacles in Bulgaria at a price considerably lower than that which its spectacles would command in the EC market. Hartlauer had bought these in Bulgaria and had reimported them into Austria. Silhouette sought to use its trade mark rights to prevent the sale of these goods.

8.59 Hartlauer argued in the Austrian courts that Silhouette's trade mark rights should be considered as exhausted by Silhouette's sale of the goods, even outside the EC, in line with the Austrian legislation. In answer to a question put to it by the Austrian courts the ECJ stated that the trade mark Directive[36] provides that the protection of a trade mark is only exhausted by a sale of a good bearing the trade mark inside the EEA, and that national law could not go beyond this to deem the protection exhausted by a sale outside the EEA.

---

[34] Joined Cases 51, 86 & 96/75 *EMI Records Ltd v CBS United Kingdom Ltd, CBS Grammofon A/S and CBS Schallplatten GmbH* [1976] ECR 811, 871 & 913.

[35] Case C–355/96 *Silhouette International v Hartlauer* [1998], judgment delivered on 16 July 1998, not yet reported.

[36] Council Directive (EEC) 89/104 of 21 December 1988 to approximate the laws of the Member States relating to trademarks [1989] OJ L40/1.

Exhaustion and Licensing under the Competition Rules

Although the majority of cases have been examined under the free movement pro- **8.60**
visions of the Treaty, the same principles apply to the relationship between intellectual property rights and the competition rules. For example in *EMI v CBS*, the
court held that 'a trade mark right as a legal entity does not possess those elements
of contract or concerted practice referred to in Article 81(1). Nevertheless, the
exercise of that right might fall within the ambit of the prohibitions contained in
the Treaty'.[37]

Once the specific subject matter of an intellectual property right has been secured, **8.61**
any further use of the rights conferred by the intellectual property law is subject to
scrutiny under the EC competition rules.

(5) Exhaustion Concept in EC Intellectual Property Legislation

The concept of exhaustion of intellectual property right protection throughout **8.62**
the EEA after a sale anywhere in the EEA has been explicitly provided for in the
EC legislation on trade marks.[38] Similar provisions on exhaustion exist in other
EC legislation conferring or harmonizing intellectual property rights. For examples, see Article 1(4)(c) of the software Directive,[39] discussed at Section F below,
or Article 9(2) of the copyright and related rights Directive.[40]

C. Licences to Manufacturers: The Technology Transfer Block Exemption

(1) Prior Case Law

Licences to manufacturers will typically be licences of some combination of **8.63**
patents and know-how, possibly in conjunction with associated other rights.
Standard technology transfer implies that a new product or process has been fully
or largely developed and that the transfer agreement is allowing it to spread to new
firms. The public benefit of this is the wider dissemination of technology, across
both new sectors of the economy, and to different geographic regions, the latter
being of particular importance within the Community.

---

[37] Cases 51, 86 & 96/75 *EMI Records Ltd v CBS United Kingdom Ltd, CBS Grammofon A/S and CBS Schallplatten GmbH* [1976] ECR 811, at paras 26 and 27.
[38] Council Directive (EEC) 89/104 of 21 December 1988 to approximate the laws of the Member States relating to trademarks [1989] OJ L40/1, at Article 7.
[39] Council Directive (EC) 91/250 on the legal protection of computer programs [1991] OJ L122/42.
[40] Council Directive (EEC) 93/98 of 29 October 1993 harmonizing the term of protection of copyright and certain related rights [1993] OJ L290/9.

8.64 Many licences of this type are therefore covered by the technology transfer block exemption, or its predecessors, the patent licence block exemption[41] and the know-how licence block exemption.[42] The approach taken in these block exemptions follows in part the precedent set by the Court's judgment in *Maize Seed*.[43]

Technology Transfer and Territorial Exclusivity: Maize Seeds

8.65 LC Nungesser KG (Nungesser) was a German limited partnership engaged in the import, production, and distribution of agricultural seeds. The Institut National de la Recherche Agronomique (INRA) was a French State-owned body which had developed certain strains of maize, the seeds of which were protected by plant breeders' rights.[44] Nungesser had entered into a licensing and distribution arrangement with INRA. On the basis of this agreement Nungesser had invoked German plant breeders' rights to prevent or limit imports into Germany of maize seed of the type covered by the arrangement.

8.66 The Commission prohibited the agreement,[45] and the Court upheld the Commission's decision only in part. The Court distinguished between two distinct factual situations which the Commission had treated together. The first, included two elements:

— By licensing a single undertaking to exploit his breeders' rights in a given territory, the licensor deprives himself for the entire duration of the contract of the ability to issue licences to other undertakings in the same territory.

— By undertaking not to produce or market the product himself in the territory covered by the contract the licensor likewise eliminates himself as a supplier in that territory.

The second:

— The fact that third parties may not import the same seed (namely the seed under licence) from other community countries into Germany, or export from Germany to other community countries, leads to market sharing and deprives German farmers of any real room for negotiation since seed is supplied by one supplier and one supplier only.

8.67 The Commission had not distinguished between these two situations in its prohibition of the agreement. The Court, however, described the first as:

---

[41] Commission Regulation (EC) 2349/84 on the application of Article 85(3) [now Article 81(3)] of the Treaty to certain categories of patent licensing agreements [1984] OJ L219/15.

[42] Commission Regulation (EC) 556/89 on the application of Article 85(3) [now Article 81(3)] of the Treaty to certain categories of know-how licensing agreements [1989] OJ L61/1.

[43] Case 258/78 *LC Nungesser KG and Kurt Eisele v Commission* [1982] ECR 2015.

[44] Plant breeders' rights are treated as patents for the purposes of the technology transfer block exemption.

[45] *Breeders' rights—maize seed* [1978] OJ L286/23.

a so-called open exclusive licence or assignment . . . [which] relates solely to the contractual relationship between the owner of the right and the licensee, whereby the owner merely undertakes not to grant other licences in respect of the same territory and not to compete himself with the licensee on that territory . . .[46]

The Court described the second form of licence as having absolute territorial protection: **8.68**

under which the parties to the contract propose, as regards the products and the territory in question, to eliminate all competition from third parties, such as parallel importers or licensees for other territories.[47]

The Court found that an open exclusive licence did not necessarily fall within   **8.69**
Article 81(1) as such a licence might be necessary to encourage innovation and the deployment of technical developments into new geographic areas.[48] By contrast, the Court, referring back to its previous case law in *Consten and Grundig*,[49] found that a licence granting absolute territorial protection which thereby controls and prevents parallel imports results in the artificial separation of national markets, contrary to Article 81(1).[50] In addition, this level of protection went beyond what could be necessary to improve production or distribution or to promote technical progress, and therefore it would not be appropriate to grant an exemption pursuant to Article 81(3).[51]

(2) Block Exemptions

Enabling Legislation.   Council Regulation 19/65[52] allows the Commission to   **8.70**
pass regulations which specify forms of agreement which can benefit from exemption without needing notification to the Commission first. This includes agreements:

which include restrictions imposed in relation to the acquisition or use of industrial property rights—in particular of patents, utility models, designs or trade marks—or to the rights arising out of contracts for assignment of, or the right to use, a method of manufacture or knowledge relating to the use or to the application of industrial processes.[53]

Such regulations increase legal certainty for commercial operators, and decrease   **8.71**
the number of requests for individual exemption made to the Commission.

---

[46] Case 258/78 *LC Nungesser KG and Kurt Eisele v Commission* [1982] ECR 201, at para 53.
[47] Case 258/78 *LC Nungesser KG and Kurt Eisele v Commission* [1982] ECR 201, at para 53.
[48] Case 258/78 *LC Nungesser KG and Kurt Eisele v Commission* [1982] ECR 201, at para 57.
[49] Joined Cases 56 and 58/64 *Consten and Grundig v Commission* [1966] ECR 299.
[50] Case 258/78 *LC Nungesser KG and Kurt Eisele v Commission* [1982] ECR 201, at para 61.
[51] Case 258/78 *LC Nungesser KG and Kurt Eisele v Commission* [1982] ECR 201, at para 77.
[52] Council Regulation (EEC) 19/65 on the application of Article 85(3) [now Article 81(3)] of the Treaty to certain categories of agreements and concerted practices [1965] OJ 36/533.
[53] Council Regulation (EEC) 19/65 on the application of Article 85(3) [now Article 81(3)] of the Treaty to certain categories of agreements and concerted practices [1965] OJ 36/533, at Article 1(b).

Typically, the Commission issues such regulations once it has dealt with a number of individual cases sufficient for it to be aware of the important issues in an area.

8.72 **Patent and know-how block exemptions.**   Prior to the adoption of the technology transfer block exemption in 1996 two block exemptions had been in force based on this part of Council Regulation 19/65. These were the patent licensing and know-how block exemptions. The patent licensing block exemption[54] covered licences to a manufacturer of patents or other similar forms of intellectual property and also of know-how provided that that know-how was essential to the exploitation of the licensed intellectual property—ie the know-how was 'ancillary' to the patent licence. The know-how licensing block exemption[55] covered pure licences of know-how. Both block exemptions were approaching renewal in 1994 and the Commission considered that it would be possible to replace them with a single Regulation covering licences of patents and/or know-how to manufacturers.

8.73 **Continued Validity.**   With the passing of the technology transfer block exemption the patent and know-how block exemptions are of decreasing commercial importance. Article 11 of the technology transfer block exemption sets out the transitional arrangements, providing that the block exemptions continued in force until 31 March 1996. The prohibition in Article 81(1) does not apply to agreements in force on that date which fulfilled the exemption requirements of the block exemptions.[56] The patent and know-how block exemptions therefore remain applicable to agreements concluded prior to 31 March 1996.

(3) The Technology Transfer Block Exemption

8.74 The technology transfer block exemption applies to licences:

— of certain types of intellectual property;

— to which only two undertakings are party;

— for the purposes of manufacturing a product or using the intellectual property in a manufacturing process;

— containing at least one of the obligatory clauses;

— which may contain one or more of the permissible clauses; and

— which may not contain any of the prohibited clauses.

---

[54] Commission Regulation (EEC) 2349/84 on the application of Article 85(3) [now Article 81(3)] of the Treaty to certain categories of patent licensing agreements [1984] OJ L219/15.

[55] Commission Regulation (EEC) 556/89 on the application of Article 85(3) [now Article 81(3)] to certain categories of know-how licensing agreements [1989] OJ L61/1.

[56] Commission Regulation (EC) 240/96 of 31 January 1996 on the application of Article 85(3) [now Article 81(3)] of the Treaty to certain categories of technology transfer agreements (text with EEA relevance) [1996] OJ L31/2.

The Commission has also indicated that where an agreement falls outside of the **8.75** terms of the block exemption, the block exemption may nevertheless 'provide criteria' for the assessment of the agreement.[57]

Types of Intellectual Property Covered by the Technology Transfer Block Exemption

In contrast to previous Commission practice where patents and know-how were **8.76** treated separately, the block exemption applies to licences of either patents, or know-how, or a combination of both, together with intellectual property rights that are ancillary to the agreement.

Definition of Patents for the Purposes of the Block Exemption

For the purposes of the block exemption, patents include:[58]   **8.77**

— *Member State patents*: each of the Member States of the EU grants patent protection to new inventions. The systems vary in detail, and some harmonization is taking place at EC level.[59]

— *European Patents*: these arise from the European Patent Convention (EPC)[60] which aims to help inventors obtain protection for their invention throughout the EC. The Convention established the European Patent Office in Munich which started to operate on 1 June 1978. A single successful application to this office provides individual national patents from as many of the signatory countries to the Convention as the applicant requests. Currently all of the EC Member States, Switzerland, and Liechtenstein are signatories.

— *Community Patents*: signed in 1975, the Community Patent Convention (CPC)[61] aims to have the European Patent Office grant a single patent covering all of the EU. The Convention has not yet come into effect due to difficulties in its ratification by Member States.

Article 8(1) of the block exemption provides that for the purposes of the **8.78** Regulation, the term patent also includes

   (a) patent applications;
   (b) utility models;
   (c) applications for registration of utility models;

---

[57] *Sicasov* [1999] OJ L4/27.
[58] Commission Regulation (EC) 240/96 of 31 January 1996 on the application of Article 85(3) [now Article 81(3)] of the Treaty to certain categories of technology transfer agreements (text with EEA relevance) [1996] OJ L31/2, at Recital 14.
[59] Directive (EC) 98/44 of the European Parliament and of the Council of 6 July 1998 on the legal protection of biotechnological inventions [1998] OJ L213/13.
[60] Convention on the grant of European patents of 5 October 1973.
[61] Convention for the European patent for the common market of 15 December 1975, [1976] OJ L17/1.

(d) topographies of semiconductor products;

(e) certificates d'utilité and certificates d'addition under French law;

(f) applications for certificates d'utilité and certificates d'addition under French law;

(g) supplementary protection certificates for medicinal products or other products for which such supplementary protection certificates may be obtained;

(h) plant breeder's certificates[.][62]

Definition of Know-How for the Purposes of the Block Exemption

8.79 Know-how is defined at Article 10 of the Regulation, as are the constituent elements of the definition:

(1) 'know-how' means a body of technical information that is secret, substantial and identified in any appropriate form;

(2) 'secret' means that the know-how package as a body or in the precise configuration and assembly of its components is not generally known or easily accessible, so that part of its value consists in the lead which the licensee gains when it is communicated to him; it is not limited to the narrow sense that each individual component of the know-how should be totally unknown or unobtainable outside the licensor's business;

(3) 'substantial' means that the know-how includes information which must be useful, ie can reasonably be expected at the date of conclusion of the agreement to be capable of improving the competitive position of the licensee, for example by helping him to enter a new market or giving him an advantage in competition with other manufacturers or providers of services who do not have access to the licensed secret know-how or other comparable secret know-how;

(4) 'identified' means that the know-how is described or recorded in such a manner as to make it possible to verify that it satisfies the criteria of secrecy and substantiality and to ensure that the licensee is not unduly restricted in his exploitation of his own technology, to be identified the know-how can either be set out in the licence agreement or in a separate document or recorded in any other appropriate form at the latest when the know-how is transferred or shortly thereafter, provided that the separate document or other record can be made available if the need arises[.][63]

8.80 The definition of know-how therefore seeks to ensure that the agreement does in fact concern confidential information, and will contribute to technological and economic progress and so meet the conditions for the grant of the exemption given by the block exemption. The requirements of being secret and substantial will normally be met, as they are drafted in relatively broad terms. As to the secrecy, it is the package of know-how as a whole that must be generally secret at

---

[62] Commission Regulation (EC) 240/96 of 31 January 1996 on the application of Article 85(3) [now Article 81(3)] of the Treaty to certain categories of technology transfer agreements (text with EEA relevance) [1996] OJ L31/2, at Article 10.

[63] Commission Regulation (EC) 240/96 of 31 January 1996 on the application of Article 85(3) [now Article 81(3)] of the Treaty to certain categories of technology transfer agreements (text with EEA relevance) [1996] OJ L31/2.

the time of communication to the licensee, rather than all individual parts of it. The requirement of 'substantial' nature appears to require only that the licensee regards it as sufficiently useful to justify entering into a licence.

The requirement that the know-how be identified ensures that the other criteria are fulfilled and that therefore the exemption is justified. **8.81**

Intellectual Property Rights that are Ancillary to the Agreement

Moving further away from the traditional distinction between different intellec- **8.82** tual property rights as a starting point for competition law analysis, the block exemption also covers licensing agreements where other types of intellectual property such as a trade mark or copyrighted software are also licensed. The reason for this extension of the scope of the block exemption is set out at Recital 6:

> It is appropriate to extend the scope of this Regulation to pure or mixed agreements containing the licensing of intellectual property rights other than patents (in particular, trademarks, design rights and copyright, especially software protection), when such additional licensing contributes to the achievement of the objects of the licensed technology and contains only ancillary provisions.[64]

This intent appears to be implemented twice in the block exemption First, in the **8.83** article setting out the obligations, at least one of which is required for the block exemption to apply, the block exemption states that 'agreements containing ancillary provisions relating to intellectual property rights other than patents' are included in the scope of the exemption.[65]

Secondly, Article 5(1)(4) makes essentially the same point in the negative, exclud- **8.84** ing 'licensing agreements containing provisions relating to intellectual property rights other than patents which are not ancillary'.[66]

Types of Agreement Covered by the Technology Transfer Block Exemption

As indicated above, the block exemption applies to licences of intellectual prop- **8.85** erty containing one of the obligations listed in Article 1(1).

Parties. The block exemption applies to intellectual property licensing agree- **8.86** ments to which only two undertakings are party.

---

[64] Commission Regulation (EC) 240/96 of 31 January 1996 on the application of Article 85(3) [now Article 81(3)] of the Treaty to certain categories of technology transfer agreements (text with EEA relevance) [1996] OJ L31/2, at Recital 6.

[65] Commission Regulation (EC) 240/96 of 31 January 1996 on the application of Article 85(3) [now Article 81(3)] of the Treaty to certain categories of technology transfer agreements (text with EEA relevance) [1996] OJ L31/2, at Article 1(1).

[66] Commission Regulation (EC) 240/96 of 31 January 1996 on the application of Article 85 (3) [now Article 81(3)] of the Treaty to certain categories of technology transfer agreements (text with EEA relevance) [1996] OJ L31/2, at Article 5(1)(4).

8.87   The Court has held in the context of the exclusive distribution block exemption that organizations which constitute a single economic unit may be regarded as one undertaking for these purposes.[67] Article 6(3) confirms this position in respect of the technology transfer block exemption.

8.88   The article also provides that agreements where some of the rights or obligations are assumed by undertakings connected[68] with the parties to the agreement also fall within the scope of the block exemption. Thus, for the purposes of the block exemption, jointly controlled companies constitute a single party.

8.89   Article 6(1) also explicitly includes agreements where the licensor is not the original owner of the intellectual property but is authorized by the original owner to enter into the agreement.

8.90   Licences and Assignments.   The distinction between a licence and an assignment may not always be clear: attempts to avoid the effect of the block exemption by drafting licensing agreements as assignments or sales of intellectual property rights rather than licences should be caught by Article 6(2). This provides that if the risk associated with the exploitation of the intellectual property remains with the assignor then the agreement is to be treated as a licence for the purposes of the Regulation. In particular if the price to be paid by the assignee is to vary in proportion to the extent to which he or she is able to successfully use the intellectual property, as a licence payment would, then the assignment is to be treated as a licence.

8.91   Manufacturing or a manufacturing process.   The agreements must be for the purposes of manufacturing a product or using the intellectual property in a manufacturing process:

> The objective being to facilitate the dissemination of technology and the improvement of manufacturing processes, this Regulation should apply only where the licensee himself manufactures the licensed products or has them manufactured for his account, or where the licensed product is a service, provides the service himself or has the service provided for his account, irrespective of whether or not the licensee is also entitled to use confidential information provided by the licensor for the promotion and sale of the licensed product.[69]

---

[67] Case 170/83 *Hydrotherm Gerätebau GmbH v Compact del Dott Ing Mario Andreoli & C Sas* [1984] ECR 299, at para 11.

[68] Defined at Article 10(14)(d): 'undertakings in which the parties to the agreement or undertakings connected with them jointly have the rights or powers listed in (a): such jointly controlled undertakings are considered to be connected with each of the parties to the agreement'.

[69] Commission Regulation (EC) 240/96 of 31 January 1996 on the application of Article 85(3) [now Article 81(3)] of the Treaty to certain categories of technology transfer agreements (text with EEA relevance) [1996] OJ L31/2, at Recital 8.

Pure sales agreements are explicitly excluded from the scope of the block exemp- **8.92**
tion,[70] given that the block exemption allows extensive restrictions on active and
passive sales. Manufacturing is not explicitly defined, although Korah has suggested[71] that the Commission's earlier interpretative Notice on Regulations
1983/83 and 1984/83 may prove useful: manufacture would therefore change the
identity of the goods or add significant value to the raw materials.[72]

Patent or know-how pools and reciprocal licences. Patent and know-how **8.93**
pools are not defined in the block exemption. Reciprocal licences are defined as:

> agreements under which one party grants the other a patent and/or know-how
> licence and in exchange the other party, albeit in separate agreements or through
> connected undertakings, grants the first party a patent, trademark or know-how
> licence or exclusive sales rights, where the parties are competitors in relation to the
> products covered by those agreements . . .

The Regulation applies to either of these types of agreements provided the parties **8.94**
are not subject to any territorial restriction within the common market with
regard to the manufacture, use, or putting on the market of the licensed products
or to the use of the licensed or pooled technologies.[73]

For any agreement to be covered by the block exemption, it has to contain at least **8.95**
one of the obligations set out in Article 1. Since all but two of the obligations
described in Article 1 have a territorial element, and since patent pools or reciprocal licensing arrangements are only covered to the extent that there is no territorial restriction, then a patent pool or reciprocal licensing agreement can only fall
within the block exemption provided that it:

— contains no territorial limits on the behaviour of the parties; and either

— requires each of them to use the other party's or the pool's get up or trade
mark; or

— only allows the parties to manufacture products for their own use.

There have been no public statements by the Commission on the application of **8.96**
these provisions.[74]

---

[70] Commission Regulation (EC) 240/96 of 31 January 1996 on the application of Article 85(3)
[now Article 81(3)] of the Treaty to certain categories of technology transfer agreements (text with
EEA relevance) [1996] OJ L31/2, at Article 5(1)(1) read in conjunction with Article 5(1)(5).
[71] V Korah, *Technology Transfer Agreements and the EC Competition Rules* (1st edn, Oxford:
Clarendon Press, 1996) at 5.1.2.3.
[72] Notice on Regulations 1983/83 and 1984/83 [1994] OJ C101/2, at para 9.
[73] Commission Regulation (EC) 240/96 of 31 January 1996 on the application of Article 85(3)
[now Article 81(3)] of the Treaty to certain categories of technology transfer agreements (text with
EEA relevance) [1996] OJ L31/2, at Article 5(1)(1) read in conjunction with Article 5(2)(2).
[74] However see V Korah, *Technology Transfer Agreements and the EC Competition Rules* (1st edn,
Oxford: Clarendon Press, 1996) at section 5.1.1 for a discussion of how this section of the new
Regulation might be interpreted in the light of previous Court and Commission decisions.

8.97 **Licences between competing undertakings to joint ventures.** The Regulation specifically excludes 'licensing agreements between competing undertakings which hold interests in a joint venture, or between one of them and the joint venture, if the licensing agreements relate to the activities of the joint venture'.[75]

8.98 This exclusion is not absolute, and the exemption may still apply where the market shares are relatively low and the licence is between a parent and the joint venture:

> under which a parent undertaking grants the joint venture a patent or know-how licence, provided that the licensed products and the other goods and services of the participating undertakings which are considered by users to be interchangeable or substitutable in view of their characteristics, price and intended use represent:
>
> — in case of a licence limited to production, not more than 20 %, and
> — in case of a licence covering production and distribution, not more than 10 %;
>
> of the market for the licensed products and all interchangeable or substitutable goods and services[.]'[76]

8.99 A licensing agreement relating to the activities of a joint venture where the principals of the joint venture are competitors can therefore fall under the block exemption Regulation provided that the combined market share of the partners and the joint venture in the product market affected by the agreement falls below certain thresholds. For agreements limited to production this threshold is 20 per cent. For agreements involving production and distribution of goods this threshold is 10 per cent.

Required Clauses

8.100 Article 1 provides that technology licences which contain *one or more* of the listed obligations can enjoy the benefit of the block exemption.[77] Recital 10 states that the obligations listed in Article 1 may not, depending on the circumstances, amount to restrictions of competition but that they are all set out in the Article for the sake of legal certainty:

> (1) an obligation on the licensor not to license other undertakings to exploit the licensed technology in the licensed territory;

---

[75] Commission Regulation (EC) 240/96 of 31 January 1996 on the application of Article 85(3) [now Article 81(3)] of the Treaty to certain categories of technology transfer agreements (text with EEA relevance) [1996] OJ L31/2, at Article 5(1)(2).

[76] Commission Regulation (EC) 240/96 of 31 January 1996 on the application of Article 85(3) [now Article 81(3)] of the Treaty to certain categories of technology transfer agreements (text with EEA relevance) [1996] OJ L31/2, at Article 5(2)(1). See also Article 5(2)(3): 'This Regulation shall continue to apply where, for two consecutive financial years, the market shares in para 2(1) are not exceeded by more than one-tenth; where that limit is exceeded, this Regulation shall continue to apply for a period of six months from the end of the year in which the limit was exceeded.'

[77] But see also Article 2(2).

(2) an obligation on the licensor not to exploit the licensed technology in the licensed territory himself;

(3) an obligation on the licensee not to exploit the licensed technology in the territory of the licensor within the common market;

(4) an obligation on the licensee not to manufacture or use the licensed product, or use the licensed process, in territories within the common market which are licensed to other licensees;

(5) an obligation on the licensee not to pursue an active policy of putting the licensed product on the market in the territories within the common market which are licensed to other licensees, and in particular not to engage in advertising specifically aimed at those territories or to establish any branch or maintain a distribution depot there;

(6) an obligation on the licensee not to put the licensed product on the market in the territories licensed to other licensees within the common market in response to unsolicited orders;

(7) an obligation on the licensee to use only the licensor's trademark or get up to distinguish the licensed product during the term of the agreement, provided that the licensee is not prevented from identifying himself as the manufacturer of the licensed products;

(8) an obligation on the licensee to limit his production of the licensed product to the quantities he requires in manufacturing his own products and to sell the licensed product only as an integral part of or a replacement part for his own products or otherwise in connection with the sale of his own products, provided that such quantities are freely determined by the licensee.[78]

8.101 Article 1(5) provides that the block exemption also applies where the agreement includes obligations of the same type as those listed above, but with a more limited scope.

Territorial Restrictions

Open exclusive licences. The Commission's interpretation of the *Maize Seed* **8.102** case is set out at Recital 10 to the block exemption:

(10) Exclusive licensing agreements, ie agreements in which the licensor undertakes not to exploit the licensed technology in the licensed territory himself or to grant further licences there, may not be in themselves incompatible with Article 85(1) [now Article 81(1)] where they are concerned with the introduction and protection of a new technology in the licensed territory, by reason of the scale of the research which has been undertaken, of the increase in the level of competition, in particular inter-brand competition, and of the competitiveness of the undertakings concerned resulting from the dissemination of innovation within the Community. In so far as agreements of this kind fall, in other circumstances, within the scope of Article

---

[78] Commission Regulation (EC) 240/96 of 31 January 1996 on the application of Article 85(3) [now Article 81(3)] of the Treaty to certain categories of technology transfer agreements (text with EEA relevance) [1996] OJ L31/2.

85(1), it is appropriate to include them in Article 1 in order that they may also benefit from the exemption.[79]

8.103 The first five restrictions set out in Article 1 correspond to an open exclusive
licence.

8.104 **Closed Exclusive licences.**[80] The fifth of the above restrictions in Article 1
allows restrictions on active sales outside the licensed territory. The sixth allows
restrictions on passive sales. Cumulatively, therefore, the first six of the above
clauses amount to a 'closed' exclusive licence as defined in the *Maize Seed* case.

8.105 The block exemption goes beyond the Court judgment in that it accepts that
there are circumstances where even a closed territorial licence may be exemptable
under Article 81(3). This is referred to at Recital 15 of the block exemption:

> (15) Provision should also be made for exemption of an obligation on the licensee
> not to put the product on the market in the territories of other licensees, the per-
> mitted period for such an obligation (this obligation would ban not just active com-
> petition but passive competition too) should, however, be limited to a few years
> from the date on which the licensed product is first put on the market in the
> Community by a licensee, irrespective of whether the licensed technology comprises
> know-how, patents or both in the territories concerned.[81]

8.106 As indicated in the Recital, there are two limits on the exclusivity which distinguish the licence allowed by the block exemption from that condemned in the
Maize Seed case:

— the licensee and licensor must supply customers in their respective territories
even if these customers intend to sell the goods purchased in another territory
(Article 3(3)). A licensee can therefore be prevented from parallel trading, but
must supply third parties even if those third parties intend to parallel trade;

— the territorial protection allowed is limited in time. The term for which the
obligation can be exempted depends on the type of agreement (patent, know-
how, or mixed), and the territory in which the obligation has its effect. It is
summarized in the Table, below.

8.107 Where the territorial restrictions extend beyond the territory of the common
market, the position of the Commission is unclear. Territorial restrictions outside
the common market can have an, at most, indirect effect on competition
within the EEA—for example, where imports into the EEA are affected by restric-

---

[79] Commission Regulation (EC) 240/96 of 31 January 1996 on the application of Article 85(3)
[now Article 81(3)] of the Treaty to certain categories of technology transfer agreements (text with
EEA relevance) [1996] OJ L31/2, at Recital 10.
[80] See also Article 2.1(14) at para 8.115 below.
[81] Commission Regulation (EC) 240/96 of 31 January 1996 on the application of Article 85(3)
[now Article 81(3)] of the Treaty to certain categories of technology transfer agreements (text with
EEA relevance) [1996] OJ L31/2, at Recital 15.

tions imposed on external territories. Recital 7 of the block exemption provides that:

> Where such pure or mixed licensing agreements contain not only obligations relating to territories within the common market but also obligations relating to non-member countries, the presence of the latter does not prevent this Regulation from applying to the obligations relating to territories within the common market. Where licensing agreements for non-member countries or for territories which extend beyond the frontiers of the Community have effects within the common market which may fall within the scope of Article 85(1) [now Article 81(1)] , such agreements should be covered by this Regulation to the same extent as would agreements for territories within the common market.

However, the block exemption's definition of a licensed territory requires that at least part of the common market is covered by the licence. As such, the block exemption does not appear automatically to exempt agreements for territories wholly outside the common market. If there appears to be a risk of such agreements infringing Article 81(1), then individual notification would be required. Such agreements would not appear to be able to benefit from the opposition procedure in Article 4 of the block exemption unless they contained one of the two obligations listed in Article 4 which do not relate to territories within the common market. **8.108**

Maximum Duration of Obligations in Required Clauses

Article 1 lists eight clauses one or more of which are required for the block exemption to apply. These obligations must be limited in time, with the maximum duration permitted by the block exemption varying depending on the type of the licence (patent, know-how, or mixed patent and know-how). The maximum duration for each of the obligations in Article 1 is set out in the following Table. **8.109**

Permissible Clauses (White List)[82]

The regulation contains a non-exhaustive list of clauses in Article 2 which are not generally considered restrictive of competition and which will not prevent a licensing agreement from benefiting from the block exemption.[83] This is explained further in Recital 18: **8.110**

> It is desirable to list in this Regulation a number of obligations that are commonly found in licensing agreements but are normally not restrictive of competition, and to provide that in the event that because of the particular economic or legal circum-

---

[82] See also paras 8.138 *et seq* below on Termination and Post-Termination issues.
[83] Commission Regulation (EC) 240/96 of 31 January 1996 on the application of Article 85(3) [now Article 81(3)] of the Treaty to certain categories of technology transfer agreements (text with EEA relevance) [1996] OJ L31/2, at Article 2(1).

Table 1: Maximum Duration of Obligations in Article 1 of Technology Transfer Block Exemption

Obligation	Duration		
	Patent Agreement	Know-How Agreement	Mixed Agreement
(1) Licensor cannot grant other licences in licensee's territory			
(2) Licensor cannot exploit the technology in licensee's territory (this includes manufacturing in the relevant territory and making active or passive sales to that territory)	While parallel patent[84] remains in force	The shorter of: (1) 10 years; and (2) the period while the know-how remains secret and substantial.	The shorter of: (1) the duration of the patents; and (2) the know-how remaining secret and substantial. Both (1) and (2) are subject to a maximum duration. The maximum duration is the longer of: (a) ten years; and b) the duration of the necessary patents.[85]
(3) Licensee cannot exploit the technology in the licensor's territory (this includes manufacturing in the relevant territory and making active or passive sales to that territory)			
((4) Licensee cannot manufacture the product or use the process licensed in another licensee's territory			
(5) Licensee cannot actively sell the licensed product in another licensee's territory			
(6) Licensee cannot passively sell the licensed product in another licensee's territory	The shorter of: (1) 5 years;[86] and (2) the term of the patent.	The shorter of: (1) 5 years; and (2) the period while the know-how remains secret and substantial.	The longer of: (1) the patent remaining in force; and (2) the know-how remaining secret and substantial. Both (1) and (2) are subject to a maximum duration of five years.
(7) Licensee must use the licensor's trade mark or get up in addition to any marks of his or her own	While parallel patent remains in force.	The shorter of: (1) 10 years; and (2) the period while the know-how remains secret and substantial.	The longer of: (1) the patent remaining in force; and (2) the know-how remaining secret and substantial.
(8) Obligation to use the licensed product only as a component in licensee's own product.			

stances they should fall within Article 85(1) [now Article 81(1)], they too will be covered by the exemption. This list, in Article 2, is not exhaustive.[87]

That the list is not exhaustive is important. Clauses with the same object as those listed in Article 2(1) may potentially be regarded as also falling within the scope of the block exemption. Logically, other clauses which do not appreciably restrict competition would similarly fall within the block exemption, although these are more difficult to predict. It may prove difficult to determine whether the block exemption applies directly, or whether a notification under the opposition procedure (see paragraph 8.141 below) would be advisable.   **8.111**

The Scope of a Licence

Sub-licences.   Article 2.1(2) allows a prohibition on the grant of sub-licences or the assignment of the licence. In *Delta Chemie*, such a clause was held not to fall within Article 81(1) as: ' it remains the sole right of the owner of the know-how to decide whether or not a third party should be granted a licence to use that know-how'.[88]   **8.112**

Field of use.   Article 2.1(8) allows a restriction on the use of the licence to one or more technical fields of application covered by the licensed technology or to one or more product markets. Again, in *Delta Chemie* such a clause was justified on the basis that: ' it constitutes the corollary to the acknowledged right of the licensor to dispose freely of his know-how and, as a result, to limit the use by third parties solely to the manufacture of the licensed products'.[89]   **8.113**

This concept is referred to in slightly different terms in Recital 22:

> An obligation on the licensee to restrict his exploitation of the licensed technology to one or more technical fields of application ('fields of use') or to one or more

---

[84] Article 10(13): ' patents which, in spite of the divergences which remain in the absence of any unification of national rules concerning industrial property, protect the same invention in various Member States'.

[85] Article 10(5)—'necesssary' patents are defined as: 'patents where a licence under the patent is necessary for the putting into effect of the licensed technology in so far as, in the absence of such a licence, the realization of the licensed technology would not be possible or would be possible only to a lesser extent or in more difficult or costly conditions. Such patents must therefore be of technical, legal or economic interest to the licensee.'

[86] Measured from the first time a licensed product is put on the market by a licensee.

[87] Commission Regulation (EC) 240/96 of 31 January 1996 on the application of Article 85(3) [now Article 81(3)] of the Treaty to certain categories of technology transfer agreements (text with EEA relevance) [1996] OJ L31/2, at Recital 18.

[88] *Delta Chemie/DDD* [1988] OJ L309/34, at para 36 (only the German and English texts are authentic). In *Davidson Rubber*, the Commission held that a prohibition on sub-licensing was necessary to maintain confidentiality: *Davidson Rubber Co* [1972] OJ L143/31 (not available in English).

[89] *Delta Chemie/DDD* [1988] OJ L309/34, at para 32 (only the German and English texts are authentic).

product markets is not caught by Article 85(1) [now Article 81(1)] either, since the licensor is entitled to transfer the technology only for a limited purpose . . .[90]

8.114 **Third party facilities.** Article 2.1(12) permits a prohibition on the use of the licensed technology to construct facilities for third parties. Restrictions on quantity produced and prices set fall within the black list since they may have the same effect as export bans and may limit the extent to which the licensee can exploit the licensed technology,[91] but:

> the licensee may lawfully be prevented from using the transferred technology to set up facilities for third parties, since the purpose of the agreement is not to permit the licensee to give other producers access to the licensor's technology while it remains secret or protected by patent[.][92]

8.115 **Patent rights and exhaustion.** Article 2.1(14) allows the licensor to reserve the right to enforce his or her patent rights to prevent the licensee exploiting the licensed technology outside the agreed territory. As it is expressed as a reservation of rights, it is likely that no restriction of competition could arise. The position may be different if the clause were to positively assert rights, or to purport to limit challenge to those rights. The utility of the exempted clause would depend on the extent to which rights would be exhausted by the first licensing.

Payment for the Licence

8.116 **Royalty payments.** Article 2.1(7) allows a licensor to oblige the licensee to continue to make agreed regular royalty payments even after the licensed know-how has become public or the term of a patent has expired, provided that, in the case of a patent, this is to facilitate payment. This is a relaxation of the position under the earlier patent and know-how block exemptions, where payment was limited to the patent remaining valid, or the know-how remaining secret.[93] The licensor can stop paying for know-how if it has become public as a result of action by the licensor. The licensor can seek extra compensation if the licensee has made the know-how public.

---

[90] Commission Regulation (EC) 240/96 of 31 January 1996 on the application of Article 85(3) [now Article 81(3)] of the Treaty to certain categories of technology transfer agreements (text with EEA relevance) [1996] OJ L31/2, at Recital 22.

[91] See Recital 24 and para 8.127 below.

[92] Commission Regulation (EC) 240/96 of 31 January 1996 on the application of Article 85(3) [now Article 81(3)] of the Treaty to certain categories of technology transfer agreements (text with EEA relevance) [1996] OJ L31/2, at Recital 24.

[93] See, respectively: Commission Regulation (EEC) 2349/84 on the application of Article 85(3) [now Article 81(3)] of the Treaty to certain categories of patent licensing agreements [1984] OJ L219/15, at Article 3(4); Commission Regulation (EEC) 556/89 on the application of Article 85(3) [now Article 81(3)] to certain categories of know-how licensing agreements [1989] OJ L61/1, at Article 3(5).

In addition Article 2.1(9) provides that the licensee can be required to pay a min- **8.117**
imum royalty or to manufacture sufficient goods or use the licensed process
enough to give rise to an agreed minimum royalty.

Use of the Licence and Restrictions on the Product

Manufacture and market.   Article 2.1(17) provides that the licensee can be **8.118**
obliged to use his best endeavours to manufacture and market the licensed product.

Production limits on second licensee.   Limits on the amount of the product **8.119**
which can be supplied to a particular customer are also permitted, by Article
2.1(13), provided that the licence was granted so that the customer would have a
second source of supply inside the licensed territory. It is clearly not obligatory to
license two companies, therefore, if a second licence is granted, it is not restrictive
of competition to allow greater restrictions to be imposed on that licensee.

Quality control.   Article 2.1(5) allows minimum quality and technical specifi- **8.120**
cations to be imposed on the licensee. Article 2.1(11) permits an obligation to be
placed on the licensee to mark licensed goods with the licensor's name or an indication of the relevant patent.

Confidentiality and Misappropriation

Article 2.1(1) allows an obligation on the licensee to maintain the confidentiality **8.121**
of the know-how, even after the agreement has expired, and Article 2.1(6) provides that a licensee can be obliged to inform the licensor of any misappropriation
of know-how or infringements of patents and to assist the licensor in taking legal
action against this.

Grant-back

A grant-back arrangement could lead to a licensee choosing to take a further **8.122**
exclusive licence from the original licensor for improvements to the original
technology. A grant-back agreement cannot be created automatically by the original licence and any exemption it enjoys will apply only to the new licence of the
new technology. Imposing an obligation in a licence to require a licensee to give
up his or her property right in technology developed by the licensee is considered
restrictive of competition and specifically prohibited by Article 3.6. However, a
mutual grant-back arrangement is specifically declared not to be restrictive of
competition: Article 2.1(4) permits clauses which oblige the licensee to grant to
the licensor a licence in respect of improvements or new applications of the
licensed technology, provided:

  — that, in the case of severable improvements, such a licence is not exclusive, so
    that the licensee is free to use his own improvements or to license them to third
    parties, in so far as that does not involve disclosure of the know-how communi-
    cated by the licensor that is still secret,

— and that the licensor undertakes to grant an exclusive or non-exclusive licence of his own improvements to the licensee[.]

8.123 Under such an agreement the licensor agrees to grant the licensee either an exclusive or non-exclusive licence to any improvements the licensor makes to the licensed technology subsequent to the original agreement. In return the licensee agrees to grant the licensor a non-exclusive licence to any improvements that the licensee makes to the licensed technology. In so far as these improvements can be used without infringing the intellectual property rights originally licensed the licensee can also license these improvements to third parties.

8.124 Article 8.3 states that a licence can be drafted in such a way that it renews automatically by the licence of improvement to the technology and still benefits from the Regulation provided that each party has a right to terminate the agreement after the expiration of the initial term. This allows the parties the administrative convenience of a single licence that automatically renews if new technology has been developed and the parties want to continue to license from each other.

Most Favoured Licensee

8.125 Article 2.1(10) permits the licensor to be obliged to amend the terms of the licence in favour of the licensee if he or she subsequently enters another licence agreement on more favourable terms than the original licence.

Prohibited Clauses (Black list)

8.126 As with other block exemption regulations a number of clauses are listed which would disqualify an agreement from benefiting from the block exemption. These are set out in Article 3. Several of these are similar to the clauses set out in Article 2, and reading the two articles together helps to clarify the extent of the prohibitions in Article 3.

Pricing

8.127 Once a licence has been granted and the licensor has received its remuneration, the intellectual property rights of the licensor are exhausted. A clause attempting to fix the pricing behaviour of either party cannot be justified, and a clause where one party is restricted in the determination of prices, components of prices or discounts for the licensed products would, according to Article 3(1) be impermissible.

Non-Competition and Business Restrictions

8.128 **Non-compete clauses.**   Notwithstanding the permissible obligation to manufacture and sell in Article 2.1(17), Article 3(2) provides that neither party can be prevented from competing in respect of research and development, use, or distribution of competing products.

However, although a licensee must be allowed to compete in respect of research **8.129** and development, use, or distribution of competing products, the licensor can ensure that certain consequences ensue from such competition. Most importantly, Article 2.1(18) provides that the licence can be terminated. In addition, Article 2.1(1) provides that the licensee can be prevented from divulging knowhow obtained under the licence even after the expiration of the agreement. Article 2.1(17) provides that it can be obliged to use its 'best endeavours' to manufacture and market the licensed goods and that the original licensor can end the exclusivity of the licence and require the licensee to prove that the licensed intellectual property is not being used in the production of competing goods.

Production restrictions. Article 3.5 similarly prohibits quantitative restrictions **8.130** on production. Recital 24 explains that these restrictions are prohibited because they can be used to achieve the same effect as a total ban on exports and parallel trade if each licensee is only allowed to produce a quantity equal to the requirements of their 'home' territory. This does not prevent licensees obtaining licences to produce goods entirely for their own use (Article 1.1(8)) or the granting of a licence to create a second source of supply for customers of the owner of the intellectual property (Article 2.1(13)).

Customer and distribution restrictions. Licences of intellectual property can- **8.131** not be used to divide up a product market between the licensor and the licensee. Where the parties were already competing manufacturers before the grant of the licence, Article 3(4) prohibits restriction on either party of the customers served, forms of distribution used, or forms of packaging. However, Article 1.1(7) provides that the licensee can be required to use the trade mark and 'get up' of the licensor.

Production limits on second licensee permitted. In addition, Article 2.1(13) **8.132** provides that if an owner of intellectual property has a customer for goods, manufactured using that intellectual property, who wishes to have the security of a second source of supply then the owner can (but is not obliged to) grant a licence to a third party. However, the licence to the third party may be limited in that it only allows that third party licensee to produce a limited quantity for that customer. Alternatively, the licensor may grant a licence to the customer that only allows the customer to manufacture or have manufactured a limited quantity of the goods for the customer's own use.

Customer and distribution restrictions should be distinguished, however, from **8.133** field of use restrictions. Although a licence agreement cannot be used to divide a given product market between the licensor and licensee, Article 2.1(8) recognizes that a given set of technology may have applications in a number of different industries. Since the owner of the intellectual property has exclusive use of the technology in all of these product markets and fields of use a licence of the technology for only one of these fields of use is not restrictive of competition.[94]

8.134 Article 2.1(5) allows a licensor to ensure that the licensee meets minimum quality standards by checking the output of the licensee and requiring the licensee to obtain certain quality specifications of product or service from the licensor or a designated third party. Article 2.1(12) allows the licensor to prohibit the licensee from constructing manufacturing facilities that use the licensed technology for third parties but provides that the licensee can extend his own facilities or construct new ones on normal commercial terms. These two provisions may mean that although a licensor can specify a list of plants, where the licensee has the approval of the licensor to manufacture the licensed goods, the licensor cannot unreasonably withhold approval from further plants except on objective technical grounds.

Territorial Restrictions and Resellers

8.135 **Parallel trading.** The Regulation exempts bans on both active and passive sales outside their territories by licensees. However, Article 3(3) protects a certain element of parallel trading by providing an alternative source of supply for customers in a licensee's territory in that it prohibits obligations on either party:

> (a) to refuse to meet orders from users or resellers in their respective territories who would market products in other territories within the common market;

> (b) to make it difficult for users or resellers to obtain the products from other resellers within the common market, and in particular to exercise intellectual property rights or take measures so as to prevent users or resellers from obtaining outside, or from putting on the market in the licensed territory products which have been lawfully put on the market within the common market by the licensor or with his consent[.][95]

8.136 Although the licensees may not be able to sell into each other's territories either actively or passively, if price differences arise between territories parallel traders will be able to obtain supplies from their local licensee and sell these goods into the territories of other licensees. After the end of the periods specified in Article 1 of the Regulation the original licensor must be free to grant further licences in the territory and the licensee must be free to operate in the territory of the original licensor or other licensees.

---

[94] See also Commission Regulation (EC) 240/96 of 31 January 1996 on the application of Article 85(3) [now Article 81(3)] of the Treaty to certain categories of technology transfer agreements (text with EEA relevance) [1996] OJ L31/2, at Recital 22.

[95] Commission Regulation (EC) 240/96 of 31 January 1996 on the application of Article 85(3) [now Article 81(3)] of the Treaty to certain categories of technology transfer agreements (text with EEA relevance) [1996] OJ L31/2, at Article 3(3).

Article 3(7) tries to ensure that this requirement cannot be avoided by including **8.137** an automatic grant of new improvements in the original licence and so automatically extending the term of the original licence.[96]

Termination

Under Article 2.1(15) and (16), the licensor can reserve the right to terminate the **8.138** licence if the licensee challenges the validity of the licensed patents, or claims that a patent is not necessary, or if the licensee challenges the secret or substantial nature of the licensed know-how or claims that a licensed patent is not necessary.

Finally, Article 2.1(18) provides that if the licensee starts to research, develop, **8.139** manufacture, distribute, or use goods that compete with the licensed goods, the licensor can:

— terminate the exclusivity of the licence;

— stop licensing improvements in the original technology to the licensee; and

— require the licensee to prove that it is not in fact using the licensed technology in the activity that competes with the activities of the licensor.

Post-Termination Restrictions

Article 2.1(3) allows a licensor to prohibit the licensee from using the licensed **8.140** patents or know-how after the termination of the agreement to the extent that the patents are still in force and the know-how is still secret. Article 2.1(1) allows an obligation on the licensee to maintain the confidentiality of the know-how, even after the agreement has expired

(4) The Opposition Procedure

Article 4 of the Regulation establishes a streamlined 'opposition procedure' for **8.141** licensing agreements that contain restrictions neither expressly allowed nor expressly prohibited by the Regulation. Parties to such an agreement can make a simplified application on Form A/B. The application need only contain the text of the agreement and the information available to the parties on the structure of the relevant markets and their position on them. It does not have to contain detailed legal arguments (Recital 25). Provided that the Commission does not raise objections to the notified agreement within four months it is deemed to be exempted under the Regulation. Article 4 mentions two types of obligation which may 'in particular' require this form of notification.

The first, set out in Article 4.2(a), is any obligation governing the manufacturing **8.142** activity of the licensee. This could include quality specifications, requirements to

---

[96] See para 8.122 above.

license additional technology, or requirements to buy specified goods and services that are not necessary to the satisfactory use of the licensed technology or to maintenance of the quality standards followed by the licensor and its other licensees. However, Article 2.1(5) expressly allows the licensor to require the licensee to meet the same minimum quality standards as the licensor and its other licensees, and to buy such specified goods from the licensor or another designated source as are necessary to meet these standards or to proper use of the licensed technology.

8.143   Article 4.2(b) also mentions prohibitions on the licensee contesting the validity of licensed know-how or patents. Although the licensor can terminate the licence agreement in the event that such a challenge is raised the licensee cannot be asked to give up its right to raise such a challenge.

(5) Withdrawal of the Block Exemption

8.144   Article 7 provides that the Commission can withdraw the benefit of the block exemption on the basis of the particular facts of an agreement that otherwise meets the conditions of the block exemption. A non-exhaustive list is provided in the article.

Elimination of Competition

8.145   In particular, the benefit can be withdrawn where the effect of the agreement is:

> to prevent the licensed products from being exposed to effective competition in the licensed territory from identical goods or services or from goods or services considered by users as interchangeable or substitutable in view of their characteristics, price and intended use, which may in particular occur where the licensee's market share exceeds 40%;

8.146   The 'licensee's market share' is defined as:

> the proportion which the licensed products and other goods or services provided by the licensee, which are considered by users to be interchangeable or substitutable for the licensed products in view of their characteristics, price and intended use, represent [of] the entire market for the licensed products and all other interchangeable or substitutable goods and services in the common market or a substantial part of it[.][97]

8.147   In drafts of the block exemption such a market share would have automatically prevented the application of the block exemption. In the adopted version parties to an agreement who have a large market share do benefit from the block exemption, but the block exemption may be withdrawn if the market share test is not met.

---

[97] Commission Regulation (EC) 240/96 of 31 January 1996 on the application of Article 85(3) [now Article 81(3)] of the Treaty to certain categories of technology transfer agreements (text with EEA relevance) [1996] OJ L31/2, at Article 10(9).

Passive Sales

There are two provisions related to parallel sales which would allow the **8.148** Commission to withdraw the benefit of the block exemption. The first, relates to a refusal by the licensee to fulfil unsolicited orders from outside the territory:

> (2) without prejudice to Article 1(1)(6), the licensee refuses, without any objectively justified reason, to meet unsolicited orders from users or resellers in the territory of other licensees[.]

The importance of this provision is likely to be limited as it does not apply if the **8.149** licensee is still subject to the limited duration ban on passive exports that can be exempted under the block exemption.[98] In addition, the licensor is also entitled to reserve any such patent rights as still exist after the licence has been granted in order to challenge such parallel trade,[99] although this second caveat is likely to prove less important than the first.

More importantly, however, the Commission can withdraw the benefit of the **8.150** block exemption if either party refuses to supply third party parallel traders or makes such parallel trade more difficult:

> (3) the parties:
>
> (a) without any objectively justified reason, refuse to meet orders from users or resellers in their respective territories who would market the products in other territories within the common market; or
> (b) make it difficult for users or resellers to obtain the products from other resellers within the common market, and in particular where they exercise intellectual property rights or take measures so as to prevent resellers or users from obtaining outside, or from putting on the market in the licensed territory products which have been lawfully put on the market within the common market by the licensor or with his consent;

Quantity Restrictions on Competing Manufacturers

A requirement in a contract that a licensee manufacture a minimum quantity of **8.151** the licensed goods or use its 'best endeavours' to exploit the licensed technology is specifically allowed by the block exemption.[100] However, the block exemption may be withdrawn if:

> (4) the parties were competing manufacturers at the date of the grant of the licence and obligations on the licensee to produce a minimum quantity or to use his best endeavours as referred to in Article 2 (1), (9) and (17) respectively have the effect of preventing the licensee from using competing technologies.

---

[98] See Article 1, at para 8.104 above.
[99] See Article 2.1(14), at para 8.115 above.
[100] See Article 2.1(17), at para 8.118 above.

D. Licences to Distributors

8.152 The commercial risks of, and consumer benefits accruing from, investment in innovation and manufacturing are clearly recognized under Community competition law, in particular by the technology transfer block exemption. Distribution arrangements are generally regarded under Community law as less in need of protection, and the permitted restrictions in agreements are consequently more limited. It is unclear whether this is because of a perception of lower commercial risk, fewer third party benefits, or the increased risks to the single market of market partitioning through territorial distribution. In any event, the degree of territorial exclusivity afforded by technology transfer block exemption appears to go beyond that which could be permitted on the basis of a trade mark licence. Whereas some absolute territorial protection for a certain period of time is now envisaged within the technology transfer block exemption, it is likely that a stricter line will continue to be taken in respect of more straightforward distribution arrangements.

(1) Licences and Assignments

8.153 **Territorial protection.** The Court established early that absolute territorial protection using trade marks was liable to infringe Article 81 in that it led to a partitioning of markets. The Court even went so far as to suggest that trade mark rights were less important than other forms of intellectual property.[101] The Court's relatively strict jurisprudence on trade mark restrictions seems to have placed an undue reliance on the importance of intra-brand competition without necessarily taking into account the existence and extent of inter-brand competition.[102]

8.154 In *Consten/Grundig*[103] Grundig had appointed Consten as its exclusive distributor in France and had assigned the GINT (Grundig International) mark to Consten. Grundig had agreed not to appoint any other distributors in France or to sell the goods itself in France. In addition it restrained its distributors outside France from selling to French customers. In return Consten agreed not to deal in goods competing with Grundig's products. Consten was able to obtain significantly higher prices for Grundig products on the French market than those prevailing in Germany. Consten used the agreements to obtain injunctions from the French courts blocking the parallel imports of Grundig products. The Court held:

> Consten's right under the contract to the exclusive use in France of the GINT trade mark, . . . is intended to make it possible to keep under surveillance and to place an obstacle in the way of parallel imports . Thus, the agreement by which Grundig, as the holder of the trade-mark by virtue of an inter-national registration, authorized Consten to register it in France in its own name tends to restrict competition.

---

[101] Case 40/70 *Sirena Srl v Eda Srl and others* [1971] ECR 69, at para 7.
[102] See, for example, Case 28/77 *Tepea BV v Commission* [1978] ECR 139, at para 43.
[103] Joined Cases 56 & 58/64 *Consten and Grundig v Commission* [1966] ECR 299.

. . .

That agreement therefore is one which may be caught by the prohibition in Article 85(1) [now Article 81(1)]. The prohibition would be ineffective if Consten could continue to use the trade-mark to achieve the same object as that pursued by the agreement which has been held to be unlawful.[104]

The Court's belief in the risks to the single market inherent in trade mark rights appears to have reduced over the years. In relation to the free movement of goods, for example, the position of the Court in respect of Article 28 in the first *Hag* case[105]—that trade marks could not be used to oppose the import of products into a Member State where the trade marks had a common origin—was abandoned in the *Hag II*[106] litigation. The current position under Article 28 is that trade mark rights cannot be used to oppose imports where the goods were put on the market by the trade mark owner, or with its consent. **8.155**

In the *Moosehead* case,[107] the Commission regarded territorial restrictions on Whitbread's activities as falling within Article 81(1). Whitbread entered into a licensing agreement to manufacture Moosehead Canadian lager in the UK. Whitbread was prevented from making active sales outside the territory. These restrictions fell within Article 81(1) as Whitbread, given its size, would otherwise have been in a position to supply other markets. However, the Commission accepted that the restrictions were exemptable in view of the benefits of the agreement. It seems safe to assume that the position on open and closed exclusive licences is essentially the same in respect of trade marks as it is in respect of other forms of intellectual property.[108] **8.156**

The Court has recently adopted a less restrictive approach in respect of assignments of trade marks to different entities in different Member States. While recognizing that this may be used as a market partitioning mechanism, the Court went on: **8.157**

> that rule and the accompanying sanction cannot be applied mechanically to every assignment. Before a trade-mark assignment can be treated as giving effect to an agreement prohibited under Article 85 [now Article 81], it is necessary to analyse the context, the commitments underlying the assignment, the intention of the parties and the consideration for the assignment.[109]

As such, it appears more likely that such clauses would fall outside Article 81(1), provided that, for example, inter-brand competition was sufficiently strong. **8.158**

---

[104] Joined Cases 56 & 58/64 *Consten and Grundig v Commission* [1966] ECR 299.

[105] Case 193/73 *Van Zuylen Frères v Hag AG* [1974] ECR 731 (Hag I).

[106] Case C10/89 *CNL Sucal v Hag GF AG* [1990] ECR I–3711 (Hag II).

[107] *Moosehead/Whitbread* [1990] OJ L100/32 (only the English text is authentic).

[108] See, inter alia, the discussion of *Maize Seeds: Breeders' rights—maize seed* [1978] OJ L286/23; Case 258/78 *LC Nungesser KG and Kurt Eisele v Commission* [1982] ECR 2015. Above, at para 8.65.

[109] Case C–9/93 *IHT Internationale Heiztechnik GmbH and Uwe Danzinger v Ideal-Standard GmbH and Wabco Standard GmbH* [1994] ECR I–278, at para 59.

8.159 **Prohibition on competing products.** In *Campari*, the Commission was prepared to exempt a ban on trade in competing goods given the consequent benefits to the distribution system, and contrasted non-competition clauses in respect of trade marks with those in respect of patents:

> Although a non-competition clause in a licensing agreement concerning industrial property rights based on the result of a creative activity, such as a patent, would constitute a barrier to technical and economic progress by preventing the licensees from taking an interest in other techniques and products, this is not the case with the licensing agreements under consideration here. The aim pursued by the parties , as is clear from the agreements taken as a whole , is to decentralize manufacture within the EEC and to rationalize the distribution system linked to it. . .
>
> The prohibition on dealing in competing products , therefore , makes for improved distribution of the relevant product in the same way as do exclusive dealing agreements containing a similar clause , which are automatically exempted by regulation no 67/67/EEC.[110]

8.160 A similar clause was exempted in the *Moosehead* case in light of the availability of competing brands.[111]

8.161 **No-challenge clauses (ownership).** The Commission has found that such a clause falls outside Article 81(1) as: 'Whether or not the licensor or licensee has the ownership of the trademark, the use of it by any other party is prevented in any event, and competition would thus not be affected.'[112]

8.162 **No-challenge clauses (validity).** In the *Moosehead* case, the Commission decided that this could potentially fall within Article 81(1) as it could contribute to the maintenance of a trade mark that could be an unjustified barrier to entry on a given market. Whether or not a particular trade mark could constitute a barrier to entry would depend on the status of the trade mark on the particular market. In this case, as Moosehead was comparatively new to the relevant market, the Commission found that the clause did not fall within Article 81(1).

8.163 As indicated above, the Commission is likely to take a stricter approach where there appears to be a risk of market partitioning,[113] or the obligation appears to have been imposed on one of the parties without justification. The Commission condemned a no-challenge clause in the *Windsurfing* case without having examined the impact of the clause on the particular market: the Commission may have been influenced in that case by the no-challenge clause being 'imposed on the

---

[110] *Campari* [1978] OJ L70/69 (only the German, Danish, French, Italian and Dutch texts are authentic).

[111] *Moosehead/Whitbread* [1990] OJ L100/32, at para 16(2) (only the English text is authentic).

[112] *Moosehead/Whitbread* [1990] OJ L100/32, at para 15(4)(only the English text is authentic).

[113] *Toltecs-Dorcet* [1982] OJ L379/19 (only the German and Dutch texts are authentic).

licensees in the agreements relating to the exploitation of the patent even though the subject-matter of the clause was quite different'.[114]

Prohibition on sub-licensing or assignment. In the *Campari* case,[115] the Commission cleared a clause prohibiting assignment of the trade mark as this was essential to ensure that the licensor could continue to select its preferred licensees. **8.164**

Quality control measures. Given the importance of maintaining the brand, the Commission has regarded quality control measures as falling outside Article 81(1).[116] **8.165**

(2) Trade Mark Delimitation Agreements

The single market increases the risks of confusion of nationally granted trade mark rights. Parties owning marks capable of being confused may wish to avoid consumer confusion by agreeing some form of territorial restrictions on the scope of use of certain trade marks. **8.166**

Market partitioning. The Commission has taken a strict line in respect of Article 81(1) where it believed that the agreements in question were being used simply to partition the market.[117] The principals can agree what trade marks they will use in various jurisdictions but they cannot agree not to compete with each other in those jurisdictions. BAT owned the German rights to the 'Dorcet' trade mark. A smaller Dutch firm, Segers, sought to export its cut tobacco to Germany under its 'Toltecs' brand name. BAT began proceedings under German law based on the fact that the two trade marks were confusingly similar. To avoid the costs of a lengthy legal battle with a larger rival, and because of the breadth of protection sometimes given to German trade marks Segers entered into a settlement with BAT. Under the terms of this settlement Segers could only export a limited number of types of tobacco to Germany under the Toltecs brand name, and could only make these exports through distributors approved by BAT. Subsequently when Segers's initial distributor ceased trading, Segers found it difficult to gain BAT's approval for a new distributor and ceased exporting their products to Germany and complained to the Commission. **8.167**

The Commission, and later the Court, held that the agreement between BAT and Segers went beyond what was necessary to avoid confusion of trade marks. The agreement served to severely limit competition to BAT from Segers. Accordingly **8.168**

---

[114] Case 193/83 *Windsurfing International Inc v Commission* [1986] ECR 61, at para 80.
[115] *Campari* [1978] OJ L70/69 (only the German, Danish, French, Italian and Dutch texts are authentic).
[116] *Moosehead/Whitbread* [1990] OJ L100/32, at para 15(2) (only the English text is authentic) and *Campari* [1978] OJ L70/69 (only the German, Danish, French, Italian and Dutch texts are authentic).
[117] *Toltecs-Dorcet* [1982] OJ L379/19 (only the German and Dutch texts are authentic). Upheld on the substance in Case 35/83 *BAT Cigaretten-Fabriken GmbH v Commission* [1985] ECR 36.

it infringed Article 81(1) and did not meet the conditions for the grant of an exemption under Article 81(3).

8.169 **Confusion of marks.**   However, where restrictions only go so far as is necessary to avoid confusion, the Commission will take a more positive view. In the *Penneys* case,[118] the Commission gave a negative clearance to an agreement to settle a range of trade mark disputes in a number of jurisdictions. The Penneys trade mark was owned both by a US clothing retailer and an Irish clothing retailer. This had given rise to a number of trade mark disputes. Under the terms of the settlement the US firm agreed not to trade as Penneys in Ireland and the Irish firm agreed to use the Penneys business name only in Ireland, and not to register it outside Ireland.

E. Content Licensing

(1) Introduction

8.170 **Community Directives relating to copyright.**   The following EC Directives have been adopted which add to or modify Member States' copyright systems.

8.171 First, Directive on semiconductor topographies[119] which introduced a form of protection for the design of products made by etching electronic circuits onto semiconducting surfaces ('chips').

8.172 Secondly, Directive on computer software[120] which extended copyright protection to computer software by providing that software should be considered as literary works. This legislation is discussed in more detail in Section F below.

8.173 Thirdly, Directive on rental lending, and neighbouring rights.[121] The emergence of a market for the sale and rental of recordings of copyright works such as films coupled with the technological possibility of making high-quality copies of these works at home, led to a need to clarify and extend copyright. This Directive clearly established a right to rent out a copy of a copyrighted work, and so to control the use of this rented copy and to prohibit the owner of a copy of a work from renting it out.

8.174 Fourthly, Directive on satellite broadcasting and cable retransmission[122] establish-

---

[118] *Penneys* [1978] OJ L60/19.
[119] Council Directive (EC) 54/87 on the legal protection of semiconductor topographies [1987] OJ L24/36.
[120] Council Directive (EC) 91/250 on the legal protection of computer programs [1991] OJ L122/42.
[121] Council Directive (EC) 92/100 on rental right and lending right and on certain rights related to copyright in the field of intellectual property [1992] OJ L346/61.
[122] Council Directive (EC) 93/83 on the co-ordination of certain rules concerning copyright and rights related to copyright applicable to satellite broadcasting and cable retransmission [1993] OJ L248/15.

ing that a copyright owner has the right to control the broadcast or transmission of their work via satellite or cable network.

Fifthly, Directive on copyright duration[123] aims to facilitate a single market in products protected by copyright by harmonizing the term of copyright protection throughout the EEA. Since the terms were harmonized upwards to the longest term granted in any Member State this had the effect of renewing the copyright protection on certain classic works. The work of an individual author is protected until seventy years after his or her death. Where the right owner is a corporate body copyright extends for fifty years.   **8.175**

Sixthly, Directive on the legal protection of databases.[124] Computer and communication technology allows the creation of ordered collections of information. This information may be the copyright of the person assembling the database or one or more third parties, non-copyrighted material in the public domain, or a mixture of the two. The creator of the database adds value by assembling the material, maintaining it, and providing facilities for searching the database. Certain Member States' copyright law would protect such an assembly of material, but in others it could not meet the requirement for originality.[125] This Directive creates a specific, *sui generis*, protection for the database.   **8.176**

Copyright in the 'Information Society'. One of the most significant trends in economic development is the shrinking importance of manufacturing and primary activities in the developed economies, and the corresponding growth in the importance of services. This has been accompanied, and partly caused, by technological advances which have vastly increased the range and quality of information and communication based services that can be provided. A major priority of EC and Member State action is trying to prepare for and promote this new 'Information Society'.   **8.177**

The Commission has published a Proposal for a Directive[126] on copyright in the Information Society. This aims to clarify the copyright protection of data in an on-line environment, covering all original works including computer programs and databases and integrating the specific legislation already in existence on satellite and cable broadcasts, rental rights, and lending rights. It will establish a single   **8.178**

---

[123] Council Directive (EC) 93/98 harmonising the term of protection of copyright and certain related rights [1993] OJ L290/9.

[124] Council Directive (EC) 96/9 on the legal protection of databases [1996] OJ L77/20.

[125] One of the issues raised in the *Magill* case was that the television listings in question were only protected by copyright due to the nature of UK and Irish copyright law. The Court of First Instance noted that the Irish courts had determined that the listings in question were in fact protected by the relevant Irish copyright law and did not need to consider the issue further. (Case T–69/89 *RTE v Commission* [1991] II–ECR 485, in particular paras 10 and 75.)

[126] Proposal for a European Parliament and Council Directive on the harmonisation of certain aspects of copyright and related rights in the Information Society COM(97) 628 final, 10 December 1997.

copyright system providing rights for the original 'author' of a work, the performer of a given fixation of a work, the producer of a given phonogram or film, and the broadcaster of a given transmission of the work. These will be given a general control over the 'making available to the public' of their work which is intended to cover existing and future ways of commercializing intellectual property, and allow them to control all of these methods of commercialization. A set of exceptions to these exclusive rights is also created for the benefit of non-commercial or educational users of the intellectual property or use in the public interest. Finally, the Directive recognizes the importance of the technical measures that a right holder may use to prevent illicit copying or reuse of their work, and the importance of the visible and hidden 'rights management' information that a right holder may include in a copy of their work. The Directive would require the Member States to introduce laws preventing the sale or use of devices that are solely intended to circumvent such technical protection, or the removal of such rights management information.

(2) Territorial Protection through Exclusive Licences

8.179   **Exclusive territory does not necessarily infringe Article 81(1).**   A licence granting the licensee exclusive rights in a particular jurisdiction is not necessarily restrictive of competition. In the *Coditel II* case,[127] the Court noted that assigning part of an exclusive right did not amount to a restrictive agreement or practice[128] and ruled that such an exclusive licence did not *in itself* breach Article 81.[129] However, there might be factual circumstances where the effect of such a licence would be to restrict competition.[130] Since the reference had not described the commercial and economic background to the case the court found that:

> it is for national courts. . .to establish whether or not the exercise of the exclusive right to exhibit a cinematographic film creates barriers which are artificial and unjustifiable in terms of the needs of the cinematographic industry, or the possibility of charging fees which exceed a fair return on investment, or an exclusivity the duration of which is disproportionate to these requirements, and whether or not, from a general point of view, such exercise within a given geographic area is such as to prevent restrict or distort competition within the common market.[131]

8.180   **Collective refusals to license.**   Refusals to licence only fall within Article 81(1) where it can be shown that the refusals are themselves part of an agreement or con-

---

[127]   Case 262/81 *Coditel v Cine-Vog* [1982] ECR 3381.
[128]   Case 262/81 *Coditel v Cine-Vog* [1982] ECR 3381, at para 15.
[129]   Case 262/81 *Coditel v Cine-Vog* [1982] ECR 3381, at para 20: 'a contract whereby the owner of the copyright in a film grants an exclusive right to exhibit that film for a specific period in the territory of a member state is not, as such, subject to the prohibitions contained in Article 85 [now Article 81] of the Treaty'.
[130]   Case 262/81 *Coditel v Cine-Vog* [1982] ECR 3381, at paras 16 and 17.
[131]   Case 262/81 *Coditel v Cine-Vog* [1982] ECR 3381, at para 19.

certed practice.[132] Horse racing in France is organized by a number of regional bodies (sociétés de course), each of which has the sole authorization to organize horse races in their area, and owns the copyright to any recordings or broadcasts of these races. Each of them had granted a firm jointly owned and controlled by them (the PMU) an exclusive licence, for France and Germany only, to broadcast the races that they organized. The PMU broadcast these races itself in France for the purpose of taking off-course bets, and licensed the German rights to a German firm, Deutscher Sportverlag Stoof GmbH & Co (DSV).

Ladbrokes operated a chain of betting shops in Belgium, and wished to show these French races in their Belgian shops in order to take bets on the races. Ladbrokes applied for a licence for these races to DSV, who informed them that they only held a licence for Germany and so could not grant licences for Belgium. Ladbrokes applied to PMU and to each of the individual 'sociétés de course'. PMU informed Ladbrokes that it only held a licence to the races for France and so could not grant the licence that Ladbrokes sought. It also informed Ladbrokes that each of the individual sociétés de course had asked it to inform Ladbrokes that they had individually decided not to license the Belgian rights to their races to Ladbrokes. **8.181**

The combination of the exclusive, limited licence from the sociétés de course to PMU, the exclusive licence from PMU to DSV, and the independent refusal of each société de course to grant a licence to Ladbrokes meant that it was not possible for Ladbrokes to broadcast French horse races and take off-course bets on them as was done in France and Germany by PMU and DSV respectively. The Court held, *inter alia*, that each of these refusals to licence did not individually or collectively infringe Article 81(1). Only if it could be shown that there was an agreement or concerted practice between the sociétés de course not to licence certain third parties would any question of a breach of Article 81(1) arise: **8.182**

> a horizontal agreement between sociétés de courses which prevented each of them from granting a licence to transmit the sound and pictures of the races which it organized to a third party such as the applicant would be liable to impede the entry of each of them on to the Belgian market in sound and pictures in general and thereby restrict such potential competition as might exist on that market, to the detriment of the interests of bookmakers and ultimate consumers. Moreover, the effect of such an agreement might be to 'limit or control . . . markets' and/or to 'share markets' within the meaning of Article 85(1)(b) and (c) [now Article 81(1)(b) and (c)] of the Treaty.[133]

Specific subject matter of copyright and Article 81(1). In *Ladbroke*, the Court allowed a system of exclusive licences with prohibitions on sub-licensing. Although prohibitions on sub-licensing are also allowed in other areas, the effect **8.183**

---

132 Case T–504/93 *Tiercé Ladbroke SA v Commission* [1997] ECR II–923.
133 Case T–504/93 *Tiercé Ladbroke SA v Commission* [1997] ECR II–92, at para 159.

in relation to copyrighted works is more severe. Whereas a patent licence would normally lead to a saleable product, the distribution of which cannot be subject to absolute territorial protection,[134] the broadcast element of copyright does not lead to such a product. The only product is in effect the broadcast transmission itself. In these circumstances, allowing the possibility of making a passive sale would largely undermine any exclusive licensing system. Copyright licensing, because of its specific subject matter, therefore allows a greater degree of territorial protection than other intellectual property rights. The Court has taken a similar approach under Article 59.[135]

8.184 Given the Court's recognition that rental rights are a distinct element of the specific subject matter of copyright, licensing sale and rental separately is not in itself a breach of Article 81.[136]

(3) Collecting Societies

Artists' Licences to a Collecting Society

8.185 An exclusive licence of copyright to a collecting society is not necessarily restrictive of competition.[137] The exclusivity merely describes the extent to which the owner of intellectual property rights has licensed those rights to another. However, as with the other types of licensing contract described above, a contract which goes beyond describing to what extent an owner of intellectual property is licensing those rights is subject to Article 81. In the *GEMA I* case, a contract between an artist and a collecting society where the artist granted the society an exclusive licence not only to his existing body of work but also to any future work infringed Article 81.

Licensing Agreements between Collecting Societies

8.186 Collecting societies tend to be organized nationally, but will often want to exploit their rights internationally. There is an obvious efficiency benefit if collecting societies grant each other licences in the work of their 'home' artists since any potential licensee can then go to their own 'home' collecting society and obtain a single licence to all of the rights they might need. The Court has therefore held that reciprocal contracts do not in themselves fall within Article 81(1), although the position might be different if the reciprocal contracts contained exclusivity clauses.[138] In addition a concerted practice between collecting societies so as to

---

[134] Save, under the technology transfer block exemption, for a limited start-up period.

[135] Case 62/79 *SA Compagnie générale pour la diffusion de la télévision, Coditel, and others v Ciné Vog Films and others* [1980] ECR 88.

[136] Case 158/86 *Warner Bros. and Metronome v Christiansen* [1988] ECR 2605.

[137] Case 125/78 *GEMA v Commission* [1979] ECR 3173.

[138] Joined Cases 110/88, 241/88 and 242/88 *François Lucazeau and others v Société des Auteurs, Compositeurs et Editeurs de Musique (SACEM) and others* [1989] ECR 281, at para 14.

restrict direct access to their repertoires from foreign users would fall within Article 81(1).[139]

Licences from Collecting Societies to Manufacturers

Collecting societies also enter into licensing arrangements with manufacturers of **8.187** recordings. Once the recordings have been manufactured and placed onto the market, the performing right society's intellectual property rights are exhausted and any term in the licensing agreement or action by the society that seeks to control the further sales of the recordings is potentially a restriction of competition subject to Article 81 of the EC Treaty.

The collecting society cannot, for example, seek to influence the retail selling price **8.188** of the product. In *BIEM/IFPI*,[140] a collecting society had granted a licence to a record manufacturer where the royalty payable by the manufacturer was expressed as a percentage of the average retail selling price of records on the market on which the manufacturer operated. This would have the effect of penalizing the manufacturer if it sold the record at a price below the average price prevailing in the market, and would consequently give the manufacturer an incentive to charge as high a price as possible. This was found to infringe Article 81 and the collecting society was required to charge a royalty calculated as a percentage of the actual prices charged by the licensee.

F. Software Licensing

(1) The Software Directive

The Software Directive[141] establishes a harmonized system of intellectual property **8.189** protection for computer software in the EC by requiring Member States to protect software by copyright as a literary work. Although it is not directly concerned with EC competition law it is a useful example of the application of the principles discussed in this chapter. In addition to the provisions of the Directive itself the Commission adopted and published a set of conclusions[142] which give further information on the application of competition law to licences of this type of intellectual property.

---

[139] Joined Cases 110/88, 241/88 and 242/88 *François Lucazeau and others v Société des Auteurs, Compositeurs et Editeurs de Musique (SACEM) and others* [1989] ECR 281, at para 17.

[140] *BIEM/IFPI, Report on Competition Policy (1983)* (Vol XIII), points 147–150.

[141] Council Directive (EC) 91/250 on the legal protection of computer programs [1991] OJ L122/42.

[142] Commission conclusions decided on the occasion of the adoption of the Commission's proposal for a Council Directive on the legal protection of computer programs [1989] OJ C91/16.

Article 81 Aspects

8.190   The Commission conclusions summarize the relationship between the intellectual property protection given by the Directive and EC competition law:

> Any arrangement or measure which goes beyond the exercise of copyright can be subject to control under the competition rules. This means that for example any attempt to extend by contractual agreements or other arrangements the scope of protection to aspects of the programs for which protection under copyright is not available, or the prohibition of any act which is not reserved for the right owner may constitute an infringement of the competition rules.

8.191   **Exclusive rights.**   The exclusive rights granted by the Directive include, with certain exceptions:[143]

> the right to do or to authorize:

> (a) the permanent or temporary reproduction of a computer program by any means and in any form, in part or in whole. Insofar as loading, displaying, running, transmision or storage of the computer program necessitate such reproduction, such acts shall be subject to authorization by the rightholder;
> (b) the translation, adaptation, arrangement and any other alteration of a computer program and the reproduction of the results thereof, without prejudice to the rights of the person who alters the program;
> (c) any form of distribution to the public, including the rental, of the original computer program or of copies thereof . . .[144]

8.192   Any agreement or concerted practice between a licensor and licensee of software that goes beyond these rights is subject to Article 81 in the same way as an agreement concerning goods not protected by intellectual property rights.

Limits on the Rights of the Author of Software in the Directive

8.193   **Exhaustion.**   Article 4(c) of the software Directive provides:

> The first sale in the Community of a copy of a program by the rightholder or with his consent shall exhaust the distribution right within the Community of that copy, with the exception of the right to control further rental of the program or a copy thereof.[145]

8.194   **Observation and decompilation.**   The Directive provides that if the owner of the rights of a piece of software does not provide interface information to its licensees so that they can design compatible pieces of software, then they have a right to decompile the licensed software to obtain this interface information.

---

[143]   Council Directive (EEC) 91/250 of 14 May 1991 on the legal protection of computer programs [1991] OJ L122/42, at Articles 5 and 6.
[144]   Council Directive (EEC) 91/250 of 14 May 1991 on the legal protection of computer programs [1991] OJ L122/42, at Article 4.
[145]   Council Directive (EEC) 91/250 of 14 May 1991 on the legal protection of computer programs [1991] OJ L122/42, at Article 4(c).

Article 5.3 gives a licensee of software the right to study the copyrighted software in various ways so as to determine the non-copyrighted ideas and methods that it expresses. Article 6.1 allows the licensee of a piece of software to 'decompile' it for the purposes of achieving interoperability of another piece of software, unless the necessary information to do this has already been made available to the licensee by the right owner.[146] These provisions guarantee third party developers certain access to the interface information necessary to produce compatible programs. However, pursuant to the Software Directive, any attempt by a licensor to limit the access of licensees to interface information contained in the licensed software, that may be used to compete without the licensor in other markets, is a potential restriction of competition.

Article 82 Aspects

The Commission conclusions referred to above also discuss the application of Article 82 to software licensing. They state that in certain circumstances the exercise of copyright, ie attempts to enforce rights that are within the copyright protection given by the software Directive, may be considered abusive. The conclusions give two related examples of where this might apply. **8.195**

The first is where an owner of copyright is dominant in a given market and is also active in a second market for compatible products. If its competitors need access to copyrighted aspects of the program to compete on the second market, refusal by the dominant firm to license its competitors this copyrighted material could constitute the abuse of using exclusive rights in one product to gain an unfair advantage in other products not covered by the rights. **8.196**

Secondly, the Commission conclusions state that a firm producing a product that competes directly with a software product that is dominant in its market may have the right to certain information about the target program or parts of it. Refusal to supply such information could constitute an abuse. **8.197**

As discussed under Article 81 aspects above, the software Directive limits the extent to which exclusive intellectual property rights limit competition to the owner of these rights, who must allow the protected program to be studied and at least tolerate access to interface information about the program. In the event that the right owner is dominant on the market for the protected software these obligations seem to be reinforced in that the exclusive rights granted by the Software Directive cannot be used to limit competition on the market for products compatible with the protected product or, more arguably, even on the market for the product itself. **8.198**

---

[146] See *IBM Undertaking, Bull EC* 7/8-1984 Point 1.1.1 and *Bull EC* 10-1984 Point 3.4.1, discussed at para 8.219 below.

8.199 The relationship between intellectual property rights and Article 82 is discussed in more detail in the following section. Similar ideas were followed by the Commission in the *IBM* case, discussed below (see paragraph 8.219). This concerned interface information about pieces of computer hardware rather than software. Notwithstanding IBM's assertion that the interface information was protected by intellectual property rights, the settlement negotiated with the Commission provided for compulsory and timely disclosure of this information to third party competitors.

(2) Microsoft's 1994 Undertaking to the Commission

8.200 In July 1994 the European Commission obtained an undertaking[147] from Microsoft which led to the closure of a case arising from a complaint made by Novell in June 1993. The undertaking highlights certain limits on the right to license computer software.

8.201 Then, as now, Microsoft had an extremely large share in the market for operating systems for microcomputers. Most microcomputers were sold with an operating system already installed, as a result of an original equipment manufacturer (OEM) licence contract between the microcomputer manufacturer and a developer of operating system software. The Commission had been investigating these OEM licences between Microsoft and microcomputer manufacturers and was concerned that certain aspects of these licences had the effect of excluding Microsoft's competitors from the market. The main practices causing concern were:

— the use of 'per processor' and 'per system' licences; (under these licences the manufactures paid a royalty to Microsoft for all or practically all of their production even if they installed non-Microsoft operating systems on some of the machines concerned);

— the inclusion of large 'minimum commitments' to pay royalties in licence contracts regardless of the number of copies used; and

— the long duration of the licence contracts.

8.202 The Commission was concerned that the cumulative effect of these would be to foreclose Microsoft's competitors from licensing operating systems to computer manufacturers.

8.203 Under the terms of the undertaking Microsoft agreed:

— to limit the term of its licences to one year;

— not to enter into per processor licences;

---

[147] See *Microsoft Undertaking, Bull EU* 7/8-1994 Point 2.4.1 and press release IP/94/653.

— to enter into per system licences only where it was clear that the manufacturer could simply name a new model of computer, and not have to pay a royalty on these machines; and

— not to impose minimum commitments on licensees.

G. Article 82

(1) Introduction

The application of Article 82 to intellectual property issues is controversial, and the existing precedents under Community law are neither comprehensive nor models of clarity. It is useful to distinguish between two main categories of case:

8.204

— those of refusals to grant licences to any third party; and

— the granting or refusal of licences on discriminatory or otherwise abusive terms.

The second category has posed relatively few difficulties from the point of view of the competition rules, but the first category has proved extremely controversial. Perhaps surprisingly, however, following the Court's judgment in *Bronner*, it now appears that the law on refusals to licence intellectual property rights is certainly clearer, and possibly more stringent, than refusals to grant access to essential facilities which are not covered by intellectual property rights.

8.205

This section looks in turn at issues of market definition, dominance, and abuse.

8.206

(2) Intellectual Property and Market Definition

It is useful to distinguish between upstream and downstream markets.

8.207

First, there may be a market for the supply to producers of the particular technology needed to produce the good in question, which may or may not be covered by intellectual property rights. Where a good could be produced using different substitutable technologies, some or all of which are protected by intellectual property, the intellectual property rights holders would compete in the supply of that intellectual property to producers. This is essentially the same position as a component manufacturer whose components are used in the manufacture of a downstream product.

8.208

Secondly, there may be the downstream market for the sale of the good produced using the intellectual property right(s).

8.209

This distinction between upstream and downstream markets has been recognized explicitly by the Commission in the related area of standardization, where the

8.210

Commission identified: 'the market for telecommunications standards and the downstream markets which use those standards'.[148]

8.211 In standardization cases, intellectual property rights holders seeking to have their intellectual property included in a standard will be doing so either implicitly or explicitly on the basis that these intellectual property rights will be licensed to third parties who wish to manufacture goods compliant with the standard. In these cases, the distinction between the upstream and downstream markets will be relatively clear.

8.212 However, the distinction between the upstream and downstream markets will not always be so apparent. Where the intellectual property holder is vertically integrated and no third party licence has been granted, whether or not the upstream market exists will depend on whether a market is defined as actual commerce, or the existence of a demand together with the potential to supply.

8.213 The Commission's decision in the *Magill* case implicitly uses this dual market analysis. In the original decision, the Commission identified two distinct products: 'the advance weekly listings of ITP and BBC regional programme services and those of RTE and also the TV guides in which these listings are published (or broadcast)'.[149] The Commission did not make it clear whether it considered the products of weekly listings and TV guides to constitute separate product markets. However, such a distinction does appear to be implicit in the decision, where the Commission referred to the parties as being: 'dominant on the market for their own listings, [and seeking to] retain for themselves also the derivative market for weekly TV guides'.[150]

(3) Intellectual Property and Dominance

8.214 Although intellectual property rights give the owner the exclusive right to use the intellectual property this does not necessarily equate to a position of dominance.[151]

8.215 An intellectual property right generally gives an exclusive right in relation to the incorporation of that right into downstream products. However, whether or not that right holder would have market power in respect of the intellectual property depends not on that exclusive right *per se*, but on the relationship between that intellectual property right and its proprietary and/or non-proprietary substitutes.

---

[148] *ETSI interim IPR policy* (Notice pursuant to Article 19(3) of Regulation 17) [1995] OJ C76/5.

[149] *Magill TV Guide/ITP, BBC and RTE* [1989] OJ L78/43, at para 20 (only the English text is authentic).

[150] *Magill TV Guide/ITP, BBC and RTE* [1989] OJ L78/43, at para 23(14) (only the English text is authentic).

[151] Joined Cases C–241/91P and C–242/91P, *Radio Telefís Eireann (RTE) and Independent Television Publications Ltd (ITP) v Commission* [1995] ECR I–74, at para 46.

Whether or not dominance arises in respect of the intellectual property depends on the extent to which substitutes for that intellectual property right which could be used to manufacture the good (or the relevant part of the good) exist. In looking at substitutability it is necessary to look at both supply and demand side issues: the downstream market may, for example, be locked into a particular technology even though competing technologies exist.

The technology transfer block exemption[152] differentiates between licences where **8.216** the parties enjoy market power and those where they do not. The Regulation states that the benefit of the block exemption may be withdrawn where the licensee is placed in a situation where it does not face competition for the goods produced under the licence. The Regulation states that this may in particular be the case where the licensee has a market share of 40 per cent or over on the market for the licensed goods and other goods considered interchangeable by consumers. Market power is being assessed by reference to the market for goods produced using the licensed intellectual property.

(4) Abuse

The distinction between the specific subject matter of an intellectual property **8.217** right, which relates to its existence and which cannot be called into question by Community law, and its exercise, which can be constrained by Community law, is set out above.

Generally, therefore, decisions on whether or not to license relate to the specific **8.218** subject matter of the right and cannot be called into question by Community competition law. The extent to which such decisions can be examined under the competition rules is a contentious area. However, the manner in which licensing is carried out (including, for example, choice of which third parties licences should be granted to) is clearly subject to competition law scrutiny.

Refusals to License Intellectual Property Rights

The IBM undertaking. In 1984 the Commission obtained an undertaking **8.219** from IBM[153] closing a case relating to IBM's practices in the market for 'mainframe' computers, particularly those compatible with IBM's 'System 370' range of mainframe computers. At the time of this case IBM's System 370 was the single most popular type of large 'mainframe' computer. Users of these computers such as banks and large commercial firms would typically have a large computer installation comprising several processor units, disk drives, and other storage

---

[152] Commission Regulation (EC) 240/96 of 31 January 1996 on the application of Article 85(3) [now Article 81(3)] of the Treaty to certain categories of technology transfer agreements (text with EEA relevance) [1996] OJ L31/2, discussed above, beginning at para 8.74.
[153] *IBM Undertaking, Bull EC* 7/8-1984 Point 1.1.1 and *Bull EC* 10-1984 Point 3.4.1.

devices all working together and sharing information because they were compatible with the IBM System 370 system. IBM's practice in the past had been to make public significant amounts of information about how the various parts of an IBM System 370 system fitted together. As a result a number of competing manufacturers such as Siemens, Hitachi, Fujitsu, and Amdahl designed and manufactured mainframe computer equipment that was compatible with System 370 and could be added to an installation built on IBM components, or could run software written for an IBM mainframe system. These manufacturers designed their own technology and merely used interface type information to design their products in such a way that they interfaced with users, information, and other computer equipment in the same way as the equivalent IBM machines. IBM then changed its commercial policy and started to withhold or delay certain of the 'interface information' required by its competitors.

8.220 After a complaint and investigation the Commission issued a statement of objections to IBM alleging breaches of Article 82 arising from its refusal of this information and from its practice of always selling mainframe processors with memory included. Before the Commission adopted a decision on the case IBM offered an undertaking to the Commission, following which the Commission was able to suspend its proceeding against IBM. IBM undertook to provide its competitors with interface information about its current and future mainframe products in accordance with a fixed timetable and format. IBM also undertook to supply on request processor products with only the memory needed for proper testing of the product. The undertaking remained in force for eleven years and during its life numerous requests were made for interface information, and a significant number of competing firms continued to offer competing products to IBM's 370 range computers and their successor products.

8.221 IBM reserved its position that the information disclosed was protected by intellectual property rights and reserved the right to charge royalties for any information it disclosed under the undertaking. The undertaking appears analogous to a know-how licence in that it provided competitors with information necessary to design competing machines in such a way that they would be compatible with IBM machines, in circumstances where this information would otherwise have been, at least, confidential to IBM and, possibly, covered by intellectual property rights. As outlined above, a similar situation is created for computer software by the software Directive, where the subject matter of the right created by the Directive does not extend to protecting information about the interfaces in a piece of Software.

8.222 *Volvo/Veng.*[154]   Veng was an importer into the UK of spare parts for Volvo cars which had been manufactured without Volvo's consent, and in respect of which

---

[154] Case 238/87 *AB Volvo v Erik Veng (UK) Ltd* [1988] ECR 6211.

Volvo held intellectual property rights. Volvo instituted proceedings against Veng for infringement of those rights. The UK High Court referred three questions to the ECJ, the latter answering only the second. The ECJ therefore avoided the difficult first question of the extent to which intellectual property rights can confer a dominant position:

> (1) If a substantial car manufacturer holds registered designs which, under the law of a Member State, confer on it the sole and exclusive right to make and import replacement body panels required to effect repair of the body of a car of its manufacture (if such body panels are not replaceable by body panels of any other design), is such a manufacturer, by reason of such sole and exclusive rights, in a dominant position within the meaning of Article 86 [now Article 82] of the EEC Treaty with respect to such replacement parts?
>
> (2) Is it prima facie an abuse of such dominant position for such a manufacturer to refuse to licence others to supply such body panels, even where they are willing to pay a reasonable royalty for all articles sold under the licence (such royalty to represent an award which is just and equitable having regard to the merits of the design and all the surrounding circumstances, and to be determined by arbitration or in such other manner as the national court shall direct)?
>
> (3) Is such an abuse likely to affect trade between Member States within the meaning of Article 86 by reason of the fact that the intending licensee is thereby prevented from importing the body panels from a second Member State?[155]

8.223 The Court held that since the right to be the only manufacturer of the protected product was part of the specific subject matter[156] of the intellectual property rights concerned, a refusal to license could not in itself be considered prima facie abusive. Other circumstances could, however, render the refusal abusive, and the Court went on to list potentially abusive conduct going beyond a simple refusal to license, provided that such conduct is liable to affect trade between Member States, such as:

— the arbitrary refusal to supply spare parts to independent repairers;

— the fixing of prices for spare parts at an unfair level; or

— a decision no longer to produce spare parts for a particular model even though many cars of that model are still in circulation.[157]

8.224 In all of these cases the intellectual property owner is limiting the use of the technology concerned (designs for car parts), to limit competition in other markets for repairs or the manufacture of new cars where the technology is not necessarily used. However, only in the third case is it the use of, or rather the refusal to use, the intellectual property right itself which is being regarded as potentially abusive.

---

[155] Case 238/87 *AB Volvo v Erik Veng (UK) Ltd* [1988] ECR 621, at para 4.
[156] Case 238/87 *AB Volvo v Erik Veng (UK) Ltd* [1988] ECR 621, at para 8.
[157] Case 238/87 *AB Volvo v Erik Veng (UK) Ltd* [1988] ECR 621, at para 9.

8.225 *Magill.* The *Magill* case arose from a refusal to license copyrighted information. Magill published a weekly magazine in Ireland containing details of television programmes to be broadcast by the three broadcasters whose programmes were widely available in Ireland at the time: BBC, the UK public broadcaster; ITV, the UK commercial broadcasting network; and RTE, the Irish national broadcaster. These listings infringed a copyright owned by the three broadcasters, each of which published a weekly magazine containing detail of their own broadcasts for the coming week. The broadcasters exercised their copyright to prevent Magill from producing its listings magazine. The Commission found by decision that this was a breach of Article 82 and required the broadcasters to grant licences.[158] The Commission's decision was upheld by the Court of First Instance and the Court of Justice.

8.226 The ECJ's judgment reiterated the position from *Volvo/Veng* cited above that a 'refusal to grant a licence, even if it is the act of an undertaking holding a dominant position, cannot in itself constitute abuse of a dominant position'.[159] However, the Court held that the exercise of an intellectual property right could, in exceptional circumstances, involve abusive conduct, and that these circumstances were present in this case. The Court therefore affirmed the decision of the Commission and the ruling of the Court of First Instance, and set out three arguments on which the CFI had based its finding, and on the basis of which the ruling of the CFI should be upheld.[160]

8.227 First, there was no actual or potential substitute for the intellectual property requested from each broadcaster.[161] As such, the refusals to license had prevented the emergence of a new product for which there was a potential consumer demand.[162] Daily or weekend guides were not an adequate substitute, and consumers would otherwise have no choice but to buy each individual weekly guide. The ECJ does not explicitly state whether this new product should be such as to fulfil demand on a new market, or whether it was sufficent for the new product to fulfil an identified but unfulfilled demand on an existing market. As a composite weekly guide would clearly compete with all of the individual weekly guides, the latter possibility appears to be the more likely.

---

[158] *Magill TV Guide/ITP, BBC & RTE* [1989] OJ L78/43.

[159] Joined Cases C–241/91P and C–242/91P *Radio Telefis Eireann (RTE) and Independent Television Publications Ltd (ITP) v Commission* [1995] ECR I–74, at para 49, citing Case 238/87 *Volvo*, paras 7 and 8.

[160] Joined Cases C–241/91P and C–242/91P *Radio Telefis Eireann (RTE) and Independent Television Publications Ltd (ITP) v Commission* [1995] ECR I–74, at paras 48–58.

[161] Joined Cases C–241/91P and C–242/91P *Radio Telefis Eireann (RTE) and Independent Television Publications Ltd (ITP) v Commission* [1995] ECR I–74, at para 52.

[162] Joined Cases C–241/91P and C–242/91P *Radio Telefis Eireann (RTE) and Independent Television Publications Ltd (ITP) v Commission* [1995] ECR I–74, at para 55.

In this, the Court deviated from the recommendation of the Advocate General, **8.228** who had argued that a refusal to supply could be abusive if the purpose of the supply was to create a new product which did not compete with the existing products and which therefore must be fulfilling a consumer demand not currently fulfilled. Where, however, the purpose of the demand was in order to be able to supply a product which did compete with existing products on the market, a refusal would not be abusive:

> Where the product is one that largely meets the same needs of consumers as the protected product, the interests of the copyright owner carry great weight. Even if the market is limited to the prejudice of consumers, the right to refuse licences in that situation must be regarded as necessary in order to guarantee the copyright owner the reward for his creative effort.[163]

Secondly, there was no objective justification based on the activities carried out by **8.229** the right owner for the refusal to license.[164]

Thirdly, the broadcasters had exercised their copyright over expressions of listings **8.230** information to reserve for themselves the secondary market for guides containing that information.[165]

The *Magill* case seems to create a limited obligation on an owner of intellectual **8.231** property to grant licences to that intellectual property. The conditions for obtaining such a licence seem to be that the licensee needs the intellectual property to create a new product for which there is potential demand.

The rationale for the judgment is not entirely clear. The Advocate General argued **8.232** that an undertaking's refusing to license intellectual property rights to ensure that its own downstream operations did not face competition from the licensed party is of the essence of intellectual property right protection. The Court appears to have agreed in part, in that the Court requires that the request for a licence be made in the context of an intention to produce a new product for which there is untapped consumer demand. It may be that the Court regarded the refusal to license as an infringement of Article 82(b) in that it limited products, markets, or technical development. This interpretation would be consistent with the position of the Advocate General in *Macrotron*:

> where national law confers an exclusive right on someone—whether in the form of a patent, a registered design or a monopoly in the provision of certain services—and he fails to produce the goods or services covered by the exclusive right, that failure

---

[163] Joined Cases C–241/91P and C–242/91P *Radio Telefís Eireann (RTE) and Independent Television Publications Ltd (ITP) v Commission* [1995] ECR I–74, Opinion of Advocate General Gulmann at para 97.

[164] Joined Cases C–241/91P and C–242/91P *Radio Telefís Eireann (RTE) and Independent Television Publications Ltd (ITP) v Commission* [1995] ECR I–74, at para 55.

[165] Joined Cases C–241/91P and C–242/91P *Radio Telefís Eireann (RTE) and Independent Television Publications Ltd (ITP) v Commission* [1995] ECR I–74, at para 56.

may amount to abuse of a dominant position, in which case the prohibition laid down in Article 86 [now Article 82] will apply.[166]

8.233 This interpretation appears consistent with the approach taken by the CFI in *Tiercé Ladbroke*.[167] In this case, Ladbroke was not only present on the Belgian market in respect of which it had requested the right, but was the leading operator. In these circumstances:

> The refusal to supply the applicant could not fall within the prohibition laid down by Article 86 [now Article 82] unless it concerned a product or service which was either essential for the exercise of the activity in question, in that there was no real or potential substitute, or was a new product whose introduction might be prevented, despite specific, constant and regular potential demand on the part of consumers.

Licensing of Intellectual Property Rights and Article 82

8.234 The main focus of attention in recent years has been on the issue of refusal to license intellectual property rights to third parties. Less controversial are the cases where the question is not whether or not there is an obligation to license third parties, but on what terms and conditions a licence can be granted to ensure that the licensing complies with Article 82.

8.235 Here, the interrelationship between the competition rules and the specific subject matter of an intellectual property right is clearer. Once an undertaking has chosen how it intends to exploit its intellectual property—for example by licensing it to a third party—then the intellectual property right has been exhausted and the competition rules apply in the normal way.

8.236 If the undertaking is dominant, therefore, a traditional Article 82 analysis can be used. Thus, for example, the following are potentially abusive exercises of intellectual property rights:

— charging or attempting to charge excessive royalties;[168]

— discriminating in the granting of licences or in the terms under which licences are granted, where such discrimination affects competition. (This may be what the Court had in mind when it referred to an 'arbitrary' refusal to license in the *Volvo* case.[169])

---

[166] Case C–41/90 *Klaus Höfner and Fritz Elser v Macrotron GmbH* [1991] ECR I–197, Opinion of Advocate General Jacobs at para 46.

[167] Case T–504/93 *Tiercé Landbroke v Commission* [1997] ECR II–923, discussed at para 8.180 above.

[168] Case 402/85 *Basset v SACEM* [1987] ECR 174,7 at para 19, and Case 395/87 *Ministère Public v Tournier* [1989] ECR 2521, at para 38.

[169] Case 238/87 *AB Volvo v Erik Veng (UK) Ltd* [1988] ECR 621, at para 9.

Conclusions on Abuses

The following summarizes the likely current state of the law: **8.237**

— *No actual or potential substitutes exist, refusal to license a competitor to produce the same products as currently exist.* This does not appear to be abusive (ECJ and the Attorney General in *Magill*), unless, perhaps, there is evidence of a failure to fulfil demand on the downstream market, possibly through lack of innovation or inefficiency leading to higher prices (*Port of Genoa, Macrotron, Ladbroke*).

— *No actual or potential substitutes exist, refusal to license a competitor to produce a new, but competing product.* This may be abusive if there is evidence of untapped consumer demand (ECJ in *Magill, Ladbroke*).

— *No actual or potential substitutes exist, refusal to license a competitor to produce a new product in a different market.* This may be abusive (Advocate General and, implicitly, ECJ in *Magill, Ladbroke*).

— *No actual or potential substitutes exist, licensing of at least one third party.* The ordinary Article 82 rules apply on discrimination, excessive pricing, etc (*Basset v SACEM, Tournier*).

— *Some actual or potential substitutes exist, refusal to license any competitor.* This is unlikely to be regarded as abusive (implicitly, ECJ and Attorney General in *Magill*).

— *Some actual or potential substitutes exist, licensing of at least one competitor.* The ordinary Article 82 rules apply to the extent that dominance can be shown.

PART III

SPECIAL SECTORS

9

FINANCIAL SERVICES

A. Introduction[1]

The Commission for a long time argued that Articles 81 and 82 (former Articles **9.01** 85 and 86) of the EC Treaty applied fully to the banking and insurance industries,[2] but it was only in the 1980s that the Court of Justice had occasion to confirm this. In the *Züchner* case,[3] the Court rejected arguments, based on Article 86 (formerly Article 90(2)) and the provisions of the Treaty then applicable to economic policy, that banks are not fully subject to Articles 81 and 82. In 1984 the Commission took its first decisions in the insurance sector; an exemption in *Nuovo CEGAM* and a prohibition in *Fire Insurance*.[4] On appeal from the latter decision in *Verband der Sacheversicherer* the applicant association of insurers argued, in a variation on the 'destructive competition' argument, that unlimited competition in the insurance industry would increase the risk of insolvency to the

---

[1] See generally on the subject of financial services, Luc Gyselen, 'EU antitrust law in the area of financial services—capita selecta for the cautious shaping of a policy' in [1996] *Proceedings of the Fordham Corporate Law Institute* 329–393.
[2] See for example *Report on Competition Policy 1972* (Vol II) points 51–57.
[3] Case 172/80 *Züchner v Bayerische Vereinsbank AG* [1981] ECR 2021, 2030.
[4] *Nuovo CEGAM* [1984] OJ L99/29; *Fire Insurance* [1985] OJ L35/20.

detriment of consumers, that co-operation between insurers was required to avoid that risk, and that special rules should therefore be adopted under Article 83 (former Article 87) to limit the applicability of Articles 81 and 82. The Court rejected those arguments: Articles 81 and 82 are fully applicable in the absence of any special rules adopted under Article 83.[5]

9.02 **Scope of this chapter.**   After considering some general issues (Section B), this chapter considers successively agreements and mergers in the banking sector (Section C), agreements and mergers in the insurance sector (Section D), and, briefly, the emerging case-law relating to the interface between the competition rules and social security systems (Section E).

B. General Issues

9.03 **Single market in banking and insurance.**   The Second Banking Directive allows credit institutions to operate throughout the EEA on the basis of a single licence from, and supervision by, their home state supervisory authorities.[6] The Third Life Directive and Third non-Life Directive have the same effect for insurers.[7] Cross-border activities can be by way of establishment or the provision of services. National markets nevertheless still exist for many products, as has been noted by the Commission in its merger decisions.

(1) Application of Articles 81 and 82 to Financial Services

9.04 **Generous scope of permitted pricing agreements.**   Horizontal agreements fixing uniform prices *vis-à-vis* customers are contrary to Article 81(1)(a) and will not be exempted; there is no equivalent in the financial services sector of the exemption of price-fixing by liner conferences in the maritime transport sector. Nevertheless, in its decisions on interbank fees in payment systems and in its insurance block exemption, the Commission has permitted horizontal agreements relating to a significant cost element making up the final price *vis-à-vis* customers.

---

[5] Case 45/86 *Verband der Sacheversicherer* [1987] ECR 405, 449–452.

[6] Second Council Directive (EEC) 89/646 of 15 December 1989 on the coordination of laws, regulations and administrative provisions relating to the taking up and pursuit of the business of credit institutions and amending Directive (EEC) 77/780 [1989] OJ L386/1.

[7] Council Directive (EEC) 92/96 of 10 November 1992 on the coordination of laws, regulations and administrative provisions relating to direct life assurance and amending Directives (EEC) 79/267 and (EEC) 90/619 (third life insurance Directive) [1992] OJ L360/1; Council Directive (EEC) 92/49 of 18 June 1992 on the coordination of laws, regulations and administrative provisions relating to direct insurance other than life assurance and amending Directives (EEC) 73/239 and (EEC) 88/357 (third non-life insurance Directive) [1992] OJ L228/1.

Characteristic of banking and insurance.   Horizontal arrangements are import-   **9.05**
ant in both the banking and insurance industries. Banks co-operate to provide
payments systems. In order to spread risks, insurers co-operate both horizontally
in pooling arrangements and vertically in reinsurance arrangements. Because of
these characteristics, it is sometimes claimed that the competition rules should be
applied differently. In *Verband der Sacheversicherer*, the Court noted that it was for
the Commission, when granting exemptions under Article 81(3), to take account
of the special characteristics of different branches of the economy and the problems peculiar to them.

Consumer protection.   In its application of the competition rules in the finan-   **9.06**
cial services sector, the Commission appears often to have put a high value on consumer protection concerns. For example, many of the standard clauses that are
'blacklisted' in the insurance block exemption regulation might seem better regulated by unfair contract terms legislation, rather than by the competition rules. As
the Commission develops an EU consumer protection policy (a Treaty basis for
which Article 153 (former Article 129a) was added by the Maastricht Treaty), it
might be expected that consumer protection regulation will replace ersatz regulation by competition policy.[8]

(2) Effect on Trade between Member States

The financial services sector contains many agreements between all or most banks   **9.07**
or insurers within a single Member State. The question arises whether such
national agreements should be considered to affect trade between Member States,
a necessary condition for the application of Articles 81 and 82.

Banking.   In *Bagnasco* the Court held that uniform bank conditions laid down   **9.08**
by the Italian Banking Association (ABI) in relation to contracts for the opening
of current account credit facilities and the provision of general guarantees were
not liable to affect trade between Member States. In reaching this conclusion the
Court had regard to the Commission's findings, made when the standard conditions had previously been notified to the Commission, that the banking service in
question involved economic activities which have a very limited impact on inter-
state trade and that there was limited participation of subsidiaries or branches of
non-Italian banks.[9] The Court did not follow its Advocate General who had proposed that the conditions in question, applied by the quasi-totality of banks operating in Italy, reduced competition between banks and should be considered
contrary to Article 81.[10] Had the Court followed the Advocate General, doubts

---

[8] See Commission Communication 'Financial services: enhancing consumer confidence'
COM(97)309 final, 26 June 1997; Commission Communication 'Boosting consumers' confidence in electronic means of payment in the single market' COM(97)353 final, 9 July 1997.

[9] Joined Cases C–215/96 and 216/96 *Bagnasco and others v Banca Popolare di Novara* [1999]
ECR I–135, at paras 49–53.

[10] Opinion of Ruiz-Jarabo AG, 15 January 1998.

could have been cast on the Commission's decisions in *Italian Banks* and *Dutch Banks* finding certain restrictive agreements not to affect inter-state trade.[11] The effect of the *Bagnasco* judgment would seem to be that it is not sufficient that an interbank agreement or payment system covers the quasi-totality of banks in a particular Member State, but that there must be some evidence of effects on access by banks from other Member States or of effects on cross-border payments. The Commission's formal decision in *Dutch Banks II* (for which an Article 19(3) notice was published in 1997)[12] should provide guidance as to how the Commission will apply the inter-state trade test.

9.09 **Insurance.**   In *Fire Insurance*, the Court upheld the Commission's two reasons for finding that the recommendation of the national association was likely to affect trade between Member States. First, the recommendation affected foreign insurers who were members of the association; it did not make any difference that at the material time foreign insurers had to operate in Germany through branch offices. Secondly, the recommendation was likely to have the effect of isolating a national market and of hindering the economic integration of the common market. Access to the German market would be made more difficult because an across-the-border increase in premiums would affect foreign insurers who could offer a more competitive service.[13]

C. Banking

(1) Price Agreements

9.10 Possible horizontal price agreements between banks include agreements on the fees to be charged to customers, or on the interest rates to be applied to customers' credits or loans. Within payment systems further forms of price agreement can exist; they are considered below.

9.11 **Customer fees.**   Agreements that set or recommend customer fees, whether fixed, maximum, or minimum fees are straightforward price-fixing agreements falling within Article 81(1)(a) and not capable of being exempted.[14] Following the

---

[11] *ABI* [1987] OJ L43/51, at paras 35–36 (restrictions included interbank fees, customer fees in the SIP telephone bills payment service, prohibition on participation in competing ATM networks, and fixing of numbers of ATMs allocated to each member), 38–40 (minimum customer fees for safe deposit and safe custody services); *Dutch Banks* [1989] OJ L253/1, at paras 58 (uniform conditions for hiring safes), 59 (interbank fee for fund-raising acceptance transfers).

[12] See para 9.20 below.

[13] *Fire Insurance* [1985] OJ L35/20, at paras 29–36; Case 45/86 *Verband der Sacheversicherer* [1987] ECR 405, 458–459.

[14] Case 172/80 *Züchner v Bayerische Vereinsbank AG* [1981] ECR 2021 (parallel conduct on customer fees could amount to concerted practice); *Uniform Eurocheques* [1985] OJ 35/43, at para 40; *Eurocheque: Helsinki Agreement* [1992] OJ 95/50, fine reduced on appeal because the agreement was as to the principle of a fee, and not also as to the amount as found in the Commission's decision:

Court's 1981 decision in the *Züchner* case,[15] the Commission investigated national agreements between banks. The Belgian, Italian, and Dutch banking associations abandoned agreement on customer fees after being sent statements of objections.[16] Recently the Commission publicized its inspections at Austrian banks to investigate suspicions that the 'Lombard Club' of Austrian banks were engaged in a price-fixing cartel.[17]

Value dates.   An agreement between banks to apply the same value dating prac-   **9.12**
tices *vis-à-vis* their customers will also fall within Article 81(1)(a) as an agreement fixing 'prices or any other trading conditions'. It is difficult to conceive of circumstances in which such an agreement would be exempted.

Interest rates. In its 1988 decision in *Van Eycke*, the Court confirmed that an   **9.13**
agreement fixing interest rates on deposits would fall within Article 81(1).[18] Until then the Commission had reserved its position on such agreements,[19] but in 1989 Commissioner Sir Leon Brittan wrote to the European Banking Federation explaining the Commission's view that interbank agreements on interest rates should be avoided or abandoned.[20] An investigation into agreements within national banking associations was ended in 1992 after all the organizations questioned confirmed that among them there were no agreements or recommendations on interest rates.[21] However, the Commission has never publicized any investigations into concerted practices on interest rates that may exist outside the framework of national banking associations.

(2) Recommended Terms and Conditions

Some national banking associations have recommended terms and conditions for   **9.14**
use by their members. In the early 1970s one association agreed to amend those of its recommended general conditions that the Commission considered unfavourable to customers.[22] In *Bagnasco* the Court held that uniform bank conditions laid down by the Italian Banking Association (ABI) in relation to contracts for the opening of current account credit facilities and the provision of general guarantees, in so far as they enable banks to change at any time the interest rate applicable to a credit facility and to do so by means of a notice displayed on their

---

Joined Cases T–39/92 & 40/92 *Groupement des Cartes Bancaires 'CB' and Europay International SA v Commission* [1994] ECR II–49.

[15] Case 172/80 *Züchner v Bayerische Vereinsbank AG* [1981] ECR 2021, 2030.

[16] *Belgische Vereniging der Banken/Association Belges des Banques* [1987] OJ 7/27, paras 17–19; *ABI* [1987] OJ L43/51, paras 14–15; *Dutch Banks* [1989] OJ L253/1, paras 17–27.

[17] IP(98)556.

[18] Case 276/86 *Van Eycke v ASPA* [1988] ECR 4769.

[19] *Irish Banks' Standing Committee* [1986] OJ L295/28, at para 10; *ABI* [1987] OJ L43/51, at para 18; *Dutch Banks* [1989] OJ L253/1, at para 15.

[20] IP(89)869; *Report on Competition Policy 1991* (Vol XXI) point 33.

[21] IP(91)520; IP(92)625.

[22] *Report on Competition Policy 1972* (vol II) point 70.

premises or in such manner as they consider most appropriate, do not restrict competition within the meaning of Article 81(1).[23] The Court seems to have recognized that the recommended condition, by providing for a variable interest rate loan, excluded the right to agree a fixed interest rate loan. Although this might at first sight seem a horizontal pricing agreement, the Court nevertheless held that there was no appreciable restrictive effect on competition since any variation of the variable interest rate depends on objective factors such as changes in the money market rate.

(3) Payment Systems: Past Approach to Pricing Issues

9.15 As stated above, agreements on customer fees are unexemptable restrictions of competition. This remains the case as between banks participating in a payment system. Payment systems also give rise to two further types of price agreement, the competition assessment of which is more contentious. First, most (but not all) systems have multilaterally agreed interbank fees paid between banks handling any particular payment within the system (so-called 'multilateral interchange fees', MIFs). Depending on the system and the type of transaction, these are expressed either as a fixed transaction fee or as a percentage of the value of the payment. Secondly, many systems include an agreement to prohibit shopkeepers and other merchants from surcharging customers for the use of a particular payment system (so-called 'no-discrimination rule', NDR).

9.16 **Uniform Eurocheques.**   In 1984 the Commission took its first decision in the banking sector, exempting the international Eurocheque system.[24] A maximum interbank commission (ie, an MIF) of 1.25 per cent paid to the payee bank from the Eurocheque issuing bank was considered to be a restriction of price competition falling within Article 81(1). For the purposes of the exemption, an important aspect of the arrangements was that the uniform Eurocheques would (subject to certain exceptions) be paid in full so that the consumer writing a Eurocheque would receive the full face value of the cheque. This was considered a benefit of the system, but not in itself identified either as a restriction of price competition between payee banks *vis-à-vis* customers or as a condition of the exemption. Because the payee banks would no longer be remunerated by customer fees, the MIF was considered as a remuneration for services provided by the payee bank to the issuing bank; its multilateral character was exempted because the alternative was considered to be bilateral agreements between the 15,000 participating banks. It was also considered as a benefit that merchants would benefit not only from the guarantee but also from the payment by the payee bank of the full amount of the cheque. The Commission did not clearly distinguish, as it probably

---

[23] Joined Cases C–215/96 and 216/96 *Bagnasco and others v Banca Popolare di Novara* 1999 [ECR] I–135, paras 35–37.
[24] *Uniform Eurocheques* [1985] OJ L35/43.

now would, between the cash distribution function of Eurocheques (involving three parties: the two banks and the customer writing a Eurocheque) and the payment function (involving four parties: the two banks, the customer writing a Eurocheque, and the merchant accepting a Eurocheque). The fourth condition of Article 81(3) was considered fulfilled in particular because of the existence of inter-system competition from other means of payment.

Belgian Banks, Italian Banks.   In *Belgian Banks*[25] the Commission exempted   **9.17**
MIFs in three agreements. In respect of each agreement a slightly different argument was put forward as to why an MIF was indispensable: the first argument, mirroring that in *Eurocheque*, was that the alternative would be bilateral agreements between eighty-four banks; the second argument was that smaller banks, which had fewer overseas correspondents and thus under the system for processing payment originating abroad paid out more than they received, would otherwise be subject to 'unfair' conditions and thus be placed at a competitive disadvantage; the third argument was that in the absence of the MIF some banks might refuse to participate in the service, which was beneficial to customers.[26] In *Italian Banks* the exempted MIFs were considered indispensable again as a necessary remuneration for interbank services, the alternative being considered bilateral negotiations between many banks (1,100 in this case).[27]

Eurocheque: Package Deal II.   The Commission did not renew the Eurocheque   **9.18**
exemption because it was concerned that the 'condition' on which the exemption was based, ie the payment of the full amount of a cheque, had not always been respected by banks.[28] In 1990 the Commission sent a statement of objections which objected that the maximum level of MIF had always been applied, and that it was systematically passed on to customers.[29] A supplementary statement of objections was sent in 1992. It nevertheless seems likely that the Commission will now renew the exemption.[30]

Helsinki Agreement.[31]   In 1992, the Commission returned to the Eurocheque   **9.19**
system in its first, and to date only, negative decision in the banking sector. In order to promote the use of payment cards in France, the French financial institutions and the Eurocheque member banks adopted the Helsinki Agreement, under which, in respect of purchases paid for by Eurocheques, members of the Groupement Carte Bleue and Eurocard France would charge their affiliated merchants a commission not exceeding the commission applicable to payments by

---

[25] *Belgische Vereniging der Banken/Association Belges des Banques* [1987] OJ L7/27.
[26] See paras 53–55.
[27] *ABI* [1987] OJ L43/51, paras 64–66.
[28] IP(88)496.
[29] IP(90)765.
[30] Gyselen (n 1 above) at 343.
[31] *Eurocheque: Helsinki Agreement* [1992] OJ L95/50.

Carte Bleue and Eurocard payments. The Commission considered this to be both an agreement to charge a commission and an agreement on the amount of the commission, and to be contrary to the full payment principle that underlay its earlier exemption of the Eurocheque system as a whole. It imposed a fine of ECU 5 million on the Groupement des cartes bancaires 'CB' and ECU 1 million on Eurocheque International. The Groupement's fine was reduced on appeal, the Court of First Instance holding that there had been an agreement to charge a commission but no agreement as to the amount of the commission.[32]

9.20 **Dutch Banks I and II.** In the *Dutch Banks* decision, the Commission noted that after it had sent a statement of objections against minimum customer fees applicable to certain payment transactions, the banks had proposed that certain of those agreed customer fees be replaced by MIFs without any accompanying agreement on the extent to which the MIFs would be passed on to customers.[33] The Commission was perhaps sceptical that MIFs were indispensable in systems that had functioned without them, and concerned that an MIF agreed in such circumstances would, even in the absence of an express agreement so to do, be likely to be passed on to customers. The Commission stated that the parties 'have not shown that such agreements on inter-bank commissions would actually be necessary for the successful implementation of certain forms of cooperation, positive in themselves, between a number of banks. The position of the Commission is that only in the exceptional cases, where such a necessity is established, may agreements on inter-bank commissions be capable of gaining an exemption under Article 81(3).'[34] In *Dutch Banks II*, the Commission in 1993 issued a statement of objections against an MIF in the Dutch GSA system (a pre-printed credit transfer system) and in 1997 published an Article 19(3) notice indicating its intention to exempt the MIF.[35] As stated above, the final decision in the *Dutch Banks II* case should give guidance on how the Commission will apply the inter-state trade test to national payment systems following the Court's *Bagnasco* judgment.[36] The developments in the Commission's services' approach to the MIF between the two *Dutch Banks* cases is considered in the next section.

---

[32] Joined Cases T–39/92 and T–40/92 *Groupement des Cartes Bancaires 'CB' and Europay International v Commission* [1994] ECR II–49.

[33] *Dutch Banks* [1989] OJ L253/1, at para 26.

[34] At para 26. The Dutch banks objected to this statement and appealed against the decision. The appeal was held to be inadmissible: Case T–138/89 *Nederlandse Bankiersvereniging and Nederlandse Vereniging van Banken v Commission* [1992] ECR II–2181.

[35] Gyselen (n 1 above) at 343. Article 19(3) Notice [1997] OJ C273/12.

[36] See para 9.08 above.

(4) Payment Systems: New Approach to Pricing Issues[37]

Since the publication of the Notice on the application of the EC competition **9.21**
rules to cross-border credit transfers in 1995,[38] there seems to have been a change
in the Commission's approach as to the competition assessment of the two most
frequent price restrictions in payment systems: MIFs and NDRs.[39] The
Commission even announced the publication in the course of 1998 of a notice
aiming at clarifying the application of competition rules to electronic payment
instruments.[40] This notice has not yet been published but the Commission has
also announced that it intends to complete its examination of a number of payment system cases, the treatment of which had been lagging for some years.[41]

Multilateral Interchange Fees

Restrictive effects. An MIF raises potential competition concerns because of its **9.22**
multilateral character. The cross-border transfers Notice explains that an MIF
may generate three types of restrictive effects. The first concerns the interbank
relationship and corresponds to the traditional approach adopted by the
Commission. An MIF is nothing other than a commonly agreed price at the interbank level and therefore a blatant price-fixing device. To this banks and payment
systems have replied that market forces do not operate at the interbank level and
that the banks are quite simply obligatory partners, with no bargaining power.
Otherwise the survival of the payment system in question would be threatened.
Banks have to co-operate to process payment orders and in relation to any particular payment the two banks involved do not choose each other. This is the result
of commercial decisions made by their respective clients. The natural conclusion
of this line of argument developed by the banking industry is then to say that
MIFs are inherent to payment systems and therefore escape the application of
competition rules. This 'inherence' argument seems questionable.[42] It can be
argued that banks always have the choice to join or not to join a payment system.
Once a member of a payment system, a bank has to agree in advance on the financial conditions under which it will proceed with payment operations on behalf of

---

[37] Gyselen (n 1 above); Henri Piffaut, Observateur de Bruxelles no 21, February 1997; Monica
Negenman, 'EU anti-trust law (Articles 81 and 82) and their potential impact on the banking sector of the Czech Republic', Fédération Bancaire de l'Union Européene (FBE)—Bruxelles—28
April 1998.
[38] Notice on the application of the EC competition rules to cross-border credit transfers [1995]
OJ C251/3.
[39] See Gyselen (n 1 above), Negenman and Piffaut (n 37 above).
[40] See COM(97)353 and IP(97)626.
[41] See *Dutch Banks II*, Article 19(3) Notice (n 35 above), and Commission's answer to Written
Questions E–1338/97, E–1339/97, E–1340/97, E–1341/97, E–1342/97, E–1343/97 and
E–1344/97 by André Fourçans, OJ C21/46, 22 January 1998.
[42] See Gyselen (n 1 above) at 346.

its clients. This was recognized by the Commission in its 23rd annual report.[43] Otherwise uncertainty would kill the co-operation at the basis of the payment system. However, this does not mean that banks have to agree multilaterally on the financial conditions to proceed with payment orders. Even if MIFs are one option, a set of bilateral interchange fees or even to leave to each bank the opportunity to levy unilateral fees are other options.

9.23 The second type of restrictive effect that an MIF might generate deals with its effect on intra-system competition. An MIF introduces some rigidity in bank-client relationships. If, say, all creditor banks have agreed to pay a certain amount for each payment operation to debtor banks, it can be expected that those creditor banks will uniformly pass on this element of cost to their clients. This results in a uniform upward effect on the prices charged to the creditor clients which use the payment system in question and therefore may restrict intra-system competition. This was an argument used by the Commission when it objected formally against the *Eurocheque Package Deal II* and *Dutch Banks II* notifications.[44] However, the Commission's cross-border transfers Notice introduces a qualification to this effect on competition. It states that there will be a restriction of competition under Article 81(1) when there is an agreement or concerted practice between banks to pass on the effect of the interchange fee in the prices they charge to their customers.[45] Accordingly, if it is found that *de facto* all banks pass on the MIF to their clients, then the MIF restricts intra-system competition.[46]

9.24 The third type of restrictive effect deals with the degree of inter-system competition. In the Notice on cross-border transfers,[47] the Commission states that sufficiently strong inter-system competition could restrain the effects of the MIF on the prices charged to the customers, provided that the competing systems do not contain similar MIFs. This analysis was applied in the *Danish Bankers' Association—cross-border transfers* case where the MIF was found not to be contrary to Article 81(1).[48]

9.25 **Exemption under Article 81(3).** Turning now to the assessment under Article 81(3), this is the area where the new approach of the Commission services has brought the most important changes. They now conclude that if a number of conditions are met, an MIF could meet all four conditions set out in Article 81(3). The Notice on cross-border transfers is not very telling on this point. The Notice focuses on justifying an exemption of an MIF where a cross-border payment system leaves all the charges to be borne by the sender of the payment. The new

---

[43] *Report on Competition Policy 1993* (vol XXIII) point 119.
[44] See for instance IP(90) 765.
[45] Notice on cross-border credit transfers (n 38 above), para 40.
[46] See Gyselen (n 1 above) at 347.
[47] Paras 41–42.
[48] *Report on Competition Policy 1996* (Vol XXVI) 130.

approach seems to have been applied in the *Dutch Banks II* case.[49] The starting point of the analysis is to note that the demand for payment system services is two-prong. This demand is a composite of a demand from a creditor and another demand from a debtor. According to the Commission services, an interchange fee, because of its passing on effect, alters the charges that both sides of the demand face. In other words an interchange fee allocates costs between the two sides of the demand for a payment system. They then argue that any multilateral interchange fee would be a more efficient way to achieve an optimal allocation of costs between the two sides of the demand than a set of bilateral interchange fees. Bilateral interchange fees would generate more transaction costs, would make it more expensive to handle payment operations (each pair of banks would then need to be identified), and it is not certain that such sets of bilateral interchange fees would lead to the same demand optimizing effects.

As to the indispensability test set out in Article 81(3), it is interpreted as a 'rea- **9.26** sonably necessary test'.[50] There are a number of ways in which interchange fees can be set up multilaterally. This could be a fixed fee applied to any pair of banks. This could also be a percentage of the amount of the payment operation or this could be the result of a uniform formula fed by bilateral parameters. Finally, there could be a few banks agreeing on bilateral interchange fees and acting as 'chefs de file' for other, smaller banks to which the 'chef de file' banks would pass on the cost of these bilateral interchange fees. The second step in the reasoning is to admit that a competition authority is unable to assess which of these alternatives would be the most efficient. Any multilaterally agreed interchange fee should therefore be considered as meeting the indispensability test as set out in the third condition of Article 81(3).

Regarding the fourth condition of Article 81(3), the Commission's services seem **9.27** to be conditioning its fulfilment to a number of requirements. First, when a payment system does not face any competition, interchange fees should be set in an objective manner and be revised regularly.[51] Secondly, there should be some transparency as to the level and existence of interchange fees for the payment system's customers.[52] Finally, there should be no restrictions on prices on any of the three other legs constituting a payment operation (ie the creditor-creditor's bank, debtor-debtor's bank, and debtor-creditor relationships). This is stating the obvious for the bank-client relationships, but is something new for the creditor-debtor relationship which was characterized in a number of payment systems by the NDR prohibiting creditors from freely price discriminating on the basis of the means of payment used. This last requirement is aimed at enabling the demand

---

[49] See Article 19(3) Notice (n 35 above).
[50] See Gyselen (n 1 above) at 353.
[51] See Article 19(3) Notice (n 35 above) at point 28.
[52] See Article 19(3) Notice (n 35 above) at point 27.

(ie creditors and debtors) to counterbalance the cost shifting mechanism put in place between the banks. If for instance, an MIF would lead to 'excessive' charges from the creditors' perspective, they could level out this excessive aspect by deciding to surcharge debtors for the use of the means of payment in question.

9.28   It must be noted that this approach departs from the requirements included in the Notice on cross-border transfers. The Notice required an MIF to be based on costs and therefore transformed the Commission into some sort of price regulator.[53] This was, however, justified by the broader context of this notice which aimed at facilitating the implementation of the then future directive on cross-border transfers.[54] This Directive promotes the offering by cross-border transfer systems of transfers free of charge for the recipient. In such a case, it is appropriate that the creditor bank be remunerated through interchange fees based on costs.

9.29   The new approach has the merit of being more process oriented in imposing requirements which aim at more competition. It should be noted, however, that if a payment system were found to hold market power and to have abused it, an exemption would not prevent the Commission from applying Article 82.

9.30   **Economic background to the new approach.**   The Commission's services have evidently been influenced by the US literature on payment systems by introducing some economic thinking in their competitive assessment of the multilateral interchange fees.[55]

9.31   Baxter argued in his seminal paper that in a four-party payment system, a service is provided jointly by the debtor bank and the creditor bank to a joint beneficiary, the debtor and the creditor. He explains that payment systems are faced with a joint demand which is the aggregation of two demands: one from the creditors and one from the debtors. In the absence of interchange fees, nothing ensures that the prices charged to their customers by each of the banks will lead to full satisfaction of each of the demands. By definition since any payment operation involves a creditor and a debtor, the satisfied demands of each of these categories of economic agents will be equal. It is very unlikely that the marginal costs of creditor banks and debtor banks will be such that the equilibrium prices and quantities will be equal with the demand expressed respectively by creditors and debtors as far as the quantities are concerned. One side of the four-party system needs to be

---

[53] Notice on cross-border credit transfers (n 38 above), at paras 51–56.

[54] Directive (EC) 97/5 of the European Parliament and of the Council of 27 January 1997 on cross-border credit transfers [1997] OJ L43/25.

[55] WF Baxter, 'Bank Interchange of transactional paper: legal and economic perspectives' (October 1983) Journal of Law and Economics; Carlton and Frankel, 'The Antitrust Economics of the Payment Card Industry' (1995) 63 Antitrust LJ 643; Evans & Schmalensee, 'Economic Aspects of Payment Card Systems and Antitrust policy towards Joint Ventures' (1995) 63 Antitrust LJ 861; Carlton and Frankel, 'The Antitrust Economics of the Payment Card Industry: reply to Evans & Schmalensee' (1995) 63 Antitrust LJ 903.

subsidized to increase the attractiveness of the system. This is achieved by the interchange fees which shift costs from one side to the other. Therefore, Baxter concludes that an interbank financial arrangement is necessary to ensure that demands expressed by creditors and debtors are fully satisfied.

Baxter goes on to argue the interchange fees must be multilaterally determined (ie, **9.32** that they be MIFs). He admits implicitly that the ideal situation would be bilaterally negotiated interchange fees, but this would be impossible for practical reasons (transaction costs). He agrees that MIFs should be default fees only, the banks having the freedom to depart from such default multilateral level. He argues that if unilaterally set interchange fees were permitted in a payment system, then the temptation on issuing banks to be a free-rider would be too great, with a consequent risk to the system as a whole.

This view has conflicted with the traditional interpretation of interchange fees as **9.33** being the remuneration for a service provided at the interbank level. Its force comes from the fact that it provides an overall picture of the working of payment systems by bringing into the analysis the two other participants, the debtor and the creditor. With the remuneration for a service argument, the analysis has to focus on an interbank 'market' (which is contested)[56] and therefore misses the obvious: the fact that this can be a tool for payment systems to exercise some market power.[57]

However, the Baxter analysis has two shortcomings. First, it fails to take into **9.34** account the fourth relationship, ie the one between the creditor and the debtor. Secondly, it does not explain convincingly why to set multilaterally the interchange fee is better from a competition point of view than to leave that to the free operation of the market.

The creditor-debtor relationship. It could be argued that the creditors and the **9.35** debtors could adjust the costs of using payment systems among themselves either instead of letting the banks do that on their behalf or in addition to the banks setting interchange fees. However, this is a rather academic discussion because the main card payment systems include an NDR prohibiting debtors and creditors from having their own settlement when they agree on a payment operation.

Carlton and Frankel argue that in a four-party payment system with no pricing **9.36** constraints such as an NDR, the level of any interchange fee is irrelevant because all of the costs of the system will be paid in the end by the customers (creditor and debtor). If there is no interchange fee, the creditor bank will pass on all its costs to the creditor in the form of a fee (which the creditor may pass on to the debtor in

---

[56] See, for example, Sousi-Roubi, *Droit bancaire européen* (Précis Dalloz, 1995).
[57] For an illustration of such market power, see for instance *The Future of the Credit Card Industry—1996 Edition* (Bernstein Research, January 1996).

the form of a surcharge). Likewise, any costs incurred by the debtor bank for the operation will also be charged to the debtor in the form of an operation fee. If the creditor bank pays an interchange fee to the debtor bank, it will then add this cost to the fee it charges to the creditor (who can correspondingly increase his surcharge to the debtor). Under normal competitive circumstances, the debtor bank should reduce or eliminate its operation charge to the debtor in line with the interchange fee it has received from the creditor bank. The precise allocation of costs between the creditor and the debtor will be determined by competition. The creditor may or may not pass on all or part of its fee to the debtor through a surcharge, depending on the competitive situation with other creditors. Likewise, the inclusion of profit margins in the commissions charged by the creditor bank and the debtor bank is not considered, as this will also be determined by competition, and is not of relevance to the model. Carlton and Frankel conclude that, given that the interchange fee is an irrelevance which complicates the transaction, it might as well not exist, and that each bank should charge its costs to its customer, that is, the creditor bank's costs should be charged to the creditor, and the debtor bank's costs should be charged to the debtor.

9.37   It seems that the Commission's services tend to agree that there is a need to counterbalance the market power that payment systems can derive from their ability to fix MIFs by also allowing creditors and debtors to allocate costs among themselves. However, an MIF does not then become irrelevant. Indeed, if the creditor-debtor segment is efficient it will offset any excessive interchange fee by a new allocation of costs between both sides. In such a case, a competition authority should not be concerned about an MIF because its effect on competition would be negligible. If, however, one assumes that, for whatever reason, the creditor-debtor segment is not fully efficient, then, first, there is a justification for an MIF and, secondly, there is a need for safeguards to be imposed to avoid any abuse of market power from payment systems.

9.38   **Multilateral versus bilateral.**   Baxter bases his justification for the multilateral character of MIFs solely on transaction costs grounds. This is not a convincing argument. On that basis any price-fixing agreement would be exempted because it brings transaction costs savings.

9.39   It could be argued that the costs to reach the social optimum are minimized when the financial arrangements are fixed multilaterally. First, this brings savings on transaction costs (ie negotiation costs to agree the bilateral interchange fees and the processing costs to handle the clearing and settlement operations of payments according to each set of bilateral agreements). Secondly, bilaterally agreed interchange fees would not lead to the achievement of the benefits outlined above. Banks participating in a payment system would have low incentives to vary from a pre-set bilateral interchange fee. For the system to work, a bank which wished to change the interchange fee it pays as a creditor bank would need to warn in advance its counterparts who would presumably retaliate by imposing similar changes when they act as creditor bank. This would not bring beneficial effects. In addition, if a bank was willing to change the level of bilateral interchange fees because it felt that this would enable joint demand and joint supply to be better satisfied, it would then need to negotiate with all the other banks and would not be certain of the outcome. This would mean incurring higher transaction costs than in a multilateral scenario and less likelihood of reaching the social optimum.

Conclusion. Overall, it would seem that the new approach of the Commission's **9.40** services aims to strike a balance between the need to trust market forces and the temptation to intervene in price setting mechanisms. The approach is process oriented. It remains to be seen to what extent the new approach will be adopted by the Commission in formal cases such as the favourable decision it has indicated would be taken in the *Dutch Banks II* case.[58]

No-Discrimination Rule

There have been few recent statements by the Commission on the NDR.[59] In the **9.41** *Abim card* case, the Commission's services objected to an NDR part of an agreement between four oil companies by which they would have allowed their cardholders to use their cards in the other companies' petrol stations.[60] In the same year, 1993, the Director-General of DG IV wrote to the Dutch competition authority to explain that in his view the NDR did not seem exemptable under Article 81(3). Shortly thereafter the Dutch authority prohibited the NDR. This decision was confirmed in May 1997 by an Administrative Appeal Court.[61] There were moreover press reports in the course of 1997 suggesting that the Commission's services were proposing that the Commission should prohibit the NDR in payment systems.[62]

The NDR can be assessed under Article 81 as follows. It could be argued that the **9.42** NDR is restrictive of competition since it weakens the bargaining power of creditors *vis-à-vis* banks when they negotiate the conditions under which they will accept the means of payment offered by a particular payment system. In the presence of an NDR, the creditor's choice is reduced to a 'take-it-or-leave-it' situation. Creditors then lose their bargaining power on the amount of the fee that any bank might charge them for the acquisition of the means of payment in question. This

---

[58] Article 19(3) Notice (n 35 above).
[59] See, for instance, Commission's answer to Written Questions E–1338/97, E–1339/97, E–1340/97, E–1341/97, E–1342/97, E–1343/97 and E–1344/97 by André Fourçans, OJ C21/46, 22 January 1998.
[60] *Report on Competition Policy 1993* (Vol XXIII) 485.
[61] See Gyselen (n 1 above) at 355.
[62] See, for example, *Les Echos* of 21 March 1997.

amounts to a lessening of intra-system competition. The same applies to inter-system competition. The creditor cannot make price competition work fully between payment systems since it can exert only limited pressure on the level of the fees charged for the acceptance of a given means of payment. Moreover, assuming that a creditor would pass on the cost of accepting different payment systems, an NDR prevents customers from getting a better picture of the relative costs of that particular means of payment. Finally, it deprives creditors of the freedom to decide whether or not to pass on to the card-using customer one component of their costs (the merchant fee).

9.43 Under this line of argument it would appear that the exemptability of an NDR under Article 81(3) is questionable. The NDR ensures predictability of costs of use of payments systems by consumers, and might therefore be considered as protecting consumers. Indeed, in the presence of an NDR consumers know in advance that they will not be charged when using the means of payment in question. The situation could become dangerous for payment systems if creditors were to abuse their freedom to surcharge by charging randomly at levels which could be deemed to be excessive. None of these scenarios, however, seem to have materialized in the countries or payment systems which do not know of an NDR.[63] Moreover, it can be argued that there are less restrictive means to achieve the benefit of consumer protection. First, merchants could be obliged to publish clearly and in advance (for example by announcements at the entrance of their premises) possible charges for particular means of payment. Secondly, in order to avoid fluctuations in the amounts charged to cardholders and to avoid abusive surcharges, a 'cap' of charges by merchants could be required. For example, merchants could be required to charge no more than the commission they have to pay to their bank. These two conditions (transparency and ceiling) have been applied in the UK where the NDR was abolished for credit cards in 1990, to the apparent satisfaction of both consumer organizations and merchant organizations. It has been suggested that in the Member States where the NDR has been abolished (the UK (1990), Sweden (1994), and The Netherlands), the negotiating position of merchants improved and merchant fees actually came down, while at the same time the use of the cards continued to increase. Therefore, on balance the positive effects on competition brought by an abolition of the NDR would offset the negative effects on consumer protection which could nevertheless be achieved through other less restrictive means.

9.44 It is striking that the Commission's services seem to have reached a position but that the Commission has not yet taken a formal decision. This contrasts sharply with the situation in Member States where this issue was tackled when the competition authorities were faced with it.

---

[63] See Gyselen (n 1 above) at 358.

Cash withdrawal operations.   Such operations involve only three parties: the   **9.45**
ATM[64] owner, the debtor bank, and the debtor. The combination of an NDR and
an MIF leads the ATM owners to earn pre-fixed income from the cash withdrawing service they provide to other banks' debtors. This seems to be a blatant price-
fixing agreement. The NDR, when the result of a multilateral agreement between
banks participating in a payment system, appears to infringe Article 81(1) and not
to meet the conditions set out in Article 81(3) since there is complete absence of
competition between the ATM owners. The same goes for the MIF: in a three-
party system it does not serve as a cost allocation device since the demand is a single entity. The MIF can therefore only be a price for using a service device for
which there can be no reason to justify multilateral price fixing. There is no reason
why ATM users cannot be charged directly by the ATM owner.[65]

(5) Payment Systems: Non-Price Issues

Five main issues have arisen in relation to payment systems: whether agreements   **9.46**
relating to the operation of a system fall with Article 81(1), under what circumstances 'essential facility' systems should be required to accept new members, and
the acceptability of territorial exclusivity for certain activities within a payment
system, prohibitions on members participating in other systems, and prohibitions
on cross-border activity. The Commission has adopted formal positions on some
of these issues in its notice on cross-border transfers and in the *SWIFT* case.

Operational Agreements

Banks can agree standards relating to the operation of a system (such as standard   **9.47**
message formats and settlement arrangements), standards on the transactions to
be processed by a system, and on security and risk management rules. Such agreements, provided they are limited to interbank arrangements, will normally fall
outside Article 81(1) or be capable of exemption under Article 81(3).[66]

In *Irish Banks*, the Commission found that an agreement between the four main   **9.48**
banks in Ireland as to their opening hours did not appreciably restrict competition.[67] The Commission would probably now be less likely to reach such a seem-
ingly surprising conclusion; the decision itself acknowledges that branch opening
hours are a factor of competition between banks. A prohibition of the agreement
between the banks would not, however, have made any practical difference as the

---

[64] ATM, or automatic teller machine, is a cash delivering machine.
[65] Such direct charges by ATM owners are widespread in the USA. In the EU, plans for a new UK
ATM network with direct charges have been announced: *Financial Times*, 11 June 1999.
[66] *Irish Banks' Standing Committee* [1986] OJ L295/28; Notice on the application of the EC
competition rules to cross-border credit transfers [1995] OJ C251/3, at paras 31–34.
[67] *Irish Banks' Standing Committee* [1986] OJ L295/28, at para 16.

opening hours were also the subject of an agreement between the banks and their employees' trade unions.[68]

Access to Payment Systems—Essential Facilities

9.49 **Essential facilities.** A payment system that constitutes an essential facility should be open to new participants. Where a system is an essential facility, it should have objectively justified and non-discriminatory membership criteria.[69] A system that is not judged to be an essential facility is free to restrict participation in its services.[70] The *SWIFT* case provides guidance on how the Commission will approach essential facilities and denial of access in the field of financial services.[71] The *GSIT* case also gives guidance as to membership criteria the Commission considers necessary in essential facility systems.[72]

9.50 **The SWIFT case.** On 13 October 1997 the Commission announced that it had suspended its investigations against SWIFT (Society for Worldwide Interbank Telecommunications sc) following SWIFT's undertaking to allow access to its network to all entities qualified to have access to EU third party fund transfer systems, and no longer to limit full access to its network and services to banks.[73]

9.51 SWIFT is a co-operative society owned by some 2,000 banks throughout the world. It owns a telecommunications network and provides an electronic message transfer system to its users, which use the SWIFT network for various types of interbank messages, including national and cross-border payment messages. Only banks and 'entities in the same type of business' had full access to the totality of the network, products, and services of SWIFT. The French Post Office, La Poste, unsuccessfully applied to become a member of SWIFT; its application was rejected by SWIFT on the advice of the Group of French SWIFT users (GUF) on the ground that La Poste did not meet the criteria for membership. The Commission, acting on a complaint from La Poste, issued a statement of objections, based on Article 82, against SWIFT.

9.52 The Commission argued that SWIFT is an essential facility holding the control of a gateway to the international transfer market for two reasons. First of all, it holds a monopolistic position in the market for international payment message transfer networks. In addition, SWIFT is the only network providing connections to

---

[68] *Irish Banks' Standing Committee,* at para 7.
[69] Notice on cross-border transfers (n 38 above), paras 26, 27.
[70] Notice on cross-border transfers (n 38 above), para 29; *IBOS, Eurogiro* 26th Report, point 109, and pp 129, 130.
[71] See also Notice on cross-border transfers (n 38 above), paras 25–28.
[72] *Groupement pour un Système Interbancaire de Télécompensation (GSIT)* (Notice pursuant to Article 19(3) of Regulation 17) [1999] OJ C64/5.
[73] IP/97/870; *Report on Competition Policy 1997* (Vol XXVII), point 68; [1997] OJ C335/3.

banks located anywhere in the world. The Commission considered that SWIFT had abused its dominant position by excluding La Poste and other entities interested and engaging in cross-border transfers from SWIFT membership without justification. SWIFT's membership criteria appeared unjustified since they related to the overall conditions under which applicants pursue their financial activities and not to their involvement in payment systems. Moreover, the Commission considered that SWIFT applied its membership criteria to La Poste in a discriminatory way.

Following the opening of proceedings by the Commission, SWIFT offered the Commission an undertaking which led the Commission to suspend its investigation. SWIFT undertook to create a new category of participants (as opposed to broadening its category of members who are also shareholders). This new category, called Non-Shareholding Financial Institution (NSFI), would be granted full access to the SWIFT network, products, and services. NSFIs are those institutions that satisfy the criteria laid down by the European Monetary Institute (the EMI), the forerunner of the European Central Bank, for access to any European payment system. To qualify as an NSFI, the entity must be authorized to hold accounts for customers; its direct participation in one or more EU fund transfer systems processing third party payments must have the approval of the central bank; and (a) its public nature must ensure little risk of failure, or (b) its financial service activities must be supervised by a recognized competent authority. **9.53**

Pending the creation of the NSFI category, SWIFT offered any institution which applied for full access and met the EMI criteria a co-operation agreement granting that institution full access to the whole range of the SWIFT network, products, and services. **9.54**

Participation requirements. The undertaking given by SWIFT gives a good example of the type of undertaking which may satisfy the Commission in essential facility cases, not forcing the company to give full access to all potentially interested applicants, and not forcing the owners to share ownership with all users. For instance, the Commission accepted that the need to avoid systemic risk and other concerns may justify refusal of network access to firms who are not qualified by their Central Bank as being entitled to direct access to EU payment systems in accordance with the EMI criteria. Such criteria are objective and proportional to the need to avoid systemic risks. To this extent, the undertaking reflects a recognition of the need to comply with the proportionality principle in essential facilities cases. **9.55**

'Essential facilities' in financial services. SWIFT argued that even assuming that it constitutes an essential facility, the non-acceptance of La Poste had no appreciable effect on the structure of competition in the French banking **9.56**

market.[74] This raises an interesting question on the application of the essential facility doctrine to the financial services industry. Most entities that are potential essential facilities are, like SWIFT, co-operatives owned by their clients (financial institutions), which offer their services (such as clearing or settlement) to numerous institutions. This is rather different from the essential facility cases in transport or telecommunications where there are a limited number of customers of the facility owner who itself is often also present on the downstream market.

9.57   Hence, if one takes the view that competition law is there to protect competition rather than competitors, then given the fact that there are numerous banks already connected to SWIFT, the addition or exclusion of La Poste from its network would have had no significant impact on the level of competition on the downstream market for international transfers. This position, adopted by the US literature and by some European commentators, aims to balance the possible short-term benefits of forcing competitors to share assets against the more long-term drawback of chilling the incentive to invest in production means.[75]

9.58   The Court had not until recently referred to essential facilities in a judgment, although the Commission has based its development of the doctrine in part on the Court's 'refusal to supply' cases. In *Bronner*, Advocate General Jacobs considered that access should be granted only in cases in which 'the dominant undertaking has a genuine stranglehold on the related [ie, downstream] market'.[76] The Court concluded that not only should a refusal to provide a service be likely to eliminate all competition in a downstream market and be incapable of being objectively justified, but also that the service in itself be indispensable to carrying on that person's business, inasmuch as there is no actual or potential substitute.[77]

9.59   The Commission does not require that the newcomer will substantially improve competition in the downstream market; it merely requires that the newcomer could not compete at all in the downstream market without access. The cross-border transfers Notice states that access should be granted where lack of access amounts to a significant barrier to entry to the downstream transfers market, which would be the case if a newcomer could not feasibly gain access to another system or create its own.[78] The Commission's telecoms access Notice requires that access to the facility in question is generally essential in order for companies to compete on a downstream market.[79]

---

[74]   IP(97)870.

[75]   Hovenkamp, 'Federal Antitrust Policy, the Law of Competition and its Practice' at section 7.7, 1994.

[76]   Case C–7/97 *Oscar Bronner v Mediaprint* Opinion of Jacobs AG, 28 May 1998, at para 65.

[77]   Case C–7/97 *Oscar Bronner v Mediaprint* [1998] ECR I–7791.

[78]   Notice on cross-border transfers (n 38 above), para 25.

[79]   Commission Notice on the application of the competition rules to access agreements in the telecommunications sector [1998] OJ C265/2.

Prohibition on Participants to Adhere to Other Payment Systems

A prohibition on members of a system from participating in other, competing, **9.60** systems is likely to fall within Article 81(1). There may be circumstances in which such a prohibition could be exempted; the cross-border transfers Notice states it might be exemptable if required to ensure that an adequate volume of transfers pass through the system.

In 1996 Visa International proposed introducing a rule that would have banned **9.61** its members from issuing some competing cards in Europe. The proposed rule was based on an existing Visa USA rule which prohibits member banks from issuing Discover or American Express cards, or 'any other card deemed competitive', but which allowed them to issue MasterCard, Diners Club and JCB cards. The Commission received complaints from American Express and Dean Witter, the issuer of the Discover Card. The EU Board of Visa International decided to drop the proposal, and as a result the complaints were withdrawn and the investigation was closed without the Commission taking any formal action.[80]

The Commission's services considered that the proposed rule, if adopted, would **9.62** have fallen within Article 81(1) because it would have restricted competition between payment card systems as well as between banks offering international general purpose cards, for two reasons. First, the proposed rule would have led to a restriction on inter-system competition. It would have substantially restricted competition between global general purpose card systems by foreclosing access to a crucial distribution channel. This rule would have impeded card systems other than Visa from licensing the vast majority of EC banks as issuers since Visa includes a substantial majority of the major European banks as its members. If the rule had been adopted, it was unlikely that any of those banks would have risked exclusion from Visa membership because they derive substantial revenue from it, and would lose substantial actual and potential sums were this membership sacrificed. Secondly, the rules would have restricted competition between banks by decreasing the broad range of products they could present to customers. Offering a range of different cards may enhance the services of banks to customers and increase their ability to target particular market segments. It should be noted that, on 7 October 1998, the US Department of Justice filed a lawsuit against Visa and MasterCard. The lawsuit charged that the two credit card systems are limiting credit card competition *inter alia* by not allowing their member banks to issue cards on the competing American Express and Discover/Novus networks.

---

[80] *Report on Competition Policy 1996* (Vol XXVI) 140–141.

Restrictions on Cross-Border Services[81]

9.63 Some payment systems restrict the freedom of their member banks to provide cross-border services, ie issuing cards to cardholders in other Member States and/or acquiring merchants for card transactions in other Member States. For example, some payment systems only allow their member banks to provide cross-border services when they have established a branch or subsidiary in the territory concerned. Moreover, in some payment systems, banks are only allowed to contract with an international merchant for all its activities within the EU (so-called central acquiring) if this merchant fall within certain limited categories, such as car rental companies and international hotels. Merchants falling outside these categories, such as large retailers and petrol companies, will have to conclude contracts with banks in several Member States. Merchants who are restricted in shopping around for a central supplier of a given payment system service of their choice will face higher transaction costs and also higher costs. If found to restrict competition in an appreciable manner (for instance, if the payment system in question holds a material market position), this geographic partitioning of markets seems difficult to justify under either Article 81 or Article 82.

Exclusive Acquisition[82]

9.64 Some payment systems banks or organizations in certain Member States hold an exclusive licence to acquire merchants within their territory. In other Member States, merchant acquirers in some payment systems hold a *de facto* monopoly because they are owned by the issuing banks. Naturally, these exclusive rights have a restrictive effect on intra-system competition.

9.65 Where there is limited inter-system competition, the granting of such an exclusive right or the establishment or maintenance of a *de facto* monopoly would appear to restrict competition, but would probably be acceptable for a start-up period.

(6) Banking Co-operation Agreements

9.66 **Banking co-operation groups.** In the 1970s several banking co-operation groups were set up by banks from different countries. The Commission decided not to open any own initiative procedures in view of the following features of such groups: the usually very loose co-operation within the groups; that the member banks remained free to extend their activities into the national markets of their partners; and that there was no exclusivity between partners for international transactions, and right of first refusal being limited to a small part of such trans-

---

[81] See Negenman (n 37 above) and Gyselen (n 1 above) at 362.
[82] See Negenman (n 37 above).

actions.[83] In 1991 the Commission announced it was sending comfort letters to agreements between European savings banks or their national associations, after seeking amendments to the following types of provisions: agreement not to enter each other's territory, agreement not to conclude similar agreements with other banks in the territory, and exclusivity granted to each partner in its home country for dealing in and distributing common products.[84]

BNP/Dresdner.[85]   In *BNP/Dresdner*, the Commission granted a ten-year   **9.67**
exemption to a wide-ranging co-operation agreement between two large full-service banks in neighbouring Member States. The agreement affected in practice all the banking and financial services markets (except insurance) on which the parties operated. In defining the market, the Commission followed its merger decisions (as to which see the following section) and identified three categories of banking services—retail banking, wholesale banking, and activities related to financial markets—each of which could be divided into a large number of individual markets. The geographic market definitions also followed those found in merger cases. Only in France (for BNP, where it ranked fourth), Germany (for Dresdner, where it ranked second) and Luxembourg (for both) did the parties have any significant activities, and the Commission examined national market shares on many specific (but unidentified in the decision) services. Both parties had low shares in retail banking services (under 10 per cent), but slightly higher shares in wholesale banking (up to 20 per cent).

The Commission found that the agreement restricted competition between the   **9.68**
two banks in France and Germany, but that any restriction on other markets would not be appreciable (including Luxembourg, where the market was very open). Nor was there any restriction on those banking markets that are international in scope; indeed the co-operation was pro-competitive as the two banks would be better able to compete in those markets.[86] The co-operation justified being exempted because consumers would benefit from the improved services that would result from the exchange of know-how between the parties and their distribution of each other's products. The agreement originally contained a wide-ranging reciprocal exclusivity clause (under which either bank could veto the other's proposed co-operation with a home country competitor of the former bank) which the Commission did not consider indispensable. At the Commission's request, the parties agreed to limit the scope of this clause to cases where such co-operation would involve the third party gaining access to know-how or business secrets which originate from the vetoing bank or arise out of the co-operation.

---

[83] *Report on Competition Policy 1972* (Vol II) point 53; *Report on Competition Policy 1978* (Vol VIII) point 33.
[84] IP(91)534.
[85] *Banque Nationale de Paris—Dresdner Bank* [1996] OJ L188/37.
[86] *Banque Nationale de Paris—Dresdner Bank* at paras 15, 16.

(7) Banking Mergers

9.69 The Commission has taken more than sixty decisions on banking mergers. All of these decisions are Article 6(1)(b) clearance decisions. Only one, *Bank Austria/Creditanstalt*,[87] has given rise to some concerns and was authorized on condition that some divestments be effected.

9.70 As can be seen from the discussion below, the Commission does not have a very developed position on the assessment of banking mergers. This contrasts sharply with the position of the American and Canadian agencies. To be fair, this contrasts as well with the application of Articles 81 and 82 where the scarcity of information publicly available makes it difficult to work out the Commission's policy. This is striking in the banking industry where, on the one hand, virtually no issue has as yet arisen in the field of merger control whereas, on the other hand, important issues have arisen in the antitrust field where there is little information available. With monetary union being implemented, it is highly likely that the European banking sector will undertake major restructuring in the next few years. The consolidation has until now taken place within national borders and most of the time has escaped the Commission's competence (the contested bids over the French Société Générale are the most striking examples of this). It is safe to predict that the Commission will be required to develop its thinking on market definition and assessment in the near future.

9.71 **Relevant product market.** In a few cases the Commission has defined with some precision relevant product markets. A relevant product market of the provision of loans to local authorities and other local public authorities was identified in three decisions.[88] The following reasons were given. The customer base is clearly identified and different from other customers such as companies. In addition, it is subject to a different set of rules and regulations. The loans are usually made for a long period of time. They are issued in the national currency and are not secured. Finally, these credits are provided by institutions which are most of the time specialized.

9.72 In one decision, the Commission considered consumer credit according to the products being bought by the debtors.[89] The same goes for leasing activities. In *John Deere Capital Corp/Lombard North Central PLC*, the Commission considered a possible product market consisting of financing leasing for agricultural machinery, equipment, and supplier and related equipment and machinery.[90] Similarly, in *Charterhouse/Porterbrook*, the Commission felt necessary in its assess-

---

[87] *Bank Austria/Creditanstalt* (Case IV/M873) (1997).

[88] *CLF CCB (Dexia)/San Paolo/Crediop* (Case IV/M910) (1997); *CCB/CLF* (Case IV/M736) (1996); and *CLF/HBB* (Case IV/M617) (1995).

[89] *Agos Italfinco* (Case IV/M907) (1997).

[90] *John Deere Capital Corp/Lombard North Central PLC* (Case IV/M823) (1996).

ment of the concentration to check whether the method of financing (with varying terms) the provision of rolling stocks to railway companies had an impact on
its conclusion.[91] In *BHF Bank/Crédit Commercial de France*, the Commission
explained that financing through leasing could be considered in isolation or
within a broader category consisting of all types of financing the purchase of
goods.[92] In *Crédit Agricole/Banque Indosuez*, the Commission also well assessed
the impact of the merger according to the projects being financed in the project
finance sector.[93]

Apart from these few examples where it has defined with some precision some **9.73**
possible relevant product markets, the Commission has in most of its banking
merger decisions limited its analysis to a list of the possible segments of banking
activities which could constitute product markets. The way the different segments have been allocated has fluctuated over the time but, broadly speaking, the
Commission has identified three categories of activities: retail banking, corporate
banking, and investment banking.

Retail banking.   In one of its early decisions, the Commission stated rather **9.74**
clearly the difficulty it faces when trying to define relevant markets in the field of
retail banking: 'each banking product is distinct, but the degree of substitutability
between different products is difficult to appreciate. There is no substitutability
between certain banking services groups but the divisions between others are far
less clear. Banks do not generally offer one type of account or loan so there is a
strong linkage between the different product groups.'[94] Retail banking has been
divided into deposit taking, lending, and payments handling.[95] Deposit taking
activities include all types of accounts and other savings instruments. The
Commission has not indicated whether these different products constitute distinct relevant markets and has always left open the question of market delineation.
Lending activities within retail banking include the provision of loans to individuals or households; these can be short-term loans, consumer credits, or mortgage
credits. Finally, payments handling deals with the issue of cheques and payment
cards which are linked to current account handling. In some cases, the
Commission has also identified some activities which could be associated with
retail banking. For instance, private banking, credit cards, securities portfolio
operations, investment management, and fund management have been singled
out.

---

[91] *Charterhouse/Porterbrook* (Case IV/M669) (1995).
[92] *BHF Bank/Crédit Commercial de France* (Case IV/M710) (1996).
[93] *Crédit Agricole/Banque Indosuez* (Case IV/M756) (1996).
[94] *Fortis/CGER* (Case IV/M342) (1993).
[95] See for example *Fortis/Mees Pierson* (Case IV/M850) (1997); *Bank Austria/Creditanstalt* (Case
IV/M873) (1997); or *Société Générale/Hambros Bank* (Case IV/M1096) (1998).

9.75 *Corporate banking.* Corporate banking deals with banking activities with non-banking organizations. It comprises in particular the following product segments:[96] payments handling (especially electronic banking services), deposit operations, lending operations, documentary business, and foreign trade financing. Lending operations as a whole can be divided basically into short-term lending (business loans) and long-term lending (investment credit). Furthermore, in view of the special conditions attaching to the granting of loans and the different legal and competitive ground rules in this field, loans with a public assistance component (development loans) may be considered separately. Obviously, this description could be refined and some decisions address more specific segments. This is the case for instance of project finance in *Crédit Agricole/Banque Indosuez*.[97] In addition, leasing or factoring activities are sometimes added in the corporate banking category or put in an 'other' category.

9.76 In some decisions, the Commission has considered that the relevant geographic markets may differ according to the category of customers to which corporate banking services are provided.[98] This might be interpreted as meaning that product markets should also be split according to the categories of customers.

9.77 *Investment banking.* Finally, investment banking comprises in particular the product segments of mergers and acquisition consultancy (sometimes more accurately described as corporate finance advisory), stock market listing, and the issue of shares and bonds (primary market).[99] Bond issuing as a whole can be divided further into the flotation of government bonds and non-bank bonds, and own issues by banks. Trading activities (such as trade in shares and bonds, derivative operations, on money markets, etc) are sometimes attributed to investment banking and sometimes assigned to a fourth category called money market and securities operations. The same goes for asset management activities such as marketing of unit trusts or provision of portfolio management.

9.78 **Relevant geographic market.** The Commission has consistently defined the geographic scope of any possible retail banking product market as being national. Some corporate banking activities may be of a national dimension while some others may be international in scope. For instance, the provision of such services to local or small and medium enterprises is deemed to be national.[100] Similarly, the provision of credits to local authorities has been found to have a national dimension. This would be due to the fact that the demand is currently met by nationally

---

[96] *Bank Austria/Creditanstalt* (Case IV/M873) (1997).
[97] *Crédit Agricole/Banque Indosuez* (Case IV/M756) (1996).
[98] See for example *Merita/Nordbanken* (Case IV/M1029) (1997).
[99] See for example *Bank Austria/Creditanstalt* (Case IV/M873) (1997) and *Swiss Bank/SG Warburg* (Case IV/M597) (1995).
[100] *Société Générale/Hambros Bank* (Case IV/M1096) (1998) or *Merita/Nordbanken* (Case IV/M1029) (1997).

based supply, that some small local authorities have not the means to look for foreign suppliers, and that local authorities are subject to national rules and regulations.[101] Conversely, the geographic market for the financing of high investments was said to be wider than national in *BHF Bank/Crédit Commercial de France* because the demand would look for the optimal solution even if it is provided across borders.[102]

As to investment banking activities, the Commission's current thinking seems to **9.79** be that some geographic markets are international and some others are national.[103] The Commission believes that the services which usually require detailed knowledge of national company law and business structures, corporate accounting, and local market characteristics, will still be required and supplied at national level for the foreseeable future. This applies to services relating to mergers and acquisitions, stock market listing, and the issue of shares and bonds and in particular to the flotation of local authority bonds. The Commission adds that government bonds are issued as a rule in the respective national currency. It is, however, difficult to understand why the nature of the currency has an impact on the geographic extent of the market. On the other hand possible product markets, such as trading activities, are considered to be international.

Comments on relevant market definition. Until now, the Commission has **9.80** never had to define thoroughly relevant markets in the banking industry. Only in the *Bank Austria/Creditanstalt* case could it have had to produce such an effort. However, the decision in that case does not include such definition, probably due to it being a first phase decision where there is little time to devote to an in-depth analysis of the extent of relevant markets. The Commission is, however, facing a number of issues as concerns relevant markets in the banking industry.

First, the Commission's decisions have fluctuated and are still fluctuating on the **9.81** list of activities covered by banking mergers. It would certainly be helpful if the contents of different banking activities were more stable.

Secondly, the Commission has never considered the issue of supply side substi- **9.82** tutability. As is the case for insurance activities, it could very well be argued that any bank could rapidly expand its presence in a given segment simply because it is already active in another segment.

Thirdly, the definition of geographic markets seems to be rather arbitrary. For **9.83** instance, it is interesting to note that, in the US, geographic markets for banking

---

[101] *CLF CCB (Dexia)/San Paolo/Crediop* (Case IV/M910) (1997); *CCB/CLF* (Case IV/M736) (1996); and *CLF/HBB* (Case IV/M617) (1995).
[102] *BHF Bank/Crédit Commercial de France* (Case IV/M710) (1996).
[103] See for example *Bank Austria/Creditanstalt* (Case IV/M873) (1997) and *Swiss Bank/SG Warburg* (Case IV/M597) (1995).

services provided to households or small companies are found to be local (based on commuting statistics).

9.84 Fourthly, the Commission has never considered the possibility of cluster markets in the banking field (ie when customers tend to purchase some services from the same provider). It might be the case for some categories of customers which tend to be captive, such as individuals for basic banking services or small and medium enterprises for a range of services. Other competition authorities have been faced with the same challenges. For instance, the assessment of bank mergers by the US Federal Reserve Board is based on a cluster of products approach, the assumption being that consumers buy bundles of banking products.[104] However, since 1986, the Department of Justice has rejected the cluster approach and has disaggregated the product market into its constituent parts.[105] Similarly, the Canadian Competition Bureau has recently published guidelines to assess bank mergers.[106] Concerning product markets, these guidelines propose to follow the Department of Justice approach. These guidelines were applied to the proposed merger of the Royal Bank of Canada and Bank of Montreal and that of the Toronto-Dominion Bank (TD) and the Canadian Imperial Bank of Commerce (CIBC) at the same time.[107] In its analysis, the Canadian Bureau concluded that the proposed mergers would have resulted in a substantial lessening of competition in a number of local markets (more than a hundred) for personal transaction accounts, personal loans/lines of credit, and residential mortgages. In addition, it identified various Provinces where there would have been substantial lessening of competition for mid-market businesses with operating loans between Canadian $1 million and Canadian $5 million. As to credit cards, the Bureau examined the impact of the mergers on the general purpose cards network services, issuing services, and acquiring services. It concluded that there might be problems in the first and the last of these services. Finally, the Bureau assessed the effects of the mergers on local markets for securities brokerage and in the national market for the underwriting of equity issues exceeding Canadian $50 million.

9.85 **Assessment of dominance.** In the *Bank Austria/Creditanstalt* case there were a number of instances where the combined market shares could have reached levels in the region of or above 30 per cent. According to the Commission, there were valid reasons to suppose that the concentration would lead to the creation or strengthening of a dominant position in two markets: retail lending and retail portfolio management. This was the case because the competitors were many

---

[104] *US v Philadelphia National Bank* 374 US 321 (1963).
[105] Michael Greenspan and Jacqueline T Coclough, 'The relevant product market for banks acquisitions' (Summer 1996) *The Antitrust Bulletin*.
[106] The Merger Enforcement Guidelines as Applied to a Bank Merger, 15 July 1998.
[107] Canadian Competition Bureau's letters to the Royal Bank and Bank of Montreal of 11 December 1998 and to the CIBC and TD Bank of 14 December 1998.

times smaller than the combined entity would have been and because the Austrian banking market revealed considerable barriers to entry. Barriers to entry would result from the need for banks to be present locally through a network of branches. In addition, customers would be very loyal due to the information and transaction costs associated with changing from one institution to another. This would be demonstrated by the low penetration achieved by foreign banks in those markets. This reasoning bears many similarities with the one presented in the *AXA/UAP* decision in the insurance sector.[108] Similar conclusions were reached in the corporate banking field regarding deposit activities, long-term lending, and documentary business. Following the undertaking by Bank Austria to the Commission that a third bank, GiroCredit controlled by Bank Austria and Credit-anstalt, would be divested, the Commission concluded that with market shares below 30 per cent the parties could not achieve dominance.

This assessment contrasts with those carried out in other cases. For instance, in **9.86** *Merita/Nordbanken*, the Commission found that market entry in corporate bank-ing markets in Finland by foreign banks is considered to be likely and easy.[109] Therefore, despite Merita holding a market share of 50 per cent for deposits and Nordbanken being one of the three main banks in a neighbouring country, the merger did not give rise to any competition concern. According to the Commission, barriers to entry would be decreasing because of the European deregulation and could further decrease thanks to the highly innovative and evolving nature of the banking market combined with the recent increase of elec-tronic banking tools.

The calculation of market shares has proved to be difficult for the Commission in **9.87** the field of investment banking activities. In the absence of any industry consen-sus on the size of the market, the Commission has relied on so-called league tables which provide a ranking of the investment banks in the provision of specific services such as mergers and acquisitions, underwriting, etc.[110] For instance, the Commission concluded that a market share for M&A advice of 60 per cent (supposedly calculated on the basis of league tables even if this is not indi-cated in the decision) in Germany would not mean the creation or strengthening of a dominant position because such shares are incidental and erratic. This would come from the absence of an active market for corporate control and the fact that in smaller economies there are a limited number of transactions. In addition, the Commission noted that there were a number of investment banks which com-peted with the notifying parties.It is worth noting that none of the Commission's decisions include an assessment of a concentration as to its effects on the creation or the strengthening of a collective dominant position. It would, however, seem

---

[108] *AXA/UAP* (Case IV/M862) (1996).
[109] *Merita/Nordbanken* (Case IV/M1029) (1997).
[110] See for example *Dresdner Bank/Kleinwort Benson* (Case IV/M611) (1995).

that this is a market which could be prone to such behaviours (mature market, homogeneous products, prices transparent, barriers to entry, etc) if the concentration ratio was high enough. Another topic which has not been dealt with as yet concerns the thresholds above which a bank might hold a dominant position. The *Bank Austria/Creditanstalt* decision has put such a threshold at 30 per cent if there were no direct competitor and if barriers to entry were high. It could also be argued that since banks refinance each other on interbank markets, the relative position of banks is of paramount importance to determine their possible market power.

D. Insurance[111]

(1) Introduction

9.88 Block exemption. As a result of the Court's *German Fire Insurance* judgment (see paragraph 9.91 below), which confirmed the application of the competition rules to the insurance sector, the Commission received over 300 notifications. In order to help deal with commonly occurring agreements that were capable of exemption the Commission has adopted a block exemption regulation, Regulation 3932/92.[112] On the basis of the experience gained from individual decisions, four categories of agreements have been block exempted: the calculation of pure premiums, the drawing up of standard policy conditions for direct insurance, pooling arrangements (co-insurance groups and co-reinsurance groups), and common rules for approving security devices.[113] The block exemption does not cover two further categories of agreement included in the Council enabling Regulation: the settlement of claims, and registers of, and information on, aggravated risks.

9.89 The Commission's block exemption Regulation entered into force on 1 April 1993 and is valid for ten years. As required by the Regulation, the Commission has prepared a report on the operation of the block exemption.[114]

---

[111] Anthony Fitzsimmons, *Insurance Competition Law* (Graham & Trotman/Martinus Nijhoff, 1994).

[112] Commission Regulation (EEC) 3932/92 of 21 December 1992 on the application of Article 81(3) of the Treaty to certain categories of agreements, decisions and concerted practices in the insurance sector [1992] OJ L398/7. The Council enabling legislation is Council Regulation (EEC) 1534/91 of 31 May 1991 on the application of Article 81(3) of the Treaty to certain categories of agreements, decisions and concerted practices in the insurance sector [1991] OJ L143/1.

[113] Titles II, III, IV, and V of the Regulation respectively.

[114] Report from the Commission to the Council and the European Parliament on the operation of Commission Regulation 3932/92, COM(1999)192 final, 12 May 1999. Hereafter, 'Block exemption report'.

(2) Horizontal Agreements on Price

Distinction between commercial premium, risk premium, and pure premium. **9.90**
A commercial premium (also known as a gross premium) is the price charged to
the policyholder. This end price can be broken down into (1) a risk premium,
itself consisting of (a) a pure premium (also known as a net premium) based on
statistical evidence from the past, and (b) an adjustment to reflect future developments; and (2) overheads, profits, and, for insurers that do not insure a spread of
risks corresponding to those upon which the pure premium is calculated, a security charge. Trade associations have often been involved in calculating pure premiums, drawing *inter alia* on data provided by their members. The basic principle
under the competition rules is that agreements on commercial premiums are prohibited, but that agreements on pure premiums can be exempted. As an exception
to this basic principle, insurers operating within co-insurance pools must necessarily agree commercial premiums and policy conditions; such pools are acceptable under certain conditions, as discussed below (see paragraphs 9.104 and
following).

Prohibition of agreements on commercial premiums. Agreements that set or **9.91**
recommend uniform commercial premiums are straightforward price-fixing
agreements falling within Article 81(1)(a) and not capable of being exempted.[115]
In *German Fire Insurance*,[116] the German Association of Property Insurers (VdS),
recommended increases in industrial fire and consequential loss insurance premiums of 10, 20, or 30 per cent in specified circumstances. Although the recommendation was stated to be non-binding, the Court held that it constituted 'the
faithful reflection of the applicant's resolve to coordinate the conduct of its members'.[117] The recommendation was stated in mandatory terms, and German reinsurers decided to treat premiums not following the recommendation as
under-insurance in the event of a claim.

In *Lloyd's Underwriters' Association and The Institute of London Underwriters*,[118] **9.92**
two agreements relating to marine hull insurance were found to infringe Article
81(1) in the following ways. The Joint Hull Understandings agreement recommended minimum increases in premiums, fixed the rate of increase in
deductibles, and fixed the rebate paid for prompt cash payment and for deferred
payment. The Respect of Lead Agreement restricted price competition by

---

[115] *Report on Competition Policy 1972* (Vol II) points 55 and 56; *Nuovo CEGAM* [1984]OJ
L99/29, para 21; *Fire Insurance* [1985] OJ L35/20, Case 45/86 *Verband der Sacheversicherer* [1987]
ECR 405, 454–455; *Lloyd's Underwriters' Association and The Institute of London Underwriters*
[1993] OJ L 4/26.
[116] *Fire Insurance* [1985] OJ L35/20, Case 45/86 *Verband der Sacheversicherer* [1987] ECR 405,
454–455.
[117] See para 32.
[118] *Lloyd's Underwriters' Association and The Institute of London Underwriters* [1993] OJ L 4/26.

prohibiting members from participating in a co-insurance contract unless there were two lead underwriters from each association, and required that the same leading underwriters were to be used upon renewal of co-insured policies. The infringing provisions were abandoned by the associations and the Commission adopted a negative clearance decision.

9.93 **Block exemption for pure premiums.**[119] Title II of the block exemption Regulation exempts the joint calculation of pure premiums, the joint establishment of frequency tables (in respect of insurance involving capitalization), and the carrying out of studies on the impact of circumstances external to the companies concerned.[120] Such agreements are considered beneficial because they improve the knowledge of risks and facilitate the individual companies' rating of risk.[121] In order to limit the co-operation to what is necessary to achieve those benefits the exemption is subject to three conditions.[122] First, any calculation, tables, or studies must include a statement that they are purely illustrative; moreover, the benefit of the exemption is expressly removed when undertakings agree not to use different calculations, tables, or studies.[123] Secondly, any calculation or tables must not include loadings for contingencies, profits, or administrative and other costs; this condition is the natural consequence of the prohibition of agreements on commercial premiums. Thirdly, the individual insurers concerned must not be identified; this condition implements the general principle that any information exchange should be limited to aggregated statistics or general studies and not extend to competitive information relating to individual undertakings.

9.94 *Calculations and studies must be genuine.*   Pure premiums and frequency tables should be the result of a genuine statistical calculation. Thus the Regulation requires that frequency tables be 'based on the assembly of data, spread over a number of risk-years chosen as an observation period, which relate to identical or comparable risks in sufficient number to constitute a base which can be handled statistically and which will yield figures on (inter alia) the number of claims during the said period, the number of individual risks insured in each risk-year . . ., the total amounts paid or payable . . . during the said period, [and] the total amount of capital insured for each risk-year . . .'.[124] A calculation not supported by any statistical data will not fall within the block exemption, nor, at the other end of the scale, will a calculation that results in a classification of types of risk that is so detailed as to go further than what is necessary to establish a reliable basis for calculating pure premiums.[125] Studies should be based on justifiable hypotheses,

---

[119] See Block exemption report, paras 4–12.
[120] Article 2.
[121] Recital (6).
[122] Article 3.
[123] Article 4.
[124] Article 2(a).
[125] Gyselen (n 1 above) 369–370.

and the Regulation expressly provides that the Commission can withdraw the benefit of the block exemption where they are not.[126]

Individual exemption.　In two individual decisions prior to the block exemp- **9.95** tion Regulation, the Commission exempted the joint fixing of pure premiums. In *Nuovo CEGAM*, an Italian association of insurers agreed to apply jointly fixed pure premiums for industrial engineering insurance.[127] This appears a more restrictive arrangement than would be allowed under the block exemption (where companies may not agree to apply the jointly agreed pure premiums). However, the members of the Nuovo CEGAM collectively had a 26 per cent market share while their largest competitor had a 25 per cent market share. The Commission found that the agreement brought new competition onto the market. The facilitation of new entry was also considered a benefit justifying the exemption in *Concordato Incendio*, even though the members of the Concordato collectively had over 50 per cent market share and its largest four members had a 28 per cent market share as against the largest four non-members' 23 per cent share.[128] The Regulation does not contain any market share threshold in relation to agreements on pure premiums.

(3) Standard Policy Conditions

Block exemption.[129]　Title III of the block exemption Regulation exempts stan- **9.96** dard policy conditions for direct insurance and, in respect of insurance involving capitalization, common models illustrating the profits to be realized.[130] Jointly agreed standard conditions and common models are considered to be beneficial because they improve the comparability of cover for the consumer and allow risks to be classified more uniformly.[131] In order to avoid the standardization of products the exemption is subject to the conditions that any standard policy conditions must include a statement that they are purely illustrative and must mention the possibility that different conditions may be agreed.[132] The benefit of the exemption is expressly removed when undertakings agree not to apply conditions other than the standard conditions.[133] The exemption is subject to the condition that common illustrative models must also be only for guidance, and the benefit of the exemption is expressly removed when the common models include only specified interest rates or include administrative costs, and when undertakings agree not to use models other than the common models.[134] In order to ensure

---

[126] Article 17.
[127] *Nuovo CEGAM* [1984] OJ L99/29.
[128] *Concordato Incendio* [1990] OJ L15/25.
[129] See Block exemption report, paras 13–24.
[130] Article 5.
[131] Recital (7).
[132] Article 6(1)(a) and (b).
[133] Article 7(2).
[134] Articles 6(2), 9(1), 9(2).

transparency *vis-à-vis* customers, and not just between insurers, standard policy conditions must be accessible and provided simply upon request.[135]

9.97 *'Black' list.* The exemption contains a long 'black' list of clauses which systematically exclude specific types of risk, or provide for an excessively long contractual period, or constitute tying clauses.[136] The exemption does not apply if the standard policy conditions contain clauses which:

(a) exclude from the cover losses normally relating to the class of insurance concerned, without indicating explicitly that each insurer remains free to extend the cover to such events;

(b) make the cover of certain risks subject to specific conditions, without indicating explicitly that each insurer remains free to waive them;

(c) impose comprehensive cover including risks to which a significant number of policyholders are not simultaneously exposed, without indicating explicitly that each insurer remains free to propose separate cover;

(d) indicate the amount of the cover or the part which the policyholder must pay himself (the 'excess');

(e) allow the insurer to maintain the policy in the event that it cancels part of the cover, increases the premium without the risk or the scope of the cover being changed (without prejudice to indexation clauses), or otherwise alters the policy conditions without the express consent of the policyholder;

(f) allow the insurer to modify the term of the policy without the express consent of the policyholder;

(g) impose on the policyholder in the non-life assurance sector a contract period of more than three years;

(h) impose a renewal period of more than one year where the policy is automatically renewed unless notice is given upon the expiry of a given period;

(i) require the policyholder to agree to the reinstatement of a policy which has been suspended on account of the disappearance of the insured risk, if he is once again exposed to a risk of the same nature;

(j) require the policyholder to obtain cover from the same insurer for different risks;

(k) require the policyholder, in the event of disposal of the object of insurance, to make the acquirer take over the insurance policy.

9.98 Although specific insurance conditions for particular social or occupational categories of the population may be established, the exemption will not apply to agreements which exclude the coverage of certain risk categories because of the characteristics associated with the policyholder.[137] Moreover, the Commission can

---

[135] Recital (9) and Article 6(1)(c).
[136] Article 7(1).
[137] Article 8.

withdraw the benefit of the block exemption where the standard policy conditions contain clauses other than those 'black' listed which create a significant imbalance between the rights and obligations arising from the contract to the detriment of the policyholder.[138]

Individual exemption. In *Concordato Incendio* the Commission exempted not only standard policy conditions, which members were free to derogate from, but also a requirement that members notify the Concordato of any such derogation that might affect the statistics used to calculate the pure premium.[139] The requirement to notify would seem likely to encourage the members to follow the standard conditions, but was held to be necessary to guarantee the reliability of the statistics. The Commission might now be less likely to accept a requirement to notify derogations given that the block exemption clearly requires standard policy conditions to be non-binding.

9.99

(4) Security Devices

Block exemption.[140] Title V of the block exemption Regulation exempts agreements on technical specifications and procedures for assessing and certifying the compliance with such specifications of *security devices* and their installation and maintenance, and rules for evaluating and approving *installation undertakings* or *maintenance undertakings*.[141] A long list of conditions are set out in order to ensure that when manufacturers of security devices and installation and maintenance undertakings apply for evaluation both the substantive specifications and the certification procedures are governed by objective, proportionate, and non-discriminatory criteria.[142] The agreed specifications and rules must be provided simply upon request, and must include a statement that insurers are free to accept devices or installation and maintenance undertakings which do not comply with those specifications and rules.[143]

9.100

European standards. The block exemption Regulation aims to promote specifications at the European level, consistent with the Commission's approach to technical harmonization and standardization considered essential to the functioning of internal markets.[144] The exemption provision itself refers to 'technical specifications, in particular technical specifications intended as future European norms'.[145] The Commission can therefore be expected to scrutinize specifications

9.101

---

[138] Article 17.
[139] *Concordato Incendio* [1990] OJ L15/25.
[140] See Block exemption report, paras 34–41.
[141] Article 14.
[142] Article 15(a), (b), (e)–(l).
[143] Article 15(d), (c).
[144] Recitals (15) and (16).
[145] Article 14.

drawn up by national associations of insurers to assess if they have the object or effect of creating entry barriers.[146]

(5) Claims Settlement[147]

9.102 Claims settlement agreements aim to simplify the settlement of claims between insurers. For example, under a 'knock for knock' agreement each insurer pays its own policyholder regardless of liability. The Commission has not taken any formal decision dealing with agreements on claims settlement. Nor did it include such agreements in the block exemption Regulation although empowered so to do by the Council enabling Regulation. The Commission has, however, sent comfort letters where such agreements have been notified.[148] Such agreements are acceptable where, first, they lead to cost savings and, secondly, they relate to small claims and are unlikely to distort commercial premiums. Insurers are only likely to enter into such an agreement when the cost benefits from simplified procedures outweigh the possibility that the agreement will result in imbalances in payments made by any particular insurer. However, such agreements should not contain provisions harming consumers, such as unjustified limitations on policyholders' legal rights.

(6) Registers of, and Information on, Aggravated Risks[149]

9.103 Registers of aggravated risks allow insurers more accurately to assess risk and therefore better calculate premiums. This is another matter which the Commission did not include in the block exemption Regulation although empowered so to do by the Council enabling Regulation. Such registers lead to an exchange of information between insurers. However, provided there are no accompanying restrictions on insurers' behaviour, such registers are unlikely to raise competition concerns.[150] An accompanying agreement to refuse insurance, or to charge higher premiums, will be an unexemptable agreement falling within Article 81(1).

(7) Co-Insurance and Co-Reinsurance Pools

9.104 The insurance industry is characterized by the spreading of risks. Policyholders pay premiums to direct insurers for their insurance policies. Direct insurers can in turn insure part or all of the risk with a reinsurer. Reinsurers can also reinsure other reinsurers, a transaction known as retrocession. Risks can also be spread by the use of pools. A pool is a group of co-insurers or co-reinsurers each of which assumes a

---

[146] Gyselen (n 1 above) 390.
[147] See Block exemption report, paras 42–46.
[148] *Report on Competition Policy 1996* (Vol XXVI), 131–132. See also Gyselen (n 1 above) 390–392.
[149] See Block exemption report, paras 47–49.
[150] Gyselen (n above) 392–393.

share of the business of the pool. Reinsurance, co-insurance, and co-reinsurance are all means by which individual insurers increase capacity to accept more risks and as such can increase the supply of insurance. Bilateral reinsurance contracts will not normally raise competition concerns in the absence of wider agreements restricting the commercial freedom of direct insurers or reinsurers. Pools, on the other hand, where they go beyond what is necessary to allow their members to provide a type of insurance that they could not provide alone, can fall within Article 81(1) but in view of the benefits they bring can be exempted under certain conditions.

9.105 In assessing the competitive impact of a particular pool, it is necessary to consider both internal competition between participants in the pool, and external competition faced by the pool from other insurers and pools.

9.106 **Applicability of Article 81(1).** Under the Commission's *de minimis* Notice a pool will not be considered appreciably to restrict competition if the combined market share of its members is below 5 per cent.[151] Furthermore, even if a pool has a higher market share, the Commission has now clarified its policy by stating that it does not consider a pool to fall within Article 81(1) if it allows its participants to enter a market they could not otherwise have entered, in particular in order to cover a sufficient number of a particular type of risk in order to reduce the potential spread between premiums and claims to a safe level.[152] Thus, a Commission inquiry into aviation insurance pools found that most covered large shares of national markets for small aviation risks and did not appear necessary in order to allow their members to be present on those markets. The Commission found there to be insufficient Community interest to bring infringement proceedings but warned the pools of the possibility of action by national competition authorities.[153]

9.107 **P&I Clubs.** The Commission has also applied its new policy to arrangements concluded within the International Group (IG) of P&I clubs. P&I clubs are mutual non-profit associations of shipowners, charterers and operators which provide their members with protection & indemnity (P&I) insurance. Such insurance provides cover against third-party liabilities such as injury or death of crew members or third parties, damage to cargo, collision damage, and pollution; the clubs within the IG represent 89 per cent of the worldwide market for P&I

---

[151] Notice on agreements of minor importance which do not fall under Article 85 [now Article 81(1)] of the Treaty establishing the European Community [1997] OJ C372/13.

[152] Block exemption report, para 28; *Report on Competition Policy 1998* (Vol XXVIII) point 112; Gyselen (n 1 above) 374, 385–387; C Esteva, 'The application of the EU competition rules to the insurance sector. Past developments and current priorities' (1997) 94 British Insurance Law Association Journal page 26.

[153] Block exemption report, para 30; *Report on Competition Policy 1998* (Vol XXVIII) points 114 and 115.

insurance. Under the Pooling Agreement, each club meets the first 4.57 million euros of any claim (called the club's 'retention'); the excess of any claim over 4.57 million euros and up to 27.42 million euros is shared between all the clubs; the IG itself purchases reinsurance for the excess of claims over claims above 27.42 million euros and up to 3.9 billion euros; any 'overspill' above 3.9 billion euros is again shared between the clubs. The mutual insurance arrangements within each club are not considered to fall within Article 81(1), but the arrangements between them concluded within the IG have caused concern.[154] In 1985, after changes were made to the then IG Agreement, in particular with the aim of easing the restrictions of members to change club, the Commission granted a ten-year exemption. When the arrangements came to an end, the Commission issued a statement of objections but, after amendments to the arrangements, adopted a new decision approving them.[155]

9.108 The Commission found that the claims sharing arrangements fell outside Article 81(1), because the level of cover could only be offered by insuring more than 50 per cent of worldwide shipping tonnage. There was therefore no room for a second viable supplier. The Commission also gave negative clearance to restrictions that were indispensable to the claims sharing, ie: provisions in the Pooling Agreement providing for a minimum level of cover (after this had been reduced from 16.5 billion euros to 3.9 billion euros, following the statement of objections), the common approval of policy conditions, and the joint purchase of reinsurance; and rules in the IG Agreement relating to release calls (claimed by a club in the event of a shipowner moving to a new club). However, two provisions of the IG Agreement in so far as they related to retention costs (ie, the costs of claims up to 4.57 million euros that are not shared) were found to fall within Article 81(1): the rules for making quotations for vessels (which restricted the freedom of clubs to compete on the rates to be quoted for vessels joining them), and rules on a minimum cost for insuring tankers. However, the Commission exempted these restrictions after the amendments to change the quotation procedures allowing clubs to compete over the part of the rate corresponding to their administrative costs; the clubs will, in addition, publish information allowing shipowners to compare the administrative costs of different clubs. The Commission also granted negative clearance under Article 82 to the notified arrangements.

9.109 In two earlier individual exemption decisions the Commission had decided that the pools under examination restricted competition within Article 81(1). Those decisions should now be read in the light of the Commission's current policy towards pools described above. In *TEKO*, a co-insurance pool for space insurance restricted competition because, even if space insurance could in general be under-

---

[154] *P&I Clubs* [1985] OJ L376/2, at para 22.
[155] *P&I Clubs* [1999] OJ L125/12.

written only on a co-insurance basis, the parties had opted for a permanent and institutionalized pool rather than co-operating on a case-by-case basis and, further, they jointly rather than individually reinsured the risks.[156]

In *TEKO* and *Assurpol*, co-reinsurance pools were considered to restrict competition again because they were permanent and institutionalized co-operation for which there were less restrictive alternatives.[157] Restrictions occurred at three levels. At the direct insurance level, the members were not required to reinsure within the pool, but if they did so they were required to follow (in *Assurpol*) or in practice did follow (in *TEKO*) the premiums calculated by the pool (pure premium plus co-reinsurance premium in *Assurpol*; minimum commercial premium in *TEKO*). That was considered to go further than the normal influence of reinsurers over direct insurers, since reinsurers generally confined themselves to checking the premiums and terms set by the direct insurers.[158] At the reinsurance level, by creating a pool the members refrained from competing with one another for reinsurance cover.[159] At the retrocession level, the members of *Assurpol* agreed not to retrocede individually their share in the co-reinsured risks; they thus refrained from competing with one another for retrocession facilities.[160]

9.110

Block exemption.[161] Title IV of the block exemption Regulation exempts agreements relating to what it calls 'co-insurance groups' and 'co-reinsurance groups'. These groups are referred to in this section as 'pools'. Pools are considered to be beneficial because they allow a greater number of insurers to enter the market and as a result increase the available capacity for covering in particular risks that are difficult to cover because of their scale, rarity, or novelty.[162] The benefit of the block exemption is not, however, limited to particular risks; instead, pools relating to all types of risk are covered, but one of the grounds on which the Commission may withdraw the benefit of the exemption is where participants in the pool would not encounter any significant difficulties in operating individually on the relevant market.[163]

9.111

The block exemption is limited to pools set up by insurers possibly, in the case of co-reinsurance pools, 'with the assistance of one or more' reinsurers.[164] Pools set up only by reinsurers are not covered by the block exemption, the Commission not having sufficient experience in the field.[165] The Regulation gives no guidance

9.112

---

[156] *TEKO* [1990] OJ L13/34, at paras 22 and 23.
[157] *TEKO* [1990] OJ L13/34, at para 20; *Assurpol* [1992] OJ L37/16, at paras 27, 30.
[158] *TEKO* [1990] OJ L13/34, at paras 18, 19; *Assurpol* [1992] OJ L37/16, at paras 28, 30.
[159] *TEKO* [1990] OJ L13/34, at paras 21, 23; *Assurpol* [1992] OJ L37/16, at paras 29, 31.
[160] *Assurpol* [1992] OJ L37/16, at paras 29, 32.
[161] See Block exemption report, paras 25–33.
[162] Recital (10).
[163] Article 17(a).
[164] Article 10(2).
[165] Recital (14).

as to the extent to which reinsurance companies can participate in block exempted pools, but in *Assurpol* the Commission granted an individual exemption to a co-reinsurance pool made up of fifty direct insurers and fourteen reinsurers; the reinsurers had 54.5 per cent of pool capacity and participated in the decision-making bodies.[166]

9.113 *Exempted restrictions.* The pool agreements may determine the nature and characteristics of the risks covered, and the shares allocated to each participant, as well as the conditions for admission to, withdrawal from, and management of the group.[167] Further restrictions are exempted in respect of each type of pool. Although there is no 'black' list of prohibited clauses, the regulation makes it clear that the exemption is limited to the restrictions expressly permitted. In particular, an obligation to bring all risks into the pool (a so-called 'obligation d'apport') is not covered by the block exemption, being considered an excessive restriction of competition.[168] Such a restriction would therefore have to be considered on its merits on an individual notification.

9.114 Co-insurance pools may agree on the following restrictions, but no others: (a) the obligations to take preventive measures into account, to use the general or specific insurance conditions accepted by the group, to use the commercial premiums set by the group; (b) the obligation to submit to the group for approval any settlement of a claim relating to a co-insured risk; (c) the obligation to entrust to the group the negotiation of reinsurance agreements on behalf of all concerned; and (d) a ban on reinsuring the individual share of the co-insured risk.[169]

9.115 Co-reinsurance pools may determine the level of retentions (the amounts which the participants do not pass on for co-reinsurance) and the cost of co-reinsurance (which includes both the pool's operating costs and the remuneration of the participants in their capacity as co-reinsurers).[170] Co-reinsurance pools may also agree on the following restrictions, but no others: (a) the obligations to take preventive measures into account, to use the general or specific insurance conditions accepted by the group, to use a common risk premium tariff for direct insurance calculated by the group, and to participate in the cost of the co-reinsurance; (b) the obligation to submit to the group for approval the settlement of claims relating to the co-reinsured risks and exceeding a specified amount, or to pass such claims on to it for settlement; (c) the obligation to entrust to the group the negotiation of retrocession agreements on behalf of all concerned; and (d) a ban on

---

[166] *Assurpol* [1992] OJ L37/16, at paras 6–12.
[167] Article 10(3).
[168] Recital (13).
[169] Article 12.
[170] Article 10(4).

reinsuring the individual retention or retroceding the individual share of the co-reinsured risk.[171]

Condition relating to market shares.   In order to ensure that pools are faced by **9.116** effective competition, the block exemption contains a market share test. The exemption applies on condition that the insurance products underwritten by the participants or on their behalf do not, on any relevant market, exceed, in the case of a co-insurance pool, 10 per cent or, in the case of co-reinsurance pools, 15 per cent.[172] There is a lower market share for co-insurance pools because the co-insurance requires agreement on commercial premiums and policy conditions with the result that residual competition between members of the pool is particularly reduced.[173]

The 10 per cent and 15 per cent limits apply to *all* products in the relevant mar- **9.117** ket underwritten by the participants, whether through the pool or individually including through 'connected undertakings'.[174] Connected undertakings include parent, subsidiary, and group companies as defined in the Regulation.[175] A derogation applies to pools which underwrite catastrophic risks where claims are both rare and large or aggravated risks where claims are more frequent because of the characteristics of the risk insured. In these cases the 10 per cent and 15 per cent limits apply only to products underwritten through the pool.[176] However, the derogation is subject to two conditions. First, none of the insurers shall participate in another pool that covers risks on the same market. Secondly, with respect to pools which cover aggravated risks, the insurance products brought into the group shall not represent more than 15 per cent of all identical or similar products underwritten by the participants or on their behalf on the relevant market. The effect of the derogation and its conditions is as follows. Participants in a (co-insurance or co-reinsurance) pool for catastrophic risks can individually underwrite as much business as they like without running the risk of losing the benefit of the block exemption, provided that the risks underwritten through the pool do not exceed the 10 per cent or 15 per cent market share limit. Participants in a (co-insurance or co-reinsurance) pool for aggravated risks must individually underwrite at least 85 per cent of their business in the relevant market outside the pool, and the risks underwritten through the pool must not exceed the 10 per cent or 15 per cent market share limit.

The Commission can withdraw the benefit of the block exemption where a **9.118** pool falling within the market share limits has such a position with respect to

---

[171] Article 13.
[172] Article 11(1)(a).
[173] Recital (11).
[174] Article 16(1).
[175] Article 16(2), 16(3).
[176] Article 11(2).

aggravated risks that the policyholders encounter considerable difficulties in finding cover outside this group.[177] This will normally not be the case where a pool
covers less than 25 per cent of those risks.[178]

9.119 *Calculation of market shares.*   The Regulation gives little guidance on market definition. Insurers and insurance supervisors are used to distinguishing between
classes of insurance, and pools typically cover one or more classes. The
Commission will apply the approach set out in its Notice on market definition to
identifying product and geographic markets,[179] and the Commission's merger
control decisions can give some guidance.[180] Relevant product markets are likely
not to be coterminous with classes of insurance; in particular, a pool covering a
single class may well cover more than one relevant product market. The result may
be that the risks covered by a pool might fall partly within and partly without the
market share limits of the Regulation. For example, a pool between national
insurers covering only catastrophe risks may well satisfy the market share test
because the relevant geographic market may well be worldwide (indeed, such a
pool might be considered not to fall within Article 81(1) at all—see paragraph
9.106 above). However, if such a pool were also to cover an ordinary risk in a
national market it might exceed the market share test and thus fall outside the
block exemption. Where a pool might exceed the market share limits on a particular type of risk it might be best advised to seek guidance from the Commission's
services and if necessary notify the pool arrangements.

9.120 *Condition relating to notice periods.*   Each participant must have the right to
withdraw from the pool, subject to a notice period of not more than six months,
without incurring any sanctions.[181]

9.121 **Networks of pools.**   Two of the grounds on which the Commission may withdraw the benefit of the block exemption are situations where links between pools
may limit competition between them. The first situation is where one or more
participants exercise a determining influence on the commercial policy of more
than one pool on the same market. The second situation is where the setting up or
operation of a pool may, through the conditions governing admission, the definition of the risks to be covered, the agreements on retrocession, or by any other
means, result in the sharing of the markets for the insurance products concerned
or for neighbouring products.[182]

---

[177] Article 17(d).
[178] Recital (19).
[179] Notice on the definition of the relevant market for the purposes of Community competition
law [1997] OJ C372/5. See also Gyselen (n 1 above) 388–389.
[180] See paras 9.128 and following, below.
[181] Article 11(1)(b).
[182] Article 17(b) and (c).

Individual exemption. Prior to its adopting the block exemption Regulation, **9.122** the Commission exempted pooling arrangements in three individual decisions. The co-insurance pool in *TEKO* was considered beneficial because it allowed the pool to develop know-how in space insurance, and enabled more favourable reinsurance terms than could be negotiated jointly.[183] The co-reinsurance pools in *TEKO* and *Assurpol* were considered beneficial for the same line of reasoning as subsequently put forward in the block exemption regulation: the pools improved the knowledge of risks and technical expertise, opened the market to insurers who would have difficulty entering alone, and enabled the pool members to obtain a more diversified and balanced portfolio of risks.[184] Although the members of the co-reinsurance pool in *TEKO* in practice applied the same commercial premiums, competition was not eliminated because the pool had a market share of 20 per cent and residual intra-pool price competition remained because the members could refund to their policyholders part of their reinsurance premium or indeed part of the commercial premium.[185] In *Assurpol* policies written within Assurpol represented 3 per cent of the relevant national market for environmental damage insurance. However, the insurer members of the pool accounted for 70–80 per cent of the national market for general liability insurance (which could include environmental damage cover); those policyholders were likely to be in the demand side for the environmental damage insurance which was reinsured within the pool. Nevertheless, competition was not eliminated. At the direct insurance level, pool members were free to set their own commercial premiums, there was competition from insurers outside the pool in the relevant geographic market (France), and if demand were to grow the relevant market would be likely to widen such that there would be competition from insurers in other Member States.[186]

(8) Distribution

The role of intermediaries, such as brokers and agents, may in some circumstances **9.123** give rise to competition concerns. The Commission has taken no formal decisions in this field, although it did in 1987 publish an Article 19(3) Notice proposing to exempt an agreement notified by the Irish Insurance Federation fixing maximum rates of commission that insurers would pay to intermediaries. The insurers wished to avoid commission rates rising (which ultimately had to be paid by consumers), and claimed that consumers would also benefit because intermediaries would be more likely to give best advice uninfluenced by the commission they

---

[183] *TEKO* [1990] OJ L13/34, at para 27.
[184] *TEKO* [1990] OJ L13/34, at para 26; *Assurpol* [1992] OJ L37/16, at para 38; Recital (10) of Regulation 3932/92.
[185] *TEKO* [1990] OJ L13/34, at paras 3, 31.
[186] *Assurpol* [1992] OJ L37/16, at para 41.

were receiving.[187] No decision was subsequently taken, and it seems unlikely that the Commission would now be persuaded to exempt this type of horizontal agreement between insurers fixing the rates of commissions to intermediaries.[188]

9.124 In its 1962 Notice on commercial agents, the Commission stated that Article 81(1) did not apply to agency agreements where the agent does not act as an independent trader.[189] Thus, insurance agents who have no more commercial autonomy *vis-à-vis* their principals than would have an employee will be regarded as part of the same economic unit as their principal. Even where agents are to be regarded as independent traders, exclusive agreements between insurers and such agents should not of themselves be regarded as falling within Article 81(1). However, on national markets where agents are an important distribution channel, insurers' exclusive agreements with agents might have the effect of foreclosing new entrants to the market. This issue is raised in a complaint lodged by an association of insurance intermediaries (BIPAR) against tied intermediary arrangements in the German market.[190] Whether such agreements fall within Article 81(1) will require a detailed market analysis to assess the nature and importance of the totality of the exclusive agreements.[191] Such an analysis would include an assessment of the development of alternative means of distribution channels such as banks and post offices, and direct telephone sales.

9.125 In *Halifax/Standard Life*, the Commission considered that the decision by the Halifax Building Society to become an agent exclusively for Standard Life fell within Article 81(1) but justified exemption. A large number of banks and building societies had decided to become tied agents as a result of the 'polarization' requirement of the UK Financial Services Act. The Commission took a favourable view after deletion of clauses preventing Standard Life from appointing other building societies as its agent and restricting Halifax from offering rebates on commissions.[192]

9.126 In the future, account should also be taken of the Commission's new policy on vertical restraints which will apply to the distribution of services as well as goods.[193]

---

[187] *Insurance Intermediaries* [1987] OJ C120/5.

[188] See for example *UIC—Distribution of railway tickets by travel agents* [1992] OJ L366/47 (infringement decision with fines for *inter alia* a standard rate of commission to travel agents; decision annulled because adopted on the basis of Regulation 17 rather than Regulation 1017/68: T–14/93 *UIC v Commission* [1995] ECR II–1503; C–245/95P *Commission v UIC* [1997] ECR I–1287).

[189] Notice on exclusive dealing contracts with commercial agents [1962] OJ C139/2921. The Commission has for many years been promising to revise this notice: see for example *Report on Competition Policy 1992* (Vol XXII) point 119.

[190] [1996] *Proceedings of the Fordham Corporate Law Institute* 450.

[191] See Case C–234/89 *Delimitis v Henninger Bräu* [1991] ECR 935.

[192] *Halifax Building Society and Standard Life Assurance Company* [1992] OJ C131/2.

[193] Green Paper on Vertical Restraints in EC Competition Policy, COM(96)721 final, 22 January 1997.

(9) *Insurance Mergers*[194]

There have been very few important decisions relating to mergers in the insurance **9.127** industry. This sector has, however, been enjoying more and more concentration in recent years and it is becoming more likely that future concentrations might raise competition concerns. For instance, Commissioner Van Miert stated recently that 'the insurance sector is starting to act a little differently now and we'll have to watch it more closely than we have in the past'.[195]

Relevant product market. The definitions of the relevant product markets in **9.128** the Commission's merger control decisions in the insurance industry show a remarkable consistency. This is no doubt due to the absence of transactions raising real doubts as to their compatibility with competition rules.

In its decisions, the Commission has distinguished between life insurance, general **9.129** (or non-life) insurance, and reinsurance. It has explained that these three categories could not be part of the same relevant market. The Commission considers that reinsurance constitutes a separate market for three reasons. First, it serves a purpose of spreading risk between insurers. Secondly, it is more specialized and conducted between insurers and reinsurers on an international basis because of the need to pool risks. Thirdly, the regulatory framework is also less stringent than for the other forms of insurance. Although the Commission has consistently distinguished between life and non-life insurance, it has never explained the reasons why these two categories could not be part of the same relevant product market.

The Commission has not yet needed to define precisely a relevant product mar- **9.130** ket. It has always been possible to conclude that, on the basis of the narrowest possible definition, the notified operation did not raise serious doubts as to its compatibility with the common market. However, the Commission has used various methods to segment or regroup relevant product markets.

Basing its reasoning on demand side considerations, it has said that life and non- **9.131** life insurance can be divided into as many product markets as there is insurance covering different kinds of risk. Their characteristics, premiums, and purposes are distinct and there is typically no substitutability for the consumer between the different risks insured. This reasoning can be found in the first merger decision relating to the insurance industry[196] and was reproduced in nearly all subsequent decisions.

In its *AXA/UAP* decision, the Commission noted that not only was it possible to **9.132** make narrower and narrower distinctions between risks and therefore between

---

[194] Guy Soussan, 'Application of the EU merger control regulation to the insurance industry', in [1996] *Proceedings of the Fordham Corporate Law Institute* 423–443.
[195] *Wall Street Journal,* 26 June 1998.
[196] *AG/Amev* (Case IV/M18) (1990).

insurance products, but that in some cases some risks could be regrouped in a single category. It provided the example of 'dommages corporels' insurance in France which covered various 'accidents corporels' risks as well as some 'general health risks'.

9.133   It was also proposed in *Abeille Vie/Viagère/Sinafer* to segment relevant markets according to the channels of distribution of life insurance products (for example direct sale, or sale through agents, brokers, or other intermediaries).[197]

9.134   In two instances the Commission has made some effort to delineate a relevant product market. These concern first the credit insurance market and second the reinsurance market.

9.135   *Credit insurance.*   In four recent decisions, the Commission examined the credit insurance market.[198] Credit insurance in general offers protection for suppliers of goods and services against the insolvency of a debtor or extended late payments. In *Allianz/Hermes* the Commission concluded that, from the supply side perspective, the credit insurance companies could cover all types of risks. A single credit insurance market was therefore defined incorporating all the above-mentioned risks. This supply side perspective was attenuated by the *Allianz/AGF* decision where the Commission examined one segment of the credit insurance activities, the 'delcredere' market (which includes domestic and export credit insurance and capital goods insurance), as one separate product market due to its special characteristics, such as the requirement of extensive knowledge of the markets, investments, and human resources.

9.136   In *Allianz/Hermes* the Commission investigated whether services offered by banks should be regarded as substitutes for credit insurance. The Commission held that, although some products offered by banks are beginning to enter the market as potential competitors to credit insurance, due to their particular characteristics and prices these products were not yet sufficiently developed to substitute for credit insurance products as such but were supplementary in nature. This view was confirmed by the investigation carried out by the Commission in *Hermes/Sampo/FGB—FCIC*, where it was concluded that bank guarantees are not, in general, considered as direct substitutes to credit insurance.

9.137   *Reinsurance.*   The Commission has traditionally stated that this type of insurance activity must be distinguished from other types of insurance activities. This is based on the following arguments.[199] First, the purpose of reinsurance is to

---

[197]   *Abeille Vie/Viagère/Sinafer* (Case IV/M919) (1997).
[198]   *Hermes/Sampo/FGB—FCIC* (Case IV/M1101) (1998), *Allianz/AGF* (Case IV/M1082) (1998), *Allianz/Hermes* (Case IV/M813) (1996), and *Allianz/Vereinte* (Case IV/M812) (1996).
[199]   *ERC/NRG Victory* (Case IV/M433) (1994); *General Re/Kölnische Rück* (Case IV/M491) (1994); *Employers Reinsurance/Frankona Rückversicherungs AG* (Case IV/M600) (1995); *Employers Reinsurance/Aachener Rückversicherungs-Gesellschafts AG* (Case IV/M601) (1995); *Schweizer Rück/Mercantile & General Reinsurance Company* (Case IV/M828) (1996).

spread risks between insurers. The reinsurer accepts either the whole or part of the direct risk insured by another insurer and thereby provides the primary insurer with the ability to increase the amount of insurance which it underwrites and to diversify its risk over time and geographic area. Secondly, reinsurance is traded between industry specialists, it is written only with other insurance companies, no premium income is derived from reinsurance sales to the public, and no channels for retail distribution are required.

In some of its decisions the Commission has examined how relevant product markets could be delineated within the reinsurance sector.[200] Hence, after having stated that reinsurance can be divided into two sectors (life and non-life), the Commission details the further possible subdivisions of the non-life sector: liability, motor, accident/sickness, fire, marine, aviation, and other. As for the credit insurance example, the Commission seems to be excluding the possibility of narrow product markets by using a supply side argument. Although some reinsurers specialize in particular types of cover, there is no reason apart from expertise why a reinsurer should not readily enter the market in any sector; there is thus a high level of supply side substitutability. Again, it has not yet been necessary for the Commission to take a position on the precise definition of relevant product markets in the reinsurance market, so this point has been left open in the merger decisions. **9.138**

Relevant geographic market. With two exceptions, the Commission has consistently defined the relevant geographic markets as being national. The two exceptions deal with the reinsurance market and some big commercial risk insurance. **9.139**

For instance, in *Commercial Union/General Accident*,[201] the Commission gave four reasons why geographic relevant markets are at present mainly national: in view of the established market structures, the need for adequate distribution channels, fiscal constraints in some cases and differing national systems of regulatory supervision. The exact meaning of 'established market structure' has never been clearly explained. It should also be noted that the *AXA/UAP* decision[202] cites consumer behaviour as one of the deciding factors for finding national markets. This is in line with the earlier *Codan/Hafnia* and *Fortis/La Caixa* decisions.[203] The *Fortis/La Caixa* decision also stated that the premiums paid varied from one country to the other. Finally, it must be added that the Commission has always tried to take into consideration the impact of the liberalization of the EU insurance markets stating that this could lead to wider relevant geographic markets in the future. **9.140**

---

[200] See for example *Mederic/URRPIMMEC/CRI/Münich Re* (Case IV/M949) (1997) and *Employers Reinsurance/Frankona Rück AG* (Case IV/M600) (1995).
[201] *Commercial Union/General Accident* (Case IV/M1142) (1998).
[202] *AXA/UAP* (Case IV/M862) (1996).
[203] *Codan/Hafnia* (Case IV/M344) (1993) and *Fortis/La Caixa* (Case IV/M254) (1992).

9.141 *Credit insurance.*   In a number of decisions, the Commission examined in some depth the geographic extent of the credit insurance relevant market. In *Allianz/Vereinte* the Commission found that, despite the fact that the market is opening up especially for industrial customers, the market structure, distribution, customer preferences and national legislation dictate that the market is national. In *Allianz/AGF* the Commission recognized the fact that markets are becoming increasingly European in scope because of the liberalization process in the European insurance markets, the worldwide reinsurance structures, and the growing internationalization of the business. The Commission noted that especially multinational corporations require a wider geographic scope in terms of servicing their group-wide operations from a single source. On the other hand, it was noted the 'delcredere' market has a national dimension, too. This can be seen in the fact that small and medium-sized companies usually seek credit insurance with domestic companies. Policies are mainly contracted on a local basis because of the need for information on the business of the insured, the financial situation of the customers, and the local economic structures. The Commission concluded that there are elements to support both international and national geographic market definition, but for the purposes of the decision the definition was left open. The Commission reached the same conclusion in *Hermes/Sampo/FGB-FCIC* stating that there were clear indications in that case that the market was evolving and there were an increasing number of foreign insurers who offer insurance policies to Finnish policy holders, also cross-border. However, it was stated that the fact that Hermes was seeking a local alliance in the Finnish market was in line with the Commission's previous findings and indicates that market entry may still require operating together with a local player.

9.142 *Large, commercial risks.*   The first exception deals with the insurance for some large risks. In its *Allianz/Vereinte* and *AXA/UAP* decisions, the Commission concluded that the relevant geographic market for insurance for large risks in transport (planes, ships and space) should be at least of a European dimension. AXA and UAP justified this definition by the fact that close to 70 per cent of insurance companies' turnover in this field is originated outside their national territory and that this percentage would increase. It is interesting to note that in *Codan/Hafnia*, the Commission, when assessing the impact on competition of market shares in the region of 38 to 56 per cent in aviation, marine and transport, and 'other commercial' insurance, found that the commercial non-life segments are open to international competition.

9.143 *Reinsurance.*   As to the geographic extent of the reinsurance market(s), the Commission has considered such markets to be international or global.[204] In

---

[204] This was for instance restated in the *Mederic/URRPIMMEC/CRI/Münich Re* (Case IV/M949) (1997).

Mederic/URRPIMMEC/CRI/Münich Re, the Commission based its reasoning on the following findings. First, because reinsurance products are traded between industry specialists and not sold to the general public, controls by national authorities over the conduct of reinsurance tend to be much less extensive than those over direct insurance. This, together with the fact that reinsurance business can be readily conducted across national borders (for example by telephone), tends to indicate that the market has a global character. Secondly, there are a number of international broking firms which mediate reinsurance on a worldwide scale. Finally, within the European Union freedom of establishment to provide reinsurance services was enacted by Directive (EEC) 225/64. This reasoning reproduced *mutatis mutandis* that included in earlier decisions.[205]

Calculation of market shares.   The calculation of market shares is not always   **9.144**
explained in the Commission's decisions. It seems that they are usually based on the total premiums earned during a year period. In a few cases the Commission has tried to refine the calculation of market shares to get a better proxy of market power, notably when revenues are the result of long-term contracts as for life insurance. This was the case in *Abeille Vie/Viagère/Sinafer* where market shares were calculated on the basis of new policies issued.[206] Similarly, in *Allianz/Vereinte*, the Commission stated that the calculation of the market shares in the health insurance markets are the result not only of present market success but mostly of turnover made with long-lasting contracts which were often closed a long time ago.[207] The longer a health insurance contract runs the more difficult it is to change the insurance company. It concluded that total turnover does not perfectly indicate the present market position of companies.

Assessment of dominance.   The Commission seems to have adopted a position   **9.145**
of principle in its *AXA/UAP* decision where it announced that a market share in the region of 30 per cent combined with an imbalance in size with the nearest competitors could lead under certain circumstances to the finding of a dominant position. This could be interpreted as meaning that given the specific market structure of the insurance market, the threshold for dominance would be lower than in other industries. In this respect it would have been useful if the Commission had indicated the specific circumstances in question. However, in its more recent *Hermes/Sampo/FGB-FCIC* decision (which centred on the credit insurance market), the Commission also stated that despite market shares in a range of 40 to 50 per cent, market shares alone did not necessarily indicate dominance given notably the rapidly changing market structure of the insurance industry which would become more and more international/European. It is therefore

---

[205] *Employers Reinsurance/Frankona Rück AG* (Case IV/M600) (1995); *ERC/NRG Victory* (Case IV/M433) (1994); *General Re/Kölnische Rück* (Case IV/M491) (1994).
[206] *Abeille Vie/Viagère/Sinafer* (Case IV/M919) (1997).
[207] *Allianz/Vereinte* (Case IV/M812) (1996).

still difficult at this stage to conclude that there would be a lower market share threshold for the assessment of dominance in the insurance industry.

9.146 In a number of cases the Commission has found possible market shares in the region of or above 30 per cent in some insurance segments.[208] It has always concluded that this would not lead to the creation or reinforcement of a dominant position. The following reasons have been used to support this conclusion.

9.147 First, the non-life insurance segments would be characterized by some degree of supply side substitutability. For instance, the Commission stated in *Commercial Union/General Accident* that insurance companies with expertise in one or more product lines are normally able to reapply those skills to enter other product areas.[209] This ability is underpinned by the fact that insurance products require a common set of skills in terms of, *inter alia*, risk assessment, administration (including IT systems), and claims management.[210]

9.148 A second argument deals with barriers to entry which, according to the Commission, would be relatively low. That would be due to the EC liberalization movement[211] and to the creation of new channels of distribution such as brokers,[212] direct telephone selling by underwriters, and marketing by banks and supermarkets.[213] It should, however, be noted that a rather sophisticated argument was adopted in its *AGF/Allianz* decision where the Commission started by noting that market entry in the 'delcredere' market required high costs in terms of heavy investments, know-how, and human resources; but then added that it could still be realized even in very mature markets as recent entrances by new competitors showed; therefore the barriers to entry in this case would be low as well.[214]

9.149 Thirdly, as a direct consequence of the first two arguments, the Commission argues that in any possible insurance market there are a number of actual and potential competitors. The potential competitors which are cited are usually

---

[208] *Codan/Hafnia* (Case IV/M344) (1993) for transport related segments of the market for commercial non-life insurance in Denmark and for credit and guarantee insurance in Denmark; *Sun Alliance/Royal Insurance* (Case IV/M759) (1996) for mortgage indemnity insurance and for engineering insurance in the UK; *Allianz/Vereinte* (Case IV/M812) (1996) for health insurance in Germany; *AXA/UAP* (Case IV/M862) (1996) for 'responsabilité civile professionnelle', for assistance, and for 'accidents du travail' in France and/or Belgium; *Allianz/AGF* (Case IV/M1082) (1998) for 'delcredere' credit insurance in a number of European countries; *GRE/PPP* (Case IV/M1090) (1998) for private medical insurance in the UK; *Hermes/Sampo/FGB-FCIC* (Case IV/M1101) (1998) for credit insurance in Finland excluding captive insurers and bank guarantees.

[209] *Commercial Union/General Accident* (Case IV/M1142) (1998).

[210] See also *Sun Alliance/Royal Insurance* (Case IV/M759) (1996).

[211] *Codan/Hafnia* (Case IV/M344) (1993); *Sun Alliance/Royal Insurance* (Case IV/M759) (1996); *Commercial Union/General Accident* (Case IV/M1142) (1998).

[212] *Codan Hafnia* (Case IV/M344) (1993); *Sun Alliance/Royal Insurance* (Case IV/M759) (1996); *Alliance/AGF* (Case IV/M1082) (1998); *Hermes/Sampo/FGB-FCIC* (Case IV/M1101) (1998).

[213] *Commercial Union/General Accident* (Case IV/M1142) (1998).

[214] *Allianz/AGF* (Case IV/M1082) (1998).

strong in other insurance product or geographic markets.[215] To support this line of argument the Commission also gives examples of new entrants or states that the market in question is still in its early stage of development.[216]

Finally, the Commission has also based its assessment on the bargaining power **9.150** held by the demand, at least for insurance products which are sold to companies instead of individuals.[217]

Collective dominance. The Commission's merger decisions in the insurance field **9.151** are all (with one exception) based on the assessment of the creation or strengthening of a dominant position of a single entity. Only the *UAP/Vinci* (1993) M384 decision explicitly excluded the risk of creation or strengthening of a collective dominant position. This can be justified by the fact that the power of the Commission to assess a notified concentration on the basis of a collective dominant position has only recently been recognized by the Court of First Instance.[218] However, when looking at the criteria set out in the *Gencor/Lonrho*[219] or *Price Waterhouse/Coopers & Lybrand*[220] decisions, it is not immediately obvious that at least some parts of the insurance industry would not present a market structure prone to the emergence of collective dominance. To cite only one example, the insurance industry is characterized by co-insurance and insurance pools arrangements which might be seen as creating structural links between insurance companies.

The Commission undertook a collective dominance assessment for the first time **9.152** in the insurance sector in its *Allianz/AGF* decision.[221] It did not actually use the words 'collective dominance', but the thrust of the analysis did not leave doubt. The market shares resulting from the addition of the shares of the respective subsidiaries for 'delcredere' credit insurance of AGF and Allianz reached around 60 per cent in Italy, around 50 per cent in the UK, and around 40 per cent in Belgium, France, and Germany. The Commission nevertheless considered that these market shares were not indicative of dominance because of the market structure of the industry, past competitive behaviour, and limited overlap between the merging entities. On the European level, the combined entity would have a market share of slightly above 40 per cent and would be three times bigger than any of

---

[215] *Sun Alliance/Royal Insurance* (Case IV/M759) (1996); *Allianz/Vereinte* (Case IV/M812) (1996); *AXA/UAP* (Case IV/M862) (1996); *GRE/PPP* (Case IV/M1090) (1998). Potential new substituting products are also mentioned in *Commercial Union/General Accident* (Case IV/M1142) (1998) and *Hermes/Sampo/FGB-FCIC* (Case IV/M1101) (1998).

[216] *Hermes/Sampo/FGB-FCIC* (Case IV/M1101) (1998) and *GRE/PPP* (Case IV/M1090) (1998).

[217] *Codan/Hafnia* (Case IV/M344) (1993); *Sun Alliance/Royal Insurance* (Case IV/M759) (1996); *AXA/UAP* (Case IV/M862) (1996).

[218] Joined Cases C–68/94 and C–30/95 *French Republic, SCPA and EMC v Commission* [1988] ECR I–1375.

[219] *Gencor/Lonrho* (Case IV/M619) (1996) [1997] OJ L11/30, at para 141.

[220] *Price Waterhouse/Coopers & Lybrand* (Case IV/M1016) (1998).

[221] *Allianz/AGF* (Case IV/M1082) (1998).

the three other significant competitors. However, the Commission found that there were instances of recent entry into the market and concluded that therefore there was evidence of enough competition to dismiss the risk of a creation of a dominant position.

9.153 The Commission then assessed the impact of the existence of structural and co-operative links between Euler, a subsidiary of AGF, and Coface. Its conclusion, when taking into account these links, was that Euler and Coface could achieve a dominant position if they continued to divide up markets and refrain from competition. This would be the case both at national level and at the European level, whatever way the relevant geographic market is defined.

9.154 Coface is an internationally active insurer specializing in export credits to the French Government. Coface holds 5 per cent of Euler's share capital. Whereas, pre-merger, Coface was controlled solely by AGF, AGF and Allianz had undertaken to reduce this stake to a level of 24.9 per cent. Moreover, personal links existed on both sides of the managing boards of Euler and Coface. Several members of the management board of AGF were members of the management or supervisory board of Coface, while members of Coface were also represented in the management board of Euler. The Commission also cited a number of commercial co-operation agreements between Coface and Euler. A second link would be the commercial and capital involvement of SCOR, a reinsurance company. SCOR is one of the main reinsurers of Euler, and the first reinsurer of Coface. In addition, it will be the main shareholder in Coface (45.2 per cent) and will hold 14 per cent in Euler. The Commission concluded that the involvement of SCOR, together with the fact that, among Coface's shareholders, only AGF and SCOR have enough expertise in 'delcredere' insurance, will be likely to lead to a *de facto* joint control of AGF and SCOR over Coface.

9.155 A similar analysis was conducted in the *AXA/GRE* case.[222] In that decision the Commission noted that the Luxembourg non-life business was characterized by the existence of two leading players, Le Foyer and La Luxembourgeoise, which hold 60 per cent of the market while AXA had so far been their only important challenger. The combined market shares of the these three companies reached 70 to 80 per cent for motor insurance, casualty, and property insurance. However, the concentration resulted in the creation of a link between AXA and Le Foyer, whereby AXA would hold a 34.8 per cent interest in Le Foyer. The Commission considered that AXA was likely to have considerably less interest to assume the role of challenger any longer. Furthermore, it concluded that, given that the remaining players' market shares were 10 to 20 times smaller than those of the two national leaders, they would not be in a position to exercise a comparable competitive pressure and that competition between the three leading companies may

---

[222] *AXA/GRE* (Case IV/M1453) (1999).

be slowed down to a large extent. The Commission therefore concluded that due to the absence of comparable competitors it cannot be excluded that the three leading non-life insurers might impose their market decisions on the remaining players or lift prices for consumers. This transaction was cleared by an Article 6(1)(b) decision with undertakings.

E. Social Security[223]

In the 1990s the Court has started to consider the possible application of the competition rules to social security schemes and the organizations that are involved in the operation of those schemes. Cases have arisen where individuals or commercial insurance companies have attacked schemes (whether obligatory or optional) whose operation is entrusted to a single, and generally not-for-profit, organization. Two questions arise from such cases: (1) whether the social security scheme in question is an economic activity whose operator is an 'undertaking' within the meaning of Articles 81 and 82; (2) whether the Member State, by entrusting the operation of the scheme to a single organization, has acted contrary to Articles 86 and 82.

9.156

Social security organizations as 'undertakings'. In *Poucet,* the Court held that organizations involved in the management of public social security systems do not pursue an economic activity and are therefore not undertakings within the meaning of Articles 81 and 82 where those organizations fulfil an exclusively social function and perform an activity based on the principle of national solidarity and which is entirely non-profit-making.[224] The schemes under consideration in *Poucet* were based on compulsory affiliation which the Court found to be indispensable for application of the principle of solidarity and the financial equilibrium of those schemes. By contrast, the 'Coreva' scheme at issue in the *FFSA* case was an optional supplementary old-age insurance *(assurance vieillesse complémentaire)* scheme for self-employed farmers. The Court held that the optional nature of the Coreva scheme and that it operated on the principle of capitalization meant that it contained only a limited degree of solidarity and was therefore an economic activity carried on in competition with life assurance companies.[225] While the Court has emphasized the degree of solidarity involved in the scheme in question,

9.157

---

[223] Francis Kessler, 'Droit communautaire de la concurrence et régimes de base de protection sociale: A la recherche d'un fondement juridique cohérent' (1997) La Semaine Juridique (JCP), Ed G, no 6–7.

[224] Joined Cases C–159/91 and C–160/91 *Poucet v AGF and Camulrac* and *Pistre v Cancava* [1993] ECR I–637.

[225] Case C–244/94 *Fédération Française des Sociétés d'Assurance and others v Ministère de l'Agriculture et de la Pêche* [1995] ECR I–4013.

the Commission appears to argue that the compulsory nature of a scheme excludes it from being an economic activity within the competition rules.[226]

9.158 The extent of the application of the competition rules should be further clarified when the Court decides on a series of preliminary references concerning Dutch supplementary old-age insurance schemes (for particular sectors or occupations) to which affiliation is compulsory but which operate on the principle of capitalization[227] and a Dutch health insurance scheme based on a sectoral agreement between the social partners.[228]

9.159 An organization that falls outside the competition rules because it participates in a compulsory, solidarity based social security system can constitute an undertaking in so far as it offers non solidarity based insurance products in competition with insurance companies.[229]

9.160 **Exclusive rights.** In the *FFSA* case, the Court of Justice did not examine the compatibility with Article 86 of exclusive rights granted to the CCMSA. Some guidance can be derived from the Court's statement that it would have to be examined whether the restrictions to which the CCMSA was subject (such as the rights and obligations of the persons insured, and restrictions to which it was subject in making its investments) could be relied upon in order to justify the exclusive right of that body to provide old-age insurance in respect of which contributions are deductible from taxable earnings.[230] The French Conseil d'Etat subsequently held that the CCMSA's exclusive right to tax-deductible contributions was an abuse within the meaning of Article 82, the restriction it brought about not being justified by the particular task assigned to the CCMSA.[231]

---

[226] Commission Notice on services of general interest in Europe [1996] OJ C281/3, at para 18.

[227] Case C–115/97 *Brentjens v Stichtin, Dedrifspensioenfonds voor de handel in bouwmaterialen*; Case C–219/97 *Drijvende Bokken v Stichting Pensioenfonds voor de vervoer- en havenbedrijven*; Joined Cases C–180/98 to 184/98 *Pavlov and others v Stichting Pensioenfonds Medische Specialisten*. The Court did not find it necessary to reply to the Dutch Hoge Raad's questions on this and the Article 86 issue in Joined Cases C–430/93 and C–431/93 *van Schijndel and van Veen v Stichting Pensioenfonds voor Fysiotherapeuten* [1995] ECR I–4705. Advocate General Jacobs delivered an Opinion on 28 January 1999 in Case C–67/96 *Albany*, Joined Cases C–115/97, C–116/97 and C–117/97 *Brentjens*, and C–219/97 *Drijvende Bokken*.

[228] Case C–222/98 *van der Woude v Stichting Beatrixoord*.

[229] Case C–244/94 *Fédération Française des Sociétés d'Assurance and others v Ministère de l'Agriculture et de la Pêche* [1995] ECR I–4013 (optional Coreva scheme at issue was managed by the same organization (CCMSA, assisted by local MSA funds) as operated the compulsory social security scheme for farmers).

[230] At para 20.

[231] CE, 8 November 1996.

10

ENERGY

A. Introduction

The energy sector is central to the achievement of the goals of the European **10.01**
Community; the coal sector has its own special Treaty (ECSC), as has the nuclear
sector (EAEC). Within the scope of the EC treaty itself, no special provision was
made for the energy sector as such. The European Court of Justice has ruled that
the energy sector is within the scope of the competition rules.[1]

---

[1] See Case 6/64 *Costa v Enel* [1964] ECR 1251, Case C–393/92 *Municipality of Almelo and others v NV Energiebedrijf Ijsselmij* [1994] ECR I–1477, Cases C–157/94 *Commission v Netherlands*, exclusive rights to import electricity for public distribution, C–158/94 *Commission v Italy*, exclusive rights to import and export electricity, C–159/94 *Commission v France*, exclusive rights to import and export gas and electricity, C–160/94 *Commission v Spain*, exclusive rights to import and export electricity [1997] ECR I–5699 *et seq*.

10.02 The Commission has sought to bring about the integration of the Member States' energy markets using a three-pronged approach. First, the Commission has sought to develop a new policy environment using Article 95 (former Article 100a) of the Treaty. Secondly, the Commission has instigated cases, using Article 226 (former Article 169) EC, to attack exclusive import and export rights. Thirdly, the competition rules have been applied.

10.03 This chapter will follow the scheme of Articles 81, 82, and 86 (former Articles 85, 86, and 90) of the Treaty, starting with general issues (market definition etc), and then moving to specific issues related to each Article in so far as these have been treated by the Commision. Most of this discussion will focus on the definition of markets, an issue that has given rise to the most debate. There will follow some general remarks about the interface between the EC Treaty rules and the special regimes (ECSC Treaty and Euratom Treaty). Lastly, the impact of the new internal market directives on the liberalization of the gas and electricity markets will be considered, in so far as these may affect the application of the competition rules. A few general remarks about the public policy domain, sector specific arguments, and the application of the competition rules preface a detailed discussion of the substantive rules, as in this sector public policy arguments are unusually forceful.

(1) The Policy Domain

10.04 **Policy is important.**   In the energy sector, the application of the competition rules cannot be done in a policy vacuum. In relation to electricity markets, application of the competition rules is complicated by the need 'to accommodate a somewhat broader range of public interest factors than is considered under contemporary competition policy'.[2] This consideration can be generalized to the energy sector. In assessing competition cases thought should be had to the policy environment and in particular the following three imperatives:

* Any change in the business environment may affect security of supply.

* Utilities in public ownership and particular tax systems provide revenues for administrations. Changes in the regulatory environment will affect revenues.

* Social equity and national social cohesion plays a major part in determining policy.[3]

The Commission values highly arguments that address these issues.

---

[2] Lee A Rau, 'Open Access in the Power Industry: Competition, Cooperation and Policy Dilemmas' (1996) 64(2) Antitrust LJ.

[3] The EC addresses this point in its overall energy policy aims: *An Overall View of Energy Policy and Actions*, section II B2, Com (97) 167 final.

(2) Risk and Historical Characteristics of the Energy Sector

Competition cases often depend on a conception of risk.   A historical charac-   **10.05**
teristic of the energy sector is the use of large capital investment. For example,
with the integration of local electricity markets and the assumption, in most cases,
by the State of responsibility for provision, economies of scale led to large-scale
investments. Investment on this scale was premised on security of consumption.
Both of these characteristics gave rise to a below-market level of risk. Publicly
owned utilities and private utilities enjoying special or exclusive rights[4] could bor-
row at below market rates, their debt akin to sovereign debt and in some cases ultimately assumed by the State.[5] Oil and gas producers selling to a monopsonist won
decent but not spectacular returns, sufficient to keep them in the market in comparison to other opportunities. Risk in the market was often reduced to political
and regulatory risk.[6]

Risk in the energy sector should be priced as in other sectors where large capital   **10.06**
investments are made. In a liberalized market, market actors should not be
allowed to argue that contractual relations be used to maintain risk at lower than
market levels as an end in itself. Otherwise investment distortions will arise as
between the energy sector and other sectors, and within the energy sector (as say
between oil exploration and wind technology). General arguments about the
nature of risk and how to deal with it in contractual relations have been made in
several cases.[7]

(3) Information Technology

Agreements that facilitate information flow *and* competition are looked upon   **10.07**
favourably.   The increased use of information technology makes sense of complex markets. In the UK electricity market, competition when introduced was
predicated on the satisfaction of half-hourly demand projections, made possible
by information technology. Retail competition in gas supply is also possible.
Competition in these sectors is possible despite the supply chain being part of a
complex system that must be 'balanced' and managed; this balancing and management is only possible, when there are a multiplicity of actors, if there is sufficient information flow among market participants.

---

[4] Commentators have made the observation that if nuclear power was funded privately, the difference between the pricing of risk in the private sector and the public sector would make the building of power stations uneconomic: see Michael Klein, 'The Risk Premium for Evaluating Public
Projects' (1997) 13(4) *Oxford Review of Economic Policy*.

[5] For example, in the UK nuclear privatization, debt was assumed by the State prior to sale and
was thus treated as State aid.

[6] For further discussion see Michael Klein, 'The Risk Premium for Evaluating Public Projects'
and Brealey, Cooper and Habib, 'Investment Appraisal in the Public Sector' both in (1997) 13(4)
Oxford Review of Economic Policy, and the accompanying essays.

[7] See for example, *Britannia gas condensate field* (EEC) 91/329 (Notice pursuant to Article 19(3)
of Regulation 17) [1996] OJ C291/10.

(4) Practice and Habit

10.08 **Habit does not equal indispensability.** Many of the established notions of the energy market are open to question because of the spread of liberalization. This has implications in the application of the law. There are often instances where the argument that only one method is feasible can be countered with a concrete example of another method working. This is especially true of joint activities done on the premise that individual action would be impossible, therefore making the participants non-competitors; large joint infrastructure and hydrocarbons developments are examples of this; many of the arguments put forward to the Commission that there is no competition to restrict between market actors have been demonstrably untrue.

(5) Stranded Costs and Adjustment

10.09 **Competition rules will have regard to stranded costs.** In order to facilitate the change from a regulated market to a liberalized one, adjustment will be necessary. In many cases, the incumbents are unlikely to suffer catastrophic loss as the result of liberalization. Where they might, devices[8] can be designed to compensate them, such as the Non Fossil Fuel Obligation (NFFO) in the United Kingdom.[9] Where security of consumption is removed, and the result could be catastrophic loss, the competition rules are unlikely to be used in a way that will prevent remedy.[10]

(6) The Interaction between Regulation and Competition Policy

10.10 **Agreements imposed as a result of the regulatory system to facilitate competition have been viewed benignly by the Commission.** In the *Pooling and Settlement Agreement Notification*,[11] the Commission accepted that an agreement between competitors imposed by the regulatory system (in this case through the operation of the licences), which facilitated the functioning of the market, was not a restrictive agreement for the purposes of Article 81(1). This position has been followed in subsequent cases, and, in some cases, has extended to agreements that would necessitate the processing of market sensitive information by a specific agent.[12]

---

[8] As in the electricity Directive (Article 26) and the gas Directive (Take or pay contracts).

[9] *Reorganisation of the electricity industry in England and Wales* (Notice pursuant to Article 19(3) of Regulation 17) [1990] OJ C191/9. It appears that the NFFO was accepted on the basis that an exemption would have benefited consumers by maintaining fuel diversity, whereas at least one of the other agreements dealt with in the same notice was considered not to 'negatively' affect trade between Member States.

[10] In this regard, reference should be made to the specific rules in the electricity and gas Directives below.

[11] *Reorganisation of the electricity industry in England and Wales* (Notice pursuant to Article 19(3) of Regulation 17) [1990] OJ C191/9.

[12] cf *British Gas plc—Network Code* (Notice pursuant to Article 19(3) of Regulation 17) [1996] OJ C93/6.

With regard to Public Service Obligations (PSOs), the Directives liberalizing the **10.11** gas and electricity sectors recognize that there are legitimate public interests that must be protected in the move to a functioning market. Agreements that implement these interests or are imposed so as to protect these interests will most likely be treated benignly. Implicit in this approach is the view that some agreements will have as their object the prevention of competition, where this competition is deemed destructive to the interests to consumers. Analogies for this can be seen in legislative approaches to the question of capital adequacy of banks, or minimun standards in the air transport sector.[13]

B. The Definition of Markets

(1) Product and Service Markets

Substitutability in Energy Markets

A specific and recurring concern in the application of the competition rules in the **10.12** energy sector is the factual definition of the market and the demand criterion that should be applied. The Commission has published analyses that indicate conflicts in approach which can be explained by reference to the demand criterion.

Interfuel competition arises from long-term demand substitution and is a func- **10.13** tion of capital retirement and incremental market growth. A nationally observed overall energy mix at any point in time and at any point in the distribution chain is the result of measurement of the use of installed capacity for each type of fuel. That this overall energy mix changes is the result of retirement of installed capacity or the building of new. Thus, bulk gas and bulk coal may be in competition in the market for fuels for power stations, though, once a choice has been made, competition for provision to that station is over.[14] This type of substitutability works only in so far as fuel types are treated equally by the regulatory and legal systems.[15] It will be limited in that several other parameters (for example the amount of investments required in each case) will have to be taken into account.

Fuel specific markets arise as the result of long-term choices. Once a fuel is cho- **10.14** sen, short-term demand substitution between fuels is zero, on the assumption that the capital expended was not negligible. However, short-term demand elasticity is in principle high between different providers of that fuel. In practice, market

---

[13] See, for example, Council Regulation (EEC) 295/91 on the establishment of common rules for denied boarding compensation, in the air traffic sector [1989] OJ L36/5.

[14] With the obvious exception of dual firing stations.

[15] Often not the case; long-term coal contracts are significantly shorter than long-term gas contracts owing to the different regulatory frameworks in some jurisdictions.

structures, such as monopolies, contract forms, and other restrictions have historically prevented this type of substitution either by prohibiting the presence of the
competitor or making switching costs prohibitively high.

10.15 The extent of the relevant market, whether it is fuel specific or more general, will
depend on fact. For example, in France, there is an argument to be made that natural gas for industrial consumers is not a separate market; the percentage of gas
sold to industrial consumers on an interruptible basis is 50 per cent,[16] so prices of
competing fuels will have an influence on gas prices.[17] Conversely, in Germany the
price of gas is often linked to the price of heavy fuel oil despite the very obvious
fact that consumers are not always free to switch.

Recent Commission Practice

10.16 The Commission, in its latest publications, analyses markets as separate parts of
the value chain from producer to consumer. This leads to the following rough distinctions which apply broadly to all of the major fuels,[18] namely production,
transmission, distribution, and retail.

10.17 In addition, the Commission takes into account the existence of different market
conditions within one and the same geographic area. This is the case, for example,
when progressive liberalization takes place and leads to the simultaneous existence
of a 'franchise market' and of a 'free market'.[19] This is also the case when general
market conditions are homogeneous (for example all customers are free to choose
their supplier) but market behaviour of some 'classes' of customers justifies further
segmentation (for example the definition of a market for sale of electricity *to distributors* in the *Electrabel* case[20] and the market for input fuels *for electricity generation* in several other cases discussed below).

10.18 These general principles apply to all cases dealt with and published by the
Commission since 1990. Some exceptions can be pointed out :

— in the *ISAB* case,[21] the Commission defined the market, without any apparent
   justification or explanation, as being that for 'bulk base load electricity'. This
   segmentation of the wholesale market for electricity into 'base load' and 'peak
   load' seems to rely exclusively on an analysis of the offer of electricity (different
   production means are used at different times of the day and of the year) rather

---

[16] International Energy Agency Annual Review 1996.
[17] The corollary of this is that the 50% of consumers with firm contracts may constitute a distinct market.
[18] cf Merger cases. *Elf/Occidental* (Case IV/M85) (1991); though in *ELF/Enterprise* (Case
IV/M88) (1991) the genesis of the new approach can be seen.
[19] cf *EDF/London Electricity* (Case IV/M1346) (1999).
[20] Commission press release IP(97)351.
[21] cf *ISAB Energy* (Notice pursuant to Article 19(3) of Regulation 17) [1996] OJ C291/10.

than on an analysis of demand substitutability (demand of electricity is usually rather inelastic);

— on several occasions, the Commission adopted a broad definition encompassing coal, gas and oil in order to create a 'market for input fuels for electricity generation': this 'market' is discussed further below;

— in the *Britannia* case,[22] the Commission adopted a dynamic approach in that it defined the market as being that for '*future* supply of natural gas by producers to the wholesale level (forward gas)'.

Market for Input Fuels

The Commission has accepted on several occasions that there was a market for 'input fuels for electricity generation'.[23] In these electricity notifications, it was commented that coal purchases are in competition with purchases of other fuels suitable for electricity generation and that the regulation of the latter are a consideration in the regulation of the former.   **10.19**

It seems that this 'market for input fuels' encompassed coal, gas, and oil although the exclusion of nuclear fuel from that list has never been justified or analysed by the Commission.

The Commission seems, on two recent occasions, to have first confirmed and then departed from this analysis :   **10.20**

— In nuclear fuel supply contracts,[24] contracts for the supply of nuclear fuel rods, and the provision of front end and back end services, for considerable periods of time have been considered. The contracts were accorded negative clearance on the basis of the effect on trade doctrine. However, the reasoning in these cases is based in part on the fact there is no conceivable long-term competition from other input fuels, on the specific types of nuclear reactors being used, and the fact that, as a function of total cost, the fuel elements are a minor cost. This analysis as to the existence of a separate market for the supply of nuclear fuel rods confirms the Commission's definition of a 'market for input fuels' excluding nuclear energy.

— In the *Britannia* case, the Commission considered a separate market for 'forward gas' and conducted an analysis exclusively under a 'gas-to-gas'

---

[22] *Britannia gas condensate field* (Notice pursuant to Article 19(3) of Regulation 17) [1996] OJ C291/10.

[23] *Electricity industry in England and Wales* (Notice pursuant to Article 19(3) of Regulation 17) [1993] OJ C281/5, *Electricity industry in Scotland* (Notice pursuant to Article 19(3) of Regulation 17) [1994] OJ C223/7, *Electricity industry in England and Wales* (Notice pursuant to Article 19(3) of Regulation 17) [1994] OJ C15/9.

[24] *Nuclear Electric plc/British Nuclear Fuels plc* and *Scottish Nuclear Ltd/British Nuclear Fuels plc* (Notice pursuant to Article 19(3) of Regulation 17) [1996] OJ C89/4.

competition perspective. This market definition took place notwithstanding the fact that 'forward gas' could be even more easily in competition with 'forward' coal or oil for the supply of future power stations than 'present' gas, coal, and oil for the supply of existing non-dual fired power plants. Hence this case departs clearly from the approach adopted since 1993 in relation to 'input fuels'.

(2) Upstream Markets

Market Share Definition

10.21 A common mistake in notifications relating to oil and gas field developments is the presentation of data with reference to the field's position in the market. It is not the position of the field that is important, but the position of the parties to the field.[25] The parties' market share is their assets' percentage of the relevant market, not of the field.

Upstream Gas Markets

10.22 The Commission has used consumer surveys to establish (*ex post*) the options available to buyers of gas fields. The result has been that the perceived availability of fields to be purchased is a subset of fields capable of development.[26] This greatly magnifies the size and importance of a single field in the market definition, though paradoxically it may mitigate the size of any one producer's market share. The parties ability to profit from the informational asymmetries that exist, namely their ability through dispersed field ownership to know which fields are within the subset, is an issue of particular concern.

10.23 It is now accepted that gas companies, in the context of long-term contracts, compete to satisfy the supply gap (incremental demand growth and unsatisfied 'old' demand), which notion was mentioned explicitly in the *BP/Sonatrach Decision.*[27]

(3) The Definition of the Relevant Geographic Market

10.24 The following definitions have been adopted by the Commission since 1990 in relation to the different stages of the value chain it has identified on the gas and electricity markets:

---

[25] *Britannia gas condensate field* (Notice pursuant to Article 19(3) of Regulation 17) [1996] OJ C291/10.

[26] Caution has been exhibited in interpreting such survey results as a small selection of alternatives may indicate satisfaction as to price (a competitive price) and the large search costs of evaluating each field.

[27] *BP/Sonatrach* (Case IV/M672) (1996).

— Production of gas and electricity and their bulk sale to big customers or to retailers have traditionally taken place at national level.[28] Legislative barriers to trade (for example import/export monopolies) or the absence of connection[29] between Member States justified this analysis. The introduction of competition, together with the increase in connection capacity[30] and the development, in some cases, of 'international' organized exchanges (for example the Nordpool for trade of electricity between Norway, Sweden, Finland, and Denmark) may lead to a new definition of that market.

— High-pressure and high-voltage transmission of gas and electricity have always been found to take place at national level.

— Distribution (ie low pressure or low-voltage transmission) is an activity taking place at local (regional or municipal) level.

— Retail has traditionally taken place at local level due to the existence, in most countries before liberalization, of exclusive distribution rights or of so-called 'demarcation' contracts by which potential competitors agreed not to enter each other's area. The Commission has already signalled its willingness to take into account recent market developments in order to extend the size of this market. Hence the Commission found that the retail market for customers of electricity above 100 kW was England and Wales whereas customers below that limit (ie domestic customers opened to competition in 1999) were active on a local market (the London Area in that case).[31] A similar conclusion was drawn in the *WATT AG (II)* merger case[32] where the Commission found that, due to the existence until very recently of so-called 'demarcation' contracts, there were only local retail markets in Germany. However, the Commission took into account the expected development of competition (and thus the likely creation of a German retail market) in its assessment of the case.

The approaches set out above led, in most cases, to 'narrow' markets and thus did not deal with transmission capacity constraints and their potential impact on market definition. However, geographic markets in a liberalized context will depend on the capacity used and therefore may vary over the demand cycle: when there is low capacity utilization, a high number of potential suppliers for

---

[28] cf, for example, *ISAB Energy* (Notice pursuant to Article 19(3) of Regulation 17) [1996] OJ C291/10; *Electricidade de Portugal/Pego project* (Notice pursuant to Article 19(3) of Regulation 17) [1993] OJ C256/3; *Northern Ireland Electricity* (Notice pursuant to Article 19(3) of Regulation 17) [1992] OJ C92/5.

[29] Either because there was no physical connection or because access to a connection was denied.

[30] Including third-party access.

[31] *EDF/London Electricity* (Case IV/M1346) (1999).

[32] *WATT AG (II)* (Case IV/M958) (1997).

incremental supply will be apparent; when there is high capacity utilization, fewer suppliers will be present.[33]

10.25 A unique approach towards the definition of an EU-wide market for electricity was made in the *WATT AG (II)* case[34] where the Commission defined a specific product market, namely 'trade of electricity' that would take place on a market of, 'at least', EU-wide dimension. The Commission must have referred in this case to the exchanges of electricity that have taken place between monopolies for several years before liberalization. It is doubtful whether this product/geographic definition would be appropriate in an era of liberalization.

10.26 Other fuel markets like the oil[35] and uranium production[36] markets are globally integrated notwithstanding apparent low levels of international trade. Indeed, low levels of international trade in some energy products is not necessarily indicative of separate geographic markets, but perhaps indicative of integrated markets. This is especially the case in oil and petroleum markets, where prices are transparent, shipping costs well known and relatively high, and opportunistic entry relatively easy.

10.27 Markets for coal are national or international but not EU-wide. This paradoxical result owes much to stark discrepancies in production costs across the EU and to national policies of subsidization and priority consumption of indigenous coal.[37] Hence purchasers of coal in most Member States tend to consume national products first before importing from third countries (for example USA, China, Canada, Australia) but not from other Member States.

(4) Appreciable Effect on Trade

10.28 The notion of appreciable effect on trade, in the past, has been used functionally to claim or disclaim jurisdiction. This interpretation arises from a close reading of official Article 19(3) Notices and decisions in cases concerning energy.

Displacement Effects

10.29 In 1990, the electricity industry in Scotland[38] was reorganized in the context of its privatization. The various agreements were notified to the Commission. In assessing the agreements, the Commission in the relevant Article 19(3) Notice remarked:

---

[33] For further examination of these issues see Lewis J Perl, 'Measuring Market Power in Electric Generation' (1996) 64 Antitrust LJ 311.

[34] *WATT AG (II)* (Case IV/M958) (1997).

[35] *Elf/Occidental* (Case IV/M85) (1991).

[36] *United Reprocessors GmbH* [1976] OJ L51/7.

[37] Commission Decision ECSC MTF 1252, 29 July 1998, *RAG-Saarbergwerke-Preussag*, not yet published.

[38] *Reorganization of the electricity industry in Scotland* (Notice pursuant to Article 19(3) of Regulation 17) [1990] OJ C245/9.

The geographical location of Scotland on the fringe of the Community and the resultant physical constraints of the system do not make electricity exchanges with other Member States very likely. Unavoidable power losses may make it uneconomic to transmit electricity over such long distances. Accordingly there is not much prospect of Scottish generated electricity displacing electricity supplies from other Member States, in particular electricity supplied from the continent to the South of England, nor of Scottish generated electricity being supplied to other Member States.

One year later the Commission wrote in a Decision:[39]

Intra-community trade is confined to that between the UK and France via the inter-connector . . . equivalent to 4% of the electricity output of England and Wales . . .

. . . the reorganisation of electricity generation in Scotland and the prospect of a medium-term increase in the transmission capacity of the interconnector . . . will help to reduce the relative isolation of the Scottish market. . . . Because of the inter-dependence of the networks, on the one hand between Scotland and England and on the other hand between England and France, and also because of the proposed development of these interconnections, the agreement is therefore likely to affect trade between Member States.

Thus the displacement effect is discussed with diametric results. In the decision, **10.30** the Commission writes that the interdependence of the systems, one with the other, will cause trade effects. Scottish electricity may displace English electricity, in turn displacing French electricity. In the Article 19(3) Notice, displacement effect is only discussed with regard to displacement of French electricity in the French market by Scottish electricity. The approach in the Article 19(3) Notice is no longer followed, and it is accepted that displacement must not be direct, so that, in this case, Scottish generated electricity may displace English generated electricity in England, and English electricity displace French electricity in France. Following this line of argument, the question whether it is economic to transmit such large amounts of power is without basis; in fact, technical advances make it likely that it is economic to transmit such amounts.

It is therefore likely that the Commission will not accept that the relative isolation of **10.31** an electricity system will lead to a lack of jurisdiction under the effect on trade test.

Appreciability

The effect on trade must be appreciable. In the *SHG* case,[40] the Commission was **10.32** prepared to intervene in a case involving a power station producing 8 to 10 million kWh per annum in France, but with only connections to Italy. This was the equivalent of around 0.002 per cent of total electricity production in France.

---

[39] (EEC) 91/329: Commission Decision of 30 April 1991 relating to a proceeding under Article 85 [now Article 81] of the EEC Treaty (IV/33.473—*Scottish Nuclear, Nuclear Energy Agreement*).
[40] Commission press release IP(92)668.

10.33   In the *Northern Ireland Electricity* case[41] (in the same year), the reorganization of the entire installed capacity in Northern Ireland and the agreements implementing this were felt not to have an effect on trade. Although a 250 MW interconnector to Scotland was planned as part of the reorganization and although connections to the Republic of Ireland were in place though subject to terrorist action, no appreciable effect on trade could be discerned. It was noted that Scotland was a net exporter of electricity. No potential displacement effects were considered, either displaced Scottish exports to Northern Ireland or increased Irish exports to Northern Ireland; the possibility of increased or decreased French imports into England was not considered.

The *Britannia* Case

10.34   In the *Britannia* case,[42] the Commission concluded that an agreement to jointly sell gas was not likely to have an appreciable effect on trade. The gas field was projected to satisfy a considerable amount of UK gas needs at peak production. The product market was defined as forward bulk gas[43] (used either by aggregators or large consumers, mainly power generators). The Commission's position in its Article 19(3) Notice leads to the following issues:

- Even if the product market definition is accepted as robust, displacement effects were not considered. Such large amounts of gas coming onto the market might have induced others to seek overseas markets, either through the interconnector with the Republic of Ireland, by then operational, or through the planned interconnector between England and Belgium, of which the Commission was aware.[44]
- In the *Scottish Power, Scottish Hydro-Electric*, and *British Coal* cases,[45] the Commission considered the Frigg pipeline connection between Norway and the UK, noting that it provided 5 per cent of UK gas consumption. No mention of this interconnector was made in the Article 19(3) Notice in the *Britannia* case.
- Effects in the electricity market were dismissed without reasoning.

---

[41] *Privatisation of the electricity energy in Northern Ireland* (Notice pursuant to Article 19(3) of Regulation 17) [1992] OJ C92/5.

[42] *Britannia gas condensate field* (Notice pursuant to Article 19(3) of Regulation 17) [1996] OJ C291/10.

[43] This product definition was also adopted in *BP/Sonatrach* (Case IV/M672) (1996).

[44] The contracts governing the use of this gas interconnector were cleared by the Commission one year before publication of the Notice in the *Britannia* case. See [1995] OJ C73/18, Commission press release IP(95)550 and *Report on Competition Policy 1995* (Vol XXV) 125.

[45] *Electricity industry in Scotland* (Notice pursuant to Article 19(3) of Regulation 17) [1994] OJ C223/8.

Market Prospection

In the *Britannia* case, the Commission looked at market prospection. The parties **10.35**
to the Britannia field had the opportunity to sell the gas produced in the field
either to the UK market or to the continental gas market. They conducted
prospection, the identification of sellers and the determination of indicative
prices, in both markets. They sold to the UK market. The Commission interpreted this as to indicate separate UK and continental markets and not to indicate
a unitary market.[46]

C. Article 81: The Prevention, Restriction, or Distortion of Competition, and Grounds for Exemption

The aim of this section is not to exhaustively describe every case that the **10.36**
Commission has dealt with, but to highlight the developments of most interest to
practitioners. This section concerns cases and instances where restrictions within
the ambit of Article 81(1) have been an issue. Where possible, we have indicated
how the cases have been dealt with, most often by means of administrative letters,
either of a negative clearance (lack of jurisdiction, no agreement, or no restriction)
or exemption type. Where possible, we have indicated the grounds for exemption.

(1) Structure and Access in Network Energy Industries

The structure of the market may take the form of a pool or be contracts based. In **10.37**
certain cases, both systems may coexist in the same geographic area with only a
limited share of gas or electricity being traded via the pool and the remaining share
being delivered according to bilateral contracts.

A pool system is an organized market for the trading of gas or electricity where a **10.38**
system operator invites bids from offerors and instructs those offerors with the
lowest bids to input gas or electricity into the network depending on the
demand.[47] For example, in the England and Wales system, all electricity traded at
a given time is paid at pool price, ie the price of the most expensive bid exercised
during that period of time. This means that each customer pays the pool price to
the pool (not to the actual supplier). In its turn the pool pays the pool price less
administrative charges to each supplier that has been instructed to run.

In a contracts based market, each supplier has to conclude contracts with cus- **10.39**
tomers before delivering electricity or gas on the network in accordance with the

---

[46] *Britannia gas condensate field* (Notice pursuant to Article 19(3) of Regulation 17) [1996] OJ
C291/10.
[47] In other pool systems, like in the Nordpool, a demand curve is built in accordance with bids
made by purchasers.

estimated offtake of these customers. The network operator has to balance the system and may instruct some suppliers to reduce or increase their deliveries to the system. In any event it is likely that the quantities input by a supplier will not match the total of the quantities offtaken by its customers (or vice versa). The difference between the contractual quantity and the actual quantity delivered to or taken from the system has to be settled between the suppliers and the network operator or between the suppliers and those suppliers which carried out the balancing process. Notifications of balancing agreements and top-up gas agreements have been made.

Restructuring the Market

10.40 The cases dealt with by the Commission in relation to structure and access agreements are:

- the reorganization of the electricity industry in England and Wales;[48]
- the reorganization of the electricity industry in Scotland;[49]
- the privatization of the electricity industry in Northern Ireland;[50]
- the Bacton/Zeebrugge gas interconnector;[51]
- the United Kingdom gas transmission network code;[52]
- the Settlement Agreement for Scotland (electricity);[53] and
- the agreement setting out the principles for tarification of electricity transmission in Germany (Verbändevereinbarung).[54]

10.41 **The Commission is positive towards agreements which have aimed at defining a competitive market.** This approach was also adopted in formal decisions granting negative clearance to market associations such as the London Potato Futures Association Limited,[55] the Petroleum Exchange of London Ltd,[56] and the London Sugar Futures Market Ltd.[57] The framework used by the Commission for the analysis of this type of agreement involves the following three headings:

---

[48] *Reorganisation of the electricity industry in England and Wales* (Notice pursuant to Article 19(3) of Regulation 17) [1990] OJ C191/9.

[49] *Reorganisation of the electricity industry in Scotland* (Notice pursuant to Article 19(3) of Regulation 17) [1990] OJ C245/9.

[50] *Privatisation of the electricity industry in Northern Ireland* (Notice pursuant to Article 19(3) of Regulation 17) [1992] OJ C92/5.

[51] [1995] OJ C73/18, Commission press release IP(95)550, and *Report on Competition Policy 1995* (Vol XXV) 125.

[52] *British Gas Network Code* (Notice pursuant to Article 19(3) of Regulation 17) [1996] OJ C93/5.

[53] Not published.

[54] Not published.

[55] *The London Potato Futures Association Limited* [1987] OJ L19/26.

[56] *Petroleum Exchange of London Limited* [1987] OJ L3/27.

[57] *Certain protection measures against foot-and-mouth diseases in Italy* [1987] OJ L341/37.

Conditions to Gain Membership of the Market

The aim of the Commission is to make sure that the rules relating to membership operate in accordance with 'objective, transparent and non-discriminatory'[58] criteria. The Commission has not so far rejected criteria on this ground. However, it is probable that restrictions of access to the market based on nationality of a candidate undertaking or on past presence in the market would be examined critically by the Commission. The Commission, however, has accepted the imposition of criteria relating to financial resources when the purpose was to ensure that undertakings can meet the obligations incumbent upon them as a result of participating in the market. **10.42**

On several occasions membership to a market access agreement was made compulsory by a Member State.[59] Undertakings wishing to operate in the electricity and gas sectors may have to conform to national regulation setting out, for example, the need to hold a licence in order to exercise certain types of activity. It is also often the case that such licence provides for the obligation to enter into an existing or forthcoming market access agreement. The Commission has not held that a market access agreement was not an 'agreement' for the purposes of Article 81 between the parties because the parties were obliged to enter into it. This approach apparently contradicts that of the Court of Justice, which ruled, for example in *Ladbroke*,[60] that Articles 81 and 82 apply only to anti-competitive conduct engaged in by undertakings on their own initiative. The Court found that if anti-competitive conduct is required by legislation, or if the legislation creates a legal framework which eliminates any possibility of competitive activity on the part of undertakings, then any restriction of competition is not attributable, as Articles 81 and 82 implicitly require, to the autonomous conduct of the undertakings. **10.43**

The Operational Rules

Operational rules will be judged *ex ante* by competitors. The Commission has used Article 19(3) Notices to give a short summary of the main operational rules set out in the agreements. The examination of these rules follows the same pattern as for the rules applicable to membership (transparent, objective, non-discriminatory). However, the size and complexity of the agreements makes difficult the *ex ante* theoretical evaluation of their potential effects and explains to a certain extent the publication, in most cases, of Notices pursuant to Article 19(3) of Council Regulation 17/62 with a view to inviting comments from market **10.44**

---

[58] This is the wording used in Article 16 (under the heading 'Organisation of access to the system') of the Directive concerning an internal market in electricity.

[59] See, for example, the Pooling and Settlement Agreement in *Reorganisation of the electricity industry in England and Wales* (Notice pursuant to Article 19(3) of Regulation 17) [1990] OJ C191/9.

[60] Joined Cases C–359 and C–379/95P *Ladbroke v Commission* [1997] ECR I–7007.

participants, as these may be in a better position to point out potential restrictions of competition.

Confidentiality

10.45 **The Commission will seek to avoid anti-competitive exchanges of information amongst members of the market.**[61]   When looking at the arrangements for the UK gas industry, parts of the agreements might have resulted in information exchanges that would have had anti-competitive effects. A solution often used in this context is the creation of an independent company in charge of aggregating data flows and administering the market.[62]

Connection and Access Agreements

10.46 This category encompasses agreements relating to the use of the network and can include provisions as to:

- technical requirements for connection;
- capacity reservation, use, and—if authorized—trading; and
- transmission fees calculation and payment.

The agreements relating to the use of the network are always entered into with the network operator whereas the agreements relating to settlement might be concluded between the users and those producers ready to provide balancing services. However, some agreements might encompass both sets of provisions in that the network operator acts as an interface between the providers of balancing services and the users of the system.

Principles of Access

10.47 **Principles used in the telecommunications sector are applicable *mutatis mutandis* in the energy sector.**   The Commission published a Notice on the application of the competition rules to access agreements in the telecommunications sector[63] setting out a framework for the analysis of access agreements or refusals of access. Such a notice is not available in the energy sector though many of the issues raised in this sector are similar to the ones dealt with in the telecommunications Notice.[64] The issues dealt with below have arisen from informal complaints and notifications.

---

[61] See, for example, *British Gas Network Code* (Notice pursuant to Article 19(3) of Regulation 17) [1996] OJ C93/5, para 15, where 'data exchange' figures among the operational rules looked at by the Commission.

[62] For example, Transco in the UK gas market and Scottish Electricity Settlement Ltd in the Scottish electricity market.

[63] Notice on the application of the competition rules to access agreements in the telecommunications sector—framework, relevant markets and principles [1998] OJ C265/2.

[64] This similarity of issues is taken into account in the Notice where para 6 reads: 'As this Notice is based on the generally applicable competition rules, the principles set out in this Notice will, to

Agreements Relating to the Reservation or Allocation of Network Capacity

The Commission has dealt with agreements relating to the reservation or alloca-   **10.48**
tion of capacity on electricity and gas networks in following cases:

- the arrangements between the National Grid Company (NGC) and Electricité
  de France (EdF) for the use of the France–United Kingdom electricity interconnector;[65]
- the National Grid Company/Scottish Interconnector Agreement relating to
  the use of the electricity connector between England and Scotland;[66]
- the agreements relating to the operation of the Belgium–United Kingdom gas
  interconnector.[67]

All these cases were dealt with before the Directives on the internal market for
electricity and on the internal market for gas were adopted. The solutions found
in these cases varied and were not in line with the most recent conclusions of the
Commission as set out in the Second Report on Harmonisation Requirements[68]
published after the entry into force of the electricity Directive.

In the UK–France electricity case, the Commission adopted a favourable position   **10.49**
on a three-year agreement between the owners of the interconnector, ie NGC and
EdF, by which EdF was granted exclusive use of the interconnector for exports to
the UK pool and for imports into the French system.

At the same time, the Commission accepted an agreement between NGC,   **10.50**
Scottish Power, and Scottish Hydro-Electric concerning the use of the high-
voltage transmission link between Scotland and England. The two latter parties
were granted exclusive use of the link under an agreement of an indefinite duration that could be terminated on five years' notice served by any party on the
others or by the national regulator for electricity.[69] This agreement was different
from the one concluded by NGC with EdF in that Scottish Power and Hydro-
Electric had the obligation to make available to third parties any part of the interconnector capacity they would not themselves require.

---

the extent that comparable problems arise, be equally applicable in other areas, such as access issues
in digital communications sectors generally. Similarly, several of the principles contained in the
Treaty will be of relevance to any company occupying a dominant position, including those in fields
other than telecommunications.'

[65] *Reorganisation of the electricity industry in England and Wales* (Notice pursuant to Article 19(3)
of Regulation 17) [1990] OJ C191/9.

[66] *Reorganisation of the electricity industry in Scotland* (Notice pursuant to Article 19(3) of
Regulation 17) [1990] OJ C245/9.

[67] [1995] OJ C73/18, Commission press release IP(95)550 and *Report on Competition Policy
1995* (Vol XXV) 125.

[68] Second Report to the Council and to the European Parliament on Harmonisation
Requirements, 16 April 1999, COM(1999) 164 final.

[69] In the UK, the then Director General of Electricity Supply.

10.51 The 'non-used contracted capacity release' *obligation* that existed in the Scottish Interconnector Arrangements was not found in the case of the UK–Belgium gas interconnector. This case, which was particular in that it concerned the *creation* of an infrastructure by nine companies, was cleared on the assumption that a secondary market for 'non-used capacity' would emerge naturally due to the relatively high number of capacity holders, ie of potential capacity sellers.

10.52 It seems that the lenient approach the Commission has adopted so far towards capacity reservation agreements will not prevail for the future. Indeed, the Commission has already indicated both in the *Report on Competition Policy 1998* (Vol XXVIII) and in the *Second Report on Harmonization Requirements* that it would concentrate on network access and more particularly on capacity reservation agreements with a view to opening up interconnectors in the Union.

10.53 The legal analysis the Commission could adopt in future cases cannot be easily inferred from past practice in the sector. However, the following elements could play a role in the assessment of a case by the Commission :

1. The extent to which capacity is reserved by way of bilateral agreements. This analysis is complex in a context where flows of opposite directions on interconnectors can balance themselves, thus leading the Commission to concentrate on the available net capacity in each direction rather than on abstract 'gross' values for reserved capacity. This approach could lead the Commission to question capacity agreements used for transmitting gas or electricity in one direction only though providing for a full reservation of an interconnector in both directions. In addition, the Commission may take into account differences in consumption patterns on the electricity or gas market when assessing the commercial interest of any free capacity that would remain uncontracted. For example, an agreement granting exclusive rights to one electricity company during winter/peak hours but leaving open free capacity in summer or at night would not be equivalent to the opposite one.

2. The duration of any capacity reservation agreement. Past practice in that respect is of limited help, with accepted durations going from three years to an indefinite period. However, one may assume that the Commission would adopt a more lenient view towards those contracts the more likely to satisfy the criteria laid down in Article 81(3) in that, for example, they would allow for the creation of new transmission capacity between Member States.

3. The provisions governing 'non-used contracted capacity'. This capacity arises when the holder of a capacity reservation agreement does not use the totality of the rights it has secured. Past practice varies between 'no provision at all', 'obligation to release', and 'natural creation of a secondary market'. The political statements of the Commission suggest that the first approach would be hardly acceptable in the context of the liberalization. The two other

options[70] seem to be still available. Technical provisions governing the release of capacity may be of importance since inappropriate rules may jeopardize the underlying objective: for example, free capacity should be released and/or offered for sale early enough to make it interesting for competitors to bid for it.

Agreement on Transmission Pricing

Transmission charges and competition between grids were dealt with in the 'Verbändevereinbarung' case. An agreement (the 'Verbändevereinbarung'— VV) was concluded in Germany on 22 May 1998 between associations of undertakings representing the industry (BDI, Bundesverband der Deutschen Industrie eV, and VIK, Verband der Industriellen Energie- und Kraftwirtschaft eV) and the electricity supply industry (VDEW, Vereinigung Deutscher Elektrizitätswerke eV).[71]   **10.54**

Under the Electricity Directive, Member States may choose between two main methods for market opening: Third Party Access (TPA) and Single Buyer. TPA can be implemented in the form of negotiated TPA (nTPA) or regulated TPA (rTPA). Under nTPA, network operators and network users have to negotiate the transmission fee whereas, under rTPA, access is granted on the basis of a published tariff. The German law provides for the implementation of nTPA[72] but the Government favoured the conclusion of a framework agreement setting out the criteria to determine transmission fees. Indeed, there are eight different network owners at high-voltage level and several hundred network owners at medium- and low-voltage level in Germany and the strict application of the nTPA principle could have created great difficulties.   **10.55**

The main features[73] of the 1998 agreement can be summarized as follows: **10.56**

- Transmissions fees are calculated according to the criteria laid down in the VV but taking into account the actual costs of each relevant network operator.[74]

- For transmissions on the high-voltage grid and over a distance of more than 100 km, a distance related fee is charged in addition to the distance independent fee charged below 100 km. The VV not only lays down this principle but also sets the level of that fee.

---

[70] Of course, other options may be possible. For example: obligation to release capacity in order to offer it for sale on a secondary market.

[71] The Commission has not opposed the VV, and the parties to the agreement and the Ministry for Economic Affairs have made public their intention to have the VV examined by the Commission.

[72] A Single Buyer regime is optional for distributors. The principles set out in the VV apply also to the tarification of the use of the Single Buyers' grids.

[73] This presentation gives a very simplified view of the agreement, leaving aside items like ancillary services, coincidence factors, practical limits for transmssion distances.

[74] With the exception of the distance related high-voltage transmission fee.

The VV is an agreement between associations of undertakings whose purpose is to fix in common price criteria and, to a limited extent, their level. The question as to whether such an agreement on prices is capable of falling under Article 81(1) because it restricts competition amounts, to a large extent, to identifying whether:

— competition is at all restricted, ie whether it was possible among network operators;

— an agreement on a pricing method is capable of falling under Article 81(1).

The analysis of the Commission[75] suggests that there is competition in the long run between electricity grid owners.

10.57 Customers (for example, power plants operators, industrial users) might take into account differences in transmission fees when assessing the profitability of new investments in certain geographic areas. In addition, customers have the possibility to build direct lines. Some customers may be in a position to choose the source of energy they use. For example, an industrial customer auto-producing electricity may decide between buying electricity or a primary fuel (for example, gas). In that case the comparative price of gas and electricity transmission could play an important role in the economic analysis. Finally, grids actually do compete in the European Union; different routes to send gas and electricity over long distances are in competition in certain geographic areas.

10.58 In addition, it seems the Commission found in that case that at least an agreement on the price of the distance related component was capable of falling under Article 81(1). It is not clear from the sole publication on the subject whether the agreement on a method was assessed in the same way.

The Commission did not undertake formal proceedings against the VV since it found that the negative aspects quoted above were counterbalanced by a certain number of beneficial effects on competitive market development.

Stranded Costs

10.59 The issue of stranded costs was dealt with in the Non Fossil Fuel Obligation (NFFO) and Non Fossil Fuel Purchasing Authority (NFPA) cases.[76] These concerned the arrangements made in the context of the privatization of the UK electricity industry for the continued functioning of the UK nuclear power stations. An obligation to purchase from nuclear installations was placed on distribution companies (regional electricity companies—RECs), with a concomitant obligation to buy from renewable sources. The RECs bought principally from Nuclear

---

[75] *Competition Policy Newsletter*, October 1998 No 3, 43.
[76] *Reorganisation of the electricity industry in England and Wales* (Notice pursuant to Article 19(3) of Regulation 17) [1990] OJ C191/9.

Electric. A fossil fuel levy was imposed, raised as a levy from sources of electricity derived from fossil fuels. These monies were passed to the RECs to compensate them for having bought higher priced nuclear or renewable generated electricity. 'Qualifying arrangements' brought a REC within the benefit of the scheme, the main part of the qualifying arrangements being made through a joint purchasing agency (NFPA).

The Commission justified these arrangements on the basis that they secured secu-   **10.60**
rity of supply through fuel diversity; these arrangments could have been equally justified through reference to the pro-competitive effect of the overall scheme of the privatization, and, indeed, the real threat of short-term severe supply disruption occasioned by financial difficulties in the nuclear industry, which supplied 17 per cent of UK electricity at that time. The real motivation may have been the fact that they enabled the orderly transition to a functioning electricity market, and compensated nuclear assets holders in a non-discriminatory way.

(2) Long-Term and Exclusive Agreements

Length of Contracts; Scottish Nuclear, Scottish Power, Hydro-Electric

Contract periods can be limited by Commission intervention.   The first case   **10.61**
which dealt with this issue concerned the restructuring of the electricity industry in Scotland in 1990. In the context of the privatization of the North of Scotland Hydro-Electric Board and of the South of Scotland Electricity Board, the Government of the United Kingdom wished to give the newly privatized companies access to a diversified generating capacity portfolio, including access to electricity generated by Scottish Nuclear Ltd, an undertaking then bound to remain in the public sector. Two contracts between Scottish Nuclear and respectively Hydro-Electric and Scottish Power were notified to the Commission in 1990 and the Commission adopted, in 1991, a Decision[77] authorizing these contracts for a duration of fifteen years.

The contracts had the following main characteristics: **10.62**

- Scottish Nuclear was not permitted, unless the contract had been terminated, to supply electricity to any other party without the consent of both Scottish Power and Hydro-Electric;

- they imposed a take-or-pay obligation on the buyers for respectively 74.9 per cent and 25.1 per cent of Scottish Nuclear's production;

- the price at which nuclear electricity was purchased was fixed under the agreements and was identical for the two companies; and

---

[77] (EEC) 91/329: Commission Decision of 30 April 1991 relating to a proceeding under Article 85 [now Article 81] of the EEC Treaty (IV/33.473—*Scottish Nuclear, Nuclear Energy Agreement*).

• the contracts were for an initial duration of thirty years.

10.63 The Commission found that the contracts restricted competition and affected trade between Member States.[78] However, the Commission decided that the contracts could benefit from an exemption under Article 81(3) after their duration had been reduced from thirty to fifteen years. The Commission accepted the other restrictions (for example exclusive sale) attached to the contracts and limited its intervention to the issue of duration.

10.64 The initial thirty-year duration was justified as follows by the Government of the United Kingdom:

> The United Kingdom Government therefore decided that the necessary restructuring should be achieved by means of contractual arrangements which create rights and obligations between the two utilities in relation to certain of the generating assets and transmission systems of each, effectively replacing ownership of these assets with long-term contractual entitlements the duration of which corresponds to the currently expected lifetime of the power stations concerned.

The Commission justified the new fifteen-year duration as follows:

> The agreement, which was originally to apply for a period equivalent to the remaining lifetime of the nuclear power stations, ie 30 years, has, at the Commission's request, been limited to 15 years. This period of validity provides the stability and guarantee necessary for long-term planning and allows the necessary adjustments to be made to the new situation after a reasonable start-up period. However, this period seems necessary to allow Scottish Nuclear to attain full profitability and become competitive.

The Commission substituted for the 'expected lifetime' criterion a duration created *ex nihilo* without providing any detailed economic justification that could have explained why precisely fifteen years were necessary. However, the Commission's aim was clearly to free up the market, while not standing in the way of the liberalization of the UK market.

Contract Length and Market Foreclosure; *Electricidade de Portugal/Pego project,*[79] *REN/Turbogás,*[80] and *ISAB Energy*[81]

10.65 **The Commission has dealt with restrictions arising from market foreclosure by limiting contract periods.**   These cases present similarities in that:

---

[78] The extent to which agreements between Scottish companies may affect trade between Member States may be open to discussion.

[79] *Electricidade de Portugal/Pego project* (Notice pursuant to Article 19(3) of Regulation 17) [1993] OJ C265/3.

[80] *REN/Turbogás* (Notice pursuant to Article 19(3) of Regulation 17) [1996] OJ C118/7.

[81] *ISAB Energy* (Notice pursuant to Article 19(3) of Regulation 17) [1996] OJ C138/3.

- they all involved power purchase agreements (PPA) concluded between a new electricity producer[82] and the incumbent monopoly;

- the PPA that were notified to the Commission were of long duration (respectively twenty-eight, twenty-five, and twenty years);

- the Commission did not accept these durations, taking into account the fact that the contracts provided for an exclusivity of supply and that the power producer would be prevented from delivering electricity to consumers other than the incumbent monopoly; and

- the contracts all got approval from the Commission for a duration reduced to fifteen years.

In the Pego project, the capacity and output of the power station was reserved **10.66** exclusively to Electricidade de Portugal for fifteen years and a 'first option' system for the remaining thirteen years of the contract, allowing the generator to sell to third parties if there is surplus capacity not required by the grid, was put in place.

Three years later, in the *REN/Turbogás* case, the same 'first option' clause was sub- **10.67** mitted to the Commission. The Commission asked the parties to amend it so as to allow the generator to opt to sell the capacity and power to third parties after fifteen years. However, the financial arrangements in that contract led to the result that the generator would receive a high price for its electricity during the first fifteen years whereas a lower price was agreed for the remaining period. As a consequence of the 'front loading' of financial costs, if the generator opts to sell to third parties after fifteen years, the contracts provide for a compensation mechanism (to the benefit of the incumbent monopoly) for the loss of the low-cost supply envisaged in the latter years of the agreement.

In the *ISAB Energy* case, the twenty-year contract was not amended but the **10.68** Commission came to the conclusion that the case should be re-examined after the first fifteen years of commercial operation.

In its examination of these agreements the Commission systematically concen- **10.69** trated on the restriction of competition arising from the exclusive supply clause which was present in all cases. The Commission imposed the fifteen-year duration as a standard in this matter though there is no apparent objective legal or economic justification for the choice of that figure. The fifteen-year figure seems to represent the Commission's compromise between what is necessary in order to provide long-term security for heavy stand-alone investments and what is an unacceptable restriction of competition in a manner contrary to the Treaty.

---

[82] Effect on trade may be open to discussion since the size of the generating plants was, in all cases, small.

Reasonable Contract Length and the Liberalization Directives;
Electrabel/Intercommunales mixtes[83]

10.70 **The Commission intervenes again to limit contract length, in anticipation of the market opening envisaged under the Electricity Directive.** In 1996, the Commission took action following the conclusion by Electrabel, a private company producing more than 90 per cent of all electricity consumed in Belgium, of new contracts (known as 'statutes') with the so-called 'intercommunales mixtes de distribution d'électricité' (mixed intercommunal distribution companies—MIDC).

10.71 MIDC are associations between communes and a private partner. In the case of distribution of electricity, the private partner is in all cases Electrabel. The seventeen MIDC represent 82 per cent of the electricity distribution in Belgium, the remaining 18 per cent being distributed by 'pure' intercommunal companies and by individual communes. Before 1996, MIDC had statutes with periods of validity until between 1998 and 2022. In 1996, new statutes were adopted simultaneously by sixteen of seventeen MIDC. These new statutes ran until dates between 2016 and 2026 (twenty to thirty years duration). A clause in the statutes granted Electrabel the exclusive right to supply the distribution company with the electricity required for resale to its final consumers. This clause was to operate for the whole duration of the new statutes, ie for twenty to thirty years.

10.72 The Commission concentrated not only on the duration of the agreements but also, in relation to the supply of electricity to the MIDC by Electrabel, on the resulting degree of exclusivity.

10.73 In particular, the Commission concluded that the statutes were agreements between undertakings (ie between the MIDC and Electrabel) providing for the exclusive supply of electricity by Electrabel throughout the whole duration of the statutes and that the cumulative effect of these agreements was to foreclose for a long period the market for the supply of electricity to MIDC.

10.74 The Commission also objected to the agreement relating to the supply by Electrabel of distribution services (the day-to-day management of the distribution company) to the MIDC for the whole duration of the statutes. Finally, the Commission objected to certain aspects of the financial arrangements entered into by Electrabel and the communes regarding the sale by Electrabel of 5 per cent of its shares to the communes participating in the new statutes.

10.75 A settlement was reached by the Commission and the parties in April 1997 and the following amendments were made:

---

[83] Commission press release IP(97)351.

- Exclusive supply of electricity by Electrabel will cease completely in 2011 (ie after fifteen years). Thereafter, all MIDC will be free to obtain supplies from the supplier of their choice. Furthermore, the financial arrangements mentioned will come to an end at the same time as Electrabel's remaining supply rights, in 2011.

- After 2006 (ie after ten years), the exclusivity will be lifted for 25 per cent of the MIDC's requirements. Each of them will have the right, after giving four years' notice, to obtain from third parties a quantity of electricity equivalent to 25 per cent of its total requirements for supply after 2006. The electricity will be constant supply ('baseload'), while Electrabel will continue to supply the balance, including peak load supplies. The security of supply for the 25 per cent, which the MIDC may source from a third party, will be guaranteed by the supplier or another producer prepared to provide this.

- Electrabel will not oppose the dissolution, with full compensation for Electrabel, of the MIDC after 2011 if the communes associated in the MIDC so decide.

Issues for the Future

All the cases mentioned above were examined by the Commission before the entry **10.76** into force of the Directive concerning common rules for the internal market in electricity. The Commission has not provided any guidance as to how it will deal with new cases presenting characteristics similar to the ones described above. However, we do.

Electricity Contracts between Generators

The market configuration that existed in most of the previous cases dealt with by **10.77** the Commission, ie the existence of a monopoly generator purchasing the totality of the electricity produced by a new entrant on the market over a long period of time, should change. Independent producers will be able to sell their electricity directly to final eligible customers.

However, it cannot be excluded that the Commission will have to examine contracts between generators, since prevalent relative market shares will not disappear in the near future. Thus, some independent producers may still have to sell their production to an incumbent monopolist because, for example, the latter would be the sole potential purchaser for some 'types' of electricity (for example, electricity that is a by-product from an industrial production process, produced in very small quantities, or on an irregular basis).

In most cases, the potential restriction of competition would arise from an exclus- **10.78** ive sale obligation imposed on the independent producer or from the long duration of the contracts.

10.79   The exclusive sale obligation would have the effect of shielding the purchaser generator from any competition by the seller. The Commission has in previous cases not objected to such agreements but this happened in a context where competition was, to a large extent, not possible because of the existence, for example, of monopoly rights. With the new framework resulting from the electricity Directive, competition between generators would be expected and the Commission may be very reluctant to give its consent to such agreements between potential competitors. However, it may be the case that the parties to these agreements can show that competition could not take place, for example because the generators do not operate on the same product market.

Electricity Contracts between Generators and Distributors

10.80   The analysis of the contracts between generators and distributors will have to take into account the new orientations proposed by the Commission in the Green Paper on vertical restraints in EC Competition Policy.[84] It is probable that contracts falling outside the regulation would be notified individually to the Commission and that the parties would point to the specificity of the sector (for example, the applicability of Article 86(2)) in their request for exemption.

10.81   The solution adopted in 'Electrabel' owed much to the particular facts and legal situation of the case. It is far from evident that the Commission would wish to apply the same solution to any other case involving distribution companies. In any event, further action may take account of an exhaustive analysis of the conditions prevailing in all the Member States in order to get a clear perception as to what is 'acceptable' for market participants. We suggest that, in the context of harmonization put in place by the Directive, comparisons between Member States may be a good way for the Commission and notifying parties to get precise answers when dealing with justifications brought by the parties either under Article 81(3) or under Article 86(2).

Electricity Contracts between Suppliers and Eligible Customers

10.82   Despite a lack of previous experience in this field, it is to be expected that the Commission will concentrate its efforts on the relations between generators or other types of electricity suppliers and final consumers. Private industrial consumers are likely to try to take advantage of the new opportunities set out in the electricity Directive. Consideration will be given to:

- the 'Delimitis' rule which will be applicable, for example, in the case of standard contracts entered into by a supplier; and

- the definition and size of the reference market. The Commission will have to take into account the degree of market opening achieved in each Member State

---

[84] COM(96)721 final.

when it comes to assess what impact an anti-competitive agreement may have in reality.

Restrictions of competition may be the result of the nature (for example, exclusive purchase) and of the duration of the contracts.

The Commission should take into account the specific nature of the product **10.83** when assessing the effect of any exclusive purchase clause included in a contract. Indeed, exclusive purchase has always been the rule in the electricity sector and, even within the framework laid down by the Directive, non-exclusive purchase will not always be technically easy, subject to the market organization[85] adopted in each Member State. If non-exclusive purchase is technically easy, the Commission would have to examine exclusive purchase clauses under Articles 81 and 82 in order to determine exactly the extent of any restriction that may exist.

The duration of the contracts may be evaluated in relation to their exclusive char- **10.84** acter and it may be the case that the Commission would accept the conclusion of exclusive contracts provided that these are of short duration. The definition of a 'right' duration is a recurrent problem for the Commission. A solution could be found in that the Commission does not try to define it *ex nihilo* but rather takes advantage of the existence and development, in some Member States, of functioning markets.

Long-Term Take or Pay or other Hydrocarbons Contracts

Long-Term Agreements

The only long-term contract that the Commission has publicly dealt with **10.85** occurred in the Mercure/Saudi Aramco merger.[86] In that, under the ancillary restraints doctrine, a long-term exclusive contract was referred for clearance under Article 81. It would have had to have been justified if it had been for investment purposes. In such a case, the term of such a contract has to be justified by reference to financing major infrastructure and to production/exploration projects. The simple reservation of the market is not enough.

Escape Clauses/Adjustment Clauses

Some take-or-pay contracts contain escape or adjustment clauses that allow the **10.86** purchaser to reduce their commitment if the seller either directly sells, or sells to a competitor of the buyer, further hydrocarbons. This restriction is not justifiable under Article 81(3), as no greater competition is engendered, and there is no benefit to the final consumer.

---

[85] See the differences between a pool and a contracts based system, for example.
[86] *Saudi Aramco/MOH* (Case IV/M574) (1995).

Pricing

10.87 **Pricing provisions may constitute a restriction of competition if there is no real-istic possibility of another supplier being able to undercut a contract price.** Advocates of long-term contracts for gas supply argue that the indeterminacy of future pricing means that suppliers will only invest if they are protected against future price falls. In some respects, UK price escalator clauses have this function as they are commonly linked to producer price indices or retail price indices.[87] These are independent of broader energy market considerations, and thus a downturn in a competing fuel will have a lesser effect than were the escalator be linked to, say, heavy fuel oil.

10.88 However, continental gas escalators allow not only price increases but decreases and are more commonly linked to competing fuels, especially heavy fuel oil. Even in the UK, there is a move away from producer or retail indices to market indices, influenced by a price obtained in a liquid market (such as the electricity pool price or gas spot prices).[88]

10.89 This state of affairs can be contrasted against the experience of other industries, where long-term prior contracting is not the norm, such as oil markets or the avi-ation sector. Clearly investments here are made with uncertain knowledge of future pricing conditions. Long-term contracting as favoured by gas and electric-ity utilities does not avoid this uncertainty when prices are indexed against com-peting fuels. A long-term gas or electricity contract with such pricing provisions does not guarantee a price, only a market. For this reason, pricing provisions will have an effect on how a long-term contract is evaluated under the scheme of Article 81 if the justification of the contract length and pricing provisions is the need to amortize expended capital.

Relationship to Security of Supply

10.90 Security of supply may be used as a justification under Article 81(3) as this may be a significant benefit for consumers that arises from the contract, or under Article 86(2) if relevant public service obligations have been imposed on one of the par-ties to a contract.

10.91 In looking at long-term contracts for fuel supply, and in this area this refers mainly to gas imports, the Commission has not given any indication of what the rela-tionship between security of supply and competition policy is. The Commission has stated that there is a relationship and has stated that there is a place for long-term take-or-pay gas contracts in securing energy supply.

---

[87] Bledyn GL Phillips, 'Examining the Future of Long-Term Take or Pay Contracts', UK Gas Industry Forum 1996.
[88] Ibid, 12.

• Political risk; this type of risk, by which is meant the type of catastrophic supply disruption occasioned by war or internal national disturbance, is rarely addressed by a specific contract. It is often proposed as an argument[89] in favour of the contract form, though, in practice, it is discounted. It played a part in the discussions on take-or-pay contracts in the gas Directive. It was invoked in the *Campus Oil* case.[90] This type of argument would have to be based on the criteria set by the ECJ in that case. In addition, it is likely that, for this type of argument to be successful, the security of supply justification must result from a specific State or community action. Thus, this type of argument will normally be addressed in the context of Article 86(2) and not Article 81(3).[91]

• Incentivizing investment; this argument arises in cases where it is argued that but for the take-or-pay agreement, the parties would not undertake investment, either individually or together. In long-term developments of new gas fields, for example, it is often argued that, without secure outlets for the product, parties would not be willing to invest either in the upstream production area, or in the transmission facilities to bring gas to end-consumers. This is an 'indispensability argument' that logically predicates a discussion of the application of Article 81(1), because in the absence of the 'restriction' neither one could have secured the market outcome. There is intense discussion about these types of argument: first, it is questioned whether this indispensability exists at all, given the empirical evidence from around the world that large-scale upstream and distribution investments are made in the absence of such restrictions, and that comparable high capital industries undertake larger investments without any security of sales; and, secondly, a signal that this argument is not valid might have the perverse effect of restricting market entry because smaller players would not be able to minimize risk, thus leaving the field open to integrated companies and larger market players. What balance to strike between these arguments will have to be arrived at in a particular case.

• Security of delivery; this arises from issues relating to the physical delivery of energy supplies to a consumer, and is usually encountered in discussion of network bound industries. Thus it played a part in the arrangements for the organization of the UK electricity supply and the Network Code for the UK gas market. In the latter case, certain minimum levels of customer service were agreed upon by competitors and, on these elements, there was an agreement not to compete. If these restrictions bring real benefits to consumers, are

---

[89] *BP/Sonatrach* (Case IV/M672) (1996).

[90] C–72/83 *Campus Oil Limited and others v Minister for Industry and Energy and others* [1984] ECR I–2727.

[91] Security of supply in this context is really the development of relations with supplier countries; for the approach on this subject see; *An Overall View of Energy Policy and Actions,* section II A1, Com (97) 167 final.

non-discriminatory, and do not increase substantially barriers to entry, they would be capable of exemption under Article 81(3). This is a form of prudential self-regulation.

- It seems that the Commission has implicitly recognized a shift from security of consumption to security of supply. This became apparent in the course of the *Electrabel* case. The communes in Belgium (MIDC) have the obligation to provide an uninterrupted supply of electricity to their customers. It follows that the MIDC were ready to enter into long-term supply agreements if these could give them sufficient guarantees as to this security. This element was new for the Commission in so far as it had concentrated, in past cases, on the 'supply side'. Indeed, the decision in *Scottish Nuclear* and the positions adopted in cases like *Pego* or *ISAB Energy* had the effect of securing output for respectively a nuclear power plant and new investors on the market. The fact that the buyers in these previous cases were producers of electricity probably made any analysis in terms of security of supply purposeless. The attention paid to security of supply in the *Electrobel* case can be inferred from the reading of the solution agreed with the parties. As of 2006, the MIDC will have the *right* to buy a part of their requirements from third parties. This means that the MIDC have got certainty as to supply by Electrabel until 2011 if they do not wish to exercise their right to buy from third parties.

(3) Upstream Co-operation

Joint Operating Agreements

10.92 In the upstream sector, production of oil and gas from reserves is usually undertaken by more than one company in any given field. The Commission has accepted the fact of multiple firm co-operation in upstream developments. In the recitals to the hydrocarbons licensing Directive, licensing is limited in time and geography to prevent 'the reservation to a single entity of an exclusive right over an area which can be prospected, explored and brought into production more efficiently by several entities'.[92] Such an approach is warranted to prevent reservation of 'blocks' to favoured companies and also not to send a policy signal that only large or integrated companies ought to develop hydrocarbons reserves.

10.93 The relationship between these companies can take many forms; the most common form though is that based on a joint operating agreement. What is considered acceptable under Article 81(1) as being non-restrictive of competition in joint operating agreements has been alluded to in the *Britannia* case Article 19(3) Notice. This reference is to the timing of development, siting of wells and infra-

---

[92] Directive (EC) 94/22 of the European Parliament and of the Council of 30 May on the conditions for granting and using authorisations for the prospection, exploration and production of hydrocarbons [1994] OJ L164/3, Article 1; 'entities' in the Directive covers consortia, a consortium being an 'entity'.

structure, etc. However, caution should be observed here as the joint operating agreement was not the object of the notification and thus joint operating agreements have not been treated by the Commission. Nevertheless, when looking at joint operating agreements, thought must be had to;

- the position of the parties on the market;

- the information requirements and confidentiality guarantees imposed as a result of it;

- the possible use that the joint operating agreement may have for equalizing the competitive positions of the parties to it; and

- the structures put in place that may restrain any of the parties from pursuing their individual interests.

In the case that a joint operating agreement creates a veto power vested in one **10.94** party on individual behaviour by another as regards selling or commercializing gas, very strong arguments would have to be adduced to consider this for exemption. The Commission has not yet seen such arguments. The definition of joint operating agreements proposed by Professor Crommelin rightly addresses the balance between common actions and common business:

> Each participant in the joint venture is undoubtedly engaged in business (that of discovery and exploitation of natural resources) with a view of profit. At the same time the participants are undertaking some common activities. *But they are not carrying on a business in common with a view of profit.* Rather they are carrying on several businesses each with a view to profit, some aspects of which are performed in common.[93][Emphasis added.]

Drafters and participants in joint operating agreements should consider carefully their effect.

Joint Selling

Joint selling has not been considered in any decisions though it was the issue in the **10.95** *Britannia* case. In that case, a consortium of gas field developers, jointly developing the Britannia gas condensate field in the United Kingdom North Sea, sought negative clearance or exemption for the practice of joint selling of their gas. The Commission concluded that the joint selling arrangement, despite the fact that the parties were able to withdraw from the arrangement at will, constituted a restriction of competition within the scope of Article 81(1).

In this case, the argument was made that but for the joint selling the parties would **10.96** not have undertaken the investment to secure production from the Britannia

---

[93] Michael Crommelin 'The mineral and petroleum joint venture in Australia', Journal of Energy and Natural Resources Law (1986) 4/68.

field; if this was correct, the withdrawal option was of no practical content. The Commission came to the view that the joint selling arrangement constituted a restriction by first concluding that the field's development might have been secured by other means. The joint selling was a means of realizing other aims and therefore it was unlikely that any party would opt out of the joint selling. The Commission, in its Article 19(3) Notice, made it quite clear that, in its opinion, the joint selling arrangement had no effect on trade, and for that reason fell outside the scope of Article 81(1).

Indispensable Restrictions

10.97 The *Britannia* case demonstrated that the Commission is open to arguments as to the indispensability of certain restrictions under Article 81(1) in the winning and commercialization of hydrocarbons.[94] These most commonly relate to joint activities with regard to infrastructure choice and development, limited commercial issues, such as swing, shutdown, *force majeure*, and timing of the realization of the project.[95] In the *Britannia* case, the Commission did not accept the indispensability of prior sales of gas for field development, although in the merger case *BP/Sonatrach* this approach was not adopted, but was also not germane to the decision.[96]

Information in Consortia

10.98 Upstream oil and gas consortia in present arrangements share great amounts of commercial information. Information about fields, pipelines, and other infrastructure is shared by reason of the disparate and dispersed nature of ownership. Shares in fields are often less than 1 per cent, which entitles the owner to full information about the intentions of co-venturers. Significantly the fact of dispersed shares across a market leads to the view that information might be abused despite confidentiality agreements. The Commission has not had the opportunity to pursue this issue; some notifications of oilfield developments have raised this issue, although the problem may not be so pronounced in oil as it is in gas.

Concerted Buying

10.99 Concerted buying (or joint buying) has been advanced as one way of ensuring security of supply. Its dismantlement is the mirror action to the dismantlement of joint selling. It can be supposed that some instances of joint buying will not fall within the scope of Article 81(1) because in the absence of the joint buying some forms of investment would not otherwise have taken place. Specifically, one can

---

[94] Similar arguments have been made and accepted with regard to oil field developments.

[95] *Britannia gas condensate field* (Notice pursuant to Article 19(3) of Regulation 17) [1996] OJ C291/10, paras 3 and 4.

[96] *BP/Sonatrach* (Case IV/M672) (1996).

point to very large, capital intensive projects which will create their specific infra-structure. However, these instances will be limited and, from the perspective of today, probably historical.

Another argument advanced in favour of joint buying is that often the buyers are **10.100** not competitors in their 'own' markets. This ignores potential competition between them and the fact that there is competition to secure gas suppplies.

The argument advanced that joint buying ought to be allowed in the case where a **10.101** buyer is facing a dominant external supplier is advanced by some advocates of this type of restriction, though it has yet to be proved that there is a dominant external supplier and low levels of competition for supply into the Community. Others think that an external buyer will seek to maximize market share as his fixed costs are high. An external supplier may be constrained by the pricing of other fuels. And the external supplier may be compelled to supply by the fiscal needs of the State in which it finds itself. In this regard reference should be made to the general guidelines on horizontal co-operation.

D. Article 82

The Commission has made limited use of Article 82 in its most recent practice in **10.102** the energy sector. Reference to this article is expressly made on two occasions only : the 'SPEGNN' and 'Verbändevereinbarung' cases. The former is dealt with under the heading 'Exclusive rights and Article 86(2)' whilst the latter is discussed below.

Despite the limited record of cases in that sector, the Commission has made clear that it was willing to use Article 82 in cases relating to access to the networks fol- **10.103** lowing the entry into force of the Directives concerning an internal market for electricity and for natural gas.

(1) Refusal of Access to a Network

Both Directives contain provisions which may influence the Commission's **10.104** **assessment of such cases.** Firstly, the Directives provide for a definition of those customers which *have to* be granted access to the network (so-called 'eligible cus-tomers'). The Commission has not yet made clear whether it would stick to the definition of the Directives or whether it would be ready to use the 'essential facil-ity doctrine' with respect to non-eligible customers. However, the latter option would appear to be adventurous in a context where the interests of the Community have been expressly defined in the Directives as including, *inter alia*, competition with regard to *eligible* customers.

Secondly, the Directives expressly provide for a limited number of reasons that **10.105** may justify a refusal of access to the system. These may relate to lack of capacity or to reciprocity. It is questionable whether the Commission would accept other justifications during the assessment of a refusal under Article 82. Furthermore, reference to the justifications laid down in the Directives may lead to a separate assessment of the behaviour of the transmission system operator that has refused access with a view to determining whether discrimination occurred (for example, if a transmission system operator were to refuse access to certain companies *only*). In addition, refusals based on 'lack of capacity' in a context where a part of the total capacity has been reserved by certain users may trigger an examination of the contracts governing the reservation and use of the capacity in question.

10.106   Lastly, the absence so far of any reference case before the Commission may be due to the provisions in the Directives relating to the designation, by each Member State, of a competent authority in charge of settling disputes relating to access to the network. This has been done and the national authorities have now dealt with several such cases.

(2) Excessive or Discriminatory Pricing

10.107   **Some of the options for network access laid down in the Directives may allow for the imposition of excessive or discriminatory transmission charges that would be prohibited under Article 82 EC.**   The Commission has touched upon incidentally the problem of transmission charges in the notification concerning the United Kingdom gas network code.[97] The code contained detailed provisions as to the charges payable for use of the system. In the notice pursuant to Article 19(3) of Council Regulation 17/62 published on that occasion, the Commission indicated that it intended to take a favourable view on the code as a whole without detailing its assessment of the charging method. The Commission, however, made an express reference to the regulation of the charges (revenue cap) by the national regulator for the gas market so that the following conclusions may be drawn:

— the Commission was satisfied that the *level* of the fees was not in breach of Article 82 because it was controlled by the national regulator; and

— in addition, the charging *method* satisfied the non-discrimination test under Article 82.

10.108   Transmission charges were central in the discussion by the Commission of the Verbändevereinbarung concluded in 1998 between three German associations of undertakings. The Commission did not publish any official statement following its assessment of that case. However, an article published in the *DG IV Competition Policy Newsletter* indicates that several elements in the Verbändevereinbarung could give rise to serious doubts under Article 82:

---

[97] *British Gas Network Code* (Notice pursuant to Article 19(3) of Regulation 17) [1996] OJ C93/5.

— The pricing method contained a distance related component which could have had discriminatory effects in that it gave an advantage to those power producers located near their customers.

— The pricing method also provided for the calculation of an average weighted distance in case of multiple feed-in/offtake points. This element could lead to a discrimination in favour of those power producers with a large number of production plants and/or a large customer base.

— Finally, the simulations showed rather high price levels resulting from the application of the criteria. An important element that must have been taken into account in that respect was the absence of a control of these price levels by a national regulator.

(3) Confidentiality

Confidentiality of the information available to the transmission system operator is required both by the Directives and by Article 82. The Commission has **10.109** not yet dealt with cases where the confidentiality of information available to a transmission system operator was directly at stake. However, the Commission has already dealt with agreements relating, *in toto* or in part, to the preservation of confidential information. Hence the Commission approved the United Kingdom gas network code which contained provisions as to the obligations of TransCo, the system operator, in terms of confidentiality. The Commission also approved the Claims Validation Services Agreement whose exclusive purpose was also to secure confidentiality of information dealt with at some of the United Kingdom gas network entry points.

E. Exclusive Rights and Article 86 (2)

(1) Ijsselcentrale Case[98]

The interest of the Community is essential in determining the application of **1.110** **Article 86, and this interest is now codified in the electricity and gas directives.** The Commission concluded that provisions in an agreement between the four electricity generating companies (the generators) in The Netherlands and a joint-venture company (SEP) that they had set up infringed Article 81(1). The Commission found that the agreement, applied in conjunction with SEP's control and influence over international supplies, had the effect of:

• restricting exports of power by industrial consumers and distributors; and

• restricting imports of power by industrial consumers.[99]

---

[98] *Ijsselcentrale and others* [1991] OJ L28/32.
[99] The restrictions on imports of power by distributors had been laid down in the Dutch Electricity Law of 1989 and fell outside the scope of the Commission's decision.

The agreement, which had a duration of twenty-five years prohibited the generators from importing and exporting other than through SEP. It also required generators to impose the same prohibition in supply agreements on distributors.

10.111 The Commission proposed that SEP put an end to the infringement and 'inform
the parties to the co-operation agreement, and purchasers, that the agreement is
to be interpreted and applied as meaning that exports of quantities of electric
power not intended for public supply, and direct imports by private industrials
consumers, are unrestricted, and will not, without good reason, be obstructed by
virtue of the ownership or operation of the power grid by SEP and the parties to
the agreement'.[100]

10.112 This remedy was limited in scope. The Commission dealt with the situation of
'private' parties such as industrial consumers and independent producers. It did
not act against the exclusive purchase obligations set out in the agreements
between the regional distributor and the local distributors (municipalities) and in
the agreements between the local distributors and their final customers. The
Commission did not act against the obligation imposed by contract on the
regional distributor not to deliver electricity to consumers located within the distribution area of a local distributor (so-called vertical demarcation).

10.113 The exception of Article 86(2) was invoked by the parties. The Commission
admitted that both SEP and its shareholders (generating companies) were
entrusted with the operation of services of general economic interest but found
that the application of the competition rules would not obstruct SEP in the performance of the tasks it had been entrusted with. Finally, the Commission found
that, even if the restrictions were necessary under the first sentence of Article
86(2), they would be unacceptable under the second sentence of Article 86(2)
because they would restrict trade within Member States in a manner contrary to
the interests of the Community. The interest of the Community was then defined
as being that of 'achieving a single market in energy'.[101] (This objective has, with
the conclusion of the Directives cited below, been modified.)

*(2) Proceedings under Article 226—Exclusive Import and Export Rights for Gas
and Electricity*[102]

10.114 **The ECJ decisions clarify the application of Article 86 (2) in the energy sector.**
On 14 June 1994, the Commission lodged applications pursuant to Article 226
before the European Court of Justice against five Member States (Ireland, Spain,

---

[100] *Ijsselcentrale and others* [1991] OJ L28/32, point 55.
[101] Ibid, point 47.
[102] Cases C–157/94 *Commission v Netherlands*, exclusive rights to import electricity for public
distribution, C–158/94 *Commission v Italy*, exclusive rights to import and export electricity,
C–159/94 *Commission v France*, exclusive rights to import and export gas and electricity, C–160/94
Commission v Spain, exclusive rights to import and export electricity [1997] ECR I–5699 *et seq.*

France, Italy, The Netherlands) to assess the exclusive import and/or export rights for gas and/or electricity that then existed.

The action against Ireland was discontinued by the Commission[103] and, on 23 October 1997, the Court of Justice ruled on the four remaining cases. The application against Spain was dismissed because the Court found that the national law did not create monopoly import and export rights for electricity. The three other applications were dismissed for the reasons outlined below.[104]   **10.115**

Grounds for Dismissal

The Commission's applications relied on Articles 28, 29, and 31 (former Articles 30, 34, and 37) EC Treaty. In each case the Court found that the exclusive imports and/or export rights infringed Article 31 and that it was thus unnecessary to consider whether they were contrary to Articles 28 and 29. Consequently, the Court held that it was unnecessary additionally to consider whether the exclusive rights might possibly be justified under Article 30 EC Treaty.[105]   **10.116**

Further, the Court found that Article 86(2) was applicable to State measures which infringe the Treaty rules on free movement of goods. Thus, it examined the arguments put forward by the Member States in order to verify whether the conditions for the application of Article 86(2) were met.   **10.117**

Main Issues

The main issues examined by the Court concerned: **10.118**

The Concept of 'Service of General Economic Interest'

The Court quoted the judgment in *Almelo*[106] accepting that uninterrupted supply of electricity throughout a territory in sufficient quantities to meet demand at any given time at uniform tariff rates, which may not vary save in accordance with objective criteria applicable to all customers, is a task of general economic interest. The Court also quoted Commission Decision 91/50 *Ijsselcentrale and others*[107] where the Commission recognized that an undertaking entrusted with the main   **10.119**

---

[103] Mainly on the basis that the legislation in question was enabling legislation (it allowed a public corporation, the Electricity Supply Board, to do certain tasks, but did not imply that other bodies could not do the same).

[104] For a detailed discussion of these cases, see Rüdiger Dohms and Christian Levasseur, 'Commentaire des arrêts de la Cour relatifs aux monopoles d'importation et d'exportation de gaz et d'électricité' (February 1998) 1 *Competition Policy Newsletter* 18.

[105] In Case C–189/95 *Franzén* [1997] ECR I–5909, decided upon the same day, the Court adopted a different view. It also found that Article 30 could not be relied upon to justify infringements to Article 31 but, nevertheless, submitted the application of Article 31 to a test of proportionality before ruling that the Swedish alcohol monopoly was lawful.

[106] Case C–393/92 *Municipality of Almelo and others v NV Energiebedrijf Ijsselmij* [1994] ECR I–1477.

[107] *Ijsselcentrale and others* [1991] OJ L28/32.

task of ensuring the reliable and efficient operation of the national electricity supply at costs which are as low as possible and in a socially responsible manner provided services of general economic interest within the meaning of Article 86(2).

The Concept of Entrustment

10.120 The Court examined in detail to what extent the particular tasks quoted by the
defendant Member States had effectively been entrusted to the national monopoly undertakings by an act of public authority. In that context the Court
repeated its former finding in *Almelo* that this does not mean that a legislative
measure or regulation is required: the grant of a concession governed by public law
may be sufficient.

The Particular Tasks Entrusted to the National Monopoly Undertakings

10.121 On the substance the Court held that obligations imposed on an undertaking
must be linked to the provision of the service of general economic interest in question and make a direct contribution to satisfying that interest.

10.122 *In fine*, the Court accepted the following as 'particular tasks'.

- the obligation to supply all customers throughout the national territory
  (France—EDF);
- the obligation to supply all customers in the areas served (France—GDF);
- ensuring continuity of supply (EDF, GDF);
- observing equal treatment between customers (EDF, GDF);
- ensuring, together with the electricity generating undertakings, the proper
  functioning of the public national electricity supply system at costs which are as
  low as possible and in a socially responsible manner (Netherlands—SEP);
- ensuring at minimum management cost the availability of electrical energy of a
  quantity and at a price appropriate to the requirements of balanced economic
  development of the country (Italy—ENEL);
- the necessity of exclusive rights.

The Necessity of Exclusive Rights

10.123 The Court tried to examine the central question in the application of Article
86(2), ie to what extent the performance of the particular tasks identified could be
achieved only through the grant of an exclusive right.

10.124 Each Member State had provided detailed considerations as to the indispensability of the exclusive rights. On the other hand the Commission had hardly considered the economic aspects but concentrated on the legal issue (the
non-applicability of Article 86(2) to State measures which infringe the Treaty
rules on free movement of goods). In a rather unusual statement, the Court held

that it was not in a position, in these proceedings, to consider whether, by maintaining the exclusive rights at issue, the Member States had in fact gone further than was necessary to enable the public undertakings to perform, under economically acceptable conditions, the tasks of general economic interest assigned to them.

This conclusion has to be compared with those of Advocate General Cosmas   **10.125**
which had suggested that the exclusive import rights were justified under Article 86(2) whereas the exclusive export rights were not.

The absence of a clear statement as to the compatibility of the exclusive rights with   **10.126**
Article 86(2) led to the dismissal of the applications (it was for the Commission to prove its case in an action lodged under Article 226).

The Interests of the Community

The exception of Article 86(2) can only be granted subject to the proviso that the   **10.127**
development of trade must not be affected to such an extent as would be contrary to the interests of the community.

The Court held that in the present circumstances it was for the Commission, sub-   **10.128**
ject to review by the Court, to define the Community interest in relation to which the development of trade must be assessed. The Court found that the only Community measure concerning trade in electricity[108] expressly states that there is increasing trade in electricity from year to year between the high-voltage electricity grids in Europe (ie between monopolists) and concluded that trade was not affected in a manner contrary to the interests of the Community.

This approach is the opposite to the one adopted by the Commission in its   **10.129**
Decision 91/50 where paragraphs 47 and 48 read:

> In view of the forgoing there is no need to consider the last sentence of Article 86(2). It is clear, however, that obstruction of imports and exports such as that deriving from Article 21 of the Co-operation Agreement does affect trade to an extent contrary to the interests of the Community. In the light of the Community's efforts to achieve a single internal market in energy such obstruction of imports and exports, which moreover is intended to continue for a period of 25 years, cannot be accepted.
> Thus this provision of Article 86(2) is in any event not satisfied either.

The Directive concerning an internal market in electricity also has to be read in the light of that judgment: its Article 3(3) provides for a definition of the Community interest including, *inter alia,* competition with regard to eligible customers. *A contrario,* full competition does not yet seem to be in the Community's interest with regard to trade in electricity.

---

[108] Council Directive (EEC) 90/547 on the transit of electricity through transmission grids [1990] OJ L313/30 as last amended by Commission Decision (EC) 95/162, [1995] OJ L107/53.

(3) Failing Monopoly Theory

The *Société Hydroélectrique de Grangevieille (SHG)* case[109]

10.130   **A monopolist must perform those tasks for which it has been granted special or exclusive rights with a minimum level of efficiency.**   This case concerned an unusual factual situation: a power station was located in the French Alps at an altitude of 1,800 metres, at a distance of 20 metres from Italian territory and cut off from the rest of France by a mountain chain rising to 3,800 metres. The legal approach adopted by the Commission was the 'failing monopoly theory' using Article 81 EC Treaty against Electricité de France (EDF) and ENEL.

10.131   Owing to the particular geographical conditions of the case, SHG was not in a position to deliver its electricity to the French grid as should have been the case under French law. As a consequence, SHG delivered its electricity to the Italian grid—ENEL—and an agreement was concluded between EDF and ENEL. The purpose of this agreement was to maintain EDF's monopoly. Under this agreement, the electricity delivered by SHG to ENEL was deemed to have been purchased by EDF at the French rate less administrative costs and then sold to ENEL at the same rate. Following the doubling of Italian rates paid to independent power producers, SHG complained to the Commission arguing that it should be allowed to sell its electricity to ENEL directly and at the Italian price.

10.132   The Commission observed that, since EDF could not perform its tasks in this part of France, it could not exercise its exclusive rights there. Therefore, the contract between EDF and ENEL which was an expression of these exclusive rights, was void under Article 81(2).

10.133   Interestingly, the Commission did not base its action on Articles 82 and 86 with regard to the French law governing EDF's exclusive rights but rather chose to attack the contract between EDF and ENEL on the basis of Article 81 solely. So far this approach has been unique.

After a settlement between the parties, the Commission decided not to pursue the matter.

The *SPEGNN* case[110]

10.134   Where a monopolist is incapable or unwilling to undertake services in consideration of which special or exclusive rights have been granted, that monopolist cannot prevent a competitor from undertaking those services through the enforcement of its special or exclusive rights.

---

[109]   *Société Hydroélectrique de Grangevieille*—Commission press release IP(92)668.
[110]   Syndicat Professionnel des Entreprises Gazières Non Nationalisées, cf Commission press release IP(99)291.

In 1992, SPEGNN lodged a complaint alleging that Gaz de France (GDF) abused **10.135** its dominant position by prohibiting independent municipal distribution undertakings from expanding in French territory in areas where GDF was not present.[111]

The legal situation in the case derived from the French nationalization law of **10.136** 1946 granting GDF a monopoly for the distribution of gas in France. A few municipal distribution undertakings that were not nationalized in 1946 still operated independently but encountered difficulties in expanding to satisfy demand in contiguous communes. GDF contended that its exclusive distribution right prohibited any extension of the municipal distributors' activities.

The Commission prepared a decision establishing that France had violated Article **10.137** 86(1) read in conjunction with Article 82 EC Treaty. The State had led GDF to abuse its dominant position, because the State prohibited independent municipal distributors from satisfying demand in cases where the monopolist was incapable or unwilling to do so. In a rather unusual procedural move, the Commission adopted the decision in principle on 9 July 1997 but delayed its execution. It seems that this position was adopted because the Commission did not wish to interfere with the negotiations of the Directive concerning an internal market in gas as these entered into their crucial phase at the end of 1997.

Following the intervention of the Commission, France adopted a new law[112] **10.138** allowing operators other than GDF—be they municipal distributors or private companies—to create new gas distribution networks in those communes where none existed before.

The *SPEGNN* case illustrates the peculiar situation of the gas distribution sector **10.139** with regard to public service obligations. Indeed, the situation in France was such that GDF would only operate a network in those communes where a business plan indicated the highest estimated rate of return. As a result, the communes in which no gas distribution network had been built and which wished to deal with independent municipal distribution undertakings or with other private operators were not the 'cherries on the pie' whose freedom to contract could have endangered the equilibrium of the monopoly undertaking in place. On the contrary, the public undertaking entrusted with the operation of services of general economic

---

[111] See, among others, *Les Echos*, 10 July 1997, 'Bruxelles demande à Paris de revoir le monopole de distribution de GDF', *La Tribune*, 9 July 1997, 'Gaz : Bruxelles incite la France à assouplir les règles de distribution', *L'Humanité*, 26 February 1998, 'Gaz : un plan de desserte explosif', *AFP*, 25 February 1998 'DDOEF: plan triennal de desserte gazière des zones non desservies'. See Assemblée Nationale, Compte-rendu analytique officiel, Session ordinaire de 1997–1998, 2ème séance of 1 April 1998, 1ère séance of 20 May 1998, and 2ème séance of 3 June 1998, and Sénat, 7 May 1998 and 27 May 1998.

[112] Article 52 of Law 98-546, 2 July 1998, *Journal Officiel de la République Française* of 3 July 1998, 10127 and Decree 99-278, 12 April 1999, *Journal Officiel de la République Française* of 14 April 1999, 5483.

interest was allowed—and even obliged—to 'cherry pick' to the detriment of the consumers located in the areas not served.

Electrabel/Intercommunales Mixte

10.140 The question in that case was to determine to what extent the exception laid down in Article 86(2) could apply to the behaviour of Electrabel, an undertaking enjoying a dominant position on the market for sale of bulk electricity in Belgium which was suspected of restricting competition by concluding long-term exclusive supply contracts with distribution companies representing a substantial part of the market

10.141 The absence of exclusive rights will lead to the full application of Articles 81 and 82, notwithstanding the situation in other Member States. It was natural for the parties to compare the situation in Belgium, where no legal monopoly rights as to supply of electricity to distribution companies was in place, with that in other Member States where such rights existed and led to foreclosure effects of similar or longer duration both on the market for electricity and on the market for distribution services. The parties and the Commission certainly did not draw the same conclusion from such comparison.

The Commission considered that, in the absence of monopoly rights, the relations between distribution companies and electricity producers were governed exclusively by private law and thus there was no obstacle to the full application of Articles 81 and 82 of the Treaty.

F. Competition Rules and the Coal and Nuclear Sectors

(1) The ECSC Treaty

10.142 The Treaty establishing the European Coal and Steel Community (ECSC) deals exclusively with the coal and steel sectors; the competition rules of the EC Treaty are not of application. The Treaty will expire in 2002. As of that date, the coal sector will be governed by the provisions of the Treaty establishing the European Economic Community.

In view of the short remaining duration of the ECSC Treaty, we will only outline the competition rules applicable under the ECSC Treaty.

10.143 However, the Commission has adopted recently a decision not to act on a complaint concerning alleged infringements of the ECSC Treaty before 1990. The Commission found that some of the competition rules of the ECSC Treaty can have retroactive effect only in order to ensure the effectiveness of the general objectives laid down in the Treaty.[113]

---

[113] (October 1998) 3 *Competition Policy Newsletter* 27.

Scheme of the Treaty

The main elements of the competition regime in the ECSC Treaty flow from the   **10.144**
general prohibitions set out under Article 4 ECSC.

Articles 65 and 66(7) ECSC are similar in their principle to respectively Articles   **10.145**
81 and 82 EC. However, some major differences have to be taken into account
when applying the provisions of the ECSC Treaty in a case involving undertakings
engaged in the production of coal within the meaning of Article 80 ECSC. These
differences are addressed briefly below.

The Exclusive Application of the Provisions of the ECSC Treaty

The Court of Justice has ruled that the ECSC deals exhaustively with discrimina-   **10.146**
tion practised by purchasers of coal and by abuses of a dominant position practised by ECSC undertakings. There is no place for the application of the EC
Treaty.

This issue arose in an action before the High Court of Justice of England and   **10.147**
Wales, in which the applicant, Hopkins,[114] alleged breach of the provisions of the
ECSC Treaty (Articles 4(b) and 63), or, in the alternative, of the EC Treaty
(Article 82) with regard to alleged discrimination practised by the Central
Electricity Generating Board (CEGB) between 1985 and 31 March 1990.

This confirmed the earlier preliminary reference ruling (*Banks*),[115] in which the   **10.148**
Court of Justice held that the legal framework of proceedings was the ECSC
Treaty and not the EC Treaty. This was because both the activity in question (the
extraction of unworked coal) and the undertakings considered (undertakings
engaged in production in the coal industry) fell within the scope of the ECSC
Treaty.

Absence of Direct Effect[116]

In *Banks* and in *Hopkins* the Court of Justice ruled that the competition provisions   **10.149**
of the ECSC Treaty do not have direct effect.

These rulings create a clear distinction between the competition rules of the EC
Treaty and those of the ECSC Treaty. Surprisingly they give the Commission sole
jurisdiction to apply the relevant provisions, notwithstanding—in the case of
Articles 65 and 66(7)—their similarity with Articles 81 and 82 EC Treaty.

---

[114] Case C–18/94 *B Hopkins and others v National Power, PowerGen* [1996] ECR I–2281.
[115] Case C–128/92 *HJ Banks and Co Ltd and others v BCC* [1994] ECR I–1209.
[116] For a detailed commentary of this aspect, see P Meunier, 'La Cour de justice des
Communautés européennes et l'applicabilité directe des règles de concurrence du Traité CECA,
Revue Trimestrielle de Droit Européen 32(2), Avril–Juin 1996, 243–258.

Effect on Trade

10.150   The ECSC Treaty differs from the EC Treaty in that 'effect on trade' is not an indispensable condition for the application of the competition rules.

10.151   Furthermore, the Court has already found[117] that restrictions of competition on a limited geographical market could affect trade between Member States if these restrictions affect a product which is used for the production of a 'secondary' product traded at EU level. This condition would be fulfilled for coal because it is mostly used as a primary fuel for electricity generation and there are exchanges of electricity between Member States.

(2) The Euratom Treaty

10.152   **The competition rules of the EC Treaty can supplement but not replace the specific rules of the Euratom Treaty.**   However, the exact delimitation between the two treaties is unaddressed, and the constituencies of the Euratom Treaty and the EC Treaty have largely avoided contact.[118]

Treaty Provisions

10.153   The nuclear industry is subject to the specific jurisdiction of the Euratom Treaty, which in its various provisions arguably creates a complete legal framework part of which is the supervision of the market by the Euratom Supply Agency (ESA). Relations between the EC Treaty, the ECSC Treaty and the Euratom Treaty are governed by Article 305 (former Article 232) of the EC Treaty.

> *1. The provisions of this Treaty shall not affect the provisions of the Treaty establishing the European Coal and Steel Community . . .*

> *2. The provisions of this Treaty shall not derogate from those of the Treaty establishing the European Atomic Energy Community.*

The difference between 'affect' and 'derogate' may be explained with reference to the fact that the ECSC Treaty was in force on the date of signature of the EC and Euratom Treaties, which were both signed on the same day; the two terms are in fact synonyms. An alternative interpretation is that the different terms indicate a different qualitative relationship as between the ECSC Treaty and the EC Treaty and the Euratom Treaty and the EC Treaty. Certainly, the practice of the Commission has been to keep the EC and ECSC regimes separate, and operating independently of one another. Cases where a choice between the Euratom and EC regimes has been made are rare.

---

[117]   For example, Case C–123/83 *BNIC v Clair* [1985] ECR 391.
[118]   Although joint ventures were looked at in the cases *United Reprocessors* and *KEWA* [1976] OJ L51/7 and 15. The circulation of radioactive materials for non-fuel purposes was looked at in *Amersham Buchler* [1982] OJ L314/34.

The Commission's practice has been one which recognized the *lex specialis* nature   **10.154**
of the Euratom Treaty, but which applied the competition rules to the nuclear sector in so far as such application would not derogate from the application of the
Euratom Treaty. The key question as to what constitutes derogation has been
looked at by the European Court of Justice in *French Republic, Italian Republic
and the United Kingdom v Commission*;[119] the European Court of Justice concluded that the onus was on a complainant, in this case France, to establish that
there is derogation. Derogation would seem to have not merely to impinge upon
the subject matter of the Euratom Treaty but also impede its application. The
Commission in its submission in that case argued that in the absence of State aid
rules in the Euratom Treaty, the State aid rules of the EC Treaty were applicable.
Therefore, secondary legislation that dealt with State aid had to expressly limit its
application if the nuclear sector was to be exempt from it.

This interpretation builds on the view that the terms used in Article 305(1) and   **10.155**
(2) [former Article 232(1) and (2)] are qualitatively different and are not synonyms. This view is reinforced when one considers that the ECSC Treaty is a complete and integrated Treaty, the functioning of which can be envisaged without
reference to the EC Treaty; the Euratom Treaty is not. Certainly the provisions of
the Euratom Treaty, when they have not been implemented, have been supplemented with powers derived from the EC Treaty.[120]

In *ENU v Commission*,[121] the Court of First Instance confirmed this approach in   **10.156**
discussing the scheme of the Euratom Treaty. Having stated that in principle the
powers of the Euratom Treaty may be supplemented by EC powers, the Court of
Justice quoted that:[122]

> the provisions of the EAEC Treaty 'reinserted in the context of the Treaty estab-
> lishing the European Economic Community . . . appear to be nothing other than
> the application, in a highly specialised field, of the legal conceptions which form the
> basis of the structure of the general common market'.

The conclusion that the Commission has drawn from this is that the EC Treaty
applies in principle to the subject matter of the Euratom Treaty except where the

---

[119] Joined Cases 188 to 190/80 *French Republic, Italian Republic and United Kingdom of Great
Britain and Northern Ireland v Commission* [1982] ECR 2545.

[120] Under Articles 93 and 94 Euratom, Member States are called upon to abolish customs duties
and quantitative restrictions in respect of materials contained in Annex IV and establish a common
customs tariff. Annex IV is divided into three lists, the third of which (List B) needs an implementing directive to be adopted. In the absence of that implementing directive, List B products have cir-
culated according to the rules of the EC Treaty. *Encyclopedia of European Law*, B5051 *et seq.*

[121] Joined Cases T–458/93 and T–523/93 *ENU v Commission* [1995] ECR II–2459.

[122] Case C–1/78 *ruling delivered pursuant to the third para of Article 103 of the EAEC Treaty, Draft
Convention of the International Atomic Energy Agency on the Physical Protection of Nuclear Materials,
Facilities and Transports* [1978] ECR 2151, para 15; the CFI, in an *obiter dicta* also observed that
since there were no anti-dumping rules in the Euratom Treaty, the anti-dumping rules of the EC
Treaty could be applied to a nuclear supply contract.

application of the EC rules would impede the application of the Euratom rules. The full panoply of the EC rules are available to remedy market distortions in the domain governed by the Euratom Treaty. This conclusion is in consonance with past Commission practice;[123] academic commentaries[124] are supportive of this view but point to the special provisions in the Euratom Treaty dealing with prices and joint ventures.

Recent Commission Practice

10.157 **Recent Commission practice might lead to the conclusion that supply and transformation contracts, dealt with under Chapter VI of the Euratom Treaty, are also justiciable under the EC Treaty.**   Two EC Commission cases concerned the arrangements for the privatization of the UK nuclear energy sector, and specifically the arrangements for fuel supply and back-end services for the newly privatized entity.[125]

10.158 The Commission, by publishing Article 19/3 Notices under Regulation 17/62, implicitly accepted that nuclear supply contracts and transformation contracts[126] are justiciable under the EC Treaty.

10.159 The nuclear supply contracts and transformation contracts are also justiciable under the Euratom Treaty; Chapter VI Euratom confers on the Euratom Supply Agency (ESA) the 'exclusive' right to conclude nuclear supply contracts, and the ESA has rights (to information but also in securing material within the Community) under Article 75 Euratom, which governs transformation contracts. Matters falling within the scope of Chapter VI of the Euratom Treaty (supply contracts) are subject to the limited competition rules contained in that Chapter; these rules are administered by the ESA, with the sanction of non-conclusion of a contract, to which the ESA is always a party. Article 75 contracts are without the scope of Chapter VI, despite being the last Article within Chapter VI.

10.160 The position of the Commission is correct in so far as it utilizes the principle established in case law and practice, namely that there is concurrent jurisdiction between the two treaties. But with regard to the supply contracts, which are governed by Article 52[127] of the Euratom Treaty, the extension of principle results in the application of the competition rules to the ESA, which legally is always the

---

[123] The only public statement of intended policy has been Response of M Vredeling to Written Question No 169/91, OJ C5/1, 21 January 1972, and concerned reprocessing.

[124] See Ritter, Rawlingson, and Braun, *EEC competition law: a practitioner's guide* (Kluwer Law and Taxation, 1991) 583; Van Bael and Bellis, *Competition Law of the European Community* (CCH Europe, 1994) 622.

[125] *Nuclear Electric plc/British Nuclear Fuels plc* and *Scottish Nuclear Ltd/British Nuclear Fuels plc* (Notice pursuant to Article 19(3) of Regulation 17) [1996] OJ C89/4.

[126] Principally retreatment, storage, and (arguably) enrichment services contracts.

[127] Excluding Article 75.

counterparty to such a contract. It cannot have been the intention of the authors of the Euratom Treaty and the EC Treaty that the ESA should be justiciable under the EC Treaty.

However, as stated Article 75 contracts are outside the scope of the supply rules in **10.161** Chapter VI of the Euratom Treaty. The position that these contracts and not supply contracts are justiciable under the EC Treaty is defensible, as Article 75 contracts relate to the fabrication and engineering associated with the provision of nuclear fuel. The limited powers granted to the ESA under Article 75 concern nuclear accounting rather than the weak competition provisions of Chapter VI. If transformation contracts were not justiciable under the EC competiton rules, they would not be subject to any competition rules. Following the reasoning that the authors' intention was for the seamless application of the competition rules, and in the absence of direct contradiction, it is reasonable to conclude that these contracts fall within the purview of the EC Treaty.

G. The Setting of a New Legal Framework

This section investigates what impact the new Directives liberalizing the electri- **10.162** city and gas markets may have on the application of the competition rules. Since both Directives are intended to make these markets more orientated to competition, there inevitably will be an impact. Moreover, parts of both Directives are either directly derived from the competition rules, or are designed to facilitate their application.

(1) Statement on Commission Policy

Determination of the Community's interest is central to resolving competition **10.163** cases in the energy sector, especially in Article 86 cases. The political background and the legal framework established under the new Directives express the Community's interest.

The political basis of Commission action is the Commission White Paper on **10.164** energy.[128] In this paper, the Commission states that 'energy policy must form part of the general aims of the Community's economic policy based on market integration, deregulation, limiting public intervention to what is strictly necessary in order to safeguard the public interest and welfare, sustainable development, consumer protection and economic and social cohesion'[129] and insists on the fact that 'market integration is the central, determining factor in the Community's energy policy'.[130]

---

[128] COM(95) 682 final.
[129] ibid, 2, para 5.
[130] ibid, 3, para 7.

10.165   In a section called 'the level playing field',[131] the Commission indicates that 'for economic operators to have full confidence in the internal energy market and to be assured that market principles prevail, it will be essential that there is a maximum of transparency and consistency in applying the competition provisions of the Treaties'. Furthermore, the Commission states that 'exemptions from this general rule [the respect of competition rules] need to be handled in a restrictive manner' and 'in particular in the energy sector where public service obligations have been imposed . . . it will be of prime importance to ensure their full transparency'.

10.166   The Commission concludes that 'it will need to be considered in the future whether general criteria need to be established to judge those cases in which the application of the competition rules of the Treaty would obstruct the achievement of such public service obligations, in order to support the application of Treaty rules in a coherent and predictable manner'.

(2) The Internal Market in Electricity

Introduction

10.167   **The electricity Directive complicates application of the competition rules.** Application of the competition rules to the electricity market will take full account of Directive 96/92/EC concerning an internal market for electricity. It will not be easy to separate the provisions of the Directive and the competition rules. The specific rules set out in the Directive derive directly from the competition rules, and the Directive aims to organize the sector transparently to facilitate the application of the competition rules.

10.168   However, the Directive clearly states that its provisions 'should not affect the full application of the Treaty, in particular the provisions concerning the internal market and competition'.[132] This principle is repeated in the particular rules applying to public undertakings or undertakings which have been granted special or exclusive rights.

10.169   The Directive sets the Community's objectives with regard to the degree of competition expected to take place and clearly defines the interest of the Community. The political objectives are distilled into technical rules with two aspects:

(1) Rules relating to the organization of the sector.

(2) Other rules in the Directive relate to ensuring the smooth running of the internal market created and organized under the first provisions. Most of the rules in this second category are drawn from the Treaty competition rules or follow the aim of facilitating their application by the competent authorities.

---

[131]   COM(95) 682 final 17–19, paras 57–63.
[132]   ibid, recital 3.

General Objectives

Only eligible customers are in a competitive market. The internal market in **10.170** electricity is to comprise an area without internal frontiers in which the free movement of goods, persons, and services is assured (recital 1). The Directive constitutes a 'further phase of liberalisation' (recital 39) following the 'first phase for the completion of the internal market in electricity' (recital 7) provided for by the transit and transparency Directives (see above). The Directive identifies an important limit to its own application: 'once it has been put into effect, some obstacles to trade in electricity between Member States will nevertheless remain in place' (recital 39). This limitation, read in combination with the objectives of the internal market in electricity, allows for a precise definition of the interests of the Community with regard to the development of trade: these interests shall include, *inter alia*, competition with regard to eligible customers (Article 3(3)).

Rules Relating to the Organization of the Sector

Generation

Rules relating to generation capacity increases must not favour incumbents, **10.171** **and must be in accordance with Articles 86 and 82.** Member States may choose between two different procedures for the construction of new generating capacity: the authorization procedure and/or the tendering procedure.

Under the authorization procedure, criteria for authorizations for construction of **10.172** generating capacity shall be stipulated . Any refusal to grant an authorization shall be on the basis of these objective, transparent, and non-discriminatory criteria. Member States which opt for the tendering procedure shall designate a body independent from electricity generation, transmission, distribution activities to be responsible for the organization, monitoring, and control of the tendering procedure and for taking all necessary steps to ensure confidentiality of the information contained in the tenders.

Finally, the option for the tendering procedure must allow for auto-producers and independent producers to obtain authorization on the basis of the criteria laid down under Articles 4 and 5 of the Directive (authorization procedure).

Contract Length under the Tendering Procedure

The tendering procedure allows for long-term supply contracts. Article 6(4), **10.173** concerning the taking into consideration of supply offers from existing generating units, favours long-term contracts. The construction of new generating capacity is an alternative to the conclusion of long-term contracts with existing generators located inside or outside the system.

The existence of a contract between the selected tenderer and the system is explic- **10.174** itly provided for and referred to under Article 6(3) (the tender specifications shall

737

contain 'a detailed description of the contract specifications and . . . a list of criteria governing the selection of tenderers and the award of the contract'), under Article 8(2) concerning the dispatching of generating plants, and under Article 20(1)(ii) (producers 'should have access to the system in order to perform the contract').

10.175 Article 6(4) refers to 'long-term guarantees from existing units' which means that the corresponding contract may be of a similar long duration. This conclusion may further be extended to the situation of a new power plant being awarded a contract after winning a call for tender: this contract too can be interpreted to be allowed to be of long duration.

It is not possible to say whether the period of the long-term contract will be coincident with the practice for evaluating contracts under Article 81 EC.

Market Opening (Article 19)

10.176 **Eligible customers will be in a fully competitive market. Thus, competition analyses may have to be predicated on an analysis of eligibility.**   Article 19 provides for a progressive market opening relying on the definition, by each Member State, of a category of customers—eligible customers—that must be able to conclude supply contracts with the supplier of their choice. The important point is that since the Directive purports to limit market opening, the application of the competition rules *de facto* becomes contingent on eligibility under the Directive.

10.177 **Definition of eligible customer.**   The degree of opening in each Member State has to equal or be greater than a minimum percentage of the total market calculated and published on an annual basis by the Commission. This figure is equal to the Community's percentage of electricity used by final consumers of a given annualized quantity of electricity (40 GWh at the entry into force of the Directive, 20 GWh three years later, and 9 GWh six years later), on a consumption site basis, including auto-production.

10.178 The Commission published,[133] in October 1998, the figure of 26.48 per cent as the minimum percentage of market opening in all Member States applicable for 1999. The minimum percentage of market opening should increase on 19 February 2000 (ie three years after the entry into force of the Directive) as a consequence of the reduction of the consumption threshold from 40 GWh to 20 GWh. Estimates show that the opening should then be around 30 per cent. The further decrease in the consumption threshold should lead, as of 19 February 2003, to a minimum percentage of market opening of around 35 per cent.

10.179 The 40, 20, and 9 GWh thresholds are for calculation purposes only and will in most cases bear no particular significance with regard to the definition of eligible

---

[133] [1998] OJ C334/16.

customers by each Member State taken individually. Hence Member States will have to start with the figure for the minimal share of market opening (for example, 26.48 per cent) before defining those customers within their territory which will be eligible.

10.180 Several approaches will be possible though the most commonly adopted will be to designate as eligible those customers with a consumption above a given 'national threshold'.[134] The national threshold will depend upon the structure of consumption for each Member State. In some cases a market opening of 27 per cent could correspond to a national threshold of 60 GWh (in Austria, for example) whereas that threshold could be 40 GWh in France or Italy.[135]

10.181 **Automatic eligibility.** Article 19(3) provides for the 'automatic' eligibility of all consumers consuming more than 100 GWh per year on a consumption site basis, including auto-production; and distribution companies, if they have not been specified already as eligible customers, but only for the volume of electricity consumed by their customers designated as eligible within their distribution system, and in order to supply those customers.

'Protection Clause'

10.182 **Eligible customers do not have total freedom of action.** The simple underlying principle of Article 19(5) is that of balanced market opening. An electricity supplier may be prevented from contracting with eligible customers located in another Member State. This can be done if those customers are not considered as eligible in both systems involved.

10.183 This provision, commonly referred to as the 'protection clause', gives rise to serious doubts as to its compatibility with the provisions or with the spirit of the EC Treaty. Indeed, reciprocity implies that restrictions (for example denial of access to the transmission system) in a Member State could serve as a base for justification of restrictions in another Member State. This approach is not accepted in other sectors when the provisions concerning the internal market are applied either by the Commission or by the Court.

As an element of secondary legislation, negative reciprocity cannot be used to vitiaite rights under Treaty provisions, and this would include the competition provisions.

---

[134] As to alternative approaches, one could think of the definition of geographic areas opened up to competition whereas other parts of the territory would be closed for competition. The compatibility of such an approach with the requirements of the Directive would have to be analysed by the Commission according to Article 19(4).

[135] The figures are *estimates* provided by the Member States in 1996 during the negotiating process and are for illustration only.

The Mechanism for Implementation

10.184 The mechanism set out under Article 19(5) can be described as follows:

(1) any contract between a supplier and an eligible customer in the system of another Member State may be prohibited if the eligible customer is not considered as eligible in both systems; and

(2) at the request of the Member State where the eligible customer is located, the Commission—taking into account the situation in the market and the common interest—may oblige the supplier to execute the requested electricity supply.

Both steps are unusual in the Community framework and the Commission will have to answer three obvious questions:

• When does a proposed contract fulfil the conditions for prohibition laid down under Article 19(5)?

• What form does the the prohibition take? and

• Can the Commission oblige anybody to execute an electricity supply contract?

Conditions for Prohibition

10.185 The first question raises practical issues with regard to the definition of eligibility in two systems in a context where Member States may choose (cf Article 19(1), (3), and (4)) their own level of market opening and their own criteria for the definition of eligible customers. These may often be incompatible.

10.186 In addition to these quantitative difficulties, eligible consumers and suppliers may have to take into account qualitative criteria when analysing the conformity of a contract with the provisions of Article 19(5). For example, some Member States may authorize the existence of supply undertakings[136] on their territory whereas others may not. A strict interpretation of Article 19(5) would deny supply undertakings established in a Member State the right to buy any amount of electricity from suppliers located in Member States where supply undertakings are not authorized, provided that an imbalance in the opening of electricity markets is avoided.

Form of the Prohibition

10.187 The second question concerning the technical implementation of the prohibition laid down in Article 19(5) has already been answered in the German Energy Law[137]

---

[136] 'Supply undertaking' means an undertaking delivering and/or selling electricity to consumers without necessarily being a producer of electricity (for example: electricity trader buying electricity from various producers in order to resell it to final consumers).

[137] Gesetz zur Neuregelung des Energiewirtschaftsrechts vom 24 April 1998, Bundesgesetzblatt Teil I Nr 23 vom 28 April 1998, 730.

where article 4§2 gives network operators the right to refuse access to the network if the purchaser of electricity is not considered as eligible in the 'exporting' Member State. Network access denial, as envisaged in Germany, certainly constitutes the most obvious way of implementing the prohibition. Other forms of prohibition may be envisaged.

Execution of the Contract

The last question, relative to the role of the Commission in the procedure laid down under Article 19(5), has to be left open in the absence of any guidelines or experience. Certainly the Commission could be called upon to exercise its powers under Article 82 by a supplier or by a consumer wishing to challenge a refusal of access to the network.[138] The Commission would have to take into account the particular framework laid down under Article 19(5) in order to assess the conformity of the refusal with the rules laid down in the Treaty.

10.188

Final Remarks

Direct lines are not affected by the 'protection clause'. The provision applies to eligible consumers located in the *system* of another Member State. This provision, read in combination with Article 21 concerning supply of electricity through direct lines, and in combination with item 12 of Article 2 setting out the definition of direct lines as being 'complementary' to the systems, must be interpreted as being not applicable to the supply of eligible customers supplied through a direct line in another Member State.

10.189

Pool systems will be equally affected. Reference is made to a 'contract' between a supplier and a consumer. However, it may be the case that electricity is sold to a 'pool' in another Member State without any contract being concluded between the supplier and a customer—eligible or not—located in the Member State where the pool operates. This particular market configuration should not prevent the Member State using the 'pool' system having recourse to Article 19(5). Indeed, the practical implementations of Article 19(5)—ie refusal of access to the network—could still be used by the 'importing' Member State.

10.190

Access to the System (Articles 16 to 18, 20 to 22)

Rules on access to the system may supersede rules on the same subject derived from the competition rules. The rules in the Directive are an elaboration of the principles contained in the competition provisions of the Treaty. The market opening provided for under Article 19 would be deprived of effects in the absence of specific rules allowing access to the networks for market participants. Two options (Third Party Access (TPA) and Single Buyer (SB)) 'must lead to equivalent

10.191

---

[138] Recital 3 and Article 20(5).

economic results in the States and hence to [a] directly comparable level of opening-up of markets and to a directly comparable degree of access to electricity markets'.[139]

10.192 Member States may choose between as many as five different options when organizing access to the market.

Table 1: Options for Access to the Market

Method	Legal base	Description
TPA—negotiated	Article 17(1)–(3)	Negotiation of access to the system(s) between customers[140] and transmission/ distribution system operator(s). Indicative average transmission prices have to be published on a yearly basis.
TPA—regulated	Article 17(4)	Eligible customers granted right of access on the basis of published tariffs for use of transmission and distribution systems.
SB—with purchase obligation	Article 18(1) and (2)	Member States designate a SB. It shall publish a tariff for the use of the transmission and distribution system. The SB is obliged to purchase electricity contracted for by eligible customers at a price equal to the SB's sale price offered to eligible customers minus the published transmission charge.[141]
SB—without purchase obligation— negotiated	Articles 18(1), (3), 17(1)–(3)	The SB is not obliged to publish a tariff for the use of the transmission and distribution system. Negotiation of access to the system(s) between eligible customers and SB.
SB—without purchase obligation— regulated	Article 18(1) and (3)	Eligible customers have access to the system on the basis of the tariffs for the use of transmission and distribution systems published by the SB.

The choice of one or another model for access to the market has no impact on the basis of a refusal of access to the distribution or transmission system. In both cases, access may only be refused if the system operator or if the SB lacks the necessary capacity.[142]

---

[139] Recital 12 and Article 3(1).

[140] Under Article 17(1), the following parties shall be able to negotiate: producers, supply undertakings (when authorized), eligible customers.

[141] In fine the eligible customer will have to pay the price for electricity agreed with its supplier plus the published transmission charge.

[142] Article 17(5) in the case of TPA and Article 18(4) in the SB model.

Besides the rules relating to TPA and SB, the Directive sets out specific provisions in relation to:

10.193

- Independent producers and auto-producers (Article 20(1)(i)): these shall be able to negotiate access to the system so as to supply their own premises or subsidiaries whatever the model for access to the market chosen and whatever the size of these premises or subsidiaries.[143]

- Direct lines (Article 21): electricity producers and supply undertakings (when authorized) shall be able to supply their own premises, subsidiaries, and eligible customers through a direct line. The authorizations for the construction of new direct lines shall be granted following objective and non-discriminatory criteria among which could figure prior refusal of system access on the basis of Article 17(5) or 18(4). Authorizations for direct lines may be refused if their granting would obstruct the provisions of Article 3.

Rules Relating to the Organization, Behaviour, and Control of Market Participants

These provisions draw upon the competition rules and aim to facilitate their application.

10.194

Management Unbundling (Article 7(6))

Management unbundling constitutes an essential element of the Directive. Its aim is to warrant the independence of the transmission system operator and thus to prevent any discrimination to the profit of an affiliate or of another group division of the operator. The Directive does not provide for any detailed requirements in that regard. However, the Commission has interpreted this provision as follows :

10.195

—managers of the transmission system should not sit on the board of directors of the company. The transmission part should act independently from the interests of the vertically integrated company;
—the transmission system operator should have all the necessary means and assets to maintain, develop and manage the network, especially if the ownership of the network remains in the hands of the vertically integrated company.[144]

Unbundling of Accounts (Article 14)

Unbundling of accounts will simplify the application of Article 82. Integrated electricity undertakings shall keep separate accounts for their generation, transmission, and distribution activities with a view to avoiding 'discrimination, cross-

10.196

---

[143] Even if these premises/subsidiaries have a consumption which is below the thresholds for eligibility defined by the Member States.

[144] Second report from the Commission to the Council and the European Parliament on state of liberalisation of the energy markets, COM(1999) 198 final, 4 May 1999, 9.

subsidization and distortion of competition'. The rules for the allocation of assets and liabilities and expenditure and income shall be specified in an annex to the accounts.

10.197   This provision draws clearly from Article 82 EC and aims at allowing the competent authorities to dispose of individual data for each type of activity in order to analyse possible infringements in relation to pricing of certain products or services. This provision may, however, prove insufficient for the application of the competition rules of the Treaty because it only provides for a 'vertical' separation of accounts whereas there is no obligation for a company dealing both with eligible customers and with 'captive' customers to hold separate accounts for both types of activity.

Confidentiality of Information

10.198   **Information guarantees will prevent abuse of sensitive information.**   Several provisions in the Directive relate to independence, confidentiality of information, and non-discrimination. All these rules are linked together in that they pursue the same aim of preventing use by an entity (as network operator) of the particular powers it has been granted or was granted as a means of favouring its parent company or subsidiaries.

Dispute Settlement and the Regulatory Authorities

10.199   **The dispute settlement authority will not replace the competition authorities in Member States nor the role of the Commission in the application of the competition rules.**   Article 20(3) provides for the designation by Member States of a 'competent authority' which must:

• be independent of the parties to the dispute; and

• settle disputes relating to contracts, negotiations and refusal of access to the network or refusal to purchase (in the case of the Single Buyer Model with obligation to purchase).

The Directive provides for a procedure in case of cross-border disputes: the dispute settlement authority shall be the one covering the system where use of or access to the system is denied.

10.200   In most Member States, there will be the creation—if it did not exist before—of National Regulatory Authorities for the electricity market.[145] In some Member States the NRA may intervene in order to settle disputes but is not empowered to apply national competition law. Cases where potential infringements of the competition law have been identified have to be forwarded to the national competi-

---

[145] In some cases the sectoral regulator is in charge of both the electricity and gas sectors (for example, the 'Autorità per l'energia elettrica e il gas' in Italy).

tion authority. In other Member States the NRA can not only settle disputes but also, if necessary, apply the relevant provisions of the national competition law.

(3) The Gas Directive

The achievement of an internal market for gas will be within the framework of the gas directive.[146]   The Directive though excludes the production phase (dealt with in the Hydrocarbons Licensing Directive[147]). **10.201**

The gas Directive provides for common rules concerning the transmission, distribution, supply, and storage of natural gas. Its aim is to introduce competition into the gas sector and allow, specifically, eligible customers to choose their supplier of gas, with the implication that non-eligible customers do not have that right. This though should be seen in the context of growing market opening. **10.202**

While formally the Directive cannot modify the application of the competition rules contained in the EC treaty, its effect may be to inhibit that application. This effect is reflected in the recitals, where it is claimed that the Directive '*should* not affect the full application of the Treaty' (emphasis added). After its adoption, 'some obstacles to trade . . . will nevertheless remain in place' (recital 32). **10.203**

The Directive can be seen to define the Community interest in the opening of the gas market, and thus it purports to limit the application of the internal market rules, such that competition is restricted to eligible customers. Article 3(3) last sentence reads: 'The interests of the Community include, inter alia, competition with regard to eligible customers in accordance with this directive and Article 90 [now Article 86] of the Treaty.' **10.204**

Progressive Market Opening

Eligible customers will be in a completely competitive environment.   Article 18 sets out the class of customers who can take advantage of the market opening provisions. After transposition of the Directive into Member States' national law, the Directive will mean that initially at least 20 per cent of the gas market in each Member State will have been opened to competition. After five years, the proportion will rise to 28 per cent and, after ten, a further increase to 33 per cent will be effected. In reality, market opening will go much further with a current projection of 70 per cent market opening on a weighted average basis in August 2000. **10.205**

---

[146] Directive (EC) 98/30 of the European Parliament and of the Council of 22 June 1998 concerning common rules for the internal market in natural gas [1998] OJ L204/1.

[147] Directive (EC) 94/22 of the European Parliament and of the Council of 30 May on the conditions for granting and using authorisations for the prospection, exploration and production of hydrocarbons [1994] OJ L164/3.

10.206 Eligible customers will be able to choose their supplier. Eligible customers are:

- 'at least' gas fired generators of electricity and combined heat and power (CHP) generators (though for CHP there is a consumption of gas threshold that can be set at levels determined by Member States); and

- other consumers on a consumption site basis consuming more than 25 million cubic metres of gas per year; after five years, this threshold will drop to 15 million cubic metres, and after 10 years to 5 million cubic metres.

If the eligible customers criterion leads to a market opening of more than 10 percentage points higher than the minimum market opening thresholds (ie 30 per cent, 38 per cent, and 43 per cent respectively), the Member State can adjust the eligible customers criterion to scale back the level of market opening. In effect, this means that the Member State may adjust the definition of eligible customers to suit the quantitative requirements (Article 18(5)). The Member State is required to include 'at least' gas fired generators and CHP generators under Article 18(2); the modification of the eligible customers criterion refers to the definition in Article 18(1) of eligible customers, a definition made by the Member State after notification to the Commission. The mandatory eligible customers under Article 18(2) constitute a subset of the State determined definition under Article 18(1). Read literally, the Directive would seem to require that no modification to the definition under Article 18(2) can be made by the Member State. If this is the case, the practical utility of Article 18(5) is reduced.

Negative Reciprocity (Article 19)

10.207 The negative reciprocity clause seeks to avoid imbalances between Member States when opening their natural gas markets. As has been remarked upon above with regard to the electricity Directive, this provision is not solidly based in Community law.

Competition Mechanisms

Third Party Access (TPA)

10.208 **The Directive codifies Third Party Access provisions that had previously been envisaged as an expression of the competition rules.** Third party access to grids will be either through negotiated third party access (NTPA) or regulated third party access, or both (Article 14).

10.209 Under NTPA, the Member State shall ensure that natural gas undertakings, that is all natural gas companies, and eligible customers are able to negotiate access to the grid system (Article 15). Either the customer and/or the supplier may negotiate with the grid operator and the negotiations must be in good faith. Main commercial terms for access shall be published by the grid owner. Regulated TPA is premised on published tariffs and other data, which shall afford the parties seeking access the necessary information to conclude a sales agreement (Article 16).

Direct Lines (Article 20)

Direct lines provisions are likely to become central to the opening of the market. This is potentially the most important competition mechanism in the Directive as there are no derogations from its provisions allowed in mature markets.[148] It will probably be used as a last resort measure by new entrants. Direct lines are transmission lines between an eligible customer and a supplier, and are thus not part of a system. Member States shall take the necessary measures to enable the building of direct lines. Conditions for building these lines must be non-discriminatory and transparent.

10.210

Authorization to build a direct line may be subject to a refusal of system access or the opening of a dispute settlement procedure (Article 20(3)). System access refusal can be on the basis of lack of capacity, the obstruction of carrying out public service obligations (PSOs), or serious difficulties arising from take-or-pay obligations. The authorization to build a direct line provision undercuts the safeguards with regard to PSOs and take-or-pay contracts, so that even if a direct line would prevent an undertaking on whom a PSO is imposed from carrying out that PSO, the direct line cannot be prevented. Similarly, obligations under take-or-pay contracts cannot prevent the building of the direct line. Article 20(3) should be construed as an attempt to prevent the proliferation of infrastructure and not as a limit to the competitive mechanism of direct lines as such.

10.211

Refusal of Access (Article 17)

Refusal of access to the system may be allowed if:

10.212

- There is lack of capacity (or, implicitly, lack of connection) in the system.

- The 'access to the system would prevent them (the system operator) from carrying out the public service obligations referred to in Art 3(2) which are assigned to them'. This is an echo of Article 86(2) of the Treaty; it is therefore likely that the jurisprudence relating to Article 86(2) will be capable of forming a basis for action under this provision. Two observations can be made with regard to this provision. First, dispute settlement procedures under Article 21 give competence (in the first instance) to adjudicate to a national authority. Secondly, the public service obligations referred to in Article 3(2) are possibly wider in scope than those admitted under Article 86(2) (see below).

- Serious economic and financial difficulties with take-or-pay contracts would arise, such that Article 25 (derogation provisions; see below) would come into play.

---

[148] Emergent markets and regions may gain derogation.

For each type of refusal, duly substantiated reasons must be given. Refusal can be contested by reference to the national authority, though this procedure does not preclude 'rights of appeal under Community law' (Article 21).

Public Service Obligations

10.213 **Public service obligations are exhaustively stipulated and, representing the Community interest, limit the future scope of Article 86(2) in this area.** Public service obligations can be imposed on natural gas undertakings by Member States. The categories of permissible PSOs are exhaustively stipulated in Article 3(3) of the Directive. They are:

- Security, including security of supply; security is defined as meaning security of supply and provision, and technical safety. Provision is thought to relate to system security, being the ability of the system to supply customers. The security of supply criterion allows the Member State to introduce long-term planning, which must take into account that third parties may wish to have access to the system. Long-term planning extends to the planning of supply and transportation capacity of natural gas undertakings (Article 2 (23)). Thus the Member State may influence future gas supply[149] and infrastructure needs of independent operators.

- Regularity; this aspect relates to system security and can be considered a synonym for security of delivery.

- Quality and price of supplies; this provision relates to the Member States' wishes to have some control on pricing and maintain 'equity' in pricing systems. Quality is an important concept because different national quality standards exist (relating to calorific value, smell, etc of gas). Thus this may have the potential to interfere with the establishment of a functioning internal gas market.

- Environmental Protection.

These PSOs must be objective, clearly defined, and non-discriminatory, and communicated to the Commission.

10.214 A further *de facto* PSO is contained in Article 9(2), whereby distribution and supply undertakings may be obliged to supply a specific geographic area or class of persons or both. Tariffs for such delivery may be regulated. The tariff may be regulated for the purposes of ensuring 'equal treatment' of the customers concerned. Other reasons for regulating the price are allowed.

---

[149] Recital 9 suggests that the Member States, based on subsidiarity, have rights to supervise supply contracts, though nowhere in the Directive is this spelt out. Recital 13 says only that Member States may monitor supply contacts.

Distribution

Distribution is included within the scope of the Directive. However, Member **10.215**
States may exempt distribution from the requirement to award authorizations for
the construction or operation of natural gas facilities, transparently and on a non-
discriminatory basis (Article 3(3) in conjunction with Article 4), if that requirement would obstruct the performance of PSOs and its removal would not affect
the development of inter-state trade to an extent that is contrary to the
Community interest.

But since Article 4 goes no further in substance than to reiterate obligations that **10.216**
derive from the EC Treaty directly, an exemption from Article 4 is somewhat perverse. The Treaty rules, notwithstanding Article 3(3) and Article 4 of the
Directive, apply directly to distribution. It would be a brave argument to make
that since distribution is by virtue of the use of Article 3(3) brought outside the
scope of Article 4, authorizations in the distribution sector can be accorded on the
basis of discriminatory criteria.[150]

Article 3(3), in that it limits exemptions from Article 4 to distribution and is based **10.217**
explicitly on Article 86(2) EC criteria, can be taken as evidence for the proposition that Member States have agreed that those criteria are not of application to
other aspects of the gas sector. The authors certainly understand it that way.

Take-or-Pay Contracts

Stranded costs in the form of long-term contracts may be protected from the **10.218**
effects that competition may have.   Take-or-pay contracts are generally long-
term commitments to buy gas, using a pricing formula indexed either to competing fuels or a wider basket of goods (either explicitly in the form of compounded
indices).

Gas undertakings that control transmission systems can apply for limited deroga- **10.219**
tions from the TPA regime if, as the result of take-or-pay contracts, the undertaking is unable to sell gas on to a final consumer *and* the result is severe economic
and financial difficulty. Severe financial difficulty is understood to mean near
bankruptcy. The derogation is a last resort measure.

Although the derogation is accorded by the Member State, the Commission has **10.220**
the final say. The criteria for the accordance of a derogation are the same whether
applied by the Commission or the Member State, and apply irrespective of the
time of conclusion of the take-or-pay contract. The most difficult of the criteria
may be that which relates to the date of conclusion of the contract and the terms
of the agreement. If the terms of agreement allow deferral in taking volumes, the

---

[150] Reference should be made to recital 15.

position of the buyer will be ameliorated. If the agreement allows for ratcheting down of the price paid by the buyer to the supplier, again the buyer will not be so disadvantaged. The Commission was pleased to note the inclusion of Article 25(3)g, a criterion introducing the concept of reasonable foresight to guide the activities of undertakings.

10.221 For agreements concluded before the entry into force of the Directive, the provisions of the Directive cannot be construed such that the undertaking has no economic means of disposing of gas it has bought (an 'economically viable outlet').

10.222 In any event, the effect of Article 25(3) final paragraph is to make that part of the market between minimum offtake guarantees[151] and maximum offtake contestable. The take-or-pay derogation cannot be accorded to protect this part of the market.

Further clarification will be made when the Commission has published a discussion note on what is meant by 'financial difficulty' and an 'economically viable outlet'.

Miscellaneous Issues

Unbundling

10.223 **Unbundling of accounts will aid in the application of Article 82.** There is unbundling of internal accounts for all integrated gas undertakings so that the dispute settlement authorities can have access to all relevant information, as may the Commission in competition cases using its powers under Regulation 17/62. The purpose of this is to 'avoid discrimination, cross-subsidisation and other distortions of competition' (recital 22).

Upstream Access Regime

10.224 **Upstream exploration has been treated benignly under t EC competition rules.**[152] There is a special upstream access regime (Artic 3) for pipelines which usually connect the transmission grid to productio eas. It is a less stringent regime than the TPA regime and allows a greater le of national discretion. The provision is intended to allow eligible customer access directly producers.

---

[151] Because take-or-pay contracts are designed to cover variable demand (inter v summer demand), they contain clauses for minimum take obligations, gas which the buy s obliged to take physical control of in order to maintain system security (a minimum offtake guar tee). Above this level, the buyer has an option essentially for further volumes.

[152] Directive (EC) 94/22 of the European Parliament and of the Council of 30 May on the conditions for granting and using authorisations for the prospection, exploration and production of hydrocarbons [1994] OJ L164/3.

Emergent Regions

Limited geographic monopolies in defined areas of Member States may be allowed (Article 26(3)).   There will be derogations from the competition mechanisms for a period not exceeding ten years. This derogation system is to allow investment in new areas. Distribution is not affected by this provision; for distribution, Article 4(4) is applicable. Article 4 relates to the transparent and non-discriminatory award of authorizations to distribute. If an authorization for distribution has been given, no further authorizations for distribution need be given for the same area if the capacity of the existing distribution network is not saturated.

The provisions on emergent regions do not elaborate primary principles of the Treaty, and thus, the application of the primary rules in these areas is unaffected.

10.225

11

COMMUNICATIONS
(TELECOMS, MEDIA, AND INTERNET)

A. Introduction

(1) Scope of the Chapter

This chapter sets out the most important issues relating to the application of **11.01**
Article 81 (formerly Article 85) and Article 82 (formerly Article 86) to the con-
verging telecommunications and media sectors.[1]

The integrated approach of this chapter in part reflects the increasing convergence **11.02**
of technology between the two sectors: this relates most clearly to issues related to
the transmission of telecommunications or media services, but is also relevant to,
for example, interface devices such as set top boxes and to retail services. With the

---

[1] This is not, however, a complete analysis of either sector: telecommunications equipment has
been excluded, as have media issues related to books and films.

development of the Internet, the overlap between content and telecommunications services is likely to become increasingly evident. Nonetheless, these similarities should not be overstated: significant differences between the sectors persist.

11.03   The second reason for writing an integrated chapter is the increasing overlap in legal issues relevant to both areas. Issues of control of bottleneck facilities and therefore requests for access have been most clearly addressed in the telecommunications sector but are increasingly relevant to the media sector, for example in relation to set top boxes. By contrast, the leveraging of market power has been an important issue in a number of formal decisions in the media sector. Although these issues are likely to prove equally relevant to the telecommunications sector, the complexities have not yet been as explicitly addressed.

11.04   Another feature shared by the two sectors is the relative paucity of formal Commission decisions, although these have been supplemented in part by policy statements from the European Commission. On many of the most important issues, there is still little in the way of Commission precedent, and even less in terms of jurisprudence.

(2) Structure of the Chapter

11.05   Section B provides a basic background to the regulatory framework of the two sectors, including an overview of telecommunications liberalization.

11.06   Section C sets out certain procedural issues that are relevant to the sectors given the existence of these overlapping regulatory environments.

11.07   Sections D to G set out the main competition issues relevant to the various levels of the value chain in the broadcast and telecommunications sectors: content, transmission, end-user interface equipment, and retail services.

11.08   Section D looks at issues related to content creation, packaging, and distribution. This is most relevant to media, but will increasingly be relevant to Internet based services.

11.09   Section E examines competition issues related to data and voice transmission, with the emphasis being mostly on the telecommunications sector. This section covers both basic infrastructure problems such as the right to build, and infrastructure related services, such as interconnection.

11.10   Section F draws together various problems related to set top boxes.

11.11   Section G looks at issues that are of particular relevance to retail services.

11.12   Inevitably, a number of legal issues such as access, discrimination, and bundling, will be relevant to more than one of the above sections. Detailed analysis of the principles is set out in the section where most relevant: for example, exclusivity is examined in Section D on content, and many of the basic Article 82 issues are set out in Section E on transmission.

B. Regulatory Framework

The sector specific regulatory frameworks of the telecommunications and broad‑   **11.13**
cast industries are quite different. There were proposals to integrate the regulatory framework at the EU level,[2] although it appears there will be no formal proposals for the time being. Issues relating to reform of the telecommunications regulatory environment will be dealt with in the context of the Commission's 1999 Review.

The traditional view of the telecommunications sector was that in order to achieve   **11.14**
certain public policy objectives—most notably universal service—a single, often State‑owned, telecommunications operator must be established in the particular State. Technical developments and, more arguably, changes in economic think‑ ing, now mean that this monopolist approach is regarded as unnecessary. The pro‑ vision of telecommunications infrastructure and services has therefore been subject to a progressive liberalization, pursuant to Article 86 (formerly Article 90) EC,[3] beginning in 1990.[4] The liberalization of the sector at the EU level was

---

[2] Green Paper on the convergence of the telecommunications, media and information techno‑ logy sectors and the implications for regulation, COM (97) 623 final, 3 December 1997, Communication to the European Parliament, the Council, the Economic and Social Committee and the Committee of the Regions, Results of the Public Consultation on the Green Paper COM(1999) 108 final.

[3] See chapter 5 above.

[4] The telecommunications sector was liberalized by Commission Directives adopted pursuant to Article 86 EC. See:

Commission Directive (EEC) 90/388 of 28 June 1990 on competition in the markets for telecommunications services [1990] OJ L192/10 (the Services Directive);

Commission Directive (EEC) 94/46 of 13 October 1994 amending Directive (EEC) 88/301 and Directive (EEC) 90/388 in particular with regard to satellite communications [1994] OJ L268/15 (the Satellite Directive);

Commission Directive (EC) 95/51 of 18 October 1995 amending Directive (EEC) 90/388 with regard to the abolition of the restrictions on the use of cable television networks for the provision of already liberalized telecommunications services [1995] OJ L256/49 (the Cable TV Directive);

Commission Directive (EC) 96/2 of 16 January 1996 amending Directive (EEC) 90/388 with regard to mobile and personal communications [1996] OJ L20/59 (the Mobile Directive);

Commission Directive (EC) 96/19 of 13 March 1996 amending Directive (EEC) 90/388 with regard to the implementation of full competition in the telecommunications markets [1996] OJ L74/13 (the Full Competition Directive).

Certain Member States were granted limited derogations from full competition in telecommuni‑ cations:

Commission Decision (EC) 97/114 of 27 November 1996 concerning the additional imple‑ mentation periods requested by Ireland for the implementation of Commission Directives (EEC) 90/388 and (EC) 96/2 as regards full competition in the telecommunications markets [1997] OJ L41/8;

Commission Decision (EC) 97/310 of 12 February 1997 concerning the granting of additional implementation periods to the Portuguese Republic for the implementation of Commission

accompanied by the introduction of a detailed sector specific regulatory regime, Open Network Provision (ONP), enacted under Article 95 (formerly 100A) EC.[5] The European Union is also party to the WTO Agreement on Basic Telecommunications Services.[6] Any consideration of the competition rules applying to companies operating in the telecommunications and interactive services sector also requires consideration of these other bodies of law.

11.15 The regulation of the Internet is very different. Although originating in a US Government research programme, it has developed without significant government support over the last five years into a worldwide data network capable of connecting anyone with a suitable computer and access to a standard telephone line. Some elements of the telecommunications and broadcast regulation could

---

Directives (EEC) 90/388 and (EC) 96/2 as regards full competition in the telecommunications markets [1997] OJ L133/19;

Commission Decision (EC) 97/568 of 14 May 1997 on the granting of additional implementation periods to Luxembourg for the implementation of Directive (EEC) 90/388 as regards full competition in the telecommunications markets [1997] OJ L234/7;

Commission Decision (EC) 97/603 of 10 June 1997 concerning the granting of additional implementation periods to Spain for the implementation of Commission Directive (EEC) 90/388 as regards full competition in the telecommunications markets [1997] OJ L243/48;

Commission Decision (EC) 97/607 of 18 June 1997 concerning the granting of additional implementation periods to Greece for the implementation of Directive (EEC) 90/388 as regards full competition in the telecommunications markets [1997] OJ L245/6.

[5] See the ONP framework:

Directive (EC) 97/13 of the European Parliament and of the Council of 10 April 1997 on a common framework for authorisations and individual licences in the field of telecommunications services [1997] OJ L117/15;

Directive (EC) 97/33 of the European Parliament and of the Council of 30 June 1997 on interconnection in Telecommunications with regard to ensuring universal service and interoperability through application of the principles of Open Network Provision (ONP) [1997] OJ L199/32;

Council Directive (EEC) 90/387 of 28 June 1990 on the establishment of the internal market for telecommunications services through the implementation of open network provision [1990] OJ L192/1, as amended by Directive (EC) 97/51 of the European Parliament and of the Council of 6 October 1997 amending Council Directives (EC) 90/387 and (EEC) 92/44 for the purpose of adaptation to a competitive environment in telecommunications [1997] OJ L295/23;

Council Directive (EEC) 92/44 on the application of open network provision to leased lines [1992] OJ L165 as amended by Directive (EC) 97/51 of the European Parliament and of the Council of 6 October 1997 amending Council Directives (EC) 90/387 and (EEC) 92/44 for the purpose of adaptation to a competitive environment in telecommunications [1997] OJ L295/23;

Directive (EEC) 95/62 of the European Parliament and of the Council of 13 December 1995, on the application of open network provision to voice telephony [1995] OJ L321/6, replaced by Directive (EC) 98/10 of the European Parliament and of the Council of 26 February 1998 on the application of open network provision (ONP) to voice telephony and on universal service for telecommunications in a competitive environment [1998] OJ L101/24;

Directive (EC) 97/66 of the European Parliament and of the Council of 15 December 1997 concerning the processing of personal data and the protection of privacy in the telecommunications sector [1998] OJ L24/1.

[6] See, as regards the Community, Council Decision (EC) 97/838, concerning the conclusion on behalf of the European Community, as regards matters within its competence, of the results of the WTO negotiations on basic telecommunications services [1997] OJ L347/45.

affect the provision of Internet services, but, more importantly, the competition rules apply automatically to the Internet.

(1) Telecommunications

Liberalization

Services liberalization.   The 1990 Services Directive provided for the liberaliza- **11.16** tion of all telecommunications services except for voice telephony,[7] though the Directive did not apply to mobile or radio telephony, satellite, paging, or telex.[8] That definition of voice telephony was not linked to a market definition, but to a technical configuration.[9] This is a source of continued difficulty, given that the set of services caught by the definition do not necessarily correspond to the set of services which are capable of meeting the demand for voice services.[10]

Relevance of voice telephony definition.   Given this disparity, it is probably not **11.17** safe to assume that this definition will prove to be a reliable basis for competition law market definition in the sector. However, the definition will continue to be relevant:

— for those countries that are permitted to continue reserving voice telephony to a particular operator, as the scope of the derogation is determined by the above definition;

— where Member States choose to establish a licensing regime, as licensing obligations may vary depending on whether a company is providing voice telephony.

This last point is a potential subject of litigation. Regulatory regimes sometimes **11.18** provide benefits to 'voice telephony' operators—such as favourable interconnection regimes—which are denied to non-voice telephony operators, or impose particular burdens on 'voice telephony' operators such as increased charges for licences. Where 'voice telephony' operators nevertheless compete with non-voice telephony operators there may be arguments that the regulatory system is

---

[7] Commission Directive (EEC) 90/388 of 28 June 1990 on competition in the markets for telecommunications services [1990] OJ L192/10, Article 2.

[8] Commission Directive (EEC) 90/388 of 28 June 1990 on competition in the markets for telecommunications services [1990] OJ L192/10, Article 1(2).

[9] Commission Directive (EEC) 90/388 of 28 June 1990 on competition in the markets for telecommunications services [1990] OJ L192/10, Article 1(1): 'the commercial provision for the public of the direct transport and switching of speech in real-time between public switched network termination points, enabling any user to use equipment connected to such a network termination point in order to communicate with another termination point'.

[10] For further analysis of the definition of voice telephony see Section G below and:

Communication by the Commission to the European Parliament and the Council on the status of implementation of Directive (EEC) 90/388 on competition in the markets for telecommunications services [1995] OJ C275/2;

Notice on the Status of Voice on the Internet under Directive 90/388 [1998] OJ C6/4.

discriminatory, contrary to Article 86 read in conjunction with Article 82. This issue is discussed further below in the discussion on competition rules and sector specific regulation.

11.19 Full liberalization. All other telecommunications services were liberalized gradually with satellite,[11] mobile,[12] and other services being liberalized over the years following the 1990 Services Directive,[13] culminating in full liberalization, including the liberalization of voice telephony, in principle on 1 January 1998.[14]

11.20 The Full Competition Directive envisaged that those Member States with less well-developed or small telecommunications networks could request a temporary derogation from the liberalization timetable of the Directive. Five derogation decisions were passed[15]—for Greece, Ireland, Luxembourg, Portugal and Spain. Derogations could be justified, for example, by the need to rebalance tariffs, to invest in infrastructure and/or the digitization of exchanges, to allow time for the telecoms operator to become market driven, or to allow time to improve the debt and cost structures of the telecoms operator. Any derogation period had to be proportionate to these aims. These decisions may be withdrawn if it is shown either that there is no longer a need for the derogation, or if a dominant position resulting from the derogation is being abused.

11.21 Infrastructure liberalization. The Cable TV Directive[16] abolished all restrictions on the supply of transmission capacity by cable TV networks and allowed the use of cable networks for the provision of telecommunications services, other than voice telephony. The Full Competition Directive then required the liberalization of all alternative infrastructure. The Directives also contain requirements

---

[11] Commission Directive (EEC) 94/46 of 13 October 1994 amending Directive (EEC) 88/301 and Directive (EEC) 90/388 in particular with regard to satellite communications [1994] OJ L268/15, Article 2. See also:
   Satellite Green Paper, COM (90) 490 final of 20 November 1990;
   Council Resolution of 19 December 1991 on the development of the common market for satellite communications services and equipment [1992] OJ C8/1.
[12] Commission Directive (EC) 96/2 of 16 January 1996 amending Directive (EEC) 90/388 with regard to mobile and personal communications [1996] OJ L20/59.
[13] See European Commission, 1992 Review of the situation in the telecommunications services sector, SEC (92) 1048, 21 October 1992. Communication to the Council and to the European Parliament on the consultation on the review of the situation in the telecommunications sector, COM (92) 159 final, 28 April 1993. Council Resolution of 22 July 1993 on the review of the situation in the telecommunication sector and the need for further development in that market, [1993] OJ C213/1.
[14] Commission Directive (EC) 96/19 of 13 March 1996 amending Directive (EEC) 90/388 with regard to the implementation of full competition in the telecommunications markets [1996] OJ L74/13.
[15] See n 4 above.
[16] Commission Directive (EC) 95/51 of 18 October 1995, amending Directive (EEC) 90/388 with regard to the abolition of the restrictions on the use of cable television networks for the provision of already liberalised telecommunications services [1995] OJ L256/49.

relating to the interconnection of networks which duplicate certain provisions found in the Interconnection Directive.

The Commission has also examined the issue of joint ownership of telecommu-   **11.22**
nications and cable networks, as the latter are important potential local infra-structure competitors for the provision of communications services. The Cable TV Directive announced that the Commission would review this situation by 1 January 1998. The Commission published a draft Directive[17] in March 1998 which suggested that if a telecoms operator also owned a cable network it should be required to hold the two operations in legally distinct companies. The position remained substantially the same in the final version of the Directive adopted by the Commission in June 1999. The Directive makes it clear that this is envisaged as a first step, and that the Commission will consider taking further action on the basis of individual cases. Divestiture of BT's very limited interests in cable televi-sion networks are therefore envisaged in the Commission's Article 19(3) Notice in the *BiB* case, discussed below.

Ensuring effective liberalization.   In addition to setting out the timetable   **11.23**
within which the telecommunications sector should be opened to competition,[18] the Directives also set out certain requirements designed to ensure the effective-ness of the liberalization. These include requirements:

— to publish technical interfaces;[19]

— to make interconnection available and publish a standard interconnection offer;[20]

[17] Notice by the Commission concerning a draft Directive amending Commission Directive (EEC) 90/388 in order to ensure that telecommunications networks and cable tv networks owned by a single operator are separate legal entities [1998] OJ C71/3;
   Draft Commission Directive amending Directive (EEC) 90/388 in order to ensure that telecom-munications networks and cable TV networks owned by a single operator are separate legal entities [1998] OJ C71/23, final version adopted 23 June 1999 (not yet published), see Commission press release IP/99/413.
[18] For those Member States which did not/do not respect this timetable, the Commission con-siders that certain provisions of the liberalization Directives have direct effect: Commission Status Report on European Union Telecommunications Policy, April 1998: 'even if not fully transposed, clear and unconditional provisions of these Directives have direct effect, and certain of the Member States concerned (Belgium, Ireland) have guaranteed provisional authorisations based on this direct effect of Community law'.
[19] Commission Directive (EEC) 90/388 of 28 June 1990 on competition in the markets for telecommunications services [1990] OJ L192/10, Article 5: 'Without prejudice to the relevant international agreements, Member States shall ensure that the characteristics of the technical inter-faces necessary for the use of public networks are published by 31 December 1990 at the latest. Member States shall communicate to the Commission, in accordance with Directive 83/189/EEC, any draft measure drawn up for this purpose.' See also the IBM Undertaking, *Bull EC* 7/8-1984 Point 1.1.1 and *Bull EC* 10-1984 Point 3.4.1.
[20] Article 4a of Directive 90/388 as amended by the Full Competition Directive. See Commission Directive (EC) 96/19 of 13 March 1996 amending Directive (EEC) 90/388 with regard to the implementation of full competition in the telecommunications markets [1996] OJ

— to establish accounting separation between their interconnect and other activities;[21] and

— in respect of contracts for telecommunications services which have more than one year to run, to give customers a right to terminate those contracts on six months' notice.[22]

11.24 A parallel can be drawn between these issues and the consideration of the joint ownership of telecommunications and cable networks referred to above. The issue of how far the Commission can proceed under Article 86 to ensure effective liberalization of the telecommunications sector is, however, unresolved.

Sector Specific Regulation

11.25 The telecommunications sector is also subject to extensive sector specific single market regulation (the ONP rules) enacted under Article 95 EC.[23] These Directives establish national regulatory authorities in each Member State with responsibility in the telecommunications sector (although it is not necessary to establish a sector specific regulator). The Directives cover the availability of and pricing for interconnection, licensing, data protection, and universal service.

L74/13, Recital 13, para 3: 'In order to allow for effective market entry and to prevent the de facto continuation of special and exclusive rights . . . Member States should ensure that, during the time period necessary for such entry by competitors, telecommunications organizations publish standard terms and conditions for interconnection to the voice telephony networks which they offer to the public, including interconnect price lists and access points, no later than six months before the actual date of liberalization of voice telephony and telecommunications transmission capacity. Such standard offers should be non-discriminatory and sufficiently unbundled to allow the new entrants to purchase only those elements of the interconnection offer they actually need. Furthermore, they may not discriminate on the basis of the origin of the calls and/or the networks.'

[21] Commission Directive (EEC) 90/388 of 28 June 1990 on competition in the markets for telecommunications services [1990] OJ L192/10, as amended by Commission Directive (EC) 96/19 of 13 March 1996 amending Directive (EEC) 90/388 with regard to the implementation of full competition in the telecommunications markets [1996] OJ L74/13, at Article 4a(4). See Full Competition Directive Recital (14): 'in order to allow the monitoring of interconnection obligations under competition law, the cost accounting system implemented with regard to the provision of voice telephony and public telecommunications networks should, during the time period necessary to allow for effective market entry, clearly identify the cost elements relevant for pricing interconnection offerings and, in particular for each element of the interconnection offered, identify the basis for that cost element, in order to ensure in particular that this pricing includes only elements which are relevant, namely the initial connection charge, conveyance charges, the share of the costs incurred in providing equal access and number-portability and of ensuring essential requirements and, where applicable, supplementary charges aimed to share the net cost of universal service, and provisionally, imbalances in voice telephony tariffs. Such cost accounting should also make it possible to identify when a telecommunications organization charges its major users less than providers of voice telephony networks.'

[22] Commission Directive (EEC) 90/388 of 28 June 1990 on competition in the markets for telecommunications services [1990] OJ L192/10, Article 8.

[23] See n 5 above.

Conditions of access to telecommunications networks must be based on objective **11.26** criteria, must be transparent (and published), and non-discriminatory. Access to networks and services can only be restricted on the basis of essential requirements such as the security of network operations, the maintenance of network integrity, and interoperability.

(2) Media

In contrast to the telecommunications sector, there is relatively little regulation of **11.27** the media sector at the European level. For the purposes of this chapter, reference is made only to EC legislation which is directly relevant to the application of the competition rules. Thus, the Television Without Frontiers Directive[24] is examined in the section on exclusive rights contracts,[25] while the Advanced Television Standards Directive[26] is dealt with in the section on set top boxes.[27]

(3) Competition Rules and Sector Specific Regulation

Depending on the facts of the case, sector specific regulation such as the ONP **11.28** regime or the TV Standards Directive, may provide more far-reaching, more detailed, or more rapid remedies for potential complainants than the competition rules. However, the mere existence of sector specific legislation does not prevent the application of the competition rules to the same area.[28] There are two areas where the relationship between sector specific regulation and competition law is not clear:

— first, to what extent do the competition rules limit the powers of national regulators;

— secondly, to what extent should sector specific regulation be taken into account in analysing a case under the competition rules?

---

[24] Council Directive (EEC) 89/552 on the coordination of certain provisions laid down by law, regulation or administrative action in Member States concerning the pursuit of television broadcasting activities [1989] OJ L298/23 as amended by Directive (EC) 97/36 of the European Parliament and of the Council [1997] OJ L202/60.

[25] See para 11.94 below.

[26] Directive (EC) 95/47 of the European Parliament and of the Council on the use of standards for the transmission of television signals [1995] OJ L281/51.

[27] See para 11.294 and following below.

[28] Notice on the Application of the Competition Rules to Access Agreements in the Telecommunications Sector [1998] OJ C265/2 at para 58, Commission Guidelines on the application of EEC competition rules in the telecommunications sector [1991] OJ C233/2, paras 15 and 16. See also *Bertelsmann/Kirch/Premiere* (Case IV/M993) [1999] OJ L53/1 and *Deutsche Telekom/BetaResearch* (Case IV/M1027) [1999] OJ L53/31.

Competition Law as a Limit on the Role of Sector Specific Regulation

11.29 An issue which may prove relevant in the future is the extent to which the competition rules can be invoked against State action in regulating a sector.[29] Where that regulation has the objective of favouring, or has the clear effect of favouring, a particular operator or class of operators, the Commission can take action under Article 86.[30] A more difficult case arises where the State action is at least overtly intended to serve another objective, such as the development or maintenance of competition. It appears possible that some such measures nevertheless risk infringing Article 86. For example, policies to encourage infrastructure investment in telecommunications, which can include differential interconnection pricing (cheaper interconnection for infrastructure operators), preventing the unbundling of local loops, and imposing line of business restrictions on dominant telecommunications companies, could potentially raise competition concerns. The impact on third party investment is also one of the arguments made in relation to a competition authority ordering access to an essential facility, although on a proper essential facilities analysis this should not arise as if investment in own infrastructure was a viable proposition then the facility cannot be deemed to be essential.

Different Interconnection Prices Risk Being Discriminatory

11.30 As regards interconnection pricing, the Interconnection Directive provides that national regulatory authorities may authorize different interconnection prices for different classes of operator.[31] This Article could be used, for example, to justify lower interconnection prices for companies owning their own infrastructure as compared to service providers who use third parties' infrastructure. This may be problematic on various grounds (Is infrastructure investment in other Member States relevant? Is the investment in infrastructure efficient? If it is efficient, is there more investment taking place than would have been the case in the absence of the policy?).

11.31 There appears to be a substantive objection to such a policy, however, on competition law grounds. Although a national regulatory authority has jurisdiction to determine certain policy objectives, this must always be subject to the provisions

---

[29] The extent to which regulatory justifications can be used to prohibit what the competition rules would allow is examined below in the section on procedure.

[30] Commission Decision of 4 October 1995 concerning the conditions imposed on the second operator of GSM radiotelephony services in Italy [1995] OJ L280/49 (only the Italian text is authentic).

[31] Directive (EC) 97/33 of the European Parliament and of the Council of 30 June 1997 on interconnection in Telecommunications with regard to ensuring universal service and interoperability through application of the principles of Open Network Provision (ONP) [1997] OJ L199/32, at Article 7.

of Articles 10 (former Article 5), 81 and 82 and 86.[32] In looking at interconnection pricing, for example, it is important to note that the Interconnection Directive itself allows differences only to the extent that there is no distortion of competition (a reiteration of the position under Article 82). In practice a distortion of competition would appear to be likely on the basis of even a small differential in price if the service being provided to two companies was equivalent, and those two companies competed on the same downstream market (or at least two closely related markets).[33]

Unbundled Local Loops

The competition issues surrounding unbundled local loops are examined in detail **11.32** in Section E. In brief, however, the bundling of separate products or services by a dominant company, where that bundling affects competition, could be regarded as abusive. A regulator can legitimately determine whether unbundled local loops *should* be provided as a matter of regulation. However, if unbundled local loops are required as a matter of competition law, it is doubtful that the national regulatory authority can cite public policy objectives to override the competition law arguments and prevent unbundling.

Different Treatment Risks Becoming a Special Right within the Meaning of Article 86

The policies described above directly or indirectly affect the rights of certain com- **11.33** panies—facilities based operators may be given preferential treatment over pure service providers. It seems arguable that this preferential treatment would constitute a special right within the meaning of Article 86, or would constitute a breach on the part of a Member State of Article 10 read in conjunction with Article 82. The following analysis looks at the possible implications of Article 86 in the context of public policy objectives.

Those public policy objectives that can legitimately be pursued by means of grant- **11.34** ing special and exclusive rights to one or more companies are limited by the provisions of Article 86, as interpreted by the liberalization Directives referred to above. For example, issues such as universal service continue to be a legitimate source for Member State intervention. Similarly, Member States can make the supply of liberalized services conditional upon licensing procedures, provided that the grant of such licences is objective, non-discriminatory and transparent, and based only on essential requirements.[34] Essential requirements are defined as follows:

---

[32] Case 66/86 *Ahmed Saeed* [1989] ECR 838.
[33] See the discussion on discriminatory pricing, below.
[34] Commission Directive (EEC) 90/388 of 28 June 1990 on competition in the markets for telecommunications services [1990] OJ L192/10, as amended by Commission Directive (EC) 96/19 of 13 March 1996 amending Directive (EEC) 90/388 with regard to the implementation of full competition in the telecommunications markets [1996] OJ L74/13 at Article 2(3).
See also Full Competition Directive, Recital 9: 'Member States may therefore only introduce

'essential requirements' means the non-economic reasons in the general interest which may cause a Member State to impose conditions on the establishment and/or operation of telecommunications networks or the provision of telecommunications services. These reasons are security of network operations, maintenance of network integrity, and, in justified cases, interoperability of services, data protection, the protection of the environment and town and country planning objectives as well as the effective use of the frequency spectrum and the avoidance of harmful interference between radio based telecommunications systems and other, space-based or terrestrial, technical systems. Data protection may include protection of personal data, the confidentiality of information transmitted or stored as well as the protection of privacy.[35]

11.35 Decisions as to the appropriate method of promoting competition clearly do not fall within this definition of essential requirements. Consequently where such decisions entail the grant of special or exclusive rights to one or more companies, they do not appear to be justifiable by reference to Article 86. As such, such decisions would only be permissible to the extent that they do not infringe the competition rules in the first place. Differential interconnection pricing would appear to risk being categorized as discriminatory.[36] Refusal to permit unbundled access to local loops could, in certain circumstances, similarly prove unlawful.[37]

11.36 If this analysis is correct, regulatory policy objectives can be used to derogate from the competition rules only to the extent that they relate to essential requirements. The Commission has also taken a clear position in the Access Notice that if a regulator infringes the competition rules it is at risk of an action for damages by a third party.[38] Regulatory intervention may also be insufficient to prevent an undertaking from itself being held liable for infringement of the competition rules.[39]

---

licensing or declaration procedures where it is indispensable to ensure compliance with the applicable essential requirements and, with regard to the provision of voice telephony and the underlying infrastructure, introduce requirements in the form of trade regulations where it is necessary in order to ensure, in accordance with Article 90(2) [now Article 86(2)] of the Treaty, the performance in a competitive environment of the particular tasks of public service assigned to the relevant undertakings in the telecommunications field and/or to ensure a contribution to the financing of universal service. Other public service requirements can be included by Member States in certain categories of licences, in line with the principle of proportionality and in conformity with Articles 56 and 66 [now Articles 46 and 55] of the Treaty.'

[35] Commission Directive (EC) 96/19 of 13 March 1996 amending Directive (EEC) 90/388 with regard to the implementation of full competition in the telecommunications markets [1996] OJ L74/13 at, Article 1.

[36] See Section E below.

[37] See Section E below.

[38] Joined Cases C–6/90 and C–9/90 *Francovich and Others* [1991] ECR I–5357, and Joined Cases C–46/93 and C–48/93 *Brasserie du Pêcheur SA v Bundesrepublik Deutschland* and *The Queen v Secretary of State for Transport, ex parte: Factortame Ltd and others* [1996] ECR I–1029, Notice on the Application of the Competition Rules to Access Agreements in the Telecommunications Sector [1998] OJ C265/2 at para 19.

[39] *AROW/BNIC* [1982] OJ L379/19.

The above analysis is based on a relatively strict interpretation of the competition **11.37**
rules. However, issues such as investment incentives are politically sensitive, and
the Commission may prove reluctant to attack Member States who espouse such
policies save in exceptional circumstances.

Relevance of Sector Specific Regulation to an Appraisal under the Competition Rules

Regulation as a mitigator of competition concerns.   Commission decisional **11.38**
practice on this issue appears to vary. Early Commission decisions in the telecommunications sector appear to have relied upon sector specific regulation more
than in recent decisions. Recent decisions have either included conditions which
mirror or build on pre-existing regulation[40] or have failed to mention the regulatory framework at all.[41]

In *BT/MCI I* the Commission did not impose non-discrimination and trans- **11.39**
parency conditions on BT given the pre-existing regulatory framework,[42]
although the Commission explicitly reserved the right to apply the competition
rules should the regulatory regime prove ineffective. The approach seems to have
altered slightly in the *Atlas* decision, where the Commission imposed certain
obligations even where the parties maintained that at least some of the conditions
reflected pre-existing national law.[43] It should be noted that in each of these cases
the regulation and conditions were not designed to address competition issues
created on the markets of the joint ventures, but were relevant to the potential
problem of the parents favouring their respective joint ventures.

This should be contrasted with the Commission's position on the **11.40**
Kirch/Bertlesmann[44] joint venture. Here, no reference is made to the TV
Standards Directive which at least in principle regulated the provision of digital
conditional access services in Germany, one of the Commission's concerns in the
case.

---

[40] *Atlas* [1996] OJ L239/23 (Atlas).
[41] *Bertelsmann/Kirch/Premiere* (Case IV/M993) (1998) [1999] OJ L53/1.
[42] *BT-MCI* [1994] OJ L223/ 36, at para 57: (*BT/MCI I*). 'The abovementioned regulatory constraints, together with the additional explanations provided by the parties, have permitted the
Commission to conclude that it is not necessary for it to take any further action as of now, including requesting the parties to make appropriate undertakings to the effect that they will neither discriminate nor cross-subsidise. However, should this conclusion prove to be wrong in the future, the
Commission will immediately apply the competition rules of the EC Treaty (and if applicable those
of the EEA Agreement) as required.'
[43] *Atlas* [1996] OJ L239/23, at para 30: 'In so far as related to existing obligations under national
or Community law, the obligations described below are intended to ensure the Parties' firm commitment to comply with the applicable legal framework.'
[44] *Bertelsmann/Kirch/Premiere* (Case IV/M993) (1998) [1999] OJ L53/1. On appeal to the
Court of First Instance.

11.41 **Regulation is irrelevant if competition is decreased.** Where sector specific regulation is intended at least in part to deal with the effects of an absence of competition, that regulation cannot be used as a justification to allow a further decrease
in competition. For example, the Interconnection Directive is intended to regulate customer access in circumstances where there is an operator with market
power. The Directive imposes on such an operator an obligation to interconnect
at cost-oriented prices. The TV Standards Directive imposes behavioural obligations on parties, and does not prevent the creation or strengthening of dominance, the relevant test under the Merger Regulation. Regulation is often
behavioural, taking as its starting point the existence of market power, and seeking to regulate the exercise of that power. If the regulation were to take as its starting point a prohibition on the creation or strengthening of market power, it is
likely that it could be taken into account under the Merger Regulation.

C. Procedural Issues

11.42 The relationship between the European Commission and national regulatory
authorities is particularly important in these sectors given the overlap between the
sector specific regulation and the competition rules. The overlap is greatest in the
telecommunications sector, and for that reason, the Commission has issued guidance on the relationship as part of the Access Notice.[45] Certain principles, however, were developed in media cases, and the principles set out below are broadly
applicable to both sectors.

(1) Notifications

11.43 **Decisions whether or not to notify.** During the discussions on the Access
Notice, the Commission wished to discourage notifications of, in particular,
interconnection agreements in the telecommunications sector as such agreements
would generally raise only limited competition concerns.[46] The Commission has
limited procedural means at its disposal under Regulation 17 to limit the number
of notifications it receives. The Commission does, however, have a certain discretion in relation to fines under Regulation 17. The Commission therefore indicated in the Access Notice that:

> where the agreement has been notified to a national regulatory authority but has not
> been notified to the Commission the Commission does not consider it would be
> generally appropriate as a matter of policy to impose a fine in respect of the agree-

---

[45] Notice on the Application of the Competition Rules to Access Agreements in the
Telecommunications Sector [1998] OJ C265/2, Part I —Framework.

[46] For a discussion of when interconnection agreements could raise competition concerns, under
Article 81, see the Notice on the Application of the Competition Rules to Access Agreements in the
Telecommunications Sector [1998] OJ C265/2, at paras 131 *et seq.*

ment, even if the agreement ultimately proves to contain conditions in breach of Article 85 [now Article 81]. A fine would, however be appropriate in some cases, for example where: —the agreement proves to contain provisions in breach of Article 86 [now Article 82] and/or the breach of Article 85 is particularly serious.[47]

Given the caveats in this statement, it is doubtful that the Commission's concession will prove significant in practice.

Regulatory jurisdiction of national authorities. Regulatory intervention to **11.44** prohibit agreements or practices that are permitted under Community competition law is possible in certain circumstances.

Article 21 of the Merger Regulation envisages regulatory scrutiny by the Member **11.45** States on the basis of public interest (non-competition) objectives. Public interest objectives could include, for example, plurality of the media.

There is no explicit comparable provision under Regulation 17. However, as **11.46** Regulation 17 explicitly precludes national authorities only from applying competition laws, national scrutiny on non-competition grounds of agreements dealt with by the Commission under Regulation 17 does appear to be permitted by Community law.

(2) Complaints

Community interest. Where other fora have potential jurisdiction over a dis- **11.47** pute, complainants should consider carefully what elements of their complaint are of Community interest, and should where possible pursue national remedies, where such Community interest is limited.

Other options available to complainants. The Access Notice notes that, as **11.48** regards complaints to the Commission, other options are often available to complainants, such as actions before national competition or regulatory authorities, or national courts. The Notice notes the directly applicable nature of Articles 81 and 82,[48] and reiterates the benefits of national court proceedings first set out in the Commission's Notice on Co-operation with National Courts.

> —national courts can deal with and award a claim for damages resulting from an infringement of the competition rules;
> —national courts can usually adopt interim measures and order the termination of an infringement more quickly than the Commission is able to do;
> —before national courts, it is possible to combine a claim under Community law with a claim under national law;
> —legal costs can be awarded to the successful applicant before a national court.[49]

---

[47] Notice on the Application of the Competition Rules to Access Agreements in the Telecommunications Sector [1998] OJ C265/2, at para 37.

[48] Access Notice, para 27, citing Case 127/73, *BRT v SABAM* [1974] ECR 51.

[49] Access Notice, para 25; Notice on cooperation between national courts and the Commission in applying Articles 85 and 86 [now Articles 81 and 82] of the EC Treaty [1993] OJ C39/6, at para 16.

11.49 **ONP procedures.** The Notice notes that the ONP Directives provide that national regulatory authorities have power to intervene and order changes in relation to both the existence and content of access agreements. National regulatory authorities must take into account 'the need to stimulate a competitive market' and may impose conditions on one or more parties, *inter alia*, 'to ensure effective competition'. Moreover, national regulatory authorities are obliged to take account of the competition rules when dealing with matters within their jurisdiction.[50]

11.50 **Commission's position.** Given the benefits of avoiding a multiplicity of proceedings, the Commission indicates that:

> Where complaints are lodged with the Commission under Article 3 of Regulation 17 while there are related actions before a relevant national or European authority or court, the Directorate-General for Competition will generally not initially pursue any investigation as to the existence of an infringement under Article 85 [now Article 81] or 86 [now 82] of the EC Treaty.[51]

11.51 **Safeguarding complainant's rights.** Just as the Commission cannot in a Notice alter the requirements of notification of restrictive agreements in Regulation 17, neither can it abrogate its responsibilities under the competition rules towards those who feel that their rights under the competition rules are being infringed. Undertakings are entitled to effective protection of their Community law rights.[52] These rights would be undermined if the Commission were to refer matters to national authorities without ensuring that those national authorities respected the Community law rights of the applicants. Although the Access Notice refers to national regulatory authorities in the telecommunications sector, it may be that similar principles will be applied in the media sector also.

11.52 The Access Notice sets out certain criteria by which this effective protection should be judged. As the Access Notice is an interpretative text these criteria are unlikely to be interpreted strictly by the Commission and each case will have to be analysed and reasoned on its merits.

11.53 **Relevance of timing to Community interest.** First, the Commission indicates that if a matter is not resolved within six months of it first being brought to the attention of the national regulatory authority, the Commission will then consider intervening.[53] This period is the same as that recommended in the ONP Directives for the resolution of disputes although this is not explicitly referred to

---

[50] Access Notice, para 19, citing Case 13/77 *GB-Inno-BM/ATAB* [1977] ECR 2115, at para 33: 'while it is true that Article 86 [now Article 82] is directed at undertakings, nonetheless it is also true that the Treaty imposes a duty on Member States not to adopt or maintain in force any measure which could deprive the provision of its effectiveness'.

[51] Access Notice, para 28.

[52] Case 14/83 *Von Colson* [1984] ECR 1891.

[53] Access Notice, para 30.

in the Notice. The Notice provides no indication of when the six-month time period will start: this is consistent with the six-month provision being more of a guideline than a strict rule. Potential complainants to the Commission would therefore be well advised to inform national regulatory authorities of their problems at the earliest possible stage.

The Notice goes on to say that timely resolution of disputes is particularly impor- **11.54**
tant in this sector given the short innovation cycles. This parallels the importance which the Commission also places on the timely provision of access by dominant operators—delay in providing access could potentially be abusive on the part of a dominant operator.[54] Resolution by the national regulatory authority could take the form of either a final determination of the action or another form of relief which would safeguard the rights of the complainant.

Cross-border/pan-European dimension.   A caveat likely to prove extremely **11.55**
significant is set out very briefly at paragraph 31 of the Access Notice:

> In addition, the Commission must always look at each case on its merits: it will take action if it feels that in a particular case, there is a substantial Community interest affecting, or likely to affect, competition in a number of Member States.

Where there is a substantial cross-border element to a particular case it is likely **11.56**
that no one national regulatory authority would have jurisdiction to act. In these circumstances it would be inappropriate for the Commission to refer matters to the national level. However, this paragraph is drafted more widely than that case would require. The paragraph also appears to envisage Commission intervention in a case where the issues are likely to recur in other Member States, even though the particular case is centred in one Member State and where that State's national regulatory authority would therefore have jurisdiction.

Interim Measures

Availability of interim measures at the national level.   The Commission also **11.57**
notes the importance of the availability in principle and in practice of interim measures at the national level. In principle the availability of interim measures at the national level should be no more difficult than before the Commission. However, given that interim measures decisions appear difficult under Community law and are therefore rarely taken by the Commission, this would not appear to be a particularly high hurdle.

Substantially the same outcome.   A principle developed in the media sector, **11.58**
but only implicit in the Access Notice, is that matters can only be appropriately referred to a national authority in circumstances where that national authority is applying rules which should lead to substantially the same outcome as an

---

[54] Access Notice, paras 95 and 125.

application of the competition rules. Where a national authority has power directly to apply Community competition law, or power to apply national competition law which is essentially the same as Community competition law, this should not prove to be an obstacle. However, for those Member States that do not have authorities with such powers, referring cases to national authorities to be dealt with under the competition rules may prove problematic.

11.59 National regulatory authorities will often be applying ONP rules in circumstances where there is an overlap with the competition rules, for example in the field of interconnection and access pricing. In such cases, this criterion will usually be satisfied. One possible area of divergence relates to obligations imposed by national regulatory authorities as a result of a company being deemed to hold significant market power under the ONP Directives. Significant market power is presumed to exist if a company has 25 per cent of the market,[55] and is calculated according to market definitions set out in the Directives. There is no requirement of market power in the economist's sense. Given that these market definitions will not necessarily correspond to those used under the competition rules, a company may be dominant without having significant market power and vice versa. This may lead to the situation, for example, where a national regulatory authority has no jurisdiction and referring a matter to that authority would be inappropriate.

11.60 Where a national competition or regulatory authority applies national rules that should lead to substantially the same outcome, but the complainant is dissatisfied with the result, the appropriate course of action would be to challenge in national proceedings the finding of the national authority. The Commission is unlikely to prove receptive to being treated as a court of appeal against decisions of national authorities, particularly in view of the Article 234 jurisdiction of the Court of Justice.

D. Content

11.61 **Scope of section.** This section will deal with the competition issues which arise in respect of the creation, packaging, and distribution of content. These categories reflect distinct economic activities but are often carried out by a single integrated company. For example, most television broadcasters are active in programme production, acquisition of the rights to further programming, packaging of channels, and their distribution or broadcasting to end-users.

11.62 Creation of content is used here to refer to the production of television programmes. Packaging of content refers to the acquisition of programming rights by broadcasters in order to create television channels. Distribution refers to the

---

[55] See Article 4(3) of the Interconnection Directive.

wholesale distribution of television channels to pay TV operators. This section thus deals only with the wholesale aspects of content distribution. Issues relating to retail end-user services (advertising-funded and pay television) are dealt with in section G on retail services.

General issue: effect on downstream markets.   Television rights are generally   **11.63** sold exclusively in respect of individual territories, and may be bought or sold collectively. Competition issues involving exclusive rights agreements, collective purchasing, and collective selling of rights are therefore common and are likely to raise issues under Article 81 EC. Analysis of the effects of such agreements, however, is primarily focused on downstream television markets as lack of access to content may constitute a barrier to entry.[56] In this respect, three issues in particular have attracted ever growing scrutiny by competition authorities at both the Community and national levels: the effects of vertical integration; the conclusion by pay television operators of series of exclusive agreements for sports and film rights; and collective selling of exclusive sports rights by sports federations or leagues. While the Commission has highlighted its concerns over the latter two points,[57] it has yet to take concrete action.

General issue: effect on trade between Member States.   The Commission has   **11.64** tended to define content product markets with regard to national, or at broadest linguistic, territories. This has not prevented it from finding agreements confined to the territory of a single Member State to have an effect on trade between Member States.[58] This seems largely to be on the basis that appreciable restrictions

---

[56] *Report on Competition Policy 1996* (Vol XXVI) at para 81: 'Steps must therefore be taken to ensure that the market is not foreclosed and that competition is not distorted . . . by difficulty in gaining access to programmes.'

[57] See, for example, *Report on Competition Policy 1996* (Vol XXVI) at para 83: 'The question of content is assuming increasing importance in the audiovisual sector. Following the introduction of digital technology, numerous special interest channels may be launched on the pay-TV market using digital compression. The pioneers on this market are currently negotiating the purchase of exclusive rights in fiction and sport—the two pillars of pay-TV—with a view to amassing vast catalogues of rights over particularly attractive programmes. The problem of content and exclusive rights in the media sector is not a new one as far as the Commission is concerned. It has already had occasion in the past to decide on the compatibility with the competition rules of agreements involving exclusive rights: while acknowledging the importance of exclusivity as a means of safeguarding the value of a programme, it takes particular care to ensure that neither the duration nor the scope of such agreements restricts third-party access to rights for too long a period or risks foreclosing the market. In relation to sports, the problem of access to rights is particularly important owing to the ephemeral nature of televised broadcasts of sports events, the concentration of rights in the hands of sports federations, thereby reducing the number of rights available on the market, and the relative inelasticity of viewer demand. Given the importance of questions to do with sports rights and the growing number of cases relating thereto, DG IV has embarked upon a wide-ranging consultation exercise involving the application of the competition rules in this area.'

[58] See, for example, *BBC/BSkyB/Premier League* (Notice pursuant to Article 19(3) of Regulation 17) [1993] OJ C94/6. Press release, IP(93)614 of 20 July 1993 and the *BDB* case referred to in the speech of JF Pons, Deputy Director-General of DGIV, 'The Future of Broadcasting' at the Institute

of competition in a national market can affect market structure, raise barriers to entry for undertakings from other countries, and thereby contribute to foreclosure of national markets.

(1) Content Creation

Market Definition

11.65 **Television programme production.** The Commission has discussed a product market for television programme production in a number of cases,[59] without having to decide definitively. In the *RTL/Veronica/Endemol* prohibition decision,[60] however, the Commission refined its previous market definition by defining, *inter alia*, a product market for independently produced Dutch television programmes, ie excluding captive in-house production by Dutch broadcasters.[61] The Commission rejected the parties' arguments that the market should include in-house production on the following grounds. First, such programmes were very rarely sold to other broadcasters. Secondly, their production involved high fixed costs which made a significant increase in the purchase of independently produced programmes a commercially unfeasible strategy. Lastly, independently produced programmes tended to be 'large-scale entertainment programmes'. Broadcasters could not easily produce such programmes in-house. This market definition has since been upheld by the Court of First Instance[62] and the Commission's reasoning confirmed.

11.66 **Geographic markets.** In the *RTL/Veronica/Endemol* case, the Commission concluded that the geographic market for independent television production was The Netherlands as there was very little trade in Dutch-language television programmes even with broadcasters in the Belgian Flanders region. This was due to cultural differences between the two areas and to the fact that programmes produced to attract Dutch audiences with well-known Dutch actors were unlikely to be attractive to Belgian audiences and vice versa. This conclusion has been confirmed by the Court of First Instance. It therefore seems likely that the Commission will continue to define national geographic markets, or depending on the facts, broader markets in respect of a homegenous cultural or linguistic area which can surpass national boundaries.[63]

---

of Economic Affairs on 29 June 1998, http:/europa.eu.int/en:comm/dg04/speech/eight/en/sp98034.

[59] *ABC/Générale des Eaux/Canal+/WH Smith TV* (Case IV/M110) (1991), *VOX (II)* (Case IV/M525) (1995), *Channel Five* (Case IV/M673) (1996).

[60] *RTL/Veronica/Endemol* (Case IV/M553) [1996] OJ L294/14.

[61] ibid, see in particular paras 24, 89, and 90.

[62] Case T–221/95 *Endemol Entertainment Holding v Commission*, judgment of 28 April 1999, not yet published.

[63] In *ABC/Générale des Eaux/Canal+/WH Smith TV* (Case IV/M110) (1991) the Commission referred to the possibility of the geographic market in question surpassing national boundaries.

Competition Issues

The only competition issues to have been examined by the Commission to date **11.67**
have arisen under the Merger Regulation and concerned television programme
markets. No significant competition concern has been identified in the majority
of these cases. The exception is the *RTL/Veronica/Endemol*[64] prohibition decision.
The main interest of this case is for its analysis of the factors relevant to dominance
and to the strengthening of that dominance through vertical integration. The
decision has been upheld on appeal by the Court of First Instance.[65]

Strengthening of dominance through vertical integration—*RTL/Veronica* **11.68**
Endemol. The case concerned the creation of a joint venture company, HMG,
by RTL, the broadcaster of two Dutch-language advertising-funded television
channels directed at The Netherlands, Veronica, the broadcaster of a third such
television channel, and Endemol, an independent producer of Dutch-language
television programmes. In addition to the structural link between Endemol and
HMG, a production agreement was concluded under the terms of which HMG
agreed to purchase a large percentage of its Dutch-language programme requirements from Endemol. The purpose of HMG was to package and supply television
and radio programmes broadcast by itself, CLT, Veronica or others to viewers in
The Netherlands and Luxembourg.

The Commission concluded that Endemol held a dominant position in the mar- **11.69**
ket for independently produced Dutch-language TV programmes and that this
position would be strengthened by its participation in the newly created joint venture, HMG. Furthermore, the Commission concluded that HMG would acquire
a dominant position on the Dutch television advertising market. The operation
was prohibited. Following this decision Endemol withdrew from HMG.[66] On
this basis, and following modifications to the programme supply agreement
between Endemol and HMG and to HMG itself, the operation was cleared.[67] The
programme supply agreement itself was then notified to the Commission under
Regulation 17.[68] There is as yet no decision.

Factors relevant to dominance in television programme production. In calcu- **11.70**
lating Endemol's pre-existing market share, the Commission concluded that the
value of programmes sold and not the volume was the most appropriate method.

---

[64] *RTL/Veronica/Endemol* (Case IV/M553) [1996] OJ L294/14.
[65] Case T–221/95 *Endemol Entertainment Holding v Commission*, judgment of 28 April 1999,
not yet published.
[66] The operation had been implemented prior its prohibition by the Commission. This was possible as it was referred by the Dutch authorities to the Commission under Article 22 of Council
Regulation (EEC) 4064/89 on the control of concentrations between undertakings [1989] OJ
L395/1 which does not provide for a suspensive effect on the operation's implementation.
[67] *RTL/Veronica/Endemol* (Case IV/M553) [1996] OJ L294/14.
[68] Notice inviting third party comment, OJ C147/5.

On this basis, Endemol had a market share which was 'clearly more than 50%'. The Court of First Instance has since confirmed the Commission's methodology. The strength of Endemol's market position was confirmed by the fact that it owned a large number of the most popular entertainment programmes, had preferential access to foreign formats which it then adapted to the Dutch audience, and had a high number of the most popular Dutch TV personalities under contract, often on an exclusive basis. Finally, Endemol's single largest competitor had a market share of less than 10 per cent, while the remainder had market shares of less than 5 per cent. The Court of First Instance has since confirmed that these factors were sufficient to establish dominance.

11.71 **Effect of downstream vertical integration.** The Commission concluded that Endemol's dominant position would be strengthened by its participation in HMG (which as stated above, was also found to hold a dominant position) as it would have 'a structural link to the future leading broadcaster in the Netherlands' and would thus secure 'a large sales basis for its product which is safe and cannot be attacked by competitors'.[69] The programme production agreement between Endemol and HMG was used as an illustration of this. *De facto* joint control of HMG would allow Endemol to 'use its influence in HMG to obtain even more orders from HMG. No other producer in the Netherlands had a similar possibility to have a safe sales basis for its production and to influence the programme acquisition of a broadcaster'.[70] Endemol's structural link with HMG would thus allow it to strengthen its position on the programme production market by foreclosing the access of its competitors to HMG. The Court of First Instance has upheld this reasoning.[71]

11.72 Importantly, even in the absence of joint control, the Commission stated that Endemol's dominant position would be strengthened. Endemol's indirect participation in HMG amounted to 23 per cent. This gave it the right to be represented in the shareholders' meeting in which the major strategic decisions relating to the commercial behaviour of HMG were taken:

> A participation of 23% in a company which is active in a downstream market has to be seen as a strategic participation, rather than a financial one. This is even more the case where this participation is combined with a substantial representation of the shareholder in the decision-making body of this company. The shareholder will be able to obtain all information on the strategic decisions and will be involved in the discussions and decision-making procedure, where it can, in particular, influence decisions related to the upstream market where it is itself active.[72]

---

[69] *RTL/Veronica/Endemol* (Case IV/M553) [1996] OJ L294/14, at para 98.
[70] ibid, at para 99.
[71] Case T–221/95 *Endemol Entertainment Holding v Commission*, judgment of 28 April 1999, not yet published, at paras 167–169.
[72] ibid, at para 100.

The Commission therefore concluded that 'through its structural link to HMG, Endemol was in a position to influence the general programming and programme acquisition policy of HMG in a manner which strengthens Endemol's current position on the market for independent production'.[73] The Court of First Instance made no reference to this argument as it concluded that HMG was jointly controlled by its shareholders.

(2) Content packaging

Market Definition

Defining product markets in respect of the acquisition of television rights by broadcasters is a complicated exercise. Measuring demand substitutability is difficult. Broadcasters' demand for individual forms of programming is a reflection of viewers' preferences. However, it is only in respect of pay television services that those preferences are directly expressed by viewers. In respect of advertising-funded television, viewer preferences are expressed by viewing shares which then determine the prices of advertising slots (as does the profile of a particular audience). Supply side substitutability between different forms of programming is limited as the producer of one form of programming cannot easily switch to produce another. The existence of both free to air and pay television broadcasters poses a further question, namely whether these different forms of broadcaster compete against each other in the acquisition of programming. **11.73**

The lack of consistency and clarity in the Commission's decisions on market definition appears to reflect these difficulties and may also explain the Commission's tendency to concentrate on differences in programme characteristics rather than on use of the hypothetical monopolist test as set out in its Notice on market definition. **11.74**

Television rights to films, TV films, and series. There is no explicit market definition in the *ARD* decision.[74] It does appear to imply, however, that the Commission considered the relevant product market to be that for the acquisition of the television rights to feature films.[75] There are no decisions in which the Commission has stated clearly whether it considers there to be a separate product market in respect of feature films or whether they are part of a broader market which includes TV films and television series.[76] The Commission appears to have **11.75**

---

[73] ibid, at para 100.

[74] *Film Purchases by German Television Stations* [1989] OJ L284/36.

[75] ibid, at para 22: 'Feature films are a particularly important component of programming. Compared with television product (ie televisions films and television series), they are in many cases on a higher artistic level and are produced with greater financial expense, are therefore often more popular and mostly achieve high ratings.'

[76] In favour of broader market: *EBU/Eurovision* [1993] OJ L179/23, *Bertelsmann/CLT* (Case IV/M779) (1996). In favour of narrower market: *BiB* (Notice pursuant to Article 19(3) of Regulation 17) [1998] OJ C322/5; *Seagram/Polygram* (Case IV/M1219) (1998).

avoided the issue on the basis that feature films would constitute the most important element of a broader market.[77] This is in contrast to decisions by national
competition authorities, which have clearly defined markets in respect of feature
films.[78]

11.76 **Narrower markets.** Rights to films are sold in respect of geographic territories
and in respect of exploitation windows: these are time periods during which the
film may be exploited for one purpose only.[79] For example, the first exploitation
window is generally theatrical release in cinemas, which is then followed by video
release, pay-per-view, pay television, and then free to air television.[80] The rights in
respect of each window and territory are also generally sold exclusively. Where the
television rights in respect of all exploitation windows are sold to a single intermediary (whether a broadcaster as in the *ARD* decision or a rights agency), there
is no need to determine whether a narrower market distinguishing exploitation
windows is appropriate. However, broadcasters may also buy rights directly from
film studios in respect of only one exploitation window, in which case the
question of whether narrower markets should be defined would arise. It would
certainly seem that separate markets exist, as there is no substitutability between
rights for individual windows. This would also appear to be the view of the
Commission.[81]

11.77 **Television rights to sports events.** In the *EBU*[82] and *Eurosport*[83] decisions, the
Commission defined product markets for the acquisition of television rights to
sports events. The *EBU* decision was annulled by the Court of First Instance but

---

[77] *TPS* [1999] OJ L90/6.

[78] See, for example, the report of the Office of Fair Trading into BSkyB's position on the wholesale pay television market in the United Kingdom of December 1996 in which separate markets in
respect of films and of sports were defined.

[79] The length of the windows varies between Member States. Indeed, in some countries, such as
France, they are determined by statute. In others, they are determined by contract.

[80] There are often sub-windows within each of these categories: for example, first and second pay
television exploitation.

[81] In the press release issued by the Commission announcing the dissolution of UIP pay TV, a
joint venture between Paramount Pictures International, MGM International, and MCA
International for the distribution of film rights to pay TV broadcasters, reference was made to 'the
market for the supply of programmes for pay-television transmission in the EU'. IP/97/227 of 17
March 1997—'The Commission imposes the dissolution of UIP Pay TV's distribution joint venture'. The following decisions also suggest that separate markets for the various windows exist:
Seagram/Polygram (Case IV/M1219) (1998) (question left open as the operation did not raise a
problem of compatibility with the Common Market); *TPS* [1999] OJ L90/6 (also left open). See
also *BiB* (Notice pursuant to Article 19(3) of Regulation 17) [1998] OJ C322/5.

[82] *EBU/Eurovision* [1993] OJ L179/23. See also *ABC/Générale des Eaux/Canal+/WH Smith TV*
(Case IV/M110) (1991): the possibility of a separate product market in respect of sports events was
raised, but not decided as even on the narrowest market definition the case raised no problems of
compatibility with the Common Market.

[83] *Screensport/EBU Members* [1991] OJ L63/32.

on grounds not related to the definition of the market.[84] In the more recent *Bertelsmann/CLT* decision[85] the Commission justified the existence of a separate market for sports rights largely on the grounds of their 'specific features', namely their popularity with audiences, appeal to advertisers and the fact that they were often acquired before the teams which were to participate in the event, and thus their attractiveness, could be determined.

Narrower markets.   There are no precedent decisions defining narrower mar-   **11.78**
kets, either in respect of rights to particular sports events or in respect of the rights to live and deferred transmission and to highlights of sports events. It appears to be the position of the Commission that narrower product markets in relation to the television rights to particular sports may need to be defined in appropriate cases.[86] The Commission also appears willing to consider distinctions in market definition between the rights to live broadcasts and to highlights or deferred transmissions.[87]

In contrast to film rights, sports rights are not always sold in accordance with   **11.79**
exploitation windows. Television rights to sports events are generally sold exclusively (subject to the distinction between live and deferred transmission and highlights) to a single broadcaster, whether for exploitation on pay or advertising-funded television. This would tend to suggest that, where this is the case, there is no justification for distinguishing between these different forms of television in defining wholesale markets.

Geographic markets.   The Commission's approach to geographic market def-   **11.80**
inition seems to be more straightforward. Television rights are protected by intellectual property and generally sold in respect of national territories or sometimes linguistic zones. The Commission has tended to conclude that the geographic market definition follows from this. In *ARD*, for example, the geographic market was said to be coterminous with the territory covered by the agreement, namely the German language territories within Europe.[88]

---

[84] Joined Cases T–528/93, T–542/93, T–543/93 and T–546/93 *Metropole television SA and Reti Televisive Italiane SpA and Gestevision Telecinco SA and Antena 3 de Television v Commission* [1996] ECR II–649.

[85] *Bertelsmann/CLT* (Case IV/M779) (1996), at para 18. However, the Commission did not take a definitive view on whether sports rights constituted a separate market as even on the narrowest market definition the case raised no problems of compatibility with the Common Market.

[86] See in particular section II of 'Broadcasting of Sports Events and Competition Law' in DGIV's *Competition Policy Newsletter*, Number 2 of 1998, which suggests that product markets in respect of certain sports and in respect of important events in a particular sport may need to be defined. See also John Temple Lang, 'Media, Multimedia and European Anti-Trust Law' which also suggests that narrower markets than that defined in the *EBU* decision will now be considered.

[87] See articles quoted in n 86 above.

[88] See also *Seagram/Polygram* (Case IV/M1219) (1998); *TPS* [1999] OJ L90/6 (also left open); and *BiB* (Notice pursuant to Article 19(3) of Regulation 17) [1998] OJ C322/5.

Competition Issues

Exclusive Rights Contracts

11.81 **Exclusivity not itself a restriction of competition.** The producer of a film owns the copyright in it and is free to exercise that copyright without contravening Community competition law (although within certain limits). Thus, exclusivity is inherent in copyright or is part of its 'specific subject matter' and exclusive rights contracts do not necessarily constitute a restriction of competition within the meaning of Article 81(1) EC.

11.82 The leading case on this issue is the *Coditel II* judgment.[89] The Court of Justice was asked for a preliminary ruling on the question of whether a contract whereby the owner of the copyright in a film grants the exclusive right to exhibit that film in cinemas within the territory of a Member State and for a given period falls within Article 81(1). The Court referred to its previous judgment in *Coditel I*,[90] in which it held that the right of the owner of the copyright in a film and his assigns to require fees for any showing of that film is part of the essential function of copyright, and then continued as follows:

> Although copyright in a film and the right deriving from it, namely that of exhibiting the film, are not, therefore, as such subject to the prohibitions contained in Article 85 [now Article 81], the exercise of those rights may, nonetheless, come within the said prohibitions where there are economic or legal circumstances the effect of which is to restrict film distribution to an appreciable degree or to distort competition on the cinematographic market, regard being had to the specific characteristics of that market.

> It must therefore be stated that it is for the national courts, where appropriate, to make such inquiries and in particular to establish whether or not the exercise of the exclusive right to exhibit a cinematographic film creates barriers which are artificial and unjustifiable in terms of the needs of the cinematographic industry, or the possibility of charging fees which exceed a fair return on investment, or an exclusivity the duration of which is disproportionate to those requirements, and whether or not, from a general point of view, such exercise within a given geographic area is such as to prevent, restrict or distort competition within the Common Market.[91]

The fact that rights owners are able by virtue of copyright to grant exclusive licences is thus not in and of itself a restriction of competition, despite the fact that there is absolute territorial protection.

11.83 **Duration and/or scope of exclusivity may constitute a restriction of competition.** In accordance with the *Coditel II* judgment, three issues are relevant to

---

[89] Case 262/81 *Coditel SA, Compagnie générale pour la diffusion de la télévision, and others v Ciné-Vog Films SA and others* [1982] ECR 3381.

[90] [1980] ECR 881.

[91] ibid, at paras 17 and 19.

consideration of whether an exclusive rights contract may fall within the ambit of Article 81(1) EC:

- the duration and scope of the exclusivity;

- the appreciability of its impact on competition between broadcasters in the acquisition of rights and on downstream television markets; and

- its effect on trade between Member States.

While it is unclear whether the owner of the television rights to sports events holds a copyright in the strictest sense,[92] the Commission has nonetheless applied the principles set out in the *Coditel II* judgment by analogy.

Commission's policy objective in respect of exclusive rights contracts. The **11.84** Commission's policy objective in seeking to limit the duration and scope of exclusive rights contracts is clear. By maintaining a fluid rights market, competition in downstream television markets is preserved. The use of exclusive rights agreements to erect barriers to entry to downstream markets has proved to be of particular relevance to pay television. Given that these markets are largely national in scope, fulfilling the criterion of effect on trade between Member States might be thought problematic. In practice, this seems unlikely to be the case: the Commission has found there to be such an effect, regardless of whether or not the parties to an exclusive agreement are situated in the same Member State.[93] However, the principles governing the Commission's application of this policy objective to individual cases are less certain. This applies, in particular, to the test for determining whether the duration and scope of a particular agreement are likely to have an appreciable effect on competition such as to fall within Article 81(1) EC. In the *ARD* decision, which is discussed below, the focus was on the proportionality of the exclusivity to the needs of the broadcaster which has acquired the rights. There is little in the way of analysis of the effect of the contract in appreciably restricting competition between ARD and its competitors on the advertising-funded television market. This fact, taken in combination with the lack of clear market definition, and the peremptory treatment of appreciability in the decision, may cast a doubt over its use as an indicator of the Commission's likely future position in relation to exclusive agreements. This section sets out the Commission's past practice with respect to exclusive rights agreements, before considering whether a development is likely in the future.

---

[92] The answer to this question may vary between Member States in view of the differences in national copyright systems. This is in contrast to the situation in the United States where federal copyright protection of live sports broadcasts is assured by the Copyright Act 1976, 17 USC paras 101–801.

[93] For example, *TPS* [1999] OJ L90/6, the exclusive rights contracts concluded in *BBC/BSkyB/Premier League* (Notice pursuant to Article 19(3) of Regulation 17) [1993] OJ C94/6. Press release, IP(93)614 of 20 July 1993.

11.85 **Past approach to applicability of Article 81(1) to exclusive rights agreements.** The Commission has adopted only one formal decision, *ARD*,[94] which dates from 1989. The Commission finally exempted the agreement, but only after having required major changes. The contract at issue was concluded between ARD (an association of German public broadcasters) and the American film studio, MGM. ARD was granted fifteen years' exclusivity in respect of each programme covered by the contract beginning with ARD's first exploitation. The contract covered both MGM's library of feature films, TV films, series, and cartoons and its future output of feature films. ARD was granted the right to choose the product it required from MGM's library and future output. MGM could grant no other licences in respect of any programme, regardless of whether ARD had chosen it. The rights granted were in respect of German-language versions of the films and covered all means of transmission: terrestrial, cable and satellite. The rights also covered both advertising-financed and pay television.[95] In terms of geographic scope, the contract covered German-speaking Europe. With one exception, ARD was free to sub-license broadcasters outside Germany. Inside Germany, ARD could only sub-license related companies. The Commission issued a statement of objections, as a result of which ARD was required to release the product which it had not chosen so that licences could be granted to third parties. To this end, windows of varying duration were created during which third parties, but not ARD, could have access to the programmes. ARD was also obliged to contribute to the costs of dubbing the product into German and to allow third parties to broadcast the product in a foreign-language version (ie not in German) throughout the contract area or to broadcast into the contract area from elsewhere (both of which were originally prohibited). Despite these changes, the Commission considered both the duration and scope of the agreement to fall within the ambit of Article 81(1) EC (although meeting the criteria of Article 81(3) EC).

11.86 **ARD: duration of agreement.** The Commission found the fifteen-year duration of the agreement beginning in respect of each programme with ARD's first exploitation to be 'disproportionate' and to result in 'an artificial barrier to trade'.[96] Two further restrictions of competition relating to the duration of the agreement were identified: first, the three-year period after conclusion of the contract during which ARD could choose the programmes it required from MGM's library and during which third parties had no access to the programmes; secondly,

---

[94] *Film Purchases by German Television Stations* [1989] OJ L284/36.

[95] In respect of pay television, however, MGM was able to license up to 25% of the films to third parties for pay TV in two pay TV windows of up to a year's duration.

[96] *Film Purchases by German Television Stations* [1989] OJ L284/36, at para 44: 'This long duration of the agreements and the extension of the exclusivity beyond the actual licence period are disproportionate within the meaning of the *Coditel II* judgment of the Court of Justice and result in an artificial barrier to trade.'

ARD's right to match the terms offered by any third party in the event that MGM wished to negotiate a similar contract with another broadcaster.

ARD: scope of agreement. The scope of rights covered by the agreement also **11.87** constituted a restriction of competition, on the grounds that:

> The stock of suitable feature films cannot be increased at will and therefore large quantities of films must not be withdrawn from the market as a result of long-term exclusive ties. The number of films involved in this case goes well beyond the normal quantity necessitated by the needs of programme acquisition and programming and also well beyond the previous acquisition practice of the ARD broadcasting organisations themselves.[97]

These restrictions were appreciable, notwithstanding the fact that the contract **11.88** concerned only 4.5 per cent of the 'total stock [of films] available worldwide' as the popularity of the films covered meant that their importance went beyond 'numeric quantity'.[98]

Sports rights. In 1993, the Commission issued an administrative letter exempt- **11.89** ing the five-year exclusive agreement to football rights between the BBC, BSkyB, and the English Football Association.[99] It said at the time that, in general, exclusive football rights contracts of a duration of more than a single season would fall within Article 81(1). In this particular case, the Commission was willing to exempt the agreements for the full five years in view of the fact that BSkyB was then a new entrant.

Development in Commission approach? In 1995, the Commission summar- **11.90** ized its approach to exclusive rights contracts as follows: 'while acknowledging the importance of exclusivity as a means of safeguarding the value of a programme, [the Commission] takes particular care to ensure that neither the duration nor the scope of such agreements restricts third-party access to rights for too long a period or risks foreclosing the market'.[100] This new emphasis on foreclosure of third party access to substitutable rights is certainly more in line with the Commission's most recent statements on its general approach to vertical restraints[101] than the *ARD* analysis. On this basis, an exclusive agreement would constitute an appreciable restriction of competition only if either its duration or scope result in foreclosure of third party access to substitutable rights. It is only in these circumstances that it could appreciably affect competition. The importance of proper market

---

[97] ibid, at para 43.
[98] ibid.
[99] Notice pursuant to Article 19(3) of Regulation 17 [1993] OJ C94/ 6. Press release, IP(93)614 of 20 July 1993.
[100] *Report on Competition Policy 1995* (Vol XXV) at para 83.
[101] Communication of 30 September 1999. Indeed, it appears likely that the expected block exemption Regulation on vertical restraints will block exempt vertical agreements provided that the supplier does not have a market share above 30%. It remains to be seen whether rights contracts will fall within the scope of this block exemption.

definition to such an analysis is crucial. Had this test been applied in *ARD*, the agreement seems unlikely to have fallen within Article 81(1) EC given that some 95 per cent of substitutable rights were unaffected by the exclusive agreement and were available for purchase by other German broadcasters.

11.91   However, there is a need to be cautious in predicting any change in the Commission's approach.[102] Even very recently, DGIV has restated the principle that an exclusive live sports rights contract with a duration exceeding a single season is likely to fall within Article 81(1) EC. It has said that the duration of a single season will depend on the sport in question: in football it would mean a year, whereas for events such as the World Cup or Olympics, a duration exceeding a single competition would seem to be justifiable.[103] There are a number of possible explanations of this stricter position in relation to sports rights. First, the Commission has indicated a willingness to consider narrow market definitions limited to particular sports, such as top national football rights. It is easier to argue that a single contract forecloses third parties in such narrow markets. Secondly, in contrast to film rights, the rights to live sports events are 'perishable' in nature. Their value plummets after the event has taken place as viewers are significantly less interested in watching a sports event on television after the fact.

11.92   **Applicability of Article 81(3).**   Again, the only formal decision is *ARD*, the pertinence of which for future practice has already been questioned above.[104] However, the 1993 comfort letter in respect of the BBC/BSkyB/English Football Association also provides some pointers. Two points in particular seem relevant to the likelihood of exemption. The first concerns the existence of 'windows' or sub-licensing schemes to attenuate concerns surrounding exclusivity, as in *ARD*. This has also been a feature of subsequent exemption decisions[105] and has been relied upon in place of a reduction in the duration of agreements. The second important point is the market position of the broadcaster acquiring the rights. In the English Football Association case, much was made of the fact that BSkyB was not only a new entrant in the pay television market but would also use a then novel means of

---

[102] See also *TPS* [1999] OJ L90/6, at paras 102–109 in relation to exclusive wholesale channel supply contracts.

[103] See in particular 'Broadcasting of Sports Events and Competition Law' in DGIV's *Competition Policy Newsletter*, Number 2 of 1998.

[104] In *Film Purchases by German Television Stations* [1989] OJ L284/36, the following benefits were said to justify exemption. First, new product was introduced to German consumers which they would not otherwise have had an opportunity to watch. Secondly, the windows system means that other broadcasters also had access to the product, sometimes even before ARD. Thirdly, buying the rights to a large number of films resulted in a lower cost per film than would have been possible with a series of smaller agreements. Fourthly, only restrictions indispensable to these objectives were maintained. Finally, competition was not likely to be eliminated as a result of the introduction of the windows system and of the fact that sufficient other films suitable for exploitation on German TV remained available.

[105] *Report on Competition Policy 1996* (Vol XXVI) at para 83.

transmission, satellite direct-to-home. However, a number of statements have since been made that, in retrospect, a five-year exemption was excessive.[106] It may therefore be that the Commission will take a stricter line in the future on the duration of exclusive sports rights contracts which meet the criteria for exemption.

Cumulation of exclusive pay television film and sports rights contracts. **11.93** Commission statements to the effect that the conclusion of a series of exclusive rights contracts can act as a barrier to entry and foreclose competition in television markets[107] have not been followed by concrete action. This may well be due to the legal difficulties which such action would involve. Not the least of the difficulties is the negative effect which such action might have on third party suppliers of film and sports rights who might find it impossible at a given time to find an alternative buyer willing to pay an equivalent sum of money. Such difficulties do not arise in the context of undertakings offered by parties as conditions of clearance of other transactions.[108] It remains to be seen whether the Commission will act independently of such related operations.

Exclusive rights to 'events of major importance for society'.   Article 3(a)[109] of   **11.94**

---

[106] See, for example, Commissioner van Miert's speech on 'Sport et Concurrence: Développements récents et action de la Commission' at the Forum Européen du Sport in Luxembourg on 27 November 1997: 'Avec le recul, la durée acceptée par la Commission était probablement trop longue parce que cette technologie de transmission [ie satellite direct-to-home] s'est implantée plus rapidement que prévu.' http:/europa.eu.int/en:comm/dg04/speech/seven/fr/ sp97069.

[107] *Report on Competition Policy 1996* (Vol XXVI) at para 83.

[108] For example, see the undertaking to sell 25% of its exclusive pay television film and sports rights offered by Kirch in an attempt to secure clearance of the merger of its and Bertelsmann's pay TV operations: *Bertelsmann/Kirch/Premiere* (Case IV/M993) [1999] OJ L53/1.

[109] '1. Each Member State may take measures in accordance with Community law to ensure that broadcasters under its jurisdiction do not broadcast on an exclusive basis events which are regarded by that Member State as being of major importance for society in such a way as to deprive a substantial proportion of the public in that Member State of the possibility of following such events via live coverage or deferred coverage on free television. If it does so, the Member State concerned shall draw up a list of designated events, national or non-national, which it considers to be of major importance for society. It shall do so in a clear and transparent manner in due and effective time. In so doing the Member State concerned shall also determine whether these events should be available via whole or partial live coverage, or where necessary or appropriate for objective reasons in the public interest, whole or partial deferred coverage.

2. Member States shall immediately notify to the Commission any measures taken or to be taken pursuant to paragraph 1. Within a period of three months from the notification, the Commission shall verify that such measures are compatible with Community law and communicate them to the other Member States. It shall seek the opinion of the Committee established pursuant to Article 23a. It shall forthwith publish the measures taken in the Official Journal of the European Communities and at least once a year the consolidated list of the measures taken by Member States.

3. Member States shall ensure, by appropriate means, within the framework of their legislation that broadcasters under their jurisdiction do not exercise the exclusive rights purchased by those broadcasters following the date of publication of this Directive in such a way that a substantial proportion of the public in another Member State is deprived of the possibility of following events

the revised Television Without Frontiers Directive[110] allows Member States to prevent pay television operators from acquiring the exclusive rights to certain events. The object is to ensure that 'events of major importance for society' are available to most of the population on 'free' television. The definition of such events, whether national or international, and whether the rights concerned are for live or deferred transmission are a matter for each Member State. However, those Member States which take advantage of this possibility remain subject to Community law. In terms of competition law, Article 82 EC is the most relevant provision. The scope of Member State action is therefore constrained.

Collective Purchasing of Television Rights

11.95 **In general.**   As stated above, broadcasters will generally acquire rights exclusively. Thus, regardless of whether the rights are purchased individually or collectively, the impact of exclusive acquisition will often be the first issue to consider. In this section collective purchasing agreements are presumed to be exclusive.

11.96 Where rights are acquired collectively, two further broad sets of issue arise. First, does collective purchasing of rights affect the vertical relationship between the seller and the buyers, that is, do the buyers have market power which would allow them to buy the rights at a price which is lower than the competitive level? In terms of rights acquisition, the scarcity of attractive content seems to make the likelihood of buyer power remote. However, the Commission has made passing reference to its existence in the sector in the past.[111] Secondly, does collective purchasing of rights appreciably affect horizontal competition between the acquiring broadcasters? This appears to be the more relevant question.

11.97 **Applicability of Article 81(1) EC.**   Horizontal competition can only be restricted if the purchasers are actual or potential competitors. If this is not the case, then there can be no negative effect on competition. However, competition in two levels of markets could be affected by collective purchasing and both require consideration: competition in upstream markets for the acquisition of television rights and competition in downstream television markets.

---

which are designated by that other Member State in accordance with the preceding paragraphs via whole or partial live coverage or, where necessary or appropriate for objective reasons in the public interest, whole or partial deferred coverage on free television as determined by that other Member State in accordance with paragraph 1.'

[110] Council Directive (EEC) 89/552 on the coordination of certain provisions laid down by law, regulation or administrative action in Member States concerning the pursuit of television broadcasting activities [1989] OJ L298/23 as amended by Directive (EC) 97/36 of the European Parliament and of the Council [1997] OJ L202/60.

[111] *Screensport* [1991] OJ L63/32, at para 65: 'the joint purchasing policy operated by the EBU through the Eurovision scheme already confers upon EBU members a certain degree of market power'. *EBU/Eurovision* [1993] OJ L179/23, collective purchasing of sports rights 'strengthened the negotiating power of the EBU and its members vis-à-vis sports organisers'.

Market definition will thus be crucial to an assessment of the effects of collective   **11.98**
purchasing agreements. In this respect, therefore, the Commission's practice in
distinguishing between separate downstream television product markets is
relevant. It has consistently defined separate downstream markets in respect of
advertising-funded television (television advertising market) and pay television
(see Section G below). As described above in the section on market definition, it
is unclear whether the same distinction will be adopted in respect of upstream
rights markets. National markets have generally been defined in respect of both
downstream and upstream markets.

In theory, therefore, a collective purchasing agreement between broadcasters
operating in different geographic markets seems unlikely to be found to have an
appreciable effect on competition as the parties are neither competitors in the
acquisition of rights nor in television markets. However, the *EBU* decision, which
is discussed below, casts some doubt on this conclusion. Whether a collective purchasing agreement between a free to air broadcaster (advertising-funded or pub-
lic-funded) and a pay television broadcaster which operate in the same geographic
market will be found to have an appreciable effect on competition will depend on
the market definition adopted in respect of upstream rights markets.[112]

Commission statement that 'in principle' Article 81(1) is applicable.   In cir-   **11.99**
cumstances in which the parties are clearly actual or potential competitors in
respect either of the acquisition of rights or on a television market, the
Commission has stated that: 'the joint acquisition or distribution of television
rights, which in principle are covered by Article 85(1) [now Article 81(1)] of the
EEC Treaty, could be exempted if they allow rationalisation, provided that they
do not prevent market access for competitors'.[113] This statement leaves a number
of questions unanswered. In the first place, it is unclear why such agreements are
'in principle' covered by Article 81(1) EC. This may be a reference to the fact that
collective agreements inevitably involve agreement on the price to be paid for the
rights in question. Article 81(1)(a) explicitly refers to agreements which directly
fix purchase prices. Secondly, it is unclear whether the Commission's concern over
competitors' access to markets concerns access to rights acquisition markets or to
television markets. In the only formal decision adopted by the Commission concerning collective rights purchasing agreements, EBU,[114] only restrictions of competition on the sports rights acquisition market were identified. Arguably,
however, the more important possible negative effect of collective purchasing
agreements would be to restrict competition on the downstream television market. Analysis of the restrictive effect of collective purchasing would therefore focus

---

[112] The issue was not raised in *BBC/BSkyB/Premier League* (Notice pursuant to Article 19(3) of
Regulation 17) [1993] OJ C94/6. Press release, IP(93)614 of 20 July 1993.
[113] *Report on Competition Policy 1990* (Vol XX) at para 82.
[114] *EBU/Eurovision* [1993] OJ L179/23.

on the market positions of the purchasers on either the television advertising or pay television market. If those positions were substantial, then co-ordination of their behaviour should give rise to concern. To date, the Commission does not appear to have considered downstream market positions to be relevant.

11.100 **EBU: facts.** The only Commission decision is *EBU*,[115] which concerned a scheme for the collective purchasing of sports rights by the members of the EBU in the context of the Eurovision system. It was annulled by the Court of First Instance[116] on the basis that the Commission had failed to properly assess whether the restrictions of competition in the collective purchasing system were indispensable within the meaning of Article 81(3)(c) as it had not examined the conditions for membership of the EBU. The Commission further erred in law by using arguments relevant to Article 86(2) EC to justify exemption under Article 81(3) EC. The judgment on appeal of the Court of Justice is pending. The Commission is currently re-examining the EBU scheme for collective acquisition of sports rights in the light of the Court of First Instance's judgment. The decision is nonetheless included here as neither the applicants before the Court of First Instance, nor the Court itself, contested the Commission's finding that the notified agreements involved appreciable restrictions of competition on the market for the acquisition of the rights to sports events.

11.101 The EBU is an international association of television broadcasters. In general terms, only one broadcaster per country meets the criteria for membership. However, there is more than one member in five Member States. The EBU's rules provided that rights to international sports events[117] might be acquired jointly by all interested EBU members, who then share the rights and related fee between them.

11.102 **EBU: applicability of Article 81(1) EC.** In its annulled decision, the Commission identified three restrictions of competition on the market for acquisition of the rights to sports events. First, the arrangements for collective purchasing of international sports rights 'greatly restricted if not, in many cases eliminated'[118] the competition which would otherwise occur between members in the acquisition of such rights. This applied in particular in those countries where more than one broadcaster was an EBU member and in respect of the acquisition of rights for transnational broadcasting. Secondly, collective purchasing by mem-

---

[115] *EBU/Eurovision* [1993] OJ L179/23.

[116] Joined Cases T–528/93, T–542/93, T–543/93 and T–546/93 *Metropole television SA and Reti Televisive Italiane SpA and Gestevision Telecinco SA and Antena 3 de Television v Commission* [1996] ECR II–649.

[117] The extent to which the rights to national events may also be acquired jointly is somewhat unclear in the decision. Paragraph 30 of the annulled decision states that the rights to national events are not 'normally' the subject of joint acquisition.

[118] *EBU/Eurovision* [1993] OJ L179/23, at para 49.

bers also strengthened the position of members in the negotiations for the acquisition of rights as against non-members. The EBU's statutes distorted competition between members and non-members in the acquisition of rights as
non-members did not benefit from the cost-savings inherent in the Eurovision
system. Finally, the fact that the consortium of EBU members active in the transnational sport channel, Eurosport, participated in the collective purchasing of
rights 'strengthened the negotiating power of the EBU and its members *vis-à-vis*
sports organisers'.

These restrictions were appreciable notwithstanding the fact that, in practice, **11.103**
only the rights to international events were acquired collectively and such rights
constituted a small proportion of all sports rights, as such rights were 'of such
widespread appeal, and of such economic importance, that their impact on the
market is not adequately reflected by their expression as a mere percentage'.[119]
Indeed, the decision states that collectively acquired rights accounted for 2 per
cent of all sports programmes shown on UK and German television and around
6.6 per cent in France.[120]

EBU: comment.   As stated above, it is now clear that the Commission's analysis **11.104**
of the EBU collective purchasing system should have included an analysis of the
criteria of membership. The reasoning as to the applicability of Article 81(1) EC
also appears open to question. In particular, it is striking that the Commission
identified restrictions of competition between broadcasters whose principal activities were in different geographic markets, both as concerns rights and television
markets. It is also difficult to understand why the issue of exclusivity was not raised
more explicitly: the principal effect on non-members flowed from the fact that
rights were acquired by EBU members exclusively. The fact that they were
acquired collectively seems to be of secondary relevance. Thirdly, the reference to
EBU's 'buyer power' *vis-à-vis* sports rights sellers appears inconsistent with the
Commission's insistence in the decision on the fact that collective acquisition of
rights by the 'public mission' broadcasters which composed EBU members
allowed them to compete with commercial broadcasters and international sports
rights agencies. Finally, the treatment of appreciability appears particularly
meagre given the very low percentage of collectively acquired rights.

Applicability of Article 81(1) to individual collective purchasing agreements. **11.105**
There are no Commission decisions concerning single collective purchasing
agreements. The most pertinent question in respect of such agreements appears
likely to be whether any restriction has an appreciable effect on competition. In
terms of rights acquisition, this will depend largely on the relative importance of

---

[119] *EBU/Eurovision* [1993] OJ L179/23, at para 57.
[120] *EBU/Eurovision* [1993] OJ L179/23, at para 30.

the rights in question within the defined market. Whether there is an appreciable effect on downstream markets will depend on the purchasers' market position.

11.106 **Applicability of Article 81(3).**   Before exempting the agreement in *EBU*, the Commission required substantial modifications on the rules governing access of non-members to sports programmes for which the exclusive rights had been acquired collectively. As amended, the Commission considered the agreement to meet the first test of Article 81(3) as the transaction costs of acquiring the rights to international sports events were reduced and cross-border broadcasting was facilitated. Consumers benefited from an increase in the broadcasting of high-quality sports programmes and from the fact that cost savings would allow money to be invested in other forms of attractive programming. The ban on individual negotiations while collective negotiations were on going was indispensable as without it the success of collective negotiations would be jeopardized. Likewise, the fact that members agree on the financial conditions and the sharing of rights in respect of each sports event was inevitable as each event was distinct. Competition was not eliminated as only a part of the market for acquisition of sports rights was affected, namely the acquisition of the rights to international events.

Collective Selling of Television Rights to Sports Events

11.107 In general terms, collective selling agreements will normally constitute a restriction of competition within the scope of Article 81(1) EC, provided that the restriction is appreciable. Such arrangements have few redeeming features from a competition point of view as they may well inflate selling prices. They will also often restrict output. As such, at first sight, they seem unlikely to meet the criteria for exemption set out in Article 81(3).

11.108 The television rights to sports events are generally sold either in respect of a particular event (for example, the rights to individual boxing matches) or in respect of all events played within the context of a competition (for example, the rights to domestic football matches in a particular league competition or to the races within the Formula One motor car series). In the case of the latter, the organizer of the competition in question often concludes a single rights contract in respect of all individual matches played in the competition.

11.109 This practice was not questioned under competition rules for many years.[121] Recently, however, the question of whether such collective selling arrangements

---

[121] For example, the issue of collective selling was neither raised nor investigated by the Commission in the context of the rights contracts concluded between BBC and BSkyB and the English Football Association, Notice pursuant to Article 19(3) of Regulation 17 [1993] OJ C94/6. Press release, IP(93)614 of 20 July 1993.

constitute restrictions of competition and whether they should be permitted has arisen at both the national[122] and Community levels.

Conflicting policy arguments?   There is certainly a clear policy argument in terms of the pay television market which militates in favour of prohibiting collective selling agreements. Acquisition of exclusive rights to sports events, in particular by pay television operators, can act as a barrier to entry. Atomizing the sellers' market would make it more difficult for a single pay television operator to acquire the rights to all individual clubs. In this way, the entry costs to the pay television market would be reduced and competition promoted.

11.110

Others argue that particular considerations should govern the application of competition law to sports. In particular, these commentators point to the need for relatively evenly balanced teams if the sport is to remain popular: to this end collective selling allows distribution of income between weaker and stronger clubs. A further argument is that collective selling allows income to be passed from the professional sport to amateur clubs. Such considerations would favour exemption of collective selling agreements.

11.111

The Commission has not yet intervened in respect of the collective selling of television rights to sports events.[123] It has said,[124] however, that it is currently examining collective selling arrangements for international motor sports. There are two issues which are particularly relevant to competition analysis of collective selling arrangements in respect of television sports rights.

11.112

Applicability of Article 81(1) EC: ownership of sports rights.   The first question to resolve is who is the owner of the television rights in question. By definition, collective selling arrangements can only be at issue if ownership of the television rights vests, at least partly, in the individual clubs or players which participate in the competition rather than in the league or association which has taken on responsibility for the selling of the rights.[125] Determination of ownership

11.113

---

[122] In Germany, the Cartel Office prohibited the German Football Association from collectively selling the television rights to home matches of German clubs playing in the UEFA Cup and the European Cup Winners' Cup. This decision was upheld by the Bundesgerichtshof, which is the highest civil court, in its judgment of 11 December 1997. In The Netherlands, the Ministry of Economic Affairs decided on 6 November 1996 that the collective selling by KNVB (Dutch Football Association) of the television rights to football matches was a cartel.

[123] However, see 'Broadcasting of Sports Events and Competition Law' in DGIV's *Competition Policy Newsletter*, Number 2, June 1998 which states that: 'If there exists an inter-state trade effect, it will be necessary to examine whether the collective selling of rights to broadcasting matches or to series of events or competitions results in an agreement restrictive of competition contrary to Article 85(1) [now Article 81(1)] of the EC Treaty and the Commission will have to examine whether the criteria for exemption could nevertheless be met by the arrangements.'

[124] 'Broadcasting of Sports Events and Competition Law' in DGIV's *Competition Policy Newsletter*, Number 2, June 1998.

[125] However, for an alternative viewpoint, see John Temple Lang's article, 'Media, Multimedia and European Anti-Trust Law' in which he suggests that the ownership of rights is irrelevant to

of rights to sports events is not a question of competition law. It must rather be determined by national civil law or statute. This issue has already arisen in a number of Member States in the context of the collective selling of football rights. Although, the approach taken has differed, there is a clear tendency towards recognizing that ownership vests in individual football clubs.[126]

11.114 Collective selling arrangements, however, are not restricted to the national arena. International sporting associations also sell television rights: for example, UEFA in respect of football or the Fédération Internationale de l'Automobile (Formula One and other motor sports events). The Commission's examination of collective selling of sports rights will inevitably involve examination of the ownership of the rights involved. National practice would certainly seem to support a finding that ownership does not vest in the association alone. On this basis, Article 81(1) would seem to be applicable provided that the restriction is appreciable. As with collective purchasing agreements, the most relevant considerations in this respect will be market definition and the relevant importance of the rights sold collectively within that market.

11.115 Effect on trade between Member States can be presumed where the association is itself an international one. However, even national collective selling agreements might well be found to affect trade between Member States given the increasing tendency for such rights to be sold in other European countries.

11.116 Membership of some sports associations is conditional upon accepting collective selling of television rights by the association. In such circumstances, it is evident that the members of the association are the proper owners of the rights. The statute which embodies the members' agreement to form the association seems likely to constitute a decision of an association of undertakings within the meaning of Article 81(1) EC.

---

the question of whether joint selling by football clubs constitutes a restriction of competition within Article 81(1) EC.

[126] In Germany, the Bundesgerichtshof held, in its judgment of 11 December 1997, that the home club is the original owner of the television rights to its matches. 'Even if the DFB [German Football Association] and UEFA set the organisational framework for competitive football, the clubs playing the football matches are the ones that render essential economic services for the marketing of the TV broadcasting rights. . . . Moreover, the home club concerned performs the necessary organisational work on site: . . . the home club is the natural market participant that is entitled to market the service produced by acting in combination with the opponent's club on a reciprocal basis agreed upon. As far as the sale of tickets . . . or the leasing of advertising space and similar commercial activities are concerned, there is no room for doubt about the home clubs' rights. The same applies in principle to the granting of film or TV rights in the stadium.' In Spain, in contrast, it has been determined by statute that ownership vests with individual football clubs. Law 10/1990 of 15 October 1990, known as the 'Sports Law', provided that the Spanish Professional Football League (LNPF) was charged with the management of all television rights to matches which it organised until the 1997/98 season. Thereafter, each club was able to manage its rights independently.

Some sports associations may go further and require members to cede ownership **11.117** of television rights as a condition of membership. Depending on the circumstances, this may be actionable under Article 82 EC where the sports association holds a dominant position. This would arguably be the case, for example, where the association has regulatory powers over the sport in question which allow it to veto the participation of a particular team in a competition, and where this approval is made conditional on the transfer of television rights. On the basis of *Télémarketing*,[127] this could be said to constitute abusive behaviour.

Applicability of Article 81(3) EC and 'special characteristics' of sport. There **11.118** appears to be a willingness to recognize the 'special characteristics' of sport which might justify exemption under Article 81(3) EC: 'these could include, for example, the need to ensure "solidarity" between weaker and stronger participants or the training of young players, which could only be achieved through redistribution of revenue from the sale of broadcasting rights. Such aims would have to be a genuine and material part of the objectives and ones which would not be achievable under less restrictive arrangements'.[128] However, it seems likely to be difficult to show that collective selling is the least restrictive means by which these benefits could be achieved.

(3) Content Distribution

Market Definition

Wholesale supply of television channels. In the *Télévision par Satéllite*[129] (*TPS*) **11.119** decision, the Commission referred to a market for 'the distribution and operation of special-interest channels' which it said were essential for the composition of a pay television service (although it also said that such channels were not confined to pay television).[130] In the *BiB* case,[131] the Commission has indicated its preliminary view that a single wholesale market exists for the supply of film and sports channels for pay-television. The Commission justified this on the grounds that such channels are significantly more expensive than others which in turn reflects the fact that the underlying pay TV rights are the most expensive. The price of the rights reflects the fact that viewers' willingness to pay for film and sports channels is higher than willingness to pay for other channels. For a pay TV operator, therefore, these channels are crucial. The Commission did not distinguish between a wholesale market for film channels and a wholesale market for sports channels for

---

[127] Case 311/84 *Centre belge d'études de marché—Télémarketing (CBEM) v SA Compagnie luxembourgeoise de télédiffusion (CLT) and Information publicité Benelux (IPB)* ECR 3261.
[128] 'Broadcasting of Sports Events and Competition Law' in DGIV's *Competition Policy Newsletter*, Number 2, June 1998, footnote 30, section IV, para 9.
[129] *TPS* [1999] OJ L90/6.
[130] ibid, at paras 37–39.
[131] *BiB* (Notice pursuant to Article 19(3) of Regulation 17) [1998] OJ C322.

pay TV, although it envisaged that such a distinction might be appropriate. The existence of separate markets does seem likely in view of the fact that the characteristics of sport and film programming are different, as are the profiles of their respective audiences. It remains to be seen whether the formal decision will reflect this reasoning. However, it does appear to be consistent with the Commission's precedents in respect of markets concerning the acquisition of film and sport rights.

11.120 **Geographic markets.**   In *TPS*, the Commission concluded that the geographic market was a national one.

Competition Issues

11.121 A notable distinction is developing in the pay TV market in the EU between retail pay TV operators, also sometimes referred to as pay TV platform operators, and suppliers of individual channels for pay TV. Pay TV operators package together a number of channels for which they charge subscribers a fee: all individual channels are not available to subscribers separately. The channels may be the property of the pay TV operator, but often also include third party channels. In the case of third party channels, therefore, wholesale supply agreements are concluded between the channel operator and the pay TV operator. The commercialization of packages of channels is not yet familiar in non-subscription-funded television. However, as the Commission pointed out in the *TPS* decision, this position may well change over time, and in particular with the introduction of digital technologies. While this section concentrates on pay television, the issues raised may increase in importance in advertising-funded television.

11.122 The tendency in pay television to commercialize packages of channels seems likely to become more pronounced with the digitization of broadcasting technologies. Digital broadcasting, and digital compression, result in a more efficient use of transmission bandwidth. A greater number of channels can therefore be provided to consumers as part of a single television service. However, to do so, the pay television operator must have access to sufficient content. This need is increasingly met by the conclusion of wholesale channel supply agreements, which may be exclusive.

11.123 The practice of acquisition of exclusive pay television rights to programmes (which are then packaged to form a channel) further contributes to this development in market structure. This applies above all to pay television film and sports channels. Where one pay television operator has acquired the majority of such rights exclusively, then it may wholesale the channels it creates to its competitors on the retail pay television market. This is the situation which has developed in the United Kingdom market and it may prove a model for other European countries.[132] The competition issues which may arise in relation to the wholesale supply of channels for pay television are varied. To date, there is little in the way of guidance from the Commission. The following discussion is therefore of necessity rather speculative.

Article 81 EC. This issue has recently been examined by the Commission in **11.124** two separate cases. Both would tend to suggest that exclusive supply agreements are likely to be found to fall within the scope of Article 81(1). The first concerns Télévision par Satellite,[133] a company established for a period of ten years to operate a digital pay television platform via satellite direct-to-home transmission in France. TPS's parent companies include three French advertising-funded terrestrial television broadcasters, namely TF1, the public broadcaster France Télévision (which broadcasts two channels, France 2 and France 3) and M6. As part of the agreement constituting TPS, these companies granted TPS the exclusive right to distribute their four channels as part of a pay television service. The poor quality of terrestrial reception in much of France makes this an attractive proposition for viewers. In addition, the parties agreed to give TPS a right of first refusal for the carriage of their special interest channels, and a right of final refusal over any programmes or services offered to third parties. TPS could choose in respect of both whether the contracts with its parents would be exclusive.

The Commission concluded that while the creation of TPS did not constitute an **11.125** appreciable restriction of competition, the exclusive distribution agreement for its parents' general interest channels was caught by Article 81(1) EC and that an exemption of three years to correspond with TPS's start-up period was appropriate. It is noteworthy that the Commission justified this conclusion solely on the basis that the exclusivity 'denied TPS's competitors access to attractive programmes' and without defining the relevant market. Moreover, there is no discussion of the appreciability of the restriction of competition. In similar terms the Commission concluded that TPS's right of first refusal over its parents' special interest channels fell within the scope of Article 81(1) as it resulted in ' a limitation of the supply of special-interest channels and television services'. Again, an exemption of three years was considered appropriate.

The issue of the wholesale supply of channels for pay television was also raised in **11.126** *British Digital Broadcasting (BDB)*,[134] which concerned the creation of a digital

---

[132] In this regard, see the undertakings sought by the Commission in *Bertelsmann/Kirch/Premiere* (Case IV/M993) [1999] OJ L53/1 and *Deutsche Telekom/BetaResearch* (Case IV/M1027) [1999] OJ L53/31 to the effect that the pay television channel, Premiere, could be marketed by independent cable operators.

[133] *TPS* [1999] OJ L90/6.

[134] See the speech of JF Pons, Deputy Director-General of DGIV 'The Future of Broadcasting' at the Institute of Economic Affairs on 29 June 1998, http://europa.eu.int/en:comm/dg04/speech/eight/en/sp98034.

terrestrial pay television operator in the United Kingdom by two advertising-funded television broadcasters, Granada and Carlton. The creation of the joint venture together with a seven-year channel supply agreement between BDB's parents and BSkyB in respect of three 'premium' channels (ie film and sport channels) and one 'basic' channel (Sky One) was notified to the Commission under Regulation 17. In contrast to the situation in *TPS*, the supply agreement between BDB and BSkyB was not exclusive: BSkyB also supplied cable operators with the same channels. Before granting an administrative letter, the Commission insisted that the duration of the programming supply agreement was reduced to a period of five years and that clauses in the agreement were deleted which could have acted as a disincentive on BDB competing with BSkyB for the acquisition of sports and film rights after the expiry of the contract. The precise nature of the Commission's concerns and the legal reasoning underlying its position is unclear. It does seem to be the case, however, that it was principally concerned by the agreement only in so far as it related to the supply of film and sports channels and its duration and terms affected BDB's future possibility to acquire the necessary rights to create such channels itself. The policy objective would be more understandable, however, if the duration of the channel supply agreement had been aligned with the duration of BSkyB's most important rights contracts. In this respect, it is noticeable that the five-year period which was exempted extended two years beyond the end of BSkyB's existing exclusive football rights contracts. At least as regards these rights, the Commission appears to have failed to meet its own declared objective.

11.127 **Article 82 EC.** The question of dominance in the markets for the wholesale supply of film and sports channels for pay television has not yet been considered by the Commission. There is thus little in the way of useful precedent. However, given the apparent importance of these forms of channels to the success of pay television operators, disputes over failure to supply or the terms of supply seem likely to arise under Article 82 EC in the future.[135] Given that the Commission now appears to define a single pay television market, without distinguishing between means of transmission, then abusive behaviour in the wholesale supply of film and sports channels would affect competition in pay television.

11.128 **Factors relevant to dominance.** In the abstract, demonstration of dominance would require an undertaking to have a persistently high share in the supply of film and sports channels and for it be improbable that this share would be significantly eroded by its competitors within a reasonable timescale. It seems likely from other precedents[136] that the Commission would adopt the value of channels, rather than their number, as the most appropriate method of calculating whole-

---

[135] In this respect, see the report of the Office of Fair Trading into BSkyB's position on the wholesale pay television market in the United Kingdom of December 1996. Conditions were imposed on BSkyB's wholesale conditions of supply of its channels to UK cable operators.

[136] See, for example, *RTL/Veronica/Endemol* (Case IV/M553) [1996] OJ L294/14.

sale market shares. If this is correct, then the percentage of total expenditure by purchasers on film and/or sports channels which is paid to the channel operator will need to be assessed. If other film and sports channels exist, then the relative numbers of subscribers might also be considered. Indeed, where the channel operator does not wholesale the film and/or sport channel in question, subscriber numbers appear to be the only available indicator of market share. In terms both of the likelihood of the market share being eroded and the endurance of dominance, consideration of the position of the channel operator in relation to the necessary programming rights will be crucial. Examination of vertical relations with content producers and owners, such as film studios or football clubs, will be relevant, as will the number, scope, and duration of exclusive rights contracts.

Obligation to supply.   There are a number of different scenarios in which the **11.129** question of obligation to supply by a dominant operator of film and/or sports channels might arise. Legally, the issues are largely the same as those analysed under refusals to supply in the section on transmission networks (see Section E below). Where the channel operator already supplies the channel to one third party, then a refusal to supply to others would require objective justification. The most appropriate ground of attack would be the unjustified discrimination between the third parties. Requiring the wholesale supply of a channel in circumstances where it has never been supplied in this way to a third party is more problematic. It would be necessary to demonstrate that the channel constituted an 'essential facility' and that failure to supply would eliminate all competition from the party requesting supply in the pay television market,[137] not merely make competition more difficult. This is an extremely high burden of proof which it would seem difficult to meet.

Terms and conditions of supply: bundling.   Bundling would seem to be clearly **11.130** prohibited by Article 82(d) EC. Thus, any attempt by a dominant operator of a film and/or sports channel to make supply of the channel conditional upon purchase of other channels would be illegal.

Terms and conditions of supply: price discrimination.   In terms of the price of **11.131** supply, on the other hand, clear guidance is more difficult. It is clear that charging different prices to third parties for the supply of the same channel must be objectively justified to avoid the prohibition of Article 82(c) EC, at least where those parties are actual or potential competitors. Differential pricing on the part of a dominant company might also result in allegations that its price is excessive.

Terms and conditions of supply: excessive pricing.   Disputes over the absolute **11.132** level of the price would be more complicated to resolve. Given that the channel operator is likely to be a competitor on the pay television market of the purchaser,

---

[137] Case C–7/97 *Oscar Bronner GMbH & Co KG*, judgment of 26 November 1998.

then complaints of excessive, rather than predatory, pricing seem to be more probable. However, there are two difficulties to be overcome if such an action were to
succeed. The first is that the Commission appears to have a general reluctance to
intervene in questions of pricing for fear of becoming a 'price regulator'. The second is that the economics of television channel production make it difficult to
assess the 'economic value of the product supplied' as against which charges of
excessive pricing must be evaluated.[138] Indeed, the fixed costs in creating a television channel may be significant, but the marginal cost of its provision are negligible, if not non-existent. In these circumstances, it is far from clear how the
appropriate price for wholesale supply of the channel can be determined.

11.133 **Terms and conditions of supply: margin squeeze.** Where the dominant channel supplier is also active on the retail pay television market, then allegations of
margin squeeze may be made. In *Napier Brown*, the Commission decided that a
firm, which is dominant in the markets for both a raw material and a derived
product, commits an abuse of a dominant position if the margin between the
prices it charges for the two products is insufficient to cover the dominant company's own costs with the result that competition in the supply of the derived
product is restricted.[139] This principle has recently been restated in the Access
Notice.[140]

11.134 The theory underlying margin squeeze may be clear: in circumstances in which
the dominant company as a whole is not making a loss, a margin squeeze means,
in effect, that the dominant company is using profit from its wholesale operation
to subsidize its retail operation. This affects competition as those downstream
competitors of the dominant company which are at least as efficient as the dominant company would nevertheless be prevented from entering the market or forced
from the market.

11.135 However, proving in practice that margin squeeze exists will be difficult. In the
Access Notice, the Commission envisages two possible ways. The first involves
examining whether the dominant company's own retail pay television arm would
be profitable if it paid the same wholesale price for channels charged to competitors. Given that in most circumstances, the accounts of the dominant firm will

---

[138] Case 26/75 *General Motors v Commission* [1975] ECR 1367.

[139] *Napier Brown/British Sugar* [1988] OJ L284/41, at para 66. 'The maintaining, by a dominant
company, which is dominant in the markets for both a raw material and a corresponding derived
product, of a margin between the price which it charges for a raw material to the companies which
compete with the dominant company in the production of the derived product and the price which
it charges for the derived product, which is insufficient to reflect that dominant company's own
costs of transformation (in this case the margin maintained by BS between its industrial and retail
sugar prices compared to its own repackaging costs) with the result that competition in the derived
product is restricted, is an abuse of a dominant position.'

[140] Notice on the Application of the Competition Rules to Access Agreements in the
Telecommunications Sector [1998] OJ C265/2, at para 92.

integrate its wholesale and retail arms, an accounting separation exercise must be conducted of the proportion of common operating costs which should be attributed to each. It is only after this cost accounting has been completed, that an evaluation can be made of whether the retail arm is able to recover both its operating costs and the transfer charges for supply of channels from the wholesale arm. (In the telecommunications sector in contrast, the general regulatory framework simplifies the task as separated accounts must in any event be produced.)

The second option to prove margin squeeze is to demonstrate that a 'reasonably **11.136** efficient' downstream competitor is unable to make a profit on the basis of the wholesale prices charged by the dominant firm. This possibility is raised in the Access Notice at paragraph 92. However, it poses two difficulties. The first is the general difficulty of defining reasonable efficiency: the appropriate marker would seem to be the efficiency of the dominant company itself. The second is that where the dominant company and its competitors use different means of transmission to provide pay television, there may be significant differences in cost structure. In other words, the means of transmission used by competitors may be less efficient, in the sense of more expensive, than that used by the dominant company. In such circumstances, it is suggested that the only appropriate way to demonstrate margin squeeze is to rely on the costs of the dominant company itself.

E. Transmission

Issues related to the transmission of information—be it voice or data, communi- **11.137** cations based or content based—are increasingly common to the telecommunications and media sectors. Unfortunately, there are few precedents on what are likely to prove the most difficult issues. This section looks briefly at issues relating to rights to build infrastructure, before turning to the main competition issues of transmission.

This section does not distinguish between the provision of access to infrastructure **11.138** and the provision of a service including access to infrastructure. The distinction underlies some discussions of telecommunications regulation, but has not so far proved useful under the competition rules.

The first subsection below provides a basic introduction to transmission net- **11.139** works, with an explanation of the types and elements of telecommunications networks. There follows a brief discussion of the issues surrounding the right to build infrastructure as a prelude to a more direct discussion of infrastructure issues.

Competition problems relating to the creation or strengthening of dominance in **11.140** transmission networks are best examined separately in relation to the separate markets of backbone transmission networks, customer access transmission networks, and networks relevant to the Internet and interactive services. Each of these markets therefore has its own subsection. Each subsection looks first at market definition issues, then issues related to the creation or strengthening of dominance on those markets.

11.141 Finally, the extent to which third parties may have rights to access and use transmission networks of dominant companies raises substantially similar issues whichever particular transmission market is being considered. As such, there is a single subsection on this topic.

(1) Introduction to Transmission Networks

11.142 Broadcast infrastructure is designed to convey the same signal simultaneously to a large number of destinations. The network does not need to be capable of directing a signal to a particular destination, although as is discussed below, when the signal is for pay TV, a system for recognizing authorized recipients of the signal (conditional access) may need to be included.

11.143 Communications infrastructure is designed to convey a number of different signals to and from a number of different destinations. The network therefore needs to be capable of directing a signal to a particular destination. There are two main ways in which this can be achieved.

Circuit Switched Networks

11.144 First, the network could dedicate part of itself to carrying the signal between two defined points (the houses of two customers who are having a telephone conversation). This is known as circuit switching—switches in the network are used to join together a dedicated line (circuit) between the two end points. For a conversation between Ireland and Greece, this would entail a dedicated line being created between the two countries for the duration of the conversation. This system is not an efficient use of the capacity of the network as the circuit between source and destination is dedicated to the conversation even if no one is speaking (no signals are being sent along the network). Telephone networks are traditionally circuit switched networks. Voice telephony under Community law is based on this circuit switching technology and is defined in part as being between two fixed points of the public switched telecommunications network.

Packet Switched Networks

11.145 Alternatively, the network can divide the data being transmitted (the telephone conversation) into smaller units (packets of data) and attach address information which describes where the data should be sent. The network then reads the address information on each packet individually and sends each packet to the destination address using whatever route is most convenient at the time. The packets of data are then reassembled into a single unit at the destination address. No two packets of data need follow the same route from source to destination. This system is known as packet switching—switches in the network (routers) are used to send packets of data to their destination. In terms of network usage, this solution is more efficient as if no one is speaking in the conversation no data is transmitted and no network capacity is used. The solution does require the data being transmitted to be in digital format. This makes packet switching well suited to the transmission of data where the source is already digital –as in the case of computer communications. Where the source is analogue—as in the case of human conversations—the data must be digitized, transmitted, and then converted back to an analogue signal. This adds to the expense, makes real-time conversations more difficult, and has affected the quality of using packet switched networks for straightforward telephone conversations. These difficulties are now being overcome.

Network Elements

Both circuit switched networks and packet switched networks are therefore comprised of transmission and switching elements. Transmission elements move the data from one place to another, and switching elements send the data to the right destination. **11.146**

Transmission elements are often further broken down into local and backbone elements. Local elements can broadly be defined as the transmission element necessary to reach an end-user (the end-user could be either the originator or the destination of a particular network transmission). Often this is taken to mean the transmission network connecting the end-user to the first switch in the network. Backbone elements can similarly broadly be defined as the transmission element necessary to connect local elements. **11.147**

For example: in a standard telephone call, the calling party picks up the phone, and dials a number. The signal from the phone is sent across the local network element to the first switch in the network (together these elements are often referred to as the local loop). The switch starts the process which establishes a circuit across the backbone network to connect to the nearest switch in the network to the called party. The signal is sent along the local network connecting the called party to the last switch. **11.148**

Local Networks and Customer Access Networks

Telecommunications access issues are often expressed in terms of local network problems—competing operators wish either to use the incumbent operator's local network to originate or to terminate traffic. The use of the term 'local' in this context is, however, potentially misleading. To take the example of the termination of **11.149**

799

international calls, the termination service being requested of the incumbent operator may often be far from local. To avoid confusion, it is probably better to refer to customer access networks.

Networks and Market Definition

11.150 An important element to consider in respect of market definition for any network is the service which is to be delivered over it. Different services place different demands on the network infrastructure: different infrastructure markets are likely to exist given these different demands.

11.151 Some of the main categories of networks are set out below, but these should not be regarded as the only relevant market definitions. Market definition in a particular case could require identification of particular technical—such as configurations or interfaces—or geographic—such as country-pairs or localized networks—aspects.

(2) Right to Build Transmission Networks

11.152 Having the right to build infrastructure is a necessary prerequisite for the establishment of competing infrastructure networks. To the extent that a right to build is denied by State action, then Article 86 could apply. Town and country planning requirements are listed as a possible essential requirement in Directive 90/388, and therefore objective and proportionate restrictions on building infrastructure are potentially legitimate under the competition rules. In these circumstances, it is likely that a State would be obliged to ensure an equitable outcome by, for example, mandating facility sharing (ducts, masts) and/or co-location of equipment.[141]

11.153 However, this could also be a private sector problem. If, for example, a railway company owned the land on which its tracks were built, that land extended across the Member State, and the company refused permission to lay cable crossing its land, this would in practice prevent the building of a nationwide telecommunications network. It would be impossible to achieve without crossing a railway track at some point. If such crossing rights could be regarded as essential to the provision of third party infrastructure, there may be arguments giving rise to access under the competition rules. The complicating factor here, however, is that the railway company may not be present on the market for which access is being sought. Although an ordering of access would appear consistent with the Commission's position on essential facilities, discussed below, and the Court's

---

[141] See, for example, Commission Decision (EC) 95/489 of 4 October 1995 concerning the conditions imposed on the second operator of GSM radio-telephony services in Italy [1995] L280/49, Article 1 where the Commission was prepared to accept remedies to counterbalance the anti-competitive effect of the licence fee.

judgment in *Magill*, ordering access where the essential facility owner is not itself present on the relevant market would be an innovation in EC competition law.

A more subtle problem is the extent to which a railway or utility (gas, electricity)   **11.154**
company could refuse to allow building along (rather than across) its property. Press reports indicate that the Commission has refused to allow exclusivity in certain joint ventures between such companies and new entrant telecoms companies. However, the Commission does not yet appear to have gone so far as to *require* such a company to allow third parties to build along its property: to do so would presumably require at the very least a finding of dominance, which would appear difficult in most cases.

(3) Backbone Transmission Markets

Market Definition

Backbone transmission networks distinguished from customer access net-   **11.155**
works.   Backbone transmission is required to move voice or data traffic from one place to another. Customer access networks are required to originate calls from or terminate calls to particular customers. The distinction can begin to break down with a sufficiently large business user where the demand for telecommunications capacity is particularly large. However in most cases, given the fundamentally different demand characteristics of backbone as opposed to local loop networks, and given the substantial cost differences between building, for example, a national backbone network as compared to a national local loop network, separate markets are likely to exist. Evidence suggests that in a relatively short period after liberalization, competing backbone networks are to a certain extent established,[142] whereas competing local loop networks are much more difficult to establish. This distinction has not been made explicitly in Commission decisions, although it is implicit. Clearer distinctions along these lines are, however, present in some national regulatory frameworks.

International Backbone Transmission Markets—BT/MCI II[143]

The relatively recent opening of telecommunications markets to competition,   **11.156**
and the consequent quasi-monopolistic market shares enjoyed by most former monopolists in many national markets has meant that dominance has sometimes been assumed rather than explicitly analysed in the relatively few Commission decisions in the sector.[144] However, when British Telecommunications sought to merge with the US operator MCI, the case raised issues of dominance over

---

[142] Although evidence from some Member States suggests that competition outside major cities can remain weak several years after liberalization.

[143] *BT/MCI (II)* [1997] OJ L336/1.

[144] *Atlas* [1996] OJ L239/23 (only the English, French and German texts are authentic).

transmission capacity between the UK and the US. Market definition and dominance were therefore examined explicitly.

11.157   Several years earlier, BT and MCI had formed a joint venture to provide telecommunications services to large corporate users. The parties had identified a number of large multinational firms whose telecommunications needs were, in the view of the parties, inadequately met by the existing nationally based telecommunications operators. This joint venture was given a mixed negative clearance and exemption by the Commission (*BT/MCI I*). The parties subsequently decided that a full merger could bring benefits beyond those afforded by the joint venture. The Commission cleared this joint venture (*BT/MCI II*) subject to certain conditions on the divestiture of backbone capacity on the transatlantic UK–US route, and some overlapping service operations in the UK. BT's merger proposal proved less attractive than a rival offer from Worldcom and the merger never in fact took place. The decision nevertheless provides some useful guidance on the analysis of backbone issues.

11.158   As indicated above the decision does not explicitly distinguish between backbone and customer access networks, and the precise products and services being analysed in the market definition are sometimes difficult to relate to the competition concern expressed. However, it is submitted that on a proper reading of the case, in particular in view of the assets divested, the Commission's concern related to a concentration of capacity on a particular backbone transmission market (transatlantic) in the hands of the merged entity.

11.159   *BT/MCI II*—**product market.**   The Commission identified a market for international voice telephony services, and appeared to narrow that market down into country-pair services: 'Interconnection between the domestic networks of any pair of countries is provided by the use of transmission capacity on the international facilities existing between the countries concerned.'[145]

11.160   The Commission then analysed in more detail the transatlantic transmission market, and considered that satellite and cable transmission capacity are not adequately substitutable for them to be considered as part of the same market. The Commission cited the inherently greater signal propagation, delay time, echo effects, and susceptibility to environmental or climatic conditions as reasons why satellite transmission cannot as yet provide an adequate substitute for cable. On the basis of demand, the relevant geographic market for international voice telephony services was defined:

> with reference to call traffic routes between any country pair, since different international routes cannot be considered as viable demand substitutes. From the supply side . . . the possibility of hubbing, ie re-routing US–UK traffic through third coun-

---

[145]   *BT/MCI (II)* [1997] OJ L336/1, at para 13.

tries, does not appear to be a viable commercial possibility at present, since under the existing system of accounting rates and proportionate return it would be more expensive than using direct routes. Furthermore, two distinct geographic markets can be identified within any international route, each comprised of the originating bilateral traffic from the countries concerned.[146]

11.161 *BT/MCI II*—**vertical integration complicated the market definition.** Market definition was complicated by the vertical integration of the companies, and particularly BT. BT operates local and backbone networks in the UK, provides local, national, and long-distance voice and data services to residential and corporate users, and has extensive international capacity. It is submitted that the Commission's emphasis on call services in analysing the market, although understandable at the time given the vertically integrated nature of the market, would no longer be appropriate.

11.162 With the emergence of carriers' carrier companies—companies seeking to build out substantial infrastructure for resale to other telecoms companies—it is likely that a more discriminating market definition would now be used were an appropriate case to arise in the future. Stripping out the vertical integration from the market definition, it would appear possible to identify a demand for transatlantic carriage independent of a demand for call termination—either because one company is present on both sides of the Atlantic, or because the operator wishes to buy transatlantic carriage from someone other than the operator that will ultimately terminate the call. There appears likely to be a number of separate markets for the provision of telecommunications capacity between States, at least in circumstances where undersea cables are used, given the substantial cost of such cable. This analysis is in fact supported by the remedies imposed by the Commission in this case: BT did not have to reduce its share of call services in the UK—the parties did, however, have to reduce their owership of transatlantic capacity. This can be contrasted with the *Worldcom/MCI* case, discussed below, where the Commission refused to accept the parties' offer to divest solely the backbone network of MCI. The Commission required that all of MCI's Internet business (backbone and customers) was divested.

11.163 *BT/MCI II*—**geographic market.** Geographic market definition of transmission networks can be problematic. *BT/MCI II* suggests that country-pair markets (such as UK–US) are appropriate, given that relaying traffic through third countries is commercially unfeasible. Such an analysis would clearly be very fact-specific and could change were international re-routing of traffic possible in a particular case.

11.164 **Carrier services.** An emerging related market for so-called carrier services (provision of services from one telecoms operator to another) was first identified formally in *Unisource/Telefonica*, where it was described as:

---

[146] *BT/MCI (II)* [1997] OJ L336/1, at para 19.

the lease of transmission capacity and the provision of related services to third-party telecommunications traffic carriers and service providers. Along with liberalisation and globalisation of telecommunications markets, demand for efficient, high-quality traffic transportation capacity has risen among old and new carriers.

. . .

Demand for carrier services is increasingly driven by alternative carriers concerned with entrusting the incumbent TO [telecoms operator] with their international traffic, for reasons such as technical dependency and commercial sensitivity of customer information.

11.165 **Competition issues—dominance in backbone transmission markets.** As indicated above, the Commission did not explicitly identify a market for transatlantic transmission capacity in *BT/MCI II*. However, the idea of such a market appears to underpin a large amount of the Commission's analysis and, in particular, the remedy imposed.

11.166 In assessing market share and dominance, however, the Commission referred to a variety of different elements:

— UK call revenue for calls to the US originating in the UK;

— UK call revenue for calls to the UK originating from the US (ie settlements paid by US correspondents on the UK–US route);

— the number of International Private Leased Circuits (IPLCs)[147] of UK companies[148] and the limited amount of spare capacity;

— UK national trunk revenue;

— UK national private circuits revenue; and

— UK local loop revenue.

11.167 The Commission found extremely high market shares in respect of all of the above, and extremely limited spare capacity on the transatlantic route. Although some of the measures appear related to BT's position in different possible UK telephony markets, the number of IPLCs in relation to the amount of spare capacity would have no direct relevance to such a market. The Commission doubted that sufficient extra capacity would be brought on stream in the foreseeable future to alleviate the capacity shortage it identified, bearing in mind the predicted high growth in demand caused at least in part by the growth of the Internet.[149]

---

[147] *BT/MCI (II)* [1997] OJ L336/1, defined at para 15 of the decision as: 'contracts for utilisation of international transmission capacity on a purchase basis, typically by either telephone operators or retail business customers with high utilisation needs. At present, IPLCs are provided and charged in half circuits. In the United Kingdom, BT or Mercury provide a UK termination, and a notional half of the international section, and a distant correspondent provides the other half-circuit and termination in its country.'

[148] At that time only BT and Mercury had international facilities licences and therefore the UK end of transatlantic cables was wholly owned between them.

[149] *BT/MCI (II)* [1997] OJ L336/1, at paras 43–51.

The decision went on to state that: **11.168**

> The high market share of BT in the provision of international voice telephony services on the UK-US route is underpinned by its current control of the local loop in the United Kingdom. Given the time leads and investments required for the development of local networks, BT's current dominant position in this market is likely to remain in place in the near future.[150]

It appears that the determination of dominance or its strengthening in respect of **11.169** these markets will be heavily dependent on the current and soon-to-be available capacity on the particular route. The Commission will apparently take a relatively strict line on this issue, being reluctant to accept future availability of capacity as sufficient to counter current market shares, at least in circumstances where demand is growing rapidly.

Relevance of vertical integration. The Commission did not simply look at the **11.170** available capacity on the transatlantic route, but went further and examined the impact of BT's vertical integration. The vertical integration between backbone and local loop transmission was illustrated particularly in the Commission's description of the accounting rate regime:

> an accounting rate is a specialised form of interconnection tariff, that treats international traffic differently from domestic traffic, in effect bundling the provision of an international half-circuit, the connection to an international gateway switching in the destination country, and the domestic termination of the call by carriers at each end.[151]

The Commission concluded that the possibility of self-corresponding (internal **11.171** termination of traffic on a network, rather than passing the traffic to a third party network for termination) provided by the parties' share of transatlantic capacity, and denied to their competitors by the absence of spare capacity, would lead to a strengthening of BT's dominant position in the market for international voice telephony services on the UK–US route.

Although dominance on an upstream market can be used to leverage market share **11.172** onto a downstream market, it is submitted that vertical integration is not a necessary prerequisite for a competition problem on a backbone market. If there is a capacity shortage—on the transatlantic route or elsewhere—then that would tend to confer market power regardless of the downstream market position of the owner of the capacity.

Divestiture of capacity. The parties provided an undertaking to the **11.173** Commission to make transatlantic cable capacity available to third parties. Moreover, capacity would be made available on an indefeasible right of use (IRU) basis. An IRU is in effect a freehold right in a cable (rather than the leasehold right

---

[150] *BT/MCI (II)* [1997] OJ L336/1, at para 26.
[151] *BT/MCI (II)* [1997] OJ L336/1, at para 28.

of an IPLC), and as such is equivalent to an asset divestiture, a common remedy in merger cases. In effect, this allowed competitors cost-based access to transatlantic capacity. The Commission considered that because the capacity would be made available at prices corresponding to BT's true cost of purchase, this would be likely to ease the entry of competitors. On this basis the merger was approved.[152]

(4) Customer Access Infrastructure

11.174 The importance of customer access infrastructure in voice telephony is clearly recognized, to the extent that a substantial part of the ONP Directives is dedicated to ensuring non-discriminatory and cost-oriented access to it. It may be as a result of this extensive regulation that relatively little recourse to the competition rules has been necessary, and, as such, market definition under the competition rules remains largely unresolved.

Product Market Definition

11.175 The Commission has expressed a preliminary view in the *BiB* Article 19(3) Notice[153] that a general customer access infrastructure market exists and describes what is sometimes known as the last mile or local loop of the telecommunications network—the network from the last switch into the home. There is no formal or informal precedent on the extent to which distinct origination and termination markets exist, or whether there is simply one customer access market. The term customer access infrastructure, although cumbersome, is preferable to the term local loop, given that the infrastructure in question may be neither local, nor configured in a loop (see above).[154]

Origination and Termination Markets

11.176 In essence, the difference between origination and termination services is the difference between making and receiving calls. The Commission has not yet ruled on a case in which the distinction between origination and termination markets would be determinant. Indeed, in the *BiB* case referred to above,[155] the Commission's Article 19(3) Notice refers solely to a customer access infrastructure market. It may be, however, that the Commission's expression of its view in the framework of the ONP Directives could serve as a guide to market definition in the future.

---

[152] There was another issue in relation to audio-conferencing on which undertakings were also provided, but this is of relatively minor significance.

[153] *BiB* (Notice pursuant to Article 19(3) of Council Regulation 17) [1998] OJ C322/6.

[154] On one analysis, the Commission's decision in *Worldcom/MCI* related to a customer access infrastructure market—the market being global and the access point often being wholly removed from the location of the customer.

[155] See also the discussion of *BiB* in Section F below.

The Commission's best practice pricing guidelines[156] are drafted on the basis that they apply to call-termination charges. The guidelines are silent as to whether call origination should be priced differently. Practice in Member States appears to vary—some national regulatory authorities mandate the same price for origination and termination, some allow (or require) differential pricing.

The main argument in favour of a single customer access infrastructure market is that the product sold is essentially the same—carriage of signals along a particular part of a network. The costs to the operator are the same no matter whether the signal originates with the customer or originates elsewhere and terminates with the customer.   **11.177**

The main argument in favour of separate markets appears to be that although the product being sold is essentially the same in both cases—the carriage of signals along a particular stretch of network—it is being sold for different purposes to different entities. Origination services are sold either to end-users (as retail telecommunications services) or to intermediate companies competing with the incumbent and wishing to use the network to sell those same services to end-users, either on a full service or, more commonly, on a market segment basis (such as international, long-distance, or Internet access). Termination services are sold to a variety of customers, including competitors originating calls on the same network or on other networks, and companies who are not competitors, for example, because they operate in different geographic markets (international termination).   **11.178**

On balance it seems highly likely that, should an appropriate case arise, the Commission would find origination and termination to occupy separate product markets. The services are fundamentally not substitutable. Given the distinction between networks which can supply different services, discussed in more detail below, it may also be the case that narrower origination and, possibly, termination markets exist. For example, it may be the case that several different networks (fixed telecom, cable, mobile) were capable of originating voice calls, but a narrower set of networks (telecom, cable) were capable of originating data calls (at least at sufficient bit-rates to provide particular services).   **11.179**

The strongest Commission precedent in favour of separate origination and termination markets results from the Internet. The market defined in *Worldcom/MCI*[157] appears to be essentially a global one for Internet termination services. The clearance of certain Internet joint ventures would appear to have been based on a market for retail Internet access for end-users (essentially an origination market) which was national. Not only, therefore, does the Commission   **11.180**

---

[156] Commission Recommendation on Interconnection in a liberalised telecommunications market [1998] OJ L73/42 (Text of Recommendation) and [1998] OJ C84/3 (Communication on Recommendation).

[157] *Worldcom/MCI* (Case IV/M1069) (1998) [1999] OJ L116/1.

appear to identify fundamentally different product markets in the two cases, but the geographic markets also appear different.

Fixed and Mobile Customer Access Infrastructure

11.181   There is no clear precedent decision under the competition rules as to the circumstances in which fixed and mobile networks occupy distinct product markets, although the Commission's decision in *GSM Italy*[158] suggests that it considers the markets separate for the moment. This case, pursuant to Article 86, related to the conditions under which the Italian Government was prepared to grant a second mobile licence in Italy. The Commission considered the conditions as granting a special and exclusive right to Telecom Italia, as the second operator was asked to pay a substantial licence fee, such fee not having been levied on Telecom Italia.

11.182   The ONP regulations refer to the national market for interconnection, and do not distinguish between termination on a fixed line network and termination on a mobile network. Companies are presumed to have significant market power if they have a market share of more than 25 per cent in relation to termination on these markets as a whole.[159]

11.183   This will not necessarily be the appropriate market definition under the competition rules. There may be grounds to hold that fixed and mobile networks occupy separate product markets, at least as long as the relevant downstream markets remain distinct. If mobile users at the retail level pay a price for mobile services significantly higher than for the comparable fixed services it is likely that fixed and mobile voice telephony services will constitute separate downstream product markets. The mobile networks capable of fulfilling this distinct downstream demand would therefore similarly occupy a distinct market.

11.184   **Residential voice telephony infrastructure.**   As originating networks, fixed and mobile networks may ultimately prove sufficiently substitutable on the basis of price for the provision of residential voice telephony services, so that for the delivery of residential voice telephony services there could be said to be only one upstream network market. This may already have occurred in some markets, such as Finland and Sweden, where the prices of fixed and mobile services are closely comparable.

11.185   Retail mobile voice services will not tend to compete with fixed voice services until the price differential becomes marginal. As such, separate markets would be likely to exist for call termination to fixed as distinct from mobile services.

---

[158] Commission Decision (EC) 95/489 of 4 October 1995 concerning the conditions imposed on the second operator of GSM radiotelephony services in Italy [1995] OJ L280/49.
[159] This also presumes that the geographic market is that of a particular Member State.

Mobile telephony infrastructure.   The Commission has previously indicated **11.186** that the operation of GSM infrastructure and the provision of GSM services constitute two separate markets.[160]

The extent to which distinct mobile network markets exist (for example **11.187** digital/analogue, GSM900/DCS1800) would appear to depend on the downstream markets. If a distinct retail product market can be identified which could only be served by a particular form of mobile infrastructure, then it is likely that that infrastructure could be regarded as constituting a separate market. One potential example would have been pan-European corporate mobile services which, it could be argued, would need use of mobile networks in each Member State. This would support digital being separate from analogue (given the lack of interoperability in analogue) and would also support GSM900 being separate from DCS1800 (given the lack of DCS1800 networks in many Member States). This last point, however, is undermined by the increasing affordability of dual-mode handsets.

Geographic Market Definition

Geographic markets in the telecommunications sector are determined by: **11.188**

> (a) . . . the extent and coverage of the network and the customers that can economically be reached and whose demands may be met; and
> (b) the legal and regulatory system and the right to provide a service.[161]

Residential markets will tend to be national, corporate markets may be national, **11.189** regional, or global. One potential issue in the future could be the identification of a geographic market which, though identifiable and distinct, is not contiguous. In the telecommunications sector, it could be argued that the conditions of competition are sufficiently different in cities compared to rural areas that separate markets should be identified. It may, for example, be commercially feasible to roll out cable or other competing networks only in areas of sufficiently high population density. If it were possible to discriminate between these areas, separate geographic markets could be identifiable.

Competitition issues.   There are as yet no precedent decisions on the creation or **11.190** strengthening of dominance on these markets, although the proposed Telia/Telenor merger, discussed below potentially raises the issue of strengthening. Issues arise most commonly in relation to the abuse of market power on these markets, for which see the subsection on Article 82 below. This section looks first

---

[160] Commission Decision (EC) 95/489 of 4 October 1995 concerning the conditions imposed on the second operator of GSM radiotelephony services in Italy [1995] OJ L280/49.
[161] *Mannesmann/Olivetti/Infostrada* (Case IV/M1025) (1998), at para 17 (only the English text is authentic).

at assessment of dominance and joint dominance on these markets, and then examines some of the issues raised by the *Telia/Telenor* case.

Dominance

11.191 **Different assessment of dominance for origination and termination markets.** It may be the case that the question of dominance would be assessed differently if these markets were distinct.

11.192 It is arguable that for full service origination markets, substitutability of alternative networks is more important than it is for termination markets. A company could therefore be regarded as non-dominant in origination markets if there were adequate alternative networks available to act as a supply side constraint. The number of connected customers and the reluctance of customers to switch would not appear relevant. For call-by-call origination services, where a particular retail demand is being addressed, market power would, by contrast, appear to be based more on the number of connected customers.

11.193 In assessing dominance on termination markets, the number of connected customers would appear to be a more accurate measure of market share. The existence of alternative networks would then be relevant to the extent that they impacted on sustainability: issues of consumer reluctance to switch networks would then beome important.

11.194 If this is correct, then termination markets, and potentially some origination markets, are perhaps best regarded as after-markets of the relevant downstream service market. The complicating factor is that access to this after market is necessary for companies to enter the downstream service market, making dominance on the downstream service market self-reinforcing.

Joint Dominance

11.195 With the ending of the legal monopolies on the provision of telecommunications services and infrastructure, and the increasing usage of mobile networks, it is likely that the former paradigm of single network dominance in the sector will become increasingly irrelevant. However, there remain significant commercial and/or technical limits to the number of competing networks likely to be present on any geographic market. The telecommunications sector is unlikely to be characterized by a large number of competing networks. As such, it may be the case that the number of networks is insufficient to ensure a competitive market, and competition problems may remain. In these circumstances it may not be possible to demonstrate that any one network operator is dominant. The continued utility of the competition rules to resolve remaining competition problems will therefore depend on the extent to which the doctrine of joint, or collective, dominance can be used.

Commission position. There are relatively few precedents in the area of joint **11.196** dominance. The Access Notice provides a strong indication that where there are a small number of network operators, but no one network operator is demonstrably dominant, the Commission will look closely at the question of joint dominance.[162]

> In addition, for two or more companies to be jointly dominant it is necessary, though not sufficient, for there to be no effective competition between the companies on the relevant market. This lack of competition may in practice be due to the fact that the companies have links such as agreements for cooperation, or interconnection agreements. The Commission does not, however, consider that either economic theory or Community law implies that such links are legally necessary for a joint dominant position to exist. It is a sufficient economic link if there is the kind of interdependence which often comes about in oligopolistic situations. There does not seem to be any reason in law or in economic theory to require any other economic link between jointly dominant companies. This having been said, in practice such links will often exist in the telecommunications sector where national TOs nearly inevitably have links of various kinds with one another.[163]

The joint dominance of two telecommunications infrastructure operators on the **11.197** same geographic market is specifically envisaged[164]—in particular:

> To take as an example access to the local loop, in some Member States this could well be controlled in the near future by two operators—the incumbent telecommunications operator and a cable operator. In order to provide particular services to consumers, access to the local loop of either the telecommunications operator or the cable television operator is necessary. Depending on the circumstances of the case and in particular on the relationship between them, neither operator may hold a dominant position: together, however, they may hold a joint monopoly of access to these facilities. In the longer term, technological developments may lead to other local loop access mechanisms being viable, such as energy networks: the existence of such mechanisms will be taken into account in determining whether dominant or joint dominant positions exist.[165]

The Commission appears to consider that given the likely limited number of rel- **11.198** evant networks, problems of, for example, refusal of access could arise across the industry as a whole even in the absence of explicit collusion. Individual operators would recognize the commercial benefit to their downstream operations should all operators on the market refuse to provide access.

---

[162] Notice on the Application of the Competition Rules to Access Agreements in the Telecommunications Sector [1998] OJ C265/2, paras 77 *et seq.*
[163] Notice on the Application of the Competition Rules to Access Agreements in the Telecommunications Sector [1998] OJ C265/2, para 79.
[164] Notice on the Application of the Competition Rules to Access Agreements in the Telecommunications Sector [1998] OJ C265/2, para 78.
[165] Notice on the Application of the Competition Rules to Access Agreements in the Telecommunications Sector [1998] OJ C265/2, para 80.

11.199 The Access Notice is written as if a single company occupied a dominant position, but references in the text to dominance should be interpreted as including references to joint dominance where appropriate.[166]

11.200 Court of First Instance. The position of the Commission has subsequently received support by a Court of First Instance judgment in a Merger Regulation case (unrelated to telecommunications). The Commission prohibited the proposed merger between Gencor and Lonrho on the basis that it risked creating an oligopoly on the relevant market. The parties contested the Commission's decision, *inter alia*, because the Commission had not proved the existence of the economic links which the Court's earlier judgment in *Italian Flat Glass*[167] had indicated as necessary. The *CFI*,[168] however, upheld the Commission's decision in *Gencor/Lonrho*,[169] concluding that a demonstration of economic links was not necessary:

> Furthermore, there is no reason whatsoever in legal or economic terms to exclude from the notion of economic links the relationship of interdependence existing between the parties to a tight oligopoly within which, in a market with the appropriate characteristics, in particular in terms of market concentration, transparency and product homogeneity, those parties are in a position to anticipate one another's behaviour and are therefore strongly encouraged to align their conduct in the market, in particular in such a way as to maximise their joint profits by restricting production with a view to increasing prices. In such a context, each trader is aware that highly competitive action on its part designed to increase its market share (for example a price cut) would provoke identical action by the others, so that it would derive no benefit from its initiative. All the traders would thus be affected by the reduction in price levels.[170]

11.201 Limited number of network operators. The economic and technical issues relating to the building of infrastructure are fundamentally different to those relating to the provision of services using that infrastructure. Even assuming widespread successful construction (roll-out) of alternative infrastructure networks, it is likely that there will be a relatively limited number of networks available. Local network construction is expensive, currently available services provided over these networks are still limited, and all alternative provision is faced with competition from an incumbent operator with substantial sunk costs in a local network often constructed in a monopoly (non-commercial) environment. The incumbent operator may also remain subject to universal service obligations and benefit from

---

[166] Notice on the Application of the Competition Rules to Access Agreements in the Telecommunications Sector [1998] OJ C265/2, para 16.
[167] Joined Cases T–68/89, T–77/89 and T–78/89 *Società Italiana Vetro SpA, Fabbrica Pisana SpA and PPG Vernante Pennitalia SpA v Commission* [1992] ECR II–1403.
[168] Case T–102/96 *Gencor v Commission* judgment of 25 March 1999, not yet reported.
[169] *Gencor/Lonrho* (Case IV/M619) (1996) [1997] OJ L11/30.
[170] Case T–102/96 *Gencor v Commission* judgment of 25 March 1999, not yet reported, at para 276.

universal service contributions. In addition to commercial problems of network roll-out, there may also be technical limits such as frequency limitations. When looking at the provision of particular services—such as high speed Internet access and video on demand—the number of usable networks is likely to be particularly limited.[171]

Such a limited number of providers may well be insufficient to provide a fully competitive market: intervention on the basis of the competition rules is likely in these markets. There are strong policy arguments against allowing the network providers (whose numbers are commercially or technically limited) from extending this limit into the service markets. If the only service providers were the down-stream arms of the network operators then: **11.202**

— there would be similar risks that the number of service providers would be insufficient to form a competitive market; and

— there would be no necessary link between ability to trade efficiently as a service provider and presence on the service provision market.

It is likely that in policy terms the Commission would seek to prevent this outcome. **11.203**

Strengthening of Dominance on Customer Access Infrastructure Markets

This could arise either through acquisitions on the relevant market, a reduction in potential competition, or through strengthening in upstream or downstream markets which could weaken the structure of the infrastructure market. These issues are discussed in the section on retail services below. **11.204**

There is no case on this issue as yet, although the proposed merger between Telia and Telenor may require the Commission to analyse the impact of the merger on the local transmission networks. As the geographic markets are different, there would appear to be strengthening through a reduction in actual competition on the customer access markets. **11.205**

Potential competition.   As each operator is already present on the market of the other, it seems possible that there could be a reduction in potential competition. Where existing networks are geographically close, it could be argued that the possibility to incrementally expand the network makes the operators important potential competitors on the market. If the Commission were to find that this reduction of potential competition was significant—and it is arguable that any reduction is significant when the incumbents have quasi-monopolistic market shares—then the Commission may seek remedies on the local transmission network markets. **11.206**

---

[171]   *BiB* (Notice pursuant to Article 19(3) of Regulation 17) [1998] OJ C322/6.

11.207 **Vertical integration.** Another issue which has not yet been addressed by the Commission is the extent to which a company's position on an infrastructure market could be strengthened by vertical integration or by a strengthening of its position on a related upstream or downstream market. Again, the *Telia/Telenor* case may prove a useful precedent on this issue.

(5) Internet and Interactive Services

Market Definition

Internet Termination—Top Level Networks

11.208 The Internet is a network of interconnected networks. In order to provide a full Internet service any company providing customers with access to the Internet (an Internet Service Provider, ISP) will need access to all, or at least the vast majority, of the networks connected to the Internet.

11.209 Market definition in this area is difficult. The distinction between competitors to whom an operator will provide reciprocal access to its customers (peering), and customers to whom an operator will provide access to all other Internet users (transit) appears more fluid than is the case in traditional telecommunications, such as voice telephony. However, as indicated above, it is possible that the traditional vertically integrated nature of voice telecommunications is breaking down, and a market structure more closely aligned to that of the Internet may be emerging. It should also be noted that some commentators predict that voice services will become a subset of the data carried on Internet networks in the medium term. It is conceivable, therefore, that voice networks may disappear in the long term as an independent market definition.

11.210 The only formal Commission precedent in this area is the decision approving the proposed merger between Worldcom and MCI.[172] The case arose shortly after the bid for MCI by BT (discussed in the *BT/MCI II* case, above). Worldcom, a relative new entrant in the telecommunications sector, had pursued an aggressive acquisition strategy over the previous years. This had provided Worldcom with operations in a number of countries, and in particular had given Worldcom a substantial presence on Internet markets. Worldcom launched a bid for MCI to counter BT's proposed bid. The main issue which emerged in the case was the position of the merged entity on the so-called 'top level networks' market for the Internet.

11.211 In order to ensure universal connectivity on the Internet, every Internet service provider network has to be connected to every other network. Direct connections from every network to every other network are clearly not technically or commercially feasible, and therefore a system of indirect connection has developed. The

---

[172] *Worldcom/MCI* (Case IV/M1069) (1998) [1999] OJ L116/1.

Commission distinguished between the two distinct services of peering and transit.

> 32 . . . the usual form of peering arrangement is one under which Network Operator A (or ISP A) agrees to accept from Network Operator B (or ISP B) all traffic originating from B's customers which is to be terminated on A's network. In return, B accepts a reciprocal obligation to terminate all traffic originating from A's customers and destined for B's network . . .

> 39 . . . The purchase of a transit service could therefore be . . . described as a right on the part of an ISP to have his traffic treated as the traffic of the transit provider's network for the purpose of exchange across a peering interface.

This distinction between peering and transit led the Commission to conclude **11.212** that there was an important distinction between two types of ISPs—essentially dividing-out top level networks.

> 41. Although ISPs may turn successively to yet larger ISPs for the provision of transit services, there is a logical limitation to the process. Traffic which is progressively defaulted to higher level networks will finally end up in the hands of an ISP who has no one else to whom to turn, and must either assume responsibility on its own account for delivering the traffic across peering interfaces, or return it undelivered. These networks (or the ISPs concerned) are referred to hereon as 'top level networks' or 'top level ISPs'.

This distinction was supported by the activities of the players on the market who **11.213** appeared to be gradually increasing the criteria which had to be fulfilled before peering were granted.[173] The Commission concluded that alternatives to the top-level networks—resellers or providers of secondary peering[174]—were not adequate substitutes.

Resellers were by definition dependent on the top-level networks for their services **11.214** and as such subject to price rises imposed by the top-level networks.[175] Secondary peering ISPs may offer some limited substitutability in terms of allowing them to access some sites without having to transit the networks of the top-level ISPs, but there will be gaps in their coverage. In no case, however, can the second tier connectivity offered by a secondary peering ISP provide a service which is a sufficient substitute for the first tier connectivity provided by the top-level network. Secondary peering ISPs who wanted to offer complete connectivity could not avoid continuing to buy some transit from the top-level networks, and their cost base is therefore captive to the extent that they continue to have to do so.

---

[173] *Worldcom/MCI* (Case IV/M1069) (1998) [1999] OJ L116/1, at para 45.
[174] Secondary peering ISPs have a collection of peering agreements, either with other similarly placed ISPs or with some, but not all, of the top-level networks.
[175] *Worldcom/MCI* (Case IV/M1069) (1998) [1999] OJ L116/1, at para 67.

Residential Internet/Interactive Services Origination Infrastructure

11.215 The majority of Internet users access the Internet via a dial-up connection using a domestic voice telephony line. However, the relevant product market for the infrastructure is not necessarily the same as that for voice telephony. As indicated above for voice services, fixed and mobile networks are likely to converge—however until the data carrying capacity of mobile networks substantially increases,[176] mobile network infrastructure will probably not be an adequate substitute for fixed line Internet access. Cable TV networks capable of carrying two-way communications are certainly substitutable for domestic telephone lines for the purpose of accessing the Internet.

Competition Issues

Strengthening of Dominance on Internet Markets

11.216 The Commission considered how to assess a strengthening of dominance in the *Worldcom/MCI* case. The Commission determined that traffic was the most appropriate means of measuring market share in the sector. Notably, the Commission rejected a simple revenue test (which the parties suggested) for determining market share on the basis that, given the vertically integrated nature of the parties' Internet operations, this would tend to understate the market share. In a co-ordinated information gathering exercise with the US authorities, the Commission conducted an extensive investigation of Internet traffic and concluded that a percentage sufficient to give rise to a presumption of dominance was carried on the networks of the merging parties.

11.217 The Commission concluded that the merger would result in the creation of a dominant position on the market for top level networks. In addition to a market share calculation, the Commission based this conclusion on:

— the importance of network effects:

> 126. Because of the specific features of network competition and the existence of network externalities which make it valuable for customers to have access to the largest network, MCI WorldCom's position can hardly be challenged once it has obtained a dominant position. The more its network grows, the less need it has to interconnect with competitors and the more need they have to interconnect with the merged entity. Furthermore, the larger its network becomes, the greater is its ability to control a significant element of the costs of any new entrant. It can achieve this by denying such entrants the opportunity to peer and insisting that they remain as customers and pay a margin accordingly for all the services they want to offer. The merger could thus have the effect of raising entry barriers still higher. Indeed, it could be argued that, as a result of the merger, the MCI WorldCom network would constitute, either immediately or in a relatively short time thereafter, an essential

---

[176] Such as with the third generation mobile.

facility, to which all other ISPs would have no choice but to interconnect (directly or indirectly) in order to offer a credible Internet access service.[177]

— the risk of a snowball effect (market tipping):

131. The merger might well create a 'snowball effect', in that MCI WorldCom would be better placed than any of its competitors to capture future growth through new customers, because of the attractions for any new customer of direct connection with the largest network, and the relative unattractiveness of competitors' offerings owing to the threat of disconnection or degradation of peering which MCI WorldCom's competitors must constantly live under. As a result, the merger might provide MCI WorldCom with the opportunity to enlarge its market share still further.[178]

— and the opportunity for incumbent operators to capture market growth:

At the oral hearing, an intervener stressed the need to avoid the error of assuming that growth could counter market dominance. Indeed, the incumbents rather than newcomers could well be the best placed to capture future growth. For example, the parties pointed to the emergence of new competitors who were engaged in laying substantial fibre networks and could therefore offer a competitive counter-force. However, entry as a top level ISP requires not only physical facilities, but also a customer base and hence traffic flow and thus access to peering interconnection. A dominant network which refused to provide peering could effectively prevent a new entrant from operating as a top level network . . .[179]

11.218 These concerns led the Commission to the conclusion that the proposed merger would have created a dominant position on the market for top-level networks. The Commission therefore determined that MCI should divest its entire Internet activities, removing all overlap between its Internet activities and those of Worldcom.

11.219 Similar concerns in relation to the power of particular networks appear to arise as with traditional telephony and interconnection. These concerns include the risks that a dominant network operator: charges supra-competitive fees for network access; seeks to reinforce its position, for example by concluding lengthy exclusive arrangements with its customers or by delaying interconnection upgrades, or otherwise favours its own operations at the expense of third parties.

11.220 **Internet connectivity as an example of termination markets.**   This decision, although in the Internet sector, is the strongest Commission precedent for there being distinct origination and termination markets. Issues relating to the downstream networks through which end-users were connected to the Internet were not considered relevant to Worldcom/MCI, indeed there could have been no allegation that the merged entity would have had any significant control over such

---

[177] *Worldcom/MCI* (Case IV/M1069) (1998) [1999] OJ L116/1, at para 126.
[178] *Worldcom/MCI* (Case IV/M1069) (1998) [1999] OJ L116/1, at para 131.
[179] *Worldcom/MCI* (Case IV/M1069) (1998) [1999] OJ L116/1, at para 134.

markets. The concern arose from the market power which the merged entity would have over competing operators, where customers of the latter wished to connect to the customers of the former. This would seem to be essentially the same issue as market power over call termination in traditional voice telephony markets.

(6) Access to Transmission Networks

11.221 Aside from avoiding the creation or strengthening of dominant positions—as in *BT/MCI II* above—a number of competition issues revolve around access to transmission facilities. This problem appears both in relation to those joint ventures or mergers where one or more parents is dominant on a relevant market and in pure Article 82 cases.

Third Party Access to Transmission Networks

11.222 A number of access issues in the telecommunications sector will be resolved by national regulatory authorities applying the provisions of the Interconnection Directive or the Full Competition Directive, which together set out a regulatory framework for interconnection issues. However, Articles 81 and 82 continue to apply and to the extent that problems emerge that do not fit fully within the pre-existing framework, competition law intervention is likely.

11.223 The Access Notice draws out general competition law principles relating to access to telecommunications facilities by third parties wishing to provide services to end-users. Access is not defined explicitly, but the Commission's intentions can be derived from Part II of the Notice, dealing with market definition. The Notice envisages markets for the provision of services to end-users, and markets in the facilities needed to provide those services to end-users.[180] Facilities are not, however, defined: any definition would risk being interpreted as limitative, whereas legally the concept cannot be limited but is relevant to any type of facility where the underlying principles are applicable. It is clear, both from the Notice and from Commission decisional practice, that the Commission envisages the concept of facility as covering a wide range of possible circumstances from physical facilities such as network infrastructure to intellectual property rights, or customer information. However, it is in the area of transmission networks that the Notice is likely to be most used.

11.224 The Notice sets out various possible abuses in the context of access to networks, examined below. Issues of third party access under Article 82 can be examined under several different legal grounds, for example essential facilities, discrimination, and bundling. The relationship between these grounds can be complex, and,

---

[180] Notice on the Application of the Competition Rules to Access Agreements in the Telecommunications Sector [1998] OJ C265/2, para 49 *et seq*.

given the very different evidential burdens each puts on complainants, an understanding of the circumstances in which each applies is particularly important.

Essential Facilities

The concept of essential facilities is a contentious one under Community law, **11.225** although it now seems clear that it is a principle of general application. The Commission devoted substantial space in the Access Notice to the concept,[181] and indicated that it will apply in circumstances where the company from whom access is being sought has not yet provided any third party with access to the facility in question. Since the publication of the Access Notice, the ECJ has delivered its judgment in *Bronner*,[182] a case involving newspaper distribution in Austria. The reasoning of *Bronner* is far from clear,[183] however, although the basic definition of what constitutes 'essential' appears consistent with the Commission's position.

The Access Notice identified five criteria which must be fulfilled before a refusal **11.226** to grant access could be characterized as abusive.

Essential. First, access to the facility in question must be essential, defined as: **11.227**

> 91 . . . It will not be sufficient that the position of the company requesting access would be more advantageous if access were granted—but refusal of access must lead to the proposed activities being made either impossible or seriously and unavoidably uneconomic . . .

This is an extremely high burden of proof, reaffirmed by Advocate General **11.228** Jacobs[184] in *Bronner*:

> 67 . . . intervention of that kind [the ordering of access], whether understood as an application of the essential facilities doctrine or, more traditionally, as a response to a refusal to supply goods or services, can be justified in terms of competition policy only in cases in which the dominant undertaking has a genuine stranglehold on the related market. That might be the case for example where duplication of the facility is impossible or extremely difficult owing to physical, geographical or legal constraints or is highly undesirable for reasons of public policy. It is not sufficient that the undertaking's control over a facility should give it a competitive advantage.

The Court provided no criteria for determining directly whether or not a facility **11.229** is essential. The Court did, however, indicate that the refusal to provide access must be likely to eliminate all competition on the part of the party requesting access.

---

[181] Notice on the Application of the Competition Rules to Access Agreements in the Telecommunications Sector [1998] OJ C265/2, paras 87–98.

[182] Case C–7/97 *Oscar Bronner GmbH & Co KG and Mediaprint Zeitungs- und Zeitschriftenverlag GmbH & Co KG, Mediaprint Zeitungsvertriebsgesellschaft mbH & Co KG, Mediaprint Anzeigengesellschaft mbH & Co KG*, judgment of 26 November 1998, not yet reported.

[183] Compare, for example, paras 35 and 43.

[184] Case C–7/97 *Oscar Bronner GmbH v Mediaprint*, Opinion of 28 May 1998, not yet reported.

11.230 AG Jacobs went on to suggest:

> 68 . . . the possibility that the cost of duplicating a facility might alone constitute an insuperable barrier to entry. That might be so particularly in cases in which the creation of the facility took place under non-competitive conditions, for example, partly through public funding.

11.231 This could clearly be relevant to the telecommunications sector where the demands of universal service required telecoms operators to connect all end-users regardless of the individual cost involved. Universal service is explicitly recognized under both the ONP rules and the Commission's liberalization Directives as a continuing issue in the sector. In those Member States where there is a continued universal service obligation imposed on a particular operator, it would appear that certain aspects of the network of that operator were by definition not commercially duplicable (and hence the need for the universal service obligation). The argument would appear barely less strong in those Member States that have imposed a universal service obligation in the past but now no longer do so.

11.232 Although the concept of an essential facility is raised in Commission practice under the analysis of abuse, it could also be regarded as essentially a market definition issue. The essential nature derives from the absence of demand or supply side substitutability. Where this essential facility is controlled by a single entity, or, in cases of joint dominance, by two or more jointly dominant entities, competition issues may arise.

11.233 **Available capacity.** Secondly, the Notice indicates that there must be '91 (b) . . . sufficient capacity available to provide access'.

11.234 There is a certain overlap between this criterion and the fifth, the absence of an objective justification, and it is not clear why in principle a capacity limit should be more important than, or considered separately from, a technical incompatibility in determining whether a refusal to provide access is abusive.

11.235 The Notice is silent as to the legal conclusion to be drawn where capacity is limited. If capacity cannot be increased, the competition rules would argue for an allocation of capacity on an objectively justifiable basis. Allocation on other than objective criteria, for example reserving capacity to the dominant operator's own downstream operations, would appear to risk charges of discrimination. However, favouring existing customers over new customers may be permissible, as may rationing between customers or simply selling to the highest bidder.

11.236 In certain circumstances there may be an obligation on the dominant operator to expand the available capacity. This would appear to be a legitimate result where only the dominant operator is in a position to expand capacity, indeed where such operator may be the only company in a position to do so, and has a guaranteed return on its investment through third parties wishing to purchase access.[185] A legitimate justification for refusing to expand capacity in those circumstances is difficult to envisage.

Effect on competition or on market development.   Thirdly, the refusal to pro-   **11.237** vide access to the facility must have an effect on the market: '91 (c) the facility owner fails to satisfy demand on an existing service or product market, blocks the emergence of a potential new service or product, or impedes competition on an existing or potential service or product market'. This criterion is relatively wide-ranging, envisaging not only direct effects on competition but the impeding of technical development by preventing the development of a new product or service. The Notice makes it clear that preventing the emergence of a completely new market would fulfil this test, but is not necessary, thus clarifying the Commission's interpretation of *Magill*.[186]

One interesting aspect is that the Notice envisages that a refusal which prevents   **11.238** the emergence of a new product market could be abusive, which by implication would mean that refusals to provide access could be abusive even where the essential facility operator is not present on the market for which access is being requested.

Non-discrimination.   Fourthly: '91 (d) the company seeking access is prepared   **11.239** to pay the reasonable and non-discriminatory price and will otherwise in all respects accept non-discriminatory access terms and conditions'.

The party requesting access must be prepared to accept non-discriminatory terms   **11.240** and conditions of access. This criterion is unlikely to prove problematic.

Objective justification.   Finally: '91 (e) there is no objective justification for   **11.241** refusing to provide access'.

There must be no other objective justification for the refusal. As indicated above,   **11.242** there is a certain overlap between this element and the question of limited capac-ity. This can be a relatively wide concept encompassing a variety of justifications such as technical incompatibilities. However, it is likely that the Commission will treat purported technical problems with a certain scepticism.

Discrimination

Discriminating between equivalent transactions where the discrimination has an   **11.243** effect on competition is specifically mentioned as an abuse under Article 82. Provision of access to a particular facility to one party while refusing that access to a third party (or providing access but at different prices, see below) could therefore

---

[185] *FAG—Flughafen Frankfurt/Main AG* [1998] OJ L72/30.
[186] Joined Cases C–241/91P and C–242/91P *Radio Telefis Eireann (RTE) and Independent Television Publications Ltd (ITP) v Commission* [1995] ECR I–743.

constitute discrimination under Article 82 provided a number of conditions are fulfilled.

11.244 **Notion of an equivalent transaction.**   For there to be a case of discrimination, there must be different treatment of equivalent transactions. In terms of transmission networks, the starting point of the analysis is to determine exactly which network elements are required in each case. It is important to note that it is the demand of the company requesting access, not the supply by the network operator that is important.

11.245 **Effect on competition.**   Discrimination can have effects on competition either on the market for the product being sold (referred to in US law as primary-line discrimination) or on the downstream market on which the product is being used (referred to in US law as secondary-line discrimination). The clearest case of an effect on competition is if the operators between whom there is discriminatory treatment compete on the same downstream market, such as that for voice telephony. Refusing to provide one with access, or supplying access at different prices will clearly affect competition. A more complex case is where the operators between whom there is discriminatory treatment operate on different downstream markets. In these circumstances, there is clearly no direct effect on actual competition. However, the Access Notice indicates that where the markets are closely related there may nevertheless be an effect on competition sufficient for the purposes of the discrimination test:

> 121 . . . Where two distinct downstream product markets exist, but one product would be regarded as substitutable for another save for the fact that there was a price difference between the two products, discriminating in the price charged to the providers of these two products could decrease existing or potential competition. For example, although fixed and mobile voice telephony services at present probably constitute separate product markets, the markets are likely to converge. Charging higher interconnection prices to mobile operators as compared to fixed operators would tend to hamper this convergence, and would therefore have an effect on competition. Similar effects on competition are likely in other telecommunications markets.

11.246 On this basis, if an operator were to discriminate in its call-termination charges depending on whether the call originates on a fixed or a mobile network this would be very likely to affect competition. A more difficult issue is where the discrimination is between different geographic markets. Clearly there is no direct effect on competition, and indirect effects on competition such as those envisaged in relation to fixed/mobile networks appear more difficult to justify. They cannot be entirely ruled out, however, as discrimination in these circumstances could be said to increase national partitioning of markets, thereby reducing potential competition between the operators on those national markets. Even if a discrimination argument cannot be used, there are strong arguments in relation to excessive pricing, see below.

Bundling

Although bundling or tying is an issue traditionally related to goods rather than   **11.247**
services, there appears to be no argument of principle that would prevent its application to services.[187] The Court in *Tetra Pak*[188] held that:

> even where tied sales of two products are in accordance with commercial usage or
> there is a natural link between the two products in question, such sales may still con-
> stitute abuse within the meaning of Article 86 [now Article 82] unless they are objec-
> tively justified . . .

Given that the telecommunications sector is characterized by former monopolist   **11.248**
operators that have not previously distinguished between their different services,
this judgment may prove to be important in relation at least to network access in
telecommunications. The Court's interpretation of the concept of bundling
appears to dispense with the possible defence that the particular unbundling
requested has never been requested. The Commission appears prepared to apply
the concept of bundling to the provision of telecommunications services.

An argument that a dominant operator is unjustifiably refusing to unbundle its   **11.249**
services carries with it a significantly lower burden of proof than an argument that
an operator is refusing to provide access to an essential facility.

In order to demonstrate bundling, it would be necessary to demonstrate: **11.250**

— dominance (note: it is not necessary to prove the existence of an essential facility);

— two or more discrete elements that are being sold together;

— an effect on competition resulting from the refusal to unbundle;

— there is, at least prima facie, no objective justification for the refusal to unbundle (technical issues could be relevant here).

Following *Tetra Pak*, there appears to be no requirement to demonstrate that the   **11.251**
elements are normally sold separately, or are sold separately elsewhere, although
such indications would clearly be beneficial to a complainant's case.

In relation to network infrastructure, a refusal to provide unbundled access to the   **11.252**
network would appear difficult to justify in many cases. Clearly, though, a dominant operator cannot be required to unbundle all elements of its network at the
request of every third party, and there must be some element of reasonableness
both in relation to the timing and content of the request for unbundling, and in
relation to all requests which it has received.

---

[187] Notice on the Application of the Competition Rules to Access Agreements in the
Telecommunications Sector [1998] OJ C265/2, para 103.
[188] Case C–333/94P *Tetra Pak International SA v Commission* [1996] ECR I–5951.

11.253   This relatively broad interpretation of the concept of bundling is consistent with the approach of the competition rules in other areas. The refusal to sell, for example, wholesale services (interconnection) without the added value of the retail services (voice telephony) could also have been characterized as monopoly leveraging using the Court's definition in *Telemarketing*[189] and *GB-Inno-BM*:[190]

> an abuse within the meaning of Article 86 [now Article 82] is committed where, without any objective necessity, an undertaking holding a dominant position on a particular market reserves to itself an ancillary activity which might be carried out by another undertaking as part of its activities on a neighbouring but separate market, with the possibility of eliminating all competition from such undertaking[191]

11.254   **Unbundled local loop.**   Unbundling in this sense means the provision of direct access to the telecommunications wire separately from that of the switch.[192] There is no precedent decision under the competition rules as to local loop unbundling, but this may prove important in the future. It should be noted, however, that this is an issue which may be resolved by sector specific regulation. The present ONP framework appears to leave this issue open, and national regulatory authorities appear divided on the point.

11.255   Unbundling the local loop is a controversial issue both in regulatory and competition law terms, although an increasing number of national telecoms regulators are requiring unbundling. The provision of unbundled access to the local loop allows the requesting company to offer both origination and termination services in respect of that line. A competitor that has the benefit of unbundled access to the local loop effectively takes over the customer from the incumbent operator and provides both origination services from and termination services to that customer.

11.256   If a dominant telecoms operator allows its competitors to use its infrastructure to provide origination services to end-users, then it is in effect allowing that competitor access to the switch and to the wire together. If that competitor wishes only to have access to the wire—for example so that the competitor can install its own switching equipment—then a refusal to provide access to the wire separately would prima facie appear to be bundling. In effect the telecoms operator would be ensuring a return on its investment in switching infrastructure in which its competitors have no interest and with which its competitors would rather compete. Similarly, given that the provision of call origination would not normally also entail the competitor being in a position to provide call termination services for

---

[189]   Case 311/84 *CBEM v CLT and IPB* [1985] ECR 3261.
[190]   Case 13/77 *GB-Inno-BM/ATAB* [1977] ECR 2115.
[191]   Case 13/77 *GB-Inno-BM/ATAB* [1977] ECR 2115, at para 18.
[192]   Unbundled local loops are known by a variety of names, including Direct Access to the Copper Loop (DACL), line-side unbundling, and, occasionally, dark copper access.

that customer, refusing to provide unbundled access can also be seen as an attempt by the dominant operator to reserve the termination market to itself.

However, it may prove to be more complicated given that unbundling is a politic-
ally sensitive issue. It can be argued that the provision of unbundled access to the local loop undermines incentives for third parties to invest in infrastructure, and some national regulatory authorities oppose unbundling on this basis. The rela-
tionship between policy objectives and the competition rules is set out above. However, particular arguments that may prove to be relevant here include whether experience in jurisdictions where unbundled access has been provided demonstrates negative effects on investment and whether there is a commercial possibility for all parts of a geographic market to be served by alternative infrastructure providers.
11.257

If the above analysis on unbundling is correct, there is no need for recourse to fur-
ther legal arguments. However, the conclusion would be strengthened if it could be demonstrated that the last wire in the network is an essential facility. This again may depend on the service for which access is being requested. On the basis of current developments it seems likely that there will be a number of possible access networks suitable for the provision of voice telephony services to end-users, but there may be a much smaller number of networks capable of providing, for example, high-speed Internet access or other on-demand services. As indicated above, where there is more than one available network, issues of joint dominance will probably prove important.
11.258

Where the regulatory authority imposes a universal service obligation on the incumbent, it may prove relatively easy to demonstrate that the local loop is essen-
tial (at least in some areas of the Member State). This conclusion may also be easy to reach where there has been a universal service obligation in the past, leading to network investment which would have been impossible otherwise to justify on commercial terms.
11.259

Self-Supply, Supply to Third Parties, and Leveraging: The Relationship between Essential Facilities, Discrimination, and Unbundling

An important element in telecommunications cases is likely to be whether self-supply—the supply by a dominant operator to its own downstream operations—is sufficient to found a case of discrimination. The Access Notice is ambiguous on this point. At paragraph 84, the Notice distinguishes between three scenarios:
11.260

a. a refusal to grant access for the purposes of a service where another operator has been given access by the access provider to operate on that services market;
b. a refusal to grant access for the purposes of a service where no other operator has been given access by the access provider to operate on that services market;
c. a withdrawal of access from an existing customer.

11.261   The distinction between (a) and (b) depends on whether an operator has been given access, but the Notice does not make it clear whether this other operator could also be the downstream operation of the dominant operator.

11.262   There are difficulties with either interpretation. For example, if self-supply is insufficient to mount a discrimination case, then the incentive placed on a dominant company is to adopt the most restrictive approach possible and to supply its own operations but no one else. As soon as it supplies to a third party, it is obliged to supply subject to the obligations of Article 82.[193]

11.263   If, on the other hand, self-supply is sufficient to mount a discrimination case, then there are risks that discrimination arguments could be used to unpick the network of the incumbent at any or all levels.

11.264   Given the ambivalence in the Access Notice on this point, it is difficult to predict the outcome of any particular case. The *Bronner* case mentioned above would tend to argue for the former interpretation. However, the impact of other Article 82 analysis, such as bundling, may avoid the issue in practice.

11.265   Where a dominant operator refuses to sell a component requested by a third party, but is prepared to sell that component combined with other components which the third party does not want, it may, as discussed above, be committing an abuse. Thus where an operator seeks to combine various network elements in a single package, access to one of those network elements may be required as a consequence of the jurisprudence on bundling. This would avoid discussions of third party supply and the notion of essential facilities, and would impose a much lower evidential burden on the complainant.

11.266   Given this, the concept of essential facilities appears to be relevant only where no form of access has been given—ie where there are no pre-existing relations between the companies. It is in these circumstances that concerns over the use of the essential facilities doctrine—most notably that it is contrary to the principle of freedom of contract[194]—are most pronounced. Where there are some contractual relations between the companies, recourse to essential facilities may well not prove to be necessary as bundling or discrimination arguments may be more easily proved.

11.267   This interpretation would also tend to the conclusion that self-supply where there are other, at least partially substitutable, contractual relations with the party requesting access is sufficient to mount a discrimination argument.

---

[193]   Subject to issues of non-discrimination, proportionality, reasonableness, etc.
[194]   But see Case C–7/97 *Oscar Bronner GmbH v Mediaprint*, Opinion of 28 May 1998, not yet reported. At para 53, which sets out the laws of a number of Member States holding that an unjustified refusal to contract may constitute an abuse of a dominant position.

Thus, for example, if access to local loop infrastructure is already granted to a third **11.268** party, then any upgrades to the local loop infrastructure—such as higher capacity switches—should be made available on a non-discriminatory basis. Supply only to the downstream operations of the incumbent operator would be likely to be discriminatory without there being any need to prove that access to the improved infrastructure was essential.

Withdrawal of Supply

The Access Notice also refers to the situation where access has been granted in the **11.269** past but has now been withdrawn. On the basis of *Commercial Solvents*,[195] and in the absence of a clear objective justification, this would appear to be a relatively straightforward case of abuse.

Access as a Remedy to a Separate Abuse

Access issues will normally arise in the context of third parties actively seeking **11.270** access to a network. Where a refusal to provide access falls within one of the categories identified above, access may be ordered under the competition rules. A slightly different access issue arose in relation to the *BiB* case, where the Commission has published an Article 19(3) Notice. This case is discussed in more detail below (see Section F), but is also of interest here given the Commission's proposed conditions in relation to BT's cable interests, and its discussion of future possible action in relation to BT's customer access infrastructure.

BiB is to provide an interactive service using broadband (and one-way) satellite **11.271** delivery, together with a standard domestic telephone line to provide interactive information. From the perspective of BT, this would allow the delivery of an interactive service with the appearance of a greater broadband communications capacity than was actually the case, thus avoiding the capacity constraints of its using its own PSTN (public switched telecommunications network).

The Commission's statements in the Article 19(3) Notice identify a concern that **11.272** in diversifying its service provision interests away from its traditional network where it was dominant, BT was reducing its incentive to invest in upgrading its own network to broadband technology. This would have effects both on competition—in that the transmission mechanisms available to competitors of the BiB service were controlled largely by BT (either in respect of the PSTN or of the broadband cable interests held by BT)—and on technical and economic progress—in that only BT is currently in a position to manage investment in the PSTN. The Commission addressed this concern in two ways: first, by requiring BT to divest its broadband cable interests; secondly, by stating that it would re-examine the development of broadband PSTN in the UK in the short to medium

---

[195] Joined Cases 6 and 7/73 *Commercial Solvents* [1974] ECR 223.

term. The Commission explicitly envisaged unbundling BT's local loop (see below) if investment in BT's broadband infrastructure could be seen to have suffered as a result of BT's investment in BiB. Given recent developments in the UK, with Oftel proposing that BT should be required to unbundle the local loop in 2001, it would appear that the Commission's concerns should be diminished and a review will in any event be unnecessary.

Access Pricing[196]

11.273 The competition rules are generally ill-suited to establishing appropriate prices for goods or services. Although the competition rules do establish parameters within which pricing issues can be analysed, detailed pricing issues are more efficiently dealt with under sector specific regulation, where available. Nevertheless, the Commission has demonstrated in a number of cases a willingness to intervene in the pricing of, for example, call-termination services.

Discriminatory Pricing

11.274 If the Commission orders access to be given to a facility, it will order access on non-discriminatory terms, including as compared to the downstream operating arm of the dominant company.[197]

11.275 The issue of non-discrimination has been referred to above. It will be important to determine which services should benefit from non-discriminatory tariffs. For example, should mobile network operators be entitled to the same interconnection rates as fixed network operators? As indicated above, even where fixed and mobile voice services are determined to occupy different downstream markets, discriminating between them is likely to affect competition. It would appear difficult to identify the effect on competition resulting from charging different prices for international as compared to national termination services, but this cannot be excluded.

11.276 Secondly, application of the non-discrimination principle may be problematic either because an effect on competition is difficult to demonstrate, or because of the absence of an appropriate cost-accounting system which would demonstrate a non-discriminatory price.

Excessive Pricing

11.277 In these circumstances, the concept of excessive pricing may prove useful. To the extent that the service performed in, for example, terminating internationally-originated calls, rather than nationally-originated calls, is essentially the same in

---

[196] Competition aspects of access by service providers to the resources of telecommunications operators, study by Cave et al, European Commission, December 1995.
[197] Notice on the Application of the Competition Rules to Access Agreements in the Telecommunications Sector [1998] OJ C265/2, para 86.

each case, a dominant operator would risk allegations of excessive pricing were it to charge substantially different prices for the provision of comparable services.

While European competition law on excessive pricing is relatively sparse,[198] the Commission has given indications that this is an area which is likely to be developed in the telecommunications sector.[199] This is a rapidly developing area—the analysis of excessive pricing in telecommunications was one of the major additions to the Access Notice between the draft and final versions. The text of the Access Notice on this point also shows the importance of the relationship between the competition rules and sector specific regulation.

11.278

The starting point for an excessive pricing analysis is the actual costs incurred in providing a good or service. This is problematic in the telecommunications sector for a number of reasons. First, telecoms operators have traditionally been heavily vertically integrated and have not identified the costs associated with various operations: although they are now obliged to provide separate accounts for the purposes of interconnection, such accounts would in many cases not yet be established and by definition would be limited to one particular type of service. Secondly, many investments in telecommunications networks would have been made in a non-commercial environment, and the extent to which these should be regarded as having been recovered is difficult to quantify. This is related to the question as to the most appropriate accounting basis on which to calculate the costs. Traditionally the Commission has accepted the accounting methodology proposed by the dominant company, but there are indications that this will not necessarily be the case in the future. The Commission may seek to bring the competition rules into line with the ONP framework which suggests that long run average incremental cost is the appropriate cost base for network access.[200] Thirdly, identifying costs of, for example, interconnection would entail detailed allocation of common costs. All of these would tend to make a cost based analysis difficult in the telecommunications sector.

11.279

In *Ahmed Saeed*, however, the Court indicated that in order to determine an excessive price, it is possible to have reference to pricing principles contained in sector specific legislation. Given that pricing principles constitute an important part of the ONP regulatory framework, this type of analysis could be extremely useful in determining an excessive price in the telecommunications sector. This position is strengthened further by the Court's judgment in *Grimaldi*, where it held that in interpreting Community law a national court should have regard to recommendations issued by

11.280

---

[198] See, for example, Case 26/75 *General Motors Continental v Commission* [1975] ECR 1367.

[199] Haag and Klotz, 'Excessive Pricing in the Telecommunications Sector', DGIV *Competition Policy Newsletter*, Summer 1998.

[200] See, for example, Notice on the Application of the Competition Rules to Access Agreements in the Telecommunications Sector [1998] OJ C265/2, discussion on predatory pricing at paras 110–116.

the Commission, especially where those guidelines were aimed at interpreting Community law.[201] If it is appropriate for a national court to rely on such recommendations, it must be similarly appropriate for the European Commission to do so. This leads to the conclusion in the Access Notice that in determining an excessive price under the competition rules, regard should be had to relevant sector specific legislation and to recommendations issued by the European Commission which interpret that legislation. This is particularly important when looking at the question of interconnection, as the European Commission has issued best practice guidelines on interconnection principles and pricing: these are referred to in the Access Notice and it is likely that, in applying Article 82, the European Commission will use these guidelines as a benchmark in determining what constitutes an excessive price.

11.281   A third possible line of argument results from the Court's judgment in *Bodson*. The Court held that in determining whether a price charged is excessive, regard can be had to prices charged in other geographic areas. This appears vulnerable to the criticism that prices can differ sharply between Member States and may, for example, be influenced by the degree of competition in the particular market—the absence of competition would tend to lead to inefficient operation, higher costs, and higher prices. Although this is logical, *Bodson* itself dealt with an activity carried out under special and exclusive rights, which could therefore be expected to suffer from these inefficiencies. If the Court nevertheless concluded that comparison with other markets was possible in that case, there appears to be reason to believe that the Court would uphold the practice in the telecommunications sector as well, particularly when full liberalization has taken place.

F. Set Top Boxes

11.282   This section addresses competition issues concerning access to set top boxes. It is therefore focused on the media sector. However, the issues which arise may also be pertinent to other sectors. For example, control of intermediate technical standards and/or equipment may be a source of problems in both the telecommunications and information technology sectors.[202]

---

[201]   Case 322/88 *Salvatore Grimaldi v Fonds des Maladies Professionnelles* [1989] ECR 4407: '18 . . . the [recommendations] in question cannot therefore be regarded as having no legal effect. The national courts are bound to take recommendations into consideration in order to decide disputes submitted to them, in particular where they cast light on the interpretation of national measures adopted in order to implement them or where they are designed to supplement binding Community provisions'.

[202]   See for example, the Symbian joint venture which was dealt with under the Merger Regulation and concerned the development of an operating system for wireless information devices combining the functions of hand-held computers and mobile telephones: IP/98/762; IP/98/1181; and IP/99/65. The decisions have not yet been made public.

This section begins with an overview of the purpose and relevance of set top boxes, **11.283** with a particular focus on digital television, before considering the applicable regulatory framework. Thereafter, it discusses the principal decisions in which the Commission has considered issues surrounding set top boxes. Both the facts and the legal reasoning in these decisions are complicated. Moreover, given the rapid developments in the technical services market, it may be that their use as precedents should be treated with caution.

(1) Overview

Analogue set top boxes have been of relevance only for television broadcasters **11.284** which are funded wholly or mainly by viewers' subscriptions. Television broadcasters which are funded by advertising revenue, public subsidy or both provide a service to all viewers who possess a television set.[203] Subscription-funded broadcasters, in contrast, must ensure that only those viewers who have paid a subscription are able to watch the television service. This is achieved by broadcasting the signal of the television service in an encrypted form. Subscribers then rent or purchase a set top box which decrypts the television signal and allows them to view the service. The collection of subscriptions is achieved by a subscriber management system.

Thus, subscription-funded television companies require a special technical infra- **11.285** structure. It is comprised of a number of basic elements, namely:

— a set top box;

— an encryption system (conditional access system) which is compatible with the set top box; and

— a subscriber management system.

We refer to the combination of these services hereafter as 'technical services'.

Implications of introduction of digital television. In contrast to analogue set **11.286** top boxes, both subscription-funded and advertising or State-funded television companies will require access to digital set top boxes, at least in the initial phase of digital broadcasting. This is because the current generation of television sets is analogue. Digital broadcast signals must be converted into an analogue form which can be displayed by current television sets. This process is known as 'demodulation'. All digital broadcasters will require demodulation of the television signal to allow viewers to watch their channels, until all viewers have bought digital television sets. Digital set top boxes will therefore typically include demodulation capabilities, in addition to the conditional access capabilities found in analogue set top boxes. The demodulation function will be included in digital set

---

[203] Subject only to any legal requirement to pay a fee for ownership of a television.

top boxes. It is likely to take a number of years before the transition to digitial tele-vision sets is complete,[204] and in the meantime, digital set top boxes will remain important.

11.287 **Proprietary set top boxes[205] and technical services.**   Conditional access systems are generally proprietary and embedded in the set top box.[206] This means that the set top box can descramble only those signals which are encrypted with that par-ticular conditional access system. There are a number of different proprietary conditional access systems operating in the EU.

11.288 The set top box may contain further proprietary elements, such as:

- an electronic programme guide (EPG—the navigational device which basically allows viewers to tune between different channels); and

- an application programming interface (API—the software which allows the features of the box to be controlled and used by broadcasters or interactive ser-vices providers; this allows, for example, interactivity in the form of broadcast icons directing viewers to 'side-channels' or interactive services).

These features can be used only by operators which have access to the underlying technology.

11.289 Access to the proprietary elements in set top boxes is controlled by the company which supplies the underlying proprietary technical services.[207] This applies equally to analogue and digital set top boxes.

11.290 **Structure of technical services market.**   There are two general points to note about the structure of the technical services market. First, in the EU, suppliers of technical services tend also to be pay TV operators. When pay TV operators entered the market, the technical services necessary for pay TV did not exist. It was therefore logical that they developed the technical services themselves. As stated above, the technology for the technical services they use is generally propri-etary. Secondly, there is a considerable first-mover advantage associated with tech-nical services. The pay TV operator which is first to market will install a base of subscribers with set top boxes. As the set top boxes are generally proprietary, they will be compatible only with that pay TV operator's conditional access system and its other technical services. A new entrant in pay TV is unlikely to find launching a second set top box to be an economic proposition. The investment required to

---

[204] The target date for ending analogue transmission of terrestrial channels is being discussed in a number of Member States. It is unlikely to take place until 2005 at the very earliest. The UK has been discussing a target date of 2008.

[205] Set top boxes (STBs) are sometimes referred to as decoders.

[206] However, this is not the case in all countries.

[207] See reference to common interface in section on Directive 95/47.

do so is substantial and consumers who have already bought a set top box would be reluctant to buy a second (at least until the retail price of set top boxes has significantly decreased).

The combination of these two facts means that a new entrant in subscription-funded television is often dependent on his incumbent competitor for supply of the technical services necessary to access consumers through existing set top boxes. All pay TV companies which wish to begin a digital service must launch digital set top boxes. In a number of European countries competing digital pay TV services have been launched contemporaneously using different conditional access systems and set top boxes.[208] However, the problem remains in that the 'dominant' digital pay TV supplier will also control the largest number of digital set top boxes in the market and, to the extent that they are proprietary, the access of competitors to those boxes.

11.291

It follows from the above that the controller of a proprietary set top box (whether analogue or digital) is in a powerful gatekeeper position. This raises competition problems in terms of foreclosure of competition in downstream markets. Just as in the telecommunications sector, access issues are therefore central.

11.292

The importance of regulating digital conditional access services has been recognized by the Community legislature. A Directive setting the regulatory framework in respect of digital conditional access services and digital set top boxes was adopted in 1995. The following section will describe the regulatory framework for the provision of digital conditional access services set out in the Directive.

11.293

(2) Regulatory Framework for Digital Conditional Access

Directive (EC) 95/47 on the use of standards for the transmission of television signals[209] (often referred to as the Advanced TV Standards Directive) contains provisions on three elements which are relevant to digital conditional access services. These are the standardization of digital transmission signals, mandatory provision of digital conditional access services, and minimum requirements with respect to the specifications and capabilities of digital set top boxes and digital television sets. It also requires Member States to establish dispute resolution procedures.[210]

11.294

Standardization of digital transmission signals. Article 2(c) of the Directive provides that '(a)ll television services transmitted to viewers in the Community

11.295

---

[208] This was the case in France with Canal Satéllite and Télévision par Satéllite (TPS) and will be the case in the United Kingdom with BSkyB, BDB, and individual cable operators.

[209] Directive (EC) 95/47 of the European Parliament and of the Council on the use of standards for the transmission of television signals [1995] OJ L281/51.

[210] Article 4(e): '. . . Member States shall ensure that any party having an unresolved dispute concerning the application of the provisions established in this Article shall have easy, and in principle inexpensive, access to appropriate dispute resolution procedures with the objective of resolving such disputes in a fair, timely and transparent manner'.

whether by cable, satellite or terrestrial means shall: . . . (c) if they are fully digital, use a transmission system which has been standardised by a recognised European standardisation body'. Standardized transmission standards exist for digital cable, digital satellite and digital terrestrial transmission and each is different. It follows from this that neither proprietary transmission signal standards nor proprietary demodulation standards are permitted.

11.296 **Provision of digital conditional access services.**   Article 4(b) of the Directive provides that: 'Conditional access systems operated on the market in the Community shall have the necessary technical capability for cost-effective transcontrol at cable head-ends allowing the possibility for full control by cable television operators at local or regional level of the services using such conditional access systems.' Article 4(c) of the Directive provides as follows:

> Member States shall take all the necessary measures to ensure that the operators of conditional access services, irrespective of the means of transmission, who produce and market access services to digital television services:
>
> — offer to all broadcasters, on a fair, reasonable and non-discriminatory basis, technical services enabling the broadcaster's digitally-transmitted services to be received by viewers authorised by means of decoders administered by the service operators, and comply with Community competition law, in particular if a dominant position appears;
> — keep separate financial accounts regarding their activity as conditional access providers.
> — Broadcasters shall publish a list of tariffs for the viewer which takes into account whether associated equipment is supplied or not.
> — A digital television service may take advantage of these provisions only if the services offered comply with the European legislation in force.

11.297 There are a number of important points to note with regard to the obligations imposed by the Directive on suppliers of conditional access services:

— A company which only self-supplies digital conditional access services is not subject to any obligations.[211]

— Member States have transposed the 'fair, reasonable and non-discriminatory' obligation into national law in widely varying degrees of detail.[212]

— The obligations are limited in scope to the provision of conditional access services for 'digital television services'. This term is not defined. However, it would appear to exclude end-user services which are not broadcast and/or are not television services. For example, a supplier of interactive services, such as home banking, which makes use of both broadcast and on-line data transmission would seem to have only limited rights under the Directive, if any.

---

[211] This may be the case of cable operators.
[212] Contrast UK implementation with France/Germany.

This would also appear to be the case for providers of digital radio services or, looking more to the future, a provider of a video-on-demand service via an upgraded telecommunications network.[213] If this interpretation is correct, it is an important lacuna as conditional access services are relevant to both these and other types of service.[214]

— The Directive requires conditional access operators to supply the 'technical services' which broadcasters require to enable viewers to view their service via the set top box. Again, the term 'technical service' is not defined. It is important to note that the supply of conditional access services alone may not allow viewers to view a particular service. For example, access to an embedded proprietary EPG or to an embedded proprietary API may also be required.[215]

— The scope of the provision on transcontrol[216] is also somewhat unclear. It is not clear whether the term 'full control' extends beyond decryption of the signal to other matters such as interoperability of embedded interactive applications.

Digital set top box specifications.   Article 4(a) provides that: **11.298**

All consumer equipment, for sale or rent or otherwise made available in the Community, capable of descrambling digital television signals, shall posses the capability:

— to allow the descrambling of such signals according to the common European scrambling algorithm as administered by a recognised European standardisation body;
— to display signals that have been transmitted in clear provided that, in the event that such equipment is rented, the rentee is in compliance with the relevant rental agreement'.

Article 4(d) provides that:

When granting licences to manufacturers of consumer equipment, holders of industrial property rights to conditional access products and systems shall ensure that this

---

[213] The capacity constraints of traditional copper pair telecommunications local loop infrastructure can be upgraded to make it suitable for the provision of such services by the installation of digital switching technology, such as asynchronous digital subscriber loop technology (ADSL) or a variant.

[214] Indeed, in transposing the Directive, the UK also extended its scope to cover such services. In that context, the provision of conditional access services for non-broadcast and non-television services has been called 'access control' services.

[215] The Commission is currently considering the extension of the scope of the Directive—Green Paper on the Convergence of the Telecommunications, Media and Information Technology Sectors, and the Implications for Regulation. Towards an Information Society Approach [COM(97)623]; Communication to the European Parliament, the Council, the Economic and Social Committee and the Committee of the Regions, Results of the Public Consultation on the Green Paper COM(1999) 108 final.

[216] Transcontrol is the process by which cable operators receive an encrypted television signal at the cable head-end which they then descramble in order to provide the television service to viewers connected to their cable network.

is done on fair, reasonable and non-discriminatory terms. Taking into account technical and commercial factors, holders of rights shall not subject the granting of licences to conditions prohibiting, deterring or discouraging the inclusion in the same product of:

— a common interface allowing connection with several other access systems, or
— means specific to another access system, provided that the licensee complies with the relevant and reasonable conditions ensuring, as far as he is concerned, the security of transactions of conditional access system operators.
— Where television sets contain an integrated digital decoder such sets must allow for the option of fitting at least one standardised socket permitting connection of conditional access and other elements of a digital television system of the digital decoder.

11.299 Two points in particular are noteworthy. First, there is no requirement that set top boxes contain demodulators (or even interface ports) for all means of transmission. Secondly, proprietary conditional access systems embedded in set top boxes are implicitly accepted, as the Directive does not impose the inclusion of a common interface[217] in set top boxes. However, it does prevent conditional access operators from preventing manufacturers either from including a common interface or a second conditional access system within set top boxes, provided that the security of the box is not affected.

11.300 **Revision of Directive linked to Convergence Green Paper.**[218] The Directive foresaw a review of its operation and scope within two years of its adoption.[219] This review has not taken place. However, in the Convergence Green Paper, the Commission raised the possibility of extending the scope of the Directive to regulate access to proprietary electronic programme guides and application programming interfaces which are embedded in set top boxes. At the time of writing, no proposal to this effect has been submitted to the Council and European Parliament by the Commission.

11.301 **Relation between Directive and competition law.** As Articles 81 and 82 are primary law set out in the Treaty, their scope cannot be limited by secondary law such as a Directive. Abiding by the terms of the Directive therefore provides no guarantee of compliance with broader competition law. However, it should be noted that, as the Directive contains dispute settlement provisions,[220] the Commission

---

[217] Inclusion of a common interface would allow the set top box to function with different conditional access systems. The absence of a common interface means that the set top box is tied to a particular conditional access system.

[218] Green Paper on the Convergence of the Telecommunications, Media and Information Technology Sectors, and the Implications for Regulation. Towards an Information Society Approach [COM(97)623]. Communication to the European Parliament, the Council, the Economic and Social Committee and the Committee of the Regions, Results of the Public Consultation on the Green Paper COM(1999) 108 final.

[219] Article 6.

[220] Article 4(e).

may well choose not to give priority to complaints surrounding the supply of technical services which are governed by the Directive,[221] at least to the extent that the dispute settlement provisions can be seen to be effective and that the requirements of the Directive are broadly comparable to those under the competition rules.

(3) *Market Definition*

Technical and administrative services for pay TV. *MSG Media Services*[222] was **11.302** the first formal Commission decision to consider issues relating to set top boxes and conditional access services. One of the markets found to be affected by the operation was that for 'administrative and technical services for pay-TV'. This market primarily concerned:

— the making available of decoders (to pay TV subscribers);
— the handling of conditional access;
— subscriber management in respect of pay TV customers; and
— settlement of accounts with programme suppliers.[223]

This market definition was followed more recently in the *Kirch/Bertelsmann/* **11.303** *Deutsche Telekom* cases,[224] which concerned the successor operation to MSG. In contrast to *MSG* which was focused on digital television, but also concerned analogue, these cases were concerned with technical services for digital television only. The market was described as including the development of conditional access technology and its supply, and the marketing of set top boxes and smart cards. The Commission did not distinguish between markets for technical services for analogue and digital pay TV.

In the *BiB* case, the Commission has indicated its provisional view[225] that one **11.304** of the markets affected by the creation of the joint venture is that for 'technical and administrative services for digital interactive TV services and retail pay TV'. In concluding that the market for technical services included those necessary for both pay TV and digital interactive TV services, the Commission noted that:

> There is a very large area of overlap between the technical and administrative services necessary for retail pay TV and the services necessary for digital interactive TV services. These services include the provision of conditional access, access to the Electronic Programme Guide (EPG) and access to the Application Programming Interface (API).

---

[221] Notice on the Application of the Competition Rules to Access Agreements in the Telecommunications Sector [1998] OJ C265/2, at paras 28 and 30.

[222] *MSG* (Case IV/M469) [1994] OJ L364/1.

[223] ibid, para 26.

[224] *Bertelsmann/Kirch/Premiere* (Case IV/M993)(1998) [1999] OJ L53/1 and *Deutsche Telekom/ BetaResearch* (Case IV/M1027) (1998) [1999] OJ L53/31.

[225] Notice pursuant to Article 19(3) of Regulation 17 [1998] OJ C322/6.

It went on to conclude that 'access control services', defined as conditional access services for on-line as opposed to broadcast services, and the technical infrastructure necessary to allow transactions to be carried out were also part of the market. Although this market definition is a provisional conclusion, it appears likely to be maintained given that it reflects the statement made in *MSG* that 'it must be assumed that there will be a single market for services relating to digital pay TV and other digital interactive television communications services'.[226]

11.305 **Narrower markets.** There is no formal decision in which a market has been defined in respect of one or more of the individual services comprising the technical services necessary for pay TV and interactive services. As the services are not substitutable, it appears likely that the Commission would identify narrower markets should it prove necessary in a particular case. The decisions cited above do indicate that the Commission would be willing to consider doing so.

11.306 The *MSG* decision states that in the future separate markets for subscriber management and conditional access services may emerge.[227] The *Kirch/Bertelsmann/Deutsche Telekom* decisions raise the possibility of separate markets in respect of technical services for cable and satellite pay TV.[228] Finally, in the Article 19(3) Notice published in the *BiB* case,[229] the Commission refers to the possibility of separate markets existing in respect of the services constituting conditional access, access to the electronic programme guide, and access to the application programming interface.

11.307 **Geographic markets.** The geographic market for the supply of technical services has been defined in light of the geographic market definition of the pay TV market for which the technical services are supplied.

(4) Competition Issues

11.308 To date, the Commission has been called upon to examine issues relating to technical services only in the context of the creation of joint ventures providing such services. In the *MSG Media Services*,[230] *Bertelsmann/Kirch/Premiere*,[231] and *Deutsche Telekom/BetaResearch*[232] decisions, adopted under the Merger Regulation, the Commission concluded that the operations would create a dom-

---

[226] *MSG* (Case IV/M469) [1994] OJ L364/1, at para 31(f).
[227] *MSG* (Case IV/M469) [1994] OJ L364/1, at paras 31(f) and 70.
[228] *Bertelsmann/Kirch/Premiere* (Case IV/M993) (1998) [1999] OJ L53/1, at paras 19–21 and *Deutsche Telekom/BetaResearch* (Case IV/M1027) (1998) [1999] OJ L53/31, at paras 16–18.
[229] The Notice pursuant to Article 19(3) of Regulation 17 [1998] OJ C322 in the *BiB* case states that conditional access comprises the inclusion of authorization signals in the broadcast data stream (entitlement control messages, entitlement management messages, and verification); and subscriber management services, including provision of smart cards compatible with a decoder population.
[230] *MSG* (Case IV/M469) [1994] OJ L364/1.
[231] *Bertelsmann/Kirch/Premiere* (Case IV/M993) (1998) [1999] OJ L53/1.
[232] *Deutsche Telekom/BetaResearch* (Case IV/M1027) (1998) [1999] OJ L53/31.

inant position in the technical services market which would, in turn, create or strengthen the parents' dominant positions in the downstream pay TV and cable networks markets. Inherently, therefore, the operations foreclosed competition from third parties in both the technical services and downstream markets.[233] The Commission's decision in *Bertelsmann/Kirch/Premiere* is currently under appeal.[234] (A further prohibition decision, *NSD*,[235] was also adopted under the Merger Regulation, but the issue of technical services arose more marginally.) In the case of the BiB joint venture, the Commission has indicated its intention to exempt the joint venture under Regulation 17.[236] The Commission thus appears to have concluded that the creation of BiB will neither create a dominant position in the technical services market, nor strengthen the position of its parents, in particular BSkyB and BT, in downstream markets. The focus of the proposed conditions in the Article 19(3) Notice has been to ensure that BiB and its parent BSkyB do not use their position in the technical services market to foreclose competition in downstream markets. Non-discriminatory access to BiB-subsidized set top boxes has thus been crucial.

11.309 The effect of vertical integration has been the central concern. Two basic issues have thus been addressed by the Commission to date: dominance on the market for technical services; and the consequent strengthening of the parents' positions on downstream markets. The parties' positions on downstream markets have been key to a finding of dominance on the technical services market; in turn the Commission has emphasized that dominance on the technical services market can be leveraged into downstream markets. Given the risk that dominance can be leveraged either up- or downstream, there is thus a certain circularity to the analysis set out in the Commission's decisions.

11.310 This section will consider the questions of dominance on the technical services market and its use to create or strengthen dominance on other markets before considering issues relating to access to set top boxes which may arise in the future under Article 82. Although there are no formal decisions dealing with the abuse of a pre-existing dominant position on the technical services market, the cases dealing with joint ventures give some indication of the Commission's likely position.

---

[233] The Commission reached the same conclusion in the *Cablevision* case. A prohibition decision was avoided as the parties withdrew the notification. See *Report on Competition Policy 1996* (Vol XXVI) at points 150 and 151.

[234] Case T–121/98 *Taurus v Commission*.

[235] *Nordic Satellite Distribution* (Case IV/M490) (1995) [1996] OJ L53/20.

[236] Notice pursuant to Article 19(3) of Regulation 17 [1998] OJ C322/5.

Dominance in the Technical Services Market

11.311 As indicated above, all of the cases examined by the Commission to date have concerned operations on the technical services market by parties with strong positions on downstream markets, and in particular on the markets for pay TV or cable networks. As the cable network market has been relevant as a means of transmission of pay TV, the downstream market essentially in cause has been the pay TV market. (Other markets may also be relevant in the future with the development of new downstream services.[237]) The positions of the suppliers of technical services on these downstream markets have been central to the Commission's finding of dominance on the technical services market. A subsidiary issue which has arisen largely as a means by which to allay a finding of dominance based on the parties' downstream positions has been the extent to which the suppliers of technical services are able to control the supply of these services to potential competitors in the technical services market.

11.312 The Commission's thesis thus appears to be that competition on the technical services market is shaped by the competitive situation on the pay TV market. In this context, it is important to distinguish between retail operators of pay TV, that is those companies which package a selection of channels for which a subscription fee is charged, and providers of individual channels. Pay TV operators may retail both their own and third party channels. This retail activity is often referred to as operation of a pay TV platform. Regardless of the ownership of the channels, it is the pay TV platform operator which will determine the technical services used. This would suggest that where a single company holds a dominant position in the pay TV market (ie as a pay TV platform operator) and is also active on the technical services market, it will also hold a dominant position there.

Importance of Parties' Positions on Downstream Markets

11.313 *Bertelsmann/Kirch/Deutsche Telekom* **decisions.** The link between dominance on the technical services market and the position of the suppliers of technical services in downstream markets is made most clear in the *Bertelsmann/Kirch/Premiere* and *Deutsche Telekom/BetaResearch* prohibition decisions.[238] These cases involved two distinct operations within the meaning of the Merger Regulation and therefore two notifications (and thus decisions) were required. However, the Commission stressed that they were closely linked as together they

---

[237] For example, in the *BiB* case one of the downstream markets in question was that for digital interactive television services: *BiB* (Notice pursuant to Article 19(3) of Regulation 17) [1998] OJ C322/5.

[238] See also *MSG* (Case IV/M469) [1994] OJ L364/1, in particular at paras 56, 61, and 72. 'Any potential competitor of MSG would therefore have to create a customer base without having the programmes of the future leading pay-TV supplier available for its technical infrastructure. This increases substantially the economic risk for an alternative service supplier.'

would form the framework for the introduction of digital television in Germany.[239] The first operation concerned the concentration of Bertelsmann and Kirch's pay television interests in Premiere, together with the acquisition of joint control of BetaDigital (until then a subsidiary of Kirch) which was to supply technical services for digital satellite television. The second concerned the acquisition of joint control in BetaResearch by Bertelsmann, Kirch, and Deutsche Telekom. BetaResearch had also been a subsidiary of Kirch. Its purpose was the supply of technical services for digital cable television. Premiere was to provide its own subscriber management services. It would use the d-box set top box which embedded BetaResearch and BetaDigital's proprietary conditional access system, electronic programme guide, and application programming interface. The latter companies would thus supply the necessary technical services to Premiere for accessing the d-box.

The Commission concluded that the concentration of Bertelsmann and Kirch's   **11.314** pay TV interests in Premiere would create a near-monopoly on the pay TV market and that Deutsche Telekom was dominant in the cable network market in Germany. The Commission further concluded that the operation would create a dominant position in the technical services market and that this would reinforce the parents' positions in the downstream markets. The downstream positions of Bertelsmann, Kirch, and Deutsche Telekom were relevant in two respects to the Commission's conclusion.

Bertelsmann/Kirch/Deutsche Telekom decisions: **Elimination of potential com-**   **11.315** **petition.**   The creation of a joint venture between the only actual or potential pay TV operators, Bertelsmann and Kirch, and the dominant cable network operator eliminated potential competition in the supply of technical services for pay TV. The possibility of pay TV operators using a different set top box and technical services in respect of pay TV transmitted either by satellite or by cable in the German-speaking area[240] was thus excluded. This conclusion appears to follow on from the Commission's statements in the *MSG Media Services* decision, that each of Bertelsmann, Kirch, and Deutsche Telekom had an interest to supply technical services and each was financially capable of doing so alone.[241]

Bertelsmann/Kirch/Deutsche Telekom decisions: **Particular importance of pay**   **11.316** **TV.**   The merger to monopoly of Bertelsmann and Kirch's pay TV interests removed any incentive for further entry into the technical services market. This being so, there were, in fact, no undertakings in respect of the supply of technical services which the parties could offer to prevent the creation of a dominant position on the technical services market. There were other barriers to entry into the

---

[239] *Bertelsmann/Kirch/Premiere* (Case IV/M993) (1998) [1999] OJ L53/1, at para 11.
[240] *Deutsche Telekom/BetaResearch* (Case IV/M1027) (1998) [1999] OJ L53/31, at para 34.
[241] *MSG* (Case IV/M469) [1994] OJ L364/1, at para 56.

pay TV market, such as the lack of attractive available pay TV programming rights. For as long as Premiere remained the only digital pay TV platform, all actual and potential content providers would be obliged to become part of the Premiere pay TV offering and there would be no alternative technical services supplier.

11.317 The only prospect of competition in the technical services market would be if a competitor to Premiere in the pay TV market emerged. Without competition in pay TV, there would be no entry into the technical services market:

> The installation of an alternative technical infrastructure for the transmission of pay-TV would require a major investment. However, other potential suppliers would be prepared to make that investment only if there were corresponding opportunities for market penetration. That would be so only if it were possible for a second pay-TV operator to set up in Germany. Such an operator could either create his own technical platform, on the basis of alternative access technology, or offer another party an opportunity of developing a technical infrastructure. But as already indicated, it is improbable that a second pay-TV operator will enter the market, given Premiere's established position, with its subscriber base and, especially, its programme resources.[242]

11.318 However, the emergence of a second pay TV operator would not necessarily mean that there would be competition in the technical services market:

> In theory, a pay-TV operator has a choice between distributing programmes via an existing decoder infrastructure or building up a new decoder infrastructure. In practice, however, a new programme supplier entering the market will have to use the services and infrastructure of the pay-TV operator already established on the market. This follows in particular from the fact that the economic risk is too great to justify installing a new infrastructure for a new programme. Households will not normally be prepared to procure another decoder in order to receive another pay-TV bouquet. This is true whether the new decoder is for sale or for hire.[243]

11.319 A subsidiary argument was that even if a second pay TV supplier did emerge, Deutsche Telekom's position in the cable market[244] would prevent it from using its own technical services. Most households in Germany received television by cable: launching a pay TV service only via satellite would not be feasible. As the private cable operators' networks were confined to the local loop, they were dependent on Deutsche Telekom's backbone cable infrastructure. In order to supply technical services other than those offered by Deutsche Telekom, investment in backbone infrastructure would be required. This was in itself an uneconomic proposition given the fact that the private cable operators' networks were spread throughout Germany.

---

[242] *Deutsche Telekom/BetaResearch* (Case IV/M1027) (1998) [1999] OJ L53/31, at para 35.
[243] *Bertelsmann/Kirch/Premiere* (Case IV/M993) (1998) [1999] OJ L53/1, at para 56.
[244] *MSG* (Case IV/M469) [1994] OJ L364/1, at para 61: Deutsche Telekom's satellite interests were also referred to and in particular the fact that it held the second largest holding in SES.

It was therefore Premiere's near-monopoly position on the pay TV market that   **11.320**
determined the market positions of BetaResearch and BetaDigital respectively on
the technical services market. There would be no new entry using technical services other than those used by Premiere as this would only be justifiable if there
was an alternative pay TV operator to Premiere. Even if such an operator were to
emerge, it was unlikely that it would choose to use technical services other than
those of Bertelsmann, Kirch, and Deutsche Telekom. The Commission therefore
concluded that BetaDigital and BetaResearch would each have monopoly positions in respect of the supply of technical services for digital satellite and digital
cable transmission respectively.

Control of Technical Services

A further issue which has been considered by the Commission in relation to dom-   **11.321**
inance in the technical services market is the extent to which the parties control
the supply of their technical services to actual or potential competitors in this market. This issue has arisen in the context of undertakings offered by parties with significant downstream positions which were designed to ensure that third parties
could supply technical services independently. However, it would also be relevant
in the absence of vertical integration as part of an analysis of barriers to entry: a
company which did not control the supply of a particular form of technical services would be unable to prevent entry by competitors using the same technology.

Proprietary Technical Services

It is clear that the owners and/or exclusive licensees of proprietary technical ser-   **11.322**
vices control their supply to third parties. In such circumstances, and in the presence of vertical integration, the Commission has concluded that the suppliers
would be unlikely to license their competitors on fair, reasonable, and non-
discriminatory terms as to do so would not be in their economic interest as it
would create competition to themselves.[245]

Bertelsmann/Kirch/Deutsche Telekom **decisions: control must be removed as a**   **11.323**
matter of fact.   The only solution, therefore, would be to remove the parties'
control over the supply of technical services. However, to be acceptable the control must be removed as a matter of fact. Thus, in the *Bertelsmann/Kirch/Deutsche
Telekom* decisions, the Commission rejected the parties' offer to open the share
capital of BetaResearch to third parties and to grant such third parties equivalent
voting rights and to license the Beta technology conditional access system and API

---

[245] See *Deutsche Telekom/BetaResearch* (Case IV/M1027) (1998) [1999] OJ L53/31, at para 39:
'BetaResearch might therefore use its licensing policy to hamper other service providers' access to
the market.' This was all the more likely given that BetaResearch was jointly controlled by a pay-TV
operator, which had no interest to promote competition to itself on the pay TV market: see *Deutsche
Telekom/BetaResearch* (Case IV/M1027) (1998) [1999] OJ L53/31, at para 38. *Bertelsmann/
Kirch/Premiere* (Case IV/M993) (1998) [1999] OJ L53/1, at para 111.

to third party broadcasters and manufacturers on standard terms with the fee to be determined, if necessary, by independent arbitration. First, it concluded first that Bertelsmann, Kirch, and Deutsche Telekom's joint control of the technology and its future development were not removed as Bertelsmann and Kirch would still be able to outvote third parties and therefore to control the set top box technology. The parties common interests would mean that they would not allow themselves to be outvoted by third parties.[246] Secondly, the Commission concluded that competition in the technical services market depended on the existence of competition in the pay TV market and that the undertakings on the technical services market were insufficient to achieve this.[247]

11.324 **MSG: common interface insufficient.** The Commission has also been unwilling to accept that dominance in the technical services market is removed by the inclusion of a 'common interface' in the set top box, at least in the presence of vertical integration. Such a common interface would allow the set top box to descramble signals using any conditional access system. This was one of the undertakings offered by the parties in the *MSG Media Services* decision. However, the Commission concluded that this undertaking would not prevent MSG from holding a dominant position 'on the separate conditional access and subscriber management market that could then in theory exist. Thanks to the business potential of Bertelsmann and Kirch in the pay-TV area, MSG will on its market probably benefit from economies of scale (subscriber base, number of programmes handled) that would make competition from other service providers much more difficult.'[248]

11.325 Any new pay TV supplier would be dependent on MSG for conditional access and subscriber management as subscribers would not want to deal with a number of different companies for technical services. The 'programme resources' of Bertelsmann and Kirch would ensure that MSG had a favoured position in the technical services market as they would be able 'most rapidly . . . and most extensively to provide the digital pay-TV market with attractive programmes'. The Commission stated that the 'suction effect' of Bertelsmann and Kirch's involvement in a technical services supplier would be countered most easily by a cable

---

[246] *Bertelsmann/Kirch/Premiere* (Case IV/M993) (1998) [1999] OJ L53/1, at para 154.

[247] *Bertelsmann/Kirch/Premiere* (Case IV/M993) (1998) [1999] OJ L53/1, at para 155. 'It is true that opening up the possibility for third parties to take a holding in BetaResearch and the simultaneous abandonment of the veto and special rights of the existing shareholders is an important concession since it will enable the structurally safeguarded control of the technology and its further development to be lifted. However, since no alternative technical platform will emerge without the chance of an alternative programme platform, the undertaking regarding BetaResearch is inadequate, even in connection with the further undertakings proposed by the parties concerning the CA licence, the API and the manufacturing licence, to prevent Premiere and BetaDigital from, in the long term, dominating the market.' *Deutsche Telekom/BetaResearch* (Case IV/M1027) (1998) [1999] OJ L53/31, at para 79.

[248] *MSG* (Case IV/M469) [1994] OJ L364/1, at para 70.

operator which supplied technical services for pay TV itself 'and possibly offered cable customers programme packages which it had itself put together'. Only Deutsche Telekom could perform this role, which led the Commission to conclude that 'as a result of Telekom's involvement in MSG, therefore, a market structure is created which suggests that MSG will have a dominant position even where a common interface is used'.[249] This decision reinforces the conclusion that dominance on the technical services and pay TV markets are fundamentally intertwined. Removing technical control of a set top box by including a common interface will therefore not necessarily prevent a finding of dominance. It is also important to note that while the inclusion of a common interface allows a set top box to function with a number of different proprietary conditional access systems, it does not address problems caused by embedded proprietary electronic programming guides or application programming interfaces. Thus, structural control of important aspects of the set top box is maintained.

Non-Proprietary Technical Services

The Commission has not yet been confronted with a situation in which the technical services which are the object of an operation are not proprietary and has not therefore had to consider the factors relevant to dominance in the supply of non-proprietary technical services. This is not surprising given that proprietary technical services are the norm in the EU. The reasoning set out above from the *MSG* decision in relation to the insufficiency of a common interface would certainly suggest that where the parties to a technical services operation hold a dominant position on the pay television market, then they will *de facto* control the technical services which are the industry standard regardless of whether the technical services are proprietary.
11.326

However, this conclusion should be treated with caution. Open standardization agreements are generally looked upon favourably under the competition rules. Indeed, Article 4(2) of Regulation 17 explicitly singles out standardization agreements for special treatment: in contrast to most other agreements, they may be exempted under Article 81(3) EC from a date prior to that of their notification. What is more, where the technical services are based on an open, non-proprietary standard then there would appear to be no barriers to entry for other suppliers of those technical services.
11.327

Relevance of Regulation of Digital Conditional Access Services to Finding of Dominance

There is no reference in the *Bertelsmann/Kirch/Deutsche Telekom* decisions to the fact that the provision of digital conditional access services is regulated. This may be due to the fact that while reliance on regulation is appropriate in respect of
11.328

---

[249] *MSG* (Case IV/M469) [1994] OJ L364/1, at para 72.

existing competition problems, it cannot be used to justify the creation of new problems.

Creation or Strengthening of Dominance on Other Markets

11.329 The creation of a joint venture to supply technical services by a company which has an interest in downstream markets for which the services are relevant (at the moment, pay TV and cable networks, although other services are likely to be relevant in the future) may well create a structural problem. Vertical integration of this sort provides the means to distort competition in downstream markets by refusing to supply technical services to downstream competitors or supplying them on less favourable terms. This is the underlying rationale of the regulation of digital conditional access services. The conflict of interest was made explicit in the *Bertelsmann/Kirch/Deutsche Telekom* decisions with reference to the pay TV market:

> If a proprietary conditional access system is to be used, there must be discrimination-free access to the system. In the Commission's view, this requires that the licenser of the decoder technology be able to conduct his business without being influenced by a programme supplier. In the present case the licenser is not independent, since BetaResearch is controlled mainly by enterprises which have their own interests as programme suppliers.[250]

Use of Technical Services to Strengthen Dominance in Pay TV

11.330 In both *MSG* and *Bertelsmann/Kirch/Premiere*, the Commission has found that the dominant positions of the parties on the pay TV market would be strengthened by the creation of dominant technical services joint ventures. The Commission has referred to the following ways in which dominance in technical services could be used to distort competition in pay TV:

- Ensuring that the terms and conditions of supply of technical services, and in particular the price, were favourable to the parent's own service and unfavourable to others;[251]

- Charging artificially high prices for technical services. This would not affect the parents' pay TV operations, as they would share in the technical services supplier's profits;[252]

---

[250] *Bertelsmann/Kirch/Premiere* (Case IV/M993) (1998) [1999] OJ L53/1, at para 111. *Deutsche Telekom/BetaResearch* (Case IV/M1027) (1998) [1999] OJ L53/31, at para 38. See also US regulation of technical services which requires provision by trusted third party without interest in content provider.
[251] *MSG* (Case IV/M469) [1994] OJ L364/1, at para 84. *Bertelsmann/Kirch/Premiere* (Case IV/M993) (1998) [1999] OJ L53/1, at para 58.
[252] *MSG* (Case IV/M469) [1994] OJ L364/1, at para 84. *Bertelsmann/Kirch/Premiere* (Case IV/M993) (1998) [1999] OJ L53/1, at para 58.

- Delaying market access of competitors through spurious technical problems;[253]

- Placing competitors' services on unattractive positions on the electronic programme guide[254] and preventing differentiation of competitors' services
through development of the EPG;[255]

- Manipulating the number of slots on smart cards to ensure that competitors
require a second smart card;[256]

- Obtaining information about competitors' programme plans, viewer profile,
and viewer preferences facilitates the development of programmes targeted at
specific groups;[257]

- Control over the development of the application programming interface and its
licensing to third parties gives information about competitors' plans and can be
used to delay them/make them more difficult.[258]

Use of Technical Services to Strengthen Dominance in Cable Networks

The Commission has found in both *MSG* and *Deutsche Telekom/BetaResearch* that **11.331**
Deutsche Telekom's dominant position on the cable network market in Germany
would be strengthened by its participation in joint ventures which would hold
dominant positions on the technical services market.[259] The arguments relied
upon by the Commission in respect of cable networks appear less convincing than
those in respect of pay TV. In particular, although the arguments raised by the
Commission are expressed in terms of the technical services market, this market is
concerned only indirectly. The arguments appear to relate more to the possible
consequences of any structural link between a dominant cable operator and a
dominant pay TV operator.

Two risks for competition in the cable network market resulting from the creation **11.332**
of a technical services joint venture between the dominant cable operator and the
dominant pay TV operator have been stressed. The first is that such an alliance
creates 'the risk that private operators could not obtain the programmes of the

---

[253] *MSG* (Case IV/M469) [1994] OJ L364/1, at para 85.

[254] *MSG* (Case IV/M469) [1994] OJ L364/1, at para 87.

[255] *Bertelsmann/Kirch/Premiere* (Case IV/M993) (1998) [1999] OJ L53/1, at paras 59, 60.

[256] *MSG* (Case IV/M469) [1994] OJ L364/1, at para 88.

[257] *MSG* (Case IV/M469) [1994] OJ L364/1, at para 89. *Bertelsmann/Kirch/Premiere* (Case IV/M993) (1998) [1999] OJ L53/1, at para 61.

[258] *Bertelsmann/Kirch/Premiere* (Case IV/M993) (1998) [1999] OJ L53/1, at paras 113–117.

[259] The use of technical services to strengthen dominance on cable network markets was also
referred to, albeit more briefly, in the *Nordic Satellite Distribution* case. NSD had plans in the future
to develop a joint Nordic encryption system and cable head-end. Transparent transmission would
be imposed on private cable operators if NSD were to adopt it. As these were future plans, the
Commission did not assess their competitive impact. It did state, however, that: 'It must be foreseen
that by controlling such a system NSD will be in a position to strengthen its function as a "gatekeeper" for broadcasters wishing to get access to Nordic cable networks' (*Nordic Satellite
Distribution* (Case IV/M490) (1995) [1996] OJ L53/20, at paras 130–131).

leading pay-TV suppliers . . . which are required for attractive programme packages, or obtained them only on unfavourable terms'.[260] This point does not appear to be directly related to the technical services market. The second is that where the dominant cable operator voluntarily renounces the possibility of direct relations with pay TV customers (that is, does not himself operate subscriber management services), then private operators are also prevented from gaining revenue from the operation of subscriber management services. The loss of this revenue prevents the private cable operators from investing in the infrastructure upgrading or building which would be necessary for competition with the dominant operator. 'It follows that Telekom's opting for the transport model has made it impossible for the private cable operators to finance an expansion of their activities, and that no such expansion will take place in the foreseeable future. This eliminates the potential competition of the private operators at network level 3, and protects and strengthens Telekom's dominant position'.[261] This point also appears to be only indirectly linked to the technical services market.

Behavioural Undertakings Likely to be Insufficient

11.333   **Rejection of behavioural undertakings.**   Where a structural problem of this nature is created, the Commission has refused to accept undertakings from the parties that limit the conduct of the dominant technical services joint venture so that it will not be used to strengthen downstream dominance. In the *MSG* decision, behavioural undertakings of this type[262] were characterized by the Commission as a 'commitment not to abuse in certain respects a dominant position held by MSG on the market for technical and administrative services to the detriment of competitors in the market for pay-TV'.[263] 'They are as a matter of principle inappropriate to solving the structural problem, namely that the creation of MSG creates or strengthens dominant positions on the markets for administrative and technical services, pay-TV and cable networks. '[264]

11.334   The fact that the creation of a dominant technical services joint venture affords the parties the possibility to distort downstream competition is sufficient. It is not

---

[260]   *MSG* (Case IV/M469) [1994] OJ L364/1, at para 93.
[261]   *Deutsche Telekom/BetaResearch* (Case IV/M1027) (1998) [1999] OJ L53/31, at para 53.
[262]   *MSG* (Case IV/M469) [1994] OJ L364/1, at para 94—promoting the sale rather than rental of decoders and not preventing the use of rented decoders for programmes not handled by MSG; 'chinese walls' preventing information on other pay TV suppliers' programmes or subscriber data from being passed to its parents; installing a neutral and non-discriminatory electronic programme guide in the decoders with an advisory committee composed of other broadcasters to ensure that this was indeed the case; charging reasonable prices and operating a transparent price policy without discrimination; and, finally, Deutsche Telekom would ensure that further digital capacity was available on its cable networks so as to avoid any shortage of channel capacity.
[263]   *MSG* (Case IV/M469) [1994] OJ L364/1, at para 95.
[264]   *MSG* (Case IV/M469) [1994] OJ L364/1, at para 99.

necessary to demonstrate in such a structural analysis that competition will be distorted, but only that distortion is made possible.

Acceptance of behavioural undertakings.   Behavioural undertakings may, however, be accepted in certain circumstances. In the *BiB* case the Commission has indicated its preliminary view that it will accept undertakings offered by the parties to provide fair, reasonable, and non-discriminatory access to the digital set top boxes to be subsidized by BiB as one of the conditions of exemption under Regulation 17.[265] BiB is a joint venture company, jointly controlled by its four parent companies, BT, BSkyB, Midland Bank, and Matsushita. Its purpose is to set up the infrastructure necessary for the provision of digital interactive TV services, including digital interactive set top boxes, to consumers in the UK and to provide such services to consumers using that infrastructure. It is clear from the Notice published pursuant to Article 19(3) of Regulation 17 that as originally notified the Commission took the view that the creation of BiB did lead to foreclosure of competition in a manner incompatible with Articles 81 and 82 EC and in particular to the strengthening of BSkyB's dominant position on the UK pay TV market. However the precise nature of the Commission's concerns will remain unclear pending the adoption of a formal decision.

11.335

BiB.   The essential difference between *BiB*, on the one hand, and *MSG* and the *Bertelsmann/Kirch/Deutsche Telekom* decisions, on the other, appears to be that BiB itself will have limited activities on the technical services market. In contrast to the cases cited above, BSkyB's technical services business has not been concentrated in BiB. The Commission has not proposed to act against the pre-existing vertical integration of BSkyB's technical services and pay TV operations. It must be assumed that the Commission felt this to fall outwith the remit of its examination of the impact of the creation of BiB. Otherwise, a structural solution of the type envisaged in the *Bertelsmann/Kirch/Premiere* decision would have been required.

11.336

Structural Solutions

Where a supplier of technical services has significant downstream interests, the clearest remedy would be a structural one: removing the downstream operators' controlling interest in the technical services joint venture. However, to be acceptable such a solution must remove the controlling interest as a matter of fact, and not only in principle. In the *Bertelsmann/Kirch/Premiere* decision, the parties offered a number of undertakings.[266] The Commission stated that the opening of

11.337

---

[265] Notice pursuant to Article 19(3) of Regulation 17 [1998] OJ C322/5.

[266] Making available 25% of Kirch and Bertelsmann's pay TV film rights to third parties; opening the share capital of BetaResearch to third parties and allowing them the same voting rights as the parties, allowing private cable operators to market Premiere's pay TV service (but not its pay-per-view services) in competition with Premiere—however, they would be obliged to package Premiere as the parties determined and would be obliged to give Premiere all relevant subscriber

BetaResearch's share capital was sufficient in principle to remove the structural problem created by the parents' conflict of interest between the markets for technical and downstream services.[267] However, in practice, given that Bertelsmann and Kirch together would retain the possibility to outvote third parties, they would still have control of BetaResearch's development. The undertaking was thus insufficient.

11.338 In the *MSG* decision, the Commission accepted that the inclusion of a common interface in the set top box which MSG would commercialize had a 'structural aspect'. However, it would not prevent MSG from holding a dominant position on the technical services market.

11.339 As for the problems raised on the cable network market, in both the *MSG* and *Deutsche Telekom/BetaResearch* cases, Deutsche Telekom offered to reserve capacity on its cable network for a pay TV supplier other than Premiere. The Commission rejected this. Indeed, in *Deutsche Telekom/BetaResearch*, the Commission appears to indicate that the only solution would be for Deutsche Telekom to begin divestiture of its cable network by accepting third party investment.[268]

11.340 **Non-proprietary technical services.** The Commission has not yet had to address whether dominance in the technical services market can be used to strengthen downstream dominance where the technology underlying the technical services is not proprietary. This will remain a theoretical question for as long as proprietary set top boxes and related set top boxes remain the norm. However, it does appear questionable that downstream dominance could be strengthened if the technical services company has no technical control over access to the set top box.

Relevance of Regulation of Digital Conditional Access Services in TV Standards Directive

11.341 As stated above, no reference is made to the Advanced Television Standards Directive in the *Bertelsmann/Kirch/Deutsche Telekom* decisions. Given the limitation of the scope of the Directive (only digital conditional access services), control of further proprietary elements, such as the electronic programme guide or application programming interface, could still be used to strengthen downstream dominance. Pre-existing regulation was therefore insufficient to address all of the means by which dominance in technical services could be leveraged into down-

---

information; Deutsche Telekom making two digital cable channels available for third party pay TV until the end 1999; and licensing the conditional access system and API to third party broadcasters and manufacturers on standard terms with the fee to be determined, if necessary, by independent arbitration.

[267] *Bertelsmann/Kirch/Premiere* (Case IV/M993) (1998) [1999] OJ L53/1, at paras 38, 79.
[268] *Deutsche Telekom/BetaResearch* (Case IV/M1027) (1998) [1999] OJ L53/31, at para 51.

stream markets. It was therefore not necessary to address the more difficult question of whether the creation of a structural competition problem can be accepted if it is subject to pre-existing regulation. Given the Commission's strict approach to behavioural undertakings, it may well be that it would not. However, the Commission's preliminary position in the *BiB* case might suggest that regulation will be relevant in respect of pre-existing problems where it is sufficient to prevent exacerbation of competition problems.

(5) Access to Set Top Boxes under Article 82

There are no decisions on this point. However, the issue seems likely to arise in the future given the fact that pay TV operators in the EU tend to be vertically integrated in the supply of technical services. **11.342**

Given the lack of precedent, the points made below are of necessity speculative. However, it should be noted that the cases cited above already give some guidance as to the types of behaviour which the Commission would consider to be abusive.[269] The factors relevant to dominance in the technical services market are set out in paragraphs 11.311 and following above. **11.343**

Bundling.   Technical services comprise a group of disparate services: for instance conditional access, subscriber management, and access to the application programming interface. It seems likely that the Commission would consider a refusal to supply any one of these services individually as bundling[270] unless it could be objectively justified. The most appropriate justification would seem to be that the security function of the set top box would be affected. In this respect, it is irrelevant that Directive (EC) 95/47 imposes an obligation only to supply digital conditional access services. Article 82 would allow the Commission to go beyond the terms of the Directive on a case-by-case basis as the Directive does not limit the scope of application of Articles 81 and 82. A further issue may arise where a company which is dominant in the wholesale supply of channels makes provision of certain technical services conditional on purchase of programming. It is difficult to imagine any acceptable justification for such behaviour. **11.344**

Excessive pricing.   There would clearly be an effect on competition if a vertically integrated company were to charge its downstream competitors an excessive price for technical services.[271] However, the Commission has been reluctant to deal with pricing issues in the past. The provisions of Directive (EC) 95/47 which require digital conditional access suppliers to keep separate accounts in respect of their **11.345**

---

[269] See in particular *MSG* (Case IV/M469) [1994] OJ L364/1, at paras 94–99. *BiB* (Notice pursuant to Article 19(3) of Regulation 17) [1998] OJ C322/5.
[270] See for example the UK regime—the separate provision of each type of service is a regulatory requirement.
[271] See *MSG* (Case IV/M469) [1994] OJ L364/1, at para 84. *Bertelsmann/Kirch/Premiere* (Case IV/M993) (1998) [1999] OJ L53/1, at para 58.

technical services and downstream operations may, if policed stringently, allow any cross-subsidization to be detected.

11.346 **Price discrimination.**   At the most rudimentary level, a company which is dominant in the supply of technical services which has agreed to supply any of those services individually to a downstream competitor or on more advantageous terms, must offer those terms to all as discrimination would be contrary to Article 82.

11.347 **'Simulcrypt'.**   In a number of Member States, competing digital pay TV platforms have been, or will be, launched together. These platforms use different proprietary conditional access systems and set top boxes. The question may therefore arise of whether the dominant technical services and pay TV operator can be obliged to enter simulcrypt agreements.[272] Refusal to do so would prevent pay TV competitors from reaching consumers who have bought or leased an incompatible set top box. Without objective justification, refusal might well be considered to constitute exclusionary and abusive behaviour. In this context, it is interesting to note that BSkyB has been required to enter such agreements as a condition of exemption of *BiB*.

G. Retail

11.348 Effects on competition in retail markets can arise either as a result of operations on upstream markets or on the retail markets themselves. The importance of upstream markets has been considered in previous sections: issues related to content, transmission networks, and interface devices, such as set top boxes, can all result in the restriction, distortion, or elimination of downstream competition. As can be seen from these sections, a number of the major competition concerns which manifest themselves in a reduction of competition at the retail level are attributable to competition problems higher up the value chain. Each of these represents a potential barrier to entry into retail markets. The existence of a bottleneck at any one level is sufficient to affect such entry.

11.349 This section focuses on activities on retail markets. In this respect, one of the most important points to note about the Commission's decisional practice is its tendency to identify narrow product and geographic markets. In the television sector, for example, advertising-funded and pay television have been considered to be

---

[272] See *BiB* (Notice pursuant to Article 19(3) of Regulation 17) [1998] OJ C322/5: the Notice indicates that one of the proposed conditions of exemption is that BSkyB enter simulcrypt agreements.

separate product markets.[273] The geographic scope of both has tended to be national, or, at the broadest, linguistic in dimension.

(1) Market Definition

Product Markets in Telecommunications

The Commission distinguishes between domestic and international voice and **11.350** data telecommunications services. The international services are likely to be sub-divisible into further geographically distinct services—the *BT/MCI II* decision discussed above seems to envisage country-pair services. The Commission also tends to distinguish between residential and corporate services given their markedly different demand characteristics. Depending on the service there will not necessarily be a clear distinction between these two markets—when looking at voice services for small office/home office users, for example, it may be difficult to determine whether these users constitute part of the corporate or part of the residential market. As a general rule, however, it seems safe to distinguish corporate and residential services when looking at most retail telecommunications markets.

Voice Telephony

Voice telephony for the purposes of Directive (EEC) 90/388 is defined as: **11.351**

> the commercial provision for the public of the direct transport and switching of speech in real-time between public switched network termination points, enabling any user to use equipment connected to such a network termination point in order to communicate with another termination point.[274]

However, the distinction between voice telephony and other voice services which **11.352** do not fall within the formal definition of voice telephony is technical, rather than economic. Services formally defined as voice telephony will sometimes compete with services which fall outside of the definition. As such it can be doubted whether liberalized voice telecommunications services would in all circumstances constitute a separate market to voice telephony services. It is therefore doubtful whether this distinction would form the basis of market definitions in the future. However, this may prove in practice to be an unnecessary complication in the early years of liberalization.

---

[273] The same distinctions in product markets have been made in respect of radio services. Thus, the Commission distinguishes between a market for radio advertising and a market for subscription-funded radio: *Bertelsmann/CLT* (Case IV/M779) (1996) (national market for radio advertising defined).

[274] Commission Directive (EEC) 90/388 of 28 June 1990 on competition in the markets for telecommunications services [1990] OJ L192/10, at Article 1.1.

11.353 **Fixed and mobile.** The Commission has distinguished between fixed and mobile infrastructure and services in several decisions,[275] and this general distinction is implicit in the Access Notice. Where at least the prices of such services are markedly different, it is likely that these should be regarded as constituting separate downstream markets. However, where, as is already the case in some Scandinavian countries, the price of fixed and mobile voice services has converged, the maintenance of separate retail markets would appear difficult to sustain.

11.354 **Internet telephony.** A further issue addressed by the Commission is the extent to which Internet telephony constitutes voice telephony within the meaning of Directive 90/388. The Commission has published a Notice on the Status of Voice on the Internet[276] which analyses the circumstances under which Internet voice could be considered as voice telephony, and the consequences which could flow from that. Taking the four elements of the definition of voice telephony from Directive 90/388:

— provided to the public: this would generally be the case as, for example, ISPs typically make their services available to the public generally;

— the subject of a commercial offer: the Notice defines this concept as 'a separate commercial activity with the intention of making a profit'. For unmetered Internet telephony provided in conjunction with a flat-rate Internet dial-up account there would therefore be no *separate* commercial activity. Metered telephony would, however, be regarded as commercial;

— to and from public switched termination points: the main example where this condition would not be fulfilled would be where Internet access was originated over leased lines;

— real-time: there is no technical definition of real-time (such as an end-to-end delay time), and the Commission notes that currently quality of service cannot be guaranteed over the Internet. This may change over time with the increase in customer access bandwidth and the possible roll-out of IPv6.

11.355 The Commission also announced that it intends to review the scope of the Notice periodically, and at the latest before 1 January 2000.

---

[275] (EC) 95/489: Commission Decision of 4 October 1995 concerning the conditions imposed on the second operator of GSM radiotelephony services in Italy (only the Italian text is authentic) [1995] OJ L280/49, at paras 7 *et seq*; (EC) 97/181: Commission Decision of 18 December 1996 concerning the conditions imposed on the second operator of GSM radiotelephony services in Spain (only the Spanish text is authentic) [1997] OJ L76/19.

[276] Notice on the Status of Voice on the Internet under Directive (EC) 90/388 [1998] OJ C6/4.

Value Added Services

Given the gradual liberalization of the sector, value added services were broadly **11.356**
regarded as those not constituting voice telephony (and therefore those that
escaped the domestic monopolies). In particular cases, more detailed market definitions will emerge, and some indications of the possible markets can already be
found in the decisions on the international alliances. *Atlas*, for example, identifies
customized package of corporate communications services[277] and packet-
switched data services,[278] explicitly noting that narrower market definitions in
respect of the latter are conceivable. *Unisource/Telefonica* echoes these definitions
and additionally identifies traveller services. Similar market definitions can be
found in other cases.[279]

Corporate Communications Services

This market is defined in the Commission's decisions on international alliances, **11.357**
discussed below. Generally large corporate customers have a demand for a range
of telecommunications services, often bought from a single supplier. The
Commission's decisions indicate that this can be further divided into national,
cross-border, regional, and international markets.

Product Markets in the Internet Sector

Despite the relatively recent emergence of Internet services, the Commission has **11.358**
issued a number of decisions which provide some guidance as to market definition. However, as these decisions are Phase I clearances, it is unlikely that the reasoning contained in the decisions will be particularly extensive.

Corporate markets. Internet access would typically be one element of the over- **11.359**
all corporate communications services market referred to above, and the
Commission decision in *Worldcom/MCI* indicates that, in some circumstances, it
may be appropriate to identify a corporate Internet access market separate from

---

[277] *Atlas* [1996] OJ L239/23, at para 5 (only the English, French and German texts are authentic).

[278] *Atlas* [1996] OJ L239/23, at para 8 (only the English, French and German texts are authentic).

[279] *BT/MCI* [1994] OJ L223/36, at para 5: 'the emerging market for value-added and enhanced
services to large multinational corporations, extended enterprises and other intensive users of
telecommunictions services provided over international intelligent networks. This market will
cover a wide range of existing global trans-border services, including virtual network services, high-
speed data services and outsourced global telecommunications solutions specially designed for individual customers requirements . . .'; *Atlas* [1996] OJ L239/23, at para 5 (only the English, French,
and German texts are authentic): 'The market comprises mostly customized combinations of a
range of existing telecommunications sevices, mainly liberalised voice services including voice communication betewen members of a closed group of users . . . high-speed data services and outsourced
telecommunications solutions specially designed for individual customer requirements . . .'

that for packaged corporate services.[280] However, if predictions as to the ubiquity of Internet based services prove realistic, then the distinction may cease to have meaning as many if not all corporate services will become Internet protocol based. Market definitions in the future, at least in the corporate sector, will therefore probably not be based on the issue of whether or not a service is Internet based, but on a definition of the type of service being provided.

11.360 **Residential services.** Looking at residential services, the Commission's decisions[281] indicate that the following markets can be identified:

— Internet access (the provision of dial-up access to the Internet for residential users);

— Internet advertising;

— paid for Internet content.

11.361 This suggests, *inter alia*, that the Commission is maintaining the advertising funded versus subscription funded distinction that it uses in the broadcasting sector.

11.362 An area that is likely to be of increasing importance in the future is the availability of Internet services or Internet-like interactive services on domestic television sets. The Commission's Article 19(3) Notice in *BiB*[282] suggests that the Commission would regard the availability of a service on a TV set, rather than on a PC, as being likely to constitute a separate product market. This conclusion appears to be based on the different price, characteristics, and use, and the consequent household penetration rates, of TVs as opposed to PCs. The Commission's preliminary view is that the interactive service to be provided by BiB is distinct from traditional broadcast television services, although it is likely that there will be an increased blurring of the boundaries between these services in the future.

11.363 **Mobile services.** Again, looking to the future, it is likely that data services will be made available over mobile telecommunications networks in the short to medium term. Given the bandwidth constraints of the present GSM/DCS1800 systems, and the price premium likely to be afforded to the UMTS (Universal Mobile Telecommunications System) networks in the future, it would appear likely that data services over UMTS will occupy a separate market to GSM based data services.

---

[280] *Worldcom/MCI* (Case IV/M1069) (1998) [1999] OJ L116/1.
[281] *Telia/Telenor/Schibsted* (Case IV/JV1) (1998), and *Cegetel/Canal+/AOL/Bertelsmann* (Case IV/JV5) (1998).
[282] *BiB* (Notice pursuant to Article 19(3) of Regulation 17) [1998]OJ C322/5.

Product Markets in the Television Sector

In defining product markets, the Commission has distinguished between televi- **11.364**
sion services which are funded by advertising and those which are funded by viewers' subscriptions. This has been a controversial and contested approach. Clarity
should be provided by the Court of First Instance's judgment in the
Bertelsmann/Kirch/Premiere appeal.

Pay Television

In the *MSG* decision,[283] the Commission concluded that pay television consti- **11.365**
tuted a separate product market from advertising-funded television and from
public television financed through fees and partly through advertising, as in the
case of pay TV there is a trade relationship between the viewer as subscriber and
the programme supplier, while in the case of advertising-funded television there is
a trade relationship only between the programme supplier and the advertising
industry. This meant that the conditions of competition were different for the two
types of television. The main parameters for competition in advertising-funded
television are audience share which determines advertising rates. In the case of pay
television, the key factors were the shaping of programmes to meet the interests of
the target groups and the level of subscription prices. In addition, the content of
pay television and advertising-funded channels differed, in that the former tended
to be of a more specialized nature.

This distinction between pay television and advertising-funded television has **11.366**
since been maintained in a series of decisions.[284] The existence of separate markets
does not mean that there is no relationship between the two types of television.
The Commission has accepted that the existence of varied and numerous free television channels in a market has an impact on the ease with which pay television
can be introduced, without, however, altering its conclusion that separate product
markets exist.[285]

Analogue and digital pay television have been found to form part of single pay **11.367**
television market.[286] However, the Commission has referred to the fact that

---

[283] *MSG* (Case IV/M469) [1994] OJ L364/1. A separate market for pay TV was first referred to
in *Kirch/Richemont/Telepiu* (Case IV/M410) (1994).

[284] Examples include *Kirch/Richemont/Multichoice/Telepiu* (Case IV/M584) (1995); *Nordic
Satellite Distribution* (Case IV/M490) (1995) [1996] OJ L53/20. In the *BiB* case, the Commission
has also indicated its preliminary conclusion that a separate market for pay TV exists in the Notice
pursuant to Article 19(3) of Regulation 17—[1998]OJ C322/5.

[285] Most recently *Bertelsmann/Kirch/Premiere* (Case IV/M993) (1998) [1999] OJ L53/1, at paras
18, 44, and 45.

[286] *Bertelsmann/Kirch/Premiere* (Case IV/M993) (1998) [1999] OJ L53/1, at para 18: 'Digital
pay TV is only a further development of analog pay TV and therefore does not constitute a separate
relevant product market. Moreover, account should be taken of the fact that in the next few years
analog broadcast pay TV will be completely superseded by digital broadcast pay TV.'

digitization may at some point in the future lead to sufficient convergence between free access and pay television for the definition of a single product market.[287] This has also been said to be the case in respect of pay TV channels which are funded partly by advertising.[288]

11.368 **Cable, satellite, and digital terrestrial pay television.** In the *MSG* and *NSD* decisions, the Commission appeared to define pay television markets in respect of cable and satellite pay television respectively. More recent decisions, however, define a single product market, regardless of the means of transmission used for delivery.[289]

11.369 **Pay per view.** There are no formal decisions concerned principally with pay-per-view, near-video-on-demand, or video-on-demand services[290] (all of which are generally subscription-funded). In the *Premiere* decision, the Commission said that pay-per-channel and pay-per-view were part of the pay TV market.[291] However, this issue was not of central importance to the case. A thorough analysis has not yet been necessary.

Television Advertising Market

11.370 The Commission has distinguished between a 'television broadcasting ' or 'viewers' market' on the one hand and a market for television advertising on the other. It has left open the question of whether the former markets in fact exist. 'In view

---

[287] *Bertelsmann/Kirch/Premiere* (Case IV/M993) (1998) [1999] OJ L53/1, at para 18 'As digitalisation continues to spread, there could admittedly, with the passage of time, be a certain convergence between pay-TV and free-TV, particularly if, at some future stage, freeTV channels too should largely be supplied in digital bouquets by pay-TV operators. However, this possible future development is not enough now to justify the acceptance of a common market for pay and free TV.'

[288] *MSG* (Case IV/M469) [1994] OJ L364/1, at para 32: 'could become blurred in the case of pay-TV programmes that are financed from a mixture of sources'. However, in *BiB* (Notice pursuant to Article 19(3) of Regulation 17) [1998] OJ C322/5, the Commission defined a single pay TV market despite the fact that BSkyB is funded partly by advertising and partly by subscription (albeit that advertising revenue is minor).

[289] *Bertelsmann/Kirch/Premiere* (Case IV/M993) (1998) [1999] OJ L53/1; *TPS* [1999] OJ L90/6; *BiB* (Notice pursuant to Article 19(3) of Regulation 17) [1998] OJ C322/5.

[290] The essential difference between near-video-on-demand and video-on-demand services is that it is only in respect of the latter that consumers have an effective choice of what programme they watch and when they watch it. Near-video-on-demand services involve, for example, a rolling schedule of particular films starting at hourly intervals.

[291] *Bertelsmann/Kirch/Premiere* (Case IV/M993) (1998) [1999] OJ L53/1, at para 18. To be contrasted with *MSG* (Case IV/M469) [1994] OJ L364/1, at para 38: 'according to what is known at present, pay-TV in the form of pay-per-channel, pay-per-view and near-video-on-demand constitutes a single market, since in such forms of viewing, the broadcaster alone determines the programme sequence and timing and the viewer has only limited choice available (in the case of near-video-on-demand, for example, a specific number of feature films is available for selection, with each being repeated at specific times of the day). Things might be different in the case of video-on-demand proper, with the customer selecting a programme of his choice from an electronic programme library. However, since this form of broadcasting will, according to the information provided by various potential market participants, probably not be achievable for technical reasons over the next few years, it need not be assigned to any particular market.'

of the fact that there is no direct trade relationship between broadcasters of "free" TV channels on the "supply side" and viewers on the "demand side", it might be argued that TV broadcasting does not constitute a market in the strict economic sense of the notion.'[292] The only economic relationship has been found to be that between advertising-funded broadcasters and advertisers or advertising agencies. However, the Commission has also said that audience shares are a determinative factor for success on the market for television advertising.[293]

The market for television advertising has been found to be separate from those for **11.371** advertising in other media, and in particular print media, on the basis that the consumers targeted through different types of advertising may vary considerably, and the techniques employed and production costs are different as is the price.[294]

There are no formal decisions in which narrower markets have been defined. **11.372** However, the Commission has referred to the possibility of defining narrower television advertising markets by reference to the target audience of the channel and advertiser.[295]

Geographic Markets

This will vary depending on the service being provided. In the telecommunica- **11.373** tions sector, the geographic market is determined by

(a) by the extent and coverage of the network and the customers that can economically be reached and whose demands may be met; and
(b) the legal and regulatory system and the right to provide a service.[296]

On this basis, the Commission has identified national markets for residential **11.374** telecommunications services, and a range of markets—national, cross-border, regional, pan-European, and global—for corporate communications services.[297] In the mobile sector, use of international roaming agreements to provide cross-border services may in time tend to break down national borders at the service level.

In respect of television services, the Commission has often identified linguistic[298] **11.375** or national markets. The Commission has generally defined national markets in

---

[292] *RTL/Veronica/Endemol* (Case IV/M553) [1996] OJ L294/14; *Canal+/UFA/MDO* (Case IV/M655) (1995).

[293] *RTL/Veronica/Endemol* (Case IV/M553) [1996] OJ L294/14, para 20.

[294] *RTL/Veronica/Endemol* (Case IV/M553) [1996] OJ L294/14, para 23. See also *Sunrise* (Case IV/M176) (1992).

[295] In *CLT/Disney/Super RTL* (Case IV/M566) (1995), the question of a television advertising market confined to children's channels was raised. However, as such a narrower market definition would not affect the competitive assessment, it was left open.

[296] *Albacom/BT/ENI/Mediaset* [1997] OJ L369/8.

[297] *Atlas* [1996] OJ L239/23 (only the English, French, and German texts are authentic).

[298] *Bertelsmann/Kirch/Premiere* (Case IV/M993) (1998) [1999] OJ L53/1.

respect of both pay and advertising-funded television. Differences in culture, language, regulatory regime, and competitive conditions have been relied upon in justification. However, the Commission has indicated a willingness to define markets with respect to areas within which the language and culture are relatively homogenous. In the *Premiere* case, it referred to the possibility of the relevant geographic market for pay TV extending beyond Germany to include all German-speaking areas within Europe. This is to be contrasted with the position in *RTL/Veronica/Endemol*,[299] in which the Commission found that the relevant geographic market for television advertising was The Netherlands and excluded Flemish-speaking Belgium.

(2) Competition Issues

11.376 As indicated above, competition problems at higher levels of the value chain often have a significant impact at the retail level. The Commission has dealt with a number of alliances in the telecoms and media sectors that were entered into by operators that were dominant on markets other than those on which the alliance was to operate.

11.377 In addition to abuses of dominance, genuinely retail issues fall into three broad categories:

— assessment of actual competition on retail markets;

— assessment of potential competition on retail markets;

— leveraging from related markets.

Telecommunications

Assessment of Actual Competition on Retail Markets

11.378 As indicated above (see Section E), many of the important issues in telecommunications cases relate to the dominant positions of the parent companies on related, often transmission, markets. However, where significant existing positions on retail markets exist—as in packet-switched data communication on the French and German markets in *Atlas*—the Commission will inevitably look at the overlap and determine whether divestiture (as in *Atlas*[300]) or prohibition might be necessary. Similarly, when looking at incumbent operator mergers such as Telia/Telenor, divestiture of actual overlapping operations on their domestic markets is likely.

11.379 **Actual competition and joint dominance.** It is possible that the Commission would also regard the divestiture of shareholdings in some operations as necessary

---

[299] *RTL/Veronica/Endemol* (Case IV/M553) [1996] OJ L294/14.

[300] *Atlas* [1996] OJ L239/23, at para 68 and Article 4(a) (only the English, French, and German texts are authentic).

even in the absence of single operator dominance. It is arguable, for example, that the frequency limitations which limit the number of mobile networks in any Member State render the mobile network market liable to joint dominance. The existence of overlapping shareholdings in more than one mobile operator could be regarded as problematic, in that it establishes economic links which would strengthen or make more likely a finding of joint dominance. If this is the case, then the Commission could object to the overlap of even relatively small minority shareholdings.

Assessment of Potential Competition on Retail Markets

Alliances addressing domestic markets.   With the liberalization of the telecom-   **11.380** munications sector in 1998, there has been a substantial number of joint venture cases notified under the Merger Regulation. These involve both companies active in other industrial areas, and telecommunications operators active in other geographic markets. The existence of a dominant player on the market meant that none of these cases raised a risk of the creation or strengthening of a dominant position. To the extent that these alliances strengthened the viability of the new entrants, there would have been no reduction in potential competition resulting from the alliance as compared to the possibility of the members of the alliance entering independently. Given that these new entrant cases raised no competition concerns, market definition issues tended to be left completely open, and the cases are therefore of little use in predicting market definition and/or competition concerns in more problematic cases in the future.

Incumbent operator mergers.   With the mixed success of international   **11.381** alliances to date, there are signs that there will be increasing consolidation between the incumbent operators. The proposed merger between Deutsche Telekom and Telecom Italia did not come to fruition, but the merger between Telia and Telenor is pending before the Commission at the time of writing. Telia and Telenor are the former monopoly telecommunications operators in Sweden and Norway respectively. They propose a full merger, however, as the parties are both State owned, the concentration is structured as a joint venture.

Mergers between incumbent operators could raise significant concerns. New   **11.382** entrant domestic alliances seek to attack the market position of the former monopolist operator and are therefore pro-competitive. Incumbent operator mergers, by contrast, can in part be seen as a defensive response to the loss of market share on domestic markets. One aspect of such mergers relates to a possible strengthening of existing positions through a reduction of potential competition. Assessing the potential competition would be difficult, but, as indicated below in the discussion of leveraging, the Commission has regarded national incumbent operators as being potential competitors to each other on certain markets. The reasons cited below would appear equally applicable as criteria for determining the extent of the reduction in potential competition:

— any overlap in their existing operations whose business scope could be extended into related markets;

— the size and domestic market share of the operators concerned;

— the geographic proximity of their respective markets;

— linguistic or other cultural issues that make their market entry in each other's markets more or less likely.

11.383 When looking at infrastructure issues, the ability to roll-out competing networks, through incremental extension of existing and geographically proximate networks, may be considered important.

11.384 This is a problematic area. Local infrastructure competition is limited, and identifying an appreciable strengthening of the parties' position through a reduction in potential competition may be difficult. A finding that there was no reduction in potential competition would, however, be significant. Looking at the Telia/Telenor notification, the parties control both the telecommunications networks and important cable networks in their respective countries. Their networks are geographically close, and the parties have proved themselves to be viable competitors on other telecommunications markets in each other's countries. To find that there is no impact on potential competition in these circumstances would appear to imply that local infrastructure is a natural monopoly and no further entrance can be expected.

11.385 **International alliances.** Operators that are well established on domestic markets appear highly likely to be considered to be at least potential competitors at the global level.[301] In the telecommunications sector, this is based at least in part, according to the Commission's decision in *Atlas*, on interconnection which allows the extension of domestic service from the national home market into another geographic market. However, given the shifting sands of international alliances, there appears no risk as yet of either an elimination of competition or the creation or strengthening of dominance on those retail markets. For the foreseeable future, therefore, competition issues in the context of international alliances are likely to revolve around an examination of the domestic positions of the parents to ensure that there is no strengthening or possibility of leveraging. The Commission's decisions in *BT/MCI I*, *Atlas/Phoenix*, and *Unisource/Uniworld* are therefore examined below.

11.386 By contrast, the Commission gave a negative clearance to International Private Satellite Partners,[302] given the need to obtain authorizations and licences, and to

---

[301] *BT/MCI* [1994] OJ L223/36, at para 34.
[302] *International Private Satellite Partners* [1994] OJ L354/75 (IPSP).

arrange the financing, construction, launch, and operation of two satellites in circumstances where none of the partners was in a position to do this alone.[303] The Commission also concluded that the joint venture could be expected to increase the level of competition in a fast-growing segment of the overall telecommunications market.[304]

Leveraging and Related Markets

Incumbent operator mergers.   The final issue which may have to be considered is whether the parties will derive additional benefits from the consolidation of their operations and from the vertical integration of their activities. The clearest consolidation benefit is likely to be the ability to self-correspond in place of national or international interconnection arrangements. While arguably a legitimate economy of scale, such benefits may prove problematic where the existing market positions of the parties are very large.   **11.387**

Such benefits could also have consequential effects on upstream or downstream markets. The reduction in interconnection costs could, for example, lead to a strengthening of the parties' position in downstream retail services markets. This in turn could undermine the viability of alternative infrastructure investment and thus strengthen the parties' position in local infrastructure.   **11.388**

International alliances.   Although the purpose of strategic alliances is usually to deliver value added retail services to corporate users, many of the most important competition issues relate to the position of the parent companies (often dominant, former monopolist telecommunications operators) on national markets. The participating companies would tend not to have substantial market presence on the relevant retail markets—at least at the global level—but the existence of dominance on national markets would raise risks of those dominant positions being used to favour the retail joint ventures.   **11.389**

International alliances between operators with strong positions on domestic markets have tended to fall under Regulation 17 rather than the Merger Regulation, although the *BT/AT&T* decision suggests that this is likely to change following the widening of the scope of the Merger Regulation.   **11.390**

The Commission has regarded the cases under Regulation 17 as falling within Article 81(1) as such operators would normally be regarded as actual or potential competitors on each other's markets, and their alliance would tend to reduce actual or potential competition between them on those markets. Clearly, a number of factors would be relevant to assessing the appreciability of this restriction of competition, including: **11.391**

---

[303] *International Private Satellite Partners* [1994] OJ L354/75, at para 53.
[304] *International Private Satellite Partners* [1994] OJ L354/75, at para 56.

— any overlap in their existing operations;

— the size of the operators concerned;

— the geographic proximity of their respective markets;

— linguistic or other cultural issues that make their market entry in each other's markets more or less likely.

11.392 *BT/MCI I.* BT and MCI entered into a joint venture to provide telecommunications services to large corporate customers whose demands could not be satisfied by national telecommunications providers. The joint venture was initially notified as a concentration, but the Commission determined that there was a risk of co-ordination of competitive behaviour of the parents of the joint venture in that:

— the joint venture would be selling to the same companies to which its parents would continue to provide other basic telecom services;

— certain products would be common to both the offerings of the parents and the joint venture, or if not actually common then in neighbouring markets and with a competitive relationship between them;

— the parents would continue to provide IPLCs (international private leased circuits) which can be used to build self-provided networks and which therefore indirectly competed with the joint venture's products; and

— for certain clients, the joint venture's services may be an alternative to the parents' national services.

The agreement was therefore re-notified as a joint venture under Regulation 17.

11.393 The competition concern was relatively limited given the limited extent to which MCI could be regarded as a significant competitor to BT on its domestic markets. In addition, the Commission recognized the existence of a strong national regulatory framework relevant to third party access to transmission facilities, and chose not to impose further conditions as part of the decision. The Commission therefore exempted the creation of the joint venture and the appointment of BT as an exclusive distributor for the joint venture's services in the EEA.

11.394 The parties later decided to merger their entire activities, leading to the Commission's decision in *BT/MCI II*. As the main issue in this case related to the availability of transatlantic capacity, this case is discussed above.

11.395 *Atlas/GlobalOne.* The Commission's decision in *BT/MCI I* contrasts markedly with its decision in *Atlas*. *BT/MCI I* was an alliance between a European and an American operator some time after the home market of the European operator had been largely liberalized (albeit with limited practical success in some areas).

Atlas involved an alliance between Deutsche Telekom and France Telecom at a time when both operators benefited from legal monopolies. The purpose of the alliance was essentially the same as that in *BT/MCI I*—the creation of a joint venture which could provide international telecommunications services to large corporate customers whose demands could not be met by national telecommunications operators. The parties in this case, however, included two European monopolists in addition to the US company Sprint. The alliance between Deutsche Telekom and France Telecom (Atlas) and the alliance between Atlas and Sprint (Phoenix) were the subject of separate notifications and therefore separate decisions. For all practical purposes, they should be regarded as a single decision.[305]

The Commission imposed significantly more extensive conditions on DT/FT **11.396** than it had on BT/MCI. These conditions sought to prevent any strengthening of DT and FT's existing market positions or favouring of the joint venture. Conditions included:

— early liberalization of the German and French markets before the joint venture was allowed to operate. The effectiveness of this liberalization was to be demonstrated by the availability and granting of licences;

— divestiture of Info AG to prevent the creation of a dominant position on the packet-switched data services market;

— non-discrimination obligations in respect of leased lines, access to PSTN/ISDN services and other reserved services;

— prohibitions on cross-subsidization of the Atlas joint venture;

— obligations to keep separate accounts identifying transfers between France Telecom and Deutsche Telekom on the one hand, and the Atlas entities on the other;

— prohibitions on bundling of France Telecom and Deutsche Telekom services with those of the Atlas entities.

Television

Assessment of Potential Competition in Television Markets

Whether analysed under the Merger Regulation or Regulation 17, agreements **11.397** between companies with largely complementary geographic activities or limited activities in neighbouring markets are unlikely to give rise to any serious

---

[305] Similar issues arose in the *Unisource/Uniworld* decisions. See *Unisource* [1997] OJ L318/1; and *Uniworld* [1997] OJ L318/24.

competition problems in television markets.[306] While such agreements are most unlikely to raise serious concerns, there is no clear line under Regulation 17 as to when they will be found to fall outside of Article 81(1) EC or whether they will be exempted under Article 81(3) EC. Relatively few cases have been examined under Regulation 17 thus making firm conclusions impossible.

11.398 **Geographic activities.** It seems to be the case that companies with activities in one geographic market will not be considered potential competitors in respect of another geographic market.[307] Given the linguistic and cultural differences between the television services offered in various countries, it appears unlikely that an operator established in one country could, or would, establish itself elsewhere without local expertise As indicated above, the Commission appears to believe that there are fewer such constraints in the telecommunications sector.

11.399 **Activities in Separate Television Markets.** It is less clear whether companies with activities in one of the television product markets (ie advertising-funded or pay television) in a single Member State would be considered potential competitors in respect of the other. The most recent formal decision under Regulation 17, *TPS*,[308] would suggest that even the most established of advertising-funded television operators would not be considered potential competitors in respect of pay television in the same country.[309] 'Télévision par Satellite' (TPS) was a company

---

[306] See the following clearance decisions under the Merger Regulation: *Kirch/Richemont/Telepiu* (Case IV/M410) (1994); *Kirch/Richemont/Multichoice/Telepiu* (Case IV/M584) (1995); *CLT/Disney/Super RTL* (Case IV/M566) (1995); *Canol+/UFA/MDO* (Case IV/M655) (1996); *RTL 7* (Case IV/M878) (1997) (creation of advertising-funded channel in Poland would not affect structure of EEA markets); *Bertelsmann/CLT* (Case IV/M779) (1996). Under Regulation 17: *TPS* [1999] OJ L90/6 (negative clearance); BDB joint venture referred to in the speech of JF Pons, Deputy Director-General of DGIV, 'The Future of Broadcasting' at the Institute of Economic Affairs on 29 June 1998, http://europa.eu.int/en:comm/dg04/speech/eight/en/sp98034 (exemption comfort letter); Channel 5 joint venture (negative clearance comfort letter) referred to in *Report on Competition Policy 1996* (Vol XXVI) 153.

[307] See, for example, the statements in *Bertelsmann/CLT* (Case IV/M779) (1996) to the effect that CLT which was mainly active in other geographic markets could not realistically be considered a potential competitor to Bertelsmann in the German pay TV market.

[308] *TPS* [1999] OJ L90/6.

[309] However, it would seem that the BDB joint venture was found to fall within Article 81(1) EC, although meeting the conditions of Article 81(3) EC. BDB was a joint venture between Carlton and Granada. It was awarded the franchise to operate digital terrestrial pay TV in the United Kingdom. Both of the parents had significant interests in the markets for advertising-funded television and programme production in the United Kingdom. Their interests in pay TV channels were relatively minor. The creation of BDB was notified to the Commission under Regulation 17, together with a programming supply agreement between Carlton and Granada on the one hand and BSkyB on the other. The Commission closed the file by means of an administrative letter exempting the BDB agreements. As such, the Commission's legal reasoning was not explained and it is unclear whether the Commission considered the creation of the joint venture itself to fall within the ambit of Article 81(1) EC or only certain of the provisions in the notified programme supply agreement. See references in the speech of JF Pons, Deputy Director-General of DGIV, 'The Future of Broadcasting' at the Institute of Economic Affairs on 29 June 1998, http://europa.eu.int/en:comm/dg04/speech/eight/en/sp98034.

established for a period of ten years to operate a digital pay television platform via satellite direct-to-home transmission in France. Its parent companies were three French advertising-funded terrestrial television broadcasters, namely TF1, the public broadcaster France Télévision (which broadcasts two channels, France 2 and France 3), and M6, the telcoms operator, France Télécom, and Suez Lyonnaise des Eaux. The Commission concluded that the creation of the company itself did not fall within Article 81(1) EC as the parents did not jointly control TPS. Any risk of spill-over effects was excluded as none of the parents were otherwise active on the French pay television market. On this basis, the Commission granted a negative clearance.[310]

There are two caveats to this apparently restrictive interpretation of potential **11.400** competition. First, in the *Eurosport* decision,[311] the Commission prohibited under Regulation 17 the creation of a joint venture between EBU members and News International's then subsidiary, Sky Television, to operate a pan-European advertising-funded sports TV channel, Eurosport. However, the reasoning in the decision appears open to question, notably on the question of the appreciability of the restriction of competition and elimination of competition which was essentially judged by the parties' intent rather than the likely effect of the agreement. Secondly, the Commission has referred to the possibility that a network of separate agreements between companies with very strong positions in individual geographic markets could ultimately give rise to concern.[312] However, this situation has not yet arisen.

Assessment of Actual Competition in Television Markets

Operations between actual competitors with significant market positions are **11.401** likely to attract close scrutiny under both Regulation 17 and the Merger Regulation. A number of prohibition decisions in respect of such agreements in television markets have been adopted by the Commission, concerning both advertising-funded and pay television. All have been examined under the Merger Regulation. The following describes the factors considered by the Commission to be relevant to dominance in the television advertising and pay television markets. The common theme is the importance attached to the effects of vertical integration. The *Premiere* decision is particularly interesting in this respect: the barriers

---

[310] As discussed above, certain clauses in the TPS agreement were found to restrict competition, although they fulfilled the conditions for exemption under Article 81(3).

[311] *Screensport/EBU Members* [1991] OJ L63/32.

[312] *Report on Competition Policy 1996* (Vol XXVI) at para 82: 'At present, more and more cross-border alliances are being planned or forged, typified by a pan-European outlook. If all these projects come to fruition, most major television distributors in Europe may well be linked through networks of alliances. The Commission will accordingly have to examine these transactions carefully. In particular, it will have to evaluate the alliances' overall impact at European level, going beyond the direct consequences for the specific national markets.' See also *Bertelsmann/CLT* (Case IV/M779) (1996), at paras 40–41.

to entry created by the parties' positions at all levels of the value chain—content, transmission networks, and technical services for pay television (set top box)— were relevant to the Commission's finding of dominance in pay television.

Dominance in Television Advertising Market

11.402 *RTL/Veronica/Endemol.*[313] The case concerned the creation of a company, HMG, by RTL, Veronica, and Endemol. The Commission concluded that, *de facto*, if not *de jure*, HMG would be jointly controlled.[314] The purpose of HMG was to package and supply advertising-funded television and radio programmes broadcast by itself, CLT, Veronica, or others to viewers in The Netherlands and Luxembourg. All of the parent companies were already active in television markets in The Netherlands. RTL operated two Dutch-language advertising-funded television channels, RTL4 and RTL 5, directed at The Netherlands. Veronica operated the third such channel in The Netherlands, having recently changed status from a public broadcasting organization to become a commercial broadcaster. Endemol was an independent producer of Dutch-language television programmes.[315]

11.403 The Commission prohibited the operation on the grounds that HMG would have a dominant position on the Dutch market for television advertising and that Endemol's existing dominant position on the market for the independently-produced Dutch-language television programmes would be strengthened.[316] The case is currently under appeal, *inter alia* on the grounds that the Commission wrongly assessed the competitive constraint to HMG which was posed by the public channels and by the then recent commercial new entrant, SBS.

11.404 *RTL/Veronica/Endemol*: **measurement of market share.** In analysing the effect of the operation on the television advertising market, the Commission stressed that viewing shares were crucial. The parties' television channels attracted the highest viewing figures. HMG would thus become the strongest broadcaster in The Netherlands, in particular in view of its link to Endemol. An econometric study was relied upon which correlated viewing share figures with advertising market shares. On this basis, the Commission concluded that HMG would have a market share of more than 60 per cent in the television advertising market. This was found to be sufficient to establish dominance.

---

[313] *RTL/Veronica/Endemol* (Case IV/M553) [1996] OJ L294/14.

[314] This conclusion has since been upheld by the Court of First Instance: Case T–221/95 *Endemol Entertainment Holding v Commission*, judgment of 28 April 1999, not yet published. In other respects, the Court of First Instance did not examine the Commission's conclusions in respect of the television advertising market as Endemol challenged the findings only in respect of the independent television programme production market which is discussed above.

[315] See Section D above.

[316] See Section D above.

RTL/Veronica/Endemol: **barriers to entry.** Various strengths of HMG were **11.405**
found to prevent public broadcasters or new entrant advertising-funded broadcasters from acting as competitive constraints. First, the target audiences of two of
the HMG channels were complementary, RTL4 and Veronica, and together covered the main target groups for advertisers. While HMG could co-ordinate programming to maximize advertising revenues, the regulatory regime prevented
public broadcasters from doing the same. HMG would also be able to negotiate
package deals with advertisers as a result of the breadth of its channels' target audiences. Secondly, prior to the operation the third HMG channel, RTL5, had had
the same target audience as Veronica. As a result of the joint venture, HMG would
be able to use RTL5 'as a fighting channel which can directly counteract the programming of competing channels and in particular the programmes of new
entrants on the market'.[317] SBS which was a recent entrant was said to be particularly vulnerable to the use of RTL5 in this way. Thirdly, the structural link to
Endemol further strengthened the position of HMG's channels. Endemol produced the most popular programmes and HMG was guaranteed preferential
access to the most successful productions made by Endemol. HMG's viewing
shares would therefore remain high.

This combination of factors meant that buyers of television advertising time **11.406**
would not be able to prevent an increase in prices by switching easily between
advertising on HMG's and other broadcasters' channels. Moreover, the combined
strength of the parents meant that 'the existence of HMG is in itself dissuasive for
the market entry of any potential newcomer'.[318] The Commission further concluded that even if there was high growth in the advertising sales markets, the
largest part of any growth would be captured by HMG.

RTL/Veronica/Endemol: **remedy.** The case was considered by the Commission **11.407**
following an Article 22 reference by The Netherlands. The operation was thus
implemented prior to the Commission prohibition decision. Subsequently,
Endemol withdrew from HMG and RTL and Veronica undertook to cease operating RTL5 as a general interest channel and instead to operate it as a news channel. This operation was re-notified,[319] and, combined with recent developments
in the market, the Commission considered the changes to be sufficient to restore
effective competition in the Dutch television advertising market. It should be
noted that the Commission rejected the parties' undertaking during the first procedure to reduce their influence in RTL5 on the basis that there was too great a risk
both that the parties would run down RTL5 prior to divestiture and that no
potential buyer would be found.

---

[317] *RTL/Veronica/Endemol* (Case IV/M553) [1996] OJ L294/14, at para 44.
[318] *RTL/Veronica/Endemol* (Case IV/M553) [1996] OJ L294/14, at para 86.
[319] Case M553 [1996] OJ L294/17.

Dominance in the Pay Television Market

11.408 The Commission has prohibited horizontal agreements between pay television competitors in two cases, *Nordic Satellite Distribution (NSD)*[320] and *Bertelsmann/ Kirch/Premiere.*[321] In both of these, the horizontal agreements formed part of broader operations involving upstream markets and this was an important element in the Commission's analysis of dominance in pay television. However, the factors relevant to dominance in pay television, and the importance of positions on upstream markets are discussed most clearly in the *Bertelsmann/Kirch/Premiere* decision.

11.409 *Bertelsmann/Kirch/Premiere*: **facts.** The *Premiere* case involved the concentration of Bertelsmann and Kirch's pay TV interests in Germany and Kirch's pay TV and pay-per-view programme rights contracts in the pay TV channel, Premiere. The parties intended to develop Premiere into a digital pay TV platform which would sell its own and third party channels in packages to viewers either via satellite direct-to-home transmission or via cable networks. As part of the operation, Bertelsmann was to acquire joint control of BetaResearch (together with Deutsche Telekom) and BetaDigital, both of which had until then been subsidiaries of Kirch. BetaResearch and BetaDigital were to supply the technical services necessary for digital pay television.

11.410 The Commission concluded that Premiere would obtain a near monopoly on the pay TV market in Germany/ the German-speaking area of Europe. The operation would also result in both BetaDigital and BetaResearch holding dominant positions in respect of the supply of technical services for pay TV. Finally, Deutsche Telekom's existing dominant position in respect of cable networks would be strengthened. The operation was prohibited. Kirch has since appealed to the Court of First Instance.

11.411 *Bertelsmann/Kirch/Premiere*: **measurement of market share.** Market share in pay television is measured by subscriber numbers. On this basis, prior to the operation the Commission found that Premiere already held a dominant position. Kirch's digital pay television service, DF1, was the only other service in Germany.

11.412 *Bertelsmann/Kirch/Premiere*: **barriers to entry.** The Commission identified barriers to entry on all relevant markets upstream of pay television. In terms of content, the extent of Bertelsmann and Kirch's exclusive pay TV and pay-per-view rights, especially to films and sports events, was found to prevent the emergence of competition to Premiere. The involvement of Deutsche Telekom further secured Premiere's market position: its future entry into pay television could be excluded. Entry by private cable operators was excluded by their lack of access to

---

[320] *Nordic Satellite Distribution* (Case IV/M490) (1995) [1996] OJ L53/20.
[321] *Bertelsmann/Kirch/Premiere* (Case IV/M993) (1998) [1999] OJ L53/1.

film and sports rights. Moreover, private cable operators had only local networks and were dependent on Deutsche Telekom for backbone transmission. The Commission considered the possibility of their investing in a second backbone cable network to be economically unfeasible. By virtue of their participation in BetaDigital and BetaResearch, Bertelsmann and Kirch (together with Deutsche Telekom) controlled the set top box infrastructure which any new entrant in pay television would require as it would be economically impossible for a new entrant to replicate this infrastructure. Moreover, control of technical services would allow the parties to steer competition in pay television to their advantage.

Bertelsmann/Kirch/Premiere: **relevance of television advertising market.** **11.413** Together, Bertelsmann and Kirch had a market share of almost 90 per cent of the television advertising market in Germany. This position could be used to strengthen Premiere's dominance in pay television. While advertising-funded and pay television constituted separate markets, the Commission stated that the more attractive the programming on advertising-funded television, the less interest viewers had in subscribing to pay TV. As Bertelsmann and Kirch had a leading position in both advertising-funded and pay TV and owned the most important programming rights in respect of both, then after the operation they would be in a position to direct the relationship between the two forms of TV. First, they would be able to buy packages of free and pay TV rights. Secondly, Bertelsmann and Kirch were in a position to co-ordinate the programming available on free TV in order to attract subscribers to Premiere. This strategy would be profitable as there was only a very limited possibility for advertisers to switch to public advertising-funded channels as these channels had restrictions on the amount of advertising they could broadcast, and, in particular, could not do so in 'prime-time'. Thus, Bertelsmann and Kirch would lose revenue if they followed such a strategy only if advertisers substituted advertising on television with other media which seemed unlikely.

It is striking that the Commission did not argue, as would have been logical, that **11.414** the parties' interest in Premiere allowed them to secure their position on the television advertising market (nor did it define television advertising as an affected market). Had the Commission done so, it would have amounted to an admission that the operation did not fall under the Merger Regulation as it led to co-ordination of Kirch and Bertelsmann's interests in a related market. This seems to be the only convincing explanation for the omission.

Bertelsmann/Kirch/Premiere: **remedies rejected.** The parties offered various **11.415** undertakings. First, making available 25 per cent of Kirch's pay TV film rights to third parties. Secondly, opening the share capital of BetaResearch to third parties and allowing them the same voting rights as the parties. Thirdly, allowing private cable operators to market Premiere's pay TV service (but not its pay-per-view services) in competition with Premiere. However, they would be obliged to package Premiere as the parties determined and would be obliged to give Premiere all relevant subscriber information. Finally, Deutsche Telekom making two digital cable channels available for third party pay television channels until the end of 1999. These were all rejected as insufficient.

Leveraging and Related Markets

11.416 The positions of the parties to an operation on a retail television market may be relevant in two respects. First, as has been stated in the introduction their positions on upstream markets can be leveraged to prevent entry to downstream markets. Secondly, as is clear from the *Bertelsmann/Kirch/Premiere* decision, the positions of the parties to an operation on one of the retail television markets on the other such market will be examined. There are two potential points of concern: first, the use of an operation on one market as a vehicle for the co-ordination of their activities on the other; secondly, the leveraging of market power from one market to another in order to foreclose competition in the latter.

12

TRANSPORT

A. Introduction

(1) Economic Significance of the Transport Sector

The value of public or commercial transport activities in the European Union in **12.01**
1996 was some ECU 270 billion. Private transport activities accounted for
another ECU 200 billion. This represented 4 per cent and 3 per cent respectively
of total GDP.

Six million people are employed in the transport service sector: this represents 4 **12.02**
per cent of total employment. In addition, two million people are employed in the
transport equipment industry and over six million in transport related industries.

Since 1970, there has been over 75 per cent growth in the transport of goods in the **12.03**
countries now making up the EU and over 110 per cent growth in the transport
of passengers. There is every reason to believe that this growth will continue and
that transport services, as other services, will remain a major dynamic force in the
European economy.

For these reasons, it is essential that transport markets are competitive and that, **12.04**
where necessary, the Community's competition rules are effectively enforced.

(2) The Treaty Rules Applicable in the Transport Sector

12.05 The environment for the application of the Community's competition rules in the transport sector cannot adequately be explained without first considering the liberalization process. The liberalization process is a transport policy issue which, so far as the Community is concerned, is governed by a specific Chapter in the Treaty.

12.06 Articles 70 to 80 (former Articles 74 to 84) of the Treaty[1] form the Transport Chapter which sets out the principles for the Community's common transport policy, one of only three common policies in the Treaty—the others being agriculture and commerce. It is focused towards rail, road, and inland waterway transport, reflecting the concerns of the six original members of the Community. Article 51 (former Article 61) of the Treaty expressly provides that the freedom to provide services in the field of transport shall be governed by the provisions of the Transport Chapter.

12.07 The Transport Chapter does not, however, lay down common principles (as was done for the Customs Union), merely setting out a procedure for the Council to adopt the necessary guidelines. In contrast to agriculture, there is no express declaration that a common transport market must be realized.

12.08 One conclusion which may be drawn from these differences is that at the time the Treaty was debated and adopted, there was no consensus as to whether transport services are public services or whether they are an economic activity to be governed by commercial principles.

12.09 So far as the legal interpretation of the Treaty is concerned, the question of the applicability of the competition rules to the transport sector was effectively laid to rest by the Court of Justice in the French Seamens' case.[2] The Court ruled that economic sectors could only be excluded from the competition rules by express provision in the Treaty as is the case with Article 36 (former Article 42) concerning agriculture.

12.10 Accordingly, Articles 81 and 82 (former Articles 85 and 86) of the Treaty are fully applicable in the transport sector and may be applied by the Commission either by means of implementing legislation or by means of Article 85 (former Article 89), both of which procedures are explained in this chapter.

---

[1] All references to 'the Treaty' are to the Treaty establishing the European Community.

[2] Case 167/73 *French Seamens'* case, [1974] ECR 359, at para 32: 'Whilst under Article 84 [now Article 80(2)], therefore, sea and air transport, so long as the Council has not decided otherwise, is excluded from the rules of Title IV of Part Two of the Treaty relating to the Common Transport Policy, it remains on the same basis as the other modes of transport, subject to the general rules of the Treaty.'

(3) Liberalization

Liberalization has developed differently in the different transport sectors. Most **12.11** transport sectors were for a long time characterized by monopoly or oligopoly on the supply side, high prices, price fixing, limitations on market access, and very little choice. For example, railways were in a monopoly position for the carriage of goods and workers because of the fact of their mechanization. They thus formed the essential infrastructure of a country and for which it was difficult to gauge profitability.

Liner Shipping

In liner shipping, national carriers and liner conferences often decided together **12.12** with governments whether to allow competitors to have access to markets. It is a highly unusual sector in that for a very long period it enjoyed the privilege of self-regulation. This has meant that economic control of maritime markets has been left in the hands of private companies. This is very different to the situation in air and rail transport markets where it was seen as being normal for governments to regulate.

It has not been clear that self-regulation in shipping has been more successful and **12.13** more beneficial to consumers than governments' regulation in other sectors.

The adoption of the 'Brussels Package' in 1979[3] was the key to the development **12.14** of Community policy in the maritime sector. From a competition policy point of view, the most important aspect of the 'Brussels Package' was that it was centred on the UNCTAD Code of Conduct for Liner Conferences and the acceptance that international liner shipping services should be provided on the basis of the conference system.

This led in 1986 to the adoption of Council Regulation 4055/86[4] applying the prin- **12.15** ciple of freedom to provide services to international maritime transport, excluding transport between ports of a single Member State. The effect of this was to require the abolition of restrictions on the carriage of certain types of cargo and to require the termination of clauses in bilateral agreements between individual Member States and third countries relating to national flag reservations and other cargo sharing arrangements. The Council adopted at the same time Regulation 4056/86.[5]

---

[3] Council Regulation (EEC) 954/79 of 15 May 1979 concerning the ratification by Member States of, or their accession to, the United Nations Convention on a Code of Conduct for Liner Conferences [1979] OJ L121/1.

[4] Council Regulation (EEC) 4055/86 of 22 December 1986 applying the principle of freedom to provide services to maritime transport between Member States and between Member States and third countries [1986] OJ L378/1.

[5] Council Regulation (EEC) 4056/86 of 22 December 1986 laying down detailed rules for the application of Articles 85 and 86 [now Articles 81 and 82] of the Treaty to maritime transport [1986] OJ L378/4.

Air Transport

12.16 European air transport markets have been characterized by a system of intergovernmental agreements and co-operation between airline companies in the framework of the Chicago Convention on International Civil Aviation.[6]

12.17 The turning point for the application of Community competition law was the *Nouvelles Frontières* case,[7] which came to the Court of Justice on the basis of an Article 234 (former Article 177) reference. In its judgment the Court made clear that, notwithstanding the absence of a common transport policy in the air transport sector, national competition authorities under Article 84 (former Article 88) of the Treaty and the Commission under Article 85 of the Treaty could take action in respect of infringements of Articles 81 and 82. In the words of one commentary, 'the agreements concerned (and particularly . . . market-sharing arrangements, profit pooling and other agreements restricting competition) . . . had become nothing less than a notorious public scandal at the expense of the travelling public'.[8]

12.18 This case gave impulse to the Commission's efforts to liberalize intra-Community air transport and to establish detailed rules for the application of Articles 81 and 82 in the air transport sector.

12.19 In December 1987, the first package of aviation measures was adopted. From the point of view of the freedom to provide services, the essential element of the first package was the establishment of third, fourth, and fifth freedom rights:

Third Freedom: the right to put down in another State passengers, freight, and mail taken up in the State in which the carrier is registered.

Fourth Freedom: the right to take on in another State passengers, freight, and mail for offloading in the State in which the carrier is registered.

Fifth Freedom: the right to undertake the commercial air transport of passengers, freight, and mail between two States, other than the State in which the Carrier is registered.

12.20 From a competition policy perspective, the essential element of the first package was the adoption of Regulation 3975/87.[9] An enabling regulation was also

---

[6] Chicago, 7 December 1944.

[7] Joined Cases 209–213/84 *Ministère Public v Asjes et al* [1986] ECR 1425.

[8] PJG Kapteyn and P Verloren Van Themaat, *Introduction to the Law of the European Communities* (2nd edn edited by Laurence W Gormley, Kluwer/Graham & Trotman, 1989) 731.

[9] Council Regulation (EEC) 3975/87 of 14 December 1987 laying down the procedure for the application of the rules on competition to undertakings in the air transport sector [1987] OJ L374/1.

adopted by the Council[10] giving the Commission the means to adopt group exemptions in the air transport sector.

In 1988, the Commission adopted three group exemptions. First, Commission Regulation 2671/88[11] relating to the joint planning and co-ordination of capacities, the sharing of revenue, consultations on tariffs on scheduled air services, and the allocation of slots at airports. Second, Commission Regulation 2672/88[12] relating to computer reservations systems. And third, Commission Regulation 2673/88[13] relating to ground handling at airports. **12.21**

In June 1990, the second liberalization package was adopted. It was designed to establish a transitional regime which would allow carriers to adapt to the more competitive environment which would result from the anticipated third package. The third package was adopted by the Council in December 1992. This consisted primarily in regulations relating to operating licences, market access, and tariffs. **12.22**

Rail

Railway activities have traditionally been operated by domestic companies enjoying exclusive rights for all or a large proportion of the national railway activities. Governments have been hesitant to liberalize the railway sector and have imposed public service obligations without compensating railway operators fully for the costs involved. Although the Commission has had detailed rules for the application of the competition rules in the rail sector since 1968,[14] this isolation from competition has prevented railway activities from benefiting from the positive effects that open-market conditions produce in terms of cost reduction, improvement of services, and development of new products and markets. **12.23**

As a result, railway's share of the transport market has substantially declined. In those countries where the railways formerly held a large share of the freight **12.24**

---

[10] Council Regulation (EEC) 3976/87 of 14 December 1987 on the application of Article 85(3) [now Article 81(3)] of the Treaty to certain categories of agreements and concerted practices in the air transport sector [1987] OJ L374/9.

[11] Commission Regulation (EEC) 2671/88 of 26 July 1988 on the application of Article 85(3) [now Article 81(3)] of the Treaty to certain categories of agreements between undertakings, decisions of associations of undertakings and concerted practices concerning joint planning and co-ordination of capacity, sharing of revenue and consultations on tariffs on scheduled air services and slot allocation at airports [1988] OJ L239/9.

[12] Commission Regulation (EEC) 2672/88 of 26 July 1988 on the application of Article 85(3) [now Article 81(3)] of the Treaty to certain categories of agreements between undertakings relating to computer reservation systems for air transport services [1988] OJ L239/13.

[13] Commission Regulation (EEC) 2673/88 of 26 July 1988 on the application of Article 85(3) [now Article 81(3)] of the Treaty to certain categories of agreements between undertakings, decisions of associations of undertakings and concerted practices concerning ground handling services [1988] OJ L239/17.

[14] Council Regulation (EEC) 1017/68 of 19 July 1968 applying rules of competition to transport by rail, road and inland waterway [1968] OJ L175/1.

market this has fallen by some 50 per cent between the 1970s and the mid-1990s. Railways have continued to lose traffic to road transport not only because road operators have been successful in reducing their real costs and improving their quality but also because road operators have not been confronted with the full costs of their activities.

12.25 This situation has started to change recently and over the last seven or eight years, in order to help EC railways adapt to single market conditions, and to increase their efficiency, the Commission has taken its first steps towards the full liberalization of railway services. However, given the special characteristics of this sector, these measures have fallen short of the liberalization measures in other transport sectors such as air transport.

12.26 Under the first package of liberalization measures adopted in 1991,[15] and supplemented in 1995,[16] Member States are required to ensure the independence of management of railway undertakings by separating the management of railway infrastructure from the provision of railway transport services.

12.27 Secondly, competition has been injected by allowing access to railway infrastructures for international services offered by international groupings of railway undertakings and railway undertakings engaged in international combined transport of goods throughout the EC.[17]

(4) Specificities of the Transport Sector

12.28 When applying the competition rules, the Commission has to take into consideration a number of specificities of the transport sector. Scheduled transport services have certain characteristics which although not specific to transport are not usually found together in other industries:

- in the absence of regulatory barriers, barriers to entry tend to be financial—the investment costs tend to be high (although not necessarily for road transport);

- scheduled services require the provision of some reserve capacity;

- demand may be seasonal and/or cyclical (for example, there are even daily and hourly fluctuations in demand for railways and flights);

- one-way demand may lead to low prices on the return, or thin, leg;

- operating costs are a small percentage of overall costs;

---

[15] Council Directive (EEC) 91/440 of 29 July 1991 on the development of the Community's railways [1991] OJ L237/25.

[16] Council Directive (EC) 95/18 of 19 June 1995 on the licensing of Railway Undertakings [1995] OJ L143/7. Council Directive (EC) 95/19 of 19 June 1995 on the allocation of railway infrastructure capacity and the charging of infrastructure fees [1995] OJ L143/75.

[17] Council Directive (EEC) 75/130 of 17 February 1975 on the establishment of common rules for certain types of combined road/rail carriage of goods between Member States [1975] OJ L48/31.

- they are *service* industries which depend on demand from manufacturing industry and private individuals; and

- they may have strategic ramifications, such as national defence.

The existence of these specificities has led some transport undertakings to seek to draw a distinction between 'fair' and 'destructive' competition. This approach is not new,[18] but has yet to be accepted by the Court of Justice. **12.29**

(5) Market Definition

The Commission's 1997 Notice on market definition is also applicable to transport.[19] **12.30**

The standard approach in defining relevant markets in the transport sector is to look at individual routes concerned by the agreement or practice and see whether other routes (including those using different modes of transport) are substitutable.[20] Thus, for international transport services the relevant market would be defined as being a particular route or (more likely in the case of the transportation of goods) a bundle of routes. **12.31**

The common practice in each of the three main transport sectors (air, sea, rail) is, as in other sectors,[21] to focus on demand substitutability rather than supply substitutability.[22] Thus, the Commission looks at the physical and technical characteristics of a transport service to see whether it is functionally interchangeable with another transport service at a given price.[23] Speed of conversion of a vessel/plane/train to provide a different service may be relevant: accordingly supply substitutability cannot be ignored. In *BA/AA*,[24] a distinction has been made between time-sensitive and other passengers on certain specified transatlantic routes. **12.32**

In some service markets (including transport markets), the place where the service is provided needs to be taken into account in determining whether the service is substitutable for other services and arriving at the definition of the relevant service market. The definition of the relevant service market therefore includes a geographic element in its own right. **12.33**

---

[18] See, for example, Case T–29/94 *SPO v Commission* [1995] ECR II–289, at point 294, where the Court of First Instance considered that no distinction could be made between normal and destructive competition. The appeal was rejected as manifestly inadmissible by Order of the Court of 25 March 1996 (Case C–137/95P [1996] ECR I–1611).

[19] Commission Notice on the definition of the relevant market for the purposes of Community competition law [1997] OJ C372.

[20] See Case 66/86 *Ahmed Saeed* [1989] ECR 803, at para 40; *LH/SAS* [1996] OJ L54/28, para 31; and *Eurotunnel* [1994] OJ L354/66, at paras 62 and 63.

[21] eg, Case T–30/89 *Hilti AG v Commission* [1991] ECR II–1439, at para 70.

[22] *Far Eastern Freight Conference* [1994] OJ L378/17, at paras 25–29.

[23] *Trans-Atlantic Agreement* [1994] OJ L376/1, at paras 35–58 (see nn 57–58).

[24] *BA/AA*, Draft Proposal adopted on 8 July 1998, not published.

12.34 However, the purchaser of the service may be located in a different place to the place where the service is provided. Since the notion of geographic market is used for the purpose of delineating the area in which market power is exercised, it follows that in some service markets the geographic market is the place where the consumer is located. This is not necessarily the place where the service is supplied. The geographic market is in fact the identification of those consumers against whom market power is exercised.

12.35 Thus, a shipper in Australia may telephone a shipping line in Singapore to arrange the transport of a container from Munich to Pittsburgh. The market power of the service supplier is not exercised in Munich, Pittsburgh, or Singapore but in Australia. The same is true of someone in Brussels who telephones a travel agent in Manchester to purchase a plane ticket on Air India from London to New York. In both these cases the number of customers outside the 'normal' catchment area may be statistically insignificant. In neither case does the location of the consumer affect the service market definition.

12.36 Identification of those against whom market power is exercised is important not only in relation to the establishment of a dominant position but also in relation to the establishment of the appreciability of the restriction of competition and the fourth condition of Article 81(3).

12.37 Finally, it is an essential part of the analysis in the transport sector to consider the possibility of market entry and consequently to assess barriers to entry/exit.[25] Although potential market entry is often exaggerated by incumbents in a market with high market shares, it is true that in certain transport markets entry can be accomplished relatively speedily although it may be expensive.

B. Procedures

(1) Regulation 17 and Regulation 141

12.38 Although Regulation 17 is of general application, Regulation 141[26] removed from its scope

> agreements, decisions and concerted practices in the transport sector which have as their object or effect the fixing of transport rates and conditions, the limitation or control of the supply of transport or the sharing of transport markets nor shall it apply to the abuse of a dominant position, within the meaning Article 86 [now Article 82] of the Treaty, within the transport market.

---

[25] *TAA* (n 23 above).
[26] Council Regulation 141/62 exempting transport from the application of Council Regulation 17 [1962] OJ L124/2751.

Following the exclusion of the transport sector from the scope of application of   **12.39**
Regulation 17, three separate procedural Regulations have been adopted, one for
each mode of transport.

There remains doubt both as to the dividing line between Regulation 17 and the   **12.40**
transport Regulations and as between the transport Regulations themselves. The
Commission's position has been that services neighbouring the transport service
itself should be dealt with under Regulation 17. Thus, decisions relating to the
following services have been adopted under Regulation 17:

— travel agency and cargo agency,[27]

— computer reservation systems,[28]

— port services,[29]

— ground handling services at airports,[30]

— express delivery cases.[31]

This approach may need to be revised in the light of the Court's decision in the   **12.41**
UIC case.[32] In appropriate cases the Commission will now be more cautious to
give parties the procedural benefits of both the applicable transport Regulation
and Regulation 17.

Prior to the *UIC* case, the Commission's practice had been to rely on the third   **12.42**
recital to Regulation 141: 'Whereas the distinctive features of transport make it
justifiable to exempt from the application of Regulation 17 only agreements, decisions and concerted practices *directly relating to the provision of transport services*'
(emphasis added).

In the *UIC* case, the Commission fined the International Railway Union (UIC)   **12.43**
for breach of Article 81(1) for issuing a leaflet recommending the way in which
member railways should appoint travel agents and setting a standard rate of commission for travel agents. The Commission applied the procedures of Regulation
17 arguing, in particular, that travel agency services are neither transport services
nor services 'directly relating' to the provision of transport services.

On appeal,[33] the Court of First Instance annulled the decision, upholding the   **12.44**
UIC's argument that the procedure of Regulation 1017/68, and not that of

---

[27] *Distribution of railway tickets by travel agents* [1992] OJ L366; *IATA Cargo Agency Programme*
[1991] OJ L258/29; *IATA Passenger Agency Programme* [1991] OJ L258/18.

[28] *London European—Sabena* [1988] OJ L317.

[29] *Sea Containers v Stena Sealink—Interim measures* [1994] OJ L15/8.

[30] *Olympic Airways* [1985] OJ L46/51; *Flughafen Frankfurt/Main AG* [1998] OJ L72/30; *Alpha Flight Services/Aéroports de Paris* [1998] OJ L230.

[31] Commission Decision of 28 January 1998 relating to a proceeding under Article 85 [now Article 81] of the EC Treaty (Case IV/36.412—*DHLI*), not published.

[32] *Distribution of railway tickets* (n 27 above).

[33] Case T–14/93 *UIC v Commission* [1995] ECR II–1503.

Regulation 17, should have been used. The Commission's appeal to the Court of Justice was rejected.[34] The Court upheld the Court of First Instance's reasoning that Article 1 of Regulation 1017/68 does not mention agreements etc 'directly' related to transport, but agreements etc 'in the transport sector which have as their object or effect the fixing of transport rates and conditions . . .'.

12.45 In considering whether the errors of law on the part of the Commission had the effect of depriving UIC of all or any of the procedural safeguards to which it was entitled, the Court of First Instance noted that there are at least three fundamental differences between Regulation 17 and Regulation 1017/68.

12.46 First, in the system of Regulation 17, prior notification to the Commission is, on the whole, an essential prerequisite for obtaining, where appropriate, a declaration under Article 81(3) of the Treaty that Article 81(1) is inapplicable. In the system of Regulation 1017/68, on the other hand, notification to the Commission is optional and does not constitute an essential prerequisite for obtaining an individual declaration under Article 5 of that regulation that Article 2 of the Regulation is inapplicable.

12.47 In the *UIC* case, even though the Commission did give a brief negative reply to the question whether the agreement in question No 130 might have been exempted under Article 81(3) of the Treaty if it had been notified, it was not certain that the Commission's reasoning would have been the same if it had found that the UIC was entitled to invoke the benefit of Article 5 of Regulation 1017/68.

12.48 Secondly, the Commission consulted the Advisory Committee provided for by Article 10(3) of Regulation 17, composed of officials of the Member States competent in the matter of restrictive practices and monopolies, and not the Advisory Committee provided for in Article 16(4) of Regulation 1017/68, composed of officials of the Member States competent in the matter of restrictive practices and monopolies in transport. Since the officials of the Member States consulted on the matter were not those specified in the Regulation which should have been applied in the case, the Court considered that it could not be assumed that the result of the consultation of the proper committee would have been the same.

12.49 Thirdly, under Article 17(1) and (2) of Regulation 1017/68, the Commission is not to give a decision in respect of which consultation of the specialist Advisory Committee referred to in Article 16 is compulsory until after the expiry of twenty days from the date on which that Advisory Committee has delivered its Opinion. During that period, any Member State may request that the Council be convened to examine with the Commission any question of principle concerning the common transport policy which it considers to be involved in the particular case for

---

[34] Case C–264/95P *Commission v UIC* [1997] ECR I–1287.

decision. If such a request is made, the Commission is not to give its decision until after the Council meeting. The Commission must also take into account the policy guidelines which emerge from the Council meeting. That provision therefore sets up a system of protection from which the addressee of the Commission's decision is entitled to benefit.

It followed that the application of Regulation 17 instead of Regulation 1017/68 **12.50** amounted to a breach of an essential procedural requirement and had the effect of depriving the UIC of the procedural safeguards to which it was entitled in the context of the application of Regulation 1017/68.

Although questions as to the scope of the other sectoral Regulations have arisen, **12.51** those Regulations are framed in more precise terms than Regulation 1017/68 and the judgment in the *UIC* case is not directly relevant in determining the scope of Regulation 4056 and Regulation 3975.

(2) The Procedural Rules of the Three Sectoral Regulations

The competition rules which are applied in the transport sector are identical to **12.52** those applied elsewhere.[35] Restrictions of competition and markets are defined in an identical manner: the only differences are procedural.

(3) Procedural Differences to Regulation 17

The detailed rules concerning the application of the competition rules have the **12.53** following main differences to the general rules:

The Commission can grant an exemption without having received a notification **12.54** (ie following a complaint or on its own initiative). The date from which the exemption takes effect may be *prior* to the date of the *decision* (and by implication before the date of the notification—assuming at that time it fulfilled the conditions for exemption). The onus is expressly placed on undertakings to ensure that their agreements comply with Community law.

The application of the *Automec*[36] principles is unclear and there is probably an **12.55** obligation[37] on the Commission to issue decisions rejecting complaints as unfounded and to issue Article 81(3) decisions (ie the Commission probably cannot issue administrative letters). On the other hand, there is no obligation to initiate procedures to terminate infringements.

Under Regulation 1017/68, the Commission may not adopt a decision until at **12.56** least twenty days following the meeting of the Advisory Committee. This is to

---

[35] *French Seamens'* case (n 2 above), at para 32; *Nouvelles Frontières* (n 7 above), at paras 42–45; *Ahmed Saeed* (n 20 above), at paras 32–33.

[36] Case T–24/90 *Automec v Commission* [1992] ECR II–2223.

[37] 'the Commission . . . *shall*' replaces the expression 'the Commission . . . *may*' ('la Commission . . . rend' 'la Commission . . . peut').

allow Member States the opportunity to request the Council to meet and consider whether the case in question raises any questions of principle. If so, the Commission is obliged to take into account in its decision any policy guidelines which emerge.

12.57 There is no express provision for negative clearance in the inland and maritime Regulations—however, it is reasonable to consider that the Commission has the power, as a general principle, to inform companies that there are no grounds for action under Community competition law.

12.58 In addition to a number of group exemptions (two in the maritime sector and two in the aviation sector), each of the transport Regulations contains *an 'objections' procedure.*

The 'objections' procedure

12.59 If an application is admissible pursuant to the relevant Regulation, if it is complete, and if the arrangement which is the subject of the application has not given rise to a complaint or to an own-initiative proceeding, the Commission publishes a summary of the request in the *Official Journal* and invites comments from interested third parties, from Member States, and, where requests relate to the EEA Agreement, from EFTA States.

12.60 Unless the Commission notifies the applicants within ninety days of the date of publication that there are serious doubts as to the applicability of Article 81(3) of the Treaty or Article 53(3) of the EEA Agreement, the arrangement will be deemed exempt for the time already elapsed and for a maximum of three years from the date of publication, in the case of applications under Regulation 1017/68, and for a maximum of six years from the date of publication in the case of applications under Regulations 4056/86 and 3975/87.

12.61 Additionally, under the group exemption for consortia, there is an 'opposition' procedure. This involves no publication and gives the Commission a time limit of six months from date of notification in which to oppose exemption.

(4) Relevance of Procedural Differences

12.62 There have only been two examples of an exemption without notification, both in the railway sector.[38] Accordingly the additional flexibility this provision might be thought to provide has had little practical value. On the other hand, it has some drawbacks: in negative decisions, the Commission is required not only to make a finding of an infringement but also a finding that the conditions for exemption

---

[38] See for example Commission Decision (EEC) 93/174 of 24 February 1993 relating to a proceeding under Article 85 [now Article 81] of the EC Treaty (Tariff Structures in the Combined Transport of Goods) [1993] OJ L73.

are not fulfilled. Secondly, national authorities cannot rely on the fact that there has been no notification to reach the conclusion that there is no possibility of exemption.

The reason why the Commission may be under the obligation to take a formal **12.63** position in transport cases is probably related to the fact that parties are not under an obligation to notify agreements in order to obtain exemption.

The provision allowing the Council to intervene following an Advisory **12.64** Committee has never been used.

C. The Application of the Substantive Rules in the Three Sectors

(1) Inland

Regulation 1017/68

Scope of Regulation 1017/68

Regulation 1017/68 applies, in the field of transport by rail, road, and inland **12.65** waterway, to:

- all agreements, decisions, and concerted practices which have as their object or effect the fixing of transport rates and conditions, the limitation or control of the supply of transport, the sharing of transport markets;

- the application of technical improvements or technical co-operation, or the joint financing or acquisition of transport equipment or supplies where such operations are directly related to the provision of transport services and are necessary for the joint operation of services by a grouping within the meaning of Article 4 of road or inland waterway transport undertakings; and

- the abuse of a dominant position on the transport market.

These provisions also apply to operations of providers of services ancillary to **12.66** transport which have any of the objects or effects listed above.

Regulation 1017/68 contains an exception for 'technical agreements' and a block **12.67** exemption for certain groups of small and medium-sized undertakings as well as provisions for the grant of individual exemption.

Dual legal basis

One of the most notable features of Regulation 1017/68 is that it contains a dual **12.68** legal basis: Articles 71 and 83 (former Article 87). The reason for this dual legal basis is not clear. If, as appears from the text, the Council intended to establish a distinct stand-alone competition regime for inland transport, why was the reference to Article 83 included?

12.69 When adopted, the Council was unwilling to recognize that Articles 81 and 82 applied to transport. It is highly questionable whether the Council may, in an implementing regulation based on Article 83, redefine the provisions of Articles 81 and 82 of the Treaty and, in any event, in 1974 the Court confirmed application to transport of the general rules of the EEC Treaty.[39]

12.70 Thus, the first question concerning Regulation 1017/68 is whether the rules applied under Regulation 1017/68 are the same as those applied under Regulation 17.

Articles 2 and 5 of Regulation 1017/68—Equivalent to Article 81

12.71 Articles 2 and 5 of Regulation 1017/68 restate Articles 81(1) and (3) of the Treaty, but with some minor differences.

12.72 The Commission's practice has been to refer to Article 81 usually together with Articles 2 and/or 5 of Regulation 1017/68. In the *Deutsche Bahn* decision,[40] the Commission referred only to Article 82 and not to Article 8 of the Regulation. The Court of First Instance[41] accepted that the aim of Article 8 of the Regulation was no different from that of Article 82. It is now the Commission's practice to refer both to Article 82 of the EC Treaty and to Article 8 of the Regulation.

12.73 It is the Commission's approach to interpret Articles 2 and 5 of Regulation 1017/68 no differently from Articles 81 and 82. In the *FEFC* decision,[42] the Commission stated that:

> Regulation (EEC) No 1017/68 applying rules of competition to transport by rail, road and inland waterway was the first regulation implementing competition rules in the transport sector. Having been adopted before the Court of Justice's express confirmation that the competition rules contained in the Treaty apply to the transport sector [in the *French Seamen's* case], Regulation (EEC) No 1017/68 reproduces with little variation the text of Articles 85 and 86 [now Articles 81 and 82] of the Treaty.

> As part of the Community's secondary legislation, Regulation (EEC) No 1017/68 cannot derogate from the provisions of the Treaty. Consequently, Regulation (EEC) No 1017/68 must be interpreted in the light of the case law of the Court, as providing the Commission with the necessary means to enforce Articles 85 and 86 of the Treaty in inland transport, without deviating from the basic competition rules contained in the Treaty.

> An agreement which does not comply with Article 85(3) cannot be exempted pursuant to Regulation (EEC) No 1017/68. Articles 2, 5, 7 and 8 of Regulation (EEC) No 1017/68 should therefore be interpreted in the same way as Articles 85 and 86, in the light of the case law, and construed as adding nothing to them.

---

[39] *French Seamens'* case (n 2 above).
[40] *HOV SVZ/MCN* [1994] OJ L104/4.
[41] Case T–229/94 *Deutsche Bahn v Commission* [1997] ECR II–1689, at para 77.
[42] *FEFC* (n 22 above), at paras 60–62.

Article 3 of Regulation 1017/68—Technical Agreements

In accordance with its approach that Regulation 1017/68 does not modify **12.74** Articles 81 and 82, the Commission has interpreted Article 3 of Regulation 1017/68, the provision relating to 'technical agreements', as follows:

> Article 3 of Regulation No 1017/68 is merely declaratory and lists a number of different kinds of agreement which do not fall within the scope of Article 85(1) [now Article 81(1)] of the Treaty when their sole object and sole effect is to achieve technical improvements or technical co-operation.[43]

The technical agreements listed in Article 3 are the following: **12.75**

(a) the standardization of equipment, transport supplies, vehicles, or fixed installations;

(b) the exchange or pooling, for the purpose of operating transport services, of staff, equipment, vehicles, or fixed installations;

(c) the organization and execution of successive, complementary, substitute, or combined transport operations, and the fixing and application of inclusive rates and conditions for such operations, including special competitive rates;

(d) the use, for journeys by a single mode of transport, of the routes which are most rational from the operational point of view;

(e) the co-ordination of transport timetables for connecting routes;

(f) the grouping of single consignments;

(g) the establishment of uniform rules as to the structure of tariffs and their conditions of application, provided such rules do not lay down transport rates and conditions.

The Court of First Instance has held that the introduction of a legal exception for **12.76** agreements of a purely technical nature cannot amount to an authorization, on the part of the Community legislature, allowing agreements to be concluded whose purpose is the joint fixing of prices.[44]

Article 4 of Regulation 1017/68—Exemption for Groups of Small and Medium-Sized Companies

Article 4 of Regulation 1017/68 provides a group exemption for agreements, **12.77** decisions and concerted practices whose purpose is:

---

[43] ibid, at para 66. This also follows from *HOV SVZ/MCN* (n 40 above) at para 91. The English language version of Article 3 of Regulation 1017/68 has omitted the word 'sole', which is included in the original language version of Regulation 1017/68 as well as in Regulations 4056/86 (Article 2) and 3975/87 (Article 2).

[44] *Deutsche Bahn* (n 41 above).

- the constitution and operation of groupings of road or inland waterway transport undertakings with a view to carrying on transport activities;

- the joint financing or acquisition of transport equipment or supplies, where these operations are directly related to the provision of transport services and are necessary for the joint operations of the aforesaid groupings.

12.78 The scope of the group exemption is limited to cases where the total carrying capacity of any grouping does not exceed 10,000 metric tons in the case of road transport or 500,000 metric tons in the case of transport by inland waterway. The individual capacity of each undertaking belonging to a grouping shall not exceed 1,000 metric tons in the case of road transport or 50,000 metric tons in the case of transport by inland waterway.

12.79 The block exemption is unlimited in time and would appear to be incapable of being withdrawn. Where there are effects which are incompatible with the requirements of Article 5 and which constitute an abuse of the exemption from the provisions of Article 2, the Council is given the power to order undertakings or associations of undertakings to make such effects cease.

Article 5 of Regulation 1017/68—Conditions for Exemption

12.80 So far as individual exemptions are concerned, the Commission has taken the position that the four conditions set out in Article 5 of Regulation 1017/68 lay down an identical test to the conditions for exemption set out in Article 81(3) of the Treaty.

12.81 **Eurotunnel.** The *Eurotunnel* case[45] concerned the individual exemption granted by the Commission on 13 December 1994 to Eurotunnel, SNCF, and BR in respect of their agreement concerning the use of the Channel Tunnel. This usage contract gave BR and SNCF 50 per cent of the capacity, per hour in each direction, of the fixed link with the remaining 50 per cent left to Eurotunnel. The usage contract was exempted for a period of thirty years beginning on 16 November 1991.

12.82 The decision identified the relevant markets as:

(1) the market in providing hourly paths for rail transport in the tunnel, and

(2) a number of markets in the international transport of passengers and freight between the United Kingdom and the Continent.

12.83 The Commission considered the arrangements restricted competition in two ways. First, they restricted competition between Eurotunnel and BR/SNCF on

---

[45] Joined Cases T–79/95 and T–80/95, *Société nationale des chemins de fer français and British Railways Board v Commission* [1996] ECR II–1491.

the transport markets since the contract provided for a division of the markets between Eurotunnel for the operation shuttles, and BR/SNCF for the operation of international trains carrying passengers and freight.

Secondly, BR and SNCF were effectively given a monopoly of those hourly paths **12.84** available for international passenger and freight trains. Accordingly, other railway undertakings could not obtain from Eurotunnel the hourly paths necessary to operate international passenger or freight trains in competition with SNCF and BR. The Commission made the exemption subject to the condition that BR and SNCF should not withhold their agreement to the sale to other railway undertakings of at least 25 per cent of the hourly capacity of the tunnel in each direction in order to run international passenger and freight trains.

On appeal, the Court of First Instance found that the Commission's statements in **12.85** the decision to the effect that half of the tunnel capacity was reserved for shuttle services and the other half for international trains and that BR/SNCF were entitled to all the capacity reserved for international trains were wrong. The assessment in the decision of the restrictive effects of the contract on competition was founded on that error. Thus, in its evaluation of those effects as regards other railway undertakings, the Commission failed to have regard to the possibility that Eurotunnel might still cede some of its own capacity to other undertakings wishing to run international trains through the tunnel.

The Court of First Instance held that if the Commission had correctly assessed the **12.86** opportunities available to other railway undertakings to obtain the hourly paths necessary to run international trains through the tunnel it might not have deemed it necessary to impose conditions on the applicants.

The circumstances of this case are clearly unusual since the annulment of the decision has meant that the usage contract remains unexempted and the conditions **12.87** on which it might be exempted have to be reconsidered in the light of a correct assessment of the facts. The case also brings out the rather obvious point that an exemption with conditions amounts to an indirect finding that the notified arrangements did not fulfil the conditions for exemption.

European Night Services. On 21 September, the Commission authorized the **12.88** European Night Services agreement between British Rail (BR), Deutsche Bahn (DB), Nederlandse Spoorwegen (NS), the Société Nationale des Chemins de Fer Français (SNCF), and the Société Nationale des Chemins de Fer Belges (SNCB), concerning the running of night passenger trains between the United Kingdom and the Continent.

BR, DB, NS, SNCF, and SNCB had set up a specialized subsidiary, European **12.89** Night Services Ltd (ENS), to organize and run night train services. The Commission took the view that this agreement was likely to restrict competition between the parties to it and between them and other operators, who would be faced with an obstacle to entering the market in question. Such an agreement also has advantages for consumers and the Commission therefore decided to authorize the agreement for eight years. However, in order not to prevent other operators from offering similar services, the Commission required the railway undertakings to sell to them the rail services they had agreed to sell to their subsidiary, on the same terms.

12.90 The *ENS* decision was annulled by the Court of First Instance in October 1998[46] on the basis that the Commission's finding that the arrangements brought about a material restriction of competition was not supported by the evidence put forward in the decision.

12.91 **Trans-European Networks (TENs).** The Trans-European Rail Freight Freeways will be a series of railway corridors on which railway operators will be granted open access on a non-discriminatory basis. These corridors will connect the main European economic centres with high density of freight traffic. Competition issues arise since rail infrastructure managers will have to co-operate in the organization of these freeways.

12.92 In essence, in assessing the Trans-European Networks transport projects under EC competition rules, the Commission has said that it will apply the following basic principles:[47]

- Where the infrastructure manager wishes to allow transport undertakings to reserve capacity as from the launch of the project, all EC undertakings that might be interested should be given the chance of doing so.

- The capacity reserved to an undertaking should be in proportion to the direct or indirect financial commitments entered into by it and should be in line with planned operational requirements over a reasonable period.

- As new infrastructure is not generally congested right from the start of operation, an operator should not be able to reserve all of the capacity available. Some of the capacity should remain available so as to allow competing services to be operated by other undertakings.

- The period covered by capacity reservation agreements must not exceed a reasonable period, to be determined on a case-by-case basis.

---

[46] Joined Cases T–374/94, T–375/94, T–384/94 and T–388/94 *European Night Services Ltd (ENS), Eurostar (UK) Ltd, formerly European Passenger Services Ltd (EPS), Union internationale des chemins de fer (UIC), NV Nederlandse Spoorwegen (NS) and Société nationale des chemins de fer français (SNCF) v Commission*, Judgment of the Court of First Instance of 15 September 1998, not yet reported.

[47] Clarification of the Commission recommendations on the application of the competition rules to new infrastructure projects, 30 September 1997, OJ C298/5.

According to the Commission, these principles are intended to reconcile the need **12.93** to maximize the financial viability of rail infrastructure projects with the provision of free and non-discriminatory access to infrastructure. By clarifying the application of the competition rules, the Commission's intention has been to provide legal guidance and thus facilitate the creation of Trans-European Networks.

Article 6 of Regulation 1017/68—Crisis Cartels

In the particular case of 'crisis cartels', Article 6 sets out a specific regime for indi- **12.94** vidual exemption. This regime does not appear to be directly based on Article 81(3) and it provides that exemption may be granted where the Council has declared a state of crisis to exist and the Commission finds that the third and fourth conditions of Article 5 of Regulation 1017/68 are fulfilled. Probably the best way to interpret this strange provision is to consider that the resolution of a state of crisis would imply that the first two conditions of Article 5 were being met.

In any event, Article 6 has never been applied and, since it is limited in time **12.95** ('Until such time as the Council, acting in pursuance of the common transport policy, introduces appropriate measures to ensure a stable transport market . . .'), it is likely that this obscure provision of community competition law will never be applied.

Article 8 of Regulation 1017/68—Equivalent to Article 82

Article 8 of Regulation 1017/68 contains provisions which are identical to those **12.96** contained in Article 82 save that they have been rewritten so as to refer expressly to transport services.

In this initial phase of rail transport liberalization, most national railway under- **12.97** takings still enjoy monopoly power for the provision of traction. Operators who want to make use of access rights are therefore obliged to purchase traction from a national monopoly. In these circumstances, railway undertakings providing traction enjoy a dominant position and must be prevented from putting into place abusive practices such as discrimination or refusal to supply traction.

In the context of Article 82, it is obviously relevant that railway infrastructure **12.98** providers are in a monopoly position. As with ports and airports (see further below), it is essential to ensure that this position is not abused if there is to be competition in the provision of train services. In particular, access rights need to be backed up by provisions on charging and capacity allocation to ensure that applicants for access are treated in a fair and non-discriminatory manner.

Deutsche Bahn. On 1 April 1988, DB, SNCB, NS, Intercontainer, and Trans- **12.99** fracht concluded the 'Maritime Container Network Agreement'. The MCN Agreement related to carriage by rail of maritime containers to or from Germany which pass through a German, Belgian, or Netherlands port. Among the German ports, referred to in the MCN Agreement as the 'northern ports', were Hamburg, Bremen, and Bremerhaven. The Belgian and Netherlands ports, known as the 'western ports', included Antwerp and Rotterdam.

12.100 The Commission found that, in view of its statutory monopoly, DB held a dominant position on the market for the supply of rail transport services in Germany. DB had abused that dominant position by acting in such a way that tariffs for carriage between a Belgian or Netherlands port and Germany were appreciably and unjustifiably higher than for carriage between points within Germany and the German ports. The Commission imposed a fine on DB of ECU 11,000,000.[48] The Commission's decision was upheld by the Court of First Instance in October 1997.[49]

(2) Maritime

Regulation 4056/86

12.101 Regulation 4056/86, like Regulation 1017/68, is based on two Treaty provisions—Articles 80(2) and 83. The reason for this is easier to justify than the dual legal basis of Regulation 1017/68 because Article 9 of Regulation 4056/86 deals with the question of conflicts of law with third countries. Since the resolution of such questions falls outside the scope of the competition Chapter of the Treaty, it was unexceptionable to include Article 80(2) as the legal base for the Regulation.

Article 1—Scope of Regulation 4056/86

12.102 Regulation 4056/86 lays down detailed rules for the application of Articles 81 and 82 of the Treaty to international maritime transport services from or to one or more Community ports, other than tramp vessel services. The scope of the Regulation also therefore excludes cabotage services. Since its adoption in 1986, the biggest controversy surrounding Regulation 4056/86 has been whether its scope is limited to maritime transport services or whether it also covers multimodal transport services including a maritime leg.

12.103 In the FEFC Decision,[50] the Commission concluded that the scope of the exemption contained in Article 3 of Regulation 4056/86 cannot be wider than the scope of Regulation 4056/86 itself, Article 1(2) of which provides that 'it shall apply only to international maritime transport services from or to one or more Community ports'.

12.104 Notwithstanding this apparently clear wording, the Commission's interpretation of the scope of the group exemption is still disputed and the Court of First

---

[48] *HOV SVZ/MCN* (n 40 above).
[49] *Deutsche Bahn* (n 41 above).
[50] *FEFC* (n 22 above).

Instance has not ruled on the application to annul the *FEFC* decision. One of the issues not yet fully addressed is where maritime transport services end and land transport services begin. In the *FEFC* decision the Commission expressly avoided taking a position on this question: 'this Decision does not address the question whether price fixing agreements relating to port handling services fall within the scope of application of Article 3 of Regulation No 4056/86'.

The possibility remains that neither the Commission nor the liner shipping industry is correct and that multimodal transport is, *sui generis*, excluded from the scope of Regulation 17 but not falling within the scope of any of the transport Regulations. This would put it into the category of cases dealt with under the Article 85 procedure about which more is written below.   **12.105**

Article 2 of Regulation 4056/86—Exception for Technical Agreements

Article 2 of Regulation 4056/86 contains a similar exception for 'technical agreements' to that found in Article 3 of Regulation 1017/68. The Commission's approach to these provisions has been the same.   **12.106**

Article 3 of Regulation 4056/86—Block Exemption for Liner Shipping Conferences

The most distinctive feature of Regulation 4056/86 is the group exemption Article 3 contains in respect of horizontal price fixing by liner shipping conferences. Exemption is also granted to the following other activities if one or more of these is carried on by the members of a liner conference in addition to fixing prices and conditions of carriage for maritime transport services: **12.107**

(a) the co-ordination of shipping timetables, sailing dates, or dates of calls;

(b) the determination of the frequency of sailings or calls;

(c) the co-ordination or allocation of sailings or calls among members of the conference;

(d) the regulation of the carrying capacity offered by each member;

(e) the allocation of cargo or revenue among members.

This is without question the most generous exemption which exists in Community competition law especially as it is unlimited in time and is granted regardless of market shares. In accordance with general principles[51] and influenced by the broad scope of the group exemption, the Commission has sought to   **12.108**

---

[51] See Case C–70/93, *BMW v ALD* [1995] ECR I–3439, at para 28 and Case C–266/93 *Bundeskartellamt v Volkswagen and VAG* [1995] ECR I–3477, at para 33 '. . . having regard to the general principle prohibiting anticompetitive agreements laid down in Article 85(1) of the Treaty, provisions in a block exemption which derogate from that principle cannot be interpreted widely and cannot be construed in such a way as to extend the effects of the regulation beyond what is necessary to protect the interests which they are intended to safeguard'.

interpret Article 3 narrowly. This general approach has been endorsed by the Court of First Instance in the *CEWAL* case.[52]

12.109 The *CEWAL* case arose out of the Commission's inquiries into the practices of the shipping conferences operating on routes between Europe and West Africa. On 23 December 1992, the Commission adopted a decision finding that three liner shipping conferences had infringed Article 81 and that the members of Associated Central West Africa Lines (CEWAL), a liner shipping conference, had infringed Article 82. The Court of First Instance upheld the Commission's decision in all respects other than as to the duration of the infringement.

12.110 The Court of First Instance stressed that group exemptions, such as that contained in Regulation 4056/86, must be strictly interpreted. In particular, the Court of First Instance said that while the aim of a shipping conference has been recognized to be beneficial and therefore justifies the granting of a group exemption, it cannot be the case that every impairment of competition brought about by shipping conferences falls outside the prohibition in principle laid down by Article 81(1) of the Treaty.

12.111 This approach has led the Commission to adopt a number of decisions in which it has found that certain practices engaged in by the members of a liner shipping conference neither fell within the scope of the group exemption nor qualified for individual exemption.

12.112 **Inland price-fixing by conferences.**   The Commission takes the view that the group exemption in Regulation 4056/86 does not allow shipowners jointly to fix prices for the inland leg of a multimodal transport operation (such as from factory to port) or door-to-door prices (such as from Munich to Pittsburgh). Conferences which fix such rates do so unlawfully and, if they have not notified their agreements to the Commission, they remain potentially liable to fines

12.113 The Commission has adopted two formal decisions prohibiting inland price-fixing: the *Trans-Atlantic Agreement* and the *Far Eastern Freight Conference*.[53]

12.114 Both the *TAA* and *FEFC* decisions have been appealed to the Court of First Instance.[54] At one time it appeared that the question whether the group exemption extends to inland price-fixing would be decided by the Court of Justice in the context of an Article 177 reference in the *SUNAG* case.[55] However, following an out-of-court settlement, the reference was withdrawn days before the Advocate General's Opinion was due to be delivered.

---

[52] Joined Cases T–24 to 26/93 and T–28/93 *Compagnie maritime belge transports SA and Compagnie maritime belge SA, Dafra-Lines A/S, Deutsche Afrika-Linien GmbH & Co. and Nedlloyd Lijnen BV v Commission* [1996] ECR II–1201.

[53] *TAA* (n 23 above) and *FEFC* (n 22 above).

[54] Case T–395/94 *ACL and others v Commission*, Case T–86/95 *CGM and others v Commission*.

[55] Case C–339/95 *Compagnia di Navigazione Maritima v CMB*.

If, as the Commission believes, the group exemption does not extend to agree- **12.115**
ments fixing prices for inland transport, then any such agreements must benefit
from an individual exemption under Article 81(3). Inland price-fixing would have
to be shown to be genuinely indispensable for the improvement in services or in
order to bring about cost reductions. The mere fact that the shipowners are offering door-to-door services, or the fact that they wish to fix prices for door-to-door
services to prevent price competition, is not in itself enough to justify exemption.

In order to assist it in assessing applications for exemption of inland price-fixing, **12.116**
the Commission established a so-called 'committee of wise men' called the
Multimodal Group. The Multimodal Group was set up by Commissioner Van
Miert for the purpose of advising him about the implementation of the new policy of the Commission concerning inland price-fixing by liner shipping conferences as set out in the Commission's Report to the Council of 8 June 1994.

The Multimodal Group was chaired by Sir Bryan Carsberg, Secretary-General of **12.117**
the International Accounting Standards Committee and former UK Director-
General of Fair Trading. The other members of the group comprised two independent experts, two executives from shipping lines, and two executives from big
EU exporters who use multimodal transport services.

The Final Report of the Multimodal Group was issued in December 1997.[56] **12.118**
Confirming its Interim Report of February 1996, the Group concluded that there
was no reason to grant an exemption to collective inland price-fixing by conferences.

In the *TACA immunity from fines* decision[57] and the *TACA* decision,[58] the **12.119**
Commission also confirmed its earlier position that inland price-fixing by liner
shipping conferences neither fell within the scope of Article 3 nor qualified for
individual exemption.

Two-tier pricing.   In the Commission's view, the scope of the group exemption **12.120**
is limited by the definition of a liner conference contained in Article 1(3)(b) of the
Regulation:

> 'liner conference' means a group of two or more vessel-operating carriers which pro-
> vides international liner services for the carriage of cargo on a particular route or
> routes within specified geographical limits and which has an agreement or arrange-
> ment, whatever its nature, within the framework of which they operate under

---

[56] Office for Official Publications of the European Communities, 1998. ISBN 92-828-2934-0.
[57] Commission Decision of 26 November 1996 relating to a proceeding pursuant to Article 85
[now Article 81] of the EC Treaty (Case IV/35.134—*Trans-Atlantic Conference Agreement*) not
published. Regulation 1017/68 is silent as to whether notification of an agreement falling within the
scope of application of the Regulation confers immunity from fines: the Commission has taken the
view that it does not.
[58] *Trans-Atlantic Conference Agreement* [1999] OJ L42.

uniform or common freight rates and any other agreed conditions with respect to the provision of liner services.

12.121 For the Commission, the key element of this definition has been the words 'uniform or common freight rates'. This has been interpreted in the *TAA*[59] and *TACA*[60] decisions as meaning that Article 3 of Regulation 4056/86 requires that the rates laid down in the tariff are to be identical for all members of a conference and that under the tariff all goods of the same category travel at the same rate.

12.122 This interpretation has been objected to on the grounds that it effectively requires the words common and uniform to be read conjunctively rather than disjunctively. Shipowners have argued for a disjunctive reading with the effect that the prices only have to be agreed in common and published in a uniform tariff. The Commission's rejection of this approach was spelt out in paragraph 349 of the *TAA* Decision:

> The reasoning of the TAA would in fact mean that every agreement on prices between shipping lines would be exempted, provided it were reached 'in common', which is an obvious feature of an agreement of any kind, and used the name 'liner conference'. Such an interpretation would be tantamount to treating Article 3 of the Regulation as an automatic derogation from Article 85(1) [now Article 81(1)] of the Treaty for every kind of agreement which provides for some kind of understanding concerning prices in the maritime sector. The very criteria which bring Article 85(1) into play would make Article 3 of the Regulation applicable automatically. Such an interpretation is impossible, as it would make Article 3 of the Regulation incompatible with Article 85(3) of the Treaty, which provides for exemption only in specified circumstances not present in this case.

12.123 The purpose of the Commission's approach has been to avoid the situations as in the TAA where the conference tariff was structured in a way that certain classes of carrier charged different prices to other carriers:

> The real purpose of the introduction of differentiated rates in a case such as that of the TAA is to bring independents inside the agreement: if they were not allowed to quote prices lower than those of the old conference members, these independents would continue as outsiders competing against the conference, notably in terms of price. The advantage to the old conference members is that this limits the activities of outsiders and thus the competition they offer. Such a system substantially reduces effective competition from outsiders, whose existence is the main safeguard for the block exemption given to liner conferences.[61]

12.124 Thus, the Commission has trodden the tightrope that it is, paradoxically, less restrictive of competition to oblige all the members of a liner conference to agree to charge the same prices than to have an agreement which would allow greater pricing flexibility. The purpose is to seek to avoid an extension of the conference's

---

[59] *TAA* (n 23 above), at para 326.
[60] *TACA* (n 58 above), at para 458.
[61] *TAA* (n 23 above), at para 341.

influence on prices to a greater part of the market: the risk is that it does just that and that consumers have no choice, at least in theory, as to the prices they pay.

The Commission's practice in this respect would appear to be equally applicable **12.125** to so-called 'tolerated outsider agreements' and 'discussion agreements'. These kinds of agreements involve if not actual price-fixing as between the members of a conference and the independent carriers operating on a given trade, then at least an understanding as to general levels of prices.

Service contracts. In the *TACA* decision, the Commission found that the group **12.126** exemption for liner conferences contained in Regulation (EEC) 4056/86 does not authorize:

(a) joint service contracts;

(b) a prohibition on individual service contracts or restrictions, whether binding or non-binding, on the contents of such contracts;

(c) a prohibition of independent action on joint service contracts.

The Commission also refused to grant individual exemption in respect of these **12.127** practices. Since the adoption of the *TACA* decision the Ocean Shipping Reform Act has come into effect in the United States. This Act amends the US Shipping Act 1984 by requiring conferences to allow their members to enter into confidential individual service contracts.

'Stabilisation agreements': capacity non-utilization agreements. The Com- **12.128** mission has also taken the view that the group exemption in Regulation 4056/86 does not allow shipowners to agree not to use capacity. An individual exemption for a capacity non-utilization agreement is not possible when, as in the *TAA* case, it is a tool for maintaining excess capacity and artificially raising freight rates. Capacity regulation could only bring benefits if there was a real withdrawal of inefficient or outdated capacity so as to bring about a reduction of costs, leading to price reductions for shippers.

In the *TAA* decision, the Commission prohibited the TAA's capacity management **12.129** programme on the westbound transatlantic trade. As regards the Europe Asia Trades Agreement capacity management programme on the Europe/Far East trades, the Commission initiated proceedings in 1994. Although the Agreement was ended in September 1997, the Commission proceeded to the adoption of a decision on 30 April 1999[62] finding that the non-utilization of capacity constituted a breach of Article 81(1) that was incapable of exemption under Article 81(3). The usual cease and desist order was imposed.

---

[62] *Europe Asia Trades Agreement* [1999] OJ L193.

Article 4 of Regulation 4056/86—Discrimination

12.130 Article 4 of Regulation (EEC) 4056/86 provides that the exemption contained in Article 3 is conditional upon the fact that differentiated rates and conditions of carriage which cause detriment to ports, transport users or carriers must be 'economically justified'. The Regulation appears to assume that discrimination without economic justification causes detriment, both to the completion of the internal market and to particular ports and regions.

12.131 This provision is based on Article 79(1) of the Treaty and would therefore appear to be included in Regulation 4056/86 for transport policy rather than competition policy reasons.

12.132 Article 4 contains an express severance clause providing that, if it can be severed, only that part of any agreement or decision not complying with the non-discrimination provision shall automatically be void pursuant to Article 81(2) of the Treaty. The question whether severance applies to other non-exempted behaviour remains open.

Article 6—Exemption for Agreements between Transport Users and Conferences

12.133 Article 6 of Regulation 4056/86 provides that agreements, decisions, and concerted practices between transport users, on the one hand, and conferences, on the other hand, and agreements between transport users which may be necessary to that end, are exempted from the prohibition laid down in Article 81(1) of the Treaty.

12.134 This exemption is limited to agreements, decisions, and concerted practices concerning the rates, conditions, and quality of liner services and loyalty agreements.

Article 7 of Regulation 4056/86—Withdrawal of the Group Exemption

12.135 According to Article 7 of Regulation 4056/86, where 'acts of a conference or a change in market conditions in a given trade . . . result in the absence of or elimination of actual or potential competition contrary to Article 85(3)(b) [now Article 81(3)(b)] of the Treaty, the Commission shall withdraw the benefit of the block exemption. At the same time it shall rule on whether and, if so, under what additional conditions and obligations an individual exemption should be granted . . .'.

12.136 The reference to Article 81(3)(b) of the Treaty makes clear that the test to be applied in determining the obligations of the Commission under Article 7 is whether the parties to the group exempted liner conference in question are afforded the possibility of eliminating competition in respect of a substantial part of the services in question.[63]

---

[63] See Case T–7/93 *Langnese* [1995] ECR II–1533, para 145. 'The Court finds, first, that it is apparent from Article 14(a) and (b) of Regulation No 1984/83 that the Commission is empowered

Although the Commission has twice stated its intention to use this provision, in **12.137** the *CEWAL* and *TACA* cases, it has never done so. It would seem that for the conditions of Article 7 to be fulfilled, the Commission would have to show that the elimination of actual or potential competition would have to be likely to continue in the future unless the benefit of the group exemption was withdrawn. Given the nature of potential competition in liner shipping markets arising from the mobility of fleets, this would appear to be a particularly onerous task.

Article 8 of Regulation 4056/86—Article 82

Article 8 of Regulation 4056/86 provides that the abuse of a dominant position **12.138** within the meaning of Article 82 of the Treaty shall be prohibited, no prior decision to that effect being required. It also gives the Commission power to withdraw the benefit of the block exemption where it finds that the group exemption brings about effects which are incompatible with Article 82 of the Treaty.

CEWAL. In the *CEWAL* case, the Court of First Instance agreed with the **12.139** Commission that the members of the CEWAL liner conference presented themselves on the market as one and the same entity. The Court of First Instance also observed that the practices described in the decision revealed an intention to adopt together the same conduct on the market in order to react unilaterally to a change, deemed to be a threat, in the competitive situation on the market on which they operated. Consequently, the Court of First Instance considered that the Commission had sufficiently shown that it was necessary to assess the position of CEWAL members on the relevant market *collectively.*

The Court of First Instance found the argument that Article 82 is inapplicable so **12.140** long as the exemption granted by Regulation 4056/86 has not been withdrawn to be based on the assertion that exemption applies to both Article 81 and Article 82. In that regard, it was sufficient to point out that, in view of the wording of Article 82 of the Treaty, no exemption may be granted in respect of an abuse of a dominant position. Moreover, in view of the principles governing the hierarchy of legislation, the grant of an exemption by means of a measure of secondary legislation cannot derogate from a provision of the Treaty, in this case Article 82. Consequently, in so far as CEWAL's argument was based on the premise that Regulation 4056/86 grants exemption in respect of Article 82 of the Treaty, it was manifestly unfounded.

As regards fines, the CEWAL parties argued that no fine could be imposed on the **12.141** conference or its members without first withdrawing the block exemption

to withdraw the benefit of the exemption provided for by that regulation, which is not conditional, by definition, upon verification that the exemption conditions laid down by Article 85(3) [now Article 81(3)] of the Treaty are in fact fulfilled, where it finds, after individual examination of a specific case, that the agreements exempted by the regulation do not fulfil all the conditions laid down by Article 85(3) of the Treaty.'

enjoyed by liner conferences and that, in so far as it ultimately fined the applicants without first withdrawing the exemption, the Commission infringed the principle of protection of legitimate expectation. This was also rejected by the Court of First Instance.

12.142   In the *TACA* decision, the Commission stated that:

> A refusal to supply can take a number of forms: it can be an outright refusal to supply, a refusal to supply otherwise than on terms which the supplier knows to be unacceptable (a constructive refusal) or a refusal to supply other than on the basis of unfair conditions. Compliance with an agreement to place restrictions on the contents of service contracts amounts to a refusal to supply services pursuant to service contracts otherwise than in accordance with the terms of that agreement and falls into the third of these three categories of refusals to supply. Compliance with an agreement to place restrictions on the availability and contents of service contracts also limits the supply of transport products. Accordingly, such behaviour falls within the scope of Article 86 [now Article 82] of the Treaty, and in particular points (a) and (b) thereof, where the supplier in question is in a dominant position.[64]

12.143   The Commission also found that the TACA parties had abused their joint dominant position by inducing potential competitors to join the TACA and thereby altering the competitive structure of the market. The TACA parties did this in a number of ways and in particular by agreeing that shipping lines which were not traditional conference members were allowed to charge a lower price in service contracts than the price charged by the traditional conference members. The purpose and effect of the TACA's agreement to enter into dual rate service contracts was to limit competition from independent shipowners by bringing them inside the conference.

12.144   Furthermore, the traditional conference members did not compete for certain contracts thereby leaving that part of the market to the shipping lines which were not traditionally conference members.

Regulation 870/95—Group Exemption for Consortia

12.145   At the time of the adoption of Regulation 4056/86, the Council invited the Commission to study the situation regarding liner shipping consortia and consider whether it was necessary to submit new proposals. The Commission presented a communication and report to the Council in June 1990[65] in which it favoured the adoption of a new group exemption for consortia agreements. The objective of consortia agreements, which are in effect joint ventures between two or more vessels operating carriers, is to bring about co-operation between the parties so as to improve the productivity and quality of the liner shipping service,

---

[64]   *TACA* (n 58 above), at para 553.
[65]   COM 90 (260) final of 18 June 1990.

encourage greater utilization of the containers, and the more efficient use of vessel capacity.

On 20 April 1995, the Commission adopted Commission Regulation 870/95[66] **2.146** on the application of Article 81(3) of the Treaty to certain categories of agreements, decisions, and concerted practices between liner shipping companies (consortia) pursuant to Council Regulation 472/92. Regulation 870/95 came into force on 22 April 1995 and is valid for a period of five years starting from the day following its publication in the *Official Journal.* That period expires on 22 April 2000. On 28 January 1999, DG IV published on its Europa web site a working document discussing the possibilities open to the Commission on the expiration of the regulation and inviting third party comment.

Co-operation between liner shipping companies can bring about benefits to ship- **12.147** pers and, in the end, the ultimate consumer in the form of lower prices. In adopting the group exemption for liner shipping consortia the Commission has shown that it recognizes that the development of container services, and the size of the investments needed for the acquisition of container vessels, may necessitate co-operation between shipowners for maritime services.

Consortia allow shipowners to organize joint services which provide users with a **12.148** better quality service. At the same time they allow carriers to rationalize their maritime transport activities, to obtain scale economies, and to reduce costs. As a result users tend to obtain a fair share of the benefits which result.

Regulation 870/95 grants a group exemption to certain categories of consortium **12.149** agreements. The group exemption seeks to establish a balance between the respective interests of shipowners and transport users. Such a balance can only be obtained if the consortia are operating in trades where they remain subject to effective competition from other shipowners.

To this end, the Regulation includes a maximum trade share condition. A con- **12.150** sortium which has a trade share higher than 50 per cent will not benefit from the group exemption. Such an agreement should be notified to the Commission and, if it fulfils the conditions of Article 81(3), it may be granted individual exemption by the Commission using the procedures under Regulation 4056/86. On the other hand, a consortium having a trade share below the first level (30 per cent or 35 per cent depending on whether or not it operates within a conference) will automatically benefit from the group exemption.

---

[66] Commission Regulation (EC) 870/95 of 20 April 1995 on the application of Article 85(3) [now Article 81(3)] of the Treaty to certain categories of agreements, decisions and concerted practices between liner shipping companies (consortia) pursuant to Council Regulation (EEC) 479/92 [1995] OJ L89.

12.151 If it has a market share of between 30 per cent or 35 per cent and 50 per cent (the second level) the consortium will come within a simplified opposition procedure in accordance with which it benefits from the group exemption unless the Commission opposes it within six months of its notification. This period is extended if the Commission considers that the notification was incomplete and starts to run again once the missing information is supplied.

12.152 The Commission has received about 30 formal notifications since October 1995, has dealt with a further 10 informal cases, and has adopted 11 positive decisions.[67] A further 9 formal cases have been closed without the adoption of a formal decision.

Mergers

12.153 At the end of 1996, the Commission approved the creation of P&O Nedlloyd Container Line Ltd pursuant to Regulation 4064/89.[68] The Commission concluded that the creation of the P&O Nedlloyd joint venture would not create or strengthen a position of dominance. The Commission reached this conclusion after examining the effect of the merger on the main trades to and from Europe on which both the parent companies carried containerized cargo on liner shipping services. The Commission also considered the effects of the liner conferences and consortia which operated on those routes.

12.154 In the light of the *CEWAL* case, in which the Court of First Instance held that members of a liner conference could under certain circumstances be jointly dominant within the meaning of Article 82, the Commission also took into account whether the P&O Nedlloyd merger could strengthen the cohesion within existing conferences or consortia in such a way as to create dominance or reinforce an existing dominance.

(3) Air

Regulation 3975/87

12.155 Council Regulation 3975/87 lays down the procedure for the application of Articles 81 and 82 in the air transport sector, and Council Regulation 3976/87 grants the Commission power to adopt group exemptions relating to certain stated activities in that sector.

Article 1—The Scope of Regulations 3975 and 3976

12.156 The geographic scope of Regulations 3975 and 3976 is limited to air transport services between Community airports, including those situated within the same

---

[67] See for example IP96/400 concerning four consortia agreements: the St Lawrence Co-ordinated Service, the East African Container Service, the Joint Mediterranean Canada Service, and the Joint Pool Agreement.
[68] *P&O/Royal Nedlloyd* (Case IV/M831) (1996).

Member State[69] provided there is the necessary effect on trade between Member States. As discussed further below, these Regulations do not apply to air transport services between the Community and third countries, with the exception of the remaining EFTA States.

Regulations 3975 and 3976 apply to all forms of air transport, including passenger and freight whether scheduled or charter. Similarly to Regulation 4056/86, Article 1 of Regulation 3975/87 makes clear that its scope is limited to air transport services and the difficulties described above in relation to the scope of Regulation 1017/68 probably do not arise. However, Regulation 3976 enables the Commission to grant group exemptions not only for agreements which relate directly to air transport services but also for those which relate to ancillary activities. **12.157**

Article 2—Exception for certain technical agreements

The Annex to Regulation 3975 contains a list of agreements, decisions, and concerted practices to which, according to Article 2 of Regulation 3975, Article 81(1) EC does not apply 'in so far as their sole object and effect is to achieve technical improvements or co-operation'. The list is said not to be exhaustive. **12.158**

Article 4(a)—Interim Measures

Article 4(a) of Regulation 3975/87 states that the Commission may order interim measures where: **12.159**

(i) it has clear prima facie evidence that certain practices are contrary to Article 81 or 82;

(ii) such practices have the object or effect of directly jeopardizing the existence of an air service; and

(iii) where recourse to normal procedures may not be sufficient to protect the air service or the airline company concerned.

Interim measures ordered by decision adopted pursuant to Article 4(a) are limited to six months renewable for three months at a time. For the initial decision, the Commission is relieved of the normal obligations formally to consult the Air Transport Advisory Committee on the basis of a draft decision. **12.160**

The question remains open whether the existence of a specific provision relating to interim measures excludes the Commission's general competence to order interim measures in appropriate cases. This issue would arise if an undertaking was threatened with grave and irreparable harm but the harm in question was not the threat to the existence of an air service. **12.161**

---

[69] This results from Council Regulation 2410/92 of 23 July 1992, Article 1 of which provided for the deletion of the word 'international' from Article 1(2) of Regulation (EEC) 3975/87.

Regulation 1617/93—Block Exemptions in Air Transport

Article 1—Group Exemptions

12.162 As part of the third package of air transport liberalization, the Commission adopted Regulation 1617/93 on 25 June 1993. Article 1 of Regulation 1617/93 grants group exemptions to agreements between undertakings in the air transport sector, decisions by associations of such undertakings, and concerted practices between such undertakings which have as their purpose one or more of the following: ˙

- joint planning and co-ordination of the schedule of an air service between Community airports,

- the joint operation of a scheduled air service on a new or on a low-density route between Community airports,

- the holding of consultations on tariffs for the carriage of passengers, with their baggage, and of freight on scheduled air services between Community airports,

- slot allocation and airport scheduling in so far as they concern air services between airports in the Community.

Article 2—Joint Planning and Co-Ordination of Schedules

12.163 Pursuant to Article 2 of Regulation 1617/93, airlines may agree to co-ordinate schedules with a view to providing service at less busy times or to facilitate connections for passengers from one airline to the other. Airlines must remain free to introduce additional services and to terminate the co-ordination on reasonable notice. Article 2 specifically excludes agreements to limit or to share capacity.

Article 3—Joint Operations

12.164 Article 3 of Regulation 1617/93 contains a block exemption enabling smaller airlines, in particular, to operate a service with marketing and financial support from another airline, thereby helping them to develop new routes or to continue service on less busy routes.

12.165 In order to maintain effective competition, the partner airlines must be free to operate independently alongside the joint operation if they wish to do so. The block exemption authorizes joint operations for three years; after that time, each joint operation must be examined on an individual basis.

Article 4—Passenger and Cargo Tariffs Consultations

12.166 Even though discussions on pricing are usually a serious restriction of competition, tariff consultations in the airline industry have been treated favourably because of the belief that they facilitate interlining. Interlining is the possibility for passengers to combine services by different airlines on a single ticket and to change reservations from one airline to another.

However, in order to maintain effective competition, the purpose of the consulta- **12.167**
tions should not be to increase fares and participating airlines may not be prevented from charging their own prices if they wish. Consultations should not
extend to further matters such as agents' remuneration.

In 1996, the Commission adopted Regulation 1523/96[70] which amended **12.168**
Regulation 1617/93 by removing tariff consultations for cargo rates from the
scope of the group exemption. The Commission is currently examining a request
for individual exemption made by IATA (International Air Transport
Association) in relation to the same activities.

Article 5—Slot Allocation and Airport Scheduling

Airlines are authorized to agree on the distribution of airport slots under a num- **12.169**
ber of conditions, essentially intended to make sure that the process is open to all
interested airlines and that slot allocation is transparent and non discriminatory.
Given the finite capacity of airports and the need to match take-off and landing
slots, it is important to seek to co-ordinate airlines' projected schedules with the
available slot capacity.

The traditional means for allocating scarce resources has been 'historical prece- **12.170**
dence', also know as 'grandfather rights'.[71] An airline keeps a slot from season to
season even if it changes the service it is offering and regardless of the type of
service. Such a system favours incumbent airlines and in saturated airports can
prevent the entry of new competitors.

The Commission therefore requires favourable treatment for new entrants in **12.171**
order to ensure that there are genuine access opportunities both at congested airports where the Council rules on the allocation of slots apply and in airports
which are not congested. Aside from conditions relating to non-discrimination,
the Regulation requires that new entrants (as defined in Article 2(b) of Council
Regulation 95/93) be allocated 50 per cent of newly created or unused slots.

Article 6—Withdrawal of the Block Exemption

Article 6 of Regulation 1617/93 allows the Commission to withdraw the benefit **12.172**
of the block exemption if it finds that the conditions of Article 81(3) are not fulfilled or that Article 82 is being infringed. It specifies the following circumstances
where that might arise:

---

[70] Commission Regulation (EC) 1523/96 of 24 July 1996 amending Regulation (EEC) 1617/93
on the application of Article 85(3) [now Article 81(3)] of the Treaty to certain categories of agreements and concerted practices concerning joint planning and coordination of schedules, joint operations, consultations on passenger and cargo tariffs on scheduled air services and slot allocation at
airports [1996] OJ L190.
[71] See Council Regulation (EEC) 95/93 on common rules for the allocation of slots in
Community airports, [1993] OJ L14. This Regulation only applies to congested airports.

(i) where there is no effective price competition on any route or group of routes which was the subject of tariff consultations,

(ii) where an air service which is jointly operated is not exposed to effective competition by direct or indirect air transport services between the two airports connected or between nearby airports, or by other modes of transport which offer speed, convenience, and prices comparable to air transport between the cities served by the two airports connected,

(iii) where new entrants have not been able to obtain such slots as may be required at a congested airport in order to establish schedules which enable those carriers to compete effectively with established carriers on any route to and from that airport, and where competition on those routes is thereby substantially impaired.

Article 7—Duration

12.173 Regulation 1617/93 expired on 30 June 1998 and a procedure to renew it is in progress at the time of writing. It is possible that Articles 2 and 3 will not be renewed.

Regulation 2672/88—Block Exemption for Computer Reservation Systems

12.174 Regulation 2672/88[72] contains a block exemption which allows airlines to set up and operate jointly owned computer reservation systems under a number of conditions, essentially intended to make sure that all interested airlines have access to these systems and that they do not discriminate against other airlines.

Exemptions for Airline Alliances

12.175 **Lufthansa/SAS.** In May 1995, Lufthansa and SAS applied to the Commission for exemption of a general co-operation agreement providing for the establishment of an integrated air transport system between the two airlines.[73] In particular, they wished to set up a joint venture for traffic between Germany and Scandinavia which would be their exclusive vehicle for operating services on those routes but each party would nevertheless retain its own commercial brand identity.

12.176 On eight routes, Lufthansa and SAS were the only airlines operating, except for one frequency per day between Frankfurt and Copenhagen operated by Singapore Airlines. In terms of the number of passengers carried, these eight routes accounted for 66 per cent of all traffic between Scandinavia and Germany.

---

[72] Council Regulation (EEC) 2672/88 on the application of Article 85(3) [now Article 81(3)] of the Treaty to certain categories of agreements between undertakings relating to computer reservation systems for air transport services [1988] OJ L239.

[73] *LH/SAS* (n 20 above).

Furthermore, at least one of the two airlines was operating on twelve other routes between Scandinavia and Germany. The new entity being set up would thus operate on twenty of the twenty-five routes between Scandinavia and Germany.

The Commission concluded that conditions needed to be imposed to ensure that **12.177** the restrictions of competition remained within the bounds of what was necessary, to safeguard the presence on the market of competing airlines, and to ensure that opportunities for market entry were available to new entrants. The Commission considered that Lufthansa and SAS should freeze the number of daily frequencies they operated on a route when a new entrant decided to serve that route. This condition was designed to prevent the airlines already present from increasing substantially their number of frequencies with a view to squeezing the new entrant from the market.

Access to routes between Scandinavia and Germany by new entrants was condi- **12.178** tional on the availability of slots at Scandinavian and German airports. Frankfurt, Dusseldorf, Stockholm, and Oslo airports were, however, saturated at certain hours of the day, and obtaining slots there by the normal allocation procedures is virtually impossible. Lufthansa and SAS were therefore required to give up, as the need arose, a sufficient number of slots at each of these airports to enable other airlines to operate competing services on certain routes. This would be called for only where the new entrant had been unable to obtain slots by the normal allocation procedure in force at each airport.

This was the first major airline case handled by the Commission. The issue of new **12.179** entry remains a key question for the Commission in dealing with airline joint ventures which involve slots at congested airports.

The Commission has also examined a number of larger airline alliances involving **12.180** EC and US airlines. At the time of writing no results have emerged although the Commission did get as far as publishing proposed remedies in the *BA/American Airlines* alliance case.[74]

Air Transport Mergers

The Commission has dealt with thirteen air transport cases under the Merger **12.181** Regulation. Twelve were not opposed (Article 6(1)(b) decisions)[75] and one was

---

[74] [1998] OJ C239.

[75] *Delta Airlines/PanAm* (Case IV/M130) (1991)' *Air France/Sabena* (Case IV/M157) (1992) OJ C272; *BA/TAT* (Case IV/M259) (1992); *BA/Dan Air* (Case IV/M278) (1993); *Swissair/Sabena* (Case IV/M616) (1995); *BA/TAT (II)* (Case IV/M806) (1996); *BA/Air Liberté* (Case IV/M857) (1997); *Lufthansa/Cityline/Bombardier/EBJS* (Case IV/M968) (1997); *KLM/Air UK* (Case IV/M967) (1997); *Hochtief/Aer Rianta/Düsseldorf Airport* (Case IV/M1035) (1997); *Maersk Air/LFV Holdings* (Case IV/M1124) (1998); *Sair Group/LTU* (Case IV/M1354) (1998).

found not to fall within the scope of the Merger Regulation (Article 6(1)(a) decision).[76] Undertakings were given to the Commission in the following three cases.

12.182 The *Air France/Sabena* case concerned the acquisition of joint control and a minority shareholding in Sabena by Air France. One of the reasons given for clearing the arrangement was that the French Government undertook to allow a competitor to Air France to create in Northern France a hub and spoke system comparable to that planned by Air France and Sabena for Brussels. The companies concerned also gave undertakings intended to facilitate the entry of competitors onto a number of routes and to limit the number of slots they controlled at Brussels airport.

12.183 In any event, the Air France/Sabena co-operation was short-lived and in 1995 Swissair replaced Air France as Sabena's partner. This co-operation created a monopoly on routes between Belgium and Switzerland to which the Community's internal regime for market liberalization did not apply. In addition, a number of the airports were congested, thereby increasing the difficulties which would be faced by any potential new entrant.

12.184 In order to remove the Commission's serious doubts as to the compatibility of the arrangement with the common market, the Belgian and Swiss Governments made declarations that they would lessen the existing regulatory barriers to entry onto the routes 'to the extent required to generate sufficient competition to Swissair and Sabena'. Secondly, Swissair and Sabena gave a number of undertakings to the Commission also intended to facilitate new entry. These related to the giving up of slots necessary for operating the main services between Belgium and Switzerland, interlining, and participation in their frequent flyer programme (FFP). Swissair also agreed to terminate its co-operation with SAS in order to ensure the potential for competition between the Lufthansa/SAS and Swissair/Sabena networks.

12.185 In the *BA/TAT (I)* case, the companies gave similar undertakings as to slots and FFPs in relation to the Gatwick/Paris and Gatwick/Lyon routes.

12.186 It is evident from the above that Regulation 4064/89 applies to air transport even in areas falling outside the scope of Regulation 3975 such as transport to third countries.

Abuses of Dominant Position

12.187 The importance of Article 82 in the air transport sector is linked to the fact that 'flag carriers' have inherited strong positions on their traditional home markets and often have considerable power to impede the development of competition, in particular from new entrants.

---

[76] *Teneo/Merill Lynch/Bankers Trust* (Case IV/M722) (1996).

In *Ahmed Saeed*,[77] the ECJ stated that the starting point for market definition in   **12.188**
air transport is the particular route which is at issue. The ECJ would then look at
possible substitutes, both from other forms of transport and from other routes to
determine the relevant market:

> In that regard two possible approaches emerged during the hearings before the
> Court: the first is that the sector of scheduled flights constitutes a separate market;
> the second that alternative possibilities, such as charter flights, the railways and road
> transport, should be taken into account as well as scheduled flights on other routes
> which might serve as substitutes.

> The test to be employed is whether the scheduled flight on a particular route can be
> distinguished from the possible alternatives by virtue of specific characteristics as a
> result of which it is not interchangeable with those alternatives and is affected only
> to an insignificant degree by competition from them.

The Commission has applied Article 82 in two air transport cases: *London*   **12.189**
European v Sabena,[78] concerning a refusal to supply computer reservation services,
and *British Midland v Aer Lingus*,[79] concerning a refusal to interline.

Aer Lingus.   Aer Lingus was the dominant airline on the London–Dublin route.   **12.190**
After British Midland announced its intention in 1989 to start its own service on that
route in competition with Aer Lingus, Aer Lingus terminated its interlining relationship with British Midland. As a result of that action, passengers holding British
Midland tickets could no longer, as of right, change flights to Aer Lingus services and
travel agents could no longer issue tickets combining flights by both airlines.

The withdrawal of interlining facilities made British Midland's flights less attract-   **12.191**
ive to travellers—in particular business travellers who prefer the higher priced
fully flexible tickets—and to travel agents. By terminating its interlining relationship, Aer Lingus made it more difficult for British Midland to compete. British
Midland was deprived of significant revenue and forced to incur higher costs in
order to overcome the handicap imposed on it.

The Commission found that Aer Lingus had abused its dominant position by ter-   **12.192**
minating its interlining agreement with British Midland. The Commission
imposed a fine of ECU 750,000 on Aer Lingus and ordered it to resume its interlining relationship with British Midland. However, it also accepted that new
entrants should not be able to rely indefinitely on frequencies and services provided by their competitors, but must be encouraged to develop their own frequencies and services. Therefore the duration of the duty to interline could be
limited to the time period which was objectively necessary for a competitor to
become established on the market. Taking into account that three years had

---

[77] Case 66/86 *Ahmed Saeed* [1989] ECR 803.
[78] *London European/Sabena* (n 28 above).
[79] *British Midland v Aer Lingus* [1992] OJ L96/34.

lapsed since British Midland started its new services, the duty to interline imposed by the decision was limited to two years, subject to review in the light of the development of competition on the relevant route.

12.193   Cases examined by the Commission concerning possible breaches of Article 82 have included the following:

- frequent flyer programmes (FFPs),

- additional commissions over and above the normal commission to travel agents (sometimes called 'override commissions'),

- excessive capacity or frequency (particularly when frequencies are increased with intention to exclude a new entrant).

D.   Transport Infrastructure—Access and Discrimination

12.194   The two main issues relating to transport infrastructure are access, to ensure that operators can get access to the necessary infrastructure to operate their services, and discrimination, to ensure that different operators are treated equally. This is especially important where an owner of essential infrastructure is also an operator of services using that infrastructure.

(1) Airports

12.195   The Commission's main concerns in airport cases have been to ensure non-discriminatory access, in particular at the level of airport charges, and to enable carriers to benefit from airport services, such as handling of luggage, catering, or registration of passengers, which are of good quality at a reasonable price. This is done mainly through opening markets for airport services.

Discriminatory Landing Fees

12.196   Examples of discrimination arise where an airport grants larger discounts from its tariff for landing fees to some airlines than to others or where landing fees are cheaper for domestic flights than for cross-border flights within the EU. Since an airport is in a monopoly position as regards the maintenance and the arrangement of runways, such discrimination is unlawful unless it can be objectively justified. Such behaviour may also be contrary to the principle of the single market.

12.197   **Zaventem.**   The *Zaventem* decision[80] concerned a complaint by British Midland (BM) about the system of discounts granted on landing fees at Brussels National

---

[80] *Zaventem* [1995] OJ L216.

Airport (Zaventem). BM considered that the system of stepped discounts, which increase in line with an airline's volume of traffic, favoured carriers with a high volume of traffic and thereby placed small carriers competing with them at a disadvantage. Moreover, according to BM, there was no objective justification in granting such discounts since the services which an arriving or departing aircraft requires are the same, however many times they are supplied.

12.198 The Commission found the Airways Authority was a public undertaking within the meaning of Article 86(1) and that the Royal Decree laying down the fees payable for the use of Zaventem, which established a system of discounts on landing fees, was a State measure within the meaning of Article 86(1).

12.199 In 1992 Sabena received final-step discounts (30 per cent) equivalent to an overall reduction of 18 per cent on its fees, whereas the other qualifying airlines (Sobelair and BA) were eligible for only a first-step discount (7.5 per cent). No other airline operating at Brussels Airport qualified for a reduction in its landing fees. This placed BM at a competitive disadvantage.

12.200 The Commission found that the Airways Authority held a dominant position in its capacity as airport authority on the market in aircraft landing and take-off services. It had not been demonstrated that handling the take-off or landing of an aircraft belonging to one airline rather than to another gives rise to economies of scale. The system of discounts on landing fees had the effect of applying dissimilar conditions to airlines for equivalent transactions linked to landing and take-off services, thereby placing some of them at a competitive disadvantage. This constituted an abuse of a dominant position within the meaning of Article 82(c).

12.201 Since this system had been established by a Member State by way of an administrative act, it constituted an infringement of Article 86, read in conjunction with Article 82 of the Treaty.

12.202 The Commission noted that Article 82 also applies to cases in which an undertaking in a dominant position discriminates against its partners for reasons other than its own interest. This may involve, for example, giving preference to another undertaking from the same State or to an undertaking which is pursuing the same general policy.

Ground Handling

12.203 The Commission has received many complaints concerning the supply by monopolies of ground-handling services of poor quality at an excessive price. The Commission's approach has been to take steps to ensure that the monopoly is broken and that second operators are allowed in on a non-discriminatory basis. This applies in particular to the level of concession fees or fees for the occupation of buildings and spaces that they must obtain from the airport.

12.204 Ground-handling services comprise all the activities performed when an aircraft stops over in respect of the aircraft itself, the passengers, and the cargo. In general, ground-handling services may be provided for airlines by the airport operator, by another airline, or by an independent specialized ground-handling company (third party handling). Air carriers may also provide their own handling services either individually (self-handling) or in a pool (joint handling).

12.205 Council Directive 96/67 of 15 October 1996 on access to the ground-handling market at Community airports[81] provides that, in the case of airports whose annual traffic is not less than three million passenger movements and of certain categories of services:

- Member States are required to take the necessary measures to ensure free access by suppliers of ground-handling services to the market for the provision of ground-handling services to third parties as from 1 January 1999 (Article 6 of the Directive); however, they may limit the number of authorized suppliers (to no fewer than two);

- Member States have to take the necessary measures to ensure the freedom to self-handle as from 1 January 1998 (Article 7 of the Directive); however, they may reserve the right to self-handle (to no fewer than two airport users), self-handling being narrowly defined.

12.206 Where specific constraints imposed by the availability of space or capacity make it impossible to open up the market and/or implement self-handling, the Member State in question may, subject to Commission approval, decide to limit the provision of ground-handling services to one supplier (for a two-year period renewable once) and to ban self-handling or to restrict it to a single airport user (for a three-year period, renewable). Member States shall notify the Commission of any exemptions they grant, at least three months before they enter into force, (Article 9(3) of the Directive).

12.207 A number of derogations have been granted to airports in accordance with the conditions set out in the Directive.

12.208 The Commission decisions in the *FAG* and *Alpha Flight Services* cases demonstrate how the Commission has applied Article 82 to cases involving the provision of ground-handling services.

12.209 **FAG.** Flughafen Frankfurt Main AG (FAG) is the company which owns and operates Frankfurt airport. The capacity of an airport is dictated essentially by three elements: the runway capacity, the capacity of the stands and the capacity of

---

[81] [1996] OJ L272/36.

the terminal buildings. FAG has one runway, an additional take-off only runway, and two terminals.

On the land side, FAG allowed air carriers the right of self-handling and/or third **12.210** party handling. As regards passengers, air carriers were allowed to self-handle their land-side activities and all airlines had the right to handle the passengers of other airlines. These services were also supplied by FAG. Independent handling opera-tors were not admitted by FAG for the provision of passenger handling services. As regards the provision of certain ramp-side activities, FAG refused to allow self-handling or to admit third party handlers. FAG was consequently the only provider of those services at Frankfurt airport.

The scope of the *FAG* decision[82] was limited to the ramp-side activities for which **12.211** FAG neither allowed self-handling nor admitted independent third party service suppliers. The Commission considered that as sole supplier of the services con-cerned, FAG held a dominant position on the market for the provision of ramp-handling services at Frankfurt airport. Potential alternative suppliers were not in a position to assail FAG's monopoly as long as the airport operator continued to deny them access to the ramp where these services have to take place.

In deciding to retain for itself the market for ramp-handling services at Frankfurt **12.212** airport, FAG extended its dominant position on the market for the provision of airport landing and take-off facilities to the neighbouring but separate market for ramp-handling services. FAG furthermore made use of its power as exclusive provider of airport facilities to deny airlines the right to self-handle. FAG thereby obliged the users of its airport facilities also to purchase from it ramp-handling services.

FAG argued that its refusal to authorize self-handling and independent ramp- **12.213** handlers was objectively justified by the lack of space at the airport. The Commission concluded that FAG's argument was not well founded. In the first place, the experts' technical reports showed that the constraints on space at Frankfurt were not such as to make it impossible to authorize self-handling or the admission of independent ramp-handlers. Secondly, even supposing that such constraints did exist, they would not be insurmountable.

The Commission therefore found that FAG had abused its dominant position in **12.214** breach of Article 82 by denying, without objective justification, potential third party handlers access to the ramp and airport users the right to self-handle, thereby reserving for itself the market for the provision of ramp-handling services at Frankfurt airport. The Commission ordered FAG to bring the infringement to an end and gave three months in which to provide a precise plan for the reorganiz-ation of the market for the provision of ramp-handling services at Frankfurt

---

[82] *Flughafen Frankfurt/Main AG* (n 30 above).

airport so as to open up market access for air carriers and independent providers of ramp-handling services.

12.215 **Alpha Flight Services.** The *Alpha Flight Services (AFS) v Aéroports de Paris (ADP)* decision[83] concerned the system of commercial fees charged by ADP in exchange for the operating licence issued to suppliers of certain categories of ground-handling services at Orly and Roissy-Charles de Gaulle airports (CDG).

12.216 AFS complained to the Commission about the difference in commercial fees which ADP charged AFS and those charged to Orly Air Traiteur (OAT), a competitor for the supply of catering services at Orly. OAT is a subsidiary of Groupe Air France. AFS considered that if the fees it paid were identical to those charged to OAT, its annual fees would be reduced by some FRF 3.5 million.

12.217 The Commission found that because of the dominant position held by ADP, the payment of a commercial fee must not create dissimilar conditions for equivalent transactions, thus placing suppliers or users engaged in the same ground-handling activity at a competitive disadvantage.

12.218 It found that in 1995, the commercial fee paid by AFS was considerably higher than the amount paid by OAT. On the basis of the turnover achieved by caterers and cleaners within the same airport, a rate that was lower by only a few per cent would lead to annual fees that were lower by several million French francs.

12.219 The Commission also considered that the zero or very low rates applied by ADP to self-handling by airlines resulted in the cost of ADP's management services supplied to all ground-handlers, including self-handlers, being passed on to suppliers of services for third parties. Ground-handling services for third parties were therefore more expensive than self-handling services.

12.220 The Commission considered that the non-imposition of a fee on airlines licensed only to self-handle gave them a discriminatory advantage in terms of costs with regard to their self-handling activities and, therefore, with regard to air transport.

12.221 The Commission concluded that the commercial fees charged by ADP for certain types of ground-handling service at Orly and CDG airports, in particular catering, aircraft cleaning, and cargo services, were applied at discriminatory rates affecting competition between the suppliers of the handling services concerned and, indirectly, between Community airlines using Orly and CDG airports. This amounted to a breach of Article 82. No fines were imposed.

---

[83] *Alpha Flight Services* (n 30 above).

(2) Ports

Ports generate the same problems of access and discrimination to those found in **12.222** airports. This is especially significant when it comes to the introduction of new ferry services but also has implications for other maritime transport services. So far as access to ports is concerned, the general principle is that the owner of an infrastructure abuses a dominant position if he refuses access to a port and thereby impedes the start up of new service.

Port Access

B&I. In the *B&I* case,[84] the Commission found that Sealink (a British ferry **12.223** operator which is also the port authority at Holyhead, Wales) had, prime facie, abused its dominant position, in breach of Article 82 EC.

In its capacity as port authority at Holyhead, Sealink permitted changes to its own **12.224** ferry sailing times which involved the movement of an additional ship past the B&I vessel while it was in its berth. B&I (an Irish ferry operator) used a berth in the mouth of the harbour. Due to the port's limitations, when a Sealink vessel passed a moored B&I ship, the water in the harbour rose. As a result, the ramp to the B&I ship had to be disconnected for safety reasons and loading or unloading of the vessel was interrupted.

B&I asked the Commission to adopt interim measures to prevent the implemen- **12.225** tation of Sealink's new schedule on the grounds that its services would be seriously disrupted due to the reduced time available in which to carry out its loading and unloading operations.

The Commission stated that a company which both owns and uses an essential **12.226** facility should not grant its competitors access on terms less favourable than those which it gives its own services and obliged Sealink to alter temporarily some of its sailing times.

Roscoff. In the *Port of Roscoff* decision,[85] the Commission granted interim mea- **12.227** sures at the request of Irish Continental Group (ICG) against the Chambre de Commerce et d'Industrie de Morlaix (CCI Morlaix), on the grounds of breach of Article 82 EC. ICG complained to the Commission that CCI Morlaix had infringed Article 82 EC by abusing its dominant position as the port authority at Roscoff by refusing access to ICG to the port facilities at Roscoff.

---

[84] Commission Decision of 11 June 1992 relating to a proceeding under Article 86 [now Article 82] of the EC Treaty (Case IV/34.174—*Sealink/B&I—Interim Measures*), not published.
[85] Commission Decision of 16 May 1995 relating to a proceeding under Article 86 [now Aritcle 82] of the EC Treaty (*Irish Continental Group/CCI Morlaix—Port of Roscoff*), not published.

12.228 The CCI Morlaix both manages the port of Roscoff (Port de Bloscon) and is a shareholder (of about 5 per cent) in Brittany Ferries, the principal user of the port of Roscoff. Brittany Ferries operates ferry services between the Irish port of Cork and the French ports of Roscoff and St Malo, and also between certain UK ports and Brittany, and between Spain and Brittany.

12.229 In its decision, the Commission concluded that the port of Roscoff was the only one providing port facilities for transport services between Brittany and Ireland, under acceptable conditions to ICG, Lorient being too far away and St Malo not providing the necessary technical facilities for large ferries. Consequently, CCI Morlaix, in its capacity as port authority, had a dominant position in the market for the provision of port facilities for passenger and car ferry services between Brittany and Ireland.

12.230 CCI Morlaix occupied a dominant position in the provision of an essential facility (ie a facility or infrastructure, without access to which competitors cannot provide services to their customers). Its refusal, without objective justification, to grant access to these facilities to a company wishing to compete with a company active in a secondary market constituted an abuse of its dominant position, even leaving aside any economic interest held by CCI Morlaix in Brittany Ferries.

12.231 A company in a dominant position which sells services must have a valid reason for refusing to sell them to a willing buyer, in particular where the company in a dominant position controls access to an essential facility. Furthermore, an undertaking which occupies a dominant position in the provision of an essential facility has an obligation to provide access on non-discriminatory terms if a refusal will cause a significant effect on competition.

12.232 The Commission considered that the unjustified behaviour of CCI Morlaix was not consistent with the obligations on an undertaking which enjoys a dominant position in relation to an essential facility.

12.233 The Commission ordered CCI Morlaix to grant ICG access to the port of Roscoff for a temporary period. The Commission added for good measure that, under Article 5 of the EC Treaty, all of the competent French authorities are obliged to take all appropriate measures to ensure fulfilment of the obligations resulting from its decision.

Discrimination

12.234 In the *Port of Genoa* decision,[86] the Commission required the Italian authorities to modify a discount system on the piloting tariffs that amounted to discrimination between maritime shipping companies for the same service.

---

[86] *Port of Genoa* [1997] OJ L301.

E. Application of Articles 84 and 85

Council Regulations 3975/87 and 3976/87 are limited in scope in that they do **12.235**
not apply to air traffic between EU Member States and third countries. There is
thus no procedural implementing regulation laying down the rules to be applied
in case of possible infringements of Articles 81 and 82 on routes with third countries. Where no procedural regulations for the application of Articles 81 and 82 by
the Commission have been adopted, the Commission, national authorities, and
industry have to rely on two transitional provisions in the Treaty, namely Articles
84 and 85. This also means that there are no block exemption regulations applying to these markets.

In all other sectors, including maritime transport (other than tramp vessel ser- **12.236**
vices), procedural implementing regulations have been adopted and are fully
applicable. Moreover, the Merger Regulation does not make a distinction
between intra-Community air traffic and air traffic between the EC and third
countries.

In the Nouvelles Frontières case[87] in 1986, the Court had already confirmed that **12.237**
in the absence of an implementing regulation based on Article 83, Articles 84 and
85 are applicable. It further said that Article 84 contains an obligation on Member
State authorities to apply Articles 81 and 82, where no such implementing regulation has been adopted by the Council.

As regards the role of national courts in applying Article 81(1) and (2), the Court **12.238**
ruled that where a Member State authority under Article 84, or the Commission
under Article 85(2) have concluded that Article 81(1) has been infringed (and the
conditions of Article 81(3) have not been met), a national court must conclude
that the agreement is null and void in accordance with Article 81(2).

In the *Ahmed Saeed* case,[88] the Court of Justice confirmed its judgment in **12.239**
Nouvelles Frontières as regards Article 81 and ruled that Article 82 is directly
applicable by national courts, even where there is no implementing regulation
under Article 83 or where neither a Member State authority nor the Commission
has acted under Article 84 or under Article 85 respectively. The Court also ruled
that a Member State is in breach of its Treaty obligations under Article 10 (former
Article 5) if it favours the conclusion of tariff agreements which infringe Article 81
or 82 or if it approves fares which result from such agreements.

Although the case law provides some guidance on the correct interpretation of **12.240**
Articles 84 and 85, the situation of uncertainty is exacerbated by the fact that the
application of these articles may give rise to legal conflicts, in particular where

---

[87] *Nouvelles Frontières* (n 7 above).
[88] *Ahmed Saeed* (n 20 above).

Member State authorities and the Commission open procedures at the same time.

12.241 The Treaty does not appear to establish a hierarchy between these two articles. It is therefore not clear if action by a Member State under Article 84, precludes action by the Commission under Article 85 or vice versa. The Commission has taken the position that parallel proceedings are possible since both articles contain clear obligations to act without establishing such a hierarchy.

12.242 As regards Article 84, the Court has ruled that it creates an obligation for the competent national authority to apply Articles 81 and 82 in the absence of a procedural implementing regulation under Article 83.[89]

12.243 First, in so far as a Member State has not granted its competent authority the power to apply Articles 81 and 82—either in general or for the specific areas which are not covered by any implementing regulation—it will not be able to act under Article 84 and it may well be in a situation of not fulfilling a Treaty obligation. At the time of writing, only eight out of the fifteen Member States have the powers to apply Articles 81 and 82 generally. Although the UK is not one of the eight, it has given itself powers to apply Articles 81 and 82 in those sectors where the Commission does not have power, namely air transport between the Community and a third country and tramp shipping.

12.244 Secondly, Article 84 stipulates that Member State authorities will also have to act 'in accordance with the law of their country'. In view of their obligation to apply, as regards the substance of a case, the Treaty provisions, this would suggest that the role of national law is one of providing the procedural framework for handling the case. This would also seem to fit with the general objective of Articles 84 and 85 which is to safeguard the application of the EC competition rules in the absence of procedural rules at Community level. Even if this reasoning is correct it cannot be excluded that the national authority and the Commission arrive at conflicting conclusions, when they both have opened procedures in the same case and both apply Community law.

12.245 Thirdly, conflicting outcomes cannot be excluded where a national authority opens its own procedure under national law, but not with a view to implementing Article 84, while the Commission acts under Article 85.

12.246 Article 85 places an obligation on the Commission to ensure the application of the principles of Articles 81 and 82 by investigating cases of suspected infringement. It creates a duty for the Commission to co-operate with the national authorities, who in turn will assist the Commission. If the Commission concludes there has been an infringement, it shall propose appropriate measures. This would

---

[89] *Nouvelles Frontières* (n 7 above).

not seem to be an act which is attackable before the Courts, in contrast to the reasoned decision referred to in the second paragraph of Article 85.

Paragraph 2 of Article 85 provides that the Commission 'may' authorize Member States to take the measures needed to remedy the situation, the conditions and details of which it shall determine. The words 'may authorize' would suggest that the Commission has a certain discretion as to whether or not to authorize a Member State to take the necessary measures. A Member State, once authorized, would not seem to have any discretion to refuse to implement the Commission's reasoned decision. A refusal would render the whole procedure under Article 85 meaningless.   **12.247**

Where the Commission has no direct enforcement powers, it must rely on Member States to assist it in its investigation. Although the Commission has applied *mutatis mutandis* the procedural rules of Regulation 3975/87 in Article 85 cases, it is not able, for example, to enforce directly any deadlines for requests for information or to carry out inspections.   **12.248**

Article 85 does not allow the Commission to grant declarations of exemption in the sense of Article 81(3). However, in order to arrive at a conclusion as to whether an infringement of the principles of Article 81 has occurred, the Commission must be able to make up its mind whether the conditions of Articles 81(3) have been satisfied or not. The reasoned decision under Article 85(2) must have as its objective the ending of the infringement and to do so it must propose effective remedies. This can take the form of a straightforward prohibition, but the wording of the last sentence, referring to 'measures, the conditions and details of which it shall determine', clearly suggests that the Commission, while arriving at the conclusion that an agreement does not qualify for exemption and must be forbidden, can describe precisely the remedies to enable an Article 81(3) decision to be taken by a Member State authority.   **12.249**

Again, depending on the nature of the conditions and the degree of detail, the risk of a conflict with a parallel Article 84 decision of a national authority cannot be excluded. Although, where parallel procedures under Articles 84 and 85 have been opened, the duty of the Commission to co-operate with national authorities in combination with the obligations on Member States under Article 10, should in principle result in outcomes which are at least compatible. Where a Member State applies its national law and the Commission acts under Article 85, Article 10 should achieve the same result.   **12.250**

In 1981, when tabling its original draft for a Council regulation laying down the procedural rules for applying the competition rules, the Commission already proposed it should cover air traffic between the Community and third countries. The Council, however, did not want to go beyond air traffic between Member States when it adopted Regulation 3975 in 1987.   **12.251**

12.252 In May 1997, the Commission tabled a proposal to extend the scope of Regulation 3975/87 to include international air transport and a proposal to enable the Commission to grant block exemptions covering EC–third country markets. The proposal to amend Regulation 3975 consists in two elements. First, the deletion of Article 1(2), which limits the scope of its application to air traffic between Community airports. The amended regulation would thus apply to passengers and goods traffic with all third countries.

12.253 The second element of the proposal deals with the situation where the application of the competition rules would lead to a conflict of law with the laws and regulations of a third country, or in relation to a bilateral agreement between a Member State and a third country. A new Article 18A would introduce a duty on the Commission to enter into consultations with the competent authority of the third country.

12.254 The second proposal would, if adopted, enable the Commission to grant block exemptions in relation to air transport between the EC and third countries. The enabling regulation would do so for agreements, decisions, and concerted practices in relation to:

- joint planning and the co-ordination of capacity and schedules,

- revenue sharing,

- tariff consultations in so far as essential for interlining,

- joint operation of services on new or less busy routes,

- and slot allocation at airports.

12.255 In comparison to the current version of Regulation 3976/87 it includes revenue sharing and the co-ordination of capacity. The proposal thus precisely reflects the original version of Regulation 3976/87. This has been done to allow the Commission to take account, at least during an initial period, of the very restrictive bilateral agreements which Member States have with certain third countries and develop its competition policy in line with the degree of liberalization of aviation markets.

12.256 For the rest, the proposal is nearly identical to the text of the existing enabling Regulation 3976/87, but for one point: the proposal contains an additional provision (Article 7(4)) to deal with the situation where breaches of conditions or obligations or effects incompatible with Article 81(3) are due to the laws or regulations of third countries or provisions in bilateral aviation agreements between a Member State and a third country. In such cases the new Article 18A (consultation process) introduced in the proposal to amend Regulation 3975/87 would be applicable.

F. Conclusions

Rail liberalization appears to have stalled in the face of persistent doubts at the **12.257** level of the Council of Ministers. In theory, this would suggest that the motor for change would most likely be found in the application of the competition rules, as in the *Deutsche Bahn* case, an area in which the Commission can act independently of the Council. However, the application of the competition rules to railway undertakings is complicated by the fact that the scope of Regulation 1017/68 remains unclear and by the fact that the existence of national monopolies limits the scope for the application of Article 81.

So far as liner shipping is concerned, every major position taken by the **12.258** Commission concerning the scope of the group exemption has been challenged before the Courts in Luxembourg. While some cases are reasonably far advanced, others remain at an early stage and legal certainty is still some way off. An important number of issues relating to the scope of the group exemption have yet to be dealt with, even by the Commission.

The aviation sector has a comprehensive regulatory framework apart from the fact **12.259** that, other than in merger cases, the Commission cannot directly apply Articles 81 and 82 to routes between the Community and third countries. When the Commission has accepted undertakings in order to clear co-operative arrangements between airlines (Lufthansa/SAS, Swissair/Sabena), it is not readily apparent that those undertakings have actually facilitated new entry. Many people would consider that fares on most city pair routes within the Community remain high. The outcome of the Commission's examination of more recent airline alliance cases is not clear at the time of writing.

Nevertheless, even if much progress remains to be made, the Commission's com- **12.260** petition policy for cases in the transport sector has been considerably advanced especially since the adoption of Regulations 4056 and 3975 in 1986 and 1987 respectively. The Commission's decisions, especially those in the liner shipping and infrastructure cases, have been highly detailed and provide a very substantial basis for future Commission activity.

INDEX